A Practical Guide to Family Proceedings: Blomfield and Brooks

A Practical Guide to Family Proceedings: Blomfield and Brooks

Seventh Edition

Edited by

His Honour Judge Christopher Simmonds

Alexander Laing
Barrister, Coram Chambers

Sophie Hill
Barrister, Coram Chambers

Edward Bennett
Barrister, Harcourt Chambers

Bloomsbury Professional

BLOOMSBURY PROFESSIONAL

Bloomsbury Publishing Plc

50 Bedford Square, London, WC1B 3DP, UK

1385 Broadway, New York, NY 10018, USA

29 Earlsfort Terrace, Dublin 2, Ireland

British Library Cataloguing-in-Publication Data

A catalogue record for this book is available from the British Library.

ISBN: PB 978 1 52652 431 7
ePDF 978 1 51652 433 1
ePub 978 1 52652 432 4

Typeset by Compuscript Ltd, Shannon
Printed and bound by CPI Group (UK) Ltd, Croydon, CR0 4YY

FSC www.fsc.org MIX Paper from responsible sources FSC® C013604

To find out more about our authors and books visit www.bloomsburyprofessional.com. Here you will find extracts, author information, details of forthcoming events and the option to sign up for our newsletters.

FOREWORD TO THE SIXTH EDITION

This invaluable practical guide, now in its sixth edition, is an established part of the essential material used in the Royal Courts of Justice, the Central Family Court and throughout the Family Court.

In his Foreword to the fifth edition, my predecessor, the late and much lamented Sir Nicholas Wall, welcomed the work the authors had done to provide guidance upon the changes resulting from the introduction in April 2011 of the Family Procedure Rules.

Time marches on, and for this edition the authors have had to accommodate the changes resulting from the creation in April 2014 of the Family Court.

The authors are to be congratulated for their clear and comprehensive exposition of the new position. I am pleased to commend it to practitioners both on and off the bench.

Sir James Munby

President of the Family Division and Head of Family Justice

PREFACE

Family law changes faster than other areas and the new, seventh edition reflects that. We cover the overhaul of divorce law, the greater focus in private law proceedings on the impact of domestic abuse in all forms and the need to ensure that vulnerable parties are able fully to participate in proceedings.

Additionally, when the Sixth Edition was written we could not have imagined the changes that would shortly take place in the Family Court, in particular the significant changes to how we operate, using technology and remote hearings, all of which are covered in this edition.

The aim of this book remains to make family law and its procedures accessible, with each chapter having a practical focus. Our aim is that, by covering such a breath of topics, family practitioners will enjoy this book as the essential starting reference point on all aspects of family law.

Family law is a hard area of law in the sense not only of its complexities but also given the effect that orders have on the lives of the people we help. We hope that this book makes your life a little easier.

Christopher Simmonds

August 2022

CONTENTS

TABLE OF CASES

TABLE OF STATUTES

TABLE OF STATUTORY INSTRUMENTS

TABLE OF EUROPEAN LEGISLATION

TREATIES AND CONVENTIONS

REGULATIONS

TABLE OF PRACTICE DIRECTIONS

TABLE OF ABBREVIATIONS

LEGISLATION

AA 1955	Army Act 1955
AEA 1971	Attachment of Earnings Act 1971
AFA 1955	Air Force Act 1955
CA 1989	Children Act 1989
CACA 1985	Child Abduction and Custody Act 1985
C(AP)O 1991	Children (Allocation of Proceedings) Order 1991, SI 1991/1677
CCA 1984	County Courts Act 1984
CCJO 2014	County Court Jurisdiction Order 2014, SI 2014/503
CCR	County Court Rules 1981, SI 1981/1687
CFA 2014	Children and Families Act 2014
CJJA 1982	Civil Jurisdiction and Judgments Act 1982
CPA 2004	Civil Partnership Act 2004
CPR 1998	Civil Procedure Rules 1998, SI 1998/3132
CSA 1991	Child Support Act 1991
DA 1869	Debtors Act 1869
DAA 2021	Domestic Abuse Act 2021
DDSA 2020	Divorce, Dissolution and Separation Act 2020
DMPA 1973	Domicile and Matrimonial Proceedings Act 1973
D(P) Regs 2000	Divorce etc (Pensions) Regulations 2000, SI 2000/1123
D(RM)A 2002	Divorce (Religious Marriages Act) 2002
FC(C&DB)R 2014	Family Court (Composition and Distribution of Business) Rules 2014, SI 2014/840
FC(CC)(P)R 2014	Family Court (Contempt of Court) (Powers) Regulations 2014, SI 2014/833
FLA 1986	Family Law Act 1986
FLA 1996	Family Law Act 1996
FLRA 1969	Family Law Reform Act 1969
FPR 2010	Family Procedure Rules 2010, SI 2010/2955
G(MP)A 2017	Guardianship (Missing Persons) Act 2017
GRA 2004	Gender Recognition Act 2004
I(PFD)A 1975	Inheritance (Provision for Family and Dependants) Act 1975

MCA 1973	Matrimonial Causes Act 1973
MC(REMO)R 1974	Magistrates' Courts (Reciprocal Enforcement of Maintenance Orders) Rules 1974, SI 1974/668
MFPA 1984	Matrimonial and Family Proceedings Act 1984
MOA 1950/1958	Maintenance Orders Act 1950/1958
MO(FE)A 1920	Maintenance Orders (Facilities for Enforcement) Act 1920
MO(RE)A 1972	Maintenance Orders (Reciprocal Enforcement) Act 1972
M(SSC)A 2013	Marriage (Same Sex Couples) Act 2013
NDA 1957	Naval Discipline Act 1957
NF(EML)A 1947	Naval Forces (Enforcement of Maintenance Liabilities) Act 1947
PDA 2013	Presumption of Death Act 2013
PHA 1997	Protection from Harassment Act 1997
RSC	Rules of the Supreme Court 1965, SI 1965/1776
TCGR 2013	Taking Control of Goods Regulations 2013, SI 2013/1894
TOLATA 1996	Trusts of Land and Appointment of Trustees Act 1996
WRPA 1999	Welfare Reform and Pensions Act 1999

PRACTICE DIRECTIONS

CPR 1998, PD 8	Practice Direction 8A – Alternative Procedure for Claims
CPR 1998, PD 20	Practice Direction 20 – Counterclaims and other Additional Claims
CPR 1998, PD 57	Practice Direction 57 – Probate and Inheritance
CPR 1998, PD 71	Practice Direction 71 – Orders to Obtain Information from Judgment Debtors
CPR 1998, PD 72	Practice Direction 72 – Third Party Debt Orders
CPR 1998, PD 73	Practice Direction 73 – Charging Orders, Stop Orders and Stop Notices
PD of 3 June 1958	Registrar's Direction (Proceeding on Answer)
PD of 17 February 1972	Practice Direction (Blood Tests) [1972] 1 WLR 353, [1972] 1 All ER 640
PD of 14 April 1986	Practice Direction (children: removal from jurisdiction) [1986] 1 WLR 475, [1986] 1 All ER 983, [1986] 2 FLR 89
PD of 19 May 2008	President's Direction (Central Index of Decree Absolute and of Final Orders for the Dissolution or Annulment of Civil Partnerships)
PD 2B	Practice Direction 2B – Allocation of Cases to Levels of Judiciary
PD 3A	Practice Direction 3A – Family Mediation Information and Assessment Meetings (MIAMS)
PD 3AA	Practice Direction 3AA – Vulnerable Persons: Participation in Proceedings and giving Evidence
PD 3AB	Practice Direction 3AB – Prohibition of Cross-Examination in Person in Family Proceedings under Part 4B of the Matrimonial and Family Proceedings Act 1984
PD 5A	Practice Direction 5A – Forms

PD 6A	Practice Direction 6A – Service Within the Jurisdiction
PD 6B	Practice Direction 6B – Service Out of the Jurisdiction
PD 6C	Practice Direction 6C – Disclosure of Addresses by Government Departments
PD 7A	Practice Direction 7A – Procedure for Applications in Matrimonial and Civil Partnership Proceedings
PD 7B	Practice Direction 7B – Medical Examinations on Applications for Annulment of a Marriage
PD 7D	Practice Direction 7D – The Gender Recognition Act 2004
PD 8A	Practice Direction 8A – Alternative Procedure for Claims
PD 9A	Practice Direction 9A – Application for a Financial Remedy
PD 10A	Practice Direction 10A – Part 4 of the Family Law Act 1996
PD 12A	Practice Direction 12A – Public Law Proceedings Guide to Case Management: April 2010
PD 12B	Practice Direction 12B – The Revised Private Law Programme
PD 12C	Practice Direction 12C – Service of Application in Certain Proceedings Relating to Children
PD 12D	Practice Direction 12D – Inherent Jurisdiction (Including Wardship) Proceedings
PD 12E	Practice Direction 12E – Urgent Business
PD 12F	Practice Direction 12F – International Child Abduction
PD 12J	Practice Direction 12J – Residence and Contact Orders: Domestic Violence and Harm
PD 12M	Practice Direction 12M – Family Assistance Orders: Consultation
PD 12N	Practice Direction 12N – Enforcement of Children Act 1989 Contact Orders: Disclosure of Information to Officers of the National Probation Service
PD 15A	Practice Direction 15A – Protected Parties
PD 16A	Practice Direction 16A – Representation of Children
PD17A	Practice Direction 17A – Statements of Truth
PD 18A	Practice Direction 18A – Other Applications in Proceedings
PD 20	Practice Direction 20 – Counterclaims and other Additional Claims
PD 22A	Practice Direction 22A – Written Evidence
PD 25	Practice Direction 25 – Experts and Assessors
PD 25A	Practice Direction 25A – Interim Injunctions
PD 25C	Practice Direction 25C – Children Proceedings – The use of Single Joint Experts and the Process leading to an Expert being Instructed or Expert Evidence being put before the Court
PD 25D	Practice Direction 25D – Financial Remedy Proceedings and other Family Proceedings (Except Children Proceedings) – The use of Single Joint Experts and the Process leading to Expert Evidence being put before the Court

PD 25E	Practice Direction 25E – Discussions between Experts in Family Proceedings
PD 26A	Practice Direction 26A – Change of Solicitor
PD 27A	Practice Direction 27A – Family Proceedings: Court Bundles (Universal Practice to be Applied in all Courts other than the Family Proceedings Court)
PD 28A	Practice Direction 28A – Costs
PD 30A	Practice Direction 30A – Appeals
PD 31A	Practice Direction 31A – Registration of Orders under the Council Regulation, the Civil Partnership (Jurisdiction and Recognition of Judgments) Regulations 2005 and under the 1996 Hague Convention
PD 33A	Practice Direction 33A – Enforcement of Undertakings
PD 34A	Practice Direction 34A – Reciprocal Enforcement of Mainenance Orders
PD 34B	Practice Direction 34B – Tracing Payers Overseas
PD 36D	Practice Direction 36D – Pilot Scheme: Procedure for using an Online System to Generate Applications in Certain Proceedings for a Matrimonial Order
PD 36Q	Practice Direction 36Q – Pilot Provision: Modification of Practice Direction 12B – Coronavirus
PD 37A	Practice Direction 37A – Applications and Proceedings in Relation to Contempt of Court
PD 40A	Practice Direction 40A – Charging Orders, Stop Orders and Stop Notices
PD 52C	Practice Direction 52C – Appeals to the Court of Appeal
PD 57	Practice Direction 57 – Probate
PD 57B	Practice Direction 57B – Proceedings under the Presumption of Death Act 2013
PD 71	Practice Direction 71 – Orders to obtain Information from Judgment Debtors
PD 72	Practice Direction 72 – Third Party Debt Orders
PD 73	Practice Direction 73 – Charging Orders, Stop Orders and Stop Notices

OTHER

BFPO	British Forces Post Office
Cafcass	Children and Family Court Advisory and Support Service
CAO	Child Arrangements Order
CAP	Child Arrangement Programme
DRA	Dispute Resolution Appointment
DVIP	domestic violence intervention programme
EEO	European Enforcement Order
FDR	Financial Dispute Resolution
FHDRA	First Hearing Dispute Resolution Appointment
IDAP	integrated domestic abuse programme

IRO	Independent Reviewing Officer
LAA	Legal Aid Agency
MIAM	Mediation Information and Assessment Meeting
MoJ	Ministry of Justice
NACC	National Association of Child Contact Centres
NOMS	National Offenders Management Service
PRFD	Principal Registry of the Family Division
Rayden	*Rayden and Jackson on Relationship Breakdown, Finances and Children* (LexisNexis, looseleaf)
REMO	Reciprocal Enforcement of Maintenance Orders
SPIP	Separated Parents Informational Programme

CHAPTER 1

THE DIVORCE APPLICATION

1.1 INTRODUCTION

FPR 2010, r 2.3(2)(a)

As from 6 April 2022, divorce proceedings are to be initiated under the Divorce, Dissolution and Separation Act 2020 (DDSA 2020), s 1 by way of an application for a divorce order.

There are significant changes to the existing law. Either party, or both parties jointly (to reduce hostility), can apply to the court for a 'divorce order', and therefore both can be the applicants, asking the court to dissolve the marriage on the sole remaining ground that the marriage has irretrievably broken down.

The applicant or applicants must provide with their application a statement that the marriage has broken down irretrievably. The statement of irretrievable breakdown will be conclusive evidence. It will replace the need for parties to provide evidence regarding the previously required facts as to adultery, unreasonable behaviour or proof of separation.

1.1.1 DDSA 2020, s 1(2)

Twenty weeks from the start of proceedings the applicant (if applying alone) or applicants will need to give confirmation to the court that they wish for the application to continue. The court will then make a 'conditional order' instead of the previous decree nisi.

Six weeks after the pronouncement of the conditional order, the applicant or applicants may apply for a 'final order' instead of the previous decree absolute. There will be some limited circumstances where it will be possible to reduce the 6-week period.

The same process will apply for the dissolution of civil partnerships.

The new reform does not provide any respondent with the ability to contest the divorce, thereby ensuring that the parties will not be forced into expensive and prolonged court proceedings to deal with a defended divorce.

Practice Direction 36X (piloting mandatory use of online divorce): this new pilot Practice Direction will mandate use of the online divorce system by applicants' legal representatives, from 13 September 2021.

All matters relating to the issue of an application and the way in which it is conducted are to be determined by the provisions of the DDSA 2020, amending the Matrimonial Causes Act 1973 (MCA 1973), and the Family Procedure Rules 2010 (FPR 2010). Both the Act and the Rules, together with annotations, will be set out in *The Family Court Practice* (LexisNexis, annual) and *Rayden & Jackson on Relationship Breakdown, Finances and Children* (LexisNexis, looseleaf) (referred to throughout this book as '*Rayden*'). The Rules and Practice Directions are also to be found at **Appendix D** of this book.

1.2 QUALIFYING CRITERIA

In order to apply for a divorce order, it is necessary to satisfy the following criteria:

(a) the parties must have been married for more than 1 year immediately preceding the application. Note that the date of the marriage must be excluded in calculating the 1-year period;

MCA 1973, s 3(1)
Butler v Butler (Queen's Proctor Intervening) [1990] FCR 336

(b) for any divorce proceedings instituted after 31 December 2020, the court no longer has jurisdiction under the Council Regulation as the UK Government has repealed Brussels IIA, including the 'Lis Pendens' rule. Therefore, the situation reverts to the pre EU 'forum conveniens' rules which exist with all other non-EU countries. As a result, cross jurisdictional EU divorces may involve lengthy and costly disputes over jurisdiction as to which EU country the divorce should take place in, as well as duplicated proceedings and potentially irreconcilable decisions. Only 12 of the existing EU Member States are signatory to the Hague 1970 divorce recognition convention and that convention, whilst helpful, may place more barriers in the way to recognising a divorce than Brussels IIA.

The EU has not yet agreed to the UK becoming a member of the 2007 Lugano Convention. As at the time of writing the European Parliament's Briefing of 18 November 2021 addresses the European Commission's current decision to block membership. If the UK does re-join the 2007

Lugano Convention, then there will be further changes to the law to include the reintroduction of 'Lis Pendens'.

(c) the marriage must have irretrievably broken down.

Note: The requirement for facts has been removed by DDSA 2020, s 1.

1.3 GROUND FOR DIVORCE

DDSA 2020, s 1(3)

Under the MCA 1973, irretrievable breakdown is the sole ground for a divorce and must be recited on the face of the application however under the DDSA 2020 no supplemental facts are to be pleaded. Instead the statement of the applicant(s) that the marriage has irretrievably broken down is conclusive evidence.

1.4 ATTEMPTS AT RECONCILIATION

DDSA 2020, Sch, Pt 1 sets out the amendments to MCA 1973, s 6

Under the provisions of the MCA 1973, s 2, the parties were permitted to attempt a period or periods of reconciliation, not exceeding in total 6 months, without it affecting their entitlement to issue an application. Under the reforms there is a requirement for 'an applicant for a divorce order to certify whether the representative has discussed with the applicant the possibility of reconciliation and given the applicant' requisite information, rather than for the representative to certify it, as before.

1.5 FORM OF THE APPLICATION

FPR 2010, r 5.1
PD 7A, para 1.1

A new Form D8 has been issued. If the applicant or respondent needs special assistance at any court hearing, it is obviously sensible practice to give the court this information.

See **Appendix A(1)** for Form D8.

1.6 STATEMENT OF TRUTH

FPR 2010, r 17.6(1)
FPR 2010, PD17A and PD22A

FPR 2010 required that a Statement of Truth is indorsed on a petition for divorce, judicial separation or dissolution of a civil partnership, or an answer to such a petition. This same requirement applies to the new divorce application Form D8. Proceedings for contempt of court may, of course, be brought against a person who makes, or causes to be made, a false statement in a document verified by a statement of truth without an honest belief in its truth.

The statement of truth must be signed by the applicant or the applicant's legal representative. If the legal representative signs, note that

> 'The individual who signs a statement of truth must sign in his or her own name and not that of his or her firm or employer'.

FPR 2010, PD 17A para 3.10

1.7 SIGNATURE

It is expected that the application should be signed by the applicant in person or by a representative of the applicant's solicitors if they are intending to place themselves on the court record.

1.8 ADDRESS FOR SERVICE

The application must give an address for service in England and Wales, to which documents for the applicant may be delivered or sent. If a solicitor is acting, this should be the solicitor's address. The solicitor's address may also be shown in a 'care of' capacity if the applicant is receiving advice under the Legal Help Scheme.

An address for service should also be provided for any respondent.

Note: See FPR 2010, r 6.11(2) regarding service on a solicitor out of the jurisdiction.

1.9 ONLINE ISSUE OF DIVORCE APPLICATIONS

The issue of proceedings online is mandatory where the applying party is represented, see **2.1** and **2.2**.

1.10 FURTHER APPLICATIONS

It is important to note that, other than with permission of the court, an applicant may not issue a second petition for divorce until the first application has been dismissed or finally determined.

FPR 2010, r 7.7(1)(a)

CHAPTER 2

REQUIREMENTS ON ISSUE OF DIVORCE APPLICATION

2.1 WHICH COURT?

HM Courts and Tribunals Service (HMCTS) announced in February 2020 that it would close some of the regional divorce centres (also referred to as regional divorce units (RDUs)) as a consequence of the move to issuing divorce proceedings online. The divorce centres shall be phased out and replaced by an online system, the use of which is mandatory in some cases. In May 2021 HMCTS announced it has opened four Courts and Tribunals Service Centres in Birmingham, Stoke-on-Trent, Loughborough and Salford.

There is no requirement to issue at the nearest divorce centre although this is encouraged. In any event, any hearing that is required will take place at the Family Court hearing centre which is most convenient for the parties. Any dispute as to the venue will be determined by a district judge in the usual way.

FPR 2010, PD 36X and PD41A

It should be noted that if the application is recorded by the court's system as being received at or after 4.31pm, it will be treated as having been *received* on the next business day; but not as being issued at that time. The Practice Direction sets out further details of the operation of the online system, and while they cannot offer legal advice, the staff at the relevant divorce centres will assist court users and their advisers in operating the system. Further information can be obtained by email for an enquiry about applying for a divorce contactdivorce@justice.gov.uk or for an existing divorce case divorcecase@justice.gov.uk or telephoning 0300 303 0642 between 8am and 5pm Monday to Friday.

From 13 September 2021 FPR 2010, PD 36X makes mandatory the use of electronic means via the online divorce system where the applicant is legally represented. Legal representatives must submit applications for divorce online, using MyHMCTS. The exceptions to this are civil partnership, judicial separation and nullity, which should continue to be processed on paper. Other than in the case of applications being filed online, documents should be sent by post to the relevant divorce centre although it is possible to deliver them by hand. There is no advantage to this other than the certainty that documents have been delivered. In urgent cases it is still possible for applications to be presented for immediate issue at the Central Family Court or any Family Court hearing centre. Circumstances which might be considered urgent would include where there is a perceived need to issue an application to secure a tactical advantage, such as a jurisdictional race or where there is a need for a financial application to be issued for the purposes of an application under the MCA 1973, s 37.

If it becomes necessary for a hearing to take place, the proceedings will be transferred to a convenient family court hearing centre for that purpose.

2.2 DOCUMENTS TO BE FILED

The following should be filed in order to issue proceedings:

(a) The application and a copy of it which will be stamped with the court seal and returned to the applicant.

(b) A copy application for service on the respondent. FPR 2010, r 7.8

(c) A statement of reconciliation in Form D6. FPR 2010, r 7.6 PD 5A MCA 1973, s 6(1)

Note: A statement of reconciliation is required only where solicitors are acting for the applicant and intending to place themselves on the court record. It should not be filed where solicitors are merely advising the client under the Legal Help Scheme created by the Access to Justice Act 1999, which came into force on 1 April 2000.

(d) the marriage certificate. Normally this must be the original or an official certified copy. FPR 2010 PD 7A, para 3.1

Note that:

(i) If not in English, a translation of the certificate will also be required. The translation must be certified by a notary public or authenticated by a statement of truth. FPR 2010 PD 7A, para 3.1(b)

(ii) In exceptional circumstances, most usually where proceedings need to be commenced urgently, the applicant may apply to the court without notice for permission to file the application without the marriage certificate or translation. FPR 2010 PD 7A, paras 3.2, 3.3 and 3.4

The court will generally require it to be filed by a specified date.

It should be noted that a formal application (accompanied by the payment of a fee or a valid application for Help with Fees) is required, seeking permission to issue the application without the marriage certificate. For marriages which took place in England and Wales, a certified copy certificate can be obtained from the General Register Office website www.gro.gov.uk/gro/content/certificates/login.asp or by writing to the General Register Office, PO Box 2, Southport, Merseyside PR8 2JD. The telephone enquiry number is 0300 123 1837.

(iii) There may be some cases in which there is no marriage certificate, for example where the parties have been married in accordance with tribal custom or where, in a war-torn country, the certificate has been lost and a copy cannot be obtained. Reference should be made to PD 7A, para 3.5 and the Evidence (Foreign Dominion and Colonial Documents) Act 1933.

(iv) if either party has formally changed their name from that which appears on the marriage certificate, a copy of the appropriate documentary evidence (such as a deed poll or statutory declaration) must be lodged. If there is an error in the marriage certificate, or a name has been changed informally, an explanation should be given, as in **2.5**, paragraph 2.

For further information see *Rayden*.

FPR 2010, PD 36E and PD36X.

Where the online system under PD36E and PD36X is being used, certain documents can be filed online rather than needing to be sent physically to the court.

2.3 OTHER CONSIDERATIONS

2.3.1 Protected parties

Special rules apply to a party to the proceedings who is a protected party, by reason of either being under the age of majority (at present 18 years) or lacking capacity under the Mental Capacity Act 2005. Reference should be made to FPR 2010, r 6.14 which clearly sets out the procedure to be followed. Care should be taken to ensure that the notice set out in PD 6A in Form D5 is endorsed on the document to be served on the protected party.

2.3.2 Court fee

At the time of issue, the appropriate court fee must be paid. If the person concerned is being advised under the Legal Help Scheme or is otherwise in receipt of State benefit, an application for Help with Fees, signed by the applicant in person, will be required.

2.3.3 Omitting applicant's address

If an applicant petitioner wishes to omit his/her address from the petition, the form should be completed referring to the fact that the address is confidential but has been disclosed to the court. Form C8 should be completed and filed with the application. FPR 2010, r 5.1

The court will lodge and retain the Form C8 on the court file in a sealed envelope. The court will not reveal the address to any person unless there is a direction otherwise. FPR 2010, r 29.1(2)

Where the applicant's address is not included in the application, care should be taken to ensure that the details of the address are not inadvertently disclosed.

2.4 ISSUE OF APPLICATION

The application is issued on the date and at the time endorsed by the court officer on the application. The court officer will also seal the application on issue. See the new Form D8 published on 6 April 2022 (**Appendix A(1)**). FPR 2010, r 5.3 FPR 2010, r 29.7

CHAPTER 3

PROCEDURE – FROM ISSUE OF DIVORCE APPLICATION TO APPLICATION FOR CONDITIONAL ORDER

3.1 SERVICE

The new Act which comes into force on 6 April 2022 allows both parties to apply jointly, so that both are 'applicants'.

3.1.1 Service generally

FPR 2010, r 7.8(1) and (2)

After the court issues the divorce application or application for a civil partnership order by way of dissolution, it will send a sealed copy with supporting documentation (if any) to the respondent at the address for service in the application unless the solicitors request that they effect service themselves.

For service within the jurisdiction see the FPR 2010, PD 6A and service out of the jurisdiction see FPR 2010, PD 6B.

Where it has been indicated that solicitors will accept service on behalf of a respondent or co-respondent, service will be effected by sending the application to those solicitors.

FPR 2010, r 6.4 as amended by The Family Procedure (Amendment) Rules 2022 PD 6A

An application may be served by any of the following methods:

(a) personal service in accordance with the FPR 2010, r 6.7;

(b) first class post, or other service which provides for delivery on the next business day, in accordance with the FPR 2010, PD 6A; or

(c) where the FPR 2010, r 6.11 applies, document exchange; or

(d) email service in accordance with rule 6.7A.

FPR 2010, r 6.7A

Email service requires that an application is served on a respondent by email by sending it to either the respondent's usual email address or the email address provided by the respondent in accordance with rule 6.12. Where an application is served by email, a notice confirming such service must be sent to the respondent's postal address, by first class post or other next business day service.

For an application to be served by a court officer, the applicant must give the court officer the respondent's usual email address (if known) and the respondent's last known or usual postal address at which the respondent is to be served in accordance with rule 6.4. FPR 2010, r 6.8

If email service has been ineffective the court officer will notify the applicant that the application was undeliverable. FPR 2010, r 6.21A

The application is served together with a notice of proceedings to which an acknowledgement of service is attached. FPR 2010, r 7.8(2)

For the need to translate documents see FPR 2010, r 6.47.

For an alternative form of service or where the respondent cannot be found, see **3.2.4**.

3.1.2 Service on a regular member of the armed forces

A regular member of the armed forces can be traced through the appropriate Service Department. If he/she is serving overseas, service can be effected by sending a sealed copy of the application and all related documents to the appropriate British Forces Post Office (BFPO). As much information as possible should be provided and, in particular, the service number, rank and last known unit of the person concerned. See the Annex to PD 6A for further details, including addresses. FPR 2010, PD 6A, Annex

3.1.3 Service on a prisoner

Where a respondent is serving a term of imprisonment in a civilian prison within the United Kingdom, service may be effected either by:

(a) post, c/o the prison governor; or

(b) personal service, by making a formal request to the governor for a process server to have a face-to-face meeting with the respondent, so that the application and the related documents can be handed directly to the respondent. However, serving a prisoner in this way, because of prison bureaucracy, can be a very time-consuming exercise. *Bland v Bland* (1875) LR 3 P&D 233

If no acknowledgment of service is received it may be necessary to apply for an order of deemed service. See **3.2.4**.

3.1.4 Service by court bailiff or process server

Personal service may also be effected, most commonly by a court bailiff or a process server instructed by solicitors.

FPR 2010, rr 6.4(a) and 6.9, PD 6A, para 11.1

The court will only consider a request for bailiff service if the address for service is in England and Wales and in normal circumstances only if postal service has been attempted.

If bailiff service is required, a formal request (in Form D89) must be made to the court, together with, if possible, a recent photograph of the person to be served. The request must be signed by the applicant in person unless solicitors are on the court record. The request, which should be accompanied by copies of the application and all other documents to be served, attracts a court fee unless the applicant is exempt from fees.

FPR 2010, PD 6A, para 11

Whenever possible, the bailiff will obtain the signature of the person being served, which can be identified in the statement leading to a conditional order in exactly the same way as an acknowledgement of service which has been personally signed by the respondent. Whether or not a signature is obtained, the bailiff will complete an endorsement of service. If service cannot be effected, the bailiff will complete an endorsement of non-service.

It should be noted that an application for bailiff service may be refused by the court where the application is made by a party who has solicitors on the record as acting. If bailiff service is refused then service will need to be attempted by a process server. This will not apply where the solicitors are advising under the Legal Help Scheme.

FPR 2010, r 6.17(3), PD 6A, para 12.1

If service is effected by a process server, such service will be proved by filing a certificate of service which must state how identification has been established.

FPR 2010, r 6.19 PD 6A, para 6

In circumstances where the current home address of the person to be served is not known, an application can be made to a district judge for an order enabling service to be attempted by an alternative mode or at an alternative address, for example his/her place of work.

It is not appropriate to seek bailiff service upon either a regular member of the armed forces or a prisoner who is in a United Kingdom civilian prison. See **3.1.2** and **3.1.3**.

3.1.5 Service by an applicant

An application must not be served personally by the applicant himself or herself. FPR 2010, r 6.5(3)

3.1.6 Respondent outside the jurisdiction

Where any respondent is to be served outside England and Wales, the appropriate time within which the acknowledgement of service is to be returned is provided for in PD 6B, para 8.1. Leave to serve an application out of the jurisdiction is not required. A court officer will not serve the application out of the jurisdiction.

FPR 2010, r 6.41A and 6.41B
FPR 2010, rr 6.43–6.46 deal with service of applications and other documents outside the jurisdiction.
FPR 2010, r 6.5(2)(b)

There are special provisions dealing with service on a party in Scotland or Northern Ireland. FPR 2010, r 6.43(2)

Where those do not apply, service may be effected through foreign government, judicial or Consular channels.

Guidance may often be obtainable from the Foreign Process Section in Room E16 at the Royal Courts of Justice, Strand, London; tel 020 7947 6691. FPR 2010, rr 6.44, 6.45 and 6.46

While there is no express provision in the FPR permitting service outside the United Kingdom by an alternative method, comparable to FPR 2010, rr 6.19 and 6.35, it has been said that FPR 2010, r 6.1(b) is wide enough to permit the court to disapply the normal rules as to service in an appropriate case, and to authorise email service on a respondent out of the jurisdiction, if there is good reason to do so. If there exists a bilateral treaty about service with that country, the court will want to know why the treaty route is not being followed; but delay or inability to pin down the respondent's location would appear to be potentially good reasons. *Maughan v Wilmot* [2016] EWHC 29 (Fam)

Note: See **3.2.1** with regard to completing the acknowledgement of service where a respondent is within the jurisdiction.

3.1.7 Time for service of application

Where the applicant serves the application, the applicant must complete the step required by the table set out in FPR 2010 r 6.6A in relation to the method of service chosen before 12.00 midnight on the day 28 days after the date of issue of the application. The applicant may apply for an order extending the time for compliance with rule 6.6A. FPR 2010, r 6.6A and 6.6B

The Act provides for a 26-week period between commencement of divorce proceedings and the final divorce order being made. Controversially, as the period runs from the date of filing the application and not from the date proceedings are served on the respondent, the respondent may have much less than the 26 week period of notice of proceedings. Provided that the respondent has been served at some stage, the applicant can apply for the conditional order any time from 20 weeks after the filing of the proceedings at court. In practice therefore, as long as the respondent is served shortly before the end of the 20 weeks, this suffices.

3.2 ACKNOWLEDGEMENT OF SERVICE

3.2.1 Completing the acknowledgement

FPR 2010, r 7.12

The requirements for acknowledgment of service has been amended to reflect the new reforms so that the respondent should within 14 working days (or such longer period where the party is living outside the jurisdiction of the court as set out in PD 6B, para 8.1) return the acknowledgement of service form to the court.

3.2.2 Signature on acknowledgement

The acknowledgement hitherto could be signed by either a respondent or, where solicitors have been instructed to act, by them on their client's behalf.

3.2.3 Address for service

FPR 2010, r 6.26

The acknowledgement also provides for the respondent to give an address for service. This address must be either the business address within the United Kingdom or any other EEA state of a solicitor (as presently contained within the rules) or an address within the United Kingdom at which the party resides or carries on business.

FPR 2010, r 6.26(4)

It should be noted, however, that a party who apart from acknowledging service does not take part in the proceedings need not give an address for service within the United Kingdom.

3.2.4 Procedure where acknowledgement of service not filed

If an acknowledgement of service is not returned to the court, other steps will have to be taken to prove that the application has been served or to seek an order from the court for leave to proceed notwithstanding that no acknowledgement has been filed.

In some circumstances, a district judge may:

(a) dispense with service, where it is likely to prove impossible to effect service upon the respondent or where, at best, it is improbable that service can be effected; FPR 2010, r 6.20 PD 6A, para 7.1

(b) deem that service has been effected, where it is likely from facts that have come to the notice of the applicant and/or solicitors (who are either on the record or merely advising) that service has taken place, for example where it can be inferred from correspondence or a conversation that the respondent has in fact received the application; or FPR 2010, r 6.16

(c) order for service by an alternative means upon the respondent. This may be done for example either:
   (i) by post at an address at which it is believed that the person receives mail;
   (ii) by way of SMS text message; or
   (iii) by way of an advertisement in a newspaper. FPR 2010, r 6.19 PD 6A, para 6

Note: If the order is one which requires postal service, it is usually the responsibility of the applicant or his/her solicitors (if they are on the court record) to effect such service. This should be done by way of first class pre-paid post or by recorded delivery, depending on the requirements of the order. Once effected, the recorded delivery slip or certificate of posting should be exhibited to a certificate of service.

Applications either to dispense with service, to deem that it has taken place or for service by an alternative method, which, by their very nature, are made without notice, must be supported by evidence which fully sets out the basis upon which such application is made. FPR 2010, r 6.6 PD 6A

Note: In some limited circumstances, an order for deemed service may be made without the need to file evidence. FPR 2010, r 6.16

In the case of an application to dispense with service, there is a standard form of statement (Form D13B). All such applications attract a court fee unless the applicant is exempt from fees.

Before ordering that service of the application be dispensed with, a district judge will often direct that enquiries be made of the Department for Work and Pensions and/or the National Health Service Central Register in an effort to trace the respondent. In accordance with a directive of the Data Protection Registrar, an order of a district judge is required before either department is prepared to effect a search for the respondent's address or, in the case of the National Health Service, the address of the health authority where the person sought is registered with a National Health Service doctor.

For the detailed procedure see PD 6C, para 3

If there are strong grounds for believing that the person sought has made a recent application for a passport enquiries may be made of the passport office.

Disclosure Orders against the Inland Revenue – Guidance from the President's Office (November 2003); FPR 2010, PD 29C www.gov.uk/hmrc-internal-manuals/information-disclosure-guide/idg40530

A disclosure order may also be made for HM Revenue and Customs to disclose information, including addresses, to the court. HM Revenue and Customs is however bound by strict statutory confidentiality obligations. To overcome this problem the President has agreed with HM Revenue and Customs that all disclosure orders must be made under the inherent jurisdiction of the High Court which must be expressed on the face of the order and signed by the judge. The suit will notionally be transferred to the District Registry at the family court hearing centre, or to the nearest District Registry.

The transfer is simply for the purpose of making the disclosure order and the suit will thereafter be transferred back to the family court. The form of order which has been agreed by the President and HM Revenue and Customs is Form EX670 **(Appendix A(2))**.

The order can be made by any of the following classes of judge:

(i) High Court judge;

(ii) Deputy High Court judge;

(iii) Section 9 judge, ie a circuit judge or recorder authorised under the Senior Courts Act 1981, s 9 to sit as a judge of the High Court;

(iv) district judge of the Principal Registry of the Family Division;

(v) district judge of any District Registry of the Family Division of the High Court.

It should be noted that any one order will give access to the records held in relation to:

(i) income tax and National Insurance contributions;

(ii) the Tax Credits office;

(iii) the Child Benefit Office;

(iv) valuation services for rating and council tax;

(v) collection of student loan repayments.

For the detailed procedure see PD 6C.

The district judge may also direct that a search be made in the national index of final divorce orders maintained by the Central Family Court. Form D440 should be used for the purpose. For each period of 10 years which is searched, a court fee is payable, unless the applicant is exempt from fees.

3.3 CONCLUSION OF PROCEEDINGS

An application for a matrimonial order may be withdrawn at any time before it is served by giving the court notice in writing. FPR 2010, r 7.9

There are some circumstances, for example if the parties are attempting a reconciliation, where the court can order a stay of the proceedings. It is stressed that this is not a final disposal of the application. MCA 1973, s 6(2)

For action to be taken following an unsuccessful attempt to reconcile, see **7.5**.

Once an application has been served, an application by either the applicant or the respondent to dismiss must be made on not less than 7 working days' notice to a district judge.

3.4 DOMICILE OR HABITUAL RESIDENCE CHALLENGED

FPR 2010, r 7.27

If there is an issue with regard to jurisdiction as set out in the application and the respondent is asserting that neither party conforms to the requirement under the Domicile and Matrimonial Proceedings Act 1973 (DMPA 1973), Part II, s 5(2) an application must be issued for a hearing inter partes, on not less than 7 working days' notice, for this preliminary issue to be determined.

Note: See **1.2**.

The application will be heard by a High Court judge or, if it is considered more appropriate, a circuit judge, but if all the parties agree it may be dealt with by the court without a hearing. FPR 2010, r 7.27(5)

The application attracts a court fee unless the applicant is exempt from fees.

If it is found that the requirement of the DMPA 1973, s 5(2) has not been fulfilled, the application must be dismissed and no further steps can be taken, other than with regard to the costs of the proceedings.

From 1 January 2021, Brussels lla Regulation no longer applies to England and Wales.

Brussels lla rules as to jurisdiction are substantially replicated by new provisions inserted into the DMPA 1973, s 5(2).

For cases instituted on or after 1 January 2021, the above grounds for jurisdiction are slightly varied by regulation 7 and paragraph 7 of the Schedule to the Regulations:

(a) both parties to the marriage are habitually resident in England and Wales;

(b) both parties to the marriage were last habitually resident in England and Wales and one of them continues to reside there;

(c) the respondent is habitually resident in England and Wales;

(d) the applicant is habitually resident in England and Wales and has resided there for at least 1 year immediately before the application was made;

(e) the applicant is domiciled and habitually resident in England and Wales and has resided there for at least 6 months immediately before the application was made;

(f) both parties to the marriage are domiciled in England and Wales; or

(g) either of the parties to the marriage is domiciled in England and Wales.

Sole domicile has been added to the primary grounds.

Marinos v Marinos [2007] EWHC 2047

Following the High Court decision in *Marinos v Marinos*, it is only necessary to be habitually resident on the day the proceedings were issued, provided there was ordinary residence for the prior 6 or 12 months, as applicable. The requirement of only habitual residence on the day of issue, rather than for the 3 months preceding the proceedings under EU law, makes it possible to bring more proceedings in England.

3.4.1 Recognition

For proceedings instituted on or after 1 January 2021, whether a divorce is automatically recognised will depend on whether the corresponding EU country is a signatory to the 1970 Hague Divorce Recognition Convention. Where they are not a signatory, recognition will depend entirely upon the national laws of that country. Legal advice should be taken from a practitioner in the law of that jurisdiction.

3.4.2 Forum

From 1 January 2021, the 'first in time' rule is no longer determinative, although the courts in England

and Wales can exercise a discretion to stay proceedings if there are proceedings taking place in another jurisdiction.

The deciding factor will be 'closest connection', and forum non conveniens will apply. This is the forum test which has been applied in England and Wales with non-EU countries.

The UK courts consider many factors to establish 'closest connection', such as:

- nationality;
- residence;
- domicile;
- where assets are held;
- the alternative court being put forward;
- where children are attending school;
- language;
- cultural background.

3.5 APPLICATION FOR A CONDITIONAL ORDER (FPR 2010, rr 7.19 AND 7.20)

If an acknowledgement of service is filed in the court office, a copy is sent to the applicant or to his/her solicitors if they are on the court record. Where an applicant is acting in person, an explanatory leaflet is also sent, together with an application for conditional order and a supporting pro forma statement.

FPR 2010, PD 6A, para 10.1

The reforms remove the option for one party to contest the application for a divorce, reflecting that each partner has the right to decide whether they want to be in the relationship or not. It removes the requirement to cross-apply.

The court may not make a conditional order without written confirmation from the applicant that they wish the application to continue in an application made by one party to the marriage only, or from both parties in the event of a joint application.

The newly introduced 20-week period of reflection allows for reconciliation or practical matters to be addressed, such as child arrangements.

3.6 JUDICIAL SEPARATION PROCEEDINGS

As will be seen later, in **Chapter 8**, applications for a judicial separation order proceed in much the same way as for divorce. However, care must be taken to ensure that the statement in support of a judicial separation order is amended so that it refers throughout to judicial separation and not divorce and also that there is no reference to the marriage having broken down irretrievably.

Note: A comprehensive checklist is to be found at **5.3**. This sets out in considerable detail all aspects of the procedure and, if followed, should eradicate most if not all of the most commonly made errors.

CHAPTER 4

PROCEDURE – AMENDED, SUPPLEMENTAL AND FURTHER APPLICATIONS

4.1 SUMMARY OF APPLICATIONS

PD 7A, paras 5A.1–5A.3

It is important to distinguish between the applications permitted in nullity proceedings and those permitted in matrimonial or civil partnership proceedings.

4.2 AMENDING AN APPLICATION

PD7A sets out that where it is necessary in some way to amend an application for a matrimonial order or a civil partnership order, there are distinctions to be drawn between an amended application, a supplemental application and a further application:

(a) an amended application might be used to make alterations or additions to the details given in the application or the orders sought;

(b) a supplemental application can only be made in nullity proceedings and might be used to add particulars, allegations or acts which occurred after the date of the original application. A supplemental application forms part of the original application and effects an amendment to it;

PD 7A, para 5A.3

(c) a further (or second) application may only be made with permission under FPR 2010, r 7.4(1)(b) except that no permission is required where the applicant has, within one year from the date of the marriage, or civil partnership, made an application for a judicial separation order or separation order and then, after that one-year period has passed, wishes to apply for a divorce or a dissolution order.

FPR 2010, rr 7.8 and 7.15 deal in detail with the amendment of an application.

An application may be amended at any time before an answer is filed subject to the provisions of FPR 2010, r 7.15.

4.3 REQUIREMENTS ON FILING AN AMENDED OR SUPPLEMENTAL APPLICATION

When filing an amended, supplemental or further application, sufficient copies for service should be lodged with the court.

A filing fee is payable unless the applicant is exempt from fees.

4.4 SERVICE OF AN AMENDED OR SUPPLEMENTAL APPLICATION

Where permission is not required to file an amended or supplemental application, a sealed copy must be served on the other party with a notice of proceedings and form of acknowledgment of service. FPR 2010, r 7.15(3)(a)

The provisions of FPR 2010, 7.7, requiring the respondent to file an acknowledgment of service (as to which, see **3.2.1**), apply after the service of the amended or supplemental application unless otherwise directed. FPR 2010, r 7.15(3)(b) FPR 2010, r 7.15(6)(b)

Where an application is amended with written consent of the parties or permission of the court, the court may give directions as to service. FPR 2010, r 7.15(6)(a)

Unless otherwise directed, it is important to ensure that the notice of proceedings and acknowledgment of service are amended throughout so that they refer to the amended or supplemental application. If the original application has not been served it should be served together with the amended application and the notice of proceedings and acknowledgement of service should be amended to refer to both pleadings throughout. FPR 2010, r 7.15(6)(b)

CHAPTER 5

JUDICIAL INVOLVEMENT LEADING TO A CONDITIONAL ORDER

5.1 APPLICATION FOR A CONDITIONAL ORDER

FPR 2010, r 7.10(2)(a)

An application for a conditional order does not attract a court fee and is considered by a district judge or legal adviser in the absence of the parties. If he/she is satisfied that the applicant has fulfilled the requirements for a divorce by establishing a case both in the application and the supporting statement, he/she will complete and sign a certificate authorising the pronouncement of the conditional order.

The certificate also deals with the costs of the divorce suit itself.

Once the district judge's certificate has been signed, the court office will fix a date and time for the pronouncement of the conditional order by a district judge and inform all parties.

There is no necessity for any party to attend unless there is an issue as to costs.

The new legislation removes the ability for a party to defend the proceedings. However, in the event of a challenge based on issues such as jurisdiction, the legal validity of the marriage, fraud, coercion and/or procedural compliance, the application may be 'disputed'.

FPR 2010, r 7.12

In a disputed case the respondent can make an application.

5.1.1 Costs

The Nuffield Foundation report made recommendations arising from its 'Finding Fault study' and analysed within the report 'Emotionally charged: costs on divorce and dissolution'. Under the new law, while the court will retain a discretion to make a costs order against either party, the circumstances in which an order for costs will be appropriate are likely to be very limited.

Appendix C(21) President's Guidance Divorce, Dissolution and Separation Act 2020: Costs in proceedings for matrimonial and civil partnership orders.

5.1.2 Arrangements for children

It should be noted that the requirement for the court to consider the arrangements for the children before finalising a divorce has been removed, with the repeal of the MCA 1973, s 41.

5.1.3 Dispensing with procedural formalities

In exceptional circumstances, the FPR 2010, r 4.1 may allow a judge to dispense with the formalities set out in this book and pronounce the conditional order immediately (DDSA 2020, s 1(8)) It must be emphasised that this is an exceptional step and it will be taken only in circumstances where:

(a) either an order which the judge considers to be of particular importance cannot be made prior to the pronouncement of the conditional order, or
(b) there is an urgent need to reduce friction and/or resolve issues as between the parties.

If the conditional order is pronounced prior to a further application being issued, an undertaking will have to be given by counsel or solicitors on behalf of the proposed application to:

(a) file an application within a specified period of time, which is unlikely to be more than 48 hours; and
(b) pay the court fee or lodge an application for help with fees at the time of issue.

Possible circumstances in which a divorce order might be expedited in this manner (given this applied to the previous decree hitherto) are:

(a) where the respondent is in the process of dissipating or disposing of family assets which need to be protected by the granting of an injunction pursuant to the MCA 1973, s 37 and where all or a part of those assets are urgently required by the applicant. A hypothetical example might be where the parties, without the benefit of legal advice, have reached agreement to separate and sell the matrimonial home, which is in the respondent's sole name, and agreed to a division of the proceeds to enable both to purchase an alternative property, only for the respondent subsequently to renege on the agreement immediately prior to the completion of the sale of the matrimonial home. In this example, it is likely that there would be an additional requirement for the applicant to be granted an expedited final order on divorce, so that a final financial remedies order could be put into immediate effect.

(b) Formalities can also be dispensed with where a party is terminally ill and there is a wish to finalise divorce and/or financial remedy proceedings prior to death.

5.2 AVOIDANCE OF BRITISH IMMIGRATION LAW

Where after the issue of an application it appears to the court that the parties have married for the purpose of avoiding British immigration law, it is likely that the court will wish to notify the Home Office. If notification has not been given by the court office of its own volition, the judge can be expected to give a direction in this regard when considering the application for conditional order or subsequently.

Information may be sought with regard to the immigration status of a party in proceedings and/or advice as to the possible effect which a court order might have upon that party's immigration status. Enquiry may be made as to whether the Secretary of State wishes to intervene, and protocols have been put in place to facilitate the Family Court communicating with the Home Office to obtain information in relation to immigration matters, and to facilitate communication between judges of the Family Court and of the Immigration and Asylum Chamber.

Note: Communicating with the Home Office in Family Proceedings (PD 12F, Annex 1), the standard form order 9.6 Disclosure Request of Home Office and the President's Guidance of May 2018 on Communicating with UK Visas and Immigration (UKVI) in Family Proceedings Form EX660.

5.3 CHECKLIST FOR APPLYING FOR A CONDITIONAL ORDER

1 Service of the application

(a) Have all parties been properly served and the appropriate acknowledgements of service filed? Although there is an obligation on the part of the court to ensure that the correct form of notice of proceedings with acknowledgement of service attached is served on the recipient, solicitors are advised to check that this has been done.

(b) Has a statement of service been filed, including details as to how the server identified the respondent?

(c) If service has been effected by court bailiff, has he/she lodged a statement of service or has the respondent signed to confirm service?

(d) If none of the above applies, has the district judge made an order dispensing with or deeming service?

2 Written confirmation of request for conditional order to be made

Form D84 is used for an application for a conditional order.

3 The statement in support of the application

(a) Is it on the correct form if required?

(b) Has it been properly completed?

(c) Have all questions been answered?

(d) Have all amendments been initialled?

(e) If an amended or supplemental application has been filed, has the statement been amended to reflect this? In the case of a supplemental application, the statement must also refer to the application.

(f) If the parties are still living together more than 6 months after the date on which irretrievable breakdown occurred, have full details of and reasons for their living arrangements been given?

(g) Does the statement ask, in the case of a divorce application, that the marriage be dissolved on the basis of irretrievable breakdown or, in the case of a judicial separation application, that the applicant may be granted a judicial separation order?

(h) Has one of the alternatives 'husband/wife' been deleted as appropriate?

(i) Is the signature on the acknowledgement of service (or other appropriate document) correctly identified?

(j) If the application has been personally served and identification is established by photograph, the applicant may be required to verify the photograph as being that of the respondent.

(k) Costs may be mentioned (depending on the implementation or otherwise of the Nuffield Foundation research recommendations).

4 Previous court orders

Have any previous court orders referred to within the application been filed?

CHAPTER 6

FINAL ORDER OF DIVORCE

6.1 APPLICATION

MCA 1973, s 1(5)
FPR 2010, r 7.19

Once 6 weeks have elapsed from the date of the conditional order, the applicant(s) can apply, as of right, for a final order of divorce.

FPR 2010, r 7.32

The application for the final order of divorce is made without notice on a standard form D36 or D36A (the latter is used in the event that the conditional order was made on a joint application but an applicant wishes to make a sole application at this stage), and must be signed by the party in person unless solicitors are on record. A fee is no longer payable (save where the petition was filed before 1 July 2013) as the fee for applying for the final order has been incorporated into the fee payable on issue of the application.

Under the reforms there is no provision in the rules for the respondent to object to the issuing of a final order after the period of 6 weeks has elapsed provided that no application to prevent a conditional order being made final has been made pursuant to FPR 2010, r 7.18.

6.2 ABRIDGING TIME

The period of 6 weeks can be abridged (shortened) by a district judge.

Such application may only be made by the party who obtained the conditional order and must be made on notice to the other party. The application attracts a court fee, unless the applicant is exempt from fees. Evidence in support is required, by way of either affidavit or statement and can be provided by either party. It is advisable to check with the court in which the suit is proceeding as to its precise requirements.

There is a general reluctance to abridge time for the granting of a final order unless there are genuinely exceptional circumstances. Judges are, however, usually more willing to expedite the pronouncement of a conditional order. Either way, an application should be supported by affidavit or evidence in writing, setting out why the matter should be viewed as urgent. In particular, if the application is being made because of the impending birth of a child, medical evidence of the expected date of confinement should be provided.

Practitioners are advised to enquire at the family court hearing centre to which the proceedings are transferred for the hearing of the application, as to whether or not an affidavit is required.

Reference should be made to PD 7A, paras 8.3–8.4, which clearly set out the procedure to be followed.

MCA 1973, s 1(5); CPA 2004, s 38(4)

6.3 APPLICATION ON NOTICE

If the applicant does not apply for the final order after the 6-week period, then, subject to any amendments of the rules, the respondent may apply once a further 3 months have elapsed.

FPR 2010, r 7.33(2)(c) MCA 1973, s 9(2); CPA 2004, s 40(2)

Such application must be made to a district judge on notice under the Part 18 procedure, using Form D11. The district judge may require an affidavit in support, or a statement verified by a statement of truth. Accordingly, applicants are advised to check with the relevant court as to local practice.

The application attracts a court fee, unless the applicant is exempt from fees.

There is no provision in the rules for the respondent to apply for the statutory period to be abridged.

MCA 1973, s 9(2)

A final order which has been erroneously obtained before the statutory period provided by the MCA 1973, s 9(2) has elapsed is null and void and, once that fact has been brought to the attention of the court, must be set aside. This is so even though one or both of the parties has remarried.

Manchanda v Manchanda [1995] 2 FLR 590, CA

Exactly the same principle will apply in circumstances where notice of a respondent's application under FPR 2010, r 7.33 has not been served upon the applicant.

Dennis v Dennis [2000] 3 WLR 1443

6.4 APPLICATION AFTER 12 MONTHS FROM CONDITIONAL ORDER

FPR 2010, r 7.32(3)

After 12 months have elapsed from the date of the conditional order, the application for final order by either the applicant or the respondent must be accompanied by an explanation in writing stating:

(a) why the application has not been made earlier;

(b) whether or not the parties have lived together since the date of the conditional order and, if so, between what dates;

(c) whether the applicant:

(i) being the female has given birth to a child since the pronouncement of the conditional order and whether it is alleged that the child is or may be a child of the family; or

(ii) if the respondent is female, whether the applicant has reason to believe that she has given birth to a child since the pronouncement of the conditional order and whether it is alleged that the child is or may be a child of the family.

FPR 2010, r 7.32(4)

The information required by FPR 2010, r 7.32(3) will usually be provided in the form of a written statement, either by the applicant or by solicitors who are on the court record. Some district judges will require the information to be incorporated in a statement verified by a statement of truth, or conceivably in an affidavit. Accordingly, applicants are advised to check with the relevant court as to local practice.

An application made by the party in whose favour the conditional order was pronounced will be considered by a district judge without giving notice to the other party; otherwise the application will be listed for hearing on notice.

6.5 THE EFFECT OF THE DIVORCE (RELIGIOUS MARRIAGES) ACT (D(RM)A) 2002 UPON A FINAL DIVORCE ORDER

D(RM)A 2002, s 1(1)
MCA 1973, s 10A

This Act provides that the court may, on the application of either party, order that the conditional order be not made final until steps have been taken to dissolve a prescribed religious marriage. The MCA 1973 is amended accordingly.

MCA 1973, s 10A(6)

Practitioners should be aware that to date the only prescribed religious marriage is one which has taken place in accordance with the usages of the Jews. Other religions can seek to be 'prescribed' within the legislation (MCA 1973, s 10A(1)(a)(ii)) by the Lord Chancellor prescribing the religion in an order after consulting the Lord Chief Justice and such an order must be made by a statutory instrument.

MCA 1973, s 10A(3)

An order preventing the conditional order being made final may only be made if the court is satisfied that in all the circumstances of the case it is just and reasonable so to do. The order may be revoked at any time.

An application for an order under the MCA 1973, s 10A(2) may be made by either party. MCA 1973, s 10A

The application is made on notice using Form D11 in accordance with the procedure set out in Part 18. The application attracts a court fee unless the applicant is exempt from fees.

Once an order has been made under the MCA 1973, s 10A(2) the order may not be made final until a declaration is produced to the court which shall: FPR 2010, r 7.30

(i) be made and signed by both parties;

(ii) give particulars of the proceedings in which the order under the MCA 1973, s 10A(2) was obtained;

(iii) confirm that such steps as are required to dissolve the marriage in accordance with the religious usages appropriate to the parties and referred to in the MCA 1973, s 10A(1)(a) have been taken;

(iv) be accompanied by a certificate from a religious authority that all such steps have been taken unless the court orders otherwise or such other documents showing the relevant steps have been taken as the court may direct.

The declaration required by FPR 2010 must be filed with the court either before or together with the application for conditional order to be made final. FPR 2010, r 7.30(1)(d)(iii)

If the certificate from the relevant religious authority is not in English it must be accompanied by a translation in English, certified by a notary public or authenticated by a statement of truth. FPR 2010, r 7.30(2)

Note: It is possible for the court to dispense with the filing of a certificate and direct that the parties file other documents to confirm that appropriate steps have been taken. FPR 2010, r 7.30(3)

Practitioners should be aware that unlike a MCA 1973, s 10 stop which is created by the filing of an application, under the provisions of the D(RM)A 2002, it is the order which places a stop on the final order.

Note: For further details of MCA 1973, s 10, see **11.3.10**.

6.6 ISSUE OF THE FINAL DIVORCE ORDER

Once the various steps set out above have been complied with, and subject to the requirements of FPR 2010, r 7.32(2), the final divorce order will be issued. FPR 2010, r 7.32(2)

The court will send a copy of the final divorce order to all parties. FPR 2010, r 7.34(b)

Practitioners should ensure that their client's copy of the final divorce order is endorsed with an original court seal.

A certificate of final divorce order which has been issued in error can be set aside. This can be done on application by either party or of the court's own motion. However, the court will exercise caution before taking such a step because of the potentially far-reaching consequences, for example, either one or both of the parties may have remarried.

FPR 2010, r 29.16

A final divorce order which contains an error or errors on the face of the certificate can be rectified.

MCA 1973, s 10(4)

A final divorce order, which has been inadvertently granted ignoring the requirements of the MCA 1973, s 10(3), is voidable.

A final divorce order which has been made after an applicant or respondent has died is a nullity and therefore of no effect. In these circumstances, the application may be abated. This could potentially be of importance where the surviving spouse is entitled to pension benefits, payable upon the death of the other spouse.

Note: For further details of abatement, see **7.3**.

FPR 2010, r 7.21

It is the final divorce order, and not the conditional order which formally ends the marriage. The date and precise time at which the divorce order is made final is endorsed on the court copy of the conditional order.

This endorsement on the conditional order provides evidence should there be a subsequent issue with regard to matters arising out of the provisions of the Inheritance (Provision for Family and Dependants) Act 1975 or, possibly, an allegation of a bigamous marriage.

FPR 2010, r 7.35(1)

A central index of final orders is maintained by the Central Family Court.

Any person is entitled to request a search of the index. Form D440 is used for the purpose. For each period of 10 years which is searched, a court fee is payable, unless the applicant is exempt from fees.

6.7 FINAL ORDER FOR USE ABROAD

FPR 2010, r 31.18

If the final divorce order is to be produced abroad, for example where a party wishes to remarry abroad, a sealed and certified copy of the final divorce order should be obtained. The certificate of authenticity should be signed by a court officer; in practice it will often be signed by a district judge.

For use in a Member State a certificate, in Form D180 as referred to in Art 39 of the Council Regulation (EC) No 2201/2003 of 27 November 2003, should be attached to the order.

The application for such a certificate must be made, without notice, to the court, which issued the order by way of witness statement or affidavit. FPR 2010, r 31.18

The witness statement or affidavit must contain the information required by FPR 2010, PD 31A, para 6.2 (and paras 6.3, 6.5)

There is no fee payable on the application.

6.8 GENDER RECOGNITION ACT 2004

See **8.2.5** for procedure where an order has been granted under the provisions of the Gender Recognition Act 2004.

CHAPTER 7

CONCLUDING APPLICATIONS OTHER THAN BY FINAL ORDER

7.1 DISMISSAL

In some circumstances, for example when an application for a matrimonial or civil partnership order is not pursued to a conclusion or where the parties have become reconciled, the application can be dismissed.

FPR 2010, rr 18.7–18.9

The application should be made under Part 18, using Form D11. Where the parties have reconciled, the application will be made by consent. If the application is, or may be, opposed, the application should be made on notice. The court will consider whether there should be a hearing.

Once an application for a divorce order has been dismissed, no further steps can be taken on it, other than any outstanding issues relating to costs. If, while there are outstanding petitions pre-dating 6 April 2022 it is the parties' intention to conclude the proceedings on the respondent's petition undefended, the application for decree nisi must be supported by a statement verified by a statement of truth in exactly the same way as would be the case if the matter were proceeding on the prayer in the petition itself.

7.2 WITHDRAWAL

FPR 2010, r 7.9

The application may be withdrawn at any time before it has been served by giving notice in writing to the court. If it has been served, the procedure at **3.3** and **7.1** must be followed.

7.3 NOTICE OF ABATEMENT UPON THE DEATH OF EITHER AN APPLICANT OR A RESPONDENT

Prior to final order, notice of abatement may be filed on the death of either the applicant or the respondent. This does not have to be on a prescribed form and no fee is payable. A precedent is to be found at **Appendix A(4)**.

There may be circumstances in which it is not appropriate to file a notice of abatement.

Once a final order has been made, the death of either party does not affect order, which remains in force for all purposes.

7.4 RESCISSION OF CONDITIONAL ORDER

There are circumstances in which a conditional divorce order or decree of nullity, or a final order of judicial separation (or their civil partnership equivalents) may be rescinded before the final order, or after a judicial separation final order or separation order has been made. For example:

(a) Either party may apply for rescission of the conditional order on the grounds that the parties are reconciled and both consent to the rescission. FPR 2010, r 7.28(2), (3)

(b) Where material facts have not been brought before the court. MCA 1973, s 9(1) CPA 2004, s 40(1)

(c) The respondent may apply if no application has been made to make a final order more than 3 months after the conditional order. MCA 1973, s 9(2) CPA 2004, s 40(2)

(d) Where there has been a change in the law and the parties agree. *S v S (Rescission of Decree Nisi and Pension Sharing Provision)* [2002] 1 FLR 457, Singer J

The divorce order must not be made final whilst an application to rescind is pending. Unless the court dispenses with a hearing, the application will be heard in open court before the same category of judge who pronounced the conditional order and where possible before the judge by whom it was pronounced.

Applications should be made under the Part 18 procedure using Form D11. Proof of consent should be provided where appropriate. The court may deal with the application without a hearing where it does not consider it appropriate, or when the parties agree and the court does not consider that a hearing would be appropriate. FPR 2010, r 18.9

Whilst rescission will usually lead to the ultimate dismissal of the application, this may not always be so. The court may give directions for the future conduct of the application.

7.5 FAILED ATTEMPT AT RECONCILIATION

If, after the pronouncement of the conditional order, an attempted reconciliation fails, in circumstances where neither the MCA 1973, s 6 nor FPR 2010 makes provision, it is suggested that either party should set out the facts in a witness statement verified by a statement of truth or affidavit and apply to a district judge for directions:

(a) as to whether the court is prepared to grant a final divorce order; or

(b) for the rescission of the conditional order and for leave to file a supplemental or further application.

Whilst rescission will usually lead to the ultimate dismissal of the application, this may not always be so. An example of circumstances where the application is unlikely to be dismissed might be where service upon a respondent has been dispensed with and that respondent subsequently makes contact with the court. The proceedings will then be determined in accordance with the procedures set out in the preceding chapters.

CHAPTER 8

OTHER MATRIMONIAL DECREES

8.1 JUDICIAL SEPARATION

8.1.1 Principles

CPA 2004, s 37(1)(d)

As with divorce proceedings, all matters relating to the issue of a judicial separation order and the way it is conducted are determined by the provisions of the MCA 1973, the DDSA 2020 and the FPR 2010. In relation to a civil partnership, the CPA 2004 provides for a separation order which is equivalent to judicial separation (see Chapter 10 for further details).

As with a divorce application, the application for a judicial separation order is issued in a divorce centre (see **2.1** and **Appendix C(1)**). Proceedings will be transferred to an appropriate Family Court hearing centre if a hearing is needed at any stage.

MCA 1973, s 17(1)

An application for judicial separation is dealt with in much the same way as set out in Chapters 1–7 with regard to a divorce application. The requirement for facts to be alleged and found has been removed by DDSA 2020, s 2.

The principal differences are as follows:

(a) an application may be presented within 12 months of the marriage. This is so because the bar contained in the MCA 1973, s 3 relates only to applications for divorce;

MCA 1973, s 17(2)

(b) the marriage may not necessarily have broken down and reference to this will not be included in the application;

(c) the application and any evidence will seek a judicial separation order;

(d) although the application is served in exactly the same way as a divorce application, the notice of proceedings and acknowledgement of service will refer to judicial separation;

(e) the judicial separation order is the only and final order; and

(f) the parties remain married after the judicial separation order is made.

8.1.2 Reasons

There are perhaps 4 reasons why a party to a marriage might issue an application for judicial separation rather than for divorce:

(a) the parties have not been married for more than 12 months;

(b) an applicant (for religious or cultural reasons) is not prepared to divorce the respondent;

(c) the applicant wishes to prevent the respondent from remarrying but at the same time is concerned to have other matrimonial matters resolved, such as the property or financial arrangements.

(d) where an applicant is concerned to preserve pension rights, which would accrue on the death of the respondent but would be lost as a result of a divorce.

8.1.3 Consequences

If an application for a judicial separation order has been presented within 12 months of the date of the marriage, it cannot, even by consent, be amended to seek a divorce order. Accordingly, once the period of 12 months has elapsed, a further application for a divorce order should be presented. It is expected that, as no facts are now required under the reforms, leave of a district judge is not required. Previously the same fact would have to be pleaded in respect of both orders sought. The issuing of the divorce application will have the effect of superseding that for judicial separation. FPR 2010, r 7.4

Where a decree of divorce, as then existed, was erroneously obtained as a result of a petition (as formerly known) filed within the 12-month period being incorrectly amended to seek a divorce, it was set aside because it contravened the mandatory statutory requirement. The court had no discretion in this regard. *Manchanda v Manchanda* [1995] 2 FLR 590, CA

Conversely, where the judicial separation application has been presented after the 12-month period, it is possible to amend that application to one of divorce. Provided no answer has been filed, or application made for an order, the amendment can be made without permission of a district judge or the written consent of the other party. FPR 2010, r 7.15

The MCA 1973, s 4 which did not preclude divorce following a judicial separation order has been removed by the DDSA 2020, s 4.

MCA 1973, s 18(2)

Practitioners' attention is also drawn to the fact that if, while a judicial separation order is in force and the separation is continuing, either of the parties dies intestate, all his/her real and personal property will devolve as if the other party to the marriage had then been dead.

8.2 NULLITY

8.2.1 Principles

CPA 2004, ss 49–54

As with divorce proceedings, all matters relating to the issue of a nullity of marriage order application and the way it is conducted are determined by the provisions of the MCA 1973 and the FPR 2010. In relation to a civil partnership, the CPA 2004 provides for equivalent nullity orders in some cases only (see Chapter 10 for further details).

MFPA 1984, s 31B

As with a divorce application, the application is issued in a divorce centre (see **2.1** and **Appendix C(1)**). Proceedings will be transferred to an appropriate family court hearing centre if a hearing is needed at any stage.

There is a prescribed form of nullity of marriage application, Form D8N.

The application is dealt with in much the same way as set out in Chapters 1 to 7 with regard to the prosecution of a divorce application, except as explained below:

(a) it may be presented within 12 months of marriage. This is because the bar contained in the MCA 1973, s 3 relates only to an application for divorce;
(b) the content will not include reference to the marriage having irretrievably broken down;
(c) the application and any evidence will seek the annulment of the marriage;
(d) although the application is served in exactly the same way as a divorce application, the notice of proceedings and acknowledgement of service will refer to nullity of marriage;

FPR 2010, r 7.1(1)

Before the introduction of the FPR 2010, the 'Special Procedure' did not apply, but now proceedings for a nullity of marriage order under the MCA 1973, s 11 or 12, are be treated in the same way as other matrimonial and civil partnership proceedings. The procedure is set out in Chapter 5.

As with divorce proceedings, a conditional order will be pronounced and, after the expiration of the statutory period of 6 weeks, an application can be made for a final order.

The general rule is that where an application for a nullity of marriage order is defended, a hearing is in public, subject to the matters set out at FPR 2010, r 7.30, which provides that a hearing, or part of it, may be in private if:

(a) publicity would defeat the object of the hearing;

(b) it involves matters relating to national security;

(c) it involves confidential information (including information relating to personal financial matters) and publicity would damage that confidentiality;

(d) a private hearing is necessary to protect the interests of any child or protected party;

(e) it is a hearing of an application made without notice and it would be unjust to any respondent for there to be a public hearing;

(f) the court considers this to be necessary, in the interests of justice.

However, in any proceedings for a nullity of marriage order, evidence on the question of sexual capacity shall be heard in camera (private) unless in any case the judge is satisfied that any such evidence shall be heard in open court. MCA 1973, s 48(2)

8.2.2 Void marriage

MCA 1973, s 11

A marriage may be annulled on the grounds that it is void or voidable. A void marriage never existed and therefore a nullity of marriage order pronounced on this basis means that the parties were never married. This is distinct from the situation where there was no marriage at all.

The grounds for presenting such an application are:

(a) the marriage was celebrated between persons who are related within the prohibited degrees (for example, brother and sister). For full details, see the Marriage Act 1949, Sch 1 (as amended by the Marriage (Prohibited Degrees of Relationship) Act 1986);

(b) the marriage was celebrated when one of the parties was under the age of 16 years when this was the age of consent, noting that the minimum age is now intended to be raised to 18 years and will be amended by the new Marriage and Civil Partnership (Minimum Age) Act 2022, which is not yet in force (it has received Royal Assent but has no commencement date at time of writing);

(c) one or more of the formalities required by law were not complied with, of which the following are more likely to arise:
   (i) a minor aged 16 or 17 years married without the consent of his/her parent or guardian, when this was the age of consent, noting that the minimum age is now raised to 18 years;
   (ii) marriage banns were not published or not published correctly;
   (iii) the marriage ceremony took place after the expiration of 3 months from the banns being published;
   (iv) the place of celebration of the marriage was not licensed;
   (v) the person celebrating the marriage was not properly licensed; or
   (vi) a party to the marriage married using a false name;

(d) a party to the marriage was already lawfully married or a civil partner (bigamy); and

(e) a polygamous marriage was entered into outside England and Wales when either party was domiciled in England and Wales at the time of the marriage and at least one party had another spouse at the time of the marriage.

8.2.3 Voidable marriage

MCA 1973, s 12

A voidable marriage is one which is valid unless annulled by a nullity of marriage order.

The grounds for presenting such an application are:

(a) the incapacity of either party to consummate the marriage. Note that an impotent man or woman can apply on the grounds of his/her own incapacity to consummate the marriage;

(b) the wilful refusal of the respondent to consummate the marriage;

Note: That these grounds do not apply to the marriage of a same sex couple.

Marriage (Same Sex Couples) Act 2013

(c) that either party to the marriage did not give a valid consent to the marriage as a consequence of duress or mistaken identity, or whilst suffering unsoundness of mind (want of consent). Note that a person of unsound mind may file his/her own application, where necessary presenting it through a litigation friend;

(d) that, at the time of the marriage, either party, though capable of giving a valid consent, was suffering from a mental disorder within the meaning of the Mental Health Act 1983 to such an extent as to be unfit for marriage;

(e) that the respondent was suffering from venereal disease, in a communicable form, at the time of the marriage; or

(f) the respondent was pregnant by another man at the time of the marriage;

(g) that an interim gender recognition certificate under the Gender Recognition Act 2004 has, after the time of the marriage, been issued to either party to the marriage – see **8.2.5**;

(h) that the respondent is a person whose gender at the time of the marriage had become the acquired gender under the Gender Recognition Act 2004 – see **8.2.5.**

Applications under the MCA 1973, s 12(1)(e) or (f) should state whether the applicant was, at the time of the marriage, ignorant of the facts alleged, as the court may not grant a nullity of marriage order unless satisfied that at the date of the marriage the applicant was ignorant of the facts alleged. MCA 1973, s 13(3)

Further, the court must not grant a nullity of marriage order on the ground that a marriage is voidable if the respondent satisfies the court that:

(a) the applicant, knowing that the marriage could be avoided, continued the relationship with the respondent in such a manner as to lead the respondent to reasonably believe that no step would be taken; and

(b) it would be unjust to the respondent to grant the decree. MCA 1973, s 13(1)

The former rule requiring the leave of a district judge when a respondent is suffering from a mental disorder has not been repeated in the FPR 2010, but the general rules contained at Part 15 as to protected parties apply, and a protected party who lacks capacity will require a litigation friend. Vulnerable parties are further protected by FPR 2010, Part 3A and PD3AA. FPR 2010, r 15.2

Where an applicant seeks a nullity of marriage order under the MCA 1973, s 12(1)(d) (mental disorder) and the respondent files an answer containing no more than a simple denial of the facts stated in the application, the respondent must, if intending to rebut the matters FPR 2010, r 7.27(2) stated in the application, give notice to the court of that intention when filing the answer.

MCA 1973, s 13(4)

Proceedings under the MCA 1973, s 12(1)(c), (d), (e) or (f) as set out above must be instituted within 3 years of the marriage unless a district judge gives leave to issue an application after this time if the applicant has at some time during that period suffered from a mental disorder within the meaning of the Mental Health Act 1983 and it would be unjust to the respondent to grant the nullity of marriage order.

FPR 2010, r 7.29
PD 7B

In a case seeking a nullity of marriage order of an opposite sex couple on the grounds of incapacity to consummate or wilful refusal to do so, the court must determine whether medical examiners should be appointed to examine the parties or either of them, but only where it is necessary for the proper disposal of the case. This will not usually be necessary where the application is not contested or defended. Application should be made by the Part 18 procedure, using Form D11.

CPA 2004, ss 49–54

Civil partnerships have different provisions for nullity – see Chapter 10.

8.2.4 Application for a conditional order using Form D84

Application for a conditional order is made using Form D84 and where it is undefended supported by a statement in Form D80F in respect of void marriages and Form D80G in respect of voidable marriages.

8.2.5 Gender Recognition Act 2004

The Gender Recognition Act 2004 provides transsexual people with legal recognition in their acquired gender. Schedules 2 and 4 to the Act amended the MCA 1973 by adding 2 new grounds of annulment under s 12 (voidable marriages). This also applies to civil partnerships. These are:

(i) that an interim gender recognition certificate under the Gender Recognition Act 2004 has, after the time of the marriage, been issued to either party to the marriage;

(ii) that the respondent is a person whose gender at the time of the marriage had become the acquired gender under the Gender Recognition Act 2004.

GRA 2004, s 21

A person who has changed gender in another country is not automatically recognised in their acquired gender in the United Kingdom. A list of approved countries and territories appears at **Appendix C(14)**.

All applications for gender recognition are determined by the Gender Recognition Panel, who may be contacted at:

PO Box 9300
Leicester LE1 8DJ
Website: www.gov.uk/apply-gender-recognition-certificate/how-to-apply

Following the coming into force of the Marriage (Same Sex Couples) Act 2013, it is possible for a marriage to continue following a change of gender by one spouse, if both spouses wish it to continue.

Under the previous law, transsexual people who were married or in a civil partnership had to end their marriage or civil partnership before a full gender recognition certificate could be issued. The Marriage (Same Sex Couples) Act 2013, Sch 5 amends the Gender Recognition Act 2004 to enable an existing marriage registered in England and Wales or outside the UK to continue where one or both parties change their legal gender and both parties wish to remain married. This is a 'protected marriage' defined in Sch 5, para 14. The Marriage (Same Sex Couples) Act 2013 also amends the Gender Recognition Act 2004 to enable a 'protected civil partnership' (defined in Sch 5, para 14 as a civil partnership under the law of England and Wales) to continue where both parties change their legal gender simultaneously and wish to remain in their civil partnership.

GRA 2004, Sch 2, paras 3 and 4

If a person who is married or in a civil partnership is granted a gender recognition certificate, the certificate will be an interim certificate only. The certificate will have a lettered prefix and a 6-digit serial number and will be sealed by the panel. The certificate is valid for a period of 6 months from the date of issue, and may only be used to enable either spouse to apply for the annulment of the marriage. This is a necessary legal precondition to obtaining a full gender recognition certificate. Once the 6 month period has elapsed it is not possible for the court to annul the marriage. It will therefore be necessary to apply for further interim gender recognition certificate.

In proceedings based on the issue of an interim gender recognition certificate, the court must, on making the final divorce order, issue a full gender recognition certificate to the person in whose favour the interim certificate was granted.

GRA 2004, s 5

FPR 2010, r 29.6(2)

Documents in proceedings concerning gender recognition must, while they are in the custody of the court, be kept in a place of special security.

8.2.6 Procedure

FPR 2010, r 7.26

The requirements for the issue of an application under the MCA 1973, s 12(1)(g) and (h) are basically the same as for any other application. The applicant to such proceedings may be the person who has acquired the new gender. It is no longer necessary to file a copy of the interim gender recognition certificate, as there is provision for the court to notify the Secretary of State. It remains good practice.

FPR 2010, r 7.26(4)(b)

If a full gender recognition certificate has been issued to the respondent, the applicant must file a copy of that full certificate with the application unless the court, on an application made without notice, directs otherwise.

GRA 2004, Sch 2, paras 3 and 4

An application based on the MCA 1973, s 12(1)(g) must be issued within 6 months of the date of issue of the gender recognition certificate.

FPR 2010, r 7.26

On the issue of an application based on an interim gender recognition certificate the court must notify the Secretary of State (care of the Gender Recognition Panel) of the issue of the proceedings, with a copy of the interim gender recognition certificate, if filed, and details of the names and parties of the marriage, the date and place of the marriage, and the last address at which the parties lived together as husband and wife (or the civil partnership equivalents) and such other information as the court officer considers appropriate.

FPR 2010, PD 7D, para 3

The title of the cause and the use of names is set out in FPR 2010, r 7, PD 7D. The application should give the name currently being used by the party followed by 'formerly known as … (married name)'. The court will use full current names, with initials only in any court list. Titles (ie Mr, Mrs, Miss etc) should be omitted.

Application for a conditional order is made in the same way as with any other nullity application.

8.2.7 Procedure after pronouncement of a conditional divorce order under the MCA 1973, s 12(1)(g)

GRA 2004, s 5

Where a conditional divorce order is pronounced on the basis of an interim gender recognition certificate the court must, within 2 days of pronouncement, notify the Secretariat to the Gender Recognition Panel and request the Panel to provide the court with an unsealed and undated full gender recognition certificate for issue together with the final divorce order.

On issue of a final divorce order under the MCA 1973, s 12(1)(g) (or its civil partnership equivalent), the court must:

(i) date, seal and issue the full gender recognition certificate and dispatch the original to the party in whose favour it has been issued. A copy must be retained on the court file;
(ii) fax a copy of the dated and sealed certificate to the Secretary of State, care of the Gender Recognition Panel. The Secretary of State will then notify the Registrar General of the issue of the certificate;
(iii) telephone the Panel on the same day to confirm that the fax has been received.

8.2.8 Correction of full gender recognition certificate

Application may be made to the court for the correction of a full gender recognition certificate. GRA 2004, s 6

The application must be made to the court which issued the certificate unless otherwise directed. FPR 2010, r 8.3

The application must be made using Form FP1 in accordance with the procedure at Part 19 of the FPR 2010. FPR 2010, r 8.1

Where the applicant is the person to whom the original certificate was issued, the Secretary of State must be a party; where the applicant is the Secretary of State, the person to whom the original certificate was issued must be a party. FPR 2010, r 8.4

Where the court issues a corrected full gender recognition certificate, a court officer must send a copy of the corrected certificate to the Secretary of State. FPR 2010, r 8.5

8.2.9 Appeals under the GRA 2004, s 8(1)

An applicant to a Gender Recognition Panel has a right to appeal to the High Court or the family court on a point of law against a decision of the panel to reject the application. This may be heard in private if the applicant so requests. The court may either allow the appeal and issue the certificate applied for, allow the appeal and refer the matter to the same or another Panel, or dismiss the appeal. GRA 2004, s 8(1)–(3)

The Secretary of State may refer an application to the High Court or the family court if it considers it was granted by fraud. The court will either GRA 2004, s 8(5)–(6)

confirm the decision, or quash it, revoke the gender recognition certificate, and make any other appropriate consequential order.

Appeals are considered under FPR 2010, Part 30 and PD 30A. While the Act provides for an appeal to the High Court or the family court, FPR 2010, r 5.4 means that the proceedings must be in the family court unless other proceedings relating to the same parties are already being heard by the High Court, or the court directs otherwise.

FC(C&DB)R 2014, r 7(1)(d)

In the family court, the appeal will be dealt with by a judge of High Court level.

Where the appeal is in the High Court, the appeal notice must be filed in the Principal Registry of the Family Division of the High Court. When the Family Court was created by the Crime and Courts Act 2013, the Principal Registry of the Family Division was superseded for most purposes by the Central Family Court. However, for certain purposes, including this one, the PRFD continues to exist. Its address is Royal Courts of Justice, Strand, London WC2A 2LL.

FPR 2010, PD 30A, paras 5.27–5.30

The appeal notice must be served on the Secretary of State and the President of the Gender Recognition Panels. The Secretary of State may appear and be heard. If the High Court issues a gender recognition certificate the court officer must send a copy of that certificate to the Secretary of State.

8.3 PRESUMPTION OF DEATH AND DISSOLUTION OF MARRIAGE

The arrangements by which a person who believes that reasonable grounds exist for presuming the death of their spouse may present an application to the court for the court to have it presumed that the other party is dead have been amended, extended and codified in the Presumption of Death Act 2013. As those arrangements now extend beyond the matrimonial relationship, they are considered separately at **9.4–9.6**.

CHAPTER 9

DECLARATORY DECREES

9.1 MARITAL OR CIVIL PARTNERSHIP STATUS

FLA 1986, s 55

A declaration may be sought from the High Court or the family court as to:

(a) the validity of a marriage at its inception;

(b) whether on a specified date the marriage subsisted;

(c) whether on a specified date the marriage did not subsist;

(d) whether a decree pronounced outside the jurisdiction should be recognised in England and Wales; or

(e) whether a decree pronounced outside the jurisdiction should not be recognised in England and Wales.

Similar powers in relation to civil partnerships are contained in the Civil Partnership Act ('CPA') 2004, s 58. See Chapter 10.

FPR 2010, r 8.18(a)

All matters relating to the issue of an application for declaration as to marital status and the way that it is conducted are governed by the Family Law Act 1986 (FLA 1986), Pt III and FPR 2010, Pt 8, Ch 5 by the Part 19 procedure.

For the content of the application see Form D70. The application concludes with a statement of truth.

The new FPR 2010, PDs 17A and 22A (statements of truth) clarify that providing false information can lead to contempt of court proceedings.

FPR 2010, r 5.1, PD 5A

A copy of any relevant marriage certificate, decree of divorce or order must be sent to the court with the application; if the document is not in English, a certified translation of it must also be supplied.

FLA 1986, s 55(3), FPR 2010, Part 8, Ch 5

It is possible for a third party to apply for a declaration as to marital status, but the court may refuse to hear the application if it considers that the applicant does not have a sufficient interest in the determination of that application.

FPR 2010, r 8.20(1)

If the application is issued by a third party, both parties to the marriage or civil partnership will be respondents.

The court has jurisdiction to consider an application for a declaration as to marital status if either party to the marriage to which the application relates:

(a) is domiciled in England and Wales at the date of presentation of the application;

(b) has been habitually resident in England and Wales throughout the period of 1 year ending with that date; or

(c) died before that date and was at death domiciled in England and Wales or had been habitually resident in England and Wales throughout the period of 1 year ending with the date of death. FLA 1986, s 55(2) FPR 2010, r 5.1

Subsequent procedure is similar to the procedure for divorce proceedings, although there are some significant differences. These include a statement setting out the circumstances and full details of all those whose interest may be affected by the proceedings. FPR 2010, r 8.20

The applicant must, when filing the application, file the written evidence on which they intend to rely. FPR 2010, r 19.7

There is also a requirement for the Treasury Solicitor, acting on behalf of the Attorney General, to be given not less than 1 month's notice of the intention to commence proceedings relating to marital status.

Note: This requirement of the Rules goes further than FLA 1986, s 59. Full details of the procedure to be followed are set out in *Rayden*, Chapter 34.13. FPR 2010, r 8.21(1) and Form D70.

The application is served on all respondents, together with any written evidence on which the applicant intends to rely, a notice of proceedings in Form FP1B, with an acknowledgement of service in Form FP5. FPR 2010, r 19.7 FPR 2010, r 8.20(1)

On receipt of the acknowledgment of service, the case should be referred to the district judge who will give directions as to any other persons who are to be made a respondent or given notice of the proceedings. FPR 2010, r 8.20(4)

Once the respondent has indicated his/her intentions with regard to the future conduct of the proceedings, the Treasury Solicitor is in a position to obtain instructions from the Attorney General as to whether or not it is his intention to intervene.

It is open to the Attorney General to intervene in any event, and reference should be made to FPR 2010, r 8.21(2), (3), (4), (5) in this regard.

A respondent wishing to defend the proceedings should give brief details in written evidence filed with the acknowledgement of service. This will be considered FPR 2010, r 19.7(3) by the district judge when the acknowledgement is referred in accordance with rule 8.20(4). If the district judge considers that a formal pleading should be filed appropriate directions will be given.

FC(C&DB)R 2014, Sch 1(3)(a)

It should be noted that, whether defended or not, directions will be given by a circuit judge, normally at a case management hearing, leading to a final hearing before a High Court or circuit judge in open court.

FLA 1986, s 60(4)

The court may direct that the application be heard in camera.

At the conclusion of the hearing, the judge will make a declaration as to whether or not there is a valid and subsisting marriage, divorce or civil partnership. The declaration is made in the form of a decree in Form D70A which is the only and final decree.

9.2 PARENTAGE

FLA 1986, s 55A(1)

Any person may apply for a declaration that the person named in the application is or was the parent of another person so named.

All matters relating to the issue of an application for a declaration of parentage and the way it is conducted are governed by the FLA 1986, Pt III and the FPR 2010, Pt 8, Ch 5.

For the content of the application see Form C63.

FPR 2010, r 5.1
Form C63

A copy of the relevant birth certificate must be sent to the court with the application, unless the court directs otherwise.

FPR 2010, r 8.20(1)

The respondents to the application will be:

(a) the person whose parentage is in issue, except where that person is a child; and

(b) any person who is, or who is alleged to be, the mother or father of the person whose parentage is in issue, unless that person is the applicant.

The court has jurisdiction to consider an application for a declaration as to parentage if the person whose parentage is in issue or the person whose parenthood is in issue:

(a) is domiciled in England and Wales on the date of the presentation of the application;

(b) has been habitually resident in England and Wales throughout the period of one year ending with that date; or

(c) died before that date and either was at death domiciled in England and Wales, or had been habitually resident in England and Wales throughout the period of one year ending with the date of death. FLA 1986, s 55A(2)

The application must conclude with a statement of truth. FPR 2010, r 5.1 FPR 2010, PD17A and PD22A

Frequently, the application will be issued on behalf of a child and thus the proceedings may have to be commenced by his/her litigation friend. FPR 2010, rr 16.6, 16.7, PD 16A

Where the mother is a respondent, an alternative litigation friend may be necessary, and accordingly, consideration will need to be given as to the appointment of another close relative, such as a grandparent, aunt or uncle.

A written consent to act, ie a certificate of suitability, must be filed by the litigation friend. If the application is presented through a litigation friend, the statement of truth will be by the litigation friend. FPR 2010, PD 16A

There is no requirement for the Treasury Solicitor, acting on behalf of the Attorney General, to be given notice of the intention to commence proceedings. FPR 2010, r 8.21(1)

The application will be served with a notice of proceedings in Form FP1B and an acknowledgement of service in Form FP5. As with an application for declaration of marital status, any respondent who wishes to defend the application should file written evidence together with the acknowledgement of service. This will be considered by a district judge on referral of the acknowledgement of service. If the district judge considers that a formal pleading should be filed appropriate directions will be given. FPR 2010, r 19.7(3)

A case management hearing will normally be fixed on receipt of the acknowledgment of service, at which the district judge may give directions as to any DNA or scientific test, the results of which will need to be available for the trial judge at the final hearing.

Note: See **Appendix B** for the procedure for obtaining these tests.

The court is required, within 21 days of the declaration being made, to notify the Registrar General by forwarding to him a copy of the declaration in Form C63A together with a copy of the application in Form C63. FPR 2010, r 8.22(2) FLA 1986, s 55A(7)

However, it is prudent to ensure that the appropriate steps have been taken by the court.

9.3 LEGITIMACY OR LEGITIMATION

A declaration may be sought that a person:

FLA 1986, s 56(1)(b)
FLA 1986, s 56(2)

(a) is a legitimate child of his/her parents;
(b) has become a legitimated person;
(c) has not become a legitimated person.

FPR 2010, r 8.18(c)

For the definition of 'legitimacy', see Legitimacy Acts of 1926 and 1976.

All matters relating to the issue of an application for a declaration of legitimacy or legitimation and the way it is conducted are governed by the FLA 1986, Pt III and the FPR 2010, Pt 8, Ch 5.

For the content of the application see Form C64.

FPR 2010, r 5.1
Form C64

A copy of the applicant's birth certificate must be sent to the court with the application unless the court directs otherwise.

FPR 2010, r 8.20(1)

The respondents to the application will be the applicant's father and mother or the survivor of them.

Where a parent is dead this may mean that the grandparents will be respondents.

The procedure to be followed is as set out at **9.1**. The family court has jurisdiction to consider an application for a declaration as to legitimacy or legitimation if the applicant:

(a) is domiciled in England and Wales on the date of the presentation of the application; or

FLA 1986, s 56(3)

(b) has been habitually resident in England and Wales throughout the period of one year ending with that date.

FPR 2010, r 5.1
Form C64

The application must conclude with a statement of truth.

FPR 2010, r 8.21(1)
FPR 2010, PD17A and PD22A

There is a requirement for the Treasury Solicitor, acting on behalf of the Attorney General, to be given not less than one month's notice of the intention to commence proceedings. As described at **9.2**, it may be necessary for a litigation friend to act for the applicant.

9.4 PRESUMPTION OF DEATH

The Presumption of Death Act 2013 (PDA 2013) came into force on 1 October 2014. It simplified, and largely codified, the procedure for seeking a declaration that a missing person is presumed to have died. Under the previous law, a number of statutes contained procedures dealing with different aspects of a missing person's affairs, and at common law a person might be presumed dead after a 7-year absence, unless other evidence showed that they were still alive.

Under PDA 2013, when the High Court makes a declaration that a person is presumed to have died, details are sent to the Registrar-General who enters details in the Register of Presumed Deaths created under the Act. Once that has been done, a certified copy of the entry in the register is treated as proof of the missing person's death in the same way as a death certificate. Presumption of Death Act 2013, Sch 1, para 4

9.4.1 Jurisdiction

When a missing person is thought to have died, or has not been known to be alive for at least 7 years, any person may apply to the High Court for a declaration that the missing person is presumed to be dead. PDA 2013, s 1(1), 1(2)

The court has jurisdiction to hear an application provided that:

(a) The *missing person* was domiciled in England and Wales on the day on which he or she was last known to be alive; or

(b) The *missing person* was habitually resident in England and Wales throughout a period of 1 year ending with that day; or PDA 2013, s 1(3)

(c) The application is made by the missing person's spouse or civil partner, and the *applicant* either is domiciled in England and Wales on the day on which the application is made; or has been habitually resident in England and Wales throughout a period of 1 year ending with that day. PDA 2013, s 1(4)

While any person may apply, if the application is not made by the missing person's spouse, civil partner, parent, child or sibling, the court must dismiss the application if it considers that the applicant does not have a sufficient interest in the determination of the application. PDA 2013, s 1(5)

9.4.2 Issue of Proceedings

Proceedings under the PDA 2013 may be issued in the Chancery Division or the Family Division of the High Court. The procedure is set out in the CPR 1998 ('CPR 1998'), rr 57.17–57.23 and Practice Direction 57B. The CPR 1998 rather than the FPR 2010 apply to the proceedings, save that the Family Procedure Rules 2010 rather than the CPR 1998, Pt 40 apply to the drawing up and service of orders. CPR 1998, r 57.18 FPR 2010, rr 29.11, 29.13, 29.14

The proceedings are issued under the CPR 1998, Pt 8. The claim form, which is the standard Part 8 claim form N208, must include or be accompanied by the following information required by Practice Direction 57B, where that information is known:

'(1) Information about the claimant

(a) the claimant's name and address;

(b) the relationship of the claimant to the missing person; and

(c) if the claimant is not the missing person's spouse, civil partner, parent, child or sibling, details of the claimant's interest in the determination of the application;

(2) Information about the missing person

(a) the missing person's name and surname, and any other names by which the missing person is or has formerly been known;

(b) the missing person's gender;

(c) the missing person's maiden surname (if any);

(d) the missing person's date and place of birth;

(e) the occupation of the missing person;

(f) the occupation, name and surname of –

(i) the missing person's spouse or civil partner (or late spouse or civil partner if the marriage or civil partnership ended on death);

(ii) where the missing person was under 16 years of age, the missing person's parents;

(g) the missing person's National Insurance number;

(h) the date on which missing person is thought to have died, or on which the missing person was last known have been alive;

(i) on which of the grounds in section 1(4) of the 2013 Act the court is considered to have jurisdiction to entertain the claim;

(j) the usual or last known address of the missing person; and

(k) the name and address of the spouse or civil partner, parents, children or siblings of the missing person (if any, and if not the claimant);

(3) Information about steps taken to trace the missing person

(a) details of any enquiries made or other steps taken to trace the missing person or confirm when the missing person was last known to be alive; and

(b) details of the results of such enquiries or other steps;

(4) Information about the missing person's property

(a) an estimate of the total value of the assets of the missing person;

(b) details of property owned by the missing person; and

(c) details of the interest of any other person in the missing person's property which it is sought to have determined by the court; and

(5) Information about advertisement and recipients of notice of the claim

(a) details of the newspaper in which the claimant proposes to advertise the claim; and

(b) details of the persons to whom the claimant is giving notice of the claim and, where notice is being given to a person under rule 57.20(1)(f), the nature of that person's interest in the claim.' CPR 1998, PD 57B

It has been said that this is a procedure without any defendants as such; rather, there is a class of potential intervenors, who must be given notice in case they wish to take part in the proceedings.

It has been suggested that the appropriate title for proceedings under this Act is '[Name], claimant, in the matter of [name of missing person]' instead of, for example, naming the missing person as defendant. *Greathead v Greathead* [2017] EWHC 1154 (Ch)

9.4.3 Service of proceedings

Notice of the claim must be given by serving a copy of it on each of the following:

(a) the spouse or civil partner of the missing person;

(b) any parent of the missing person;

(c) any child of the missing person;

(d) any sibling of the missing person;

(e) if there are no persons within sub-paragraphs (a) to (d), the nearest relative of the missing person known to the claimant; and

CPR 1998, r 57.20(1)

(f) any other person (including in particular any insurance company) appearing to the claimant to have an interest in the claim.

CPR 1998, r 57.19(4); PD 57B para 1.3

9.4.4 Issue of claim form without serving notice

Where the claimant believes there to be no person within the above categories, the claimant may apply to the court for permission to issue a claim form without serving notice on any person. The application must explain why the claimant believes that there is no such person.

9.4.5 Advertising the claim

The claimant must within 7 days of issue of the claim, ensure that notice of it is published (in the form set out in CPR PD 57B) in at least one newspaper circulating in the vicinity of the last known address of the missing person.

CPR 1998, r 57.21

The claimant must, at least 5 days before the hearing, file a copy of the page of the newspaper bearing the advertisement and the date on which it was published.

9.4.6 Interveners

The Attorney General may intervene in proceedings under the PDA 2013. The court may at any stage direct that the papers relating to the matter be sent to the Attorney General. It may so order on the application of a party or on its own initiative.

The spouse, civil partner, parent, child, or sibling of the missing person may intervene.

Any other person may intervene only with the permission of the court.

Intervention for this purpose includes arguing any question before the court or seeking a determination under the PDA 2013, s 4 or 7.

PDA 2013, ss 10, 11 CPR 1998, r 57.22

Where permission to intervene is given, it may be given on conditions and the court may give case management directions.

9.4.7 Orders to provide information

At any stage of an application under the PDA 2013, the court may order a person who is not a party to the proceedings to provide information relevant to the question of whether the missing person is alive or dead.

Such an order may only be made where it is necessary to do so. It may be made on the application of a party or without such an application (but in any event prior notice of the intention to make the order must be given to any person who the court considers is likely to be affected by it). Notice of an application for such an order must be served at least 14 days before the hearing of the application.

An order may not require the provision of information:

(a) which is permitted or required to be withheld on grounds of public interest immunity;

(b) which a person is entitled to refuse to provide on grounds of legal professional privilege;

(c) the provision of which might incriminate the person providing it, or their spouse or civil partner.

PDA 2013, s 12
CPR 1998, r 57.23

9.4.8 Case management

The claim (whether for a declaration of presumed death or for a variation order: see **9.5**) must be listed for case management directions at least 28 days after issue. The Practice Direction states that 'where practicable' this should be no later than 56 days after issue, but that depends on the resources of the Court Service.

A longer period is prescribed if the claim form has been served out of the jurisdiction

The court must notify all those who have filed notice of intention to intervene (or applied for permission to intervene) of the date of the directions hearing.

CPR 1998, PD 54B, para 1.4

9.4.9 Declaration under the Act

The court must make a declaration under the PDA 2013 if it is satisfied that the missing person

(a) has died or

(b) has not been known to be alive for a period of at least 7 years.

The declaration must include a finding as to the date and time of the missing person's death.

PDA 2013, s 2(2)

The PDA 2013, s 2(3) and (4) prescribe the findings to be made where:

(a) the court is satisfied that the missing person has died but is uncertain as to the precise time of death, or

(b) the court is not satisfied that the missing person has died but is satisfied that the missing person has not been known to be alive for at least 7 years.

9.4.10 Effect of Declaration

Provided that it has not been appealed against and the period for bringing an appeal has expired, a declaration under the PDA 2013:

(a) is conclusive of the missing person's death and of the date and time of it;

PDA 2013, s 3

(b) is effective against all persons and for all purposes, including the acquisition of an interest in property, and the ending of a marriage or civil partnership to which the missing person was a party.

When making a declaration under the PDA 2013, the court may determine any question relating to an interest in property which arises as a result of the declaration, and may determine the domicile of the missing person at the time of his or her presumed death.

The court may make such order as it considers reasonable in relation to any interest in property acquired as a result of the declaration. Such an order may direct that the value of any interest in property acquired as a result of the declaration shall not be recoverable if the court makes a variation order. It may direct that the value of the interest:

(a) is not to be recoverable in any circumstances; or

(b) is not to be recoverable where conditions specified in the order are met.

9.4.11 Register of Presumed Deaths

PDA 2013, s 15, Sch 1

A Register of Presumed Deaths is maintained by the Registrar-General, and may be searched in the same way as the registers of births, deaths and marriages. Entries in the Register of Presumed Deaths are cross-referenced to the corresponding entries in the register of deaths.

PDA 2013, Sch 1, paras 1(1), 2(1)

When the court makes a declaration under the Act, it must send a copy of the declaration to the Registrar-General, together with certain prescribed information; similarly if the court makes a variation order: see **9.5**.

9.5 VARIATION AND FURTHER ORDERS

9.5.1 Variation order

Although a declaration under the PDA 2013 is stated to be conclusive, the High Court may make a subsequent order varying or revoking it (a 'variation order').

The commonest situation where a variation order is likely to be appropriate is where the missing person reappears, having been missing for over 7 years and consequently having been declared to be presumed dead.

The High Court must refuse to hear an application for a variation order if it considers that the applicant does not have a sufficient interest in the outcome.

9.5.2 Procedure

The application for a variation order is made in the same way as the application for a declaration (see **9.4.2–9.4.5**).

Practice Direction 57B requires the claim form for a variation order to include or be accompanied by the following (where known) –

'(1) Information about the claimant

(a) the claimant's name and address;

(b) the relationship of the claimant to the missing person; and

(c) details of the claimant's interest in the determination of the application;

(2) Information about previous claim and missing person's property

(a) details of the declaration of presumed death or (as the case may be) previous variation order which it is sought to have varied or revoked;

(b) details of the circumstances which are claimed to justify a variation order, and evidence of the enquiries made and other steps taken to verify them and their outcomes; and

(c) details of any interest in property acquired as a result of the declaration of presumed death or (as the case may be) previous variation order which it is sought to have varied or revoked; and

(3) Information about advertisement and recipients of notice of the claim

(a) details of the newspaper in which the claimant proposes to advertise the claim; and

(b) details of the persons to whom the claimant is giving notice of the claim and, where notice is being given to a person under rule 57.20(2)(g), the nature of that person's interest in the claim.'

9.5.3 Effect of a variation order

PDA 2013, s 6(1)
A variation order does not of itself affect any interest in property acquired as a result of a declaration under the Act (but see the court's powers under the PDA 2013, s 7 – **9.5.4**).

PDA 2013, s 6(2)
A variation order does not revive a marriage or civil partnership that was brought to an end by the declaration.

When it makes a variation order, the court may

(a) determine any question which relates to an interest in property and arises as a result of the variation order, and

PDA 2013, s 7(1)
(b) determine the domicile of the missing person at the time of his or her presumed death.

9.5.4 Further orders as to property interests

PDA 2013, s 7(2)
When making a variation order, the court must make such further order (if any) as it considers reasonable in relation to any interest in property acquired as a result of the declaration varied or revoked by the order ('the original declaration')

but:

PDA 2013, s 7(3)
it must not make an order under the PDA 2013, s 7(2) if the application for the variation order was made after the end of the period of 5 years beginning with the day on which the original declaration was made, unless it considers that there are exceptional circumstances which make it appropriate to do so;

PDA 2013, s 7(5)
the order does not affect income that accrued in the period between the making of the original declaration and the making of the variation order;

the order does not affect or provide grounds to challenge –

(a) a related good faith transaction, or

(b) an interest in property acquired under such a transaction.

A 'related good faith transaction' for these purposes is a transaction under which a person acquires an interest in property in good faith and for value from –

(a) a person who acquired an interest in the property (or any part of it) as a result of the original declaration, or

PDA 2013, s 7(6)
PDA 2013, ss 7(2), (4), 8(2)–(4)
(b) a person who acquired an interest in the property (or any part of it) from a person described in paragraph (a), whether directly or indirectly.

Where property acquired as a result of the original declaration is held on trust, the court may order that a person who but for the PDA 2013, s 6(1) would have an interest in the relevant property should have the property still in the hands of the trustees (or its value, if the trust property has been distributed) made over to him.

Where an insurer has paid a capital sum as a result of the original declaration (other than by way of annuity or periodical payment) and the facts justify such an order, the court may order that the whole or part of the capital sum should be repaid to the insurer. PDA 2013, ss 7(2), (4), 8(5)–(7)

Accordingly, the court may direct the trustees of a trust affected by a declaration under the Act to take out an insurance policy against any claim arising as a result of an order under the PDA 2013, s 7(2). PDA 2013, s 13(1)

The premium payable in respect of such a policy may be paid out of the trust property. PDA 2013, s 13(3)

Similarly, before paying out a capital sum as a result of a declaration under the Act, insurers may require the recipient to take out an insurance policy in respect of any claim which might arise in the event of a variation order being made. PDA 2013, s 14

9.6 RESIDUAL JURISDICTION AS TO CIVIL PARTNERS

It is possible that a party to an English civil partnership may be missing but the English courts lack jurisdiction under the PDA 2013. This may occur if a civil partnership is registered in England and Wales but the civil partners subsequently move abroad.

To deal with this situation, an amendment to the CPA 2004 provides that the court has jurisdiction to entertain proceedings for a presumption of death order if, and only if, at the time the application is made:

(a) the High Court does not have jurisdiction to entertain an application by the surviving civil partner under the PDA 2013, s 1; and
(b) the 2 people concerned registered as civil partners of each other in England and Wales; and
(c) it appears to the court to be in the interests of justice to assume jurisdiction in the case. CPA 2004, s 222(ba), (c) PDA 2013, s 16, Sch 2, para 3

'The court' for the purposes of the CPA 2004, s 222 means the High Court or the family court. CPA 2004, s 220

However, it is suggested that it would normally be appropriate for proceedings under this section to be instituted in the High Court.

9.7 MISSING PERSONS WHO CANNOT BE PRESUMED DEAD

Following the disappearance of Claudia Lawrence in 2009, it was recognised that the law did not adequately deal with the situation where a person is missing but cannot be presumed to have died. This has The Guardianship (Missing Persons) Act 2017 ('G(MP)A 2017'), which, remarkably, began as a Ten-Minute Rule Bill, received the Royal Assent in April 2017 and came into force on 31 July 2019. Certain details, notably as to whether applications under the Act are to be heard by the High Court or the Court of Protection, remain to be addressed in regulations to be made under the Act, and codes of practice remain to be prepared and issued.

G(MP)A 2017, s 22(1)

It is important to note that a guardianship order is distinct from a declaration of presumption of death. Guardianship is intended to enable families to manage and maintain a missing loved one's practical affairs including property in the hope that they may return, whereas presumption of death allows for them to be resolved on the basis that the missing person will never return.

9.7.1 Application for a guardianship order

On the assumption that Parliament brings the Act into force as it stands (in the modern fashion, there is scope for certain provisions of the Act itself to be amended by regulation; see for example the G(MP)A 2017, s 3(5)), it is possible to offer the following summary of the Act's provisions.

G(MP)A 2017, s 1

A person is 'missing' if he or she is absent from their usual place of residence or usual day to day activities, and either: their whereabouts are not known at all, or not known sufficiently to enable them to be contacted to allow their financial affairs to be dealt with; or they are unable to make decisions relating to their property and financial affairs for reasons beyond their control other than illness, injury or lack of mental capacity.

G(MP)A 2017, s 3

The court may make a guardianship order if a person has been missing throughout a period of 90 days ending with the date of the application, a suitable guardian or guardians (as defined by the G(MP)A 2017, s 4) is available, and the appointment of a guardian is in the missing person's best interests.

The details of the procedure for making such an application remain to be set out in regulations and rules of court. Rules will specify who is to be given notice of the application and how it is to be advertised. An applicant will need to have a sufficient interest in the missing person's property or financial affairs.

G(MP)A 2017, ss 19(1), 20,

9.7.2 Effect of a guardianship order

G(MP)A 2017, ss 6, 8(1), 18

A guardianship order will give the guardian the power to deal with the missing person's property or financial affairs to the extent specified in the order and subject to any conditions or restrictions set out in the order. While a guardianship order may authorise the guardian to make a gift out of the missing person's property, it may not empower the guardian to execute a will on the missing person's behalf. The guardian must act in what he or she reasonably believes to be the missing person's best interests.

A guardianship order will last for a period not exceeding 4 years, but a further guardianship order can be made thereafter if appropriate.

G(MP)A 2017, s 7

A guardian is entitled to be reimbursed their reasonable expenses, and the court may authorise that a guardian be remunerated for acting as guardian. A guardian must keep records of the exercise of their functions, including accounts.

G(MP)A 2017, s 9

Guardians will be supervised by the office of the Public Guardian, PO Box 16185 Birmingham B2 2WH (telephone 0300 456 0300).

G(MP)A 2017, s 17(2), inserting a new subsection 58(2A) into the Mental Capacity Act 2005

9.7.3 Revocation of a guardianship order

A guardianship order may be revoked (the term used in the Act, though 'discharged' would probably have been more accurate) by the court if the person the subject of the order is no longer missing, or revocation is in all the circumstances in their best interests. It will automatically be revoked on the death of the missing person or of the guardian, or on the making of a declaration of presumed death.

G(MP)A 2017, ss 13, 14

CHAPTER 10

CIVIL PARTNERSHIP

10.1 INTRODUCTION

CPA 2004, s 1

The Civil Partnership Act 2004 ('CPA 2004') came into force on 5 December 2005. The Act defines a civil partnership as a relationship between 2 people ('civil partners') which is:

(a) formed when they register as civil partners of each other in England and Wales (under the CPA 2004, Pt 2), in Scotland (Pt 3) and in Northern Ireland (Pt 4), or

(b) formed outside of the United Kingdom under an Order in Council made under the CPA 2004, Pt 5, Ch 1, or

(c) treated under the CPA 2004, Pt 5, Ch 2 as having been formed by virtue of registration as an overseas relationship;

(d) results from the conversion under Northern Irish 2020 regulations of their marriage.

The formation of a civil partnership is beyond the scope of this book and accordingly this chapter is solely concerned with the powers of the court to deal with the consequences of the breakdown of a civil partnership.

CPA 2004, s 1(3)

A civil partnership ends only on death, dissolution or annulment; or in the case of a civil partnership registered in England or outside the UK under the CPA 2004, s 1(a)(i) or (iv), on the conversion of the civil partnership into a marriage under the Marriage (Same Sex Couples) Act 2013 (M(SSC)A 2013), s 9. Note that in this case the marriage will be treated as having subsisted since the date of the civil partnership.

CPA 2004, s 71

The M(SSC)A 2013, s 9(6) makes provision for the effect of the ending of a civil partnership for the purposes of wills and intestacy.

CPA 2004, s 73

A civil partnership does not have effect as a contract giving rise to legal rights. No action lies for breach of a civil partnership in England and Wales, whatever the law applicable to the agreement.

FPR 2010, r 7.1
FPR 2010, r 9.4(a)

Although some changes were necessary, in particular with regard to terminology, broadly the law in respect of civil partnership adopted the same procedures as those which apply to divorce, judicial separation and nullity. As such, the Family Procedure Rules 2010 (FPR 2010) generally deal with civil partnerships in the same way as marriages, both as to procedure (Part 7) and applications for a financial order (Part 9).

10.1.1 Jurisdiction

In the implementation of Brexit, jurisdiction was changed. Pursuant to the CPA 2004, s 219, the Lord Chancellor may by regulations ('section 219 regulations') make provision as to the jurisdiction of courts in England and Wales in proceedings for the dissolution or annulment of a civil partnership or for legal separation of the civil partners in cases.

The s 219 regulations are the Civil Partnership (Jurisdiction and Recognition of Judgments) Regulations 2005 (as amended), which provide in Part 1 that the courts in England and Wales shall have jurisdiction in relation to proceedings for the dissolution or annulment of a civil partnership or for the legal separation of civil partners where on the date of the application:

(a) both civil partners are habitually resident in England and Wales;
(b) both civil partners were last habitually resident in England and Wales and one of the civil partners continues to reside there;
(c) the respondent is habitually resident in England and Wales;
(d) the applicant is habitually resident in England and Wales and has resided there for at least one year immediately before the application was made;
(e) the applicant is domiciled and habitually resident in England and Wales and has resided there for at least six months immediately before the application was made; or
(f) both civil partners are domiciled in England and Wales.

Pursuant to CPA 2004, s 221, the court has jurisdiction to entertain proceedings for a dissolution order or a separation order if (and only if):

(a) the court has jurisdiction under section 219 regulations;
(b) no court has, or is recognised as having, jurisdiction under section 219 regulations and either civil partner is domiciled in England and

Wales on the date when the proceedings are begun; or

(c) the following conditions are met—
   (i) the two people concerned registered as civil partners of each other in England or Wales;
   (ii) no court has, or is recognised as having, jurisdiction under section 219 regulations; and
   (iii) it appears to the court to be in the interests of justice to assume jurisdiction in the case.

The court has jurisdiction to entertain proceedings for a nullity order if (and only if):

(a) the court has jurisdiction under section 219 regulations;
(b) no court has, or is recognised as having, jurisdiction under section 219 regulations and either civil partner—
   (i) is domiciled in England and Wales on the date when the proceedings are begun; or
   (ii) died before that date and either was at death domiciled in England and Wales or had been habitually resident in England and Wales throughout the period of 1 year ending with the date of death; or
(c) the following conditions are met—
   (i) the two people concerned registered as civil partners of each other in England or Wales;
   (ii) no court has, or is recognised as having, jurisdiction under section 219 regulations; and
   (iii) it appears to the court to be in the interests of justice to assume jurisdiction in the case.

Also, at any time when proceedings are pending in respect of which the court has jurisdiction by virtue of CPA 2004, s 221(1)–(2), the court also has jurisdiction to entertain other proceedings, in respect of the same civil partnership, for a dissolution, separation or nullity order, even though that jurisdiction would not be exercisable under s 221(1)–(2).

10.2 DISSOLUTION

10.2.1 Procedure and grounds

The CPA 2004 mirrors, to a large extent, the provisions contained in MCA 1973, Pt 1 in relation to the dissolution of marriages. Practitioners should refer to the changes introduced by the Divorce, Dissolution and Separation Act 2020 (DDSA 2020) which are discussed in Chapters 1–8 of this book in respect of divorce. Those changes have served to remove important distinctions between the dissolution of civil partnerships and the dissolution of marriages (such as the inclusion of the 'adultery ground' in marriage dissolutions but not in civil partnership dissolutions).

10.3 NULLITY

10.3.1 Introduction

The power to make a nullity order is to be found at the CPA 2004, s 37.

The court can make a nullity order which annuls a civil partnership which is void or voidable. The CPA 2004, s 49 sets out the grounds upon which a partnership can be declared void and s 50 the grounds upon which it can be declared voidable (see below). CPA 2004, ss 37–38

Unlike the situation where a partnership is declared null and void, a declaration that it is voidable annuls it only from the date upon which the order is made final. The civil partnership is treated, despite the order, as existing up to that time.

The fundamental changes introduced by the DDSA 2020 do not apply to nullity.

10.3.2 Procedure

The procedure for annulling a civil partnership is similar to that for annulling a marriage. Reference should be made to Chapters 1–8 of this book, except as explained below:

(a) The petition may be presented within the first year of the date of registration of the civil partnership but not more than 3 years after, though the court has power to grant leave to present a petition after the 3-year period. It must where appropriate be presented within 6 months of the date of a Gender Recognition Certificate.

(b) The content should not contain a reference to the civil partnership as having broken down irretrievably.

(c) The prayer will seek the annulment of the civil partnership.

(d) Although the petition is served in exactly the same way as a petition for divorce or dissolution of a civil partnership, the notice of proceedings and acknowledgement of service will refer to civil partnership nullity.

Details of the procedure for applying for a conditional order are identical to those in respect of divorce and will be found in Chapter 5 of this book.

10.3.3 Grounds on which civil partnership is void

CPA 2004, s 49

A civil partnership is void if:

(a) at the time the parties register as civil partners they are not eligible to do so under the CPA 2004, s 3. This will, of course, include a situation where either of them is already married or in a civil partnership;

(b) at the time of the registration of the civil partnership both parties knew that:

   (i) due notice of the proposed civil partnership had not been given;

   (ii) the civil partnership document had not been duly issued;

CPA 2004, ss 17(3) and 27(2)

   (iii) the civil partnership document was void because the time for registering had expired;

   (iv) the place of registration is a place other than that specified in a notice of proposed civil partnership and the civil partnership document;

   (v) there was no civil partnership registrar present; or

   (vi) the place of registration is not one approved under the provisions of the CPA 2004, s 6(3A)(a);

(c) the civil partnership document is void under of the CPA 2004, Sch 2, para 6(5) (civil partnership between a child and another person is forbidden).

10.3.4 Grounds on which civil partnership is voidable

CPA 2004, s 50

A civil partnership is voidable if:

(a) either of the parties did not validly consent, whether by reason of duress, mistake, unsoundness of mind or otherwise;

(b) at the time of its formation either of them, though capable of giving a valid consent, was suffering (whether continuously or intermittently) from mental disorder of such a kind or to such an extent as to be unfit for civil partnership;

(c) at the time of the registration of the civil partnership the respondent was pregnant by some person other than the applicant;

Note: This provision appears to reproduce the MCA 1973, s 12(1)(f), but there is no provision in the CPA 2004 corresponding to the MCA 1973, s 12(1)(e), that 'the respondent was suffering from venereal disease in a communicable form'.

(d) an interim gender recognition certificate under the Gender Recognition Act 2004 has, after the time of its formation, been issued to either civil partner;

(e) the respondent is a person whose gender at the time of the formation of the civil partnership had become acquired under the Gender Recognition Act.

As to paragraphs (d) and (e), note at **8.2.5** concerning the situation where both parties change their legal gender simultaneously and wish to remain in their civil partnership.

10.3.5 Bars to relief where civil partnership voidable

These are set out in the CPA 2004 as follows: CPA 2004, s 51

(a) the court must not make a nullity order where the civil partnership is voidable if the respondent satisfies the court that the applicant, with knowledge that it was open to him to obtain a nullity order, conducted himself in relation to the respondent in such a way as to lead the respondent reasonably to believe that he would not seek to do so, and it would be unjust to the respondent to make the order; CPA 2004, s 51(3)

(b) in relation to **10.3.4(a), (b), (c)** and **(d)** above and without prejudice to the generality of (a) above, the court will not make a nullity order unless the proceedings were begun within 3 years of the formation of the civil partnership or leave has been granted on the limited grounds set out in the Act.

10.3.6 Power to validate civil partnership

The Lord Chancellor has power to validate retrospectively civil partnerships which would otherwise be void under the CPA 2004, s 49(b) (for want of any of the formalities set out at **10.3.3(b)** above). CPA 2004, s 53

10.4 SEPARATION ORDERS

The court has power to make a separation order on the application of either civil partner. This is the equivalent of a decree of judicial separation and, as with divorce, the DDSA 2020 removes the need for factual grounds to obtain a separation order.

10.5 DECLARATIONS

10.5.1 Introduction

CPA 2004, s 58

A declaration may be sought under the CPA 2004, s 58:

(a) that a civil partnership was at its inception valid;

(b) that a civil partnership subsisted on a date specified in the application;

(c) that the civil partnership did not subsist on a date so specified;

(d) that the validity of a dissolution, annulment or legal separation obtained outside England and Wales in respect of the civil partnership is entitled to recognition in England and Wales;

(e) a declaration that the validity of a dissolution, annulment or legal separation so obtained in respect of the civil partnership is not entitled to legal recognition.

These powers are akin to those which apply under the FLA 1986, s 55 in respect of marital status.

10.5.2 Jurisdiction

CPA 2004, s 224

The jurisdiction of the court is set out at the CPA 2004, s 224 as follows:

(a) if either of the civil partners in the civil partnership to which the application relates:

  (i) is domiciled in England and Wales on the date of the application,

  (ii) has been habitually resident in England and Wales throughout the period of 1 year ending with that date, or

  (iii) died before that date and either was at death domiciled in England and Wales or had been habitually resident in England and Wales throughout the period of 1 year ending with the date of death, or

(b) if the 2 people concerned registered as civil partners of each other in England and Wales and it appears to the court to be in the interests of justice to assume jurisdiction in the case.

It should be noted that the jurisdiction differs from that which applies to dissolution, separation, nullity and presumption of death.

10.5.3 Procedure

The procedure is the same as for declarations of marital status under the FLA 1986, which are considered at **9.1**. CPA 2004, s 220

They are covered by the FPR 2010, Pt 8, Ch 5, rr 8.18–8.21. A copy of the application must be sent to the Attorney General at least 1 month before making the application; he may decide to intervene in the proceedings. It is possible for a third party to apply for a declaration as to the status of a civil partnership but the court may refuse to hear the application if it considers that the applicant does not have a sufficient interest in determination of that application. FPR 2010, r 8.18 FPR 2010, r 8.21 CPA 2004, s 58(2)

10.6 FINANCIAL RELIEF

10.6.1 Scope of orders

The provisions of the CPA 2004 enable the court in cases of separation, dissolution or annulment to make equivalent orders to those it can make in relation to marriage. The detailed provisions are contained in Sch 5, the basic structure of which is as follows: CPA 2004, s 72 and Sch 5

(a) Part 1 contains the financial provision orders;

(b) Part 2 contains the property adjustment orders;

(c) Part 3 contains the sale of property orders;

(d) Part 4 contains the pension sharing orders;

(e) Part 5 contains the matters to which the court is to have regard when dealing with an application;

(f) Part 6 deals with pension attachment orders;

(g) Part 7 deals with the Pension Protection Fund;

(h) Part 8 deals with maintenance pending outcome;

(i) Part 9 mirrors the provisions of the MCA 1973, s 27 (failure to maintain);

(j) Part 10 mirrors the provisions of the MCA 1973 on ancillary relief, ss 26, 28 and 29 dealing with the commencement and duration of certain orders;

(k) Part 11 deals with variation of orders and is comparable to the MCA 1973, s 31;

(l) Part 12 deals with arrears and repayments;

(m) Part 13 deals with consent orders and maintenance agreements; and

(n) Part 14 deals with avoidance of disposition orders and is the equivalent to the MCA 1973, s 37.

An excellent and easily understood table is to be found in 'At a Glance' setting out how the provisions of Sch 5 correspond to the same provisions in the Matrimonial Causes Act 1973, the Domestic Proceedings and Magistrates Court Act 1978 and the Matrimonial and Family Proceedings Act 1984.

10.6.2 Procedure and points to note

CPA 2004, Sch 5, para 3(4)

The FPR 2010 apply equally to marriages and civil partnerships, and the procedure is identical to that which applies to financial applications following divorce, judicial separation and nullity.

The factors to be taken into account in dealing with financial applications are set out in the CPA 2004, Sch 5 at paras 21 and 22.

CPA 2004, Sch 5, Pt 8

Note that in relation to a civil partnership the court has the power to make orders for interim periodical payments (known as maintenance pending outcome of proceedings) and legal services orders.

CPA 2004, Sch 5, Pt 7

Practitioners should note the specific provisions dealing with Pension Protection Fund Compensation.

10.6.3 Application of other enactments

In a number of instances the CPA 2004 applies older law to civil partners in relation to their disputes as follows:

CPA 2004, ss 66, 67 and 68

(a) there are provisions dealing with contributions by a civil partner to property improvement which mirror the Matrimonial Proceedings and Property Act 1970, s 37;

CPA 2004, s 68

(b) the Married Women's Property Act 1882, s 17 is applied to certain defined policies of life assurance.

10.7 PRESUMPTION OF DEATH AND DISSOLUTION OF CIVIL PARTNERSHIP

The arrangements by which a person who believes that reasonable grounds exist for presuming the death of their civil partner may present a claim to the court for the court to have it presumed that the other party is dead have been amended, extended and codified in the Presumption of Death Act 2013. As those arrangements now extend beyond the partnership relationship, they are considered separately in **9.4**.

10.8 CHILDREN

CPA 2004, s 75(2)
Children Act 1989, s 4A(1)

A civil partner may acquire parental responsibility for the child of the other civil partner by agreement or by application to the court in the same way as a step-parent in a marriage.

A civil partner is entitled to make an application for residence and/or contact in respect of a child of the family. CPA 2004, s 77 Children Act 1989, ss 10(4)(aa), 10(5)(aa)

A civil partner may apply for financial provision for a child of the family under the provisions of the Children Act 1989, Sch 1. See Chapter 13 and especially **13.2** and **13.6** for further details. CPA 2004, s 78

10.9 DOMESTIC VIOLENCE

Civil partners have the same right to occupy the civil partnership home as do spouses to occupy the former matrimonial home. CPA 2004, ss 81 and 82

The protection from domestic violence afforded by the FLA 1996 is extended to civil partners, who can therefore apply for non-molestation and occupation orders.

See Chapter 23 for further details.

CHAPTER 11

APPLICATIONS FOR A FINANCIAL ORDER WITHIN PROCEEDINGS UNDER THE MATRIMONIAL CAUSES ACT 1973 AND THE CIVIL PARTNERSHIP ACT 2004

11.1 INTRODUCTION

This chapter is concerned with applications for a financial order.

FPR 2010, r 9.4

An application for a financial order, formerly known as 'ancillary relief', may be made in an application for a matrimonial or civil partnership order or at any time thereafter.

FPR 2010, r 2.3(1)

A 'financial order' means:

(a) an avoidance of disposition order;
(b) an order for maintenance pending suit;
(c) an order for maintenance pending outcome of proceedings;
(d) an order for periodical payments or lump sum provision as mentioned in the MCA 1973, s 21(1), except an order under s 27(6) of that Act (failure to maintain);
(e) an order for periodical payments or lump sum provision as mentioned in para 2(1) of Sch 5 to the CPA 2004, Sch 5, para 2(1), made under Part 1 of Sch 5 to that Act;
(f) a property adjustment order;
(g) a variation order;
(h) a pension sharing order; or
(i) a pension compensation sharing order.

A 'financial remedy' is wider, including a financial order, and also orders under the Children Act 1989, Sch 1, orders for financial relief after an overseas divorce under the Matrimonial and Family Proceedings Act 1984 (except applications for permission to apply), failure to maintain, alteration of maintenance agreements, orders under the Domestic Proceedings and Magistrates Courts Act 1978 and applications to consider the position of the respondent under the MCA 1973, s 10(2) and their civil partnership equivalents.

11.2 SCOPE OF THE COURT'S JURISDICTION

A financial order can potentially deal with:

(a) the matrimonial home;

(b) all other assets including, by way of example, land, contents of the matrimonial home, life policies, stocks and shares and motor vehicles;

(c) accrued pension benefits;

(d) maintenance for either party (also referred to as periodical payments);

(e) in limited circumstances, maintenance for a child of the family. The majority of such cases now come under the jurisdiction of the Child Maintenance Service.

Maintenance can potentially include provision for the payment of school or college fees.

The court has very wide powers to order:

(a) A transfer of property from one party to the other or of joint property into the sole name of one party.

(b) A transfer of a tenancy from one party to the other or a joint tenancy to the sole name of one party.

(c) A sale of property owned by one or both of the parties and a related distribution of the proceeds to either one or both of the parties.

(d) A payment of a lump sum from one party to the other or to a relevant child of the family.

(e) A future payment of a lump sum or maintenance to one party out of monies which are due to be received by the other party upon retirement or death in service. These are referred to as 'pension attachment orders'.

(f) A variation of a party's pension provision for the benefit of the other. This is referred to as a 'pension sharing order'.

(g) A variation of any financial agreement made before or after the marriage.

(h) A charge in favour of one party over the assets of the other.

(i) Secured provision in respect of maintenance.

11.2.1 Lump sum order

MCA 1973, s 23(1)(c) MCA 1973, s 23(3)(c) A lump sum referred to at (d) above can be payable by instalments and could include, for example, a payment to be made out of capital which is due to the other party upon retirement or upon a life policy maturing.

Although the total amount of a lump sum order once made is incapable of being varied, where it is payable by instalments, the court may, in exceptional circumstances, consider a variation as to the size of the instalments and/or the dates upon which they are due to be paid.

11.2.2 Secured provision in respect of maintenance

MCA 1973, s 23(1)(b), (e) The order for this type of relief at (i) above provides for the paying party to transfer, at the direction of the court, an income-bearing asset, for example shares or premises which have been let, such transfer to be for a specified period of time in order to secure maintenance payments for the benefit of a party or a child.

11.2.3 Maintenance orders

MCA 1973, s 23(1)(d) Maintenance payments must always have a commencement date, and the order must be clear as to the duration and as to the rate and frequency of payments.

Where maintenance payments are made in respect of a child of the family, they will be expressed to be payable until a defined point. It is important, in order to avoid future uncertainty and the possibility of a further application to the court, to make it clear whether the payments will come to an end once the child finishes either secondary or tertiary education.

The specified duration of the order for a spouse will be for such term as the court thinks fit, subject to the following limitations:

(a) The term cannot begin earlier than the date of the application for the order. An application for this purpose is either a prayer, in a petition or answer, for a financial order or an application in Form A.

(b) The term cannot extend beyond the death of either party or the remarriage or the entry into a civil partnership of the party in whose favour the order was made.

MCA1973, s 28(1A) The court also has power to direct that, upon the expiry of a maintenance order, which is limited in duration, the receiving party shall not be entitled to apply under the MCA 1973, s 31 for an extension of the term which is specified in that order.

11.2.4 Interim maintenance

Maintenance prior to the final decree is referred to as maintenance pending suit for a spouse and as interim periodical payments. In civil partnership proceedings, maintenance prior to the financial order is referred to as maintenance pending outcome of proceedings. After the final order interim maintenance is referred to as interim periodical payments until the final financial order has been made, after which they are simply referred to as periodical payments.

Once financial proceedings have been commenced by the issue of Form A, an application for interim maintenance can be made by way of an application notice in form D11, a copy of which must be served on the respondent at least 14 days before the date fixed for the hearing of the application. The Part 18 procedure applies. FPR 2010, rr 9.7(2) and 18.8(1)(b)(i)

Where an application is made before a party has filed Form E, the written evidence in support must: FPR 2010, r 9.7(3)

(a) explain why the order is necessary;

(b) give up to date information about that party's financial circumstances. FPR 2010, r 9.7(4)

Unless the respondent has already filed a financial statement (Form E), not less than 7 days before the date fixed for the hearing, the respondent must file with the court and serve on the applicant a statement of his means. Even where a financial statement has been filed, a short supplemental statement dealing with the immediate need can often be helpful.

A party who has an order in his/her favour for maintenance pending suit or maintenance pending outcome of proceedings may upon conditional order apply for a periodical payments order at the same rate by way of application notice, using the Part 18 procedure. If the order has been drafted so as to provide for continuity, this will not be necessary. FPR 2010, r 9.8

11.3 PROCEDURE

The rules in the FPR 2010, part 9, which are summarised from **11.3.1–11.3.7**, should since 11 January 2022 be read alongside the Statement on the Efficient Conduct of Financial Remedy Hearings Proceeding in the Financial Remedies Court below High Court Judge Level. This builds on and extends the revised 1 February 2016 Statement on the Efficient Conduct of Financial Remedy Hearings Allocated to a High Court Judge whether Sitting at the Royal Courts of Justice or Elsewhere.

FPR 2010, PD27A

Bundles of documents for use at all hearing should be prepared in accordance with the FPR 2010, PD 27A. This deals with the responsibility for preparation, the contents, format, and timetable for lodging. Unless the court has specifically directed otherwise the bundle shall be limited to no more than 350 sheets of A4 paper (para 5.1). The Practice Direction also deals with time estimates and taking cases out of the list.

11.3.1 Pre-application Protocol

FPR 2010, PD 3A

Prior to issuing any application for a financial order the court will expect the Pre-application Protocol for Mediation Information and Assessment to have been complied with. This is to be found at Practice Direction 3A. Practitioners should note the requirement to complete and fill Form FM1 at the same time as filing the financial application. The Form is to be found at **Appendix A(10)**.

FPR 2010, PD 9A

There is also a Pre-Application Protocol annexed to FPR PD9A which deals with the responsibilities of solicitors conducting litigation, including First Letter, Negotiation and Settlement, the general principles of the overriding objective at rules 1.1 to 1.4 to obtain a just outcome without costs being unreasonably incurred, taking account of the needs of any children and with minimum distress and promoting as good a continuing relationship as is possible in the circumstances. It also refers to Identifying the Issues, Disclosure and Correspondence, the aim being to assist the parties to resolve their differences speedily and fairly and at least narrow the issues or assist the court to do so.

11.3.2 Issuing and serving an application

In order to commence proceedings, a party must issue an application in Form A, which is filed with the court together with a copy for service and the appropriate court fee unless the applicant is exempt from fees. An applicant with the benefit of a legal aid certificate must pay the full court fee.

The application should set out all forms of financial relief which are being sought by the applicant and/or on behalf of a relevant child of the family and should include specific details of any order sought pursuant to the MCA 1973, s 24B, 25B or 25C (and civil partnership equivalent).

Where an application is for a property adjustment or an avoidance of disposition order, relating to land, the notice in Form A must identify the land by description and, where appropriate, the Land Registry registration number and give particulars of any known mortgagee. FPR 2010, PD 9A, para 1.3

Form A must be signed by solicitors if they are on the record for the purposes of financial relief, whether or not the applicant is legally aided. Otherwise the form must be signed by the litigant in person.

Upon issue the court will allocate a date for a first appointment not less than 12 weeks and not more than 16 weeks after the filing of the notice of application. The details will appear in the notice of first appointment in Form C. FPR 2010, r 9.12(1)(a)

The date fixed for the first appointment and any subsequent hearing date cannot be adjourned except with the court's permission and only to a further fixed date. FPR 2010, r 9.12(3)

The copy of Form A, sealed by the court, and the related Form C must be served upon the respondent to the application within 4 days of the date upon which the notice was filed. The court will effect service unless the applicant notifies the court that he/she wishes to serve. FPR 2010, r 9.12(1)(b)

Where the applicant indicates to the court he/she wishes to serve, the court will return to the applicant the copy of the application and the notice in Form C and the applicant must serve these documents on the respondent within 4 days of receipt. The applicant must file a certificate of service with the court at or before the first appointment. FPR 2010, r 9.12(2)

11.3.3 Procedure before the first appointment

Not less than 35 days before the date of the first appointment, the parties must simultaneously file and exchange a completed Form E (financial statement). FPR 2010, r 9.14(1)

The Form E must be verified by a statement of truth. Whilst it is not sworn, this does not reduce the party's obligation to the court to be truthful when completing the Form E. FPR 2010, r 9.14(2)(a)

Proceedings for contempt of court may be brought against a person who makes, or causes to be made, FPR 2010, r 17.6(1) a false statement in a document verified by a statement of truth without an honest belief in its truth.

FPR 2010, r 9.14(2)(b) Documents accompanying a Form E must be restricted to those prescribed by rule. They are:

(a) any document required by the Form E itself;
(b) any other documentation necessary to explain or clarify any of the information contained in the Form E;
(c) any documents provided to the party producing the Form E by a person responsible for a pension arrangement or following a request for information referred to in the Pensions on Divorce etc (Provision of Information) Regulations 2000, reg 2(2);
(d) any notification or other document relating to a pension scheme that is in an assessment period.

FPR 2010, r 9.14(3) Where a party is unavoidably delayed or prevented from sending any document required by Form E, that party must at the earliest opportunity:

(a) serve copies on the other party; and
(b) file a copy with the court together with an explanation for the delay.

The comprehensive disclosure required by Form E should make it possible for practitioners to start negotiations, without delay, with a view to reaching an early settlement.

No disclosure should be sought or given between the issue of Form A and the first appointment, except:

(a) for copy documents sent with Form E; or
(b) in accordance with the questionnaire referred to below.

If disclosure has not already been provided, practitioners should ensure that a matrimonial or other caution or notice and restriction, which a party has registered at the Land Registry, is disclosed to the other side when Form E is served.

FPR 2010, r 9.14(5) At least 14 days before the date of the first appointment each party shall file and serve on the other:

(a) a concise statement of issues;
(b) a chronology;
(c) a questionnaire setting out by reference to the concise statement of issues any further information and documents requested from the other party or a statement that the information and documents are required;

(d) a notice stating whether that party will be in a position at the first appointment to proceed on that occasion to an FDR appointment.

Additionally, not less than 14 days before the first appointment the applicant must file with the court and serve on the respondents, confirmation of the names of all the persons served in accordance with the FPR 2010, r 9.13(1) and (3) – ie where the claim includes an application for an order for a variation of settlement, the trustees of the settlement and the settlor, if living, and where the claim includes an application relating to land, the mortgagee. FPR 2010, r 9.14(6)

At every hearing, including the first appointment, each party must produce to the court in Form H an estimate of the costs incurred by that party up to the date of that hearing or appointment. FPR 2010, r 9.27(1)

Although not a requirement of the rules, the parties should, additionally, if possible, exchange and file with the court: FPR 2010, PD 9A, para 4.1

(a) a summary of the case agreed between the parties;

(b) a schedule of assets agreed between the parties;

(c) details of any directions they seek.

11.3.4 The first appointment

The main purpose of the first appointment is to define the issues and save costs. FPR 2010, r 9.15(1)

The court will determine the extent to which information and documentation requested by questionnaire must be provided. FPR 2010, r 9.15(2)

11.3.5 The financial dispute resolution appointment

The financial dispute resolution (FDR) appointment is governed by the FPR 2010, r 9.17. It is a meeting held for the purpose of discussion and negotiation. FPR 2010, r 9.17(1)

Such meetings have developed as a means of reducing the tension which inevitably arises in family disputes and facilitating the settlement of such disputes. Parties attending the appointment are required by rule to use their best endeavours to reach an agreement on matters in issue between them. FPR 2010, r 9.17(6)

Between the first appointment and the FDR a party is not entitled to the production of any further documents except in accordance with directions given at the first appointment or with the permission of the court. Though sometimes ignored, there could be consequences with regard to costs. FPR 2010, r 9.16(1)

FPR 2010, r 9.17(3)

Not less than 7 days before the FDR appointment the applicant must file with the court details of all offers and proposals, and responses to them. Experience shows that where offers have been filed this is a considerable aid to settlement.

Where the court directs at first appointment that there should be an FDR appointment, the court will serve the notice of the appointment by way of Form D with any order made on the first appointment.

Both parties should attend the FDR personally unless the court directs otherwise and they must use their best endeavours to reach agreement on matters at issue between them. It should be noted that the court will be reluctant to excuse attendance as settlement is more likely if the parties attend and are involved.

11.3.6 Preparation for the final hearing

FPR 2010, r 9.27(2)

Not less than 14 days before the date fixed for the final hearing both parties must file with the court and serve on each other a statement giving full particulars of all costs incurred or expected to be incurred to enable the court to take account of the parties' liabilities for costs when deciding what order, if any, to make.

FPR 2010, r 9.28

Both parties must file with the court and serve on each other an open statement which sets out concise details including the amounts involved of the orders which they propose to ask the court to make. The applicant's statement must be filed and served not less than 14 days before the date fixed for the final hearing and the respondent must file and serve his statement not more than 7 days after the service of the applicant's statement.

It is usual for the court to direct the parties to exchange statements dealing with the matters in dispute by reference to the criteria in the MCA 1973, s 25 to stand as evidence in chief.

11.3.7 The final hearing

FPR 2010, r 9.27A

Where at an FDR appointment the court does not make an appropriate consent order or direct a further FDR appointment, each party must file with the court and serve on each other party an open proposal for settlement by such date as the court directs or, where no such direction is given, within 21 days after the date of the FDR appointment. Where no FDR appointment takes place, each party must file with the court and serve on each other party an open proposal for settlement by such date as the court directs or, where no such direction is given, not less than 42 days before the date fixed for final hearing.

The final hearing will not be before the judge who has already conducted an FDR appointment in the matter, because what is said during such an appointment is privileged and, in the absence of the parties' consent (ie waiving privilege), should not be referred to during the final hearing. FPR 2010, r 9.17(2)

Unless otherwise ordered by the court, both the applicant and the respondent should attend the court for the purpose of cross-examination.

Advocates should adopt a realistic approach and arguments in their respective openings to the trial judge, for example, with regard to alternative accommodation for the parties. Lengthy cross-examination on matters of a historical nature should be avoided except, for example, in a case where it is alleged that a party has dissipated significant matrimonial assets.

The judge is likely to be concentrating on what is now available to distribute between the parties and how best to achieve a fair division, based on the needs of both parties. The judge will take into account a number of important factors including the future ability of the parties to provide for themselves, their respective pension provisions (if any) and any significant medical problems. Generally judges do not want the parties to dwell on the past but are anxious to concentrate on what can be constructively achieved to secure the future of both parties and any relevant child of the family.

As with the FDR appointment, a party may be represented by counsel, a solicitor or a legal executive, and preferably by the same person who appeared at the earlier hearing(s).

Not less than one day before every hearing or appointment, with the exception of the final hearing (in respect of which the rule is not less than 14 days: **12.1.7**) each party must file with the court and serve on each other party an estimate of the costs incurred by the party up to the date of that hearing or appointment. Not less than one day before the first appointment and the FDR appointment each party must file with the court and serve on each other party an estimate of the costs that each party expects to incur if a settlement is not reached up to, respectively, the FDR appointment and the final hearing. FPR 2010, r 9.27(1)–(4)

11.3.8 Consent orders

Financial aspects of a suit are often agreed between the parties. Once the form of the agreement and consent order have been approved by both parties, the draft should be lodged at court for a judge to consider making the order.

FPR 2010, r 9.26(1)(a) PD 9A

The draft must be:

(a) Filed in duplicate by the applicant, one of which must be endorsed with a statement signed by the respondent to the application signifying agreement. Where a solicitor is on the record as acting for a party the agreement may be signed by that solicitor. However, where the consent order applied for contains undertakings, it should be signed by the party giving the undertakings as well as that party's solicitor.

FPR 2010, r 9.26(2) and (3)

(b) Accompanied by a financial statement in Form D81 completed by both parties. The Form D81 was updated in February 2022 and is now fuller than previously. Where each party's statement is contained on the same form, it must be signed by both the applicant and the respondent to certify that they have read the contents of the other party's statement. Where each party's statement is in a separate form, the form of each party must be signed by the other party to certify that they have read the contents of the statement contained in that form.

(c) Accompanied by a Form A completed by or on behalf of the respondent to the application (even if only for dismissal purposes) unless he/she has previously filed an application for a financial order. It is noted that not all courts insist upon Form A being filed solely for the purposes of dismissal.

Practitioners should ensure that the order itself contains only provisions which, if not complied with, are capable of being enforced by the court. If incapable of enforcement in this way, such provisions should be made the subject of recitals or undertakings.

It is important to ensure that the following matters are dealt with when lodging a draft minutes of agreement and consent order for approval:

(a) where there is an apparent inequality in the terms of the settlement, that the reason(s) is/are fully explained in the Form D81 or in a covering letter;

(b) where a party who is not working is to provide for the payment of a lump sum, that an explanation is given as to the source of such moneys;

(c) that all assets which are referred to in the draft are detailed in the Form D81, in particular, the value of collateral life policies, which are frequently omitted.

11.3.9 Final order after divorce

Although the substantive order cannot be made until after pronouncement of the conditional order or judicial separation, it is not unusual for the application to be filed and directions orders made before the conditional order. MCA 1973, ss 23(1) and 24(1) *K v K (Financial Remedy: Final Order Prior to Decree nisi)* [2016] EWFC 23

A substantive order inadvertently made before pronouncement of the conditional order must be set aside by a judge. It cannot be amended under the provisions of the slip rule. However, a judge can approve an order to be made after the conditional order has been pronounced.

Accordingly, therefore, it may be considered advisable not to lodge a draft consent order for approval until after the conditional order has been pronounced. It should also be noted that the information which must be provided in a statement to the court pursuant to FPR 2010, r 9.26 should be current as at the date when the draft order is submitted. It follows that if there is any inordinate delay between lodging the draft and the pronouncement of the conditional order, the court may require confirmation that the parties' circumstances are unchanged. This will inevitably lead to unnecessary work and further delay.

Whilst the substantive order can be made after the conditional order and before the final divorce order it cannot take effect until, at the earliest, the date of the final divorce order. Exceptionally, a judge may expedite the conditional order and/or final divorce order where there is an urgent need to conclude all outstanding financial matters, but will usually require the pronouncement to be listed and heard in open court.

See **5.1.3** for dispensing with formalities.

11.3.10 Pension sharing or attachment orders

At the outset, it is important to note that practitioners involved in cases concerning pensions would be well advised carefully to read A Guide to the Treatment of Pensions on Divorce, The Report of the Pension Advisory Group, July 2019.

When the court fixes a first appointment as required by the FPR 2010, r 9.12(1)(a), the party with pension rights shall, within 7 days after receiving notification of the FPR 2010, r 9.30(1) and (2) date of that appointment, request the person responsible for each pension arrangement under which he has or is likely to have benefits to furnish the information referred to in the Pensions on Divorce etc (Provision of Information) Regulations 2000, reg 2(2).

FPR 2010, r 9.30(3)

Within 7 days of receiving the above information, the party with pension rights shall send a copy of it to the other party, together with the name and address of the person responsible for each pension arrangement.

FPR 2010, r 9.30(4)

A request under the FPR 2010, r 9.30(1) need not be made where the party with pension rights is in possession of, or has requested, a relevant valuation of the pension rights or benefits accrued under the pension arrangement in question. Generally this will have been provided annually.

FPR 2010, r 9.31

Upon making an application for a financial order, including provision to be made under the MCA 1973, s 24B (pension sharing) or upon adding a request for such provision to an existing application for a financial order, the applicant shall send to the person responsible for the pension arrangement concerned a copy of Form A.

FPR 2010, r 9.33(1)

Upon making an application for a financial order, including provision to be made under of the MCA 1973, s 24B or 25C (pension attachment) or upon adding a request for such provision to an existing application, the applicant shall send to the person responsible for the pension arrangement concerned:

(a) a copy of Form A;

(b) an address to which any notice which the person responsible is required to serve on the applicant under the Divorce etc (Pensions) Regulations 2000 (D(P) Regulations 2000) or the Dissolution etc (Pensions) Regulations 2005, as the case may be, is to be sent;

(c) an address to which any payment which the person responsible is required to make to the applicant is to be sent; and

(d) where the address in sub-paragraph (c) is that of a bank, a building society or the Department of National Savings, sufficient details to enable payment to be made into the account of the applicant.

A person responsible for a pension arrangement on whom a copy of a notice under the FPR 2010, r 9.33(1) is served may, within 21 days after service, require the applicant to provide him with a copy of the section of that person's Form E that relates to pension rights and benefits under that arrangement. The applicant must then provide that person with the copy of that section of the statement within the time specified by the FPR 2010, r 9.33(4), or 21 days after being required to do so, whichever is the later.

A person responsible for a pension arrangement who files a statement in answer pursuant to the FPR 2010, r 9.33(6) shall be entitled to be represented at the first appointment, and the court must, within 4 days of the date of filing of the statement in answer, give the person notice of the date of the first appointment. FPR 2010, r 9.33(2)

Where the parties have agreed on the terms of an order including provision under the MCA 1973, s 25B or 25C (pension attachment) then unless service has already been effected under the FPR 2010, r 9.33(1), they shall serve on the person responsible for the pension arrangement concerned:

(a) the notice of application for a consent order;

(b) a draft of the proposed order under r 9.26(1), complying with r 9.35; and

(c) the particulars set out at r 9.33(1).

No consent order that includes a pension attachment order shall be made unless either: FPR 2010, r 9.34(3)

(a) the person responsible has not made any objection within 21 days after the service on him of such notice; or

(b) the court has considered any such objection,

and for the purpose of considering any objection the court may make such direction as it sees fit for the person responsible to attend before it or to furnish written details of his objection.

The Rules are in mandatory form. They are often not complied with, but solicitors are warned that failure to do so could cause major problems at a later stage.

Pension sharing order

A pension sharing order creates a separate pension fund for the applicant and reduces the respondent's fund by the same amount. Orders for pension sharing can be made within applications for financial orders in proceedings for divorce, dissolution or annulment but not in separation proceedings.

When an order is made, varied or discharged which contains pension sharing provision, it must comply with the FPR 2010, r 9.35(a) and must be accompanied by an annex in Form P1 containing the information set out in r 9.35. When completing the annex, practitioner should have reference in particular to Appendix F of the July 2019 Report of the Pension Advisory Group. When the application is lodged as a consent order, this annex, completed by the solicitors acting, should be lodged with the application for the order. If the order is the result of a contested hearing, the annex should, at the end of the hearing, be completed by the solicitors for the applicant.

The order takes effect no earlier than 21 days from the making of the order or from decree absolute, whichever is the later. Page 1 of the annex needs to have that date inserted in the box marked 'THIS ORDER TAKES EFFECT FROM'. Practitioners need to check that the correct date has been entered.

FPR 2010, r 9.35(b)

Practitioners should note that a separate annex is required for each pension referred to in the order.

FPR 2010, r 9.36(4)

Where a pension sharing order is made, the following documents must be sent to the person responsible for each pension arrangement within 7 days beginning with the date the order was made or decree absolute, final order or separation order where made, whichever be the later:

(a) a copy of the financial order;

(b) a copy of the annex;

(c) a copy of the decree of divorce or nullity; and

(d) a copy of the decree absolute.

FPR 2010, r 9.36(1)

The court will either send the documents or direct one of the parties to send them.

Pension attachment order

A pension attachment order requires a payment or payments to be made to the applicant directly from the pension fund manager. It is a form of security for payment. These can be made within applications for financial orders in divorce, nullity and separation proceedings.

The order, which must comply with the FPR 2010, r 9.35(a), must be accompanied by an annex in Form P2. When the application is lodged as a consent order, the solicitors acting should lodge the annex with the application for the order. In consent cases, confirmation that notice of the application for the order has been given to the pension provider is required on the back of Form P2 and must be completed by the court.

This information should be in Form D81, which accompanies the draft consent order. If the order is the result of a contested hearing, the annex should, at the end of the hearing, be completed by the solicitors for the applicant. Care should be taken to ensure that the date the order was made is inserted at page 1 of the annex.

Practitioners should note that a separate annex is required for each pension referred to in the order. FPR 2010, r 9.35(b)

Where a pension attachment order is made, the following documents must be served on the person responsible for the pension arrangement within 7 days beginning with the date of the order or the decree absolute, final order or separation order where made, whichever is the later:

(a) a copy of the financial order;
(b) a copy of the annex;
(c) a copy of the decree absolute or the decree of judicial separation. FPR 2010, r 9.36(4)

11.3.11 Application to vary or discharge a maintenance order

Once a final maintenance order has been made, any application to vary or discharge it is dealt with under the FPR 2010, Pt 9, Ch 5 (or 'fast-track procedure') which envisages a shorter procedure than for financial orders with the aim of early resolution. Applicants are required to attend a mediation information assessment meeting (MIAM) before making the application, subject to exceptions. See **11.3.1** above.

If the application to vary is being made as a matter of urgency, for example where a paying party's financial circumstances have taken a dramatic turn for the worse, it may be appropriate to include an application for an interim order, but the procedure will be the same to the first hearing.

Practitioners should be aware that it is essential that an application to vary periodical payments be issued prior to the expiration of the existing order. *G v G (Periodical Payments)* [1997] 1 All ER 272, CA

If the parties are able to reach agreement, then the procedure for consent orders set out at **11.3.8** should be followed.

Where an application has been issued the court will fix a hearing date within 6 to 10 weeks, and serve on the respondent a copy of the application, unless the applicant wishes to effect service and notifies the court, in which case the applicant must within 4 days serve a FPR 2010, r 9.18 (1)–(2)

copy of the application, the notice of the date of the first hearing, and a certificate of service must be filed before the first hearing

FPR 2010, r 9.18A The applicant may seek a direction from the court that the procedure in Chapter 4 (the procedure for a financial order) should apply instead, giving reasons and the court will determine without notice to the parties and before the first hearing which procedure should apply, and notify the parties of the decision and any consequential directions. This is likely to be appropriate where a full investigation is required, with the information required by Form E, and the exchange of questionnaires. Factors will include the length of time since the original order was made, whether evidence of capital is required for capitalisation purposes, or if there are complex issues. The court may adjourn the decision to the first hearing.

FPR 2010, r 9.19 Not more than 21 days after the date of the issue of the application both parties must simultaneously exchange and file with the court a financial statement E2, verified by a statement of truth and containing only the documents required by the financial statement and any other documents necessary to explain or clarify any of the information contained in it.

FPR 2010, r 9.20 Unless the court is able to determine the application at the first hearing the court may direct that further evidence may be filed and set a date for a directions hearing or appointment or final hearing. In practice this means that the court will chose whatever procedure is most appropriate.

11.4 COSTS

11.4.1 General rule

FPR 2010, r 28.3(5) The general rules in the financial remedy proceedings listed below is that the court will not make an order requiring one party to pay the costs of another party. This rule applies to proceedings for:

- a financial order (see **11.1**) except proceedings for an order for maintenance pending suit, maintenance pending outcome of proceedings, an interim periodical payments order or any other form of interim order for the purposes of FPR 2010, r 9.7(1)(a), (b), (c) and (e);
- an order under the Matrimonial and Family Proceedings Act 1984, Pt 3;

- an order under the Civil Partnership Act 2004, Sch 7;
- an order under the MCA 1973, s 10(2);
- an order under the Civil Partnership Act 2004, s 48(2). FPR 2010, r 28.3(4)

However, the court may make an order for costs in such proceedings at any stage where it considers it appropriate to do so because of the conduct of a party in relation to the proceedings (whether before or during them). FPR 2010, r 28.3(6)

11.4.2 Factors to consider

In deciding whether to make an order for costs the court must have regard to:

- any failure by a party to comply with the rules, and order of the court or any practice direction which the court considers relevant;
- any open offer to settle made by a party;
- whether it was reasonable for a party to raise, pursue or contest a particular allegation or issue;
- the manner in which a party has pursued or responded to the application or a particular allegation or issue;
- any other aspect of a party's conduct in relation to which the court considers relevant; and
- the financial effect on the parties of any costs order. FPR 2010, r 28.3(7)

In considering the conduct of the parties the court will have regard in particular to the FPR 2010, PD28A para 4.4 considerations, which include a refusal openly to negotiate reasonably and responsibly and, in a 'needs' case, where the applicant litigates unreasonably resulting in the costs incurred by each party become disproportionate to the award made by the court. Where an order for costs is made at an interim stage the court will not usually allow any resulting liability to be reckoned as a debt in the computation of the assets. FPR 2010, PD28A, para 4.4

11.4.3 Application of CPR costs rules

Where, notwithstanding the general rule, the court decides to make an order, CPR 1998, r 44.3(6) to (9) shall apply so that the order may provide for a party to pay:

- a proportion of another party's costs;
- a stated amount in respect of another party's costs;

- costs from or until a certain due date only;
- costs incurred before proceedings have begun;
- costs relating only to a distinct part of the proceedings;
- interest on costs from or until a certain date before judgment.

FPR 2010, r 28.3(3)

FPR 2010, PD28A, para 4.5 and CPR 1998 PD44, para 9.5(4)

Parties who intend to seek a costs order against another party should ordinarily make this plain before the date of the hearing, and in any case where summary assessment would be appropriate are under an obligation to file a statement of costs in CPR Form N260, not less than 24 hours before the hearing.

11.4.4 Proceedings for a variation order and interim variation order

FPR 2010, PD28A, para 4.4

Proceedings for a variation order and interim variation order are excluded from the definition of financial remedy proceedings in FPR 2010, r 28.3. This means that the general rule does not apply. In such cases, the court's regard to the obligation of the parties to help the court to further the overriding objective (FPR 2010, rr 1.1 and 1.3), and the court will take into account the nature, importance and complexity of the issues in the case, as it will in all cases. In variation cases this may be of particular significance where there is a risk of the costs becoming disproportionate to the amounts in dispute.

11.4.5 Without prejudice correspondence

FPR 2010, r 28.3(8)

There is nothing in the rules to remove the normal obligation to parties to seek to settle their proceedings by agreement with the assistance of 'without prejudice' negotiations. Indeed, there is an obligation to bring such correspondence to an FDR appointment. Subject to that, no offer to settle which is not an open offer to settle shall be admissible at any stage of the proceedings, except in accordance with r 9.17(3)–(4) (ie at the FDR appointment).

11.4.6 Other proceedings for a financial remedy

It should be noted that the general rule does not apply to the following proceedings for a financial remedy because of the different forensic dynamic at play in such proceedings:

- an order under the Children Act 1989, Sch 1;
- an order under the MCA 1973, s 27;

- an order under the Civil Partnership Act 2004, Sch 5, Pt 9;
- an order under the MCA 1973, s 35;
- an order under the Civil Partnership Act 2004, Sch 5, para 69;
- an order under Part I of the Domestic Proceedings and Magistrates' Courts Act 1978;
- an order under the Civil Partnership Act 2004, Sch 6.

CHAPTER 12

OTHER FINANCIAL APPLICATIONS

12.1 THE MCA 1973, s 27: FAILURE TO PROVIDE REASONABLE MAINTENANCE

The MCA 1973, s 27 provides the mechanism for a spouse to apply to the court for a maintenance order in circumstances where no other matrimonial proceedings have been issued.

Note: The pre-application protocol for mediation and assessment contained in PD 3A applies to these proceedings. See **11.3.1** for further information.

12.1.1 The nature of the relief

Either husband or wife (and this includes parties who have been judicially separated) can apply for maintenance from the other party on the grounds that he/she has failed to provide reasonable maintenance for the applicant or failed to make a proper contribution towards the maintenance of any child of the family.

The range of the orders which the court is empowered to make are set out in the MCA 1973, s 27(6)(a)–(f).

MCA 1973, s 27(1)

Unlike the MCA 1973, s 23, under the provisions of s 27 a child of the family cannot apply on his/her own behalf and consequently is reliant upon a parent to make the application.

MCA 1973, s 27(5)

Where there is an urgent need for immediate assistance, it is possible to apply to the court for an interim order.

For the purposes of the MCA 1973, s 27 the grounds of jurisdiction are that:

(a) one of the parties is domiciled in England and Wales on the date of the application;

(b) the applicant has been habitually resident in England and Wales throughout the period of one year ending with that date;

(c) the respondent is resident there on that date.

Where the application comes within the subject-matter jurisdiction of Art 18 of the 2007 Hague Convention (the modification or replacement of existing maintenance decisions) the court may only entertain the application if permitted to by the jurisdiction rules contained within Art 18.

12.1.2 Best practice generally

The rules in the FPR 2010, Pt 9, which are summarised from **12.1.3–12.1.9**, should since 11 January 2022 be read alongside the Statement on the Efficient Conduct of Financial Remedy Hearings Proceeding in the Financial Remedies Court below High Court Judge Level. This builds on and extends the revised 1 February 2016 Statement on the Efficient Conduct of Financial Remedy Hearings Allocated to a High Court Judge whether Sitting at the Royal Courts of Justice or Elsewhere (in respect of both, see Chapter 11).

12.1.3 Application: issue and service

The procedure is governed by the FPR 2010, Pt 9 which provide that an order under the MCA 1973, s 27 is a financial remedy. FPR 2010, r 2.3(1)

Proceedings are commenced in the family court as a free standing application using Form D50C unless there are already proceedings for a matrimonial order in the High Court. FPR 2010, r 9.5(1)

The procedure follows that prescribed for a financial order (see Chapter 11). Upon issue the court shall fix a first appointment not less than 12 weeks and not more than 16 weeks after the date of the filing of the application. FPR 2010, r 9.12(1)

The court officer will serve a copy of the application on the respondent and give notice of the date of the first appointment to both parties within 4 days from the date of the filing of the application, unless the applicant informs the court that (s)he wishes to serve the respondent. Where the applicant wishes to serve, the court officer will return a copy of the application for service to the applicant together with the notice of the first appointment. These must be served on the respondent within 4 days of the applicant receiving them from the court. FPR 2010, r 9.12(2)

Where service has been carried out by the applicant, a certificate of service must be filed at or before the first appointment. FPR 2010, r 9.12(2)(c)

12.1.4 Procedure before the first appointment

Not less than 35 days before the first appointment both parties must simultaneously exchange with each other and file with the court a financial statement in Form E1. This must be verified by a statement of truth. Form E1 FPR 2010, r 9.14(1), PD5A is less detailed than the Form E used for applications for a financial order. This reflects the more limited scope of the court's powers under the MCA 1973, s 27.

FPR 2010, r 9.14(2)

The Form E1 must be accompanied only by any documents required by the form and any other documents necessary to explain or clarify any other information the financial statement contains.

FPR 2010, r 9.14(3)

Where a party is unable to send any document required by Form E1, that party must serve a copy of any such document at the earliest opportunity and file a copy with the court together with a written explanation of the failure to send it with the financial statement.

Not less than 14 days before the hearing of the first appointment, each party must file with the court and serve on the other party:

(a) a concise statement of the issues between the parties;

(b) a chronology;

(c) a questionnaire setting out by reference to the concise statement of issues any further information and documents requested from the other party or a statement that no information and documents are required; and

FPR 2010, r 9.14(5)

(d) a notice stating whether that party will be in a position at the first appointment to proceed on that occasion to a financial dispute resolution (FDR) appointment.

There shall be no other disclosure or inspection of documents requested or given between the filing of the application and the first appointment.

12.1.5 The first appointment and subsequent steps

The duties of the court at the first appointment are prescribed by the FPR 2010, r 9.15.

Where the court directs that there be an FDR appointment, a party is not entitled to the production of any further documents except in accordance with direction made at the first appointment or with the permission of the court.

A party may apply at any stage for further directions or for an FDR appointment. Similarly, the court may at any stage give further directions or direct that parties attend an FDR appointment.

12.1.6 Procedure before the Financial Dispute Resolution appointment

Not less than 7 days before the FDR appointment the applicant must file with the court details of all offers and proposals and responses to them. At the conclusion of the hearing, these documents will be returned to the applicant on request (and must not be retained on the court file).

Both parties must personally attend the FDR appointment unless the court otherwise directs. The parties must use their best endeavours to reach agreement on matters in issue between them.

The FDR appointment shall be treated as a meeting held for the purposes of discussion and negotiation. Where the parties reach an agreement, the court may make an appropriate consent order.

If the parties fail to reach an agreement, the court will give directions for the future course of proceedings including, where appropriate, the filing of evidence and the fixing of a final hearing date.

Note: See Chapter 26 for the requirement for bundles: FPR 2010, PD 27A. FPR 2010, r 9.17

12.1.7 Before the final hearing

Where at the FDR appointment the court does not make an appropriate consent order or direct a further FDR appointment, or where there has been no FDR appointment, each party must file with the court and serve on each other party an open proposal for settlement within 21 days from the date of the FDR appointment or by such other date as the court directs or, where there has been no FDR appointment, not less than 42 days before the date fixed for final hearing or by such other date as the court directs. FPR 2010, r 9.27A

Not less than 14 days before the date fixed for the final hearing, unless otherwise directed:

(i) Each party must file and serve a statement giving full particulars of all costs in respect of the proceedings which the filing party has incurred or expects to incur. FPR 2010, r 9.27(1)

(ii) The applicant must file and serve an open statement which sets out concise details, including the amounts involved, of the orders which the applicant proposes to ask the court to make. FPR 2010, r 9.28(1)

Not more than 7 days after service of the applicant's statement under (ii) above, the respondent must file and serve a similar statement. FPR 2010, r 9.28(2)

12.1.8 Costs

FPR 2010, r 9.27(1)–(4)

Not less than one day before every hearing or appointment, with the exception of the final hearing (in respect of which the rule is not less than 14 days: **12.1.7**) each party must file with the court and serve on each other party an estimate of the costs incurred by the party up to the date of that hearing or appointment. Not less than one day before the first appointment and the FDR appointment each party must file with the court and serve on each other party an estimate of the costs that each party expects to incur if a settlement is not reached up to, respectively, the FDR appointment and the final hearing.

FPR 2010, r 28.3
PD28A para 4.2

The costs rule under FPR 2010, r 28.3 does not apply. The court may exercise its discretion with a 'clean sheet' in accordance with CPR 1998, r 44.2 except paras (2) and (3) of that rule.

12.1.9 Civil partnership

The procedure for an order under the Civil Partnership Act 2004 ('CPA 2004)', Sch 5, Pt 9 shall follow the procedure described above for an equivalent order under the MCA 1973, s 27.

12.2 INJUNCTIONS UNDER THE MCA 1973, s 37

12.2.1 The nature of the relief

The MCA 1973, s 37 provides the means for a party to matrimonial proceedings, who has issued an application for a financial order, to apply to the court for an order (injunction) restraining the other spouse from attempting to defeat a claim for a financial order.

An application will usually be made for an order preventing a disposition under the MCA 1973, s 37(2)(a) or an avoidance of disposition order under s 37(2)(b) or (c) of the Act.

Applications will usually be made within existing proceedings for a financial order. In cases of extreme urgency the court may grant an immediate order even though no application for a financial order has been made. However, in such circumstances, the court will require the applicant to undertake to issue proceedings for a financial order within a specified period.

Note: For procedure for urgent applications, please refer to Chapter 24.

12.2.2 Procedure

An application for an order preventing a disposition will be made under the procedure prescribed by FPR 2010, Part 18 (Procedure for other applications in proceedings). FPR 2010, r 9.6(1)

Proceedings will be commenced by the filing of an application notice unless the court dispenses with this requirement. Any written evidence in support must be verified by a statement of truth. FPR 2010, r 18.4

An application may be made without giving notice where there is exceptional urgency or if permitted by the court. FPR 2010, PD 18A, para 5.1

Where service of the application is required, service will be undertaken by the applicant unless the court is requested to serve. FPR 2010, r 6.24, as applied by r 18.8(1)

Where an application is made without notice, the court may make an interim order and fix an early return date. An order in the form of an injunction must be served personally on the respondent.

Where an application is made for an avoidance of disposition order, the applicant must serve copies of the application on the person in whose favour the disposition is alleged to have been made and the applicant must file a certificate of service at or before the first appointment. FPR 2010, r 9.13(2)

Any person so served may request from the court in writing, within 14 days beginning with the date of service of the application, a copy of the applicant's financial statement or any relevant part of that statement. FPR 2010, r 9.13(4)

The applicant is heard before a district judge but where a worldwide freezing order is sought, the application may be transferred to a High Court judge.

12.2.3 Undertakings

FPR 2010, PD 33A

As an alternative to the court granting an injunction, it may be appropriate in some circumstances for the respondent to the application to give an undertaking in respect of a part or all of the assets in question. The form of undertaking will be endorsed with a notice setting out the consequences of disobedience. The person signing the undertaking must make a signed statement to the effect that he or she understands the terms of the undertaking being given and the consequences of failing to comply with it.

12.2.4 Civil partnership

Proceedings for an order preventing a disposition under the CPA 2004, Sch 5, para 74(2) and for an avoidance of disposition order under Sch 5, para 74(3) or (4) will follow the procedure described above for the equivalent relief in matrimonial proceedings.

12.3 APPLICATION FOR FINANCIAL RELIEF AFTER OVERSEAS DIVORCE, ETC

MFPA 1984, s 12(1)

The Matrimonial and Family Proceedings Act 1984 ('MFPA 1994') provides that where a marriage has been dissolved or annulled in an overseas country or where the parties to a marriage have been legally separated by means of judicial or other proceedings, and if the divorce, annulment or legal separation is recognised as valid in England and Wales, it is possible for either party to the marriage to apply to the court in England and Wales for financial relief.

MFPA 1984, s 12(2)

If, however, either party has re-married, that party shall not be entitled to make such application.

MFPA 1984, s 17

The court may make any one of the orders which it could make under the MCA 1973, Pt II but subject to the MFPA 1984, s 20.

MFPA 1984, s 13(1)

Before the application for financial relief can be issued, permission must first be obtained.

12.3.1 Application for leave under the MFPA 1984, s 13

FPR 2010, rr 8.23–8.27
Barnett v Barnett [2014] EWHC 2678 (Fam), Holman J
FPR 2010, 9.26(6)

An application for permission may be heard by a district judge, even if contested.

The application for financial remedy may be heard at the same time as the application for permission if it is by consent and evidence of the respondent's consent is filed with the application.

FPR 2010, r 8.23
MFPA 1984, s 13 (2)

The application for permission must be made by way of an application notice on Form D50E in accordance with the procedure prescribed by Part 18 of FPR 2010. The application is made without notice, though it is sometimes appropriate to give informal notice. The court may direct a without notice hearing to consider whether leave should be given, and if so, give directions as to the hearing of an application under section 12. Leave may be granted subject to such conditions as the court thinks fit.

12.3.2 Application for financial relief under the MFPA 1984, s 12

An application for financial relief under Part 3 is made in the family court in Form D50F.

The application follows the same procedure as for an application for a financial order within domestic matrimonial or civil partnership proceedings.

Note: The pre-application protocol for mediation and assessment contained in PD3A applies to these proceedings. See **11.3.1** for further information.

12.4 THE MARRIED WOMEN'S PROPERTY ACT 1882, s 17

12.4.1 The nature of the relief

Proceedings under the Married Women's Property Act 1882, s 17 (and the equivalent provisions in relation to civil partners under the CPA 2004, s 66) are considered here, although it should be noted that such proceedings are not proceedings for a financial remedy as defined by the FPR 2010. Applications involve the determination of property rights rather than the exercise of discretion, so different procedures apply.

An application under s 17 of the 1882 Act can be filed by either party to marriage, at any time during the marriage or within 3 years of the date of decree absolute for:

(a) a declaration as to their respective equitable interests in any land or other property which they jointly own; and
(b) an order for sale, or in the case of chattels, a distribution as between the parties.

By virtue of the Matrimonial Causes (Property and Maintenance) Act 1958, s 7, these remedies are also available to those who have been engaged, providing proceedings are instituted within 3 years of the termination of the agreement to marry (or enter into a civil partnership).

12.4.2 Procedure

FPR 2010, r 8.13–14, PD 8A

Where there are no existing proceedings for a financial order, an application may be made in the High Court or a family court on Form D50 using the FPR 2010, Part 19 procedure. However, if matrimonial or civil partnership proceedings have been started or are intended, the application must be made on Form D11 using the FPR 2010, Part 18 procedure in the same court as those proceedings, if in the family court, in the same Designated Family Judge area.

Whichever procedure is used, the application must be supported by a statement verified by a statement of truth.

FPR 2010, r 19.5(1)
FPR 2010, r 19.5(3)(a)

Where the application is proceeding under the Part 19 procedure, the copy of the application in Form D50 and statement in support will be served with a notice of proceedings and form of acknowledgment of service in Form D50A. Within 14 days beginning with the date on which the application is served the respondent must file and serve a copy of the acknowledgment on the applicant and any other party. The respondent must state in the acknowledgment whether the application is contested.

FPR 2010, r 8.15(1)
FPR 2010, r 8.15(2)

Where particulars of a mortgage are provided with the application, the applicant must serve a copy of the application on the mortgagee, who within 14 days beginning with the date on which the application was received may file an acknowledgment of service and be heard on the application. The court must direct that a mortgage be made a party to the proceedings where the mortgagee requests to be one.

At the first hearing directions will usually be given as to the conduct of the proceedings. The final hearing will normally be heard in private before a district judge and accordingly counsel, a solicitor or a legal executive has the right of audience.

If the parties have been married, wherever possible the applicant for financial and property orders will use the provisions of the MCA 1973, ss 24 and 24A, rather than those provided by s 17 of the MWPA 1882. This is because under the MCA 1973 the court:

(a) has the very much wider powers; and

(b) can make an order or orders under ss 24 and 24A even though a previous order or orders have been made under s 17 of the 1882 Act.

CHAPTER 13

CHILDREN AND FINANCIAL APPLICATIONS

13.1 FINANCIAL ORDERS

Financial orders are covered by the MCA 1973, ss 23 and 24.

A child of the family can apply to the court for a financial order in much the same way as either a petitioner or a respondent.

The application can be made on behalf of a child by:

(a) a parent, guardian or special guardian;

(b) any person in who is named in a child arrangement order as a person with whom a child is to live; or

(c) any other person entitled to apply for a child arrangement order as to where the child should live; or

(d) a local authority, where an order has been made placing a child in its care; or

(e) the Official Solicitor, if appointed as children's guardian of the child pursuant to FPR 2010, r 16.24; or

FPR 2010, r 9.10(1), (1A)

(f) a child of the family who has been given permission to apply, save that no permission is required where the application is for a variation of an order for periodical payments in respect of a child, with the application made by the child in question, in circumstances in which the child is 16 or over.

In all other respects, the procedure for an application under ss 23 and 24 is identical to that set out in Chapter 11 with regard to an application for a financial remedy by either a petitioner or a respondent. However, it should be noted that the power to make a property adjustment order, pursuant to s 24, will be exercised only very rarely in favour of a child of the family.

CA 1989, Sch 1, para 2

13.2 FINANCIAL PROVISION ORDERS UNDER THE CA 1989, Sch 1

Subject to the provisions of the Child Support Act 1991 ('CSA 1991'), the Children Act 1989 ('CA 1989'), s 15,

Sch 1 empower the High Court or family court to order a parent of a child to make financial provision to or for the benefit of that child in one or more of the following ways:

(a) periodical payments;

(b) secured periodical payments;

(c) lump sum;

(d) settlement of property;

(e) transfer of property.

The whole focus of Schedule 1 proceedings and provision is for the benefit of the child; the fact that that parent with care may/will benefit is incidental. The parent with care, provided finances allow, needs to be able to care both financially and generally.

Ideally, where there are existing divorce proceedings, or matrimonial proceedings in the family court, involving the parent or parents of a child, any financial matters concerning that child should be dealt with as part of those proceedings. Where there has been a clean break in financial proceedings the circumstances for the court to make a further award have to be exceptional and there is a very high hurdle to overcome.

PK v BC (Financial Remedies: Schedule 1) [2012] 2 FLR 1426

Practitioners should note that an application to vary an existing order is treated as a new application and the procedure to be followed is as set out at **11.3.1**.

FPR 2010, PD9A, para 1.2

Jurisdiction is provided for in Sch 1, para 14. In respect of 'para 1 orders' the court has jurisdiction if any of the following persons are domiciled or habitually resident in England and Wales on the date of the application:

(a) a parent of the child;

(b) a guardian or special guardian of the child;

(c) a person who is named in a child arrangements order as a person with whom the child is to live;

(d) the child.

Turning to 'para 2 orders', the court has jurisdiction if the applicant or a parent against whom the order is sought or made is domiciled or habitually resident in England and Wales on the date of the application.

13.3 MAINTENANCE

13.3.1 Periodical payments orders

At any time prior to the final disposal of the application, the court may make an interim periodical payments order. The order can potentially include

CA 1989, Sch 1, para 9(1)(a)
CF v KM [2011] 1 FLR 208

provision for the payment of school or college fees or even costs of preparing for CA 1989 proceedings.

CA 1989, Sch 1, para 3(1)(a) and (b) and para 3(2)

The order can commence from the date of making the application and unless the court thinks it appropriate in the circumstances of a case, a periodical payments order will not, in the first instance, extend beyond the 17th birthday of a child and in any event not beyond the 18th birthday unless: (a) the child is, or will be, or if an order were made without complying with that paragraph would be receiving instruction at an educational establishment or undergoing training for a trade, profession or vocation, whether or not while in gainful employment; or (b) there are special circumstances which justify the making of an order without complying what that paragraph.

13.3.2 The CSA 1991

CSA 1991, s 8

The CSA 1991 substantially restricts the power of the court to order maintenance for a child and, before making an application, practitioners should check to ensure that it is within the residual jurisdiction of the court.

The court has no power to make an order for child maintenance unless:

(a) parents agree in writing to the court making a consent order;

CSA 1991, s 8(5)(a)

(b) the absent parent's income exceeds a specific sum (the current figure should be checked before making an application) and the court is being asked to 'top up' the assessment

(c) the application is for a variation of an existing court order;

CSA 1991, s 8(7)(a)

(d) a child is or will be receiving instruction at an educational establishment or undergoing training for a trade, profession or vocation, whether or not in gainful employment;

CSA 1991, s 8(8)

(e) a child is disabled;

CSA 1991, s 44(1)(c)

(f) the absent parent is habitually resident outside the United Kingdom.

CSA 1991, s 55(1) and (2)

If there is an issue as to whether or not a child falls within the scope of the CSA 1991, it may be necessary, in the first instance, to consider the statutory meaning of 'child'.

Where an agreement is reached for the payment of maintenance, that agreement can be made the subject of a consent order, which will be enforceable in the same way as any other maintenance order.

Even if the parties reach agreement and an order is made either party is permitted, after one year, to apply to the Child Maintenance Service for an assessment and once an assessment is made the order ceases and CMS assume jurisdiction. That only applies if the parties and child are in the UK. If one is not then CMS does not have jurisdiction.

13.3.3 Members of the armed forces

Where the respondent to an application for maintenance is a regular member of the armed forces it is possible to apply to his/her unit commander for a compulsory allotment of the respondent's pay. This will be simpler and quicker than proceeding through the CMS for an assessment or seeking a court order.

Note: A list of armed forces contact addresses is to be found at **Appendix C(2)**.

NF(EML)A 1947, AA 1955, s 150 and AFA 1955, s 150

13.4 LUMP SUM ORDERS

A lump sum order may include provision for payment of a sum in respect of expenses relating to the birth of the child or monies otherwise incurred prior to a final order being made.

CA 1989, Sch 1, para 5(1) and (2)

Lump sums can be awarded for furnishings to furnish the home pursuant to any order, to repay debts or a car.

Whereas the MCA 1973 allows one lump sum order to be made in favour of a party to the proceedings, the CA 1989 permits the court to make a second or subsequent order, provided that the child concerned has not reached the age of 18 before the date of the application.

CA 1989, Sch 1, para 1(5)(a)

An order for the payment of a lump sum, whether interim or final, can be made to be payable by instalments.

CA 1989, Sch 1, para 5(5)

13.5 TRANSFER OF PROPERTY ORDERS

An application for a transfer of property order can be used, inter alia, as a means of asking the court to transfer a tenancy as between parents, for the benefit of a child.

Unlike the position with regard to lump sum provision, the court is restricted to making only one transfer of property or settlement order. The jurisdiction to make only one order applies even if it can be clearly shown

Philips v Pearce [2005] 2 FLR 1212

that the housing needs of the child have changed considerably.

The transfer is for the benefit of the child (ie the child's needs for a home during its minority are met) and therefore on the child's majority the need for a home no longer exists and the property will revert back to the transferor.

CA 1989, Sch 1, para 1(5)(b)

There is nothing in the Act that prevents the property being transferred in perpetuity. However, there is no reported case where the court has either transferred the property absolutely or granted the parent with care an interest that extends beyond tertiary education as to do so might be though to be outside the statutory provision 'for the benefit of the child'.

13.6 PARTIES TO AN APPLICATION AND SCOPE OF ORDERS

CA 1989, Sch 1, para 1(1)

CA 1989, Sch 1, para 16(2)

An application can be made by a parent, guardian or special guardian of a child or by any person in whose favour a child arrangement 'live with' order is in force. The application must be made against a parent.

CA 1989, Sch 1, para 1(2)

If an application is granted, the resultant order can be expressed to be made either to the applicant for the benefit of a child or direct to that child.

CA 1989, Sch 1, para 16(2)

An order can be sought against one or both of a child's birth or adopted parents, or a person who, during the course of a marriage or civil partnership, has treated the child as a child of the family. However, as explained at the end of this section, an application, pursuant to the CA 1989, Sch 1, para 2(1), by a child over the age of 18 is much more restricted in its ambit.

CA 1989, s 3(4)

In view of the wide definition of the CA 1989, Sch 1, para 16(2) referred to above, it is clear that a putative father is included and the fact that he does not have parental responsibility is irrelevant.

CA 1989, Sch 1, para 4(2)(c)

Whilst, as explained above, a person who has treated a child as a child of the family can be ordered to receive financial provision, it should always be borne in mind that there is a continuing responsibility on the part of a birth parent and this is a factor which the court may properly be asked to take into account.

CA 1989, Sch 1, para 2(1)(a)

Unlike under the MCA 1973, there is no provision under the CA 1989 for a child under the age of 18 to make an application on his/her own behalf. However, once a child has reached the age of 18, he/she can then make an application in circumstances where he/she is or will be receiving instruction at an educational establishment or undergoing training for a trade, profession or vocation, whether or not while in gainful employment. Such application has to be made against a parent and does not include a party to a marriage or civil partnership.

An application can also be made by a person over 18 years where there are special circumstances which justify the making of an order, for example where the person concerned has a mental or physical impairment and as a result is unable to work. The Court of Appeal has examined this in detail in *UD v DN (Schedule 1, Children Act 1989; Capital Provision)*.

UD v DN (Schedule 1, Children Act 1989; Capital Provision) [2021] EWCA Civ 1947

CA 1989, Sch 1, para 2(1)(b)

Whilst the court is granted the power to make an order in favour of a child who has reached the age of 18, that power is limited to making periodical payments and lump sum orders.

CA 1989, Sch 1, para 2(2)

The court is also prevented from making an order under the provisions of Sch 1, para 2 in circumstances where:

(a) there was already a periodical payments order in force immediately prior to a child reaching the age of 16; or

(b) the parents of that child are living together in the same household.

CA 1989, Sch 1, para 2(3) and (4)

13.7 FACTORS FOR THE COURT TO CONSIDER

In making an order pursuant to the CA 1989, Sch 1, the court must have regard to all the circumstances of the case and the factors set out in Sch 1, para 4. Whilst not identical, the principles are very similar to those provided in the MCA 1973, s 25.

> '4(1) In deciding whether to exercise its powers under paragraph 1 or 2, and in so in what manner, the court shall have regard to all the circumstances including;
>
> (a) The income, earning capacity, property and other financial resources which each relevant person mentioned in sub-paragraph (4) has or is likely to have in the foreseeable future;
>
> (b) The financial needs, obligations and responsibilities which each person has or is likely to have in the foreseeable future;
>
> (c) The financial needs of the child;

(d) The income, earning capacity (if any) of the child

(e) any physical or mental disability of the child;

(f) The manner in which the child was being, or was expected to be, educated or trained.'

When compared with the MCA 1973, s 25 factors, is the following are not included:

(a) The standard of living enjoyed by the parties prior to the breakdown of the relationship;
(b) Age of the parties and length of the relationship;
(c) Contributions made or likely to be made in the future;
(d) Loss of future benefits (eg pension, inheritance);
(e) Conduct.

CA 1989, Sch 1, para 4(1) and (2)

However, para 4(1) includes 'all the circumstances' and a reference to s 25 factors may be relevant in any application.

13.8 NO CLEAN BREAK

CA 1989, Sch 1 para 1(3)

In financial proceedings under the MCA 1973 the concept of a clean break is familiar; for parties to settle their finances and be able to plan for the future subject to any variation application if there is ongoing obligation. The concept of clean break does not apply to Schedule 1 applications and therefore an applicant can apply to vary a maintenance order and, more importantly, apply for a further lump sum although not a further property order. There is also no capitalisation provision of periodical payments as there is available under the MCA 1973, s 31.

13.9 PRACTICAL CONSIDERATIONS

The leading case remains *Re P* and if a Schedule 1 application is being considered this case is required reading. There are a number of relevant points that can be derived from *Re P*:

(a) The carer parent should be able to raise the child in circumstances that have some relationship to the other parent's resources;
(b) The parent with care should control the budget;
(c) The budget should be set to meet reasonable needs; not aspirations;

(d) The starting point is housing needs; assessment of lump sum and periodical payment needs follow that assessment. *Re P* [2003] 2 FLR 865

13.10 PROCEDURE

As an application under the CA 1989, Sch 1 is a financial remedy the rules at the FPR 2010, Pt 9 apply. FPR 2010, r 2.3

Pursuant to the FPR 2010, Pt 3 parties will be expected to follow pre-action protocol to include attending mediation (MIAMS) and the court will consider adjourning proceedings to allow parties to attempt out of court settlement.

The application is commenced by issuing Form A1. An application pursuant to Schedule 1, if only seeking periodical payments under Sch 1, para 1(2)(a), (b) or 2(2)(a), falls into the list in FPR 2010, r 9.18(A1)(a) and therefore the Chapter 5 (or 'fast-track procedure') should be followed. In the previous chapters concerning proceedings under the Chapter 4 ('standard procedure') have been considered. The main differences are:

- Once issued the court will list a first hearing date not less than 4 weeks and not more than 8 weeks after the date of the filing of the application; and
- Within 4 days beginning on the date on which the application was filed, the court will: (a) serve a copy of the application on the respondent; (b) give notice of the date of the first hearing; and (c) send a blank financial statement to both parties
- Both parties should file and exchange Forms E1 (with slightly less demanding requirements than Form E) no more than 14 days after the issue date. FPR 2010, r 9.19(1)
- There is no provision in the rules for questionnaires. FPR 2010, r 9.19(4)
- There is no provision in the rules for a financial dispute resolution appointment ('FDR').

Even in these circumstances, unless the case is straightforward on issue an application might wish to be made that the case be transferred to the Chapter 4 ('standard procedure') (as above) to allow for an FDR. Such application needs to state:

(a) That the applicant seeks a direction that the procedure in FPR 2010, r 9.12 (Chapter 4 procedure) should apply; and

(b) The applicant's reasons for seeking such direction

FPR 2010, r 9.18(A)

The court will then determine the application on the papers and notify the parties without the need for the parties to attend.

An application pursuant to Schedule 1 seeking other relief does not fall into the list in the FPR 2010, r 9.18(A1)(a) and so the Chapter 4 ('standard procedure') applies.

13.11 INHERITANCE (PROVISION FOR FAMILY AND DEPENDANTS) ACT 1975

The Inheritance (Provision for Family and Dependants) Act 1975 (I(PFD)A 1975), s 2 provides the mechanism for an application by a child for financial support out of the estate of a parent, in circumstances where it is alleged that no or insufficient provision has been made for that child in the parent's will or, where there is no will, by operation of the laws of intestacy.

I(PFD)A 1975, s 1(1)(c) and (d)

A child for the purposes of an application under the I(PFD)A 1975, s 2 includes a birth or adopted child of the deceased, or otherwise one who has been treated as a child of the family.

CPR 1998, r 8.2

The application will be commenced under the provisions of the CPR 1998, Pt 8 using Form N208.

CPR 1998, r 21.2

If, at the time of the application, the child is still a minor, it will be necessary to appoint a litigation friend unless the court makes an order under CPR 1998, r 21.2(3). Where there is a conflict with the surviving parent in relation to the distribution of the estate, an alternative litigation friend will have to be sought.

If the child has reached the age of majority, the application will be commenced in the usual way.

The court has unfettered power to make an order in respect of a child in any of the forms of financial relief set out in the I(PFD)A 1975, s 2. However, the court will have to carefully weigh in the balance any competing claims of a surviving spouse of the deceased.

Any possible conflict between a child and a surviving spouse should be resolved as quickly as possible and, in such a situation, practitioners should apply to the court for directions at an early stage.

Note: For fuller details and the procedure to be followed, see Chapter 14.

CHAPTER 14

FINANCIAL APPLICATIONS GOVERNED BY THE CIVIL PROCEDURE RULES 1998

All aspects of the proceedings which are dealt with in this chapter are governed by the Civil Procedure Rules 1998 ('CPR1998'), as subsequently modified by Part 57 in relation to claims under the Inheritance (Provision for Family and Dependants) Act 1975, rather than the FPR 2010.

14.1 INHERITANCE (PROVISION FOR FAMILY AND DEPENDANTS) ACT 1975

The Act enables a claim for capital and/or income to be brought by:

(a) the spouse or civil partner of the deceased;

I(PFD)A 1975, s 1

(b) a former spouse or civil partner of the deceased but not one who has formed a subsequent marriage or civil partnership; or

(c) a child of the deceased; or

(d) a person who, whilst not a child of the deceased, was treated at any time as a child of the family in relation to a marriage or civil partnership to which the deceased was a party;

(e) a person who, immediately before the death of the deceased, was being maintained either wholly or partly, by the deceased. The sole ground for the claim being that the deceased's will/or the laws on intestacy do not make reasonable provision for the claimant.

Sections 2 and 3 of the Act respectively set out the orders that can be made and the factors to be taken into account by the court.

14.1.1 Jurisdiction

The claim can be commenced in:

(a) a county court:

  (i) for the district in which the defendant or one of them lives or carries on business; or

  (ii) where the property is situated,

(b) the High Court in the Chancery Division or Family Division (but not in the Queen's Bench Division). The Central Family Court does not have jurisdiction, but the District Judges of the Principal Registry of the Family Division may hear Inheritance Act claims, sitting in the High Court. CPR 1998, r 57.15(1), PD 2B, para 1.1C

Note: There is no financial limit to the county court jurisdiction.

14.1.2 Requirements on issue

A claim must be made under the CPR 1998, Part 8, using Form N208 and attracts a court fee unless the claimant is fees exempt. The content of the claim form must be verified by a statement of truth. CPR 1998, rr 8.2 and 57.16

Sufficient copies of the claim form and written evidence of the claimant should be filed for service on every defendant.

On filing the claim the claimant must, at the same time, file the written evidence upon which it is intended to rely. Exhibited to that written evidence must, save in circumstances in which no grant of probate has been obtained, be: CPR 1998, r 8.5

(a) a copy of the grant of probate or letters of administration; and

(b) a copy of all testamentary documents in respect of which the grant of probate or letters of administration were granted. CPR 1998, r 57.16(3)–(3A)

It may be appropriate to seek a representation order in relation to any beneficiary with the same interest. CPR 1998, r 19.6

Where the claimant is a minor or otherwise under a disability, the claim must be made by a litigation friend acting on behalf of the claimant, who must sign and file a certificate in Form N235. CPR 1998, r 21.2

14.1.3 Time limit for commencement

The claim must be brought within 6 months of a grant of representation or letters of administration. I(PFD)A 1975, s 4

The 6-month period can be extended with the permission of the court. However, an application in this respect must be included in the claim form. This is a discretionary power and the court in exercising its discretion will take all the circumstances into account. They include:

(a) the explanation for the delay;

(b) any efforts made to reduce the delay;

(c) whether there have been any efforts to negotiate the claim;
(d) whether the estate has been distributed and whether it was done so in the knowledge of the claim or potential claim;
(e) possible professional negligence implications;
(f) any hardship that might arise; and
(g) the overall merits of the claim.

An application for leave to apply out of time may be heard separately from any substantive hearing.

14.1.4 Contents of the claim form

CPR 1998, rr 8.2 and 8.5

The claim form, supported by a statement of truth or affidavit, must state:

(a) the question which the claimant wants the court to decide; or
(b) the remedy which the claimant is seeking and the legal basis for the claim to that remedy;
(c) if the claim is made under an enactment, what that enactment is;
(d) if the claimant is claiming in a representative capacity, what that capacity is; and
(e) if the defendant is sued in a representative capacity, what that capacity is.

CPR 1998, r 57.16

In addition the claim form must include the matters listed in the note to CPR 1998, r 57.16. An official copy of the grant of probate or letters of administration must be exhibited to the written evidence filed and served by the claimant, save in circumstances in which no grant of probate has been obtained.

The defendants should be:

(a) the personal representatives;
(b) the beneficiaries;
(c) other persons affected by the claim; and
(d) any other person directed by the court to be added.

14.1.5 Service

Each defendant must be served with:

(a) a copy of the claim form;

CPR 1998, r 8.5(2)

(b) a copy of the claimant's statement and other written evidence filed with the claim form;
(c) an acknowledgement of service in Form N210;

(d) notes of guidance in Form N208C; and
(e) notice of the place, date and time of the first directions hearing, if already fixed.

A defendant will be served by the court by first class post, unless solicitors have indicated that they will effect service in accordance with CPR 1998, r 6.4.

A claim form must be served within 4 months of issue. CPR 1998, r 7.5(1)

The claimant may apply for an order extending the period for service of the claim form. CPR 1998, r 7.6

The general rule is that an application to extend the time for service must be made:

(a) within the period for serving the claim form specified by CPR 1998, r 7.5; or
(b) where an order has been made under r 7.6 within the time for service specified by that order.

If the claimant applies for an order to extend the time for service of the claim form after the end of the period specified by r 7.5 or r 7.6, the court may make such an order only if: CPR 1998, r 7.6(3)

(a) the court has been unable to serve the claim form; or
(b) the claimant has taken all reasonable steps to serve the claim form but has been unable to do so; and
(c) in either case the claimant has acted promptly in making the application.

The application preferably in Form N244 for an order extending the time for service:

(a) must be supported by evidence; and
(b) may be made without notice. CPR 1998, r 7.6(4)

A court fee is payable unless a claimant is exempt from fees.

For service out of the jurisdiction reference should be made to Chapter 4, CPR 1998, Pt 6.

14.1.6 Acknowledgement of service

The time within which a defendant must file and serve:

(a) an acknowledgement of service; and
(b) any written evidence,

is not more than 21 days after service. CPR 1998, rr 8.3 and 57.16

The acknowledgement must state: CPR 1998, r 8.3

(a) whether the defendant contests the claim; and

(b) if the defendant seeks a different remedy from that set out in the claim, what that remedy is.

The acknowledgement must comply with CPR 1998, r 10.5. An acknowledgement in Form N210 should be filed.

Practitioners are reminded of the rules in relation to the filing of an acknowledgement of service where the claim form has been served out of the jurisdiction as set out at the CPR 1998, rr 6.35, 6.12(3), 6.37(5) and 10.3.

CPR 1998, r 10.4

On receipt of the acknowledgement the court must notify the claimant in writing. This is usually done by sending the claimant or his solicitors a copy of the acknowledgement of service.

CPR 1998, PD 57, para 15

Where a defendant who is a personal representative wishes to remain neutral, and agrees to abide by any decision of the court, he should state this in Section A of the acknowledgement of service.

CPR 1998, r 8.4

A defendant who has failed to file an acknowledgement of service and in respect of whom the time for so doing has expired, may attend the hearing of the claim but may not take part unless the court gives permission. The application for permission may be made at the commencement of the hearing.

14.1.7 Allocation and management

CPR 1998, r 8.9(c)

As the claim is made as a CPR 1998, Pt 8 claim in the county court it is automatically allocated to the multi-track. A district judge has jurisdiction in relation to all hearings.

CPR 1998, 8APD.6

The court may give directions immediately the claim is issued or it will give directions as soon as practically possible after the defendant has filed an acknowledgement of service or the time for doing so has expired.

CPR 1998, Pt 3 and the court's normal case management powers apply.

CPR 1998, r 8.5(1) and (2), 8APD.7.1

The claimant must file any written evidence upon which it is intended to rely when the claim form is filed. That evidence must be served on the defendant with the claim form.

CPR 1998, r 8.5(3) and 8APD.7.3

The defendant must file any written evidence on which he relies with the acknowledgement of service and at the same time serve the other parties.

CPR 1998, 8APD.6.2

When the court receives the acknowledgement of service, it will consider what, if any, directions are needed at that stage.

The claimant then has 14 days in which to file further written evidence in reply and at the same time serve all other parties. CPR 1998, r 8.5(5)

No evidence may be given at trial unless: CPR 1998, r 8.6

(a) it has been served as above; or

(b) the court has given permission.

The court may require or permit a party to give oral evidence at the hearing. CPR 1998, r 8.6(2)

The court has power to give directions requiring the attendance for cross-examination of a witness who has given written evidence. CPR 1998, r 8.6(3)

Part 20 claims (counterclaims and other additional claims) may only be brought with the permission of the court. For further information, see **14.3.1**.

The court may on the hearing date proceed to hear the case and dispose of the claim, or give case management directions. CPR 1998, r 8.1

Practitioners should note the following:

(a) A witness statement from personal representatives should include all the matters set out in CPR PD 57, para 16.

(b) Although a defendant has a 21-day period within which to file an acknowledgement of service, the rules give the court power to order an interim hearing within that period where it is just so to do. I(PFD)A 1975, s 5

(c) The court has power to make interim orders where appropriate.

(d) A copy of every substantive order which is made by the court must be sent to the Probate Department of the Principal Registry, together with the original grant. This is to enable a memorandum of the order to be endorsed on the probate or letters of administration under which the estate is being administered. I(PFD)A 1975, s 19(3) CPR 1998, PD 57, para 18.3

(e) On the hearing of the claim, the personal representatives must produce to the court the original grant of representation.

(f) If, whilst a decree of separation is in force and the separation is continuing, either of the parties dies intestate all his/her real or personal property will devolve as if the other party to the marriage had then been dead.

14.1.8 Rights of audience

Substantive hearings will, unless otherwise directed, be in open court before a district judge but may, if there are complex or other significant issues, be heard before a circuit judge or even a High Court judge. Practitioners may therefore wish to check with the court as to the level of judge before making a decision as to who is to appear. There is specific provision to enable any proceedings under the Act to be disposed of in private if the court so directs.

14.2 TRUSTS OF LAND AND APPOINTMENT OF TRUSTEES ACT 1996

The Act enables a trustee or beneficiary of the proceeds of sale of land (including buildings on the land) to apply for an order in relation to the exercise by the trustees of any of their powers and discretions. A claimant can seek a declaration of his/her interest in a trust and the court can also regulate the occupation of the property, if need be on a long-term basis.

There is no requirement for the joint owners to have been married or engaged.

If the parties have been married, wherever possible the applicant for financial and property orders will use the MCA 1973, ss 24 and 24A rather than the Trusts of Land and Appointment of Trustees Act 1996 ('TOLATA 1996'), s 14. This is because under the provisions of the MCA 1973 the court:

(a) has the very much wider powers set out in Chapter 11; and
(b) can make an order or orders under the MCA 1973, ss 24 and 24A even though a previous order or orders have been made under the TOLATA 1996, s 14.

The provisions of the TOLATA 1996, s 14 are also used to enforce a charging order by sale. Full details of the procedure in this respect are set out at **15.5.3**.

14.2.1 Jurisdiction

CCA 1984, s 23, County Court Jurisdiction Order 2014, Art 3

The claim can be commenced in a county court which has jurisdiction, subject to the county court equity jurisdiction limit, £350,000.

If the proceedings are brought in the county court they must be brought in:

(a) the court for the district in which the defendant or one of them lives or carries on business; or

(b) where the property is situated.

If there is a divorce or a relevant application under the Children Act 1989 pending in another court, the claim should either be issued in that court or transferred there.

The Family Court, including the Central Family Court, has no jurisdiction to hear cases under this Act, but the District Judges of the Principal Registry of the Family Division do, sitting in the High Court. Any related application under the Children Act 1989 can be transferred to the High Court, Family Division, to enable all matters to be dealt with simultaneously.

Arising from the restrictions on the orders that are available to the court under the Children Act 1989, Sch 1 practitioners may wish to issue simultaneously proceedings under TOLATA 1996.

14.2.2 Requirements on issue

A claim should normally be commenced as a CPR 1998, Pt 8 action in Form N208 and attracts a civil procedure fee unless the claimant is exempt from fees. CPR 1998, r 8.2

The claim form, together with a signed statement of truth, must be supported by a witness statement of the claimant. CPR 1998, r 8.5

Where the claimant is a minor or otherwise under a disability, the claim must be made through a litigation friend acting on behalf of the claimant and a certificate in Form N235, signed by the litigation friend, must be filed. CPR 1998, r 21.2

Sufficient copies of the claim form and written evidence of the claimant should be filed for service on every defendant.

14.2.3 Contents of the claim form

The claim form supported by a statement of truth must state: CPR 1998, rr 8.2 and 8.5

(a) the question which the claimant wants the court to decide; or

(b) the remedy which the claimant is seeking and the legal basis for the claim to that remedy;

(c) if the claim is made under an enactment, what that enactment is;

(d) if the claimant is claiming in a representative capacity, what that capacity is; and

(e) if the defendant is sued in a representative capacity, what that capacity is.

14.2.4 Service

CPR 1998, r 8.5(2)

Each defendant must be served with:

(a) a copy of the claim form;

(b) a copy of the claimant's statement and other written evidence filed with the claim form;

(c) an acknowledgement of service in Form N210;

(d) notes of guidance in Form N208C; and

(e) notice of the place, date and time of the first directions hearing, if already fixed.

A defendant will be served by the court by first class post, unless solicitors have indicated that they will effect service in accordance with CPR 1998, r 6.4.

A claim form must be served within 4 months of issue.

CPR 1998, r 7.5(2)

Note: If the proceedings are being served out of the jurisdiction, CPR 1998, r 7.5(2) provides that the claim form must be served within 6 months of the date of issue: ie the time for serving the proceedings is extended from 4 months to 6.

CPR 1998, r 7.6(1)

The claimant may apply for an order extending the period within which the claim form may be served.

CPR 1998, r 7.6(2)

The general rule is that an application to extend time for service must be made:

(a) within the period for serving the claim form specified by the CPR 1998, r 7.5; or

(b) where an order has been made under r 7.6 within the time for service specified by that order.

CPR 1998, r 7.6(3)

If the claimant applies for an order to extend the time for service of the claim form after the end of the period specified by r 7.5 or r 7.6, the court may make such an order only if:

(a) the court has been unable to serve the claim form; or

(b) the claimant has taken all reasonable steps to serve the claim form but has been unable to do so; and

(c) in either case the claimant has acted promptly in making his application.

CPR 1998, r 7.6(4)

The application, preferably, in Form N244 for an order extending the time for service:

(a) must be supported by evidence; and

(b) may be made without notice.

A court fee is payable unless a claimant is exempt from fees.

For the procedure concerning an application for service out of the jurisdiction, reference should be made to the CPR 1998, Pt 6, Ch 4.

14.2.5 Acknowledgement of service

The time within which a defendant must file and serve: CPR 1998, r 8.3

(a) an acknowledgement of service; and

(b) any written evidence,

is not more than 14 days after service.

The acknowledgement must state: CPR 1998, r 8.3

(a) whether the defendant contests the claim; and

(b) if the defendant seeks a different remedy from that set out in the claim, what that remedy is.

The acknowledgement must comply with CPR 1998, r 10.5. The use of Form N210 is to be preferred.

Practitioners are reminded of the rules in relation to the filing of an acknowledgement of service where the claim form has been served out of the jurisdiction as set out at rr 6.22 and 6.23.

On receipt of the acknowledgement the court must notify the claimant in writing. This is usually done by sending the claimant or his solicitors a copy of the acknowledgement of service. CPR 1998, r 10.4

A defendant who has failed to file an acknowledgement of service and in respect of whom the time for so doing has expired, may attend the hearing of the claim but may not take part unless the court gives permission. CPR 1998, r 8.4

14.2.6 Allocation and management

As the claim is made as a CPR 1998, Pt 8 claim PD 8A applies, including the court's power on a hearing to hear the case and dispose of the claim, or give specific case management decisions which may include specific allocation of a case to a track. CPR 1998, 8APD.8 CPR 1998, Part 3 and the court's normal case management powers apply

The claimant must file any written evidence upon which it is intended to rely when the claim form is filed. CPR 1998, r 8.5(1) and (2)

That evidence must be served on the defendant with the claim form.

The defendant must file any written evidence on which he relies with his acknowledgement of service and at the same time serve other parties. CPR 1998, r 8.3(3)

CPR 1998, r 8.8(2) When the court receives an acknowledgement of service, it will consider what, if any, directions are needed at that stage.

CPR 1998, r 8.5(5) The claimant then has 14 days in which to file further written evidence in reply and at the same time serve all other parties.

CPR 1998, r 8.6 No evidence may be given at trial unless:

(a) it has been served as above; or

(b) the court has given permission.

CPR 1998, r 8.7 Part 20 claims (counterclaims or other additional claims) may only be brought with the permission of the court.

CPR 1998, r 8.6(2) The court may require or permit a party to give oral evidence at the hearing.

CPR 1998, r 8.6(3) The court has power to give directions requiring the attendance for cross-examination of a witness who has given written evidence.

14.2.7 Rights of audience

Substantive hearings will, unless otherwise directed, be in open court before a district judge but may, if there are complex or other significant issues, be heard before a circuit judge or even a High Court judge. Practitioners may therefore wish to check with the court as to the level of judge before making a decision as to whom is to appear.

14.3 ADDITIONAL (PART 20) CLAIMS

CPR 1998, r 20.2 An Additional (Part 20) claim is any claim other than a claim by a claimant against a defendant and includes:

(a) a counterclaim by a defendant against the claimant or against the claimant and some other person;

(b) a claim by a defendant against any person for contribution or indemnity or other remedy; and

(c) where an Additional (Part 20) claim has been made against a person who is not already a party, any claim by that person against any other person.

14.3.1 Requirements on issue

CPR 1998, r 8.7 In the case of proceedings under CPR 1998, Pt 8 the permission of the court is needed to issue an Additional (Part 20) claim save as set out below (see PD 20).

CPR 1998, r 20.4(2) A defendant can make a counterclaim without permission of the court if he files it with his defence.

The claim should be made on Form N211. CPR 1998, r 20.7(5)

The contents of the claim form should be supported by a statement of truth. CPR 1998, PD 20, para 4.1

An application for permission may be made without notice, unless the court orders otherwise. CPR 1998, r 20.7(5)

An application for permission should comply with CPR 1998, PD 20 and must be supported by evidence stating: CPR 1998, PD 20, para 2.1

(a) the stage which the action has reached;

(b) the nature of the claim to be made or details of the question or issue which needs to be decided;

(c) a summary of the facts on which the Additional (Part 20) claim is based; and

(d) the name and address of the proposed Additional (Part 20) defendant.

14.3.2 Service

Where the court gives permission to make an Additional (Part 20) claim it will at the same time give directions as to service. CPR 1998, r 20.8(3)

The court will decide the mode of service. Part 6 sets out the differing methods of service and the dates by which it will be deemed to have taken place. CPR 1998, r 6.3(2)

Each defendant must be served with:

(a) a copy of the claim form;

(b) a copy of the claimant's statement and any other written evidence;

(c) an acknowledgement of service in Form N213;

(d) notes for guidance in Form N211C; and

(e) notice of the place, date and time of the first directions appointment, if already fixed.

The acknowledgement of service is governed by Part 10.

But a defendant wishing to defend a counterclaim does not have to file an acknowledgement of service. CPR 1998, r 20.4(3)

Sufficient copies should be lodged for service on all other parties.

The effect of service is that the person upon whom Additional (Part 20) proceedings is served becomes a party to the proceedings if not one already. CPR 1998, r 20.10

Part 15 applies to any defence filed in response to an Additional (Part 20) claim.

CPR 1998, r 20.12

Practitioners should bear in mind the special rules that apply where an Additional (Part 20) claim is served on a person who is not already a party to the proceedings.

14.3.3 Management

A Part 20 claim is treated exactly the same as any other claim, so that the CPR 1998 are applied.

The exceptions to this general rule are contained within CPR 1998, r 20.3(2), (3) and (4).

Once a defence has been filed to an Additional (Part 20) claim other than a counterclaim, the court will fix a directions hearing and give notice to each party. The court may:

(a) treat the hearing as a summary judgment hearing;

(b) order that the Additional (Part 20) proceedings be dismissed;

(c) give directions as to the manner in which the claim or a part of the claim should be dealt with;

(d) give directions as to the part the Additional (Part 20) defendant may play at the trial of the claim;

(e) give directions as to the extent the Additional (Part 20) defendant is to be bound by any judgment or decision to be made in the claim.

CPR 1998, r 20.9

There are separate rules dealing with matters relevant to the question as to whether an Additional (Part 20) claim should be separated from the main claim. These apply when the court is considering whether:

(a) to permit the Additional (Part 20) claim to be made;

(b) to dismiss the Additional (Part 20) claim; or

(c) to require the Additional (Part 20) claim to be heard separately from the main claim.

This is a discretionary decision and at CPR, r 20.9(2) are listed some of the matters the court may take into account.

CPR 1998, r 20.11

Practitioners should note that there is no provision for default judgments on an Additional (Part 20) claim except for counterclaims in respect of which r 10.2 applies the normal rules set out in Part 12.

Part 24 is however applicable to all Additional (Part 20) claims and practitioners are referred to the special provisions in that connection.

14.3.4 Rights of audience

Substantive hearings will, unless otherwise directed, be in open court before a district judge but may, if there are complex or other significant issues, be heard before a circuit judge or even a High Court judge. Practitioners may therefore wish to check with the court as to the level of judge before making a decision as to who is to appear.

CHAPTER 15

PROCEDURES FOR THE ENFORCEMENT OF FINANCIAL AND COSTS ORDERS

15.1 INTRODUCTION

FPR 2010, r 33.3(1)

Where a party has obtained a financial order which has not been fully complied with, there is a variety of steps which can potentially be taken with a view to enforcement. When an application is issued for the enforcement of an order governed by the FPR 2010 made in the High Court or the Family Court for the payment of money to any person, it must be accompanied by a statement verified by a statement of truth stating the amount due under the order and showing how that amount was arrived at.

FPR 2010, r 33.3(2)

The application for an enforcement order may either specify the method of enforcement or may seek an order for such method of enforcement as the court may consider appropriate.

FPR 2010, r 33.2; CPR 1998, r 70.2(2)

The creditor may pursue more than one means of enforcement at the same time, but must inform the court, or the enforcement officer in the case of a High Court writ of execution, if any payment is made by the judgment debtor.

15.2 MAINTENANCE ARREARS

15.2.1 Maintenance arrears in excess of 12 months

MCA 1973, s 32(1)

Leave of the court is required to enforce arrears of maintenance if those arrears became due more than 12 months prior to the issue of the enforcement proceedings.

The application for leave should be made by way of Form D11 application notice in accordance with the FPR 2010, Pt 18.

15.2.2 Interest

Re TW & TM (Minors) [2015] EWHC 3054 (Fam)

Interest cannot be charged on arrears of periodical payments.

15.3 APPLICATION FOR AN ORDER FOR SUCH METHOD OF ENFORCEMENT AS THE COURT MAY CONSIDER APPROPRIATE

In an attempt to improve the effectiveness of enforcing financial orders, the FPR 2010 introduced a procedure whereby a judgment creditor may apply to the court for such method of enforcement as the court may consider appropriate. This procedure is aimed particularly at parties in person who might not know which type of enforcement would be suitable in the circumstances of their case.

15.3.1 Form of application

The application is made on Form D50K verified by a statement of truth and will lead to an order for the judgment debtor to attend court producing such documents as are identified in the order and to answer on oath such questions as the court may require. The order will warn the debtor that a failure to comply with it may lead to committal.

Precedent order 4.6 '*Order to Attend for Questioning (Made on Papers)*', for example (promulgated on 16 November 2020 by the President and Mostyn J) includes, at para 7, a useful list of information and supporting documentation which the debtor can be directed to produce and practitioners should refer to it.

15.3.2 If the debtor fails to attend?

The FPR are unclear as to the court's powers if the debtor fails to attend. Although the CPR 1998, r 71.2(6) and (7) are incorporated into the FPR 2010, r 33.3(3), the CPR 1998, r 71.8 is not, and it does not appear, therefore, that the summary power for a circuit judge or High Court judge to make a suspended committal order is available.

The most appropriate course for the court to be invited to take is to issue a warrant for the debtor's arrest. The matter is discussed in detail in *Family Court Practice* in the commentary to FPR 2010, r 33.3, to which readers are referred, and the High Court has expressly approved that analysis.

Westwood v Knight [2012] EWPCC 14; *Re K (REMO – Power of Magistrates to Issue Bench Warrant)* [2017] EWFC 27

15.3.3 The powers of the court

If the debtor fails to produce documents which he has been ordered to produce, or refuses to answer questions which are properly put to him, it appears that this may

Deutsche Bank AG v Sebastian Holdings Inc [2016] EWHC 3222 (Comm)

be treated as a contempt of court and punished as such. However, a separate application would have to be made seeking the debtor's committal, particularising the alleged failures to comply with the court's orders.

JSC BTA Bank v Solodchenko & Ors [2011] EWCA Civ 1241

It may be appropriate to draw the debtor's attention to the view expressed in the Court of Appeal that where there is a continuing failure to disclose relevant information, the court should consider imposing a long sentence, 'possibly even the maximum of 2 years, in order to encourage future co-operation by the contemnor'.

Kaur v Randhawa [2015] EWHC 1592 (Fam)

It is important to remember that the application under FPR 2010, r 33.3(2) is an application for 'an order for such method of enforcement as the court may consider appropriate'. Accordingly, at the conclusion of a hearing under this procedure the court may make a charging order, attachment of earnings order or third party debt order, or direct the issue of a warrant of control, without further formality and without requiring a separate application for that form of enforcement.

FC(C&DB)R 2014, Sch 2, Table 1
Mohan v Mohan [2014] 1 FLR 717

There are 2 limitations on this. First, a family court consisting of lay justices may not grant enforcement remedies other than an attachment of earnings order, so if one of those other forms of enforcement is considered appropriate the case must be referred to an appropriate level of judge. Secondly, information extracted from the debtor under compulsion under this procedure cannot be used as the basis for a judgment summons, because this would breach the debtor's right not to incriminate himself. Documents produced under this procedure, however, can be used in that way.

15.4 ORDER TO OBTAIN INFORMATION FROM A JUDGMENT DEBTOR

FPR 2010, r 33.23

An order to obtain information from a judgment debtor may be a useful means of enabling a judgment creditor to establish:

(a) the ability or otherwise of the judgment debtor to meet the substantive order and any related order for costs; and
(b) the most appropriate method of enforcement;

Watson v Sadiq [2015] EWHC 3403 (QB) (son of judgment debtor)
FPR 2010, r 33.23

although in family proceedings it will normally be preferable to take advantage of the procedure under the FPR 2010, r 33.3(2) (see **15.3**), not least because it avoids further court fees becoming payable in respect of each substantive form of enforcement. Note that there is no jurisdiction to require anyone other than the judgment debtor (or an officer of a company judgment debtor) to attend court under this provision.

The application is made by way of application notice in Form N316 to the court which made the order it is sought to enforce, unless proceedings have since been transferred to a different court, in which case it should be issued to the latter court. If granted, the application will lead to an order for the judgment debtor to attend court at a specified date and time to provide information about his/her means or any other matter about which information is needed to enforce the order. CPR 1998, r 71.2

The hearing must be fixed sufficiently far ahead to allow time for service of the order.

A copy of the order must be served personally on the judgment debtor not less than 14 days before the hearing. Where the order is to be served by the judgment creditor he must inform the court not less than 7 days before the hearing if he has been unable to serve it. CPR 1998, r 71.3

The judgment debtor may ask the judgment creditor for a reasonable sum to cover travelling expenses to and from court; the judgment creditor must pay such a sum, if requested. CPR 1998, r 71.4

An affidavit of service must be filed not less than 2 days before the hearing or be produced at the hearing. This affidavit (or a separate affidavit) should also state whether travelling expenses were requested and paid and should state how much of the debt under the order remains unpaid.

Note: That this is one of the relatively few situations in which the use of an affidavit is required, rather than a witness statement verified by a statement of truth. CPR 1998, r 71.5

15.4.1 The hearing

If the High Court made the order which it is sought to enforce, the application must be issued in the High Court. Otherwise, the application is made to the family court for the Designated Family Judge area within which the order was made. If, however, the proceedings have since been transferred to another court or another Designated Family Judge area, the application must be issued in that area.

Generally the order will provide for the judgment debtor to attend the family court hearing centre for the district in which he resides or carries on business, unless a judge decides otherwise. CPR 1998, PD 71, para 2.1

CPR 1998, PD 71, paras 4.1 and 4.2

A court officer or, where there are compelling reasons to do so, a district judge, will conduct the hearing. Where the court officer conducts the hearing a standard series of questions will be asked and the judgment creditor may attach to the application notice additional questions to be put to the judgment debtor.

CPR 1998, r 71.6; PD 71, para 5.1

Where the hearing takes place before a district judge the questioning will be conducted by the judgment creditor or his representative.

Broomleigh Housing Association v Okonkwo [2010] EWCA Civ 1113

Failure to attend an oral examination may result in a suspended committal order being made against the judgment debtor. The procedure is set out in CPR 1998 r 71.8. It has been said that the making of such an order should not be regarded as routine.

Deutsche Bank AG v Sebastian Holdings Inc [2016] EWHC 3222 (Comm)

Refusal to answer legitimate questions may be punished as a contempt of court. The existence of what has been described as a streamlined or summary power of committal under the CPR 1998, r 71.8 does not exclude the general powers of the family court to enforce its orders under the FPR 2010, r 37.4(1) by means of committal proceedings.

FC(C&DB)R 2014, r 14
FC(CC)(P)R 2014, r 4

If committal proceedings are taken, the FPR 2010, r 37.4 must be carefully observed, and in particular the grounds on which the application is made must be set out and each act of contempt alleged must be identified. Although in the civil jurisdiction such a committal application would be listed before a circuit judge or High Court judge, in the family court, any level of judge may deal with it, though FC(CC)(P)R 2014, r 4 limits the committal power of lay justices to 2 months.

15.5 FAILURE TO COMPLY WITH FINANCIAL ORDERS OTHER THAN THOSE RELATING TO CURRENT PERIODICAL PAYMENTS

15.5.1 Charging order

A charging order can potentially protect the receiving party in respect of unpaid lump sum or sums, accumulated arrears of periodical payments and costs orders, by imposing a charge on an asset or assets owned by the judgment debtor.

FPR 2010, Pt 40

In the family court, applications for charging orders are governed by the FPR 2010, Pt 40 which is similar, but not identical, to the CPR 1998, Pt 73 which applies in the civil courts.

Interim charging order

The application for an interim charging order is made by way of application notice in Form FE6 (in the case of land) or FE7 (in the case of securities) verified by a statement of truth to a district judge without giving notice to the other party. Per r 40.4, the application must contain all the information required by the FPR 2010, PD 40A, para 1.3. The application is made to the family court or, if the order it is sought to enforce is an order of the High Court exercising family jurisdiction, to the High Court.

Where the asset is land or buildings erected upon the land, which has or have been registered at the Land Registry, almost all district judges will insist on official copies of the entries on the register being lodged with the application. These copies of a registered title can straightforwardly be obtained from HM Land Registry. Comprehensive guidance notes are available on the gov.uk website under Housing and local services > Owning and renting a property > Search for property information from Land Registry.

The court may make an interim charging order imposing a charge over the judgment debtor's interest in the asset to which the application relates. That order is normally made without notice to the judgment debtor. The order will also fix a hearing to consider whether to make a final charging order. FPR 2010, r 40.5(2)

Copies of the interim charging order, application notice and any supporting documents shall be served by the creditor not less than 21 days before the hearing on the judgment debtor and those other persons listed in the FPR 2010, r 40.6(3). The district judge will need to be satisfied that the judgment debtor and other interested parties have been served. Note that service of the interim order and related documents is explicitly the responsibility of the creditor. FPR 2010, r 40.6(1)

Final charging order

If any person objects to the making of a final charging order, the rules stipulate that written evidence stating the grounds for objection must be filed and served by the objecting person on the applicant not less than 7 days before the hearing. FPR 2010, r 40.8(1)

At the hearing the court may: FPR 2010, r 40.8(2)

(a) make a final charging order confirming that the charge imposed by the interim charging order shall continue, with or without, modification;

(b) discharge the interim charging order and dismiss the application;

(c) decide any issues in dispute between the parties or between any of the parties and any other person who objects to the making of the final order; or

(d) direct a trial of any such issues and if necessary give directions; or

(e) make such other order as it considers appropriate.

FPR 2010, r 40.8(4)

A copy of the order should then be served by the creditor in such a way so as to ensure that the interest of the judgment creditor is recorded on the appropriate register, for example at HM Land Charges Registry, the Land Registry or with a company registry (in respect of a stock or share holding).

Failure on the part of a solicitor to ensure that a charging order is promptly registered on property which is subsequently sold would almost certainly be viewed as negligence. Accordingly, all aspects of such an application should be conducted with the absolute minimum of delay.

A charging order is not of itself a means of enforcement but it may be enforced by an order for sale in separate proceedings (see **15.5.3**).

15.5.2 Charging order on the making of an order

Green v Adams [2017] EWFC 24

In a case where the evidence satisfied the court that the paying party would 'do all in his power to frustrate' the order the court was making, and where the party's title to property had been fully examined in the course of the hearing, the High Court has asserted the power to make a final charging order at the conclusion of the initial hearing without requiring the receiving party to make a separate application and without requiring compliance with the FPR 2010, Pt 40. Such cases are presumably likely to be exceptional.

15.5.3 Enforcement of charging order by sale

If, following the granting of a final charging order, the judgment debtor still fails to pay the amount due, either under the original substantive order or any subsequent variation, an application can be made for the property to be sold or, where property can conveniently be divided, for the sale of a sufficient part.

If the charged property is owned by the debtor together with others, or the debtor only has a partial beneficial interest in it, an order for sale must be sought under the provisions of the Trusts of Land and Appointment of Trustees Act 1996, as to which see **14.2**. Because of the wording of the CPR 1998, r 73.10C(1), it is not unknown for a badly advised creditor to seek an order for sale of a jointly owned property without even naming the other joint owners as defendants.

If the charged property is owned by the debtor alone, an application for an order for sale will be commenced using the procedure provided by the CPR 1998, Pt 8. The claim form must be accompanied by a copy of the final charging order and be supported by written evidence as set out in the CPR 1998, PD 73, para 4.3. The Part 8 claim form N208 can be issued in either a county court or in the Chancery Division of the High Court. If the proceedings are issued in the High Court they must be started in Chancery Chambers at the Royal Courts of Justice, or a Chancery district registry. (There are Chancery district registries at Birmingham, Bristol, Caernarfon, Cardiff, Leeds, Liverpool, Manchester, Mold, Newcastle upon Tyne and Preston.) CPR 1998, r 73.10C

If the debt secured exceeds £350,000 at the date of issue of the proceedings the application must be issued in the High Court, unless the defendant consents to the county court having jurisdiction. CCJO 2014 (SI 2014/503), art 3 CCA 1984, ss 23, 24

The High Court may transfer the proceedings to the county court irrespective of the size of the debt. It was said (admittedly at a time when the county court jurisdiction limit was only £30,000) that 'If, on consideration of the circumstances of an individual case, the High Court decides that it is suitable for determination by a county court, it is in keeping with the modern policy of assigning cases to the appropriate tier in the court system that it should transfer it, irrespective of the county court limit'. *National Westminster Bank Plc v King* [2008] EWHC 280 (Ch)

If the application is commenced in the county court, it should be issued in the county court hearing centre for the district in which the defendant resides or carries on business. The family court does not have jurisdiction to make an order for sale.

The claim form must be served within 4 months after the date of issue, unless service is required out of the jurisdiction, in which case the period is extended to 6 months. CPR 1998, r 7.5

For procedure concerning service out of the jurisdiction reference should be made to the CPR 1998, Pt 6. The claimant may apply for an order extending the period within which the claim form may be served.

Note: See **14.2.4** for further information concerning an application to extend time.

The defendant has 14 days from service of the claim form in which to file an acknowledgement of service and accordingly the court will usually fix a hearing date not less than 28 days ahead to take account of service by post.

Prior to the hearing, it is advisable to obtain a valuation of the property in question for presenting to the court. This is because the judge who hears the application will, if an order for sale is made, need to fix a minimum sale price. In the first instance, the proportionate approach will generally be to seek a 'drive-by' valuation. Occasionally, courts are invited to treat figures from websites such as Zoopla as evidence of value. This is quite inappropriate.

A copy of the claim form should be served on the defendant together with:

(a) notice of the hearing date;

(b) a copy of the witness statement in support of the application;

(c) acknowledgement of service;

(d) a copy of a valuation if one has been obtained as suggested above.

If a valuation has taken place after service has been effected, a copy of the valuation should be sent to the defendant without delay.

CPR 1998, r 8.3(1)

The rules stipulate that the defendant must file a completed acknowledgement of service not more than 14 days after service of the claim form and must serve a copy on the claimant and any other party.

The acknowledgement of service must state:

(a) whether the defendant contests the claim;

CPR 1998, r 8.3(2)

(b) if the defendant seeks some other remedy to the claim.

CPR 1998, r 8.4(2)

If a defendant fails to do so but attends the hearing, he may nonetheless seek permission to advance any seriously arguable ground of opposition to the claim. Such permission is likely to be granted although the court may make the defendant pay any costs which are thrown away as a result of his procedural failure.

It has been said that to order the sale of the debtor's home is a draconian step. It is likely to be ordered in a case of deliberate neglect or refusal to pay or in a case where in reality without a sale the debt will not be paid, and most district judges will wish to afford the defendant an opportunity to deal with the debt rather than making an order for sale at the first hearing.

The duty to have respect for the debtor's home under Art 8 of the European Convention on Human Rights may mean that the court should satisfy itself that to order a sale would be a proportionate step. For this reason, although not mentioned in PD 73 para 4.3, it is sensible for the claimant's evidence in support of the application to address the question of proportionality. *Zehentner v Austria* [2009] ECHR 1119

15.5.4 Third party debt order

A third party debt order freezes assets of a judgment debtor which are in the possession of a third party in order to enforce a judgment for money owed to the judgment creditor.

The CPR 1998, Pt 72, with minor modification, applies to applications for third party debt orders in the family court. FPR 2010, r 33.24

Examples of a 'third party' are high street banks and building societies; but a third party debt order can equally be made against an individual. Note that a third party debt order cannot be made against the Crown (ie against a Government department, including the National Savings Bank), but an equivalent procedure is available under the Crown Proceedings Act 1947, s 27, as to which see the CPR 1998, r 66.7. Note also that a third party debt order can only be made in respect of something recognised in law as a debt owed to the judgment debtor. See the notes to the CPR 1998, r 72.2 in *Family Court Practice*.

Interim third party debt order

An application for a third party debt order must be made by filing an application notice in Form N349. The application notice must contain the information required by the CPR 1998, PD 72, para 1.2 and be verified by a statement of truth. It may be made without notice and must be issued in the court which made the order that it is sought to enforce unless proceedings have subsequently been transferred to a different court, in which case it must be issued in the latter court. CPR 1998, r 72.3 FPR 2010, r 33.24(1A)

The application will initially be dealt with by a district judge without a hearing. The district judge may make an interim third party debt order and fix a hearing to consider whether to make a final third party debt order. The interim order will direct that until the hearing the third party must not make any payment which reduces CPR 1998, r 72.4(2) the amount made to the judgment debtor to less than the amount specified in the order.

CPR 1998, r 72.4(5)

The date of the hearing of the application must not be less than 28 days after the interim third party debt order has been made.

The third party must be served with the interim order, the application notice and any supporting documents not less than 21 days before the date fixed for the hearing. The judgment debtor must be served at least 7 days after the order has been served on the third party and at least 7 days before the hearing. Although the court can be asked to effect service, because of the need for haste it will almost always be more sensible for the creditor to do so.

CPR 1998, r 72.5

Where the judgment creditor serves, he must either file a certificate of service not less than 2 days before the hearing or produce a certificate of service at the hearing.

Where a judgment debtor or his family is suffering hardship in meeting ordinary living expenses as a result of being prevented from withdrawing money from his bank or building society account as a result of a third party debt order, an application for a hardship payment order may be made. The procedure is set out in the CPR 1998, r 72.7 and the CPR 1998, PD 72, paras 5.1–5.5. Note that this procedure is only available where the order is against a bank or building society.

A third party debt order can be a particularly potent weapon where it is known that moneys are to be paid into a bank or building society on a particular day. In these circumstances, the timing of the application is obviously vital and, where necessary, the application should be made by a practitioner in person and not by post. Having issued the application, the practitioner should ask to go before a district judge and, if the interim third party debt order is made, should request the court to draw the order immediately so that service can then be effected on the third party without delay.

All aspects of a third party debt order application should be conducted expeditiously since any unreasonable delay on the part of a solicitor which results in failure to secure funds, which are subsequently withdrawn from an account after instructions have been received, could well be viewed as negligence. In particular, it is important to remember that a third party is not bound by the terms of the order until the order has been served.

Final third party debt order

If the judgment debtor or the third party objects to the making of a final third party debt order, he must file and serve written evidence stating the grounds for the objections. Written evidence must also be filed where there is a dispute between the third party and the judgment creditor as to the amount owed to the judgment debtor.

At the final hearing the court may: CPR 1998, r 72.8(6)

(i) make a final third party debt order;
(ii) discharge the interim third party debt order and dismiss the application;
(iii) decide any issues in dispute between the parties or between any of the parties and any other person who has a claim to the money specified in the interim order; or
(iv) direct a trial of any such issues and if necessary give directions.

A final third party debt order shall be enforceable as an order to pay money. CPR 1998, r 72.9(1)

15.5.5 Matrimonial judgment summons

A matrimonial judgment summons may result in the family court committing to prison a judgment debtor who wilfully fails to pay. Debtors Act 1869, s 5

Orders which are enforceable by this means are orders for periodical payments (where there are accumulated arrears), lump sums and, in some circumstances, those for costs.

An order for the payment of school fees direct to a school can also be enforced by judgment summons.

A judgment summons may be heard by any level of judge in the family court, including lay justices; however, an order for committal may only be made by a judge of at least the same level as the judge who made the original order. FC(C&DB)R 2014, rr 14, 17(5)

Failure to attend an adjourned hearing may of itself result in the judgment debtor being committed to prison for a period not exceeding 14 days. County Courts Act 1984, s 110(2)

The application may be issued in the case of an order of: FPR 2010, r 33.10(1)(a)

(a) The High Court:
    (i) in the Principal Registry of the Family Division;
    (ii) in a district registry;

(iii) in the family court (and if to the family court in whichever Designated Family Judge area is, in the opinion of the judgment creditor, most convenient), whichever in the opinion of the judgment creditor is most convenient;

FPR 2010, r 33.10(1)(b)
FPR 2010, r 33.10(1)(c)

(b) In the case of an order of the family court, to the family court in whichever Designated Family Judge area is, in the opinion of the judgment creditor, most convenient having regard in either case to the place where the judgment debtor resides or carries on business and irrespective of the court or registry in which the order was made.

FPR 2010, r 33.10(2)

The application must be made by filing a request in Form D62 together with a statement showing the amount due under the order and how the amount was arrived at, and all written evidence on which the creditor intends to rely. The statement must be verified by a statement of truth and have exhibited to it a copy of the order it is sought to enforce.

FPR 2010, rr 33.11(3), (5), (6).

The judgment summons and written evidence must be served on the debtor not less than 14 days before the day fixed for the hearing. It may, if the judgment creditor wishes, be served by post, unless the court specifically orders personal service.

FPR 2010, rr 33.13, 33.14A
Iqbal v Iqbal [2017] EWCA Civ 19

If the judgment debtor fails to attend the hearing, the court can order him to attend an adjourned hearing. Notice of the date and time of the adjourned hearing (which must make the purpose of the hearing clear, and specifically that the debtor is at risk of being sent to prison), together with copies of the judgment summons and the documents mentioned in the FPR 2010, r 33.10(3) must be personally served on the judgment debtor, and conduct money (a sum reasonably sufficient to cover the expenses in travelling to and from the court) must be paid or tendered to the judgment debtor. Curiously, although the judgment debtor cannot be committed under the County Courts Act 1984, s 110(2) for failure to attend an adjourned hearing unless travelling expenses have been paid or offered to him, the tender of travelling expenses no longer appears to be a pre-requisite to a committal order under the 1869 Act.

FPR 2010, r 33.16(1)

At the hearing, the judge may:

(a) where the order is for a lump sum provision or costs; or

(b) where the order is for maintenance pending suit, maintenance pending outcome of proceedings or for other periodical payments and it appears to the court that the order would have been varied or suspended if the debtor had made an application for that purpose,

make an order for payment of the amount due under the original order, together with the costs of the judgment summons either at a specified time or by instalments.

No order for committal may be made on a judgment summons unless it is made under the County Courts Act 1984, s 110(2) or the judgment creditor proves that the debtor: (i) has or has had since the date of the order the means to pay the sum in respect of which he had made default; and (ii) has refused or neglected or refuses or neglects to pay that sum. The debtor may not be compelled to give evidence, and the judgment creditor must consider carefully whether he or she is in a position to prove (to the criminal standard) that the judgment debtor has indeed wilfully refused or neglected to pay. See the discussion of the FPR 2010, r 33.14 in *Family Court Practice*.

FPR 2010, r 33.14
Mubarak v Mubarak [2001] 1 FLR 698, CA

Where an order for committal is made, the court may direct its execution be suspended on terms that the debtor pays to the judgment creditor the amount due, the costs of the judgment summons and any sums accruing under the original order, either at a specified time or by instalments.

FPR 2010, r 33.16(2)

A suspended order must not be executed until the judgment creditor has filed a statement of default on the part of the debtor.

FPR 2010, r 33.16(4)(b)

Even when a judgment debtor is committed to prison, it will not have the effect of extinguishing the judgment debt.

DA 1869, s 5.

The maximum sentence which can be imposed is 6 weeks' imprisonment. It has been known for courts to overlook this and to purport to sentence judgment debtors for longer periods.

Zuk v Zuk [2012] EWCA Civ 1871 (9 months imposed in proceedings 'riddled with errors')

Such a blunder may potentially give rise to a claim for damages against the Government.

LL v The Lord Chancellor [2017] EWCA Civ 237

15.5.6 Warrant of control

The procedure in respect of a warrant of control (formerly known as a warrant of execution) is governed by CPR 1998, Pt 83, sections I, II and IV, and Pt 84, the Taking Control of Goods Regulations 2013 and the Taking Control of Goods (Fees) Regulations 2014. The warrant authorises a county court bailiff to seize goods belonging to a judgment debtor and to sell them in order to satisfy a sum of money, including costs, due under a court order. The application for a warrant is made by way of Form N323 supported by a statement of truth, showing the amount due under the order and how the amount was arrived at.

TCGR 2013, reg 6

Unless a district judge directs otherwise on application by the creditor, the bailiff must give the judgment debtor 7 days' notice of intention to levy.

If the debt remains unpaid at the end of this 7-day period, the warrant is executed by the court bailiff against goods owned by the judgment debtor.

A bailiff is empowered to seize and sell items sufficient to cover the value of the debt, although any excess monies not required to satisfy the debt are repaid to the debtor.

15.5.7 Writ of Control

A similar procedure exists in the High Court where a creditor can apply for a writ of control (formerly known as a writ of fieri facias).

Note: Some goods are exempt from levy: see TCGR 2013, regs 4–5.

FPR 2010, r 33.4(5)

It is possible to transfer certain orders of the family court to the High Court for the purpose of enforcement, following which the order will have the same effect as if it had originally been made in the High Court. Note that orders for periodical payments, and for the recovery of arrears under such orders, may not be transferred to the High Court for enforcement.

With the introduction of the Courts Act 2003, s 99 and the High Court Enforcement Officers Regulations 2004 on 15 March 2004 the forms were amended and High Court writs are no longer addressed to the Sheriff of a particular county but to an enforcement officer.

Application is made by filing a request (formerly called a praecipe) in Form PF86A, supported by a statement showing the amount due under the order and how the amount has been arrived at, supported by a statement of truth and a prepared writ in Form PF53 for sealing by the court. The request must be signed by a solicitor if acting in full or by the creditor in person.

It is the responsibility of the creditor to nominate an Enforcement Officer. Unlike a Sheriff, the Enforcement Officer is not restricted to a particular county and may be authorised to enforce in different areas across England and Wales. There are 104 districts for the purposes of enforcement.

The High Court Enforcement Officers Association publishes a directory of High Court Enforcement Officers on its website at www.hceoa.org.uk/choosing-a-hceo/find-a-member.

If the creditor is unable to nominate an Enforcement Officer he or she should arrange for the writ to be addressed to: 'The enforcement officers authorised to enforce writs of execution from the High Court who are assigned to the district (enter location such as London W) in England and Wales' and should forward the sealed writ to the National Information Centre for Enforcement (c/o Registry Trust Ltd, 153–157 Cleveland Street, London W1T 6QW) DX 134211 Tottenham Court Road 2. They may be contacted by telephone on 020 7391 7299. Information may also be obtained from the website of the High Court Enforcement Officers Association at https://www.hceoa.org.uk/home.

It should be noted that a writ or warrant of control is valid in the first instance for a period of 12 months from the date of issue. CPR 1998, r 83.3(3)

15.6 FAILURE TO COMPLY WITH PERIODICAL PAYMENTS ORDERS

15.6.1 Attachment of earnings

An attachment of earnings order requires the employer of a judgment debtor to make deductions from the debtor's earnings and make regular payments direct to the court, for subsequent transmission to the judgment creditor. It should be noted that an attachment of earnings order cannot be made against a member of HM Forces, but a deduction from pay in similar terms can be sought under the Armed Forces (Forfeitures and Deductions) Regulations 2009, SI 2009/1109.

Where an attachment of earnings order is sought in the High Court or the family court to secure payments under a maintenance order, the procedure is governed by the Attachment of Earnings Act 1971 ('AEA 1971') and the FPR 2010, Pt 39. 'Maintenance order' for this purpose has an extended definition (set out at length in the AEA Act 1971, Sch 1) which includes orders for the payment of lump sums under the MCA 1973, and orders for costs awarded on the making of a maintenance order. Where an attachment of earnings order is sought to enforce an order other than a maintenance order, the CPR 1998, Pt 89 applies. It provides a code, largely delegated to court staff, for the making of orders without a hearing. Reference should be made to the notes to the CPR 1998, Pt 89 in *Civil Court Service*. The following summary deals with the enforcement of maintenance orders.

MCA 1973, s 32

It should be noted that leave of the court will be required to enforce payment of any arrears which have been outstanding for more than 12 months.

The application for an attachment or earnings order is made on the prescribed Form FE15, and must be issued in the court in which the maintenance order was made; in the case of a High Court order, to the District Registry for the district in which the debtor resides, in the family court, to the family court in the Designated Family Judge area within which the order was made. The application must be supported by a statement verified by a statement of truth showing the amount due under the order to be enforced and how that amount was arrived at. Unlike other enforcement applications, there is no requirement for any arrears to have accrued. However, where there are no arrears the order may be refused.

FPR 2010, r 39.6(1)

Once the application is issued, it is endorsed with the date and time of a hearing. Notice of the application and a reply form (FE17) will be served on the debtor by the court.

FPR 2010, rr 39.5(3), 39.8

Applications for attachment of earnings orders in respect of maintenance orders differ from those in respect of county court judgments in that they are listed for a private hearing, in chambers, before a district judge.

The application, endorsed with the details of the hearing, will be served on the judgment debtor together with a form of reply, in Form FE17, which requires the debtor to provide to the court full financial disclosure, information which will subsequently be passed to the judgment creditor.

FPR 2010, r 39.6(2)

The debtor is required to complete and file the Form FE17 within 8 days of being served.

A copy of any reply form received from the debtor will be sent by the court to the creditor.

FPR 2010, r 39.6(3)(c)

If the debtor complies and provides comprehensive information concerning both income and expenditure, the district judge will then be able to calculate fairly the appropriate deduction to be made from the debtor's earnings (referred to as the normal deduction rate) and fix a protected earnings rate. Protected earnings are, as the term implies, a level of earnings below which no deductions can properly be made by an employer. It, in effect, guarantees a minimum take-home pay.

The attachment of earnings order may be suspended in circumstances where there is a good reason to believe that the judgment debtor will make regular payments in future, and where an immediate order may have a detrimental effect on future employment.

A copy of the order which sets out the information given above should be sent by the court to the debtor's employer, without delay, together with an explanatory leaflet. If the order is not complied with and the employer fails to provide a satisfactory reason, a fine may be imposed.

The employer has a duty to notify the court, within 10 days, of any person bound by an attachment of earnings order ceasing to be in their employ.

Where the debtor leaves his employment the order shall lapse unless and until the court directs it to a new employer.

An attachment of earnings order in respect of maintenance takes priority over other attachment of earnings orders which may have been made against the judgment debtor or any which are subsequently made and should be endorsed accordingly. The court which makes the order has a duty to send a copy of that order to the Court Officer for the district in which the debtor resides.

If the debtor fails to disclose details of his/her financial position or details of his/her employer, an adjourned hearing will be listed, at which the court will consider whether an offence has been committed under the AEA 1971, s 23(2)(c), and whether the debtor should be imprisoned (for up to 14 days) or fined as a result. Notice of such a hearing must be personally served on the debtor not less than 5 days before the hearing. FPR 2010, r 39.9(3)

As an alternative to a fine or a sentence of imprisonment, the court may simply make an attachment of earnings order on the basis of such information as is available. The normal deduction rate may be in excess of what would have otherwise been ordered had the relevant information been provided (and the protected earnings figure may be lower). However, in these circumstances it is always open to the judgment debtor to apply to the court for a variation order, and at the same time provide full and proper financial disclosure.

The provision set out above applies equally in circumstances where the judgment debtor fails to attend an attachment of earnings hearing and, having been given an opportunity to explain that failure, does not take that opportunity or otherwise does not provide a satisfactory reason as to why a fine or a period of imprisonment should not be imposed.

FPR 2010, r 39.7

Where details of the employer have been disclosed, the court can require the employer to disclose full details of the debtor's earnings using Form N338.

FPR 2010, r 39.5(1)

It is also possible for a judgment debtor to apply on his/her own behalf for an attachment of earnings order either at the time a maintenance order is made or on any subsequent variation.

The attachment of earnings order will usually make provision for the payment of the instalments required under the order, together with a further instalment in respect of any accumulated arrears.

Where the attachment of earnings order relates to maintenance for a minor child, it may be prudent for a practitioner who is acting for the debtor to ask the court to request the creditor to provide an undertaking to notify the court when the child concerned has ceased full-time education. Without this, child maintenance orders are difficult to monitor.

15.7 JUDICIAL AUTHORITY TO SIGN DOCUMENTS

A party may decline or otherwise be unable to sign a document, for example a contract or a deed, required in connection with the sale or transfer of property pursuant to a court order. The Senior Courts Act 1981, s 39 (applied to the family court by virtue of the Matrimonial and Family Proceedings Act 1984, s 31E(1)(a)) empowers a judge to sign the document on behalf of that party or alternatively direct another person to sign.

An application may be made at the time the substantive order is made, where there is little prospect of co-operation. Otherwise, a subsequent application on notice may be made, in respect of which a court fee is payable unless the applicant is exempt from paying fees. A draft form of order is precedent order 4.4 '*Order for Execution of a Document*' (promulgated on 16 November 2020 by the President and Mostyn J).

A deed should be endorsed as follows:

Signed by District Judge	[name]	[*signature of district judge*]
on behalf of	[name] pursuant	
to section 39 of the Senior Courts Act 1981		
and pursuant to an order of the [name]		
Court dated the	day of	

Before me,
[*signature of witness*]

[*address of witness*]

[*occupation of witness*]

Note: The form and wording will require some variation, for example where the document to be signed is a contract.

CHAPTER 16

RECIPROCAL ENFORCEMENT OF MAINTENANCE ORDERS

16.1 RECIPROCAL OR INTERNATIONAL ENFORCEMENT

Sometimes, one party to a relationship is resident in England and Wales, and the other party is resident in another jurisdiction – another part of the United Kingdom, the European Union, or a country further afield than that. This raises issues for the determination and enforcement of financial claims – for one country cannot directly enforce its orders in the territory of another.

This Chapter will seek to offer a brief introduction to the complex subject of Reciprocal Enforcement of Maintenance Orders ('REMO'), which it is hoped will be sufficient to assist the reader when a REMO situation is encountered. When that occurs, careful examination of the helpful Procedural Guides contained in the *Family Court Practice* should be the next step, accompanied by consideration of the relevant rules, statutes and international conventions. It is not advisable to attempt to conduct a REMO case using this book as your sole procedural guide.

Much of the necessary procedural guidance is contained in the Family Procedure Rules 2010 (FPR 2010), PD 34A, but this Practice Direction cannot be read in isolation.

It is necessary to consider separately maintenance orders (which in some circumstances includes orders for the payment or transfer of capital) and other financial orders such as those for the payment of lump sums or costs.

16.2 CONVENTIONS AND LEGISLATION

A comprehensive list of the conventions and related primary legislation dealing with the enforcement of maintenance orders is to be found at **Appendix C(16)**.

The main provisions are:

(a) the Maintenance Orders (Facilities for Enforcement) Act 1920 ('MO(FE)A) 1920');

(b) the Maintenance Orders (Reciprocal Enforcement) Act 1972 ('MO(RE)A 1972');

(c) the Civil Jurisdiction and Judgments Act 1982 (as amended) ('CJJA 1982');

(d) The Convention on the International Recovery of Child Support and Other Forms of Family Maintenance (The Hague Convention 2007), brought into effect by The International Recovery of Maintenance (Hague Convention 2007 etc) Regulations 2012, SI 2012/2814;

(e) Council Regulation (EC) 4/2009 (The Maintenance Regulation).

Note: Some countries are governed by more than one Act.

The first attempt at reciprocal enforcement of maintenance orders was in MO(FE)A 1920, which now applies only to those Commonwealth countries which have not been designated as reciprocating countries under MO(RE)A 1972. Under this Act a 'maintenance order' is an order for the periodical payment of sums of money.

MO(FE)A 1920, s 10.

The principal legislation dealing with REMO is the MO(RE)A 1972.Under this Act, a 'maintenance order' is 'an order which provides for the payment of a lump sum or the making of periodical payments' towards a person's maintenance. Broadly, the MO(RE)A 1972, Pt 1 applies to certain Commonwealth countries, to countries which are party to the Hague Convention 1973 (distinct from the Hague Convention 2007), and (until 2017) the USA. The MO(RE)A 1972, Pt II applies to certain countries which have ratified the 1956 UN Convention on the Recovery Abroad of Maintenance.

MO(RE)A 1972, s 21(1)

CJJA 1982 provides for maintenance orders governed by the Hague Convention 2007, the Brussels Conventions (the forerunners of the Maintenance Regulation) and the Lugano Convention (which applies to Iceland, Switzerland and Norway) to be recognised and enforced in the courts of the UK. Less than helpfully, the Act defines a maintenance order as 'a maintenance judgment within the meaning of the 1968 [Brussels] Convention or, as the case may be, the Lugano Convention'; but a decision of the European Court has clarified that not only periodical payments but a lump sum or transfer of property may be regarded as 'maintenance' if it is intended to ensure the support of a spouse. (If, however, it serves only the purpose of division of the assets, it will not be treated as maintenance).

CJJA 1982, ss 2(1), 5(4), 5A(3), 15(1)
Van den Boogaard v Laumen (1997) ECR I-1147 (CJEU); *Moore v Moore* [2007] EWCA Civ 361

Since the coming into force of the Maintenance Regulation on 18 June 2011, that Regulation governed reciprocal enforcement between the UK and other Member States of the European Union. The interpretation of 'maintenance' under the Maintenance Regulation is the same as that under the Brussels Convention. Post-Brexit, the Maintenance Regulation applies to those cases whose proceedings were instituted prior to 11pm on 30 December 2020, but not to those which postdate that.

The Hague Convention 2007 was ratified by the EU in 2014 and it entered into force in the EU Member States, including the UK, on 1 August 2014. It closely resembles the Maintenance Regulation. Its importance was increased when on 1 January 2017 it entered into force in the USA. Note that the Hague Conventions 1973 and 2007 are quite distinct from the better known Hague Convention 1980 which deals with international child abduction.

16.3 RECIPROCATING COUNTRIES

A comprehensive list of those countries with which England and Wales have reciprocal arrangements for the enforcement of maintenance orders is to be found at **Appendix C(16)**.

16.4 MAINTENANCE ENFORCEMENT BUSINESS CENTRES

REMO work is administered through 3 Maintenance Enforcement Business Centres. The London MEBC is at the Central Family Court, First Avenue House, 42–49 High Holborn, London WC1V 6NP. That for the rest of England is at Bury St Edmunds MEBC, Triton House, St Andrews Street, Bury St Edmunds IP33 1TR. The MEBC for Wales is at The Port Talbot Justice Centre, Port Talbot, South Wales SA13 1SB.

16.5 INCOMING ORDERS – 1920 ACT AND 1972 ACT

Pilcher v Pilcher [1955] P 318

The foreign court which made the original order should be asked to arrange for a certified copy of the order to be transmitted to the Lord Chancellor (in practice, the REMO Unit, Official Solicitor & Public Trustee Office, Victory House, 30–34 Kingsway, London WC2B 6EX). An order to be registered under the 1920 Act will be sent to the Principal Registry, now located in the Family Division of the High Court (if an order of the superior courts) or to the relevant MEBC for the area in which the debtor lives. Registration is an administrative act and the payer cannot object to it.

An order to be registered under the 1972 Act will be sent to the relevant MEBC for the area in which the debtor lives or has assets.

If the payer is not resident in the country making the order, the order will be a provisional order and a hearing will be listed in the High Court or the family court at which that order may be confirmed with or without modification, after giving the payer the opportunity to make representations. In that situation, the legislation lists further material which must be sent to the court which is to deal with the matter:

- the depositions from the hearing in the foreign court (under MO(FE)A 1920) or a note or authenticated summary of the evidence at that hearing (under MO(RE)A 1972);
- a certified copy of the order; and
- a statement of the grounds on which the making of the order might have been opposed in the original court (normally, the respondent will only be able to challenge the provisional order on those grounds). MO(FE)A 1920, s 4; MO(RE)A 1972, s 7

Obviously the REMO Unit should also be supplied with:

- information as to the identity of the respondent and his whereabouts;
- a photograph of the respondent, if available.
- a marriage certificate; and
- birth certificates of any children for whom maintenance has been ordered.

16.6 VARIATION OF ORDERS REGISTERED UNDER THE MO(RE)A 1972 OR THE LUGANO CONVENTION

Where a foreign maintenance order has been registered under the MO(RE)A 1972 (but not the MO(FE)A 1920 or the Maintenance Regulation) the registering court has the same power to vary or revoke the order as if it had been made by the registering court. Normally the variation or revocation will be by a provisional order. This will not apply if both parties are residing at the time in the United Kingdom, or the application is made by the payee. It will also not apply if the variation is a reduction in the rate of payments on the ground of a change in the payer's circumstances and the courts in the reciprocating country do not have power to confirm provisional orders.

M v V [2010] EWHC 1453 (Fam)

Where an order is registered under the Lugano Convention, the English courts cannot review it as to its substance. However, it has been said that the payer can apply to vary the order in England if there has been a change of circumstances.

16.7 INCOMING ORDERS – THE MAINTENANCE REGULATION

Regulation (EC) 4/2009, art 41(1); *MS v PS* ECJ 9 Feb 2017; *AB v JJB* [2015] EWHC 192, Fam; Regulation (EC) 4/2009, preamble, para (17)

An incoming order will be sent to the Lord Chancellor and forwarded to the relevant MEBC. However, as the Regulation states that it must be enforced under the same conditions as a decision given in the Member State of enforcement, the ***payee*** may send it directly to the family court in the relevant area without the delays inherent in involving the Central Authorities in the respective states and the MEBC. It has previously been held that this does not allow the ***payer*** to register in the English court without going through the Central Authorities, with a view to seeking a modification of a European order; note in any event that such a modification cannot be sought if the payee is still resident in the country whose courts made the original order.

16.8 OUTGOING ORDERS – MO(FE)A 1920 AND MO(RE)A 1972

16.8.1 Application

MO(RE)A 1972, s 2(3)

An application must be made to the court which made the order by the person to whom payments should be made. This is made by way of an affidavit setting out:

FPR 2010, r 34.14; PD 34A, para 4.2

(a) the reason that the applicant has for believing that the payer under the maintenance order is residing in the reciprocating country; and

(b) the amount of any arrears due to the applicant under the order, the date to which those arrears have been calculated and the date on which the next payment under the order falls due.

In addition a statement should be provided giving:

(a) such information as the applicant has as to the whereabouts of the payer; and

(b) such information as the applicant has for facilitating the identification of the payer (including, if known to the applicant, the name and address of any employer of the payer, his/her occupation and the date and place of issue of any passport of the payer).

A photograph of the payer would also assist and a certified copy of the maintenance order must also be provided.

Note: The certificate must be signed by the district judge of the relevant court.

Once a practitioner has identified the country in which the order is to be enforced, reference should be made to Practice Direction 34A, paras 4.3–4.11 as some countries require additional information to that set out above.

As a general rule, only final orders will be considered for reciprocal enforcement, and given the delays inherent in the procedure it may not be sensible to apply it to interim orders.

It is understood that the REMO Unit of the Ministry of Justice require that all documents should be provided in triplicate.

If a district judge approves the application he/she will complete and sign a certificate confirming:

(a) that the maintenance order is enforceable in the United Kingdom;

(b) that the arrears of maintenance are as set out in the affidavit;

(c) the date of birth of any child referred to in the maintenance order;

(d) that the applicant's statement contains the information in the possession of the court as to the whereabouts and the identification of the payer. MO(RE)A 1972, s 2(4)

In addition, if registration is sought in a Hague Convention 1973 country, the certificate must also state: MO(RE)A 1972, s 2(4) as shown in Sch 3

(a) whether the payer has been served with the proceedings;

(b) whether he/she has appeared at any hearing and, if they have not;

(c) that they were served with notice of the application; and

(d) whether the payee has received legal aid either within the proceedings or in connection with the application to enforce.

The court will then forward, in triplicate, the affidavit, statement, certificate and certified copy of the relevant order, to the REMO Unit of the Ministry of Justice for onward transmission to the appropriate authority in the reciprocating country.

MO(RE)A 1972, Pt 1

The REMO Unit will provide any necessary translation free of charge.

The REMO Unit will subsequently act as a form of intermediary, forwarding mail between the originating court and the reciprocating court.

16.8.2 Variation

MO(FE)A 1920, s 4A; MO(RE)A 1972, s 5

Registration in a reciprocating country does not preclude the originating court from subsequently varying the order; but in the case of an order registered under the MO(RE)A 1972, if the variation increases the payments, the order will be a provisional order only unless the application was served on the payer and both parties attended at the hearing.

16.8.3 Claims for maintenance

MO(RE)A 1972, s 26(1), (2), (3), (4)

The MO(RE)A 1972, Pt II also provides for dealing with claims for maintenance (as opposed to orders) by persons resident in the UK against persons resident in a designated country. The REMO Section will offer assistance in completing an application which will comply with the law of the reciprocating country, and will arrange for the application to be transmitted to that country together with any necessary supporting documents. The application will then be considered in the reciprocating country. Similar arrangements exist for the transmission of applications for the variation of orders made in the reciprocating country.

16.8.4 Documentation required by the REMO Unit

The documentation which will normally be required by the REMO Unit will include:

(a) the birth certificate of any relevant child;

(b) a marriage certificate if applicable;

(c) a recent photograph of the payer;

(d) copies of any previous orders;

(e) a power of attorney which authorises the authorities in the reciprocating country to take all necessary steps to enforce the order;

(f) a certificate by the designated officer of the family court in accordance with the MO(RE)A 1972, s 26(3A).

In addition, as much information as possible to trace the address of the payer.

16.9 OUTGOING ORDERS – THE MAINTENANCE REGULATION

16.9.1 Application

An application to enforce in another EU Member State a maintenance decision made in a court in England and Wales is made in the form at Annex VI to the Regulation, accompanied by a certified copy of the order to be enforced.

The application will be made to the court which made the order and court staff will complete the form at Annex II to the Regulation, which must be signed, sealed and dated before the papers are submitted to the REMO Section (the Central Authority for the purpose of the Regulation).

It should be noted that if the respondent is resident in another Member State, a claim for maintenance may have been made in the English courts on the basis of the applicant's habitual residence; and, of course, vice versa in the case of an applicant resident in another Member State who sought maintenance from a respondent who is resident in England and Wales. Regulation (EC) 4/2009, Art 3(b)

If an order is made and the payee continues to be habitually resident in the country where the order was originally made, only that country's courts have jurisdiction to vary or revoke it. Regulation (EC) 4/2009, Art 8(1)

There is a very limited right for the payer to seek a review if he did not appear before the court which granted the order. This is subject to a strict time limit of 45 days from when the payer became aware of the decision, and 'no extension may be granted on account of distance'.

16.9.2 Hague Conventions and the Republic of Ireland

Where EU Member States are also Hague Convention 1973 Countries, the Maintenance Regulation and not the Hague Convention will, in circumstances in which both are available, apply, except for transitional cases.

The Hague Conventions 1973 and 2007 apply to maintenance matters between the UK and parties to the Convention outside the EU (including, since January 2017, the USA) and to matters which postdate 11pm on 30 December 2020.

16.10 RATE OF EXCHANGE

MO(RE)A 1972, s 16

Incoming orders will, of course, be converted to sterling. It is important to note that the exchange rate at the date of registration will continue to apply thereafter, unless the order is varied.

16.11 OTHER FINANCIAL ORDERS

Harrop v Harrop [1920] 3 KB 386.

Arrears under foreign maintenance orders can generally not be pursued as a debt in the English courts. However as discussed above, arrangements have been made with a number of countries for their reciprocal enforcement.

Colt Industries Inc v Sarlie (No 2) [1966] 1 WLR 1287

A money judgment of a foreign court can be the basis of an action in the English courts in which summary judgment will usually be granted.

However, a number of pieces of legislation allow judgments from certain foreign countries to be registered for enforcement in the English courts, and English judgments to be directly enforced in foreign courts. CPR 1998, Pt 74 and its accompanying PDs set out the relevant procedural rules. The text of Part 74 with detailed annotation and the PDs are set out in *Civil Court Service* (Jordan Publishing/LexisNexis).

It is important to realise that unless the case falls within the scope of one of them, there is no power to register a foreign money judgment for enforcement.

The Administration of Justice Act 1920 provides for reciprocal enforcement of High Court judgments in certain Commonwealth countries.

The Foreign Judgments (Reciprocal Enforcement) Act 1933 made further provision for reciprocal enforcement of judgments with a number of countries. The only non-Commonwealth countries to which the 1933 Act is still relevant are Israel, Surinam and Tonga. The debtor may apply to set aside the registration of a foreign judgment under this Act within a limited period.

The Civil Jurisdiction and Judgments Act 1982 gave effect to the Brussels Convention (to which the EEC countries were parties) and, as amended, gives effect to the similar Lugano Conventions of 1988 and 2007 signed by Iceland, Switzerland and Norway. The grounds on which registration may be set aside are very limited.

Council Regulation (EU) No 1215/2012 ('the Judgments Regulation') replaced Regulation (EC) No 44/2001 from 10 January 2015, but only in relation to judgments in proceedings instituted on and after that date and it has come to an end with Brexit. It made judgments of the courts of Member States directly enforceable without further formality.

16.12 TRACING THE WHEREABOUTS OF A PAYER

Where the payer is residing outside the United Kingdom but a precise address is not known, PD 34B suggests that it may be possible to trace his/her whereabouts if he/she is in Australia, Canada, New Zealand or South Africa.

The Practice Direction envisages that a questionnaire in Form D312 (Principal Registry of the Family Division) (sic) or Form D85 (in the Family Court), will be completed and lodged with the relevant court, with no fee being payable. These forms are being reviewed; and the guidance offered by the REMO Unit suggests that Australia (if the Territory is known), Canada (if the Province is known), New Zealand and the United States (if the State is known) will trace debtors but makes no such suggestion concerning South Africa.

Practice Note of 10 February 1976, now contained in FPR 2010, PD 34B

Solicitors may be required to give an undertaking that they will not disclose the address provided to the applicant or use it otherwise than for the purpose of the enforcement proceedings.

16.13 HIGH COURT OR FAMILY COURT?

Some countries (eg Hong Kong and Singapore) will accept only a High Court order for enforcement purposes and, accordingly, practitioners may think it prudent to check with the legal department of the High Commission or Embassy of the country in question. It is possible to transfer a family court order, other than a periodical payments order, to the High Court for the purpose of enforcement; but that may not necessarily cause it to be treated by the foreign country as 'a High Court judgment'.

Re Hardwick [1995] Jersey LR 245; FPR 2010, r 33.4(5)

If the order to be enforced is for periodical payments, the suit must be transferred to the High Court. Note that this will require an order of a High Court judge as set out in the FPR 2010, r 29.17(4).

16.14 PENSION ATTACHMENT

Practitioners should note that there is no provision for the reciprocal enforcement of pension attachment orders, whether made within the jurisdiction or within a foreign jurisdiction. However, the court has the power

MFPA 1984, s 17
WRPA 1999, Sch 12

to make an order for financial relief after an overseas divorce, to include a pension sharing element. It may therefore be possible in some circumstances to obtain a mirror order under the MFPA 1984, s 12 reflecting the terms of a pension sharing order made abroad and then seek to enforce that order in England and Wales.

Note: For further details as to MFPA 1984, ss 12 and 13, see **12.3**.

16.15 COSTS ORDERS

Costs orders within divorce and related matters whether in the High Court or family court are also subject to enforcement under the Civil Jurisdiction and Judgments Act 1982 as set out in **16.11**.

16.16 RECIPROCAL ENFORCEMENT IN OTHER PARTS OF THE UNITED KINGDOM

The Maintenance Orders Act 1950 provides for the enforcement of orders made in different parts of the United Kingdom.

16.16.1 Registration in London of orders made in Scotland or Northern Ireland

It is possible for the Principal Registry of the Family Division (now located in the Family Division of the High Court) to register an order made in the Court of Session in Scotland or the Supreme Court of Northern Ireland.

FPR 2010, r 32.7

The application is made to the originating court by way of affidavit or statutory declaration. Once approved, the officer of that court will forward the application to the Principal Registry together with a certified copy of the order.

On receipt of a certified copy of the order and accompanying documents, the court will:

(a) enter particulars of the order in Part 2 of the register;
(b) notify the clerk of the Court of Session or the registrar in Northern Ireland as the case may be, that the order has been registered; and

FPR 2010, r 32.7

(c) file the certified copy of the order and any statutory declaration, affidavit or statement as to the amount of arrears under the order.

It is possible for the order, once registered in London, to be re-registered in the family court pursuant to the MOA 1958.

Note: It is not possible for the Principal Registry to register an order made in the Sheriff Court in Scotland or in a Court of Summary Jurisdiction in Northern Ireland. (These orders must be registered in the family court.) MOA 1950, s 17(3)(b)

16.16.2 Registration of an English order in Scotland or Northern Ireland

It is possible to register a Maintenance Order made in the High Court in the Court of Session in Scotland or the Supreme Court of Jurisdiction in Northern Ireland. FPR 2010, r 32.3 and MOA 1950, Part II

Maintenance Orders made in the family court must be registered in the Sheriff Court in Scotland or in the Court of Summary Jurisdiction in Northern Ireland. FPR 2010, r 32.6

The application is made by sending to the court which made the order a copy of the order and a statement, which sets out:

(a) the address in the United Kingdom and the occupation of the payer;
(b) the date on which that order was served on the person, or if the order has not been served, the reason why this has not been done;
(c) the reason why it is convenient for the order to be enforced in either Scotland or Northern Ireland;
(d) the amount of any arrears due under the order;
(e) that the order is not already registered.

The statement must be verified by a statement of truth. FPR 2010, r 32.3(1)

Note: An order can be registered in one court only at any given time.

If the court is satisfied that the payer is resident in either Scotland or Northern Ireland, it will direct that a certified copy of the order, together with a copy of the statement, be sent to the appropriate court in that country for registration to be effected there.

16.17 FINAL THOUGHTS

Once an order has been registered, enforcement can potentially be effective, but practitioners should be aware, and make their clients aware at the outset, that the process of reciprocal enforcement can take many months to complete. Delay can potentially be encountered both within the Ministry of Justice and in the receiving country.

The level of success may, to a large extent, depend upon the degree of co-operation provided by the country in which enforcement is sought.

Clients should also be informed that the amount which is eventually enforced may not be the same as the amount ordered by the court in England and Wales, because a judge of the country in which the enforcement is sought may have the jurisdiction to order a variation, although this would be subject to confirmation by the originating court.

Should the payer move to another country, the frustrating process will then have to start all over again.

CHAPTER 17

JURISDICTION IN CHILDREN PROCEEDINGS

17.1 INTRODUCTION

The aim of this chapter is to provide an overview of jurisdiction in children proceedings. It is not a comprehensive guide to what is a complex and ever changing area of law. For a more detailed analysis please refer to *Hershman and McFarlane: Children Law and Practice* (Bloomsbury Professional)

Jurisdiction means the court's ability to hear and resolve the issue in question and is a question of fact; the court either does or does not have jurisdiction. If it does not have substantive jurisdiction, then it must decline to intervene save in a limited way where urgent temporary orders are required to safeguard a child's welfare. If it does have substantive jurisdiction, there is the question of whether and, if so, how, to exercise it.

In most cases the issue of jurisdiction is straightforward; the parties live and have always lived in England and Wales and jurisdiction is not in doubt. In other cases it may not be so straight forward in that one party may be from another country/they have lived in another country or the parties who are international may be trying to issue in different jurisdictions for tactical reasons.

The duty is on the court to examine jurisdiction at the outset of each case and the decision should normally be recorded on the face of the order.

Re F [2014] EWCA Civ 789

The court's jurisdiction is conferred under:

(a) The Family Law Act 1986;

(b) 1996 Hague Convention on Jurisdiction, Applicable Law, Recognition, Enforcement and Co-operation in Respect of Parental Responsibility and Measures for the Protection of Children;

(c) Council Regulation (EC) 2201/2003 (Brussels IIR) for proceedings commenced before 11pm UK time on 31 December 2021; and

(d) the High Court's inherent jurisdiction.

The 1996 Hague Convention has replaced Brussels IIR as the primary source for determining the court's jurisdiction and will be the focus of this chapter although it is important to consider the other methods to confer jurisdiction.

It is also important to note that there are important differences, including conceptual differences, between Brussels IIR and the 1996 Hague Convention, despite the former having been based on the latter. It should **not** be assumed that Brussels IIR concepts or case law on its provisions which have some similarity to those in the 1996 Hague Convention should be followed through parity of reasoning absent careful consideration.

17.2 WHICH JURISDICTIONAL RULES TO APPLY

Save for those legacy cases issued prior to 11pm UK time on 31 December 2021 where Brussels IIR remains relevant, apply the following rules:

- Where the 1996 Hague Convention applies, its rules must be followed;
- Where the 1996 Hague Convention does not apply, follow the rules in the FLA 1986; and
- In all intra-UK cases, follow the rules in the FLA 1986.

For those legacy cases referred to above where Brussels IIR remains relevant:

- Apply Brussels IIR wherever it applies;
- If Brussels IIR does not apply but the 1996 Hague Convention does, apply the 1996 Hague Convention;
- If neither Brussels IIR nor the 1996 Hague Convention applies, apply the FLA 1986; and
- In all intra-UK cases, apply the FLA 1986.

17.3 1996 HAGUE CONVENTION

The Convention was established to create a unified approach between Contracting States to matters of jurisdiction and applicable law and cross boarder cooperation, recognition and enforcement of orders. Whereas Brussels IIR is limited to members of the European Union the Hague Convention applies to a wider number of states that have ratified or acceded its terms.

The 1996 Convention's objects include determining the law applicable to parental responsibility, determining the State whose authorities have jurisdiction to take measures directed to the protection of the person or property of the child, and to provide for the recognition and enforcement of such measures of protection in all Contracting States, see Articles 1(1)(a)–(c).

It applies to children up to the age of 18 years, Article 2. A non-exhaustive list of 'measures of protection' is set out in Article 3.

It includes most (but not all) typical children law welfare orders (such as child arrangements orders). It does not include those matters specified in Article 4 such as the establishment or contesting of a parent-child relationship, or decisions on adoption, or disputes concerning the name and forenames of a child.

Warrington Borough Council v W (Care Proceedings: Jurisdiction) [2021] EWFC 68; *London Borough of Hackney v P & Ors* [2022] EWHC 1981 (Fam)

Some authority is suggestive of the 1996 Hague Convention applying as between Contracting States and non-Contracting States. However, this issue should not be regarded as settled. Practitioner works such as *Clarke Hall & Morrison* have previously argued that it should not (see Division 1, Chapter 8 § 935.1 for the reasoning), not least because the 1996 Hague Convention is simply an international treaty designed to regulate matters between Contracting States, and does not, like Brussels IIR, emanate from a supra-national political and economic structure with underlying supra-national principles.

17.4 HABITUAL RESIDENCE

A key concept in determining jurisdiction under the 1996 Hague Convention (and Brussels IIR and the FLA 86 for that matter) is where a child is habitually resident as at a relevant date.

A v A (Children: Habitual Residence) [2013] UKSC 60, [2014] AC 1; *Re KL (Abduction: Habitual Residence: Inherent Jurisdiction)* [2013] UKSC 75, [2014] AC 1017; *Re LC (Abduction: Habitual Residence: State of Mind)* [2014] UKSC 1, [2014] AC 1038; *Re R (Children)* [2015] UKSC 35, [2016] AC 76; *Re B (A Child)* [2016] UKSC 4, [2016] AC 606; *M (Children: Habitual Residence: 1980 Hague Child Abduction Convention)* [2020] EWCA Civ 1105; and *B (A Child) (Abduction: Habitual Residence)* [2020] EWCA Civ 1187

The current law on what constitutes a child's habitual residence is set out in 5 Supreme Court and 2 Court of Appeal authorities.

The following principles can be extracted from the key authorities:

- The habitual residence of a child corresponds to the place which reflects **some degree of integration** by the child in a social and family environment.
- The test is essentially a factual one which should not be overlaid with legal sub-rules or glosses. It must be emphasised that the factual inquiry must be centred throughout on the circumstances of the child's life that is most likely to illuminate his habitual residence.
- Its meaning is 'shaped in the light of the best interests of the child, in particular on the criterion of proximity'. Proximity in this context means 'the

practical connection between the child and the country concerned'.

- It is possible for a parent unilaterally to cause a child to change habitual residence by removing the child to another jurisdiction without the consent of the other parent.
- A child will usually but not necessarily have the same habitual residence as the parent(s) who care for him or her. The younger the child the more likely the proposition, however, this is not to eclipse the fact that the investigation is child focused. It is the child's habitual residence which is in question and, it follows the child's integration which is under consideration.
- Parental intention is relevant to the assessment, but not determinative.
- It will be highly unusual for a child to have no habitual residence. Usually a child lose a pre-existing habitual residence at the same time as gaining a new one.
- It is the *stability* of a child's residence as opposed to its *permanence* which is relevant, though this is qualitative and not quantitative, in the sense that it is the integration of the child into the environment rather than a mere measurement of the time a child spends there.
- The relevant question is whether a child has achieved *some degree* of integration in social and family environment; it is not necessary for a child to be *fully* integrated before becoming habitually resident.
- The requisite degree of integration can, in certain circumstances, develop quite quickly. It is possible to acquire a new habitual residence in a single day.
- Habitual residence was a question of fact focused upon the situation of the child, with the purposes and intentions of the parents being merely among the relevant factors. It was the stability of the residence that was important, not whether it was of a permanent character. There was no requirement that the child should have been resident in the country in question for a particular period of time, let alone that there should be an intention on the part of one or both parents to reside there permanently or indefinitely.
- It is unlikely, but not impossible, for a child to have no habitual residence.

When considering the issue therefore consideration needs to be given to the factual realities of the child's residence; it should be determined on a factual basis and not 'glossed with legal meanings'. You need to look carefully at all the circumstances, whether the child is integrated into a social and family environment and with young children, the primary care's place of habitual residence.

Habitual residence is not lost because of a temporary absence (eg a holiday) or where a person is ambiguous about their plans. Habitual residence requires a degree of stability although as seen from the above quote it is not full integration.

OL v PQ CJEU case C-111/17 PPU 8 June 2017 judgment

You cannot, even with a newborn baby, have habitual residence without some physical presence during the child's lifetime.

Re B (A Minor: Habitual Residence) [2016] EWHC 2174 (Fam)

Hayden J In *Re B* highlighted the need for a real and detailed consideration of a child's day to day activities, the family environment, interests and hobbies, friends and an appreciation of what adults are most important.

In summary: focus on the key issues that establish where habitual residence lies remembering the factual nature of the enquiry.

17.5 THE GENERAL JURISDICTIONAL RULE UNDER THE 1996 HAGUE CONVENTION

Article (5)1 provides that a court of the Contracting State of the habitual residence of the child has jurisdiction to take measures directed to the protection of the child's person or property.

Re NH (1996 Child Protection Convention: Habitual Residence) [2016] 1 FCR 16; *Warrington Borough Council v W (Care Proceedings: Jurisdiction)* [2022] 2 WLR 299; *H v R & Anor* [2022] EWHC 1073 (Fam)

Dicta suggests that the relevant date is assessed as at the date of the hearing.

If a child's habitual residence changes during the course of proceedings, save in cases of child abduction (Article 7), jurisdiction shifts to the new Contracting State.

Beware though, that where jurisdiction has shifted, a court is not precluded from exercising substantive jurisdiction by virtue of the seisin provisions in Article 13.

17.6 JURISDICTIONAL RULES UNDER THE 1996 HAGUE CONVENTION: NO HABITUAL RESIDENCE

If the general rule in Article 5 does not apply, a court may still have jurisdiction.

- *Article 6*: if a child's habitual residence cannot be established, or if they are a refugee or internationally displaced, the court where that child is physically present at the relevant date will have jurisdiction.
- *Article 7*: in cases of child abduction, the courts of the jurisdiction of a child's habitual residence prior to the wrongful removal or retention shall retain jurisdiction save in prescribed limited circumstances which are beyond the scope of this chapter.
- *Articles 8 and 9*: a court of a Contracting State with jurisdiction can request that a court of another Contracting State assume jurisdiction. Likewise, a court of a Contracting State without jurisdiction can request that the courts of the Contracting State with jurisdiction transfer that jurisdiction to it (see below).
- *Article 10*: in cases where proceedings for divorce or legal separation are ongoing in one Contracting State, the parties can elect for the courts of that State to exercise substantive jurisdiction in relation to a child where: (a) at least one parent is habitually resident in that state; (b) one of the child's parents has parental responsibility for that child; and (c) both parents agree. Jurisdiction will end on the conclusion of the divorce/legal separation proceedings.

17.7 URGENT/PROVISIONAL PROTECTIVE MEASURES

If the court has yet to establish whether it has substantive jurisdiction, or whether it has concluded that substantive jurisdiction lies elsewhere, if a child (or its property) is physically present in the jurisdiction, the court can exercise either urgent or provisional jurisdiction to secure a child's welfare. The measures taken are temporary and designed to support the court with primary jurisdiction under the 1996 Hague Convention.

A court can take **urgent measures** under Article 11 if the following four conditions are met:

- The child must be physically present in, or have property located in, the jurisdiction;
- The order sought must be a 'protective measure' for the purpose of the 1996 Hague Convention;

- The measure must be necessary; and
- The case must be urgent.

Re J (a child) [2015] UKSC 70

The higher courts have chosen not to be prescriptive over what measures can be taken under Article 11. They could include any order under the CA 1989, s 8. They could include a summary return order requiring the return of a child to another Contracting State. They could include an Interim Care Order.

B v B [2014] EWHC 1804 (Fam)

Article 11 has extra-territorial effect. The classic example where it is used in an extra-territorial manner is in abduction cases, where, on a summary return, protective measures to secure the short term protection of the child are used, such measures to last until the first hearing in the courts of the jurisdiction of a child's habitual residence.

Measures taken under Article 11 lapse where:

(a) the courts of a Contracting State with substantive welfare jurisdiction under the 1996 Hague Convention have taken measures required by the situation; or
(b) the courts of a non-Contracting State (of the child's habitual residence) have taken measures required of the situation *and* are recognised by the Contracting State which has taken the Article 11 measures in question.

Re S (A Child) [2022] EWHC 2053 (Fam) is an example of the court taking provisional measures under Article 12

Under Article 12, a court can take measures of a provisional character for the protection of the person or property of a child in whose territory the child or property belonging to the child is present. Such measures cannot be incompatible with measures already taken by the courts with substantive jurisdiction. Unlike with Article 11, the need for the measure does not require urgency.

Note: see also the HCCH Practical Guide to the Operation of the 1996 Hague Convention (2014), Chapter 7 (Provisional Measures) and the Explanatory Report on the 1996 Hague Convention by Prof. Paul Lagarde, Paragraphs 74–76.

Unlike with Article 11, these measures have a territorial effect limited to the state in question.

Measures taken under Article 12 lapse in the same circumstances as those taken under Article 11 (above).

17.8 TRANSFER TO A BETTER PLACED COURT

See also FPR 2010, r 12.68

Where the courts of two Contracting States have jurisdiction concerning a child under the 1996 Hague

Convention and are ongoing, *Article 13*, a seisin provision, operates so as to prohibit the court effectively second seised from exercising substantive welfare jurisdiction.

The principle way this conflict is typically resolved is through the court originally seised declining jurisdiction, either of its own accord, or through an exchange via Central Authorities or, where appropriate (and in England & Wales' case, only if sanctioned by the International Family Justice Office), international judicial liaison.

In contrast pursuant to *Articles 8 and 9*, where a Contracting State with jurisdiction considers that the courts of another Contracting State without jurisdiction is better placed to hear the case, it can request that the case is transferred to it. Likewise, where a Contracting State without jurisdiction considers that it is better placed to hear a case than the Contracting State with substantive jurisdiction, it can request that that court transfers the case to it.

A court of a Contracting State without jurisdiction under the 1996 Hague Convention makes a request to the courts of the Contracting State with jurisdiction under Article 9. In order to make a request, the following criteria have to be satisfied:

- The requesting state has to be either:
  - i a state of which the child is a national;
  - ii a state in which the property of the child is located;
  - iii a state whose authorities are seised of an application for divorce or legal separation of the child's parents, or for annulment of their marriage; and
  - iv a state with which the child has a substantial connection.
- The proceedings to be transferred have to be proceedings within the scope and remit of the 1996 Hague Child Protection Convention.
- The requesting state considers that it is better placed to assess a child's best interests.

JA v TH [2016] EWHC 2535 (Fam), [2017] 2 FLR 250; *Re D (a child) (Care Proceedings 1996 Hague Convention: Article 9 request)* [2021] EWHC 1970 (Fam), [2022] 1 FLR 922

A request can either be made directly by the requesting court, either through Central Authorities and/or international judicial liaison (subject to the approval of the International Family Justice Office). Alternatively, the court may invite the parties to make the request to the other court.

The final decision lies with the court receiving the request. Experience suggests it is helpful to set realistic timeframes to receive answers from foreign jurisdictions.

CFA (Ireland) v Mother [2021] EWHC 1774 (Fam)

The process and criteria similar where the court of substantive jurisdiction wishes to consider whether a court of a Contracting State without jurisdiction would be better placed to hear a case (*Article 8*).

Standard Form Precedent Orders have been issued dealing with incoming transfer requests.

The procedure for both Article 8 and 9 applications is set out in Chapter 6 of Part 12 FPR 2010.

Note: see, in particular, FPR 2010, rr 12.61–12.64 concerning Article 8 and FPR 2010, r 12.65 concerning Article 9. Article 9 applications are heard in the High Court.

FLA 1986, 2(1)

17.9 THE FAMILY LAW ACT 1986

The main purpose of the FLA 1986 was to prevent conflicts of jurisdiction within the UK and applies to private law orders made in England, Wales, Scotland and Northern Ireland and applies in respect of children under the age of 18. It provides that at any one time the courts of only one jurisdiction in the UK will have jurisdiction to make orders in respect of a child except in emergencies.

FLA 1986, s 25(1)

Note: Although recognition and enforcement is limited to children under the age of 16.

It is only when the court does not have jurisdiction under the Hague Convention 1996 or, for legacy cases, Brussels IIR, that the court will consider whether it has jurisdiction to make CA 1989, s 8 orders under the FLA 1986 if the conditions pursuant to s 2(1) are satisfied which include;

(a) there are ongoing matrimonial proceedings or civil partnership proceedings and the conditions of section 2A are satisfied namely the proceedings are continuing; or

(b) The child is habitually resident in England and Wales or present in England and Wales on the relevant date and not habitually resident in any other part of the UK

FLA 1986, s 7. There is dicta to the effect that an oral application would not constitute an application for the purposes of s.7(c)(i) FLA 86, see *Re S (A Child) (Jurisdiction)* [2022] EWHC 1720 (Fam)

The relevant date is the date of the application.

17.10 INHERENT JURISDICTION OF THE HIGH COURT

Consideration must first be given as to whether jurisdiction is governed by the 1996 Hague Convention or, for those remaining legacy cases, Brussels IIR. If *neither* applies then the High Court may be able to exercise its inherent jurisdiction as a source of jurisdiction. The inherent jurisdiction derives from 'the right and duty of the Crown as *parens patriae* to take care of those who are not able to take care of themselves'.

Re L (and infant) [1968] 1 All ER 20. Article 14 of Brussels IIR provided that, if the courts of no Member State had jurisdiction under the general jurisdiction provisions of that Regulation, jurisdiction was to be determined by local law. This opened the door to the use of the inherent jurisdiction as a source of jurisdiction in Brussels IIR cases. The position is different in relation to the 1996 Hague Convention. There is a closed jurisdictional scheme, and, where a case concerns two Contracting States, there is no scope for the English court to found jurisdiction under the inherent jurisdiction, see *Re I-L (Children) (1996 Hague Child Protection Convention: Inherent Jurisdiction)* [2019] EWCA Civ 1956.

Jurisdiction may be exercised only with respect of a child who is:

(a) a British subject whether or not in the jurisdiction;

(b) physically present in England and Wales; or

(c) habitually resident in England and Wales.

17.11 COUNCIL REGULATION (EC) 2201/2003 (BRUSSELS II REVISED REGULATIONS)

Brussels IIR came into force on 1 August 2004 and became applicable in UK law on 1 March 2005. It applies in all Member States of the European Union save Denmark. The scope of the Regulation is wide and Article 1(1) provides for it to apply in cases concerning divorce, legal separation or marriage annulment and the attribution, exercise, delegation, restriction or termination of parental responsibility (both private and public law proceedings).

For both matrimonial and children matters the crucial issue is habitual residence; Article 8 provides the general rule that the most appropriate forum to determine matters of parental responsibility is the relevant court of the Member State where the child is habitually resident.

17.12 BRUSSELS IIR: URGENT PROTECTIVE MEASURES

Where a child is physically present in the jurisdiction and it is necessary to take urgent steps to safeguard the child's welfare the court can accept limited jurisdiction pursuant to Article 20. This allows the court in urgent cases to take 'provisional, including protective, measures'. By way of example this may include an order for a prohibited steps order preventing the removal of a child from the jurisdiction for a short period to allow the court to consider the position of jurisdiction.

Care must always be taken in the court exercising its jurisdiction, a return date should always be listed as soon as possible after the initial hearing and the court's limited jurisdiction should be made plain on the face of the court.

17.13 BRUSSELS IIR: TRANSFER TO A BETTER PLACED COURT

Where another court is better placed to determine the entire case or any part of it then the court seized with the case may transfer it to another Member State pursuant to Art 15.

Article 15 applies where the court of origin has jurisdiction on the basis that the child is habitually resident there but determines that it is in the best interests of the child to transfer the case to another Member State.

Transfer is subject to the child having a particular connect with the other member state. Art 15(3) sets out 5 situations where such connection exists:

(i) the child has acquired habitual residence in the new Member State after the court of origin was seized;

(ii) the other Member State is the former habitual residence of the child;

(iii) it is the place of the child's nationality;

(iv) it is the habitual residence of a holder of parental responsibility; or

(v) the child owns property in the other Member State and the case concerns measures for the protection of the child relating to the administration, conservation or disposal of this property.

Both courts must be of the opinion that the transfer is in the bests interests of the child and there should be liaison between the 2 courts to achieve this.

Any application to transfer may be made by a party, the courts own motion or on the application of a court of another member state if at least one party agrees.

When the court is faced with an application it can either stay the case and invite the parties to introduce a request before the court in the Member State it is proposed the case be transferred to or it may directly request the court in the other Member State to take over the case.

CHAPTER 18

CHILDREN – PRIVATE LAW ISSUES

18.1 THE CHILDREN ACT 1989, PTS I AND II

The Children Act 1989 ('CA 1989') is concerned with all aspects of the welfare and general upbringing of a child. The CA 1989, Pts I and II relate to private law matters, that is to say proceedings brought by one individual against another individual or individuals. Parts III to XI concern public law matters, that is to say proceedings brought by a local authority against an individual or individuals. Part XII deals with both private and public law matters. The public law aspects of the CA 1989 are outside the scope of this book but an overview of what you need to know as a private law practitioner is included in Chapter 22.

CFA 2014, s 1(2A)

In making an order under the various provisions of Parts I and II, the court must have regard to the provisions of the CA 1989, s 1(3). These provisions are commonly referred to as the welfare checklist. However, it should be noted that it is a basic principle of the CA 1989 that no order should be made unless it would be in the best interest of a child to make one. This is generally referred to as the 'non-intervention principle'. The Children and Families Act 2014 made numerous changes to the CA 1989 which included the presumption that unless the contrary is shown, the involvement of a parent in the life of the child concerned will further the child's welfare. The term 'involvement' means 'involvement of some kind, either direct or indirect, but not any particular division of the child's time'.

18.1.1 Pre-proceedings

CFA 2014, s 10(1)
FPR 2010, r 3.6

It is a requirement that before making an application the applicant is required to attend a mediation information and assessment meeting (MIAM) unless they fall within one of the MIAM exemptions or a mediator's exemption applies.

Mediation should take place within 15 business days of contacting the mediator and be within 15 miles of the applicant's home. If no appointment is available within that time or within that distance, then an exemption applies and you can apply immediately to the court.

As to cost; if one of the parties is eligible for public funding on means grounds then the cost of the initial mediation meeting can be met by the Legal Aid Agency ('LAA'). If neither is eligible for funding then the costs are to be agreed with the mediator.

Only an authorised family mediator can conduct a MIAM, The first meeting is intended to allow the parties, separate or together, to meet with the mediator who will: FPR 2010, r 3.9 PD3A

- provide information about mediation and other forms of out of court resolution
- try and clarify what is in dispute and how issues can be resolved
- identify possible sources of support
- provide more information about services, to include mediation, that encourage the reaching of agreement
- assess the parties' suitability for mediation
- assess risk of domestic violence and assess any risk to the child (this is not a risk assessment and nor is there any statutory authority to undertake a risk assessment)

If agreement is reached the mediator will draft a memorandum of understanding.

An online database of authorised family mediators can be found at www.familymediationcouncil.org.uk.

Note: Mediation is confidential. Information about what is discussed in mediation is not to be given to the court; the parties will have signed an agreement to mediate which confirms, inter alia, that: (a) the mediation is confidential; (b) will not be referred to in evidence in any court proceedings about the same issue; and (c) will not be used in statements. The court is not able to require mediators to disclose information as to what has been discussed in mediation. The parties of course can waive this confidentiality by mutual consent.

18.1.2 Exemptions from the requirement to mediate

These are set out fully in the FPR 2010, r 3.8 but in summary are:

(a) Domestic violence

(b) Child protection concerns

(c) Urgency

(d) Previous MIAM in the last 4 months and this application relates to the same or substantially the same dispute

(e) Other (which includes not sufficient contact details for the respondent)

FPR 2010, r 3.8

(f) An authorised family mediator confirms that he/she is satisfied is not suitable for mediation.

If mediation is not appropriate then this must be set out in the application. If a MIAM exemption is claimed inappropriately the court either at the allocation or at the first hearing will:

(a) direct the applicant, or direct the parties to attend a MIAM; and

FPR 2010, r 3.10

(b) if necessary adjourn the proceedings to enable a MIAM to take place.

Re K and K [2022] EWCA Civ 468

The Court of Appeal have highlighted the importance of MIAM compliance and the duty on the court to carefully scrutinise any exemption claims.

18.1.3 Parenting plan

FPR 2010, PD 12B, para 2.4

A parenting plan is a tool for separating parents to identify and agree, in writing, the arrangements for their child and is a useful tool pre-proceedings in an attempt to reach agreement or at least narrow the issues. A copy can be obtained at www.cafcass.gov.uk/grown-ups/parents-and-carers/divorce-and-separation/parenting-together/parenting-plan/#:~:text=The%20Parenting%20Plan%20is%20a,having%20to%20go%20to%20court.

Note: Practitioners should consider using a parenting plan as part of early negotiations as this can assist in enabling agreement.

18.1.4 Who can apply?

The following persons are entitled to apply to the court for any CA 1989, s 8 order with respect to a child:

(a) any parent, guardian or special guardian of the child;

(b) any person who by virtue of the CA 1989, s 4(A) (see below) has parental responsibility for the child;

CA 1989, s 10(4)(a), (aa) and (ab)

(c) any person who is named, in a child arrangements order that is in force with respect to the child, as a person with whom the child is to live.

The following persons are entitled to apply for a child arrangements order with respect to a child:

(a) any party to a marriage (whether or not subsisting) in relation to whom the child is a child of the family;

(b) any civil partner in a civil partnership (whether or not subsisting) in relation to whom the child is a child of the family;

(c) any person with whom the child has lived for a period of at least 3 years; where that person is a relative then the time period is reduced to 1 year provided the application relates to with whom the child concerned is to live or when the child is to live with any person;

(d) any person who: CA 1989 s10 (5B)

(i) in any case where a child arrangements order in force with respect to the child, regulates arrangements relating to with whom the child is to live or when the child is to live with any person, has the consent of each of the persons named in the order as a person with whom the child is to live;

(ii) in any case where the child is in the care of a local authority, has the consent of that local authority; or

(iii) in any other case, has the consent of each of those (if any) who have parental responsibility for the child.

(e) Any person who has parental responsibility for the child by virtue of provision made under the CA 1989, s 12(2A) (see below). CA 1989, s 10(5)(a) to (d)

Where a child is placed with a local authority foster parent for at least 1 year or has lived with a relative for a period of one year that person may apply. CA 1989, s 10(5A) and (5B)

If a person is not automatically able to apply an application for leave may be made. When applying for leave the court shall, in deciding whether or not to grant leave have regard to:

(a) the nature of the proposed application for the CA 1989, s 8 order;

(b) the applicant's connection with the child;

(c) any risk there might be o that proposed application disrupting the child's life to such an extent he would be harmed by it; and

(d) where the child is being looked after by a local authority:

(i) the authority's plans for the child's future; and

(ii) the wishes and feelings of the child's parents. CA 1989, s 10(6)

18.1.5 Application

Proceedings are commenced by issuing an application using Form C100, which must conclude with a statement of truth and include confirmation of attendance at a MIAM or otherwise. Sufficient copies of the application must be sent to the court, together with the court fee, unless the applicant is exempt from fees. In existing proceedings you use Form C2.

Note: Four copies are usually required; one for the applicant, one for the respondent, one for Cafcass and one for the court. The family court is moving away from the paper based process to becoming fully electronic working. At the time of preparing this book this has not happened in private law but has in public law.

FPR 2010, r.5.1, PD3A PD5A and PD12B

If an application alleges harm or domestic violence supplemental information is required in Form C1A.

The application Forms C100 and C1A should be confined to relevant factual information. The forms make it clear that there will be an opportunity to file a detailed statement if one is needed. Parties should continue to avoid unnecessary inflammatory language or allegations.

FPR 2010, r 29.1

If the applicant, or any other party, does not wish to reveal his/her address or that of a relevant child, a Form C8 must be completed. Once filed at court, the address should not be disclosed to any person other than by direction of the court. The form will be placed, in a sealed envelope, on the court file which will be marked accordingly.

FPR 2010, PD 12C, para 1.3

Where the application is in respect of more than one child, all the children are to be included in the one application.

Once the application has been filed, it cannot be withdrawn without leave of the court.

18.1.6 Gatekeeping

FPR 2010, PD 12B, para 9.2

Within one working day of receipt of the application by the court the application shall be considered by the nominated gatekeeper. This is either a nominated legal advisor and/or District Judge. In most courts gatekeeping is undertaken by both a legal advisor and District Judge working together.

Gatekeeping is undertaken in accordance with the guidance issued by the President on Allocation and Gatekeeping for Proceedings under the CA 1989, Pt II.

Note: See **Appendix C(8)** for President's Guidance issued 22 April 2014 which replaces Practice Direction, 3 November 2008.

The Allocation and Gatekeeping team will consider the application carefully and allocate the case and give directions in accordance with the President's Guidance issued 22 April 2014. The application will be thoroughly scrutinised, the facts considered, together with any previous files or orders that have been obtained and the application will be allocated in accordance with:

(a) the need to make the most effective and efficient use of the local judicial resources;
(b) the need to avoid delay;
(c) the need for judicial continuity;
(d) the location of the parties (and transfer the case to the most suitably located court); and
(e) complexity, in accordance with the Schedule to the guidance.

From that the initial allocation is made but will be kept under review and can be reconsidered with further information (ie on receipt of the safeguarding report) or a party may ask the court to reconsider allocation at the first or further hearing. FPR 2010, r 29.19

At the gatekeeping stage careful consideration will be given to attendance at a MIAM and if the parties have not attended, the reason why. If there has been non-attendance and no reason is provided, or the exemption does not appear to apply, attendance can be directed before the First Hearing Dispute Resolution Appointment ('FHDRA').

The gatekeeping team can also give any urgent and necessary directions. Any such directions should be set out in a covering letter. FPR 2010, PD12B para 9.4(2)

18.1.7 Service

Unless the applicant or solicitors request to serve or have been ordered to do so, the court will serve a copy of the application together with notice of hearing on Form C6 allowing for the time specified in the Practice Direction; that is 14 days prior to the hearing. FPR 2010, r 12.8, PD 12C

The respondents to the application are every person with parental responsibility, any person with parental responsibility before a care order was made and, on an application to discharge or vary an order, the parties to those proceedings. FPR 2010, r.12.3, PD12B

Every respondent will receive a Form C1A, even where the applicant has not raised matters of abuse, violence or harm. The respondent can use this form either to raise matters of abuse, violence or harm or to respond to matters raised by the applicant.

Both Forms C100 and C1A provide for the applicant or respondent to indicate whether or not they need an FPR 2010, PD 12C, para 3.1

interpreter or whether they have a disability for which either special assistance or special facilities are required.

If there is a requirement to serve a person who is not a party to the proceedings, for example a relative with whom a child resides, or a local authority who are providing accommodation the notice will be in Form C6A and not C6.

FPR 2010, rr 6.44–6.46

Forms C6 or C6A will be endorsed with the time and date of the first hearing or directions appointment.

If a respondent to the application is residing overseas at the time of the application, the time for service will be extended by reference to the provisions of the FPR 2010, r 6.42 and PD 6B, taking account of the fact that the time for service within the jurisdiction is 14 days.

For service on a respondent who is a member of the armed forces, see PD 6A, para 5.1 and the Annex.

Note: For a list of armed forces contact addresses, see **Appendix C(2)**.

FPR 2010, r 4.1(3)(i)

Wherever possible, a further application, by any party, relating to the same child or a sibling of that child will be listed on the same day and at the same time as the original application. This will invariably mean that the time for service on any respondent will need to be abridged. The applicant will need to apply without notice, by way of Form C2, to a district judge for such an order. The application attracts a court fee unless the applicant is exempt from fees.

Note: Service is made by delivery to the party's address for service which is normally by post. However, service can be by electronic means. If this is more appropriate you should seek an order at the commencement of proceedings and set out why

18.1.8 Action following service upon a respondent

FPR 2010, r 12.32

Within 14 days of service of the application or, where the respondent is outside the jurisdiction, such additional period as has been allowed by the court, the respondent is required to file a completed acknowledgement of service (Form C7) and an answer to the application and serve a copy on all other parties.

The respondent also has the opportunity to complete Form C1A if appropriate.

FPR 2010, r 29.1

If any respondent does not wish to disclose his/her address, a Form C8 should be completed and lodged at court by or on behalf of that party. Once filed at court the Form C8 will be placed in a sealed envelope on the court file, which will be marked accordingly. Similarly, if the address of a child who is the subject of the proceedings is to remain confidential a Form C8 should be completed on behalf of that child.

Once a Form C8 has been lodged with the court, the address of the person concerned must not be disclosed other than by order of the court.

18.1.9 Where a party is in prison

If the presence of a party who is in prison is reasonably required at a hearing, it may be necessary to apply to the court for an order directing the governor of the relevant prison to produce the prisoner to give evidence at that hearing (this is referred to as a production order). County Courts Act 1984, s 57

An application for a production order is normally made on notice to the prison governor, to enable objections to be made to the court in circumstances where, for example, the prisoner is violent or would otherwise pose a threat. The application should be made on Form C2, in respect of which a fee is payable unless the applicant is exempt from fees.

Care should be taken to ensure that the production order specifies a particular hearing and is not couched in general terms.

With the increase in availability of video links in courts and in prisons enquiries should first be made to ascertain if the prisoner could attend by this method before personal attendance is considered. Most prisons are able to arrange for a prisoner to attend via CVP.

18.1.10 Safeguarding report

The court shall send to The Children and Family Court Advisory and Support Service ('Cafcass') a copy of the Form C100 (and the Form C1A if supplied) and the Form C6 Notice of Hearing no later than 2 working days after the date of issue. FPR 2010, PD12B, para 8.9

All applications on issue go to the national centre who then seek information from the local teams including: FPR 2010, PD 12B, para 13

(a) considering information from the Local Authority;
(b) considering information from the police;
(c) assessing any recent offending and any patterns of offending; and
(d) speaking to the parties (this can only be done if the contact information is provided. Therefore, it is essential that telephone numbers are included in any application).

Cafcass will then set out the above in the safeguarding letter to assist the court; the information is for the purposes of safeguarding NOT trying to resolve the issues in the case.

FPR 2010, PD12B, para 13

The safeguarding letter should be received 3 working days before the hearing; this allows the parties to consider the contents and the court to check that the case has been allocated to the correct level of judiciary.

Note: the safeguarding letter is essential for the first hearing. Where it is not available and there are no other reliable safeguarding information the court must adjourn the FHDRA until the safeguarding results are available – PD12J para 12

18.1.11 Covid-19 pandemic

This chapter is written on the basis that, with time, proceedings will return to some form of normality. Although some case management hearings may remain remote most hearings to include FHDRA's and DRA's are likely to return to in person hearings.

PD36Q modifies PD12B to allow individual courts to modify their approach to proceedings and process to manage the workload.

18.1.12 Emergency applications

See Chapter 24.

FPR 2010, PD 12B, para 14.3

18.1.13 Seeking an order on issue

Parties sometimes agree the terms of the child arrangements but, for various reasons, wish to put this in an order. Applications are therefore issued attaching a draft order and seeking that order be made without the parties' attendance on the basis that they have reached agreement. The obvious question of course is why an order is required if there is agreement but, even if that is overcome the court cannot make an order on issue. Before making any order safeguarding checks must be undertaken.

Note: If this course of action is being considered the court should be asked to list the hearing but with the parties' attendance excused. This will allow the court to consider the application, draft order and safeguarding report and decide whether or not the order can be made without the parties' attendance.

FPR 2010, PD12J, para 6

The court must not make a child arrangements order by consent, or give permission for an application for a child arrangements order to be withdrawn, unless the parties are present in court, all initial safeguarding checks have been obtained by the court, and an officer of Cafcass or of Cafcass Cymru has spoken to the parties separately, except where it is satisfied that there is no risk of harm to the child and/or the other parent in so doing.

18.1.14 Welfare of the child

When the court determines any question about the upbringing of a child then the child's welfare shall be the court's paramount consideration and the principle applies in full to all the applications outlined in this chapter. CA 1989, s 1(1)

In determining any question about a child's upbringing the court shall have regard to the general principle that any delay in determining the question is likely to prejudice the child's welfare (no-delay principle). CA 1989, s 1(2)

The court should not intervene and make an order unless it considers that doing so would be better for the child than making no order at all (non-intervention principle). CA 1989, s1 (5)

Where the court is considering making, varying or discharging a section 8 order the court shall have regard to (the welfare checklist):

(a) the ascertainable wishes and feelings of the child concerned (considered in the light of his age and understanding);

(b) the child's physical, emotional and educational needs;

(c) the likely effect on the child of any change in his circumstances;

(d) the child's age, sex, background and any characteristics of his which the court considers relevant;

(e) any harm which the child has suffered or is at risk of suffering;

(f) how capable each of the child's parents, and any other person in relation to whom the court considers the question to be relevant, is of meeting his needs; and

(g) the range of powers available to the court under this Act (CA 1989) in the proceedings in question. CA 1989, s 1(3)

When the court is faced with an application it is to presume, unless the contrary is shown, that involvement of that parent in the life of the child concerned will further the child's welfare. CA 1989, s 1(2A)

The term 'involvement' means involvement of some kind, either direct or indirect, but not any particular division of a child's time. CA 1989, s 1(2B)

Note: PD12J provides that the court in every case must consider carefully whether the statutory presumption applies, having particular regard to the allegation or admission of harm by domestic abuse to the child or parent or any evidence indicting such harm or risk of harm (para 7).

18.2 SECTION 8 ORDERS

When the Children and Families Act 2014 came into force on 22 April 2014 the terminology that was used changed, and residence and contact orders were replaced with child arrangement orders. Prohibited steps and specific issue orders remained unchanged.

CA 1989, s 9(6)

A section 8 order can be made in respect of a child which means a person under the age of 18 although, unless the court is satisfied there are exceptional circumstances, the court should not make an order that has effect after the child has reached the age of 16.

18.2.1 Child arrangements orders

A child arrangements order means an order regulating arrangements relating to any of the following:

CA 1989, s 8(1)(a) and (b)

(a) with whom a child is to live, spend time or otherwise have contact; and

(b) where a child is to live, spend time or otherwise have contact with any person.

Any order made must include a warning notice setting out the consequences of not complying with the order (see Chapter 19).

18.2.2 Prohibited steps order

An order that provides specified steps shall not be taken by any person without the consent of the court.

A prohibited steps order can be made against any person (and is therefore not just limited to parents) and that person does not need to be a party to the proceedings (although the court should join them if it makes an order). The prohibition may only relate to a step that could be taken by a parent in meeting his parental responsibility and if outside of that cannot be made. An example is an order that attempts to prohibit adults meeting; the order can prevent the child coming into contact with a specified adult but not the adults themselves meeting without the child present.

The most common type of applications are:

(a) To prevent a child coming into contact with a named individual. This could be where a parent is insisting on bringing a child into contact with a family member who has a conviction for an offence against a child. The order cannot exclude a parent from their home.

(b) To prevent the removal of a child from the UK (this could include for a holiday that is not agreed).

(c) To prevent the change of a child's school or religious upbringing.

These provide examples of an act in exercise of parental responsibility the court can prevent.

No court may make a prohibited steps order with a view to achieving a result that could be achieved by making a child arrangements order. CA 1989, s 9(5)

Any order should be clear, setting out in plain terms what has been ordered (not to remove from the jurisdiction, from school, etc) and the duration of the order. *Re A and B (Prohibited Steps Order as DRA)* [2015] EWFC 816

18.2.3 Specific issue order

An order giving directions for the purpose of determining a specific question which has arisen, or which may arise, in connection with any aspect of parental responsibility for a child.

This is the opposite of the prohibited steps order and allows for the determination of a specific single issue that the parties are unable to agree.

This can include:

(a) What school the child attends or their religious upbringing.

(b) Whether a child should undergo any medical treatment (which could include blood transfusion or circumcision).

(c) The child's surname.

(d) A holiday.

The above list gives examples only but a specific issue application cannot be used to determine where a child should live or to seek the removal of a child from the jurisdiction. The application should be limited to a specific issue. CA 1989, s 9(5)

18.3 INTERIM ORDERS

Where a court has power to make a section 8 order, it may do so at any time during the course of the proceedings in question even though it is not in a position to dispose finally of those proceedings. CA 1989, s 11(3)

18.4 WITHDRAWAL

FPR 2010, r 29.4

Once issued the application can only be withdrawn with permission of the court.

FPR 2010, PD12J, para 6

Such permission should not be given until the court has scrutinised the reason for the withdrawal.

18.5 CHILD ARRANGEMENTS PROGRAMME

The Child Arrangements Programme came into force on 22 April 2014 and is contained in FPR 2010, PD12B. It sets out the process that the court follows to resolve disputes concerning children. Practitioners should read PD12B carefully and this section is an outline of the main issues and principles that apply with practical considerations.

18.6 THE FIRST HEARING DIRECTIONS RESOLUTION APPOINTMENT (FHDRA)

This is a key stage in the process and all those involved need to be proactive.

FPR 2010, PD12B, paras 14.1 and 14.2

The hearing should take place between weeks 5 and 6 of the proceedings being issued, allowing Cafcass to undertake its safeguarding checks and the respondent to have at least 10 days' notice.

Although a FHDRA is not mediation all those involved should try to narrow the issues and the court specifically needs to consider:

Whether the applicant has attended a MIAM and if not whether the proceedings should be adjourned to allow this.

- Whether the respondent should attend a MIAM with the applicant or alone.
- Whether the parties should attend in court or out of court mediation.
- Whether the parties should attend a Separated Parents Informational Programme ('SPIP').
- The safeguarding report, any concerns and whether a finding of fact hearing is required and whether they are any allegations of domestic abuse.
- The child's wishes and feelings to include how the child is going to be involved in the proceedings and informed of the outcome.
- If the matter cannot be resolved finally on the day the steps to be taken – to include:
  - interim orders;
  - directions to include statements;

- steps towards a finding of fact hearing;
- any investigation required (Cafcass report etc); and
- allocation.

Both parties are required to attend the hearing and anything said in the hearing is not privileged. FPR 2010, r 12.14 and PD12B, para 14.4

A Cafcass officer will attend and speak to the parties before the hearing and the Cafcass officer and the judge will then assist the parties in their attempt to reach agreement. FPR 2010, PD12B, para 14.9 FPR 2010, PD12B para 14.11

Where the results of Cafcass or Cafcass Cymru safeguarding checks are not available at the FHDRA, and no other reliable safeguarding information is available, the court **must** adjourn the FHDRA until the results of safeguarding are available. FPR 2010, PD12J, para 12

The court has template Child Arrangement Programme ('CAP') orders which the court should be able to access electronically to allow parties to leave court with a copy of the Order. The Order must set out:

(a) who the case is allocated to;
(b) issues resolved and outstanding;
(c) how the outstanding issues are to be resolved;
(d) interim arrangements;
(e) a statement as to any facts relating to risk or safety; in so far as they are resolved the result will be stated and, in so far as not resolved, the steps to be taken to resolve them will be stated;
(f) timetable for the child and proceedings;
(g) any activity direction(s) that would assist the parties; and
(h) date for next hearing and what type of hearing (finding of fact, dispute resolution appointment or final hearing).

18.7 McKENZIE FRIEND

A litigant in person may take another person with them in court to support them and to take notes. That person is known as a McKenzie friend. For guidance see Practice Guidance: *McKenzie Friends* (Civil and Family Courts) issued by the Master of the Rolls and the President of the Family Division, 12 July 2010 (see **Appendix C(10)**).

18.8 OTHER MATTERS TO CONSIDER AT THE FHDRA

18.8.1 Section 7 report

CA 1989, s 7(1)

Where parties are unable to reach agreement and the court requires further information it may direct a section 7 report which is a report to the court on such matters relating to the welfare of that child.

The report should provide the court with information; assessment and advice as to what (if any) orders should be made to promote the child's welfare.

Protocol for Allocating Responsibilities for Court Reporting in Private Law

This is normally from Cafcass although where the local authority are involved, or have recently been involved, the order can be for them to report.

FPR 2010, PD12B, para 14.13

The request for a report should specifically set out the issues the court wants the report to address and although a general report can be ordered this is discouraged.

The time to prepare reports differs in accordance with local practice but usually reports should be completed within 8 to 12 weeks from the date of order and the date the report is required must be included in the order, which should be served by the court 'forthwith'.

Note: With a backlog in courts sending orders out it is generally good practice to send the order issued by the judge to Cafcass immediately after the hearing to prevent delay. The time for completing reports is extending in most areas and a timeframe of 16 weeks is not uncommon.

18.8.2 Section 37 report

See Chapter 22.

18.8.3 Risk assessments

CA 1989, s 16A(1) and (2)

The CA 1989, s 16A imposes a duty on Cafcass when carrying out its functions where an officer is given cause to suspect the child concerned is at risk of harm to make a risk assessment and provide that risk assessment to the court.

18.8.4 Appointing a guardian and representation of the child(ren)

FPR 2010, r 16.2(1)

In the most difficult cases the court may consider joining a child as a party to the proceedings and, depending on their age and understanding, appointing a guardian for them. The test is a simple one; the court may make a child a party to proceedings if it considers it is in the best interests of the child to do so.

The guidance makes it clear, though, that this is a step the court will take only in the most complex, and therefore the minority of, cases. The decision is always exclusively that of the court and guidance is offered as to the circumstances in which the court would make an order.

FPR 2010, PD16A 7.2 (a) to (j)

18.8.5 Out of court options

Mediation or other out of court options need to be considered and the court may invite parties to attempt mediation or other options and the case adjourned for this. The adjournment can be for such period as it considers appropriate to enable the parties to obtain information and advice and, where the parties agree, to enable non-court dispute resolution to take place.

FPR 2010, r 3.4

If there are allegations, or other evidence, of domestic abuse the court should not expect the parties to engage in conciliation or other forms of dispute resolution which are not suitable and/or safe.

FPR PD12J para 9

18.8.6 DNA reports

From 23 November 2015 Cafcass are able to arrange and fund DNA testing provided that it is ordered by the court under the Family Law Reform Act 1969, s 20. DNA testing will be funded where:

(a) an application has been made pursuant to the CA 1989, s 8;

(b) the application cannot be resolved until the issue of paternity is resolved; and

(c) the parent or person with care is willing to cooperate with the testing.

The court, on making the order, needs to follow the template in the CAP order and complete the form BD1. The order must state who is responsible for bringing the child for testing and they should be given an information leaflet. For a detailed explanation and draft precedents go to www.gmfcf.org/uploads/5/5/4/0/55401763/himct_court_guidance. CAFCASS warn courts that there is restricted capacity for such reports and should be ordered only when critical for the case progression.

18.8.7 Allegations of domestic abuse

A Definition of Domestic Abuse and Victims

The Domestic Abuse Act 2021 ('DAA 2021'), s 1 introduces a new definition of 'domestic abuse':

'(2) Behaviour of a person ("A") towards another person ("B") is "domestic abuse" if—

(a) A and B are each aged 16 or over and are personally connected to each other, and

(b) the behaviour is abusive.

(3) Behaviour is "abusive" if it consists of any of the following—

(a) physical or sexual abuse;

(b) violent or threatening behaviour;

(c) controlling or coercive behaviour;

(d) economic abuse (see subsection (4));

(e) psychological, emotional or other abuse;

and it does not matter whether the behaviour consists of a single incident or a course of conduct.

(4) "Economic abuse" means any behaviour that has a substantial adverse effect on B's ability to—

(a) acquire, use or maintain money or other property, or

(b) obtain goods or services.

(5) For the purposes of this Act A's behaviour may be behaviour "towards" B despite the fact that it consists of conduct directed at another person (for example, B's child).'

'Personally connected' in defined in the DAA 2021, s 2 as:

'(1) For the purposes of this Act, two people are "personally connected" to each other if any of the following applies—

(a) they are, or have been, married to each other;

(b) they are, or have been, civil partners of each other;

(c) they have agreed to marry one another (whether or not the agreement has been terminated);

(d) they have entered into a civil partnership agreement (whether or not the agreement has been terminated);

(e) they are, or have been, in an intimate personal relationship with each other;

(f) they each have, or there has been a time when they each have had, a parental relationship in relation to the same child (see subsection (2));

(g) they are relatives.

(2) For the purposes of subsection (1)(f) a person has a parental relationship in relation to a child if—

(a) the person is a parent of the child, or

(b) the person has parental responsibility for the child.

(3) In this section—

"child" means a person under the age of 18 years;

"civil partnership agreement" has the meaning given by section 73 of the Civil Partnership Act 2004;

"parental responsibility" has the same meaning as in the Children Act 1989 (see section 3 of that Act);

"relative" has the meaning given by section 63(1) of the Family Law Act 1996.'

The DAA 2021, s 3 defines children living in a household in which domestic abuse is perpetrated as primary victims of domestic abuse, whether or not they were directly subject to abuse by the perpetrator parent:

'3 Children as victims of domestic abuse

(1) This section applies where behaviour of a person ("A") towards another person ("B") is domestic abuse.

(2) Any reference in this Act to a victim of domestic abuse includes a reference to a child who—

(a) sees or hears, or experiences the effects of, the abuse, and

(b) is related to A or B.

(3) A child is related to a person for the purposes of subsection (2) if—

(a) the person is a parent of, or has parental responsibility for, the child, or

(b) the child and the person are relatives.

(4) In this section—

"child" means a person under the age of 18 years;

"parental responsibility" has the same meaning as in the Children Act 1989 (see section 3 of that Act);

"relative" has the meaning given by section 63(1) of the Family Law Act 1996.'

These three sections of the 2021 Act have been incorporated into Practice Direction 12J (PD12J) by Practice Direction Update (No 5 of 2021).

Sections 1 and 2 of the 2021 Act (definitions of domestic abuse and personally connected) are now found in para 2A of PD12J. Para 2B of PD12J adds:

> 'For the avoidance of doubt, it should be noted that "domestic abuse" includes, but is not limited to, forced marriage, honour-based violence, dowry-related abuse and transnational marriage abandonment.'

The DAA 2021, s 3 (children included in the definition of victims of domestic abuse) has been added to the definitions in para 3 of PD12J. Para 4 of PD12J, which explains the ways in which children may be harmed or put at risk of harm by domestic abuse has been amended accordingly:

> 'Domestic abuse is harmful to children, and/or puts children at risk of harm, including where they are victims of domestic abuse for example by witnessing one of their parents being violent or abusive to the other parent, or living in a home in which domestic abuse is perpetrated (even if the child is too young to be conscious of the behaviour). Children may suffer direct physical, psychological and/or emotional harm from living with and being victims of domestic abuse, and may also suffer harm indirectly where the domestic abuse impairs the parenting capacity of either or both of their parents.'

In addition, paras 21 (section 7 reports) and 25 (interim orders) of PD12J have been amended to incorporate the definition of the child as a victim of domestic abuse.

When considering allegations of abuse you need to consider the relevance of the allegations to the application before the court and the lives experience of the child/carer.

In respect of allegations of coercive and controlling behaviour the focus must be on the pattern which is not going to be demonstrated easily (or at all) in a limited schedule. Further the fact that an allegation of violence is historic does not mean that it is irrelevant. The act may have created the conditions of fear that allowed controlling behaviour to take place.

See – para 52 H-N

18.8.8 Finding of fact hearing

FPR 2010, PD12J, para 9

Where any information provided to the court indicates that there are issues of domestic abuse which may be relevant to the court's determination, the court must ensure that the issues are addressed at the hearing.

In general terms the question to ask is are there allegations of violence, harm or other actions that would pose a risk to the child(ren) that need to be resolved? Can the court make a welfare decision without findings? The court is looking at future welfare risks.

FPR 2010, PD12J, para 16–20
FPR 2010, PD 12J, para 6

The court must, at all stages of the proceedings, and specifically at the FHDRA, consider whether domestic abuse is raised as an issue, either by the parties or Cafcass or otherwise and if so must:

'(a) identify at the earliest opportunity (usually at the FHDRA) the factual and welfare issues involved;

(b) consider the nature of any allegation, admission or evidence of domestic abuse, and the extent to which it would be likely to be relevant in deciding whether to make a child arrangements order and, if so, on what terms;

(c) give directions to enable contested relevant factual and welfare issues to be tried as soon as possible and fairly

(d) ensure that where domestic abuse is admitted or proven, that any child arrangements order in place protects the safety and wellbeing of the child and the parent with whom the child is living, and does not expose either of them to the risk of further harm; and

(e) ensure that any interim child arrangement order (ie considered by the court before determination of the facts, and in the absence of admission) is only made having followed the guidance in paragraphs 25–27 below.'

FPR 2010, PD12J, para 5

It is unlikely that the court, at the first hearing, will have all the information necessary to determine if a finding of fact hearing is necessary. The court at the first hearing will give directions for evidence and then list a hearing to determine the issue.

Re H-N and Others (Children) (Domestic Abuse: Findings of Fact Hearings) [2021] EWCA Civ 448

The Court of Appeal in *Re H-N and Others (Children) (Domestic Abuse: Findings of Fact Hearings)* gave guidance on dealing with these cases considering 4 linked appeals and gave judgment of 4 main issues:

(a) whether there should be a finding of fact hearing (see below);

(b) the challenged presented by Scott schedules (see below);

(c) the approach to controlling and coercive behaviour (see above);

(d) the relevance of criminal concepts.

www.bailii.org/ew/cases/EWCA/Civ/2021/448.html.

Re K and K [2022] EWCA Civ 468

The Court of Appeal in *Re K and K* revisited *Re H-N* to provide general guidance on the proper approach to fact finding hearings. The court highlighted the need for the court to first identify the relevance of the findings (if made) to the welfare issues in the case, that the purpose must be assist in assessing future risk and any hearing must be proportionate.

The decisions in *Re H-N* and *Re K* have then been distilled into guidance from the President, May 2022.

FPR 2010, PD12J, para 15

18.8.9 Admissions

Where at any hearing an admission of domestic violence or abuse towards another person or the child is made by a party, the admission should be recorded in writing by the judge and set out as a Schedule to the relevant order. The court office must arrange for a copy of any order containing a record of admissions to be made available as soon as possible to any Cafcass officer or local authority officer preparing a report under the CA 1989, s 7.

Note: Consider whether the admissions are sufficient. Do they cover the issues being raised and are they enough to form the basis of a risk assessment? If the allegations are of serious and ongoing violence and the admission is one incident of violence then that is unlikely to be enough?

FPR 2010, PD12J, para 17

The following is a summary of the factors to be considered when deciding whether a Fact Finding Hearing is required:

(a) The views of the parties and Cafcass.

(b) Whether the admissions form a sufficient factual basis on which to proceed.

(c) If a party is in receipt of LAA whether the evidence required for that is sufficient to provide a sufficient factual basis on which to proceed.
(d) Whether there is other factual evidence which is sufficient to proceed.
(e) Whether the factor in paras 36 and 37 can be determined without a fact finding hearing
(f) Whether the case can be resolved fairly without the need for the fact to be determined.
(g) The nature of the evidence required.
(h) Whether the allegations, if proved, would be relevant to the issues before the court.
(i) Whether a finding of fact hearing would be proportionate.

If a hearing is not necessary the decision needs to be recorded on the order and if it is necessary then directions must be given to that hearing considering all the matters in paragraph 19.

FPR 2010, PD12J, para 18
FPR 2010, PD12J, para 19

Where the court considers that a fact-finding is necessary, it must give directions as to how the proceedings are to be conducted to ensure that the matters in issue are determined as soon as possible, fairly and proportionately, and within the capabilities of the parties. In particular it should consider:

(a) What are the key facts in dispute;
(b) Whether it is necessary for the fact-finding to take place at a separate (and earlier) hearing than the welfare hearing;
(c) Whether the key facts in dispute can be contained in a schedule of table (known as a Scott schedule) which sets out what the applicant complains of or alleges, what the respondent says in relation to each individual allegation or complaint; the allegations in the schedule should be focused on the factual issues to be tried; and if so, whether It is practicable for this schedule to be completed at the first hearing, with the assistance of the judge;
(d) What evidence is required in order to determine the existence of coercive, controlling or threatening behaviour, or of any other form of domestic abuse;
(e) Directing the parties to file written statements giving details of such behaviour and of any response;
(f) Whether documents are required from third parties and if so, giving directions for the filing of written statements form such third parties;

(g) Whether oral evidence may be required from third parties and if so, giving directions for the filing of written statements from such third parties;

(h) Where (for example in cases of abandonment) third parties from whom documents are to be obtained are abroad, how to obtain those documents in good time for the hearing, and who should be responsible for the costs of obtaining those documents;

(i) Whether any other evidence is required to enable the court to decide they key issues and giving directions for that evidence to be provided;

(j) What evidence the alleged victim of domestic abuse is able to give and what support the alleged victim may require at the fact-finding hearing in order to give that evidence;

(k) In cases where the alleged victim of domestic abuse is unable for reasons beyond their control to be present at the hearing (for example, abandonment cases where the abandoned spouse remains abroad), what measures should be taken to ensure that that person's best evidence can be put before the court. Where video-link is not available, the court should consider alternative technological or other methods which may be utilised to allow that person to participate in the proceedings;

(l) What support the alleged perpetrator may need in order to have a reasonable opportunity to challenge the evidence; and

FPR 2010, PD12J, para 19

(m) Whether pre-hearing review would be useful prior to the fact-finding hearing to ensure directions have been complied with and all the required evidence is available.

Where the court fixings a fact finding hearing it must also list a dispute resolution appointment to follow.

18.9 IS A FACT FINDING HEARING NECESSARY?

In determining whether a fact finding hearing is necessary you apply PD12J, paras 16 and 17.

In *H-N* (above) the P said this

'i) The first stage is to consider the nature of the allegations and the extent to which it is likely to be relevant in deciding whether to make a child arrangements order and if so in what terms (PD12J.5).

ii) In deciding whether to have a finding of fact hearing the court should have in mind its purpose (PD12J.16) which is, in broad terms, to provide a basis of assessment of risk and therefore the impact of the alleged abuse on the child or children.

iii) Careful consideration must be given to PD12J.17 as to whether it is 'necessary' to have a finding of fact hearing, including whether there is other evidence which provides a sufficient factual basis to proceed and importantly, the relevance to the issue before the court if the allegations are proved.

iv) Under PD12J.17 (h) the court has to consider whether a separate fact-finding hearing is 'necessary and proportionate'. The court and the parties should have in mind as part of its analysis both the overriding objective and the President's Guidance as set out in '*The Road Ahead*.''

The key question is, is the determination of the facts necessary to determine the welfare issues of this child?

Not all cases require a fact find. The Court of Appeal noted in *Re L* that 'few relationships lack instances of bad behaviour on the part of one or both parties at some time and it is a rare family case that does not contain complaints by one party against the other, and often complaints are made by both'.

Re L Relocation (second appeal) [2017] EWCA Civ 2121

18.9.1 Evidence

The issue of how the allegations are presented remains a difficult one. Schedules are what parties are used to although they fail to allow for patterns of behaviour to be properly pleaded. This was highlighted by Peel J:

FG v HI and JK [2021] EWHC 1367 (Fam)

> 'Since Scott Schedules had been prepared and the case has been managed by reference to them, I did not dispense with them but, at my invitation, the parties prepared short narrative summaries of their respective cases about the allegedly coercive and/or controlling behaviour of the other. The summaries were very different in style and illustrated the complexities involved in presenting allegations for a finding of fact hearing such as this one where there are overlapping allegations by the mother against the father of coercion and control, physical violence against the mother, physical violence against the child, and allegations by the father against the mother

> of control, fabrication, and abduction. How can the party alleging a pattern of coercion and control over a relationship that has lasted several years present that case for a finding of fact hearing in a way that is proportionate and manageable, and without giving a day-by-day account of the whole relationship?'

And Hayden J:

F v M [2021] EWFC 4

> 'An intense focus on particular and specified incidents may be a counterproductive exercise. It carries the risk of obscuring the serious nature of harm perpetrated in a pattern of behaviour. This was the issue highlighted in the final report of the expert panel to the Ministry of Justice: '*Assessing Risk of Harm to Children and Parents in Private Law Children Cases*' (June 2020). It is, I hope, clear from my analysis of the evidence in this case, that I consider Scott Schedules to have such severe limitations in this particular sphere as to render them both ineffective and frequently unsuitable. I would go further, and question whether they are a useful tool more generally in factual disputes in Family Law cases. The subtleties of human behaviour are not easily receptive to the confinement and constraint of a Schedule. I draw back from going further because Scott Schedules are commonly utilised and have been given much judicial endorsement. I do not discount the possibility that there will be cases when they have real forensic utility. Whether a Scott Schedule is appropriate will be a matter for the judge and the advocates in each case unless, of course, the Court of Appeal signals a change of approach.'

It was suggested by Poole J in *GK v PR* that:

GK v PR [2021] EWFC 106

> 'the risk of applying the Scott Schedule technique is that the judge approaches the case in a formulaic, incident by incident way which detracts from the holistic overview necessary to determine fluid and nuanced patterns. It also runs the risk that incidents which may appear trivial are overlooked and not relied upon'.

Although there is no definitive guidance it is suggested that statements should be directed to allow the case to be fully put and to avoid the pitfalls identified above. There will be cases where a Scott Schedule will remain appropriate, a number of very specific incidents for example.

The judge may direct the matters to be dealt with in the statement but a suggested template which you can then suggest to the court is:

- Limited to 15 sides of A4.
- All paragraphs must be numbered.
- Respondent to reply using the same numbered paragraphs.
- If the Respondent is making allegations then they adopt the same process as the applicant and each respond to the others.
- How long has the applicant known the respondent?
- When did they become a couple (roughly)?
- Have you ever cohabited and if so, for how long?
- When did they stop being a couple?
- When did they stop cohabiting?
- Identify each child of the relationship, ages, where they are educated and any particular features (such as a disability).
- Identify any other child who live/d with the couple during the relationship/cohabitation.
- Was the respondent always abusive or did the behaviour change after the relationship began – if so when?
- Was the abusive behaviour directed at the applicant alone or do it target the child/ren or a particular child?
- Did this behaviour continue after the relationship/cohabitation was at an end?
- Describe behaviours where were coercive/controlling and cannot be pinned down to one incident? Suggest use one paragraph for each sort of behaviour.

For each behaviour answer the following questions:

- What happened?
- What was the impact on the applicant's health, safety and well-being or on the children?
- Did the applicant tell anyone about this behaviour at the time or later and if so who?
- Attach any supporting documents such as a medical report.

Looking at specific incidents:

- What was the first incident of abusive behaviour? Date? What happened? Effect on the applicant and the children? Did they tell anyone? Supporting material?

- What was the worst incident? Date? What happened? Effect on the applicant and the children? Did they tell anyone? Supporting material?
- What was the most recent incident? Date? What happened? Effect on the applicant and the children? Did you tell anyone? Supporting material?
- Is there anything else you think that the court needs to know and take into account about you? (Physical disability/mental health problems/ learning problems/convictions.)
- Is there anything else you think that the court needs to know and take into account about the respondent? (Physical disability/mental health problems/learning problems/convictions.)

K v L [2022] EWHC 986 (Fam)

If your client seeks to rely on intimate images they should not be filed as evidence without a written application having first ben made.

FPR 2010, PD12J, paras 25–27

18.10 INTERIM ORDERS PENDING A FACT FINDING HEARING

In reality is it a balance between any harm the child/ carer will suffer if the order is made and the harm the child may suffer if there is no contact. Each case is different and will be resolved on its facts.

Paragraph 25 of Practice Direction 12J provides that the court should not make an interim child arrangements order unless it is satisfied that it is in the interests of the child to do so and that the order would not expose the child or the other parent to an unmanageable risk of harm.

Paragraph 26: in deciding any interim child arrangements question pending a full hearing the court should:

(a) take into account the matters set out in the CA 1989, s 1(3) or the Adoption and Children Act 2002, s 1(4) as appropriate; and

(b) give particular consideration to the likely effect on the child, and on the care given to the child by the parent who has made the allegation of domestic abuse, of any contact and any risk of harm, whether physical, emotional or psychological, which the child and that parent is likely to suffer as a consequence of making or declining to make an order.

Paragraph 27 sets out the additional considerations as to safety, venue etc if contact is to be ordered pending determination of the allegations.

Note: Paragraph 38 provides that where a risk assessment has concluded that a parent poses a risk to a child or to the other parent, contact via a supported contact centre, or contact supported by a parent or relative, is not appropriate. It is hard to see therefore, as there is no risk assessment and the allegations are serious, how such considerations would not apply to interim contact.

18.11 ACTIVITY DIRECTIONS AND CONDITIONS

An activity direction is made when the court is considering making, varying or discharging an order and an activity condition is made when the court makes a final order. CA 1989, s 11A(3)

An activity direction is a direction requiring an individual who is a party to the proceedings to take part in an activity that would, in the court's opinion, help to establish, maintain or improve either that person's involvement in the child's life or the involvement of another party to the proceedings.

When considering making an order the child's welfare is the court's paramount consideration. CA 1989, s 11A(9)

18.11.1 Separated Parents Information Programme (SPIP)

How the programme is run depends on the provider in that it lasts for 4 hours but may be made up of one session of 4 hours or 2 sessions of 2 hours. The parents do not attend the same course and the programme is delivered by way of group sessions which are a mix of applicants and respondents. Provided it is directed by the court it is free to attend.

If a contact activity direction/condition is made for the parties to attend a SPIP the court will complete the necessary referral and will then send the parties details and a copy of the court order to the local providers who will then contact the parties to arrange for their attendance.

The service is due to be recommissioned and a replacement programme is due in April 2023 with a better digital support offer.

18.11.2 Mediation Information and Assessment Meeting (MIAM)

See above at **18.8.5**.

18.11.3 Domestic Violence Perpetrators Programme

Also called Integrated Domestic Abuse Programme depending on the provider. The programme is run in groups (usually between 8 and 12 people) and over approximately 26 weeks. Its aim is to develop a person's skill and understanding to reduce the risk of violence, develop safe and positive parenting, increase their awareness of their behaviour and help them to resolve conflicts non-abusively. This is free when ordered by the court (it is funded by the Department for Education) and delivered by an approved provider.

Note: If English is not the participant's first language then funding for an interpreter will need to be secured from Cafcass as the Department for Education will not fund this. Such course should be directed as an activity direction as otherwise the court has no control if: (a) they are not accepted; (b) means of monitoring attendance; or (c) resolving contact after the conclusion of the course.

CA 1989, s 11A(6)

A contact activity direction or condition cannot require a party to undergo medical or psychiatric examination, assessment or treatment or take part in mediation.

The direction must specify: (a) who is to attend; (b) what the activity is; and (c) who is providing it.

Before making a contact activity direction or condition the court must satisfy itself that:

(a) it is appropriate in the circumstances of the case;

(b) the provider is suitable to provide the activity;

(c) it will take place in an area where the participant can reasonably be expected to travel; and

(d) the court has sufficient information on the person to be subject to the direction/condition as to the effect of the direction/condition on him.

The court would normally ask Cafcass to provide this information. This can be easily achieved if a Cafcass officer is at court or it is a recommendation in a report. In cases where there has been domestic violence then a party may be considered suitable to attend a domestic violence intervention programme (DVIP) or an integrated domestic abuse programme (IDAP). A referral can be made on the advice of Cafcass without the need for an expert risk assessment and is ordered by way of a contact activity direction.

For a case to be suitable for a contact activity direction without a specialist risk assessment then the perpetrator needs to be low to medium risk which means:

– they have no history of high risk/potentially lethal behaviour;

– there are no complications (ie drug or alcohol addiction);
– they are motivated; and
– they accept responsibility.

If perpetrators fall into the high risk group then a referral without a risk assessment is pointless as they will be deemed unsuitable for the programme and time will simply have been wasted. In those circumstances a risk assessment will need to be undertaken and one of the recommendations arising from that may be attendance on a prevention programme. The difficulty is that such an assessment is not free.

If the criteria are met and Cafcass has recommended it then an order can be made for the party to attend a suitability assessment and, if suitable, the course itself.

The provider will send to Cafcass the suitability report and, if the party is accepted on the programme, a midway assessment report (at the 12-week stage) and a completion report. These will then be annexed to the Cafcass report and therefore a separate order for them to be filed and served is not required.

The report will focus on the party's progress and engagement. It does not provide an assessment of risk or contact arrangements. For this Cafcass is required.

The court may also wish the party's progress monitored and to report to the court if there is a failure to comply. CA 1989, s 11G

The monitoring provision can also be used at the conclusion of the proceedings with the court requiring Cafcass to monitor the compliance of an individual with a child arrangements order although this cannot extend beyond a term of 12 months. During the period of monitoring Cafcass will report to the court on matters specified in the order (usually that contact has broken down) This is an underused provision but helpful in cases where there has been a long history of problems and where the court has made a final order but there are likely to be further complications, particularly in light of the limited role of the court. CA 1989, s 11H(6) CA 1989, s 11H

Note: The Covid-19 pandemic has significantly reduced the number of courses and delays have been reported at between 12–15 months. Before the court makes directions, practitioners should establish what the delay is in your area

18.11.4 Contact centres

Where contact is agreed or ordered but there is a need for this to be in a neutral or safe environment contact can take place in a contact centre. Such centres can offer supported contact (a person is present but not monitoring what is said) or supervised contact (where a person is watching and taking notes) and can ensure that parents don't meet. Such centres have an initial referral fee and if supervised and ongoing hourly rate for supervision.

Any court order must set out:

(a) who must inform the centre co-ordinator of the contents of the order and when by;

(b) who must complete the referral form for the centre co-ordinator and provide with that a copy of any order (and any injunctions or undertakings in place);

(c) who is to take and collect the child from the centre;

(d) who is responsible for the fees.

FPR 2010, PD 12B(10) sets out where a party can go for advice about contact centres. A list of contact centres can be found at www.naccc.org.uk

G v G [2022] EWHC 113

If there have been findings of abuse it would only be in exceptional circumstances that the victim of that abuse should be asked to contribute to the costs of contact (*G v G*).

18.12 DISPUTE RESOLUTION APPOINTMENTS

This hearing should follow the section 7 report or the parties attending a SPIP or some other event that allows the case to resolve.

The Dispute Resolution Appointment ('DRA') should be approached in a similar way to a Financial Dispute Resolution hearing but what is said is **NOT PRIVILEGED**.

FPR 2010, PD12B, para 19.2

The author of the section 7 report is not required to attend unless directed by the court.

FPR 2010, PD12B, para 19.3

The court's aim is to:

(a) identify the key issues and either resolve or narrow them;

(b) consider whether a final order can be made;

(c) hear evidence if necessary to narrow or resolve issues;

(d) identify what evidence needs to be heard; and

(e) give case management directions to a final hearing.

18.13 THE FINAL HEARING

This is limited to the issues that need to be resolved but the onus remains on the parties to make many of the decisions. The case should limit the issues at the Dispute

Resolution Appointment ('DRA') and parties should expect robust case management.

Given the overriding objective, the court's case management powers and the new culture encapsulated in the Child Arrangement Programme (and the single Family Court) this means:

FPR 2010, rr 1.1, 1.4

(a) a duty to resolve by promoting agreement;
(b) a duty to identify the issues;
(c) a duty to manage the case in accordance with the overriding objective;
(d) a power to direct such investigation as necessary;
(e) a power to control the filing of evidence;
(f) a power to limit oral evidence and to control cross examination;
(g) a power to strike out applications for a lack of merit; and
(h) the ability to make an order whether a party has applied or not if that order is required in the child's interests.

Parties should ensure compliance with the court bundle (see Chapter 26) and then file the following preliminary documents by 11am the day before the hearing:

FPR 2010, PD27A, para 6.4

(a) An up to date case summary of the background to the hearing confirmed to those matters which are relevant to the hearing and the management of the case and limited, if practicable, to 4 A4 pages.
(b) A statement of the issue or issues to be determined at the final hearing.
(c) A position statement by each party including a summary of the order or directions sought by that party (2) at the final hearing.
(d) An up to date chronology, if it is a final hearing.
(e) Skeleton arguments if appropriate.
(f) A list of essential reading for the hearing.
(g) The time estimate.

FPR 2010, PD27A, para 4.3

18.14 ORDER OF EVIDENCE

Subject to any directions given by the court the order of evidence is:

(a) The applicant.
(b) Any party with parental responsibility for the child.
(c) Other respondents.

(d) The children's guardian.

FPR 2010, r 12.21

(e) Any child if the child is a party to the proceedings and there is no children's guardian.

18.15 EXTERNAL AND INTERNAL RELOCATION

Re C (International Relocation) [2015] EWCA Civ 1305 and *Re R (a child)* [2016] EWCA Civ 1016

In an increasingly globalised world, there have recently been more applications regarding the relocation of children and thus a marked increase in appeal decisions over where children reside both internationally and internally within England and Wales and, as a result, a development of the law. Whilst the factual elements of the relocations are different, the legal approach is the same.

K v K [2011] EWCA Civ 793

The only legal principle that applies in all of these cases is that the welfare of the child is paramount. Where a parent wishes to move (internationally or within England and Wales), that is part of the facts of the case, but nothing more.

Payne v Payne [2001] EWCA Civ 166
Re C (above) per Bodey J

The guidance in cases such as *Payne v Payne* is guidance and assistance on how to interpret the welfare decision; it is not a straightjacket.

> 'a judge is likely to find helpful some or all of the considerations referred to in Payne v Payne; but not as a prescriptive blueprint; rather as a checklist of the sort of factors which will or may need to be weighed in the balance when determining which decision would better serve the welfare of the child.'

See *Re R* (above)

On internal relocation the concept of summary return which apply to abduction cases cannot be imported.

18.16 CHANGE OF NAME AND REMOVAL FROM JURISDICTION

CA 1989, s 13(1)

Where a Child Arrangements Order (CAO) is in force that regulates with whom a child is to live and when a child is to live with any person, no person may cause the child to be removed from the United Kingdom or be known by another surname without either the written consent of every person who has parental responsibility or the leave of the court.

CA 1989, s 13(2)

A person named in a CAO as the person with whom the child lives may remove a child from the United Kingdom for a period of less than one month without consent.

CA 1989, s 13(3)

The court, on making a CAO can grant leave to remove for a holiday generally or specifically.

Note: This is a useful tool when dealing with repeat holiday applications when the other party has made clear they will always object.

Any application to remove a child permanently from the jurisdiction is therefore pursuant to section 13(1)(b) and is a freestanding application that follows the Part 18 procedure.

Note: 'Part 18' refers to Part 18 of the FPR 2010. FPR 2010, PD5A provides a list of forms to be used in making any particular application (Form C2 in existing proceedings and C100 if free standing) and Part 18 sets out the procedure to be followed.

18.17 FAMILY ASSISTANCE ORDER

Where, in any family proceedings, the court has the power to make an order (this includes section 8 orders) it may make an order requiring:

(a) an officer of the service (Cafcass); or

(b) a local authority

to advise, assist and (where appropriate) befriend any person named in the Order (a family assistance order). CA 1989, s 16(1)

The persons who may be named in the order are:

(a) any parent, guardian or special guardian;

(b) any person with whom the child is living or who is named in a child arrangements order as a person with whom the child is to live, spend time or otherwise have contact; or

(c) the child himself. CA 1989, s 16(3)

The court cannot make an order unless everyone named in the order (except the child) consents and cannot make an order against a local authority unless they agree or the child concerned lives or will live within their area. Consent can be given orally or otherwise. CA 1989, s 16(3) CA 1989, s 16(7) FPR 2010, r 12.29

Before making a family assistance order the court must have obtained the opinion of the officer from the organisation the order is to be made against (ie Cafcass) as to whether such an order would be in the best interests of the child, how the order would operate and for how long. All those to be named in the order must also be given the opportunity to comment. FPR 2010, PD12M

A family assistance order can be for any length of time but cannot last beyond 12 months. CA 1989, s 16(5)

18.18 PROHIBITION ON FURTHER APPLICATIONS

On disposing of any application the court may (whether or not it makes any other order in response to the CA 1989, s 91(14)

application) order that no application for an order of any specified kind may be made with respect to the child concerned by any person named in the order without leave of the court.

Re P [1999] 2 FLR 420. *Re A* [2021] EWCA Civ 1749

The leading case is *Re P* and practitioners should follow the guidance set out. *Re P* is though now over 20 years old. The Court of Appeal in *Re A* looked at the guidance with the changing legal landscape.

E v M [2015] EWCA Civ 1313

Note: Practitioners should approach these applications with caution and ensure they are not made without proper notice and a fair procedure is followed.

See FPR 2010, PD12Q

The fact there has been coercive or controlling behaviour or other domestic abuse towards the victim is also grounds for the court making an order and the court should give early and ongoing consideration to this even when an application has not been made.

18.19 PARENTAL RESPONSIBILITY

18.19.1 Definition

The CA 1989, s 3 defines parental responsibility as being all the rights, duties, powers, responsibilities and authority which by law a parent has in relation to the child and his/her property.

CA 1989, s 2(1)

Upon birth the mother automatically has parental responsibility for a child whether or not she was married to the father.

Adoption and Children Act 2002, s 111

Where the parents were married to each other at the date of the birth, the father also by operation of law automatically has parental responsibility for that child.

Where the parents of a child were not married to each other at the date of birth, the father will acquire parental responsibility for that child if the birth was registered after 1 December 2003 (irrespective of the date of birth) and he is registered as the father in accordance with the provisions of the Births and Deaths Registration Act 1953.

CA 1989, s 2(1); s 2(1A)

Where the child has two female parents as a result of the operation of the Human Fertilisation and Embryology Act 2008 ('HFEA 2008'), s 42 or 43 the parent who is not the child's legal mother (the parent who did not give birth) is treated in the same way as a father in respect of PR for the child.

CA 1989, s 4(1) and (2)

Where the parents were not married to each other at the date of birth and the father is not registered as such in accordance with the provisions of the Births and Deaths

Registration Act 1953 but he nevertheless wishes to assume parental responsibility he may:

(a) apply to the court for a parental responsibility order; or

(b) enter into a parental responsibility agreement with the mother.

In the event of an application to the court, a fee is payable. There is no fee payable when a parental responsibility agreement is entered into.

The form for parental responsibility agreement is Form C(PRA1)

The courts have recently shown a much greater willingness to grant a parental responsibility order. In deciding whether or not to grant parental responsibility the court will principally have in mind the 3 factors:

(a) commitment to the child;

(b) attachment to the child; and

(c) reason for making the application.

These factors are not an exhaustive list and the court must take into account all the circumstances and the CA 1989, s 1 which applies.

Re H (Parental Responsibility) [1998] 1 FLR 855

Where more than one person has parental responsibility for a child each of them may act alone save where an enactment requires the consent of the other. However, it would be usual for people to consult as was held in *Re W* 'it will be the duty of one parent to ensure that the rights of the other parent are respected, and vice versa, for the benefit of the child'.

Re W (Direct Contact) [2013] 1 FLR 494

18.19.2 Acquisition of parental responsibility by a second female parent

Where a child has a parent by virtue of the HFEA 2008, s 43 and is not a person to whom the Family Law Reform Act 1987, s 1(3) applies, that parent shall acquire parental responsibility for the child if:

(a) she becomes registered as a parent of the child;

(b) she enters into a parental responsibility agreement with the mother (see below for form and procedure); or

(c) she applies to the court for a parental responsibility order

CA 1989, s 4ZA

18.19.3 Requirements

CA 1989, s 4(2)

The requirements and form of a parental responsibility agreement are contained in the Parental Responsibility Agreement Regulations 1991. A copy of the blank form of agreement is found in Form C(PRA1). Particular note should be taken of the fact that the signature of the mother, father or second female parent can only be witnessed by a Justice of the Peace, a justice's clerk or an authorised officer of the court. A solicitor is not empowered to sign as a witness. Any agreement must comply with and be in the form prescribed.

Where more than one child is involved, a separate form of agreement is required in respect of each child.

CA 1989, s 12(1)

Where the court makes a child arrangements order in favour of an unmarried father or a woman who is a parent by virtue of the HFEA 2008 naming him/her as the person the child is to live with it must, at the same time, make a parental responsibility order if that person would not otherwise have parental responsibility.

CA 1989, s 12(1A)

The automatic requirement to make a parental responsibility order applies to any person with whom the child is to live but If the order is for the father/woman to spend time with them the court can make a parental responsibility order at the same time it the court considers it appropriate for them to have PR although it is not automatic.

The court can also made an order for parental responsibility to any person it makes a child arrangements order for the child to live with that person but by reason of the CA 1989, s 12(2) a person who is not a parent of the child, has parental responsibility only whilst that order remains in force.

18.19.4 Acquisition of parental responsibility by a step-parent

CA 1989, s 4A

A step-parent may acquire parental responsibility for a child where the step-parent is either married to or has entered into a civil partnership with a parent of the child who has parental responsibility.

This can be achieved in 1 of 2 ways:

CA 1989, s 4A(1)(a) and (b)

(a) an agreement between the step-parent and the parent(s) who has/have parental responsibility for the child (using Form C (PRA2) (see **Appendix A(10)**); or

CA 1989, s 4A(2)

(b) an order of the court.

An agreement under this provision is also a 'parental responsibility agreement' and the provisions of the CA 1989, s 4(2) apply to such an agreement as they do to an agreement under s 4.

An application to the court under the CA 1989, s 4A(1)(b) by a step-parent is dealt with in exactly the same manner as an application is made pursuant to s 4.

A parental responsibility agreement under the CA 1989, s 4A(1)(a) may only be brought to an end by an order of the court made on the application of: CA 1989, s 4A(3)

(a) any person who has parental responsibility for the child: or

(b) with the leave of the court, the child, if the court is satisfied that the child has sufficient understanding. CA 1989, s 4A(4)

The application is therefore made, or leave sought, as under the CA 1989, s 4.

There are therefore no new procedures introduced. The Agreement and/or the application to the court in respect of 'step-parent' acquisition fall to be dealt with in accordance with the previous procedures for an agreement and/or application to the court.

Once executed, a parental responsibility agreement must be sent to the Central Family Court who will record the agreement (address on the form). The agreement will not take effect until it has been received and recorded at the Central Family Court.

Forms of Parental Responsibility Agreements for both parents and step-parents and second female parent are to be found at **Appendices A(5)–A(7)**.

The CA 1989, s 12 was amended by the Children and Families Act 2014 ('CFA 2014')and together with the usual provisions for parental responsibility to be granted when the court makes an order that a child is to live with a father without parental responsibility, it also makes provision for the court to grant parental responsibility to a person named as having contact. CFA 2014, s 12, Sch 2

This allows the court to give limited parental responsibility to, say, a grandparent during their time with the child. The notes in the *Family Court Practice* suggest that; 'it is envisaged that this power would be exercised rarely' but the ability is there and in some cases may be very useful if the relationship between the adults is poor or they live a considerable distance apart.

18.20 SPECIAL GUARDIANSHIP ORDERS

18.20.1 Introduction

CA 1989, s 14A(1)

A special guardianship order appoints a person or persons to be the special guardian(s) of a child. The special guardian is able to exercise parental responsibility to the exclusion of any other person with parental responsibility. It is intended to operate in cases where adoption is either not possible or in the interest of the child but where nonetheless permanence and security are needed whilst at the same time preserving the link with the birth parents.

These provisions apply to both private and public proceedings but the information that follows deals solely with the private law aspects.

18.20.2 A preliminary matter

CA 1989, s 14A(7)

At least 3 months before making an application to the court any person wishing to apply for a special guardianship order must inform the local authority in writing of their intention.

CA 1989, s 14A(7), (8)

If the child is being looked after by a local authority, the notice must be given to that local authority. Otherwise the notice should be given to the local authority where the applicant resides.

CA 1989, s 14A(11)

The local authority must, during that time, prepare a report for the court concerning the suitability of the applicant and any other relevant matters. A date for the filing of such report will be given at the first directions hearing. No special guardianship order can be made without such a report.

Note: Where an applicant needs the permission of the court to make the application, the obligation on the part of the local authority does not arise unless and until such permission has been obtained.

FPR 2010, r 12.18

The court can restrict the disclosure of the report or parts of it (such as a person's address or financial circumstances to another party).

Message from the President 15 June 2020 18.19.3

The issue of Special Guardianship Orders was considered by the Public Law Working Group whose recommendations were endorsed by the President by way of Practice Guidance. Although this is aimed at public law proceedings the guidance emphasises the need for any assessment to be robust and comprehensive, for the child to have lived with the applicants before making any final order so that any support plan and needs can to tailored to the child's lived experience and for any contact needs to include what support will be needed to ensure the placement is supported.

18.20.3 Who may apply?

CA 1989, s 14A(5)

The following are entitled to apply for an order:

(i) a guardian of the child;

(ii) a person who is named in a CAO as a person with whom the child is to live;

(iii) a person with whom the child has lived for 3 out of the last 5 years;

(iv) a person who has the agreement of anyone who has a residence order in respect of the child;

(v) a person who has the agreement of all the people with parental responsibility for the child;

(vi) a local authority foster parent with whom the child has been living for at least one year immediately preceding the application; and

(vii) a person who has the permission of the court.

But in every instance a special guardian must be aged 18 or over and must not be a parent of the child in question. CA 1989, s 14A(2)

Practitioners should note that the provisions which apply to obtaining permission to make an application under the CA 1989, s 8 also apply to special guardianship orders. CA 1989, s 14A(4)

Where the person making the application is the child, the court will only grant permission if it is satisfied that the child has sufficient understanding to make the application for an order. CA 1989, s 14A(12)

Where the person making the application is not the child the court must have particular regard to the normal factors applicable to any application for permission to make a section 8 application. CA 1989, s 10(9)

The court also has power to make a special guardianship order in any other family proceedings in which a question arises with respect to the welfare of a child if: CA 1989, s 14A(6)

(a) an application has been made by a person who falls within (i)–(vii) above; or

(b) the court considers that a special guardianship order should be made even though no such application has been made. CA 1989, s 14A(5)

18.20.4 Commencement of proceedings

An application for special guardianship is a free standing application and made on Form C1 and must also be accompanied by a completed form C13A. A fee is payable unless the applicant is exempt from fees. Attendance at a MIAM is still required but is not included in Form C1 so a form FM1 (Family Mediation Information and Assessment Form) is also required.

18.20.5 The Local Authority

Once notice has been given to the local authority of a potential application the local authority most investigate and prepare a report dealing with:

(a) the suitability of the applicant to be a special guardian;

(b) each of the factors set out in the schedule to the SGR 2005;

(c) the implications of making the order on the child and wider family;

(d) the merits of the orders open to the court;

(e) any other matters relevant.

The report should also come with a support plan.

CA 1989, s 14A(8)(9)

The court is only able to make an order when it has a report from the local authority.

18.20.6 The order

CA 1989, s 14B(2)

On making a special guardianship order, the court may also:

(i) give leave for the child to be known by a new surname; and

(ii) grant the leave required by s 14(3)(b), either generally or for specified purposes to enable the child to be removed from the United Kingdom.

CA 1989, s 14B(1)

When making an order the court must consider whether:

(i) a child arrangement order containing contact provision: and

(ii) any section 8 order in force with respect to the child should be varied or discharged.

CA1989, 1989, s 14B(1)

Before making a special guardianship order the court must consider the issue of contact between the child and its family.

18.20.7 Effect of an order for special guardianship

Whilst an order is in force:

CA 1989, s 14C

(i) a special guardian has parental responsibility for the child in respect of whom the order is made;

(ii) subject to any other orders in force, a special guardian may exercise parental responsibility to the exclusion of any other person with parental responsibility for the child, except another special guardian;

(iii) the making of a special guardianship order discharges any existing care order; and

(iv) a care order and a live with order may be made while a special guardianship order is in force.

Practitioners should however note the following:

(i) a special guardianship order does not affect the operation of any enactment or rule of law which requires the consent of more than one person with parental responsibility in a matter affecting the child; CA 1989, ss 14C(2)(a), (b), 91(5A)

(ii) a special guardianship order does not affect any rights which a parent of the child has in relation to the child's adoption or placement for adoption;

(iii) whilst a special guardianship order is in force no person may:

(a) cause the child to be known by a new surname; or CA 1989, s 14C(3), (4)

(b) remove him from the United Kingdom, except that a special guardian may so remove the child for a period of up to 3 months;

(iv) in the event that the child dies whilst the order is in force the special guardian must take reasonable steps to inform: CA 1989, s 14C(5)

(a) each parent of the child with parental responsibility; and

(b) each guardian of the child; and CA 1989, s 14F

A support plan will be included as part of the special guardianship report. Every local authority must make arrangements for the provision of special guardianship support services together with ancillary responsibilities. This can include a support allowance and it is important for the plan to be considered and agreed before the final order is made.

18.20.8 Variation and discharge of an order

An application to vary or discharge may be made by: CA 1989, s 14D(1)

(i) the special guardian or one of them if there is more than one;

(ii) any parent or guardian of the child;

(iii) any person in whose favour there is a live with child arrangements order in respect of the child;

(iv) any person not being one mentioned in (i) or (iii) above who has or had immediately before the making of the special guardianship order parental responsibility for the child;

(v) the child; or

(vi) the local authority designated in a care order with respect to the child.

CA 1989, s 14D(2)

The court may, of its own volition, in any family proceedings in respect of the child may vary or discharge an order for special guardianship, even though no application has been made to that effect.

CA 1989, s 14D(3)

The following must obtain the leave of the court before making an application to vary or discharge an order:

(a) the child;

(b) any parent or guardian;

(c) any step-parent who has acquired, and has not lost, parental responsibility pursuant to the CA 1989, s 4; and

(d) any person being someone who is mentioned in (i) and (iii) above and who immediately before the making of the special guardianship order had, but no longer has, parental responsibility for the child.

CA 1989, s 14D(5)

Note: (i) The court may only grant leave to a child if satisfied that he has sufficient understanding to make the proposed application; (ii) the court may not grant leave to a person mentioned in (c) and (d) above unless satisfied that there has been a significant change of circumstances since the making of the special guardianship order; (iii) special provisions apply in relation to a timetable and directions following an application to vary or discharge an order for special guardianship.

CA 1989, s 14E

The court is required when considering the making, varying or discharging a special guardianship order to draw up a timetable for the application in order to avoid delay and to give directions to achieve this.

Re M (Special Guardianship Order; Leave to Apply) [2021] EWCA Civ 442

The court may not grant leave to a person falling within (b) (c) or (d) above unless it is satisfied that there has been a significant change in circumstances since the making of the special guardianship order. The Court of Appeal has held that the word 'significant' was an important term in the test; what is being proposed is the disruption of an intended long-term placement and as such any change must be 'significant' for leave to be granted.

CHAPTER 19

ENFORCEMENT OF CHILDREN ACT ORDERS

19.1 INTRODUCTION

The fact that a party is considering making an application to enforce an order indicates that there is a problem. Previous editions of this work have referred to research that shows that that cases fall within 4 categories:

(a) Conflicted – where there is a high level of mistrust and the parents are unable to work together to implement the order

(b) Risk/Safety – where safeguarding issues are raised

(c) Refusing – an older child refused to attend contact usually centring around some behaviour/lack of sensitivity by the non-resident parent

(d) Implacable hostility/Alienation – unreasonable resistance to contact by the resident parent and such resistance not being for safeguarding issues. This can include the parent influencing the child

From the research most cases fell within (a) to (c) and only 4% fell into category (d). What this infers is that most problems can be managed by the court's swift intervention and that practitioners should consider, if matters cannot be resolved quickly, a swift application to the court before the matter becomes entrenched.

FPR 2010, PD 12B
Re A and B (Contact) (No 4) [2015] EWHC 2839 (FAM)

The Child Arrangement Programme in its explanation of terms for enforcement states 'making sure that the order is complied with' and that defines enforcement. When those judgments are read the systematic failings in case management can be seen, the lack of judicial continuity, delay and the reality that people's personalities cannot be changed. The family court is a blunt instrument and has blunt tools at its disposal.

D v D (Access: Contempt: Committal) [1991] 2 FLR 34

From the authorities a theme emerges as to the need for early court intervention, the need for judicial continuity (and for cases to go back to the original judge if at all possible), robust case management and to avoid drift and delay.

See *Re L-W (Enforcement and Committal: Contact); CPL v CH-W and others* [2011] 1 FLR 1095 for an example of a provision being held not to be enforceable against a parent

There is a clear obligation on the court to enforce orders but practitioners have an obligation to ensure that orders drafted are clear, defined and therefore enforceable.

19.2 CHILD ARRANGEMENTS PROGRAMME

Paragraph 21 of the Child Arrangement Programme provides that any application for enforcement of a child arrangement order, the court shall;

- Consider whether the facts relevant to the alleged non-compliance are agreed, or whether it is necessary to conduct a hearing to establish the facts
- Consider the reasons for non-compliance
- Consider how the wishes and feelings of the child are to be ascertained
- Consider what advice is required from Cafcass
- Assess and manage any risks of making further or other chid arrangement orders
- Consider whether a SPIP or referral for dispute resolution is appropriate
- Consider whether an enforcement order may be appropriate, and
- Consider the welfare checklist. FPR 2010, PD 12B

Paragraph 21 provides an overview of all the issues the court shall consider when faced with an enforcement application and practitioners should be prepared to address each of those factors before the court.

The court shall (in the absence of agreement between the parties about the relevant facts) determine the facts in order to establish the cause of the alleged failure to comply. FPR 2010, PD12B, para 21.7

19.3 THE WARNING NOTICE

Where the court makes (or varies) a child arrangements order it is to attach to it a notice, warning of the consequences of failing to comply with the order. The warning reads: CA 1989, s 11I

> 'Where a contact order is in force: if you do not comply with this contact order –
>
> (i) you may be held in contempt of court and be committed to prison or fined; and/or
>
> (ii) the court may make an order requiring you to undertake unpaid work ('an enforcement order') and/or an order that you pay financial compensation.'

The 'warning notice' is not the same as a 'penal notice' (see Chapter 25). *CH v CT* [2018] EWHC 1310 (Fam); [2018] 4 WLR 122

19.4 THE APPLICANT

CA 1989, s 10(1)(a) and (2)

Where a child arrangements order has been made and it is alleged that a party has failed to comply with the order, an application for an enforcement order may be made. The application can be a freestanding application or an application within ongoing proceedings.

CA 1989, s 11J(5)

An application for an enforcement order may be made by:

(a) the person with whom the child concerned lives;

(b) the person whose contact with the child concerned is provided for in the child arrangements order;

(c) an individual who is subject to a contact activity direction or a condition imposed on a section 8 order pursuant to s 11(7)(b) of the 1989 Act; or

(d) the child concerned.

CA 1989, s 11J(6)
CA 1989, s 11J(7)

Where the child is the applicant they require leave of the court and the court will only grant leave if satisfied the child has sufficient understanding to make the proposed application.

19.5 PROCEDURE

FPR 2010, r 12.3

An application for an enforcement order shall be filed in form C79 with sufficient copies for service on each respondent. The court shall fix a hearing date on form C6. The applicant shall serve a copy of form C79, C6 and a form of acknowledgment in form C7 on each respondent at least 14 days prior to the hearing and before the hearing shall file a statement of service.

The application attracts a court fee unless the applicant is exempt from fees.

FPR 2010, rr 12.35(3) and 33.7(2)(a)

Where an enforcement order is made, the applicant shall serve a copy of the order personally on the person against whom the order has been made, unless otherwise directed.

As soon as practicable the court shall serve a copy of the order on:

(a) the parties (except the person against whom the order was made);

FPR 2010, r 12.35(2)

(b) the officer of the Service or Welsh family proceedings officer who is obliged to comply with a request to monitor or arrange for the monitoring of the person's compliance with the unpaid work requirement; and

(c) the responsible officer (ie of the National Offenders Management Service (NOMS)) in the local justice area where the unpaid work requirement is to be carried out.

In appropriate cases the court can abridge the time for service and the time limits generally. This is particularly useful in ongoing proceedings where contact has just commenced and any delay would prevent the next scheduled contact taking place.

FPR 2010, rr.4(1)(3)(a) and 12.12

19.6 GATEKEEPING

The application should be listed before the original judge if possible. If that judge is not available them to the same level of the judiciary and should be heard within 20 working days of issue.

FPR 2010, PD 12B, paras 21.2 and 21.3

If the child was a party then service of any application should also be on the guardian.

FPR 2010, PD 12C, para 1.1

The gatekeeping judge should also consider whether further safeguarding checks are required and if they are direct Cafcass to do so and give such other directions of its own initiative as maybe necessary to include; timetable, evidence and transfer.

FPR 2010, PD 12B, para 21.4
FPR 2010, r 12.12

Note: Limited time is allowed for gatekeeping and practitioners should send any application with a covering letter setting out: (a) the requirement for the matter to be heard within 20 days of listing; and (b) any directions considered necessary to make that hearing effective.

19.7 ENFORCEMENT

Enforcement is contained in the CA 1989, ss 11J onwards. For the court to make an enforcement order it must be satisfied beyond reasonable doubt that a person has failed to comply with a provision of the child arrangements order. If satisfied it may impose an unpaid work requirement but the court may not make an enforcement order if it is satisfied that the person had a reasonable excuse for failing to comply. The burden of proof as to reasonable excuse is on the person claiming it and the standard of proof is the balance of probabilities.

CA 1989, s 11J(2)
CA 1989, s 11J(3)
CA 1989, s 11J(4)

The changing standards of proof are noteworthy and practitioners need to be aware of the higher standard to prove the breach yet the lower standard to prove reasonable excuse.

The court can only make an enforcement order if before the breach the person in breach had been given or otherwise informed of the terms of the order and the order contained a warning notice (as set out above).

CA 1989, s 11K

The court cannot make an enforcement order if the person the application is against is under the age of 18 or is no longer habitually resident in England and Wales.

CA 1989, s 11K

Note: If they are no longer habitually resident in England and Wales then the order (if enforceable) has to be enforced in the new jurisdiction they are habitually resident in.

19.8 MAKING OF THE ORDER

Before making an enforcement order the court must be satisfied that:

(a) Making the enforcement order proposed is necessary to secure the person's compliance with the child arrangements order or any child arrangements order that has effect in its place; and

CA 1989, s 11L(1)

(b) The likely effect on the person of the enforcement order proposed to be made is proportionate to the seriousness of the breach.

CA 1989, s 11L(2) and (3)
CA 1989, s 11L(5)

The court must satisfy itself that provision of any unpaid work can be made in the area the person lives and also has information about the person who the order is against and the effect it will have upon them. The information includes any conflict with their religious beliefs and impact on work, education etc. The court can ask Cafcass to provide this information.

CA 1989, 3 11L(7)

Before making any order the court must take into account the welfare of the child although the child's welfare is not the court's paramount consideration.

FPR 2010, PD 12N

Any unpaid work is provided via the National Probation Service and the Cafcass officer will liaise with the local office to see what is available. To achieve this the court should make an order providing for disclosure to probation and give leave for the Cafcass officer to disclose and discuss the proceedings as necessary.

CA 1989, Sch A1 (3) and (4)
CA 1989, Sch A1, para 7

Any unpaid work is for a minimum of 40 hours and a maximum of 200 hours and must be performed within 12 months of the order although the period of 12 months can be extended.

19.9 MONITORING ORDER

CA 1989, s 11M

On the making of an enforcement order the court can ask Cafcass to monitor a person's compliance with the unpaid work, to report if there are any matters of compliance or whether the person becomes unsuitable to perform the work requirement.

In reality this is done by the probation service who then report matters to Cafcass.

19.10 WARNING NOTICE ATTACHED TO ENFORCEMENT ORDERS

When the court makes an enforcement order it must attach to the order a warning notice explaining the consequences of failing to comply with the order. CA 1989, s 11N

19.11 COMPENSATION FOR FINANCIAL LOSS

If the court is satisfied that an individual has failed to comply with the provision of the child arrangement order, and a person has suffered financial loss it may make an order requiring that person to pay the other compensation in respect of financial loss. CA 1989, s 11O(1)(a) and (b)

The court will not make an order if satisfied the person had reasonable excuse for failing to comply and the burden is on them to show that. CA 1989, s 11O(3) and (4)

The amount of compensation is determined by the court but cannot exceed the applicant's actual financial loss and the court will take into account an individual's financial circumstances before making the order. CA 1989, s 11O(9) CA 1989, s 11O(10)

The order should set out how the payment is to be made and such payment is recoverable as a civil debt. CA 1989, s 11O(11)

The person in breach must have been given a copy or otherwise was informed of the order and a warning notice was attached and not against a person under the age of 18. CA 1989, s 11P

Note: This would cover any fares to contact and then contact not taking place and could include the cost of a holiday where one parent has failed to make the child available for that contact. If calculating loss for a car journey the writer would suggest the MOJ rate of 45p per mile. There is no guidance on the amount but this appears to be generally accepted.

19.12 AMENDMENT AND REVOCATION OF AN ENFORCEMENT ORDER

The court may revoke the enforcement order if it appears to the court that:

(a) in all the circumstances no enforcement order should have been made,

(b) having regard to circumstances which have arisen since the enforcement order was made, it would be appropriate for the enforcement order to be revoked, or

(c) having regard to the person's satisfactory compliance with the [child arrangements] or any [child arrangements] order that has effect in its place, it would be appropriate for the enforcement order to be revoked. CA 1989, Sch A1, Pt 4(2)

CA 1989, Sch A1, Pt 4(3)

Such revocation can be on application or by the court's own motion.

In deciding whether to revoke the enforcement order the court shall take into account:

(a) the extent in which the person subject to the enforcement order has complied with it; and

(b) the likelihood that the person will comply with the [child arrangement] order or any [child arrangements] order that has effect in its place in the absence of the enforcement order.

CA 1989, Sch A1, Pt 4(4)(2)

Where the court is considering revoking or amending the order on the basis of a person's compliance it is to take into account the likelihood that person will comply with the order in the absence of the enforcement order.

CA 1989, Sch A1, Pt 6(1), (2) and (3)

The court can also amend and reduce the number of hours of unpaid work but the court must be satisfied that the effect on the person of the enforcement order as proposed to be amended is no more that is required to secure compliance.

19.13 COMMITTAL

There remains a power to commit for breach of a child arrangement order. See Chapter 25 for the procedure to be followed when making application for committal.

19.14 SUSPENDED ORDER

CA 1989, s 11J(9)

The court may suspend an enforcement order for such period as it thinks fit.

19.15 THE ORDERS

The court orders are:

- Enforcement
- Revocation or Amendment
- Financial Compensation Order

19.16 COSTS

Re P (Costs: Contact Enforcement) [2012] 1 FLR 445

The usual rule that there are no costs orders in Children Act proceedings does not fully apply in enforcement proceedings and the court has a discretion to make a costs order and there is no presumption against it.

Given the standard of proof is the criminal standard if a non-resident parent has been able to prove the breach to that standard then there is a real chance the costs should follow.

CHAPTER 20

LOCATING THE WHEREABOUTS OF A CHILD

20.1 PROCEDURE FOR LOCATING A CHILD

20.1.1 Family Law Act 1986

FLA 1986, s 33(1) and FPR 2010, r 12.16

If the whereabouts of a child is not known, an application can be made to the court in proceedings for or relating to a Part I order (for a definition of a Part I order, see below) for an order requiring any person who it has reason to believe may have relevant information to disclose it to the court. An order can be against any person including a legal advisor or the police (although against the police should not be routinely made). The order is for disclosure to a named officer of the court not the other party and will specify how the information should be given, eg in writing.

Note: The Order is Order 9.3 in Vol 2 Compendium of Standard Orders. As at the time of writing, the Compendium of Standard Orders is being revised, such that the order reference numbers may change in the not too distant future.

FPR 2010, r 12.16(2)
FPR 2010, PD 6C

The application is made by way of Form C4 and may be made with or without notice. If it is made on notice and is related to an application for an order pursuant to the FLA 1986, Pt I, the period of that notice will be 14 clear days, otherwise it will be 7 clear days. Whether made with or without notice the application attracts a court fee unless the applicant is exempt from fees. The application should be supported by a statement.

The FLA 1986 (as amended by the CA 1989) provides the definition of a Part I order.

An application in Form C4 will only be considered without notice in circumstances where the criteria for the making of an order without notice is made out. In lay terms, these include where the whereabouts of the respondent is not known, or where there is a perceived real urgency or emergency.

If the court makes an order, the named person or body will be directed to give the information which they have, to a named official of the court and in a specified manner, usually in writing. The court will then decide what to do with the information. In practice the file will be referred to a judge on provision of the information to give directions. In order to save time at any application a judge may be invited to give additional directions to include the court serving the respondent and listing the matter for an urgent inter-parties hearing.

The order will be endorsed with a penal notice to allow the applicant to enforce the order, if necessary, by committal. See Chapter 19 for the procedure to follow where the order is subsequently breached.

It is also possible, in connection with a Part I order, to apply to the court pursuant to the FLA 1986, s 34 in Form C3 for an order authorising a search for, taking charge of and delivery of a child. In view of the nature of the application, it will relatively frequently be made without notice. The application attracts a court fee unless the applicant is exempt from fees.

FLA 1986, s 34
FPR 2010, r 12.16(4)

Note: The Order is Order 7.9 in Volume 2 Compendium of Standard Orders. As at the time of writing, the Compendium of Standard Orders is being revised, such that the order reference numbers may change in the not too distant future.

FLA 1986, s 34
FPR 2010, r 12.16

Where the court makes an order requiring a person to hand over a child to another person and that order is not complied with, the court may make a further order in an attempt to force compliance. The order is addressed to all police constables and authorises them to search for, take charge of and deliver the child to a person specified in the order. Such an order confers wide powers to ensure compliance.

A Part I order can be registered in another part of the United Kingdom and, once registered, can be enforced in exactly the same way as in England and Wales.

FLA 1986, s 27

Similarly, a Part 1 order made in another part of the United Kingdom can be registered in England and Wales, at the Principal Registry of the Family Division, and thereafter enforced as though made within the jurisdiction.

FLA 1986, s 27
FPR 2010, r 32.26

20.1.2 Child Abduction and Custody Act 1985

In incoming child abduction cases engaging the 1980 Hague Child Abduction Convention or other cases engaging the 1980 European Convention, the court's power to make orders for the location of a child is grounded in the Child Abduction and Custody Act 1985, s 24A.

20.1.3 Inherent jurisdiction

Separately, the High Court can exercise its inherent jurisdiction to make location orders, passport orders and collection orders.

20.2 SURRENDER OF PASSPORTS

FLA 1986, s 37

Where there is in force a prohibited steps order or other order restricting the removal of a child from the UK the court may require a person to surrender any UK passport which has been issued to or contains particulars of the child.

FPR 2010, PD 12F, para 4.9

This section is limited to any UK passport and limited to the passport of or one that contains the particulars of the child.

The High Court may exercise its inherent jurisdiction to require the surrender of any non-UK passport.

20.3 PORT ALERT

Where there is a possibility of a child being imminently removed from the United Kingdom, it may be appropriate to request a port alert.

The police have the power to initiate a port alert absent a court order in cases of children under 16 where their threat of removal is real and imminent (FPR 2010, Pt 4, PD12F). Home Office Circular 21/1986 stated that the terms 'imminent' and 'real' means within the next 24 or 48 hours and was not being sought as a means of insurance.

The Family Court has jurisdiction to make free-standing Port Alert orders in relation to all children under 18. The allocation rules do not specify which tier of judge should hear such cases but authority suggests judges of Circuit Judge level. Free standing orders on a without notice basis should only be made where the applicant demonstrates with clear evidence that there is a real and imminent risk that the children in question will be removed from England and Wales. When assessing that risk the court will not demand proof that it is more likely than not that the children will be removed; it will, nonetheless, still expect proof of a degree of probability not far short of that standard.

A v B [2021] EWHC 1716 (Fam), [2021] 4 WLR 108

The default position should be that a free-standing Port Alert order should last for only 28 days in the first instance and that any extension of that period should only be ordered on a subsequent inter partes hearing.

A port alert is automatically attached to any High Court location order, passport order or collection order.

CHAPTER 21

WARDSHIP AND CHILD ABDUCTION

21.1 WARDSHIP

21.1.1 The process of wardship

The High Court's wardship jurisdiction is part of, and not separate from the court's inherent jurisdiction. The issuing of an application in Form C66 for wardship vests in the High Court rights and obligations in respect of all significant aspects of the upbringing of a child. Accordingly, once a child is warded, no step of importance can be taken with regard to him/her without first obtaining the leave of the court.

Re F (in Utero) [1988] Fam 122, [1988] 2 All ER 193
C v C [1990] 1 FLR 462, CA

A child may be made a ward of court immediately upon birth but not prior to birth.

In the matter of NY (A Child) [2019] UKSC 49

Wardship proceedings should not be commenced unless the issue concerning the child cannot be resolved under the CA 1989. Even if the issue cannot be resolved under the CA 1989, a party will still have to justify why it is necessary for the child to be made a ward, as opposed to simply seek relief under the inherent jurisdiction more generally. For a review of the relevant case law and principles, see *In the matter of NY (A Child)*.

FPR 2010, PD 12D, para 1.2

The most obvious examples of circumstances in which wardship may still be appropriate are:

(a) to restrain publicity;
(b) to prevent undesirable association;
(c) orders relating to medical treatment;
(d) orders to protect abducted children, or children where the case has another substantial foreign element;
(e) orders for the return of children to and from another state.

Note: For abduction matters generally see **21.2**.

In the exercise of its inherent jurisdiction the High Court has jurisdiction only if the child is habitually resident in England and Wales or is present in England and Wales and is not habitually resident in any other part of the UK and provided that jurisdiction is not excluded by FLA 1986, s 3(2).

The court may also exercise its wardship jurisdiction in respect of a child who is a British national in exceptional circumstances, see *Re B (A Child) (Habitual Residence: Inherent Jurisdiction)*. However, this exceptional course, which necessitates the inherent jurisdiction being a source of jurisdiction, is not available in cases engaging the 1996 Hague Child Protection jurisdictional scheme, see *Re I-L (Children) (1996 Hague Child Protection Convention: Inherent Jurisdiction)*.

Re B (A Child) (Habitual Residence: Inherent Jurisdiction) [2016] 1 FLR 561, SC
Re I-L (Children) (1996 Hague Child Protection Convention: Inherent Jurisdiction) [2019] EWCA Civ 1956

21.1.2 Procedure

Procedure is governed by FPR 2010, Chapter 5 and is clearly set out in PD 12D to which reference should be made.

FPR 2010, r 12.36(1)

See *In the matter of a Ward of Court* for a full review of the relevant case law and principles.

In the matter of a Ward of Court [2017] EWHC 1022 (Fam)

Wardship proceedings are commenced by issuing an application in Form C66 in the High Court (which includes District Registries of the High Court Family Division). A court fee is payable unless the applicant is exempt from fees.

The application and the statement of case must be verified by a statement of truth.

FPR 2010, r 17.2, 'statement of case' defined by r 4.1(1)

Although the family court does not have jurisdiction to deal with applications that a child be made or cease to be made a ward of court, consideration will be given to transferring the case in whole or in part to a family court where wardship has been confirmed.

FPR 2010, r 12.36(2)
FPR 2010, PD12D, paras 2.1–2.3

Wherever possible, the child's birth certificate and, if appropriate, a certified copy of the relevant entry in the Adopted Children's Register must be lodged with the court. Where the child was born or adopted in England and Wales, a certified copy certificate can be obtained from the General Register Office, PO Box 2, Southport, Merseyside PR8 2JD. There are also regional offices in Greater Manchester, Birmingham, Bridgend, Newcastle and Plymouth. The telephone enquiry numbers is 0300 123 1837. Further information is also available on the website www.gro.gov.uk.

FPR 2010, r 5.1
Form C66

If proper proof of the date of birth cannot be immediately obtained, the direction of the court should be sought at the first hearing.

FPR 2010, r 5.1

The full name of the child should appear in the title of the action. If a baby has not yet been named, his/her gender should be given, for example 'Baby Smith, a male'.

In addition to the name and, where possible, the date of birth of the child, the application should also provide:

(a) the full name of each party to the application together with the relationship to or other interest in the child;

(b) if known, the whereabouts of the child or otherwise a statement to confirm that they are not known;

FPR 2010, r 5.1
FPR 2010, r 12.39

(c) a notice to each respondent informing him/her of the requirement to keep the court informed as to the whereabouts of the minor, unless a respondent is unaware of the details.

FPR 2010, r 12.37(1) and (2)

A child must not be made a respondent to wardship proceedings without the permission of the court.

The application must conclude with a statement of truth.

Sufficient copies of the application must be lodged for service upon each respondent, together with the appropriate court fee unless the applicant is exempt from fees.

Each respondent must be served with:

(a) a sealed copy of the application;

(b) a notice of the proceedings;

(c) acknowledgement of service.

The applicant is responsible for service of the above documents upon each respondent. This is usually undertaken by a process server.

FPR 2010, r 6.41

Leave is not required to serve the application out of the jurisdiction.

All substantive hearings will be before a High Court judge. Whilst all hearings will be in chambers, because of the nature of these proceedings, it may be thought appropriate for either counsel or a solicitor to appear as an advocate.

21.1.3 The effect of proceedings

Senior Courts Act 1981, s 41(2) and (2A) as inserted by CA 1989, Sch 13, para 45(2). See also CA 1989, s 108(5)

Immediately upon the issue of the application, the minor will become a ward of court unless he is the subject of a care order.

FPR 2010, PD 12D, para 4.1

No ward of court may be removed from the jurisdiction, by any person, without the permission of the court.

FPR 2010, PD12F Part 4 para 4.4

Where the child is a ward and permission has not been given to remove a child from the jurisdiction and a person seeks police assistance they must produce evidence that the child is a ward.

Particulars of all applications issued for wardship will be recorded in the Register of Wards, which is maintained by the Principal Registry of the Family Division.

FPR 2010, r 12.38

Wardship, once confirmed by a court order, remains in force throughout the minority of a child unless previously discharged by order of the court.

Senior Courts Act 1981, s 41(3)

21.2 CHILD ABDUCTION

Child abduction in all its various facets is far too substantial to be dealt with in any great detail in a book of this nature. However, a comprehensive account is to be found in *Clarke Hall & Morrison*, *Rayden* and (the more dated but invaluable and peerless) Lowe & Nicholls' *International Movement of Children: Law, Practice and Procedure* (2nd edition). Those texts also deal with those cases for which Brussels IIA still applies.

The applications the court is typically faced with where a child has been removed from one jurisdiction to another without appropriate consent having been given include:

a an application for a child's summary return to a foreign jurisdiction;

b an application to the appropriate English court for a declaration for ultimate use in a foreign court in child abduction proceedings there;

c an application in the English court for a specific issues order or similar order for the purposes of recognising and enforcing that order abroad;

d an application to the English court for the recognition and enforcement of a foreign order.

This work confines itself to some brief comments in relation to the following areas:

a Child abduction within England & Wales;

b Child abduction between this jurisdiction and Scotland and this jurisdiction and Northern Ireland;

c Incoming international child abduction; and

d Outgoing international child abduction.

21.2.1 Child abduction within England & Wales

It is not unusual in a domestic private law children case to be faced with a scenario where:

(i) prior to any proceedings commencing, one parent decamps with the child to another part of the country which, however far from the left behind parent, significantly impacts upon his or her ability to spend time with their child; and

(ii) by the time the matter gets to court, the move, from a welfare perspective, is effectively a *fait accompli*.

The test to be applied is that set out by the Court of Appeal in *Re R (Internal Abduction)*. See Black LJ's judgment:

Re R (Internal Abduction) [2016] EWCA Civ 1016 at [47]

> 'In short, in a domestic abduction case, as in a non-Convention international abduction case, the judge must derive the answer by applying section 1(1) of the Children Act to the particular facts of the case before him, having regard to all the relevant features, including the matters listed in section 1(3) (whether because the circumstances are within section 1(4) of the Act or otherwise by analogy).'

E Devereux, R George and E Bennett, *Domestic Child Abduction: Legal Responses*, Family Law Week (2017)

The court is entitled in an appropriate case to approach this welfare assessment in a summary manner (without waiting for full statements or a Cafcass report, for example, if there is other evidence before the judge which gives enough information to make interim decisions about return or otherwise). However, there are no presumptions or glosses on the welfare enquiry.

The application is for an order under the CA 1989, s 8 and may be made on an urgent basis. If without notice orders are made, provision should be made for a rapid return date hearing.

Re R (Children: Peremptory Return) [2011] EWCA Civ 558, [2011] 2 FLR 863

In cases where a child is removed from the care of his/her primary carer and has applied for relief (or the matter is before the court) very shortly after such a removal (ie a matter of hours or days), it is possible, again within the CA 1989, s 8 framework, to seek what is termed a 'peremptory return' of the child, ie an order for immediate return to restore the status quo prior to a final determination.

In order for an application for the peremptory return of a child to be effective:

- There should be no safeguarding issues in the case;
- An application should be made rapidly (ie within 24–48 hours if possible, or as quickly after the removal as possible) to the urgent applications judge of the appropriate Family Court or Family Division of the High Court; and
- It should be clear that the applicant is either the primary carer, or a parent who is obviously sharing care of the child.

21.2.2 Intra-UK child abduction

If a child has been removed from England & Wales by a parent to Scotland or Northern Ireland, there are three steps to take:

a obtain a specific issues order under the CA 1989, s 8 for the child's return to England & Wales (or other s 8 order to like effect);

b apply to the English court to have that order registered in the relevant other jurisdiction; and

c apply in the Scottish or Northern Irish court to enforce the registered order (in addition to any further relief Scottish or Northern Irish lawyers may advise is appropriate).

The FLA 1986 governs jurisdiction in private law children cases between England & Wales, Scotland and Northern Ireland. Amongst other matters, it provides for the registration, recognition and enforcement of 'Part 1 Orders' which include CA 1989, s 8 orders. Such a s 8 order should be sought on an urgent basis and the court will apply the same criteria than a similar application in relation to a domestic English abduction, or a non-Hague Convention international abduction. FLA 1986, ss 1(1)(a), 27

21.2.3 Registration

The procedure for the registration of a Part 1 order is set out in the FPR 2010, r 32.25. The application can be made to either the Family Court or the High Court.

Any person on whom rights are conferred by a Part 1 order may apply. FLA 1986, s 27

The application to register is made in the first instance to the court that made the order. An application to register a High Court order (in Scotland or Northern Ireland) must be made to the High Court. An application to register a Family Court order must be made to the court which made it. FPR 2010, r 32.25(1)

Applications to register a High Court order should be made in the Principal Registry, to the family proceedings manager. Applications to register a Family Court order should be made to the court manager of the relevant court. FPR 2010, r 32.23

The application is made on Form C2. It should be accompanied by:

a A certified copy of the order;

b A copy of the any order which has varied the terms of the original order;

c A statement which:

i contains the name and address of the applicant and the applicant's interest under the order;

ii contains the name and date of birth of the child in respect of whom the order was made;

iii addresses the whereabouts or suspected whereabouts of the child;

iv contains the name of any person with whom the child is alleged to be;

v contains the name and address of any other person who has an interest under the order and states whether the order has been served on that person;

vi states in which jurisdiction the order is to be registered;

vii gives details of any order known to the applicant which affects the child and is in force in the jurisdiction in which the order is to be registered;

viii annexes any document to the application; and

ix is verified by a statement of truth.

FPR 2010, r 32.25(1)

The court officer will then send the documents to the appropriate court in the appropriate jurisdiction for registration.

FPR 2010, r 32.25(4)–(5)

If the court officer refuses to send the documents, the court officer must notify the applicant within 14 days and the applicant has the right to apply to a judge for an order that the documents be sent to the appropriate court.

FPR 2010, r 32.26

Where the appropriate papers are sent to the English court to register a Scottish or Northern Irish order, the prescribed officer registers the order and notifies the applicant. If the order is registered in the High Court, the Clerk of the Rules has traditionally written a letter to the applicant or his or her solicitors confirming the registration.

21.2.4 Enforcement

FPR 2010, PD5A

Where a registered order is being enforced in England & Wales, the application is made on Form FP1, under the FPR 2010, Part 19 to the court at which the order has ultimately been registered.

Where an ordered is registered under the FLA 1986, s 27 the court has the same powers for enforcing the order as it would have if it itself made the order including dismissing or staying the enforcement proceedings and orders including:

a Collection and location orders;

b Disclosure of whereabouts, Child Abduction and Custody Act 1985, s 24A;

c Attendance order;

d Surrender of UK Passport, FLA 1986, s 37 (only the High Court has the power, under the inherent jurisdiction to require the surrender of a non UK Passport);

e Port alert;

f Flight information;

g Injunction prohibiting further removal and removal from the UK;

h Injunction freezing assets;

i Any other direction for securing the welfare of the child or preventing changes in the circumstances relevant to the determination of the application: FLA 1986, s 29(2);

j Child Arrangements Order: CA 1989, s 8.

21.2.5 Incoming international child abduction

Incoming child abduction cases usually fall into the following categories:

a Those to which the 1980 Hague Convention applies;

b Those to which the 1980 Hague Convention does not apply but the 1996 Hague Convention applies;

c Those to which neither the 1980 Hague Convention nor the 1996 Hague Convention apply but the 1980 European Convention applies (a vanishingly rare category of cases);

d Those to which no international treaty applies;

e Those where the relief sought is recognition and enforcement under the 1996 Hague Convention of an order made in a Contracting State.

21.3 WHERE THE 1980 HAGUE CONVENTION APPLIES

The 1980 Hague Child Abduction Convention was ratified and implemented by the Child Abduction and Custody Act 1985.

The broad schema of the act is that a child, under the age of 16 years old, who is removed from the jurisdiction of their habitual residence to another Contracting State, should be returned there forthwith, absent the establishment of a limited number of defences.

21.3.1 Procedure

Procedure is governed by FPR 2010, Ch 6 and PD12F and the President's Practice Guidance on Case Management and Mediation of International Child Abduction Proceedings. Pursuant to the CACA 1985, Sch 1, para 11, proceedings from issuing of proceedings to final determination should take no longer than six weeks.

FPR 2010, r 12.45

Proceedings can only be issued in the High Court Family Division. The application is made on Form C67 and should include the information set out in the FPR 2010, PD12F, para 2.11 and the documents set out in PD12F Para 2.12. The heading on the application form must comply with the High Court Family Division. The application is made on Form C67 and should include the information set out in FPR 2010, PD12F, para 2.14. The statement must be verified by a statement of truth in the amended form set out in FPR 2010, r 17A and not as set out in FPR 2010, PD12F, para 12.13. A court fee is payable on the issue of the application unless the applicant is exempt from fees.

If the child has been the subject of previous proceedings, copies of all relevant documents must also be lodged with the court.

A copy of the application should be provided for service on each respondent. Each respondent will be served with:

FPR 2010, r 12.48

(a) a copy of the application, with the hearing date endorsed;
(b) acknowledgement of service.

Practitioners should note that FPR 2010, r 12.3 sets out a list of persons who should be made respondents.

FPR 2010, r 12.49

Once served, a respondent may file and serve an answer to the application within a period of 7 days, unless the court has made provision for a longer period.

FPR 2010, r 12.48(1)(a)

The court may however dispense with service of any summons in any proceedings under the CACA 1985.

FPR 2010, r 12.51

Whilst the court may adjourn the first or any subsequent hearing, the period of such adjournment may not exceed a period of 21 days at any one time.

FPR 2010, r 12.47
CACA 1985, ss 5 and 19

Where the case is one of urgency, the court may consider an application without notice.

Note: See PD12E re urgent business procedure.

All hearings of a substantive nature in relation to abduction matters are before a High Court judge and will be in chambers unless otherwise directed.

FPR 2010, r 12.45(b)

21.4 WHERE THE 1980 HAGUE CONVENTION DOES NOT APPLY BUT THE 1996 HAGUE CONVENTION APPLIES

Examples include:

a where a child is between the ages of 16–18; or

b where the 1996 Hague Convention is in force between this jurisdiction and the other state, but the 1980 Hague Convention is not.

The procedure to be followed is as with an application for the summary return of a child under the Inherent Jurisdiction (Form C66) (see below).

There is a separate procedure for the recognition and enforcement of court orders under the 1996 Hague Convention (see below).

21.5 WHERE THE 1980 HAGUE CONVENTION AND THE 1996 HAGUE CONVENTION DO NOT APPLY BUT THE 1980 EUROPEAN CONVENTION DOES APPLY

The European Convention was ratified and given effect by the CACA 1985. Its schema is for the recognition and enforcement of custody orders made by Contracting States.

Given the current prevalence of the 1996 Hague Convention, the 1980 European Convention is only likely to be used in a vanishingly rare number of cases.

Note: *AA v TT (Recognition & Enforcement)* [2015] 2 FLR 1 and *Re O-C (A Child) (Abduction: European Convention)* [2013] Fam Law 658 are perhaps the most recent reported cases and these pre-date the more widespread use of the 1996 Hague Convention, which takes precedence where states are Contracting States to both.

The procedure is the same as for an application under the 1980 Hague Convention.

21.6 WHERE NEITHER THE 1980 HAGUE CONVENTION, NOR THE 1996 HAGUE CONVENTION, NOR THE 1980 EUROPEAN CONVENTION APPLY

An application for the child's summary return can be made in the exercise of either the CA 1989 or the inherent jurisdiction. The procedure is the same as for wardship (see above). In some cases, it will be

See, in particular, FPR 2010, PD12D, 12F and 12E.

appropriate to ward the child. In others not. The application is made on Form C66.

AB v EM (Jurisdiction: Foreign Custody Order) [2020] 2 FLR 107 at [42]–[42].

If, in the context of summary return proceedings, recognition and enforcement is sought of a foreign custody order (non 1996 Hague Convention and non 1980 European Convention), the weight to be given to that order will depend on the circumstances of each case.

21.7 RECOGNITION AND ENFORCEMENT UNDER THE 1996 HAGUE CONVENTION

In some cases, in the abduction context, litigants choose to apply to recognise and enforce a foreign custody order under the 1996 Hague Convention, if that order was made in a Contracting State and is of a nature that engages the Convention, ie a child arrangements order equivalent. Reasons for this include the scope for resisting recognition under Article 23 is more limited than the defences open to a defendant in a 1980 Hague Convention.

Recognition is dealt with on the papers in the first instance by a District Judge of the Principal Registry, sitting at the Central Family Court. An appeal lies to a High Court Judge sitting in the Family Division.

Recognition and enforcement applications are notorious for being technical, and for requiring scrupulous and rigid adherence to all procedural rules to succeed. The rules in depth should be checked when making an application, as opposed to simply the summary below.

21.7.1 Procedure

The rules are set out in FPR 2010, Part 31 and PD31A.

FPFO 2008 fee 1.1

The Part 19 procedure is to be followed subject to FPR 2010, rr 31.8-44. A fee of £245 is payable.

FPR 2010, rr 31.4(1), 31.3(1) and 31.4(2)(a)

Any interested party may apply to a district judge of the Principal Registry.

FPR 2010, PD 31A, para 4.2

The application must contain all documents relevant to the court considering whether the criteria for refusing recognition in Article 23 of the 1996 Hague Convention are met. The application should, further, contain: (a) a statement addressing all those matters dealt with at FPR PD31A, para 4.3; and (b) an address within the jurisdiction for service on the applicant and stating in so far as is known to the applicant, the name and usual or last known address or place of business of the person in whose favour judgment was given, FPR PD31A, para 4.3(b).

The court serves the application on the person against whom registration is sought.

The court may direct that the judgment be recognised or alternatively that it should be treated as an application for enforcement and order that the judgment be registered for enforcement provided that the requirement for the filing of the relevant documents and information ahs been satisfied. FPR 2010, r 31.10

An appeal must be made to a judge of the High Court within 1 month of the date of service of the notice of registration or in the case of an appellant habitually resident in another Contracting State within 2 months of the date of service of notice of registration, or refusal to recognise or to register for enforcement. FPR 2010, r 31.15(1)–(2)

21.8 OUTGOING INTERNATIONAL CHILD ABDUCTION

A litigant may seek to apply under the CA 1989 for a s 8 order requiring the return of a child to England and Wales with a view to seeking that this order is recognised and enforced abroad. That application can be made in the Family Court or the High Court.

Equally, a litigant may seek an order for a child's return to England and Wales under the Inherent Jurisdiction. That application is made in the High Court, on Form C66, on the same basis as for an incoming return order.

On occasion, a litigant will apply to the High Court for a declaration under the CACA 1985, s 8 (incorporating Article 15 of the 1980 Hague Convention) that a child has been wrongfully removed or retained away from the United Kingdom. Usually, the purpose of obtaining such a declaration will be to use it in foreign 1980 Hague Convention proceedings. The procedure for seeking such a declaration is the same as for an incoming child abduction under the 1980 Hague Convention (see above), the only difference being that the details of the relevant legal proceedings in respect of which the declaration is sought (if any), including a copy of any order made relating to the application, should be included in the documentation. FPR 2010, PD12F, para 2.15

On occasion, it is necessary to seek the assistance of British Embassies and High Commissions abroad. The President has issued guidance on when and where this is appropriate, and, where so, the procedure to adopt for liaison with them, see *Liaison between Courts in England and Wales and British Embassies and High Commissions Abroad* (14 March 2022).

CHAPTER 22

PUBLIC LAW FOR THE PRIVATE LAW PRACTITIONER

22.1 INTRODUCTION

In many private law cases the local authority will be involved or become involved. It is therefore essential that a private law practitioner has a rudimentary knowledge of public law proceedings and the duties upon local authorities.

Public law proceedings are outside the scope of this book and this chapter is aimed at providing an overview of the essential sections of the CA 1989 that practitioners should be aware of. For a more detailed account please refer to *Hershman and McFarlane: Children Law and Practice*.

22.2 GENERAL DUTIES OF A LOCAL AUTHORITY TO CHILDREN IN NEED

CA 1989, s 17(1)

The CA 1989, s 17 imposes a general duty on local authorities to provide a range and level of services to children in their area to safeguard and promote the welfare of those children and, so far as is consistent with that duty, to promote the upbringing of such children by their family.

The term 'in need' is defined in s 17(10) as:

(a) the child is unlikely to achieve or maintain or to have the opportunity of achieving or maintaining, a reasonable standard of health or development without the provision for him of services by a local authority;

(b) the child's health or development is likely to be significantly impaired, or further impaired, without the provision for him of such services; or

(c) the child is disabled.

CA 1989, Sch 2

The assessment of whether a child is in need is one of evaluated judgement by the local authority and is subject to judicial review. It is therefore for the local authority to determine the question and only when they have do the provisions of the CA 1989, s 17 apply.

The range of services that a local authority can provide are wide ranging and are set out in the CA 1989, Sch 2.

They include the provision of accommodation for a person causing ill treatment to the child; so for example if it is said the problem is mother's new partner who has moved in the authority can assist that person in finding alternative accommodation. Steps to maintain the family home (a deep clean) and the provision of a family centre in the area and services there (for example parenting classes or support workers) are other examples. The services to be provided should also be aimed at preventing care proceedings.

The services can be in kind or in cash so would allow the provision of funds to purchase baby milk or even pay a deposit on rented accommodation (although this is rare).

CA 1989, s 17(6)

The local authority can impose conditions on the provision of services which could include cooperation or for repayment although the local authority cannot request repayment if a person is in receipt of benefits.

CA 1989, s 17(7)
CA 1989, s 17(8)

Before providing any services the local authority, as far as they are able, shall obtain the wishes and feeling of the child and give consideration to those wishes and feelings.

CA 1989, s 17(4A)

Although the duty under the CA 1989, s 17 is wide ranging it does not impose a duty on the local authority to meet the assessed needs of a child. That is the case even if those services are deliverable by the local authority within its resources.

R (G) v Barnet London Borough council; R (W) v Lambeth London Borough council; R (A) v Lambeth London Borough council [2004] 1 FLR 454

Note: CA 1989, s 17 is therefore a useful section when acting for a client that is involved with social services and needs help and support. In any letters to the local authority the duty under s 17 should be quoted. An enquiry should be made as to whether there has been or will be an assessment of the child as a child in need and also refer to the services available under Sch 2.

22.3 CHILD PROTECTION CONFERENCES

A Child Protection Conference is a significant step and normally follows a strategy discussion and a CA 1989, s 47 enquiry (see below). It is therefore a serious step by local authority when they are of the view that a child is suffering or likely to suffer significant harm and consideration is being given to the possibility that a plan may be required to support the child.

The decision to convene a child protection conference is made at team manager level and the conference should be held within 15 working days of a strategy meeting

The conference brings together all those with knowledge of the child or family and therefore includes health professionals, teachers, police and anyone else working with the family. If a professional is unable to attend they normally provide a written report.

The conference will be chaired by an Independent Reviewing Officer (IRO) who should be a social worker experienced at management level or above but will be independent of the case management in respect of the family.

Before the conference starts the normal structure is that the chair will meet with the parents and/or child to go through the conference process and then when the conference starts the chair should explain the purpose of the meeting, introduce all participants and note any apologies. Professionals will then be asked to develop and contribute anything that they wish to add to their report and the family of course will be asked their views. Solicitors who attend, attend to observe and support the family; they are not able to ask questions although they may be able (with the permission of the chair) to seek clarification or play some role.

Note: Clarification should be sought from the chair before the conference of the role to be taken.

At the end of the discussion it is for the chairperson to decide whether the child is made subject to a child protection plan but in doing so they must take into account the views of other professionals; although they are not bound by them. If the parents disagree, then they may follow a complaints procedure. In determining that the child should be subject to a child protection plan the chair should determine what category of abuse or neglect it is said the child is suffering (physical, emotional, sexual) and that should also be recorded.

If the child is to be made subject to a plan, that plan should be compiled by the allocated social worker and must be initially reviewed after 3 months and thereafter reviewed at regular intervals of no more than 6 months.

If the decision is taken not to make the child subject to a child protection plan, then the conference and the family should consider whether there is any further help or assistance that could be given to the family to help them and also whether any assessments should be undertaken.

A clear record of the conference proceedings should be taken and that should be sent to all those who attended (and had been invited) within 15 working days of the conference and any amendments should be received by one week thereafter.

22.4 LOCAL AUTHORITY'S DUTY TO INVESTIGATE

Where a local authority is informed that a child in its area: (a) is subject to police protection or an emergency protection order; (b) is in contravention of a curfew; or (c) the local authority has reasonable cause to suspect that a child who lives or is found within their area is suffering, or likely to suffer significant harm, it shall make or cause to be made inquiries to decide what action (if any) it should take to safeguard the child.

Any assessment should be in accordance with the guidance and any assessment must conclude within 45 working days.

Working Together to Safeguard Children (HM Government, March 2015) Chapter 1; Assessing Needs and Providing Help

The assessment will be led by social workers but with contributions from other professionals and at the conclusion of the assessment the local authority should conclude whether they need to take convene a core group meeting within 10 days or an Initial Child Protection Conference (see above) or take no further action.

22.5 PROVISION OF ACCOMMODATION

The CA 1989, s 20 provides that a local authority shall provide accommodation to a child in its area where:

(a) there is no person with parental responsibility for the child.

(b) the child is lost or has been abandoned; or

(c) the person who has been caring for the child is prevented (whether or not permanently, and for whatever reason) from providing him with suitable accommodation or care.

CA 1989, s 20(1)

Every local authority shall also provide accommodation for a child in need who has reached the age of 16 and whose welfare the authority considers is likely to be seriously prejudiced if they do not provide him with accommodation.

CA 1989, s 20(3)

Accommodation can only be provided if there is a person with parental responsibility and that person consents. Such consent must be valid. Valid consent means that the person with parental responsibility needs to have the capacity to consent and if the social worker has any doubts they should stop seeking consent and, if necessary, apply to the court for public law orders.

CA 1989, s 20(7)

A local authority may not provide accommodation if any person with parental responsibility is willing and able to provide accommodation for the child or able to arrange for accommodation to be provided for him.

CA 1989, s 20(8) A person with parental responsibility may remove the child from accommodation provided by the local authority at any time.

However where the child is subject to a 'live with' or special guardianship order then it is that person who gives the consent pursuant to the CA 1989, s 20(7) and any other person with parental responsibility but not named in the order cannot remove or accommodate the child. An application would need to be made to the court.

Note: In many circumstances CA 1989, s 20 is used where the local authority has concerns but wishes time to work with the family before issuing court proceedings and the family agree to the child going into foster care (or care with another family member or friend) whilst this happens. It could be that the parent(s) are subject to bail conditions which prevent them caring for the child. CA 1989, s 20 should be for a short period and should not be used to avoid care proceedings. If the local authority conclude that a child can't return home they should apply to the court.

Although the CA 1989, s 20(8) provides that a person with parental responsibility may remove the child at any time, in practice there is usually an agreement with the local authority to provide notice (usually 7 days) which then allows the local authority to apply to court if they disagree with the return.

22.6 SECTION 37 INVESTIGATION

CA 1989, s 37 If the court in any family proceedings considers that it may be appropriate to make a care or supervision order it can direct a local authority to undertake an investigation of the child's circumstances. The court takes this step of its own initiative but with sufficient evidence and usually it is recommended by Cafcass at the first hearing from its safeguarding enquiries.

CA 1989, s 37(4) Such investigation must be undertaken within an 8-week period and the local authority in their report to the court should inform the court as to whether they should:

CA 1989, s 37(2)

(a) apply for a care order or for a supervision order in respect of the child;
(b) provide services or assistance to the child or his family; or
(c) take any other action with respect to the child.

If the local authority decide not to take any action their report must set out:

(a) the reason for their decision;

(b) services or assistance which they have provided or intend to provide to the child and his family; and

(c) any other action which they have taken, or propose to take, with respect to the child. CA 1989, s 37(3)

The court on making a section 37 direction can make an interim care or supervision order and also appoint a guardian although to appoint a guardian the proceedings must be specified proceedings and the court, on making the section 37 direction, must therefore either make an interim care order or be considering making such order. CA 1989, s 38(1)(b) CA 1989, s 41(1) CA 1989, s 41(6)(b)

A section 37 report must not be used to obtain a general welfare report; there must be a possibility on the facts that the local authority need to take proceedings (see below). If the local authority are involved with the family then an order can be made for them to prepare a section 7 report (see **18.8.1**).

On giving a section 37 direction the court, in its order, should set out in detail the reasons for making the order and provide for the local authority to receive the court papers and the order as quickly as possible. FPR 2010, r 12.17

22.7 POLICE PROTECTION

The Children Act 1989, s 46 provides for a police officer who has reasonable cause to believe that a child would otherwise be likely to suffer significant harm, to:

(a) remove the child to suitable accommodation and keep him there; or

(b) take such steps as are reasonable to ensure that the child's removal from any hospital or other place in which he is then being accommodated is prevented.

On taking such steps the officer should immediately inform the local authority who should commence a section 47 investigation (see above). CA 1989, s 46

Police protection lasts for 72 hours. CA 1989, s 46(6)

Police protection does not confer parental responsibility but those with care can take such steps as is necessary to promote the child's welfare. CA 1989, s 46(9)

Police protection concerns emergency situations where the police, as part of their investigations, become aware of a child who is suffering harm (for example being found home alone) or where a child has been brought to hospital with an injury that is considered to be non-accidental and the parents wish to remove the child from hospital and the hospital/social services consider the child should remain for further tests and there is not time for the local authority to apply to the court for an emergency protection order.

Note: This is an emergency step taken by the police. It is the exception and not the rule. If social services are already involved and there is time an application should be made for an Emergency Protection Order which then allows the matter to be scrutinised by the court (see below).

22.8 EMERGENCY PROTECTION ORDER

An emergency protection order is a draconian, urgent order that is used sparingly. It is for emergency situations where there is reasonable cause to believe that a child is likely to suffer significant harm:

(a) if he is not removed to accommodation provided by or on behalf of the local authority, or does not remain in the place where he is accommodated; and

(b) the local authority are being unreasonably refused access to a child

CA 1989, s 44(1) and (4)

Although the CA 1989, s 44(1) permits any person to make an application this is usually the local authority and s 44(1) confers on the local authority parental responsibility and will be applied for in very similar circumstances as police protection. The differences are: (a) this is ordered by the court; and (b) it confers parental responsibility.

Such applications are usually made and heard on the same day and although they can be made without notice, in practice the parents are usually given a little notice and the court will, whenever possible, list the hearing in the afternoon.

A guardian should be immediately appointed for the child on issue of the application.

CA 1989, s 45(1)
CA 1989, s 45(5)

Any order lasts for a maximum period of 8 days and can be renewed only once for a further period of up to 7 days.

22.9 THRESHOLD CRITERIA

The core principle to making any public law order is that the threshold criteria are met. The court must find that the threshold criteria are met to have jurisdiction to make an order.

The threshold criteria are set out in the CA 1989, s 31(2):

> 'A court may only make a care order or supervision order if it is satisfied that:
>
> (a) the child concerned is suffering or is likely to suffer significant harm; and
>
> (b) that the harm or likelihood of harm, is attributable to:
>
> (i) the care given to the child, or likely to be given to him if the order were not mad, not being what it would be reasonable to expect a parent to give him or
>
> (ii) the child's being beyond parental control.' CA 1989, s 31(2)

The relevant time for this assessment is at the date of the application or when the local authority took protection measures (ie the child was accommodated pursuant to section 20). CA 1989, s 20

The term 'harm' is defined by s 31(9) as:

> '"Harm" means ill treatment or the impairment of health or development including for example impairment suffered from seeing or hearing the ill treatment of another; "development" means physical, intellectual, emotional, social or behavioural development, "health" means physical or mental health; and "ill treatment" includes sexual abuse and forms of ill treatment which are not physical.' CA 1989, s 31(9)

The term 'significant' is not defined in the act and is clearly fact specific. The Supreme Court in *Re B* concluded that 'significant' meant something more than commonplace failure or human inadequacy and something considerable, noteworthy or important. It does not have to be intentional or deliberate; the test is whether factually it is made out. The parent with significant mental health problems that impact on the child it not intentionally or deliberately causing the child significant harm but the child, nevertheless, is suffering such harm. *Re B (Care Proceedings; Appeal)* [2013] 2 FLR 1075

The term 'likely to suffer' was considered by the Supreme Court In *Re B* (see above) to mean 'a real possibility, a possibility that cannot be sensibly ignored having regard to the gravity of the feared harm in the particular case'. This must be established on the basis of evidence not assumptions or speculation.

The satisfaction of the threshold criteria means that the court has jurisdiction to make an order. It does not automatically follow that the court will then make an order. Threshold is stage one and if crossed the court, having jurisdiction to make an order, will then consider whether or not to make an order (and what type of order) in accordance with the child's welfare, applying the CA 1989, s 1(1) and the welfare checklist in s 1(3). In doing this the court looks at the holistic welfare needs of the child and the realistic options available for the child and which option (giving full weight to the importance of family placements) is most proportionate and best meets the needs of the child.

22.10 THE PUBLIC LAW OUTLINE

FPR 2010, PD 12A

All applications for care or supervision orders are subject to the Public Law Outline which is contained in PD12A. This sets out the key stages within the proceedings, the hearings and what is expected at each hearing. If public law proceedings are being considered/ to be issued this is essential reading.

22.11 DURATION OF PROCEEDINGS

CA 1989, s 32; FPR 2010, PD 12A, para 5.1

Public law proceedings should be concluded within 26 weeks and the court, at the first hearing, should draw up a timetable to ensure the matter is concluded without delay.

CA 1989, s 32(7); FPR 2010, PD 12A, para 6.1

The court can extend the proceedings beyond 26 weeks only on the basis that it is in the child's best interests and is required to resolve the case justly. Any extension should be for no more than a period of 8 weeks although there can be multiple extensions.

22.12 INTERIM CARE ORDERS

B v B (Interim Contact with Grandparents) [1993] Fam Law 393

An interim care order invests parental responsibility in the local authority and its purpose is to hold the balance so as to cause the least possible harm to the child and is not an advanced judgment of the final outcome of the case. It is an order that 'holds the ring' pending final determination.

At the start of the proceedings the court will not be in a position to dispose of the case but may conclude that there are reasonable grounds for believing that the threshold criteria is met (see above) and that it is in the child's welfare for it to be in the care of the local authority.

The question as to whether or not the court makes an interim care order is in 2 stages; the first is set out in the CA 1989, s 38(2): CA 1989, s 38(2)

> '(2) A court shall not make an interim care order or interim supervision order under this section unless it is satisfied that there are *reasonable grounds* for believing that circumstances with respect to the child are as mentioned in section 31(2).' (see above, emphasis added)

This is not a final order. The court therefore is considering whether, on the facts, there are *reasonable grounds* for believing the threshold is met. It is not a final determination of threshold and the court will not usually make findings of fact.

An interim care order has effect for such period as specified in the order which is normally until further order or disposal of the application. CA 1989, s 38(4)

If the interim threshold is met the court will then consider whether or not to grant an interim care order having regard for the welfare checklist with the welfare of the child being paramount. CA 1989, s 1(3) CA 1989, s 1(1)

There are numerous authorities from the higher courts as to how to approach this second stage of the court's determination, the purpose of which is to establish a holding position pending a full hearing.

In *Re H* 2 propositions were extracted:

> 'that the decision taken by the court on an interim care order application must necessarily be limited to issues that cannot await the fixture and must not extend to issues that are being prepared for determination at that fixture'

and

> 'that separation is only to be ordered if the child's safety demands immediate separation.'

Re H (a Child) (Interim Care Order) [2003] 1 FCR 350

Such removal should not be sanctioned at an interim stage unless the child's safety requires interim protection.

Re M (Interim Care Order; Removal) [2006] 1 FLR 1043

22.13 CONTACT

Where a child is in the care (to include interim care) of a local authority they (the local authority) are under a duty to promote reasonable contact between the child and its parents or any person who before the making CA 1989, s 34 of an order had an order for contact or parental responsibility.

If contact cannot be agreed then the court, on application, or on making an interim or final order, can make an order for contact.

CA 1989, s 34(6)
CA 1989, s 34(4)

If the local authority consider that contact is not in the best interests of the child they can stop contact for a period of up to 7 days and then apply to the court for an order to refuse contact.

22.14 CARE ORDERS

A care order is a final order. The court has to find threshold and also that it is in the child's best interests to make a final order (see above). The order vests parental responsibility in the local authority and also the power to determine the extent to which a parent or any other person with parental responsibility may meet their parental responsibility. It lasts until the child reaches the age of 18 unless discharged before that date.

CA 1989, s 31A
CA 1989, s 34(11)

Before making a care order the court is required to consider the plan of the local authority as to the long term placement plans for the child and also contact.

22.15 SUPERVISION ORDER

A supervision order does not vest parental responsibility in the local authority but a duty to:

(a) advise, assist and befriend the supervised child;

(b) take steps as are reasonably necessary to give effect to the order; and

(c) where:

   (i) the order is not wholly complied with; or

   CA 1989, s 35(1)

   (ii) the supervisor considers that the only may no longer be necessary; to consider whether or not to apply to the court for variation or discharge.

CA 1989, Sch 3, Part II, para 6

To make a supervision order the court has to find the threshold criteria are met as otherwise it does not have jurisdiction. A supervision order can only be made for a period of 12 months and although it can be extended it may not be extended so as to run beyond the end of the period of 3 years beginning the date on which it was made. The court cannot initially make an order for 3 years. The extensions are by application only.

CHAPTER 23

FAMILY HOMES AND DOMESTIC VIOLENCE

23.1 INTRODUCTION

The Family Law Act 1996 ('FLA 1996'), Pt IV sets out the law relating to the occupation of a family home, domestic violence and related matters, save for stalking, which is covered by the Protection from Harassment Act 1997 ('PHA 1997'). The Domestic Violence, Crime and Victims Act 2004 brought in a number of developments to the law, including criminalising the breach of non-molestation orders made under the FLA 1996, and its provisions were extended to civil partnerships by the Civil Partnership Act 2004, Sch 5. The relevant rules are now to be found at the FPR 2010, Pt 10, supplemented by Practice Direction 10A.

23.2 WHICH COURT?

Proceedings may be commenced in:

(a) the High Court;

(b) the Family Court.

In practice, this is nearly always in the Family Court.

23.3 POWERS OF THE COURT

FLA 1996, ss 33–38

Subject to the limitations referred to below, the court has wide powers with regard to:

(a) rights of occupation in respect of a dwelling;

(b) regulate the occupation of part of the dwelling by each party;

(c) the exclusion of a party from all or a part of a dwelling;

(d) the protection of a party from domestic violence (a non-molestation order).

An order in the form of (b) and (c) above can include a restriction on a party from approaching within a set distance of the dwelling in question, or a specified locality. Such an order is commonly termed a 'zonal non-molestation order'.

FLA 1996, Pt IV also makes provision for a court to order the transfer of certain tenancies upon the pronouncement of a decree of divorce, nullity or judicial separation, or upon the separation of cohabitants or at any time when it has the power to make a property adjustment order under the Civil Partnership Act 2004, Sch 5, Pt 2 with respect to civil partnership.

A comprehensive account of the provisions of the FLA 1996, ss 33 and 36–38, with regard to rights of occupation and the scope of the orders which the court can make is to be found in *Rayden*.

The court is also able to impose one or more of a number of additional provisions when making an occupation order under any one of s 33, 35 or 36, for example:

(a) requiring a party to pay outgoings in respect of a dwelling-house or to repair and maintain it;

(b) in some circumstances, requiring a party to make periodical payments to the other party concerning expenditure in respect of the occupation of a dwelling-house;

(c) with regard to the use and security of a dwelling-house and its contents.

However, the true value of one of the financial orders referred to above has been put in doubt by a decision of the Court of Appeal in which it has been made clear that the court has no related power of enforcement, and this remains the case.

Nwogbe v Nwogbe [2000] 2 FLR 744

23.4 DOMESTIC VIOLENCE HELPLINES

A list of useful contact telephone numbers and websites is to be found at **Appendix C(18)**.

23.5 FACTORS TO BE CONSIDERED

In considering an application for an occupation order under any of the FLA 1996, s 33, 35 or 36, the court must have regard to all the circumstances of the case, taking particular account of the statutory factors set out in the FLA 1996. Practitioners should note these differ in respect of each section.

A court when considering whether to make an occupation order should also consider whether to make a non-molestation order.

FLA 1996, s 42 (4A)

In deciding whether to grant a non-molestation order under the FLA 1996, s 42, the court must have regard to all the circumstances of the case, including the need to secure the health, safety and well-being of the applicant and of any relevant child.

FLA 1996, s 63
FLA 1996, s 45

For the purposes of s 42, health includes physical or mental health.

Section 45 sets out the factors to which the court must have regard in deciding whether or not to make a without notice order.

See **23.7** and **23.7.1** with regard to a without notice application and order. It would be exceptional to make an occupation order without notice. The Practice Guidance Family Court – Duration of Ex Parte (Without Notice) Orders, revised by the President of the Family Division and re-issued on 18 January 2017, sets out the law and procedure for without notice orders, particularly at paragraphs 5 and 6 in respect of orders under the FLA 1996.

The term molestation is not defined in the act. In common law molestation has been held 'implies some quite deliberate conduct which is aimed at a high degree of harassment of the other party, so as to justify the intervention of the court'.

C v C (Non-Molestation Order; Jurisdiction) [1998] 1 FLR 554

It will of course include all forms of domestic abuse which is defined in the Domestic Abuse Act 2021 which provides a wide definition incorporating psychological, physical, sexual, financial and emotional abuse.

23.6 PARTIES TO THE PROCEEDINGS

23.6.1 Non-molestation orders

Where the remedy sought is an injunction to protect the applicant from domestic violence, the applicant can seek an order against a person with whom he/she is associated.

FLA 1996, s 62(3)(a)–(g)

For the purpose of the FLA 1996, Pt IV, a person is associated with another person if:

'(a) they are or have been married to each other;

(aa) they are or have been civil partners of each other;

(b) they are cohabitants or former cohabitants (2 persons who are neither married to each other nor civil partners of each other but are living together as husband and wife or as if they were civil partners);

(c) they live or have lived in the same household, other than merely by reason of one of them being the other's employee, tenant, lodger or boarder;

(d) they are relatives;

(e) they have agreed to marry one another (whether or not that agreement has been terminated) (see below as to proof);

(eza) they have entered into a civil partnership agreement (as defined by the Civil Partnership Act 2004, s 73), whether or not that agreement has been terminated (see below as to proof);

(ea) they have or have had an intimate personal relationship with each other which is or was of significant duration;

(f) in relation to any child, both are either the parent or has or has had parental responsibility for the child in question;

(g) they are parties to the same family proceedings (other than proceedings under Part IV), for example, under the CA 1989.'

Two persons are also associated if they have both been involved in the adoption of a child.

Evidence of agreements to marry or create a civil partnership is required. FLA 1996, s 62(5) FLA 1996, s 44

Although the term relative is broad and includes step-parents and children the High Court has held it is no so broad as to include a step-nephew. *M v D* [2021] EWHC 1351

23.6.2 Occupation orders

Where the remedy sought is an occupation order and the dwelling house is, or at some time has been, the parties' home, any of the following persons can apply:

(a) those who are or have been married or civil partners to each other;

(b) those who are cohabitants or former cohabitants; or

(c) an associated person, not falling within (a) and (b) above, who is already entitled to occupy the property which is the subject of the application.

Practitioners will need to check carefully under which section they are bringing their client's application, the FLA 1996, s 33 where the applicant has estate or interest or has home rights, s 35 where former spouse or civil partner has no existing right to occupy, s 36 where one cohabitant or former cohabitant has no existing right to occupy, s 37 where neither spouse or civil partner is entitled to occupy, or s 38 where neither cohabitant or former cohabitant is entitled to occupy.

23.6.3 Relevant children

FLA 1996, s 62(2)

An order may be made for the benefit or protection of a relevant child, such child being:

(a) any child who is living with or might reasonably be expected to live with either party to the proceedings;

(b) any child in relation to whom an order under the Adoption Act 1976, the Adoption and Children Act 2002 or the CA 1989 is in question in the proceedings;

(c) any other child whose interest the court considers relevant.

FLA 1996, s 43(1), (2) FPR 2010, PD 10A, para 2.1 FC(CDB)R 2014, r 16(5)

However, other than with leave of the court, a child under the age of 16 may not apply for occupation or non-molestation orders, and the court may grant leave only if satisfied that the child has sufficient understanding to make the proposed application. Such an application may be made to the first available judge of the Family Court other than lay justices, and made under the Part 18 procedure.

FPR 2010, r 16.6(1)(b)

A litigation friend is not required for such an application.

23.7 PROCEDURE

The application must be issued in Form FL401.

The proceedings can be commenced either by way of a free-standing application or within existing proceedings. If issued as a free-standing application reference should be made to the existence of the other proceedings.

FPR 2010, r 29.1(2)

If the applicant does not wish to reveal his/her address or that of a relevant child, Form C8 should be completed, giving notice of those particulars to the court, and the particulars will not be revealed to any person unless the court directs otherwise. The form will be placed in a sealed envelope on the court file, marked accordingly.

FPR 2010, r 10.2(1)

An application for an occupation order must be supported by a witness statement. It is good practice to provide the court with a draft of the order which is sought, particularly where an application is made without notice.

FPR 2010, r 10.2(4)

An application in the first instance can be made without notice to the respondent or on notice (inter parties). Where made without notice, the witness statement in support must state the reasons why notice has not been given.

The court may make a non-molestation or an occupation order without the respondent having notice if it just and convenient, having regard to all the circumstances, including:

(a) any risk of significant harm to the applicant or a relevant child attributable to the conduct of the respondent if the order is not made immediately;

(b) whether it is likely that the applicant will be deterred or prevented from pursuing the application if an order is not made immediately;

(c) whether there is reason to believe that the respondent is deliberately evading service and there is reason to believe that the applicant or a relevant child will be seriously prejudiced by the delay in effecting service.

The Practice Guidance Family Court – Duration of Ex Parte (Without Notice) Orders makes it clear that a without notice application will normally be appropriate only if:

(a) there is an emergency or other great urgency, so that it is impossible to give any notice, however short or informal, or

(b) there is a real risk that, if alerted to what is proposed, if 'tipped off' the respondent will take steps in advance of the hearing to thwart the court's order of otherwise to defeat the ends of justice. In an appropriate case this can justify the grant of a non-molestation injunction without notice, less the respondent, having been served with an application, further molests his (or her) victim or exerts pressure on her (him) to abandon the proceedings. FLA 1996, s 45

An application made on notice must be served together with any statement in support and notice of any hearing or directions appointment set by the court. It must be served on the respondent personally not less than 2 days before the hearing, or within such period as the court may direct. An applicant acting in person may request the court officer to serve the application on the respondent. The applicant must file a certificate of service in Form FL415 to confirm that service has been effected before the hearing. FPR 2010, r 10.3

Any hearing relating to an application for an occupation order or a non-molestation order will be in private unless the court orders otherwise. FPR 2010, r 10.5

FPR 2010, rr 6.23, 6.35

The court may authorise alternative methods of service in an appropriate case.

Note: For the procedure to follow with regard to an emergency application see Chapter 22.

FLA 1996, s 42(2)(b)

The court can, when dealing with other family proceedings, make an order of its own initiative.

23.7.1 Action following a court order

FPR 2010, r 10.6

When an order is made on an application without notice the applicant must serve on the respondent a copy of the order, any statement supporting it, and where an order has been made by lay justices, a copy of the record of the reasons for a decision. Where the order is made on notice, the applicant must serve a copy of the order on the respondent, subject to any order of the court. No injunctive order is enforceable unless it is proved that the respondent is aware of it.

It will often be expedient to arrange for the respondent to be served with a copy of the order before leaving court. Not only will this be quicker and cheaper, but it will also avoid the necessity of the respondent having to be pursued by a process server.

FPR 2010, r 10.6(1A)

Where the applicant is acting in person, or the order is made on the initiative of the court, service of the prescribed documents must be made by the court.

FLA 1996, s 45(3)

If the court makes an order without notice it must afford the respondent an opportunity to make representations at a full hearing, as soon as it is just and convenient. Many judges consider that it is sufficient to make an order for a fixed term on the basis that there is a return date within 14 days so that the respondent can seek a review if he wishes to contest the proceedings – see the Practice Guidance Family Court – Duration of Ex Parte (Without Notice) Orders.

23.7.2 Procedure where property mortgaged or leased

FPR 2010, r 10.3(3), (4)
FPR 2010, r 10.6(3)

Where the property subject to an application for an occupation order under s 33, 35 or 36 is mortgaged or rented, notice must be given to the mortgagee or landlord, who must be served (following FPR 2010, r 6.23 or 6.35) with a copy of the application and notice of the right to make representations in writing or orally at any hearing.

The applicant must file a certificate of service after serving the application. The applicant must also serve a copy of any order on the mortgagee or landlord.

The court may direct that a hearing may be held in order to consider any representations from a mortgagee or landlord. FPR 2010, r 10.7

23.7.3 Transfer of tenancy

An application may be made under the FLA 1996, s 55, Sch 7 for the transfer of certain tenancies on divorce or termination of a civil partnership. Application should be made on Form D50B, which provides for acknowledgement of service in Form FP5. Notice must be served on the spouse, civil partner or cohabitant and on the landlord. Any person who has been served is entitled to be heard on the application.

The court must have regard to all the circumstances of the case, including the circumstances in which the tenancy was granted or either or both became tenants; the factors set out at FLA 1996, s 33(6)(a)–(c), (e)–(h) where relevant; and the suitability of the parties as tenants. FLA 1996, Sch 7, para 5

Practitioners should be aware that a respondent can potentially frustrate such an application by surrendering the tenancy or giving notice to quit without consulting the applicant, and may consider it prudent to seek an injunction to prevent the tenancy being surrendered. Any such injunction, or written undertaking given to the court in lieu of an injunction, should be served on the landlord. *Bater v Greenwich LBC* [1999] 2 FLR 993

If the parties are married or in a civil partnership, an order for transfer of tenancy only takes effect on final decree; this obviously does not apply if they are, or have been cohabitants. An order for transfer of tenancy made under FLA 1996 takes effect 'without further assurance' and may be more effective than an order made in financial proceedings. FLA 1996, Sch 7

23.7.4 Actions by mortgagees

The FLA 1996, ss 55 and 56 set out the steps which are to be taken in circumstances where a mortgagee commences possession and/or enforcement proceedings in respect of a dwelling which is the subject of a Part IV application.

23.8 DURATION OF ORDERS

As a general rule, the court can be expected to grant an exclusion or non-molestation order for a period of 6 to 12 months. If, at the end of the period ordered, the matter has not been satisfactorily resolved, an application FLA 1996, s 42(7) can be made for an extension. In cases of serious violence a judge may be prepared to grant a non-molestation order for up to 2 years, or until further order.

FLA 1996, s 42(8)

A non-molestation order which is made in other family proceedings ceases to have effect if those proceedings are withdrawn or dismissed. Although the FLA 1996, s 42 makes no reference to an exclusion order, as a matter of logic, such an order will similarly cease to have effect.

FLA 1996 s 36(10)

An occupation order under s 36, by a cohabitant or former cohabitant who has no existing rights of occupation, may be made for a maximum period of 6 months and may be renewed on only one occasion.

An occupation order under the FLA 1996, ss 37 and 38 may be made for a maximum period of 6 months, renewable on one or more occasions. However, where a s 38 order is made as between cohabitants or former cohabitants, it may be renewed on only one occasion.

In any event, where the parties are married and there are separate proceedings pending for divorce, nullity, or judicial separation, or in respect of a civil partnership, it will sometimes be more appropriate for issues relating to the parties' home to be determined in financial proceedings.

23.9 VARIATION OF AN ORDER

FPR 2010, r 10.8

An application to vary, extend or discharge a Part IV order is made on Form FL403. The same rules as to privacy, service and representations by a mortgagee or landlord apply.

23.10 UNDERTAKINGS

Where the court has power to make an occupation or non-molestation order, it may accept an undertaking from any party to the proceedings.

FLA 1996, s 46(1), (2)

No power of arrest may be attached to any undertaking.

FLA 1996, s 46(3)

The court shall not accept an undertaking instead of making an occupation order where a power of arrest would otherwise be attached to the order, and shall not accept an undertaking instead of making a non-molestation order where it appears to the court that:

(a) the respondent has used or threatened violence against the applicant or a relevant child; and

FLA 1996, s 46(3A)

(b) for the protection of the applicant or child it is necessary to make a non-molestation order so that any breach may be punishable under the FLA 1996, s 42A (as a criminal offence).

An undertaking given to the court is enforceable in the same way as a court order. A warrant of arrest under s 47(8) may be sought to enforce an undertaking.

An undertaking should generally be given on Form N117 and signed by the person giving it. A copy should be served on that person, preferably before leaving the court.

Note: See below with regard to the power of arrest.

23.11 POWER OF ARREST

23.11.1 Attaching a power of arrest

FLA 1996, s 47(3)

Where the court makes an occupation order and it appears that the respondent has used or threatened violence against the applicant or a relevant child, it is required to attach a power of arrest to that order unless satisfied that, in all the circumstances of the case, the applicant or child will be adequately protected without such a power. The power of arrest is confined to occupation orders, as breach of a non-molestation order is a criminal offence.

Accordingly, there is a general presumption in favour of attaching the power, although where, pursuant to s 45(1), an order is made without notice, the Act is less emphatic and states that the court *may* attach the power.

PD 10A, paras 3.1 and 3.2

The power of arrest must be pronounced in open court. If the person to whom it was addressed did not have notice and was not present, the terms of the order and the name of the person to whom it addressed shall be announced in open court at the earliest opportunity.

It may be for a shorter period than the substantive order, and may be extended on one or more occasions on an application to vary or discharge.

FLA 1996, s 47(6)

The power of arrest authorises a police officer to arrest, without warrant, a person whom he/she has reasonable cause for suspecting is in breach of any part of an order to which the power attaches.

Once an order has been made with a power of arrest attached, it is important that the respondent be served personally, without delay.

23.11.2 Service on the police

FPR 2010, r 10.10

Where the court makes an occupation order with a power of arrest attached, or a non-molestation order, a copy of the order must be delivered to the officer for the time being in charge of the police station for the applicant's address or such other police station as the court may specify.

It must be accompanied by a statement showing that that the respondent has been served with the order or informed of its terms (whether by being present when the order was made or by telephone or otherwise).

The documentation must be delivered by the applicant (or solicitors representing them), or the court officer, if requested by an applicant acting in person, if the order was made on the court's own initiative, or on a variation or discharge of the order.

It is advisable for the police to be provided with details of:

(a) the applicant's name, address and telephone number;

(b) the applicant's solicitor's name, address and telephone number, including any emergency number;

(c) the name and address of the person against whom the order is made; and

(d) information as to how to contact the court in the event of an arrest being made outside normal business hours. For further information on the subject, see Chapter 24 and **Appendix C(3)**.

Breach of a non-molestation order is a criminal offence. As the maximum penalty is 5 years' imprisonment, the offence is an arrestable one pursuant to the Police and Criminal Evidence Act 1984, s 24(1). This enables the police to arrest for breach of a non-molestation order without the need to attach a power of arrest.

23.12 PENAL NOTICE

23.12.1 Attached to a court order

All non-molestation and occupation orders should have a penal notice endorsed on the face of the order. The notice warns the respondent that if the order is not obeyed he/she may be committed to prison for contempt. The notice attached to a non-molestation order also warns the respondent that if he/she does anything which is forbidden in the order, without reasonable excuse, he/she will be committing a criminal offence and may be liable on conviction to a term of imprisonment not exceeding 5 years or to a fine or both.

Once the order has been served a statement of service should be served on the police and filed with the court.

23.12.2 Attached to an undertaking

An undertaking will similarly have a penal notice endorsed on the face of the document (this is referred to as 'Important Notice' on the standard form of undertaking). This notice warns the person giving the undertaking that a failure to keep the promise that has been given to the court may result in a period of imprisonment for contempt.

The judge who accepts the undertaking should explain its nature and the consequences of breaking the promise. If the judge does not do so, it is appropriate to provide a discreet reminder.

Although there is no formal requirement to serve an undertaking, for the purposes of enforcement it is usually necessary. Therefore, in order to save unnecessary expense and inconvenience, it is usually appropriate to ask the person concerned to wait in the court so that a sealed copy may be served there and then.

23.13 ACTION WHERE AN ORDER HAS BEEN BREACHED

Where there has been a breach of an exclusion requirement in an occupation order, the matter can be dealt with in one of the following ways:

(a) by the activation of a power of arrest;

(b) as a result of a warrant issued pursuant to the FLA 1996, s 47(8) (where there is no power of arrest);

(c) by way of an application to commit.

Where there has been a breach of a non-molestation order the matter can be dealt with in one of the following ways:

(a) as a criminal offence (such proceedings would not be family proceedings and are therefore outside the scope of this book);

(b) as a result of a warrant issued pursuant to the FLA 1996, s 47(8).

23.13.1 Activating a power of arrest

Where a police officer activates a power of arrest, the person who has been arrested must be brought before a court within the period of 24 hours from the time of the arrest. In calculating the period of 24 hours, no account is to be taken of Christmas Day, Good Friday or any Sunday.

FLA 1996, s 47(7)
FPR 2010, r 10.11(2)

Once the matter is brought before it, the court can either deal with the breach forthwith and determine whether the facts, and the circumstances which led to the arrest, amount to disobedience of the order, or adjourn the proceedings.

FPR 2010, r 10.11(3), (4)

Where the proceedings are adjourned and the arrested person is released the matter must be dealt with within 14 days beginning with the date of arrest unless the court directs otherwise, and the arrested person must be given at least 2 days' notice of the hearing. If it is not dealt with within this time, an application seeking the committal of the arrested person for contempt of court may be issued.

FPR 2010, PD 10A, paras 5.2, 5.3

The attendance of the arresting officer will not be necessary, unless the arrest itself is in issue. A written statement will normally be sufficient. If the arresting officer was a witness to the events leading to the arrest and his evidence is required, arrangements should be made for him to attend a subsequent hearing.

The court may remand the person arrested in custody or on bail. In the High Court, Family Court or county court this is governed by the FLA 1996, Sch 5; in the magistrates' court, by ss 128 and 129 and by rules made under the Magistrates' Courts Act 1980, s 144.

In ordering a remand on bail, the court may require a recognizance (with or without sureties) to be given. Details of the information required for a bail application is contained at PD10A, paras 6.1–6.5.

FLA 1996, s 48(1)–(3)

The broad rule is that the period of remand should not exceed 8 clear days, unless by consent or in the case of a remand for medical reports, when an adjournment of not more than 4 weeks at any time may be ordered, or not more than 3 weeks if the person has been remanded in custody.

Where the person remanded is suffering from mental illness or severe mental impairment, the court has the same power as it would have under the Mental Health Act 1983, s 35 to make a hospital order.

The court may adjourn the hearing for consideration of the penalty to be imposed for any contempt of court found proved and such a hearing may be restored if the respondent does not comply with any conditions specified by the court.

FLA 1996, s 47(8)

23.13.2 Arrest warrant

Even where a power of arrest has not been attached to an order, where the applicant considers that the respondent has failed to comply with that order, an application may be made to the court for the issue of a warrant for the arrest of the respondent. A court fee is payable unless the applicant is exempt. Application is by Form FL407.

An undertaking may now be enforced in the same way. FLA 1996, s 46(4)

The application must be substantiated on oath, and the relevant judicial authority must have reasonable grounds for believing that the respondent has failed to comply with the order. FLA 1996, s 47(9)

The police will then arrest the respondent and bring him before the court.

23.13.3 Application to commit

Alternatively, the applicant can apply to commit the respondent to prison under the FPR 2010, Part 37. See Chapter 25 for details.

23.14 COMMITTAL HEARINGS

At a committal hearing, for breach of an order or undertaking or one which takes place following the activation of a power of arrest, the person who is alleged to have breached the order is answerable to the court. However, the person in whose favour the original order was granted or undertaking given may be required to give evidence at the hearing and indeed it will often be crucial where it is that person whose allegations give rise to the hearing. The burden of proof is the criminal standard, and the respondent is entitled to cross examine and call witnesses.

Where the police have not witnessed the relevant events, the attendance of the arresting officer will not be necessary, unless the arrest itself is in issue. A written statement from the arresting officer as to the circumstances of the arrest should normally be sufficient.

Where the arresting officer was also a witness to the events leading to the arrest, and his evidence regarding those events is required, arrangements should be made for his attendance at a subsequent hearing to give evidence. FPR 2010, PD 10A

Note: In the magistrate's court, rules under the Magistrates' Courts Act 1980, s 144.

Hale v Tanner [2000] 2 FLR 879

If the breach is not considered serious, it may be dealt with by way of a warning, adjournment, fine or suspended order. If the breach is serious, an immediate committal order is more likely to be made. Should the contemnor repeat the contempt, it can be anticipated that increasingly longer sentences will be passed.

The maximum sentence which can be imposed for contempt of court in respect of a breach of a Part IV order is 2 years' imprisonment (including the activation of a suspended sentence). Such sentence will be subject to remission for good conduct.

See also Chapter 25 in respect of committal generally, and FPR 2010, Part 37 and PD 37A.

23.15 PURGING CONTEMPT

CCR Ord 29, r 3

Where a contemnor shows genuine remorse, it is possible for the court to allow that person to purge their contempt.

The application is made by notice of application, or a letter from prison attested by the prison governor. No fee is required. The person at whose instance the warrant or order was issued should have at least one day's notice.

Generally, an application to purge is made to the judge who passed the sentence, but it may be heard by another judge, and unless directed otherwise, in the county court may be made to a district judge.

23.16 ALLOCATION OF HEARINGS

FPR 2010, r 10.5

All hearings, whether without notice or otherwise in respect of Part IV orders will be heard in private unless the court directs otherwise.

Such hearings may be before any level of judge, both full and part time, and counsel, solicitors and legal executives will have the right of audience.

However, committals or applications for a warrant of arrest are heard in open court, before a judge other than a deputy district judge. In the Central Family Court such applications are usually heard by a circuit judge.

23.17 STALKING AND PROTECTION FROM HARASSMENT

The Protection from Harassment Act 1997 ('PHA 1997') makes provision for the protection of a person from harassment and similar conduct. The Act provides both criminal and civil remedies; only the civil aspects are considered here.

23.17.1 Jurisdiction

Proceedings can be issued in either a county court or the High Court Queen's Bench Division, but not the Family Court because they are not family proceedings. PHA 1997, s 3

23.17.2 Procedure

An application should be commenced as a Part 8 action in Form N 208, and attracts a court fee unless the claimant is exempt.

Note: For full details of the Part 8 procedure, see Chapter 14.

23.17.3 Detailed provisions of the PHA 1997

A person must not pursue a course of conduct which:

(a) amounts to harassment of another; and

(b) which that person knows or ought to know amounts to harassment of that other person. PHA 1997, s 1(1)

Note*:* PHA 1997, s 1A extends the definition to include 2 or more people and intending to persuade someone not to do something or to do something they were not under any obligation to do.

For the purposes of the PHA 1997: PHA 1997, s 7

(a) harassment includes alarming a person or causing distress;

(b) a course of conduct must involve offending conduct on at least 2 occasions to a single person or on one occasion to 2 or more persons;

(c) conduct includes speech.

The person whose conduct is in question ought to know that it amounts to harassment of another if a reasonable person in possession of the same information would think the course of action amounts to harassment. PHA 1997, s 1(2)

A course of conduct will not amount to harassment if: PHA 1997, s 1(3)

(a) it was pursued for the purpose of preventing or detecting crime;

(b) it was pursued under any enactment or rule of law;

(c) in the particular circumstances the course of conduct was reasonable.

An actual or apprehended breach of the PHA 1997, s 1 may be the subject of a civil claim by the person who is or may be the victim of the conduct in question. PHA 1997, s 3(2)

Where the court makes a finding that harassment has taken place it may grant an injunction restraining the defendant from pursuing the offending course of conduct and/or make an award in damages.

It is likely that the claimant will be more concerned with obtaining an injunction than seeking financial compensation in most cases.

Practitioners are advised to check with the court of issue as to whether the matter is to be heard in private or in open court and as to the level of judiciary before deciding who should appear as advocate.

23.17.4 Action on a breach

PHA 1997, s 3(3)

Where an injunction has been breached, the claimant may apply for the issue of a warrant for the arrest of the defendant.

The warrant application in Form N139 must:

(a) state that it is an application for the issues of a warrant for the arrest of the defendant;

(b) set out the grounds for making the application, which must be supported by an affidavit or evidence on oath;

(c) state whether the claimant has informed the police of the defendant's conduct;

(d) state whether to the claimant's knowledge, criminal proceedings are being pursued.

PHA 1997, s 3(4)(a) and (b)

An application for a warrant must be made to a High Court judge where the injunction was granted by a judge of that court. Where granted by a county court, the application should be to a judge or district judge of that or any other county court.

A judge or district judge may issue a warrant only if:

PHA 1997, s 3(5)(a) and (b)

(a) the application is substantiated on oath; and

(b) he/she has reasonable grounds for believing that the defendant has done anything which he/she is prohibited by the injunction from doing.

Following the arrest of the defendant, the resultant committal proceedings will be brought before either a High Court judge or circuit judge who may:

(a) adjourn the proceedings for a maximum period of 14 days from the date of arrest. Where the matter is adjourned the defendant must be released and given not less than 2 days' notice of the adjourned hearing;

(b) make an immediate custodial order;

(c) make a suspended custodial order;

(d) dismiss the application.

See **23.14** and Chapter 25 in respect of committal proceedings

23.17.5 Restraining order

The Domestic Violence, Crime and Victims Act 2004 extends the circumstances in which a restraining order can be made under the PHA 1997 following criminal proceedings. Courts can consider making a restraining order when a person has been acquitted of an offence where the court believes that such an order is necessary to protect a person from harassment.

CHAPTER 24

EMERGENCY APPLICATIONS

24.1 PROCEDURE

24.1.1 Without notice applications

All courts have arrangements to deal with urgent applications during court hours. In the Family Division of the High Court, where there is an urgent applications judge, contact should be made with the Clerk of the Rules. In the Central Family Court there is an urgent business judge, and other courts have their own arrangements. Wherever possible, urgent applications should be made during court hours.

24.1.2 Out of hours contacts

In cases of real emergency, a judge may be prepared to make an order outside normal court hours. Every court area will have an Urgent Court Business Officer for the group of courts for the area. All practitioners who specialise in a sphere of law where this may be necessary should keep a record of relevant telephone numbers. Police Stations should have a number for the Officer. If this cannot be obtained, contact should be made with the security office at the Royal Courts of Justice (020 7947 6000 or 020 7947 6260) who will refer the matter to the Urgent Business Officer, who may in turn contact the duty judge at the appropriate level of court.

24.1.3 Out of hours guidance

Practice Direction 12E – Urgent Business supplements FPR 2010, Pt 12 which deals with applications in respect of children to the Family Division of the High Court.

The principles should be taken to apply to applications to other courts as appropriate. An Information Sheet is to be found at **Appendix C(3)**. This covers injunctions, Children Act applications and other urgent applications where an individual's personal safety, well-being, business or assets may be at risk.

24.1.4 What is urgent

The High Court Out of Hours system operates between 16.15 and 10.30 the following morning, and over weekends. The county court guidance only operates until 8.30 in the morning, but courts will generally be helpful in the case of a true emergency. When the court is not sitting, a service is provided day and night.

Urgent is defined as cases in which an order of the court is required to regulate the position between the moment the order is made and the next available sitting of the court in normal court hours. It must be capable of being reduced to a faxed sheet of A4 or its email equivalent and a short telephone conversation. The judge should not be required to consider substantial documentation unless absolutely necessary. Whether or not a case is urgent will always be a matter for the judge. President's Guidance 18 November 2010, paras 2, 4

Where appropriate, consultation should take place with the Official Solicitor, Cafcass or Cafcass Cymru, whose contact numbers are to be found at para 14 of the Practice Note.

24.1.5 Conduct of out of hours hearing

If the judge decides to make a without notice order, there will need to be provision for service on any respondent, and for when the matter is to be heard during normal court hours.

A hearing may be arranged either in court or elsewhere if necessary, but more usually will take place by telephone, in which case it should be by tape recorded telephone conference call arranged and paid for in the first instance by the applicant's solicitors. All parties, especially the judge, should be informed that the case is being recorded. The applicant's solicitors should obtain a transcript from their service provider or prepare a note for approval by the judge. FPR 2010, PD 12E, para 1.5

Necessary respondents should have the opportunity to have access to independent legal advice, or at least support or counselling.

It is good practice to provide a draft of the order sought.

24.1.6 Misuse

It is important that this system is only used when necessary, and a judge who has concerns that the facility is being abused may require a representative to attend at a subsequent directions hearing to provide an explanation. In extreme cases, there could be wasted costs orders or reports to professional bodies for serious professional misconduct. Presidents Guidance 18 November 2010, para 6

CHAPTER 25

PENAL NOTICES, UNDERTAKINGS AND COMMITTAL APPLICATIONS

25.1 COMMITTAL

In some circumstances, an order made by the court, or a promise given to the court, may be enforced by committing a disobedient party to prison, fining him or sequestrating his assets.

Where the order in question is made in family proceedings, the relevant rules will be found in FPR 2010, Pt 37. The current rules have been updated and simplified and came into force on 1 October 2020. Where it is made in civil proceedings (for example under the Trusts of Land and Appointment of Trustees Act 1996 ('TOLATA 1996')), the relevant rules are in CPR 1998, Pt 81.

Before contemplating committal proceedings or the threat of them, it is sensible to consider whether other means of securing compliance may be more effective in the particular circumstances, for example:

- an order that an act be done by the applicant or some other person appointed by the court, at the expense of the disobedient party;
- CPR 1998, r 70.2A, applied to family proceedings by FPR 2010, r 33.2; and
- an order that the court will 'exclude an issue from consideration' so that unless particular steps are taken the final hearing will proceed on the assumption that, eg the respondent has net earnings of not less than £X per annum, or free capital of £Y.

FPR 2010 r 4.1(3)(l)

Al-Baker v Al-Baker [2016] EWHC 2510 (Fam)

In exceptional cases, where the disobedient party is seeking to appeal against the order, or applying to vary it, an application to the court may be made for an order that he should not be permitted to proceed with his variation application or appeal until he has complied with the existing court order (a '*Hadkinson* Order' (*Hadkinson v Hadkinson*)). Such an order is draconian in its effect because it goes directly to a litigant's right of access to a court, and should be regarded as a case management order of last resort where a litigant is in wilful contempt.

Hadkinson v Hadkinson [1952] P 285; *Assoun v Assoun [No 1]* [2017] EWCA Civ 21; and see *Mubarak v Mubarak* [2006] EWHC 1260 (Fam), as explained in *J (Children)* [2015] EWCA Civ 1019, and the cases there cited. See also *De Gafforj (Appeal – Hadkinson Order)* [2018] EWCA Civ 2070 and *HR v DS* [2019] EWHC 2425 (Fam)

25.2 PENAL NOTICES

If an order is to be enforceable by committal (or sequestration of assets), a penal notice must appear on the front of the order. The former FPR 2010, PD 37A prescribed the wording of a penal notice as

> 'If you the within-named [insert name] do not comply with this order you may be held to be in contempt of court and imprisoned or fined, or your assets may be seized'

There is no longer a prescribed form of words but it is suggested that this wording, or wording to the same effect, can be used.

but the form of words is not mandatory and may be adapted to suit the particular case, so long as the meaning is clear and all essential elements are included.

FPR 2010, r 37.2. *Iberian Trust Ltd v Founders Trust and Investment Co. Ltd* [1932] 2 KB 87

Leicester City Council v Saracen Dyers Ltd [2002] EWHC 2068 (QB) *Newman, Re* [2014] EWHC 3136 (Fam) *CH v CT* [2018] EWHC 1310 (Fam) where the omission of a penal notice was fatal to the committal application

Note that the requirement is that the penal notice should appear on the front of the order, that is, on the front page. If an order is drawn up in the court office it should be checked carefully to see that this requirement has been followed. The court tends to insist on strict compliance with procedural requirements in this area because the respondent faces the loss of his liberty, and committal applications have failed where the penal notice has not been endorsed on the front page of the order.

Sometimes, a penal notice is endorsed on an order that has already been made. A common instance of this is when a party to financial proceedings fails to file Form E or fails to answer a questionnaire. It is important to check that the time for compliance stated in the endorsed order has not expired. Thus if the original order requires an act to be done by 30th June and the penal notice is indorsed on 7th July, a new time for compliance also needs to be stated. Simply endorsing a penal notice on the original order achieves nothing; the endorsed order should make the time for compliance unambiguously clear. 'By 4 pm on 14th July 2017' is acceptable, as is 'within 14 days of service of this order'. 'Within 14 days', which is often seen, is meaningless and ineffective. Does it mean 14 days from the making of the order, the sealing of the order or the service of the order? As long ago as 1986 O'Connor LJ said:

> '… we have been told (and indeed it is the experience of both Neill LJ and myself) that there are very many 'unless' orders which are made in this form. They are, on the authorities which I have cited, bad'.

Hitachi Sales (UK) v Mitsui Osk Lines [1986] 2 Lloyd's Rep. 574, CA
CA 1989, s 11I

Three to four decades later, people are still getting this wrong.

25.3 UNDERTAKINGS

An undertaking, a solemn promise to the court intended to be enforceable in the same way as an order of the court, must normally carry a penal notice.

It is suggested that the person giving the undertaking sign an acknowledgment substantially in the following broad terms:

> 'I understand the undertaking that I have given and that if I break any of my promises to the court I may be sent to prison, or fined, or my assets may be seized, for contempt of court'

The acknowledgment does not need to be given before the court. It may be endorsed on the court copy of the undertaking or contained in a separate document such as a letter.

In the case of an undertaking to pay money that has the same effect as an order under the MCA 1973, Pt 2 (ie an undertaking contained in consent order for financial relief), there is still standard form wording and it is:

> 'If you fail to pay any sum of money which you have promised the court that you will pay, a person entitled to enforce the undertaking may apply to the court for an order. You may be sent to prison if it is proved that you
>
> (a) Have, or have had since the date of your undertaking, the means to pay the sum; and
>
> (b) Have refused or neglected, or are refusing or neglecting, to pay that sum'

FPR 2010, PD 33A, para 2.2

In this case, the acknowledgment which must be signed will be in the following terms

FPR 2010, PD 33A, para 2.2

> 'I understand the undertaking that I have given and that if I break my promise to the court to pay any sum of money, I may be sent to prison'

Cutler v Wandsworth Stadium Ltd [1945] 1 All ER 103; *Birch v Birch* [2017] UKSC 53

It is open to a person who has given an undertaking to ask the court to release them from it, and such an application may be accompanied by an offer of a further undertaking in different terms. The court may decide to accept the further undertaking and, in the light of it, to grant the application for release. It may indicate that it will grant the application for release only on condition that an undertaking in other terms is offered. In either event the court's actual power is to grant or refuse the application for release; and, although exercise of that power may result in something which looks like 'a variation of an undertaking', it is the product of a different process of reasoning.

It goes without saying that unless and until a party is released from his or her undertaking (either unconditionally or on terms) it remains binding and enforceable by committal. A request to 'vary' an undertaking made in response to an application for committal is unlikely to be sympathetically received. Compare the position with appeals at **29.3.2**.

25.4 SERVICE

Normally, if a judgment or order is to be enforceable by committal, a copy of it must have been served on the person affected. FPR 2010, rr 37.4(2)(c)

In the case of a judgment or order requiring a person to do an act, it is advisable that the copy must be served before the end of the time fixed for doing the act, together with a copy of any order fixing that time. Where the time for doing the act has been varied by a subsequent order, it is advisable that a copy of that subsequent order must also have been served; and where the judgment or order was made pursuant to an earlier judgment or order requiring the act to be done, it is advisable that a copy of that earlier judgment or order must also have been served.

The court may dispense with service of a copy of the judgment or order but presumably, given the consequences for the respondent, must have good reasons for it.

It has been said that where the court is satisfied that the respondent knew what the order said and knew the consequences of disobedience, a failure to dispense with service would encourage offenders to use technicalities to defeat the purpose of the order. But this should be regarded as very much a last resort; even though since *Nicholls v Nicholls* the courts have moved away from an over-strict attitude to procedural formalities, it remains the case that committal proceedings concern the liberty of the subject and procedural rules are there for a reason. *Nicholls v Nicholls* [1996] EWCA Civ 1271

It has traditionally been regarded as not strictly necessary for a copy of an undertaking to be served on the person giving the undertaking; 'he must be presumed *Callow v Young* (1886) 55 LT 543 to have known that he had given his undertaking', as was said in 1886.

However, in family cases it has been the practice since at least 1986 to ensure that the person giving the undertaking has a copy of it.

25.5 COMMITTAL APPLICATIONS

25.5.1 FPR 2010, Pt 37

FPR 2010, r 37.3(1). NB For contempt in relation to alleged interference with the due administration of justice, see r 37.3(3) where applications are made under Part 19.

A committal application is made by an application notice using the Part 18 procedure in the proceedings in which the judgment or order was made or the undertaking was given, whether or not the application is made against a party to those proceedings. Form FC600 is the appropriate application form (committal for disobedience of an injunctive order or breach of an undertaking in the Family Court and High Court). Unless and to the extent that the court directs otherwise, the application must be supported by written evidence given by affidavit or affirmation.
The application must include statements of all of the following:

(a) the nature of the alleged contempt;

(b) the date and terms of any order allegedly breached or disobeyed;

(c) confirmation that any such order was personally served, and the date it was served, unless the court or the parties dispensed with personal service;

(d) if the court dispensed with personal service, the terms and date of the court's order dispensing with personal service;

(e) confirmation that any order allegedly breached or disobeyed included a penal notice;

(f) the date and terms of any undertaking allegedly breached;

(g) confirmation of the applicant's belief that the person who gave any undertaking understood its terms and the consequences of failure to comply with it;

(h) a brief summary of the facts alleged to constitute the contempt, set out numerically in chronological order;

(i) that the respondent has the right to be legally represented in the contempt proceedings;

(j) that the respondent is entitled to a reasonable opportunity to obtain legal representation and to apply for legal aid which may be available without any means test;

(k) that the respondent is entitled to the services of an interpreter;

(l) that the respondent is entitled to reasonable time to prepare for the hearing;

(m) that the respondent is entitled but not obliged to give written and oral evidence in their defence;

(n) that the respondent has the right to remain silent and to decline to answer any question the answer to which may incriminate the respondent;

(o) that the court may proceed in the respondent's absence if they do not attend but (whether or not they attend) will only find the respondent in contempt if satisfied beyond reasonable doubt of the facts constituting contempt and that they do constitute contempt;

(p) that if the court is satisfied that the respondent has committed a contempt, the court may punish the respondent by a fine, imprisonment, confiscation of assets or other punishment under the lay;

(q) that if the respondent admits the contempt and wishes to apologise to the court, that is likely to reduce the seriousness of any punishment by the court;

(r) that the court's findings will be provided in writing as soon as practicable after the hearing; and

(s) that the court will sit in public, unless and to the extent that the court orders otherwise, and that its findings will be made public. FPR 2010, r 37.4(2)

Unless the court directs otherwise in accordance with the FPR 2010, Pt 6 a contempt application and evidence in support must be served on the respondent personally save for one exception. FPR 2010, r 37.5(10)

That exception is that where a legal representative is on the record in the proceedings in which, or in connection with which, an alleged contempt is committed, the application and evidence in support may be served on the representative for the respondent unless the representatives objects in writing within 7 days of receipt of the application and evidence in support.

If the representative does not object in writing, they must at once provide to the respondent a copy of the application and supporting evidence and take all reasonable steps to ensure the respondent understands them.

FPR 2010, r 37.5(2)

If the representative objects in writing, the issue of service shall be referred to a judge of the court dealing with the contempt application, who will deal with the question on the papers on receipt of written submissions from the parties, unless an oral hearing is deemed more appropriate.

FPR 2010, r 37.6

Separate rules apply to cases where no application is made (such as contempt in the face of the court) and to other forms of committal (see below).

Grounds for striking out a committal application are set out in PD 37A, para 2.

25.5.2 The committal hearing

FPR 2010, r 37.8(1)

Particular note should be taken that: an application for committal is one of the few family matters which is heard in open court, although, where the alleged breach relates to proceedings involving a child, and in certain other circumstances it may be heard in private. Advocates must accordingly appear robed and have appropriate rights of audience;

See r.37.7(3) FPR 2010, r 37.7(3); *Morris v Morris* [2016] EWCA Civ 812 and *LL v The Lord Chancellor* [2017] EWCA Civ 237 (successful claim for damages where the court's procedural failings were 'obvious and gross')

The alleged contemnor cannot be compelled to give evidence; for this reason, the committal hearing should not be listed together with a substantive hearing (and the court's listing section must be challenged if this happens).

The alleged act(s) of contempt must be proved to the criminal standard, in other words beyond reasonable doubt rather than on a balance of probability.

In L (A Child) [2016] EWCA Civ 173

In *In L (A Child)*, the Court of Appeal allowed an appeal from a committal order sentencing the appellant to 6 months' imprisonment for breach of a collection order which had been made over 11 years previously.

Theis J set out a 'useful checklist' (at paragraph 78) for use in cases where the court is hearing a committal application, whether for a contempt in the face of the court or for breach of an order. She said that the court should ensure that the following matters are at the forefront of its mind:

'(1) There should be complete clarity at the start of the proceedings as to precisely what the foundation of the alleged contempt is: contempt in the face of the court, or breach of an order.

(2) Prior to the hearing the alleged contempt should be set out clearly in a document or application that complies with FPR rule 37 and which the person accused of contempt has been served with.

(3) If the alleged contempt is founded on breach of a previous court order, the person accused had been served with that order, and that it contained a penal notice in the required form and place in the order.

(4) Whether the person accused of contempt has been given the opportunity to secure legal representation, as they are entitled to. [Note that the alleged contemnor may also be entitled to legal aid under the criminal legal aid scheme].

Brown v London Borough of Haringey [2015] EWCA Civ 483 (especially at [26]–[36])

(5) Whether the judge hearing the committal application should do so, or whether it should be heard by another judge.

(6) Whether the person accused of contempt has been advised of the right to remain silent.

(7) If the person accused of contempt chooses to give evidence, whether they have been warned about self-incrimination.

(8) The need to ensure that in order to find the breach proved the evidence must meet the criminal standard of proof, of being sure that the breach is established.

(9) Any committal order made needs to set out what the findings are that establish the contempt of court, which are the foundation of the court's decision regarding any committal order.'

25.6 THE COURT'S POWERS

The court's powers are set out in the FPR 2010, r 37.9 and can include a period of imprisonment (an order for committal), a fine, a confiscation of assets or other punishment permitted under the law.

A judge of the Family Court of district judge level or above generally has the power to impose a sentence of up to 2 years' imprisonment or a fine of up to £5,000 (Level 5). A High Court judge may impose an unlimited fine.

Lay justices have the power to impose a sentence of up to 2 months' imprisonment or a fine of up to £5,000.

Al-Baker v Al-Baker [2015] EWHC 3229 (Fam)

Note that where the contempt in question is the failure to pay a sum of money, the court's powers are constrained by the Debtors Act 1869 (DA 1869) and the maximum sentence which may be imposed is 6 weeks' imprisonment (see DA 1869, s 5). Other forms of contempt in relation to financial proceedings may attract longer sentences, eg *Al-Baker v Al-Baker* (9 months' imprisonment for non-disclosure).

Criminal Justice Act 2003, s 258

Thompson v Mitchell [2004] EWCA Civ 1271

The contemnor will in fact serve one half of the sentence imposed and will be released unconditionally thereafter.

FC(CC)(P)R 2014, SI 2014/833, read with MFPA 1984, ss 31A–31P. Pursuant to Contempt of Court Act 1981, s 14(4B), ss.14(1)–(4A) of that act do not apply to the Family Court, save for the limited exceptions mentioned.

25.7 OTHER FORMS OF CONTEMPT, ETC

The FPR 2010, r 37 deals separately with:

- Contempt in the face of the court (FPR 2010, r 37.6 and Part 3 of PD 37A). Note that a judge of the Family Court below circuit judge level may only impose a sentence of up to one month's imprisonment for such contempt (Family Court (Contempt of Court) (Powers) Regulations 2014);
- Committal for interference with the due administration of justice (FPR 2010, rr 37.3–37.5);
- Committal for making a false statement of truth (FPR 2010, rr 37.5). Note that permission of (in the family court) a judge of the Family Division (in the High Court) the court dealing with the matter is required to bring such an application.

Separately, the FPR 2010, rr 33.9–33.18 deals with committal by way of judgment summons.

Harris v Harris [2002] 1 FLR 248

Sequestration (CPR 1998, r 83).

General rules relating to committal proceedings (FPR 2010, rr 37 and PD 37A). Note particularly the provisions of the FPR 2010, r 37.10 concerning an application by the contemnor to purge his contempt.

CHAPTER 26

COURT BUNDLES

26.1 INTRODUCTION

FPR 2010, PD 27A: Family Proceedings; Court Bundles (Universal Practice to be applied in the High Court and Family Court)

Practice Direction 27A's aim is to achieve consistency across the country in the Family Courts and Family Division of the High Court. It applies to all hearings, including without notice and whether for directions or for substantive relief. The requirements and the penalty for failing to comply are clearly set out in the Practice Direction. The main points are highlighted in this chapter.

FPR 2010, PD 27A, para 2.4

Note: The PD does not apply to urgent hearings if and to the extent that it would be impossible to comply with.

26.1.1 E-bundles

The President issued guidance on the 21 December 2021 for the use of electronic bundles in the family court. This guidance does not modify the requirements in PD27A and supplements the general guidance given on the 29 November 2021. The main issues to know are:

(a) e-bundles must be provided in pdf format;

(b) all pages in an e-bundle must be numbered by computer not hand (at the time of preparing this section this part of the general guidance was suspended in public law proceedings);

(c) each entry in the index must be hyperlinked to the indexed document;

(d) all pages must be subject to optical character recognition;

(e) the resolution should not be greater than 300 dpi.

26.2 RESPONSIBILITY

FPR 2010, PD 27A, para 3.1

A bundle shall be provided by the party in the position of applicant at that hearing (and if there are cross applications by the person whose application is first in time). If the applicant is a litigant in person then the responsibility passes to the first listed respondent who is not a litigant in person.

Where all parties are litigants in person then, unless the court directs otherwise, none are obliged to provide a bundle.

26.3 CONTENTS

The bundle shall be paginated using Arabic numbering and be agreed by all parties if possible. For e-bundles (save in public law) the general guidance provides for computer generated numbering.

FPR 2010, PD 27A, para 3.2 – for public law see para 4.2

Paragraph 4.1 PD 27A sets out what the bundle shall contain 'only those documents which are relevant to the hearing' and shall not include such things as correspondence, contact notes etc.

FPR 2010, PD 27A, paras 4.1(a)–(g)

The documents shall be in chronological order, paginated individually and divided into separate sections:

(a) Preliminary documents and any other case management documents required by any other practice direction.
(b) Applications and orders.
(c) Statements and affidavits (which must be dated in the top right corner of the front page) but without exhibiting or duplicating documents referred to in para 4.1.
(d) Care plans (where appropriate).
(e) Expert and other reports (including those of the guardian, children's guardian and litigation friend).
(f) Other documents, divided into further sections as may be appropriate.

All statements, affidavits, care plans, expert reports and other reports included in the bundle must be copies of the originals which have been signed and dated.

FPR 2010, PD 27A, para 4.2

Any skeleton argument or essential reading list shall be inserted at the commencement of the bundle.

FPR 2010, PD 27A, para 4.3

26.4 FORMAT

The bundle shall be in A4 format, in a font no smaller than 12 point and no more than 350 single sided sheets. For e-bundles the default view for all pages should be 100%.

FPR 2010, PD 27A, paras 5.1 and 5.2

26.5 TIMETABLE

The paginated bundle shall be provided to the other parties not less than 4 working days before the hearing, be delivered to counsel (if instructed) no less than 3 working days before the hearing and lodged with the court no less than 2 working days before the hearing (or as specified by the court) and preliminary documents shall be lodged with the court no later than 11am on the day before the hearing.

FPR 2010, PD 27A, paras 6.1–6.4

26.6 RETAIN OR RE-LODGE

FPR 2010, PD 27A, paras 9.1 and 9.2

Unless the court wishes to retain the bundle the bundle should be removed at the end of the hearing and then re-lodged.

If bundles are not removed at the end of the hearing they must be removed within 5 days and if not the court may destroy the bundle.

Note: If the judge retains the bundle check how the bundle is to be updated.

26.7 LODGING THE BUNDLE AND FAILURE TO LODGE

FPR 2010, PD 27A, para 7.1
FPR 2010, PD 27A, para 12.1

The bundle must be lodged at the appropriate office and if lodged at the wrong place the court may treat the bundle as having not been lodged.

If a bundle has not been lodged (or lodged wrongly) the court may remove the case from the list, adjourn it to later in the day or make a wasted costs order or some other adverse costs order.

It is important for practitioners to know the local practice for the filing of e-bundles. Public Law bundles are likely to be filed via the portal and financial remedy bundles via the DCCS.

26.8 THE FINANCIAL DISPUTE RESOLUTION APPOINTMENT ('FDR')

FPR 2010, r 9.17(5)

The requirements for the FDR bundle are somewhat different and should comply with the FPR 2010, r 9.17(3), (4) and therefore enclose parties' offers and responses. At the conclusion of the hearing those documents must be returned by the court to the parties and not retained on the court file.

CHAPTER 27

EXPERT WITNESSES IN FAMILY PROCEEDINGS

27.1 INTRODUCTION

FPR 2010, Pt 25

The need to comply with the Rules and Practice Directions when applying to instruct an expert is essential in achieving a successful outcome. The Family Procedure Rules 2010, Pt 25 which governs experts and applies to all family proceedings was significantly amended on 31 January 2013 and this chapter is written to provide an overview of what is required. In respect of children proceedings the instruction of experts is governed by the Children and Families Act 2014, s 13. Part 25 should be read in conjunction with s 13 as much of it was lifted from Part 25.

The court has made clear the need for compliance with Part 25:

Re: W (A Child) Re: H (Children) [2013] EWCA Civ 1177

> 'The court is entitled to expect and from now on family courts will demand strict compliance with all such orders. Non-compliance with orders should be expected to have and will usually have a consequence.'

Re C (A Child) (Procedural Requirements of a Part 25 Application) [2016] 1 FLR 707

> 'A failure to comply with the [procedural] code is regarded as being sufficiently important that by rule 25.5(1A) it is given enhanced status as a prescribed matter to be taken into account by the court when it considers an application which is not in compliance with the Rules.'

The President of the Family Division has noted the reduction in medical experts willing to give evidence in the Family Court and in the Autumn of 2018 he asked Williams J to convene a working group to suggest solutions. Their final report with 22 recommendations was published on the 5 November 2020. At the time of writing those recommendations remain with the FJC sub-committee. The President has also noted that the instruction of an expert is the primary reason for delay in the Family Court.

27.2 INITIAL CONSIDERATIONS

Instructing an expert is a time-consuming and costly exercise. Most cases do not require an expert and the information required can be obtained in a cost-effective manner (eg through estate agent valuations). Before embarking on any instructions, consideration should be given as to whether an expert is required, if the evidence can be provided elsewhere, what steps can be taken before instruction and who is to be instructed. There are of course many other questions (and issues that need to be addressed in accordance with the FPR 2010 in any application as set out below) but if, for example, the business is an income stream only or a sole trader then why value the business? If in private law Children Act proceedings the issue is the frequency of contact why instruct an Independent Social Worker when Cafcass can provide a report?

It is also important to remember that the prospect of being the subject to scrutiny, direct observation and being interviewed by an expert is not a neutral act. Children who are at the centre of high conflict disputes, with divided loyalties to parents, are particularly at risk. The potential advantages of instruction need to be weighed against the disadvantages.

Finally, as to who to instruct it is essential before making an application that parties do their research. If a party does not have experience of an expert attempts should be made to find someone who has and can comment on their work. It is the responsibility of the instructing solicitor to ensure that the expert meets the standards and that includes professional registration with bodies such as the GMC, etc. All registers can be checked on line with the relevant professional body.

27.3 PRINCIPLES TO BE APPLIED

On the 4 October 2021, the President issued a memorandum on experts in the Family Court seeking to explain the principles applied when considering authorising or admitting expert evidence.

Unlike other witnesses an expert may give evidence of their opinions and the admissibility of that are governed by four criteria:

Kennedy v Codia (Services) LLP (Scotland) [2016] UKSC 6

(a) whether the proposed expert evidence will assist the court in its task;
(b) whether the witness has the necessary knowledge and experience;
(c) whether the witness is impartial in his or her presentation and assessment of the evidence; and
(d) whether there is a reliable body of knowledge or experience to underpin the expert's evidence.

In the Family Court you then of course have to add the further requirement as necessary. That does not apply in cases governed by the CPR 1998 such as the Trusts of Land and Appointment of Trustees Act 1996.

27.4 PRELIMINARY ENQUIRIES OF THE EXPERT

FPR 2010, PD 25C, paras 3.2 and 3.5 (children)
FPR 2010, PD 25D, paras 3.3 and 3.4 (financial proceedings)

In good time for the information to be available at the hearing the party or parties intending to instruct shall approach the expert and provide them with brief details of the proceedings and to then obtain from the expert confirmation that the work is within their area of expertise, their availability and ability to comply with any timescales and costs.

Note: It is essential to clarify the questions for the expert to address. This will ensure the correct expert is consulted and will give a realistic sense of the length of time the assessment will take.

27.5 THE APPLICATION

In all proceedings any application to adduce expert evidence must be made by way of a Part 18 application notice (in Children Act proceedings would be on Form C2, in financial proceedings, Form D11) and the notice must state:

(i) the field in which the expert evidence is required;

(ii) where practicable, the name of the proposed expert;

(iii) the issues to which the expert evidence is to relate;

(iv) whether the expert evidence could be obtained from a single joint expert;

(v) the other matters set out in PD 25C (children) or PD25D (financial remedy proceedings); and

(vi) a draft of the order including the matters required in PD 25C or 25D.

In addition to the above it is expected that the information obtained from preliminary enquiries of the expert will be provided, this is to include timescales and fees and in respect of children proceeding a draft letter of instruction as the court will need to approve the questions to the expert (see below).

FPR 2010, PD 25C, para 3.8
FPR 2010, PD 25D, para 3
FPR 2010, rule 25.6

The application to instruct an expert should be made as soon as possible.

That generally means at the first hearing so in private law proceedings at the FHDRA and in financial proceeding at the first appointment.

In financial proceeding the court at the first appointment *must* give directions where appropriate about: (a) the valuation of assets (including the joint instruction of joint experts); and (b) obtaining and exchanging expert evidence if required.

FPR 2010, rr 9.15 and 25.6

27.6 THE OVERRIDING OBJECTIVE AND THE COURT'S POWER TO CONTROL EXPERT EVIDENCE

The court's power to restrict expert evidence is set out in Rule 25.4 in respect of all proceedings save children proceedings and those controls are contained in the Children and Families Act 2014 ('CFA 2014'), s 13. A person may not without permission of the court put expert evidence (in any form) before the court.

FPR 2010, r 25.4
CFA 2014, s 13(5)

In children proceedings a person may not without permission of the court instruct a person to provide expert evidence for use in those proceedings.

CFA 2014, s 13(1)

Any application pursuant to Part 25 is governed by the overriding objective Rule 1.1(1) (dealing with cases justly) which include (at 1.1(2)):

> '(a) ensuring that it is dealt with expeditiously and fairly;
>
> …
>
> (d) saving expense; and
>
> (e) allotting to it an appropriate share of the court's resources, while taking into account the need to allot resources to other cases.'

The parties are required to help the court to further the overriding objective and that includes the instruction of an expert and whether it is necessary.

FPR 2010, r 1.3

The timing of an application has already been dealt with (as soon as possible) and the court's case management powers includes timing of the application as the court, as part of its active case management, shall:

> '(b) identify at an early stage:
>
> (i) the issues;
>
> (c) decide promptly –
>
> (i) which issues need full investigation and hearing and which do not;
>
> …
>
> (e) control the use of expert evidence;
>
> …
>
> (m) give directions to ensure that the case proceeds quickly and efficiently.'

FPR 2010, r 1.4

27.7 THE TEST

FPR 2010, r 25.4

In proceedings other than children proceedings the court may give permission only if of the opinion that the expert evidence '*is necessary to assist the court to resolve the proceedings*'.

CFA 2014, s 13(6)

In children proceedings the court may give permission only if the court is of the opinion that the expert evidence '*is necessary to assist the court to resolve the proceedings justly*'.

Re TG (Care Proceedings. Case Management. Expert Evidence) [2013] 1 FLR 1250, FD per Sir James Munby P at [30]
Re H-L (Expert Evidence: Test for Permission) [2013] 2 FLR 1434, FD per Sir James Munby P

The question of what is meant by the word *necessary* has been considered by the President of the Family Division and means *necessary*, rather than being merely reasonable, desirable or of assistance.

When deciding whether to give permission the court is to have regard to:

(a) the issues to which the expert evidence would relate;
(b) the questions which the court would require the expert to answer;
(c) the impact which giving permission would be likely to have on the timetable, duration and conduct of the proceedings;
(d) any failure to comply with the FPR 2010, r 25.6 or any direction of the court about expert evidence, and
(e) the cost of the expert evidence.

FPR 2010, r 25.5

In addition with children proceedings the court must also consider:

(a) any impact which giving permission would be likely to have on the welfare of the children concerned, including in the case of permission as mentioned in the CFA 2014, s 13(3) any impact which any examination or other assessment would be likely to have on the welfare of the child who would be examined or otherwise assessed;
(b) what other expert evidence is available (whether obtained before or after the start of proceedings); and
(c) whether evidence could be given by another person on the matters on which the expert would give evidence.

CFA 2014, s 13(7)

27.8 SINGLE JOINT EXPERT

Parties are encouraged to have one expert that they both instruct and send an agreed joint letter. If the letter cannot be agreed then the court can settle the terms of the letter or, on rare occasions, the court can permit both parties to send separate letters to the expert. FPR 2010, r 25.12

A Single Joint Expert is a witness to the court where there can be no objection to the expert being cross-examined by either party. *F v F (Financial Remedies: Pre-Marital Wealth)* [2012] 2 FLR 1212

27.9 THE DUTY OF THE EXPERT

The duty of the expert is to help the court on matters within the expert's expertise and that duty overrides any duty to those instructing or paying them. The duties are set out in PD25B. The Annex to PD25B sets out the standards for expert witnesses which they must comply. FPR 2010, r 25.3

27.10 LETTER OF INSTRUCTION

The order granting permission will set the date on which the report is to be received. FPR 201, r 25.8(1)

In children proceedings the court should at the hearing giving permission also approve the questions which the expert is required to answer and also specify the date on which the expert should receive the letter of instruction. FPR 2010, r 25.8(2)

In other cases the letter of instruction should be agreed and filed with the court within 5 business days after the hearing.

Note: It is important that the letter of instruction reflects what has been initially agreed with the expert. Letters of instruction are often used as a starting point for any assessment and should be understood by the persons who are the subject of the letter. FPR 2010, PD 25, para 4.1

The Law Society provides template letters of instruction which are a useful starting point; http://www.lawsociety.org.uk/support-services/family-court-resources/family-law--templates-for-instructing-experts/.

27.11 WRITTEN QUESTIONS

Experts should not attend final hearings to give oral evidence unless directed by the court. The court will only direct an expert to attend if it is necessary to do so in the interest of justice.

Parties are able to put questions to the expert to seek clarification of an issue within 10 days of the report being served on them. Such questions must be proportionate and only put once and must be copied to the other party. The rules provide no date for the expert to reply but the order directing the report will normally set out the timetable for questions and answers.

FPR 2010, r 25.10

If a party puts an extensive list of questions or strays beyond clarification the court may need to settle the questions.

FPR 2010, r 25.10(3)(b)

The expert's answers are treated as part of the expert's report.

27.12 DISCUSSION BETWEEN EXPERTS

If there are more than one expert instructed the court may direct discussion between the experts to:

(a) identify and discuss the expert issues in the proceedings; and

FPR 2010, r 25.16(1)

(b) where possible, reach an agreed opinion on the issues.

Following the discussion the experts must prepare a statement for the court setting out those issues on which:

(a) they agree; and

FPR 2010, r 25.16(3)

(b) they disagree; with a summary of their reasons for disagreeing.

The whole purpose of this discussion is to further the overriding objective, to narrow the issues and to avoid experts from attending court. The discussion does not need to be in person and can be by telephone (which is usually easier to arrange and also cheaper). How the discussion is organised is set out in PD25E which includes (subject to any directions by the court):

(a) The arrangements should be made within 15 business days after the expert's reports have been filed and copied to the other parties.

(b) Where experts are from different disciplines there can be a global discussion.

(c) Five business days prior to a discussion the person charged with organising the meeting (whose identify should be clear from the order) should formulate an agenda including a list of questions to be considered and should be circulated amongst the parties.

(d) The agenda and list of questions should be sent to the experts not later than 2 business days before the discussion.

(e) The discussion should be chaired by the person charged with arranging the discussion, a minute taken (if by telephone a transcript can be obtained).

(f) An agreed statement (see above) should be served and filed not later than 5 business days after the discussions.

27.13 ALTERNATIVE EXPERT

Where a party is dissatisfied with the report form the Single Joint Expert an application can be made for another report. The test to be applied was set out by Lord Woolf MR in *Daniels v Walker*:

Daniels v Walker [2000] 1 WLR 1382

> '[27] … Where a party sensibly agrees to a joint report and the report is obtained as a result of joint instructions in the manner which I have indicated, the fact that a party has agreed to adopt that course does not prevent that party being allowed facilities to obtain a report from another expert, or, if appropriate, to rely on the evidence of another expert.
>
> [28] In a substantial case such as this, the correct approach is to regard the instruction of an expert jointly by the parties as the first step in obtaining expert evidence on a particular issue. It is to be hoped that in the majority of cases it will not only be the first step but the last step. If, having obtained a joint expert's report, a party, for reasons which are not fanciful, wishes to obtain further information before making a decision as to whether or not there is a particular part (or indeed the whole) of the expert's report which he or she may wish to challenge, then they should, subject to the discretion of the court, be permitted to obtain that evidence.
>
> [29] In the majority of cases, the sensible approach will not be to ask the court straight away to allow the dissatisfied party to call a second expert. In many cases it would be wrong to make a decision until one is in a position to consider the position in the round. You cannot make generalisations, but in a case where there is a modest sum involved a court may take a more rigorous approach. It may be said in a case where there is a modest amount involved that it would be disproportionate to obtain a second report in any circumstances. At most what should be allowed is merely to put a question to the expert who has already prepared a report.'

The court will only order an alternate expert if the reasons are not fanciful and a party has first raised questions to the expert (pursuant to the FPR 2010, r 25.10 (above). Further that another expert report is proportionate given the issues in the case.

27.14 EXPERT EVIDENCE OBTAINED WITHOUT THE PERMISSION OF THE COURT

Re M (Children) [2018] EWCA Civ 607

Expert evidence cannot be adduced without the permission of the court. If a party has obtained such evidence they will need to seek the court's permission to adduce it. The Court of Appeal has made it clear that the court should as a matter of principle be slow to admit expert evidence that has been irregularly obtained.

CHAPTER 28

VULNERABLE WITNESSES IN FAMILY PROCEEDINGS

28.1 INTRODUCTION

There is no doubt the family legal system was behind the criminal legal system in its approach to vulnerable witnesses and parties attending court, participating in proceedings and giving evidence.

[2014] Fam Law 978, 981

In light of this the President of the Family Division in June 2014 set up the Children and Vulnerable Witnesses Working Group chaired by Hayden J and Russell J.

[2014] Fam Law 1217
[2015] Fam Law 443

The interim report was published in August 2014 and its final report in February 2015 which set out proposals for a New Rule and Practice Directions with a hope that they would be in force towards the end of that year. The New Rule 3A 'Vulnerable Persons; Participation in Proceedings and Giving Evidence' and new Practice Direction 3AA came into force on 27 November 2017 and has been subsequently amended by the Domestic Abuse Act 2021.

28.2 PARTICIPATION

FPR 2010, r 3A.4

The court must consider whether a party's participation in the proceedings (other than by way of giving evidence) is likely to be diminished by reason of vulnerability and, if so, whether it is necessary to make one or more participation directions.

FPR 2010, r 3A.5

The court must consider whether the quality of evidence given by a party or witness is likely to be diminished by reason of vulnerability and, if so, whether it is necessary to make one or more participation directions. Before making such direction the court must consider any views expressed by the party or witness about giving evidence.

FPR 2010, PD 3AA para 1.4

All parties and their representatives are required to work with the court and each other to ensure that each party or witness can participate in proceedings without the quality of their evidence being diminished and without being put in fear or distress by reason of their vulnerability with reference to the circumstances of each person and to the nature of the proceedings.

Where a person is, or is at risk of being, a victim of domestic abuse the court must assume that their participation and evidence will be diminished by reason of vulnerability. FPR 2010, r3A2A

The provisions of FPR 2010, r 3A and PD3AA are mandatory. Even when a party is represented the obligation to consider vulnerability is on the court. Failure by a party's representative to apply to the rule do not relieve the court of its responsibility. *Re M (A Child)* [2021] EWHC 3225

28.3 IDENTIFYING VULNERABILITY

There is no simple answer or definition; a series of risk factors have to be considered and assessed as to whether those factors bring a person within the definition. An allegation of domestic abuse creates a presumption of vulnerability. 'Domestic abuse' and 'victims' are defined in the Domestic Abuse Act 2021, s 1.

Once a risk factor has been identified consideration needs to be given as to how that factor will impact on a party or witnesses' ability to give complete, coherent and accurate evidence. This includes how it may impact on their ability to physically attend the hearing and as a party, to participate in and comprehend the proceedings (to include being able to give instructions) and whether that participation/comprehension is likely to be diminished without help.

The duty to identify if any party or witness is vulnerable is on the court and all parties and should be identified at the earliest possible stage (see *Re M* above). FPR 2010, rr 1.1(2), 1.2, 1.3, 1.4 and 3A.3

Even if there is no simple definition the importance, at the earliest possible stage, of identifying and putting in place measures to assist a party cannot be underestimated; that is regardless of whether its public, private or financial proceedings. *Re X, Y, Z (Minors)* [2011] EWHC 402 (Fam) per Baker J

FPR 2010, r 3A.7 and PD 3AA, paras 2.1 and 3.1 set out factors that the court must have regard to when deciding whether to make one or more participation directions.

28.3.1 Risk factors

There is no exhaustive list or definition but these include:

– being a child

– suffering a mental disorder

– lack of fluency in the English language

- illiteracy
- learning disabilities
- hearing impairment
- speech (or language) impairment
- forced marriage
- being the subject of violence or sexual abuse
- being an alleged victim of domestic abuse
- coercive and/or financial control

To this should be added circumstances which give rise to a person suffering fear or distress and the factors contained in FPR 2010, r 3A.7 and PD 3AA, paras 2.1 and 3.1.

Most people that fall within the definition will present with a combination of risk factors and the issue is then how that combination (not each factor taken separately) impacts.

Re H-L [2013] EWCA Civ 655

When considering the definition of the word 'necessary' the President in *Re H-L* gave the answer: 'the short answer is that necessary means necessary. It is, after all, an ordinary English word'.

Adopting such a test 'vulnerability' means that the person is:

> 'Exposed to the possibility of being attacked or harmed, either physically or emotionally (of a person) in need of special care, support or protection, because of age, disability, or risk of abuse or neglect'.

28.3.2 What to ask

Questions about their school history, medication they may be taking, literacy or how they manage day to day, etc may elicit information that alerts the advocate to explore the issue further.

The Advocate's Gateway (www.theadvocatesgateway.org) provides advocates with good practice examples of questions that might help to identify risk factors;

- Do you/did you get any extra help at school from a person just for you?
- Do you need extra help managing money?
- Do you need any extra help with listening, speaking or reading?
- Do you need any extra help to stay calm?

Those specific questions are more likely to provide accurate information than 'do you have a learning disability?'

With a client there may also be the opportunity to look at other behaviours and characteristics that may suggest vulnerability which can then be further explored.

If a party is not represented then it is much harder to identify vulnerability because people are seen for only a short period and in what for them is a strange and daunting environment and at a time of distress, pressure and anxiety.

It will be necessary to rely on information provided by the client, reading the papers, observing the party in and outside of court, considering the above factors, the views of others, the view of anyone who has attended to support them, from professionals working with the family (social workers, Cafcass, etc) or from any other available reports.

It will be difficult without reason when first talking to someone as the advocate for the other party (or the judge) to start asking them about their schooling and support they may have received!

The *Vulnerable and Intimidated Witnesses Guide* identified characteristics and behaviour that might suggest a person is vulnerable:

- has no speech or limited speech
- is difficult to understand
- finds it difficult to communicate without assistance
- communicates via signs and gestures
- appears to have difficulty in understanding questions
- responds inappropriately or inconsistently to questions
- focuses on the irrelevant
- appears to have a short attention span
- cannot read or write
- is unable to tell the time or recall key dates/facts such as a birthday, age or address
- appears over eager to please
- repeats what is said to them
- appears uninterested/withdrawn or confused
- expresses strange ideas

A Police Service Guide 2011

There is other behaviour that may warrant further investigation:

– angling head for viewing
– failing to search for someone visually
– hesitancy in movement
– uncontrollable muscular movement

There are also circumstances that may warrant further investigation; the person is:

– in receipt of disability living allowance
– in sheltered accommodation or work placement
– on certain mediation
– receiving support from a carer/social worker/ mental health team

28.3.3 Expert evidence

If there is uncertainty about the existence, type or impact of a person's vulnerability expert advice should be taken. This can include a psychological report or a report from an intermediary who can carry out an assessment of the communication needs and abilities of the party. As will be set out below intermediaries are not experts in capacity or understanding; it is limited to communication.

For benefits see *Newcastle City Council v WM and Others* [2015] EWFC 42

Such instruction will also assist in your considering what special measures, if any, are required; if there is a need for a ground rules hearing or any other adjustments that are necessary to ensure that the hearing is fair.

Note: See FPR 2010, PD3AA para 5.2 re Ground Rules Hearings: see **28.5**.

28.3.4 Be proactive

The Advocate's Gateway Toolkit 10

'Advocates and Judges should **be proactive** in identifying the need for an assessment of potential vulnerability and responding to it. If it appears that the adjustments or special measures are necessary to safeguard the witness or defendant or to ensure they give their best evidence and participate effectively, the advocate should consider inviting the judge to impose these, even if the witness/defendant says that they do not wish to have them'.

28.4 MEASURES TO BE TAKEN

The court building where the hearing is taking place may dictate the measures available. In some courts there are no facilities to have a separate waiting room or a video link and the best on offer is a screen.

The court has a duty to implement the measures required to assist and promote participation and, if they are not available at the court, enquires should be made of other courts that the parties could travel to where they are.

FPR 2010, PD 12J, para 10
FPR 2018, r 3A.8

Any application for directions may be made on the application form initiating the proceedings or during the proceedings. The court can make a participation direct of its own initiative.

FPR 2010, rr 3A.10 and 3A.11

Any application shall contain the following information:

(a) Why the party or witness would benefit from assistance;

(b) The measure or measures that would be likely to maximise as far as practicable the quality of that evidence;

(c) Why the measure or measures sought would be likely to improve the person's ability to participate in the proceedings; and

(d) Why the measure or measures sought would be likely to improve the quality of the person's evidence.

And should follow, if free standing, the Part 18 procedure (see **27.4**).

FPR 2010, PD 3AA, para 6.1

When the court makes, varies or revokes a direction it must record its reasons.

FPR 2010, r 3A.9

The measures that should be considered to assist participation are:

(a) taking steps to prevent a party or witness from seeing another party – this can include a separate entrance, waiting room and screens in court;

(b) allowing participation via video link – if the court does not have a video link room then most chambers do and arrangements can usually be made for the party to attend and participate from that venue;

(c) interpreter – to include sign language interpreters and relay interpreters. It is important to ascertain what is required and also to try and achieve continuity of interpreters. If it is a trial how many interpreters do you require (for example sign language interpreters require 3 – 1 to interpret, 1 to check and 1 resting);

(d) devices to help communication; for example a person with hearing loss who can't sign may require a person to type the evidence for them to read;

(e) limiting questions to be put or who will put the questions to a witness;

(f) giving evidence before the trial date by way of recording;

(g) timing of the hearing and length of the court day;

(h) Breaks – when and for how long. This can change for different parts of the hearing in that fewer breaks may be required when listening to evidence as opposed to when giving evidence;

(i) Intermediaries;

(j) such other directions under the court's general case management powers as it considers appropriate to facilitate a party's participation (PD 3AA para 4.2).

The role of the intermediary is to assist with communication between the court, advocates and the witness or party.

The Youth Justice and Criminal Evidence Act 1999, s 29(2) sets out the function of an intermediary for a witness in criminal proceedings as to communicate;

(a) to the witness, questions put to the witness; and

(b) to any person asking such questions, the answers given by the witness in reply to them, and to explain such questions or answers as so far as necessary to enable them to be understood by the witness or person in question.

The intermediary is not an expert witness: they cannot say if someone can recall an event accurately or whether they have capacity. Their role is not as an interpreter where English is not the primary language, nor a support worker or advisor. They support effective communication and help the court in achieving that. For those reasons many intermediaries will only act when a person is represented as otherwise they may be put in a difficult position of being asked to assist/support/advise which is not their role. Further, if they are being asked to provide communication support for a party then they have to provide that support throughout the hearing not just when they are giving evidence. The argument is that how can a party who has trouble communicating give evidence when they have not fully comprehended the earlier evidence?

An intermediary is instructed by the court and funding is via HMCTS for their role at court. There will be a need for an assessment and this can be undertaken at court with a hearing as to whether an intermediary is necessary to follow in the afternoon. In these circumstances there will not be a written report but the intermediary will provide an oral report to the court.

If it is considered that any measures are required to assist an application can be made following the Part 18 procedure (see **27.4**). Any application should explain why assistance is required, how it will assist in participation or the person's (see PD) ability to give evidence and who should/could provide it (ie separate entrance and room/the formality of language used in court etc). FPR 2010, PD 3AA, para 4.2

When considering any measure required it is important to discuss them with the witness or party and obtain their views; they may not want assistance.

28.5 THE GROUND RULES HEARING

Prior to any trial involving a vulnerable person the court should list a short 'ground rules hearing' to establish and set out how a party or witness is going to participate/ give evidence and how any measures necessary are going to be implemented. The ground rules hearing does not need to be a separate hearing to any other hearing in the proceedings so could be considered at the Dispute Resolution Hearing for example. FPR 2010, PD 3AA, para 5.2

The court should invite representation on how any measures necessary for a witness or party to participate should be implemented and give directions accordingly. If an intermediary is involved it is normal to invite the intermediary to assist and the judge and the intermediary should be encouraged to speak directly as to their recommendations on communication, questions, breaks etc.

If a person is to give oral evidence the court must consider the best way in which the person should give evidence, including considering whether the person's oral evidence should be given at a point before the hearing, recorded and, if the court so directs, transcribed, or given at the hearing with, if appropriate, participation directions being made. FPR 2010, PD 3AA, para 5.4

Any ground rules should be recorded on the face of the order.

28.6 REMOTE AND HYBRID HEARINGS

The Family Justice Council has issued guidance on Safety from Domestic Abuse and Special Measures in Remote and Hybrid Hearings: https://www.judiciary.uk/wp-content/uploads/2020/11/Safety-from-Domestic-Abuse-and-Special-Measures-in-Remote-and-Hybrid-Hearings-Family-Justice-Council-guidance.pdf. The guidance covers all aspects of the process including arranging the hearing and the format of the hearing; personal protection; special measures and participation directions; delivering the court's decision; urgent and without notice hearings; fact-finding hearings; and the service of protective orders. It includes the following checklist of considerations for proceedings in which domestic abuse is an issue:

- In what environment will the victim be appearing?
- In what environment will the victim be preparing themselves for and dealing with the aftermath of the hearing?
- What will be visible to the court and any other participant in the proceedings? What will be visible to the victim?
- What kind of environment and level of visibility is necessary in order to ensure physical and emotional safety for the victim and any children involved?
- What kind of environment and level of visibility is necessary to enable the victim to give their best evidence?
- What kind of environment is necessary to enable the victim to prepare themselves mentally and emotionally for the hearing and to cope after the hearing?
- What kind of environment is necessary for the court to deal justly with the case having regard to any welfare issues involved?

28.7 THE ADVOCATE'S GATEWAY

It cannot be stressed how well written and beneficial the tool kits contained in the Advocate's Gateway are and how essential it is for anyone dealing with a case involving a vulnerable witness/party to read them. They draw on considerable research and experience and although mainly focused on the criminal court still provide best practice. They included detailed tool kits on ground rule hearings, questioning a person with a learning disability or autism, how to question a person via remote link and Tool Kit 13 deals specifically with family proceedings. FPR 2010, PD 3AA, para 5.7 makes clear that all advocates (including those who are litigants in person) are expected to be familiar with them.

The site can be accessed at www.theadvocatesgateway.org.

28.8 CROSS EXAMINATION OF A VULNERABLE PARTY OR WITNESS

Where it is proposed that a vulnerable party or witness is to be cross examined the court must consider whether to make participation directions, including prescribing the manner in which the person is to be cross-examined. The court must consider whether to direct that:

(a) any questions that can be asked by one advocate should not be repeated by another without the permission of the court;

(b) questions or topics to be put in cross-examination should be agreed prior to the hearing;

(c) questions to be put in cross-examination should be put by one legal representative or advocate alone, of, if appropriate, by the judge; or

(d) the taking of evidence should be managed in any other way.

FPR 2010, PD3AA, para 5.5

The court must also consider whether a vulnerable party or witness has previously given evidence or been cross-examined in criminal proceedings and whether that was pre-recorded. Or if they have given an interview which was recorded but not used in previous criminal or family proceedings and, if so – and such recordings are available, the court should consider their being used in the family proceedings.

FPR 2010, PD3AA, para 5.6

28.9 CROSS EXAMINATION OF THE ALLEGED VICTIM

If a party is represented this is not an issue. However the rise of litigants in person given the limitations on public funding has made this a more common event and has given rise to considerable debate.

Women's Aid report 'Nineteen Child Homicides' January 2016

The Domestic Abuse Act 2021, s 65 inserts a new Part 4B into the Matrimonial and Family Proceedings Act 1984 (MFPA 1984) (ss 31Q–31Z). This Part makes detailed provision for the prohibition of cross-examination in person either of or by a victim or alleged victim of domestic abuse in family proceedings. The Part further specifies the alternative arrangements to be made where a party appearing in person is prohibited from conducting cross-examination in person. The procedure is set out in PD3AB and came into force on 21 July 2022 and covers all proceedings that were commenced **on or after 21 July 2022**. *It provides the court power to appoint a qualified legal representative to conduct cross-examination in certain circumstances. Statutory Guidance has also been issued the Lord Chancellor and provided a clear overview of the principles and limitations of the role of the qualified legal representative.*

It is important to note that where both parties are unrepresented and where the cross-examination provisions apply the court will be able to appoint two court appointed advocates.

Further that the application of these provisions does not affect the court's duty to a vulnerable party or the provisions available under PD3AA.

HMCTS will maintain a list of suitably qualified advocates who have undertaking the necessary training or have sufficient experience.

The rules provide for 2 scenarios. The automatic prohibition to cross examination and the discretionary.

The automatic prohibition applies to parties (acting in person) that have been cautioned or convicted of an offence set out in the Regulations (the Prohibition of Cross Examination in Person (Civil and Family Proceedings) Regulations 2022, SI 2022/568) or who have been made subject of an in person protective injunction (which remains in force) or where there is specific evidence adduced of domestic abuse – the evidence requires is set out in the Regulation (above) (see MFPA 1984, ss 31R–31T).

Where the automatic provisions arise then the duty is on the court to consider making a direction – the same as FPR 2010, r 3AA provisions. The court must in deciding whether to grant or refuse to make a direction set out its reasons (PD3AB, para 3.6).

To be able to do this the court will invite the parties to complete forms EX740 (by the person making the allegations) and EX741 (by the person accused of abuse). The C100 (page 16) has been amended to provide a pointer to these forms.

The MFPA 1984, s 31U provides (discretionary) for the prohibition of cross examination in family proceedings where none of the above applies but it appears to the court that: (i) the quality condition or significant distress condition is met; and (ii) it would not be contrary to the interests of justice to give the direction.

The 'quality condition' is met if the quality of evidence given by the witness on cross-examination: (a) is likely to be diminished if the cross-examination (or continued cross-examination) is conducted by the party in person; and (b) would be likely to be improved if a direction were given under this section.

The 'significant distress condition' is met if: (a) the cross examination (or continued cross-examination) of the witness by the party in person would be likely to cause significant distress to the witness or party; and (b) that distress is likely to be more significant that would be the case if the witness were cross-examined other than by the party in person.

In considering these conditions the court applies the factors set out at the MFPA 1984, s 31U(5).

The direction to prohibit the cross-examination can be made either by way of application or by the court of its own motion.

Before making an order the court has to consider the alternatives. The judge asking questions is not an alternative (PD3AB, para 5.3). These alternatives include whether the evidence could be given by other means and/or invite the party to obtain their own representation and give them time to arrange. If neither option is available the court has to consider whether in the interests of justice a qualified legal representative is appointed for the purposes of cross-examination and if so to duly appoint.

When making direction for a Court-Appointed Qualified Legal Representative the court shall (para 7):

(a) specify the witness or witnesses that are to be cross-examined by the court-appointed qualified legal representative;
(b) provide for the court-appointed qualified legal representative to be given access to the full court bundle or such parts of the court bundle as the court directs;
(c) specify the date by when the court-appointed qualified legal representative is be given access to the court bundle under paragraph (b); and

(d) where there is no court bundle—

(i) provide for the court to prepare and provide the court-appointed qualified legal representative with a court bundle; and

(ii) specify the date by when the bundle should be provided

The directions the court gives may specify which hearing or hearings or which part or parts of any hearing the court-appointed qualified legal representative is required to attend.

The court may give such further directions as are necessary to assist the court-appointed qualified legal representative to carry out the cross-examination.

Before making any such directions, the court may invite representations from the party and the witness in writing or at a hearing.

The qualified legal representative is not a representative of the court even though the court has appointed them nor are they responsible to the party they are appointed for and don't have the traditional lawyer/client relationship and are not there to advance the party's case generally or act as an advocate to the court. Their duty is to cross-examine in the interests of the party and similar to the role of advocates appointed in the criminal court. Although they should ascertain the case from the prohibited party their duty is to cross-examine to enable information to be before the court to reach a conclusion on the issues. The guidance provides for the court to set this out at the start to the prohibited party.

The guidance provides for the qualified legal representative to meet the prohibited party in advance to understand their case, have access to the papers and recommends they prepare a brief position statement to help focus cross-examination.

Where the prohibited party does not cooperate with the qualified legal representative they should then confine their questions to what the judge directs as relevant/apparent from the case papers. If there is any issue as to a party's capacity they must inform the court.

At the end of the court appointed legal representative should be informed of the outcome either by them receiving the order, written reasons or copy of the judgment.

Where the proceedings commenced before 21 July 2022 then the MFPA 1984 and PD12J continue to apply in relation to direct cross-examination. The MFPA 1984, s 31G(6) provides:

Where in any proceedings in the family court it appears to the court that a party to the proceedings, who is not legally represented is unable to cross-examine a witness effectively, the court is to:

(a) ascertain from that party the matters about which the witness may be able to depose or on which the witness ought to be cross-examined; and
(b) put, or cause to be put, to the witness such questions in the interests of that party as may appear to the court to be proper.

PD12J, para 19 specifies that:

Where the court considers that a fact-finding hearing is necessary, it must give directions as to how the proceedings are to be conducted to ensure that the matters in issue are determined as soon as possible, fairly and proportionately, and within the capabilities of the parties. In particular it should consider what support the alleged perpetrator may need in order to have a reasonable opportunity to challenge the evidence.

PD12J, para 28 states:

While ensuring that the allegations are properly put and responded to, the fact-finding hearing or other hearing can be an inquisitorial (or investigative) process, which at all times must protect the interests of all involved. At the fact-finding hearing or other hearing –

- each party can be asked to identify what questions they wish to ask of the other party, and to set out or confirm in sworn evidence their version of the disputed key facts; and
- the judge should be prepared where necessary and appropriate to conduct the questioning of the witnesses on behalf of the parties, focusing on the key issues in the case.

These provisions must now be read in light of the amendments deeming victims or alleged victims of domestic abuse automatically to be vulnerable witnesses, whether or not the court has made findings of fact in relation to domestic abuse. Consequently, the court should always consider the making of participation directions to prevent direct cross-examination by or of a victim or alleged victim of domestic abuse.

They could consider asking the solicitor for the child or a 'McKenzie friend' to ask questions. However, both have problems. The solicitor for the child may have a positive case and putting question on behalf of a party would be difficult or may wish to ask the 'catch all' questions at the end. To allow a 'McKenzie friend' the ability to ask questions changes their role. This is usually not appropriate, and they may not be comfortable with the role.

This therefore leaves one option and that is the judge as the questioner. Before embarking on this course of action it is necessary to:

(a) consider each of the options in court, their pros and cons, and what is the best option on the facts of the case

(b) ensure that all parties agree the way forward

(c) there is a clear explanation of who is asking questions and why they are doing it

(d) If it is the child's solicitor or the Judge a clear explanation to both parties that they does not mean they have taken sides, now representing that party or with the judge made up their mind

(e) the alleged perpetrator knows what is expected of them – they need to write questions down to be asked

(f) there is proper court time for questions to be written, put and any additional questions added.

As with special measures there may be merit in having a ground rules hearing or pre-trial hearing to consider these matters and set a proper timetable for the questions to be written.

When considering special measures and judges asking questions of alleged perpetrators it is important to underline the word *alleged* and remind the respondent that this does not in any way mean the court (or the guardian) believes the allegations. The perception of alleged perpetrators when they say the allegations are false yet see the court taking these measures can send the wrong message; it is important that the reasons are explained and they understand why the court is acting as it is. If acting for the alleged perpetrator it is always helpful to raise this.

CHAPTER 29

APPEALS

29.1 INTRODUCTION

In family proceedings as elsewhere, a litigant who is dissatisfied with a decision may wish to appeal. This chapter is intended to offer a brief introduction to the subject. It is not a comprehensive guide – for example, it does not deal with a respondent's cross-appeal – and should not be used as the sole procedural reference when contemplating or conducting an appeal.

For the sake of brevity, in the discussion which follows the court or judge making the original decision will be referred to as 'the lower court'; the court dealing with the appeal will be referred to as 'the appeal court' (even though most appeals will in fact be to a single judge).

The rules governing appeals in family proceedings will be found in the FPR 2010, Pt 30, together with the accompanying Practice Direction, which should be carefully studied.

FPR 2010, r 30.2

It is important to note that all parties to an appeal must comply with the relevant Practice Direction 30A.

29.2 THE NATURE OF AN APPEAL

FPR 2010, r 30.12(1), (2). For the extreme rarity of it being in the interests of justice to hold a re-hearing, see *Ealing LBC v Richardson* [2005] EWCA Civ 1798 and the cases there cited

It is important to recognise that, save in the very exceptional case where the appeal court considers that it would be in the interests of justice to hold a re-hearing, an appeal will be limited to a review of the decision of the lower court. The appeal court will not normally receive oral evidence, or evidence which was not before the lower court.

V v V [2005] 2 FLR 697

The approach to an appeal hearing was summarised by Coleridge J in *V v V*:

> '… it is right to start by recording, of course, that this is an appeal; it is not a hearing de novo in which I carry out the same task as the District Judge. It is vital for all to appreciate that …. my function in relation to this appeal is the same as in relation to any other such appeal; namely, to review the process undertaken by the District Judge to determine whether or not he fell into error in the steps which he took and in the analysis which he brought to bear. I do not start from scratch …'.

FPR 2010, r 30.12(3) sets out the basic rule: that an appeal will be allowed where the decision of the lower court was:

(a) wrong; or

(b) unjust because of a serious procedural or other irregularity in the proceedings in the lower court.

An appeal should not normally be issued where the matters in question would be better dealt with on an application to set aside a financial remedy order under FPR 2010, r 9.9A.

FPR 2010, PD 30A, para 4.1B

29.2.1 The approach to appeals

Munby (then P) in *Re F (Children)* summarised the approach to appeals:

Re F (Children) [2016] EWCA Civ 546

> '22. Like any judgment, the judgment of the Deputy Judge has to be read as a whole, and having regard to its context and structure. The task facing a judge is not to pass an examination, or to prepare a detailed legal or factual analysis of all the evidence and submissions he has heard. Essentially, the judicial task is twofold: to enable the parties to understand why they have won or lost; and to provide sufficient detail and analysis to enable an appellate court to decide whether or not the judgment is sustainable. The judge need not slavishly restate either the facts, the arguments or the law. To adopt the striking metaphor of Mostyn J in *SP v EB and KP* [2014] EWHC 3964 (Fam), [2016] 1 FLR 228, para 29, there is no need for the judge to "incant mechanically" passages from the authorities, the evidence or the submissions, as if he were "a pilot going through the pre-flight checklist."
>
> 23. The task of this court is to decide the appeal applying the principles set out in the classic speech of Lord Hoffmann in *Piglowska v Piglowski* [1999] 1 WLR 1360. I confine myself to one short passage (at 1372):
>
> > "The exigencies of daily court room life are such that reasons for judgment will always be capable of having been better expressed. This is particularly true of an unreserved judgment such as the judge gave in this case … These reasons should be read on the assumption that, unless he has demonstrated the contrary, the judge knew how he should perform his functions and which matters he should take into account. This is particularly true when the matters in question are

so well known as those specified in section 25(2) [of the Matrimonial Causes Act 1973]. An appellate court should resist the temptation to subvert the principle that they should not substitute their own discretion for that of the judge by a narrow textual analysis which enables them to claim that he misdirected himself.

It is not the function of an appellate court to strive by tortuous mental gymnastics to find error in the decision under review when in truth there has been none. The concern of the court ought to be substance not semantics. To adopt Lord Hoffmann's phrase, the court must be wary of becoming embroiled in 'narrow textual analysis'."'

29.2.2 Where the decision was wrong

KW & Ors v Rochdale Metropolitan Borough Council (Rev 3) [2015] EWCA Civ 1054

The clearest instance of the judgment of the lower court being wrong will be where the lower court has failed to follow binding authority, as happened for example in the remarkable case of *KW & Ors v Rochdale Metropolitan Borough Council (Rev 3)* or there has been an error of law. It is worth reiterating that the fact that a party disagrees with a decision does not, without more, mean that the decision is wrong.

Royal Bank of Scotland v Carlyle [2015] UKSC 13

The court reached a conclusion on the facts which was not open to the court on the evidence before it (see *Royal Bank of Scotland v Carlyle*).

It has been said that:

Henderson v Foxworth Investments Ltd [2014] UKSC 41

> 'It does not matter, with whatever degree of certainty, that the [appeal] court considers that it would have reached a different conclusion. What matters is whether the decision under appeal is one that no reasonable judge could have reached.'

29.2.3 Discretionary decisions

Many decisions in family proceedings involve the exercise of a discretion by the lower court. Familiar examples are:

- The making of an order in financial relief proceedings. The lower court will have to consider the weight to be given to the various factors in MCA 1973, s 25;
- The making of an order concerning children. The lower court will have to consider the various factors in the 'welfare checklist' of CA 1989, s 1.

It is important to note that the fact that had it been hearing the matter the appeal court might have arrived at a different conclusion from the lower court is not a valid ground of appeal. As was said by the Court of Appeal as long ago as 1948:

> 'We are here concerned with a judicial discretion, and it is of the essence of such a discretion that on the same evidence 2 different minds might reach widely different decisions without either being appealable. It is only where the decision exceeds the generous ambit within which reasonable disagreement is possible, and is, in fact, plainly wrong, that an appellate body is entitled to interfere'.

Bellenden (formerly Satterthwaite) v Satterthwaite [1948] 1 All ER 343

Only if the appeal court concludes that the lower court's decision was wrong *in principle*, or vitiated because the lower court took into account a matter which was legally irrelevant or failed to take into account something that was legally significant, is the appeal court in a position to interfere. The appeal court may find itself obliged to direct a rehearing, but in some cases may be able to exercise the discretion afresh. That is the only respect in which an appeal can amount to a 'second bite of the cherry'.

29.2.4 Where the decision was unjust

This provision of the rules is frequently misunderstood. If a litigant is ordered to pay 'too much' to his former spouse, or is afforded 'too little' time with his child under a Child Arrangements Order, that litigant may well perceive the decision as unjust but, if the lower court's decision was within the 'generous ambit' referred to in **29.2.1**, there will not be the basis for an appeal.

If, on the other hand, the judge appears to have closed his mind to a relevant issue, the hearing may be regarded as unjust and a rehearing may be directed.

P (A Child) (Rev 1) [2014] EWCA Civ 888

A process has been adopted which is procedurally irregular and unfair to an extent that it renders the decision unjust.

Re S-W (Care Proceedings; Case Management Hearing) [2015] 2 FLR 136

A failure to give due weight to some very significant matter or has given undue weight to some matter.

B v B (Residence Orders; Reasons for Decision) [1997] 2 FLR 602

29.2.5 Proportionality

The appeal court may, exceptionally, decline to hear an appeal on the basis that the cost of further litigation is disproportionate to the issues, or the amount at stake in the case.

Cook v Plummer [2008] EWCA Civ 484; *HH v BLW* [2012] EWHC 2199 (Fam)

29.3 THE REQUIREMENT FOR PERMISSION

FPR 2010, rr 30.3(1B), (2)

Generally, permission is required for an appeal. That requirement does not apply to an appeal from lay justices. Neither does it apply to an appeal against a committal order, a secure accommodation order, or a refusal to grant habeas corpus in relation to a minor.

FPR 2010, rr 30.3(3), (4)
FPR 2010, r 30.3(5A)

Permission should be sought from the lower court at the hearing, or from the appeal court. If the lower court refuses permission, a further application may be made to the appeal court in an appeal notice.

In the first instance the appeal court will consider the application for permission on paper, and generally the prospective appellant can ask for a refusal to be reconsidered at a hearing; but a High Court judge or Designated Family Judge may, if satisfied that the prospective appeal is totally without merit, order that the application may not be renewed at an oral hearing.

FPR 2010, PD30A para 4.10

The court will notify the parties of any decision made without attendance.

Re R (A Child) [2019] EWCA Civ 895
FPR 2010, r 30.3(7)

Permission to appeal may only be given where the court considers that the appeal would have a real prospect of success, or where there is some other compelling reason why the appeal should be heard. The term real prospect of success means that there must be a realistic, as opposed to fanciful, prospect of success. There is no requirement that success should be probable or more likely than not.

FPR 2010, r 30.3(8); PD 30A para 4.18

The court may grant permission to appeal on some issues only. In that case it will either refuse permission on the remaining issues, or reserve the question of permission on those issues to the court hearing the appeal. In the latter case, the appellant must notify the appeal court and the respondent whether he intends to pursue the reserved issues.

29.4 AN APPEAL DOES NOT AUTOMATICALLY OPERATE AS A STAY

There is a widely held belief that appealing against a decision automatically puts that decision 'on hold'. Indeed, it commonly appears to be supposed that simply seeking permission to appeal has the same effect.

The belief is wholly wrong. The FPR 2010, r 30.8 could not be more explicit:

> 'Unless the appeal court or the lower court orders otherwise, an appeal does not operate as a stay of any order or decision of the lower court.'

If the decision is one in which the refusal of a stay would make an appeal futile, the lower court, when being asked for permission to appeal, should also be specifically asked to stay the decision pending the appeal. If, as will commonly be the case, the lower court declines to give permission and indicates that an application for permission must be made to the appeal court, the lower court should be invited to grant a stay 'for a period of 21 days from today, and if application is made for permission to appeal, until that application is determined by the appeal court'. The appeal court should be invited not only to give permission for the appeal but to continue the stay.

Mostyn J in *NB v London Borough of Haringey* at para 7 has drawn together existing authorities as to the court's powers to stay and summarised them as this: *NB v London Borough of Haringey* [2011] EWHC 3544 (Fam)

> 'I derive the following five principles in relation to the application before me. First, the Court must consider all the circumstances of the case. Second, a stay is the exception rather than the general rule. Third, the party seeking a stay should provide cogent evidence that the appeal will be stifled or rendered nugatory unless a stay is granted. Fourth, in exercising its discretion the court applies what is in effect a balance of harm test in which the likely prejudice to the successful part must be carefully considered. Fifth, the Court should consider the prospects of the appeal succeeding. Only where strong grounds of appeal or a strong likelihood of success is shown should a stay be considered.'

29.5 TIME FOR APPEALING

FPR 2010, rr 30.4(2),(3)

Normally the time for appealing is 21 days after the decision appealed from, but the lower court can extend or abridge that period. The normal period for appealing from a case management decision is 7 days beginning with the date of the lower court's decision.

29.6 THE ROUTE OF APPEAL

Care must be taken to follow the correct route of appeal. A lengthy table appears in the FPR 2010, PD 30A para 2.1. It is not proposed to set out its provisions in detail: the basic principle is that appeals from lay justices or district judges go to a circuit judge; appeals from a circuit judge and a district judge of the Principal Registry of the Family Division go to a High

Court judge; appeals from a High Court judge go to the Court of Appeal. There are, however, exceptions to the general principle and the Practice Direction must be studied with care.

29.7 REQUIREMENTS ON ISSUE OF APPEAL

The appellant must file with the court an appeal notice in the appropriate form as specified in Practice Direction 5A and a skeleton argument, together with copies for service on each respondent. The appeal notice must set out the grounds for the appeal.

FPR 2010, r 30.6

A fee is payable unless the appellant is exempt from fees.

FPR 2010, r 30(4), PD 30A para 5.1

FPR 2010, PD 30A paras 5.8–5.22; CPR 1998, PD 52C

An appeal bundle must be filed, again with a copy for service on each respondent. The requirements as to what documents must be included in the appeal bundle differ depending on whether the appeal is to the family court, to the High Court, or to the Court of Appeal. The relevant paragraphs of the Practice Directions must be studied with care to ensure that the appropriate documents (and, especially in the case of appeals to the High Court or Court of Appeal, no superfluous documents) are included.

FPR 2010, PD 30A para 5.23

In virtually every case, a transcript or approved note of the judgment of the lower court will be required. If a written judgment was delivered, a copy endorsed by the judge should be used; lay justices will provide written reasons for their decision. Many hearings will be officially recorded and a transcript of any judgment can be obtained on payment of a prescribed fee. If there is no official recording a note of the judgment should be agreed between the advocates and submitted to the judge for approval. Where the appellant is unrepresented it is the duty of any opposing advocate to make his note of the judgment available promptly and without charge.

FPR 2010, PD 30A para 5.24

The transcript may not be available within the time limit for appealing. In that case the appellant must complete the appeal notice as best they can on the information available, and seek permission to amend it subsequently if appropriate.

FPR 2010, PD 30A, paras 4.19, 6.6

If the appellant is legally represented, the appeal court must be notified in writing of the advocate's time estimate for the hearing of the appeal. If the appellant intends to pursue issues which were reserved when permission to appeal was granted, the time estimate must include a specific time estimate for the reserved issues.

29.8 SECOND APPEALS

There are even more stringent limits on a 'second appeal', that is, an appeal to the Court of Appeal from a decision of the county court, the Family Court or the High Court where that decision was itself made on appeal. CPR 1998, r 52.7(1)

Permission for a second appeal may only be given by the Court of Appeal (not by the court hearing the first appeal) and only if the Court of Appeal considers that:

(a) the appeal would
 (i) have a real prospect of success; and
 (ii) raise an important point of principle or practice; or

(b) there is some other compelling reason for the Court of Appeal to hear the appeal.

Note: That under paragraph (a) both requirements must be satisfied. CPR 1998, r 52.7(1)

CHAPTER 30

THE COURT RECORD

30.1 DETAILS RELATING TO THE COURT RECORD

Solicitors who sign either:

(a) a document which initiates court proceedings;

(b) an acknowledgement of service; or

(c) a document which operates as a defence,

automatically put themselves on the court record as acting for the party on whose behalf the document has been signed and filed.

Signing a subsequent application will also probably have the effect of solicitors being put on the court record, but see **30.2** for the correct procedure to adopt.

Going on the court record results in the solicitors concerned receiving copies of all the following: documents from the court which are for personal service, copies of all documents filed by other parties to the proceedings and any correspondence to the parties which is generated by the court. Whilst on the record, solicitors are obliged to accept service of all documents and it will be presumed that they will remain on the record until the conclusion of the matter.

It also results in the solicitors being responsible for the payment of all court fees, whether or not their client is in receipt of Public Funding.

Conversely, if the document initiating or defending proceedings is signed by a litigant in person, the documents referred to above will be sent direct to that litigant. It also follows that the litigant will be personally responsible for all court fees unless exempt from paying fees.

However, it is permissible in some circumstances for a litigant in person to use a solicitors' address as a care of address. Examples of such circumstances are where:

FPR 2010, r 29.1(2)

(a) a litigant does not wish to reveal their home address and has given notice of their address to the court; or

(b) solicitors are advising in divorce proceedings under the provisions of the Legal Help Scheme.

Unlike the situation where a litigant is in receipt of public funding, where solicitors are merely advising under the Legal Help Scheme, no court fees are payable on behalf of the client.

A solicitor who is appointed solely for advocacy is exempt from going on the record. FPR 2010, r 26.2(1)(b)

30.2 AMENDING THE COURT RECORD

Solicitors can go on record in place of a litigant in person, at any stage in the course of proceedings, and this is achieved simply by filing a notice of change of acting with the court and by serving a copy on all parties. The notice filed with the court should confirm that the notice has been served in accordance with the rules. FPR 2010, r 26.2(2), PD26A

The form of notice of change (form FP8) is prescribed by the FPR 2010. FPR 2010, PD5A

Similarly, if a litigant wishes to conclude proceedings acting in person, rather than continuing with the services of solicitors, a notice of change must be filed at court and served on all parties. A solicitor remains on the record until this is done.

If either solicitors or a litigant in person change address, telephone number or any other details relevant to the proceedings, a notice of such change must be filed at court and served on all parties.

The reason for filing a notice of change of details is to ensure that at all times the court and other parties to the proceedings can promptly receive relevant documents or be contacted, for example, as a matter of urgency should there be a late adjournment of a court hearing.

If solicitors wish to be removed from the court record, other than with the consent of their client, they will need to apply on notice supported by evidence. FPR 2010, r 26.3(2)

It is the client who is the respondent to the application. The other parties to the matter must not be served unless the court directs.

The application and evidence must be served on the party for whom the solicitor is acting on not less than 7 days' notice. FPR 2010, r 18.8(1)(b)(ii)

An application to be removed from a court record may not necessarily be an automatic process and permission may be refused; particularly in circumstances where a client has already paid significant monies on account of costs. The application attracts a court fee.

FPR 2010, r 26.2(6)(a)

Where a litigant has the benefit of public funding and subsequently has that certificate discharged or revoked, the solicitor who acted will cease to be the solicitor acting in the case as soon as the retainer is determined under the Civil Legal Aid (Procedure) Regulations 2012, reg 24 or 41.

FPR 2010, r 26.2(6)(b)(ii), PD26A para 2.5

Where the party subsequently wishes to appoint a solicitor, a notice of change must be filed. Where the party wishes to act in person, the party must give an address for service that is within the United Kingdom. Reference should be made to the FPR 2010, r 6.26.

In circumstances where solicitors have been merely advising under the Legal Help Scheme but are no longer providing advice it will be sufficient to inform the court of that fact and, where possible, to provide an alternative contact address. It is not appropriate to issue an application to be removed from the court record.

30.3 INSPECTING THE COURT FILE

Inspection of the court file is governed by the FPR 2010, r 29.12.

FPR 2010, r 29.12(1)

The court file is confidential but a party to the proceedings or their legal representative, children's guardian or litigation friend may have a search made for, and may inspect or take a copy of, any document filed or lodged in the court office in those proceedings.

FPR 2010, r 29.12(1), (2)

This does not apply to an address of a party supplied to the court where the party has indicated they do not wish to reveal their address or other contact details in accordance with the FPR 2010, r 29.1(2). No document on the court file will be open to inspection to anybody else without permission from the court, except for a copy of a decree or order made in open court.

FPR 2010, r 7.36(3)

Decrees nisi and absolute in matrimonial proceedings and conditional orders and final orders in civil partnership proceedings are public records and anyone is entitled to inspect these document or be provided with a copy.

FPR 2010, r 29.1

The FPR 2010, r 7.20(8) also permits any person to inspect, within 14 days after the making of the decree nisi or conditional order, the district judge's certificate and the evidence filed under r 7.19(4), that is the statement filed in support of an undefended application for a decree nisi or conditional order. This provision does not apply to proceedings for a decree of nullity on the basis that a party to the marriage or civil partnership has been issued with an interim gender recognition certificate since the date of the marriage or civil partnership.

A party who does not wish their home address or other contact details, or those of a child, to be revealed must give notice of the address or other contact details to the court and such particulars will not be revealed to any person unless the court directs otherwise.

Any person who attempts to inspect court documents when he knows that permission is required for that purpose is guilty of contempt of court.

30.4 McKENZIE FRIEND

Guidance with regard to the status of a McKenzie Friend may be found at **Appendix C(11)**.

Appendices

APPENDIX A

PRECEDENTS AND FORMS

Other matrimonial pleadings

(1) Application for a divorce, dissolution or (judicial) separation (D8)

Matrimonial applications and orders

(2) Order to HM Revenue and Customs to disclose address

Sundry documentation

(3) Certificate Referred to in Article 39 of Council Regulation (EC) No 2201/2003 (D180) (Annex I certificate)

(4) Sample Notice of abatement

(5) Parental responsibility agreement

(6) Step-parent parental responsibility agreement

(7) Parental responsibility agreement (acquisition of parental responsibility by second female parent)

(8) Pension Sharing Annex under Section 24B of the Matrimonial Causes Act 1973/Paragraph 15 of Schedule 5 to the Civil Partnership Act 2004

(9) Pension Attachment Annex under Section 25B or 25C of the Matrimonial Causes Act 1973/Paragraph 25 or 26 of Schedule 5 to the Civil Partnership Act 2004

(10) Family Mediation Information and Assessment Form

1 Application for a divorce, dissolution or (judicial) separation (D8)

You can apply online
Divorce – www.gov.uk/apply-for-divorce
Dissolution – www.gov.uk/end-civil-partnership

Application for a divorce or dissolution (ending a civil partnership)

HMCTS USE ONLY

You can only make an application for divorce or dissolution if you have been in your marriage or civil partnership for at least one year.

If there are exceptional reasons why your application should be dealt with urgently then please set those reasons out in a covering letter.

Legal representatives are required to apply digitally through the My HMCTS Solicitor Portal for a Divorce or Dissolution. You can find more information at: https://www.gov.uk/guidance/myhmcts-online-case-management-for-legal-professionals

Section 1 – Your application

1.1 What application are you making?

☐ **Divorce** on the ground that the marriage has broken down irretrievably

☐ **Dissolution** on the ground that the civil partnership has broken down irretrievably

1.2 Are you applying as a sole applicant or joint applicants?

☐ **A sole application** – I am applying on my own.

You will complete this application on your own before you submit it to the court. The court will send a copy of your application to your spouse/civil partner.

You will be referred to as the sole applicant, and your spouse/civil partner will be referred to as the respondent in this application.

☐ **A joint application** – We are applying together.

You and your spouse/civil partner will complete this application jointly before you submit to the court.

You will be referred to as applicant 1 and your spouse/civil partner as applicant 2 in this application.

Applicant 2 must complete section 3 and the statement of truth.

Relationship support and child arrangements
Where it may be helpful (and safe) to recieve relationship support, you can find information at: https://www.nhs.uk/Service-Search/other-services/Relationship%20counselling/LocationSearch/400

You can also find information on making child arrangements if you divorce or separate at: https://www.gov.uk/looking-after-children-divorce

Note: If you entered into a religious marriage as well as a civil marriage, these divorce proceedings may not dissolve the religious part of your marriage. It is important that you contact the relevant religious authority and seek further guidance if you are unsure.

Note 1.2: How you divide your money and property is dealt with separately. You may wish to consider taking legal advice.

It should not affect your decision on whether to do a sole or a joint application.

Any application for costs should be made using form **D11** application notice. This is available on the gov.uk website.

D8 Application for a divorce or dissolution (ending a civil partnership) (04.22)

1.3 What documents are you supplying to support your application?

☐ Your marriage or civil partnership certificate or a certified copy of the certificate from where you got married or entered into a civil partnership (a photocopy will **not** be accepted).

☐ A translation that has been certified by a notary public or authenticated by a statement of truth by the person who did the translation. This should be provided if your marriage or civil partnership certificate (or a similar document issued under the law in the country you registered your marriage or civil partnership) is not in English.

For marriages/civil partnerships in England and Wales you can order a copy of the certificate at www.gro.gov.uk/gro/content/certificates. You will need to pay for each copy.

In cases of urgency it may be possible for you to make an application to allow you to deliver the original or a certified copy of the marriage/civil partnership certificate to the court at a later date, if the document is unavailable. To do this, you will need to complete and file the **D11** application notice. This is available at https://www.gov.uk/government/publications/form-d11-application-notice

Section 2 – About you
(the sole applicant or applicant 1)

2.1 Full name of the sole applicant or applicant 1

First name(s)

Middle name(s)

Last name

Is this either your married name or the name shown on your marriage or civil partnership certificate?

☐ Yes

☐ No. Please attach your change of name deed/statutory declaration or if this is not applicable, explain why your name has changed

Note 2.1: This can be different to the one on your marriage or civil partnership certificate. This can be your last name, your spouse/civil partner's last name or a double barrelled last name that combines the two.
If you have changed your name, other than through your marriage, since you got married you must attach a copy of your change of name deed or otherwise explain why your name has changed.

2.2 Do you wish to keep your contact details confidential from your spouse or civil partner?

☐ Yes. Please keep my details confidential.

☐ No

Note 2.2: If you do not wish to disclose your contact details to the respondent, please tick 'Yes' and complete question 2.3 below.

2.3 What is your address and contact details?

Building and street

Second line of address

Town or city

County (optional)

Country

Postcode

Phone number (if you have one)

Email (if you have one)

Note 2.3: You should give a home address in the UK, if you have one. The court will send papers to your home address, or you can provide a business address in the UK. If you want to supply an address outside of the UK, different rules may apply about documents being sent to you. You may wish to seek legal advice.

Remember information contained in this form will be sent to your spouse/civil partner. If you do not want them to know your current contact details, please make sure you have ticked 'Yes' at question 2.2, the court will not disclose these details.

If you have not provided an email address, the court will send a copy of the issued application to your postal address.

2.4 Do you have a solicitor?

☐ Yes. **Complete the following questions (2.5 – 2.8)**

☐ No. **Go to Section 3.**

Note 2.4: For a solicitor completing this application: references to 'solicitor' in this form includes any person who, for the purposes of the Legal Services Act 2007, is an authorised person in relation to an activity which constitutes the conduct of litigation (within the meaning of that Act)

2.5 The solicitor's name

2.6 The solicitor's reference number (if applicable)

2.7 Name of the solicitor's firm

2.8 Address of solicitor's firm

Building and street

Second line of address

Town or city

County (optional)

Country

Postcode

DX address (if applicable)

Phone number

Email

Section 3 – About the respondent or applicant 2

If you are applying as a sole applicant, complete this section with the respondent's details.

If applying jointly, applicant 2 must complete this section. Applicant 1 should continue to complete the form at Section 4.

3.1 Full name

First name(s)

Middle name(s)

Last name

Note: For applicant 2, this can be different to the one on your marriage or civil partnership certificate. This can be your last name, your spouse/civil partner's last name or a double barrelled last name that combines the two.

If you have changed your name, other than through your marriage, since you got married you must attach a copy of your change of name deed or otherwise explain why your name has changed.

3.2 Is this either the married name or the name shown on the marriage or civil partnership certificate?

☐ Yes

☐ No. Please attach the change of name deed/statutory declaration or if this is not applicable, explain why the name has changed

3.3 What is the address of the respondent or applicant 2?

Building and street

Second line of address

Town or city

County (optional)

Country

Postcode

Phone number (if there is one)

Please insert the respondent's usual email address or an email address provided by the respondent for service (for example, their solicitor's email address). You should avoid using a work email address, as this may not be confidential.

Email (if there is one)

☐ For the respondent's email address only – I confirm that to the best of my knowledge only the respondent has access to the above email account

If this is a joint application please go to question 3.7

Note 3.3: Where the application is to be served by the court this will be served by email with a notice confirming service sent to the respondent's postal address.

Note: You should use the email address actively used by the respondent for personal emails. Where the respondent has a solicitor who is instructed to accept service of the application, please insert the solicitor's email address here instead.

The email address should not be the same as the one given for the sole applicant/ applicant 1.

3.4 Is the application to be served on the respondent outside England and Wales?

☐ Yes. You must arrange service of this application on the respondent. **Go to question 3.6.**

☐ No

Note 3.4: If the respondent to a sole application is not in England and Wales the applicant must arrange to serve this application on the respondent. Special rules about service may apply and you may wish to seek legal advice.

3.5 The court will serve the application on the respondent by email and a notice sent by post unless you tick the box below

☐ Please serve this application by post only

☐ I will arrange service on the respondent

3.6 Has the respondent provided a different address for the court documents to be sent to?

☐ Yes, please complete the address details below

☐ No. **Go to Section 4.**

Note 3.6: Alternative addresses or solicitor addresses should be provided at question 3.10.

3.7 The solicitor's name for the respondent or applicant 2 (if applicable and if known)

3.8 The solicitor's reference number (if applicable and if known)

3.9 Name of the solicitor's firm (if applicable and if known)

3.10 The solicitor's or other address they have provided

Note 3.10: The court will send documents to this address.

Building and street

Second line of address

Town or city

County (optional)

Country

Postcode

DX address (if applicable)

Phone number

Section 4 – Details of marriage/civil partnership

You should attach your marriage or civil partnership certificate to this application, together with a certified translation in English if necessary (the court will usually keep your documents and not return them). If you do not have the original certificate and cannot get a copy of it, you will have to make a separate application, alongside this application, to issue this form without it.

Note: If you are applying without your marriage/civil partnership certificate you will need to make a separate application on form **D11** (Application notice) and pay another court fee. It is recommended that you seek legal advice if you are unsure of how to do this.

4.1 Did your marriage/civil partnership take place outside of the UK?

☐ Yes

☐ No

4.2 Are you making a separate application to issue without your marriage or civil partnership certificate?

☐ Yes

☐ No

If you answered 'Yes', to either question 4.1 or 4.2 above, please give the place where the marriage/civil partnership was formed, as it appears on your marriage/civil partnership certificate (if any)

[ ]

4.3 Date of marriage or civil partnership

Day

Month

Year

Note 4.3: You can only apply for a divorce/dissolution if you have been in your marriage or civil partnership for at least one year.

4.4 Your full name as shown on your certificate

[ ]

Your spouse/civil partner's full name as shown on your certificate

[ ]

4.5 Are the details set out in your marriage or civil partnership certificate correct?

☐ Yes

☐ No. Please explain why

Section 5 – Why this court can deal with your case (Jurisdiction)

The court needs to understand why you think it has the legal power (jurisdiction) to deal with your application.

Please complete section 5.1 or if that section does not apply to you then complete section 5.2.

Important: If you need help deciding which reasons apply to you then you should consider seeking legal advice, particularly if you live outside England and Wales.

5.1 The usual basis for the court to have jurisdiction is where one or both parties are habitually resident in England and Wales.

Habitual Residence

Your habitual residence is the place in which your life is mainly based. You must be settled there and intend to stay settled there. Some of the following may apply: you work there, own property, have your children in school there, and your main family life takes place there.

Domicile

Your domicile is the place of your permanent home in which you live, or to which you intend to return.

When you were born you will have acquired your parents' domicile (for example, your father's if they were married, or your mother's if they weren't married or if your father died before you were born). If you have since moved to another country and made that your permanent home then your domicile may have moved there.

If you were born in England or Wales, lived your entire life here, and intend to stay here, then it is very likely that you'll be **both habitually resident and domiciled** here.

As the court will need to know the reason(s) for why you think it has jurisdiction to deal with the application, please tick the reason(s) from the list over the page.

Please tick the reasons that apply:

- [ ] both parties to the marriage/civil partners are habitually resident in England and Wales;
- [ ] both parties to the marriage/civil partners were last habitually resident in England and Wales and one of them continues to reside there;
- [ ] the respondent is habitually resident in England and Wales;
- [ ] this is a joint application and either
  - [ ] applicant 1

  or
  - [ ] applicant 2

  is habitually resident in England and Wales;
- [ ] the applicant is habitually resident in England and Wales and has resided there for at least one year immediately before the application was made;
- [ ] the applicant is domiciled and habitually resident in England and Wales and has resided there for at least six months immediately before the application was made;
- [ ] both parties to the marriage/civil partners are domiciled in England and Wales; **or**
- [ ] only
  - [ ] applicant/applicant 1
  - [ ] applicant 2
  - [ ] respondent

  is domiciled in England and Wales.

OR for civil partners or same sex marriage only

5.2 If the options in section 5.1 do not apply to you, please consider if below is applicable:

- [ ] the parties registered as civil partners of each other in England or Wales or, in the case of a same sex couple, married each other under the law of England and Wales and it would be in the interests of justice for the court to assume jurisdiction in this case.

Section 6 – Statement of irretrievable breakdown (the legal reason for your divorce or dissolution)

6.1 You must state that your marriage or civil partnership has broken down irretrievably in order for the court to make an order.

If a joint application applicant 1 and applicant 2 must each make a statement by ticking the box that applies to them.

Sole applicant or applicant 1

☐ I confirm that my marriage or civil partnership has broken down irretrievably

Applicant 2 (if a joint application)

☐ I confirm that my marriage or civil partnership has broken down irretrievably

Section 7 – Existing or previous court cases

7.1 Are there any existing or previous court proceedings relating to your marriage/civil partnership or affecting its validity (including any existing or concluded court proceedings overseas)?

☐ Yes, please give details below

☐ No

Note 7: Joint applicants are to complete the details together in the same box provided.

Case number(s)

Summary of the existing or previous court proceedings

Section 8 – Dividing your money and property – Orders which are sought

You can apply to the court about how your money, property, pensions and other assests are to be split. These are called financial orders and may include

- an order for maintenance pending suit/outcome
- periodical payments order
- secured provision order
- lump sum order
- property adjustment order
- Pension sharing/compensation sharing/attachment order

You can apply for orders for yourself, and/or, if appropriate for your children.

If you agree with your spouse or civil partner about how your property, money, pensions and other assets will be split, and want it to be legally binding, you can apply for a financial order to be made by consent.

If you disagree with your spouse or civil partner about how your property, money, pensions and other assets will be split, then you can ask the court to decide for you.

8.1 Do you want to apply for a financial order?

Sole applicant or applicant 1

☐ Yes, I want to apply for a financial order for (select all that apply)

☐ myself

☐ the children

☐ No

Applicant 2

☐ Yes, I want to apply for a financial order for (select all that apply)

☐ myself

☐ the children

☐ No

Money and property when you divorce or separate
You may be able to solve your financial and other arrangements outside of court, for example through mediation. You can find more information on mediation at https://www.gov.uk/money-property-when-relationship-ends/mediation

If you answer 'Yes' to question 8.1 the court will take no action at this stage. To formally start financial proceedings, you will also need to complete a separate application **Form A** or **Form A1** and pay another court fee.

You can find more guidance on financial orders and how to get help agreeing on any issues at www.gov.uk/money-property-when-relationship-ends/apply-for-a-financial-order

If you answer 'No' to question 8.1 you can still apply for a financial order in the future, but only **until you remarry or form** another **civil partnership**. This restriction does not apply to pension sharing or pension compensation sharing orders.

If you are unsure what to do here it is recommended you seek legal advice.

Please note that decisions regarding child maintenance are usually made by agreement or by the Child Maintenance Service and the court can only make these orders under certain circumstances.

Section 9 – Summary of what is being applied for (the prayer)

The sole applicant or the joint applicants apply for the following:

9.1 The application

That the

☐ marriage be dissolved

☐ civil partnership be dissolved

The sole applicant or applicant 1 wishes to apply for the following

9.2 Financial Order (if you ticked 'Yes' to the question at 8.1 and wish to make an application for a Financial Order)

That a financial order may be granted for:

☐ The sole applicant or applicant 1

☐ For the children

Applicant 2 wishes to apply for the following

9.3 Financial Order (if you ticked 'Yes' to the question at 8.1 and wish to make an application for a Financial Order)

That a financial order may be granted for:

☐ Applicant 2

☐ For the children

Section 10 – Statement of truth

10.1 Sole applicant or applicant 1

I understand that proceedings for contempt of court may be brought against anyone who makes, or causes to be made, a false statement in a document verified by a statement of truth without an honest belief in its truth.

☐ **I believe** that the facts stated in this form and any continuation sheets are true.

☐ **The applicant** believes that the facts stated in this form and any continuation sheets are true. **I am authorised** by the applicant to sign this statement.

Signature

☐ Applicant

☐ Applicant's legal representative (as defined by FPR 2.3(1))

Date

Day Month Year

Full name

Name of applicant's legal representative's firm

If signing on behalf of firm or company give position or office held

10.2 Applicant 2

I understand that proceedings for contempt of court may be brought against anyone who makes, or causes to be made, a false statement in a document verified by a statement of truth without an honest belief in its truth.

☐ **I believe** that the facts stated in this form and any continuation sheets are true.

☐ **The applicant** believes that the facts stated in this form and any continuation sheets are true. **I am authorised** by the applicant to sign this statement.

Signature

☐ Applicant

☐ Applicant's legal representative (as defined by FPR 2.3(1))

Date

Day Month Year

Full name

Name of applicant's legal representative's firm

If signing on behalf of firm or company give position or office held

Court fee

What you need to pay

the court fee is

☐

How to pay the court fee

Sole or applicant 1

☐ **I have not included payment because**

☐ I have applied for Help with Fees online and my reference number is

H	W	F						

☐ I am applying for Help with Fees, see attached form **EX160**

☐ Other – please explain why

Applicant 2

☐ **I have not included payment because**

☐ I have applied for Help with Fees online and my reference number is

H	W	F						

☐ I am applying for Help with Fees, see attached form **EX160**

☐ Other – please explain why

☐ **A debit or credit card payment**

☐ I will pay over the phone.

☐ please email me details on how to pay, my email address is

☐ I attach a **cheque or postal order,** made payable to 'HMCTS'

Court fee
You can find the current fee in leaflet EX50 Civil and Family Court Fees which can be downloaded from: https://hmctsformfinder.justice.gov.uk

If you cannot afford the court fee
You may not have to pay a fee, or you may get some money off it if you only have a small amount of savings and investments, receive certain benefits or are on a low income.

You can apply for help with court and tribunal fees online at www.gov.uk/help-with-court-fees or through the 'EX160 Apply for help with fees' form and 'EX160A – How to apply for help with fees' guidance.

If applying jointly, both applicant 1 and applicant 2 must qualify for HWF, or the full fee will be payable by one applicant only. You can decide how you wish to share the cost of the fee. Then you must agree who will make the payment to the court.

A debit or credit card payment. To pay the court fee over the phone, you should call the payment line **10 days after** you submit the application to court on 0300 303 0642 (Monday to Friday: 8am to 6pm, Saturday 8am to 2pm)

When returning your form, you must include:

- **One original or certified** copy of your marriage/civil partnership certificate or a similar document issued under the law in force in the country where the marriage or civil partnership registration took place (photocopies will not be accepted). If your certificate is not in English then a certified translation must also be provided. The court will keep the documents you send. If you want them back you will need to apply for their return.
- **The court fee**
  You can find the current fee in leaflet **EX50** Civil and Family Court Fees which can be downloaded from: https://www.gov.uk/government/collections/court-and-tribunal-forms

  If you cannot afford to pay a court fee, you may be eligible for a fee remission or a reduced fee. The form **EX160** Apply for help with fees and the **EX160A** guidance booklet gives you further information – https://www.gov.uk/get-help-with-court-fees

Please send your application and the items listed above to

HMCTS Divorce and Dissolution service
PO Box 13226
Harlow
CM20 9UG

Phone: 0300 303 0642
Monday to Friday: 8am to 6pm
Saturday 8am to 2pm

email: divorcecase@justice.gov.uk

Cheque payments only

If you are paying by cheque, remember to include it with your application and make it payable to 'HMCTS'.

You must send your completed application and cheque to:

Bury St Edmunds Regional Divorce Unit
Triton House
St Andrew's Street North
Bury St Edmunds
IP33 1TR

2 Order to HM Revenue and Customs to Disclose Address

In the High Court of Justice **No:**
Family Division
Sitting at [place]

THE CHILD ABDUCTION AND CUSTODY ACT 1985
COUNCIL REGULATION (EC) No. 2201/2003
THE SENIOR COURTS ACT 1981
THE CHILDREN ACT 1989
Delete or Adapt as appropriate

The Child(ren)	**AA (a boy/girl born on dd/mm/yyyy)**
	BB (a boy/girl born on dd/mm/yyyy)
	CC (a boy/girl born on dd/mm/yyyy)

After hearing *[name the advocate(s) who appeared]….*
After consideration of the documents lodged by the applicant
After reading the statements and hearing the witnesses specified in paragraph 6 of the Recitals below

DISCLOSURE ORDER MADE BY [NAME OF JUDGE] ON [DATE] SITTING IN PRIVATE

The Parties

1. The applicant is XX
   The respondent is YY
   Specify any additional respondents
   Specify if any adult party acts by a litigation friend
   Specify if the children or any of them act by a children's guardian

Recitals

2. This order was made at a hearing without notice to the respondent. The reason why the order was made without notice to the respondent was [*set out*]

3. The Judge read the following affidavits/witness statements [*set out*] and heard oral testimony from [*name*].

4. This order is made pursuant to the inherent jurisdiction of the High Court.

Undertakings to the court by the applicant's solicitor LL on behalf of himself and his partners in the firm KKK (*delete if information is to be disclosed to the Court)*

5. To use any information received by them as a consequence of this order solely for the purposes of (a) assisting in the location of the children named in this order, and (b) in the conduct of these proceedings.

6. Not to disclose any information received by them as a consequence of this order to [ ].

7. To keep any record of information received by them as a consequence of this order in a separate file marked confidential and with a note that its contents are subject to undertakings to the court and not to copy or provide that information to others save for the purposes (a) assisting in the location of the children named in this order, and (b) in the conduct of these proceedings.

8. To obtain a written undertaking in the terms of the first two undertakings given by him/her above from any person provided with information received by them as a consequence of this order.

IT IS ORDERED THAT:

9. *[If the proceedings have not already been commenced in or transferred to the High Court].* The application for this order is transferred to the High Court. Otherwise, the proceedings shall remain in the Family Court.

10. HM Revenue & Customs, by its officers, servants or agents shall disclose, in writing, as soon as practicable to *either* [an officer of this court namely *specify the officer giving address*] *or* [to the applicant's solicitor LL (whose direct telephone number is [ ] and whose email address is [ ])] all information in its knowledge or control concerning the whereabouts of AA, BB and CC.

11. HM Revenue & Customs shall not disclose the content of this order, or any action they take pursuant to it, to [ ].

12. HM Revenue & Customs may apply to vary or discharge this order upon 24 hours notice.

13. *[Where the disclosure is to be made to the court]* Any information received by the court under this order
(a) [will be confidential to the court and may not be disclosed to the parties without permission of the court] / [may be disclosed to the parties].
(b) may be used only for the purposes of locating AA, BB and CC.
Adapt as appropriate

14. Costs reserved

Dated

Notice pursuant to PD 33A para 1.4

You LL may be sent to prison for contempt of court if you break the promise that have been given to the court

Statements pursuant to PD 33A para 1.5

I understand the undertakings that I have given, and that if I break any of my promises to the court I may be sent to prison for contempt of court

………

LL

3 BIIa Annex 1 Certificate

Clear your text here

Certificate referred to in Article 39 of Council Regulation (EC) No. 2201/2003 of 27 November 2003[1] concerning judgments on parental responsibility

In the * [County Court] * [Principal Registry of the Family Division]	
Case number (Always quote this)	
Applicant's Solicitors reference	
Respondent's Solicitors reference	

1. Member State of origin ....

2. Court or authority issuing the certificate

 2.1. Name ....

 2.2. Address ....

 2.3. Tel./Fax/E-mail ....

3. Person(s) with rights of access

 3.1. Full name ....

 3.2. Address ....

 3.3. Date and place of birth (where available)..........

4. Holders of parental responsibility other than those mentioned under 3[2]

 4.1. 4.1.1. Full name ....

 4.1.2. Address ....

 ....

 4.1.3. Date and place of birth (where available)..........

 4.2. 4.2.1. Full name ....

 4.2.2. Address ....

 ....

 4.2.3. Date and place of birth (where available)..........

 4.3. 4.3.1. Full name ....

 4.3.2. Address ....

 ....

 4.3.3. Date and place of birth (where available)..........

(1) Council Regulation (EC) No 2201/2003 of 27 November 2003 concerning jurisdiction and the recognition and enforcement of judgments in matrimonial matters and the matters of parental responsibility, repealing Regulation (EC) No 1347/2000.

(2) In cases of joint custody, a person already mentioned under item 3 may also be mentioned under item 4.

C60 Certificate referred to in Article 39 of Council Regulation (EC) No. 2201/2003 concerning judgments on parental responsibility (03.05) Printed by Publications Branch

5. Court which delivered the judgment

5.1. Name of Court ....

5.2. Place of Court ....

6. Judgment

6.1. Date ....

6.2. Reference number ....

6.3. Was the judgment given in default of appearance?

6.3.1. No ☐

6.3.2. Yes [1] ☐

7. Children who are covered by the judgment [2]

7.1. Full name and date of birth ....

7.2. Full name and date of birth ....

7.3. Full name and date of birth ....

7.4. Full name and date of birth ....

8. Names of parties to whom legal aid has been granted ....

9. Attestation of enforceability and service

9.1. Is the judgment enforceable according to the law of the Member State of origin?

9.1.1. Yes ☐

9.1.2. No ☐

9.2. Has the judgment been served on the party against whom enforcement is sought?

9.2.1. Yes ☐

9.2.1.1. Full name of the party ....

9.2.1.2. Address ....

....

9.2.1.3. Date of service ....

9.2.2. No ☐

[1] Documents referred to in Article 37(2) must be attached.

[2] If more than four children are covered, use a second form.

10. Specific information on judgments on rights of access where 'exequator' is requested under Article 28. This possibility is foreseen in Article 40(2).

10.1. Practical arrangements for exercise of rights of access (to the extent stated in the judgment)

10.1.1. Date and time ....

10.1.1.1. Start ....

10.1.1.2. End ....

10.1.2. Place ....

10.1.3. Specific obligations on holders of parental responsibility ....

10.1.4. Specific obligations on the person with right of access...

10.1.5. Any restrictions attached to the exercise of rights of access ....

11. Specific information for judgments on the return of the child in cases where the 'exequator' procedure is requested under Article 28. This possibility is foreseen in Article 40(2).

11.1. The judgment entails the return of the child ....

11.2. Person to whom the child is to be returned (to the extent stated in the judgment) ....

....

11.2.1. Full name ....

11.2.2. Address ....

....

Done at .... date .... signature and/or stamp

4 Sample Notice of Abatement

No.

Between Applicant/Applicant 1

and Respondent/Applicant 2

Take notice that owing to the death of

the Applicant/Applicant 1/Respondent/Applicant 2 herein on the day of 20 this divorce application has now abated.

Dated

5 Parental Responsibility Agreement

Click here to reset form | Click here to print form

Parental Responsibility Agreement

Section 4(1)(b) Children Act 1989

Keep this form in a safe place

Date recorded at The Central Family Court:

Read the notes on the other side before you make this agreement.

This is a Parental Responsibility Agreement regarding

the Child *Full Name* ______

Gender ______ *Date of birth* ______ *Date of 18th birthday* ______

Between

the Mother *Name* ______

Address ______

and the Father *Name* ______

Address ______

We declare that we are the mother and father of the above child and we agree that the child's father shall have parental responsibility for the child (in addition to the mother having parental responsibility).

Signed **(Mother)** ______ Signed **(Father)** ______

Date ______ Date ______

Certificate of witness

The following evidence of identity was produced by the person signing above:	The following evidence of identity was produced by the person signing above:
Signed in the presence of:	Signed in the presence of:
Name of Witness	*Name of Witness*
Address	*Address*
Signature of Witness	*Signature of Witness*
[A Justice of the Peace] [Justices' Clerk] [An assistant to a justices' clerk] [An officer of the court authorised by the judge to administer oaths]	[A Justice of the Peace] [Justices' Clerk] [An assistant to a justices' clerk] [An Officer of the Court authorised by the judge to administer oaths]

C(PRA1) (08.14) Click here to print form

Notes about the Parental Responsibility Agreement

Read these notes before you make the agreement.

About the Parental Responsibility Agreement

The making of this agreement will affect the legal position of the mother and the father. You should both seek legal advice before you make the Agreement. You can obtain the name and address of a solicitor from the Children Panel (020 7242 1222)

or from
- a local office of the family court
- a Citizens Advice Bureau
- a Law Centre
- a local library.

You may be eligible for legal aid.

When you fill in the Agreement

Please use black ink (the Agreement will be copied). Put the name of one child only. If the father is to have parental responsibility for more than one child, fill in a separate form for each child. **Do not sign the Agreement.**

When you have filled in the Agreement

Take it to a local office of the family court, or The Central Family Court (the address is below).

A justice of the peace, a justices' clerk, an assistant to a justices' clerk, or a court official who is authorised by the judge to administer oaths, will witness your signature and he or she will sign the certificate of the witness. **A solicitor cannot witness your signature.**

To the mother: When you make the declaration you will have to prove that you are the child's mother so take to the court the child's full birth certificate.

You will also need evidence of your identity showing a photograph and signature (for example, a photocard, official pass or passport). **Please note that the child's birth certificate cannot be accepted as sufficient proof of your identity.**

To the father: You will need evidence of your identity showing a photograph and signature (for example, a photocard, official pass or passport).

When the Certificate has been signed and witnessed

Make 2 copies of the Agreement form. You do not need to copy these notes.

Take, or send, this form and the copies to **The Central Family Court, First Avenue House, 42-49 High Holborn, London, WC1V 6NP**.

The Court will record the Agreement and keep this form. The copies will be stamped and sent back to each parent at the address on the Agreement. The Agreement will not take effect until it has been received and recorded at The Central Family Court.

Ending the Agreement

Once a parental responsibility agreement has been made it can only end
- by an order of the court made on the application of any person who has parental responsibility for the child
- by an order of the court made on the application of the child with permission of the court
- when the child reaches the age of 18.

6 Step-Parent Parental Responsibility Agreement

Click here to reset form | Click here to print form

Step-Parent Parental Responsibility Agreement

Section 4A(1)(a) Children Act 1989

Keep this form in a safe place

Date recorded at The Central Family Court:

Read the notes on the other side before you make this agreement.

This is a Step-Parent Parental Responsibility Agreement regarding

the Child *Full Name*

Gender *Date of birth* *Date of 18th birthday*

Between

Parent A *Name*

Address

and

*the other parent (with parental responsibility) *Name*

Address

and

the step-parent *Name*

Address

We declare that we are the parents and step-parent of the above child and we agree that the above mentioned step-parent shall have parental responsibility for the child (in addition to those already having parental responsibility).

Signed **(Parent A)**	*Signed **(Other Parent)**	Signed **(Step-Parent)**
Date	Date	Date

Certificate of witness

The following evidence of identity was produced by the person signing above:	The following evidence of identity was produced by the person signing above:	The following evidence of identity was produced by the person signing above:
Signed in the presence of: *Name of Witness*	Signed in the presence of: *Name of Witness*	Signed in the presence of: *Name of Witness*
Address	*Address*	*Address*
Signature of Witness	*Signature of Witness*	*Signature of Witness*
[A Justice of the Peace] [Justices' Clerk] [An assistant to a justices' clerk] [An Officer of the Court authorised by the judge to administer oaths]	[A Justice of the Peace] [Justices' Clerk] [An assistant to a justices' clerk] [An Officer of the Court authorised by the judge to administer oaths]	[A Justice of the Peace] [Justices' Clerk] [An assistant to a justices' clerk] [An Officer of the Court authorised by the judge to administer oaths]

*If there is only one parent with parental responsibility, please delete this section.

C(PRA2) (08.14)

Click here to print form

Notes about the Step-Parent Parental Responsibility Form

Read these notes before you make the Agreement

About the Step-Parent Parental Responsibility Agreement

The making of this agreement will affect the legal position of the parent(s) and the step-parent. You should seek legal advice before you make the Agreement. You can obtain the name and address of a solicitor from the Children Panel (020 7242 1222) or from:

- a local office of the family court,
- a Citizens Advice Bureau,
- a Law Centre,
- a local library.

You may be eligible for legal aid.

When you fill in the Agreement

Please use black ink (the Agreement will be copied). Put the name of one child only. If the step-parent is to have parental responsibility for more than one child, fill in a separate form for each child. **Do not sign the Agreement.**

When you have filled in the Agreement

Take it to a local office of the family court, or The Central Family Court (the address is below).

A justice of the peace, a justices' clerk, an assistant to a justices' clerk, or a court official who is authorised by the judge to administer oaths, will witness your signature and he or she will sign the certificate of the witness. **A solicitor cannot witness your signature.**

To Parent A and the Other Parent with parental responsibility:

When you make the declaration you will have to prove that you have parental responsibility for the child. You should therefore take with you to the court one of the following documents:

- the child's full birth certificate and a marriage certificate or civil partnership certificate to show that the parents were married to each other or were in a civil partnership with each other at the time of birth or subsequently,
- a court order granting parental responsibility,
- a registered Parental Responsibility Agreement Form between the child's mother and father or other parent,
- if the birth was registered after the 1 December 2003, the child's full birth certificate showing that the parents jointly registered the child's birth.

You will also require evidence of your (both parents') identity showing a photograph and signature (for example, a photocard, official pass or passport) **(Please note that the child's birth certificate cannot be accepted as sufficient proof of your identity.)**

To the step-parent: When you make the declaration you will have to prove that you are married to, or the civil partner of, a parent of the child so take to the court your marriage certificate or certificate of civil partnership.

You will also need evidence of your identity showing a photograph and signature (for example, a photocard, official pass or passport).

When the Certificate has been signed and witnessed

Make sufficient copies of the Agreement Form for each person who has signed the form. You do not need to copy these notes.

Take, or send, the original form and the copies to: **The Central Family Court, First Avenue House, 42-49 High Holborn, London, WC1V 6NP.**

The Court will record the Agreement and retain the original form. The copies will be stamped with the seal of the court and sent back to every person with parental responsibility who has signed the Agreement Form and to the step-parent. The Agreement will not take effect until it has been received and recorded at The Central Family Court.

Ending the Agreement

Once a step-parent parental responsibility agreement has been made it can only end:

- by an order of the court made on the application of any person who has parental responsibility for the child,
- by an order of the court made on the application of the child with permission of the court,
- when the child reaches the age of 18.

7 Parental Responsibility Agreement (Acquisition of Parental Responsibility by Second Female Parent)

Click here to reset form | Click here to print form

Parental Responsibility Agreement

Section 4ZA Children Act 1989 (Acquisition of parental responsibility by second female parent)

Read the notes on the other side before you make this agreement.

Keep this form in a safe place

Date recorded at The Central Family Court:

This is a Parental Responsibility Agreement regarding

the Child *Full Name*

Gender *Date of birth* *Date of 18th birthday*

Between

the Mother *Name*

Address

and other parent *(Second female parent)* *Name*

Address

We declare that that we are the parents of the above child and we agree that the above mentioned parent shall have parental responsibility for the child (in addition to the mother having parental responsibility for the child).

Signed **(Mother)** Signed **(Other parent)**

Date Date

Certificate of witness

The following evidence of identity was produced by the person signing above: The following evidence of identity was produced by the person signing above:

Signed in the presence of: *Name of Witness* Signed in the presence of: *Name of Witness*

Address *Address*

Signature of Witness *Signature of Witness*

[A Justice of the Peace] [Justices' Clerk] [An assistant to a justices' clerk] [An officer of the court authorised by the judge to administer oaths]

[A Justice of the Peace] [Justices' Clerk] [An assistant to a justices' clerk] [An Officer of the Court authorised by the judge to administer oaths]

Notes about the Parental Responsibility Agreement

Read these notes before you make the agreement.

This form is for use by **a mother** and **a woman** who is a parent of the child by virtue of section 43 of the Human Fertilisation and Embryology Act 2008 (the 'other parent').

About the Parental Responsibility Agreement

The making of this agreement will affect the legal position of the mother and other parent. You should both seek legal advice before you make the Agreement. You can obtain the name and address of a solicitor from the Children Panel (020 7242 1222)

or from

- a local office of the family court
- a Citizens Advice Bureau
- a Law Centre
- a local library.

You may be eligible for legal aid.

When you fill in the Agreement

Please use black ink (the Agreement will be copied). Put the name of one child only. If the other parent is to have parental responsibility for more than one child, fill in a separate form for each child. **Do not sign the Agreement.**

When you have filled in the Agreement

Take it to a local office of the family ourt, or The Central Family Court (the address is below).

A justice of the peace, a justices' clerk, an assistant to a justices' clerk, or a court official who is authorised by the judge to administer oaths, will witness your signature and he or she will sign the certificate of the witness. **A solicitor cannot witness your signature.**

To the mother: When you make the declaration you will have to prove that you are the child's mother so take to the court the child's full birth certificate.

You will also need evidence of your identity showing a photograph and signature (for example, a photocard, official pass or passport). **Please note that the child's birth certificate cannot be accepted as sufficient proof of your identity.**

To the other parent: You will need evidence of your identity showing a photograph and signature (for example, a photocard, official pass or passport).

When the Certificate has been signed and witnessed

Make 2 copies of the Agreement form. You do not need to copy these notes, please send a copy of the child's full birth certificate with the two copies of the Agreement.

Take, or send, this form and the copies to **The Central Family Court, First Avenue House, 42-49 High Holborn, London, WC1V 6NP**.

The Court will record the Agreement and keep this form. The copies will be stamped and sent back to each parent at the address on the Agreement. The Agreement will not take effect until it has been received and recorded at The Central Family Court.

Ending the Agreement

Once a parental responsibility agreement has been made it can only end

- by an order of the court made on the application of any person who has parental responsibility for the child
- by an order of the court made on the application of the child with permission of the court
- When the child reaches the age of 18.

C(PRA3) (Notes) (08.14)

8 Pension Sharing Annex under section 24B of the Matrimonial Causes Act 1973/Paragraph 15 of Schedule 5 to the Civil Partnership Act 2004

Print form | Reset form

Pension Sharing Annex under [section 24B of the Matrimonial Causes Act 1973] [paragraph 15 of Schedule 5 to the Civil Partnership Act 2004]

In the Family Court sitting at	
*[Principal Registry of the Family Division]	
Case No. (Always quote this)	
Transferor's Solicitor's reference	
Transferee's Solicitor's reference	

Between ____________________ **(Petitioner)**

and ____________________ **(Respondent)**

Take Notice that:

On ____________ the court *(delete as appropriate)

- made a pension sharing order under Part IV of the Welfare Reform and Pensions Act 1999.
- [varied] [discharged] an order which included provision for pension sharing under Part IV of the Welfare Reform and Pensions Act 1999 dated D D / M M / Y Y Y Y .

This annex to the order provides the person responsible for the pension arrangement with the information required by virtue of rules of court:

A. Transferor's details

(i) The full name by which the Transferor is known:

(ii) All names by which the Transferor has been known:

(iii) The Transferor's date of birth: D D / M M / Y Y Y Y

(iv) The Transferor's address:

(v) The Transferor's National Insurance Number:

B. Transferee's Details

(i) The full name by which the Transferee is known:

(ii) All names by which the Transferee has been known:

(iii) The Transferee's date of birth: D D / M M / Y Y Y Y

(iv) The Transferee's address:

(v) The Transferee's National Insurance Number:

(vi) If the Transferee is also a member of the pension scheme from which the credit is derived, or a beneficiary of the same scheme because of survivor's benefits, the membership number:

C. Details of the Transferor's Pension Arrangement

(i) Name of the arrangement:

(ii) Name and address of the person responsible for the pension arrangement:

(iii) Reference Number:

(iv) If appropriate, such other details to enable the pension arrangement to be identified:

(v) The specified percentage of the member's CEV to be transferred: __ . __ %

(vi) Where State Pension is to be shared, if the transferor reaches his/her state pension age on or after 6 April 2016 and divorce or dissolution proceedings start on or after that date, then insert the shared weekly amount of State Pension which is payable. For the definition of the shared weekly amount of State Pension please see section 49A(3) of the Welfare Reform and Pensions Act 1999.

D. Pension Sharing Charges

It is directed that: (*delete as appropriate)

*The pension sharing charges be apportioned between the parties as follows:

or

*The pension sharing charges be paid in full by the Transferor.

E. Have you filed Form D81 (Statement of Information for a Consent Order for a financial remedy)? ☐ Yes ☐ No

If 'Yes' delete the text opposite.

The parties certify that:

(i) they have received the information required by Regulation 4 of the Pensions on Divorce etc (Provisions of Information) Regulations 2000; and

(ii) it appears from that information that there is power to make an order including provision under [section 24B of the Matrimonial Causes Act 1973] [paragraph 15 of Schedule 5 to the Civil Partnership Act 2004].

F. In cases where the Transferee has a choice of an internal or external transfer, if the Transferee has indicated a preference, indicate what this is. ☐ Internal transfer ☐ External transfer

G. In the case of external transfer only (recommended but optional information)

(i) The name of the qualifying arrangement which has agreed to accept the pension credit:

(ii) The address of the qualifying arrangement:

(iii) If known, the Transferee's membership or policy number in the qualifying arrangement and reference number of the new provider:

(iv) The name, or title, business address, phone and fax numbers and email address of the person who may be contacted in respect of the discharge of liability for the pension credit on behalf of the Transferee:
(This may be an Independent Financial Advisor, for example, if one is advising the Transferee or the new pension scheme itself.)

(v) Please attach a copy of the letter from the qualifying arrangement indicating its willingness to accept the pension credit ☐

Please complete boxes H to J where applicable

H. Where the credit is derived from an occupational scheme which is being wound up, has the Transferee indicated whether he wishes to transfer his pension credit rights to a qualifying arrangement? ☐ Yes ☐ No

I.	**Where the pension arrangement has requested details of the Transferor's health, has that information been provided?**	☐ **Yes**	☐ **No**
J.	**Where the pension arrangement has requested further information, has that information been provided?**	☐ **Yes**	☐ **No**

Note: Until the information requested in A, B, (and as far as applicable G, H, I and J) is provided the pension sharing order cannot be implemented although it may be made. Even if all the information requested has been provided, further information may be required before implementation can begin. If so, reasons why implementation cannot begin should be sent by the pension arrangement to the Transferor and Transferee within 21 days of receipt of the pension sharing order and this annex.

THIS ORDER TAKES EFFECT FROM the later of

a. the date on which the Decree Absolute of Divorce or Nullity of marriage is granted, or the Final Order of Dissolution or Nullity of civil partnership is made;

b. 28 days from the date of this order or, where the court has specified a period for filing an appeal notice, 7 days after the end of that period;

c. where an appeal has been lodged, the effective date of the order determining that appeal.

To the person responsible for the pension arrangement:

*(delete as appropriate)

*1. Take notice that you must discharge your liability within the period of 4 months beginning with the later of:
- the day on which this order takes effect; or
- the first day on which you are in receipt of –

a. the pension sharing order including this annex (and where appropriate any attachments);

b. in a matrimonial case, a copy of the decree absolute of divorce or nullity of marriage;

c. in a civil partnership case, a copy of the final order of dissolution or order of nullity of civil partnership;

d. the information specified in paragraphs A, B and C of this annex and, where applicable, paragraphs G to J of this annex; and

e. payment of all outstanding charges requested by the pension scheme.

*2. The court directs that the implementation period for discharging your liability should be determined by regulations made under section 34(4) or 41(2)(a) of the Welfare Reform and Pensions Act 1999, in that:

9 Pension Attachment Annex under Section 25B or 25C of the Matrimonial Causes Act 1973/Paragraph 25 or 26 of Schedule 5 to the Civil Partnership Act 2004

Pension Attachment Annex under [section 25B or 25C of the Matrimonial Causes Act 1973] [paragraph 25 or 26 of Schedule 5 to the Civil Partnership Act 2004]

In the Family Court sitting at	
	***[Principal Registry of the Family Division]**
Case No. (Always quote this)	
Applicant's Solicitor's reference	
Respondent's Solicitor's reference	

Between __________ **(Petitioner)**

and __________ **(Respondent)**

Take Notice that:

On __________ the court ***(delete as appropriate)**

- made an order including provision under [section [25B][25C]* of the Matrimonial Causes Act 1973]* [paragraph [25][26]* or Schedule 5 to the Civil Partnership Act 2004]*.
- [varied] [discharged] an order which included provision under [section [25B][25C]* of the Matrimonial Causes Act 1973] [paragraph [25][26] of Schedule 5 to the Civil Partnership Act 2004]* and dated D D / M M / Y Y Y Y

This annex to the order provides the person responsible for the pension arrangement with the information required by virtue of rules of court:

1. Name of the party with the pension rights:
2. Name of the other party:
3. The National Insurance Number of the party with pension rights:
4. Details of the Pension Arrangement:
   (i) Name and address of the person responsible for the pension arrangement:

   (ii) Policy Reference Number:

   (iii) if appropriate, such other details to enable the pension arrangement to be identified:

5A. **(i) To be completed where a Periodical Payments Order is made under s.25B of the Matrimonial Causes Act 1973.**

The specified percentage of any payment due to the party with the pension rights that is to be paid for the benefit of the other party: __ . __ %

(ii) To be completed where the court orders that the party with pension rights commutes a percentage of his pension to a tax free lump sum on retirement under s.25B of the Matrimonial Causes Act 1973.

(a) the specified percentage of the maximum lump sum available that is to be commuted: __ . __ %

(b) the specified percentage of the commuted sum which is to be paid to the spouse or the former spouse of the party with pension rights: __ . __ %

(iii) To be completed where the court orders, under s.25C of the Matrimonial Causes Act 1973, that all or part of a lump sum payable to the party with pension rights in respect of his death be paid to the other party.

(a) the percentage of the lump sum to be paid by the person responsible for the pension arrangement to the other party: __ . __ %

(b) the percentage of the lump sum payable (in accordance with a nomination by the party with pension rights) to the other party: __ . __ %

(c) the percentage of the lump sum to be paid by the person responsible for the pension arrangement for the benefit of the other party: __ . __ %

5B. **(i) To be completed where a Periodical Payments Order is made under paragraph 25 of Schedule 5 to the Civil Partnership Act 2004.**

The specified percentage of any payment due to the civil partner with the pension rights that is to be paid for the benefit of the other civil partner: __ . __ %

(ii) To be completed where the court orders that the civil partner with pension rights commutes a percentage of his pension to a tax free lump sum on retirement under paragraph 25 of Schedule 5 to the Civil Partnership Act 2004.

(a) the specified percentage of the maximum lump sum available that is to be commuted: __ . __ %

(b) the specified percentage of the commuted sum which is to be paid to the civil partner or the former civil partner of the civil partner with pension rights: __ . __ %

(iii) To be completed where the court orders, under paragraph 26 of Schedule 5 to the Civil Partnership Act 2004, that all or part of a lump sum payable to the civil partner with pension rights in respect of his death be paid to the other civil partner.

(a) the percentage of the lump sum to be paid by the person responsible for the pension arrangement to the other civil partner: __ . __ %

(b) the percentage of the lump sum payable (in accordance with a nomination by the civil partner with pension rights) to the other civil partner: __ . __ %

(c) the percentage of the lump sum to be paid by the person responsible for the pension arrangement for the benefit of the other civil partner: __ . __ %

To the person responsible for the pension arrangement:
*(delete if this information has already been provided to the person responsible for the pension arrangement)

1. *You are required to serve any notice under the Divorce etc. (Pensions) Regulations 2000 or the Dissolution etc. (Pensions) Regulations 2005 on the other party at the following address:

2. *You are required to make any payments due under the pension arrangement to the other party at the following address:

3. *If the address at 2. above is that of a bank, building society or the Department of National Savings the following details will enable you to make payment into the account of the other party (e.g. Account Name, Number, Bank/Building Society/etc. Sort code):

Note: Where the order to which this annex applies was made by consent the following section should also be completed.

The court also confirms: *(delete as appropriate)

- *That notice has been served on the person responsible for the pension arrangement and that no objection has been received.
- *That notice has been served on the person responsible for the pension arrangement and that the court has considered any objection received.

10 Family Mediation Information and Assessment Form

Print form Reset form

Family Mediation Information and Assessment Meeting (MIAM)

To be completed by the court
The Family Court sitting at
Case reference

Before completing this form please read the information notes at the end of the form. This form is only to be used when making an application to the court on form C1 or C2 for one of the orders shown below.

Before completing this form please also read the leaflet 'CB1 – Making an application – Children and the Family Courts' and the leaflet CB7 - Guide for separated parents: children and the family courts. These leaflets are available from your local court or online at hmctsformfinder.justice.gov.uk

Full name of applicant(s)

Full name of respondent(s)

If you are making an application on form C1 or C2 for any of the following types of Children Act 1989 order, you must first attend a Mediation, Information and Assessment Meeting (MIAM):

- A parental responsibility order (sections 4(1)(c), 4ZA(1)(c) or 4A(1)(b) of the Children Act 1989) or an order terminating parental responsibility (sections 4(2A), 4ZA(5) or 4A(3) of that Act).
- An order appointing a child's guardian (section 5(1) of the Children Act 1989) or an order terminating the appointment (section 6(7) of that Act).
- An order giving permission to change a child's surname or remove a child from the United Kingdom (sections 13(1) or 14C of the Children Act 1989).
- A special guardianship order or an order varying or discharging such an order (section 14D of the Children Act 1989).

This completed FM1 form must be sent to the family court, together with the relevant completed application form C1 or C2. This FM1 form is not an application form for a court order.

1. Requirement to attend a Mediation, Information and Assessment Meeting (MIAM)

Before making an application for a

- A parental responsibility order (sections 4(1)(c), 4ZA(1)(c) or 4A(1)(b) of the Children Act 1989) or an order terminating parental responsibility (sections 4(2A), 4ZA(5) or 4A(3) of that Act).
- An order appointing a child's guardian (section 5(1) of the Children Act 1989) or an order terminating the appointment (section 6(7) of that Act).
- An order giving permission to change a child's surname or remove a child from the United Kingdom (sections 13(1) or 14C of the Children Act 1989).
- A special guardianship order or an order varying or discharging such an order (section 14D of the Children Act 1989).

you must first attend a Mediation, Information and Assessment Meeting (MIAM). At the MIAM an authorised family mediator will consider with you (and the other party if present) whether family mediation, or another form of non-court dispute resolution, would be a more appropriate alternative to court. The mediator will also be able to sign post you to other help and support services.

You **must** have attended a MIAM before making this application **unless** the requirement to attend a MIAM does not apply because the Children Act 1989 order you are applying for:

- is for a consent order; **or**
- concerns a child who is the subject of separate ongoing emergency proceedings, care proceedings or supervision proceedings (or is already the subject of an emergency, care or supervision order); **or**
- you are exempt from the requirement to attend a MIAM. (Some exemptions you can claim yourself, others must be certified by an authorised family mediator).

In special cicumstances such as where domestic violence is involved you may not need to attend a MIAM. However, you will be asked to provide the judge with evidence (such as a police report to prove domestic violence has taken place) and should bring it to the first hearing.

All applicants must complete section 1 and sign section 3 of this form.

In addition, you must tick one of the boxes below and ensure that you, your solicitor or a family mediator completes (and where indicated signs) the relevant section(s) of this form as shown.

1a. Are there previous or onging proceedings for child(ren) for an emergency protection, care or supervision order?	☐ Yes	☐ No	**If Yes,** to provide additional details on form C1 or C2 where shown. **Sections 2 or 4 of the FM1 form should be left blank.** If No, please **answer question 1b.**
1b. Are you claiming exemption from the requirement to attend a MIAM?	☐ Yes	☐ No	**If Yes, complete section 2.** **If No**, please **answer question 1c.**
1c. Has a family mediator informed you that a mediator's exemption applies, and you do not need to attend a MIAM?	☐ Yes	☐ No	**If Yes,** you must ensure that the **family mediator completes and signs section 4a.** **If No**, please **answer question 1d.**
1d. Have you attended a MIAM?	☐ Yes	☐ No	**If Yes,** you must ensure that **the family mediator completes and signs section 4b.** **If No, you cannot make the application on form C1 or C2.**

2. Applicant claims exemption(s) from attendance at a Mediation, Information and Assessment Meeting (MIAM)

(To be completed by the person intending to make a court application or their solicitor)

The applicant has not attended a MIAM because the following MIAM exemption(s) applies:

- ☐ Domestic violence (you must complete **section 2a**)
- ☐ Child protection concerns (you must complete **section 2b**)
- ☐ Urgency (you must complete **section 2c**)
- ☐ Previous MIAM attendance or previous MIAM exemption (you must complete **section 2d**)
- ☐ Other (you must complete **section 2e**)

Now complete the relevant section 2a, b, c, d or e by ticking the appropriate box(s)

Further details of MIAM exemption(s) claimed by the applicant

If you have claimed a MIAM exemption above you must also tick the relevant box(s), as shown below to confirm that you have the necessary evidence to support your ground(s) for exemption and should bring it to the first hearing. Where you are asked to provide additional details you must do so.

Section 2a - Domestic violence evidence

The applicant confirms that there is evidence of domestic violence, as specified below:

- ☐ evidence that a prospective party has been arrested for a relevant domestic violence offence;
- ☐ evidence of a relevant police caution for a domestic violence offence;
- ☐ evidence of relevant criminal proceedings for a domestic violence offence which have not concluded;
- ☐ evidence of a relevant conviction for a domestic violence offence;
- ☐ a court order binding a prospective party over in connection with a domestic violence offence;
- ☐ a domestic violence protection notice issued under section 24 of the Crime and Security Act 2010 against a prospective party;
- ☐ a relevant protective injunction;
- ☐ an undertaking given in England and Wales under section 46 or 63E of the Family Law Act 1996 (or given in Scotland or Northern Ireland in place of a protective injunction) by a prospective party, provided that a cross-undertaking relating to domestic violence was not given by another prospective party;
- ☐ a copy of a finding of fact, made in proceedings in the United Kingdom, that there has been domestic violence by a prospective party;
- ☐ an expert report produced as evidence in proceedings in the United Kingdom for the benefit of a court or tribunal confirming that a person with whom a prospective party is or was in a family relationship, was assessed as being, or at risk of being, a victim of domestic violence by that prospective party;
- ☐ a letter or report from an appropriate health professional confirming that-

  (i) that professional, or another appropriate health professional, has examined a prospective party in person; and

Section 2a - Domestic violence evidence - **continued**

(ii) in the reasonable professional judgment of the author or the examining appropriate health professional, that prospective party has, or has had, injuries or a condition consistent with being a victim of domestic violence;

☐ a letter or report from-

(i) the appropriate health professional who made the referral described below;

(ii) an appropriate health professional who has access to the medical records of the prospective party referred to below; or

(iii) the person to whom the referral described below was made;

confirming that there was a referral by an appropriate health professional of a prospective party to a person who provides specialist support or assistance for victims of, or those at risk of, domestic violence;

☐ a letter from any person who is a member of a multi-agency risk assessment conference (or other suitable local safeguarding forum) confirming that a prospective party, or a person with whom that prospective party is in a family relationship, is or has been at risk of harm from domestic violence by another prospective party;

☐ a letter from an independent domestic violence advisor confirming that they are providing support to a prospective party;

☐ a letter from an independent sexual violence advisor confirming that they are providing support to a prospective party relating to sexual violence by another prospective party;

☐ a letter from an officer employed by a local authority or housing association (or their equivalent in Scotland or Northern Ireland) for the purpose of supporting tenants containing-

(i) a statement to the effect that, in their reasonable professional judgment, a person with whom a prospective party is or has been in a family relationship is, or is at risk of being, a victim of domestic violence by that prospective party;

(ii) a description of the specific matters relied upon to support that judgment; and

(iii) a description of the support they provided to the victim of domestic violence or the person at risk of domestic violence by that prospective party;

☐ a letter which-

(i) is from an organisation providing domestic violence support services, or a registered charity, which letter confirms that it-

(a) is situated in England and Wales,

(b) has been operating for an uninterrupted period of six months or more; and

(c) provided a prospective party with support in relation to that person's needs as a victim, or a person at risk, of domestic violence; and

(ii) contains-

(a) a statement to the effect that, in the reasonable professional judgment of the author of the letter, the prospective party is, or is at risk of being, a victim of domestic violence;

(b) a description of the specific matters relied upon to support that judgment;

(c) a description of the support provided to the prospective party; and

Section 2a - Domestic violence evidence - **continued**	(d) a statement of the reasons why the prospective party needed that support;
	☐ a letter or report from an organisation providing domestic violence support services in the United Kingdom confirming- (i) that a person with whom a prospective party is or was in a family relationship was refused admission to a refuge; (ii) the date on which they were refused admission to the refuge; and (iii) they sought admission to the refuge because of allegations of domestic violence by the prospective party referred to in paragraph (i);
	☐ a letter from a public authority confirming that a person with whom a prospective party is or was in a family relationship, was assessed as being, or at risk of being, a victim of domestic violence by that prospective party (or a copy of that assessment);
	☐ a letter from the Secretary of State for the Home Department confirming that a prospective party has been granted leave to remain in the United Kingdom under paragraph 289B of the Rules made by the Home Secretary under section 3(2) of the Immigration Act 1971, which can be found at https://www.gov.uk/guidance/immigration-rules/immigration-rules-index;
	☐ evidence which demonstrates that a prospective party has been, or is at risk of being, the victim of domestic violence by another prospective party in the form of abuse which relates to financial matters.
Section 2b – Child protection concerns	**The applicant confirms that a child would be the subject of the application and that child or another child of the family who is living with that child is currently—**
	☐ the subject of enquiries by a local authority under section 47 of the Children Act 1989 Act; or
	☐ the subject of a child protection plan put in place by a local authority.
Section 2c – Urgency	**The applicant confirms that the application must be made urgently because:**
	☐ there is risk to the life, liberty or physical safety of the prospective applicant or his or her family or his or her home; or
	☐ any delay caused by attending a MIAM would cause— ☐ a risk of harm to a child; or ☐ a risk of unlawful removal of a child from the United Kingdom, or a risk of unlawful retention of a child who is currently outside England and Wales; or ☐ a significant risk of a miscarriage of justice; or ☐ unreasonable hardship to the prospective applicant; or ☐ irretrievable problems in dealing with the dispute (including the irretrievable loss of significant evidence); or
	☐ there is a significant risk that in the period necessary to schedule and attend a MIAM, proceedings relating to the dispute will be brought in another state in which a valid claim to jurisdiction may exist, such that a court in that other State would be seized of the dispute before a court in England and Wales.

Section 2d – Previous MIAM attendance or MIAM exemption

The applicant confirms that one of the following applies:

☐ in the 4 months prior to making the application, the person attended a MIAM or participated in another form of non-court dispute resolution relating to the same or substantially the same dispute; or

☐ at the time of making the application, the person is participating in another form of non-court dispute resolution relating to the same or substantially the same dispute; or

☐ in the 4 months prior to making the application, the person filed a relevant family application confirming that a MIAM exemption applied and that application related to the same or substantially the same dispute; or

☐ the application would be made in existing proceedings which are continuing and the prospective applicant attended a MIAM before initiating those proceedings; or

☐ the application would be made in existing proceedings which are continuing and a MIAM exemption applied to the application for those proceedings.

Section 2e – Other exemptions

The applicant confirms that one of the following other grounds for exemption applies:

☐ the prospective applicant does not have sufficient contact details for any of the prospective respondents to enable a family mediator to contact any of the prospective respondents for the purpose of scheduling the MIAM.

☐ the application would be made without notice (Paragraph 5.1 of Practice Direction 18A sets out the circumstances in which applications may be made without notice.)

☐ (i) the prospective applicant is or all of the prospective respondents are subject to a disability or other inability that would prevent attendance at a MIAM unless appropriate facilities can be offered by an authorised mediator; (ii) the prospective applicant has contacted as many authorised family mediators as have an office within fifteen miles of his or her home (or three of them if there are three or more), and all have stated that they are unable to provide such facilities; and (iii) the names, postal addresses and telephone numbers or e-mail addresses for such authorised family mediators, and the dates of contact, can be provided to the court if requested.

☐ the prospective applicant or all of the prospective respondents cannot attend a MIAM because he or she is, or they are, as the case may be (i) in prison or any other institution in which he or she is or they are required to be detained; (ii) subject to conditions of bail that prevent contact with the other person; or (iii) subject to a licence with a prohibited contact requirement in relation to the other person.

☐ the prospective applicant or all of the prospective respondents are not habitually resident in England and Wales.

☐ a child is one of the prospective parties by virtue of Rule 12.3(1).

☐ (i) the prospective applicant has contacted as many authorised family mediators as have an office within fifteen miles of his or her home (or three of them if there are three or more), and all of them have stated that they are not available to conduct a MIAM within fifteen business days of the date of contact; and (ii) the names, postal addresses and telephone numbers or e-mail addresses for such authorised family mediators, and the dates of contact, can be provided to the court if requested.

☐ there is no authorised family mediator with an office within fifteen miles of the prospective applicant's home.

3. Signature of applicant/applicant's solicitor

*delete as appropriate *I am duly authorised by the applicant to sign this form.

Print full name

Name of applicant solicitor's firm

Signed

Dated D D / M M / Y Y Y Y

(Applicant) (Applicant's solicitor)

Position or office held (If signing on behalf of firm or company)

4. Mediator certifies that the prospective applicant is exempt from attendance at Mediation Information and Assessment Meeting (MIAM) or confirms MIAM attendance

(To be completed and signed by the authorised family mediator)
(tick the boxes that apply)

4a. The following MIAM exemption(s) applies:

☐ An authorised family mediator confirms that he or she is satisfied that -

☐ (a) mediation is not suitable as a means of resolving the dispute because none of the respondents is willing to attend a MIAM; or

☐ (b) mediation is not suitable as a means of resolving the dispute because all of the respondents failed without good reason to attend a MIAM appointment; or

☐ (c) mediation is otherwise not suitable as a means of resolving the dispute.

4b. The prospective applicant attended a MIAM:

☐ The prospective applicant only attended a MIAM.

☐ The prospective applicant and respondent party(s) attended the MIAM together.

☐ The prospective applicant and respondent(s) have each attended a separate MIAM.

☐ The prospective respondent party(s) has/have made or is/are making arrangements to attend a separate MIAM.

Mediation or other form of Dispute Resolution is not proceeding because:

☐ The applicant has attended a MIAM alone and

- the applicant does not wish to start or continue mediation; or
- the mediator has determined that mediation is unsuitable; or
- the respondent did not wish to attend a MIAM

☐ Both the applicant and respondent have attended a MIAM (separately or together) and

- the applicant does not wish to start or continue mediation; or
- the respondent does not wish to start or continue mediation; or
- the mediator has determined that mediation is unsuitable

☐ Mediation has started, but has:

- broken down; or
- concluded with some or all issues unresolved

Signed	

Authorised Family Mediator
(a family mediator who is authorised to undertake MIAMs)

FMC Registration no.	
Family Mediation Service name	
Sole trader name	
Address	

Dated D D / M M / Y Y Y Y

General information for completing this form

1. You need to complete this form and send it to the court with a completed application form C1 or C2 if you want to ask the court to make an (or change an existing) order about a child(ren) and your application is for:
   - A parental responsibility order (sections 4(1)(c), 4ZA(1)(c) or 4A(1)(b) of the Children Act 1989) or an order terminating parental responsibility (sections 4(2A), 4ZA(5) or 4A(3) of that Act).
   - An order appointing a child's guardian (section 5(1) of the Children Act 1989) or an order terminating the appointment (section 6(7) of that Act).
   - An order giving permission to change a child's surname or remove a child from the United Kingdom (sections 13(1) or 14C of the Children Act 1989).
   - A special guardianship order or an order varying or discharging such an order (section 14D of the Children Act 1989).

Requirement to attend a Mediation, Information and Assessment Meeting

2. It is now a legal requirement that, unless an exemption applies, a person who wishes to apply to court for one or more of the orders listed at paragraph 1 of these notes must first attend a Mediation, Information and Assessment Meeting (a MIAM). At the stage before proceedings the other party (the respondent) is expected to attend either the same MIAM or a separate MIAM.
3. At the MIAM, a trained family mediator will give you (the applicant) and the other person if present (the respondent) information about family mediation and other types of non-court dispute resolution. They will consider with you whether non-court dispute resolution would be an appropriate way to resolve the dispute. It is then for the applicant and respondent to decide whether or not to do so.
4. The requirement for the applicant to attend a MIAM does not apply if a Children Act 1989 order is being applied for and:
   - the other person is in agreement about what you are asking the court to order (the order is a "consent order"); or
   - there is an ongoing case about the child(ren) who would be the subject of the new Children Act 1989 application and that case concerns an emergency protection order, a supervision order or a care order, or if one of those orders has previously been made.
5. You must tick the relevant box in Section 1 of this form so that the court knows whether the MIAM requirement applies, whether an exemption applies (and why) or whether you have attended a MIAM.

MIAM exemptions and MIAM attendance

6. As the applicant you are expected to have contacted an authorised family mediator in order to make arrangements to attend a MIAM unless :
   - the MIAM requirement does not apply for one of the reasons explained at paragraph 4 of these notes, or
   - you are claiming a MIAM exemption, or a family mediator certifies that a mediator's exemption applies.
7. You can find an authorised family mediator by using the 'Find your local mediator' search facility available at: www.familymediationcouncil.org.uk
8. You should give the mediator the contact details of the other person so that the family mediator can contact them to check their willingness to attend a MIAM. If the other persons (or none of the other persons if there is more than one respondent) is or are unwilling to attend a MIAM this is a ground for the family mediator to exempt you from attending a MIAM.
9. If you or your solicitor believe that you have grounds for claiming exemption from MIAM attendance you or your solicitor must tick the relevant box in Section 1 of this form and complete Section 2.
10. If a family mediator wishes to certify that a mediator's exemption applies, so that you do not need to attend a MIAM, you must ask the family mediator to complete Section 4a of this form and sign it where shown.
11. If you have attended a MIAM you must ask the family mediator who conducted the MIAM to complete Section 4b of this form and sign it where shown.
12. If you claim a MIAM exemption and make an application to the court, the court will inquire into the grounds for exemption. The court may ask you to produce written evidence (see Section 2 of this form for details against each exemption shown).
13. If the court determines that the exemption was not validly claimed it may direct you, or you and the other party, to attend a MIAM and, if the case has already progressed to the first hearing, may adjourn the case to enable you to make arrangements to attend a MIAM.

14. The detailed procedure relating to the MIAM requirement and MIAM exemptions and attendance is set out in Part 3 of the Family Procedure Rules and in supporting Practice Direction 3A (judicial guidance). These are available online at: www.justice.gov.uk/courts/procedure-rules/family/practice_directions/pd_part_03a

Paying for MIAM attendance or for family mediation

15. Legal aid is available for MIAMs and for family mediation. If you are eligible for legal aid you could receive both the MIAM and mediation sessions free of charge, as well as some advice from a solicitor to support you in the mediation process.
16. If you, or the prospective respondent, is eligible for Legal Aid then the total cost of MIAM attendance can be met by the Legal Aid Agency, whether you and the prospective respondent attend the same MIAM or separate MIAMs.
17. If neither you nor the respective respondent is eligible for Legal Aid then the mediator will agree with you how the cost of MIAM attendance is to be met.
18. See paragraph 28 below on how to find out whether you are eligible for Legal Aid.

Safety and MIAM attendance

19. Please note: the family mediator will discuss with you and with the other person whether you wish to attend the MIAM separately or together. Family mediators have a responsibility to ensure the safety and security of all concerned and will always check with each of you that attending together is your individual choice and is safe.

Information about mediation

20. If suitable, mediation can be a better way of resolving issues about arrangements for children when you and your partner separate or divorce. Mediation can be less expensive than going to court and much less stressful for all the family. It can also help you as parents to focus on your child(ren)'s needs in making decisions about them.
21. Family Mediation is an impartial process that involves an independent third person who assists both parties involved in a family dispute to reach a resolution. Family mediation can be used to settle any or all of the following issues:
    - Arrangements for children
    - Financial arrangements and dividing up property
    - Any combination of these
    - Any other disputes to do with separation and divorce.
22. Family Mediation is not just for divorcing or separating couples – it is a means for resolving a range of family disputes, whether they arise from divorce or the separation of cohabiting parents. Family Mediation could also help resolve issues with wider family members such as grandparents.
23. The family mediator helps the process of negotiation between the parties to agree their own arrangements by way of a Memorandum of Understanding. You can ask a solicitor, if you have one, to check the Memorandum of Understanding.
24. If both parties agree, you can ask the court to endorse what you have agreed by issuing a consent order. The mediator will help you to decide whether your case is complicated and does in fact need the court to consider your situation and make an order. The mediator should also tell you about other local services and options for resolving your dispute.
25. A statutory Mediation Information and Assessment Meeting (MIAM) is reserved for "authorised mediators" under the Family Procedure Rules. "Authorised family mediator" means a person identified by the Family Mediation Council as qualified to conduct a MIAM. "Qualified to conduct a MIAM" is interpreted as holding current Family Mediation Council accreditation (FMCA). FMCA mediators are issued with a unique FMC registration number. Authorised mediators are requested to enter this number in the box provided.

Further information and sources of help

26. General information about family mediation is available from the Family Mediation Council website at: www.familymediationcouncil.org.uk
27. The family mediator who undertakes the MIAM for you must be a member of a national mediation organisation which adheres to the Family Mediation Council's Code of Conduct and the mediator must be authorised to conduct MIAMs. The service finder will help you find such a local mediator.
28. You can find out more about legal aid for family matters, including whether you may eligible for legal aid, on the Legal Aid Information Service on the Gov.UK site at: www.gov.uk/check-legal-aid or you can telephone the Civil Legal Advice direct helpline 0345 345 4345.
29. For general advice on separation services and options for resolving disputes: www.sortingoutseparation.org.uk
30. For general advice about sorting out arrangements for children, the use of post-separation mediation, and/or going to court: www.advicenow.org.uk; www.advicenow.org.uk/guides/survival-guide-sorting-out-arrangements-your-children

31. For general advice about sorting out arrangements for children: www.theparentconnection.org.uk/
32. For advice about Contact Centres, which are neutral places where children of separated families can enjoy contact with their non-resident parents and sometimes other family members, in a comfortable and safe environment; and information about where they are: www.naccc.org.uk
33. For help with taking a case to court without a solicitor, the Personal Support Unit: www.thepsu.org/
34. For guidance on representing yourself at court, including a list of commonly used terms that you may come across: http://www.barcouncil.org.uk/using-a-barrister/representing-yourself-in-court/
35. For advice about finding and using a family law solicitor see: Law Society www.lawsociety.org.uk, and Resolution (family law solicitors): www.resolution.org.uk
36. For advice about finding using a family law barrister: see http://www.barcouncil.org.uk/using-a-barrister/find-a-barrister/ and for arrangements for using a barrister directly see http://www.barcouncil.org.uk/using-a-barrister/how-to-instruct-a-barrister/
37. Judicial guidance that sets out the approach of the courts to deciding child arrangements is available online at: www.justice.gov.uk/courts/procedure-rules/family/practice_directions/pd_part_12b

Online videos

38. There are several videos explain more about the mediation process, making your application, what will happen in court and will help you prepare for the hearing. To watch the videos visit www.bit.ly/guides_for_separating_parents

APPENDIX B

BLOOD AND DNA TESTS

(1) Scientific tests – direction form (BD1)

(2) Blood Tests (Evidence of Paternity) Regulations 1971, SI 1971/1861

(3) Report by Tester (BD2)

(4) Sample Clause in an Order for blood or DNA tests

(5) List of laboratories approved by the Ministry of Justice to test bodily samples in cases of disputed parentage

1 Scientific tests – direction form (BD1)

FORM BD1

Direction form

Family Law Reform Act 1969

....

V

....

Reference No of direction .. ..

Full name and date of birth of person to be tested to whom this form relates.

....

(Insert title of proceedings.)

PART I

Notification of direction

The ....*(name and address of court)*

on .... day of .... 20..... directed that scientific tests be carried out in respect of the persons whose names are set out below for the purpose of ascertaining the parentage of .... *(name of person whose parentage is in dispute)*

and that bodily samples be obtained from the persons named below on or before the .... day of .... 20....

The name of the person appearing to the court to have the care and control of the person to whom this form relates who is under 16/a protected party*, is ....

....(Signed)

....(Print)

Proper Officer of the Court.

Name	Address	Age

**(Delete as appropriate.)*

PART II

Request to sampler to obtain sample

To ....*(name and address of sampler).* You are hereby requested to obtain a bodily sample from ....
(name of person to whom form relates).

The sample is to be obtained notwithstanding the refusal to consent of the person with care and control of ....*(name of person to whom form relates). (Delete if not applicable)*

You are further requested to send the sample obtained to ....
....
(name and address of accredited body) (Delete if sampler is also tester)

Other samples will be obtained as follows:--

Name of person from whom sample will be obtained ....
Name, address and telephone number of sampler
....
....

....(Signed)
....(Print)

(To be completed where all the samples from the parties named in Part I are not to be obtained by the same sampler.)

Being unable to comply with the request set out above, I have nominated ....*(name and address of nominee)* to obtain the sample.

....(Signed)]
....(Print)

(For use where sampler named above nominates another sampler.)

PART III

Photograph

Below, or attached to this form, is a photograph of the person to whom this form relates.

PART IV

(To be completed by sampler where sample is of blood)

I have questioned *(Insert name of person to whom this form relates or, in the case of a person under 16 or a protected party, person accompanying that person.)* ……………………………………………………………………………………

……………………………………………………………………………………

and it appears that he/she/the party to whom this form relates --

has/has not* been transfused with blood in the last three months;*

has not been injected with a blood product or plasma substitute;* has been injected with a blood product/ blood plasma* on or about ……………… ………..and that the value of any tests will thereby be/not be affected.*

……………………………….(Signed)

……………………………….(Print)

(Sampler)

**(Delete as appropriate.)*

PART V

Declaration

(To be completed where the person to whom the form relates has attained the age of sixteen years and is not a protected party.)

I ………………………………………………………………………………..*(insert full name and address of person to whom the form relates)* declare that the photograph attached to this form is a photograph of me and that I am a person in respect of whom the above-named court gave a direction that [scientific tests] be made. I hereby consent/do not consent* to a bodily sample being obtained from me for the purpose of such tests.

I do not consent because …………………………………..

(To be deleted unless the person making the declaration withholds consent and wishes to record the reason for so doing.)

I understand that it is a serious offence punishable by imprisonment to personate another person for the purpose of providing a bodily sample.

Date …………………………

……………………………….(Signed)

……………………………….(Print)

The above was explained to the declarant who stated that he/she understood it and signed it in my presence.

Date …………………………

……………………………….(Signed)

……………………………….(Print)

(Sampler)

**(Delete as appropriate.)*

PART VI

Declaration

(To be completed where the person to whom the form relates has not attained the age of sixteen years or is a protected party.)

I ....(*full name and address of person accompanying the subject)* [*being the person having the care and control of .... *(name of person to whom form relates)*] declare that the person whom I identify to .... *(insert name of sampler)* and whose photograph is attached to this form is, to the best of my knowledge and belief ....) who is the son/daughter of ....*(insert the name of mother of person identified.)*

**Delete as appropriate*

I, being the person having the care and control of the person to whom this form relates, consent/do not consent *(Delete as appropriate)* to a sample being obtained. I do not consent because:--

(To be completed if the person making the declaration withholds consent and wishes to record the reason for so doing.)

I understand that it is a serious offence punishable by imprisonment to personate another person for the purpose of providing a bodily sample or to proffer the wrong child for that purpose.

Date ....

....(Signed)

....(Print)

The above was explained to the declarant who stated that he/she understood it and signed it in my presence.

Date ....

....(Signed)

....(Print)

(Sampler)

***(Delete if not applicable.)**

PART VII

(To be completed by sampler)

I have today obtained a bodily sample from .... to whom this form relates, whose [apparent] age is .... years. I identified him/her from the photograph attached to this form. He/She was also identified to me by ....*(Delete as appropriate)*

Date ....

....(Signed)

....(Print)

(Sampler)

OBSERVATIONS

(Any observations by the sampler, which may assist the tester, shall be inserted here)

PART VIII

(To be completed by sampler) (Delete if inappropriate)

The person to whom this form relates did not attend on the date originally arranged or on a new date arranged by me.

His/Her reasons given to me for failing to attend were as follows:

Date ....

....(Signed)

....(Print)

(Sampler)

PART VIIIA

Request to accredited body to carry out tests

To .... *(name and address of accredited body).*

You are hereby requested to carry out scientific tests on a bodily sample from ....*(name of person to whom form relates).*

PART IX

(To be completed by tester)

I have today received at .... *(insert place of receipt)* the sample referred to in Part VII of this form.

It was received by recorded signed for delivery/international* signed for delivery *(*Delete as appropriate)*

It was handed to me by ....

Date ....

....(Signed)

....(Print)

2 Blood Tests (Evidence of Paternity) Regulations 1971

SI 1971/1861

1 Citation and commencement

These Regulations may be cited as the Blood Tests (Evidence of Paternity) Regulations 1971 and shall come into operation on 1st March 1972.

2 Interpretation

(1) In these Regulations, unless the context otherwise requires,—

'the Act' means the Family Law Reform Act 1969;

'court' means a court which gives a direction for the use of [scientific tests][1] in pursuance of section 20(1) of the Act;

'direction' means a direction given as aforesaid;

'direction form' means Form 1 in Schedule 1 to these Regulations;

'photograph' means a recent photograph, taken full face without a hat, of [at least][2] the size required for insertion in a passport;

['protected party' means a person who lacks capacity, within the meaning of the Mental Capacity Act 2005, to consent to tests;][3]

['sample' means bodily fluid or bodily tissue taken for the purpose of scientific tests;][1]

['sampler' has the meaning given in paragraph (4) and is subject to the provisions of paragraphs (5) and (6);][4]

'subject' means a person from whom a court directs that [bodily samples][1] shall be taken;

['tester' means an individual employed to carry out tests by a body which has been accredited for the purposes of section 20 of the Act either by the Lord Chancellor or by a body appointed by him for those purposes and which has been nominated in a direction to carry out tests;][1];

'tests' means [scientific tests][1] carried out under Part III of the Act and includes any test made with the object of ascertaining the inheritable [characteristics of bodily fluids or bodily tissue][1].

(2) …[5]

(3) The Interpretation Act 1889 shall apply to the interpretation of these Regulations as it applies to the interpretation of an Act of Parliament.

[(4) In these Regulations, subject to the provisions of paragraphs (5) and (6), 'sampler' means—

(a) a registered medical practitioner;

(b) a person who is under the supervision of a registered medical practitioner and who is—

(i) a registered nurse; or

(ii) a registered biomedical scientist;

(c) a tester;

(d) an officer of the Service, within the meaning given by section 11(3) of the Criminal Justice and Court Services Act 2000;

(e) a Welsh family proceedings officer, within the meaning given by section 35(4) of the Children Act 2004; or

(f) a person, not being someone within sub-paragraphs (a) or (b), who is appointed by a tester to be a sampler.

(5) A sampler who is within sub-paragraph (d) or (e) in the definition of 'sampler' in paragraph (4) may only be involved in the obtaining of samples where—

(a) the court has given a direction of its own initiative in proceedings for a child arrangements order under section 8 of the Children Act 19891;

(b) the sampler has been trained by a tester, or under arrangements made by a tester, in relation to the requirements of these Regulations; and

(c) the sample is to be obtained by way of a mouth swab.

(6) A sampler who is within sub-paragraph (f) in the definition of 'sampler' in paragraph (4) may only be involved in the obtaining of samples where—

(a) the sampler has been trained by a tester, or under arrangements made by a tester, in relation to the requirements of these Regulations; and

(b) the sample is to be obtained by way of a mouth swab.][2]

Amendments

1 Substituted by the Blood Tests (Evidence of Paternity) (Amendment) Regulations 2001, SI 2001/773, regs 2, 4(a), (b), (d)–(f).
2 Inserted by the Blood Tests (Evidence of Paternity) (Amendment) Regulations 2015, SI 2015/1834, reg 2(1), (2)(a)(i), (b).
3 Inserted by the Blood Tests (Evidence of Paternity) (Amendment) Regulations 2008, SI 2008/972, reg 4(a).
4 Substituted by the Blood Tests (Evidence of Paternity) (Amendment) Regulations 2015, SI 2015/1834, reg 2(1), (2)(a)(ii).
5 Repealed by the Blood Tests (Evidence of Paternity) (Amendment) Regulations 2008, SI 2008/972, reg 4(b).

3 Direction form

A sampler shall not [obtain][1] a sample from a subject unless Parts I and II of the direction form have been completed and the direction form purports to be signed by the proper officer of the court or some person on his behalf.

Amendments

1 Substituted by the Blood Tests (Evidence of Paternity) (Amendment) Regulations 2015, SI 2015/1834, reg 2(1), (3).

4 [Subject who is under 16 or a protected party to be accompanied to sampler][1]

A subject who is [under 16 or a protected party][1] who attends a sampler for [a sample to be obtained][2] shall be accompanied by a person of full age who shall identify him to the sampler.

Amendments

1 Substituted by the Blood Tests (Evidence of Paternity) (Amendment) Regulations 2008, SI 2008/972, regs 5, 6.
2 Substituted by the Blood Tests (Evidence of Paternity) (Amendment) Regulations 2015, SI 2015/1834, reg 2(1), (4).

5 [Obtaining][1] samples

(1) Without prejudice to the provisions of rules of court, a sampler may make arrangements for [samples to be obtained][1] from the subjects or may change any arrangements already made and make other arrangements.

(2) Subject to the provisions of these Regulations, where a subject attends a sampler in accordance with arrangements made under a direction, the sampler [must on that

occasion act in accordance with paragraph (2A), (2B) or (2C), as applicable to that sampler][1].

[(2A) Where the sampler is a person within sub-paragraph (a), (b) or (c) of the definition of 'sampler' in regulation 2(4), the sampler must take a sample from the subject.

(2B) Where the sampler is a person within sub-paragraph (d) or (e) of the definition of 'sampler' in regulation 2(4), the sampler must supervise the taking of the sample—

(a) by the subject; or

(b) where the subject is under 16 or a protected party, by the person of full age who has accompanied the subject.

(2C) Where the sampler is a person within sub-paragraph (f) of the definition of 'sampler' in regulation 2(4), the sampler must—

(a) take the sample; or

(b) supervise the taking of the sample—

(i) by the subject; or

(ii) where the subject is under 16 or a protected party, by the person of full age who has accompanied the subject.][2]

(3) A sampler shall not [obtain][1] a sample from a subject if—

(i) [in the case of a blood sample,][3] he has reason to believe that the subject has been transfused with blood within the three months immediately preceding the day on which the sample is to be [obtained][1]; or

(ii) in his opinion, tests on a sample [obtained][1] at that time from that subject could not effectively be carried out for the purposes of and in accordance with the direction; or

(iii) in his opinion, [obtaining][1] a sample might have an adverse effect on the health of the subject.

(4) A sampler may [obtain][1] a sample from a subject who has been injected with a blood product or blood plasma if, in his opinion, the value of any tests done on that sample would not be thereby affected, but shall inform the tester that the subject was so injected.

(5) Where a sampler does not [obtain][1] a sample from a subject in accordance with arrangements made for [obtaining][1] that sample and no other arrangements are made, he shall return the direction form relating to that subject to the court, having stated on the form his reason for [not obtaining][1] the sample and any reason given by the subject (or the person having the care and control of the subject) for any failure to attend in accordance with those arrangements.

(6) A subject who attends a sampler [to give][1] a sample may be accompanied by his legal representative.

Amendments

1 Substituted by the Blood Tests (Evidence of Paternity) (Amendment) Regulations 2015, SI 2015/1834, reg 2(1), (5)(a)–(c), (e)–(h).

2 Inserted by the Blood Tests (Evidence of Paternity) (Amendment) Regulations 2015, SI 2015/1834, reg 2(1), (5)(d).

3 Inserted by the Blood Tests (Evidence of Paternity) (Amendment) Regulations 2001, SI 2001/773, regs 2, 6.

6 Sampling procedure

(1) A sampler shall comply with the provisions of this Regulation, all of which shall be complied with in respect of one subject before any are complied with in respect of any other subject; so however that a report made in accordance with the provisions of section 20(2) of the Act or any other evidence relating to the samples or the tests made on the samples shall not be challenged solely on the grounds that a sampler has not acted in accordance with the provisions of this Regulation.

[(2) The sampler shall ensure that a photograph of the subject is attached to the direction form relating to him before he [obtains][1] a sample from that subject.][2]

(3) Before a sample is [obtained][1] from a subject, he, or where he is [under 16 or a protected party][2] the person of full age accompanying him, shall complete the declaration in Part V of the direction form (that that subject is the subject to whom the direction form relates and, where a photograph is [attached][1] to the direction form, that the photograph is a photograph of that subject) which shall be signed in the presence of and witnessed by the sampler.

(4) …[3]

(5) A sample shall not be [obtained][1] from any subject unless—

(a) he or, where he is [under 16 or a protected party][2], the person having the care and control of him, has signed a statement on the direction form that he consents to the sample being [obtained][1]; or

(b) where he is [under 16 or a protected party][2] and is not accompanied by the person having the care and control of him, the sampler is in possession of a statement in writing, purporting to be signed by that person that he consents to the sample being [obtained][1] [; or][4]

[(c) where he is under the age of sixteen years, and the person with care and control of him does not consent, the court has nevertheless ordered that a sample be [obtained][1].][4]

(6) The sampler shall [attach][1] to the direction form any statement referred to in sub-paragraph (b) of the preceding paragraph.

(7) If a subject or, where he is [under 16 or a protected party][2], the person having the care and control of him, does not consent to [a sample being obtained][1], he may record on the direction form his reasons for withholding his consent.

(8) When the sampler has [obtained][1] a sample he shall place it in a suitable [, tamper-proof,][5] container and shall affix to the container a label giving the full name, age and sex of the subject from whom it was [obtained][1] and the label shall be signed by the sampler …[3].

(9) The sampler shall state in Part VII of the direction form that he has [obtained][1] the sample and the date on which he did so.

Amendments

1 Substituted by the Blood Tests (Evidence of Paternity) (Amendment) Regulations 2015, SI 2015/1834, reg 2(1), (6).

2 Substituted by the Blood Tests (Evidence of Paternity) (Amendment) Regulations 2008, SI 2008/972, regs 7, 8.

3 Repealed by the Blood Tests (Evidence of Paternity) (Amendment) Regulations 2001, SI 2001/773, regs 2, 7(b), (d).

4 Inserted by the Blood Tests (Evidence of Paternity) (Amendment) Regulations 2001, SI 2001/773, regs 2, 7(c).

5 Inserted by the Blood Tests (Evidence of Paternity) (Amendment) Regulations 2008, SI 2008/972, reg 9.

7 Despatch of samples to tester

(1) When a sampler has [obtained][1] samples, he shall, where he is not himself the tester, pack the containers together with the relevant direction forms and shall despatch them forthwith to the tester by post by [recorded signed for delivery or international signed for delivery][2] or shall deliver them or cause them to be delivered to the tester by some person other than a subject or a person who has accompanied a subject to the sampler.

(2) If at any time a sampler despatches to a tester samples from some only of the subjects and has not previously despatched samples [obtained][1] from the other subjects, he shall inform the tester whether he is expecting to [obtain][1] any samples from those other subjects and, if so, from whom and on what date.

Amendments

1 Substituted by the Blood Tests (Evidence of Paternity) (Amendment) Regulations 2015, SI 2015/1834, reg 2(1), (7).

2 Substituted by the Blood Tests (Evidence of Paternity) (Amendment) Regulations 2008, SI 2008/972, reg 10.

8 Procedure where sampler nominated is unable to [obtain][1] the samples

(1) Where a sampler is unable himself to [obtain][1] samples from all or any of the subjects, he may nominate another [sampler][2] to [obtain][1] the samples which he is unable to [obtain][1].

(2) The sampler shall record the nomination of the other sampler on the relevant direction forms and shall forward them to the sampler nominated by him.

Amendments

1 Substituted by the Blood Tests (Evidence of Paternity) (Amendment) Regulations 2015, SI 2015/1834, reg 2(1), (8).

2 Substituted by the Blood Tests (Evidence of Paternity) (Amendment) Regulations 2001, SI 2001/773, regs 2, 9.

[8A Accreditation

[(1) Subject to paragraph (2), a body shall not be eligible for accreditation for the purposes of section 20 of the Act unless it is accredited to ISO/IEC17025 by—

(a) a Full Member of the International Laboratory Accreditation Cooperation ('ILAC'); or

(b) a body that is a signatory to an ILAC Recognised Regional Cooperation Body.][1]

(2) A body which employs a person who at the date of the coming into force of the Blood Tests (Evidence of Paternity) (Amendment) Regulations 2001 was a tester appointed by the Lord Chancellor shall, until three years after that date, be eligible for accreditation for the purposes of section 20 of the Act notwithstanding that it does not comply with paragraph (1).][2]

Amendments

1 Substituted by the Blood Tests (Evidence of Paternity) (Amendment) Regulations 2008, SI 2008/972, reg 11.

2 Inserted by the Blood Tests (Evidence of Paternity) (Amendment) Regulations 2001, SI 2001/773, regs 2, 10.

9 Testing of samples

(1) Samples [obtained][1] for the purpose of giving effect to a direction shall (so far as practicable) all be tested by the same tester.

(2) A tester shall not make tests on any samples for the purpose of a direction unless he will, in his opinion, be able to show from the results of those tests (whether alone or together with the results of tests on any samples which he has received and tested or expects to receive subsequently) that a subject is or is not excluded from being [the father or mother of the person whose parentage falls to be determined][2].

Amendments

1 Substituted by the Blood Tests (Evidence of Paternity) (Amendment) Regulations 2015, SI 2015/1834, reg 2(1), (9).

2 Substituted by the Blood Tests (Evidence of Paternity) (Amendment) Regulations 2001, SI 2001/773, regs 2, 11.

10 Report by tester

On completion of the tests in compliance with the direction, the tester shall forward to the court a report in Form 2 in Schedule 1 to these Regulations, together with the appropriate direction forms.

11 Procedure where tests not made

If at any time it appears to a tester that he will be unable to make tests in accordance with the direction, he shall inform the court, giving his reasons, and shall return the direction forms in his possession to the court.

[12

[(1) A sampler may charge [£37.90][1] for making the arrangements to [obtain][2] a sample.

(2) The charge in paragraph (1) is payable whether or not a sample is [obtained][2].][3]

[(3) This regulation does not apply where regulation 2(5) applies in a given case.][4]][5]

Amendments

1 Substituted by the Blood Tests (Evidence of Paternity) (Amendment) Regulations 2008, SI 2008/972, reg 12.

2 Substituted by the Blood Tests (Evidence of Paternity) (Amendment) Regulations 2015, SI 2015/1834, reg 2(1), (10)(a), (b).

3 Substituted by the Blood Tests (Evidence of Paternity) (Amendment) Regulations 2004, SI 2004/596, regs 3, 4.

4 Inserted by the Blood Tests (Evidence of Paternity) (Amendment) Regulations 2015, SI 2015/1834, reg 2(1), (10)(c).

5 Substituted by the Blood Tests (Evidence of Paternity) (Amendment) Regulations 1989, SI 1989/776, reg 3.

Schedule 1

Regulations 2(1) and 10

Form 1 Direction form

Family Law Reform Act 1969

.... Insert title of proceedings

v.

....

Reference No. of direction ....

Full name and date of birth of person to be tested to whom this form relates.

....

Part I
Notification of direction

The .... (*name and address of court*) on .... day of .... 19... directed that [scientific tests][1] be carried out in respect of the persons whose names are set out below for the purpose of ascertaining the paternity of .... (*name of person whose paternity is in dispute*) and that [bodily samples][1] be [obtain][2] from the persons named below on or before the .... day of .... 19...

The name of the person appearing to the court to have the care and control of the person to whom this form relates who is under 16 /[a protected party][3], is .... *Delete as appropriate

.... (Signed)

[.......................... (Print)][4]

Proper Officer of the Court.

Name	Address	Age
....	....	....
....	....	....
....	....	....
....	....	....
....	....	....

Part II
Request to sampler to take sample

To ……………………… (*name and address of sampler*).

You are hereby requested to [obtain][2] a [bodily sample][1] from ……………………… (*name of person to whom form relates*).

[[*The sample is to be [obtained][2] notwithstanding the refusal to consent of the person with care and control of ……………………… (*name of person to whom form relates*).]] — *Delete if not applicable][5]

You are further requested to send the sample [obtained][2] to ……………………… ([*name and address of accredited body]*[1]) […[6]]. — Delete if sampler is also tester

[Other samples will be [obtained][2] as follows:–

Name of person from whom sample will be [obtained][2]	Name, address and telephone number of sampler
………………………	………………………
………………………	………………………
………………………	………………………]

To be completed where all the samples from the parties named in Part I are not to be [obtained][2] by the same sampler.

……………………… (Signed)

[……………………… (Print)][4]

[Being unable to comply with the request set out above, I have nominated ……………………… (*name and address of nominee*) to [obtain][2] the sample. — For use where sampler named above nominates another sampler.

……………………… (Signed)]

[……………………… (Print)][4]

Part III
Photograph

Below[, or attached to this form,][7] is a photograph of the person to whom this form relates …[8].

………………………

Part IV

(*To be completed by sampler [where sample is of blood][5]*)

I have questioned* ……………………… and it appears that he/she/the party to whom this form relates—

has/has not† been transfused with blood in the last three months;†

has not been injected with a blood product or plasma substitute;†

has been injected with a blood product/blood plasma† on or about ……………………… and that the value of any tests will thereby be/not be affected.†

……………………… (Signed))

[……………………… (Print)][4]
(Sampler

*Insert name of person to whom form relates or, in the case of person under 16 or [a protected party][4], person accompanying that person.

†Delete as appropriate.

Part V
Declaration

(*To be completed where the person to whom the form relates has attained the age of sixteen years and is not [a protected party]*[3]*.*)

I ……………………… (*insert full name and address of person to whom the form relates*) declare that the photograph [attached to][2] this form is a photograph of me and that I am a person in respect of whom the above-named court gave a direction that [scientific tests][1] be made. I hereby consent/do not consent* to [a bodily sample being obtained][2] from me for the purpose of such tests.

*Delete as appropriate.

[I do not consent because ………………………][†]

I understand that it is a serious offence punishable by imprisonment to personate another person for the purpose of providing a [bodily sample][1].

†To be deleted unless the person making the declaration withholds consent and wishes to record the reason for so doing.

Date ……………………… ……………………… (Signed)

[……………………… (Print)][4]
(Sampler)

The above was explained to the declarant who stated that he/she understood it and signed it in my presence.

Date ……………………… ……………………… (Signed)

[……………………… (Print)][4]
(Sampler)

Part VI
Declaration

(*To be completed where the person to whom the form relates has not attained the age of sixteen years or is [a protected party]*[3]*.*)

I ……………………… (*full name and address of person accompanying the subject*) [*being the person having the care and control of ……………………… (*name of person to whom form relates*)] declare that the person whom I identify to ……………………… (*insert name sampler*) [†and whose photograph is [attached to][2] this form] is, to the best of my knowledge and belief ………………………] who is the son/daughter of ……………………… (*insert the name of mother of person identified.*)]

*Delete if no applicable

†Delete as appropriate.

I, being the person having the care and control of the person to whom this form relates, consent/do not consent[†] to [a sample being obtained][2]. [I do not consent because:—[‡]

I understand that it is a serious offence punishable by imprisonment to personate another person for the purpose of providing a [bodily sample][1] or to proffer the wrong child for that purpose.

‡To be completed if the person making the declaration withholds consent and wishes to record the reason for so doing.

Date ……………………… ……………………… (Signed)

[……………………… (Print)][4]
(Sampler)

The above was explained to the declarant who stated that he/she understood it and signed it in my presence.

Date ……………………… ……………………… (Signed)

[……………………… (Print)][4]
(Sampler)

Part VII

(*To be completed by sampler*)

I have today [obtained][2] a [bodily sample][1] from ……………………… to whom this form relates, whose [apparent] age is ……………………… years. [I identified him/her from the photograph [attached][2] to this form.] [He/She was [also] identified to me by ………………………] — Delete as appropriate.

Date ……………………… ……………………… (Signed)

[……………………… (Print)][4]
(Sampler)

OBSERVATIONS

(*Any observations by the sampler which may assist the tester shall be inserted here.*)

Part VIII

(*To be completed by sampler*)

The person to whom this form relates did not attend on the date originally arranged.[or on a new date arranged by me]. — Delete if inappropriate.

His/Her reasons given to me for failing to attend were as follows:—

Date ……………………… ……………………… (Signed)

[……………………… (Print)][4]
(Sampler)

[Part VIIIA
Request to accredited body to carry out tests

To ……………………… (*name and address of accredited body*).

You are hereby requested to carry out scientific tests on a bodily sample from ……………………… (*name of person to whom form relates*).][5]

Part IX

(*To be completed by tester*)

I have today received at ……………………… (*insert place of receipt*) the sample referred to in Part VII of this form. — Delete as appropriate.

[It was received by [recorded signed for delivery/international signed for delivery][3].]

[It was handed to me by ………………………]

Date ……………………… ……………………… (Signed)

[……………………… (Print)][4]
(Tester)

Amendments

1 Substituted by the Blood Tests (Evidence of Paternity) (Amendment) Regulations 2001, SI 2001/773, regs 2, 12, 13(b).
2 Substituted by the Blood Tests (Evidence of Paternity) (Amendment) Regulations 2015, SI 2015/1834, reg 2(1), (11)(a), (b), (d)–(f).
3 Substituted by the Blood Tests (Evidence of Paternity) (Amendment) Regulations 2008, SI 2008/972, reg 13(a), (c)–(e).
4 Inserted by the Blood Tests (Evidence of Paternity) (Amendment) Regulations 2008, SI 2008/972, reg 15.

5 Inserted by the Blood Tests (Evidence of Paternity) (Amendment) Regulations 2001, SI 2001/773, regs 2, 13(a), 14, 15.
6 Repealed by the Blood Tests (Evidence of Paternity) (Amendment) Regulations 2001, SI 2001/773, regs 2, 13(c).
7 Inserted by the Blood Tests (Evidence of Paternity) (Amendment) Regulations 2015, SI 2015/1834, reg 2(1), (11)(c), (b).
8 Repealed by the Blood Tests (Evidence of Paternity) (Amendment) Regulations 2008, SI 2008/972, reg 13(b).

Form 2 Report by tester

Ref. No. of Proceedings ……………………

Family Law Reform Act 1969

To:—

(…………………… High Court of Justice, Strand, London W.C.2.

([Court Manager][1], …………………… County Court

([Justices' Chief Executive][1], …………………… Magistrates' Court.(1)

…………………… v ……………………(2)

Part I

I, ……………………, [being employed to carry out scientific tests [by …………………… (*name of accredited* body) being a body][2] which has been accredited for the purposes of section 20][1] of the Family Law Reform Act 1969, certify that I have carried out [[scientific tests][1] (the details of which are given in Part II of this Report) on samples provided by][3] the persons named in this direction, viz.,

From the results obtained …[4] …………………… is excluded/is not excluded from possible [parentage][1] of ……………………

Reason for conclusion:—

Comments on value, if any, of tests in determining whether any person tested is the father [or mother][5] of the person whose [parentage][1] is in dispute:—

…………………… Signed

[…………………… Print][6]

…………………… Status

…………………… Address

Part II
[Report of Scientific Tests][1]

(1) Complete as appropriate.

(2) Insert title of proceedings.

Amendments

1 Substituted by the Blood Tests (Evidence of Paternity) (Amendment) Regulations 2001, SI 2001/773, regs 2, 17(a)–(d), (f), (h).
2 Substituted by the Blood Tests (Evidence of Paternity) (Amendment) Regulations 2008, SI 2008/972, reg 14.
3 Substituted by the Blood Tests (Evidence of Paternity) (Amendment) Regulations 1989, SI 1989/776, reg 4.
4 Repealed by the Blood Tests (Evidence of Paternity) (Amendment) Regulations 2001, SI 2001/773, regs 2, 17(e).

5 Substituted by the Blood Tests (Evidence of Paternity) (Amendment) Regulations 2001, SI 2001/773, regs 2, 17(g).

6 Inserted by the Blood Tests (Evidence of Paternity) (Amendment) Regulations 2008, SI 2008/972, reg 15.

Schedule 2

…[1]

Amendments

1 Repealed by the Blood Tests (Evidence of Paternity) (Amendment) Regulations 2004, SI 2004/596, regs 3, 5.

3 Report by Tester (BD2)

FORM BD2

Report by Tester

Family Law Reform Act 1969

Ref No of Proceedings ………………………………

To: High Court of Justice, Strand, London WC2.

Court Manager……………………………………………………………County Court

(Designated Officer) ………………………………………………the Family court sitting at…………………………………

I ……………………………………………………………………………… being employed to carry out scientific tests by ……………………………………………(*name of accredited body*) being a body which has been accredited for the purposes of section 20 of the Family Law Reform Act 1969, certify that I have carried out scientific tests (the details of which are given in Part II of this Report) on samples provided by the persons named in this direction, viz.,

From the results obtained ………………………………………is excluded/is not excluded from possible parentage of ………………………………

Reason for conclusion:-

Comments on value, if any, of tests in determining whether any person tested is the father or mother of the person whose parentage is in dispute:-

……………………………………………Signed

……………………………………………Print

……………………………………………Status

……………………………………………Address

……………………………………………

PART II

Report of Scientific Tests

(1)Complete as appropriate.

BD2 - Report by tester (11.14)

4 Sample Clause in an Order for blood or DNA tests

Paternity testing

1. The court needs a report to find out whether [*name*] is the father of [*name*]. A tester needs samples from [*name*] and [*name*] so that tests can be carried out and a report prepared.
2. As the dispute regarding parentage has arisen in relation to an application for a child arrangement order and as the court has made the above direction for a report on parentage of its own motion, a test is considered necessary to resolve the proceedings:

(TESTING THROUGH CAFCASS/CAFCASS CYMRU)

a. The court officer must complete Parts I and II of form BD1 and send this to:
   i. **[(WHERE THE CHILD WHOSE PARENTAGE IS IN DISPUTE IS RESIDENT IN ENGLAND)** DNA Requests, CAFCASS National Business Centre, Millburn Hill Road, University of Warwick Science Park, Coventry CV4 7JJ (DNArequests@cafcass.gsi.gov.uk and inboundpost@cafcass.gsi.gov.uk; telephone number 0300 456 4000)]
   ii. **[(WHERE THE CHILD WHOSE PARENTAGE IS IN DISPUTE IS RESIDENT IN WALES)** Central Administrative Team, Welsh Government Rhydycar Business Park, Merthyr Tydfil CF48 1UZ (CafcasscymruCAT@wales.gsi.gov.uk)].

b. an officer of [Cafcass] / [CAFCASS Cymru] must then make arrangements with [*name*] for mouth swab samples to be given by [*name*], supervised by a trained officer of [Cafcass] / [CAFCASS Cymru];
c. [*name*] must allow the officer of [Cafcass] / [CAFCASS Cymru] to take photographic identity of [his] / [her] identity at the time the sample is taken;
d. the officer of [Cafcass] / [CAFCASS Cymru] must send the samples to the tester to arrive by no later than [*date*];
e. the tester must send the written test report to the court and [Cafcass] / [CAFCASS Cymru] by [*date*];
f. the costs of the sampling, testing and report will be paid for by Cafcass in respect of proceedings in England and by the Ministry of Justice in respect of proceedings in Wales.

(TESTING NOT THROUGH CAFCASS/CAFCASS CYMRU)

a. The court office must complete Parts I and II of form BDI and send this to [*name*];
b. [*Name*] must contact an accredited tester and make arrangements for an appropriate sampler to obtain samples by [*date*];
c. At the time the samples are obtained the person giving the samples must provide to the sampler the completed form BD1, a copy of this order and photo identity;
d. The sampler must send the samples to the tester by [*date*];
e. The tester must send the written test report to the court and [Cafcass] / [CAFCASS Cymru] by [*date*];
f. The costs of sampling, testing and reporting must be paid by [*name*].

5 List of Laboratories Approved by the Ministry of Justice to Test Bodily Samples in Cases of Disputed Parentage

List of bodies that may carry out court-directed parentage tests under section 20 of the Family Law Reform Act 1969

The Ministry of Justice is responsible for accrediting bodies which may carry out scientific tests for parentage in accordance with a direction made by a court pursuant to section 20 of the Family Law Reform Act 1969. A list of bodies currently accredited by the Ministry of Justice appears below. This list replaces all previous lists. The list is updated at http:/ www.justice.gov.uk/courts/paternity-testing/paternity-test

NAME & CONTACT DETAILS		
Alpha BioLaboratories Ltd	**Tel no:**	0333 600 1300
14 Webster Court	**Email:**	info@alphabiolabs.com
Carina Park	**Website:**	www.alphabiolabs.co.uk
Warrington, WA5 8WD		
Anglia DNA Services	**Tel no:**	01603 358 161
33 Scottow Enterprise Park	**Fax no:**	01603 298 071
Badersfield	**Email:**	office@angliadna.co.uk
Norwich		
NR10 5FB		
Complement Genomics Ltd	**Tel no:**	0808 145 5789
(*trading as dadcheck*®)	**Fax no:**	0871 231 1282
Park House	**Email:**	sales@dadcheck.com
Station Road	**Website:**	http://dadcheck.com
Lanchester		
Co Durham DH7 0EX		
DDC Laboratories, Inc	**Tel no:**	0845 408 2084
Britannia House	**Fax no:**	020 8563 1858
11 Glenthorne Road		
London W6 0LH		
DNA Analysis at King's	**Tel no:**	020 7848 4130
Franklin Wilkins Building	**Fax no:**	020 7848 4129
150 Stamford Street	**Email:**	dna.analysis@kcl.ac.uk
London SE1 9NH		
Endeavor DNA Laboratories	**Tel no:**	01273 951 195
Phoenix House,	**Email:**	info@endeavordna.co.uk
32 West Street, Brighton,		
East Sussex BN1 2RT		

Eurofins Medigenomix GmbH K10 The Courtyard Jenson Ave Commerce Park Frome BA11 2FG	**Tel no:** **Website:**	020 3199 7408 www.dnalegal.com
Genetrack Biolabs	**Tel no:** **Email:**	0800 092 8060 info@genetrack.co.uk
Key Forensic Services Ltd University of Warwick Science Park Sir William Lyons Road Coventry West Midlands CV4 7EZ	**Tel** **Email** **Web:**	02477 712246 sales@keyforensic.co.uk www.keyforensic.co.uk
Paternity for Life	**Tel no:** **Fax no:** **Email:** **Website:**	08002461760 Enquires@paternityforlife.co.uk www.paternityforlife.co.uk
Northgene Ltd International Centre for Life Newcastle upon Tyne NE1 4EP	**Tel no:** **Email:**	0870 803 0999 info@northgene.co.uk
Orchid Cellmark Ltd 16 Blacklands Way Abingdon Business Park Abingdon Oxon OX14 1DY	**Tel no:** **Fax no:** **Email:**	0800 4702522 info@cellmarkforensics.co.uk

APPENDIX C

OTHER INFORMATION

(1) HMCTS divorce centres: contact details

(2) List of armed forces contact addresses

(3) Urgent court business – information for court users

(4) President's Guidance of 18 November 2010 in relation to Out of Hours Hearings

(5) Practice Note of 28 July 2006 (Official Solicitor, CAFCASS and the National Assembly for Wales: Urgent and Out of Hours Cases in the Family Division of the High Court)

(6) Official Solicitor's Practice Note of 30 January 2017

(7) Family Court (Composition and Distribution of Business) Rules 2014, SI 2014/840

(8) President's Guidance of 22 April 2014 (Allocation and Gatekeeping of Care, Supervision and other Proceedings under Part IV of the Children Act 1989 (Public Law))

(9) President's Guidance of 22 April 2014 on Allocation and Gatekeeping for Proceedings Under Part II of the Children Act 1989 (Private Law)

(10) President's Guidance of 22 April 2009 (Applications Consequent upon the Attendance of the Media in Family Proceedings)

(11) Practice Guidance of 12 July 2010 (*McKenzie Friends* (Civil and Family Courts))

(12) President's Guidance of October 2014 (Communicating with Home Office in Family Proceedings)

(13) Protocol on communications between judges of the Family Court and Immigration and Asylum Chambers of the First-tier Tribunal and Upper Tribunal

(14) Approved countries and territories – Gender Recognition Act 2004, SI 2011/1630

(15) Hague Convention Countries

(16) European Convention Countries

(17) Conventions and legislation relating to reciprocal enforcement of maintenance orders

(18) Domestic violence lifelines

(19) President's Direction of 19 May 2008

(20) Civil Partnership (Jurisdiction and Recognition of Judgments) Regulations 2005, SI 2005/3334

(21) President's Guidance of 28 March 2022 (Divorce, Dissolution and Separation Act 2020: Costs in proceedings for matrimonial and civil partnership orders)

(22) Fact finding Hearings and Domestic Abuse in Private Law Children Proceedings – Guidance for Judges and Magistrates 5th May 2022

1 HMCTS divorce centres: contact details

London and South East

Bury St Edmunds Divorce Centre
Write to:
Bury St Edmunds Divorce Centre
Triton House
St Andrew's St North
Bury St Edmunds
Suffolk
IP33 1TR
DX: 97640 Bury St Edmunds 3
Opening hours: court counter open 10.00am to 4.00pm by appointment
Email: divorceunitbse@hmcts.gsi.gov.uk
Phone: 0344 892 4000

South West

South West Regional Divorce Centre
Write to:
South West Regional Divorce Centre
PO Box 1792
Southampton
Hampshire
SO15 9GG
DX: 135986 Southampton 32
Opening hours: telephone enquiries from Monday to Friday 9am to 5pm
Email: sw-region-divorce@hmcts.gsi.gov.uk
Phone: 023 8038 4200
Fax: 01264 758162

Midlands

West Midlands Divorce Unit
Write to:
PO Box 3650
Stoke-on-Trent
Staffordshire
ST4 9NH
Opening hours: telephone enquiries from: 9am to 4pm
Email: westmidlandsdivorce@hmcts.gsi.gov.uk
Phone: 0300 123 5577

East Midlands Divorce Unit

Write to:
PO Box 10447
Nottingham
Nottinghamshire
NG2 9QN
Opening hours: telephone enquiries from: 9am to 4pm
Email: eastmidlandsdivorce@hmcts.gsi.gov.uk
Phone: 0115 955 8266

North West

Liverpool Civil and Family Court

Write to:
Liverpool Civil and Family Court Hearing Centre
35 Vernon Street
Liverpool
Merseyside
L2 2BX
DX: 702600 Liverpool 5
Opening hours: court building open Monday to Friday 8:30am to 5pm, counter open by prior appointment only
Email: family@liverpool.countycourt.gsi.gov.uk
Phone: 0151 296 2604

North East

Durham County Court and Family Court

Write to:
Durham Family Court
Green Lane
Old Elvet
Durham
DH1 3RG
DX: 65115 Durham 5
Opening hours: court building open Monday to Friday 9am to 5pm, counter open 10am to 2pm
Email: divorce.durham@hmcts.gsi.gov.uk
Phone: 0191 3751 810
Fax: 0870 739 5954

Doncaster Magistrates' Court and Family Court

Write to:
Doncaster Magistrates' Court and Family Court
P.O. Box 49
The Law Courts
College Road
Doncaster
South Yorkshire
DN1 3HT
DX: 742840 Doncaster 20

Opening hours: Monday to Friday 9am to 5pm, counter open: 9am to 5pm
Email: family@doncaster.countycourt.gsi.gov.uk
Phone: 01302 366 711
Fax: 01264 347 977

Bradford Combined Court Centre

Write to:
Bradford Law Courts
Exchange Square
Drake Street
Bradford
West Yorkshire
BD1 1JA
DX: 702083 Bradford 2
Opening hours: Monday to Friday 8am to 5pm, counter open 10am to 4pm by prior appointment only
Email: divorcecentrebradf@hmcts.gsi.gov.uk
Phone: 01274 840 274
Fax: 01264 785 015

Wales

Newport (Gwent) County Court and Family Court

Write to:
Newport (Gwent) Civil and Family Court
5th Floor
Clarence House
Clarence Place
Newport
Gwent
NP19 7AA
DX: 99480 Newport (South Wales) 4
Opening hours: court building open 8:30am to 5pm, counter open 10am to 2pm
Email: newportdivorce@hmcts.gsi.gov.uk
Phone: 01633 245 040
Fax: 0870 324 0309

Neath and Port Talbot County Court and Family Court

Write to:
Neath and Port Talbot Family Court
Forster Road
Neath
South Wales
SA11 3BN
DX: 99550 Neath 2
Opening hours: Monday to Friday 10am to 4pm, counter open: 10am to 2pm
Email: family@neath.countycourt.gsi.gov.uk
Phone: 01639 642 267
Fax: 0870 739 5985

Wrexham County Court and Family Court

Write to:
The Law Courts
Bodhyfryd
Wrexham
Denbighshire
LL12 7BP
DX: 745320 Wrexham 9
Opening hours: 9:00am to 4:30pm (4pm Friday), counter: enquiries 10am to 2pm
Email: family@wrexham.countycourt.gsi.gov.uk
Phone: 01978 317 400
Fax: 01264 347955

2 List of armed forces contact addresses

Armed forces manning and records offices

Naval Pay and Pension Executive Office
Centurion Building
Grange Road
Gosport
Hants
PO13 9XA

Pension Division
Army Personnel Centre
Kentigern House
65 Brown Street
Glasgow
G2 8EX
RAF Pensions Office
AFPAA
RAF Innsworth
Gloucester
GL3 1EZ

Postal and Courier Services

Defence Mail and Courier Services
BFPO
Frith Lane
Mill Hill
London
NW7 1PX

3 Urgent court business – information for court users

Introduction

Not all the incidents which may require the attention of a judge occur within normal office hours, and some are too urgent to wait until the next day that a court is open. In order to cater for such emergencies, the Court Service provides a system known as 'urgent court business'. This system enables court users to contact an experienced member of staff at any time during the night, weekends or public holidays. If the circumstances are serious enough, the urgent court business officer will arrange a hearing with a judge. The following gives a basic guide to urgent court business, how it operates, the work it covers and how you can contact an officer in an emergency.

Nature of work covered

- Injunctions;
- Children Act applications; and
- other urgent applications where an individual's personal safety, well-being, business or assets may be at risk.

Times when the system operates

- Between 4 pm and 8.30 am each workday;
- between 4 pm on Friday until 8.30 am on Monday for each weekend; and
- from 4 pm on the last day preceding a public holiday or privilege holiday that the court is open until 8.30 am on the day the court is next open.

Publicity for the scheme

Details of the scheme must be given, locally, to:

- Police;
- Citizens Advice Bureau(x);
- the local authority social services department;
- law centres;
- the local Law Society;
- the local Bar.

Some Circuits/Group Manager's Offices also give the information to other organisations.

How it operates

Urgent court business officers all carry a radio pager. Anybody with a touch tone telephone who needs to contact one of them simply telephones the pager number provided and leaves their telephone number. **Note: the system will not accept verbal messages. When asked for your message you simply tap in your telephone number on which you wish to be contacted.** Anyone without a touch tone telephone will need to contact the Security Office at the Royal Courts of Justice on 0207 947 6000. The caller will be required to leave a contact number and the name of their local court. The Security Officer will then telephone the pager number for the area of the local court. In either case, the urgent court business officer will telephone you back and ask for details of the case. It would be of great assistance if solicitors could have any relevant orders to hand when contacting the court office. The officer will then discuss the case with a member of the judiciary who will decide whether a hearing is necessary. All urgent court business officers in a particular region, such as South Wales, will have a pager with the same number. The number therefore always remains the same.

If you have any queries about urgent court business or would like more information about how it works, please contact the Group Manager's Office for the relevant region.

4 President's Guidance of 18 November 2010

Citations: [2011] 1 FLR 303

Out of Hours Hearings

1 It is perhaps not sufficiently appreciated by the general public that there is always a High Court judge of the Family Division on duty "out of hours" – that is to say every day of the year including all holiday periods either: (1) between 16.15 on day one and 10.30 am on day two of a normal court sitting; or (2) between 16.15 on any given Friday and 10.30 the following Monday. In vacations, when the court is not sitting, a similar service is provided at any time of the day or night.

2 It is of the utmost importance that this service is used for its intended purposes and is not abused. It is designed for urgent cases. In this context "urgent" has a specific meaning. It means cases in which an order of the court is required to regulate the position between the moment the order is made and the next available sitting of the court in conventional court hours – that is, usually, 10.30 on the following morning.

3 Judges of the Family Division have no complaint, for example, if, in the middle of the night, they are asked to sanction life saving medical treatment, or if they have to visit a hospital at such a time in order to decide whether a given individual should undergo urgent and specific treatment.

4 Any application that is "urgent" within the definition set out in paragraph 2 above must be capable of being reduced to a faxed sheet of A4 (or its email equivalent), or a short telephone conversation. Whether or not a case is "urgent" will always be a matter for the judge.

5 What is unacceptable is an application which can plainly wait until the normal sitting of the court and/or which involves a substantial amount of documentation. A judge cannot and should not be expected either to receive or to assimilate a substantial volume of documentation in an urgent, out of hours application unless both are absolutely essential to a proper understanding of the order which the judge is being asked to make. Equally, judges who are on duty out of hours should not be expected to make arrangements to sit in court unless such a sitting is strictly necessary to enable an order to be made. The profession should also remember that the judge on duty, whilst always available on the telephone, will be at home, and that "home" may not be in London.

6 Lawyers who abuse the system, particularly those who seek to take advantage of an order not made on notice and out of hours with a speedy return date in hours may not only be the subject of orders for wasted costs, but may find themselves reported to their professional bodies for serious professional misconduct. The profession is thus reminded of the definition of "urgent" set out in paragraph 2 of this note.

7 Nothing in this note supersedes any previous Guidance or Practice Note relating to out of hours applications.

Sir Nicholas Wall

President of the Family Division

5 Practice Note of 28 July 2006

Citations: [2006] 2 FLR 354

Official Solicitor, CAFCASS and the National Assembly for Wales: Urgent and Out of Hours Cases in the Family Division of the High Court

1 This Practice Note is issued jointly by the Official Solicitor, the Chief Executive of CAFCASS, and the Chief Executive of CAFCASS Cymru on behalf of the National Assembly for Wales. It describes the procedure to be followed in respect of urgent and out of hours cases in which a decision is sought by a judge of the Family Division of the High Court. It is issued with the approval of the President of the Family Division.

2 In some cases, urgent or out of hours applications become necessary because applications to the court have not been pursued sufficiently promptly. This is undesirable, in particular because urgent applications may be founded on incomplete evidence, inquiries and underprepared advocacy, and should be avoided where possible. A judge who has concerns that the urgent or out of hours facilities may have been abused may require a representative of the claimant to attend at a subsequent directions hearing to provide an explanation.

3 Whenever possible, urgent applications should be made within court hours. The earliest possible liaison is required with the Clerk of the Rules. It will usually be possible to accommodate a genuinely urgent application (at least for initial directions) in the Family Division applications court, from which the matter may, if necessary and possible, be referred to another judge.

4 When it is not possible to apply within court hours, contact should be made with the security office at the Royal Courts of Justice (020 7947 6000) who will refer the matter to the urgent business officer. The urgent business officer can contact the duty judge. The judge may agree to hold a hearing, either convened at court or elsewhere, or by telephone. When the hearing is to take place by telephone it should be by tape-recorded conference call arranged (and paid for in the first instance) by the claimant's solicitors. Solicitors acting for NHS Trusts or other potential claimants should have standing arrangements with their telephone service providers under which such conference calls can be arranged. All parties (especially the judge) should be informed that the call is being recorded by the service provider. The claimant should order a transcript of the hearing from the service provider.

Adult medical treatment and welfare cases

5 The Official Solicitor will act in urgent cases under the inherent jurisdiction concerning medical treatment to, or the welfare of, an adult who lacks capacity to make decisions for himself or herself. His office should be contacted at the earliest possible opportunity if an urgent application is envisaged. Where cases arise out of hours the urgent business officer will be able to contact him or his representative. As with cases dealt with on a less urgent basis, evidence is required of incapacity and as to best interests. When written evidence is not available, oral evidence of incapacity must be available. When there is a telephone hearing, oral evidence must be given as part of the conference call.

6 When final evidence either as to capacity or best interests is not available, the court may be willing to grant an interim declaration (r 25.1(1)(b) of the Civil Procedure

Rules 1998 (CPR) – *NHS Trust v T (Adult Patient: Refusal of Medical Treatment)* [2004] EWHC 1279 (Fam), [2005] 1 All ER 387). Evidence establishing on the balance of probability that the patient is under incapacity and that the treatment proposed is in his or her best interest must be adduced. An interim injunction to restrain treatment may be granted *Re C (Adult) (Refusal of Treatment)* [1994] 1 WLR 290, [1994] 1 FLR 31.

7 An adult patient must be a party and must be represented through a litigation friend (r 21.3 of the CPR). Notice of an application must be given to the patient (or his or her litigation friend). The claimant may be an NHS Trust, local authority, relative, carer, or the patient. The Official Solicitor stands ready to accept appointment as litigation friend (usually for the patient as defendant) if the conditions for his appointment are shown (either on an interim or final basis) to exist. Should a declaration be made without notice, it is of no effect and may be set aside – *St George's Healthcare NHS Trust v S; R (S) v Collins and Others* [1999] Fam 26, [1998] 2 FLR 728.

Children medical treatment and welfare cases

8 It may be desirable for a child who is the subject of such proceedings to be made a party and represented through a guardian ad litem (usually an officer of CAFCASS or a Welsh Family Proceedings Officer). CAFCASS and CAFCASS Cymru stand ready to arrange for an officer to accept appointment as guardian ad litem. They should be contacted at the earliest opportunity where an urgent application is envisaged. For urgent out of hours applications, the urgent business officer is able to contact a representative of CAFCASS. CAFCASS Cymru is not able to deal with cases that arise out of office hours and those cases should be referred to CAFCASS who will deal with the matter on behalf of CAFCASS Cymru until the next working day. A child of sufficient understanding to instruct his or her own solicitor should be made a party and given notice of any application.

9 Interim declarations/orders under the wardship jurisdiction (or the Children Act 1989) may be made on application either by an NHS trust, a local authority, an interested adult (where necessary with the leave of the court) or by the child if he or she has sufficient understanding to make the application.

General issues

10 Parents, carers or other necessary respondents should be given the opportunity to have independent legal advice or at least to have access to support or counselling.

11 In suitable cases, application may be made for direction providing for anonymity of the parties and others involved in the matter in any order or subsequent listing of the case. Exceptionally, a reporting restriction order may be sought – see the *President's Practice Direction (Applications for Reporting Restriction Orders)* [2005] 2 FLR 120 issued on 18 March 2005.

12 Either the Official Solicitor or CAFCASS, as the case may be, may be appointed by the court as advocate to the court – see Memorandum from the Lord Chief Justice and the Attorney-General reproduced in *The White Book Service 2006, Civil Procedure* (Sweet & Maxwell, 2006) at 39.8.2, especially at 39.8.5.

13 Draft standard form orders for use in urgent and out of hours medical treatment cases are annexed to this note. They should be adapted to suit the individual circumstances of each case.

Consultation with CAFCASS, CAFCASS CYMRU and Official Solicitor

14 Members of the Official Solicitor's legal staff, CAFCASS, and CAFCASS Cymru are prepared to discuss medical cases before proceedings are issued. In all cases in which the urgent and out of hours procedures are to be used it would be helpful if the Official Solicitor, CAFCASS or CAFCASS Cymru have had some advance notice of the application and its circumstances. Inquiries about adult medical and welfare cases should be addressed to a family and medical litigation lawyer at the office of the Official Solicitor, 81 Chancery Lane, London, WC2A, telephone 0207 911 7127, fax number: 0207 911 7105, email: inquiries@offsol.gsi.gov.uk. Inquiries about children medical cases should be directed to the duty lawyer at CAFCASS, 8th Floor, South Quay Plaza 3, 189 Marsh Wall, London, E14 9SH, telephone: 0207 510 7000, fax number: 0207 510 7104. Inquiries about children medical cases in Wales should be directed to the Social Care Team, Legal Services, National Assembly for Wales, Cathays Park, Cardiff, CF10 3NQ, telephone: 02920 826813, fax no: 02920 823834.

Laurence Oates
Official Solicitor

Anthony Douglas
Chief Executive
CAFCASS

Dafydd Ifans
Chief Executive
CAFCASS CYMRU
National Assembly for Wales

Annex
Out of Hours Adult Interim Declaration and Directions

****

6 Official Solicitor's Practice Note of 30 January 2017

The Official Solicitor to the Senior Courts: Appointment in family proceedings and proceedings under the inherent jurisdiction in relation to adults

Introduction

1. This Practice Note replaces the Practice Note dated March 2013 issued by the Official Solicitor.
2. It concerns:
   (a) the appointment of the Official Solicitor as 'litigation friend' of a 'protected party' or child in family proceedings, where the Family Division of the High Court is being invited to exercise its inherent jurisdiction in relation to a vulnerable adult[1] or where proceedings in relation to a child aged 16 or 17 are transferred into the Court of Protection;
   (b) requests by the court to the Official Solicitor to conduct *Harbin v Masterman*[2] enquiries; and
   (c) requests by the court to the Official Solicitor to act as, or appoint counsel to act as, an advocate to the court.[3]

The Note is intended to be helpful guidance, but is always subject to legislation including the Rules of Court, to Practice Directions, and to case law.

In this Note 'FPR 2010' means Family Procedure Rules 2010, 'CPR 1998' means Civil Procedure Rules 1998 and 'CoPR 2007' means Court of Protection Rules 2007.

3. For the avoidance of doubt, the Children and Family Court Advisory and Support Service (CAFCASS) has responsibilities in relation to a child in family proceedings in which their welfare is or may be in question (Criminal Justice and Court Services Act 2000, section 12). Since 1 April 2001 the Official Solicitor has not represented a child who is the subject of family proceedings (other than in very exceptional circumstances). In cases of doubt or difficulty, staff of the Official Solicitor's office will liaise with staff of CAFCASS Legal Services to avoid duplication and ensure the most suitable arrangements are made.

Appointment of a litigation friend for a protected party

4. A 'protected party' requires a litigation friend. In family proceedings this requirement appears in Part 15 of the FPR 2010, in proceedings in the Family Division of the High Court of Justice under the court's inherent jurisdiction it appears in Part 21 of the CPR 1998 and in proceedings in the Court of Protection it appears in Part 17 of the CoPR 2007.

5. In family proceedings, a 'protected party' means a party, or an intended party, who lacks capacity (within the meaning of the Mental Capacity Act 2005) to conduct the proceedings: FPR 2010, rule 2.3; and in proceedings under the inherent jurisdiction the expression has the same meaning: CPR 1998, rule 21.2. The following should be noted:
   (a) there must be undisputed evidence the party, or intended party, lacks capacity to conduct the proceedings;

1 In this context a 'vulnerable adult' is a person who has mental capacity in respect of the decisions in question but who lacks litigation capacity.
2 [1896] 1 Ch 351.
3 See the Attorney-General's Memorandum of 19 December 2001: 'Requests for the appointment of an advocate to the court'. [2002] Fam Law 229.

(b) that evidence, and what flows from the party, or intended party, being a protected party, should have been disclosed to, and carefully explained to, the party or intended party;

(c) the party, or intended party, is entitled to dispute an opinion that they lack capacity to conduct the proceedings; there may be cases where the party's, or intended party's, capacity to conduct the proceedings is the subject of dispute between competent experts. In either case a formal finding by the court under FPR 2010, rule 2.3, or CPR 1998, rule 21.2 is required.

Vulnerable adult

6. Applications made under the inherent jurisdiction in respect of a 'vulnerable' adult are made to the Family Division of the High Court but are not family proceedings; the CPR 1998 apply to proceedings under the inherent jurisdiction in respect of adults and the application should be made on a Part 8 claim form using the Part 8 alternative procedure.

7. Difficult questions may arise if the 'vulnerable' adult despite having capacity to make the decision or decisions in question nonetheless lacks capacity to conduct the proceedings.

8. A litigation friend is only required if the 'vulnerable' adult does lack capacity to conduct the proceedings and is therefore a protected party as defined in CPR 1998, rule 21.2.

Court of Protection

9. The Court of Protection was established by section 45 Mental Capacity Act 2005. Court of Protection proceedings are not family proceedings. 'P' in Court of Protection proceedings is any person (other than a protected party) who lacks or, so far as consistent with the context, is alleged to lack capacity to make a decision or decisions in relation to any matter that is the subject of an application to the Court of Protection (CoPR 2007, rule 6).

10. A 'protected party' is a party or an intended party (other than P or a child) who lacks capacity to conduct the proceedings (CoPR 2007, rule 6).

Children who require a litigation friend in proceedings

11. Non-subject child: a child who is not the subject of family proceedings may nevertheless be a party and subject to FPR 2010 rule 16.6 (see paragraph 7), requires a litigation friend in family proceedings. The most common examples are:

(a) a child who is also the parent of a child, and who is a respondent to a Children Act 1989 or Adoption and Children Act 2002 application;

(b) a child who wishes to make an application for a Children Act 1989 order naming another child (typically a child arrangements order for contact with a sibling);

(c) a child who has been joined as an intervener in a public law children case to respond to allegations;

(d) a child intervenor in financial remedy proceedings;

(e) a child party to applications for declarations of status under Part III Family Law Act 1986 other than section 55A applications;

(f) a child applicant for, or respondent to, an application for an order under Part IV (Family Homes and Domestic Violence) or Part 4A (Forced Marriage) of the Family Law Act 1996;

12. Child parties to applications for declarations of parentage under section 55A Family Law Act 1986: subject to FPR 2010 rule 16.6, in section 55A cases

(a) any child whose parentage is in dispute and who has been joined as party under FPR 2010 rule 16.2 would have a children's guardian appointed under rule 16.4;
(b) a child party whose parentage is not in dispute requires a litigation friend.

13. FPR 2010 Part 16 makes provision for the representation of children.
    (a) Rule 16.6 sets out the circumstances in which a child does not need a children's guardian or litigation friend. A child party to proceedings under the Children Act 1989, section 55A Family Law Act 1986, Part 4A Family Law Act 1996, applications in adoption, placement and related proceedings, or proceedings relating to the exercise of the court's inherent jurisdiction with respect to children, may rely on the provisions of rule 16.6.
    (b) However this rule does not apply to those children who are the subject of and party to specified proceedings or proceedings to which Part 14 applies.

14. Children aged 16–17 years: the Mental Capacity Act 2005 (Transfer of Proceedings) Order 2007 (SI 2007/1899) makes provision for the transfer of proceedings from the Court of Protection to a court having jurisdiction under the Children Act 1989. The Order also makes provision for the transfer of the whole or part of the proceedings from a court having jurisdiction under the Children Act 1989 to the Court of Protection where it considers that in all circumstances, it is just and convenient to transfer the proceedings:
    (a) Article 3(3) of the Order lists those factors to which the court must have regard when making a determination about transfer to the Court of Protection either on an application or of its own initiative;
    (b) proceedings transferred under Article 3 are to be treated for all purposes as if they were proceedings under the Mental Capacity Act 2005 which had been started in the Court of Protection;
    (c) as Court of Protection proceedings are not family proceedings transfer of proceedings into the Court of Protection means any involvement by CAFCASS in those proceedings will end;
    (d) there should be reason to believe that the child lacks capacity (within the meaning of the Mental Capacity Act 2005) in relation to a matter or matters concerning their own welfare and that it is likely that they will still lack capacity to make decisions in respect of that matter when they reach 18.

15. Rules 141(4)–(5) of the CoPR 2007 make provision for a child to be permitted to conduct proceedings in the Court of Protection without a litigation friend. However if the child is 'P' within the meaning of rule 6 of the CoPR 2007 reference should be made to rule 141(1) and rule 147 of those Rules in relation to the appointment of a litigation friend.

The role of a litigation friend

16. The case law and the Rules provide that a litigation friend must fairly and competently conduct the proceedings in the protected party's or child's best interests,[4] and must

4 Sir Robert Megarry V-C said in *Re E (mental health patient)* [1984] 1 All ER 309 at pages 312–3

> 'The main function of a [litigation] friend appears to be to carry on the litigation on behalf of the plaintiff and in his best interests. For this purpose the [litigation] friend must make all the decisions that the plaintiff would have made, had he been able … the [litigation] friend … is responsible to the court for the propriety and the progress of the proceedings. The [litigation] friend does not, however, become a litigant himself …'

have no interest in the proceedings adverse to that of the protected party or child. The procedure and basis for the appointment of a litigation friend and the duty of a litigation friend are contained in Part 15 (Representation of Protected Parties) FPR 2010 and Part 16 (Representation of Children and Reports in Proceedings Involving Children) FPR 2010 and the associated Practice Directions.

The Official Solicitor's criteria for consenting to act as litigation friend

17. The Official Solicitor is the litigation friend of last resort. No person, including the Official Solicitor, can be appointed to act as litigation friend without their consent. The Official Solicitor will not accept appointment where there is another person who is suitable and willing to act as litigation friend. The Official Solicitor's criteria for consenting to act as litigation friend are:
   (a) in the case of an adult that the party or intended party is a protected party;[5]
   (b) there is security for the costs of legal representation of the protected party which the Official Solicitor considers satisfactory. Sources of security may be:
      (i) the Legal Aid Agency where the protected party or child is eligible for legal aid;
      (ii) the protected party's or child's own funds where they have financial capacity or where they do not where the Court of Protection has given him authority to recover the costs from the adult's or child's funds;
      (iii) an undertaking from another party to pay his costs;
   (c) the case is a last resort case.

Invitations to the Official Solicitor: new cases

18. Solicitors who have been consulted by a child or a protected party (or by someone acting on their behalf, or concerned about their interests) should write to the Official Solicitor setting out the background to the proposed case and explaining the basis on which the Official Solicitor's criteria for acting are met.

Invitations to the Official Solicitor: pending proceedings

19. Where a case is already before the court, an order inviting the Official Solicitor to act should be expressed as being made subject to his consent. The Official Solicitor cannot consent to act unless and until he is satisfied that his criteria are met.

20. If so satisfied, he will allocate public law children cases to a case manager within 2 working days of his criteria being met; all other cases will be allocated within 5 working days. The position in relation to allocation may be subject to change from time to time.

Public law children cases

21. Allocation to a case manager does not preclude the need for the case manager to be given sufficient time to become familiar with the facts of, and issues in the case before the Official Solicitor, as litigation friend of the protected party or child, is able to give instructions. The case manager will have existing cases and must make decisions about priorities. Allocation to a case manager in close proximity to a hearing may require that the hearing be re-listed.

5 The Official Solicitor is able to provide a pro forma certificate of capacity to conduct proceedings and guidance notes. The pro forma is also available on www.gov.uk.

22. To enable the Official Solicitor promptly to consider the invitation to him to act, he should be sent as soon as possible the completed referral form for public law children cases (available at www.gov.uk[6]) and the documents that form refers to.

All other cases

23. In all other cases the Official Solicitor should be provided with the following as soon as possible:
    (a) the sealed court order inviting him to act as litigation friend (with a note of the reasons approved by the Judge if appropriate);
    (b) (adult party):
        (i) a copy of the letter of instruction to the expert by which an opinion was sought as to the party's capacity to conduct the proceedings;
        (ii) the opinion on capacity (the Official Solicitor's pro forma certificate of capacity to conduct proceedings may be requested from his office for the purpose of obtaining an opinion and is available on www.gov.uk[7]);
    (c) a full explanation as to how the costs of legal representation are to be paid (including any relevant supporting documents) – it is a matter for the Official Solicitor whether the proposed security for costs is satisfactory;
    (d) confirmation that there is no other person suitable and willing to act as litigation friend (including enquiries made about this);
    (e) the court file (provision of the court file may not be necessary if the court directs a party to provide a full indexed copy of the bundle to the Official Solicitor on a timely basis).

Litigants in person

24. If one or more of the parties is or are litigants in person, and there is reason to believe that a litigant in person may lack capacity to conduct the proceedings, the court will need to consider, and if necessary give directions as to:
    (a) who is to arrange for assessment of their capacity to conduct the proceedings;
    (b) how the cost of that assessment is to be funded;
    (c) how any invitation to act as litigation friend is to be made either to any suitable and willing person or to the Official Solicitor so as to provide the proposed litigation friend with the documents and relevant information (including information to enable enquiries necessary to establish whether or not funding for legal costs is available);
    (d) any resulting timetabling: where the Official Solicitor is being invited to be litigation friend regard should be had to the Official Solicitor's need to investigate whether his acceptance criteria are met including the possibility that an application to the Court of Protection (for authority to pay the costs out of the protected party's or child's funds) may be necessary.

25. The Official Solicitor will notify the court in the event he expects a delay in accepting appointment either because it is not evident that his criteria are met or for any other reason. The court may wish to consider:
    (a) making enquiries of the parties as to the steps being taken by them to establish that the Official Solicitor's criteria for acting are met;
    (b) whether directions should be made to ensure that the parties progress such enquiries on a timely basis;
    (c) fixing a further directions appointment.

6 https://www.gov.uk/government/publications/official-solicitor-referral-form-for-children-act-public-law-proceedings.

7 https://www.gov.uk/government/publications/certificate-as-to-capacity-to-conduct-proceedings.

26. If, at any time, another litigation friend is appointed before the Official Solicitor is in a position to accept the invitation to him to act, the Official Solicitor should be notified without delay.

Where the Official Solicitor has accepted appointment as litigation friend

27. Once the Official Solicitor is able to accept appointment as litigation friend he will need time to prepare the case on behalf of the protected party or child and may wish to make submissions about any substantive hearing date.

28. In all cases to avoid unnecessary delay in progression of the case, he requires from the solicitors he appoints for the protected party or child:
(a) a reading list identifying the material documents;
(b) identification of the issues including those which require consideration on behalf of the protected party or child;
(c) a summary of the background to, and major steps in the proceedings;
(d) advice as to the steps the Official Solicitor, as litigation friend, should now take in the proceedings on behalf of the protected party or child;
(e) copies of <u>all</u> notes of attendance on the protected party or child (so that the Official Solicitor is properly informed as to the views and wishes expressed by the protected party or child to date);
(f) confirmation of the protected party's or child's ascertainable present views and wishes in relation to the proceedings.

Advising the court: Harbin v Masterman *enquiries and Advocate to the Court*

29. Where the Official Solicitor is invited, with his consent, to conduct enquiries under *Harbin v Masterman* and it appears to the Official Solicitor that any public body wishes to seek the assistance of the court but is unwilling to carry out the enquiries itself, the Official Solicitor may seek an undertaking from that public body to indemnify him in respect of his costs of carrying out those enquiries.

30. The Official Solicitor may be invited by the court to act or instruct counsel as a friend of the court (advocate to the court) if it appears to the court that such an invitation is more appropriately addressed to him rather than (or in addition to) CAFCASS Legal Services or to the Attorney-General. It is a matter for him whether he accepts that invitation.

Contacting the Official Solicitor

31. It may be helpful to discuss the question of appointment with the Official Solicitor or one of his staff by telephoning 020 3681 2755 (General enquiries: public law family cases) 020 3681 2754 (General enquiries: private law family cases including divorce), or 020 3681 2751 (General enquiries: Court of Protection healthcare & welfare). In particular:
(a) if in doubt about whether the Official Solicitor's acceptance criteria are met, or
(b) to request a copy of the Official Solicitor's pro forma certificate of capacity to conduct proceedings and guidance notes.[8]

32. Enquiries about the appointment of the Official Solicitor as litigation friend in family proceedings should be addressed:
(a) (in private law family cases) to the Team Leader, Family Litigation (Private Law);
(b) (in public law family cases) to the Team Leader, Family Litigation (Public Law).

8 Also available online by navigating from: https://www.gov.uk/government/organisations/official-solicitor-and-public-trustee.

All other enquiries should be addressed to a family lawyer.

The contact details are:

Office of the Official Solicitor to the Senior Courts

Victory House
30-34 Kingsway
London WC2B 6EX

DX 141423 Bloomsbury 7

Fax: 020 3681 2762

E-mail: enquiries@offsol.gsi.gov.uk

Alastair Pitblado, Official Solicitor

January 2017

https://www.gov.uk/government/organisations/official-solicitor-and-public-trustee

7 Family Court (Composition and Distribution of Business) Rules 2014

SI 2014/840

PART 1
INTRODUCTORY PROVISIONS

Citation, commencement and interpretation

1

These Rules may be cited as the Family Court (Composition and Distribution of Business) Rules 2014 and come into force on 22nd April 2014.

2

(1) In these Rules—

'the 1991 Act' means the Child Support Act 1991;

'appeal' includes an application seeking permission to appeal and an application in the course of the appeal proceedings;

'assistant to a justices' clerk' has the meaning given in section 27(5) of the Courts Act 2003;

'authorised', except in the context of references to an authorised court officer, means authorised by the President of the Family Division or nominated by or on behalf of the Lord Chief Justice to conduct particular business in the family court, in accordance with Part 3;

'authorised court officer' has the meaning assigned to it by rule 44.1 of the Civil Procedure Rules 1998 as applied to family proceedings by rule 28.2(1) of the Family Procedure Rules 2010;

'costs judge' means—

(a) the Chief Taxing Master;

(b) a taxing master of the Senior Courts; or

(c) a person appointed to act as deputy for the person holding office referred to in paragraph (b) or to act as a temporary additional officer for any such office;

'financial remedy' has the meaning assigned to it by rule 2.3 of the Family Procedure Rules 2010;

'judge of circuit judge level' means—

(a) a circuit judge who, where applicable, is authorised;

(b) a Recorder who, where applicable, is authorised;

(c) any other judge of the family court authorised to sit as a judge of circuit judge level in the family court;

'judge of district judge level' means—

(a) the Senior District Judge of the Family Division;

(b) a district judge of the Principal Registry of the Family Division;

(c) a person appointed to act as deputy for the person holding office referred to in paragraph (b) or to act as a temporary additional officer for any such office;

(d) a district judge who, where applicable, is authorised;

(e) a deputy district judge appointed under section 102 of the Senior Courts Act 1981 or section 8 of the County Courts Act 1984 who, where applicable, is authorised;

(f) an authorised District Judge (magistrates' Courts);
(g) any other judge of the family court authorised to sit as a judge of district judge level in the family court.

'judge of High Court judge level' means—
(a) a deputy judge of the High Court;
(b) a puisne judge of the High Court;
(c) a person who has been a judge of the Court of Appeal or a puisne judge of the High Court who may act as a judge of the family court by virtue of section 9 of the Senior Courts Act 1981;
(d) the Senior President of Tribunals;
(e) the Chancellor of the High Court;
(f) an ordinary judge of the Court of Appeal (including the vice-president, if any, of either division of that court);
(g) the President of the Queen's Bench Division;
(h) the President of the Family Division;
(i) the Master of the Rolls;
(j) the Lord Chief Justice;

'judge of the family court' means a judge referred to in section 31C(1) of the Matrimonial and Family Proceedings Act 1984;

'justices' clerk' has the meaning given in section 27(1) of the Courts Act 2003; and

'lay justice' means an authorised justice of the peace who is not a District Judge (magistrates' Courts).

(2) In these Rules, references to provisions of the Adoption and Children Act 2002 include, as applicable, references to those provisions as modified by the Human Fertilisation and Embryology (Parental Orders) Regulations 2010.

PART 2
COMPOSITION OF THE FAMILY COURT

Composition: general

3

(1) Subject to rules in this Part, the family court shall be composed of—
(a) one of the following—
(i) a judge of district judge level;
(ii) a judge of circuit judge level; or
(iii) a judge of High Court judge level; or
(b) two or three lay justices.

(2) Where paragraph (1)(b) applies, the court shall include, so far as is practicable, both a man and a woman.

Composition: allocation decision

4

When making a decision on allocation to which rule 20 applies, the family court shall be composed of one or more of the following —

(a) a judge of district judge level;
(b) a judge of circuit judge level.

Composition: appeals heard by a judge of district judge level

5

(1) Subject to rule 7, the family court shall be composed of a judge of district judge level when hearing an appeal from the decision of the Secretary of State where an appeal is brought under—
   (a) regulation 25AB(1) of the Child Support (Collection and Enforcement) Regulations 1992 (Appeals);
   (b) section 20(1) (a) or (b) of the 1991 Act to a court by virtue of article 3 of the Child Support Appeals (Jurisdiction of Courts) Order 2002 (Parentage appeals to be made to courts).

(2) The family court may be composed of a judge of district judge level when hearing applications in the course of appeal proceedings against decisions of persons referred to in rule 6(2)(b) to (d) or decisions of the court referred to in rule 6(3).

(3) The family court shall be composed of a costs judge or a district judge of the High Court when hearing an appeal against the decision of an authorised court officer.

Composition: appeals heard by a judge of circuit judge level or a judge of High Court level

6

(1) Subject to rule 7, when hearing an appeal from the decisions of persons referred to in paragraph (2) or the court referred to in paragraph (3), the family court shall be composed of—
   (a) a judge of circuit judge level; or
   (b) a judge of High Court level where there is a need for such a level of judge to hear the appeal to make most effective and efficient use of local judicial resource and the resource of the High Court bench.

(2) The persons referred to in paragraph (1) are—
   (a) a judge of district judge level;
   (b) two or three lay justices;
   (c) a lay justice; or
   (d) a justices' clerk or an assistant to a justices' clerk.

(3) The court referred to in paragraph (1) is a magistrates' court where an appeal is brought under section 111A of the magistrates' Courts Act 1980 (appeals on ground of error of law in child support proceedings).

Composition: appeals heard by a judge of High Court level

7

(1) The family court shall be composed of a judge of High Court level when hearing an appeal from the decision of—
   (a) the Senior District Judge of the Family Division in financial remedy proceedings;
   (b) …[1]
   (c) a costs judge; or
   (d) the Gender Recognition Panel where an appeal is brought under section 8(1) of the Gender Recognition Act 2004 (Appeals etc.).

(2) The family court shall be composed of a judge of High Court level (instead of a judge of district judge level or a judge of circuit judge level) where there is—

(a) an appeal against a decision referred to in rules 5 and 6; and
(b) the Designated Family Judge or a judge of High Court level considers that the appeal would raise an important point of principle or practice.

Amendments

1 Revoked by the Family Court (Composition and Distribution of Business) (Amendment) Rules 2021, SI 2021/505.

Composition: matters part heard

8

(1) Paragraph (2) applies where a hearing—
(a) was before two or three lay justices; and
(b) was part heard.
(2) The court which resumes the hearing shall, wherever possible, be composed of the same lay justices as dealt with the previous part of the hearing.

PART 3
AUTHORISATIONS

Powers to grant authorisations

9

(1) Paragraph (2) applies to business in such categories as may be specified from time to time by the President of the Family Division.
(2) A judge of district judge level or a judge of circuit judge level may conduct business to which this paragraph applies in the family court only if authorised by the President of the Family Division to do so.
(3) The President of the Family Division may specify the matters referred to in paragraph (1) in directions, after consulting the Lord Chancellor.
(4) A lay justice may conduct business in the family court only if authorised by the Lord Chief Justice to do so.

PART 4
LAY JUSTICES: CHAIRMANSHIP OF THE FAMILY COURT

[Interpretation of this Part

10

In this Part, '2016 Rules' means the Justices of the Peace Rules 2016.][1]

Amendments

1 Substituted by the Justices of the Peace Rules 2016, SI 2016/709, r 36(1), (2).

Chairman

11

(1) When the family court is composed of two or three lay justices, it shall sit under the chairmanship of a lay justice who [has been approved to preside in accordance with the 2016 Rules][1].

(2) A lay justice may preside before being [approved to preside in accordance with the 2016 Rules][1] only if that lay justice is—
  (a) under the supervision of another authorised lay justice who is [approved to preside in accordance with the 2016 Rules][1]; and
  (b) has completed the training course required by [rule 19 of the 2016 Rules][1].

(3) …[2]

(4) This rule and rule 12 are subject to sections 18(1) and (2) of the Courts Act 2003.

Amendments

1 Substituted by the Justices of the Peace Rules 2016, SI 2016/709, r 36(1), (3)(a)–(d).
2 Repealed by the Justices of the Peace Rules 2016, SI 2016/709, r 36(1), (3)(e).

Absence of authorised lay justice entitled to preside

12

(1) The lay justices present may appoint one of their number to preside in the family court to deal with any case in the absence of a lay justice entitled to preside under rule 11 if—
  (a) before making such appointment the lay justices present are satisfied as to the suitability for this purpose of the lay justice proposed; and
  (b) expect as mentioned in paragraph (2), the lay justice proposed has completed or is undergoing a chairman training course in accordance with [rule 19(f) of the 2016 Rules][1].

(2) The condition in paragraph (1)(b) does not apply if by reason of illness, circumstances unforeseen when the lay justices to sit were chosen, or other emergency, no lay justice who complies with that condition is present.

Amendments

1 Substituted by the Justices of the Peace Rules 2016, SI 2016/709, r 36(1), (4).

PART 5
DISTRIBUTION OF BUSINESS OF THE FAMILY COURT

[Interpretation of this Part

12A

In this Part—

'incoming protection measure' means a protection measure that has been ordered in a Member State of the European Union other than the United Kingdom or Denmark;

'protection measure' has the meaning given to it in the Protection Measures Regulation;

'Protection Measures Regulation' means Regulation (EU) No 606/2013 of the European Parliament and of the Council of 12th June 2013 on mutual recognition of protection measures in civil matters.][1]

Amendments

1 Inserted by the Family Court (Composition and Distribution of Business) (Amendment) Rules 2014, SI 2014/3297 rr 2, 3.

General

13

(1) This Part makes provision for the distribution of business of the family court among the judges of the family court.

(2) Rules 15 and 20 are subject to rule 17.

(3) Rules 15, 16, 17, 18, 19 and 20 make provision regarding the level of judge of the family court to which a matter is to be allocated initially.

(Rule 29.19 of the Family Procedure Rules 2010 makes provision for a judge of the family court to determine that a matter should be heard by a different level of judge of the family court.)

Persons who may exercise jurisdiction of the family court

14

Subject to the provisions of this Part or of any other enactment, any jurisdiction and powers conferred by any enactment on the family court, or on a judge of the family court, may be exercised by any judge of the family court.

Allocation of proceedings in Schedule 1

15

(1) An application in a type of proceedings listed in the first column of the table in Schedule 1 shall be allocated to be heard by a judge of the level listed in the second column of that table.

(2) Paragraph (1) and the provisions of Schedule 1 are subject to the need to take into account the need to make the most effective and efficient use of local judicial resource and the resource of the High Court bench that is appropriate given the nature and type of the application.

Allocation of emergency applications

16

(1) In this rule—

'the 1986 Act' means the Family Law Act 1986;
'the 1989 Act' means the Children Act 1989; and
'the 1996 Act' means the Family Law Act 1996.

(2) An application of a type referred to in paragraph (3) shall be allocated to the first available judge of the family court who—

- (a) where applicable, is authorised to conduct the type of business to which the application relates; and
- (b) would not be precluded by Schedule 2 from dealing with the application.

(3) The types of applications are those—

- (a) under—
  - (i) section 33 of the 1986 Act (disclosure of information as to the whereabouts of a child);
  - (ii) section 34 of the 1986 Act (order authorising the taking charge and delivery of a child);

(iii) section 44(1) of the 1989 Act (emergency protection order);
(iv) section 44(9)(b) of the 1989 Act (varying a direction in an emergency protection order given under section 44(6) of the 1989 Act);
(v) section 45(4) of the 1989 Act (extending the period during which an emergency protection order is to have effect);
(vi) section 45(8) of the 1989 Act (to discharge an emergency protection order);
(vii) section 45(8A) of the 1989 Act (to vary or discharge an emergency protection order in so far as it imposes an exclusion requirement on a person who is not entitled to apply for the order to be discharged);
(viii) section 45(8B) of the 1989 Act (to vary or discharge an emergency protection order in so far as it confers powers of arrest attached to an exclusion requirement);
(ix) section 48(9) of the 1989 Act (warrant to assist in discovery of children who may be in need of emergency protection);
(x) section 50 of the 1989 Act (recovery of abducted children);
(xi) section 102(1) of the 1989 Act (warrant for a constable to assist in the exercise of certain powers to search for children or inspect premises);
(xii) Part 4 of the 1996 Act which are made without notice, except where the applicant is under 18 or where an application for an occupation order under section 33 of that Act requires a determination of a question of property ownership;
(xiii) section 41 of the Adoption and Children Act 2002 (recovery order); …[1]
(xiv) section 79 of the Childcare Act 2006 (warrant for a constable to assist in the exercise of powers of entry); …[1]
[(xv) the Protection Measures Regulation made within or in connection with an application under sub-paragraph (xii); or
(xvi) Article 11 of the Protection Measures Regulation for adjustment of an incoming protection measure except where the applicant is aged under 18; or][2]

(b) which are not referred to in paragraph (a) but which require the immediate attention of the court.

(4) An application of a type listed in paragraph (5) shall be allocated to the first available judge of the family court, other than lay justices, who, where applicable, is authorised to conduct the type of business to which the application relates.

(5) The types of application are those under—
(a) Part 4 of the 1996 Act which are made without notice and where the applicant is aged under 18 or where an application for an occupation order under section 33 of that Act requires a determination of a question of property ownership;
(b) Part 4A of the 1996 Act which are made without notice[;][3]
[(c) the Protection Measures Regulation made within or in connection with an application under sub-paragraph (a) or (b);
(d) Article 11 of the Protection Measures Regulation for adjustment of an incoming protection measure where the applicant is aged under 18[;][4]][1]
[(e) Part 1 of Schedule 2 to the Female Genital Mutilation Act 2003 which are made without notice.][5]

Amendments

1 Repealed by the Family Court (Composition and Distribution of Business) (Amendment) Rules 2014, SI 2014/3297 rr 2, 4(a)(i).

2 Inserted by the Family Court (Composition and Distribution of Business) (Amendment) Rules 2014, SI 2014/3297 rr 2, 4(a)(ii), (b)(ii).
3 Substituted by the Family Court (Composition and Distribution of Business) (Amendment) Rules 2014, SI 2014/3297 rr 2, 4(b)(i).
4 Substituted by the Family Court (Composition and Distribution of Business) (Amendment) Rules 2015, SI 2015/1421, rr 2, 3(a).
5 Inserted by the Family Court (Composition and Distribution of Business) (Amendment) Rules 2015, SI 2015/1421, rr 2, 3(b).

Allocation: applications in existing proceedings or in connection with proceedings that have concluded

17

(1) Subject to paragraphs (3) to (5), an application made within existing proceedings in the family court shall be allocated to the level of judge who is dealing with the existing proceedings to which the application relates.

(2) Subject to paragraphs (3) to (5), an application made in connection with proceedings in the family court that have concluded shall be allocated to the level of judge who last dealt with those proceedings.

(3) In Schedule 2—

(a) the remedies listed in tables 1, 2 and 3 may not be granted by lay justices;

(b) the remedies listed in tables 2 and 3 may not be granted by a judge of district judge level;

(c) the remedies listed in table 3 may not be granted by a judge of circuit judge level, subject to any exception stated in that table.

(4) Where the effect of Schedule 2 is that an application for a particular remedy may not be granted by the level of judge referred to in paragraph (1) or (2), then that application shall be allocated to a level of judge who is able to grant that remedy.

(5) Any power of the family court to make an order for committal in respect of a breach of a judgment, order or undertaking to do or abstain from doing an act may only be made by a judge of the same level as, or of a higher level than, the judge who make the judgment or order, or who accepted the undertaking, as the case may be.

Allocation: costs

18

Subject to any direction of the court, an application for detailed assessment of a bill of costs shall be allocated to an authorised court officer, a district judge or a costs judge.

Allocation: appeals

19

An appeal shall be allocated to a judge in accordance with rules 5 to 7.

Allocation: all other proceedings

20

(1) An application of a type not referred to in other rules in this Part or in Schedule 1 or Schedule 2 shall be allocated by one or more of the persons referred to in rule 4.

(2) When deciding which level of judge to allocate such an application to, the decision must be based on consideration of the relative significance of the following factors—
   (a) the need to make the most effective and efficient use of the local judicial resource and the resource of the High Court bench that is appropriate, given the nature and type of application;
   (b) the need to avoid delay;
   (c) the need for judicial continuity;
   (d) the location of the parties or of any child relevant to the proceedings; and
   (e) complexity.

PART 6
GUIDANCE

Guidance on distribution of business of the family court

21

(1) The President of the Family Division may, after consulting the Lord Chancellor, issue guidance on the application or interpretation of Part 5.
(2) Where the Lord Chancellor determines that the guidance has significant implications for resources, it may only be issued with the agreement of the Lord Chancellor.
(3) If the Lord Chancellor does not agree the guidance, the Lord Chancellor must provide the President of the Family Division with written reasons why the Lord Chancellor does not agree the guidance.

Schedule 1
Allocation

Rule 15

Type of proceedings	*Level of judge*
1 Proceedings under— (a) the Maintenance Orders (Facilities for Enforcement) Act 1920; (b) the Marriage Act 1949; (c) the Maintenance Orders Act 1950; (d) the Maintenance Orders Act 1958; (e) the Maintenance Orders (Reciprocal Enforcement) Act 1972; (f) the Domestic Proceedings and magistrates' Courts Act 1978; (g) the Civil Jurisdiction and Judgments Act 1982; (h) the Family Law Act 1986, section 55A (declarations of parentage); (i) the Child Support Act 1991, except section 32L or appeals; (j) the Crime and Disorder Act 1998, section 11 (child safety order);	Lay justices.

	(k) Council Regulation (EC) No.44/2001 (known as the Judgments Regulation); (l) section 34 of the Children and Families (Wales) Measure 2010; (m) Schedule 6 to the Civil Partnership Act 2004; (n) the Childcare Act 2006, except section 79; (o) the Human Fertilisation and Embryology Act 2008, section 54, where the child's place of birth was in England and Wales and where all respondents agree to the making of the order; (p) Council Regulation (EC) No. 4/2009 (known as the Maintenance Regulation)[;][1] [(q) the Protection Measures Regulation for enforcement of an incoming protection measure.][2]	
2	Proceedings under— (a) the Married Women's Property Act 1882; (b) the Matrimonial Causes Act 1973; (c) the Matrimonial and Family Proceedings Act 1984 sections 13 and 12 (permission and substantive application) …;[3] (d) the Children Act 1989, Schedule 1; (e) the Gender Recognition Act 2004, except appeals under section 8(1) and referrals to the court under section 8(5); (f) the Civil Partnership Act 2004, except under— (i) Schedule 6 (financial provision corresponding to provision made by the Domestic Proceedings and magistrates' Courts Act 1978); and[4]	Judge of district judge level
3	Proceedings under— (a) the Family Law Act 1986 section 55 (declarations as to marital status), 56 (declarations as to legitimacy or legitimation) or 57 (declarations as to adoptions effected overseas); (b) the Child Support Act 1991 under section 32L (orders preventing avoidance); (c) the Human Fertilisation and Embryology Act 2008, section 54, where the child's place of birth was in England and Wales but where not all respondents agree to the making of the order.	Judge of circuit judge level.

4	Proceedings under— (a) …[5] (b) the Adoption and Children Act 2002, section 60(3) (order to disclose or to prevent disclosure of information to an adopted person); (c) the Adoption and Children Act 2002, section 79(4) (order for Registrar General to give information); (d) …[6] (e) referrals to the court under section 8(5) of the Gender Recognition Act 2004; (f) the Human Fertilisation and Embryology Act 2008, section 54, where the child's place of birth was outside of England and Wales[;][1] [(g) Article 13 of the Protection Measures Regulation.][2]	Judge of High Court judge level
5	Proceedings under the Adoption and Children Act 2002 under— (a) section 21 (placement order); (b) section 23 (order varying a placement order); (c) section 24 (order revoking a placement order); (d) section 26 (contact order); (e) section 27 (order varying or revoking a contact order); (f) section 28(2) or (3) (order permitting the child's name to be changed or the removal of the child from the United Kingdom); (g) section 46 (adoption order) except where— (i) a local authority is a party to the application; (ii) the application is for an overseas adoption within the meaning given in section 87 of the Adoption and Children Act 2002; or (iii) the application is for a Convention adoption within the meaning given in section 66(1)(c) of the Adoption and Children Act 2002; (h) section 51A(2)(a) or (b) (post-adoption contact); (i) section 55 (revocation of adoption on legitimation); (j) paragraph 4 of Schedule 1 (amendment of orders).	Level of judge who is dealing with, or has dealt with, proceedings relating to the same child or, if there are or were no such proceedings, to lay justices.
6	Proceedings under the Adoption and Children Act 2002 under section 46 (adoption order) where — (a) a local authority is a party to the application; (b) the application is for an overseas adoption within the meaning given in section 87 of the Adoption and Children Act 2002; or (c) the application is for a Convention adoption within the meaning given in section 66(1)(c) of the Adoption and Children Act 2002.	Level of judge who is dealing with, or dealt with, proceedings relating to the same child or, if there are or were no such proceedings, to a judge of district judge level.

Amendments

1 Substituted by the Family Court (Composition and Distribution of Business) (Amendment) Rules 2014, SI 2014/3297 rr 2, 5(a)(i), (b)(i).
2 Inserted by the Family Court (Composition and Distribution of Business) (Amendment) Rules 2014, SI 2014/3297 rr 2, 5(a)(ii), (b)(ii).
3 Words omitted revoked by the Family Court (Composition and Distribution of Business) (Amendment) Rules 2021, SI 2021/505.
4 Sub-para (ii) revoked by the Family Court (Composition and Distribution of Business) (Amendment) Rules 2021, SI 2021/505.
5 Sub-para (a) revoked by the Family Court (Composition and Distribution of Business) (Amendment) Rules 2021, SI 2021/505.
6 Sub-para (d) revoked by the Family Court (Composition and Distribution of Business) (Amendment) Rules 2021, SI 2021/505.

Schedule 2
Remedies

Rule 17

Table 1
Remedies which may not be granted by lay justices in the family court

1 Charging order.
2 Order (known as a 'freezing injunction') restraining a party from:
(a) removing from the jurisdiction assets located there;
(b) dealing with any assets whether located in the jurisdiction or not.
3 Interim injunction.
4 Interim declaration.
5 Order under section 34Senior Courts Act 1981 or section 53County Courts Act 1984, as applied to the family court under section 31EMatrimonial and Family Proceedings Act 1984, for disclosure of documents or inspection of property against a non-party.
6 Order for a specified fund to be paid into court where there is a dispute over a party's right to the fund.
7 Order permitting a party seeking to recover personal property to pay money into court pending the outcome of the proceedings and directing that, if money is paid into court, the property must be given to that party.
8 Order directing a party to provide information about the location of relevant property or assets or to provide information about relevant property or assets, which are or may be the subject of an application for a freezing injunction.
9 Order directing a party to prepare and file accounts relating to the dispute.
10 Order directing an account to be taken or enquiry to be made by the court.
11 Third party debt order.
12 Order for—
(a) detention, custody or preservation of relevant property;
(b) inspection of relevant property;
(c) taking of a sample of relevant property;
(d) carrying out an experiment on or with relevant property;
(e) sale of relevant property which is of a perishable nature or which for any other good reason it is desirable to sell quickly;
(f) the payment of income from relevant property until an application is decided.

13 Order authorising a person to enter any land or building in the possession of a party for the purposes of carrying out an order referred to in paragraph 12.
14 Warrant of delivery.
15 Warrant of control.
16 Warrant for the possession of land.
17 Order to deliver up goods under section 4 of the Torts (Interference with Goods) Act 1977.

Table 2

Remedies which may not be granted by lay justices or judges of district judge level in the family court

1 Civil restraint order (limited).

Table 3

Remedies which may not be granted by lay justices, judges of district judge level or judges of circuit judge level in the family court

1 Civil restraint order (extended or general), except that such orders may be granted by a Designated Family Judge or a deputy Designated Family Judge.
2 Search order requiring a party to admit another party to premises for the purposes of preserving evidence etc (section 7 Civil Procedure Act 1997).
3 Claims in respect of a judicial act under the Human Rights Act 1998.
4 Action in respect of the interference with the due administration of justice.
5 Warrants of sequestration to enforce a judgment, order or undertaking in the family court.
[6 Order under Article 13 of the Protection Measures Regulation refusing to recognise or enforce an incoming protection measure.][1]

Amendments

1 Inserted by the Family Court (Composition and Distribution of Business) (Amendment) Rules 2014, SI 2014/3297 rr 2, 6.

8 President's Guidance on Allocation and Gatekeeping for Care, Supervision and other Proceedings under Part IV of the Children Act 1989 (Public Law)

Issued in accordance with rule 21 of the Family Court (Composition and Distribution of Business) Rules 2014

Issued 22 April 2014

Introduction

1. This Guidance is issued by the President of the Family Division and applies to all care, supervision and other Part IV proceedings commencing on and after 22 April 2014. It is issued following consultation with, and where applicable the agreement of, the Lord Chancellor, in accordance with rule 21 of the Family Court (Composition and Distribution of Business) Rules 2014, and is to be read with those Rules and PD12A (PLO 2014).
2. This Guidance applies to the allocation of all relevant proceedings to judges of the Family Court, including allocation to lay justices working with Justices' Clerks or Assistant Justices' Clerks (referred to in this guidance as "legal advisers"). The purpose of the Guidance is to ensure that all new care, supervision and other Part IV proceedings are allocated to the appropriate level of judge and, where appropriate, to a named case management judge (or case manager) who shall provide continuity for the proceedings in accordance with the President's Guidance on Judicial Continuity and Deployment (Public Law).

Gatekeeping teams

3. Each Designated Family Judge (DFJ) will lead a gatekeeping team in each Designated Family Centre. A gatekeeping team will consist of the Designated Family Judge, his nominated deputy, the Justices 'Clerk (or his nominated legal adviser) and an equal number of District Judges nominated by the Designated Family Judge, and legal advisers who will be identified by the Justices' Clerk in agreement with the Designated Family Judge. The number of legal advisers and District Judges is to be consistent with the needs of the business and the expertise of those who are available. Members of the gatekeeping team are referred to in this guidance as "gatekeepers".
4. All applications for care, supervision and other Part IV orders which are received for issue by 4.00 pm will be issued by HMCTS and placed before gatekeepers for their joint consideration on the next working day. Applications that are considered urgent will be allocated to the first available judge of the Family Court (in accordance with rule 16 of the Family Court (Composition and Distribution of Business) Rules 2014).
5. Local Authority applicants are to complete the Allocation Proposal section of the C110A application form when issuing proceedings. The Allocation Proposal section is to be used by the gatekeepers to record their allocation decision.
6. Members of the gatekeeping team are to be available at fixed times on each weekday to allocate jointly all relevant proceedings that have been issued. It is recommended that if they do not sit together at a fixed time in a court list for this purpose, they have a listed time for discussion between each other, for example, an hour at the beginning of the day. The gatekeepers will have access to information about existing allocated case volumes in the family court to help inform allocation decisions, as

well as information about when and where Case Management Hearings can be listed. They will consider the file in each new application that has been issued on the preceding day and any outstanding applications and determine, in accordance with the Family Court (Composition and Distribution of Business) Rules 2014 and this guidance, the level of judge, and where possible the identity of the judge to which the proceedings are to be allocated. They will record their allocation decision on the Allocation Proposal section of the C110A application form.

7. When the allocation decision has been made, the case management judge or case manager will issue the Standard Directions on Issue and Allocation (SDO) in accordance with PD12A (PLO 2014) together with any appropriate Notice of Hearing. Court staff will notify by e-mail the relevant local authority of the date, time, location and identity of the allocated case management judge (or case manager) for the case management hearing and will list the case management hearing before an identified case management judge or case manager in accordance with the guidance of the DFJ and the allocation decision that has been made.

8. If the gatekeepers cannot agree on an allocation decision or they require further guidance, they must refer the allocation decision to the Designated Family Judge or his nominated deputy.

9. An allocation decision made by the gatekeepers does not prevent the possibility of a party to the proceedings making a subsequent application for a review of the decision.

10. If a care or supervision application is issued by a local authority as "urgent" with a request for an early hearing to authorise the removal of a child and permission to abridge time to serve the parties, the application for expedition and any consequential directions will be considered by the gatekeepers. These are exceptional cases which may include newborn babies who are about to be discharged from hospital where the issue of care and supervision order applications is part of planned pre-proceedings involvement with the family. In all other cases where there is an identified real and immediate safety risk to the child, the expectation is that an application will be made for an Emergency Protection Order. This Guidance does not affect the existing procedures for dealing with Emergency Protection Order applications.

11. The Designated Family Judge shall monitor the allocation and gatekeeping process with a consultation group comprising: a Circuit Judge, a District Judge, a District Judge (Magistrates Court), the Justices' Clerk or his nominated deputy, a legal adviser and two members of the administration in the Designated Family Centre. The consultation group will meet at least once a month to identify any allocation questions upon which the advice of the Designated Family Judge or the Family Division Liaison Judge is required to ensure that there is consistency of allocation, effective use of resources and the identification of specific questions, the answers to which will be used as local guidance by the gatekeepers.

Principles

12. Allocation decisions must be made in accordance with the Family Court (Composition and Distribution of Business) Rules 2014.

13. This Guidance is consistent with those Rules, the guidance issued by the President of the Family Division in accordance with PD12A (PLO 2014), and decisions of the superior courts. It is intended to reflect the wide variation in the level of experience and expertise in the Family Court. Cases should be allocated to judges (including lay justices) and case managers with the appropriate level of experience to ensure that judicial resources are used most effectively.

14. In determining allocation, the gatekeepers shall consider each application having regard to the information provided on and with the C110A application form and shall determine the appropriate level of judge of the Family Court, in accordance with the requirements of rule 20 of the Family Court (Composition and Distribution of Business) Rules 2014:
    (a) the need to make the most effective and efficient use of the local judicial resources that is appropriate, given the nature and type of application;
    (b) the need to avoid delay;
    (c) the need for judicial continuity;
    (d) the location of the parties or of any child relevant to the proceedings; and
    (e) complexity.
15. In the Family Court, no distinction is to be drawn between proceedings which may be heard by District Judges and District Judges (Magistrates Courts) ('judges of 'district judge level'). There is an expectation that judges of district judge level will assume personal responsibility for all case management hearings in proceedings allocated to them, in accordance with the President's Guidance on Judicial Continuity and Deployment (Public Law).

Allocation Guidance

16. The factors set out at paragraph (14) above, include at (a) the judicial and HMCTS resources available in each court location, at (b) the needs of the parties to ensure that cases are listed before the appropriate level of judge with the minimum of delay, so that all proceedings are heard within the Timetable for the Child and within a maximum of 26 weeks or any extended Timetable for the Proceedings, as directed by the case management judge, at (c) the President's Guidance on Judicial Continuity and Deployment (Public Law) and at d) a location that is suitable for the parties, particularly if special requirements or circumstances exist.
17. The schedule to this Guidance sets out matters which are likely to be relevant to the consideration of the "complexity" factor referred to at paragraph (14)(e) above.
18. Subject to the guidance given below, all care, supervision and other Part IV proceedings may be heard by any judge of the Family Court (including lay justices) who has been authorised or nominated to conduct care and supervision proceedings and may be case managed by any judge or legal adviser who has likewise been authorised or nominated.
19. It is not expected that proceedings described in the schedule to this Guidance will be allocated to lay justices or the legal adviser acting as their case manager unless specifically approved by the Justices' Clerk (or his nominated deputy) in consultation with the Designated Family Judge. There is also an expectation that magistrates will not hear any contested hearing where the ELH is in excess of 3 days without the same having been approved from time to time by the Justices' Clerk (or his nominated deputy) in consultation with the Designated Family Judge.
20. It is expected that proceedings described in column 1 of the schedule to this Guidance will be allocated to a judge of district judge level.
21. It is expected that proceedings described in column 2 of the schedule to this Guidance will be allocated to a judge of circuit judge level or a judge of High Court judge level and will not be allocated to a judge of district judge level unless specifically released by the Designated Family Judge or one of his nominated deputies.
22. Proceedings described in paragraph H of column 2 of the schedule to this Guidance are to be issued in the Family Division of the High Court of Justice.

9 President's Guidance on Allocation and Gatekeeping for Proceedings under Part II of the Children Act 1989 (Private Law)

Issued in accordance with rule 21 of the Family Court (Composition and Distribution of Business) Rules 2014

Issued 22 April 2014

Introduction

1. This Guidance is issued by the President of the Family Division and applies to all private law proceedings under Part II of the Children Act 1989 (hereinafter referred to as 'private law proceedings') from 22 April 2014. It is issued following consultation with, and where applicable with the agreement of, the Lord Chancellor, in accordance with rule 21 of the Family Court (Composition and Distribution of Business) Rules 2014, and is to be read with those Rules and PD12B FPR (CAP 2014)).
2. The purpose of the Guidance is to ensure that all new private law proceedings are allocated to the appropriate level of judge and, where appropriate to a named case management judge (or case manager in those cases allocated to lay justices) who shall provide continuity for the proceedings in accordance with the President's Guidance on Judicial Continuity and Deployment (Private Law).
3. This Guidance applies to the allocation of all relevant proceedings to all judges of the Family Court (including lay justices sitting with assistant justices' clerks (referred to in this Guidance as legal advisers). During the implementation and consolidation of arrangements for the Family Court, this includes allocation to legal advisers conducting FHDRAs in court centres where:
   (i) there is agreement between the Designated Family Judge ('DFJ'), HMCTS Head of CFT, the justices' clerk and the relevant Panel Chair(s) that available judicial resources locally require that FHDRAs continue to be listed before the legal advisers; or
   (ii) in areas where the practice does not currently take place, where there is agreement between the DFJ, HMCTS Head of CFT, the justices' clerk and the relevant Panel Chair(s), and specific permission granted from the President of the Family Division and the HMCTS Director for Civil Family and Tribunals, that it be extended to facilitate the appropriate allocation of cases;

   And in any event

   (iii) provided that such allocation does not restrict the court's ability to make substantive orders on the day of the hearing (i.e. by using parallel or back-to-back lists, so that lay justices or judges are available to consider the case and, where appropriate, make a substantive order).

Allocation and Resources

4. In some DFJ's areas, full implementation of this guidance may result in a significant shift of caseload between levels of the judiciary. Before implementation it will therefore be necessary for the DFJ in consultation with the local judiciary, the justices' clerk, and HMCTS to review the available resources, in terms of courtrooms, court staff and judiciary including lay justices and legal advisers. The extent and timescale of implementation of the guidance should take these

factors into account alongside any shift in allocation of public law cases following the implementation of the President's Guidance on Allocation Gatekeeping for Care Supervision and other Proceedings under Part IV of the Children Act 1989 (Public Law). The overarching intention should be to avoid delay in all children's proceedings wherever possible.

Allocation and listing schedules

5. The DFJ in consultation with the judiciary, the justices' clerk and HMCTS should review the family listing schedules in place within the DFJ's area taking into account the plans for the implementation of the Family Court. Where feasible and practical, consideration should be given to arranging listing schedules so that First Hearing Dispute Resolution Appointments (FHDRAs) are taking place in parallel lists (i.e. on the same day and ideally in the same building) before District Judges and lay justices (sitting with a legal adviser), or where appropriate (in accordance with paragraph 3 above) before legal advisers sitting alone. This will allow for re-allocation to be considered up to and including the date of the hearing of the case, so that an alternative judicial level to that selected by the Gatekeeper(s) (see paragraph 6 below) can be arranged if necessary (in particular, should receipt of the Cafcass Safeguarding checks or interview with the parties raise matters of particular significance which justify a revised allocation decision).

Gatekeeping teams

6. Each DFJ will lead a gatekeeping team responsible for private law gatekeeping in each of the Family Hearing Centres that are nominated by the President to be Designated Family Centres. The team will consist of the DFJ and the justices' clerk with as many legal advisers and District Judges as the DFJ considers necessary to carry out the gatekeeping role depending on local demand and conditions. The DFJ in consultation with the District Judges and the justices' clerk will determine whether gatekeeping decisions are to be made by the District Judges or legal advisers acting alone, or together. The District Judge and legal advisers when making gatekeeping and allocation decisions are referred to as 'the Gatekeeper(s)' in this guidance.
7. All applications for private law orders which are received by 4.00 pm will be issued by HMCTS and placed before the Gatekeeper(s) for their consideration on the next working day, except where they are (or have been) dealt with as an urgent application. The Gatekeeper(s) should consider the application on the basis of the information provided in the application, and shall determine the appropriate level of judiciary in accordance with this guidance, and the requirements of the Family Court (Composition and Distribution of Business) Rules 2014, based on consideration of the relative significance of:
   (a) The need to make the most effective and efficient use of the local judicial resources that is appropriate, given the nature and type of application;
   (b) The need to avoid delay;
   (c) The need for judicial continuity;
   (d) The location of the parties or of any child relevant to the proceedings; and
   (e) Complexity.

   The judiciary including lay justices and legal advisers have an ongoing duty to keep allocation decisions under review particularly:
   (a) when any response to the application is received;
   (b) the safeguarding checks are received; and
   (c) at the FHDRA when further information has been ascertained from the parties and Cafcass or CAFCASS Cymru at court.

9. When making an allocation decision the Gatekeepers will enquire into whether a MIAM exemption has been validly claimed, to the extent possible at this stage. If the MIAM exemption has not been validly claimed, the Gatekeepers shall give directions in accordance with rule 3.10(2)/(3) FPR 2010.

10. Prior to making an allocation decision the Gatekeeper(s) shall consider whether to allocate the application to a different location for hearing within the DFJ area, or to transfer the application to another DFJ area, where it appears that the parties, and/or the child(ren) who are the subject of the application, reside(s) in an area other than that covered by the DFJ.

11. Gatekeeper(s) are to be made available for a period of time on each weekday to allocate all private law proceedings which have been issued. Gatekeeper(s) will consider the file in each new application which has been issued on the preceding day and any urgent applications which are outstanding, and determine to which level of judge the proceedings should be allocated, i.e. to lay justices, a judge at District Judge level, a judge at Circuit Judge level or judge at High Court level sitting in the Family Court:

(a) Based on consideration of the relative significance of the matters set out in paragraph 7(a)–(e) (above),

and

(b) When considering complexity, by reference to the schedule to this guidance.

The Gatekeeper(s) will record their allocation decision and reasons on the case papers and make any appropriate arrangements for transfer (between courts) as necessary. In addition, where it appears that a case needs an urgent listing, the Gatekeeper(s) will ensure that the case is listed as a matter of urgency, and will give directions to abridge time for service if necessary.

12. The DFJ shall make arrangements to ensure the swift allocation of all cases within the Family Court to a named case manager so that it can be listed (in accordance with this Guidance and the Family Court (Composition and Distribution of Business) Rules 2014) in week 5 or 6 after issue, for an FHDRA, or sooner if an FHDRA is not appropriate.

13. If any Gatekeeper requires further guidance on a particular case, they should refer the allocation decision to the DFJ or his nominated deputy.

14. An allocation decision made by the Gatekeepers does not prevent a party to the proceedings applying for a review of the decision

15. The DFJ shall monitor the allocation and gatekeeping practices in the DFJ area to ensure that there is consistency of allocation, effective use of resources and the capacity to list cases at the earliest opportunity to avoid delay. He/she may issue local guidance to the Gatekeepers from time to time to reflect local circumstances and ensure the best use of resources. The allocation of work between the Circuit Bench, the District Bench, the lay justices and, where appropriate and agreed, the legal advisers may be subject to local directions by the DFJ.

Directions on Issue

16. Gatekeepers shall be able to issue Directions on Issue on Form CAP01 in the following circumstances:

(a) where the Gatekeeper finds on the basis of the information provided that the exemption from attending a MIAM has not validly been claimed, the Gatekeeper will direct the applicant, or will direct the parties, to attend a MIAM before the FHDRA, unless the Gatekeeper considers that in all the circumstances of the case the MIAM requirement should not apply to the application in question; the Gatekeeper will have regard to the matters set out in rule 3.10(3) FPR when making this decision;

(b) where it appears that an urgent issue requires determination, the Gatekeeper may give directions for an accelerated hearing;
(c) exceptionally, where it appears that directions need to be given for the service and filing of evidence, he/she may give directions for the filing of evidence.

Principles of Allocation

17. Allocation decisions must be made in accordance with the Family Court (Composition and Distribution of Business) Rules 2014.
18. This Guidance identifies criteria which are intended to be consistent with the Family Court (Composition and Distribution of Business) Rules 2014, and the decisions of superior courts.
19. In determining allocation, judicial continuity is an important consideration and the President's Guidance on Judicial Continuity and Deployment (Private Law) is to be followed.
20. In determining allocation consideration must be given to the matters set out in paragraph 7(a)–(e) above, in particular the need to avoid delay and provide the earliest possible hearing dates consistent with the welfare of the subject child(ren).
21. No distinction is to be drawn between proceedings which may be heard by District Judges and District Judges (Magistrates' Courts). There is an expectation that District Judges will assume personal responsibility for all case management hearings in proceedings allocated to them in accordance with the President's Guidance on Judicial Continuity and Deployment (Private Law).

Allocation Guidance

22. Subject to the guidance given below, all private law proceedings may be heard by any judge who has been authorised or nominated to conduct such proceedings, and may be case managed by the same judge or legal adviser.
23. When considering specifically the complexity of a case (see paragraph 7(e) above), it is envisaged that all relevant family applications (as defined in CAP paragraph 23) will be heard by lay justices (or at the FHDRA by legal advisers) unless they are of the type set out in the Schedule to this Guidance (see paragraphs 25 and 26 below). Additionally, a relevant family application may:
    (a) be allocated to be heard by lay justices where specifically approved by the justices' clerk (or his nominated deputy) in consultation with the DFJ, or
    (b) be re-allocated to be heard by lay justices where, at FHDRA or other hearing, it appears to the judge that the case does not fall, or no longer falls, within the Schedule.
24. There is an expectation that lay justices will not hear any contested private law application where the estimated length of the hearing is in excess of 3 days without the same having been approved by the justices' clerk in consultation with the DFJ.
25. When considering specifically the complexity of a case (see paragraph 7(e) above), it is envisaged that:
    (c) proceedings described in Part 1 of the schedule to this Guidance will be allocated to a District Judge, or a District Judge (Magistrates' Court). If, on allocation it appears to the District Judge that the particular circumstances of the individual case justify allocation to a Circuit Judge, the District Judge shall so allocate it.
    (d) subject to paragraph 27 (below), proceedings described in Part 2 of the schedule to this Guidance will be allocated to either a District Judge, District Judge (Magistrates' Court) or to a Circuit Judge or a High Court Judge.

26. Where the Gatekeeper allocates proceedings described in Part 2 of the schedule to a Circuit Judge or to a High Court Judge sitting in the Family Court, the FHDRA for that case shall be listed before a District Judge or District Judge (Magistrates' Court) unless the Gatekeeper considers (in discussion with the DFJ) that the FHDRA should be conducted by the Circuit Judge or High Court Judge (as appropriate).

27. Proceedings described in Part 3 of the schedule to this Guidance are to be issued in the High Court, not the Family Court. If they are received in the Family Court, then they must be identified and transferred to the Family Division of the High Court.

28. Where it appears to a Court that the issues in a case have developed from the point of initial allocation in such a way as to justify re-allocation, the court shall consider re-allocation in accordance with this Guidance and Schedule, having regard to the matters set out in paragraph 7(a)–(e) above, and taking account to the extent appropriate the principle of judicial continuity, and the need to avoid delay.

Urgent hearings

29. Urgent applications are those in which the applicant for a private law family order invites the court by application C2 either to (a) list the application for a hearing without notice to the respondent, or (b) reduce the normal (14 days) time-limit for service of an application and list a hearing at short notice.

30. If the application is considered by the Gatekeeper(s), they are to have regard generally to the guidance in paragraph 12.1–12.5 of the CAP in relation to the making of without notice orders when considering how to allocate an application that is presented for allocation as 'urgent'.

31. When presented with an application said to be urgent, the Gatekeeper(s) shall upon receipt:
    (a) allocate the application to the appropriate level of judiciary in accordance with rule 16 of the Family Court (Composition and Distribution of Business) Rules 2014, and
    (b) determine whether the application requires
        (i) a hearing on that day, or
        (ii) requires an early hearing in advance of the FHDRA, with a reduced time for service of the application.

    If an application for an urgent hearing is refused, reasons shall be given in writing and the application listed for FHDRA; the Gatekeeper may issue further directions in accordance with paragraph 16 above.

Schedule to the Allocation and Gatekeeping Guidance – Private Law

NOTE THAT

When, on allocation, Gatekeepers are considering specifically the issue of complexity, it is envisaged that they will allocate all relevant family applications (as defined in the Child Arrangements Programme paragraph 23) to the lay justices (or at the FHDRA by legal advisers) UNLESS they are of the type set out in this Schedule (below) (See paragraph 23 Guidance on Allocation & Gatekeeping for Proceedings under Part II of the Children Act 1989 (Private Law Proceedings))

Part 1 – District Judge (unless in the opinion of the allocated District Judge, the particular characteristics of the individual case justify transfer to a Circuit Judge)	Part 2 – District Judge but may be by Circuit Judge (or at most serious level by High Court Judge)	Part 3 – High Court and Inherent Jurisdiction
Allegations of significant physical, emotional or sexual abuse, or behaviours which have caused, or are at risk of causing, significant harm to the relevant child.	Cases involving significant factual disputes (including allegations of abuse, violence, alleged or proven criminal activity, gravely inappropriate behaviours, sexual abuse, complex physical and/or mental health issues in relation to relevant adults or children) particularly where a fact finding hearing of 3 days or more is a real possibility and/or where it is likely that more than one expert (not including CAFCASS and/or social worker) will be involved.	Inherent jurisdiction of the court relating to minors Application to make a child a ward of court, or to bring such an order to an end. Proceedings under the Child Abduction & Custody Act 1985, and other international abduction cases Proceedings with an international element relating to or enforcement of Orders, conflict or comity of laws which have exceptional immigration/ asylum status issues. Declarations of incompatibility under the Human Rights Act 1998
Cases where significant factual matters are in issue (including substance misuse, domestic abuse, paternity, physical and/or mental health of relevant adults or children) such that a fact-finding hearing lasting more than one day is likely and the necessity for expert evidence (i.e. beyond the expertise of CAFCASS and/or social worker) is likely to arise.	Cases where there are particularly difficult and unusual immigration or jurisdictional issues.	Applications for Declaratory Relief
	Cases involving leave to remove (permanently or temporarily) from the jurisdiction to Hague Convention and/or EU countries which are factually or legally complex.	Registration of foreign judgments under Part 1 of the Foreign Judgments (Reciprocal Enforcement) Act 1920
	Cases which appear to involve, or have the potential to involve, intractable opposition to contact.	Registration of judgments given in a different part of the UK under Part 2 of the Civil Jurisdiction and Judgments Act 1982

Part 1 – District Judge (unless in the opinion of the allocated District Judge, the particular characteristics of the individual case justify transfer to a Circuit Judge)	Part 2 – District Judge but may be by Circuit Judge (or at most serious level by High Court Judge)	Part 3 – High Court and Inherent Jurisdiction
Cases where the capacity of one of the parents is, or is likely to be, raised as an issue. Cases where there is a real possibility that the child will have to be joined as a party (see guidelines under rule 16.4 FPR 2010) &/or may be called to give evidence.	Cases seeking enforcement of existing Orders made by a Circuit Judge or Recorder or in cases where a Circuit Judge or Recorder has previously made orders in relation to the same parties. Allocation should be to the same Circuit Judge or Recorder where practicable.	Registration of custody (Part 1) orders made in a court in another part of the UK under the Family Law Act 1986, section 32(1) Parental Responsibility order prior to adoption abroad (Adoption and Children Act 2002, section 84(1))
Cases where there is, or is likely to be, a significant issue in relation to disclosure of documents to or from third parties or outside agencies. Cases where immigration issues are likely to be relevant and significant	Circuit Judge (not District Judge): Cases seeking leave to remove from the jurisdiction [permanently or temporarily] outside of the Hague Convention/ the EU. Where there are particular factual or legal complexities, the cases should ordinarily be allocated to the High Court following consultation with the DFJ.	Application for direction that section 67(3) of the Adoption and Children Act 2002 (status conferred by adoption) does not apply. Application for annulment of overseas or Convention adoption under Adoption and Children Act 2002, section 89
Cases involving leave to remove children (permanently or temporarily) from the jurisdiction to Hague Convention and/or EU countries.		Issuance of letter of request for person to be examined out of the jurisdiction. Applications under Article 15 of the 2201/2003 Council Regulation and Article 9 of the 1996 Hague Convention (request for transfer of jurisdiction).

Part 1 – District Judge (unless in the opinion of the allocated District Judge, the particular characteristics of the individual case justify transfer to a Circuit Judge)	Part 2 – District Judge but may be by Circuit Judge (or at most serious level by High Court Judge)	Part 3 – High Court and Inherent Jurisdiction
Cases which involve significant issues to be determined in relation to the disclosure of information to one or other of the parties (e.g. where the Cafcass officer seeks to withhold information contained in a Safeguarding letter).		Applications under Article 16 of the 1996 Hague Convention for a declaration as to the extent or existence of parental responsibility. Applications under Part 31 of the FPR (registration of orders under the 2201/2003 Council Regulation, the 1996 Hague Convention and the Civil Partnership (Jurisdiction and Recognition of Judgments) Regulations 2005).
Cases involving the enforcement of existing orders made by a District Judge or cases where a District Judge has previously made orders in relation to the same parties. Allocation should be to the same District Judge where practicable.		Cases which require the jurisdiction of the Administrative Court to be invoked
Cases where there is a real possibility that Public Law Orders will be required, where the issues arising are of a type described in Part 1 or Part 2 of the Schedule to the President's Guidance on Allocation and Gatekeeping for Care, Supervision and other Part 4 proceedings.		

10 President's Guidance of 22 April 2009

Citation: [2009] 2 FLR 167

Applications Consequent upon the Attendance of the Media in Family Proceedings

1 The Government's announcement about the attendance of the media at hearings in family proceedings (see *Family Justice in View* Cm 7502, December 2008) has been implemented by a change to the Family Proceedings Rules made by *The Family Proceedings (Amendment) (No 2) Rules 2009* SI 2009 No 857 (county court and High Court) and *The Family Proceedings Courts (Miscellaneous Amendments) Rules 2009* SI 2009 No 858 (magistrates' courts) and two Practice Directions *Attendance of Media Representatives at Hearings in Family Proceedings* dated 20th April 2009 made by the President to support the rule changes in the respective courts.

2 In the county court and High Court media attendance is implemented by the change to FPR Rule 10.28. (to which the Practice Direction applies). Change regarding media attendance in the family proceedings courts is introduced through amendment to the Family Proceedings Courts (Children Act 1989) Rules 1991, with the insertion of rule 16A.

3 In broad terms the changes for the county court and the High Court relating to media attendance permit duly accredited representatives of news gathering and reporting organisations, and any other unaccredited person whom the court permits, to be present at hearings of all family proceedings (defined by s 32 Matrimonial and Family Proceedings Act 1984) except hearings conducted for the purposes of judicially assisted conciliation or negotiation. They also provide that the court can exclude media representatives

4 For the county court and the High Court, the change relates to most of the proceedings which are for the time being heard in private. It therefore covers a wide range of proceedings including for example public and private law proceedings under the Children Act 1989 and claims for ancillary relief under the Matrimonial Causes Act 1973.

5 Representatives of newspapers or news agencies are admitted to the family proceedings courts under section 69 (2) Magistrates' Courts Act 1980. Media attendance will now be regulated by the insertion of rule "16A Restrictions on presence of persons at directions appointment and hearing". Duly accredited representatives of news gathering and reporting organisations are not entitled to be present at hearings conducted for the purposes of judicially assisted conciliation or negotiation. They may also be excluded for reasons set out in rule 16A(3).

6 In respect of the county court and the High Court the new Part 11 of the FPR, and in respect of the family proceedings court the new Part 11C of the Family Proceedings Courts (Children Act 1989) Rules 1991 as amended, regarding communication of information only apply to proceedings concerning children. In particular, they do not apply to proceedings for ancillary relief. Nor do they <u>expressly</u> cover communication of information to representatives of the media.

7 As appears from the Practice Direction governing the county court and High Court, it is a premise of the change for these courts that the proceedings remain proceedings held in private and that therefore the existing position relating to the publication of matters relating to proceedings which are so heard continues to apply, both whilst the proceedings continue and when they have ended (see the Practice Direction paras 2.4 and 2.5)

8 Useful summaries of the position relating to the publication of matters relating to proceedings heard in private can be found in: *Clayton v Clayton* [2006] EWCA Civ 878 [2007] 1 FLR 11 (in particular at paragraphs 23 to 60, 82 to 85, 92 to 104 and 118 to 136 and *Re B (A Child) (Disclosure)* [2004] EWHC 411 (Fam), [2004] 2 FLR 142 (in particular at paragraphs 62 to 82 (on s 12 AJA 1960) and 83 to 107 (on the jurisdiction to relax or increase the statutory restrictions on publication). Other useful cases are listed in the footnote to this paragraph.[1]

1 Re S (A Child) (Identification: Restrictions on Publication) [2004] UKHL 47, [2005] 1 AC 593; Pelling v Bruce-Williams (Secretary of State for Constitutional Affairs Intervening) [2004] EWCA Civ 845, [2004] Fam 155, [2004] 2 FLR 823; Re Webster; Norfolk County Council v Webster and Others (No 1) [2006] EWHC 2733 (Fam), [2007] 1 FLR 1146; Re Webster; Norfolk County Council v Webster and Others (No 2) [2006] EWHC 2898 (Fam), [2007] 2 FLR 415; Re B; X Council v B [2007] EWHC 1622 (Fam), [2008] 1 FLR 482; Re B; X Council v B (No 2) [2008] EWHC 270 (Fam), [2008] 1 FLR 1460; BBC v Cafcass [2007] EWHC 616 (Fam), [2007] 2 FLR 765; Oldham Metropolitan Borough Council v GW & PW [2007] EWHC 136 (Fam), [2007] 2 FLR 597.

9 It is to be noted that the above decisions all concern the interests and welfare of children and that the approach in ancillary relief proceedings (which are also likely to be productive of media applications) has not been the subject of similar judicial consideration and guidance.

10 The new Rules and the Practice Directions include provisions relating to the exclusion of media representatives but are silent on the approach to be taken by the courts to the exercise of their discretion in respect of other issues which may well arise as a consequence of the attendance of media representatives at hearings in family proceedings. In this respect the Government declined to adopt the recommendation of the High Court judges to address the detail of such issues when introducing the change. It is therefore left to the courts to determine how such issues are to be approached and decided. It is clear that a principled approach to such issues should be applied by the courts and that this can only properly be developed by the courts with the benefit of full argument from the interested parties.

11 The change to admit media representatives to hearings in family proceedings in county courts and the High Court is likely to give rise to a number of issues relating to the exercise of discretion by all levels of court. In particular it is likely that courts will quickly be faced with applications for the provision of documents to media representatives present in court to enable them the better to follow the substance of the proceedings. If minded to grant such application, the court will need to consider the terms of any restriction relating to the use (and in particular the publication) of information contained in any such documents provided to media representatives as a condition of their being so provided.

12 In cases involving children, applications, whether by the media or the parties, are also likely to raise issues as to

(i) The proper application of the existing statutory provisions restricting the publication of the identity of children and information relating to proceedings heard in private;

(ii) the adequacy of the protection afforded in children cases by Section 12 of the Administration of Justice Act 1960 ('AJA 1960') which, inter alia, does not extend to the identity of the parties or witnesses;

(iii) the effect of the publication of any anonymised judgment;

and whether or not injunctive relief may be required upon a wider basis.

13 In relation to the need for injunctive relief in cases affecting children, particularly in local courts, it may be necessary to consider how far it is appropriate to protect from identification not only the children and the parties, but also witnesses and others whose identities will be known locally as associated with the child or his family.

14 Finally, there will be issues over the need on child welfare grounds for protection to extend beyond the end of the hearing (see paragraph 2.5 of the respective Practice Directions).

15 No doubt the basic opposing arguments in relation to the question of access to documents will be, on the one hand, that the Government has sought to retain the basic structure and rationale of the long standing policy of privacy in relation to children proceedings, while at the same time admitting the press, to avoid charges of "secret justice" and to promote better understanding of the working of the family courts. For these purposes, however, access to court documents is not generally necessary or desirable having regard to their confidential nature.

16 On the other hand, the media may argue that, particularly in those cases where there is not a formal oral opening, they should be enabled to see statements and documents filed in order fully to understand the nature and progress of the proceedings, and so as to be able to publish articles, within appropriate reporting constraints, about the cases which they attend. In this connection, it is likely, if not inevitable, that in individual cases of high interest to the media, courts at all levels and all over the country will be faced with detailed legal argument relating to rival Convention Rights, public and private interests, the welfare of children, and the construction and application of the primary and secondary legislation.

17 Inconsistency of approach in children cases as to the principles to be applied to the determination of such issues on the part of the courts, parties, witnesses, other persons involved in the relevant events (eg social workers and doctors) and the media could well give rise to justified criticism on grounds of uncertainty. It would not promote the public interest in the proper administration of justice and could be damaging to children.

18 So far as ancillary relief proceedings are concerned, policy, privacy and Convention issues may also arise for decision, albeit the interests of children may not be engaged.

19 The purpose of this guidance is therefore to try to avoid, or at least to minimise, inconsistency by providing that decisions are made by the High Court (and the Appellate Courts) as soon as possible as to the principled approach to be taken. Its purpose is also to provide that, until that is done, delay in decision making in individual cases, (particularly those concerning children) should be avoided. It is to be hoped that the media will co-operate in these aims.

20 Pending the availability of formal judicial guidance from the High Court or Court of Appeal as to the principled approach to be adopted, all County Courts and Magistrates' Courts hearing family proceedings should carefully consider adopting the following course:

(i) The court should deal in accordance with the Rules and Practice Directions with any application made for exclusion of the media from the proceedings or any part of them on any of the grounds set out in the Practice Directions.

(ii) Where a representative of the media in attendance at the proceedings applies to be shown court documents, the court should seek the consent of the parties to such representative being permitted (subject to appropriate conditions as to anonymity and restrictions upon onward disclosure) to see such summaries, position statements and other documents as appear reasonably necessary to a broad understanding of the issues in the case.

(iii) If the objection of any of the parties is maintained, then in any case where the objecting party demonstrates reasonably arguable grounds for resisting disclosure of the document or documents sought, no order for disclosure should be made, but the following course of action should be considered.

(iv) If considered necessary or appropriate the court should transfer (or, in the case of a family proceedings court, take the first step to bring about an urgent transfer of) the proceedings to the High Court for the determination of any disclosure and/or reporting issues.

(v) Alternatively, in order to avoid delay in decision making on the substantive issues in the case, the court should adjourn determination of any disclosure and/or reporting issues pending a decision by the High Court (or the Appellate Courts) on the principled approach to be taken to them and should make any necessary interim orders in accordance with the argument mentioned in paragraph 15 above in order to secure the position meanwhile.

(vi) Similarly, if a representative of the media applies for reporting restrictions to be lifted during the currency of a case, in the absence of agreement between the parties the court should consider following one or the other of the alternative steps set out in sub-paragraphs (iv)–(v) above.

(vii) If injunctive relief is sought restraining publication based on Convention rights rather than statutory provisions, the matter should in any event be transferred to the High Court to be dealt with under the *President's Practice Direction (Applications for Reporting Restriction Orders)* 18 March 2005 and the *Practice Note (Official Solicitor: Deputy Director of Legal Services CAFCASS: Applications for Reporting Restriction Orders* [2005] 2 FLR 111 and, if interim injunctive relief appears necessary under threat of publication before such application can be dealt with by a High Court judge, the county court should comply with s 12(2) of Human Rights Act 1998.

21 The underlying aim of this guidance is to seek to ensure that the principled approach to be taken is determined by the High Court (and the Appellate Courts) as soon as possible and that in the interim changes of practice do not take place which may not accord with that principled approach. Though this may result in delayed rulings on some early contested applications involving arguments such as those mentioned in paragraphs 15 and 16 above, it may be considered desirable, in the absence of legislative guidance, that such rulings should only be made on the basis of authoritative judicial guidance following proper determination, with the benefit of full argument, of the relevant principled approach for the longer term.

22 To assist in the early determination of the principled approach:

(i) Arrangements will be made in the High Court to identify appropriate test cases and for their early determination, and

(ii) Arrangements will be made to seek to ensure that directions are given as soon as is practicable in any proceedings that are transferred to the High Court because they raise substantial issues arising from the attendance of media representatives

(iii) Proceedings which are transferred to the High Court other than in the PRFD should be put before a family High Court Judge on circuit or, failing the presence on circuit of a High Court Judge, before the Family Division Liaison Judge as an urgent application for directions.

Sir Mark Potter
President of the Family Division

11 Practice Guidance of 12 July 2010

Citation: [2010] 2 FLR 962

McKenzie Friends (Civil and Family Courts)

1 This Guidance applies to civil and family proceedings in the Court of Appeal (Civil Division), the High Court of Justice, the County Courts and the Family Proceedings Court in the Magistrates' Courts.[1] It is issued as guidance (**not** as a Practice Direction) by the Master of the Rolls, as Head of Civil Justice, and the President of the Family Division, as Head of Family Justice. It is intended to remind courts and litigants of the principles set out in the authorities and supersedes the guidance contained in *Practice Note (Family Courts: McKenzie Friends) (No 2)* [2008] 1 WLR 2757, which is now withdrawn.[2] It is issued in light of the increase in litigants-in-person (litigants) in all levels of the civil and family courts.

1 References to the judge or court should be read where proceedings are taking place under the FPC(MP etc)R 1991, as a reference to a justices' clerk or assistant justices' clerk who is specifically authorised by a justices' clerk to exercise the functions of the court at the relevant hearing. Where they are taking place under the FPC(CA 1989)R 1991 they should be read consistently with the provisions of those Rules, specifically rule 16A(5A).

2 *R v Leicester City Justices, ex parte Barrow* [1991] 260, *Chauhan v Chauhan* [1997] FCR 206, *R v Bow County Court, ex parte Pelling* [1999] 1 WLR 1807, *Attorney-General v Purvis* [2003] EWHC 3190 (Admin), *Clarkson v Gilbert* [2000] CP Rep 58, *United Building and Plumbing Contractors v Kajla* [2002] EWCA Civ 628, *Re O (Children) (Hearing in Private: Assistance)* [2005] 3 WLR 1191, *Westland Helicopters Ltd v Sheikh Salah Al-Hejailan (No 2)* [2004] 2 Lloyd's Rep 535. *Agassi v Robinson (Inspector of Taxes) (No 2)* [2006] 1 WLR 2126, *Re N (A Child) (McKenzie Friend: Rights of Audience) Practice Note* [2008] 1 WLR 2743.

The Right to Reasonable Assistance

2 Litigants have the right to have reasonable assistance from a layperson, sometimes called a McKenzie Friend (MF). Litigants assisted by MFs remain litigants-in-person. MFs have no independent right to provide assistance. They have no right to act as advocates or to carry out the conduct of litigation.

What McKenzie Friends may do

3 MFs may: i) provide moral support for litigants; ii) take notes; iii) help with case papers; iv) quietly give advice on any aspect of the conduct of the case.

What McKenzie Friends may not do

4 MFs may not: i) act as the litigants' agent in relation to the proceedings; ii) manage litigants' cases outside court, for example by signing court documents; or iii) address the court, make oral submissions or examine witnesses.

Exercising the Right to Reasonable Assistance

5 While litigants ordinarily have a right to receive reasonable assistance from MFs the court retains the power to refuse to permit such assistance. The court may do so where it is satisfied that, in that case, the interests of justice and fairness do not require the litigant to receive such assistance.

6 A litigant who wishes to exercise this right should inform the judge as soon as possible indicating who the MF will be. The proposed MF should produce a short curriculum vitae or other statement setting out relevant experience, confirming that

he or she has no interest in the case and understands the MF's role and the duty of confidentiality.

7 If the court considers that there might be grounds for circumscribing the right to receive such assistance, or a party objects to the presence of, or assistance given by a MF, it is not for the litigant to justify the exercise of the right. It is for the court or the objecting party to provide sufficient reasons why the litigant should not receive such assistance.

8 When considering whether to circumscribe the right to assistance or refuse a MF permission to attend the right to a fair trial is engaged. The matter should be considered carefully. The litigant should be given a reasonable opportunity to argue the point. The proposed MF should not be excluded from that hearing and should normally be allowed to help the litigant.

9 Where proceedings are in *closed court*, i.e. the hearing is in chambers, is in private, or the proceedings relate to a child, the litigant is required to justify the MF's presence in court. The presumption in favour of permitting a MF to attend such hearings, and thereby enable litigants to exercise the right to assistance, is a strong one.

10 The court may refuse to allow a litigant to exercise the right to receive assistance at the start of a hearing. The court can also circumscribe the right during the course of a hearing. It may be refused at the start of a hearing or later circumscribed where the court forms the view that a MF may give, has given, or is giving, assistance which impedes the efficient administration of justice. However, the court should also consider whether a firm and unequivocal warning to the litigant and/or MF might suffice in the first instance.

11 A decision by the court not to curtail assistance from a MF should be regarded as final, save on the ground of subsequent misconduct by the MF or on the ground that the MF's continuing presence will impede the efficient administration of justice. In such event the court should give a short judgment setting out the reasons why it has curtailed the right to assistance. Litigants may appeal such decisions. MFs have no standing to do so.

12 The following factors should not be taken to justify the court refusing to permit a litigant receiving such assistance:

(i) The case or application is simple or straightforward, or is, for instance, a directions or case management hearing;
(ii) The litigant appears capable of conducting the case without assistance;
(iii) The litigant is unrepresented through choice;
(iv) The other party is not represented;
(v) The proposed MF belongs to an organisation that promotes a particular cause;
(vi) The proceedings are confidential and the court papers contain sensitive information relating to a family's affairs.

13 A litigant may be denied the assistance of a MF because its provision might undermine or has undermined the efficient administration of justice. Examples of circumstances where this might arise are: i) the assistance is being provided for an improper purpose; ii) the assistance is unreasonable in nature or degree; iii) the MF is subject to a civil proceedings order or a civil restraint order; iv) the MF is using the litigant as a puppet; v) the MF is directly or indirectly conducting the litigation; vi) the court is not satisfied that the MF fully understands the duty of confidentiality.

14 Where a litigant is receiving assistance from a MF in care proceedings, the court should consider the MF's attendance at any advocates' meetings directed by the court, and, with regard to cases commenced after 1.4.08, consider directions in accordance with paragraph 13.2 of the Practice Direction Guide to Case Management in Public Law Proceedings.

15 Litigants are permitted to communicate any information, including filed evidence, relating to the proceedings to MFs for the purpose of obtaining advice or assistance in relation to the proceedings.

16 Legal representatives should ensure that documents are served on litigants in good time to enable them to seek assistance regarding their content from MFs in advance of any hearing or advocates' meeting.

17 The High Court can, under its inherent jurisdiction, impose a civil restraint order on MFs who repeatedly act in ways that undermine the efficient administration of justice.

Rights of audience and rights to conduct litigation

18 MFs do **not** have a right of audience or a right to conduct litigation. It is a criminal offence to exercise rights of audience or to conduct litigation unless properly qualified and authorised to do so by an appropriate regulatory body or, in the case of an otherwise unqualified or unauthorised individual (i.e., a lay individual including a MF), the court grants such rights on a case-by-case basis.[3]

3 Legal Services Act 2007 s 12–19 and Schedule 3.

19 Courts should be slow to grant any application from a litigant for a right of audience or a right to conduct litigation to any lay person, including a MF. This is because a person exercising such rights must ordinarily be properly trained, be under professional discipline (including an obligation to insure against liability for negligence) and be subject to an overriding duty to the court. These requirements are necessary for the protection of all parties to litigation and are essential to the proper administration of justice.

20 Any application for a right of audience or a right to conduct litigation to be granted to any lay person should therefore be considered very carefully. The court should only be prepared to grant such rights where there is good reason to do so taking into account all the circumstances of the case, which are likely to vary greatly. Such grants should not be extended to lay persons automatically or without due consideration. They should not be granted for mere convenience.

21 Examples of the type of special circumstances which have been held to justify the grant of a right of audience to a lay person, including a MF, are: i) that person is a close relative of the litigant; ii) health problems preclude the litigant from addressing the court, or conducting litigation, and the litigant cannot afford to pay for a qualified legal representative; iii) the litigant is relatively inarticulate and prompting by that person may unnecessarily prolong the proceedings.

22 It is for the litigant to persuade the court that the circumstances of the case are such that it is in the interests of justice for the court to grant a lay person a right of audience or a right to conduct litigation.

23 The grant of a right of audience or a right to conduct litigation to lay persons who hold themselves out as professional advocates or professional MFs or who seek to exercise such rights on a regular basis, whether for reward or not, will however only be granted in exceptional circumstances. To do otherwise would tend to subvert the will of Parliament.

24 If a litigant wants a lay person to be granted a right of audience, an application must be made at the start of the hearing. If a right to conduct litigation is sought such an application must be made at the earliest possible time and must be made, in any event, before the lay person does anything which amounts to the conduct of litigation. It is for litigants to persuade the court, on a case-by-case basis, that the grant of such rights is justified.

25 Rights of audience and the right to conduct litigation are separate rights. The grant of one right to a lay person does not mean that a grant of the other right has been made. If both rights are sought their grant must be applied for individually and justified separately.

26 Having granted either a right of audience or a right to conduct litigation, the court has the power to remove either right. The grant of such rights in one set of proceedings cannot be relied on as a precedent supporting their grant in future proceedings.

Remuneration

27 Litigants can enter into lawful agreements to pay fees to MFs for the provision of reasonable assistance in court or out of court by, for instance, carrying out clerical or mechanical activities, such as photocopying documents, preparing bundles, delivering documents to opposing parties or the court, or the provision of legal advice in connection with court proceedings. Such fees cannot be lawfully recovered from the opposing party.

28 Fees said to be incurred by MFs for carrying out the conduct of litigation, where the court has not granted such a right, cannot lawfully be recovered from either the litigant for whom they carry out such work or the opposing party.

29 Fees said to be incurred by MFs for carrying out the conduct of litigation after the court has granted such a right are in principle recoverable from the litigant for whom the work is carried out. Such fees cannot be lawfully recovered from the opposing party.

30 Fees said to be incurred by MFs for exercising a right of audience following the grant of such a right by the court are in principle recoverable from the litigant on whose behalf the right is exercised. Such fees are also recoverable, in principle, from the opposing party as a recoverable disbursement: CPR 48.6(2) and 48(6)(3)(ii).

Personal Support Unit & Citizen's Advice Bureau

31 Litigants should also be aware of the services provided by local Personal Support Units and Citizens' Advice Bureaux. The PSU at the Royal Courts of Justice in London can be contacted on 020 7947 7701, by email at cbps@bello.co.uk or at the enquiry desk. The CAB at the Royal Courts of Justice in London can be contacted on 020 7947 6564 or at the enquiry desk.

Lord Neuberger of Abbotsbury
Master of the Rolls

Sir Nicholas Wall
President of the Family Division

12 Communicating with the Home Office in Family Proceedings

Originally issued December 2002
Re-issued March 2013

(1) The 'Communicating with the Home Office in Family Proceedings' protocol enables the family courts to communicate with the Home Office (UK Visas & Immigration/ HM Passport Office) to obtain immigration, visa and passport information for family court proceedings.

(2) This guidance has been reissued to replace & amalgamate previous guidance issued in 2002, 2004, 2006, 2010 and 2014 (including the Communicating with the Passport Service 2004) to reflect the new contact details for the Home Office Liaison Officer who has responsibility for administering requests made under the Protocol. It does not alter the nature or purpose of the Protocol.

(3) Where an order is made against the Home Office in Family Proceedings, the court shall draw up the relevant order. The HMCTS form EX660 should be fully completed (including specifying the details of the relevant family members and their relationship to the child). Parties should provide details of *both* mother and father if known, whether or not they are involved in the proceedings.

(4) The sealed order and the completed EX660 should be sent immediately to:

Home Office Liaison Officer

Her Majesty's Courts and Tribunal Service

Arnhem House

PO Box 6987

Leicester

LE1 6ZX

Email: homeofficeliaison@hmcts.gsi.gov.uk

Telephone: 0116 249 4177

Fax: 0116 249 4302

(5) Please note that all information provided in the EX660 will be forwarded to the Home Office. Parties should ensure that any additional information, such as a case synopsis, which it wishes the Home Office to view, has the required leave of the court, set out in the order, to be disclosed to the Home Office. (Note that it is a contempt of court to disclose this information otherwise).

(6) Where the query relates to the proposed adoption of a foreign national minor, the Home Office Liaison Officer can advise as to the additional information which will be required.

(7) The order and EX660 should clearly state the time by which the information is required. In order to comply with the agreed four (4) week period in for the Home Office to provide a response to the court, parties and court staff should ensure that the Home Office Liaison Officer receives the court order on the day the order is made.

(8) Where it will not be possible for court to send the sealed order to the Home Office Liaison Officer on the day it is made, the court when stating the required date of receipt by the court of the information should allow any additional time necessary for the preparation and sending of the order. This is in order to ensure that Home

Office has 4 weeks to provide a response from the time it receives the order from the Home Office Liaison Officer. Any reduction in this period may result in a request by the Home Office for further time in which to reply.

(9) The request or order should identify the questions it wishes to be answered by the Home Office.

(10) Parties should provide the name and contact details of someone who has agreed and is able to provide further information should it be needed.

(11) The order and EX660 should be forwarded to the Home Office Liaison Officer together with such information as is sufficient to enable the Home Office to understand the nature of the case, to identify whether the case involves an adoption, and to identify whether the immigration issues raised might relate to an asylum or non-asylum application.

(12) The Home Office Liaison Officer will then send to an appropriate officer in the Home Office the enquiry, together with a copy of any order made. The Home Office official will be personally responsible for either:

(a) answering the query themselves, by retrieving the file and preparing a statement for the court; or

(b) forwarding the request to a caseworker or relevant official with carriage of that particular file.

(13) The Home Office Liaison Officer will follow up as required in order to ensure that the information is received by the court in time, and will receive the information before forwarding it on as instructed by the judge or court making the request.

(14) Attached is a sample court order and completed EX660 which should provide further useful guidance.

In the Central Family Court

Case Number: FD05C00345

The full name(s) of the child(ren)	Date(s) of Birth
Child Y	12.02.05

Order

Children Act 1989

UPON HEARING Counsel for all parties

IT IS ORDERED THAT:-

1. In accordance with the President's Protocol of December 2002 the Home Office is requested to provide the following information (also detailed in the attached form EX660) to the court by 4pm on 25 November 2005:
   a. What is the current immigration status of the father, *adult Y*?
   b. Does *adult Y* have any outstanding applications pending before the Home Office?
2. There be leave to disclose the case synopsis/summary/background to the Home Office.
3. There be permission granted for any information received from the Home Office to be disclosed to the parties.

Ordered by Mrs Justice Bloggs this 14th day of October 2014.

13 Protocol on communications between judges of the Family Court and Immigration and Asylum Chambers of the First-tier Tribunal and Upper Tribunal

Issued 19 July 2013

Introduction

1. This protocol has been issued by the Senior President of Tribunals and the President of the Family Division and Head of Family Justice
2. This protocol applies where an immigration appeal is pending before the Tribunal[1] and the welfare of a child in the United Kingdom is likely to be affected by the decision in those proceedings and there are family proceedings in existence relating to that child. It applies to all family proceedings in the High Court, a County Court or a Family Proceedings Court and (once the Family Court has been established) in the High Court or the Family Court. For ease of reference, these courts are all referred to hereafter as the Family Court.
3. It is anticipated that judges in the Tribunal and the Family Court will be assisted by knowing of the existence of the proceedings in the other jurisdiction, the issues arising, the procedure and time scale for determining them and any information disclosed in the other jurisdiction that may be of relevance to the respective immigration or family court decision.
4. This protocol is designed to enable judges in each jurisdiction to communicate in order to obtain information about proceedings in their respective jurisdictions which may affect the outcome of the proceedings before them and to make better informed decisions.
5. The timeline of the respective proceedings is likely to be of assistance to each jurisdiction. Regard should be had to the guidance in *Re M and N (Parallel Family and Immigration Proceedings)* [2008] EWHC Fam 2281, [2008] 2 FLR 2030.[2]
6. It is not the role of the judges in either jurisdiction to predict the outcome of the proceedings in the other jurisdiction. Where the decision in the Family Court is likely to be a weighty consideration in the immigration decision, it is anticipated that it will normally be necessary for the Tribunal to wait until the Family Court judge has reached a decision on the issue relevant to the immigration appeal.[3] If so, either the appeal will be allowed by the Tribunal in anticipation of a short period of leave being granted or the hearing will be adjourned, depending on the anticipated timescale of the family proceedings.

1 In this Protocol the Tribunal means the Immigration and Asylum Chamber (IAC) of either the First-tier Tribunal (FtT) and on appeal on a point of law, the Upper Tribunal (UT).

2 Approved by the Court of Appeal in *Re C (A Child)* [2013] EWCA Civ 431 at [26].

3 In the decision of *RS (India)* [2012] UKUT 218 IAC the UT indicated that the Tribunal should either adjourn the immigration appeal or grant a period of limited leave where there are Family Court proceedings the outcome of which is likely to be material to the immigration decision, unless it appears that those proceedings have only been instituted to delay immigration action or removal is otherwise inevitable: see also *Nimako-Boateng* [2012] UKUT 216 IAC. The Court of Appeal endorsed the approach in *RS* in *Mohan v SSHD* [2012] EWCA Civ 1363. Reported decisions of the Upper Tribunal can be found on BAILII under United Kingdom and also on the UT's own web site at http://www.justice.gov.uk/tribunals/ immigration-asylum-upper/decisions.

Disclosure of documents and directions

A. Directions

7. Documents in family proceedings cannot be disclosed to third parties including judges in the Tribunal without an order of the Family Court Judge.[4] There are no formal constraints on disclosure of material supplied for the purpose of an appeal in the Tribunal; a direction is sufficient to respond to a request from the Family Court. The First-tier Tribunal's powers to give directions do not include the power to direct disclosure from the parties or third parties although it may issue a witness summons but the Upper Tribunal has such a power where necessary for the fair hearing of the appeal.[5]
8. Where it appears to a judge that there are or may be relevant proceedings pending in another court or Tribunal directions may be issued at case management stage requiring disclosure by the relevant party of the court reference numbers of any past or current immigration proceedings or any past or current family proceedings that have involved any of the parties.
9. The kind of information likely to be relevant that may be held by either jurisdiction is indicated at Annex 1 to this Protocol.

B. Communication

10. A request for disclosure of documents in the immigration proceedings may be sought at the instigation of the family judge using the form of order set out in Annex 2 part 1.
11. An application for disclosure of documents in family proceedings should be directed to the Designated Family Judge[6] and should state clearly the date by which such information is to be needed which should ideally be no longer than four weeks.
12. A request for disclosure of information or documents in the family proceedings may be sought either by one of the parties direct or at the instigation of the Tribunal judge using the form set out in Annex 2 part 3.
13. A request for the supply of information or documents from the Tribunal should be directed to the Resident Judge of the relevant Tribunal Chamber.[7]

C. Supply of information

14. A draft direction of the Tribunal judge responding to the application of the Family judge is set out in Annex 2 part 2.
15. Where a judge of the family court decides that information can be supplied to a judge in the Tribunal, the judge shall inform the Resident Judge of this fact and at the same time indicate any conditions on the use of the material that are necessary in the circumstances. A draft order is set out in Annex 2 part 4.

4 See Family Procedure Rules 2010, rules 12.73 and 12.75 and Practice Direction 12G.
5 The FtT is still governed by Asylum and Immigration Tribunal (Procedure) Rules 2005 rule 45, and rule 50(l)(b) and (c) while the UT operates under the Tribunal Procedure (Upper Tribunal) Rules 2008 rule 5.
6 The names and details of the Designated Judges of the Family Court can be found at Annex 4.
7 The Resident Judge is the lead Tribunal judge of one the FTT(IAC)'s main hearing centres. The Principal Resident Judge is the lead administrative Judge in the UT(IAC) based at Field House, London. The names and details of these can be found at Annex 3.

16. Directions providing for the anonymity of children and where necessary other parties in both family and immigration proceedings will be considered by the judge in accordance with the joint guidance issued by the President of the Family Division, the Judicial College and the Society of Editors in July 2011 (see 17) and Anonymity Directions in the First-tier Tribunal (IAC) Presidential Guidance Note No2 of February 2011 (see 18).
17. http://www.judiciary.gov.uk/publications-and-reports/guidance/2011/family- courts-media-access-reporting
18. http://waww.justice.gov.uk/downloads/tribunals/immigration-and-asylum/lower/guidance-2-2011 -.pdf

Signed

Sir James Munby President of the Family Division and Head of Family Justice

Sir Jeremy Sullivan Senior President of Tribunals

Date: 19 July 2013

Annex 1

Part One

Suggested case management by the Tribunal judge where there are or may be family proceedings

1. Direct the appellant disclose court reference numbers of any family court proceedings in which s/he was a party or involved.
2. Give consideration to seeking an order for disclosure from the family court judge of;
   (a) any interim or final fact finding judgment
   (b) care plan
   (c) guardian/CAFCASS report
   (d) directions
   (e) timetable of hearings
   (f) other documentation as specified.

Part Two

Suggested case management by the family court judge where there are or may be immigration proceedings.

1. Grant permission for disclosure by the Family Court judge to the Tribunal judge of specific documents, with any specific directions as regards disclosure to third parties attached.
2. Consider giving instructions in the production of ' the guardian/CAFCASS report to include that the report consider the implications for, and effect, on the child(ren) of the removal/deportation of the adult in question and the effects of restricted contact eg during school holidays only or through Skype etc.
3. Consider requesting disclosure from the relevant Tribunal of:
   (a) determinations by the Tribunal of immigration appeals in which any of the parties have been an appellant/respondent;
   (b) decision letter of the Home Office;
   (c) witness statements, grounds of appeal or skeleton arguments filed in pending immigration proceedings;

(d) any case management directions in pending immigration proceedings;
(e) date of substantive hearing;
(f) other documentation as specified.

4. Consider requesting disclosure direct from the Home Office in accordance with the Guidance reissued in March 2013 by the President of the Family Division.[8]

Annex 2

Part 1

In the Court No:

Sitting at [Place]

The [name of statute] Act [year]

The Immigration and Asylum Acts

The Marriage/Civil Partnership/Relationship/Family of XX and YY

The Children **AA (a boy/girl born on dd/mm/yyyy)**

BB (a boy/girl born on dd/mm/yyyy)

CC (a boy/girl born on dd/mm/yyyy)

Adapt as appropriate

After hearing ….

After consideration of the documents lodged by the Parties

ORDER MADE BY [NAME OF JUDGE] ON [DATE] SITTING IN OPEN COURT/PRIVATE

The Parties

1. The applicant is XX
The respondent is YY
The second respondent is ZZ
Specify if any party acts by a litigation friend
The third respondent is AA (acting by his/her guardian FF)
The third respondent is BB (acting by his/her guardian FF)
The fourth respondent is CC (acting by his/her guardian FF)
Delete or Adapt as appropriate

Recitals

2. This is a request made to Resident Judge [name of Judge see Annex 3 below] of the FtT/Upper Tribunal Immigration and Asylum Chamber sitting at [name of centre see Annex 3 below] for information to be provided to this court by the [First Tier Tribunal (IAC)] / [Upper Tribunal (IAC)] in accordance with the Protocol made between President of the Family Division and the Senior President of Tribunals dated 19 July 2013

8 'Communicating with the Home Office in Family Proceedings' [2013] Fam Law 762.

3. The name of the appellant in the immigration proceedings is …. and the file number of the appeal is ….[9]
4. The reason that this request for information is made is *[specify.]*

Request

5. This court requests that the following information be provided by the [First Tier Tribunal (IAC)] / [Upper Tribunal (IAC)]:
The following are examples
   (a) What immigration decision has been made and in respect of who?
   (b) What nationality is the child concerned with the immigration proceedings and his/her parents or carers?
   (c) What possible outcomes are there as a result of the appeal and what immigration rules are in point?
   (d) What stage has the hearing reached?
   (e) When is the next hearing?
6. The information should be supplied to *[specify]* by *[date and time – allow a minimum of 2 weeks]*.
7. If the [First Tier Tribunal (IAC)] / [Upper Tribunal (IAC)] requires any further information it should contact *[specify with telephone number and email address]*.

IT IS ORDERED (BY CONSENT):

8. For the purposes of enabling the [First Tier Tribunal (IAC)] / [Upper Tribunal (IAC)] to consider this request fully the following documents shall be disclosed to it *[specify the documents and any redactions which are considered necessary]*.
9. The documents listed in para 8 shall be disclosed by *[name person or body]* by *[date and time]*. They shall be returned by the [First Tier Tribunal (IAC)] / [Upper Tribunal (IAC)] when the requested information is supplied.
10. The requested information when supplied may be used only for the purposes of these proceedings and must not be disclosed to any third party without the express permission of this court.

Dated

Annex 2

Part 2

Direction of the Immigration and Asylum Chamber

First-tier/Upper Tribunal (delete as appropriate)
(Immigration and Asylum Chamber) Appeal Number:

THE IMMIGRATION ACTS

Heard at Field House (or insert as appropriate)

On (date of response)

……………………………………

9 In the absence of the file number please contact the Resident Judge in your locality with any other information eg Home Office reference number, other names or dates of birth to enable the IAC to carry out a search on its data base.

Between

Appellant

And

THE SECRETARY OF STATE FOR THE HOME DEPARTMENT

Respondent

Representation:

For the Appellant:

For the Respondent:

RESPONSE TO REQUEST FOR INFORMATION FROM THE FAMILY COURT

UPON the request of Judge XX of the XX Court IT IS DIRECTED THAT:-

1. The information sought by the Family Court shall be copied from the appeal file and provided forthwith subject to the following modifications (if any).
2. The following additional information set out in the schedule attached to this direction shall also be copied and provided.

Resident Judge …….

Date

Schedule

Answer the request for information

List documents supplied

Indicate whether an anonymity order has been made in the Immigration and Asylum Chamber

Annex 2

Part 3

First-tier Tribunal/Upper Tribunal (IAC) request for Information to Family Court

First-tier/Upper Tribunal (delete as appropriate)
(Immigration and Asylum Chamber) Appeal Number:

THE IMMIGRATION ACTS

Heard at Field House (or insert as appropriate)

On (date of request)

…………………………………

Between

Appellant

And

THE SECRETARY OF STATE FOR THE HOME DEPARTMENT

Respondent

Representation:

For the Appellant:

For the Respondent:

REQUEST FOR INFORMATION MADE TO THE COURT

Each of the following fields should be completed by the requesting judge to assist the Court to find the relevant records.

Once completed pass the form to your Resident Judge who will, if appropriate produce the formal request seeking the information to be sent to the Court attaching the information provided on this form.

The form must be sent without delay, together with the court order, to the relevant Designated Family Judge

To the Designated Judge of .... Family Court

1. Tribunal judge X requests the information set out in the forms attached in accordance with the provisions of the Protocol made between the President of the Family Division and the Senior President of Tribunals dated 19 July 2013
2. Name of parties to the family proceedings:-
3. Reference number of the Family Proceedings
4. Date by which requesting court would like the information (allow a minimum of four weeks)
5. Name and contact details of Resident Judge of the IAC who is making the application:
   Name of Resident Judge:
   Address
6. Name of Designated Judge[10] and court centre who is to respond to the Request
7. Reason for request

The information sought will be disclosed to the parties to the Tribunal proceedings on terms that the information is used only for the purpose of those proceedings and will not be disclosed to third parties without the prior written consent of the Family court.

Is any other order sought in terms of disclosure or the use that be made of the information?

INFORMATION REQUESTED BY THE TRIBUNAL

A. The information sought from the receiving court is:
B. Documents sought from the receiving court
C. Details of any other Direction required by the receiving court in connection with disclosure
D. Contact details of person from whom additional information can be sought:

<u>Direction to the Court Clerk</u>

Please send this document together with the order and any attached documents, without delay to;

Designated Family Judge ....

Address ....

e-mail ....

Telephone number ....

10 The names and details of the Designated Judges of the Family Court can be found at Annex 4.

Annex 2

Part 4

In the Court No:

Sitting at [Place]

The [name of statute] Act [year]

The Immigration and Asylum Acts

The Marriage/Civil Partnership/Relationship/Family of XX and YY

The Children AA (a boy/girl born on dd/mm/yyyy)

BB (a boy/girl born on dd/mm/yyyy)

CC (a boy/girl born on dd/mm/yyyy)

Adapt as appropriate

After hearing ….

After consideration of the documents lodged by the Parties

ORDER MADE BY [NAME OF JUDGE] ON [DATE] SITTING IN OPEN COURT/ PRIVATE

The Parties

1. The applicant is XX
The respondent is YY
The second respondent is ZZ
Specify if any party acts by a litigation friend
The third respondent is AA (acting by his/her guardian FF)
The third respondent is BB (acting by his/her guardian FF)
The fourth respondent is CC (acting by his/her guardian FF)
Delete or Adapt as appropriate

Recitals

2. This court has received a request for disclosure by the [First Tier Tribunal (IAC)] / [Upper Tribunal (IAC)].
3. The reason that this request has been made is *[specify]*.
4. This court has decided to grant the request, subject to the conditions set out at paras 6–8 below, for the following reasons *[specify]*.
5. If the [First Tier Tribunal (IAC)] / [Upper Tribunal (IAC)] requires any further information it should contact *[specify with telephone number and email address]*.

IT IS ORDERED (BY CONSENT):

6. The following information and documents shall be disclosed to the [First Tier Tribunal (IAC)] / [Upper Tribunal (IAC)] *[specify the documents and any redactions which are considered necessary]*.
7. The information and documents listed in para 6 shall be disclosed to *[name person or body]* by *[name person or body]* by *[date and time]*. They shall be returned by the [First Tier Tribunal (IAC)] / [Upper Tribunal (IAC)] when the proceedings in that tribunal have been concluded.

8. The information and documents listed in para 6 may be used only for the purposes of those proceedings and must not be disclosed to any third party without the express permission of [this court] / [the [First Tier Tribunal (IAC)] / [Upper Tribunal (IAC)]].

Dated

Annex 3

Names and details of Resident Judges of FT/UT IAC

TITLE	NAME	CENTRE	PAs	TELEPHONE
UPPER TRIBUNAL				
Principal Resident Judge	**Paul Southern**	**UTIAC** Field House 15–25 Breams Buildings, London, EC4A1DZ	Elaine Walker Elaine.walker@ hmcts.gsi.gov.uk	0207 073 4221 (F) 0207 073 0345
FIRST TIER TRIBUNAL				
Resident Judge	**Donald Conway**	**Hatton Cross** York House 2–3 Dukes Green Avenue Feltham, Middlesex TW14 OLS	Carole North Carole.north@ hmcts.gsi.gov.uk	0208 831 3545 (F) 0208 890 7647
Resident Judge	**Francis Pinkerton**	**Taylor House** Taylor House 88 Rosebery Road Islington London, EC1R 4QU	Sheron Brown Sheron.Brown2@ hmcts.gsi.gov.uk	0207 862 4322 (F) 0207 862 4323
Resident Judge	**Nigel Poole**	**Newport** Columbus House Chepstow road Langstone business Park Newport south Wales NP18 2LX	Christine Cotton Christine.cotton@ hmcts.gsi.gov.uk	01633 416 791 (F) 01633 416 732

TITLE	NAME	CENTRE	PAs	TELEPHONE
Resident Judge	**Mungo Deans**	**Glasgow** 4th floor Eagle Building 215 Bothwell Street Glasgow G2 7EZ	Joan Wilson Joan. wilson@hmcts.gsi. gov.uk	0141 242 7576 (F) 0141 242 7555
Resident Judge	**Christine Martin**	**Manchester** 1st floor Piccadily Exchange 2 Piccadilly Plaza Manchester M14AH	Jacky Lawrence Tacky.lawrence@ hmcts.gsi.gov.uk	0161 234 2073 - (F) 0161 234 2074
Resident Judge	**Nicholas Renton**	**Birmingham** 3rd floor Sheldon Court 1 Wagon Lane Birmingham B26 3DU	Allison Whitehead Allison. whitehead@hmcts. gsi.gov.uk	0121 722 7911 (F) 0121 722 7948
Resident Judge	**Christine Martin**	**Stoke** Bennett House Town Road Hartley Stoke on Trent ST1 2QB	Joanne Shaw Toanne.shaw@ hmcts.gsi.gov.uk	01782 200 163 (F) 01782 200 165
Resident Judge	**Christine Roberts**	**Bradford** Phoenix house Rushton Avenue Thornton Bradford BD3 7BH	Michelle Lumb Michelle.lumb@ hmcts.gsi.gov.uk	01274 267 048 (F) 01274 267 049
Resident Judge	**Mungo Deans**	**North Shields** Kings Court Royal Quays Earl Grey Way North Shields Tyne and Weir NE 29 6AR	Susan Goggin Susan.goggin@ justice.gsi.gov.uk	0191 298 2202 (F) 0870 761 7692

Annex 4

Names and details of Designated Family Judges of the Family Court

Name	**Base Court (Care Centre)**	**Address (1)**	**Address (2)**	**Address (3)**
SOUTH EASTERN CIRCUIT				
His Honour Judge John Altman	Principal Registry of the Family Division (PRFD)	First Avenue House, 42–49 High Holborn, London WC1V 6NP DX 160010 Kingsway 7 PRFD. Familygeneralenquiries@hmcts.gsi.gov.uk		
Her Honour Judge Claire Jakens	Brighton County Court	William Street, Brighton, East Sussex, BN2 ORF DX 98070 Brighton 3 family@brighton.countycourt.gsi.gov.uk		
His Honour Judge Richard Polden	Canterbury Combined Court Centre / Medway County Court	The Law Courts, Chaucer Road, Canterbury, Kent CTI 1ZA DX 99710 Canterbury 3 family@canterbury.countycourt.gsi.gov.uk	Anchorage House 47–67 High Street Chatham Kent ME4 4DW DX 98180 Chatham 4 family@medway.countycourt.gsi.gov.uk	
His Honour Judge Roderick Newton	Chelmsford County Court / Ipswich County Court	Priory Place, New London Road, Chelmsford, Essex CM2 OPP DX97660 Chelmsford 4 family@chelmsford.countycourt.gsi.gov.uk	8 Arcade Street, Ipswich, Suffolk, IP1 1EJ DX 97730 Ipswich 3 family@ipswich.countycourt.gsi.gov.uk	
His Honour Judge Peter Greene	Cambridge County Court / Peterborough Combined Court Centre	197 East Road Cambridge CB1 1BA DX97650 Cambridge cambridgecountyfamily@hmcts.gsi.gov.uk	Crown Buildings, Rivergate, Peterborough, Cambridgeshire PE1 1EJ DX 702302 Peterborough 8 family@peterborough.countycourt.gsi.gov.uk	
His Honour Judge Peter Nathan	Guildford County Court	The Law Courts, Mary Road, Guildford, Surrey, GU1 4PS DX 97860 Guildford 5 guildctycsm@hmcts.gsi.gov.uk		

Name	Base Court (Care Centre)	Address (1)	Address (2)	Address (3)
His Honour Judge Gavyn Arthur	Luton County Court	2nd Floor Cresta House, Alma Street, Luton, Beds.LUI 2PU DX 97760 Luton 4 enquiries@luton. countycourt.gsi.gov.uk		
His Honour Judge Antony Hughes	Milton Keynes County Court / Oxford Combined Court Centre	351 Silbury Boulevard, Witan Gate East, Central Milton Keynes, Bucks, MK9 2DT DX 136266 Milton Keynes 6 family@miltonkeynes. countycourt.gsi.gov.uk	St Aldates, Oxford, Oxfordshire, 0X1 1TL DX 96450 Oxford 4 family@ oxford.countycourt. gsi.gov.uk	
His Honour Judge Jeremy Richards	Norwich Combined Court Centre	The Law Courts, Bishopsgate, Norwich, Norfolk NR3 1UR DX 97385 Norwich 5 family@norwich. countycourt.gsi.gov.uk		
His Honour Judge Simon Oliver	Reading County Court	160–163 Friar Street, Reading, Berks, RG1 1HE DX 98010 Reading 6 family@reading. countycourt.gsi.gov.uk		
His Honour Judge Peter Wright	Watford County Court	3rd Floor, Cassiobury House, 11–19 Station Road, Watford, Herts, WD17 1EZ DX 122740 Watford 5 enquiries@watford. countycourt.gsi.gov.uk		
MIDLAND CIRCUIT				
Her Honour Judge Estella Hindley QC	Birmingham Civil Justice Centre and Family Courts	Priory Courts, 33 Bull Street, Birmingham, B4 6DS DX 701987 Birmingham 7 family@birmingham. countycourt.gsi.gov.uk		
Her Honour Judge Hilary Watson	Coventry Combined Court Centre	140 Much Park Street, Coventry, West Midlands, CV1 2SN DX 701580 Coventry 5 family@coventry. countycourt.gsi.gov.uk		

Name	Base Court (Care Centre)	Address (1)	Address (2)	Address (3)
His Honour Judge James Orrell	Derby Combined Court Centre	Mortledge, Derby, Derbyshire. DE1 2XE DX 724060 Derby 21 family@derby. countycourt.gsi.gov.uk		
His Honour Judge Clifford Bellamy	Leicester County Court	90 Wellington Street, Leicester, Leicestershire LE1 6HG DX 17401 Leicester 3 family@leicester. countycourt.gsi.gov.uk		
Her Honour Judge Heather Swindells QC	Lincoln County Court	360 High Street, Lincoln, Lincolnshire LN5 7PS DX 703231 Lincoln 6 family@lincoln. countycourt.gsi.gov.uk		
His Honour Judge Anthony Rumbelow QC	Northampton Crown and Countv Court	85–87 Lady's Lane, Northampton, NN1 3HQ DX 725380 Northampton 21 family@northampton. countycourt.gsi.gov.uk		
His Honour Judge Jeremy Lea	Nottingham County Court	60 Canal Street, Nottingham, NG1 7EJ DX 702380 Nottingham 7 family@nottingham. countycourt.gsi.gov.uk		
His Honour Judge Ross Duggan	Stoke-on-Trent Combined Court	Bethesda Street, Hanley, Stoke-on-Trent, Staffordshire ST1 3BP DX 703360 Hanley 3 family@stoke. countycourt.gsi.gov.uk		
Her Honour Judge Helen Hughes	Telford County Court / Wolverhampton Combined Court Centre	Telford Square, Malinsgate Town Centre, Telford, Shropshire, TF3 4JP DX 701976 Telford 3 family@telford. countycourt.gsi.gov.uk	Pipers Row, Wolverhampton, West Midlands WV1 3LQ DX 702019 Wolverhampton 4 family@ wolverhampton. countycourt.gsi. gov.uk	
His Honour Judge Richard Rundell	Worcester Combined Court	The Shirehall, Foregate Street, Worcester, WR1 1EQ DX 721120 Worcester 11 family@worcester. countycourt.gsi.gov.uk		

Name	Base Court (Care Centre)	Address (1)	Address (2)	Address (3)
NORTH EAST CIRCUIT				
His Honour Judge John Dowse	Kingston-upon-Hull Combined Court Centre	Lowgarte, Humberside, HU1 2EZ DX703010 Hull 5 family@kingstonuponhull.countycourt.gsi.gov.uk		
Her Honour Judge Nancy Hillier	Leeds Combined Court Centre	The Courthouse, 1 Oxford Row, Leeds, LS1 3BG DX 703016 Leeds 6 family@leeds.countycourt.gsi.gov.uk		
Her Honour Judge Judith Moir	Newcastle upon Tyne Combined Court Centre / Sunderland County Court	The Law Courts, The Quayside, Newcastle-upon-Tyne & Wear, NE1 3LA DX 65127 Newcastle upon Tyne 2 family@newcastle.countycourt.gsi.gov.uk	44 John Street, Sunderland, Tyne & Wear, SR1 1RB DX 65149 Sunderland 2 family@sunderland.countycourt.gsi.gov.uk	
Her Honour Judge Annabel Carr QC	Sheffield Combined Court Centre	The Law Courts, 50 West Bar, Sheffield, S3 8PH DX 703028 Sheffield 6 family@sheffield.countycourt.gsi.gov.uk		
His Honour Judge Michael Taylor	Teesside Combined Court Centre	Russell Street, Middlesbrough, Cleveland, TS1 2AE DX65152 Middlesbrough 2 family@middlesbrough.countycourt.gsi.gov.uk		
Her Honour Judge Angela Finnerty	York County Court	Piccadilly House, 55 Piccadilly, York, North Yorkshire, Y01 9WL DX 65165 York 4 family@york.countycourt.gsi.gov.uk		
NORTH WEST CIRCUIT				
His Honour Judge Jeremy Rawkins	Blackburn County Court / Lancaster County Court	64 Victoria Street, Blackburn, Lancs, BB1 6DJ DX 702650 Blackburn 4 blackburn.cty.cm@hmcts.gsi.gov.uk	2nd Floor, Mitre House, Church Street, Lancaster, LA1 1UZ DX145880 Lancaster 2 family@lancaster.countycourt.gsi.gov.uk	

Name	Base Court (Care Centre)	Address (1)	Address (2)	Address (3)
Her Honour Judge Barbara Forrester	Carlisle Combined Court Centre	Courts of Justice, Earl Street, Carlisle, Cumbria CA1 1DJ DX 65331 Carlisle 2 enquiries@carlisle.countycourt.gsi.gov.uk		
Her Honour Judge Margaret de Haas QC	Liverpool Civil and Family Court / Warrington County Court / Chester	35 Vernon Street, Liverpool, Merseyside L2 2BX DX 702600 Liverpool 5 family@liverpool.countycourt.gsi.gov.uk	Law Courts, Legh Street, Warington, Cheshire WA1 1UR DX 702501 Warrington 3 family@warrington.countycourt.gsi.gov.uk	Chester Civil Justice Centre, Trident House, Little St John Street, Chester CH1 1SN DX 702460 Chester 4 family@chester.countycourt.gsi.gov.uk
His Honour Judge lain Hamilton	Manchester County Court	Manchester Civil Justice Centre, 1 Bridge Street West, Manchester, M60 9DJ DX 724783 Manchester 44 family@manchester.countycourt,gsi.gov.uk		
SOUTH WEST CIRCUIT				
His Honour Judge Richard Bond	Bournemouth and Poole County Court	Ccurts of Justice, Deansleigh Road, Bournemouth, Dorset, BH7 7DS DX 98420 Bournemouth 4 family@bournemouth.countycourt.gsi.gov.uk		
His Honour Judge Stephen Wildblood QC	Bristol Civil Justice Centre	Bristol Civil Justice Centre, 2 Redcliff Street, Bristol, BS1 6GR DX 95903 Bristol 3 family@bristol.countycourt.gsi.gov.uk		
His Honour Judge David Tyzack QC	Exeter Combined Court Centre	Exeter Combined Court Centre, Southernhay Gardens, Exeter EX1 1UH DX98440 Exeter 2 family@exeter.countycourt.gsi.gov.uk		

Name	Base Court (Care Centre)	Address (1)	Address (2)	Address (3)
Her Honour Judge Miranda Robertshaw	Plymouth Combined Court	The Law Courts, 10 Armada Way, Plymouth, Devon PL1 2ER DX 98470 Plymouth 7 family@plymouth.countycourt.gsi.gov.uk		
His Honour Judge Andrew Levey	Portsmouth Combined Court Centre	The Courts of Justice, Winston Churchill Avenue, Portsmouth, Hampshire P01 2EB DX 98490 Portsmouth 5 family@portsmouth.countycourt.gsi.gov.uk		
Her Honour Judge Katharine Marshall	Swindon Combined Court	The Law Courts, Islington Street, Swindon, Wiltshire SN1 2HG DX 98430 Swinton 5 swindon.cty.fly@hmcts.gsi.gov.uk		
His Honour Judge Richard Bromilow	Taunton County Court	The Shire Hall, Taunton, Somerset TA1 4EU DX 98410 Taunton 2 family@taunton.countycourt.gsi.gov.uk		
His Honour Judge Nick Vincent	Truro County Court	Courts of Justice, Edward Street, Truro, Cornwall TR1 2PB DX 135396 Truro 2 FamilySection.TruroCountyCourt@hmcts.gsi.gov.uk		
HMCTS WALES				
His Honour Judge Gareth D Jones	Caernarfon County Court / Rhyl County Court	Llanberis Road, Caernarfon, Gwynedd, Wales LL55 2DF DX 702483 Caernarfon 2 enquiries@caernarfon.countycourt.gsi.gov.uk	The Courthouse, Clwyd Street, Rhyl, Denbighshire, Wales LL18 3LA DX 702489 Rhyl 2 enquiries@rhyl.countycourt:gsi.gov.uk	
Her Honour Judge Isabel Parry	Cardiff Civil Justice Centre / Pontypridd County Court	2 Park Street, Cardiff, South Wales CF10 1ET DX 99500 Cardiff 6 enquiries@cardiff.countycourt.gsi.gov.uk	The Courthouse, Courthouse Street, Pontypridd Rhondda Cynon Taf, Wales CF37 1JR DX 99620 Pontypridd 2 family@Pontypridd.countycourt.gsi.gov.uk	

Name	Base Court (Care Centre)	Address (1)	Address (2)	Address (3)
His Honour Judge Mark Furness	Newport (Gwent) Civil and Family Court	5th floor, Clarence House, Clarence Place, Newport, Gwent, Wales NP19 7AA DX 99480 Newport (South Wales) 4 enquiries@newportgwent.countycourt.gsi.gov.uk		
His Honour Judge Terence John	Swansea Civil Justice Centre	Caravella House, Quay West, Quay Parade, Swansea, South Wales SA1 1SP DX 99740 Swansea 4 enquiries@swansea.countycourt.gsi.gov.uk		

14 Approved countries and territories – Gender Recognition Act 2004

(SI 2011/1630)

APPROVED COUNTRIES AND TERRITORIES FOR PURPOSES OF GENDER RECOGNITION ACT 2004

The Australian territories of Australian Capital Territory and Northern Territory and the states of New South Wales, Queensland, South Australia, Tasmania, Victoria and Western Australia
Austria
Belgium
Bulgaria
The Canadian provinces of Alberta, British Columbia, Manitoba, New Brunswick, Newfoundland and Labrador, Nova Scotia, Ontario, Prince Edward Island, Quebec and Saskatchewan and the Yukon Territory
Croatia
Republic of Cyprus
Czech Republic
Denmark
Estonia
Finland
France
Germany
Greece
Iceland
Italy
Japan
Liechtenstein
Luxembourg
Malta
The Federal District of Mexico
Moldova
Netherlands
New Zealand
Norway
Poland
Romania
Russian Federation
Serbia

Singapore
Slovakia
Slovenia
South Africa
South Korea
Spain
Sweden
Switzerland
Turkey
Ukraine
The District of Columbia and all of the states of the United States of America except for Idaho, Ohio, Tennessee and Texas
Uruguay

15 Hague Convention Countries

CONVENTION ON THE CIVIL ASPECTS OF INTERNATIONAL CHILD ABDUCTION, THE HAGUE, 25TH OCTOBER 1980

Contracting States to the Convention	*Territories specified in Declarations under Article 39 or 40 of the Convention*	*Date of Coming into Force as between the United Kingdom and the State or Territory*
Argentina	—	1st June 1991
Australia	Australian States and mainland Territories	1st January 1987
Austria	—	1st October 1988
The Bahamas	—	1st January 1994
Belarus	—	1st October 2003
Belgium	—	1st May 1999
Belize	—	1st October 1989
Bosnia and Herzegovina	—	1st December 1991
Brazil	—	1st March 2005
Bulgaria	—	1st May 2009
Burkina Faso	—	1st November 1992
Canada	Ontario	1st August 1986
	New Brunswick	1st August 1986
	British Columbia	1st August 1986
	Manitoba	1st August 1986
	Nova Scotia	1st August 1986
	Newfoundland and Labrador	1st August 1986
	Prince Edward Island	1st August 1986
	Quebec	1st August 1986
	Yukon Territory	1st August 1986
	Saskatchewan	1st November 1986
	Alberta	1st February 1987
	Northwest Territories	1st April 1988
	Nunavut	1st January 2001
Chile	—	1st May 1994
China	Hong Kong Special Administrative Region	1st September 1997
	Macau Special Administrative Region	1st March 1999
Columbia	—	1st March 1996

Contracting States to the Convention	*Territories specified in Declarations under Article 39 or 40 of the Convention*	*Date of Coming into Force as between the United Kingdom and the State or Territory*
Costa Rica	—	1st May 2009
Croatia	—	1st December 1991
Cyprus	—	1st February 1995
Czech Republic	—	1st March 1998
Demark	—	1st July 1991
Ecuador	—	1st April 1992
El Salvador	—	1st May 2009
Estonia	—	1st September 2003
Fiji	—	1st September 2003
Finland	—	1st August 1994
France	—	1st August 1986
Georgia	—	1st October 1997
Germany	—	1st December 1990
Greece	—	1st June 1993
Honduras	—	1st March 1994
Hungary	—	1st September 1986
Iceland	—	1st November 1996
Republic of Ireland	—	1st October 1991
Israel	—	1st December 1991
Italy	—	1st May 1995
Latvia	—	1st September 2003
Lithuania	—	1st March 2005
Luxembourg	—	1st January 1987
Macedonia	—	1st December 1991
Malta	—	1st March 2002
Mauritius	—	1st June 1993
Mexico	—	1st September 1991
Monaco	—	1st February 1993
Montenegro	—	1st December 1991
Netherlands	—	1st September 1990
New Zealand	—	1st August 1991
Norway	—	1st April 1989
Panama	—	1st December 1991
Peru	—	1st September 2003
Poland	—	1st November 1992

Contracting States to the Convention	*Territories specified in Declarations under Article 39 or 40 of the Convention*	*Date of Coming into Force as between the United Kingdom and the State or Territory*
Portugal	—	1st August 1986
Romania	—	1st February 1993
San Marino	—	1st June 2011
Serbia	—	27th April 1992
Slovakia	—	1st February 2001
Slovenia	—	1st June 1994
South Africa	—	1st October 1997
Spain	—	1st September 1987
St Kitts and Nevis	—	1st August 1994
Sweden	—	1st June 1989
Switzerland	—	1st August 1986
Turkey	—	1st August 2001
Turkmenistan	—	1st March 1998
Ukraine	—	1st June 2011
United States of America	—	1st July 1988
Uruguay	—	1st September 2003
Uzbekistan	—	1st September 2003
Venezuela	—	1st January 1997
Zimbabwe	—	1st July 1995

16 European Convention Countries

EUROPEAN CONVENTION ON RECOGNITION AND ENFORCEMENT OF DECISIONS CONCERNING CUSTODY OF CHILDREN AND ON THE RESTORATION OF CUSTODY OF CHILDREN, LUXEMBOURG, 20TH MAY 1980

Contracting States to the Convention	*Territories specified in Declarations under Article 24 or 25 of the Convention*	*Date of Coming into Force of Convention as between the United Kingdom and the State or Territory*
Austria	—	1st August 1986
Belgium	—	1st August 1986
Bulgaria	—	1st October 2003
Cyprus	—	1st October 1986
Czech Republic	—	1st July 2000
Denmark	—	1st August 1991
Estonia	—	1st September 2001
Finland	—	1st August 1994
France	—	1st August 1986
Germany	—	1st February 1991
Greece	—	1st July 1993
Hungary	—	1st June 2004
Iceland	—	1st November 1996
The Republic of Ireland	—	1st October 1991
Italy	—	1st June 1995
Latvia	—	1st August 2002
Liechtenstein	—	1st August 1997
Lithuania	—	1st March 2005
Luxembourg	—	1st August 1986
Macedonia	—	1st March 2003
Malta	—	1st February 2000
Moldova	—	1st May 2004
Montenegro	—	6th June 2006
Netherlands	—	1st September 1990
Norway	—	1st May 1989
Poland	—	1st March 1996
Portugal	—	1st August 1986
Romania	—	1st September 2004
Serbia	—	1st May 2002
Slovakia	—	1st September 2001

Contracting States to the Convention	*Territories specified in Declarations under Article 24 or 25 of the Convention*	*Date of Coming into Force of Convention as between the United Kingdom and the State or Territory*
Spain	—	1st August 1986
Sweden	—	1st July 1989
Switzerland	—	1st August 1986
Turkey	—	1st June 2000

17 Conventions and legislation relating to reciprocal enforcement of maintenance orders

CONVENTION	LEGISLATION
Brussels	Civil Jurisdiction and Judgments Act 1982
Commonwealth 1920	Maintenance Orders (Facilities for Enforcement) Act 1920
Commonwealth – Part I	Part I of the Maintenance Orders (Reciprocal Enforcement) Act 1972
Hague	Part I of the Maintenance Orders (Reciprocal Enforcement) Act 1972 – as amended by the Reciprocal Enforcement of Maintenance Orders (Hague Convention Countries) Order 1993
Irish	Part I of the Maintenance Orders (Reciprocal Enforcement) Act 1972 – as amended by the Reciprocal Enforcement of Maintenance Orders (Republic of Ireland) Order 1993
Lugano	Civil Jurisdiction and Judgments Act 1982
UN	Part II of the Maintenance Orders (Reciprocal Enforcement) Act 1972
US	Part I of the Maintenance Orders (Reciprocal Enforcement) Act 1972

COUNTRIES	CONVENTIONS
Alberta†	Commonwealth – Part 1
Algeria	UN
Anguilla	Commonwealth – Part 1
Antigua	Commonwealth 1920
Australia	
Australian Capital Territory‡	Commonwealth – Part 1
Austria§	UN, Brussels, Lugano
Bahamas	Commonwealth 1920
Barbados	Commonwealth – Part 1, UN
Belgium	UN, Brussels, Lugano
Belize	Commonwealth 1920
Bermuda	Commonwealth – Part 1
Bosnia and Herzegovina	UN
Botswana	Commonwealth 1920
Brazil	UN
British Columbia	Commonwealth – Part 1
British Solomon Islands	Commonwealth 1920

COUNTRIES	CONVENTIONS
Brunei	Commonwealth 1920
Canada	
Cayman Islands	Commonwealth 1920
Central African Republic	UN
Chile	UN
Croatia	UN
Cyprus	Commonwealth 1920
Czech Republic	UN, Hague
Denmark	UN, Brussels, Hague
Dominica	Commonwealth 1920
Ecuador	UN
Estonia	Hague
Falkland Islands	Commonwealth – Part 1
Fiji	Commonwealth – Part 1
Finland§	UN, Hague, Brussels
France	UN, Hague, Brussels
Gambia	Commonwealth 1920
Germany	UN, Hague, Brussels, Lugano
Ghana*	Commonwealth – Part 1
Gibraltar	Commonwealth – Part 1
Gilbert and Ellice Islands	Commonwealth 1920
Greece§	UN, Brussels
Grenada	Commonwealth 1920
Guatemala	UN
Guernsey	Commonwealth 1920
Guyana	Commonwealth 1920
Haiti	UN
Holy See	UN
Hong Kong	Commonwealth – Part 1
Hungary	UN
India*	Commonwealth – Part 1
Ireland – The Republic of	Irish, Brussels
Isle of Man	Commonwealth – Part 1
Israel	UN
Italy	UN, Hague, Brussels
Jamaica	Commonwealth 1920
Jersey	Commonwealth 1920

COUNTRIES	CONVENTIONS
Kenya*	Commonwealth – Part 1
Kiribati	Commonwealth 1920
Lesotho	Commonwealth 1920
Luxembourg	UN, Hague, Brussels
Macedonia – former Yugoslav Republic of	UN
Malawi	Commonwealth 1920
Malaysia	Commonwealth 1920
Malta	Commonwealth – Part 1
Manitoba	Commonwealth – Part 1
Mauritius	Commonwealth 1920
Monaco	UN
Montserrat	Commonwealth 1920
Morocco	UN
Naura	Commonwealth – Part 1
Netherlands	UN, Hague, Brussels
New Brunswick*	Commonwealth – Part 1
New South Wales‡	Commonwealth – Part 1
New Zealand†	Commonwealth – Part 1
Newfoundland and Prince Edward Island	Commonwealth 1920
Niger	UN
Nigeria	Commonwealth 1920
Norfolk Island‡	Commonwealth – Part 1
Northern Territory‡	Commonwealth – Part 1
Northwest Territories*	Commonwealth – Part 1
Norway	UN, Hague, Lugano
Nova Scotia‡	Commonwealth – Part 1
Ontario	Commonwealth – Part 1
Pakistan	UN
Papua New Guinea	Commonwealth – Part 1
Philippines	UN
Poland	UN, Hague
Portugal§	UN, Hague, Brussels
Queensland‡	Commonwealth – Part 1
Saskatchewan†	Commonwealth – Part 1
Serbia and Montenegro	UN
Seychelles	Commonwealth 1920
Sierra Leone	Commonwealth 1920
Singapore	Commonwealth – Part 1

COUNTRIES	CONVENTIONS
Slovakia	UN, Hague
Slovenia	UN
South Africa*	Commonwealth – Part 1
South Australia‡	Commonwealth – Part 1
Spain§	UN, Brussels
Sri Lanka	UN, Commonwealth 1920
St Christopher (Kitts) and Nevis	Commonwealth 1920
St Helena	Commonwealth – Part 1
St Lucia	Commonwealth 1920
St Vincent	Commonwealth 1920
Surinam	UN
Swaziland Protectorate	Commonwealth 1920
Sweden§	UN, Hague, Brussels
Switzerland	UN, Hague, Lugano
Tanzania (except Zanzibar)*	Commonwealth – Part 1
Tasmania‡	Commonwealth – Part 1
Territory of Christmas Island	Commonwealth 1920
Territory of Cocos Islands	Commonwealth 1920
Trinidad and Tobago	Commonwealth 1920
Tunisia	UN
Turkey	UN, Hague
Turks and Caicos Islands*	Commonwealth – Part 1
Tuvalu	Commonwealth 1920
Uganda	Commonwealth 1920
United States*	US
Upper Volta	UN
Victoria‡	Commonwealth – Part 1
Virgin Islands	Commonwealth 1920
Western Australia‡	Commonwealth – Part 1
Yugoslavia (see under new names)	UN
Yukon Territory	Commonwealth 1920
Zambia	Commonwealth 1920
Zanzibar	Commonwealth 1920
Zimbabwe*	Commonwealth – Part 1

* Not affiliation orders.
† Not provisional affiliation orders.
‡ Not orders obtained by or in favour of a public authority.
§ Although these countries are party to the Brussels Convention through accession to the EU, there is doubt whether they will enforce maintenance orders under it.

18 Domestic violence lifelines

England	Refuge's National Domestic Abuse Helpline	0808 2000 247 Online live chat Web form
Northern Ireland	Domestic and Sexual Abuse Helpline	0808 802 1414 Online live chat help@dsahelpline.org
Scotland	Domestic Abuse and Forced Marriage Helpline	0800 027 1234 Online live chat helpline@sdafmh.org.uk
Wales	Live Fear Free	0808 80 10 800 Online live chat Text info@livefearfreehelpline.wales
UK-wide	The Men's Advice Line run by Respect is a confidential helpline specifically for male victims.	0808 801 0327 info@mensadviceline.org.uk

19 President's Direction of 19 May 2008

CENTRAL INDEX OF DECREES ABSOLUTE AND OF FINAL ORDERS FOR THE DISSOLUTION OR ANNULMENT OF CIVIL PARTNERSHIPS

Introduction

1. This Practice Direction takes effect from 16th June 2008 and replaces the Registrar's Directions of 3rd November 1980 and 20th January 1992, which are revoked from that date.
2. The Principal Registry of the Family Division is required by the Family Proceedings Rules 1991, rule 2.51(3) to retain a central index of decrees absolute and by rule 2.51A(3) to retain a central index of final orders for the dissolution and annulment of civil partnerships. Since January 1981 information has been provided to the Principal Registry by computer in conjunction with the Office of Population Censuses and Surveys, now the Office for National Statistics ('ONS'). Courts create a computer input form 105 (see Annex 1) for each relevant decree absolute and, since 5th December 2005, a form 106 (see Annex 2) for each relevant final order for the dissolution or annulment of a civil partnership. The completed form is forwarded to the ONS and the ONS then creates the index, which is sent to and kept under the control of the Principal Registry.
3. The procedures set out in this Direction are to be followed in completing form 105 and form 106, and in dealing with the despatch of forms and the resolution of queries.
4. Form 105 should be completed in respect of decrees absolute only, i.e. for decrees of divorce or nullity, and not for decrees of judicial separation. Form 106 should be completed in respect of final orders for the dissolution or annulment of civil partnerships and not for separation orders.
5. In the case of a marriage, where cross-petitions are involved, the forename(s) and surname(s) of the spouse who obtained the decree absolute should be entered in the box 'Forename(s) and Surname(s) of spouse obtaining decree'. In the case of a civil partnership, where cross-petitions are involved, the forename(s) and surname(s) of the civil partner who obtained the final order for dissolution or annulment should be entered in the box 'Forename(s) and Surname(s) of the Civil Partner obtaining order'.
6. For both forms 105 and 106 staff must ensure that the correct date of petition is supplied in the 'date of Petition' box.

Instructions for Completing Form 105

7. The following procedure will apply to completion of Form 105:

7.1 The form must be produced on white paper.

7.2 The boxes marked 'ONS code' and 'ONS number' appearing at the head of the form are solely for ONS use and must be left blank.

7.3 The Court name must appear on the form. It is not necessary to add the words 'County Court';

7.4 The surname of marriage is the name by which both parties were known during the subsistence of the marriage. Where the parties did not share a common surname the surname of the petitioner should be inserted. All surnames must include any necessary hyphens or apostrophes, and in multi-element names without hyphens (e.g. de la Rue) a space left between each element;

7.5 The case number should be completed as follows:

Divorce Reference						
0	8	D	4	3	2	1
Year			Number of case			

7.6 The dates for filing petition, decree absolute and marriage should be completed as in the following example for 1st January 2008:

D		M		Y	
0	1	0	1	0	8

7.7 The class of decree, or combination of classes should be inserted commencing in the left hand box for husband or wife as appropriate. Codings for the class of decree are A=Adultery, B=Behaviour, C=Desertion, D=Separation – 2 years Consent, E=Separation 5 years and N=Nullity.

H Decree			
A	B		

Where the decree was granted on the ground of presumption of death, the word

D	E	A	D

should be inserted as an alternative to the classes of decree listed on the form.

7.8 Where the age of the parties is not stated in years in the marriage certificate or where the decree relates to a foreign marriage and the ages of the parties are not know the box should be left blank.

7.9 The status of the parties at the time of the marriage (bachelor, spinster, widow/widower or divorced) are abbreviated to 'B', 'S', 'W' and 'D' respectively and should be inserted accordingly. Where the marriage certificate describes a party as P.M.D. (Previous Marriage Dissolved) the letter 'D' should be inserted. If the information is not know the box should be left blank. For marriages taking place after the 5 December 2005 the code S (for single) should be used in place of B and S. In addition, the codes C for civil partnership dissolved and X for civil partner deceased may appear.

7.10 The information relating to children should be completed according to the situation at the date of filing the petition. However, in the event of a child being born to the parties between the date of filing the petition and the date of the decree absolute the date of birth of that child should also be included. It is essential that the dates of birth of the children are shown with the eldest child first and the youngest last.

7.11 The alternative or present name boxes are to be completed where either party has used or adopted a different surname or forename since the date of the marriage or is known by an alias.

7.12 Full details relating to the parties' occupations should be extracted from the petition.

Instructions for Completing Form 106

8. Form 106 is in most respects similar to form 105. The form should be produced on blue paper; if for any reason it is not possible to use blue paper, the form may be produced on paper of a different colour, provided that it is not white or yellow and

that it is of a different colour to that used for form 105. The following instructions apply to those parts of the form which differ from form 105.

8.1 The gender of the couple involved in the dissolution or annulment of a civil partnership should be recorded with the code M for male or F for female.

8.2 Form 105 collects age. However form 106 collects date of birth, which mirrors the collection of date of birth at the formation of a civil partnership. The date should be completed as in the following example for 1st January 1968:

D		M		Y			
0	1	0	1	1	9	6	8

8.3 The case number should be completed as follows:

Dissolution Reference						
0	8	D	1	2	3	4
Year			Number of case			

8.4 The class of order, or combination of classes should be inserted commencing in the left hand box for civil partner 1 or civil partner 2 as appropriate. Codings for the class of order are, **B=Behaviour, C=Desertion, D=Separation -2 years Consent, E=Separation 5 years and N=Annulment**.

Where the final order was granted on the ground of presumption of death, the word

D	E	A	D

should be inserted as an alternative to the classes of order listed on the form.

8.5 The status of the parties at the time of the civil partnership (single, widow/widower, divorced, civil partnership dissolved or civil partnership, partner deceased) are abbreviated to 'S', 'W', 'D', 'C' and 'X' respectively and should be inserted accordingly. If the information is now known the box should be left blank.

Despatch of the completed forms 105 or 106

9. The completed forms 105 and 106 should be collected and despatched *each Friday* and addressed to:

The Office for National Statistics,
Marriages and Divorces Section,
Room 2200
Segensworth Road,
Titchfield,
Fareham,
Hants,
PO15 SRR
Telephone: 01329 813771.

Query resolution

10. It has been agreed with the ONS that where any query arises about information provided by the court in form 105 or 106, there should be direct contact between the court submitting the completed forms and the ONS. The court may telephone the ONS to amend earlier data which subsequently requires correction, and the

ONS may send the court queries which have arisen concerning the consistency of information which has been supplied in the forms. The contact address and telephone number for the ONS are given in paragraph 9.

11. Any queries on forms 105 or 106 raised with the court by the ONS should be dealt with promptly and returned with the following week's return of forms.

Issued by the President of the Family Division as the nominee of the Lord Chief Justice, with the agreement of the Lord Chancellor.

The Right Honourable Sir Mark Potter
President of the Family Division and Head of Justice

20 Civil Partnership (Jurisdiction and Recognition of Judgments) Regulations 2005

SI 2005/3334

Citation and commencement

1

These Regulations may be cited as the Civil Partnership (Jurisdiction and Recognition of Judgments) Regulations 2005 and shall come into force on 5 December 2005.

Extent

2

(1) Except as provided by this regulation, these Regulations extend to England and Wales and Northern Ireland.
(2) Regulations 4 and 11(1) extend to England and Wales only.
(3) Regulations 5 and 11(2) extend to Northern Ireland only.

Application

3

(1) These Regulations apply to proceedings for the dissolution or annulment of an overseas relationship entitled to be treated as a civil partnership, or the legal separation of the same, as they apply to proceedings for the dissolution or annulment of a civil partnership or the legal separation of civil partners.
(2) Regulations 7 and 8, in respect of recognition and non-recognition of a judgment, apply to all judgments even if the date of the judgment is earlier than the date on which section 219 of the Civil Partnership Act 2004 and these Regulations come into force.

PART 1
JURISDICTION

Jurisdiction: England and Wales

4

The courts in England and Wales shall have jurisdiction in relation to proceedings for the dissolution or annulment of a civil partnership or for the legal separation of civil partners where—

(a) both civil partners are habitually resident in England and Wales;
(b) both civil partners were last habitually resident in England and Wales and one of the civil partners continues to reside there;
(c) the respondent is habitually resident in England and Wales;
(d) the petitioner is habitually resident in England and Wales and has resided there for at least one year immediately preceding the presentation of the petition; or
(e) the petitioner is domiciled and habitually resident in England and Wales and has resided there for at least six months immediately preceding the presentation of the petition.

Jurisdiction: Northern Ireland

5

The courts in Northern Ireland shall have jurisdiction in relation to proceedings for the dissolution or annulment of a civil partnership or for the legal separation of civil partners where—

(a) both civil partners are habitually resident in Northern Ireland;
(b) both civil partners were last habitually resident in Northern Ireland and one of the civil partners continues to reside there;
(c) the respondent is habitually resident in Northern Ireland;
(d) the petitioner is habitually resident in Northern Ireland and has resided there for at least one year immediately preceding the presentation of the petition; or
(e) the petitioner is domiciled and habitually resident in Northern Ireland and has resided there for at least six months immediately preceding the presentation of the petition.

PART 2
RECOGNITION AND REFUSAL OF RECOGNITION OF JUDGMENTS

Definitions for Part 2

6

(1) In this Part 'judgment' means an order for the dissolution or annulment of a civil partnership or the legal separation of civil partners, pronounced by a court of a Member State, however termed by that State.
(2) A 'court of a Member State' referred to in paragraph (1) means all the authorities, whether judicial or administrative, in Member States with jurisdiction in those matters falling within the scope of these Regulations.
(3) The 'Member States' referred to in paragraph (1) are any of the following States—Belgium, Cyprus, Czech Republic, Denmark, Germany, Greece, Spain, Estonia, France, Hungary, Ireland, Italy, Latvia, Lithuania, Luxembourg, Malta, Netherlands, Austria, Poland, Portugal, Slovakia, Slovenia, Finland and Sweden.

Recognition of a judgment

7

(1) Where a judgment is (or has been) given in respect of a civil partnership, that judgment shall, without any special formalities, be recognised in England and Wales or Northern Ireland.
(2) Any interested party may, in accordance with the procedure set out in rules, apply for a judgment to be, or not to be, recognised.
(3) Where the recognition of a judgment is raised as an incidental issue in proceedings before the court, that court may determine the issue.

Refusal of recognition of a judgment

8

(1) Recognition of the validity of a judgment may be refused in England and Wales or Northern Ireland if the judgment was obtained at a time when it was irreconcilable

with a decision determining the question of the subsistence or validity of the civil partnership—

(a) previously given by a court of civil jurisdiction in that part of the United Kingdom, or

(b) previously given by a court elsewhere and recognised or entitled to be recognised in that part of the United Kingdom.

(2) Recognition of the validity of a judgment may be refused in England and Wales or Northern Ireland if the judgment was obtained at a time when, according to the law of that part of the United Kingdom, there was no subsisting civil partnership.

(3) Recognition of the validity of a judgment may be refused if—

(a) in the case of a judgment obtained by means of proceedings, it was obtained—

(i) without such steps having been taken for giving notice of the proceedings to a civil partner as, having regard to the nature of the proceedings and all the circumstances, should reasonably have been taken, or

(ii) without a civil partner having been given (for any reason other than lack of notice) such opportunity to take part in the proceedings as, having regard to those matters, he should reasonably have been given, or

(b) in the case of a judgment obtained otherwise than by means of proceedings—

(i) there is no official document certifying the judgment is effective under the law of the country in which it was obtained, or

(ii) where either civil partner was domiciled in another country at the relevant date, there is no official document certifying that the judgment is recognised as valid under the law of that other country, or

(c) in either case, recognition of the judgment would be manifestly contrary to public policy.

(4) In this regulation—

'official', in relation to a document certifying that a judgment is effective, or is recognised as valid, under the law of any country, means issued by a person or body appointed or recognised for the purpose under that law;

'the relevant date' means—

(a) in the case of a judgment obtained by means of proceedings, the date of the commencement of the proceedings;

(b) in the case of a judgment obtained otherwise than by means of proceedings, the date on which it was obtained.

Jurisdiction and review

9

The court may not review the jurisdiction of the court which issued the judgment.

10

A judgment may not be reviewed as to its substance.

Differences in applicable law

11

(1) The recognition of a judgment in England and Wales may not be refused because the law of England and Wales would not allow dissolution, annulment or legal separation on the same facts.

(2) The recognition of a judgment in Northern Ireland may not be refused because the law of Northern Ireland would not allow dissolution, annulment or legal separation on the same facts.

Stay of proceedings

12

Where recognition is sought of a judgment given in a Member State and an appeal against that judgment has been lodged in a Member State, the court may stay the proceedings.

21 President's Guidance on Divorce, Dissolution and Separation Act 2020: Costs in proceedings for matrimonial and civil partnership orders

Issued 28 March 2022

Introduction

(1) The Divorce, Dissolution and Separation Act 2020 ("the 2020 Act") amends the Matrimonial Causes Act 1973 and the Civil Partnership Act 2004 to remove fault-based concepts in proceedings for divorce, dissolution and (judicial) separation. This is a fundamental change which will affect the way in which the courts deal with applications and the purpose of this guidance is to explain the impact of this change on the court's approach to costs. The amendments made by the 2020 Act take effect from 6 April 2022 and this guidance applies to applications issued on or after that date.

(2) The great majority of applications are likely to be undisputed and cases will not involve any consideration by the court of the reasons for or responsibility for the breakdown of the marriage or civil partnership. Even where an application is disputed, the grounds for opposition will be limited to issues about the court's jurisdiction to hear the case or about the validity or subsistence of the marriage or civil partnership. It follows that, while the court will retain a discretion to make a costs order against either party, the circumstances in which an order for costs will be appropriate are likely to be very limited.

The governing principles

(3) The exercise of the court's discretion to make a costs order in proceedings for a matrimonial or civil partnership order is governed by the relevant provisions of the Civil Procedure Rules, as applied to family proceedings by rule 28.2(1) of the Family Procedure Rules, and in particular CPR rule 44.2 (excluding r 44.2(2) and (3)).

(4) CPR rule 44.2(4) provides that, in deciding what order (if any) to make about costs, the court will have regard to all the circumstances, including–

(a) the conduct of all the parties;

(b) whether a party has succeeded on part of its case, even if that party has not been wholly successful; and

(c) any admissible offer to settle made by a party which is drawn to the court's attention, and which is not an offer to which costs consequences under Part 36 apply.

(5) By CPR r 44.2(5), the conduct of the parties includes –

(a) conduct before, as well as during, the proceedings and in particular the extent to which the parties followed the Practice Direction – Pre-Action Conduct or any relevant pre-action protocol;

(b) whether it was reasonable for a party to raise, pursue or contest a particular allegation or issue;

(c) the manner in which a party has pursued or defended its case or a particular allegation or issue; and

(d) whether a claimant who has succeeded in the claim, in whole or in part, exaggerated its claim.

(6) The effect of these provisions is that in proceedings for a matrimonial or civil partnership order the court has a wide discretion in relation to the award of costs. There is no general rule that costs are awarded to a successful party; the court must consider all the circumstances. However, these provisions must be considered in the context of the court's role in the proceedings.

The approach under the new law

(7) Under the new process the court's decision about whether to make a divorce order, dissolution order or (judicial) separation order does not depend on any findings about the responsibility of either party for the breakdown of the relationship. There is therefore no scope for the court to consider the conduct of the parties in that respect. The parties' conduct in relation to the proceedings (whether before or during the proceedings or in the manner in which a case has been pursued or defended) will remain relevant; in particular, if the court concludes that the conduct of a party has been unreasonable (for example by attempting to evade service or raising spurious or irrelevant arguments) and that costs have been incurred or increased as a result, an award of costs in favour of the other party may be appropriate.

(8) Equally, the concept of 'success' will be of limited application. In a standard case, where the court has not been required to determine any dispute between the parties, it is not appropriate to regard either party as having succeeded in the outcome. In a disputed case, different considerations may apply, depending on the nature of the dispute and the issues raised by the parties, but bearing in mind the limited grounds for opposing an application: see below.

(9) These considerations mean that in the great majority of cases, including joint applications, where an application for an order for divorce, dissolution or (judicial) separation is not disputed and the parties have conducted the proceedings in a reasonable manner, a costs order would be inappropriate.

(10) Where a divorce or dissolution application is disputed on the ground that the court does not have jurisdiction to hear it, for example because the marriage or civil partnership has already been dissolved overseas, or because the marriage or civil partnership does not validly subsist, there will likely be a separate hearing to determine that issue. If the defending party is unsuccessful the court will consider whether the pursuit of the defence was unreasonable. If the court determines that it was, it will normally determine that it would be appropriate to order that the unsuccessful defending party should pay the costs of the successful party. If the court determines that the pursuit of that defence was not unreasonable, it will nonetheless consider whether to make an order for costs in any event in favour of the successful party to reflect the court's decision on the specific issue.

(11) The changes made by the 2020 Act do not affect the grounds for seeking a nullity order or the court's approach to making a costs order in nullity proceedings, but the procedure for seeking a costs order is changed as described below.

Procedure

(12) The forms of application for a matrimonial or civil partnership order do not include any provision for making an application for a costs order. In a disputed case any application for costs may be made at the hearing of the application: see FPR, r 7.32(1). In a standard case, any application for costs should be made by application notice: see FPR, r 7.32(2); the procedure is set out in Practice Direction 7A. This procedure applies to proceedings for a nullity order as well as to proceedings for divorce, dissolution or (judicial) separation. 4

(13) In a standard case, the application notice or written evidence in support must set out the grounds on which a costs order is sought. In the case of proceedings for divorce, dissolution or (judicial) separation the applicant should have regard to the guidance above and set out clearly any conduct in relation to the proceedings which is said to justify the making of a costs order. Wherever possible the applicant should specify the amount of costs claimed, showing how the amount has been calculated; Form N260 (Statement of Costs for Summary Assessment) is not required unless directed by the court. A respondent who opposes the making of a costs order or disputes the amount of costs claimed must file a witness statement in response and the court will normally deal with the application without a hearing, on the basis of the parties' written statements.

28 March 2022

22 Fact Finding Hearings and Domestic Abuse in Private Law Children Proceedings – Guidance for Judges and Magistrates

Introduction

In March 2022 I invited Lady Justice Macur to form a small group with the task of producing short, clear and practical guidance for judges and magistrates concerning fact finding hearings and domestic abuse in Private Law children proceedings in the Family Court. I am extremely grateful to Macur LJ and her team who have, in the short time available, conducted a useful survey of salaried and fee-paid judges before producing this guidance, which I now approve and publish.

Sir Andrew McFarlane

President of the Family Division

5th May 2022

General

1. Make every hearing count. Do not sanction short hearings or agree to insufficient preparation time for the first or other case management hearings on the basis that things can be 'sorted out' next time. Seize the opportunity to probe. Remain 'in control' throughout. Strive to achieve judicial continuity and take ownership of the case. Remember delay is inimical to child welfare.
2. As the judge or magistrate, you have the relevant expertise and competence to analyse and determine the necessity for a fact-finding hearing, and if so, the extent of the hearing and the evidence that will be required. The views of the parties, the CAFCASS officer or the advocates may be persuasive, but they are not determinative; interrogate their reasoning.
3. There is a time and a place to determine allegations of domestic abuse, but it may not be in your court. Unless it will be relevant to, and necessary for, your decision regarding the welfare of the child, do not allow the court to be used to litigate such allegations.

At the FHDRA/first directions appointment/to be considered at gatekeeping

4. Non-court dispute resolution and MIAMs:
   a. Has a MIAM taken place? If not, why not? Should it now be required? The court has a duty to consider non-court dispute resolution: FPR r3.3.
   b. If a MIAM exemption has been claimed on the ground of domestic abuse, check that evidence exists as specified at FPR PD3A [20]. Is the exemption valid? FPR r.3.10.
   c. If appropriate, invite an authorised family mediator to advise whether mediation is possible with adaptations such as shuttle diplomacy or protective measures.
5. Identify the real issues in the case. Is one parent denying contact per se or seeking to add conditions for or in relation to contact arrangements? What are the questions pertaining to the child's welfare?
6. What exactly is alleged in terms of domestic abuse and by whom? Consider the definitions at FPR PD 12J [2A] and [3] in addition to PD 12J [14].

7. Has a Form C1A been completed? Is there a response?
   a. If so, ensure the forms are considered in their entirety. Are there admissions? Does the form and/or response suggest a possible way forward to the satisfaction of the court that will permit safe continuation of relationships with the child and avoid conflict with other adults?
   b. If not, why not? Is it appropriate to obtain a verbal summary of any allegations and/or response during the hearing in order for progress to be made?
8. Collectively, does the information already before the court (for example, the C100, C1A and any safeguarding report) contain sufficient detail to avoid the necessity of directing further evidence/documentation to determine the issue?
9. If further evidence/documentation is required to determine the issue, what is necessary in the fact specific circumstances of the case? The judgment in *Re H-N* [2021] EWCA Civ 448 (paras 41-49) cautioned against allowing a Scott Schedule to distort the fact finding process (by becoming the sole focus of a hearing), but the Court of Appeal did not rule out the use of a schedule as a structure to assist in analysing specific allegations.
10. In determining what further evidence/documentation is needed, the nature of the allegations will be important. Allegations that can be clearly defined (such as specific incidents of physical abuse) may be suitable for reduction to a schedule. Other allegations that require the court to take a broad overview and look at patterns of behaviour (such as coercive and controlling behaviour) are likely to require a statement. A hybrid of the two, dividing types of abuse into clusters to provide an overview akin to a threshold document in public law proceedings might be appropriate. However, do not consider only the nature of the allegations, but also practicality and expediency bearing in mind the parties before you. Require a like for like document in response from the alleged perpetrator.
11. Ensure that you obtain the essential information in respect of any allegation at an early stage. What, when, where? What was the effect on the child and the parent? Were there witnesses? What other evidence might be available? Is the behaviour complained of because of the breakdown of the relationship rather than a/the cause of the breakdown?

Is a fact-finding hearing required?

12. When determining whether to order a fact-finding hearing, consider:
    a. the nature of the allegations and the extent to which those allegations are likely to be relevant to the making of a child arrangements order;
    b. that the purpose of a fact finding is to allow assessment of the future risk to the child and the impact of any abuse on the child;
    c. whether fact-finding is necessary or whether other evidence suffices; and,
    d. whether fact-finding is proportionate.
13. The fundamentals are relevance, purpose, and proportionality. Consider FPR PD 12J [14] and [17].
14. Allegations that require the assessment of a pattern of behaviour, such as controlling and coercive behaviour, do not justify a different approach. The court only needs to determine allegations of such behaviour to the extent that it is relevant and necessary to determine issues as to a child's future welfare. Even then, the court is only required to assess the overarching issue, rather than every single subsidiary factual allegation that may also be raised.

15. Always consider whether the allegations (at their highest) go to safeguarding in general or to particular circumstances that could be mitigated by supervision of contact or some other measures. If the latter and mitigations are available, why is it said that a fact-finding hearing is required?
16. If your conclusion is that the allegations, if proved and however serious, would not be relevant to the decision, then no fact-finding hearing is required.
17. Record brief reasons for your decision whether or not a fact-finding hearing is necessary on the face of the order.

Case management if a fact-finding hearing is required

18. When determining the specific allegations to be tried, consider relevance, purpose, and proportionality.
19. Robust case management is required from the outset. Remember your case management responsibilities and powers: FPR r1.1, r1.4, r.4.4.
20. It is the court that controls the evidence in the case: FPR r.22.1.
21. Only order third party disclosure where it is necessary and proportionate to do so. Require justification for any requests and refuse fishing exercises. In what respect is it said the proposed evidence supports or undermines an allegation? Ensure that any orders are targeted and precise. For example, is it possible to direct specific disclosure from the police, as opposed to a 'catch all' order? Will a GP summary suffice instead of a party's full GP records?
22. If a party seeks to rely on a witness of fact, only allow evidence that goes to an issue to be determined. Test with the parties and decide what, if any, real value is likely to be brought to your enquiry by the evidence of third parties.
23. No case should be timetabled to a fact-finding hearing without a properly completed witness template. This will assist the parties and manage their expectations.
24. Consider participation directions. Section 63 Domestic Abuse Act 2001 establishes a presumption that where a party or witness is or at risk of being a victim of domestic abuse from a party to the proceedings, the quality of their evidence and / or their participation as a party is likely to be diminished by reason of vulnerability. Consideration of FPR r.3A and PD 3AA are mandatory and the obligation to consider vulnerability is the court's, regardless of whether a party is represented or if participation directions are sought.
25. At the fact-finding hearing itself, control the hearing and keep the parties and advocates on point. Keep in mind the issues / previously identified allegations. Do not permit irrelevant diversions.
26. Always ensure that any summary of findings you have made is fairly and accurately recorded in the order or a document attached to it.

Re-visiting a decision not to have a fact-finding hearing

27. The court must, at all stages in the proceedings, consider whether domestic abuse is raised as an issue: FPR PD 12J [5]. However, guard against attempts to re-argue the question once a decision has been made. What is said to have changed to undermine the original analysis? Proceedings should have judicial continuity, wherever possible, and a consistent approach.
28. If 'new' evidence relating to past events is presented, ask why it was not available or disclosed before. If no good reason is advanced, then you may refuse to admit it. The more significant the evidence is said to be, the more compelling the explanation needs to be for its late receipt.

APPENDIX D

RULES AND SUPPLEMENTARY PRACTICE DIRECTIONS

FAMILY PROCEDURE RULES 2010

SI 2010/2955

TABLE OF ARRANGEMENTS

Chapter 3

Family Mediation Information and Assessment Meetings (MIAMs)

PART 3A

VULNERABLE PERSONS: PARTICIPATION IN PROCEEDING AND GIVING EVIDENCE

PART 4

GENERAL CASE MANAGEMENT POWERS

PART 5

FORMS, START OF PROCEEDINGS AND COMMUNICATION WITH THE COURT

PART 6
SERVICE

Chapter 1
Scope of this Part and interpretation

Chapter 2
Service of the application for a matrimonial order or civil partnership order in the jurisdiction

Chapter 3
Service of documents other than an application for a matrimonial order or civil partnership order in the United Kingdom

Chapter 4

Service out of the jurisdiction

PART 7

PROCEDURE FOR APPLICATIONS IN MATRIMONIAL AND CIVIL PARTNERSHIP PROCEEDINGS

Chapter 1

Application and interpretation

Chapter 2

Rules about starting proceedings

Chapter 3

Standard case

Chapter 4

Disputed case

Chapter 5

Proceedings after conditional order (standard and disputed case)

Chapter 8

Pensions

Chapter 9

Pension Protection Fund compensation

Chapter 10

Communication of information from financial remedy proceedings

PART 10

APPLICATIONS UNDER PART 4 OF THE FAMILY LAW ACT 1996

PART 11

APPLICATIONS UNDER PART 4A OF THE FAMILY LAW ACT 1996 OR PART 1 OF SCHEDULE 2 TO THE FEMALE GENITAL MUTILATION ACT 2003

PART 12

CHILDREN PROCEEDINGS EXCEPT PARENTAL ORDER PROCEEDINGS AND PROCEEDINGS FOR APPLICATIONS IN ADOPTION, PLACEMENT AND RELATED PROCEEDINGS

Chapter 1

Interpretation and application of this Part

Chapter 2

General rules

Chapter 3

Special provisions about public law proceedings

PART 14

PROCEDURE FOR APPLICATIONS IN ADOPTION, PLACEMENT AND RELATED PROCEEDINGS

PART 15

REPRESENTATION OF PROTECTED PARTIES

PART 16
REPRESENTATION OF CHILDREN AND REPORTS IN PROCEEDINGS

PART 19

ALTERNATIVE PROCEDURE FOR APPLICATIONS

PART 20

INTERIM REMEDIES AND SECURITY FOR COSTS

Chapter 1

Interim remedies

Chapter 2

Security for costs

PART 21

MISCELLANEOUS RULES ABOUT DISCLOSURE AND INSPECTION OF DOCUMENTS

PART 22

EVIDENCE

Chapter 1

General rules

PART 26

CHANGE OF SOLICITOR

PART 27

HEARINGS AND DIRECTIONS APPOINTMENTS

PART 28

COSTS

PART 32

REGISTRATION AND ENFORCEMENT OF ORDERS

Chapter 1

Scope and interpretation of this Part

Chapter 2

Registration etc. of orders under the 1950 Act

Section 1

Interpretation of this Chapter

Section 2

Registration etc of High Court and family court orders

Section 3

Registration etc. of Scottish and Northern Irish orders

Chapter 3

Registration of maintenance orders under the 1958 Act

Chapter 2

Committal by way of judgment summons

Chapter 3

Attachment of earnings

Chapter 4

Warrant of control

Chapter 5

Court's power to appoint a receiver

Chapter 6

Orders to obtain information from judgment debtors

Chapter 7

Third party debt orders

Chapter 8

Charging order, stop order, stop notice

PART 34

RECIPROCAL ENFORCEMENT OF MAINTENANCE ORDERS

Chapter 1

Enforcement of maintenance orders under the Maintenance Orders (Facilities for Enforcement) Act 1920

Chapter 3

Enforcement of maintenance orders under the 2007 Hague Convention

Section 1

Registration and enforcement in a magaistrates' court of maintenance order made in a State bound by the 2007 Hague Convention

Section 2

Reciprocal enforcement in a Contracting State of orders of a court in England and Wales

PART 35

…

PART 36

TRANSITIONAL ARRANGEMENTS AND PILOT SCHEMES

PART 37

APPLICATIONS AND PROCEEDINGS IN RELATION TO CONTEMPT OF COURT

PART 38

RECOGNITION AND ENFORCEMENT OF PROTECTION MEASURES

Chapter 1

Scope and interpretation of this Part

Chapter 2

…

Chapter 3

Incoming protection measures

PART 39

ATTACHMENT OF EARNINGS

Chapter 1

General

Chapter 2

Securing payments under a maintenance order in the family court – attachment of earnings order

Chapter 3

Securing payments under a maintenance order in the High Court – attachment of earnings order

PART 40

CHARGING ORDER, STOP ORDER, STOP NOTICE

Chapter 1

General

Practice Direction – Practice Directions relating to family proceedings in force before 6th April 2011 which support the Family Procedure Rules 2010

1.1 The Family Procedure Rules 2010 ('the FPR 2010') come into force on 6th April 2011. The purpose of this practice direction is to inform court users of the practice directions relating (only) to family proceedings which date from before 6th April 2011 ('existing Practice Directions') but will continue to apply after that date.

1.2 The table in the Annex to this practice direction lists those existing Practice Directions which will continue to apply. The listed existing Practice Directions will apply to family proceedings on and after 6th April 2011–

(a) with the modifications outlined in the Annex (in particular that the numbering of the existing Practice Directions will be as set out in column one of the table in the Annex) and any other modifications necessary in consequence of the FPR 2010 coming into force; and

(b) subject to the FPR 2010 and any other practice directions supporting those rules.

Application of Practice Direction 23B of the Civil Procedure Rules 1998

2.1 Paragraphs 1.1, 1.2, 1.4 and 1.5 of CPR Practice Direction 23B apply to applications under Part lll of the Family Law Reform Act 1969 for the use of scientific tests to determine parentage. These applications will be made using the procedure in Part 18 of the FPR 2010 (Procedure for Other Applications in Proceedings).

Annex

Number	Title	Date	Court	Updated Rule References
Practice Direction 6C	Practice Direction (Disclosure of Addresses by Government Departments) • (amending Practice Direction of 13th February 1989) • (NB this practice direction does not apply to requests for disclosure from HMRC and related agencies which are covered by 'Disclosure Orders against the Inland Revenue-Guidance from the President's Office (November 2003)'	20 July 1995	High Court, county court and magistrates' court	
Practice Direction 7D	Gender Recognition Act 2004	5th April 2005	High Court and county court	

Number	Title	Date	Court	Updated Rule References
Practice Direction 12A	Public Law Proceedings Guide to Case Management: April 2010	April 2010	High Court, county court and magistrates' court	
Practice Direction 12B	The Revised Private Law Programme	April 2010	High Court, county court and magistrates' court	
Practice Direction 12I	Applications for Reporting Restriction Orders (nb this practice direction applies to information about children and protected parties)	18 March 2005	High Court	
Practice Direction 12J	Residence and Contact Orders: Domestic Violence and Harm	14th January 2009	High Court, county court and magistrates' court	In paragraph 10, for 'the Family Proceedings Rules 1991, rule 4.17AA and by the Family Proceedings Courts (Children Act 1989) Rules 1991, rule 17AA', substitute, 'rule 12.34 of the Family Procedure Rules 2010'
Practice Direction 12K	President's Direction (Children Act 1989: Exclusion Requirement)	17th December 1997	High Court, county court and magistrates' court	
Practice Direction 12L	Children Act 1989: Risk Assessments under Section 16A	3rd September 2007	High Court, county court and magistrates' court	
Practice Direction 12M	Family Assistance Orders: Consultation	3rd September 2007	High Court, county court and magistrates' court	
Practice Direction 12N	Enforcement of Children Act 1989 Contact Orders: Disclosure of Information to Officers of the National Probation Service (High Court and county court)	6th November 2008	High Court and county court (The Lord Chief Justice issued a Practice Direction on this subject for the magistrates' courts mirroring the one for the High Court and county courts)	

Number	Title	Date	Court	Updated Rule References
Practice Direction 12O	Practice Direction (Arrival of Child in England by Air)	18th January 1980	High Court and county court	
Practice Direction 12P	Registrar's Direction (Removal from jurisdiction: issue of Passports)	15th May 1987	High Court and county court	
Practice Direction 14A	Who Receives a Copy of the Application Form for Orders in Proceedings		High Court, county court and magistrates' court	In the heading, for 'Part 5, rule 24(1)(b)(ii) of the Family Procedure (Adoption) Rules 2005', substitute 'Part 14, rule 14.6(1)(b)(ii) of the Family Procedure Rules 2010'
Practice Direction 14B	The First Directions Hearing-Adoptions with a Foreign Element		High Court, county court and magistrates' court	In the heading, for 'Part 5, rule 26(3) of the Family Procedure (Adoption) Rules 2005', substitute 'Part 14, rule 14.8(3) of the Family Procedure Rules 2010'; and in paragraph 2, for 'rule 26(1)', substitute 'rule 14.8(1)'
Practice Direction 14C	Reports by the Adoption Agency or Local Authority		High Court, county court and magistrates' court	In the heading for 'Part 5, rule 29(3) of the Family Procedure (Adoption) Rules 2005', substitute 'Part 14, rule 14.11(3) of the Family Procedure Rules 2010'

Number	Title	Date	Court	Updated Rule References
Practice Direction 14D	Reports by a Registered Medical Practitioner ('Health Reports')		High Court, county court and magistrates' court	In the heading for 'Part 5, rule 30(2) of the Family Procedure (Adoption) Rules 2005', substitute 'Part 14, rule 14.12(2) of the Family Procedure Rules 2010'; and in paragraph 1.1, for 'rule 30(1)', substitute 'rule 14.12(1)'
Practice Direction 14E	Communication of Information Relating to the Proceedings		High Court, county court and magistrates' court	In the heading for 'Part 8, rule 78(1)(b) of the Family Procedure (Adoption) Rules 2005', substitute 'Part 14, rule 14.14(b) of the Family Procedure Rules 2010'; and in paragraph 1.1, for 'rule 78', substitute 'rule 14.14'
Practice Direction 14F	Disclosing Information to an Adopted Adult		High Court, county court and magistrates' court	In the heading for 'Part 8, rule 84(1)(d) of the Family Procedure (Adoption) Rules 2005', substitute 'Part 14, rule 14.18(1)(d) of the Family Procedure Rules 2010'; in paragraphs 1,1 and 1.2, for 'rule 84', substitute 'rule 14.18'; and in paragraph 1.2, for 'rule 17', substitute 'rule 5'
Practice Direction 27A	Family Proceedings: Court Bundles (Universal Practice to be applied in All Courts other than the Family Proceedings Court)	27th July 2006	High Court and county court	

Number	Title	Date	Court	Updated Rule References
Practice Direction 27B	Attendance of Media Representatives at Hearings in Family Proceedings (High Court and county courts) (This practice direction should be read as if amended by Re X (a child)(residence and contact: rights of media attendance) (2009) EWHC 1728 (Fam) [87])	20th April 2009	High Court and county courts	For references to 'rule 10.28 of the Family Proceedings Rules 1991', substitute 'rule 27.11 of the Family Procedure Rules 2010'; • in paragraph 2.2 for 'paragraphs (4) to (6)', substitute 'paragraphs (3) to (5)'; • in paragraph 2.3, for 'Part 11 of the Family Proceedings Rules 1991', substitute 'Part 12, Chapter 7 of the Family Procedure Rules 2010 and Practice Direction 12G'; • in paragraph 4.2, for 'paragraph (8)',substitute 'paragraph (7)'; • in paragraph 4.3, for 'paragraph (3)(f)', substitute 'paragraph 2(f)' and for 'paragraph 3(g)', substitute 'paragraph (2)(g)'; • in paragraph 5.1, for paragraph(4), substitute paragraph (3);

Number	Title	Date	Court	Updated Rule References
				• in paragraph 5.2, for 'paragraph (4)', substitute 'paragraph (3)' and for 'paragraph (4) (a)', substitute 'paragraph 3(a)'; • in paragraph 5.3, for 'paragraph 4(a) (iii)', substitute 'paragraph 3(a) (iii)'; • in paragraph 5.4, for 'paragraph 4(b)', substitute 'paragraph 3(b)'; and • in paragraph 6.1, for 'paragraph (6)' substitute 'paragraph (5)'
Practice Direction 27C	Attendance of Media Representatives at Hearings in Family Proceedings (Family Proceedings Court) (This practice direction should be read as if amended by Re X (a child) (residence and contact: rights of media attendance) (2009) EWHC 1728 (Fam) at [87]	20th April 2009	Magistrates' courts	In paragraph 1.1, for 'rule 16A of the Family Proceedings Courts (Children Act 1989) Rules 1991 ('the Rules')', substitute 'rule 27.11 of the Family Procedure Rules 2010 ('the Rules')'; • in paragraph 2.1, for references to 'rule 16A(2)' where it occurs, substitute 'rule 27.11(1)' and for 'paragraphs (3) to (5) of rule16A',substitute; 'paragraphs (3) to (5) of rule 27.11';

Number	Title	Date	Court	Updated Rule References
				• in paragraph 2.2, for 'rule 16A(2)', substitute 'rule 27.11(1)'; • in paragraph 2.3 for 'Part 11C (rules relating to disclosure to third parties)', substitute 'Part 12, Chapter 7 of the Family Procedure Rules 2010 and Practice Direction 12G'; • in paragraph 2.4, for 'rule 16A', substitute 'rule 27.11'; and • in paragraph 4.3, for 'paragraph (1)(f)', substitute 'paragraph 2(f)' and for 'paragraph (1)(g)' substitute 'paragraph 2(g)'
Practice Direction 29B	Human Rights Act 1998	24th July 2000	High Court, county court and magistrates' court	
Practice Direction 34B	Practice Note Tracing Payers Overseas	10th February 1976	High Court and county court	

PART 1
OVERRIDING OBJECTIVE

1.1 The overriding objective

(1) These rules are a new procedural code with the overriding objective of enabling the court to deal with cases justly, having regard to any welfare issues involved.

(2) Dealing with a case justly includes, so far as is practicable—

(a) ensuring that it is dealt with expeditiously and fairly;
(b) dealing with the case in ways which are proportionate to the nature, importance and complexity of the issues;

(c) ensuring that the parties are on an equal footing;
(d) saving expense; and
(e) allotting to it an appropriate share of the court's resources, while taking into account the need to allot resources to other cases.

1.2 Application by the court of the overriding objective

The court must seek to give effect to the overriding objective when it—

(a) exercises any power given to it by these rules; or
(b) interprets any rule.

1.3 Duty of the parties

The parties are required to help the court to further the overriding objective.

1.4 Court's duty to manage cases

(1) The court must further the overriding objective by actively managing cases.

[(2) Active case management includes—

(a) setting timetables or otherwise controlling the progress of the case;
(b) identifying at an early stage—
  (i) the issues; and
  (ii) who should be a party to the proceedings;
(c) deciding promptly—
  (i) which issues need full investigation and hearing and which do not; and
  (ii) the procedure to be followed in the case;
(d) deciding the order in which issues are to be resolved;
(e) controlling the use of expert evidence;
(f) encouraging the parties to use [a non-court dispute resolution][1] procedure if the court considers that appropriate and facilitating the use of such procedure;
(g) helping the parties to settle the whole or part of the case;
(h) encouraging the parties to co-operate with each other in the conduct of proceedings;
(i) considering whether the likely benefits of taking a particular step justify the cost of taking it;
(j) dealing with as many aspects of the case as it can on the same occasion;
(k) dealing with the case without the parties needing to attend at court;
(l) making use of technology; and
(m) giving directions to ensure that the case proceeds quickly and efficiently.][2]

Amendments

1 Substituted by the Family Procedure (Amendment No 3) Rules 2014, SI 2014/843, rr 2, 3.
2 Substituted by the Family Procedure (Amendment) (No 5) Rules 2012, SI 2012/3061, rr 2, 3.

[1.5 The Welsh language

(1) Nothing in the overriding objective undermines the principles provided by section 1 of the Welsh Language (Wales) Measure 2011 that the Welsh language has official status in Wales or by section 22 of the Welsh Language Act 1993 that in any legal proceedings in Wales the Welsh language may be used by any person who desires to use it.

(2) The parties are required to assist the court to put into effect the principles set out in paragraph (1).][1]

Amendment

1 Inserted by the Family Procedure (Amendment No 2) Rules 2018, SI 2018/1172, rr 2, 3.

PART 2
APPLICATION AND INTERPRETATION OF THE RULES

[2.1 Application of these Rules

Unless the context otherwise requires, these rules apply to family proceedings in—

(a) the High Court; and
(b) the family court.][1]

Amendment

1 Substituted by the Family Procedure (Amendment No 3) Rules 2013, SI 2013/3204, rr 2, 3.

2.2 The glossary

(1) The glossary at the end of these rules is a guide to the meaning of certain legal expressions used in the rules, but is not to be taken as giving those expressions any meaning in the rules which they do not have in the law generally.

(2) Subject to paragraph (3), words in these rules which are included in the glossary are followed by 'GL'.

(3) The word 'service', which appears frequently in the rules, is included in the glossary but is not followed by 'GL'.

2.3 Interpretation

(1) In these rules—

['the 1958 Act' means the Maintenance Orders Act 1958;][1]

'the 1973 Act' means the Matrimonial Causes Act 1973;

'the 1978 Act' means the Domestic Proceedings and Magistrates' Courts Act 1978;

'the 1980 Hague Convention' means the Convention on the Civil Aspects of International Child Abduction which was signed at The Hague on 25 October 1980;

'the 1984 Act' means the Matrimonial and Family Proceedings Act 1984;

'the 1986 Act' means the Family Law Act 1986;

'the 1989 Act' means the Children Act 1989;

'the 1990 Act' means the Human Fertilisation and Embryology Act 1990;

'the 1991 Act' means the Child Support Act 1991;

'the 1996 Act' means the Family Law Act 1996;

'the 1996 Hague Convention' means the Convention on Jurisdiction, Applicable Law, Recognition, Enforcement and Co-Operation in Respect of Parental Responsibility and Measures for the Protection of Children;

'the 2002 Act' means the Adoption and Children Act 2002;

'the 2004 Act' means the Civil Partnership Act 2004;

'the 2005 Act' means the Mental Capacity Act 2005;

['the 2007 Hague Convention' means the Convention on the International Recovery of Child Support and other forms of Family Maintenance done at The Hague on 23 November 2007;][2]

'the 2008 Act' means the Human Fertilisation and Embryology Act 2008;

['the 2014 Act' means the Children and Families Act 2014;][3]

'adoption proceedings' means proceedings for an adoption order under the 2002 Act;

…[4]

…[5]

'application form' means a document in which the applicant states his intention to seek a court order other than in accordance with the Part 18 procedure;

'application notice' means a document in which the applicant states his intention to seek a court order in accordance with the Part 18 procedure;

['Article 11 form' means a form published by the Permanent Bureau of the Hague Conference under Article 11(4) of the 2007 Hague Convention for use in relation to an application under Article 10 of that Convention, and includes a Financial Circumstances Form as defined in rule 9.3(1) which accompanies such an application;][2]

'Assembly' means the National Assembly for Wales;

'bank holiday' means a bank holiday under the Banking and Financial Dealings Act 1971—

(a) for the purpose of service of a document within the United Kingdom, in the part of the United Kingdom where service is to take place; and
(b) for all other purposes, in England and Wales.

'business day' means any day other than—

(a) a Saturday, Sunday, Christmas Day or Good Friday; or
(b) a bank holiday;

'care order' has the meaning assigned to it by section 31(11) of the 1989 Act;

'CCR' means the County Court Rules 1981, as they appear in Schedule 2 to the CPR […[6]][7];

'child' means a person under the age of 18 years who is the subject of the proceedings; except that—

(a) in adoption proceedings, it also includes a person who has attained the age of 18 years before the proceedings are concluded; and
(b) in proceedings brought under …[8] the 1980 Hague Convention or the European Convention, it means a person under the age of 16 years who is the subject of the proceedings;

['child arrangements order' has the meaning given to it by section 8(1) of the 1989 Act;][3]

'child of the family' has the meaning given to it by section 105(1) of the 1989 Act;

'children and family reporter' means an officer of the Service or a Welsh family proceedings officer who has been asked to prepare a welfare report under section 7(1)(a) of the 1989 Act or section 102(3)(b) of the 2002 Act;

'children's guardian' means—

(a) in relation to a child who is the subject of and a party to specified proceedings or proceedings to which Part 14 applies, the person appointed in accordance with rule 16.3(1); and
(b) in any other case, the person appointed in accordance with rule 16.4;

'civil partnership order' means one of the orders mentioned in section 37 of the 2004 Act;

'civil partnership proceedings' means proceedings for a civil partnership order;

…[4]

'civil restraint order' means an order restraining a party—

(a) from making any further applications in current proceedings (a limited civil restraint order);

(b) from making certain applications in specified courts (an extended civil restraint order); or
(c) from making any application in specified courts (a general civil restraint order);

…[9]

'consent order' means an order in the terms applied for to which the respondent agrees;

…[5]

…[8]

'court' means, subject to any rule or other enactment which provides otherwise, the High Court [or the family court][10]; (rule 2.5 relates to the power to perform functions of the court.)

…[4]

'court officer' means [a member of court staff][10];

'CPR' means the Civil Procedure Rules 1998;

'deputy' has the meaning given in section 16(2)(b) of the 2005 Act;

…[4]

'detailed assessment proceedings' means the procedure by which the amount of costs is decided in accordance with Part 47 of the CPR;

'directions appointment' means a hearing for directions;

…[4]

…[4]

…[4]

'the European Convention' means the European Convention on Recognition and Enforcement of Decisions concerning Custody of Children and on the Restoration of Custody of Children which was signed in Luxembourg on 20 May 1980;

'filing', in relation to a document, means delivering it, by post or otherwise, to the court office;

'financial order' means—

(a) an avoidance of disposition order;
(b) an order for maintenance pending suit;
(c) an order for maintenance pending outcome of proceedings;
(d) an order for periodical payments or lump sum provision as mentioned in section 21(1) of the 1973 Act, except an order under section 27(6) of that Act;
(e) an order for periodical payments or lump sum provision as mentioned in paragraph 2(1) of Schedule 5 to the 2004 Act, made under Part 1 of Schedule 5 to that Act;
(f) a property adjustment order;
(g) a variation order;
(h) a pension sharing order; …[11]
(i) a pension compensation sharing order[; or
(j) an order for payment in respect of legal services;][12]

('variation order', 'pension compensation sharing order' and 'pension sharing order' are defined in rule 9.3.)

'financial remedy' means—

(a) a financial order;
(b) an order under Schedule 1 to the 1989 Act;
(c) an order under Part 3 of the 1984 Act [except an application under section 13 of the 1984 Act for permission to apply for a financial remedy][13];
(d) an order under Schedule 7 to the 2004 Act [except an application under paragraph 4 of Schedule 7 to the 2004 Act for permission to apply for an order under paragraph 9 or 13 of that Schedule][13];

(e) an order under section 27 of the 1973 Act;
(f) an order under Part 9 of Schedule 5 to the 2004 Act;
(g) an order under section 35 of the 1973 Act;
(h) an order under paragraph 69 of Schedule 5 to the 2004 Act;
(i) an order under Part 1 of the 1978 Act;
(j) an order under Schedule 6 to the 2004 Act;
(k) an order under section 10(2) of the 1973 Act; or
(l) an order under section 48(2) of the 2004 Act;

'hearing' includes a directions appointment;

'hearsay' means a statement made, otherwise than by a person while giving oral evidence in proceedings, which is tendered as evidence of the matters stated, and references to hearsay include hearsay of whatever degree;

['incoming protection measure' means a protection measure that has been ordered in a Member State of the European Union other than …[8] Denmark;][14]

'inherent jurisdiction' means the High Court's power to make any order or determine any issue in respect of a child, including in wardship proceedings, where it would be just and equitable to do so unless restricted by legislation or case law; (Practice Direction 12D (Inherent Jurisdiction (including Wardship Proceedings)) provides examples of inherent jurisdiction proceedings.)

['judge' means—

(a) in the High Court, a judge or a district judge of that court (including a district judge of the principal registry) or a person authorised to act as such; and
(b) in the family court, a person who is—
  (i) the Lord Chief Justice;
  (ii) the Master of the Rolls;
  (iii) the President of the Queens Bench Division;
  (iv) the President of the Family Division;
  (v) the Chancellor of the High Court;
  (vi) an ordinary judge of the Court of Appeal (including the vice-president, if any, of either division of that court);
  (vii) the Senior President of Tribunals;
  (viii) a puisne judge of the High Court;
  (ix) a deputy judge of the High Court;
  (x) a person who has been a judge of the Court of Appeal or a puisne judge of the High Court who may act as a judge of the family court by virtue of section 9 of the Senior Courts Act 1981;
  (xi) the Chief Taxing Master;
  (xii) a taxing master of the Senior Courts;
  (xiii) a person appointed to act as a deputy for the person holding office referred to in sub-paragraph (xiii) or to act as a temporary additional officer for any such office;
  (xiv) a circuit judge;
  (xv) a Recorder;
  (xvi) the Senior District Judge of the Family Division;
  (xvii) a district judge of the principal registry;
  (xviii) a person appointed to act as a deputy for the person holding office referred to in sub-paragraph (xvii) or to act as a temporary additional office holder for any such office;
  (xix) a district judge;
  (xx) a deputy district judge appointed under section 102 of the Senior Courts Act 1981 or section 8 of the County Courts Act 1984;

(xxi) a District Judge (Magistrates' Courts);
(xxii) a lay justice;
(xxiii) any other judge referred to in section 31C(1) of the 1984 Act who is authorised by the President of the Family Division to conduct particular business in the family court;][15]

'jurisdiction' means, unless the context requires otherwise, England and Wales and any part of the territorial waters of the United Kingdom adjoining England and Wales;

['justices' legal adviser' means a person authorised to exercise functions under section 67B of the Courts Act 2003 who has such qualifications as are prescribed by the Authorised Court Staff (Legal Advice Functions) Qualifications Regulations 2020;][16]

['lay justice' means a justice of the peace who is not a District Judge (Magistrates' Courts);][17]

'legal representative' means a—

(a) barrister;
(b) solicitor;
(c) solicitor's employee;
(d) manager of a body recognised under section 9 of the Administration of Justice Act 1985; or
(e) person who, for the purposes of the Legal Services Act 2007, is an authorised person in relation to an activity which constitutes the conduct of litigation (within the meaning of the Act),

who has been instructed to act for a party in relation to proceedings;

'litigation friend' has the meaning given—

(a) in relation to a protected party, by Part 15; and
(b) in relation to a child, by Part 16;

[…[8]][1]

'matrimonial cause' means proceedings for a matrimonial order;

'matrimonial order' means—

(a) a [divorce order][18] made under section 1 of the 1973 Act;
(b) a [nullity of marriage order][18] made on one of the grounds set out in [section 11, 12 or 12A][19] of the 1973 Act;
(c) a [judicial separation order][18] made under section 17 of the 1973 Act;

['non-court dispute resolution' means methods of resolving a dispute, including mediation, other than through the normal court process;][3]

'note' includes a record made by mechanical means;

'officer of the Service' has the meaning given by section 11(3) of the Criminal Justice and Court Services Act 2000;

'order' includes directions of the court;

'order for maintenance pending outcome of proceedings' means an order under paragraph 38 of Schedule 5 to the 2004 Act

'order for maintenance pending suit' means an order under section 22 of the 1973 Act;

['order for payment for legal services' means an order under section 22ZA of the 1973 Act or an order under paragraph 38A of Part 8 of Schedule 5 to the 2004 Act;][20]

'parental order proceedings' has the meaning assigned to it by rule 13.1;

'parental responsibility' has the meaning assigned to it by section 3 of the 1989 Act;

'placement proceedings' means proceedings for the making, varying or revoking of a placement order under the 2002 Act;

'principal registry' means the principal registry of the Family Division of the High Court;

'proceedings' means, unless the context requires otherwise, family proceedings as defined in section 75(3) of the Courts Act 2003;

'professional acting in furtherance of the protection of children' includes—

(a) an officer of a local authority exercising child protection functions;

(b) a police officer who is—

(i) exercising powers under section 46 of the Act of 1989; or

(ii) serving in a child protection unit or a paedophile unit of a police force;

(c) any professional person attending a child protection conference or review in relation to a child who is the subject of the proceedings to which the information regarding the proceedings held in private relates[;][21]

(d) an officer of the National Society for the Prevention of Cruelty to Children; [or][13]

[(e) a member or employee of the [Disclosure and Barring Service][22], being the body established under [section 87(1) of the Protection of Freedoms Act 2012][22];][13]

'professional legal adviser' means a—

(a) barrister;

(b) solicitor;

(c) solicitor's employee;

(d) manager of a body recognised under section 9 of the Administration of Justice Act 1985; or

(e) person who, for the purposes of the Legal Services Act 2007, is an authorised person in relation to an activity which constitutes the conduct of litigation (within the meaning of that Act),

who is providing advice to a party but is not instructed to represent that party in the proceedings;

'property adjustment order' means—

(a) in proceedings under the 1973 Act, any of the orders mentioned in section 21(2) of that Act;

(b) in proceedings under the 1984 Act, an order under section 17(1)(a)(ii) of that Act;

(c) in proceedings under Schedule 5 to the 2004 Act, any of the orders mentioned in paragraph 7(1); or

(d) in proceedings under Schedule 7 to the 2004 Act, an order for property adjustment under paragraph 9(2) or (3);

'protected party' means a party, or an intended party, who lacks capacity (within the meaning of the 2005 Act) to conduct proceedings;

['protection measure' has the meaning given to it in the Protection Measures Regulation;

'Protection Measures Regulation' means the Regulation (EU) No 606/2013 of the European Parliament and of the Council of 12th June 2013 on mutual recognition of protection measures in civil matters;][14]

'reporting officer' means an officer of the Service or a Welsh family proceedings officer appointed to witness the documents which signify a parent's or guardian's consent to the placing of the child for adoption or to the making of an adoption order or a section 84 order;

'risk assessment' has the meaning assigned to it by section 16A(3) of the 1989 Act;

...[4]

'RSC' means the Rules of the Supreme Court 1965 as they appear in Schedule 1 to the CPR [...[6]][7];

'section 8 order' has the meaning assigned to it by section 8(2) of the 1989 Act;

'section 84 order' means an order made by the High Court under section 84 of the 2002 Act giving parental responsibility prior to adoption abroad;

'section 89 order' means an order made by the High Court under section 89 of the 2002 Act—

(a) annulling a Convention adoption or Convention adoption order;

(b) providing for an overseas adoption or determination under section 91 of the 2002 Act to cease to be valid; or

(c) deciding the extent, if any, to which a determination under section 91 of the 2002 Act has been affected by a subsequent determination under that section;

'Service' has the meaning given by section 11 of the Criminal Justice and Court Services Act 2000;

…[8]

'specified proceedings' has the meaning assigned to it by section 41(6) of the 1989 Act and rule 12.27;

'welfare officer' means a person who has been asked to prepare a report under section 7(1)(b) of the 1989 Act;

'Welsh family proceedings officer' has the meaning given by section 35(4) of the Children Act 2004.

(2) In these rules a reference to—

(a) an application for a matrimonial order or a civil partnership order is to be read as a reference to [an application][18] for—

(i) a matrimonial order; [or][14]

(ii) …[23]

(iii) a civil partnership order,

and includes [an application][18] by a respondent asking for such an order;

(b) 'financial order' in matrimonial proceedings is to be read as a reference to 'ancillary relief';

(c) 'matrimonial proceedings' is to be read as a reference to a matrimonial cause …[23]

(3) [Where][15] these rules apply the CPR, they apply the CPR as amended from time to time.

[(4) …[6]][7]

Amendment

1 Inserted by the Family Procedure (Amendment) Rules 2011, SI 2011/1328, rr 2, 3, 4.
2 Inserted by the Family Procedure (Amendment No 4) Rules 2012, SI 2012/2806, rr 2, 3, 4.
3 Inserted by the Family Procedure (Amendment No 3) Rules 2014, SI 2014/843, rr 2, 4(a), (c), (d).
4 Repealed by the Family Procedure (Amendment No 3) Rules 2013, SI 2013/3204, rr 2, 4(a).
5 Repealed by the Family Procedure (Amendment No 3) Rules 2014, SI 2014/843, rr 2, 4(b), (e).
6 Repealed by the Family Procedure (Amendment No 2) Rules 2014, SI 2014/667, rr 2, 3(a)(i), (c).
7 Inserted by the Family Procedure (Amendment No 3) Rules 2012, SI 2012/2046, rr 2, 3(a), (c).
8 Repealed by the Family Procedure Rules 2010 and Court of Protection Rules 2017 (Amendment) (EU Exit) Regulations 2019, SI 2019/517, rr 2, 3.
9 Repealed by the Public Bodies (Child Maintenance and Enforcement Commission: Abolition and Transfer of Functions) Order 2012, SI 2012/2007, art 3(2), Schedule, para 125(a).
10 Substituted by the Family Procedure (Amendment No 3) Rules 2013, SI 2013/3204, rr 2, 4(b), (c).
11 Repealed by the Family Procedure (Amendment No 2) Rules 2013, SI 2013/1472, rr 2, 3(a)(i).
12 Substituted by the Family Procedure (Amendment No 2) Rules 2013, SI 2013/1472, rr 2, 3(a)(ii).
13 Inserted by the Family Procedure (Amendment) Rules 2012, SI 2012/679, rr 2, 3(a), (b)(ii), (iii).
14 Inserted by the Family Procedure (Amendment No 4) Rules 2014, SI 2014/3296, rr 2, 3(a), (b)(i)(aa).

15 Substituted by the Family Procedure (Amendment No 2) Rules 2014, SI 2014/667, rr 2, 3(a)(iii), (b).
16 Substituted by the Family Procedure (Amendment) Rules 2020, SI 2020/135, rr 2, 3.
17 Inserted by the Family Procedure (Amendment No 2) Rules 2014, SI 2014/667, rr 2, 3(a)(ii).
18 Substituted by the Family Procedure (Amendment) Rules 2022, SI 2022/44, rr 2, 3.
19 Substituted by the Family Procedure (Amendment) Rules 2015, SI 2015/913, rr 2, 3.
20 Inserted by the Family Procedure (Amendment No 2) Rules 2013, SI 2013/1472, rr 2, 3(b).
21 Substituted by the Family Procedure (Amendment) Rules 2012, SI 2012/679, rr 2, 3(b)(i).
22 Substituted by the Protection of Freedoms Act 2012 (Disclosure and Barring Service Transfer of Functions) Order 2012, SI 2012/3006, art 30.
23 Repealed by the Family Procedure (Amendment No 4) Rules 2014, SI 2014/3296, rr 2, 3(b)(i)(bb), (ii).

2.4 Modification of rules in application to serial numbers etc.

If a serial number has been assigned under rule 14.2 or the name or other contact details of a party is not being revealed in accordance with rule 29.1—

(a) any rule requiring any party to serve any document will not apply; and
(b) the court will give directions about serving any document on the other parties.

2.5 Power to perform functions conferred on the court by these rules and practice directions

(1) Where these rules or a practice direction provide for the court to perform any function then, except where any rule or practice direction [or any other enactment][1], provides otherwise, that function may be performed—

(a) in relation to proceedings in the High Court or in a district registry, by any judge or district judge of that Court including a district judge of the principal registry;
[(b) in relation to proceedings in the family court—
 (i) by the court composed in accordance with rules made under section 31D of the 1984 Act; or
 (ii) where Practice Direction 2A applies, by a single lay justice who is authorised as specified in rules made under section 31D of the 1984 Act.][2]
(c) …[3]

[…[4]][1]

[(1A) The functions of the family court or a judge of the family court listed in Practice Direction 2C may be exercised by a justices' legal adviser.][5]

(2) A deputy High Court judge and a district judge, including a district judge of the principal registry, may not try a claim for a declaration of incompatibility in accordance with section 4 of the Human Rights Act 1998.

Amendment

1 Substituted by the Family Procedure (Amendment No 3) Rules 2013, SI 2013/3204, rr 2, 5(a), (b), (d).
2 Substituted by the Family Procedure (Amendment No 2) Rules 2014, SI 2014/667, rr 2, 4.
3 Repealed by the Family Procedure (Amendment No 3) Rules 2013, SI 2013/3204, rr 2, 5(c).
4 Repealed by the Family Procedure (Amendment) Rules 2020, SI 2020/135, rr 2, 4(a).
5 Inserted by the Family Procedure (Amendment) Rules 2020, SI 2020/135, rr 2, 4(b).

2.6 Powers of the single justice to perform functions under the 1989 Act, the 1996 Act, the 2002 Act and the Childcare Act 2006

(1) [A single lay justice who is authorised as specified in rules made under section 31D of the 1984 Act may perform the functions of the family court—][1]

(a) where an application without notice is made under sections 10, 44(1), 48(9), 50(4) and 102(1) of the 1989 Act;
(b) subject to paragraph (2), under sections 11(3) or 38(1) of the 1989 Act;

(c) under sections 4(3)(b), 4A(3)(b), 4ZA(6)(b), 7, 34(3)(b), 41, 44(9)(b) and (11)(b)(iii), 48(4), 91(15) or (17) or paragraph 11(4) of Schedule 14 of the 1989 Act;
(d) …[2]
(e) where an application without notice is made under section 41(2) of the 2002 Act (recovery orders);
(f) where an application without notice is made for an occupation order or a non molestation order under Part 4 of the 1996 Act; or
(g) where an application is made for a warrant under section 79 of the Childcare Act 2006;

(2) A single [lay justice][1] may make an order under section 11(3) or 38(1) of the 1989 Act where—

(a) a previous such order has been made in the same proceedings;
(b) the terms of the order sought are the same as those of the last such order made; and
(c) a written request for such an order has been made and—
  (i) the other parties and any children's guardian consent to the request and they or their legal representatives have signed the request; or
  (ii) at least one of the other parties and any children's guardian consent to the request and they or their legal representatives have signed the request, and the remaining parties have not indicated that they either consent to or oppose the making of the order.

(3) The proceedings referred to in paragraph [(1)(a) and (c)][1] are proceedings which are prescribed for the purposes of section 93(2)(i) of the 1989 Act.

Amendment

1 Substituted by the Family Procedure (Amendment No 2) Rules 2014, SI 2014/667, rr 2, 5(a)(i), (b) (c).
2 Repealed by the Family Procedure (Amendment No 2) Rules 2014, SI 2014/667, rr 2, 5(a)(ii).

[2.7 Single lay justice: power to refer to the family court

Where a single lay justice—

(a) is performing a function of the family court in accordance with rule 2.5(1)(b)(ii) or rule 2.6(1) or (2); and
(b) considers, for whatever reason, that it is inappropriate to perform the function,

the single lay justice must refer the matter to the family court.][1]

Amendment

1 Substituted by the Family Procedure (Amendment No 2) Rules 2014, SI 2014/667, rr 2, 6.

2.8 Court's discretion as to where it deals with cases

The court may deal with a case at any place that it considers appropriate.

2.9 Computation of time

(1) This rule shows how to calculate any period of time for doing any act which is specified—

(a) by these rules;
(b) by a practice direction; or
(c) by a direction or order of the court.

(2) A period of time expressed as a number of days must be computed as clear days.

(3) In this rule 'clear days' means that in computing the numbers of days—

(a) the day on which the period begins; and
(b) if the end of the period is defined by reference to an event, the day on which that event occurs, are not included.

(4) Where the specified period is 7 days or less and includes a day which is not a business day, that day does not count.

(5) When the period specified—

(a) by these rules or a practice direction; or
(b) by any direction or order of the court,

for doing any act at the court office ends on a day on which the office is closed, that act will be in time if done on the next day on which the court office is open.

2.10 Dates for compliance to be calendar dates and to include time of day

(1) Where the court makes an order or gives a direction which imposes a time limit for doing any act, the last date for compliance must, wherever practicable—

(a) be expressed as a calendar date; and
(b) include the time of day by which the act must be done.

(2) Where the date by which an act must be done is inserted in any document, the date must, wherever practicable, be expressed as a calendar date.

(3) Where 'month' occurs in any order, direction or other document, it means a calendar month.

Practice Direction 2A – Functions of the court in the Family Procedure Rules 2010 and practice directions which may be performed by a single justice of the peace (applicable to applications issued by the court on or after 6 April 2022)

This PD applies to applications issued by the court on or after 6 April 2022. For applications issued by the court before 6 April 2022 see [https://webarchive.nationalarchives.gov.uk/ukgwa/20211201113823/https://www.justice.gov.uk/courts/procedure-rules/family/practice_directions/pd_part_02a].

See also Part 2

This Practice Direction supplements FPR Part 2, rule rule 2.5(1)(b)(ii) (Power to perform functions conferred on the court by these rules and practice directions)

1.1 Where the FPR or a practice direction provide for the court to perform any function, that function may be performed by single lay justice who is authorised as specified in rules made under section 31D of the 1984 Act except that such a justice cannot perform the functions listed in –

(a) column 2 of Table 1 in accordance with the rules listed in column 1; and
(b) column 2 of Table 2 in accordance with the paragraph of the practice direction listed in column 1.

1.2 For the avoidance of doubt, unless a rule, practice direction or other enactment provides otherwise, a single lay justice cannot make the decision of the family court at the final hearing of an application for a substantive order. For example, a single lay justice cannot make a child arrangements order on notice, placement order, adoption or care order. However, a single lay justice can discharge the functions of the family court under the statutory provisions listed in rule 2.6 of the FPR.

Table 1

Rule	Nature of function
3.10	Determining whether a MIAM exemption has been validly claimed.
4.1(3)(g)	Stay the whole or part of any proceedings or judgment either generally or until a specified date or event
4.1(3)(l)	Exclude an issue from consideration
4.1(3)(m)	Dismiss or give a decision on an application after a decision on a preliminary issue
4.1(4)(a)	When the court makes an order, making that order subject to conditions
4.1(6)	Varying and revoking an order (other than directions which the court has made)
4.3(1)	Ability of the court to make orders (other than directions) of its own initiative
4.3(7)	Recording a decision to strike out a statement of case or dismiss an application (including an application for permission to appeal) and considering whether it is appropriate to make a civil restraint order where the court considers that the application is totally without merit.
4.4, 4.5 and 4.6	All the powers of the family court under these rules (power to strike out statement of case, sanctions have effect unless defaulting party obtains relief from sanctions)
Part 7	The duties and powers of the family court in this Part.
Part 8	The duties and powers of the family court in this Part otherwise than specified in rule 8.20(4) and except in relation to applications for a declaration of parentage under section 55A of the 1986 Act.
8.20(4)	A direction that a child should be made a respondent to the application for a declaration of parentage under section 55A of the Family Law Act 1986, except where the parties consent to the child being made a respondent
9.11 (2)	Direction that a child be separately represented on an application
9.12(1)	The duties of the family court upon the issue of an application for financial remedies for children.
9.15	The duties and powers of the family court in respect of the first appointment relating to applications for financial remedies for children.
9.16(1)	Giving permission for the production of further documents between the first appointment and FDR appointment in applications for financial remedies for children.
9.16(2)	Giving further directions or directing that parties attend an FDR appointment.

Rule	Nature of function
9.17(8)	Making an appropriate consider order at the conclusion of an FDR appointment.
9.17(9)	Giving directions for the future course of proceedings for financial remedies for children where it does not make an appropriate consent order.
9.17(10)	Giving directions that the parties need not personally attend an FDR appointment.
9.18A(5)(a)	Determining whether the standard procedure or the fast-track procedure should apply to an application for a financial remedy
9.22	All the powers of the family court under this rule (relating to proceedings by or against a person outside England and Wales for variation or revocation of orders under section 20 of the 1978 Act or paragraphs 30 to 34 of Schedule 6 to the 2004 Act)
9.26B	The powers of the family court in respect of adding parties to, or removing parties from, proceedings for a financial remedy.
9.33(6)	Giving notice of the date of the first appointment or other hearing in an application for a financial remedy where the applicant or respondent is the party with pension rights.
9.34(3)(b)	Giving directions that a person objecting to a consent order for pension attachment attends court of furnish written details of the objection.
9.36	The duties of the family court in respect of making a pension sharing order or a pension attachment order.
10.11(2)	Determining, following an arrest, whether the facts and circumstances leading to an arrest amount to breach of an occupation order or non-molestation order and deciding whether to adjourn proceedings.
10.14	Adjourning hearings for consideration of the penalty to be imposed for contempt of court.
10.17(1)	The taking of recognizance.
Part 11	The duties and powers of the family court in this Part.
12.3(2)	Where the person with parental responsibility is a child, a direction for that child be made a party, except where the parties consent to that child being made a party
12.3(3)	Direction that a child be made a party to proceedings or that a child who is a party be removed, except where the parties consent to the child being made a party or to the removal of that party
12.3(4)	Consequential directions following the addition or removal of a party except where a single justice is able to make such a direction under rule 12.3(2) and (3)
12.8(2)	Directing that an applicant effect service in section 8 private law proceedings.
12.22	Drawing up a timetable for public law proceedings.
12.25	The duties and powers of the family court in respect of case management hearings.

Rule	Nature of function
12.26	The duties and powers of the family court in respect of discussions between advocates.
12.26C(1)	Giving reasons for, and an explanation of the impact on the welfare of the child of, decisions to extend time limits.
12.61(1) and (2)	Considering the transfer of proceedings to the court of another contracting state, directions in relation to the manner in which parties may make representations and power to deal with question of transfer without a hearing with the consent of parties
12.64(1)	Exercising court's powers under Article 8 of the 1996 Hague Convention
12.68(1)	Staying the proceedings
12.68(3)	Giving reasons for the court's decision, making a finding of fact and stating a finding of fact where such a finding has been made
12.70(1)	Contemplating the placement of a child in another contracting state
12.70(3)	Sending request directly to the central authority or other authority having jurisdiction in the other State
12.70(4)	Sending request to Central Authority for England and Wales for onward transmission
12.70(5)	Considering the documents which should accompany the request
13.3(3)	Where the person with parental responsibility is a child, a direction for that child be made a party, except where the parties consent to that child being made a party
13.3(4)	Direction that a child be made a party to proceedings or that a child who is a party be removed, except where the parties consent to the child being made a party or to the removal of that party
13.3(5)	Consequential directions following the addition or removal of a party except where a single justice is able to make such a direction under rule 13.3(3) and (4)
13.9(7)	Variation or revocation of direction following transfer, except where a single justice would be able to make the direction in question under rule 13.9(1)
13.15(3)	Determination of the probable date of the child's birth
13.20(1)	Specifying a later date by which a parental order takes effect
14.2(4)	Giving directions regarding the removal of serial numbers.
14.3(2)	Direction that a child be made a respondent, except where the parties consent to the child being made a respondent
14.3(3)(b)	Direction that a child who is a party be removed, except where the parties consent to the child being made a respondent
14.3(4)	Consequential directions following the addition or removal of a party except where a single justice is able to make such a direction under rule 14.3(2) and (3)

Rule	Nature of function
14.8(3)	Any of the directions listed in PD14B in proceedings for – (a) a Convention adoption order (b) a section 84 order (c) a section 88 direction (d) a section 89 order; or (e) an adoption order where section 83(1) of the 2002 Act applies (restriction on bringing children in)
14.16(8)	Making an adoption order under section 50 of the 2002 Act after personal attendance of one only of the applicants if there are special circumstances
14.16(9)	Not making a placement order unless the legal representative of the applicant attends the final hearing
14.17(4)	Determination of the probable date of the child's birth
14.25(1)	Specifying a later date by which an order takes effect
15.3(1)	Permission to a person to take steps before the protected party has a litigation friend
15.3(2)	Permission to a party to take steps (where during proceedings a person lacks capacity to continue to conduct proceedings) before the protected party has a litigation friend
15.3(3)	Making an order that a step taken before a protected party has a litigation friend has effect
15.6(1)	Making an order appointing a person as a litigation friend
15.6(6)	Court may not appoint a litigation friend unless it is satisfied that the person complies with the conditions in rule 15.4(3)
15.7	Direction that a person may not act as a litigation friend, termination of an appointment, appointment of a litigation friend in substitution for an existing one
16.2	Power of court to make a child a party to proceedings if it considers it is in the best interests of the child to do so
16.6(3)(a)	Permission to a child to conduct proceedings without a children's guardian or litigation friend
16.6(6)	Power of the court to grant an application under paragraph (3)(a) or (5) if the court considers that the child has sufficient understanding to conduct the proceedings
16.6(7)	Power of the court to require the litigation friend or children's guardian to take such part in proceedings (referred to in paragraph (6)) as the court directs
16.6(8)	Power of the court to revoke permission granted under paragraph (3) in specified circumstances
16.6(10)	Power of the court, in specified circumstances, to appoint a person to be the child's litigation friend or children's guardian
16.8(2)	Permission to a person to take steps before the child has a litigation friend

Rule	Nature of function
16.8(3)	Making an order that a step taken before the child has a litigation friend has effect
16.11(1)	Making an order appointing a person as a litigation friend
16.12	Direction that a person may not act as a litigation friend, termination of an appointment, appointment of a litigation friend in substitution for an existing one
16.23(2)	Permission to a person to take steps before the child has a children's guardian
18.3(1)(c)	Direction that a child be a respondent to an application under Part 18
18.9(1)(a)	Power of court to deal with a Part 18 application without a hearing
18.12	Power of the court to proceed in absence of a party, except where a single justice has the power to make the relevant order applied for
19.8(2)	The court's power to require or permit a party to give oral evidence at the hearing
Part 20	The duties and powers of the family court in this Part.
21.3	Power of court relating to withholding inspection or disclosure of a document
22.1(2) to (4)	Power to exclude evidence that would otherwise be admissible, power to permit a party to adduce evidence, or to seek to rely on a document, in respect of which that party has failed to comply with requirements of Part 22 and power to limit cross examination
22.6	Court's powers relating to use at final hearing of witness statements which have been served
22.12	Power of court to require evidence by affidavit instead of or in addition to a witness statement
22.15(4)	Permission for a party to amend or withdraw any admission made by that party on such terms as the court thinks just
22.20(3)(a)	Permission for a witness statement in proceedings in the family court under Part 9 to be used for a purpose other than the proceedings in which it is served
25.4	Giving permission to put expert evidence before the family court.
25.5(1)	Having regard to any failure to comply with rule 25.6 or any direction of the family court about expert evidence when deciding whether to give permission mentioned in section 13(1), (3) or (5) of the 2014 Act or to give a direction under section 38(6) of the 1989 Act.
25.6(1)	Giving directions in respect of permission mentioned in section 13(1), (3) or (5) of the 2014 Act or rule 25.4(2).
27.5	Granting applications to set aside judgments or orders following failure to attend.
27.10(1)(b)	Direction that proceedings to which the Rules apply will not be held in private, expect that a single justice may give such a direction in relation to a hearing which that single justice is conducting
27.11(2)(g)	Power of the court to permit any other person to be present during any hearing, except that a single justice may give such permission in relation to a hearing which that single justice is conducting

Rule	Nature of function
27.11(3)	Direction that persons within rule 27.11(2)(f) shall not attend the proceedings or any part of them
28.3(6)	Making an order requiring one party to pay the costs of another party.
29.8(1)	Court's opinion that it would be prevented by section 8 or 9 of the Child Support Act 1991 from making an order
29.8(2)	Court's consideration of the matter without a hearing
29.8(10)	Power of the court to determine that it would be prevented by sections 8 or 9 of the 1991 Act from making an order, and to dismiss the application
29.8(11)	The court must give written reasons for its decision
29.9(2)	Direction that the document will be treated as if it contained the application and directions as the court considers appropriate as to the subsequent conduct of the proceedings
29.12(1)	Permission for inspection of a document, except where no party to the proceedings to which that document relates objects
29.13(1)	Direction for a court officer not to serve a copy of an order (other than directions that the single justice has made) to every party affected by it
29.15	Specifying alternative date for an order to take effect, except an order which the single justice has made
29.16	Correcting an accidental slip or omission in an order, except where that order was made by a single justice
29.17	Functions in relation to the transfer of proceedings to another court.
29.19(3)	Giving directions in respect of requests for reconsideration of decisions on the allocation of proceedings.
29.91(5)	Reconsidering decisions in respect of allocation of proceedings.
Part 30	Any power of the magistrates' court (where it is the lower court) to grant or refuse permission to appeal, except where a single justice has the power to make the order which is subject to the appeal
31.9	Power for court to stay the proceedings
32.22B	Powers in relation to methods of payment for means of payment orders.
32.22C(2)	Notifying interested parties of the outcome of an application for a variation of a method of payment.
32.22C(3)	Recording variations of methods of payment on the order to which the variation relates.
Part 33	The duties and powers of the family court in this Part.
Part 34	The duties and powers of the family court in this Part in so far as they relate to enforcement.
Part 37	The duties and powers of the family court in this Part.
Part 38	Recognition and Enforcement of Protection Measures.
Part 39	The duties and powers of the family court in this Part.
Part 40	The duties and powers of the family court in this Part.

Table 2

PD 3A – Family Mediation Information and Assessment Meetings (MIAMS) – Paragraphs 7, 36 and 37	Under paragraph 7 if an applicant claims a MIAM exemption, the family court will issue proceedings but will inquire into the exemption claimed. At the first hearing the family court may review any supporting evidence in order to ensure that the MIAM exemption was validly claimed. If a MIAM exemption has not been validly claimed, the family court may direct the applicant or the parties to attend a MIAM, and may adjourn proceedings for that purpose. Under paragraph 36 the family court may adjourn proceedings where evidence is not available or may give directions about how and when evidence is to be filed. Under paragraph 37, if the family court determines that the MIAM exemption was not validly claimed, the court may direct the applicant, or the parties, to attend a MIAM and may adjourn proceedings pending MIAM attendance.
PD 4B – Civil Restraint Orders	Generally, the family court's functions in respect of applications for civil restraint orders.
PD 7A – Procedure for Applications in Matrimonial and Civil Partnership Proceedings – Paragraphs 3.4, 5.3 and 7.1	Under paragraph 3.4 the family court may give permission to file an application without the required documentation. Under paragraph 5.3 the family court may direct a period within which a party must file with the court an amended application for a matrimonial or civil partnership order or an amended answer. Under paragraph 7.1 the family court may made an order for the disclosure of documents under rule 7.17(2)(c) where an application for a matrimonial or civil partnership order is not being dealt with as a standard case.
PD 7B – Medical Examinations on Applications for Annulment of a Marriage – Paragraph 1.1	Under paragraph 1.1 where a defended application is made for the annulment of a marriage based on the incapacity of one of the parties to consummate, the family court should not appoint a medical examiner unless it appears necessary to do so for the proper disposal of the case.
PD 7C–Polygamous Marriages– paragraph 2.4	Under paragraph 2.4 the family court may give an additional spouse notice of any of the proceedings to which this practice direction applies and make an additional spouse a party to such proceedings.
PD8A – Where to Start Certain Proceedings – Paragraph 1.2	Under paragraph 1.2 the family court may make a direction in respect of whether a matter will be heard in the same location of the family court as existing (or proposed) proceedings.
PD 12J – Child Arrangements and Contact Order: Domestic Violence and Harm.	Generally, the family court's functions in respect of applications in respect of child arrangements orders, about where a child should live or about contact between a child and a parent or other family member except the functions in the first three bullets points in paragraph 6 and paragraphs 8, 15 and 21.

PD 12M – Family Assistance Orders: Consultation – paragraphs 1.2, 1.3 and 1.5	Under paragraph 1.2 the family court must have obtained the opinion of the appropriate officer about whether it would be in the best interests of the child in question for a family assistance order to be made and, if so, how the family assistance order could operate and for what period Under paragraph 1.3 the family court decides on the category of officer required to be made available under the family assistance order Under paragraph 1.5 the family court must give to the person it proposes to name in the order an opportunity to comment
PD 14B – The First Directions Hearing – adoptions with a Foreign Element – Paragraph 2	Under paragraph 2 the court's consideration of – (a) whether the requirements of the Adoption and Children Act 2002 and the Adoptions with a Foreign Element Regulations 2005 (S.I. 2005/392) appear to have been complied with and, if not, consider whether or not it is appropriate to transfer the case to the High Court; (b) whether all relevant documents are translated into English and, if not, fix a timetable for translating any outstanding documents; (c) whether the applicant needs to file an affidavit setting out the full details of the circumstances in which the child was brought to the United Kingdom, of the attitude of the parents to the application and confirming compliance with the requirements of The Adoptions with a Foreign Element Regulations 2005; and (d) give directions about – (i) the production of the child's passport and visa; (ii) the need for the Official Solicitor and a representative of the Home office to attend future hearings; and (iii) personal service on the parents (via the Central Authority in the case of an application for a Convention Adoption Order) including information about the role of the Official Solicitor and availability of legal aid to be represented within the proceedings; and (e) consider fixing a further directions no later than 6 weeks after the date of the first directions appointment and timetable a date by which the Official Solicitor should file an interim report in advance of that further appointment
PD 15A – Protected Parties – Paragraph 4.2(b)	Under paragraph 4.2 (b) court directions on service on protected party
PD16A – Representation of Children – Paragraph 6.8	Under paragraph 6.8 the children's guardian must – (a) unless the court otherwise directs, file a written report advising on the interests of the child in accordance with the timetable set by the court; and

	(b) in proceedings to which Part 14 applies, where practicable, notify any person the joining of whom as a party to those proceedings would be likely, in the opinion of the children's guardian, to safeguard the interests of the child, of the court's power to join that person as a party under rule 14.3 and must inform the court (i) of any notification; (ii) of anyone whom the child's guardian attempted to notify under this paragraph but was unable to contact; and (iii) of anyone whom the children's guardian believes may wish to be joined to the proceedings Under paragraph 7.5 the court may, at the same time as deciding whether to join the child as a party, consider whether the proceedings should be transferred to another court taking into account the provisions of Part 3 of the Allocation and Transfer of Proceedings Order 2008
PD18A – Other Applications in Proceedings – Paragraphs 4.1 to 4.4(a)	Under paragraph 4.1 on receipt of an application notice containing a request for a hearing, unless the court considers that the application is suitable for consideration without a hearing, the court officer will, if serving a copy of the application notice, notify the applicant of the time and date fixed for the hearing of the application
	Under paragraph 4.2 on receipt of an application notice containing a request that the application be dealt with without a hearing, the court will decide whether the application is suitable for consideration without a hearing
	Under paragraph 4.3 where the court considers that the application is suitable for consideration without a hearing but is not satisfied that it has sufficient material to decide the application immediately it may give directions for the filing of evidence and will inform the applicant and the respondent(s) of its decision
	Under paragraph 4.4 (a) where the court does not consider that the application is suitable for consideration without a hearing it may give directions as to the filing of evidence
PD 20A – Interim Remedies	Generally, the family court's functions in respect of applications for interim remedies.
PD22A – Written Evidence – Paragraphs 1.6, 14.1 and 14.2	Under paragraph 1.6 the court may give a direction under rule 22.12 that evidence shall be given by affidavit instead of or in addition to a witness statement on its own initiative; or after any party has applied to the court for such a direction
	Under paragraph 14.1 where an affidavit, a witness statement or an exhibit to either an affidavit or a witness statement does not comply with Part 22 or PD 22A in relation to its form, the court may refuse to admit it as evidence and may refuse to allow the costs arising from its preparation

	Under paragraph 14.2 permission to file a defective affidavit or witness statement or to use a defective exhibit may be obtained from the court where the case is proceeding
PD27A – Family Proceedings: Court Bundles (Universal Practice to be Applied in all Courts other than the Family Proceedings Court)	Generally, the family court's functions in respect of court bundles.
PD 27B – Attendanceof Media Representatives at Hearings in Family Proceedings	Generally the family court's discretion to exclude media representatives from attending hearings or part of hearings (other than where a Single Lay Justice is conducting the hearing).
PD 37A – Applications and Proceedings in relation to contempt of court	Generally, the family court's functions in respect of applications and proceedings in relation to contempt of court.
PD 40A – Charging Orders, Stop Orders and Stop Notices	Generally, the family court's functions in respect of applications and proceedings for charging orders, stop orders and stop notices.

Practice Direction 2B – References in the Rules to actions done by the court or by a court officer

In the past, where the Rules have provided for an action to be done by the court or by a court officer, they have often provided that the court or court officer 'will' do that action.

From and including 11th January 2015, and including amendments coming into force on that date, where an amendment is made to these Rules to insert a new provision or alter an existing one, and that amendment provides for an action to be done by the court, or by a court officer, the Rules will generally provide that the court or court officer 'must' do the action, rather than 'will'. This is to make it clearer where an obligation lies with the court or court officer to do something. Occasionally in the future, it may still be appropriate to use the word 'will', for example in a statement of future intent, and on those occasions, 'will' will be used.

This does not affect the meaning of 'will' and 'must' in the Rules before 11th January 2015.

Practice Direction 2C – Justices' legal adviser (applicable to applications issued by the court on or after 6 April 2022)

This PD applies to applications issued by the court on or after 6 April 2022. For applications issued by the court before 6 April 2022 see [https://webarchive.nationalarchives.gov.uk/ukgwa/20211201113601/https://www.justice.gov.uk/courts/procedure-rules/family/practice_directions/practice-direction-2c-justices-legal-adviser].

This Practice Direction supplements FPR Part 2, rule 2.5(1A).

Functions which may be carried out by a justices' legal adviser

1. The functions of the family court or a judge of the family court that may be carried out by a justices' legal adviser are the functions of the family court or of a judge of the court specified in the provisions listed in column 1 of the table subject to the exceptions or restrictions specified in column 2 in relation to particular functions.

Duty to refer if inappropriate to carry out function

2. When considering a function specified in the table—

a) a justices' legal adviser must consider whether in the particular circumstances it would be inappropriate to carry out the function; and
b) if a justices' legal adviser determines that it would be inappropriate to carry out the function, the justices' legal adviser must refer the matter to the court.

Table

Column 1	**Column 2**
FPR rule 3.3	
FPR rule 3.4	
FPR rule 3.10	
FPR rule 4.1(3)(a)	Except any extensions in public law proceedings that would have the effect that disposal of the application would occur later than the end of twenty-six weeks beginning with the day on which the application was issued.
FPR rule 4.1(3)(b), (c), (d), (f), (h), (j), (k), (n), (o)	
FPR rule 4.3(2)	
FPR rule 4.3(5)	
FPR rule 4.7(a) and (b)	
FPR rule 6.14(4) and (6)	
FPR rule 6.16(1)	
FPR rule 6.19	
FPR rule 6.20	
FPR rule 6.24(2)	
FPR rule 6.26(5)	
FPR rule 6.32	
FPR rule 6.36	
the 1973 Act, sections 1(3) 1(4) and 1(5)	Only in standard cases, and only the making of final conditional orders of divorce
the 1973 Act, section 6(2)	Only where the parties consent to the adjournment
the 1973 Act, sections 10A(2) and (3)	Only in an application under section 10A(2) to which the other party consents

Column 1	Column 2
the 1973 Act, section 17(1B)	Only in standard cases
the 2004 Act, section 37(1)(a) and (d)	Only in standard cases, and only the making 'final' of such orders
the 2004 Act, section 42(3)	Only where the parties consent to the adjournment
the 2004 Act, sections 44 and (4)	Only in standard cases
FPR rule 7.8(3)(b)	
FPR rule 7.8(4)	
FPR rule 7.10(2)	
FPR rule 7.10(3)	
FPR rule 7.10(4)	
FPR rule 7.23(1)(d)(ii) and (3)	Only where the application under section 10A(2) was made on consent
FPR 7.19(4)	
FPR rule 8.20(4)	Only where the parties consent to the person being made a respondent and where the person is not a child
FPR rule 9.18	
FPR rule 9.20	
FPR rule 9.26	
FPR rule 9.46(2)	
FPR rule 10.3(1)	
FPR rule 10.6(2)	
FPR rule 10.7	
FPR rule 12.3(2)	
FPR rule 12.3(3)	Only where the parties consent to the person being made a respondent and where the person is not a child
FPR rule 12.3(4)	Only where otherwise authorised to add or remove the person as a party
FPR rule 12.4(5)	Only where the parties consent to the person being made a respondent and where the person is not a child
FPR rule 12.5(1)	
the 1989 Act, section 32(1)	
the 1989 Act, section 32(4)	Except that the carrying out of such function must not have the direct or indirect effect of extending the timetable for the proceedings with the effect that the disposal of the application would occur later than the end of twenty-six weeks beginning with the day on which the application was issued

Column 1	Column 2
FPR rule 12.5(2)	Except at an Issues Resolution Hearing for which Practice Direction 12A makes provision, and except the carrying out of any function that has the direct or indirect effect of extending the timetable for the proceedings with the effect that the disposal of the application would occur later than the end of twenty-six weeks beginning with the day on which the application was issued
FPR rule 12.6(a)-(c)	
the 1989 Act, section 7(1) and FPR rule 12.6(d)	
FPR rule 12.12	Except at an Issues Resolution Hearing for which Practice Direction 12A makes provision, and except any direction in public law proceedings that has the direct or indirect effect of extending the timetable for the proceedings with the effect that the disposal of the application would occur later than the end of twenty-six weeks beginning with the day on which the application was issued
FPR rule 12.13	Except that in any public law proceedings, the carrying out of such function must not have the direct or indirect effect of extending the timetable for the proceedings with the effect that the disposal of the application would occur later than the end of twenty-six weeks beginning with the day on which the application was issued
FPR rule 12.14(3) and (4)	
FPR rule 12.15	Except any direction in a public law proceeding that has the direct or indirect effect of extending the timetable for the proceedings with the effect that the disposal of the application would occur later than the end of twenty-six weeks beginning with the day on which the application was issued
FPR rule 12.16(6)	
FPR rule 12.16(7)	
FPR rule 12.19(2) and (3)	
FPR rule 12.21(1)	
FPR rule 12.22	
FPR rule 12.73(1)(b)	
Practice Direction 12G, paragraph 1.2	
Practice Direction 12J, paragraph 6, first three bullet points only	
Practice Direction 12J, paragraph 8	

Column 1	Column 2
Practice Direction 12J, paragraph 15	
Practice Direction 12J, paragraph 21	
FPR rule 12.24	
FPR rule 12.25(1), (2) and (5)	
FPR rule 12.26	
FPR rule 12.29	
FPR rule 12.30	
the 1989 Act, section 41	
the 1989 Act, sections 10(1) and (2)	Only where – (a) a previous such order has been made in the same proceedings; (b) the terms of the order sought are the same as those of the last such order made; (c) the order is an order in the course of proceedings and does not dispose finally of the proceedings; and (d) a written request for such an order has been made and – (i) the other parties and any children's guardian consent to the request and they or their legal representatives have signed the request; or (ii) at least one of the other parties and any children's guardian consent to the request and they or their legal representatives have signed the request, and the remaining parties have not indicated that they either consent to or oppose the making of the order.
the 1989 Act, section 38(1)	Only where – (a) a previous such order has been made in the same proceedings; (b) the terms of the order sought are the same as those of the last such order made; and (c) a written request for such an order has been made and – (i) the other parties and any children's guardian consent to the request and they or their legal representatives have signed the request; or (ii) at least one of the other parties and any children's guardian consent to the request and they or their legal representatives have signed the request, and the remaining parties have not indicated that they either consent to or oppose the making of the order.
FPR rule 12.31	

Column 1	Column 2
FPR rule 13.3(3)	
FPR rule 13.3(4)	
FPR rule 13.3(5)	
FPR rule 13.5	
FPR rule 13.9(1)	Except 13.9(1)(e) and (f)
FPR rule 13.9(3)	
FPR rule 13.9(6)	
FPR rule 13.9(8)	
FPR rule 13.9(9)	
FPR rule 13.11(1)	
FPR rule 13.14	
FPR rule 13.16	
FPR rule 13.17	
FPR rule 13.21(1)	
FPR rule 13.21(4)	
FPR rule 13.22(4)	
FPR rule 14.2(3)	Only where the applicant consents to the removal
FPR rule 14.3(2)	Only where the parties consent to the child being made a respondent
FPR rule 14.3(3)	Only where the parties consent to the person or body being made a respondent or to a party being removed, as the case may be, and only where the person being made a respondent or being removed as a party is not a child
FPR rule 14.3(4)	Only where such directions are consequential on directions made under FPR rule 14.3(2) or (3)
FPR rule 14.5(2)(b) and (3)	
FPR rule 14.6(1)	
FPR rule 14.6(2)(a)	
FPR rule 14.6(2)(b)	
FPR rule 14.6(3)(b)	
FPR rule 14.6(4)	
FPR rule 14.7	
the 2002 Act, section 51B(3)	
FPR rule 14.8(1)	Except 14.8(1)(d)
FPR rule 14.8(4)	
FPR rule 14.8(6)	
FPR rule 14.8(7)	
FPR rule 14.9(4)(b)	

Column 1	Column 2
FPR rule 14.10(2)	
FPR rule 14.14	
FPR rule 14.16(4) and (7)	
FPR rule 14.18	
FPR rule 14.20	
FPR rule 14.26(1)	
FPR rule 14.27(2)	
Practice Direction 14E, paragraph 1.2	
FPR rule 15.6(3)	
FPR rule 15.6(5)	
FPR rule 15.8(1)(b)	
FPR rule 15.9	
Practice Direction 15B	
FPR rule 16.3(1)	
FPR rule 16.3(2), (3) and (4)	Only in relation to specified proceedings as defined in the 1989 Act, section 41(6)
FPR rule 16.4	
FPR rule 16.11(3)	
FPR rule 16.11(5) and (6)	
FPR rule 16.21	
FPR rule 16.24	
FPR rule 16.30	
FPR rule 16.33	
FPR rule 16.34	
FPR rule 17.3(2)	
FPR rule 17.4	
FPR rule 17.5	
FPR rule 18.3(1)(c)	Only where the parties consent to the person being made a respondent and where the person being made a respondent is not a child
FPR rule 18.4(2)(b)	
FPR rule 18.5(2)(c)	
FPR rule 18.8(4)	
FPR rule 18.9(1)	Only where authorised by this Practice Direction to deal with the application with a hearing
Practice Direction 18A, paragraph 8.1	

Column 1	Column 2
Practice Direction 18A, paragraph 10.1	
Practice Direction 18A, paragraph 11.2	
FPR rule 19.1(3)	
FPR rule 19.4(4)	
FPR rule 19.6(2)	
FPR rule 19.8(1)(b)	
FPR rule 19.8(3)	
FPR rule 19.9(2)	
Practice Direction 19A, paragraphs 4.1 and 4.4	
FPR rule 21.2(3)	Only where the parties consent to the application for disclosure
Practice Direction 21A, paragraph 2.4	
FPR rule 22.1(1)	
FPR rule 22.3	
FPR rule 22.5	
FPR rule 22.7(1)	
FPR rule 22.9	
FPR rule 22.10	
Practice Direction 22A, paragraph 5.3	
FPR rule 23.4(1)	
FPR rule 23.6(8)	
the 1984 Act, section 31G(2)	
FPR rule 23.9	
FPR rule 24.3	
FPR rule 24.4(2)	
FPR rule 24.7	
FPR rule 24.8	
FPR rule 24.9	
FPR rule 24.10	
FPR rule 24.11(3)	
FPR rule 24.13	
the 2014 Act, section 13	
FPR rule 25.4	

Column 1	Column 2
FPR rule 25.8	
FPR rule 25.9	
FPR rule 25.10(2)	
FPR rule 25.10(3)	
FPR rule 25.10(4)	
FPR rule 25.11	
FPR rule 25.12	
FPR rule 25.13	
FPR rule 25.16	
FPR rule 25.17	
FPR rule 25.18	
FPR rule 25.19	
Practice Direction 25A, paragraph 2.1	
Practice Direction 25B, paragraphs 10.1 and 10.2	
Practice Direction 25E, paragraph 4.1	
FPR rule 26.3	
FPR rule 26.4	
FPR rule 27.3	
FPR rule 27.4	
FPR rule 27.7	
FPR rule 29.1	
FPR rule 29.4	
FPR rule 29.11	
FPR rule 29.14	
FPR rule 29.15	Only where the order in question is one which the justices' legal adviser made
FPR rule 29.16	Only where the order in question is one which a justices' legal adviser made
FPR rule 29.19(5)	
FPR rule 37.9(3)	
The Family Court (Composition and Distribution of Business) Rules 2014, rule 20	

[PART 3
NON-COURT DISPUTE RESOLUTION

Chapter 1
Interpretation

3.1

In this Part—

'allocation' means allocation of proceedings other than appeal proceedings to a level of judge;

['authorised family mediator' means a person identified by the Family Mediation Council as qualified to conduct a MIAM;][1]

'domestic violence' means any incident, or pattern of incidents, of controlling, coercive or threatening behaviour, violence or abuse (whether psychological, physical, sexual, financial or emotional) between the prospective applicant and another prospective party;

'family mediation information and assessment meeting' has the meaning given to it in section 10(3) of the 2014 Act.

'harm' has the meaning given to it in section 31 of the Children Act 1989;

'mediator's exemption' has the meaning given to it in Rule 3.8(2);

'MIAM' means a family mediation information and assessment meeting;

'MIAM exemption' has the meaning given to it in Rule 3.8(1);

'MIAM requirement' is the requirement in section 10(1) of the 2014 Act for a person to attend a MIAM before making a relevant family application;

'private law proceedings' has the meaning given to it in Rule 12.2;

'prospective applicant' is the person who is considering making a relevant family application;

'prospective party' is a person who would be likely to be a party to the proceedings in the relevant family application;

'prospective respondent' is a person who would be a likely respondent to the proceedings in the relevant family application; and

'relevant family application' has the meaning given to it in section 10(3) of the 2014 Act.][1]

Amendment

1 Substituted by the Family Procedure (Amendment No 3) Rules 2015, SI 2015/1868, rr 2, 3.
2 Substituted by the Family Procedure (Amendment No 3) Rules 2014, SI 2014/843, rr 2, 5.

[Chapter 2
The Court's Duty and Powers Generally

3.2 Scope of this Chapter

This Chapter contains the court's duty and powers to encourage and facilitate the use of non-court dispute resolution.][1]

Amendment

1 Substituted by the Family Procedure (Amendment No 3) Rules 2014, SI 2014/843, rr 2, 5.

[3.3 The court's duty to consider non-court dispute resolution

(1) The court must consider, at every stage in proceedings, whether non-court dispute resolution is appropriate.

(2) In considering whether non-court dispute resolution is appropriate in proceedings which were commenced by a relevant family application, the court must take into account—

(a) whether a MIAM took place;

(b) whether a valid MIAM exemption was claimed or mediator's exemption was confirmed; and

(c) whether the parties attempted mediation or another form of non-court dispute resolution and the outcome of that process.][1]

Amendment

1 Substituted by the Family Procedure (Amendment No 3) Rules 2014, SI 2014/843, rr 2, 5.

[3.4 When the court will adjourn proceedings or a hearing in proceedings

(1) If the court considers that non-court dispute resolution is appropriate, it may direct that the proceedings, or a hearing in the proceedings, be adjourned for such specified period as it considers appropriate—

(a) to enable the parties to obtain information and advice about[, and consider using,][1] non-court dispute resolution; and

(b) where the parties agree, to enable non-court dispute resolution to take place.

(2) The court may give directions under this rule on an application or of its own initiative.

(3) Where the court directs an adjournment under this rule, it will give directions about the timing and method by which the parties must tell the court if any of the issues in the proceedings have been resolved.

(4) If the parties do not tell the court if any of the issues have been resolved as directed under paragraph (3), the court will give such directions as to the management of the case as it considers appropriate.

(5) The court or court officer will—

(a) record the making of an order under this rule; and

(b) arrange for a copy of the order to be served as soon as practicable on the parties.

(6) Where the court proposes to exercise its powers of its own initiative, the procedure set out in rule 4.3(2) to (6) applies.][2]

Amendment

1 Inserted by the Family Procedure (Amendment No 4) Rules 2014, SI 2014/3296, rr 2, 4.

2 Substituted by the Family Procedure (Amendment No 3) Rules 2014, SI 2014/843, rr 2, 5.

[Chapter 3

Family Mediation Information and Assessment Meetings (MIAMs)

3.5 Scope of this Chapter

This Chapter contains Rules about the requirement in section 10(1) of the 2014 Act to attend a MIAM.][1]

Amendment

1 Substituted by the Family Procedure (Amendment No 3) Rules 2014, SI 2014/843, rr 2, 5.

[3.6 Applications to which the MIAM requirement applies

(1) The MIAM requirement applies to any application to initiate the proceedings specified in paragraph (2), unless a MIAM exemption or a mediator's exemption applies.

(2) The specified proceedings are—

(a) the private law proceedings relating to children specified in Practice Direction 3A; and

(b) the proceedings for a financial remedy specified in Practice Direction 3A.][1]

Amendment

1 Substituted by the Family Procedure (Amendment No 3) Rules 2014, SI 2014/843, rr 2, 5.

[3.7 Making an application

An application to initiate any of the proceedings specified in Rule 3.6 must contain, or be accompanied by, a form containing, either—

(a) a confirmation from an authorised family mediator that the prospective applicant has attended a MIAM;

(b) a claim by the prospective applicant that one of the MIAM exemptions applies; or (A list of MIAM exemptions is set out in Rule 3.8(1) below.)

(c) a confirmation from an authorised family mediator that a mediator's exemption applies.

(A list of mediator's exemptions is set out in Rule 3.8(2) below.)][1]

Amendment

1 Substituted by the Family Procedure (Amendment No 3) Rules 2014, SI 2014/843, rr 2, 5.

[3.8 Circumstances in which the MIAM requirement does not apply (MIAM exemptions and mediator's exemptions)

The MIAM requirement does not apply if—

(1) a prospective applicant claims in the relevant form that any of the following circumstances (a 'MIAM exemption') applies—

Domestic violence

(a) there is evidence of domestic violence, as specified in Practice Direction 3A; or

Child protection concerns

(b)

(i) a child would be the subject of the application; and

(ii) that child or another child of the family who is living with that child is currently—

(aa) the subject of enquiries by a local authority under section 47 of the 1989 Act; or

(ab) the subject of a child protection plan put in place by a local authority; or

Urgency

(c) the application must be made urgently because—

(i) there is risk to the life, liberty or physical safety of the prospective applicant or his or her family or his or her home; or

(ii) any delay caused by attending a MIAM would cause—

(aa) a risk of harm to a child;

(ab) a risk of unlawful removal of a child from the United Kingdom, or a risk of unlawful retention of a child who is currently outside England and Wales;

(ac) a significant risk of a miscarriage of justice;

(ad) unreasonable hardship to the prospective applicant; or

(ae) irretrievable problems in dealing with the dispute (including the irretrievable loss of significant evidence); or

(iii) there is a significant risk that in the period necessary to schedule and attend a MIAM, proceedings relating to the dispute will be brought in another state in which a valid claim to jurisdiction may exist, such that a court in that other State would be seised of the dispute before a court in England and Wales; or

Previous MIAM attendance or MIAM exemption

(d) —

(i) in the 4 months prior to making the application, the person attended a MIAM or participated in another form of non-court dispute resolution relating to the same or substantially the same dispute; or

(ii) at the time of making the application, the person is participating in another form of non-court dispute resolution relating to the same or substantially the same dispute; or

(e) —

(i) in the 4 months prior to making the application, the person filed a relevant family application confirming that a MIAM exemption applied; and

(ii) that application related to the same or substantially the same dispute; or

(f) —

(i) the application would be made in existing proceedings which are continuing; and

(ii) the prospective applicant attended a MIAM before initiating those proceedings; or

(g) —

(i) the application would be made in existing proceedings which are continuing; and

(ii) a MIAM exemption applied to the application for those proceedings; or

Other

(h) —

(i) there is evidence that the prospective applicant is bankrupt, as specified in Practice Direction 3A; and

(ii) the proceedings would be for a financial remedy; or

(i) the prospective applicant does not have sufficient contact details for any of the prospective respondents to enable a family mediator to contact any of the prospective respondents for the purpose of scheduling the MIAM; or

(j) the application would be made without notice; or

(Paragraph 5.1 of Practice Direction 18A sets out the circumstances in which applications may be made without notice.)

(k) —

(i) the prospective applicant is or all of the prospective respondents are subject to a disability or other inability that would prevent attendance at a MIAM unless appropriate facilities can be offered by an authorised mediator;

(ii) the prospective applicant has contacted as many authorised family mediators as have an office within fifteen miles of his or home (or three of them if there are three or more), and all have stated that they are unable to provide such facilities; and

(iii) the names, postal addresses and telephone numbers or e-mail addresses for such authorised family mediators, and the dates of contact, can be provided to the court if requested; or

(l) the prospective applicant or all of the prospective respondents cannot attend a MIAM because he or she is, or they are, as the case may be—

(i) in prison or any other institution in which he or she is or they are required to be detained;

(ii) subject to conditions of bail that prevent contact with the other person; or

(iii) subject to a licence with a prohibited contact requirement in relation to the other person; or

(m) the prospective applicant or all of the prospective respondents are not habitually resident in England and Wales; or

(n) a child is one of the prospective parties by virtue of Rule 12.3(1); or

(o) —

(i) the prospective applicant has contacted as many authorised family mediators as have an office within fifteen miles of his or her home (or three of them if there are three or more), and all of them have stated that they are not available to conduct a MIAM within fifteen business days of the date of contact; and

(ii) the names, postal addresses and telephone numbers or e-mail addresses for such authorised family mediators, and the dates of contact, can be provided to the court if requested; or

(p) there is no authorised family mediator with an office within fifteen miles of the prospective applicant's home; or

(2) an authorised family mediator confirms in the relevant form (a 'mediator's exemption') that he or she is satisfied that—

(a) mediation is not suitable as a means of resolving the dispute because none of the respondents is willing to attend a MIAM; or

(b) mediation is not suitable as a means of resolving the dispute because all of the respondents failed without good reason to attend a MIAM appointment; or

(c) mediation is otherwise not suitable as a means of resolving the dispute.][1]

Amendment

1 Substituted by the Family Procedure (Amendment No 3) Rules 2014, SI 2014/843, rr 2, 5.

[3.9 Conduct of MIAMs

(1) Only an authorised family mediator may conduct a MIAM.

(2) At the MIAM, the authorised family mediator must—

- (a) provide information about the principles, process and different models of mediation, and information about other methods of non-court dispute resolution;
- (b) assess the suitability of mediation as a means of resolving the dispute;
- (c) assess whether there has been, or is a risk of, domestic violence; and
- (d) assess whether there has been, or is a risk of, harm by a prospective party to a child that would be a subject of the application.][1]

Amendment

1 Substituted by the Family Procedure (Amendment No 3) Rules 2014, SI 2014/843, rr 2, 5.

[3.10 MIAM exemption not validly claimed

(1) If a MIAM exemption has been claimed, the court will, if appropriate when making a decision on allocation, and in any event at the first hearing, inquire into whether the exemption was validly claimed.

(2) If a court finds that the MIAM exemption was not validly claimed, the court will—

- (a) direct the applicant, or direct the parties to attend a MIAM; and
- (b) if necessary, adjourn the proceedings to enable a MIAM to take place;

unless the court considers that in all the circumstances of the case, the MIAM requirement should not apply to the application in question.

(3) In making a decision under Rule 3.10(2), the court will have particular regard to—

- (a) any applicable time limits;
- (b) the reason or reasons why the MIAM exemption was not validly claimed;
- (c) the applicability of any other MIAM exemptions; and
- (d) the number and nature of issues that remain to be resolved in the proceedings.][1]

Amendment

1 Substituted by the Family Procedure (Amendment No 3) Rules 2014, SI 2014/843, rr 2, 5.

Practice Direction 3A – Family Mediation Information and Assessment Meetings (MIAMs)

See also Part 3

Summary

1 The purpose of this Practice Direction is to supplement the MIAM Rules in the Family Procedure Rules and to set out good practice to be followed by prospective respondents who are expected to also attend a MIAM.

2 Under section 10(1) of the Children and Families Act 2014, it is now a requirement for a person to attend a MIAM before making certain kinds of applications to obtain a court order. (A list of these applications is set out in Rule 3.6 and in paragraphs 12 and 13 below.) The person who would be the respondent to the application is expected to attend the MIAM. The court has a general power to adjourn proceedings in order for non-court

dispute resolution to be attempted, including attendance at a MIAM to consider family mediation and other options.

3 A MIAM is a short meeting that provides information about mediation as a way of resolving disputes. A MIAM is conducted by a trained mediator who will assess whether mediation is appropriate in the circumstances. A MIAM should be held within 15 business days of contacting the mediator.

4 There are exemptions to the MIAM requirement. These are set out in the MIAM Rules (see Chapter 3 to Part 3 of the Family Procedure Rules), and are explained in more detail in this Practice Direction.

5 The effect of the MIAM requirement and accompanying Rules is that a person who wishes to make certain kinds of applications to the court must first attend a MIAM unless a 'MIAM exemption' or a 'mediator's exemption' applies. These exemptions are set out in Rule 3.8.

6 When making certain kinds of applications (see paragraphs 12 and 13 below), an applicant must therefore provide on the application form, or on a separate form, one of the following –

(i) confirmation from a mediator that she or he has attended a MIAM;
(ii) confirmation from a mediator that a 'mediator's exemption' applies; or
(iii) a claim that a MIAM exemption applies. An applicant who claims an exemption from the MIAM requirement is not required to attach any supporting evidence with their application, but should bring any supporting evidence to the first hearing.

7 If an applicant claims a MIAM exemption, the court will issue proceedings but will inquire into the exemption claimed, either at the stage at which the case is allocated or at the first hearing. At the first hearing, the court may review any supporting evidence in order to ensure that the MIAM exemption was validly claimed. As set out in more detail below, if a MIAM exemption has not been validly claimed, the court may direct the applicant or the parties to attend a MIAM, and may adjourn proceedings for that purpose.

Background: Consideration of mediation and other non-court dispute resolution

8 The adversarial court process is not always best suited to the resolution of family disputes. Such disputes are often best resolved through discussion and agreement, where that can be managed safely and appropriately.

9 Family mediation is one way of settling disagreements. A trained mediator can help the parties to reach an agreement. A mediator who conducts a MIAM is a qualified independent facilitator who can also discuss other forms of dispute resolution if mediation is not appropriate.

10 Attendance at a MIAM provides an opportunity for the parties to a dispute to receive information about the process of mediation and to understand the benefits it can offer as a way to resolve disputes. At that meeting, a trained mediator will discuss with the parties the nature of their dispute and will explore with them whether mediation would be a suitable way to resolve the issues on which there is disagreement.

The applications to which the MIAM requirement applies

11 In accordance with section 10 of the 2014 Act, and Rule 3.6, the proceedings to which the MIAM requirement applies are the private law proceedings relating to children listed in paragraph 12 and the proceedings for a financial remedy listed in paragraph 13 below.

Private law proceedings relating to children

12(1) The private law proceedings relating to children referred to in paragraph 11 are proceedings for the following orders, unless one of the circumstances specified in sub-paragraph (2) applies –

(a) a child arrangements order and other orders with respect to a child or children under section 8 of the Children Act 1989;

(b) a parental responsibility order (under sections 4(1)(c), 4ZA(1)(c) or 4A(1)(b) of the Children Act 1989) or an order terminating parental responsibility (under sections 4(2A), 4ZA(5) or 4A(3) of that Act);

(c) an order appointing a child's guardian (under section 5(1) of the Children Act 1989) or an order terminating the appointment (under section 6(7) of that Act);

(d) an order giving permission to change a child's surname or remove a child from the United Kingdom (under sections 13(1) or 14C of the Children Act 1989);

(e) a special guardianship order; and

(f) an order varying or discharging such an order (under section 14D of the Children Act 1989).

(2) The circumstances referred to in sub-paragraph (1) are that the proceedings –

(a) are for a consent order;

(b) are for an order relating to a child or children in respect of whom there are ongoing emergency proceedings, care proceedings or supervision proceedings; or

(c) are for an order relating to a child or children who are the subject of an an emergency protection order, a care order or a supervision order.

Proceedings for a financial remedy

13(1) The proceedings for a financial remedy referred to in paragraph 11 are proceedings for the following orders, unless one of the circumstances specified in sub-paragraph (2) applies –

(a) the following financial orders –

(i) an order for maintenance pending suit;

(ii) an order for maintenance pending outcome of proceedings;

(iii) an order for periodical payments or lump sum provision as mentioned in section 21(1) of the Matrimonial Causes Act 1973, except an order under section 27(6) of that Act;

(iv) an order for periodical payments or lump sum provision as mentioned in paragraph 2(1) of Schedule 5 to the Civil Partnership Act 2004, made under Part 1 of Schedule 5 to that Act;

(v) a property adjustment order;

(vi) a variation order;

(vii) a pension sharing order; or

(viii) a pension compensation sharing order;

(b) an order for financial provision for children (under Schedule 1 to the Children Act 1989);

(c) an order for financial provision in a case of neglect to maintain (under section 27 of the Matrimonial Causes Act 1973 or under Part 9 of Schedule 5 to the Civil Partnership Act 2004);

(d) an order for alteration of a maintenance agreement (under section 35 of the Matrimonial Causes Act 1973 or under paragraph 69 of Schedule 5 to the 2004 Act);

(e) an order for financial provision for failure to maintain for parties to a marriage and children of the family (under Part 1 of the Domestic Proceedings and Magistrates' Courts Act 1978 or an order under Schedule 6 to the Civil Partnership Act 2004); and

(f) an order for special protection for respondent in certain separation cases (under section 10(2) of the Matrimonial Causes Act 1973 or under section 48(2) of the Civil Partnership Act 2004).

(2) The circumstances referred to in sub-paragraph (1) are that the proceedings –

(a) are for a consent order; or

(b) are for enforcement of any order made in proceedings for a financial remedy or of any agreement made in or in contemplation of proceedings for a financial remedy.

Making an application

14 An application to the court in any of the proceedings specified above must be on the relevant court form which must contain either: (a) a confirmation from a mediator that the applicant has attended a MIAM; (b) a claim by the applicant that a MIAM exemption applies (the list of MIAM exemptions is set out in Rule 3.8(1)); or (c) a confirmation from a mediator that a mediator's exemption applies (the list of circumstances that qualify for a mediator's exemption is in Rule 3.8(2)).

15 Relevant application forms are available from the HMCTS form finder service at www.justice.gov.uk/forms/hmcts. For matters concerning children you can find out which form to use by reading the leaflet CB1 – Making an application – Children and the Family Courts'. Leaflet CB7 – Guide for separated parents: children and the family courts also provides guidance on the court process.

16 The relevant form can be completed either by the applicant or his or her legal representative. Any reference in this Practice Direction or in the Rules to completion of the form by an applicant includes a reference to completion by a legal representative.

MIAM exemptions

17 FPR Rule 3.8(1) sets out the circumstances in which the MIAM requirement does not apply. These are called MIAM exemptions.

18 In order to claim that a MIAM exemption applies, an applicant will need to tick the appropriate MIAM exemption boxes on the relevant form.

19 Applicants should note that some of the MIAM exemptions require that certain evidence is available. The next section of the Practice Direction specifies those forms of evidence. This evidence does not need to be provided with the application but applicants should bring such evidence to the first hearing because the court will inquire into such evidence in order to determine whether the MIAM exemption has been validly claimed.

MIAM exemption – Domestic violence

20 The forms of evidence referred to in Rule 3.8(1)(a) are–

(a) evidence that a prospective party has been arrested for a relevant domestic violence offence;

(b) evidence of a relevant police caution for a domestic violence offence;

(c) evidence of relevant criminal proceedings for a domestic violence offence which have not concluded;

(d) evidence of a relevant conviction for a domestic violence offence;
(e) a court order binding a prospective party over in connection with a domestic violence offence;
(f) a domestic violence protection notice issued under section 24 of the Crime and Security Act 2010 against a prospective party;
(g) a relevant protective injunction;
(h) an undertaking given in England and Wales under section 46 or 63E of the Family Law Act 1996 (or given in Scotland or Northern Ireland in place of a protective injunction) by a prospective party, provided that a cross-undertaking relating to domestic violence was not given by another prospective party;
(i) a copy of a finding of fact, made in proceedings in the United Kingdom, that there has been domestic violence by a prospective party;
(j) an expert report produced as evidence in proceedings in the United Kingdom for the benefit of a court or tribunal confirming that a person with whom a prospective party is or was in a family relationship, was assessed as being, or at risk of being, a victim of domestic violence by that prospective party;
(k) a letter or report from an appropriate health professional confirming that-
    (i) that professional, or another appropriate health professional, has examined a prospective party in person; and
    (ii) in the reasonable professional judgment of the author or the examining appropriate health professional, that prospective party has, or has had, injuries or a condition consistent with being a victim of domestic violence;
(l) a letter or report from-
    (i) the appropriate health professional who made the referral described below;
    (ii) an appropriate health professional who has access to the medical records of the prospective party referred to below; or
    (iii) the person to whom the referral described below was made;
    confirming that there was a referral by an appropriate health professional of a prospective party to a person who provides specialist support or assistance for victims of, or those at risk of, domestic violence;
(m) a letter from any person who is a member of a multi-agency risk assessment conference (or other suitable local safeguarding forum) confirming that a prospective party, or a person with whom that prospective party is in a family relationship, is or has been at risk of harm from domestic violence by another prospective party;
(n) a letter from an independent domestic violence advisor confirming that they are providing support to a prospective party;
(o) a letter from an independent sexual violence advisor confirming that they are providing support to a prospective party relating to sexual violence by another prospective party;
(p) a letter from an officer employed by a local authority or housing association (or their equivalent in Scotland or Northern Ireland) for the purpose of supporting tenants containing-
    (i) a statement to the effect that, in their reasonable professional judgment, a person with whom a prospective party is or has been in a family relationship is, or is at risk of being, a victim of domestic violence by that prospective party;
    (ii) a description of the specific matters relied upon to support that judgment; and
    (iii) a description of the support they provided to the victim of domestic violence or the person at risk of domestic violence by that prospective party;

(q) a letter which-
  (i) is from an organisation providing domestic violence support services, or a registered charity, which letter confirms that it-
    (aa) is situated in England and Wales,
    (bb) has been operating for an uninterrupted period of six months or more; and
    (cc) provided a prospective party with support in relation to that person's needs as a victim, or a person at risk, of domestic violence; and
  (ii) contains-
    (aa) a statement to the effect that, in the reasonable professional judgment of the author of the letter, the prospective party is, or is at risk of being, a victim of domestic violence;
    (bb) a description of the specific matters relied upon to support that judgment;
    (cc) a description of the support provided to the prospective party; and
    (dd) a statement of the reasons why the prospective party needed that support;

(r) a letter or report from an organisation providing domestic violence support services in the United Kingdom confirming-
  (i) that a person with whom a prospective party is or was in a family relationship was refused admission to a refuge;
  (ii) the date on which they were refused admission to the refuge; and
  (iii) they sought admission to the refuge because of allegations of domestic violence by the prospective party referred to in paragraph (i);

(s) a letter from a public authority confirming that a person with whom a prospective party is or was in a family relationship, was assessed as being, or at risk of being, a victim of domestic violence by that prospective party (or a copy of that assessment);

(t) a letter from the Secretary of State for the Home Department confirming that a prospective party has been granted leave to remain in the United Kingdom under paragraph 289B of the Rules made by the Home Secretary under section 3(2) of the Immigration Act 1971, which can be found at https://www.gov.uk/guidance/immigration-rules/immigration-rules-index;

(u) evidence which demonstrates that a prospective party has been, or is at risk of being, the victim of domestic violence by another prospective party in the form of abuse which relates to financial matters.

MIAM exemption – Bankruptcy

21 The forms of evidence referred to in Rule 3.8(1)(h) are –

(a) application by the prospective applicant for a bankruptcy order;
(b) petition by a creditor of the prospective applicant for a bankruptcy order; or
(c) a bankruptcy order in respect of the prospective applicant.

Finding an authorised family mediator

22 As set out in Rule 3.9, a MIAM must be conducted by an authorised family mediator. Under that rule, an authorised family mediator is a person identified by the Family Mediation Council as qualified to conduct a MIAM.

23 A list of authorised family mediators, including their location, can be found using the 'Find your local mediator' search engine at: www.familymediationcouncil.org.uk

24 The expectation is that a prospective applicant should be able to find an authorised family mediator within 15 miles of his or her home. As stated in Rule 3.8(1)(o) a MIAM exemption is available if –

(i) the prospective applicant has contacted as many authorised family mediators as have an office within fifteen miles of his or her home (or three of them if there are three or more), and all of them have stated that they are not available to conduct a MIAM within fifteen business days of the date of contact; and
(ii) the names, postal addresses and telephone numbers or e-mail addresses for such authorised family mediators, and the dates of contact, can be provided to the court if requested.

25 Rule 3.8(1)(p) also provides an exemption if there is no authorised family mediator with an office within fifteen miles of the prospective applicant's home.

26 To determine whether a mediator is within the distance of 15 miles from their home, applicants can use the 'Find your local mediator' search engine to type in their own post code and then use the distance option to display only family mediators within a 15 mile distance.

27 The applicant will need to be prepared to produce at the first hearing the names, contact information and details of the dates of contact with the authorised family mediators.

28 Information about the Family Mediation Council, including its code of conduct can also be found at www.familymediationcouncil.org.uk

Funding attendance at a MIAM

29 The cost of attending a MIAM will depend on whether the prospective parties attend separately or together and whether at least one of the prospective parties is eligible for Legal Aid. If at least one party is eligible for Legal Aid then the total cost of MIAM attendance can be met by the Legal Aid Agency, whether the parties attend the same MIAM or separate MIAMs.

30 If neither party is eligible for Legal Aid then the mediator will agree with the prospective parties how the cost of MIAM attendance is to be met.

31 Parties can find out whether they are eligible for Legal Aid by using the calculator tool available at www.gov.uk/legal-aid

Attending a MIAM

32 Prospective respondents are expected to attend a MIAM, either with the prospective applicant or separately. A respondent may choose to attend a MIAM separately but this should usually be with the same authorised family mediator.

33 The prospective applicant should provide contact details for the prospective respondent to an authorised family mediator for the purpose of the mediator contacting them to discuss their willingness to attend a MIAM and, if appropriate, to schedule their attendance at a MIAM.

34 If the mediator contacts the prospective respondent and determines that he or she is unwilling to attend a MIAM, a prospective applicant should ask the mediator to confirm this as a ground for MIAM exemption in the relevant section of the application form, which should then be returned signed to the applicant.

MIAM exemption: Inquiries by the court

35 Where a MIAM exemption requires that certain evidence is available, the evidence does not need to be provided with the application form. Applicants should instead bring any such evidence to the first hearing because the court will inquire into such evidence in order to determine whether the MIAM exemption was validly claimed.

36 The court may if appropriate adjourn proceedings where such evidence is not available or may give directions about how and when such evidence is to be filed with the court.

37 If the court determines that the MIAM exemption was not validly claimed, the court may direct the applicant, or the parties, to attend a MIAM and may adjourn proceedings pending MIAM attendance.

Definitions

38 For the purpose of this Practice Direction –

'appropriate health professional' means-

(a) a medical practitioner licensed to practise by the General Medical Council;
(b) a health professional who is registered to practise in the United Kingdom by-
    (i) the Nursing and Midwifery Council; or
    (ii) the General Dental Council; or
(c) a paramedic, practitioner psychologist, radiographer or social worker registered to practise in the United Kingdom by the Health and Care Professions Council;

'care order' has the meaning given to it in Rule 2.3 of the FPR;
'care proceedings' has the meaning given to it in Rule 12.2 of the FPR;
'consent order' has the meaning given to it in Rule 2.3 of the FPR;
'domestic violence offence' has the meaning given in the list published by the Lord Chancellor which can be viewed at https://www.gov.uk/government/publications/domestic-violence-and-child-abuse-offences;
'emergency proceedings' has the meaning given to it in Rule 12.2 of the FPR;
'emergency protection order' has the meaning given to it in Rule 12.2 of the FPR;
'expert report' means a report by a person qualified to give expert advice on all or most of the matters that are the subject of the report;
'FPR' means the Family Procedure Rules 2010;
'financial order' has the meaning given to it in Rule 2.3 of the FPR;
'financial remedy' has the meaning given to it in Rule 2.3 of the FPR;
'housing association' has the same meaning as in section 1(1) of the Housing Associations Act 1985;
'local authority' means a county council, a district council, a London borough council or a parish council but, in relation to Wales, means a county council, county borough council or community council;
'health professional' means a registered –

(a) medical practitioner who holds a licence to practise;
(b) nurse;
(c) midwife; or
(d) practitioner psychologist who holds a licence to practise;

'mediator's exemption' has the meaning given to it in Rule 3.1 of the FPR;
'MIAM' means a family mediation information and assessment meeting;

'MIAM exemption' has the meaning given to it in Rule 3.1 of the FPR;
'MIAM requirement' has the meaning given to it in Rule 3.1 of the FPR;
'non-court dispute resolution' has the meaning given to it in Rule 2.3 of the FPR;
'pension compensation sharing order' has the meaning given in Rule 9.3 of the FPR;
'pension sharing order' has the meaning given in Rule 9.3 of the FPR;
'private law proceedings' has the meaning given to it in Rule 12.2 of the FPR;
'prospective applicant' has the meaning given to it in Rule 3.1 of the FPR;
'prospective party' has the meaning given to it in Rule 3.1 of the FPR;
'prospective respondent' has the meaning given to it in Rule 3.1 of the FPR;
'protective injunction' means an order made by the court–

(a) in respect of persons who are in a family relationship with each other, containing any of the following provisions-
  (i) protecting a person from harm, intimidation, threats or harassment;
  (ii) protecting a person from being forced into a marriage or from any attempt to be forced into a marriage;
  (iii) prohibiting a person from contacting, or communicating with, another;
  (iv) concerning entry or access to, or the use or occupation of, property;
(b) for the protection from female genital mutilation under paragraph 1 or 18 of Schedule 2 to the Female Genital Mutilation Act 2003; or
(c) in respect of a violent offender within the meaning of section 98 of the Criminal Justice and Immigration Act 2008,

but does not include an order made without notice to the respondent that was subsequently set aside by the court;
'public authority' has the same meaning as in section 6 of the Human Rights Act 1998;
'registered charity' means a charity which is registered in accordance with section 30 of the Charities Act 2011;
'refuge' means-

(a) a refuge established for the purpose of providing accommodation for victims of, or those at risk of, domestic violence; or
(b) a residential home established and maintained by a public body for any other purpose that also provides accommodation to the victims of, or those at risk of, domestic violence;

'relevant' in paragraph 20 of this Practice Direction means that the evidence–

(a) identifies a person with whom a prospective party is or was in a family relationship as being, or at risk of being, the victim of domestic violence; or
(b) is-
  (i) in a form described in paragraph 20(1)(a) to (d);
  (ii) identifies a prospective party as the person arrested for, cautioned with, charged with, or convicted of the domestic violence offence; and
  (iii) relates to a domestic violence offence which does not identify the victim;

'supervision order' has the meaning given to it in Rule 12.2 of the FPR;
'supervision proceedings' has the meaning given to it in Rule 12.2 of the FPR; and
'variation order' has the meaning given to it in Rule 9.3 of the FPR.

39(1) For the purposes of paragraph 20, there is a family relationship between two people if they are associated with each other. A person is associated with another person if-

(a) they are or have been married to each other;
(b) they are or have been civil partners of each other;
(c) they are cohabitants or former cohabitants;
(d) they live or have lived in the same household, otherwise than merely by reason of one of them being the other's employee, tenant, lodger or boarder;
(e) they are relatives;
(f) they have agreed to marry one another (whether or not that agreement has been terminated);
(g) they have entered into a civil partnership agreement (as defined by section 73 of the Civil Partnership Act 2004) (whether or not that agreement has been terminated);
(h) they have or have had an intimate personal relationship with each other which is or was of significant duration;
(i) in relation to any child, they are both persons falling within sub-paragraph (3); or
(j) they are parties or prospective parties to the same family proceedings.

(2) For the purposes of sub-paragraph (1)–

(a) 'cohabitants' are two persons who are neither married to each other nor civil partners of each other but are living together as husband and wife or as if they were civil partners, and
(b) 'cohabit' and 'former cohabitants' are to be read accordingly, but the latter expression does not include cohabitants who have subsequently married each other or become civil partners of each other.

(3) A person falls within this sub-paragraph in relation to a child if—

(a) the person is a parent of the child; or
(b) the person has or has had parental responsibility for the child.

(4) If a child has been adopted or falls within sub-paragraph (6), two persons are also associated with each other for the purposes of sub-paragraph (1) if—

(a) one is a natural parent of the child or a parent of such a natural parent; and
(b) the other is the child or any person—
  (i) who has become a parent of the child by virtue of an adoption order or has applied for an adoption order, or
  (ii) with whom the child has at any time been placed for adoption.

(5) A body corporate and another person are not, by virtue of sub-paragraph (1)(i) or (j), to be regarded as associated with each other.

(6) A child falls within this sub-paragraph if—

(a) an adoption agency, within the meaning of section 2 of the Adoption and Children Act 2002, has power to place him for adoption under section 19 of that Act (placing children with parental consent) or he has become the subject of an order under section 21 of that Act (placement orders), or
(b) the child is freed for adoption by virtue of an order made—
  (i) in England and Wales, under section 18 of the Adoption Act 1976, or
  (ii) in Northern Ireland, under Article 17(1) or 18(1) of the Adoption (Northern Ireland) Order 1987, or
(c) the child is the subject of a Scottish permanence order which includes provision granting authority to adopt.

(7) In sub-paragraph (6)(c) 'Scottish permanence order' means a permanence order under section 80 of the Adoption and Children (Scotland) Act 2007 (including a deemed permanence order having effect by virtue of article 13(1), 14(2), 17(1) or 19(2) of the Adoption and Children (Scotland) Act 2007 (Commencement No 4, Transitional and Savings Provisions) Order 2009).

(8) For the avoidance of doubt, where paragraph 20 refers to a person with whom a prospective party is in a family relationship, that person could be (but need not necessarily be), another prospective party.

[PART 3A
VULNERABLE PERSONS: PARTICIPATION IN PROCEEDING AND GIVING EVIDENCE

3A.1 Interpretation

In this Part—

'child' means a person under the age of 18 years whether or not the child is the subject of the proceedings, except that—

- (a) in adoption proceedings, it also includes a person who is the subject of proceedings and has attained the age of 18 years before the proceedings are concluded; and
- (b) in proceedings brought under …[1] the 1980 Hague Convention or the European Convention, it means a person under the age of 16 years who is the subject of proceedings;

['domestic abuse' has the meaning given in section 1 of the Domestic Abuse Act 2021;][2]

'intermediary' means a person whose function is to—

- (a) communicate questions put to a witness or party;
- (b) communicate to any person asking such questions the answers given by the witness or party in reply to them; and
- (c) explain such questions or answers so far as is necessary to enable them to be understood by the witness or party or by the person asking such questions;

'live link' means a live television link or other arrangement whereby a witness or party, while absent from the courtroom or other place where the proceedings are being held, is able to see and hear a person there and to be seen and heard by the judge, legal representatives acting in the proceedings and other persons appointed to assist a witness or party;

'mental disorder' has the meaning given in section 1 of the Mental Health Act 1983;

'participation direction' means—

- (a) a general case management direction made for the purpose of assisting a witness or party to give evidence or participate in proceedings; or
- (b) a direction that a witness or party should have the assistance of one or more of the measures in rule 3A.8; and

['relative' has the meaning given by section 63(1) of the 1996 Act;

'victim' includes a child to whom section 3(2) of the Domestic Abuse Act 2021 applies; and][2]

references to 'quality of evidence' are to its quality in terms of completeness, coherence and accuracy; and for this purpose 'coherence' refers to a witness's or a party's ability in giving evidence to give answers which address the questions put to the witness or the party and which can be understood both individually and collectively.][3]

Amendment

1 Repealed by the Family Procedure Rules 2010 and Court of Protection Rules 2017 (Amendment) (EU Exit) Regulations 2019, SI 2019/517, rr 2, 4.
2 Inserted by the Family Procedure (Amendment No 2) Rules 2021, SI 2021/875, rr 2, 3.
3 Inserted by the Family Procedure (Amendment No 3) Rules 2017, SI 2017/1033, rr 2, 3.

[3A.2 Application of provisions in this Part

(1) Rule 3A.4 does not apply to a party who is a child.

(2) Rules 3A.3 to 3A.5 do not apply to a party who is a protected party.

[(3) Rules 3A.3 to 3A.5 do not apply to a party or witness who—
(a) falls within the assumption set out at rule 3A.2A(1); and
(b) has not made a request of a kind referred to in rule 3A.2A(2).][1]][2]

Amendment

1 Inserted by the Family Procedure (Amendment No 2) Rules 2021, SI 2021/875, rr 2, 4.
2 Inserted by the Family Procedure (Amendment No 3) Rules 2017, SI 2017/1033, rr 2, 3.

[3A.2A Court's duty to consider making participation directions: victims of domestic abuse

(1) Subject to paragraph (2), where it is stated that a party or witness is, or is at risk of being, a victim of domestic abuse carried out by a party, a relative of another party, or a witness in the proceedings, the court must assume that the following matters are diminished—

(a) the quality of the party's or witness's evidence;
(b) in relation to a party, their participation in the proceedings.

(2) The party or witness concerned can request that the assumption set out in paragraph (1) does not apply to them if they do not wish it to.

(3) Where the assumption set out in paragraph (1) applies, the court must consider whether it is necessary to make one or more participation directions.][1]

Amendment

1 Inserted by the Family Procedure (Amendment No 2) Rules 2021, SI 2021/875, rr 2, 5.

[3A.3 Court's duty to consider vulnerability of [other parties or witnesses][1]

(1) When considering the vulnerability of a party or witness as mentioned in rule 3A.4 or 3A.5, the court must have regard in particular to the matters set out in paragraphs (a) to (j) and (m) of rule 3A.7.

(2) Practice Direction 3AA gives guidance about vulnerability.][2]

Amendment

1 Substituted by the Family Procedure (Amendment No 2) Rules 2021, SI 2021/875, rr 2, 6.
2 Inserted by the Family Procedure (Amendment No 3) Rules 2017, SI 2017/1033, rr 2, 3.

[3A.4 Court's duty to consider how a party can participate in the proceedings

(1) The court must consider whether a party's participation in the proceedings (other than by way of giving evidence) is likely to be diminished by reason of vulnerability and, if so, whether it is necessary to make one or more participation directions.

(2) Before making such participation directions, the court must consider any views expressed by the party about participating in the proceedings.][1]

Amendment

1 Inserted by the Family Procedure (Amendment No 3) Rules 2017, SI 2017/1033, rr 2, 3.

[3A.5 Court's duty to consider how a party or a witness can give evidence

(1) The court must consider whether the quality of evidence given by a party or witness is likely to be diminished by reason of vulnerability and, if so, whether it is necessary to make one or more participation directions.

(2) Before making such participation directions, the court must consider any views expressed by the party or witness about giving evidence.][1]

Amendment

1 Inserted by the Family Procedure (Amendment No 3) Rules 2017, SI 2017/1033, rr 2, 3.

[3A.6 Protected parties

(1) The court must consider whether it is necessary to make one or more participation directions to assist—

- (a) the protected party participating in proceedings; or
- (b) the protected party giving evidence.

(2) Before making such participation directions, the court must consider any views expressed by the protected party's litigation friend about the protected party's participation in the proceedings or that party giving evidence.

(Part 15 contains rules about representation of a protected party. Practice Direction 15B contains provisions about the ability of a protected party to give evidence.)][1]

Amendment

1 Inserted by the Family Procedure (Amendment No 3) Rules 2017, SI 2017/1033, rr 2, 3.

[3A.7 What the court must have regard to

When deciding whether to make one or more participation directions the court must have regard in particular to—

- (a) the impact of any actual or perceived intimidation, including any behaviour towards the party or witness on the part of—
  - (i) any other party or other witness to the proceedings or members of the family or associates of that other party or other witness; or
  - (ii) any members of the family of the party or witness;
- (b) whether the party or witness—
  - (i) suffers from mental disorder or otherwise has a significant impairment of intelligence or social functioning;
  - (ii) has a physical disability or suffers from a physical disorder; or
  - (iii) is undergoing medical treatment;

(c) the nature and extent of the information before the court;
(d) the issues arising in the proceedings including (but not limited to) any concerns arising in relation to abuse;
(e) whether a matter is contentious;
(f) the age, maturity and understanding of the party or witness;
(g) the social and cultural background and ethnic origins of the party or witness;
(h) the domestic circumstances and religious beliefs of the party or witness;
(i) any questions which the court is putting or causing to be put to a witness in accordance with section 31G(6) of the 1984 Act;
(j) any characteristic of the party or witness which is relevant to the participation direction which may be made;
(k) whether any measure is available to the court;
(l) the costs of any available measure; and
(m) any other matter set out in Practice Direction 3AA.][1]

Amendment

1 Inserted by the Family Procedure (Amendment No 3) Rules 2017, SI 2017/1033, rr 2, 3.

[3A.8 Measures

(1) The measures referred to in this Part are those which—

(a) prevent a party or witness from seeing another party or witness;
(b) allow a party or witness to participate in hearings and give evidence by live link;
(c) provide for a party or witness to use a device to help communicate;
(d) provide for a party or witness to participate in proceedings with the assistance of an intermediary;
(e) provide for a party or witness to be questioned in court with the assistance of an intermediary; or
(f) do anything else which is set out in Practice Direction 3AA.

(2) If the family court makes a direction for a measure which is not available where the court is sitting, it may direct that the court will sit at the nearest or most convenient location where the family court sits and the measure is available.

(3) If the High Court makes a direction for a measure which is not available where the court is sitting, it may direct that the court will sit at the nearest or most convenient location where the High Court sits and the measure is available.

(4) Nothing in these rules gives the court power to direct that public funding must be available to provide a measure.

(5) If a direction for a measure is considered by the court to be necessary but the measure is not available to the court, the court must set out in its order the reasons why the measure is not available.][1]

Amendment

1 Inserted by the Family Procedure (Amendment No 3) Rules 2017, SI 2017/1033, rr 2, 3.

[3A.9 When the duties of the court apply and recording reasons for decisions made under this Part

(1) The court's duties under rules 3A.3 to 3A.6 apply as soon as possible after the start of proceedings and continue until the resolution of the proceedings.

(2) The court must set out its reasons on the court order for—

(a) making, varying or revoking directions referred to in this Part; or
(b) deciding not to make, vary or revoke directions referred to in this Part, in proceedings that involve a vulnerable person or protected party.][1]

Amendment

1 Inserted by the Family Procedure (Amendment No 3) Rules 2017, SI 2017/1033, rr 2, 3.

[3A.10 Application for directions under this Part

(1) An application for directions under this Part may be made on the application form initiating the proceedings or during the proceedings by any person filing an application notice.

(2) The application form or application notice must contain the matters set out in Practice Direction 3AA.

(3) Subject to paragraph (2), the Part 18 procedure applies to an application for directions made during the proceedings.

(4) This rule is subject to any direction of the court.][1]

Amendment

1 Inserted by the Family Procedure (Amendment No 3) Rules 2017, SI 2017/1033, rr 2, 3.

[3A.11 Procedure where the court makes directions of its own initiative

Where the court proposes to make a participation direction of its own initiative the procedure set out in rule 4.3(2) to (6) applies.][1]

Amendment

1 Inserted by the Family Procedure (Amendment No 3) Rules 2017, SI 2017/1033, rr 2, 3.

[3A.12 Functions of officers of the Service and Welsh family proceedings officers

Nothing in this Part gives the court power to direct that an officer of the Service or a Welsh family proceedings officer should perform any function beyond the functions conferred upon such officers by any other enactment.][1]

Amendment

1 Inserted by the Family Procedure (Amendment No 3) Rules 2017, SI 2017/1033, rr 2, 3.

[3A.13 Prohibition of cross-examination in person under Part 4B of the 1984 Act

A practice direction may make provision in relation to the prohibition of cross-examination in person under Part 4B of the 1984 Act.][1]

Amendment

1 Inserted by the Family Procedure (Amendment) Rules 2022, SI 2022/44, rr 2, 4.

Practice Direction 3AA – Vulnerable persons: participation in proceedings and giving evidence

This Practice Direction supplements FPR Part 3A.

1 Preamble and interpretation

1.1 Part 3A FPR makes provision in relation to vulnerable persons (parties and witnesses), including protected parties, in family proceedings.

Rule 3A.2A FPR sets out the assumption that where it is stated that a party or witness is, or is at risk of being, a victim of domestic abuse carried out by a party, relative of another party, or a witness in the proceedings, they are vulnerable. Where the assumption applies, the court must consider whether it is necessary to make a participation direction.

Rule 3A.4 FPR places a duty on the court to consider whether a party's participation in the proceedings is likely to be diminished by reason of vulnerability and, if so whether it is necessary to make one or more participation directions (as defined in rule 3A.1 FPR). Rule 3A.4 FPR does not apply to a child or to a party who is a protected party, or to those who fall within the assumption at rule 3A.2A FPR.

Rule 3A.5 FPR places a duty on the court to consider whether the quality of evidence given by a party or witness is likely to be diminished by reason of vulnerability and, if so whether it is necessary to make one or more participation directions. Rule 3A.5 FPR does not apply to a party who is a protected party, or to those who fall within the assumption at rule 3A.2A FPR.

Rule 3A.6 FPR places a duty on the court to consider whether it is necessary to make one or more participation directions to assist a protected party in proceedings, or a protected party giving evidence.

1.1A For the avoidance of doubt, it should be noted that the assumption that a person is vulnerable, as referred to in rule 3A.2A FPR and in paragraph 1.1 above, only applies for the purposes of the court considering whether it is necessary to make a participation direction and not for any other purpose.

1.2 This Practice Direction sets out the procedure and practice to be followed to achieve a fair hearing by providing for appropriate measures to be put in place to ensure that the participation of parties and the quality of the evidence of the parties and other witnesses is not diminished by reason of their vulnerability.

1.3 It is the duty of the court (under rules 1.1(2); 1.2 & 1.4 and Part 3A FPR) and of all parties to the proceedings (rule 1.3 FPR) to identify any party or witness who is a vulnerable person at the earliest possible stage of any family proceedings.

1.4 All parties and their representatives are required to work with the court and each other to ensure that each party or witness can participate in proceedings without the quality of their evidence being diminished and without being put in fear or distress by reason of their vulnerability as defined with reference to the circumstances of each person and to the nature of the proceedings.

1.5 In applying the provisions of Part 3A FPR and the provisions of this Practice Direction, the court and the parties must also have regard to all other relevant rules and Practice Directions and in particular those referred to in the Annex to this Practice Direction.

2 Factors to which the court has to have regard when considering the vulnerability of a party or witness mentioned: rule 3A.3(1) FPR

2.1 Rule 3A.3 FPR makes clear that when considering the vulnerability of a party or witness for the purposes of rule 3A.4 FPR (the court's duty to consider how a vulnerable party other than a child can participate in the proceedings) or rule 3A.5 FPR (the court's duty to consider how a vulnerable party or witness can give evidence), the court must have regard in particular to the matters set out in paragraphs (a) to (j) and (m) of rule 3A.7 FPR. Where rule 3A.7(d) refers to questions of abuse, this includes any concerns arising in relation to any of the following-

a) domestic abuse,
b) sexual abuse;
c) physical and emotional abuse;
d) racial and/or cultural abuse or discrimination;
e) forced marriage or so called 'honour based violence';
f) female genital or other physical mutilation;
g) abuse or discrimination based on gender or sexual orientation; and
h) human trafficking.

2.2 As provided by rule 3A.2A FPR, where it is stated that a party or witness is, or as at risk of being, a victim of domestic abuse carried out by certain third parties, it is to be automatically assumed for the purposes of Part 3A FPR that they are vulnerable. For such parties and witnesses, the court should proceed directly to a consideration of whether a participation direction is necessary.

3 Guidance about vulnerability: rule 3A.3(2) FPR

3.1 Rule 3A.3 FPR requires the court to have regard in particular to the matters set out in paragraphs (a) to (j) and (m) of rule 3A.7 FPR when considering the vulnerability of a party or witness other than a protected party or victim of domestic abuse. The court should require the assistance of relevant parties in the case when considering whether these factors or any of them may mean that the participation of any party or witness in the case is likely to be diminished by reason of vulnerability. When addressing this question, the court should consider the ability of the party or witness to-

a) understand the proceedings, and their role in them, when in court;
b) put their views to the court;
c) instruct their representative/s before, during and after the hearing; and
d) attend the hearing without significant distress.

4 Participation directions: participation other than by way of giving evidence

4.1 This section of the Practice Direction applies where the assumption at rule 3A.2A FPR applies to a party, or where a court has concluded that a party's participation in proceedings (other than by way of giving evidence) is likely to be diminished by reason of vulnerability, including cases where a party might be participating in proceedings by way of asking questions of a witness.

4.2 The court will consider whether it is necessary to make one or more participation directions, as required by rule 3A.4 and rule 3A.2A. The court may make such directions for the measures specified in rule 3A.8. In addition, the court may use its general case management powers as it considers appropriate to facilitate the party's participation. For example, the court may decide to make directions in relation to matters such as the structure and the timing of the hearing, the formality of language to be used in the court and whether (if facilities allow for it) the parties should be enabled to enter the court building through different routes and use different waiting areas.

5 Participation directions: the giving of evidence by a vulnerable party, vulnerable witness or protected party

5.1 This section of the Practice Direction applies where a court has concluded that a vulnerable party, vulnerable witness or protected party (including those deemed vulnerable by virtue of the assumption at rule 3A.2A FPR should give evidence. In reaching its conclusion as to whether a child should give evidence to the court, the court must apply the guidance from relevant caselaw and the guidance of the Family Justice Council in relation to children giving evidence in family proceedings.

Ground rules hearings

5.2 When the court has decided that a vulnerable party, vulnerable witness or protected party should give evidence there shall be a 'ground rules hearing' prior to any hearing at which evidence is to be heard, at which any necessary participation directions will be given-

a) as to the conduct of the advocates and the parties in respect of the evidence of that person, including the need to address the matters referred to in paragraphs 5.3 to 5.7, and
b) to put any necessary support in place for that person.

The ground rules hearing does not need to be a separate hearing to any other hearing in the proceedings.

5.3 If the court decides that a vulnerable party, vulnerable witness or protected party should give evidence to the court, consideration should be given to the form of such evidence, for example whether it should be oral or other physical evidence, such as through sign language or another form of direct physical communication.

5.4 The court must consider the best way in which the person should give evidence, including considering whether the person's oral evidence should be given at a point before the hearing, recorded and, if the court so directs, transcribed, or given at the hearing with, if appropriate, participation directions being made.

5.5 In all cases in which it is proposed that a vulnerable party, vulnerable witness or protected party is to be cross-examined (whether before or during a hearing) the court must consider whether to make participation directions, including prescribing the manner in which the person is to be cross-examined. The court must consider whether to direct that-

a) any questions that can be asked by one advocate should not be repeated by another without the permission of the court;
b) questions or topics to be put in cross-examination should be agreed prior to the hearing;
c) questions to be put in cross-examination should be put by one legal representative or advocate alone, or, if appropriate, by the judge; and
d) the taking of evidence should be managed in any other way.

5.6 The court must also consider whether a vulnerable party, vulnerable witness or protected party has previously-

a) given evidence, and been cross-examined, in criminal proceedings and whether that evidence and cross-examination has been pre-recorded (see sections 27 and 28 of the Youth Justice and Criminal Evidence Act 1999); or

b) given an interview which was recorded but not used in previous criminal or family proceedings.

If so, and if any such recordings are available, the court should consider their being used in the family proceedings.

5.7 All advocates (including those who are litigants in person) are expected to be familiar with and to use the techniques employed by the toolkits and approach of the Advocacy Training Council. The toolkits are available at www.theadvocatesgateway.org/toolkits. Further guidance for advocates is available from the Ministry of Justice at http://www.justice.gov.uk/guidance.htm.

6 Matters to be included in an application form for directions: rule 3A.10(2) FPR

6.1 An application for directions under Part 3A FPR should contain the following information, as applicable:

a) why the party or witness would benefit from assistance;
aa) whether the party or witness falls within the assumption at rule 3A.2A FPR 177057
b) the measure or measures that would be likely to maximise as far as practicable the quality of that evidence;
c) why the measure or measures sought would be likely to improve the person's ability to participate in the proceedings; and
d) why the measure or measures sought would be likely to improve the quality of the person's evidence.

Annex

As noted at paragraph 1.5, in applying the provisions of Part 3A FPR and the provisions of this Practice Direction, the court and the parties must also have regard to all other relevant rules and Practice Directions and in particular-

Part 1 FPR (Overriding Objective);
Part 4 FPR (General Case Management Powers);
Part 12 FPR and Practice Direction 12J
Part 15 FPR (Representation of Protected Parties) and Practice Direction 15B (Adults Who May Be Protected Parties and Children Who May Become Protected Parties in Family Proceedings);
Part 18 FPR (Procedure for Other Applications in Proceedings);
Part 22 FPR (Evidence);
Part 24 FPR (Witnesses, depositions generally and taking of evidence in Member States of the European Union);
Part 25 FPR (Experts) and the Experts Practice Directions;
Rule 27.6 FPR and Practice Direction 27A (Court Bundles);
Part 30 FPR (Appeals) and Practice Direction 30A (Appeals).

PART 4
GENERAL CASE MANAGEMENT POWERS

4.1 The court's general powers of management

(1) In this Part, 'statement of case' means the whole or part of, an application form or answer.

(2) The list of powers in this rule is in addition to any powers given to the court by any other rule or practice direction or by any other enactment or any powers it may otherwise have.

(3) Except where these rules provide otherwise, the court may—

(a) extend or shorten the time for compliance with any rule, practice direction or court order (even if an application for extension is made after the time for compliance has expired);
(b) make such order for disclosure and inspection, including specific disclosure of documents, as it thinks fit;
[(bb) direct that any proceedings in the High Court be heard by a Divisional Court of the High Court;][1]
(c) adjourn or bring forward a hearing;
(d) require a party or a party's legal representative to attend the court;
(e) hold a hearing and receive evidence by telephone or by using any other method of direct oral communication;
(f) direct that part of any proceedings be dealt with as separate proceedings;
(g) stay[(GL)] the whole or part of any proceedings or judgment either generally or until a specified date or event;
(h) consolidate proceedings;
(i) hear two or more applications on the same occasion;
(j) direct a separate hearing of any issue;
(k) decide the order in which issues are to be heard;
(l) exclude an issue from consideration;
(m) dismiss or give a decision on an application after a decision on a preliminary issue;
(n) direct any party to file and serve an estimate of costs; and
(o) take any other step or make any other order for the purpose of managing the case and furthering the overriding objective.

(Rule 21.1 explains what is meant by disclosure and inspection.)

[(Rule 37.15(6)(b) makes specific provision in relation to Divisional Courts.)][1]

(4) When the court makes an order, it may—

(a) make it subject to conditions, including a condition to pay a sum of money into court; and
(b) specify the consequence of failure to comply with the order or a condition.

[(4A) Where the court has made a direction in accordance with paragraph (3)(bb) the proceedings shall be heard by a Divisional Court of the High Court and not by a single judge.][1]

(5) Where the court gives directions it will take into account whether or not a party has complied with any relevant pre-action protocol[(GL)].

(6) A power of the court under these rules to make an order includes a power to vary or revoke the order.

(7) Any provision in these rules—

(a) requiring or permitting directions to be given by the court is to be taken as including provision for such directions to be varied or revoked; and
(b) requiring or permitting a date to be set is to be taken as including provision for that date to be changed or cancelled.

(8) The court may not extend the period within which [an application for][2] a section 89 order must be made.

Amendment

1 Inserted by the Family Procedure (Amendment) Rules 2018, SI 2018/440, rr 2, 3.
2 Inserted by the Family Procedure (Amendment) Rules 2012, SI 2012/679, rr 2, 4.

4.2 Court officer's power to refer to the court

Where a step is to be taken by a court officer—

(a) the court officer may consult the court before taking that step;
(b) the step may be taken by the court instead of the court officer.

4.3 Court's power to make order of its own initiative

(1) Except where an enactment provides otherwise, the court may exercise its powers on an application or of its own initiative.

(Part 18 sets out the procedure for making an application.)

(2) [Subject to rule 29.17, where][1] the court proposes to make an order of its own initiative—

(a) it may give any person likely to be affected by the order an opportunity to make representations; and
(b) where it does so it must specify the time by and the manner in which the representations must be made.

(3) Where the court proposes—

(a) to make an order of its own initiative; and
(b) to hold a hearing to decide whether to make the order,

it must give each party likely to be affected by the order at least 5 days' notice of the hearing.

(4) The court may make an order of its own initiative without hearing the parties or giving them an opportunity to make representations.

(5) Where the court has made an order under paragraph (4)—

(a) a party affected by the order may apply to have it set aside(GL), varied or stayed(GL); and
(b) the order must contain a statement of the right to make such an application.

(6) An application under paragraph (5)(a) must be made—

(a) within such period as may be specified by the court; or
(b) if the court does not specify a period, within 7 days beginning with the date on which the order was served on the party making the application.

(7) If [the court][2] of its own initiative strikes out a statement of case or dismisses an application (including an application for permission to appeal) and it considers that the application is totally without merit—

(a) the court's order must record that fact; and
(b) the court must at the same time consider whether it is appropriate to make a civil restraint order.

Amendment

1 Substituted by the Family Procedure (Amendment No 3) Rules 2013, SI 2013/3204, rr 2, 6.

4.4 Power to strike out a statement of case

(1) Except in proceedings to which Parts 12 to 14 apply, the court may strike out(GL) a statement of case if it appears to the court—

(a) that the statement of case discloses no reasonable grounds for bringing or defending the application;

(b) that the statement of case is an abuse of the court's process or is otherwise likely to obstruct the just disposal of the proceedings;

(c) that there has been a failure to comply with a rule, practice direction or court order; or

(d) in relation to applications for matrimonial and civil partnership orders and answers to such applications, that the parties to the proceedings consent.

[(1A) When the court is considering whether to exercise the power to strike out a statement of case, it must take into account any written evidence filed in relation to the application or answer.][1]

(2) When the court strikes out a statement of case it may make any consequential order it considers appropriate.

(3) Where—

(a) the court has struck out an applicant's statement of case;

(b) the applicant has been ordered to pay costs to the respondent; and

(c) before paying those costs, the applicant starts another application against the same respondent, arising out of facts which are the same or substantially the same as those relating to the application in which the statement of case was struck out,

the court may, on the application of the respondent, stay(GL) that other application until the costs of the first application have been paid.

(4) Paragraph (1) does not limit any other power of the court to strike out (GL) a statement of case.

(5) If [the court][2] strikes out an applicant's statement of case and it considers that the application is totally without merit—

(a) the court's order must record that fact; and

(b) the court must at the same time consider whether it is appropriate to make a civil restraint order.

Amendment

1 Inserted by the Family Procedure (Amendment) Rules 2016, SI 2016/355, rr 2, 3.

2 Substituted by the Family Procedure (Amendment No 3) Rules 2013, SI 2013/3204, rr 2, 7.

4.5 Sanctions have effect unless defaulting party obtains relief

(1) Where a party has failed to comply with a rule, practice direction or court order, any sanction for failure to comply imposed by the rule, practice direction or court order has effect unless the party in default applies for and obtains relief from the sanction.

(Rule 4.6 sets out the circumstances which the court may consider on an application to grant relief from a sanction.)

(2) Where the sanction is the payment of costs, the party in default may only obtain relief by appealing against the order for costs.

(3) Where a rule, practice direction or court order—

(a) requires a party to do something within a specified time; and
(b) specifies the consequence of failure to comply,

the time for doing the act in question may not be extended by agreement between the parties.

4.6 Relief from sanctions

(1) On an application for relief from any sanction imposed for a failure to comply with any rule, practice direction or court order the court will consider all the circumstances including—

(a) the interests of the administration of justice;
(b) whether the application for relief has been made promptly;
(c) whether the failure to comply was intentional;
(d) whether there is a good explanation for the failure;
(e) the extent to which the party in default has complied with other rules, practice directions, court orders and any relevant pre-action protocol[(GL)];
(f) whether the failure to comply was caused by the party or the party's legal representative;
(g) whether the hearing date or the likely hearing date can still be met if relief is granted;
(h) the effect which the failure to comply had on each party; and
(i) the effect which the granting of relief would have on each party or a child whose interest the court considers relevant.

(2) An application for relief must be supported by evidence.

4.7 General power of the court to rectify matters where there has been an error of procedure

Where there has been an error of procedure such as a failure to comply with a rule or practice direction—

(a) the error does not invalidate any step taken in the proceedings unless the court so orders; and
(b) the court may make an order to remedy the error.

4.8 Power of the court to make civil restraint orders

Practice Direction 4B sets out—

(a) the circumstances in which [the court][1] has the power to make a civil restraint order against a party to proceedings;
(b) the procedure where a party applies for a civil restraint order against another party; and
(c) the consequences of the court making a civil restraint order.

Amendment

1 Substituted by the Family Procedure (Amendment No 3) Rules 2013, SI 2013/3204, rr 2, 8.

Practice Direction 4A – Striking out a statement of case

See also Part 4, Practice Direction 4B

This Practice Direction supplements FPR Part 4, rule 4.4 (Power to strike out a statement of case)

Introduction

1.1 Rule 4.4 enables the court to strike out the whole or part of a statement of case which discloses no reasonable grounds for bringing or defending the application (rule 4.4 (1)(a)), or which is an abuse of the process of the court or otherwise likely to obstruct the just disposal of the proceedings (rule 4.4(1)(b)). These powers may be exercised on an application by a party or on the court's own initiative.

1.1A Before exercising these powers the court must take into account any written evidence filed in relation to the application or answer (rule 4.4(1A)). For example, the court must take into account the financial statement (Form E) filed in relation to an application for a property adjustment order, pension sharing order and other financial orders.

1.2 This practice direction sets out the procedure a party should follow to make an application for an order under rule 4.4.

Examples of cases within the rule

2.1 The following are examples of cases where the court may conclude that an application falls within rule 4.4(1)(a)–

(a) those which set out no facts indicating what the application is about;

(b) those which are incoherent and make no sense;

(c) those which contain a coherent set of facts but those facts, even if true, do not disclose any legally recognisable application against the respondent.

2.2 An application may fall within rule 4.4(1)(b) where it cannot be justified, for example because it is frivolous, scurrilous or obviously ill-founded.

2.3 An answer may fall within rule 4.4(1)(a) where it consists of a bare denial or otherwise sets out no coherent statement of facts.

2.4 Omitted.

2.5 The examples set out above are intended only as illustrations.

2.6 Where a rule, practice direction or order states 'shall be struck out or dismissed' or 'will be struck out or dismissed' this means that the order striking out or dismissing the proceedings will itself bring the proceedings to an end and that no further order of the court is required.

Applications which appear to fall within rule 4.4(1)(a) or (b)

3.1 A court officer who is asked to issue an application form but believes the application may fall within rule 4.4(1)(a) or (b) should issue the application form, but may then consult the court (under rule 4.2) before returning the form to the applicant or taking any other step to serve the respondent. The court may of its own initiative make an immediate order designed to ensure that the application is disposed of or (as the case may be) proceeds in a way that accords with the rules.

3.2 The court may allow the applicant a hearing before deciding whether to make such an order.

3.3 Orders the court may make include–

(a) an order that the application be stayed until further order;
(b) an order that the application form be retained by the court and not served until the stay is lifted;
(c) an order that no application by the applicant to lift the stay be heard unless the applicant files such further documents (for example a witness statement or an amended application form) as may be specified in the order.

3.4 Where the court makes any such order or, subsequently, an order lifting the stay, it may give directions about the service on the respondent of the order and any other documents on the court file.

3.5 The fact that the court allows an application referred to it by a court officer to proceed does not prejudice the right of any party to apply for any order against the applicant.

Answers which appear to fall within rule 4.4(1)(a) or (b)

4.1 A court officer may similarly consult the court about any document filed which purports to be an answer and which the officer believes may fall within rule 4.4 (1)(a) or (b).

4.2 If the court decides that the document falls within rule 4.4(1)(a) or (b) it may on its own initiative make an order striking it out. Where the court does so it may extend the time for the respondent to file a proper answer.

4.3 The court may allow the respondent a hearing before deciding whether to make such an order.

4.4 Alternatively the court may make an order requiring the respondent within a stated time to clarify the answer or to give additional information about it. The order may provide that the answer will be struck out if the respondent does not comply.

4.5 The fact that the court does not strike out an answer on its own initiative does not prejudice the right of the applicant to apply for any order against the respondent.

General provisions

5.1 The court may exercise its powers under rule 4.4(1)(a) or (b) on application by a party to the proceedings or on its own initiative at any time.

5.2 Where the court at a hearing strikes out all or part of a party's statement of case it may enter such judgment for the other party as that party appears entitled to.

Applications for orders under rule 4.4(1)

6.1 Attention is drawn to Part 18 (Procedure for Other Applications in Proceedings) and to the practice direction that supplements it. The practice direction requires all applications to be made as soon as possible.

6.2 While many applications under rule 4.4(1) can be made without evidence in support, the applicant should consider whether facts need to be proved and, if so, whether evidence in support should be filed and served.

Practice Direction 4B – Civil restrain orders

See also Part 4, Practice Direction 4a

This Practice Direction supplements FPR rule 4.8

Introduction

1.1 This practice direction applies where the court is considering whether to make–

(a) a limited civil restraint order;
(b) an extended civil restraint order; or
(c) a general civil restraint order,

against a party who has made applications which are totally without merit.

Rules 4.3(7), 4.4(5) and 18.13 provide that where a statement of case or application is struck out or dismissed and is totally without merit, the court order must specify that fact and the court must consider whether to make a civil restraint order. Rule 30.11(5) makes similar provision where the appeal court refuses an application for permission to appeal, strikes out an appellant's notice or dismisses an appeal.

The powers of the court to make civil restraint orders are separate from and do not replace the powers given to the court by section 91(14) of the Children Act 1989.

Limited civil restraint orders

2.1 A limited civil restraint order may be made where a party has made 2 or more applications which are totally without merit.

2.2 Where the court makes a limited civil restraint order, the party against whom the order is made–

(a) will be restrained from making any further applications in the proceedings in which the order is made without first obtaining the permission of a judge identified in the order;
(b) may apply for amendment or discharge of the order, but only with the permission of a judge identified in the order; and
(c) may apply for permission to appeal the order and if permission is granted, may appeal the order.

2.3 Where a party who is subject to a limited civil restraint order–

(a) makes a further application in the proceedings in which the order is made without first obtaining the permission of a judge identified in the order, such application will automatically be dismissed–
    (i) without the judge having to make any further order; and
    (ii) without the need for the other party to respond to it; and
(b) repeatedly makes applications for permission pursuant to that order which are totally without merit, the court may direct that if the party makes any further application for permission which is totally without merit, the decision to dismiss the application will be final and there will be no right of appeal, unless the judge who refused permission grants permission to appeal.

2.4 A party who is subject to a limited civil restraint order may not make an application for permission under paragraphs 2.2(a) or (b) without first serving notice of the application on the other party in accordance with paragraph 2.5.

2.5 A notice under paragraph 2.4 must–

(a) set out the nature and grounds of the application; and
(b) provide the other party with at least 7 days within which to respond.

2.6 An application for permission under paragraphs 2.2(a) or (b)–

(a) must be made in writing;
(b) must include the other party's written response, if any, to the notice served under paragraph 2.4; and
(c) will be determined without a hearing.

2.7 Omitted

2.8 Where a party makes an application for permission under paragraphs 2.2(a) or (b) and permission is refused, any application for permission to appeal–

(a) must be made in writing; and
(b) will be determined without a hearing.

2.9 A limited civil restraint order–

(a) is limited to the particular proceedings in which it is made;
(b) will remain in effect for the duration of the proceedings in which it is made, unless the court orders otherwise; and
(c) must identify the judge or judges to whom an application for permission under paragraphs 2.2(a), 2.2(b) or 2.8 should be made.

Extended civil restraint orders

3.1 An extended civil restraint order may be made where a party has persistently made applications which are totally without merit.

3.2 Unless the court orders otherwise, where the court makes an extended civil restraint order, the party against whom the order is made–

(a) will be restrained from making applications in any court concerning any matter involving or relating to or touching upon or leading to the proceedings in which the order is made without first obtaining the permission of a judge identified in the order;
(b) may apply for amendment or discharge of the order, but only with the permission of a judge identified in the order; and
(c) may apply for permission to appeal the order and if permission is granted, may appeal the order.

3.3 Where a party who is subject to an extended civil restraint order–

(a) makes an application in a court identified in the order concerning any matter involving or relating to or touching upon or leading to the proceedings in which the order is made without first obtaining the permission of a judge identified in the order, the application will automatically be struck out or dismissed–
    (i) without the judge having to make any further order; and
    (ii) without the need for the other party to respond to it; and
(b) repeatedly makes applications for permission pursuant to that order which are totally without merit, the court may direct that if the party makes any further application for permission which is totally without merit, the decision to dismiss the application will be final and there will be no right of appeal, unless the judge who refused permission grants permission to appeal.

3.4 A party who is subject to an extended civil restraint order may not make an application for permission under paragraphs 3.2(a) or (b) without first serving notice of the application on the other party in accordance with paragraph 3.5.

3.5 A notice under paragraph 3.4 must–

(a) set out the nature and grounds of the application; and
(b) provide the other party with at least 7 days within which to respond.

3.6 An application for permission under paragraphs 3.2(a) or (b)–

(a) must be made in writing;
(b) must include the other party's written response, if any, to the notice served under paragraph 3.4; and
(c) will be determined without a hearing.

3.7 Omitted

3.8 Where a party makes an application for permission under paragraphs 3.2(a) or (b) and permission is refused, any application for permission to appeal–

(a) must be made in writing; and
(b) will be determined without a hearing.

3.9 An extended civil restraint order–

(a) will be made for a specified period not exceeding 2 years;
(b) must identify the courts in which the party against whom the order is made is restrained from making applications; and
(c) must identify the judge or judges to whom an application for permission under paragraphs 3.2(a), 3.2(b) or 3.8 should be made.

3.10 The court may extend the duration of an extended civil restraint order, if it considers it appropriate to do so, but the duration of the order must not be extended for a period greater than 2 years on any given occasion.

General civil restraint orders

4.1 A general civil restraint order may be made where, the party against whom the order is made persists in making applications which are totally without merit, in circumstances where an extended civil restraint order would not be sufficient or appropriate.

4.2 Unless the court otherwise orders, where the court makes a general civil restraint order, the party against whom the order is made–

(a) will be restrained from making any application in any court without first obtaining the permission of a judge identified in the order;
(b) may apply for amendment or discharge of the order, but only with the permission of a judge identified in the order; and
(c) may apply for permission to appeal the order and if permission is granted, may appeal the order.

4.3 Where a party who is subject to a general civil restraint order–

(a) makes an application in any court without first obtaining the permission of a judge identified in the order, the application will automatically be struck out or dismissed–
 (i) without the judge having to make any further order; and
 (ii) without the need for the other party to respond to it; and

(b) repeatedly makes applications for permission pursuant to that order which are totally without merit, the court may direct that if the party makes any further application for permission which is totally without merit, the decision to dismiss that application will be final and there will be no right of appeal, unless the judge who refused permission grants permission to appeal.

4.4 A party who is subject to a general civil restraint order may not make an application for permission under paragraphs 4.2(a) or (b) without first serving notice of the application on the other party in accordance with paragraph 4.5.

4.5 A notice under paragraph 4.4 must–

(a) set out the nature and grounds of the application; and
(b) provide the other party with at least 7 days within which to respond.

4.6 An application for permission under paragraphs 4.2(a) or (b)–

(a) must be made in writing;
(b) must include the other party's written response, if any, to the notice served under paragraph 4.4; and
(c) will be determined without a hearing.

4.7 Omitted

4.8 Where a party makes an application for permission under paragraphs 4.2(a) or (b) and permission is refused, any application for permission to appeal–

(a) must be made in writing; and
(b) will be determined without a hearing.

4.9 A general civil restraint order–

(a) will be made for a specified period not exceeding 2 years;
(b) must identify the courts in which the party against whom the order is made is restrained from making applications; and
(c) must identify the judge or judges to whom an application for permission under paragraphs 4.2(a), 4.2(b) or 4.8 should be made.

4.10 The court may extend the duration of a general civil restraint order, if it considers it appropriate to do so, but he duration of the order must not be extended for a period greater than 2 years on any given occasion.

General

5.1 The other party or parties to the proceedings may apply for any civil restraint order.

5.2 An application under paragraph 5.1 must be made using the procedure in Part 18 unless the court otherwise directs and the application must specify which type of civil restraint order is sought.

PART 5
[FORMS, START OF PROCEEDINGS AND COMMUNICATION WITH THE COURT][1]

[5.A.1 Application

(1) This Part is subject to any provision made by or pursuant to Part 41 (proceeding by electronic means).][2]

Amendment

1 Substituted by the Family Procedure (Amendment) Rules 2020, SI 2020/135, rr 2, 5.
2 Inserted by the Family Procedure (Amendment) Rules 2020, SI 2020/135, rr 2, 6.

5.1 Forms

(1) Subject to rule 14.10(2) and (3), the forms referred to in a practice direction, shall be used in the cases to which they apply.

(2) A form may be varied by the court or a party if the variation is required by the circumstances of a particular case.

(3) A form must not be varied so as to leave out any information or guidance which the form gives to the recipient.

(4) Where these rules require a form to be sent by the court or by a party for another party to use, it must be sent without any variation except such as is required by the circumstances of the particular case.

[(5) …[1].][2]

[(6) Nothing in this rule requires a party to reveal any particulars referred to in rule 29.1(1) if notice of those particulars is given to the court in accordance with rule 29.1(2).][3]

Amendment

1 Repealed by the Family Procedure Rules 2010 and Court of Protection Rules 2017 (Amendment) (EU Exit) Regulations 2019, SI 2019/517, rr 2, 5(1), (2).
2 Inserted by the Family Procedure (Amendment) Rules 2011, SI 2011/1328, rr 2, 3, 5.
3 Inserted by the Family Procedure (Amendment) Rules 2012, SI 2012/679, rr 2, 5.

5.2 Documents to be attached to a form

Subject to any rule or practice direction, unless the court directs otherwise, a form must have attached to it any documents which, in the form, are—

(a) stated to be required; or
(b) referred to.

5.3 Proceedings are started by issue of application form

(1) Proceedings are started when a court officer issues an application at the request of the applicant.

(2) An application is issued on the date entered in the application form by the court officer.

(Rule 29.7 requires an application form to be authenticated with the stamp of the court when it is issued)

[(3) Where the application is made …[1] under Article 10 of the 2007 Hague Convention, the applicant is deemed to have requested the issue of the application by virtue of making the application for establishment or modification of a maintenance decision forwarded on his or her behalf by the Lord Chancellor.

(The Lord Chancellor is the Central Authority for England and Wales in relation to the 2007 Hague Convention …[1])][2]

Amendment

1 Repealed by the Family Procedure Rules 2010 and Court of Protection Rules 2017 (Amendment) (EU Exit) Regulations 2019, SI 2019/517, rr 2, 5(1), (3).
2 Inserted by the Family Procedure (Amendment No 4) Rules 2012, SI 2012/2806, rr 2, 3, 6.

[5.4 Where to start proceedings

(1) Where both the family court and the High Court have jurisdiction to deal with a matter, the proceedings relating to that matter must be started in the family court.

(2) Paragraph (1) does not apply where—

(a) proceedings relating to the same parties are already being heard in the High Court;
(b) any rule, other enactment or Practice Direction provides otherwise; or
(c) the court otherwise directs.][1]

Amendment

1 Inserted by the Family Procedure (Amendment No 3) Rules 2013, SI 2013/3204, rr 2, 9.

[5.5 Filing documents with and sending documents to the court by e-mail

(1) A practice direction may make provision for documents to be filed with or sent to the court by e-mail.

(2) Any such practice direction may—

(a) provide that only particular categories of documents may be filed with or sent to the court by such means;
(b) provide that particular provisions only apply in specified courts or court offices; and
(c) specify the requirements that must be fulfilled for any document filed with or sent to the court by such means.][1]

Amendment

1 Inserted by the Family Procedure (Amendment No 3) Rules 2015, SI 2015/1868, rr 2, 4.

[5.6 Documents in the Welsh language

(1) Any document placed before the court in family proceedings in or having a connection with Wales may be in the English or Welsh language.

(2) It is the responsibility of any party if acting in person or of that party's legal representative to inform the court as soon as practicable if documents in the Welsh language will or may be placed before the court, so that appropriate arrangements can be made.][1]

Amendment

1 Inserted by the Family Procedure (Amendment No 2) Rules 2018, SI 2018/1172, rr 2, 4.

[5.7 Communications with the court

(1) Any communication between a party to proceedings and the court must be disclosed to, and if in writing (whether in paper or electronic format) copied to, the other party or parties or their representatives.

(2) Paragraph (1) applies to any communication in which any representation is made to the court on a matter of substance or procedure but does not apply to communications that are purely routine, uncontentious and administrative.

(3) A party is not required under paragraph (1) to disclose or copy a communication if there is a compelling reason for not doing so, and provided that any reason is clearly stated in the communication.

(4) A written communication required under paragraph (1) to be copied to the other party or parties, or their representatives, must state on its face that it is being copied to that person or those persons, stating their identity and capacity.

(5) Unless the court directs otherwise, a written communication which does not comply with paragraph (4) will be returned to the sender without being considered by the court, with a brief explanation of why it is being returned.

(6) In addition to returning a communication under paragraph (5), where a party fails to comply with paragraph (1) the court may, subject to hearing the parties, exercise its case management powers under Part 4.

(7) Paragraph (1) does not apply to communications authorised by a rule or practice direction to be sent to the court without at the same time being provided to the other party or parties or their representatives.][1]

Amendment

1 Inserted by the Family Procedure (Amendment) Rules 2020, SI 2020/135, rr 2, 7.

[5.8 Provision in relation to bulk scanning of documents

(1) A practice direction may make provision for the bulk scanning of documents that are to be filed with, or otherwise sent to, the court.

(2) The practice direction may modify or disapply any provision of these rules.][1]

Amendment

1 Inserted by the Family Procedure (Amendment) Rules 2022, SI 2022/44, rr 2, 5.

Practice Direction 5A – Forms (applicable to applications issued by the court on or after 6 April 2022)

This PD applies to applications issued by the court on or after 6 April 2022. For applications issued by the court before 6 April 2022 see [https://webarchive.nationalarchives.gov.uk/ukgwa/20211201113607/https://www.justice.gov.uk/courts/procedure-rules/family/practice_directions/pd_part_05a].

See also Part 5

This Practice Direction supplements FPR Part 5, rule 5.1 (Forms)

Scope and interpretation

1.1 This Practice Direction lists the forms to be used in family proceedings on or after 6th April 2011. Table 1 lists the forms against the part of the FPR to which they are relevant, and Table 2 lists the forms individually with their description.

1.2 The forms may be –

(a) modified as the circumstances require, provided that all essential information, especially information or guidance which the form gives to the recipient, is included;

(b) expanded to include additional pages where that may be necessary, provided that any additional pages are also verified by a statement of truth.

1.3 Any reference in family proceedings forms to a Part, rule or Practice Direction is to be read as a reference to the equivalent Part, rule or Practice Direction in the FPR and any reference to a Practice Direction in any CPR form used in family proceedings is to be read as a reference to the equivalent Practice Direction in the FPR.

2.1 Omitted

Application notices

2.2 Where an application under the Part 18 procedure is to be made by application notice, the forms to be used are –

(i) subject to sub-paragraph (ia), Form C2 where the application is made in the course of or in connection with proceedings under Part 12;

(ia) Form C650 where the application is to vary or set aside an order made in relation to children where a toxicology test error has been identified and the applicant asserts that this has materially or significantly affected the order;

(ii) Subject to sub-paragraphs (iii) and (iv), Form D11 where the application is made in the course of or in connection with proceedings under Parts 7, 8 or 9;

(iii) Form D650 where the application is to vary or set aside a financial order where a Form E calculator error has been identified in an online HMCTS FormFinder Form E and the applicant asserts that this has materially or significantly affected the order;

(iv) Form D651 where the application is to vary or set aside an order made in financial remedy proceedings where a Form E1 calculator error has been identified in an online HMCTS FormFinder Form E1 and the applicant asserts that this has materially or significantly affected the order;

(v) Form N244 where the application is made in the course of or in connection with appeal proceedings in the family court;

(vi) Form FP244 where the application is made in the course of or in connection with appeal proceedings in the High Court;

(vii) Form FP2 in any other case.

Other Forms

3.1 Other forms may be authorised by practice directions.

Table 1
Index to forms

FPR Part	Forms
Part 3 Alternative Dispute Resolution (Family Mediation)	FM1
Part 6 Service	C9, D5, D89, FL415, FP6
Part 7 Matrimonial and Civil Partnership Proceedings	D6, D8, D8B, D8BN, D8D, D8D Notes, D8N, D8S, D9B, D11, D13B, D20, D36, D36A, D36N, D81,D84, D84NV, D84NVA

FPR Part	Forms
Part 8 Miscellaneous Applications	D50, D50A, D50B, D50C, D50D, D50E, D50F, D50G, D50H, D50J, D50K
Part 8 Chapter 5 Applications for declarations	C63, C64, C65, D70
Part 9 Applications for a Financial Remedy	Form A, Form A1, Form B, Form E, Form E Notes,Form E1, Form E2, Form F, Form I, Form P, Form P1, Form P2, Form PPF, Form PPF1, Form PPF2
Part 10 Applications under Part 4 of the Family Law Act1996	FL401, FL403, FL407, FL415
Part 11 Applications under Part 4A of the Family Law Act 1996 or Part 1 of Schedule 2 to the Female Genital Mutilation Act 2003	FGM001, FGM003, FGM005, FGM006, FGM007, FL401A, FL403A, FL407A, FL430, FL431
Part 12 Applications in respect of children	C1, C1A, C2, C3, C4, C5, C8, C9, C12,C13A, C14, C15, C16, C18, C19, C20,C66, C67, C68, C78, C79, C100, C110A, C(PRA1), C(PRA2) C(PRA3), PLO8, PLO9, PLP10(PLO8 and PLO9 do not apply to Part 4 proceedings)
Part 13 Applications under section 54 of Human Fertilisation and Embryology Act 2008	C51, C52, A64A, A101A
Part 14 Adoption	A4, A5, A50, A51, A52, A53, A54, A55, A56, A57 A58, A59, A60, A61, A62, A63, A50 Notes, A51 Notes, A52 Notes, A53 Notes, A54 Notes, A55 Notes, A56 Notes, A57 Notes, A58 Notes, A59 Notes, A60 Notes, A61 Notes, A62 Notes, A63 Notes, A64, A65, A100, A101, A102, A103, A104, A105, A106, A107
Part 15 Representation of Protected Parties	FP9
Part 16 Representation of children	FP9
Part 18 Applications in proceedings	C2, C650, D11, D650, D651, FP2
Part 19 Alternative Procedure for applications	FP1, FP1A, FP1B, FP3, FP5
Part 22 Evidence	N285
Part 24 Witnesses	FP25
Part 26 Notification of change of solicitor	FP8
Part 28 Costs	D252, D254, D258, D258A, D258B, D258C, D259, Form H, Form H1, N260
Part 30 Appeals	FP161, FP161A, FP162, FP162A, N161, N161A, N161B, N161D, N162, N162A, N162, N164

FPR Part	Forms
Part 31 Registration of Orders under the Hague Convention 1996	C69
Part 32 Registration and Enforcement of Orders	D151
Part 33 Enforcement	D62, N323, N349
Part 34 Reciprocal Enforcement of Maintenance Orders	REMO 1, REMO 2
Part 37 Applications and proceedings in relation to contempt of court	FC600
Part 39	FE15, FE16, FE17
Part 40	FE6, FE7

Table 2

List of Forms

Number	*Name*
A4	Application For Revocation Of An Order Freeing A Child For Adoption
A5	Application For Substitution Of One Adoption Agency For Another
A50	Application for a placement order Section 22 Adoption and Children Act 2002
A51	Application for variation of a placement order Section 23 Adoption and Children Act 2002
A52	Application for revocation of a placement order Section 24 Adoption and Children Act 2002
A53	Application for a contact order Section 26 of the Adoption and Children Act 2002 or an order for contact or prohibiting contact under section 51A of the Adoption and Children Act 2002
A54	Application for variation or revocation of a contact order Section 27(1)(b) or Section 51B(1)(c) Adoption and Children Act 2002
A55	Application for permission to change a child's surname Section 28 Adoption and Children Act 2002
A56	Application for permission to remove a child from the United Kingdom Section 28 Adoption and Children Act 2002
A57	Application for a recovery order Section 41 Adoption and Children Act 2002
A58	Application for an adoption order Section 46 Adoption and Children Act 2002
A59	Application for a Convention adoption order Section 46Adoption and Children Act 2002
A60	Application for an adoption order (excluding a Convention adoption order) where the child is habitually resident outside the British Islands and is brought into the United Kingdom for the purposes of adoption Section 46 Adoption and Children Act 2002

Number	*Name*
A61	Application for an order for parental responsibility prior to adoption abroad Section 84 Adoption and Children Act 2002
A62	Application for a direction under section 88(1) of the Adoption and Children Act 2002
A63	Application for an order to annul a Convention adoption or Convention adoption order or for an overseas adoption or determination under section 91 to cease to be valid Section 89 Adoption and Children Act 2002
A50 Notes	Application for a placement order Section 22 Adoption and Children Act 2002 – Notes on completing the form
A51 Notes	Application for variation of a placement order Section 23 Adoption and Children Act 2002 – Notes on completing the form
A52 Notes	Application for revocation of a placement order Section 24 Adoption and Children Act 2002 – Notes on completing the form
A53 Notes	Application for a contact order Section 26 Adoption and Children Act 2002 or an order under section 51A of the Act – Notes on completing the form
A54 Notes	Application for variation or revocation of a contact order Section 27(1)(b) or section 51B(1)(c) Adoption and Children Act 2002 – Notes on completing the form
A55 Notes	Application for permission to change a child's surname Section 28 Adoption and Children Act 2002 – Notes on completing the form
A56 Notes	Application for permission to remove a child from the United Kingdom Section 28 Adoption and Children Act 2002 – Notes on completing the form
A57 Notes	Application for a recovery order Section 41 Adoption and Children Act 2002 – Notes on completing the form
A58 Notes	Application for an adoption order Section 46 Adoption and Children Act 2002 – Notes on completing the form
A59 Notes	Application for a Convention adoption order Section 46 Adoption and Children Act 2002 – Notes on completing the form
A60 Notes	Application for an adoption order (excluding a Convention adoption order) where the child is habitually resident outside the British Islands and is brought into the United Kingdom for the purposes of adoption Section 46 Adoption and Children Act 2002 – Notes on completing the form
A61 Notes	Application for an order for parental responsibility prior to adoption abroad Section 84 Adoption and Children Act 2002 – Notes on completing the form
A62 Notes	Application for a direction under section 88(1) of the Adoption and Children Act 2002 – Notes on completing the form
A63 Notes	Application for an order to annul a Convention adoption or Convention adoption order or for an overseas adoption or determination under section 91 to cease to be valid Section 89 Adoption and Children Act 2002 – Notes on completing the form

Number	*Name*
A64	Application to receive information from court records Section 60(4) Adoption and Children Act 2002
A64A	Application to receive information from court records about a parental order Section 60(4) Adoption and Children Act 2002
A65	Confidential information
A100	Consent to the placement of my child for adoption with any prospective adopters chosen by the Adoption Agency Section 19 of the Adoption and Children Act 2002
A101	Consent to the placement of my child for adoption with identified prospective adopters Section 19 of the Adoption and Children Act 2002
A101A	Agreement to the making of a parental order in respect of my child Section 54 of the Human Fertilisation and Embryology Act 2008
A102	Consent to the placement of my child for adoption with identified prospective adopter(s) and, if the placement breaks down, with any prospective adopter(s) chosen by the adoption agency Section 19 of the Adoption and Children Act 2002
A103	Advance Consent to Adoption Section 20 of the Adoption and Children Act 2002
A104	Consent to Adoption The Adoption and Children Act2002
A105	Consent to the making of an Order under Section 84 of the Adoption and Children Act 2002
A106	Withdrawal of Consent Sections 19 and 20 of the Adoption and Children Act 2002
A107	Consent by the child's parent to adoption by their partner The Adoption and Children Act 2002
C1	Application for an Order
C1A	Allegations of harm and domestic violence (Supplemental information form)
C2	Application For permission to start proceedings For an order or directions in existing proceedings To be joined as, or cease to be, a party in existing family proceedings under the Children Act1989
C3	Application for an order authorising search for, taking charge of and delivery of child
C4	Application for an order for disclosure of a child's whereabouts
C5	Local Authority application concerning the registration of a child-minder or a provider of day care
C8	Confidential contact details
C9	Statement of service
C12	Supplement for an application for a warrant to assist a person authorised by an Emergency Protection Order

Number	*Name*
C13A	Supplement for an application for a Special Guardianship Order Section 14A Children Act 1989
C14	Supplement for an application for authority to refuse contact with a child in care
C15	Supplement for an application for contact with a child in care
C16	Supplement for an application for a Child Assessment Order
C18	Supplement for an application for a Recovery Order
C19	Application for a warrant of assistance
C20	Supplement for an application for an order to hold a child in Secure Accommodation
C51	Application for a Parental Order Section 54 Human Fertilisation and Embryology Act 2008
C52	Acknowledgement of an application for a Parental Order
C63	Application for declaration of parentage under section55A of the Family Law Act 1986
C64	Application for declaration of legitimacy or legitimation under section 56 (1) (b) and (2) of the Family Law Act 1986
C65	Application for declaration as to adoption effected overseas under section 57 of the Family Law Act 1986
C66	Application for inherent jurisdiction order in relation to children
C67	Application under the Child Abduction and Custody Act 1985
C68	Application for international transfer of jurisdiction to or from England and Wales
C69	Application for registration, recognition or nonrecognition of a judgment under the 1996 Hague Convention
C78	Application for attachment of a warning notice a child arrangements order
C79	Application related to enforcement of a child arrangements order
C100	Application under the Children Act 1989 for a a child arrangements, prohibited steps, specific issue section 8 order or to vary or discharge a section 8 order
C110A	Application for a Care or Supervision Order and other orders under Part 4 of the Children Act 1989 or an Emergency Protection Order under section 44 of the Children Act 1989
C650	Application notice to vary or set aside an order in relation to children (drug and/or alcohol toxicology test after 2010)
C(PRA1)	Parental Responsibility Agreement
C(PRA2)	Step Parent Parental Responsibility Agreement
C(PRA3)	Parental Responsibility Agreement Section 4ZA Children Act 1989 (Acquisition of parental responsibility by second female parent)
D5	Notice to be indorsed on documents served in accordance with rule 6.14
D6	Statement of Reconciliation

Number	*Name*
D8	Application for a divorce or dissolution (ending a civil partnership)
D8B	Answer to a divorce/dissolution/(judicial) separation or application
D8BN	Answer to a nullity application
D8D	Petition for a presumption of death order and dissolution of a civil partnership
D8D Notes	Supporting notes for guidance on completing a petition for a presumption of death order and dissolution of a civil partnership
D8N	Nullity application
D8S	Application for a (judicial) separation
D9B	Particulars of person whose address is being sought where details are unknown
D11	Application Notice
D13B	Statement in support of a request to dispense with service of the divorce/ dissolution /nullity/ (judicial) separation application on the Respondent
D20	Medical Examination: statement of parties & examiner
D36	Notice of Application for Conditional Order to be made final
D36A	Notice of application for a conditional order to be made final (Where the conditional order was made on a joint application, but you wish to make a sole application at this stage)
D36N	Notice of application for a conditional order of nullity to be made final
D50	Notice of application under section 17 of the Married Women's Property Act 1882/section 66 of the Civil Partnership Act 2004
D50A	Notice of proceedings and acknowledgement of service under section 17 of the Married Women's Property Act 1882/section 66 of the Civil Partnership Act 2004
D50B	Application under section 17 of the Married Women's Property Act 1882/section 66 of the Civil Partnership Act 2004/Application to transfer a tenancy under the Family Law Act 1996
D50C	Application on ground of failure to provide maintenance
D50D	Application for alteration of maintenance agreement after the death of one of the parties,under section 36 of the Matrimonial Causes Act 1973/ paragraph 73 of Schedule 5to the Civil Partnership Act 2004
D50E	Application for permission to apply for financial relief after overseas divorce/dissolution etc under section 13 of the Matrimonial and Family Proceedings Act 1984/paragraph 4 of Schedule 7 to the Civil Partnership Act 2004
D50F	Application for financial relief after overseas divorce etc under section 12 of the Matrimonial and Family Proceedings Act1984/paragraph 4 to Schedule 7 to the Civil Partnership Act 2004
D50G	Application to prevent transactions intended to defeat prospective applications for financial relief
D50H	Application for alteration of maintenance agreement during parties lifetime

Number	*Name*
D50J	D50J Application for an order preventing avoidance under section 32L of the Child Support Act 1991
D50K	Notice of Application for Enforcement by such method of enforcement as the court may consider appropriate
D62	Request for issue of Judgment Summons
D70	Application for Declaration of Marital/Civil Partnership Status
D81	Statement of information for a Consent Order in relation to a financial remedy
D84	Application for a conditional order or(judicial) separation order
D84NV	Application for a conditional order of nullity – void marriage/civil partnership
D84NVA	Application for a conditional order of nullity – voidable marriage/civil partnership
D89	Request for personal service by a court bailiff
D151	Application for registration of maintenance order in the family court
D252	Notice of commencement of assessment of bill of costs
D254	Request for a default costs certificate
D258	Request for a detailed assessment of hearing
D258A	Request for detailed assessment (legal aid only)
D258B	Request for detailed assessment (Costs payable out of a fund other than the Community Legal Service Fund)
D258C	Request for detailed assessment hearing pursuant to an order under Part III of the Solicitors Act 1974
D259	Notice of appeal against a detailed assessment(divorce)
D650	Notice of application to vary or set aside a financial order (Form E calculator error)
D651	Notice of application to vary or set aside a financial remedy (Form E1 calculator error)
FC600	Contempt application
FE6	Application for a charging order on land or property
FE7	Application for a charging order on securities
FE15	Request for attachment of earnings order
FE16	Request and result of search in the attachment of earnings index
FE17	Form for replying to an attachment of earnings application (statement of means)
FGM001	Application for a Female Genital Mutilation (FGM) Protection Order
FGM003	Application to vary, extend or discharge a Female Genital Mutilation (FGM) Protection Order
FGM005	Application for a warrant of arrest Female Genital Mutilation Protection Order

Number	*Name*
FGM006	Application for leave to apply for a Female Genital Mutilation (FGM) Protection Order
FGM007	Application to be joined as, or cease to be, a party to a Female Genital Mutilation (FGM) Protection Order
FL401	Application for a non molestation order/an occupation order
FL401A	Application for a Forced Marriage Protection Order
FL403	Application to vary, extend or discharge
FL403A	Application to vary, extend or discharge Forced Marriage Protection Orders
FL407	Applications for warrant of Arrest
FL407A	Application for warrant of arrest for a Forced Marriage Protection Order
FL415	Statement of service
FL430	Application for leave to apply for a Forced Marriage Protection Order
FL431	Application to join/cease as a party to Forced Marriage Protection Proceedings
FM1	Family Mediation Information and Assessment Form FM1
Form A	Notice of [intention to proceed with] a financial application to which the standard procedure applies
Form A1	Notice of [intention to proceed with] a financial application to which the fast-track procedure applies
Form B	Notice of an application to consider the financial position of the Respondent after the divorce/dissolution
Form E	Financial statement For a financial order (other than a variation order) under the Matrimonial Causes Act 1973/Civil Partnership Act 2004 For financial relief after an overseas divorce etc under Part 3 of the Matrimonial and Family Proceedings Act 1984/Schedule 7 to the Civil Partnership Act 2004
Form E Notes	Form E (Financial Statement for a financial order (other than a variation order) or for financial relief after an overseas divorce or dissolution etc) Notes for guidance
Form E1	Financial Statement for a financial remedy (other than a financial order or financial relief after an overseas divorce/dissolution etc) in the family or high court
Form E2	Financial Statement for a variation of an order for a financial remedy
Form F	Notice of allegation in proceedings for financial remedy
Form H	Estimate of costs (financial remedy)
Form H1	Statement of Costs (financial remedy)
Form I	Notice of request for periodical payments order at the same rate as order for interim maintenance pending outcome of proceeding
Form P	Pension inquiry form

Number	*Name*
Form P1	Pension sharing annex
Form P2	Pension attachment annex
Form PPF	Pension Protection Fund Inquiry Form
Form No. 67	Writ of sequestration
Form PPF 1	Pension Protection Fund sharing annex
Form PPF 2	Pension Protection Fund attachment annex
FP1	Application under Part 19 of the Family Procedure Rules 2010
FP1A	Application under Part 19 of the Family Procedure Rules 2010 Notes for applicant on completing the application (Form FP1)
FP1B	Application under Part 19 of the Family Procedure Rules 2010 Notes for respondent
FP2	Application notice Part 18 of the Family Procedure Rules 2010
FP3	Application for injunction (General form)
FP5	Acknowledgment of service Application under Part 19 of the Family Procedure Rules 2010
FP6	Certificate of service
FP8	Notice of change of solicitor
FP9	Certificate of suitability of litigation friend
FP25	Witness Summons
FP161	Appellant's Notice
FP161A	Guidance Notes on completing the FP161 – Appellant's Notice
FP162	Respondent's Notice
FP162A	Guidance Notes on completing the FP162 – Respondent's Notice
FP244	Application Notice
FP244A	Application Notice (FP244) – Notes for Guidance
N161	Appellant's Notice
N161A	Guidance Notes on Completing the Appellant's Notice
N161B	Important Notes for Respondents
N161D	Guidance Notes on completing the form N161 – Appellant's notice (all family proceedings appeals in the Court of Appeal (Civil Division) and the family court)
N162	Respondent's Notice
N162A	Guidance Notes for Completing the Respondent's Notice
N163	Skeleton Argument
N164	Appellant's Notice
N244	Application Notice
N260	Statement of costs (summary assessment)

Number	*Name*
N285	General Affidavit
N323	Request for Warrant of Execution
N349	Application for a third party debt order
PLO8	Standard Directions on Issue
PLO9	Standard Directions at First Appointment
PLP10	Order Menu – Directions Revised Private Law Programme
REMO 1	Notice of Registration
REMO 2	Notice of Refusal of Registration.

Practice Direction 5B – Communication and filing of documents by e-mail

This Practice Direction supplements FPR Part 5, rule 5.5

Chapter 1
Scope and interpretation

1.1 This practice direction provides for communication and filing of documents with the court by e-mail.

1.2 Chapter 2 applies to specified organisations.

1.3 Chapter 3 applies to persons other than specified organisations.

1.4 Chapters 4, 5 and 6 apply to all persons, including specified organisations.

1.5 In this practice direction—

(a) 'specified document' is a document that is—
  (i) related to any family proceedings other than adoption proceedings; and
  (ii) listed in the e-mail guidance on Her Majesty's Courts and Tribunals Service website as a document that may be sent by e-mail to a specified e-mail address;
  (The e-mail guidance can be found at: https://www.justice.gov.uk/courts/email-guidance#canfile)

(b) 'specified e-mail address' is the e-mail address for a court office which has been listed on the Courts and Tribunals Finder website at: https://courttribunalfinder.service.gov.uk/courts/

(c) 'specified organisation' is any of—
  (i) a local authority;
  (ii) Cafcass;
  (iii) CAFCASS Cymru; and

(d) 'urgent application' means an application in which—
  (i) there is risk to the life, liberty or physical safety of a person who is the subject of the application or his or her family or his or her home;
  (ii) any delay in issuing the application could cause—
    (aa) a risk of harm to a child;
    (bb) a risk of unlawful removal of a child from the United Kingdom, or a risk of unlawful retention of a child who is currently outside England and Wales;

(cc) a significant risk of a miscarriage of justice;
(dd) unreasonable hardship to the applicant; or
(ee) irretrievable problems in dealing with the dispute (including the irretrievable loss of significant evidence).

1.6 References in this practice direction to e-mailing a court mean e-mailing a court office at its specified e-mail address.

Chapter 2
Specified organisations and adoption agencies

2.1 Subject to this Chapter, a specified organisation may e-mail a court at the court's specified e-mail address and may attach or include one or more specified documents to or in that e-mail.

2.1A Subject to this Chapter-

(a) a specified organisation;
(b) an adoption agency (other than a local authority) which has taken part at any stage in the arrangements for the adoption of the child; or
(c) a legal representative of a specified organisation or of an adoption agency referred to in sub-paragraph (b),

may email a court at the court's specified email address and attach or include one or more documents related to adoption proceedings.

2.1B Paragraph 2.1A does not apply to an application for an adoption order (section 46 of the 2002 Act).

2.2 If a fee is payable in order for a document to be filed with or accepted by the court, then subject to paragraph 2.3, the specified organisation must, when e-mailing the court—

(a) both-
(i) provide a Fee Account number which the person emailing the court has authority to charge for the applicable fee; and
(ii) authorise the court to charge the applicable fee to that Fee Account; or
(b) outline the preferred method of payment (credit or debit card) and provide the court with a contact number to take payment over the telephone.

2.3 When a specified organisation is e-mailing an urgent application to the court, the specified organisation may undertake to take the steps specified at paragraph 2.2(a) and (b) on the next business day.

(A list of applicable fees can be found here: http://www.justice.gov.uk/courts/fees)

(Further information about using the Fee Account service can be found at: https://www.justice.gov.uk/courts/fees/payment-by-account)

2.4 A court officer must refuse any application or other document, including any attachment, sent to the court by e-mail if—

(a) it does not comply with this Chapter; or
(b) a fee is payable and—
(i) the sender has not complied with paragraph 2.2;
(ii) the sender has complied with paragraph 2.2 but the court has not been able to charge or take the fee; or
(iii) in the case of an urgent application, the sender has not provided the undertaking specified in paragraph 2.3.

Chapter 3
Persons other than specified organisations

3.1 Subject to paragraphs 3.2 – 3.4, a person other than a specified organisation may e-mail the court or attach a specified document to an e-mail to the court.

3.2 If a fee is payable in order for an e-mailed document to be filed with or accepted by the court, the person must, when e-mailing the court—

(a) both-
  (i) provide a Fee Account number which the person has authority to charge for the applicable fee; and
  (ii) authorise the court to charge the applicable fee to that Fee Account; or
(b) outline the preferred method of payment (credit or debit card) and provide the court with a contact number to take payment over the telephone.

(A list of applicable fees can be found here: http://www.justice.gov.uk/courts/fees)

3.3 A person may e-mail the court or attach one or more specified documents to an e-mail to the court provided that—

(a) when printed out on both sides of A4 paper, the following documents together do not exceed 25 sheets of paper in total—
  (i) the e-mail;
  (ii) the attachments, including any document or e-mail embedded in any attachment; and
  (iii) copies of documents in (i) and (ii) that the court would be required to serve, if service by the court is requested or required under the rules;
(b) if the e-mail, including any attachments, is being sent to take a step in proceedings, that step is being taken by only that e-mail and attachments, and no other e-mail or hard copy is being sent as part of that step; and
(c) the total size of the e-mail, including any attachments, does not exceed 10.0 megabytes.

3.4 A court officer must refuse any application or other document, including any attachment, sent to the court by e-mail if—

(a) it does not comply with this Chapter; or
(b) a fee is payable and-
  (i) the sender has not complied with paragraph 3.2; or
  (ii) the sender has complied with paragraph 3.2 but the court has not been able to charge or take the fee.

Chapter 4
Technical specifications

4.1 An e-mail sent to the court must—

(a) contain the name of the sender and an address for contact, which can be an e-mail address; and
(b) be in plain text or rich text format rather than HTML.

(Rule 29.1 specifies the information that a party is not required to reveal, and makes provision for notice by a party to the court where a party does not wish for particulars to be revealed by the court to another person.)

4.2 Subject to this practice direction, correspondence and documents may be sent as either text in the body of an e-mail, or as one or more attachments. Any notice given to the court under rule 29.1 (personal details not to be disclosed) must be sent as a separate attachment to the email and not as part of another attachment.

4.3 Completed forms that are prescribed by a rule or practice direction must be sent as attachments.

4.4 Where a prescribed form requires that one or more documents must be attached to that form, that document or documents must be attached to the e-mail to which the form is attached.

Court forms may be downloaded from HMCTS website at: http://hmctsformfinder.justice.gov.uk/HMCTS/FormFinder.do

4.5 Attachments must be sent in a format supported by the software used by the court to which it is sent.

The format or formats which may be used in sending attachments to a particular specified court are listed in the e-mail guidance on Her Majesty's Courts and Tribunals website. The e-mail guidance can be found at: https://www.justice.gov.uk/courts/email-guidance#canfile

4.6 Where an e-mail relates to existing proceedings, the person sending the e-mail must include the following information in the subject line of the e-mail, to the extent that space allows—

(a) the case number, if one exists;
(b) the parties' names (abbreviated if necessary);
(c) the name of the judge or other person before whom the case has been listed, if known by the person sending the e-mail; and
(d) if applicable, the date and time of any hearing to which the e-mail relates.

Chapter 5
Further provisions

5.1 Where a person sends an e-mail to the court, that person must not send a hard copy of that e-mail or any attachment to the court.

5.3 An application that has been e-mailed to the court is lodged with the court on the date and at the time that HMCTS e-mail software records the e-mail as received, provided that –

(a) the e-mail has been sent in accordance with this practice direction; and
(b) the application is subsequently issued by the court.

5.3A A document, other than an application, that has been e-mailed to the court is filed with or otherwise received by the court on the date and at the time that HMCTS e-mail software records the email as received, provided that the email has been sent in accordance with this practice direction.

5.4 Where a time limit applies to the receipt or filing of a document or application, and the document or application is e-mailed to the court, it remains the responsibility of the person subject to that time limit to ensure that the document or application is sent within applicable time limits taking into account the operation of the practice direction.

5.5 A court officer may reply by e-mail to an e-mail received at a specified e-mail address, where the e-mail or any attachment received relates to proceedings which are not adoption proceedings.

5.6 If a document sent by e-mail requires urgent attention, the sender should contact the court by telephone.

Chapter 6
Statements of truth

6.1 Where a person wishes to file a specified document containing a statement of truth by e-mail, that person should retain the document containing the original signature and file with the court a version of the document satisfying one of the following requirements—

(a) the name of the person who has signed the statement of truth is typed underneath the statement; or

(b) the person who has signed the statement of truth has applied a facsimile of their signature to the statement in the document by mechanical means.

6.2 The court may require a person to produce the document containing the original signature.

Practice Direction 5C – Communications with the court

This practice direction supplements Part 5 of the Family Procedure Rules 2010

1 Rule 5.7(1) FPR 2010 makes provision in relation to the requirement to disclose and, if in writing, to copy any communication with the court to the other parties or their representatives. Exceptions to the requirement are specified in rule 5.7(2), (3) and (7) FPR 2010. This practice direction supplements rule 5.7(7) FPR 2010.

2 Unless the court directs otherwise, the requirement in rule 5.7(1) FPR 2010 does not apply where a communication is sent by a party to proceedings to the court and paragraph 3, 4 or 5 applies.

3 This paragraph applies where the communication relates to proceedings under-

(a) the following provisions of the 2002 Act-
   (i) section 42(6) (permission to apply for an adoption order)
   (ii) section 46 (application for an adoption order);
   (iii) section 51 (adoption by one person);
   (iv) section 51A (post-adoption contact); or
   (v) section 84 (giving parental responsibility prior to adoption abroad);

(b) Part 4A of the 1996 Act (forced marriage); or

(c) Part 1 of Schedule 2 to the Female Genital Mutilation Act 2003.

4 This paragraph applies where the party sending the correspondence has not been provided with an address at which another party may be served with documents relating to the proceedings.

5 This paragraph applies where the party sending the correspondence is prevented by law from contacting another party and that other party is not legally represented. This might be as a result of a requirement imposed on the party sending the correspondence by, for example, a non-molestation order or a restraining order. If the other party is legally represented, then the correspondence must be sent to that legal representative.

6 Where a party relies on an exception to rule 5.7(1) FPR 2010 which is specified in this practice direction, the party must state in the correspondence with the court-

(a) which exception in this practice direction is being relied on; and

(b) why the party considers that the exception applies.

Practice Direction 5D – Procedure for bulk scanning of certain documents

PLEASE NOTE THIS PD COMES INTO FORCE ON 3 APRIL 2022

This Practice Direction supplements rule 5.8 of the Family Procedure Rules 2010

Scope and interpretation

1.1 This Practice Direction makes provision for the bulk scanning by a specified third-party company of certain documents which are required to be filed with or otherwise sent to the court.

1.2 This Practice Direction comes into force on 3 April 2022.

1.3 This Practice Direction applies where all of the following conditions are met-

(a) a document is to be filed with or otherwise sent to the family court;
(b) Her Majesty's Courts and Tribunals Service indicates (whether via information given online, in correspondence or otherwise) that the document must be filed with or sent to the court by sending it to a specified third-party company; and
(c) the document is filed or sent on or after 3 April 2022.

1.4 In this Practice Direction-

'document' means anything in which information of any description is recorded and includes (but is not limited to) an application, a notice, a statement or a letter; and
'specified third-party company' means-

(a) Exela Technologies Limited.

Modification or disapplication of the FPR and Practice Directions, and application of this Practice Direction

2.1 Where this Practice Direction applies, the FPR and the Practice Directions supporting the FPR apply-

(a) subject to the provisions of this Practice Direction; and
(b) as modified by paragraphs 5.1 to 7.1.

Sending documents to a specified-third party company

3.1 Where this Practice Direction applies, subject to paragraph 3.7, any document to be filed with, or otherwise sent to, the court must be sent by post to the address for a specified third-party company to which Her Majesty's Courts and Tribunals Service has indicated that the document should be sent.

(The indication from Her Majesty's Courts and Tribunals Service of the address to which a document should be sent may be via information provided online, in correspondence, or otherwise.)

3.2 An application sent to a specified third-party company in accordance with paragraph 3.1 is treated as lodged with the court on the date of receipt recorded by the specified third-party company, provided that the application is subsequently issued by the court.

3.3 A document other than an application sent to a specified third-party company in accordance with paragraph 3.1 is treated as filed with or otherwise received by the court on the date of receipt recorded by the specified third-party company.

3.4 If a person fails to send a document to a specified third-party company in accordance with paragraph 3.1 and instead sends a document to the court (other than by way of email in accordance with rule 5.5 FPR and Practice Direction 5B), the court may send the document to the specified third-party company.

3.5 The court may also send a document to the specified third-party company where the court considers it appropriate to do so.

3.6 Where paragraph 3.4 or 3.5 applies and the court sends a document to the specified third-party company, paragraphs 3.2 and 3.3 do not apply.

3.7 Nothing in this Practice Direction precludes a document being sent to the court by email, where that is permitted under rule 5.5 FPR and Practice Direction 5B.

3.8 When a document is sent to a specified third-party company in accordance with paragraph 3.1, only one copy of the document should be sent, even if provision in the FPR or another PD requires more than one copy to be sent.

Documents scanned by a specified third-party company

4.1 A scan of a document from a specified third-party company shall be treated by the court as a true copy of the original document.

Modification of rule 2.3(1) of the FPR

5.1 Where this Practice Direction applies, in rule 2.3(1) of the FPR, the definition of 'filing' is modified by inserting after 'office'-

> '(or, where Practice Direction 5D applies, to the address to which HMCTS indicates that a document should be sent)'.

Modification of rule 9.26 of the FPR

6.1 Where this Practice Direction applies, for rule 9.26(1)(a) of the FPR substitute-

'(a) the applicant must file a copy of a draft of the order in the terms sought, endorsed with a statement signed by the respondent to the application signifying agreement; and'.

Modification of Practice Direction 27A – Family Proceedings: Court Bundles (Universal Practice to be applied in the High Court and Family Court)

7.1 Where this Practice Direction applies, Practice Direction 27A is modified as follows-

(a) in paragraph 7.1, for 'The bundle' substitute 'Subject to paragraph 7.2A, the bundle';
(b) in paragraph 7.2(b), for 'Unless' substitute 'Subject to paragraph 7.2A, unless';
(c) after paragraph 7.2, insert-

'7.2A Where Practice Direction 5D applies, if Her Majesty's Courts and Tribunals Service has indicated to a litigant in person that the bundle should be sent to an address for a specified third-party company, the bundle shall be lodged with the court by sending it to that address.'; and

(d) after paragraph 7.3 insert-

'7.3A Any bundle lodged in accordance with paragraph 7.2 shall show the date and place of the hearing on the bundle.'

PART 6
SERVICE

Chapter 1
Scope of this Part and interpretation

6.1 Part 6 rules about service apply generally

This Part applies to the service of documents, except where—

(a) another Part, any other enactment or a practice direction makes a different provision; or
(b) the court directs otherwise.

6.2 Interpretation

In this Part 'solicitor' includes any person who, for the purposes of the Legal Services Act 2007, is an authorised person in relation to an activity which constitutes the conduct of litigation (within the meaning of that Act).

Chapter 2
Service of the application for a matrimonial order or civil partnership order in the jurisdiction

6.3 Interpretation

In this Chapter, unless the context otherwise requires, a reference to an application—

(a) is a reference to an application for a matrimonial or civil partnership order; and
(b) includes an application by a respondent …[1].

[('Jurisdiction' is defined in rule 2.3.)][2]

(Part 7 deals with applications in matrimonial or civil partnership proceedings.)

Amendment

1 Repealed by the Family Procedure (Amendment) Rules 2022, SI 2022/44, rr 2, 6(a).
2 Inserted by the Family Procedure (Amendment) Rules 2022, SI 2022/44, rr 2, 6(b).

6.4 Methods of service

An application may be served by any of the following methods—

(a) personal service in accordance with rule 6.7;
(b) first class post, or other service which provides for delivery on the next business day, in accordance with Practice Direction 6A; …[1]
(c) where rule 6.11 applies, document exchange[; or][2]
[(d) email service in accordance with rule 6.7A.][3]

Amendment

1 Repealed by the Family Procedure (Amendment) Rules 2022, SI 2022/44, rr 2, 7(a).
2 Substituted by the Family Procedure (Amendment) Rules 2022, SI 2022/44, rr 2, 7(b).
3 Inserted by the Family Procedure (Amendment) Rules 2022, SI 2022/44, rr 2, 7(c).

6.5 Who is to serve the application

(1) Subject to the provisions of this rule, an application may be served by—

(a) [a court officer][1]; or
(b) [the applicant][1], if so requested by the applicant.

[(2) A court officer will not serve the application if the party to be served is—

(a) a child or protected party; or
(b) out of the jurisdiction.][1]

(3) An application must not be served personally by the applicant himself or herself.

(Rule 6.14 deals with service of the application on children and protected parties.)

Amendment

1 Substituted by the Family Procedure (Amendment) Rules 2022, SI 2022/44, rr 2, 8.

6.6 …[1] Respondent to be served

The application must be served on [the][2] respondent.

Amendment

1 Repealed by the Family Procedure (Amendment) Rules 2022, SI 2022/44, rr 2, 9(a).
2 Substituted by the Family Procedure (Amendment) Rules 2022, SI 2022/44, rr 2, 9(b).

[6.6A Time for serving an application by the applicant

Where the applicant serves the application, the applicant must complete the step required by the following table in relation to the method of service chosen before 12.00 midnight on the day 28 days after the date of issue of the application.

Method of service	*Step required*
First class post, document exchange or other service which provides for delivery on the next business day	Posting, leaving with, delivering to or collection by the relevant service provider
Personal service under rule 6.7, by someone other than the applicant personally	Leaving it with the person to be served
Email service under rule 6.7A	Sending the application by e-mail and sending the notice required by rule 6.7A(2) by posting, leaving with, delivering to or collection by the relevant service provider][1]

Amendment

1 Inserted by the Family Procedure (Amendment) Rules 2022, SI 2022/44, rr 2, 10.

[6.6B Extension of time for serving the application

(1) The applicant may apply for an order extending the time for compliance with rule 6.6A.

(2) The general rule is that an application under paragraph (1) must be made—

(a) within the period for service specified by rule 6.6A; or
(b) where an order has been made under this rule, within the period specified by that order.

(3) Where an applicant asserts that they have a good reason for not making an application under paragraph (1) within a period specified in paragraph (2) an application under paragraph (1) may be made—

(a) after the period for service specified by rule 6.6A; or
(b) where an order has been made under this rule, after the period specified by that order.

(4) On an application under paragraph (1), the court must consider all the circumstances including whether—

(a) the court has failed to serve the application;
(b) the applicant has taken reasonable steps to comply with rule 6.6A; and
(c) the applicant has acted promptly.

(5) An application for an order extending the time for compliance with rule 6.6A—

(a) must be supported by evidence; and
(b) may be made without notice.

(6) Where an order is made without notice—

(a) a copy of the order; and
(b) a copy of the application for an order extending time together with any statement supporting it,

must be served on the respondent when the application for a matrimonial or civil partnership order is served.][1]

Amendment

1 Inserted by the Family Procedure (Amendment) Rules 2022, SI 2022/44, rr 2, 10.

6.7 Personal service

An application is served personally on a respondent by leaving it with that respondent.

[6.7A Email service

(1) Subject to paragraph (2), an application is served on a respondent by email by sending it to—

(a) the respondent's usual email address; or
(b) the email address provided by the respondent in accordance with rule 6.12.

(2) Where an application is served by email, a notice confirming such service must be sent to the respondent's postal address, by first class post or other service which provides for delivery on the next business day.][1]

Amendment

1 Inserted by the Family Procedure (Amendment) Rules 2022, SI 2022/44, rr 2, 11.

[6.8 Service of application by the court

(1) Where the application is to be served by a court officer, the applicant must give the court officer—

(a) the respondent's usual email address (if known); and
(b) the respondent's last known or usual postal address,

at which the respondent is to be served in accordance with rule 6.4.

(2) Subject to paragraph (3), a court officer will serve the application by email in accordance with rule 6.7A.

(3) Where—

(a) an email address for service on the respondent is not provided; or
(b) the applicant does not seek email service on the respondent,

a court officer will serve the application by first class post or other service which provides for delivery on the next business day.

(4) Where the court officer has sent to the applicant a notification of failure of service in accordance with rule 6.21 (postal service) or 6.21A (email service), the applicant may request the court officer to serve the document on the respondent at an alternative address.

(5) Where the court officer has served the respondent following a request in accordance with paragraph (4), the court will not try to serve the application again.][1]

Amendment

1 Substituted by the Family Procedure (Amendment) Rules 2022, SI 2022/44, rr 2, 12.

6.9 Service by the bailiff

(1) An applicant may request that an application be served by a bailiff delivering a copy of the application to the respondent personally.

(2) The request must be made in accordance with Practice Direction 6A.

(3) Where the bailiff is unable to serve the application, the applicant may apply to the court for an order under rule 6.19 (service by an alternative method or at an alternative place).

(Practice Direction 6A contains provision about when a request under this rule is appropriate.)

(Rule 6.22 provides for notice of non-service by a bailiff.)

6.10 Where to serve the application – general provisions

(1) The application must be served within the jurisdiction except as provided for by Chapter 4 of this Part (service out of the jurisdiction).

[(2) The applicant must include in the application—

(a) an email address (if this is known); and
(b) a postal address,

at which the respondent may be served.][1]

(3) Paragraph (2) does not apply where an order made by the court under rule 6.19 (service by an alternative method or at an alternative place) specifies the place or method of service of the application.

Amendment

1 Substituted by the Family Procedure (Amendment) Rules 2022, SI 2022/44, rr 2, 13.

6.11 Service of the application on a solicitor within the jurisdiction …[1]

(1) Where a solicitor acting for the respondent has notified the applicant in writing that the solicitor is instructed by the respondent to accept service of the application on behalf of the respondent at a business address within the jurisdiction, the application must be served at the business address of that solicitor.

(2) …[1]

('Solicitor' has the extended meaning set out in rule 6.2 …[1].)

Amendment

1 Repealed by the Family Procedure Rules 2010 and Court of Protection Rules 2017 (Amendment) (EU Exit) Regulations 2019, SI 2019/517, rr 2, 6(1), (2).

6.12 Service of the application where the respondent gives an address at which the respondent may be served

Subject to rule 6.13, the respondent may be served with the application at an [email address in accordance with rule 6.7A or at a postal][1] address within the jurisdiction which the respondent has given for the purpose of being served with the proceedings.

Amendment

1 Inserted by the Family Procedure (Amendment) Rules 2022, SI 2022/44, rr 2, 14.

6.13 Service of the application where the respondent does not give an address at which the respondent may be served

(1) This rule applies where—

(a) rule 6.11 (service of application on solicitor); and
(b) rule 6.12 (respondent gives address at which respondent may be served),

do not apply and the applicant does not wish the application to be served personally under rule 6.7.

[(2) Subject to paragraphs (3) to (5) the application must be served on the respondent—

(a) if the respondent's usual email address is known, at that address in accordance with rule 6.7A; or
(b) if that usual email address is not known, or if the applicant does not seek email service on the respondent, at the respondent's usual or last known postal address.][1]

(3) Where the applicant has reason to believe that the respondent no longer resides at his usual or last known [postal][2] address, [or no longer has access to the usual email address,][2] the applicant must take reasonable steps to ascertain the current [postal and email][2] address of the respondent.

(4) Where, having taken the reasonable steps required by paragraph (3), the applicant—

(a) ascertains the respondent's current [email and postal][2] address, the application must be served [in accordance with paragraph (2)][1]; or

(b) is unable to ascertain the respondent's current [email and postal][2] address, the applicant must consider whether there is—
 (i) an alternative place where; or
 (ii) an alternative method by which,

service may be effected.

(5) If, under paragraph (4)(b), there is such a place where or a method by which service could be effected, the applicant must make an application under rule 6.19.

Amendment

1 Substituted by the Family Procedure (Amendment) Rules 2022, SI 2022/44, rr 2, 15(a), (c)(i)(bb).
2 Inserted by the Family Procedure (Amendment) Rules 2022, SI 2022/44, rr 2, 15(b), (c)(i)(aa), (ii).

6.14 Service of the application on children and protected parties

(1) Where the respondent is a child, the application form must be served on—

(a) one of the child's parents or guardians; or
(b) if there is no parent or guardian, an adult with whom the child resides or in whose care the child is.

(2) Where the respondent is a protected party, the application must be served on—

(a) one of the following persons with authority in relation to the protected party—
 (i) the attorney under a registered enduring power of attorney;
 (ii) the donee of a lasting power of attorney; or
 (iii) the deputy appointed by the Court of Protection; or
(b) if there is no such person, an adult with whom the protected party resides or in whose care the protected party is.

(3) Any reference in this Chapter to a respondent or party to be served includes the person to be served with the application form on behalf of a child or protected party under paragraph (1) or (2).

(4) The court may make an order permitting an application form to be served on a child or protected party, or on a person other than the person specified in paragraph (1) or (2).

(5) An application for an order under paragraph (4) may be made without notice.

(6) The court may order that, although an application form has been sent or given to someone other than the person specified in paragraph (1) or (2), it is to be treated as if it had been properly served.

(7) Where a document is served in accordance with this rule—

(a) it must be endorsed with the notice set out in Practice Direction 6A; and
(b) the person commencing the proceedings must file a witness statement by the person on whom the application form was served stating whether—
 (i) the contents of the application form; or
 (ii) the purpose and intention of the application,

were communicated to the child or protected party and, if not, why not.

(8) Paragraph (7)(b) does not apply where the Official Solicitor is, as the case may be—

(a) the litigation friend of the protected party; or
(b) the litigation friend or children's guardian of the child.

6.15 Deemed service – receipt of acknowledgment of service

(1) Subject to paragraph (2), an application is deemed to be served if the acknowledgment of service, signed by the party served or the solicitor acting on that party's behalf, is returned to the court office.

(2) Where the signature on the acknowledgment of service purports to be that of the other party to the marriage or civil partnership, the applicant must prove that it is the signature of that party by—

(a) giving oral evidence to that effect at the hearing; or
(b) if the application is [not disputed][1], confirming it to be so in the [statement][2] the applicant files under rule [7.9(4)][1].

Amendment

1 Substituted by the Family Procedure (Amendment) Rules 2022, SI 2022/44, rr 2, 16.
2 Substituted by the Family Procedure (Amendment) Rules 2012, SI 2012/679, rr 2, 6.

6.16 Deemed service by post or alternative service where no acknowledgment of service filed

(1) Subject to paragraph (2), if—

(a) an application has been served on a respondent by [email in accordance with rule 6.7A or by][1] post or other service which provides for delivery on the next business day;
(b) no acknowledgment of service has been returned to the court office; and
(c) the court is satisfied that the respondent has received the application,

the [court][2] may direct that the application is deemed to be served.

(2) …[3]

Amendment

1 Inserted by the Family Procedure (Amendment) Rules 2022, SI 2022/44, rr 2, 17(a).
2 Substituted by the Family Procedure (Amendment No 3) Rules 2013, SI 2013/3204, rr 2, 10.
3 Repealed by the Family Procedure (Amendment) Rules 2022, SI 2022/44, rr 2, 17(b).

6.17 Proof of personal service where no acknowledgment of service filed

(1) This rule applies where—

(a) an application has been served on a respondent personally; and
(b) no acknowledgment of service has been returned to the court office.

(2) The person serving the application must file a certificate of service stating the date and time of personal service.

(Practice Direction 6A makes provision for a certificate of service by a bailiff.)

(3) If the respondent served was the other party to the marriage or civil partnership, the certificate of service must show the means by which the person serving the application knows the identity of the party served.

6.18 Proof of service by the court etc.

(1) Where a court officer serves an application by post, or other service which provides for delivery on the next business day, the court officer must note in the court records the date of—

(a) posting; or
(b) leaving with, delivering to or collection by the relevant service provider.

[(1A) Where a court officer serves an application by email in accordance with rule 6.7A, the court officer must note in the court records the date and time of the email and the date on which the accompanying notice was posted.][1]

(2) A record made in accordance with paragraph (1) is evidence of the facts stated in it.

(3) This rule does not affect the operation of [section 31N of the 1984 Act][2].

> ([Section 31N of the 1984 Act][2] provides that where a summons or other process issued from [the family court][2] is served by an officer of a court, service may be proved by a certificate in a prescribed form.)

Amendment

1 Inserted by the Family Procedure (Amendment) Rules 2022, SI 2022/44, rr 2, 18.
2 Substituted by the Family Procedure (Amendment No 3) Rules 2013, SI 2013/3204, rr 2, 11.

6.19 Service of the application by an alternative method or at an alternative place

(1) Where it appears to the court that there is a good reason to authorise service by a method or at a place not otherwise permitted by this Part, the court may direct that service is effected by an alternative method or at an alternative place.

(2) On an application under this rule, the court may direct that steps already taken to bring the application form to the attention of the respondent by an alternative method or at an alternative place is good service.

(3) A direction under this rule must specify—

(a) the method or place of service;
(b) the date on which the application form is deemed served; and
(c) the period for filing an acknowledgment of service or answer.

6.20 Power of the court to dispense with service of the application

(1) The court may dispense with service of the application where it is impracticable to serve the application by any method provided for by this Part.

(2) An application for an order to dispense with service may be made at any time and must be supported by evidence.

(3) The court may require the applicant to attend when it decides the application.

6.21 Notification of failure of [postal][1] service by the court

Where—

(a) the court serves the application by post or other service which provides for delivery on the next business day; and
(b) the application is returned to the court,

the court will send notification to the applicant that the application has been returned.

Amendment

1 Inserted by the Family Procedure (Amendment) Rules 2022, SI 2022/44, rr 2, 19.

[6.21A Notification of failure of email service by the court

Where—

(a) the court officer serves the application by email in accordance with rule 6.7A; and

(b) the court is notified that the email was undeliverable,

the court officer will send notification to the applicant that the application was undeliverable.][1]

Amendment

1 Inserted by the Family Procedure (Amendment) Rules 2022, SI 2022/44, rr 2, 20.

6.22 Notice of non-service by bailiff

Where—

(a) the bailiff is to serve an application; and
(b) the bailiff is unable to serve it on the respondent,

the court officer will send notification to the applicant.

Chapter 3

Service of documents other than an application for a matrimonial order or civil partnership order in the United Kingdom

6.23 Method of service

A document may be served by any of the following methods—

(a) personal service, in accordance with rule 6.25;
(b) first class post, document exchange or other service which provides for delivery on the next business day, in accordance with Practice Direction 6A;
(c) leaving it at a place specified in rule 6.26; or
(d) fax or [e-mail][1] in accordance with Practice Direction 6A.

(Rule 6.35 provides for the court to permit service by an alternative method or at an alternative place.)

Amendment

1 Substituted by the Family Procedure (Amendment No 3) Rules 2015, SI 2015/1868, rr 2, 5.

6.24 Who is to serve

(1) A party to proceedings will serve a document which that party has prepared, or which the court has prepared or issued on behalf of that party, except where—

(a) a rule or practice direction provides that the court will serve the document; or
(b) the court directs otherwise.

(2) Where a court officer is to serve a document, it is for the court to decide which method of service is to be used.

(3) Where the court officer is to serve a document prepared by a party, that party must provide a copy for the court and for each party to be served.

6.25 Personal service

(1) Where required by another Part, any other enactment, a practice direction or a court order, a document must be served personally.

(2) In other cases, a document may be served personally except where the party to be served has given an address for service under rule 6.26(2)(a).

(3) A document is served personally on an individual by leaving it with that individual.

6.26 Address for service

(1) A party to proceedings must give an address at which that party may be served with documents relating to those proceedings.

(2) Subject to paragraph (4), a party's address for service must be—

(a) the business address …[1] within the United Kingdom …[1] of a solicitor acting for the party to be served; or

(b) where there is no solicitor acting for the party to be served, an address within the United Kingdom at which the party resides or carries on business.

…[1]

(3) Where there is no solicitor acting for the party to be served and the party does not have an address within the United Kingdom at which that party resides or carries on business, the party must, subject to paragraph (4), give an address for service within the United Kingdom.

(4) A party who—

(a) has been served with an application for a matrimonial or civil partnership order outside the United Kingdom; and

(b) apart from acknowledging service of the application, does not take part in the proceedings,

need not give an address for service within the United Kingdom.

(5) Any document to be served in proceedings must be sent, or transmitted to, or left at, the party's address for service unless it is to be served personally or the court orders otherwise.

(6) Where, in accordance with Practice Direction 6A, a party indicates or is deemed to have indicated that they will accept service by fax, the fax number given by that party must be at the address for service.

(7) Where a party indicates in accordance with Practice Direction 6A, that they will accept service by [e-mail][2], the e-mail address …[3] given by that party will be deemed to be …[3] the address for service.

(8) This rule does not apply where an order made by the court under rule 6.35 (service by an alternative method or at an alternative place) specifies where a document may be served.

Amendment

1 Repealed by the Family Procedure Rules 2010 and Court of Protection Rules 2017 (Amendment) (EU Exit) Regulations 2019, SI 2019/517, rr 2, 6(1), (3).
2 Substituted by the Family Procedure (Amendment No 3) Rules 2015, SI 2015/1868, rr 2, 6(a).
3 Repealed by the Family Procedure (Amendment No 3) Rules 2015, SI 2015/1868, rr 2, 6(b), (c).

6.27 Change of address for service

Where the address for service of a party changes, that party must give notice in writing of the change, as soon as it has taken place, to the court and every other party.

6.28 Service of an application form commencing proceedings on children and protected parties

(1) This rule applies to the service of an application form commencing proceedings other than an application for a matrimonial or civil partnership order.

(2) An application form commencing proceedings which would otherwise be served on a child or protected party must be served—

(a) where the respondent is a child, in accordance with rule 6.14(1); and
(b) where the respondent is a protected party, in accordance with rule 6.14(2).

6.29 Service of other documents on or by children and protected parties where a litigation friend has been or will be appointed

(1) This rule applies to—

(a) a protected party; or
(b) a child to whom the provisions of rule 16.5 and Chapter 5 of Part 16 apply (litigation friends).

(2) An application for an order appointing a litigation friend where a protected party or child has no litigation friend must be served in accordance with rule 15.8 or rule 16.13 as the case may be.

(3) Any other document which would otherwise be served on or by a child or protected party must be served on or by the litigation friend conducting the proceedings on behalf of the child or protected party.

6.30 Service on or by children where a children's guardian has been or will be appointed under rule 16.4

(1) This rule applies to a child to whom the provisions of rule 16.4 and Chapter 7 apply.

(2) An application for an order appointing a children's guardian where a child has no children's guardian must be served in accordance with rule 16.26.

(3) Any other document which would otherwise be served on or by a child must be served on or by the children's guardian conducting the proceedings on behalf of the child.

6.31 Service on or by children where a children's guardian has been appointed under rule 16.3

(1) This rule applies where a children's guardian has been appointed for a child in accordance with rule 16.3.

(2) Any document which would otherwise be served on the child must be served on—

(a) the solicitor appointed by the court in accordance with section 41(3) of the 1989 Act; and
(b) the children's guardian.

(3) Any document which would otherwise be served by the child must be served by—

(a) the solicitor appointed by the court in accordance with section 41(3) of the 1989 Act or by the children's guardian; or
(b) if no solicitor has been appointed as mentioned in paragraph (a), the children's guardian.

6.32 Supplementary provisions relating to service on children and protected parties

(1) The court may direct that a document be served on a protected party or child or on some person other than a person upon whom it would be served under rules 6.28 to 6.31 above.

(2) The court may direct that, although a document has been sent or given to someone other than a person upon whom it should be served under rules 6.28 to 6.31 above, the document is to be treated as if it had been properly served.

(3) This rule and rules 6.28 to 6.31 do not apply where the court has made an order under rule 16.6 allowing a child to conduct proceedings without a children's guardian or litigation friend.

6.33 Supplementary provision relating to service on children

(1) This rule applies to proceedings to which Part 12 applies.

(2) Where a rule requires—

(a) a document to be served on a party;
(b) a party to be notified of any matter; or
(c) a party to be supplied with a copy of a document,

in addition to the persons to be served in accordance with rules 6.28 to 6.32, the persons or bodies mentioned in paragraph (3) must be served, notified or supplied with a copy of a document, as applicable, unless the court directs otherwise.

(3) The persons or bodies referred to in paragraph (2) are—

(a) such of the following who are appointed in the proceedings—
  (i) the children's guardian (if the children's guardian is not otherwise to be served);
  (ii) the welfare officer;
  (iii) the children and family reporter;
  (iv) the officer of the Service, Welsh family proceedings officer or local authority officer acting under a duty referred to in rule 16.38; and
(b) a local authority preparing a report under section 14A(8) or (9) of the 1989 Act.

6.34 Deemed service

A document, other than an application for a matrimonial or civil partnership order, served in accordance with these rules or a practice direction is deemed to be served on the day shown in the following table—

Method of service	Deemed day of service
First class post (or other service which provides for delivery on the next business day)	The second day after it was posted, left with, delivered to or collected by the relevant service provider, provided that day is a business day; or, if not, the next business day after that day.
Document exchange	The second day after it was left with, delivered to or collected by the relevant service provider, provided that day is a business day; or, if not, the next business day after that day.
Delivering the document to or leaving it at a permitted address.	If it is delivered to or left at the permitted address on a business day before 4.30 p.m., on that day; or in any other case, on the next business day after that day.
Fax.	If the transmission of the fax is completed on a business day before 4.30 p.m., on that day; or, in any other case, the next business day after the day on which it was transmitted.
Other electronic method.	If the e-mail or other electronic transmission is sent on a business day before 4.30 p.m., on that day; or in any other case, on the next business day after the day on which it was sent.
Personal service	If the document is served personally before 4.30 p.m. on a business day, on that day; or, in any other case, on the next business day after that day.

(Practice Direction 6A contains examples of how the date of deemed service is calculated.)

6.35 Service by an alternative method or at an alternative place

Rule 6.19 applies to any document in proceedings as it applies to an application for a matrimonial or civil partnership order and reference to the respondent in that rule is modified accordingly.

6.36 Power to dispense with service

The court may dispense with the service of any document which is to be served in proceedings.

6.37 Certificate of service

(1) Where a rule, practice direction or court order requires a certificate of service, the certificate must state the details set out in the following table—

Method of service	*Details to be certified*
Personal service.	Date and time of personal service and method of identifying the person served.
First class post, document exchange or other service which provides for delivery on the next business day.	Date of posting, leaving with, delivering to or collection by the relevant service provider.
Delivery of document to or leaving it at a permitted place.	Date and time when the document was delivered to or left at the permitted place.

Method of service	*Details to be certified*
Fax.	Date and time of completion of transmission.
Other electronic method	Date and time of sending the email or other electronic transmission.
Alternative method or place permitted by court	As required by the court.

(2) An applicant who is required to file a certificate of service of an application form must do so at or before the earlier of—

(a) the first directions appointment in; or
(b) the hearing of,

the proceedings unless a rule or practice direction provides otherwise.

(Rule 17.2 requires a certificate of service to contain a statement of truth.)

6.38 Notification of outcome of service by the court

Where—

(a) a document to be served by a court officer is served by post or other service which provides for delivery on the next working day; and
(b) the document is returned to the court,

the court officer will send notification to the party who requested service that the document has been returned.

6.39 Notification of non-service by bailiff

Where—

(a) the bailiff is to serve a document; and
(b) the bailiff is unable to serve it,

the court officer must send notification to the party who requested service.

Chapter 4
Service out of the jurisdiction

6.40 Scope and interpretation

(1) This Chapter contains rules about—

(a) service of application forms and other documents out of the jurisdiction; and
(b) the procedure for service.

('Jurisdiction' is defined in rule 2.3.)

(2) In this Chapter—

'application form' includes an application notice;

'Commonwealth State' means a State listed in Schedule 3 to the British Nationality Act 1981; and

'the Hague Convention' means the Convention on the service abroad of judicial and extrajudicial documents in civil or commercial matters signed at the Hague on November 15, 1965.

6.41 Permission to serve not required

Any document to be served for the purposes of these rules may be served out of the jurisdiction without the permission of the court.

[6.41A Time for serving an application for a matrimonial or civil partnership order out of the jurisdiction

(1) The applicant must complete the step required by the table in paragraph (2) or (3), as applicable, in relation to the method of service chosen before 12.00 midnight on the day 28 days after the date of issue of the application.

(2) Where service of an application for a matrimonial or civil partnership order is to be effected on a party in Scotland or Northern Ireland—

Method of service	*Step required*
First class post, document exchange or other service which provides for delivery on the next business day	Posting, leaving with, delivering to or collection by the relevant service provider
Personal service under rule 6.7, by someone other than the applicant personally	Leaving it with the person to be served
Email service under rule 6.7A	Sending the application by e-mail and sending the notice required by rule 6.7A(2) by posting, leaving with, delivering to or collection by the relevant service provider

(3) Where service of an application for a matrimonial or civil partnership order is to be effected on a respondent out of the United Kingdom—

Method of service	*Step required*
Where service is to be effected by a method provided for by rule 6.45	The steps required by rule 6.46(2)
Where service is to be effected by another method permitted by the law of the country in which it is to be served	Sending or delivering the application to, or leaving it with, the person to be served or taking such other such steps to effect service as are permitted by the law of the country in which it is to be served][1]

Amendment

1 Inserted by the Family Procedure (Amendment) Rules 2022, SI 2022/44, rr 2, 21.

[6.41B Extension of time for serving the application for a matrimonial or civil partnership order

(1) The applicant may apply for an order extending the time for compliance with rule 6.41A.

(2) The general rule is that an application under paragraph (1) must be made—

(a) within the period for service specified by rule 6.41A; or
(b) where an order has been made under this rule, within the period specified by that order.

(3) Where an applicant asserts that they have a good reason for not making an application under paragraph (1) within the periods specified in paragraph (2) an application under paragraph (1) may be made—

(a) after the period for service specified by rule 6.41A; or
(b) where an order has been made under this rule, after the period specified by that order.

(4) On an application under paragraph (1), the court must consider all the circumstances including whether—

(a) the applicant has taken reasonable steps to comply with rule 6.41A; and
(b) the applicant has acted promptly.

(5) An application for an order extending the time for compliance with rule 6.41A—

(a) must be supported by evidence; and
(b) may be made without notice.][1]

Amendment

1 Inserted by the Family Procedure (Amendment) Rules 2022, SI 2022/44, rr 2, 21.

6.42 Period for acknowledging service or responding to application where application is served out of the jurisdiction

(1) This rule applies where, under these rules, a party is required to file—

(a) an acknowledgment of service; or
(b) an answer to an application,

and sets out the time period for doing so where the application is served out of the jurisdiction.

(2) Where the applicant serves an application on a respondent in—

(a) Scotland or Northern Ireland; or
(b) …[1] Hague Convention country within Europe,

the period for filing an acknowledgment of service or an answer to an application is 21 days after service of the application.

(3) Where the applicant serves an application on a respondent in a Hague Convention country outside Europe, the period for filing an acknowledgment of service or an answer to an application is 31 days after service of the application.

(4) Where the applicant serves an application on a respondent in a country not referred to in paragraphs (2) and (3), the period for filing an acknowledgment of service or an answer to an application is set out in Practice Direction 6B.

Amendment

1 Repealed by the Family Procedure Rules 2010 and Court of Protection Rules 2017 (Amendment) (EU Exit) Regulations 2019, SI 2019/517, rr 2, 6(1), (4).

6.43 Method of service – general provisions

(1) This rule contains general provisions about the method of service of an application for a matrimonial or civil partnership order, or other document, on a party out of the jurisdiction.

Where service is to be effected on a party in Scotland or Northern Ireland

(2) Where a party serves an application form or other document on a party in Scotland or Northern Ireland, it must be served by a method permitted by Chapter 2 (and references to 'jurisdiction' in that Chapter are modified accordingly) or Chapter 3 of this Part and rule 6.26(5) applies.

Where service is to be effected on a respondent out of the United Kingdom

(3) Where the applicant wishes to serve an application form, or other document, on a respondent out of the United Kingdom, it may be served by any method—

[(a) provided for by rule 6.45 (service through foreign governments, judicial authorities and British Consular authorities); or][1]
(b) permitted by the law of the country in which it is to be served.

(4) Nothing in paragraph (3) or in any court order authorises or requires any person to do anything which is contrary to the law of the country where the application form, or other document, is to be served.

Amendment

1 Substituted by the Family Procedure (Amendment) Rules 2021, SI 2021/155, rr 2, 3.

6.44 …[1]

…[1]

Amendment

1 Repealed by the Family Procedure Rules 2010 and Court of Protection Rules 2017 (Amendment) (EU Exit) Regulations 2019, SI 2019/517, rr 2, 6(1), (6).

6.45 Service through foreign governments, judicial authorities and British Consular authorities

(1) Where the applicant wishes to serve an application form, or other document, on a respondent in any country which is a party to the Hague Convention, it may be served—

(a) through the authority designated under the Hague Convention in respect of that country; or
(b) if the law of that country permits—
 (i) through the judicial authorities of that country; or
 (ii) through a British Consular authority in that country.

(2) Where the applicant wishes to serve an application form, or other document, on a respondent in any country which is not a party to the Hague Convention, it may be served, if the law of that country so permits—

(a) through the government of that country, where that government is willing to serve it; or
(b) through a British Consular authority in that country.

(3) Where the applicant wishes to serve an application form, or other document, in—

(a) any Commonwealth State which is not a party to the Hague Convention;
(b) the Isle of Man or the Channel Islands; or
(c) any British Overseas Territory,

the methods of service permitted by paragraphs (1)(b) and (2) are not available and the applicant or the applicant's agent must effect service on a respondent in accordance with rule 6.43 unless Practice Direction 6B provides otherwise.

(4) …[1]

(A list of British overseas territories is reproduced in Practice Direction 6B.)

Amendment

1 Repealed by the Family Procedure Rules 2010 and Court of Protection Rules 2017 (Amendment) (EU Exit) Regulations 2019, SI 2019/517, rr 2, 6(1), (7).

6.46 Procedure where service is to be through foreign governments, judicial authorities and British Consular authorities

(1) This rule applies where the applicant wishes to serve an application form, or other document, under rule 6.45(1) or (2).

(2) Where this rule applies, the applicant must file—

- (a) a request for service of the application form, or other document, by specifying one or more of the methods in rule 6.45(1) or (2);
- (b) a copy of the application form or other document;
- (c) any other documents or copies of documents required by Practice Direction 6B; and
- (d) any translation required under rule 6.47.

(3) When the applicant files the documents specified in paragraph (2), the court officer will—

- (a) seal[(GL)], or otherwise authenticate with the stamp of the court, the copy of the application form or other document; and
- (b) forward the documents to the Senior Master of the Queen's Bench Division.

(4) The Senior Master will send documents forwarded under this rule—

- (a) where the application form, or other document, is being served through the authority designated under the Hague Convention, to that authority; or
- (b) in any other case, to [the Foreign, Commonwealth and Development Office][1] with a request that it arranges for the application form or other document to be served.

(5) An official certificate which—

- (a) states that the method requested under paragraph (2)(a) has been performed and the date of such performance;
- (b) states, where more than one method is requested under paragraph (2)(a), which method was used; and
- (c) is made by—
  - (i) a British Consular authority in the country where the method requested under paragraph (2)(a) was performed;
  - (ii) the government or judicial authorities in that country; or
  - (iii) the authority designated in respect of that country under the Hague Convention,

is evidence of the facts stated in the certificate.

(6) A document purporting to be an official certificate under paragraph (5) is to be treated as such a certificate, unless it is proved not to be.

Amendment

1 Substituted by the Transfer of Functions (Secretary of State for Foreign, Commonwealth and Development Affairs) Order 2020, SI 2020/942, art 9, Schedule, para 18(a).

6.47 Translation of application form or other document

(1) Except where paragraphs (4) and (5) apply, every copy of the application form, or other document, filed under rule 6.45 (service through foreign governments, judicial authorities and British Consular authorities) must be accompanied by a translation of the application form or other document.

(2) The translation must be—

(a) in the official language of the country in which it is to be served; or
(b) if there is more than one official language of that country, in any official language which is appropriate to the place in the country where the application form or other document is to be served.

(3) Every translation filed under this rule must be accompanied by a statement by the person making it that it is a correct translation, and the statement must include that person's name, address and qualifications for making the translation.

(4) The applicant is not required to file a translation of the application form, or other document, filed under rule 6.45 where it is to be served in a country of which English is an official language.

(5) The applicant is not required to file a translation of the application form or other document filed under rule 6.45 where—

(a) the person on whom the document is to be served is able to read and understand English; and
(b) service of the document is to be effected directly on that person.

…[1]

Amendment

1 Repealed by the Family Procedure Rules 2010 and Court of Protection Rules 2017 (Amendment) (EU Exit) Regulations 2019, SI 2019/517, rr 2, 6(1), (8).

6.48 Undertaking to be responsible for expenses of the Foreign and Commonwealth Office

Every request for service filed under rule 6.46 (procedure where service is to be through foreign governments, judicial authorities etc.) must contain an undertaking by the person making the request—

(a) to be responsible for all expenses incurred by [the Foreign, Commonwealth and Development Office][1] or foreign judicial authority; and
(b) to pay those expenses to [the Foreign, Commonwealth and Development Office][1] or foreign judicial authority on being informed of the amount.

Amendment

1 Substituted by the Transfer of Functions (Secretary of State for Foreign, Commonwealth and Development Affairs) Order 2020, SI 2020/942, art 9, Schedule, para 18(b).

Practice Direction 6A – Service within the jurisdiction (applicable to applications issued by the court on or after 6 April 2022)

This PD applies to applications issued by the court on or after 6 April 2022. For applications issued by the court before 6 April 2022 see [https://webarchive.nationalarchives.gov.uk/ukgwa/20211201114143/https://www.justice.gov.uk/courts/procedure-rules/family/practice_directions/pd_part_06a].

See also Part 6, Practice Direction 6B, Practice Direction 6C

This Practice Direction Supplements FPR Part 6, Chapters 2 and 3

General Provisions

Scope of this Practice Direction

1.1 This Practice Direction supplements the following provisions of Part 6 –

(a) Chapter 2 (service of the application for a matrimonial order or civil partnership order in the jurisdiction);
(b) Chapter 3 (service of documents other than an application for a matrimonial order or civil partnership order in the United Kingdom); and
(c) rule 6.43(2) in relation to the method of service on a party in Scotland or Northern Ireland.

(Practice Direction B supplementing Part 6 contains provisions relevant to service on a party in Scotland or Northern Ireland, including provisions about the period for responding to an application notice.)

When service may be by document exchange

2.1 Subject to the provisions of rule 6.4 (which provides when an application for a matrimonial or civil partnership order may be served by document exchange) service by document exchange (DX) may take place only where –

(a) the address at which the party is to be served includes a numbered box at a DX; or
(b) the writing paper of the party who is to be served or of the solicitor acting for that party sets out a DX box number; and
(c) the party or the solicitor acting for that party has not indicated in writing that they are unwilling to accept service by DX.

How service is effected by post, an alternative service provider or DX

3.1 Service by post, DX or other service which provides for delivery on the next business day is effected by –

(a) placing the document in a post box;
(b) leaving the document with or delivering the document to the relevant service provider; or
(c) having the document collected by the relevant service provider.

Service by fax or e-mail

4.1 Paragraphs 4.2 to 4.6 apply to the service by the court or by a party of a document other than an application for a matrimonial or civil partnership order and documents in adoption proceedings and parental order proceedings.

4.2 Subject to the provisions of rule 6.26(6) and (7), where a document is to be served by fax or e-mail –

(a) the party who is to be served or the solicitor acting for that party must previously have indicated in writing to the court or party serving, whichever is applicable –
  (i) that the party to be served or the solicitor is willing to accept service by fax or e-mail; and
  (ii) the fax number or e-mail address to which it must be sent; and
(b) the following are to be taken as sufficient written indications for the purposes of paragraph 4.2(a) –
  (i) a fax number set out on the letterhead or website of the solicitor acting for the party to be served;
  (ii) an e-mail address set out on the letterhead or website of the solicitor acting for the party to be served but only where it is stated that the e-mail address may be used for service;
  (iii) a fax number or e-mail address set out on a statement of case or an answer to a claim filed with the court by the party to be served; or
  (iv) an e-mail or other correspondence from the party to be served, to the court or party serving, confirming that they are willing to accept service by e-mail.

4.3 Where a party intends to—

(a) serve a document by e-mail; or
(b) request that the court serve a document by e-mail that party must first ask the party who is to be served whether there are any limitations to the recipient's agreement to accept service by such means (for example, the format in which documents are to be sent and the maximum size of attachments that may be received).

4.4 Where a document is served by e-mail, the party serving the document need not in addition send or deliver a hard copy.

4.5 Where a party requests the court to serve a document by e-mail and has received notification of limitations to the recipient's agreement to accept service pursuant to paragraph 4.3, that party must communicate those limitations to the court when requesting the court to serve.

4.6 Where limitations have been communicated by a party pursuant to paragraph 4.3, service on that party must comply with those limitations.

Service by email of an application for a matrimonial order or civil partnership order in the jurisdiction under rule 6.7A

4A.1 Where the respondent does not provide an email address rule 6.7A provides for email service by sending it to the respondent's usual email address. This is generally considered to be the email address actively used by the respondent for personal emails. Email service to a respondent's business email address should be avoided where possible

Service on members of the Regular Forces and United States Air Force

5.1 The provisions that apply to service on members of the regular forces (within the meaning of the Armed Forces Act 2006) and members of the United States Air Force are annexed to this practice direction.

Application for an order for service by an alternative method or at an alternative place

6.1 An application for an order under rule 6.19 may be made without notice.

6.2 Where an application for an order under rule 6.19 is made before the document is served, the application must be supported by evidence stating –

(a) the reason why an order is sought;
(b) what alternative method or place is proposed; and
(c) why the applicant believes that the document is likely to reach the person to be served by the method or at the place proposed.

6.3 Where the application for an order is made after the applicant has taken steps to bring the document to the attention of the person to be served by an alternative method or at an alternative place, the application must be supported by evidence stating –

(a) the reason why the order is sought;
(b) what alternative method or alternative place was used;
(c) when the alternative method or place was used; and
(d) why the applicant believes that the document is likely to have reached the person to be served by the alternative method or at the alternative place.

6.4 Examples –

(a) an application to serve by posting or delivering to an address of a person who knows the other party must be supported by evidence that if posted or delivered to that address, the document is likely to be brought to the attention of the other party;
(b) an application to serve by sending a SMS text message or leaving a voicemail message at a particular telephone number saying where the document is must be accompanied by evidence that the person serving the document has taken, or will take, appropriate steps to ensure that the party being served is using that telephone number and is likely to receive the message.

Applications for an order to dispense with service

7.1 An application for an order under rule 6.36 (power to dispense with service) may be made without notice.

Deemed service of a document other than an application for a matrimonial or civil partnership order

8.1 Rule 6.34 contains provisions about deemed service of a document other than an application for a matrimonial or civil partnership order. Examples of how deemed service is calculated are set out below.

Example 1

8.2 Where the document is posted (by first class post) on a Monday (a business day), the day of deemed service is the following Wednesday (a business day).

Example 2

8.3 Where the document is left in a numbered box at the DX on a Friday (a business day), the day of deemed service is the following Monday (a business day).

Example 3

8.4 Where the document is sent by fax on a Saturday and the transmission of that fax is completed by 4.30p.m. on that day, the day of deemed service is the following Monday (a business day).

Example 4

8.5 Where the document is served personally before 4.30p.m. on a Sunday, the day of deemed service is the next day (Monday, a business day).

Example 5

8.6 Where the document is delivered to a permitted address after 4.30p.m. on the Thursday (a business day) before Good Friday, the day of deemed service is the following Tuesday (a business day) as the Monday is a bank holiday.

Example 6

8.7 Where the document is posted (by first class post) on a bank holiday Monday, the day of deemed service is the following Wednesday (a business day).

Service of application on children and protected parties

9.1 Rule 16.14(1) and (2) are applied to service of an application form (other than an application for a matrimonial or civil partnership order) commencing proceedings on children and protected parties by rule 6.28. Rule 6.14(7) makes provision as to how an application form must be served where the respondent is a child or protected party. A document served in accordance with rule 6.14(7) must be endorsed with the following notice which is set out in Form D5 –

Important Notice

The contents or purport of this document are to be communicated to the Respondent

[or as the case may be], [full name of Respondent]

if s/he is over 16 [add if the person to be served lacks capacity within the meaning of the Mental Capacity Act 2005 to conduct the proceedings] unless you are satisfied [after consultation with the responsible medical officer within the meaning of the Mental Health Act 1983 or, if s/he is not liable to be detained or subject to guardianship under that Act, his/her medical attendant]* that communication will be detrimental to his/her mental condition].

Provisions Relating to Applications for Matrimonial and Civil Partnership Orders

Acknowledgment of service to be sent to applicant

10.1 Where the court office receives an acknowledgment of service the court officer must send a photographic or scanned copy of it to the applicant.

Personal service of application by bailiff

11.1 The court will only consider a request for personal service of the application by a bailiff if the address for service is in England and Wales.

11.2 In normal circumstances, a request should only be made if email service (if applicable) and postal service has been attempted. In this case, if –

(a) a signed acknowledgment of service is not returned to the court within 14 days after posting; and
(b) the applicant reasonably believes the respondent is still living at the stated address,

the applicant may make a request to the court for personal service by a bailiff.

11.3 A request for personal service by a bailiff should be made in writing to the court officer on the prescribed form and accompanied by the relevant fee. The request should also be accompanied by –

(a) evidence that email service (if applicable) and postal service has been attempted and failed; or
(b) if postal service has not been attempted, an explanation as to why postal service is not considered appropriate in the circumstances of the case.

11.4 A request will rarely be granted where the applicant is legally represented and it will be necessary for the representative to show why service by bailiff is required rather than by a process server.

Proof of personal service by bailiff

12.1 Once service of the application has been effected or attempted by the bailiff he must file a certificate of service in the issuing court.

12.2 If the respondent fails to sign and return an acknowledgment of service to the court office and –

(a) the certificate contains a signature of receipt of the application by the respondent; or
(b) the identity of the respondent is to be proved by a photograph supplied by the applicant,

the applicant must prove the signature or photograph in the statement filed by the applicant under rule 7.19(4).

13.1 Omitted

Service of application on children and protected parties

14.1 A document served in accordance with rule 6.14(7) must be endorsed with the notice contained in paragraph 9.1.

Annex

Service on Members of the Regular Forces

1 The following information is for litigants and legal representatives who wish to serve legal documents in civil proceedings in the courts of England and Wales on parties to the proceedings who are (or who, at the material time, were) members of the regular forces (as defined in the Armed Forces Act 2006).

2 The proceedings may take place in the family court or the High Court, and the documents to be served may be claim forms, interim application notices and pre-action application notices. Proceedings for divorce or maintenance and proceedings in the Family

Courts generally are subject to special rules as to service which are explained in a practice direction issued by the Senior District Judge of the Principal Registry on 26 June 1979.

(now see Practice Direction 1 Maintenance Orders:Service Personnel:2 Disclosure of Addresses (1995)2FLR 813.)

3 In this Annex, the person wishing to effect service is referred to as the 'claimant' and the member of the regular forces to be served is referred to as 'the member'; the expression 'overseas' means outside the United Kingdom.

Enquiries as to address

4 As a first step, the claimant's legal representative will need to find out where the member is serving, if this is not already known. For this purpose the claimant's legal representative should write to the appropriate officer of the Ministry of Defence as specified in paragraph 10 below.

5 The letter of enquiry should in every case show that the writer is a legal representative and that the enquiry is made solely with a view to the service of legal documents in civil proceedings.

6 In all cases the letter must give the full name, service number, rank or rate, and Ship, Arm or Trade, Regiment or Corps and Unit or as much of this information as is available. Failure to quote the service number and the rank or rate may result either in failure to identify the member or in considerable delay.

7 The letter must contain an undertaking by the legal representative that, if the address is given, it will be used solely for the purpose of issuing and serving documents in the proceedings and that so far as is possible the legal representative will disclose the address only to the court and not to the claimant or to any other person or body. A legal representative in the service of a public authority or private company must undertake that the address will be used solely for the purpose of issuing and serving documents in the proceedings and that the address will not be disclosed so far as is possible to any other part of the legal representative's employing organisation or to any other person but only to the court. Normally on receipt of the required information and undertaking the appropriate office will give the service address.

8 If the legal representative does not give the undertaking, the only information that will be given is whether the member is at that time serving in England or Wales, Scotland, Northern Ireland or overseas.

9 It should be noted that a member's address which ends with a British Forces Post Office address and reference (BFPO) will nearly always indicate that the member is serving overseas.

10 The letter of enquiry should be addressed as follows –

(a) Royal Navy and Royal Marine Officers, Ratings and Other Ranks

Director Naval Personnel
Fleet Headquarters
MP 3.1
Leach Building
Whale Island
Portsmouth
Hampshire
PO2 8BY

Army Officers and other Ranks –

Army Personnel Centre
Disclosures 1
MP 520
Kentigern House
65 Brown Street
Glasgow
G2 8EX

Royal Air Force Officers and Other Ranks –

Manning 22E
RAF Disclosures
Room 221B
Trenchard Hall
RAF Cranwell
Sleaford
Lincolnshire
NG34 8HB

Assistance in serving documents on members

11 Once the claimant's legal representative has ascertained the member's address, the legal representative may use that address as the address for service by post, in cases where this method of service is allowed by the Civil Procedure Rules. There are, however, some situations in which service of the proceedings, whether in the High Court or in the family court, must be effected personally; in these cases an appointment will have to be sought, through the Commanding Officer of the Unit, Establishment or Ship concerned, for the purpose of effecting service. The procedure for obtaining an appointment is described below, and it applies whether personal service is to be effected by the claimant's legal representative or the legal representative's agent or by a court bailiff, or, in the case of proceedings served overseas (with the leave of the court) through the British Consul or the foreign judicial authority.

12 The procedure for obtaining an appointment to effect personal service is by application to the Commanding Officer of the Unit, Establishment or Ship in which the member is serving. The Commanding Officer may grant permission for the document server to enter the Unit, Establishment or Ship but if this is not appropriate the Commanding Officer may offer arrangements for the member to attend at a place in the vicinity of the Unit, Establishment or Ship in order that the member may be served. If suitable arrangements cannot be made the legal representative will have evidence that personal service is impracticable, which may be useful in an application for service by an alternative method or at an alternative place.

General

13 Subject to the procedure outlined in paragraphs 11 and 12, there are no special arrangements to assist in the service of legal documents when a member is outside the United Kingdom. The appropriate office will, however, give an approximate date when the member is likely to return to the United Kingdom.

14 It sometimes happens that a member has left the regular forces by the time an enquiry as to address is made. If the claimant's legal representative confirms that the proceedings result from an occurrence when the member was in the regular forces and the legal

representative gives the undertaking referred to in paragraph 7, the last known private address after discharge will normally be provided. In no other case, however, will the Ministry of Defence disclose the private address of a member of the regular forces.

Service on Members of United States Air Force

15 In addition to the information contained in the memorandum of 26 July 1979, and after some doubts having been expressed as to the correct procedure to be followed by persons having civil claims against members of the United States Air Force in England and Wales, the Lord Chancellor's Office (as it was then) issued the following notes for guidance with the approval of the appropriate United States authorities.

16 Instructions have been issued by the United States authorities to the commanding officers of all their units in England and Wales that every facility is to be given for the service of documents in civil proceedings on members of the United States Air Force. The proper course to be followed by a creditor or other person having a claim against a member of the United States Air Force is for that person to communicate with the commanding officer or, where the unit concerned has a legal officer, with the legal officer of the defendant's unit requesting the provision of facilities for the service of documents on the defendant. It is not possible for the United States authorities to act as arbitrators when a civil claim is made against a member of their forces. It is, therefore, essential that the claim should either be admitted by the defendant or judgment should be obtained on it, whether in the High Court or the family court. If a claim has been admitted or judgment has been obtained andthe claimant has failed to obtain satisfaction within a reasonable period, the claimant's proper course is then to write to: Office of the Staff Judge Advocate, Headquarters, Third Air Force, R.A.F. Mildenhall, Suffolk, enclosing a copy of the defendant's written admission of the claim or, as the case may be, a copy of the judgment. Steps will then be taken by the Staff Judge Advocate to ensure that the matter is brought to the defendant's attention with a view to prompt satisfaction of the claim.

Practice Direction 6B – Service out of the jurisdiction

See also Part 6, Practice Direction 6A, Practice Direction 6C

Scope of this Practice Direction

1.1 This Practice Direction supplements Chapter 4 (service out of the jurisdiction) of Part 6.

(Practice Direction 6A contains relevant provisions supplementing rule 6.43(2) in relation to the method of service on a party in Scotland or Northern Ireland.)

Documents to be filed under rule 6.46(2)

3.1 A duplicate of –

(a) the application form or other document to be served under rule 6.45(1) or (2);
(b) any documents accompanying the application or other document referred to in paragraph (a); and
(c) any translation required by rule 6.47;

must be provided for each party to be served out of the jurisdiction, together with forms for responding to the application.

3.2 Some countries require legalisation of the document to be served and some require a formal letter of request which must be signed by the Senior Master. Any queries on this should be addressed to the Foreign Process Section (Room E02) at the Royal Courts of Justice.

Service in a Commonwealth State or British Overseas Territory

4.1 The judicial authorities of certain Commonwealth States which are not a party to the Hague Convention require service to be in accordance with rule 6.45(1)(b)(i) and not 6.45(3). A list of such countries can be obtained from the Foreign Process Section (Room E02) at the Royal Courts of Justice.

4.2 The list of British overseas territories is contained in Schedule 6 to the British Nationality Act 1981. For ease of reference these are –

(a) Anguilla;
(b) Bermuda;
(c) British Antarctic Territory;
(d) British Indian Ocean Territory;
(e) Cayman Islands;
(f) Falkland Islands;
(g) Gibraltar;
(h) Montserrat;
(i) Pitcairn, Henderson, Ducie and Oeno Islands;
(j) St. Helena, Ascension and Tristan da Cunha;
(k) South Georgia and the South Sandwich Islands;
(l) Sovereign Base Areas of Akrotiri and Dhekelia;
(m) Turks and Caicos Islands;
(n) Virgin Islands.

Period for responding to an application form

5.1 Where rule 6.42 applies, the period within which the respondent must file an acknowledgment of service or an answer to the application is the number of days listed in the Table after service of the application.

5.2 Where an application is served out of the jurisdiction any statement as to the period for responding to the claim contained in any of the forms required by the Family Procedure Rules to accompany the application must specify the period prescribed under rule 6.42.

Service of application notices and orders

6.1 The provisions of Chapter 4 of Part 6 (special provisions about service out of the jurisdiction) also apply to service out of the jurisdiction of an application notice or order.

6.2 Where an application notice is to be served out of the jurisdiction in accordance with Chapter 4 of Part 6 the court must have regard to the country in which the application notice is to be served in setting the date for the hearing of the application and giving any direction about service of the respondent's evidence.

Period for responding to an application notice

7.1 Where an application notice or order is served out of the jurisdiction, the period for responding is 7 days less than the number of days listed in the Table.

Further information

8.1 Further information concerning service out of the jurisdiction can be obtained from the Foreign Process Section, Room E02, Royal Courts of Justice, Strand, London WC2A 2LL (telephone 020 7947 6691).

Place or country	Number of days
Afghanistan	23
Albania	25
Algeria	22
Andorra	21
Angola	22
Anguilla	31
Antigua and Barbuda	23
Antilles (Netherlands)	31
Argentina	22
Armenia	21
Ascension Island	31
Australia	25
Austria	21
Azerbaijan	22
Azores	23
Bahamas	22
Bahrain	22
Balearic Islands	21
Bangladesh	23
Barbados	23
Belarus	21
Belgium	21
Belize	23
Benin	25
Bermuda	31
Bhutan	28
Bolivia	23
Bosnia and Herzegovina	21
Botswana	23
Brazil	22
British Virgin Islands	31
Brunei	25
Bulgaria	23
Burkina Faso	23

Place or country	Number of days
Burma	23
Burundi	22
Cambodia	28
Cameroon	22
Canada	22
Canary Islands	22
Cape Verde	25
Caroline Islands	31
Cayman Islands	31
Central African Republic	25
Chad	25
Chile	22
China	24
China (Hong Kong)	31
China (Macau)	31
China (Taiwan)	23
China (Tibet)	34
Christmas Island	27
Cocos (Keeling) Islands	41
Colombia	22
Comoros	23
Congo (formerly Congo Brazzaville or French Congo)	25
Congo (Democratic Republic)	25
Corsica	21
Costa Rica	23
Croatia	21
Cuba	24
Cyprus	31
Czech Republic	21
Denmark	21
Djibouti	22
Dominica	23
Dominican Republic	23
East Timor	25
Ecuador	22
Egypt	22
El Salvador	25

Place or country	Number of days
Equatorial Guinea	23
Eritrea	22
Estonia	21
Ethiopia	22
Falkland Islands and Dependencies	31
Faroe Islands	31
Fiji	23
Finland	24
France	21
French Guyana	31
French Polynesia	31
French West Indies	31
Gabon	25
Gambia	22
Georgia	21
Germany	21
Ghana	22
Gibraltar	31
Greece	21
Greenland	31
Grenada	24
Guatemala	24
Guernsey	21
Guinea	22
Guinea-Bissau	22
Guyana	22
Haiti	23
Holland (Netherlands)	21
Honduras	24
Hungary	22
Iceland	22
India	23
Indonesia	22
Iran	22
Iraq	22
Ireland (Republic of)	21
Ireland (Northern)	21

Place or country	Number of days
Isle of Man	21
Israel	22
Italy	21
Ivory Coast	22
Jamaica	22
Japan	23
Jersey	21
Jordan	23
Kazakhstan	21
Kenya	22
Kiribati	23
Korea (North)	28
Korea (South)	24
Kosovo	21
Kuwait	22
Kyrgyzstan	21
Laos	30
Latvia	21
Lebanon	22
Lesotho	23
Liberia	22
Libya	21
Liechtenstein	21
Lithuania	21
Luxembourg	21
Macedonia	21
Madagascar	23
Madeira	31
Malawi	23
Malaysia	24
Maldives	26
Mali	25
Malta	21
Mariana Islands	26
Marshall Islands	32
Mauritania	23

Place or country	Number of days
Mauritius	22
Mexico	23
Micronesia	23
Moldova	21
Monaco	21
Mongolia	24
Montenegro	21
Montserrat	31
Morocco	22
Mozambique	23
Namibia	23
Nauru	36
Nepal	23
Netherlands	21
Nevis	24
New Caledonia	31
New Zealand	26
New Zealand Island Territories	50
Nicaragua	24
Niger (Republic of)	25
Nigeria	22
Norfolk Island	31
Norway	21
Oman (Sultanate of)	22
Pakistan	23
Palau	23
Panama	26
Papua New Guinea	26
Paraguay	22
Peru	22
Philippines	23
Pitcairn, Henderson, Ducie and Oeno Islands	31
Poland	21
Portugal	21
Portuguese Timor	31
Puerto Rico	23

Place or country	Number of days
Qatar	23
Reunion	31
Romania	22
Russia	21
Rwanda	23
Sabah	23
St. Helena	31
St. Kitts and Nevis	24
St. Lucia	24
St. Pierre and Miquelon	31
St. Vincent and the Grenadines	24
Samoa (U.S.A. Territory) (See also Western Samoa)	30
San Marino	21
Sao Tome and Principe	25
Sarawak	28
Saudi Arabia	24
Scotland	21
Senegal	22
Serbia	21
Seychelles	22
Sierra Leone	22
Singapore	22
Slovakia	21
Slovenia	21
Society Islands (French Polynesia)	31
Solomon Islands	29
Somalia	22
South Africa	22
South Georgia (Falkland Island Dependencies)	31
South Orkneys	21
South Shetlands	21
Spain	21
Spanish Territories of North Africa	31
Sri Lanka	23

Place or country	Number of days
Sudan	22
Surinam	22
Swaziland	22
Sweden	21
Switzerland	21
Syria	23
Tajikistan	21
Tanzania	22
Thailand	23
Togo	22
Tonga	30
Trinidad and Tobago	23
Tristan Da Cunha	31
Tunisia	22
Turkey	21
Turkmenistan	21
Turks & Caicos Islands	31
Tuvalu	23
Uganda	22
Ukraine	21
United Arab Emirates	22
United States of America	22
Uruguay	22
Uzbekistan	21
Vanuatu	29
Vatican City State	21
Venezuela	22
Vietnam	28
Virgin Islands – U.S.A	24
Wake Island	25
Western Samoa	34
Yemen (Republic of)	30
Zaire	25
Zambia	23
Zimbabwe	22

Practice Direction 6C – Disclosure of addresses by government departments (applicable to applications issued by the court on or after 6 April 2022)

See also Part 6, Practice Direction 6A, Practice Direction 6B

This PD applies to applications issued by the court on or after 6 April 2022. For applications issued by the court before 6 April 2022 see [https://webarchive.nationalarchives.gov.uk/ukgwa/20211201113608/https://www.justice.gov.uk/courts/procedure-rules/family/practice_directions/pd_part_06c].

See also Part 6, Practice Direction 6A, Practice Direction 6B

13 February 1989 [as amended by Practice Direction 20 July 1995]

The arrangements set out in the Registrar's Direction, Disclosure of Addresses by Government Departments of 26 April 1988 ([1988] 2 FLR 183; [1988] Fam. Law 360; [1988] 2 All ER 573; [1988] 1 WLR 638), whereby the court may request the disclosure of addresses by government departments have been further extended.

These arrangements will now cover –

(a) tracing the address of a person in proceedings against whom another person is seeking to obtain or enforce an order for financial provision either for himself or herself or for the children of the former marriage; and,

(b) tracing the whereabouts of a child, or the person with whom the child is said to be, in proceedings under the Child Abduction and Custody Act 1985 or in which a custody order, as defined in Part I of the Family Law Act 1986, is being sought or enforced.

Requests for such information will be made officially by the registrar. The request, in addition to giving the information mentioned below, should certify –

(1) In financial provision applications either (a) that a financial provision order is in existence, but cannot be enforced because the person against whom the order has been made cannot be traced; or (b) that the applicant has filed or issued a notice, application or originating summons containing an application for financial provision which cannot be served because the respondent cannot be traced.

A 'financial provision order' means any order made under ss. 23, 24, 24A and 27 of the Matrimonial Causes Act 1973 or the variations of any order made under s. 31 of the 1973 Act, and any periodical payments or lump sum order made under s. 6 of the Family Law Reform Act 1969, the Guardianship of Minors Act 1971, s. 34 of the Children Act 1975 and any order registered in the High Court under the Maintenance Orders (Facilities for Enforcement) Act 1920, the Maintenance Orders Act 1950 and the Maintenance Orders Act 1958, and any order made under s. 17 of the Matrimonial and Family Proceedings Act 1984.

(2) In wardship proceedings that the child is the subject of wardship proceedings and cannot be traced, and is believed to be with the person whose address is sought.

(3) In custody proceedings that the child is the subject of custody proceedings and cannot be traced, and is believed to be with the person whose address is sought.

The following notes set out the information required by those departments which are likely to be of the greatest assistance to an applicant.

Department of Social Security

1 The department most likely to be able to assist is the Department of Social Security, whose records are the most comprehensive and complete. The possibility of identifying one person amongst so many will depend on the particulars given. An address will not be supplied by the department unless it is satisfied from the particulars given that the record of the person has been reliably identified.

The applicant or his solicitor should therefore be asked to supply as much as possible of the following information about the person sought –

(i) National Insurance number;
(ii) surname;
(iii) forenames in full;
(iv) date of birth (or, if not known, approximate age);
(v) last known address, with date when living there;
(vi) any other known address(es) with dates;
(vii) if the person sought is a war pensioner, his war pension and service particulars (if known);

and in applications for financial provision –

(viii) the exact date of the marriage and the wife's forenames.

Enquiries should be sent by the registrar to:

Department of Social Security
N1CB
Special Section A
Newcastle upon Tyne
NE98 1YU

The department will be prepared to search if given full particulars of the person's name and date of birth, but the chances of accurate identification are increased by the provision of more identifying information. Second requests for records to be searched, provided that a reasonable interval has elapsed, will be met by the Department of Social Security.

Supplementary Benefit/Income Support

Where, in the case of applications for financial provision, the wife is or has been in receipt of supplementary benefit income support, it would be advisable in the first instance to make enquiries of the manager of the local Social Security office for the area in which she resides in order to avoid possible duplication of enquiries.

Passport Office

2 If all reasonable enquiries, including the aforesaid methods, have failed to reveal an address, or if there are strong grounds for believing that the person sought may have made a recent application for a passport, enquiries may be made to the Passport Office. The applicant or his solicitor should provide as much of the following information about the person as possible –

(i) surname;
(ii) forenames in full;
(iii) date of birth (or, if not known, approximate age);
(iv) place of birth
(v) occupation;

(vi) whether known to have travelled abroad, and, if so, the destination and dates;
(vii) last known address, with date living there;
(viii) any other known address(es), with dates.

The applicant or his solicitor must also undertake in writing that information given in response to the enquiry will be used solely for the purpose for which it was requested, i.e. to assist in tracing the husband in connection with the making or enforcement of a financial provision order or in tracing a child in connection with custody or wardship proceedings, as the case may be.

Enquiries should be sent to:

The Chief Passport Officer
Passport Department
Home Office
Clive House
Petty France
London
SW1H 9HD

Ministry of Defence

3 In cases where the person sought is known to be serving or to have recently served in any branch of H.M. Forces, the solicitor representing the applicant may obtain the address for service of financial provision or custody and wardship proceedings direct from the appropriate service department.

In the case of army servicemen, the solicitor can obtain a list of regiments and of the various manning and record offices from the Officer in Charge, Central Manning Support Office, Higher Barracks, Exeter, EC4 4ND.

The solicitor's request should be accompanied by a written undertaking that the address will be used for the purpose of service of process in those proceedings and that so far as is possible the solicitor will disclose the address only to the court and not to the applicant or any other person, except in the normal course of the proceedings.

Alternatively, if the solicitor wishes to serve process on the person's commanding officer under the provisions contained in s. 101 of the Naval Act 1957, s. 153 of the Army Act 1955 and s. 153 of the Air Force Act 1955 (all of which as amended by s. 62 of the Armed Forces Act 1971) he may obtain that officer's address in the same way.

Where the applicant is acting in person the appropriate service department is prepared to disclose the address of the person sought, or that of his commanding officer, to a registrar on receipt of an assurance that the applicant has given an undertaking that the information will be used solely for the purpose of serving process in the proceedings.

In all cases, the request should include details of the person's full name, service number, rank or rating, and his ship, arm or trade, corps regiment or unit or as much of this information as is available. The request should also include details of his date of birth, or, if not known, his age, his date of entry into the service and, if no longer serving, the date of discharge, and any other information, such as his last known address. Failure to quote the service number and the rank or rating may result in failure to identify the serviceman or at least in considerable delay.

Enquiries should be addressed as follows –

(a)	
Officers of Royal Navy and Women's Royal Naval Service	The Naval Secretary Room 161 Victory Building HM Naval Base Hants PO1 3LS
Ratings in the Royal Navy WRNS Ratings QUARNNS Ratings	Captain Naval Drafting Centurion Building Grange Road Gosport, Hants PO13 9XA
RN Medical and Dental Officers	The Medical Director General (Naval) Room 114 Victory Building HM Naval Base Portsmouth Hants PO1 3LS
Officers of Queen Alexandra's Royal Naval Nursing Service	The Matron-in-Chief QARNNS Room 129 Victory Building HM Naval Base Portsmouth Hants PO1 3LS
Naval Chaplains	Director General Naval Chaplaincy Service Room 201 Victory Building HM Naval Base Portsmouth Hants PO1 3LS

(b)	
Royal Marine Officers	The Naval Secretary Room 161 Victory Building HM Naval Base Portsmouth Hants PO1 3LS
Royal Marine Ranks	HQRM (DRORM) West Battery Whale Island Portsmouth Hants PO2 8DX
(c)	
Army Officers (including WRAC and QARANC)	Army Officer Documentation Office Index Department Room F7 Government Buildings Stanmore Middlesex
Other Ranks, Army	The Manning and Record Office which is appropriate to the Regiment or Corps.
(d)	
Royal Air Force Officers and other Ranks Women's Royal Air Force Officers and Other Ranks (including PMRAFNS)	Ministry of Defence RAF Personnel Management 2b1 (a) (RAF) Building 248 RAF Innsworth Gloucester GL3 1EZ

General Notes

Records held by other departments are less likely to be of use, either because of their limited scope or because individual records cannot readily be identified. If, however, the circumstances suggest that the address may be known to another department, application may be made to it by the registrar, all relevant particulars available being given.

When the department is able to supply the address of the person sought to the registrar, it will be passed on by him to the applicant's solicitor (or, in proper cases, direct to the applicant if acting in person) on an understanding to use it only for the purpose of the proceedings.

Nothing in this practice direction affects the service in matrimonial causes of petitions which do not contain any application for financial provision, etc. The existing arrangements whereby the Department of Social Security will at the request of the solicitor forward a letter by ordinary post to a party's last known address remain in force in such cases.

The Registrar's Direction Disclosure of Addresses by Government Department, of 26 April 1988, is hereby revoked.

[PART 7
PROCEDURE FOR APPLICATIONS IN MATRIMONIAL AND CIVIL PARTNERSHIP PROCEEDINGS

Chapter 1
Application and interpretation

7.1 Application and interpretation

(1) The rules in this Part apply to matrimonial and civil partnership proceedings.

(2) This Part is subject to any provision made by or pursuant to Part 41 (proceeding by electronic means).

(3) In this Part—

'disputed case' means—

(a) nullity proceedings in which—
 (i) an answer has been filed opposing the grant of an order on the application, and has not been struck out; or
 (ii) the respondent has filed an application for a matrimonial or civil partnership order in accordance with rule 7.24 and neither party's application has been disposed of; or
 (iii) rule 7.27(2) applies (in light of paragraph (1) of that rule), notice has been given of intention to rebut and that notice has not been withdrawn,

 and in which no matrimonial or civil partnership order has been made; and

(b) matrimonial or civil partnership proceedings (excluding nullity proceedings) in which—
 (i) an answer has been filed disputing—
  (aa) the validity or subsistence of the marriage or civil partnership; or
  (ab) the jurisdiction of the court to entertain the proceedings,

 and has not been struck out; or
 (ii) the respondent has filed an application for a matrimonial or civil partnership order in accordance with rule 7.12(1) and neither party's application has been disposed of,

 and in which no matrimonial or civil partnership order has been made;

'nullity proceedings' means proceedings for a nullity order or nullity of marriage order; and

'standard case' means matrimonial proceedings or civil partnership proceedings other than a disputed case.

(4) In this Part—

(a) a reference to a conditional order is a reference to a matrimonial order or civil partnership order (other than a judicial separation order or separation order) which has not been made final; and

(b) a reference to a final order is a reference to a conditional order which has been made final.][1]

Amendment

1 Substituted by the Family Procedure (Amendment) Rules 2022, SI 2022/44, rr 2, 22, Schedule.

[Chapter 2
Rules about starting proceedings

7.2 Who the parties are

The parties to matrimonial proceedings or civil partnership proceedings are—

(a) the parties to the marriage or civil partnership concerned; and

(b) any other person who is to be a party in accordance with a provision of the rules in this Part.][1]

Amendment

1 Substituted by the Family Procedure (Amendment) Rules 2022, SI 2022/44, rr 2, 22, Schedule.

[7.3 Statement of reconciliation

(1) Where the applicant is, or in the case of joint applications either or both of the applicants are, legally represented, the legal representative must, unless the court directs otherwise, complete and file with the application a statement in the form for this purpose referred to in Practice Direction 5A, certifying whether the legal representative has discussed with the applicant the possibility of a reconciliation and given the applicant the names and addresses of persons qualified to help effect a reconciliation.

(2) This rule applies to an application for—

(a) a divorce order made under section 1 of the 1973 Act;

(b) a judicial separation order made under section 17 of the 1973 Act;

(c) a dissolution order as mentioned in section 37(1)(a) of the 2004 Act; or

(d) a separation order as mentioned in section 37(1)(d) of the 2004 Act.][1]

Amendment

1 Substituted by the Family Procedure (Amendment) Rules 2022, SI 2022/44, rr 2, 22, Schedule.

[7.4 Limitation on applications in respect of same marriage or civil partnership

(1) Subject to paragraph (2), a person may not make more than one application for a matrimonial or civil partnership order in respect of the same marriage or civil partnership unless—

(a) the first application has been dismissed or finally determined; or

(b) the court gives permission.

(2) Where a person—

(a) has, within one year of the date of the marriage or civil partnership, made an application for a judicial separation order or separation order; and

(b) then, after that one-year period has passed, wishes to apply for a divorce or a dissolution order,

that person does not need the court's permission to make the application referred to in sub-paragraph (b).][1]

Amendment

1 Substituted by the Family Procedure (Amendment) Rules 2022, SI 2022/44, rr 2, 22, Schedule.

[7.5 Service of application

(1) After an application for a matrimonial or civil partnership order has been issued by the court, a copy of it must be served on any respondent.

(Rule 6.5 provides for who is to serve an application for a matrimonial or civil partnership order; where the applicant serves the application, rule 6.6A and 6.41A provide a time limit of 28 days from the date of issue for taking the prescribed steps to serve the respondent.)

(2) When the application is served on a respondent it must be accompanied by—

(a) a form for acknowledging service; and
(b) a notice of proceedings.

(3) When the parties to the marriage or civil partnership have made a joint application for a matrimonial or civil partnership order (other than a nullity order) the court must send a copy of the notice of proceedings to both parties.][1]

Amendment

1 Substituted by the Family Procedure (Amendment) Rules 2022, SI 2022/44, rr 2, 22, Schedule.

[7.6 Withdrawal of application before service

An application for a matrimonial or civil partnership order, made by one party to the marriage or civil partnership, may be withdrawn at any time before it has been served, by giving notice in writing to the court.][1]

Amendment

1 Substituted by the Family Procedure (Amendment) Rules 2022, SI 2022/44, rr 2, 22, Schedule.

[7.7 What the respondent must do on receiving the application

(1) The respondent must file an acknowledgment of service within 14 days beginning with the date on which the application for a matrimonial or civil partnership order was served.

(2) This rule is subject to rule 6.42 (which specifies how the period for filing an acknowledgment of service is calculated where the application is served out of the jurisdiction).

(3) The acknowledgment of service must—

(a) be signed by the respondent or the respondent's legal representative;
(b) include the respondent's address for service; and
(c) indicate whether or not the respondent intends to dispute the proceedings.

(4) Where a notice of proceedings is sent to joint applicants under rule 7.5(3) each joint applicant must acknowledge receipt of the notice of proceedings within 14 days of receipt of such notice.

(5) A respondent who wishes to dispute proceedings must file and serve an answer within 21 days beginning with the date by which the acknowledgment of service is required to be filed.

(6) A respondent may file an answer even if the intention to do so was not indicated in the acknowledgment of service.][1]

Amendment

1 Substituted by the Family Procedure (Amendment) Rules 2022, SI 2022/44, rr 2, 22, Schedule.

[Chapter 3
Standard case

7.8 Amending an application

(1) A party making an application for a matrimonial or civil partnership order may amend the application at any time before an application is made under rule 7.9(1) or (2).

(2) Where an amendment to the application is made under paragraph (1)—

(a) it must be served in accordance with rule 7.5; and
(b) rule 7.7 applies.

(3) Where an application has been made under rule 7.9(1) or (2), an amendment may not be made to an application except—

(a) with the written consent of all the other parties; or
(b) with the permission of the court.

(4) Where paragraph (3) applies, the court may give directions as to—

(a) the service of the amended application and the service of any accompanying documents;
(b) the joining of any additional parties; and
(c) the extent to which rule 7.7 must be complied with in respect of any amended application.

(Practice Direction 7A contains information on amending applications.)][1]

Amendment

1 Substituted by the Family Procedure (Amendment) Rules 2022, SI 2022/44, rr 2, 22, Schedule.

[7.9 Applications for conditional order

(1) An application may be made to the court for it to consider the making of a conditional order of divorce or dissolution in the proceedings at any time after the end of the period of 20 weeks from the date on which the application was issued provided that—

(a) the time for filing the acknowledgment of service has expired and no party has filed an acknowledgement of service indicating an intention to dispute the proceedings; and
(b) in any other case, the time for filing an answer to every application for a matrimonial or civil partnership order made in the proceedings has expired.

(2) An application may be made to the court for it to consider the making of a conditional order of nullity of marriage or nullity, a judicial separation order or a separation order in the proceedings—

(a) at any time after the time for filing the acknowledgment of service has expired, provided that no party has filed an acknowledgment of service indicating an intention to dispute the proceedings; and

(b) in any other case, at any time after the time for filing an answer to every application for a matrimonial or civil partnership made in the proceedings has expired.

(3) An application under paragraph (1) or (2) may be made—

(a) by the applicant; or

(b) in a joint application, by both parties; or

(c) in a joint application that is to proceed as an application by one party only, by that party.

(4) An application under this rule must be accompanied by a statement—

(a) stating whether there have been any changes in the information given in the application;

(b) confirming that, subject to any changes stated, the contents of the application are true; and

(c) where the acknowledgment of service has been signed by the other party to the marriage or civil partnership, confirming that party's signature on the acknowledgment of service.

(5) A statement under paragraph (4) must be verified by a statement of truth.

(6) A copy of the application made under paragraph (3)(c) must be served on the other party to the marriage or civil partnership.][1]

Amendment

1 Substituted by the Family Procedure (Amendment) Rules 2022, SI 2022/44, rr 2, 22, Schedule.

[7.10 What the court will do on an application for a conditional order, a judicial separation or a separation order

(1) This rule applies where an application is made under rule 7.9(1) or (2).

(2) If at the relevant time the case is a standard case, the court must—

(a) if satisfied that the applicant is, or applicants are, entitled to—

(i) in matrimonial proceedings, a conditional order or a judicial separation order (as the case may be); or

(ii) in civil partnership proceedings, a conditional order or a separation order (as the case may be),

so certify and direct that the application be listed before a judge for the making of that order at the next available date;

(b) if not so satisfied, direct—

(i) that any party to the proceedings provide such further information, or take such other steps, as the court may specify; or

(ii) that the case be listed for a case management hearing.

(3) If the applicant has applied for costs, the court may, on making a direction under paragraph (2)(a), make directions in the costs application.

(4) The court may, when giving a direction under paragraph (2)(b), direct that the further information provided be verified by a statement of truth.

(5) The court must not give directions under this rule unless at the relevant time it is satisfied—

- (a) that a copy of each application for a matrimonial or civil partnership order has been properly served on each party on whom it is required to be served; and
- (b) that—
  - (i) in matrimonial proceedings, the application for a conditional order or a judicial separation order; or
  - (ii) in civil partnership proceedings, the application for a conditional order or separation order,

  was made at a time permitted by rule 7.9(1) or (2).

(6) In this rule, 'the relevant time' means the time at which the court is considering an application made under rule 7.9(1) or (2).

(7) Where an order is made in accordance with a certificate under paragraph (2)(a), any person may, within 14 days after the making of the order, inspect the certificate and the statement filed under rule 7.9(4) and may obtain copies.][1]

Amendment

1 Substituted by the Family Procedure (Amendment) Rules 2022, SI 2022/44, rr 2, 22, Schedule.

[7.11 What the court must do for the case management hearing

(1) At a hearing that has been directed under rule 7.10(2)(b)(ii), the court must—

- (a) consider what further evidence is required properly to dispose of the proceedings and give directions about the filing and service of such evidence;
- (b) give directions for the further conduct of the proceedings, including—
  - (i) giving a direction that on compliance with any directions under sub-paragraph (a) a further application may be made under rule 7.9(1) or (2) for the proceedings to be dealt with under rule 7.10(2)(a); or
  - (ii) giving a direction that the case is not suitable for determination under that rule.

(2) Where the court gives a direction under paragraph (1)(b)(ii), it may also give directions under rule 7.17 or direct that the case be listed for a further hearing at which such directions will be given.

(3) Any party to proceedings which are not being dealt with under rule 7.10(2)(a) may apply to the court for further directions at any time.

(Part 4 sets out the court's general case management powers.)][1]

Amendment

1 Substituted by the Family Procedure (Amendment) Rules 2022, SI 2022/44, rr 2, 22, Schedule.

[Chapter 4
Disputed case

7.12 How the respondent can make an application

(1) Subject to rule 7.27—

(a) a respondent may not make an application for a matrimonial or civil partnership order for the same relief in respect of the same marriage or civil partnership unless—
  (i) the first application has been dismissed or finally determined; or
  (ii) the court gives permission.

(b) a respondent who wishes to make an application for a matrimonial or civil partnership order, other than an order for the same relief, must make the application for that order within 21 days beginning with the date by which the respondent's acknowledgment of service is required to be filed, unless the court gives permission to make the application after that time has passed.

(2) Where the respondent makes an application under this rule, that application is to be treated as an application in the same proceedings for the purposes of this Part.][1]

Amendment

1 Substituted by the Family Procedure (Amendment) Rules 2022, SI 2022/44, rr 2, 22, Schedule.

[7.13 References to respondents

Where a respondent makes an application for a matrimonial order or a civil partnership order, unless the context otherwise requires, the rules in this Part shall apply with necessary modifications as if the reference to a respondent is a reference to the applicant in the other party's application for a matrimonial order or a civil partnership order.][1]

Amendment

1 Substituted by the Family Procedure (Amendment) Rules 2022, SI 2022/44, rr 2, 22, Schedule.

[7.14 Case management hearing

Where a respondent—

(a) files an answer under rule 7.7(5);
(b) obtains permission to file an application under 7.12(1)(a)(ii); or
(c) files an application for a matrimonial or civil partnership order under rule 7.12(1)(b) or 7.24,

the case must be listed for a case management hearing within 6 weeks of the date on which the answer is filed, or permission is granted, or the application is filed under rule 7.12(1)(b) or 7.24.][1]

Amendment

1 Substituted by the Family Procedure (Amendment) Rules 2022, SI 2022/44, rr 2, 22, Schedule.

[7.15 Amendment of application and answer

(1) Unless paragraph (2) applies—

(a) a party making an application for a matrimonial or civil partnership order may amend the application at any time before an answer to it has been filed;
(b) a party who has filed an answer may amend the answer.

(2) No amendment to an application for a matrimonial or civil partnership order or to an answer may be made under paragraph (1) if an application under rule 7.9(1) or (2) has been made in relation to the marriage or civil partnership concerned.

(3) Where an amendment to the application is made under paragraph (1)—

(a) it must be served in accordance with rule 7.5; and
(b) rule 7.7 applies.

(4) Where an answer has been filed, or an application has been made under rule 7.9(1) or (2), an amendment may not be made to an application except—

(a) with the written consent of all the other parties; or
(b) with the permission of the court.

(5) Where an answer has been filed and an application has been made under rule 7.9(1) or (2), an amendment may not be made to the answer except—

(a) with the written consent of all the other parties; or
(b) with the permission of the court.

(6) Where paragraph (4) or (5) applies, the court may give directions as to—

(a) the service of the amended application or the amended answer and the service of any accompanying documents;
(b) the extent to which rule 7.7 must be complied with in respect of any amended application.

(Practice Direction 7A contains information regarding amending applications, making supplemental applications and making second (or further) applications.)][1]

Amendment

1 Substituted by the Family Procedure (Amendment) Rules 2022, SI 2022/44, rr 2, 22, Schedule.

[7.16 Further information about the contents of the application and the answer

(1) The court may at any time order a party—

(a) to clarify any matter which is in dispute in the proceedings; or
(b) to give additional information in relation to any such matter,

whether or not the matter is contained or referred to in the application for a matrimonial or civil partnership order, acknowledgment of service or in the answer.

(2) Paragraph (1) is subject to any rule of law to the contrary.

(3) Where the court makes an order under paragraph (1), the party against whom it is made must—

(a) file the reply to the order made under paragraph (1); and
(b) serve a copy of it on each of the other parties,

within the time specified by the court.

(4) The court may direct that information provided by a party to another party (whether given voluntarily or following an order made under paragraph (1)) must not be used for any purpose except for the proceedings in which it is given.][1]

[7.17 What the court must do for the case management hearing

(1) This rule applies to a case in which the court has listed a case management hearing under rule 7.14.

(2) At a hearing which has been listed under rule 7.14 the court must—

(a) decide where the hearing in the case should take place;
(b) set a timetable for the filing and service of evidence;
(c) make such order for the disclosure and inspection of documents as it considers appropriate; and
(d) give directions as to the conduct of the final hearing and the attendance of witnesses.

(Rule 21.1 explains what is meant by disclosure and inspection.)

(3) Any party to proceedings which are not being dealt with under rule 7.10(2)(a) may apply to the court for further directions at any time.

(Part 3 sets out the court's powers to encourage the parties to use non-court dispute resolution and Part 4 sets out the court's general case management powers.)][1]

Amendment

1 Substituted by the Family Procedure (Amendment) Rules 2022, SI 2022/44, rr 2, 22, Schedule.

[Chapter 5
Proceedings after conditional order (standard and disputed case)

7.18 Applications to prevent conditional orders being made final

(1) This rule applies to an application under section 8 or 9 of the 1973 Act or under section 39 or 40 of the 2004 Act to prevent a conditional order being made final.

(2) An application to which this rule applies must be made using the Part 18 procedure, subject to paragraphs (3) to (6) of this rule.

(3) The person making an application to which this rule applies must within 28 days of filing the application apply to the court to give directions for the hearing of the application.

(4) Where the person making an application to which this rule applies does not apply for directions under paragraph (3), then the person, or persons, in whose favour the conditional order was made may do so.

(5) Rule 7.17(2) applies to an application to which this rule applies as it applies to an application for a matrimonial or civil partnership order.

(6) Where an application to which this rule applies is made by the Queen's Proctor—

(a) the Queen's Proctor may give written notice, to the court and to the party or parties in whose favour the conditional order was made, of the Queen's Proctor's intention to make an application to prevent conditional order being made final; and
(b) where the Queen's Proctor does so the application under paragraph (1) must be made within 21 days beginning with the date on which the notice is given.][1]

Amendment

1 Substituted by the Family Procedure (Amendment) Rules 2022, SI 2022/44, rr 2, 22, Schedule.

[7.19 Making conditional orders final by giving notice

(1) Unless rule 7.20 applies —

(a) a party in whose favour a conditional order has been made may give notice to the court that they wish the conditional order to be made final;

(b) both parties in whose favour a conditional order has been made may jointly give notice to the court that they wish the conditional order to be made final; or

(c) subject to paragraph (2) below, where the conditional order is in favour of both parties, but the application is to proceed as a notice by one party only, that party may give notice to the court that they wish the conditional order to be made final.

(2) The party giving notice to the court under paragraph (1)(c) must first give the other party to the marriage or civil partnership 14 days' notice of their intention to give notice to the court that they wish the conditional order to be made final.

(3) The party giving notice under paragraph (2) must file a certificate of service after serving the notice.

(4) Subject to paragraphs (5) and (6), where the court receives a notice under paragraph (1) it will make the conditional order final if it is satisfied that—

(a) no application for rescission of the conditional order is pending;

(b) no appeal against the making of the conditional order is pending;

(c) no order has been made by the court extending the time for bringing an appeal of the kind mentioned in sub-paragraph (b), or if such an order has been made, that the time so extended has expired;

(d) no application for an order of the kind mentioned in sub-paragraph (c) is pending;

(e) no application to prevent the conditional order being made final is pending;

(f) the provisions of section 10(2) to (4) of the 1973 Act or section 48(2) to (4) of the 2004 Act do not apply or have been complied with;

(g) any order under section 10A(2) of the 1973 Act has been complied with; and

(h) where the conditional order was made on the ground in section 12(1)(g) of, or paragraph 11(1)(e) of Schedule 1 to, the 1973 Act, or was made under section 12A(3) of the 1973 Act in a case where section 12(1)(g) of the 1973 Act applies, or the conditional order was made under section 50(1)(d) of the 2004 Act—

(i) there is not pending a reference under section 8(5) of the Gender Recognition Act 2004, or an application under section 8(5A) of that Act, in respect of the application on which the interim gender recognition certificate to which the application relates was granted;

(ii) that interim certificate has not been revoked under section 8(6)(b) of that Act; and

(iii) no appeal is pending against an order under section 8(6)(a) of that Act.

(5) Where the notice is received more than 12 months after the making of the conditional order, it must include or be accompanied by an explanation in writing stating why the application has not been made earlier.

(6) Where paragraph (5) applies, the court may—

(a) require the applicant to verify the explanation with a statement of truth; and

(b) make such order on the application as it thinks fit, but where it orders the conditional order to be made final that order is not to take effect until the court is satisfied that none of the matters mentioned in paragraph (4)(a) to (h) applies.][1]

Amendment

1 Substituted by the Family Procedure (Amendment) Rules 2022, SI 2022/44, rr 2, 22, Schedule.

[7.20 Applications to make conditional orders final

(1) An application must be made for the conditional order to be made final, where the conditions set out in paragraph (2) apply.

(2) The conditions referred to in paragraph (1) are—

(a) the Queen's Proctor gives notice to the court under rule 7.18(6)(a) and has not withdrawn that notice;

(b) there are other circumstances which ought to be brought to the attention of the court before the application is granted; or

(c) the application is made by the party against whom the conditional order was made.

(3) An application under this rule to which paragraph (2)(a) applies must be served on the Queen's Proctor.

(4) Where the court orders a conditional order to be made final under this rule, that order is not to take effect until the court is satisfied about the matters mentioned in rule 7.19(4)(a) to (h).][1]

Amendment

1 Substituted by the Family Procedure (Amendment) Rules 2022, SI 2022/44, rr 2, 22, Schedule.

[7.21 What the court officer must do when a conditional order is made final

Where a conditional order is made final the court officer must—

(a) endorse that fact on the conditional order together with the precise time at which the order was made final; and

(b) send the final order to the applicant or applicants, any respondent and any other party.][1]

Amendment

1 Substituted by the Family Procedure (Amendment) Rules 2022, SI 2022/44, rr 2, 22, Schedule.

[7.22 Applications under section 10(2) of 1973 Act or section 48(2) of 2004 Act

Where the court makes—

(a) in the case of divorce, a final order following an application under section 10(2) of the 1973 Act; or

(b) in the case of dissolution, a final order following an application under section 48(2) of the 2004 Act,

it must make a written record of the reasons for deciding to make that final order.][1]

Amendment

1 Substituted by the Family Procedure (Amendment) Rules 2022, SI 2022/44, rr 2, 22, Schedule.

[7.23 Orders under section 10A(2) of the 1973 Act

(1) Where the court has made an order under section 10A(2) of the 1973 Act, the declaration referred to in that section must—

- (a) be made and signed by both parties to the marriage concerned;
- (b) give particulars of the proceedings in which the order was obtained;
- (c) confirm that the steps required to dissolve the marriage in accordance with the religious usages appropriate to the parties have been taken;
- (d) be accompanied by—
  - (i) a certificate from a relevant religious authority that all such steps have been taken; or
  - (ii) such other documents showing the relevant steps have been taken as the court may direct; and
  - (iii) be filed at the court either before or together with an application to make the conditional order final, under rule 7.19 or 7.20.

(2) Where the certificate referred to in paragraph (1)(d)(i) is not in English it must be accompanied by a translation of that certificate into English, certified by a notary public or authenticated by statement of truth.

(3) The court may direct that the declaration need not be accompanied by the material mentioned in paragraph (1)(d).

(4) In this rule a religious authority is 'relevant' if the party who made the application for the order under section 10A(2) of the 1973 Act considers that authority competent to confirm that the steps referred to in paragraph (1)(c) have been taken.][1]

Amendment

1 Substituted by the Family Procedure (Amendment) Rules 2022, SI 2022/44, rr 2, 22, Schedule.

[Chapter 6

Provisions specific to nullity proceedings

7.24 Respondent to nullity application

(1) A respondent to a nullity application who wishes to make an application for a matrimonial or civil partnership order must make the application for that order within 21 days beginning with the date by which the respondent's acknowledgment of service is required to be filed, unless the court gives permission to make the application after that time has passed.

(2) Where the respondent makes an application under this rule, that application is to be treated as an application in the same proceedings for the purposes of this Part.][1]

Amendment

1 Substituted by the Family Procedure (Amendment) Rules 2022, SI 2022/44, rr 2, 22, Schedule.

[7.25 Supplemental applications

In nullity proceedings rule 7.8 and 7.15 apply to supplemental applications as they apply to amended applications.][1]

Amendment

1 Substituted by the Family Procedure (Amendment) Rules 2022, SI 2022/44, rr 2, 22, Schedule.

[7.26 Nullity: interim and full gender recognition certificates

(1) Where the application is for—

(a) nullity of marriage under section 12(1)(g) of, or paragraph 11(1)(e) of Schedule 1 to, the 1973 Act;

(b) nullity of marriage under section 12A(3) of the 1973 Act in a case where section 12(1)(g) of the 1973 Act applies; or

(c) an order of nullity of civil partnership under section 50(1)(d) of the 2004 Act,

the court officer must send to the Secretary of State a notice in writing that the application has been made.

(2) Where a copy of an interim gender recognition certificate has been filed with the application, that certificate must be attached to the notice.

(3) Where no copy of an interim gender recognition certificate has been filed the notice must also state—

(a) in matrimonial proceedings—

(i) the names of the parties to the marriage and the date and place of the marriage, and

(ii) the last address at which the parties to the marriage lived together as a married couple;

(b) in civil partnership proceedings—

(i) the names of the parties to the civil partnership and the date on, and the place at which, the civil partnership was formed, and

(ii) the last address at which the parties to the civil partnership lived together as civil partners of each other; and

(c) in either case, such further particulars as the court officer considers appropriate.

(4) Where—

(a) the application is for—

(i) a nullity of marriage order under section 12(1)(h) of the 1973 Act;

(ii) a nullity of marriage order under section 12A(3) of the 1973 Act in a case where section 12(1)(h) of the 1973 Act applies; or

(iii) an order of nullity of civil partnership under section 50(1)(e) of the 2004 Act; and

(b) a full gender recognition certificate has been issued to the respondent,

the applicant must file a copy of that full certificate with the application unless the court, on an application made without notice, directs otherwise.

(In relation to paragraphs (1)(b), (3)(a) and (4)(a)(ii), section 9(6) of the Marriage (Same Sex Couples) Act 2013 provides that where a civil partnership is converted into a marriage, the civil partnership ends on the conversion, and the resulting marriage is to be treated as having subsisted since the date the civil partnership was formed.)][1]

Amendment

1 Substituted by the Family Procedure (Amendment) Rules 2022, SI 2022/44, rr 2, 22, Schedule.

[7.27 Nullity: filing an answer

(1) Paragraph (2) applies where—

(a) the application is for—

(i) nullity of marriage under section 12(1)(d) of the 1973 Act;

(ii) nullity of marriage under section 12A(3) of the 1973 Act in a case where section 12(1)(d) of the 1973 Act applies; or

(iii) nullity of civil partnership under section 50(1)(b) of the 2004 Act; and

(b) the respondent files an answer containing no more than a simple denial of the facts stated in the application.

(2) The respondent must, if intending to rebut the matters stated in the application, give notice to the court of that intention when filing the answer.

(The form of the answer is referred to in Practice Direction 5A.)

(In relation to paragraph (1)(a)(ii), section 9(6) of the Marriage (Same Sex Couples) Act 2013 provides that where a civil partnership is converted into a marriage, the civil partnership ends on the conversion, and the resulting marriage is to be treated as having subsisted since the date the civil partnership was formed.)][1]

Amendment

1 Substituted by the Family Procedure (Amendment) Rules 2022, SI 2022/44, rr 2, 22, Schedule.

[7.28 Nullity – inspection of certificate of entitlement

Rule 7.10(7) does not apply to a certificate which relates to—

(a) a nullity of marriage order under section 12(1)(g) of, or paragraph 11(1)(e) of Schedule 1 to, the 1973 Act;

(b) a nullity of marriage order under section 12A(3) of the 1973 Act in a case where section 12(1)(g) of the 1973 Act applies; or

(c) an order for nullity of civil partnership under section 50(1)(d) of the 2004 Act,

unless the court has given permission.][1]

Amendment

1 Substituted by the Family Procedure (Amendment) Rules 2022, SI 2022/44, rr 2, 22, Schedule.

[7.29 Medical examinations in proceedings for nullity of a marriage of an opposite sex couple

(1) Where the application is for a nullity of marriage order of an opposite sex couple on the ground of incapacity to consummate or wilful refusal to do so, the court must determine whether medical examiners should be appointed to examine the parties or either of them.

(2) The court must only appoint medical examiners under paragraph (1) where it considers that it is necessary for the proper disposal of the case.

(3) The person to be examined must, in the presence of the medical examiner, sign a statement identifying that person as the party to whom the order for examination applies.

(4) The medical examiner must certify on the same statement that it was signed in his or her presence by the person who has been examined.

(5) The person who carries out the examination must prepare a report and file it with the court by the date directed by the court.

(6) Either party is entitled to see a copy of a report filed under paragraph (5).][1]

Amendment

1 Substituted by the Family Procedure (Amendment) Rules 2022, SI 2022/44, rr 2, 22, Schedule.

[Chapter 7
General provisions

7.30 General rule – hearing to be in public

(1) The general rule is that a hearing to which this Part applies is to be in public.

(2) The requirement for a hearing to be in public does not require the court to make special arrangements for accommodating members of the public.

(3) A hearing, or any part of it, may be in private if—

(a) publicity would defeat the object of the hearing;
(b) it involves matters relating to national security;
(c) it involves confidential information (including information relating to personal financial matters) and publicity would damage that confidentiality;
(d) a private hearing is necessary to protect the interests of any child or protected party;
(e) it is a hearing of an application made without notice and it would be unjust to any respondent for there to be a public hearing; or
(f) the court considers this to be necessary, in the interests of justice.

(4) A hearing of an application for rescission of an order by consent under rule 7.34 is, unless the court directs otherwise, to be in private.

(5) The court may order that the identity of any party or witness must not be disclosed if it considers non-disclosure necessary in order to protect the interests of that party or witness.][1]

Amendment

1 Substituted by the Family Procedure (Amendment) Rules 2022, SI 2022/44, rr 2, 22, Schedule.

[7.31 Notice of hearing

The court officer will give notice to the parties—

(a) of the date, time and place of every hearing which is to take place in a case to which they are a party; and
(b) in the case of a hearing following a direction under rule 7.10(2)(a), of the fact that, unless the person wishes or the court requires, the person need not attend.][1]

Amendment

1 Substituted by the Family Procedure (Amendment) Rules 2022, SI 2022/44, rr 2, 22, Schedule.

[7.32 Further provisions about costs

(1) In a disputed case any party to matrimonial or civil partnership proceedings may be heard on any question as to costs at the hearing of the proceedings.

(2) In a standard case, any application for costs should be made using the Part 18 procedure.][1]

Amendment

1 Substituted by the Family Procedure (Amendment) Rules 2022, SI 2022/44, rr 2, 22, Schedule.

[7.33 Stay of proceedings

(1) Where—

(a) the court is considering an application in accordance with rule 7.10 or gives directions under rule 7.11 or 7.17;
(b) it appears to the court that there are proceedings continuing in any country outside England and Wales which are in respect of the marriage or civil partnership in question or which are capable of affecting its validity or subsistence; and
(c) the court considers that the question whether the proceedings should be stayed under paragraph 9 of Schedule 1 to the Domicile and Matrimonial Proceedings Act 1973 or, for civil partnership proceedings, under rules made under sections 75 and 76 of the Courts Act 2003 ought to be determined by the court,

the court must give directions for the hearing of that question.

(2) The court may, if all parties agree, deal with any question about the jurisdiction of the court without a hearing.

(3) For the purposes of paragraph 5 of Schedule 1 to the Domicile and Matrimonial Proceedings Act 1973—

(a) proceedings in another jurisdiction shall include such proceedings which are not instituted in a court of that jurisdiction, if they are instituted before a tribunal or other authority having power under the law having effect there to determine questions of status; and
(b) proceedings which are continuing in another jurisdiction are proceedings which have been begun and have not been finally disposed of.][1]

Amendment

1 Substituted by the Family Procedure (Amendment) Rules 2022, SI 2022/44, rr 2, 22, Schedule.

[7.34 The circumstances in which an order may be set aside (rescission)

Either party to the marriage or civil partnership concerned may apply—

(a) after the conditional order has been made but before it has been made final; or
(b) after a judicial separation order or separation order has been made,

for the rescission of the order on the grounds that the parties are reconciled and both consent to the rescission.][1]

Amendment

1 Substituted by the Family Procedure (Amendment) Rules 2022, SI 2022/44, rr 2, 22, Schedule.

[7.35 Records of decrees absolute and final orders

(1) A central index of decrees absolute and final orders must be kept under the control of the principal registry.

(2) Any person may require a search to be made of that index and to be provided with a certificate showing the results of that search.

(3) Any person who requests it must be issued with a copy of the decree absolute or final order.][1]

Amendment

1 Substituted by the Family Procedure (Amendment) Rules 2022, SI 2022/44, rr 2, 22, Schedule.

Practice Direction 7A – Procedure for applications in matrimonial and civil partnership proceedings (applicable to applications issued by the court on or after 6 April 2022)

This PD applies to applications issued by the court on or after 6 April 2022. For applications issued by the court before 6 April 2022 see [https://webarchive.nationalarchives.gov.uk/ukgwa/20211201114117/https://www.justice.gov.uk/courts/procedure-rules/family/practice_directions/pd_part_07a].

See also Part 7, Practice Direction 7B, Practice Direction 7C, Practice Direction 7D

This Practice Direction supplements FPR Part 7

Applications for matrimonial and civil partnership orders: general

1.1 An application for a matrimonial or civil partnership order must be made in the form referred to in Practice Direction 5A. The application form sets out the documents which must accompany the application.

1.2 The application for a matrimonial order or a civil partnership order must be completed according to the detailed notes which accompany the form.

(a) in matrimonial proceedings, a dissolution or annulment of the marriage or a decree of judicial separation;

(b) in civil partnership proceedings, a dissolution or annulment of the civil partnership or a separation order.

The particulars should, however, be as concise as possible consistent with providing the necessary evidence.

2.1 Omitted

Proof of marriage or civil partnership to accompany the application

3.1 The application form for a matrimonial order or a civil partnership order sets out the documents which must accompany the application. Where the existence and validity of a marriage or civil partnership is not disputed, its validity will be proved by the application being accompanied by –

(a) one of the following –

  (i) a certificate of the marriage or civil partnership to which the application relates; issued under the law in force in the country where the marriage or civil partnership registration took place;

  (ii) a similar document issued under the law in force in the country where the marriage or civil partnership registration took place; or

  (iii) a certified copy of such a certificate or document obtained from the appropriate register office; and

(b) where the certificate, document or certified copy is not in English (or, where the court is in Wales, in Welsh), a translation of that document certified by a notary public or authenticated by a statement of truth.

Filing without accompanying proof of marriage or civil partnership

3.2 If –

(a) the applicant cannot produce –

  (i) the certificate, similar document or a certified copy; and

  (ii) (where necessary) an authenticated translation;

at the time of filing the application; and

(b) it is urgent that the application be filed,

the applicant may apply to the court without notice for permission to file the application without the certificate, document, certified copy or authenticated translation.

3.3 The applicant or the applicant's solicitor must in such a case file with the application a statement explaining why –

(a) the required document is not available; and
(b) the application is urgent.

3.4 The court may give permission to file the application without the required document if the applicant gives an undertaking to file that document at the very earliest opportunity and within any time limit set by the court.

3.4A In the case of a joint application the references in paragraphs 3.2 and 3.3 to 'the applicant' shall be taken to mean either applicant.

Other methods of proof of the marriage or civil partnership

3.5 The requirements of this Practice Direction do not prevent the existence and validity of a marriage, or of an overseas relationship which is not a marriage, being proved in accordance with –

(a) the Evidence (Foreign, Dominion and Colonial Documents) Act 1933; or
(b) any other method authorised in any other Practice Direction, rule or Act.

Information required where evidence of a conviction or finding is to be relied on

4.1 An applicant in nullity proceedings who wishes to rely on evidence –

(a) under section 11 of the Civil Evidence Act 1968 of a conviction of an offence; or
(b) under section 12 of that Act of a finding or adjudication of adultery or paternity,

must include in the application form a statement to that effect and give the following details –

(i) the type of conviction, finding or adjudication and its date;
(ii) the court or Court-Martial which made the conviction, finding or adjudication; and
(iii) the issue in the proceedings to which it relates.

Supplemental applications and amendments to applications and answers

5.1 An application for permission, where required, to file a supplemental application in nullity proceedings or to amend an application or answer may be dealt with at a hearing.

5.2 When making an application for permission for the purposes of paragraph 5.1, the applicant should file at court –

(a) the notice of application for permission; and
(b) the proposed supplemental application or a copy of the application for a matrimonial or civil partnership order or the answer showing the proposed amendments.

5.3 Where permission has been given for the purposes of paragraph 5.1, the applicant should within 14 days of the date of the order, or within such other period as the court directs, file with the court the amended application for a matrimonial or a civil partnership order, the amended answer or, in nullity proceedings, the supplemental application.

5.4 A supplemental application should be made on form D8. It should contain the same details of the parties as the original application, set out the supplemental allegations the party seeks to rely upon, state that 'The [Petitioner/ Respondent] prays as before', include an address for service and be dated.

Summary of applications etc. which may be made

5A.1 In nullity proceedings an applicant may make (i) an application (ii) an amended application (iii) a supplemental application (iv) a further (or second) application. By virtue of being served with such applications, a respondent may file (i) an answer (ii) an answer to an amended application (iii) an answer to a supplemental application (iv) an answer to a further (or second) application. Separately, a respondent may file an amended answer. Rule 7.14 sets out when a respondent may make an application.

5A.2 In matrimonial and civil partnership proceedings (other than nullity proceedings) an applicant may make (i) an application (including a joint application) (ii) an amended application (iii) a further (or second) application. A respondent when disputing proceedings may file (i) an answer (ii) an answer to an amended application (iii) an answer to a further (or second) application. Separately, a respondent may file an amended answer. Rule 7.12 sets out when a respondent may make an application.

5A.3 Where it is necessary in some way to amend an application for a matrimonial order or a civil partnership order, there are distinctions to be drawn between an amended application, a supplemental application and a further application –

(a) an amended application might be used to make alterations or additions to the details given in the application or the orders sought;

(b) a supplemental application can only be made in nullity proceedings and might be used to add particulars, allegations or acts which occurred after the date of the original application. A supplemental application forms part of the original application and effects an amendment to it;

(c) a further (or second) application may only be made with permission under FPR 2010, r 7.4(1)(b) except that no permission is required where the applicant has, within one year from the date of the marriage, or civil partnership, made an application for a judicial separation order or separation order and then, after that one-year period has passed, wishes to apply for a divorce or a dissolution order.

5A.4 A respondent may only make an application for a matrimonial or civil partnership order seeking the same relief as the applicant if the applicant's application has been dismissed or finally determined or if the court gives permission (FPR 2010, r 7.12(1)). Where, for example, an applicant has applied for a divorce or dissolution order and the application has not been pursued, but has not been dismissed or withdrawn, the respondent would require the court's permission to make an application for a divorce or dissolution order in respect of their marriage or civil partnership. On the other hand, the court's permission would not be required where, for example, the applicant has applied for a judicial separation order or a separation order and the respondent wishes to apply for a divorce order or dissolution order (where a period of at least one year has expired since the date of the marriage or civil partnership).

Requests for further information under rule 7.16 (further information)

6.1 Before making an application under rule 7.16, the party seeking clarification or information ('the requesting party') should first serve a written request for it on the party from whom the clarification or information is sought, giving a date by which a reply should be served. The date should be such as to allow the requested party a reasonable time to respond.

6.2 A request should be made by letter or in a separate document, should contain no other subject matter, and should make clear that it is made under rule 7.16. It must be concise and confined to matters which are reasonably necessary and proportionate to enable the requesting party to prepare his or her own case or understand the case of the party to whom the request is directed.

6.3 The reply to the request must be in writing, dated and signed by the requested party or that party's legal representative.

6.4 The reply may be made by letter or in a separate document, should contain no other subject matter, and should make clear that it is a reply to the request concerned. It should repeat each request together with the reply to it. It must be served on every party to the proceedings.

6.5 A party who objects to replying to all or part of a request under rule 7.16, or who is unable to do so, must inform the requesting party promptly, and in any event within the time within which a reply has been requested, and give reasons for objecting or being unable to reply (as the case may be).

Disclosure and inspection

7.1 Where an application for a matrimonial or civil partnership order is disputed the court may make an order for the disclosure of documents under rule 7.17(2)(c).

7.2 When an order for disclosure is made, the disclosing party must, in order to comply, make a reasonable search for the documents required to be disclosed. The extent of the search will depend upon the circumstances of the case and parties should bear in mind the overriding principle of proportionality.

7.3 Documents should be disclosed in a list which should normally list the documents in date order, numbering them consecutively and giving each a concise description. Where there are a large number of documents falling into a particular category they may be grouped together (e.g. 50 bank statements relating to x account from y date to z date).

7.4 The obligations imposed by a disclosure order continue until the proceedings come to an end. If, after the list of documents has been prepared and served, the existence of further documents to which the order applies comes to the attention of the disclosing party, that party must prepare and serve a supplemental list.

7.5 A list of documents must contain the following statement:

I, [insert name] state that I have carried out a reasonable and proportionate search to locate all the documents which I am required to disclose under the disclosure order made by the court on [insert date]. [I did not search for [insert here any limitations on search by reference to date, location, nature of documents etc]]. I understand the duty of disclosure and to the best of my knowledge I have carried out that duty. I certify that the list above is a complete list of all the documents which are or have been in my control and which I am obliged under the order to disclose.

7.6 If the disclosing party wishes to claim a right or duty to withhold inspection of a document or part of a document, that party must indicate in writing in the disclosure statement that such a right or duty is claimed, and the grounds on which it is claimed.

Final orders: need for expedition

8.1 Omitted

8.2 Omitted

8.3 Where a party in an application for a matrimonial or civil partnership order has grounds for expediting the making of the final order, that party should ordinarily seek directions with a view to an early hearing of the case. Where such an application has not been possible, an application should be made to the district judge making the conditional order for the time between the conditional and final order to be shortened.

(Section 1(8) of the Matrimonial Causes Act 1973 provides that the court may, in a particular case, by order shorten the period that would otherwise be applicable.)

8.4 Where the need for expedition only becomes obvious after the making of the conditional order, or where (exceptionally) it arises in a standard case, an application, on notice to the other parties to the proceedings, should be made using the procedure in Part 18 for an order shortening the time before which the final order may be made.

Joint applications

9.1 A joint application must be completed in accordance with the notes that accompany the form. If a joint application is progressed by one applicant only it becomes a sole application. A joint application can proceed as a sole application only when applying for a conditional order or final order.

9.2 In a joint application where the conditional order has been made in favour of both parties, but the application for final order is made by one party only that party must first give prior notice to the other party of their intention in accordance with r 7.19(2).

Disputed cases

10.1 An answer cannot be filed disputing the irretrievable breakdown of the marriage or civil partnership. An answer to an application can be filed disputing the validity or subsistence of the marriage or civil partnership or the jurisdiction of the court to entertain proceedings.

Other proceedings

11.1 An applicant (whether a sole or joint applicant) for a matrimonial or civil partnership order must give details in the application of any existing or concluded proceedings known to the applicant in respect of the marriage or civil partnership, or which may have affected its validity or subsistence. This includes any proceedings in England and Wales or in any country outside England and Wales. A respondent to an application must give details of any such existing or concluded proceedings in the acknowledgment of service and in any answer to the application.

11.2 Where, on considering an application in accordance with rule 7.10 or giving directions under rule 7.11 or 7.17, it appears to the court that there are proceedings continuing in any country outside England and Wales which are in respect of the marriage or civil partnership or which are capable of affecting its validity or subsistence, the court must consider whether it is necessary to give directions under rule 7.33 (consideration of whether the proceedings should be stayed under paragraph 9 of Schedule 1 to the Domicile and Matrimonial Proceedings Act 1973 or, for civil partnership proceedings, under rule 4 of the Family Procedure (Civil Partnership: Staying of Proceedings) Rules 2010).

11.3 Any application by a party for matrimonial or civil partnership proceedings to be stayed under paragraph 9 of Schedule 1 to the Domicile and Matrimonial Proceedings Act 1973 or rule 4 of the Family Procedure (Civil Partnership: Staying of Proceedings) Rules 2010) must be made using the Part 18 procedure.

11.4 Where at any stage it appears to the court, whether by virtue of information provided under para 11.1 or otherwise, that proceedings have been concluded in any country outside England and Wales which were in respect of the marriage or civil partnership or which may have affected its validity or subsistence and no answer has been filed disputing the validity or subsistence of the marriage or civil partnership, the court must consider whether to direct:

(i) that any party to the proceedings provide such further information, or take such other steps, as the court may specify; or
(ii) that the case be listed for a case management hearing.

Procedure for costs applications: standard cases

12.1 In a standard case, any application for an order in respect of the costs of the proceedings should generally be made no later than the application for a conditional order under r.7.9, but must in any event be made before the date on which the conditional order is made final.

12.2 The applicant must set out in the application notice or in any written evidence in support, the grounds on which the order is sought and, where costs are sought in a specified amount, a summary showing how the amount has been calculated.

12.3 The applicant must serve the application notice and any written evidence in support on the respondent within 7 days after the application has been issued and must file a certificate of service within 7 days thereafter.

12.4 A respondent who opposes the making of a costs order or who disputes the amount of costs claimed must, within 14 days after service of the application, file with the court and serve on the applicant a witness statement setting out the grounds on which the application is opposed.

12.5 The court will normally deal with an application for a costs order under r 7.32(2) without a hearing but may direct a hearing of the application if it considers that a hearing would be appropriate.

12.6 Paragraphs 12.1 to 12.5 do not affect the power of the court to make an order about costs on any other application made in the course of the proceedings.

Practice Direction 7B – Medical examinations on applications for annulment of a marriage (applicable to applications issued by the court on or after 6 April 2022)

This PD applies to applications issued by the court on or after 6 April 2022. For applications issued by the court before 6 April 2022 see [https://webarchive.nationalarchives.gov.uk/ukgwa/20211201113525/https://www.justice.gov.uk/courts/procedure-rules/family/practice_directions/pd_part_07b].

See also Part 7, Practice Direction 7A, Practice Direction 7C, Practice Direction 7D

This Practice Direction supplements FPR Part 7, rule 7.29 (Medical examinations in proceedings for nullity of marriage)

1.1 Where an application is made for the annulment of a marriage based on the incapacity of one of the parties to consummate, it will not usually be necessary to appoint a medical examiner where the application is in a standard case. Where the application is disputed the court should not appoint a medical examiner unless it appears necessary to do so for the proper disposal of the case.

1.2 A medical examination ordered under rule 7.29 must, if the party to be examined so requests, be conducted by a doctor of the same gender as the person to be examined. Unless both parties are to be examined, each by a doctor of their own gender, it should not normally be necessary to appoint more than one medical examiner.

1.3 The costs of any medical examination ordered under rule 7.29 will be borne, in the first instance, by the party on whose application the medical examiner is appointed. Such costs form part of the costs of the proceedings.

1.4 It is the responsibility of the party on whose application the medical examiner is appointed to address, at the case management hearing, the question of whether any medical examiner is required to attend the final hearing of the proceedings. A medical examiner who is to give evidence at the proceedings is to be treated as an expert witness and the relevant rules in Part 25 (Experts and Assessors) will apply. The relevant rules in Part 25 will also apply to the medical examiner's report.

1.5 Nothing in this Practice Direction or in rule 7.29 affects the parties' right to adduce other evidence relevant to the proper disposal of the case. Such evidence must be verified by a statement of truth.

Practice Direction 7C – Polygamous marriages (applicable to applications issued by the court on or after 6 April 2022)

This PD applies to applications issued by the court on or after 6 April 2022. For applications issued by the court before 6 April 2022 see [https://webarchive.nationalarchives.gov.uk/ukgwa/20211201113613/https://www.justice.gov.uk/courts/procedure-rules/family/practice_directions/pd_part_07c].

See also Part 7, Practice Direction 7A, Practice Direction 7B, Practice Direction 7D

This Practice Direction supplements FPR Part 7 (procedure for applications in matrimonial and civil partnership proceedings), Part 9 (applications for a financial remedy) and Part 18 (procedure for other applications in proceedings)

Scope of this Practice Direction

1.1 This practice direction applies where an application is made for –

(a) a matrimonial order;
(b) an order under section 27 of the 1973 Act;
(c) an order under section 35 of the 1973 Act;
(d) an order under the 1973 Act which is made in connection with, or with proceedings for any of the above orders; or
(e) an order under Part 3 of the 1984 Act,

and either party to the marriage is, or has during the course of the marriage, been married to more than one person (a polygamous marriage).

Polygamous marriages

2.1 Where this practice direction applies the application must state –

(a) that the marriage is polygamous;
(b) whether, as far as the party to the marriage is aware, any other spouse (that is, a spouse other than the spouse to whom the application relates) of that party is still living (the 'additional spouse'); and
(c) if there is such an additional spouse –
  (i) the additional spouse's name and address;
  (ii) the date and place of the marriage to the additional spouse.

2.2 A respondent who believes that the marriage is polygamous must include the details referred to in paragraph 2.1 above in the acknowledgment of service if they are not included in the application.

2.3 The applicant in any proceedings to which this practice direction applies must apply to the court for directions as soon as possible after the filing of the application or the receipt of an acknowledgment of service mentioning an additional spouse.

2.4 On such an application or of its own initiative the court may –

(a) give the additional spouse notice of any of the proceedings to which this practice direction applies; and
(b) make the additional spouse a party to such proceedings.

2.5 In any case where the application or acknowledgment of service states that the marriage is polygamous (whether or not there is an additional spouse) a court officer must clearly mark the file with the words 'Polygamous Marriage'. The court officer must also check whether an application under paragraph 2.4 has been made in the case and, where no application has been made, refer the file to the court for consideration.

References in orders to section 47 of the 1973 Act

3.1 Every conditional order and final order which is made in respect of a polygamous marriage must refer to the fact that the order is made with reference to section 47 of the 1973 Act.

Practice Direction 7D – The Gender Recognition Act 2004

See also Part 7, Practice Direction 7A, Practice Direction 7B, Practice Direction 7C

Introduction

1.1 The Gender Recognition Act 2004 ('the Act') provides transsexual people with the opportunity to obtain legal recognition in their acquired gender. Legal recognition follows from the issue of a full gender recognition certificate by a Gender Recognition Panel. Section 4 of the Act requires that where a Panel has granted an application to a married applicant, the gender recognition certificate that it must issue shall be an interim gender recognition certificate. The interim certificate may then be used by either party to the marriage as evidence in support of an application to annul the marriage under Section 12(g) of, or paragraph 11(1)(e) of Schedule 1 to, the Matrimonial Causes Act 1973 ('that an interim gender recognition certificate has, after the time of the marriage, been issued to either party to the marriage').

Application

2.1 This Practice Direction applies to proceedings for divorce, judicial separation and annulment of marriage commenced on or after 4th April 2005.

2.2 Where proceedings for divorce, judicial separation or annulment of marriage have been commenced prior to this date, paragraphs 3.2 to 3.5 below shall also apply to those proceedings if, but only if, the court acquires protected information (as defined by Section 22 of the Act) in respect of a party to those proceedings.

Title of the Cause

3.1 When a party to a matrimonial cause has changed his or her name since marriage, by deed poll or otherwise, the name currently being used by the party should appear first on any petition, answer and statement of arrangements followed by 'formerly known as .... (married name)'.

3.2 Subject to paragraph 3.3, when describing the parties in any Decree, Order, Notice or other document issued by the court, the parties should be described by their full current names only.

3.3 When giving details of the parties in any court list (including a special procedure cause list) they should be described by the initials and surname of their current names only. (For example, A B Jones v C D Jones).

3.4 For the sake of clarity, in any document or court list mentioned in paragraphs 3.2 and 3.3 above party titles (i.e. Mr, Mrs, Miss, etc.) should be omitted.

3.5 The Practice Note of 2nd May 1940 (Title of Cause) shall cease to have effect.

Evidence at trial of cause

4.1 This part of the Practice Direction applies where the following conditions are met–

(a) proceedings for annulment of marriage are brought under Section 12(g) of, or paragraph 11(1)(e) of Schedule 1 to, the Matrimonial Causes Act 1973 and under no other ground under Sections 11 or 12 of, or paragraph 11 of Schedule 1 to, that Act; and
(b) the cause is an undefended cause.

4.2 Any party requesting directions for trial may, in addition to the requirements of FPR rule 2.25(2), state in their request that they would wish to give their evidence at the trial of the cause in accordance with the provisions of this Practice Direction; and in that event, the request must be accompanied by an affidavit setting out the information required by the appendix to this Practice Direction.

4.3 Where directions for trial are given in accordance with FPR rule 2.24(5) in respect of a request to which paragraph 4.2 applies, a direction may also be given under Rule 2.28(3) that the affidavit lodged with the request for directions shall be treated as the evidence of that party at the trial of the cause (unless otherwise directed).

4.4 In the case of an undefended cause proceeding on the respondent's answer, this part of the Practice Direction and the contents of the appendix shall apply with appropriate modifications.

4.5 The appendix sets out a form of affidavit that may be used for the purposes of paragraph 4.2.

Appendix

A form of affidavit for the purposes of paragraph 4.2

Affidavit by Petitioner in support of petition for annulment under Section 12(g) of the Matrimonial Causes Act 1973

No. of matter:

* Delete as appropriate.

IN THE COUNTY COURT*
[PRINCIPAL REGISTRY OF THE FAMILY DIVISION*]

Between (Petitioner)
and (Respondent)
and (Co-Respondent)

QUESTION	ANSWER
About the Petition	
1. Have you read the petition in this case?	
2. Do you wish to alter or to add to any statement in the petition? If so, state the alterations or additions.	
3. Subject to these alterations or additions (if any) is everything stated **in your petition** true? If any statement is not within your own knowledge, indicate this and say whether it is true to the best of your information and belief.	
About the interim gender recognition certificate	
4. State the date on which the interim gender recognition certificate was issued: State the serial number of the interim certificate: State the name of the person to whom the certificate has been issued: State the date on which you commenced proceedings to annul your marriage: **You must attach a copy of the interim gender recognition certificate to this form.**	
About other proceedings	

5. To the best of your knowledge and belief has there been or is there continuing any of the following proceedings;

- an application to amend an error in the interim certificate;
- an appeal against a decision to amend (or not to amend) an error in the interim certificate;
- a reference under section 8(5) of the Gender Recognition Act 2004; or
- an appeal against a decision made following a reference under section 8(5)?

If so, please give details of those proceedings and any order made. (You should also attach copies of any orders made).

About the children of the family

6. Has a Statement of Arrangements been filed in this case?

If so, answer questions 7, 8 and 9.

---

7. Have you read the Statement of Arrangements filed in this case?

---

8. Do you wish to alter anything in the Statement of Arrangements or add to it?

If so, state the alterations or additions.

---

9. Subject to these alterations and additions (if any) is everything stated in the **Statement of Arrangements** true?

If any statement is not within your own knowledge, indicate this and say whether it is true and correct to the best of your information and belief.

I, (full name)

of (full residential address)

(occupation)

make oath and say as follows:-

1. I am the petitioner in this cause.

2. **The answers to Questions 1 to 9 above are true.**

3.(1) I identify the signature ……………………………………………………………… (2) appearing in the copy acknowledgement of service now produced to me and marked "A" as the signature of my husband / wife, the respondent in this cause.

l) Delete if the cknowledgement is signed y a solicitor.

2) Insert name of the espondent exactly as it ppears on the cknowledgement signed by im or her.

3) If you have answered Yes" to question 5, exhibit

4. I exhibit marked "B" a copy of the interim gender recognition certificate issued to myself / the respondent in this cause.

5. (3)

6. I identify the signature.. (2) appearing at Part IV of the Statement of Arrangements dated................................... now produced to me and marked "C" as the signature of the respondent.

7. I ask the court to grant a decree annulling my marriage with the respondent on the ground stated in my petition [and to order the respondent / co-respondent to pay the costs of this suit]. (4)

Sworn at

In the County of

this day of 20

Before me, ...

(5) Delete as the case may be.

A Commissioner for Oaths (5)
Officer of the Court appointed by the Judge to take Affidavits

PART 8
PROCEDURE FOR MISCELLANEOUS APPLICATIONS

Chapter 1
Procedure

8.1 Procedure

Subject to rules 8.13 and 8.24, applications to which this Part applies must be made in accordance with the Part 19 procedure.

Chapter 2
Application for corrected gender recognition certificate

8.2 Scope of this Chapter

The rules in this Chapter apply to an application under section 6(1) of the Gender Recognition Act 2004 for the correction of a full gender recognition certificate issued under section 5(1) or 5A(1) of that Act.

8.3 Where to start proceedings

The application must be made to the court which issued the original certificate unless the court directs otherwise.

8.4 Who the parties are

Where the applicant is—

(a) the person to whom the original certificate was issued, the Secretary of State must be a respondent;

(b) the Secretary of State, the person to whom the original certificate was issued must be a respondent.

8.5 Delivery of copy certificate to Secretary of State

Where the court issues a corrected full gender recognition certificate, a court officer must send a copy of the corrected certificate to the Secretary of State.

Chapter 3
Application for alteration of maintenance agreement after death of one party

8.6 Scope of this Chapter

The rules in this Chapter apply to an application under section 36 of the 1973 Act or paragraph 73 of Schedule 5 to the 2004 Act to alter a maintenance agreement after the death of one of the parties.

8.7 ...[1]

...[1]

Amendment

1 Repealed by the Family Procedure (Amendment No 3) Rules 2013, SI 2013/3204, rr 2, 16.

8.8 Who the parties are

(1) Where the applicant is—

(a) the surviving party to the agreement, the personal representative of the deceased must be a respondent;
(b) the personal representative of the deceased, the surviving party to the agreement must be a respondent.

(2) The court may at any time direct that—

(a) any person be made a party to proceedings; or
(b) a party be removed.

8.9 Representative parties

(1) The court may, before or after the application has been filed at court, make an order appointing a person to represent any other person or persons in the application where the person or persons to be represented—

(a) are unborn;
(b) cannot be found;
(c) cannot easily be ascertained; or
(d) are a class of persons who have the same interest in an application and—
  (i) one or more members of that class are within sub-paragraphs (a), (b) or (c); or
  (ii) to appoint a representative would further the overriding objective.

(2) An application for an order under paragraph (1) may be made by—

(a) any person who seeks to be appointed under the order; or
(b) any party to the application.

(3) An application for an order under paragraph (1) must be served on—

(a) all parties to the application to alter the maintenance agreement, if that application has been filed at court;
(b) the person sought to be appointed, if that person is not the applicant or a party to the application; and
(c) any other person as directed by the court.

(4) The court's approval is required to settle proceedings in which a party is acting as a representative.

(5) The court may approve a settlement where it is satisfied that the settlement is for the benefit of all the represented persons.

(6) Unless the court directs otherwise, any order made on an application in which a party is acting as a representative—

(a) is binding on all persons represented in the proceedings; and
(b) may only be enforced by or against a person who is not a party with the permission of the court.

(7) An application may be brought by or against trustees, executors or administrators without adding as parties any persons who have a beneficial interest in the trust or estate and any order made on the application is binding on the beneficiaries unless the court orders otherwise.

8.10 Acknowledgment of service

(1) A respondent who is a personal representative of the deceased must file with the acknowledgment of service a statement setting out—

(a) full particulars of the value of the deceased's estate for probate after providing for the discharge of the funeral, testamentary and administration expenses, debts and liabilities (including inheritance tax and interest); and
(b) the people (including names, addresses and details of any persons under disability) or classes of people beneficially interested in the estate and the value of their interests so far as ascertained.

(2) The respondent must file the acknowledgment of service and any statement required under this rule within 28 days beginning with the date on which the application is served.

8.11 Hearings may be in private

The court may decide to hear any application to which this Chapter applies in private.

Chapter 4
Application for question as to property to be decided in summary way

8.12 Scope of this Chapter

The rules in this Chapter apply to an application under section 17 of the Married Women's Property Act 1882 or section 66 of the 2004 Act.

8.13 Procedure

Where an application for an order under section 17 of the Married Women's Property Act 1882 or section 66 of the 2004 Act is made in any proceedings for a financial order, the application must be made in accordance with the Part 18 procedure.

[8.14 Where to start proceedings

Where any matrimonial proceedings or civil partnership proceedings have been started, or are intended to be started, by the applicant or the respondent, the application must be made in the same court as those matrimonial proceedings or civil partnership proceedings.

(Practice Direction 8A makes provision in respect of the particular location where the application should be made.)][1]

Amendment

1 Substituted by the Family Procedure (Amendment No 3) Rules 2013, SI 2013/3204, rr 2, 17.

8.15 Mortgagees as parties

(1) Where particulars of a mortgage are provided with the application—

(a) the applicant must serve a copy of the application on the mortgagee; and
(b) the mortgagee may, within 14 days beginning with the date on which the application was received, file an acknowledgment of service and be heard on the application.

(2) The court must direct that a mortgagee be made a party to the proceedings where the mortgagee requests to be one.

8.16 Injunctions

(1) The court may grant an injunction(GL) only if the injunction(GL) is ancillary or incidental to the assistance sought by the applicant.

(2) Applications for injunctive relief must be made in accordance with the procedure in rule 20.4 (how to apply for an interim remedy) and the provisions of rule 20.5 (interim injunction(GL) to cease if application is stayed(GL)) apply.

8.17 Application of other rules

Rule 9.24 applies where the court has made an order for sale under section 17 of the Married Women's Property Act 1882 or section 66 of the 2004 Act.

Chapter 5
Declarations

8.18 Scope of this Chapter

The rules in this Chapter apply to applications made in accordance with—

(a) section 55 of the 1986 Act (declarations as to marital status) and section 58 of the 2004 Act (declarations as to civil partnership status);
(b) section 55A of the 1986 Act (declarations of parentage);
(c) section 56(1)(b) and (2) of the 1986 Act (declarations of legitimacy or legitimation); and
(d) section 57 of the 1986 Act (declarations as to adoptions effected overseas).

8.19 …[1]

…[1]

Amendment

1 Repealed by the Family Procedure (Amendment No 3) Rules 2013, SI 2013/3204, rr 2, 18.

8.20 Who the parties are

(1) In relation to the proceedings set out in column 1 of the following table, column 2 sets out who the respondents to those proceedings will be.

Proceedings	*Respondent*
Applications for declarations as to marital or civil partnership status.	The other party to the marriage or civil partnership in question or, where the applicant is a third party, both parties to the marriage or civil partnership.
Applications for declarations of parentage.	[(i) The person whose parentage is in issue [except where that person is a child][1]; and (ii) any person who is or is alleged to be the parent of the person whose parentage is in issue, except where that person is the applicant [or is a child][1].][2]
Applications for declarations of legitimacy or legitimation.	The applicant's father and mother or the survivor of them.
Applications for declarations as to adoption effected overseas.	The person(s) whom the applicant is claiming are or are not the applicant's adoptive parents.

[(Under rule 16.2 the court may make a child a party to certain proceedings (including applications for declarations of parentage) where it considers that to be in the best interests of the child.)][1]

(2) The applicant must include in his application particulars of every person whose interest may be affected by the proceedings and his relationship to the applicant.

(3) The acknowledgment of service filed under rule 19.5 must give details of any other persons the respondent considers should be made a party to the application or be given notice of the application.

(4) Upon receipt of the acknowledgment of service, the court must give directions as to any other persons who should be made a respondent to the application or be given notice of the proceedings.

(5) A person given notice of proceedings under paragraph (4) may, within 21 days beginning with the date on which the notice was served, apply to be joined as a party.

(6) No directions may be given as to the future management of the case under rule 19.9 until the expiry of the notice period in paragraph (5).

Amendment

1 Inserted by the Family Procedure (Amendment No 2) Rules 2016, SI 2016/901, rr 2, 3.
2 Substituted by the Family Procedure (Amendment) Rules 2012, SI 2012/679, rr 2, 15.

8.21 The role of the Attorney General

(1) The applicant must, except in the case of an application for a declaration of parentage, send a copy of the application and all accompanying documents to the Attorney General at least one month before making the application.

(2) The Attorney General may, when deciding whether to intervene in the proceedings, inspect any document filed at court relating to any family proceedings mentioned in the declaration proceedings.

(3) If the court is notified that the Attorney General wishes to intervene in the proceedings, a court officer must send the Attorney General a copy of any subsequent documents filed at court.

(4) The court must, when giving directions under rule 8.20(4), consider whether to ask the Attorney General to argue any question relating to the proceedings.

(5) If the court makes a request to the Attorney General under paragraph (4) and the Attorney General agrees to that request, the Attorney General must serve a summary of the argument on all parties to the proceedings.

8.22 Declarations of parentage

(1) If the applicant or the person whose parentage or parenthood is in issue, is known by a name other than that which appears in that person's birth certificate, that other name must also be stated in any order and declaration of parentage.

(2) A court officer must send a copy of a declaration of parentage and the application to the Registrar General within 21 days beginning with the date on which the declaration was made.

Chapter 6
Application for permission to apply for a financial remedy after overseas proceedings

8.23 Scope of this Chapter

Subject to rule 9.26(6), the rules in this Chapter apply to an application for permission to apply for a financial remedy under section 13 of the 1984 Act and paragraph 4 of Schedule 7 to the 2004 Act.

(Rule 9.26(6) enables the application for permission to apply for a financial remedy under section 13 of the 1984 Act or paragraph 4 of Schedule 7 to the 2004 Act to be heard at the same time as the application for a financial remedy under Part 3 of the 1984 Act or Schedule 7 to the 2004 Act where that application is an application for a consent order.)

[(The Family Court (Composition and Distribution of Business) Rules 2014 make provision in relation to the allocation of the proceedings to which this Chapter applies to a specified level of judge in the family court.)][1]

Amendment

1 Inserted by the Family Procedure (Amendment No 2) Rules 2017, SI 2017/741, rr 2, 3.

[8.24 How to start proceedings

The application must be made in accordance with the Part 18 procedure.][1]

Amendment

1 Substituted by the Family Procedure (Amendment No 3) Rules 2013, SI 2013/3204, rr 2, 19.

[8.25 Application without notice

(1) The application must be made without notice to the respondent.

(2) Subject to paragraph (3), the court must determine the application without notice.

(3) The court may direct that the application be determined on notice to the respondent if the court considers that to be appropriate.][1]

Amendment

1 Substituted by the Family Procedure (Amendment No 2) Rules 2017, SI 2017/741, rr 2, 4.

8.26 Notification of hearing date

The court officer must—

(a) fix a date, time and place for the hearing of the application …[1]; and
(b) give notice of the date of the hearing to the applicant.

Amendment

1 Repealed by the Family Procedure (Amendment No 4) Rules 2014, SI 2014/3296, rr 2, 8.

8.27 Hearings to be in private unless the court directs otherwise

An application under this Chapter must be heard in private unless the court directs otherwise.

8.28 …[1]

…[1]

Amendment

1 Repealed by the Family Procedure (Amendment No 2) Rules 2017, SI 2017/741, rr 2, 5.

Chapter 7
Application for the transfer of a tenancy under section 53 of, and Schedule 7 to, the 1996 Act

8.29 Scope of this Chapter

This Chapter applies to an application for the transfer of a tenancy under section 53 of, and Schedule 7 to, the 1996 Act.

[8.30 Where to start proceedings

Where any matrimonial proceedings or civil partnership proceedings have been started by the applicant or the respondent, the application must be made in the same court as those matrimonial proceedings or civil partnership proceedings.

(Practice Direction 8A makes provision in respect of the particular location where the application should be made.)][1]

Amendment

1 Substituted by the Family Procedure (Amendment No 3) Rules 2013, SI 2013/3204, rr 2, 21.

8.31 Service of the application

(1) The court will serve a copy of the application on—

(a) the respondent; and
(b) the landlord (as defined by paragraph 1 of Schedule 7 to the 1996 Act),

unless the court directs that the applicant must do so.

(2) Where service is effected by the applicant, the applicant must file a certificate of service.

8.32 Who the parties are

The court will direct that a landlord be made a party to the proceedings where the landlord requests to be one.

8.33 Orders for disclosure

Any party may apply to the court under rule 21.2 for an order that any person must attend an appointment before the court and produce any documents that are specified or described in the order.

8.34 Injunctions

(1) The court may grant an injunction(GL) only if the injunction(GL) is ancillary or incidental to the assistance sought by the applicant.

(2) Applications for injunctive relief must be made in accordance with the procedure in rule 20.4 (how to apply for an interim remedy) and the provisions of rule 20.5 (interim injunction(GL) to cease if application is stayed(GL)) apply accordingly.

Chapter 8
Applications for orders preventing avoidance under section 32L of the Child Support Act 1991

8.35 Scope of this Chapter

Subject to rule 8.40, the rules in this Chapter apply to applications made under section 32L (1) and (2) of the 1991 Act.

8.36 Interpretation

In this Chapter—

'child support maintenance' has the meaning assigned to it in section 3(6) of the 1991 Act;

'reviewable disposition' has the meaning assigned to it in section 32L(5) of the 1991 Act.

8.37 …[1]

…[1]

Amendment

1 Repealed by the Family Procedure (Amendment No 3) Rules 2013, SI 2013/3204, rr 2, 22.

8.38 Who the parties are

(1) The applicant to the proceedings is the [Secretary of State][1] and the respondent is the person who has failed to pay child support maintenance.

(2) The court may at any time direct that—

(a) any person be made a party to proceedings; or

(b) a party be removed from the proceedings.

Amendment

1 Substituted by the Public Bodies (Child Maintenance and Enforcement Commission: Abolition and Transfer of Functions) Order 2012, SI 2012/2007, art 3(2), Schedule, para 125(b).

8.39 Service of the application

(1) The applicant must serve the application and a copy of the applicant's written evidence on—

(a) any respondent;
(b) the person in whose favour the reviewable disposition is alleged to have been made; and
(c) such other persons as the court directs.

(2) Where an application includes an application relating to land, the applicant must serve a copy of the application on any—

(a) mortgagee;
(b) trustee of a trust of land or settlement; and
(c) other person who has an interest in the land,

of whom particulars are given in the application.

(3) Any person served under paragraph (2) may make a request to the court in writing, within 14 days beginning with the date of service of the application, for a copy of the applicant's written evidence.

(4) Any person who—

(a) is served with copies of the application and the applicant's written evidence under paragraph (1); or
(b) receives a copy of the applicant's written evidence following a request under paragraph (3),

may, within 14 days beginning with the date of service or receipt, file a statement in answer.

(5) A statement in answer filed under paragraph (4) must be verified by a statement of truth.

8.40 Applications without notice

(1) This rule applies to an application under section 32L(1) of the 1991 Act.

(2) The court may grant an application made without notice if it appears to the court that there are good reasons for not giving notice.

(3) If the applicant makes an application without giving notice, the evidence in support of the application must state the reasons why notice has not been given.

(4) If the court grants an application under paragraph (2)—

(a) the order must include a provision allowing any respondent to apply to the court for an order to be reconsidered as soon as just and convenient at a full hearing; and
(b) the applicant must, as soon as reasonably practicable, serve upon each respondent a copy of the order and a copy of the written evidence in support of the application.

Chapter 9
Application for consent to marriage of a child or to registration of civil partnership of a child

8.41 Scope of this Chapter

The rules in this Chapter apply to an application under—

(a) section 3 of the Marriage Act 1949; or
(b) paragraph 3, 4 or 10 of Schedule 2 to the 2004 Act.

8.42 Child acting without a children's guardian

The child may bring an application without a children's guardian, unless the court directs otherwise.

8.43 Who the respondents are

Where an application follows a refusal to give consent to—

(a) the marriage of a child; or
(b) a child registering as the civil partner of another person,

every person who has refused consent will be a respondent to the application.

Practice Direction 8A – Where to start certain proceedings

See also Part 8

This Practice Direction supplements rules 8.14 and 8.30 FPR.

1.1 Provision for the court (that is, the family court or the High Court) in which proceedings should be started is made in–

(a) rule 8.14 FPR as regards an application under section 17 of the Married Women's Property Act 1882 or section 66 of the 2004 Act; and
(b) rule 8.30 FPR as regards an application for the transfer of a tenancy under section 53 of, and Schedule 7 to, the 1996 Act.

1.2 Where rule 8.14 or rule 8.30 FPR means that an application must be made in the family court, then–

(a) the application must be made to the same Designated Family Judge area as the existing (or proposed) matrimonial proceedings or civil partnership proceedings; and
(b) subject to any direction of the court, the matter will be heard in the same location of the family court as those existing (or proposed) proceedings.

PART 9
APPLICATIONS FOR A FINANCIAL REMEDY

Chapter 1
Application and interpretation

[9.1 Application

(1) The rules in this Part apply to an application for a financial remedy.

(2) This Part is subject to any provision made by or pursuant to Part 41 (proceeding by electronic means).

('Financial remedy' and 'financial order' are defined in rule 2.3.)][1]

Amendment

1 Inserted by the Family Procedure (Amendment) Rules 2020, SI 2020/135, rr 2, 9.

9.2 …[1]

…[1]

Amendment

1 Repealed by the Family Procedure (Amendment No 2) Rules 2014, SI 2014/667, rr 2, 7.

9.3 Interpretation

(1) In this Part—

'avoidance of disposition order' means—

(a) in proceedings under the 1973 Act, an order under section 37(2)(b) or (c) of that Act;
(b) in proceedings under the 1984 Act, an order under section 23(2)(b) or 23(3) of that Act;
(c) in proceedings under Schedule 5 to the 2004 Act, an order under paragraph 74(3) or (4); or
(d) in proceedings under Schedule 7 to the 2004 Act, an order under paragraph 15(3) or (4);

'the Board' means the Board of the Pension Protection Fund;
['fast-track procedure' means the procedure set out in Chapter 5;][1]
'FDR appointment' means a Financial Dispute Resolution appointment in accordance with rule 9.17;
['Financial Circumstances Form' means the Financial Circumstances Form published by the Permanent Bureau of the Hague Conference under Article 11(4) of the 2007 Hague Convention for use in relation to applications under Article 10 of that Convention;][2]
'order preventing a disposition' means—

(a) in proceedings under the 1973 Act, an order under section 37(2)(a) of that Act;
(b) in proceedings under the 1984 Act, an order under section 23(2)(a) of that Act;
(c) in proceedings under Schedule 5 to the 2004 Act, an order under paragraph 74(2); or
(d) in proceedings under Schedule 7 to the 2004 Act, an order under paragraph 15(2);

'pension arrangement' means—

(a) an occupational pension scheme;
(b) a personal pension scheme;
(c) shareable state scheme rights;
(d) a retirement annuity contract;

(e) an annuity or insurance policy purchased, or transferred, for the purpose of giving effect to rights under an occupational pension scheme or a personal pension scheme; and
(f) an annuity purchased, or entered into, for the purpose of discharging liability in respect of a pension credit under section 29(1)(b) of the Welfare Reform and Pensions Act 1999 or under corresponding Northern Ireland legislation;

'pension attachment order' means—

(a) in proceedings under the 1973 Act, an order making provision under section 25B or 25C of that Act;
(b) in proceedings under the 1984 Act, an order under section 17(1)(a)(i) of that Act making provision equivalent to an order referred to in paragraph (a);
(c) in proceedings under Schedule 5 to the 2004 Act, an order making provision under paragraph 25 or paragraph 26; or
(d) in proceedings under Schedule 7 to the 2004 Act, an order under paragraph 9(2) or (3) making provision equivalent to an order referred to in paragraph (c);

'pension compensation attachment order' means—

(a) in proceedings under the 1973 Act, an order making provision under section 25F of that Act;
(b) in proceedings under the 1984 Act, an order under section 17(1)(a)(i) of that Act making provision equivalent to an order referred in to paragraph (a);
(c) in proceedings under Schedule 5 to the 2004 Act, an order under paragraph 34A; and
(d) in proceedings under Schedule 7 to the 2004 Act, an order under paragraph 9(2) or (3) making provision equivalent to an order referred to in paragraph (c);

'pension compensation sharing order' means—

(a) in proceedings under the 1973 Act, an order under section 24E of that Act;
(b) in proceedings under the 1984 Act, an order under section 17(1)(c) of that Act;
(c) in proceedings under Schedule 5 to the 2004 Act, an order under paragraph 19A; and
(d) in proceedings under Schedule 7 to the 2004 Act, an order under paragraph 9(2) or (3) making provision equivalent to an order referred to in paragraph (c);

'pension sharing order' means—

(a) in proceedings under the 1973 Act, an order making provision under section 24B of that Act;
(b) in proceedings under the 1984 Act, an order under section 17(1)(b) of that Act;
(c) in proceedings under Schedule 5 to the 2004 Act, an order under paragraph 15; or
(d) in proceedings under Schedule 7 to the 2004 Act, an order under paragraph 9(2) or (3) making provision equivalent to an order referred to in paragraph (c);

'pension scheme' means, unless the context otherwise requires, a scheme for which the Board has assumed responsibility in accordance with Chapter 3 of Part 2 of the Pensions Act 2004 (pension protection) or any provision in force in Northern Ireland corresponding to that Chapter;

'PPF compensation' has the meaning given to it—

(a) in proceedings under the 1973 Act, by section 21C of the 1973 Act;
(b) in proceedings under the 1984 Act, by section 18(7) of the 1984 Act; and
(c) in proceedings under the 2004 Act, by paragraph 19F of Schedule 5 to the 2004 Act;

'relevant valuation' means a valuation of pension rights or benefits as at a date not more than 12 months earlier than the date fixed for the first appointment which has been furnished or requested for the purposes of any of the following provisions—

(a) the Pensions on Divorce etc (Provision of Information) Regulations 2000;
(b) regulation 5 of and Schedule 2 to the Occupational Pension Schemes (Disclosure of Information) Regulations 1996 and regulation 11 of and Schedule 1 to the Occupational Pension Schemes (Transfer Value) Regulations 1996;
(c) section 93A or 94(1)(a) or (aa) of the Pension Schemes Act 1993;
(d) section 94(1)(b) of the Pension Schemes Act 1993 or paragraph 2(a) (or, where applicable, 2(b)) of Schedule 2 to the Personal Pension Schemes (Disclosure of Information) Regulations 1987;
(e) the Dissolution etc. (Pensions) Regulations 2005;

['standard procedure' means the procedure set out in Chapter 4;][1]

'variation order' means—

(a) in proceedings under the 1973 Act, an order under section 31 of that Act; or
(b) in proceedings under the 2004 Act, an order under Part 11 of Schedule 5 to that Act.

(2) …[3]

[(3)

(a) …[4]

[(aa) Where an application for establishment or modification of maintenance is made under Article 10 of the 2007 Hague Convention, references in this Part to 'financial statement' apply to the applicant as if for 'financial statement' there were substituted 'Financial Circumstances Form'.][2]

(b) [Sub-paragraph (aa) does][5] not apply where the relief sought includes relief which is of a type to which …[4] […[4] the 2007 Hague Convention …[4]][2] does not apply.][6]

Amendment

1 Inserted by the Family Procedure (Amendment) Rules 2018, SI 2018/440, rr 2, 4.
2 Inserted by the Family Procedure (Amendment No 4) Rules 2012, SI 2012/2806, rr 2, 3, 7(a), (b)(i), (ii)(bb).
3 Repealed by the Family Procedure (Amendment No 3) Rules 2013, SI 2013/3204, rr 2, 22.
4 Repealed by the Family Procedure Rules 2010 and Court of Protection Rules 2017 (Amendment) (EU Exit) Regulations 2019, SI 2019/517, rr 2, 8(1), (2)(a), (b)(ii), (iii).
5 Substituted by the Family Procedure Rules 2010 and Court of Protection Rules 2017 (Amendment) (EU Exit) Regulations 2019, SI 2019/517, rr 2, 8(1), (2)(i).
6 Inserted by the Family Procedure (Amendment) Rules 2011, SI 2011/1328, rr 2, 3, 7.

Chapter 2
Procedure for applications

9.4 When an Application for a financial order may be made

An application for a financial order may be made—

(a) in an application for a matrimonial or civil partnership order; or
(b) at any time after an application for a matrimonial or civil partnership order has been made.

9.5 Where to start proceedings

(1) An application for a financial remedy must be filed—

(a) if there are proceedings for a matrimonial order or a civil partnership order which are proceeding in [the family court][1], in that court; or
(b) if there are proceedings for a matrimonial order or a civil partnership order which are proceeding in the High Court, in the registry in which those proceedings are taking place.

(2) …[2]

(3) …[3]

Amendment

1 Substituted by the Family Procedure (Amendment No 3) Rules 2013, SI 2013/3204, rr 2, 23(a).
2 Repealed by the Family Procedure (Amendment No 3) Rules 2013, SI 2013/3204, rr 2, 23(b).
3 Repealed by the Family Procedure (Amendment No 2) Rules 2017, SI 2017/741, rr 2, 6.

9.6 Application for an order preventing a disposition

(1) The Part 18 procedure applies to an application for an order preventing a disposition.

(2) An application for an order preventing a disposition may be made without notice to the respondent.

('Order preventing a disposition' is defined in rule 9.3.)

9.7 Application for interim orders

(1) A party may apply at any stage of the proceedings for—

(a) an order for maintenance pending suit;
(b) an order for maintenance pending outcome of proceedings;
(c) an order for interim periodical payments;
(d) an interim variation order;
[(da) an order for payment in respect of legal services; or][1]
(e) any other form of interim order.

[(2) An application for an order mentioned in paragraph (1) shall be made using the Part 18 procedure.][1]

(3) Where a party makes an application before filing a financial statement, the written evidence in support must—

(a) explain why the order is necessary; and
(b) give up to date information about that party's financial circumstances.

(4) Unless the respondent has filed a financial statement, the respondent must, at least 7 days before the court is to deal with the application, file a statement of his means and serve a copy on the applicant.

(5) An application for an order mentioned in paragraph (1)(e) may be made without notice.

Amendment

1 Substituted by the Family Procedure (Amendment No 2) Rules 2013, SI 2013/1472, rr 2, 4.

9.8 Application for periodical payments order at same rate as an order for maintenance pending suit

(1) This rule applies where there are matrimonial proceedings and—

(a) a [conditional order][1] of divorce or nullity of marriage has been made;
(b) at or after the date of the [conditional order][1] an order for maintenance pending suit is in force; and
(c) the spouse in whose favour the [conditional order][1] was made has made an application for an order for periodical payments.

(2) The spouse in whose favour the [conditional order][1] was made may apply, using the Part 18 procedure, for an order providing for payments at the same rate as those provided for by the order for maintenance pending suit.

Amendment

1 Substituted by the Family Procedure (Amendment) Rules 2022, SI 2022/44, rr 2, 23.

9.9 Application for periodical payments order at same rate as an order for maintenance pending outcome of proceedings

(1) This rule applies where there are civil partnership proceedings and—

(a) a conditional order of dissolution or nullity of civil partnership has been made;
(b) at or after the date of the conditional order an order for maintenance pending outcome of proceedings is in force;
(c) the civil partner in whose favour the conditional order was made has made an application for an order for periodical payments.

(2) The civil partner in whose favour the conditional order was made may apply, using the Part 18 procedure, for an order providing for payments at the same rate as those provided for by, the order for maintenance pending the outcome of proceedings.

[9.9A Application to set aside a financial remedy order

(1) In this rule—

(a) 'financial remedy order' means an order or judgment that is a financial remedy, and includes—
  (i) part of such an order or judgment; or
  (ii) a consent order; and
(b) 'set aside' means—
  (i) in the High Court, to set aside a financial remedy order pursuant to section 17(2) of the Senior Courts Act 1981 and this rule;
  (ii) in the family court, to rescind or vary a financial remedy order pursuant to section 31F(6) of the 1984 Act.

(2) A party may apply under this rule to set aside a financial remedy order where no error of the court is alleged.

(3) An application under this rule must be made within the proceedings in which the financial remedy order was made.

(4) An application under this rule must be made in accordance with the Part 18 procedure, subject to the modifications contained in this rule.

(5) Where the court decides to set aside a financial remedy order, it shall give directions for the rehearing of the financial remedy proceedings or make such other orders as may be appropriate to dispose of the application.][1]

Amendment

1 Inserted by the Family Procedure (Amendment No 2) Rules 2016, SI 2016/901, rr 2, 4.

[9.9B Standard and fast-track procedures for financial remedy proceedings

(1) In this rule 'order for periodical payments' means an order under—

(a) section 23(1)(a), (b), (d) or (e) of the 1973 Act;
(b) section 27(5) or (6)(a), (b), (d) or (e) of the 1973 Act;
(c) paragraph 1(2)(a) or (b), 2(2)(a) or 9 of Schedule 1 to the 1989 Act;
(d) paragraph 2(1)(a), (b), (d) or (e) of Schedule 5 to the 2004 Act;
(e) paragraph 40 or 41(1)(a), (b), (d) or (e) of Schedule 5 to the 2004 Act.

(2) Subject to paragraph (3), an application for a financial remedy must be dealt with under the standard procedure.

(3) The fast-track procedure applies to—

(a) any application where the financial remedy sought is only for an order for periodical payments;
(b) any application made under—
  (i) the 1978 Act;
  (ii) Schedule 6 to the 2004 Act;
  (iii) …[1] or
  (iv) Article 10 of the 2007 Hague Convention;
(c) any application for the variation of an order for periodical payments, except where the applicant seeks the dismissal (immediate or otherwise) of the periodical payments order and its substitution with one or more of a lump sum order, a property adjustment order, a pension sharing order or a pension compensation sharing order.

(4) At any stage in the proceedings the court may order that an application proceeding under the fast-track procedure must proceed under the standard procedure.

(Rule 9.18A provides for specific occasions when the court may direct that a case should proceed under the standard procedure.)][2]

Amendment

1 Repealed by the Family Procedure Rules 2010 and Court of Protection Rules 2017 (Amendment) (EU Exit) Regulations 2019, SI 2019/517, rr 2, 8(1), (3).
2 Inserted by the Family Procedure (Amendment) Rules 2018, SI 2018/440, rr 2, 5.

Chapter 3
Applications for financial remedies for children

9.10 Application by parent, guardian etc for financial remedy in respect of children

(1) The following people may apply for a financial remedy in respect of a child—

(a) a parent, guardian or special guardian of any child of the family;
(b) any person [who is named in a child arrangements order as a person with whom a child of the family is to live][1], and any applicant for such an order;
(c) any other person who is entitled to apply for [a child arrangements order which names that person as a person with whom a child is to live][1];
(d) a local authority, where an order has been made under section 31(1)(a) of the 1989 Act placing a child in its care;
(e) the Official Solicitor, if appointed the children's guardian of a child of the family under rule 16.24; and
(f) [subject to paragraph (1A),][2] a child of the family who has been given permission to apply for a financial remedy.

[(1A) Where the application is—

(a) for the variation of an order under section 2(1)(c), 6 or 7 of the 1978 Act or paragraph 2(1)(c) of, or Part 2 or 3 of, Schedule 6 to the 2004 Act for periodical payments in respect of a child;
(b) the application is made by the child in question; and
(c) the child in question is aged 16 or over,

the child does not require permission to make the application.][2]

(2) …[3]

Amendment

1 Substituted by the Family Procedure (Amendment No 3) Rules 2014, SI 2014/843, rr 2, 13(a).
2 Inserted by the Family Procedure (Amendment No 3) Rules 2013, SI 2013/3204, rr 2, 24.
3 Repealed by the Family Procedure (Amendment No 3) Rules 2014, SI 2014/843, rr 2, 13(b).

9.11 Children to be separately represented on certain applications

(1) Where an application for a financial remedy includes an application for an order for a variation of settlement, the court must, unless it is satisfied that the proposed variation does not adversely affect the rights or interests of any child concerned, direct that the child be separately represented on the application.

(2) On any other application for a financial remedy the court may direct that the child be separately represented on the application.

(3) Where a direction is made under paragraph (1) or (2), the court may if the person to be appointed so consents, appoint—

(a) a person other than the Official Solicitor; or
(b) the Official Solicitor,

to be a children's guardian and rule 16.24(5) and (6) and rules 16.25 to 16.28 apply as appropriate to such an appointment.

Chapter 4
[Standard procedure][1]

9.12 Duties of the court and the applicant upon issuing an application

(1) When an application under this Part is issued[, except where Chapter 5 of this Part applies][2]—

(a) the court will fix a first appointment not less than 12 weeks and not more than 16 weeks after the date of the filing of the application; and
(b) subject to paragraph (2), within 4 days beginning with the date on which the application was filed, a court officer will—
  (i) serve a copy of the application on the respondent; and
  (ii) give notice of the date of the first appointment to the applicant and the respondent.

(2) Where the applicant wishes to serve a copy of the application on the respondent and on filing the application so notifies the court—

(a) paragraph (1)(b) does not apply;
(b) a court officer will return to the applicant the copy of the application and the notice of the date of the first appointment; and
(c) the applicant must,—
  (i) within 4 days beginning with the date on which the copy of the application is received from the court, serve the copy of the application and notice of the date of the first appointment on the respondent; and
  (ii) file a certificate of service at or before the first appointment.

(Rule 6.37 sets out what must be included in a certificate of service.)

(3) The date fixed under paragraph (1), or for any subsequent appointment, must not be cancelled except with the court's permission and, if cancelled, the court must immediately fix a new date.

[(4) In relation to an application to which …[3] […[3] the 2007 Hague Convention][4] applies, where the applicant does not already know the address of the respondent at the time the application is issued, paragraph (2) does not apply and the court will serve the application in accordance with paragraph (1).][5]

Amendment

1 Substituted by the Family Procedure (Amendment) Rules 2018, SI 2018/440, rr 2, 6.
2 Substituted by the Family Procedure (Amendment No 3) Rules 2013, SI 2013/3204, rr 2, 26.
3 Repealed by the Family Procedure Rules 2010 and Court of Protection Rules 2017 (Amendment) (EU Exit) Regulations 2019, SI 2019/517, rr 2, 8(1), (4).
4 Inserted by the Family Procedure (Amendment No 4) Rules 2012, SI 2012/2806, rr 2, 3, 8.
5 Inserted by the Family Procedure (Amendment) Rules 2011, SI 2011/1328, rr 2, 3, 8.

9.13 Service of application on mortgagees, trustees etc

(1) Where an application for a financial remedy includes an application for an order for a variation of settlement, the applicant must serve copies of the application on—

(a) the trustees of the settlement;
(b) the settlor if living; and
(c) such other persons as the court directs.

(2) In the case of an application for an avoidance of disposition order, the applicant must serve copies of the application on the person in whose favour the disposition is alleged to have been made.

(3) Where an application for a financial remedy includes an application relating to land, the applicant must serve a copy of the application on any mortgagee of whom particulars are given in the application.

(4) Any person served under paragraphs (1), (2) or (3) may make a request to the court in writing, within 14 days beginning with the date of service of the application, for a copy of the applicant's financial statement or any relevant part of that statement.

(5) Any person who—

(a) is served with copies of the application in accordance with paragraphs (1), (2) or (3); or
(b) receives a copy of a financial statement, or a relevant part of that statement, following an application made under paragraph (4),

may within 14 days beginning with the date of service or receipt file a statement in answer.

(6) Where a copy of an application is served under paragraphs (1), (2) or (3), the applicant must file a certificate of service at or before the first appointment.

(7) A statement in answer filed under paragraph (5) must be verified by a statement of truth.

9.14 Procedure before the first appointment

(1) Not less than 35 days before the first appointment both parties must simultaneously exchange with each other and file with the court a financial statement in the form referred to in Practice Direction 5A.

(2) The financial statement must—

(a) be verified by [a statement of truth][1]; and
(b) accompanied by the following documents only—
  (i) any documents required by the financial statement;
  (ii) any other documents necessary to explain or clarify any of the information contained in the financial statement; and
  (iii) any documents provided to the party producing the financial statement by a person responsible for a pension arrangement, either following a request under rule 9.30 or as part of a relevant valuation; and
  (iv) any notification or other document referred to in rule 9.37(2), (4) or (5) which has been received by the party producing the financial statement.

[(2ZA) Paragraph (2A) applies where the court has determined that the procedure in this Chapter should apply to an application under …[2] Article 10 of the 2007 Hague Convention.][3]

[[(2A) The requirement of paragraph (2)(a) relating to verification by a statement of truth does not apply to the financial statement of either party where the application has been made under—

(a) …[2]
(b) Article 10 of the 2007 Hague Convention, using the Financial Circumstances Form,

and the relief sought is limited to a type to which [that Convention][4] applies, but the court may at any time direct that the financial statement of either party shall be verified by a statement of truth.][5][6]

(3) Where a party was unavoidably prevented from sending any document required by the financial statement, that party must at the earliest opportunity—

(a) serve a copy of that document on the other party; and
(b) file a copy of that document with the court, together with a written explanation of the failure to send it with the financial statement.

(4) No disclosure or inspection of documents may be requested or given between the filing of the application for a financial remedy and the first appointment, except—

(a) copies sent with the financial statement, or in accordance with paragraph (3); or
(b) in accordance with paragraphs (5) and (6).

(Rule 21.1 explains what is meant by disclosure and inspection.)

(5) Not less than 14 days before the hearing of the first appointment, each party must file with the court and serve on the other party—

(a) a concise statement of the issues between the parties;
(b) a chronology;
(c) a questionnaire setting out by reference to the concise statement of issues any further nformation and documents requested from the other party or a statement that no information and documents are required; and
(d) a notice stating whether that party will be in a position at the first appointment to proceed on that occasion to a FDR appointment.

(6) Not less than 14 days before the hearing of the first appointment, the applicant must file with the court and serve on the respondent confirmation—

(a) of the names of all persons served in accordance with rule 9.13(1) to (3); and
(b) that there are no other persons who must be served in accordance with those paragraphs.

Amendment

1 Substituted by the Family Procedure (Amendment) Rules 2012, SI 2012/679, rr 2, 16.
2 Repealed by the Family Procedure Rules 2010 and Court of Protection Rules 2017 (Amendment) (EU Exit) Regulations 2019, SI 2019/517, rr 2, 8(1), (5)(a), (b)(i).
2 Inserted by the Family Procedure (Amendment No 2) Rules 2014, SI 2014/667, rr 2, 8.
4 Substituted by the Family Procedure Rules 2010 and Court of Protection Rules 2017 (Amendment) (EU Exit) Regulations 2019, SI 2019/517, rr 2, 8(1), (5)(b)(ii).
5 Substituted by the Family Procedure (Amendment No 4) Rules 2012, SI 2012/2806, rr 2, 3, 9.
6 Inserted by the Family Procedure (Amendment) Rules 2011, SI 2011/1328, rr 2, 3, 8.

9.15 Duties of the court at the first appointment

(1) The first appointment must be conducted with the objective of defining the issues and saving costs.

(2) At the first appointment the court must determine—

(a) the extent to which any questions seeking information under rule 9.14(5)(c) must be answered; and
(b) what documents requested under rule 9.14(5)(c) must be produced,

and give directions for the production of such further documents as may be necessary.

(3) The court must give directions where appropriate about—

(a) the valuation of assets (including the joint instruction of joint experts);
(b) obtaining and exchanging expert evidence, if required;
(c) the evidence to be adduced by each party; and
(d) further chronologies or schedules to be filed by each party.

[(4) The court must direct that the case be referred to a FDR appointment unless—

(a) the first appointment or part of it has been treated as a FDR appointment and the FDR appointment has been effective; or
(b) there are exceptional reasons which make a referral to a FDR appointment inappropriate.][1]

(5) If the court decides that a referral to a FDR appointment is not appropriate it must direct one or more of the following—

(a) that a further directions appointment be fixed;
(b) that an appointment be fixed for the making of an interim order;
(c) that the case be fixed for a final hearing and, where that direction is given, the court must determine the judicial level at which the case should be heard.

([Under Part 3][2] the court may also direct that the case be adjourned if it considers that [non-court dispute resolution][2] is appropriate.)

(6) In considering whether to make a costs order under rule 28.3(5), the court must have particular regard to the extent to which each party has complied with the requirement to send documents with the financial statement and the explanation given for any failure to comply.

(7) The court may—

(a) where an application for an interim order has been listed for consideration at the first appointment, make an interim order;
(b) having regard to the contents of the notice filed by the parties under rule 9.14(5)(d), treat the appointment (or part of it) as a FDR appointment to which rule 9.17 applies;
(c) in a case where a pension sharing order or a pension attachment order is requested, direct any party with pension rights to file and serve a Pension Inquiry Form, completed in full or in part as the court may direct; and
(d) in a case where a pension compensation sharing order or a pension compensation attachment order is requested, direct any party with PPF compensation rights to file and serve a Pension Protection Fund Inquiry Form, completed in full or in part as the court may direct.

(8) Both parties must personally attend the first appointment unless the court directs otherwise.

Amendment

1 Substituted by the Family Procedure (Amendment No 2) Rules 2017, SI 2017/741, rr 2, 7.
2 Substituted by the Family Procedure (Amendment No 3) Rules 2014, SI 2014/843, rr 2, 14.

9.16 After the first appointment

(1) Between the first appointment and the FDR appointment, a party is not entitled to the production of any further documents except—

(a) in accordance with directions given under rule 9.15(2); or
(b) with the permission of the court.

(2) At any stage—

(a) a party may apply for further directions or a FDR appointment;
(b) the court may give further directions or direct that parties attend a FDR appointment.

9.17 The FDR appointment

(1) The FDR appointment must be treated as a meeting held for the purposes of discussion and negotiation.

(2) The judge hearing the FDR appointment must have no further involvement with the application, other than to conduct any further FDR appointment or to make a consent order or a further directions order.

(3) Not less than 7 days before the FDR appointment, the applicant must file with the court details of all offers and proposals, and responses to them.

(4) Paragraph (3) includes any offers, proposals or responses made wholly or partly without prejudice(GL), but paragraph (3) does not make any material admissible as evidence if, but for that paragraph, it would not be admissible.

(5) At the conclusion of the FDR appointment, any documents filed under paragraph (3), and any filed documents referring to them, must, at the request of the party who filed them, be returned to that party and not retained on the court file.

(6) Parties attending the FDR appointment must use their best endeavours to reach agreement on matters in issue between them.

(7) The FDR appointment may be adjourned from time to time.

(8) At the conclusion of the FDR appointment, the court may make an appropriate consent order.

(9) If the court does not make an appropriate consent order as mentioned in paragraph (8), the court must give directions for the future course of the proceedings including, where appropriate—

(a) the filing of evidence, including up to date information; …[1]
(b) fixing a final hearing date[; and][2]
[(c) any necessary directions for the filing of open proposals for settlement under rule 9.27A or rule 9.28.][3]

(10) Both parties must personally attend the FDR appointment unless the court directs otherwise.

Amendment

1 Repealed by the Family Procedure (Amendment) Rules 2020, SI 2020/135, rr 2, 10(a).
2 Substituted by the Family Procedure (Amendment) Rules 2020, SI 2020/135, rr 2, 10(b).
3 Inserted by the Family Procedure (Amendment) Rules 2020, SI 2020/135, rr 2, 10(c).

Chapter 5
[Fast-track procedure][1]

9.18 Duties of the court and the applicant upon filing an application

[(A1) This Chapter applies where, in accordance with rule 9.9B, the fast-track procedure applies to an application for a financial remedy.][1]

(1) [Where an application is issued][2]—

(a) the court will fix a first hearing date not less than [6 weeks and not more than 10][1] weeks after the date of the filing of the application; and
(b) subject to paragraph (2), within 4 days beginning with the date on which the application was filed, a court officer will—
(i) serve a copy of the application on the respondent; [and][3]
(ii) give notice of the date of the first hearing to the applicant and the respondent[.][1]
(iii) …[4]

(2) Where the applicant wishes to serve a copy of the application on the respondent and, on filing the application, so notifies the court—

(a) paragraph (1)(b) does not apply;
(b) a court officer will return to the applicant the copy of the application and the notice of the date of the first hearing; and
(c) the applicant must—
(i) within 4 days beginning with the date on which the copy of the application is received from the court, serve the copy of the application and notice of the date of the first hearing on the respondent; [and][3]
(ii) …[4]
(iii) file a certificate of service at or before the first hearing.

(3) The date fixed under paragraph (1), or for any other subsequent hearing or appointment must not be cancelled except with the court's permission and, if cancelled, the court must immediately fix a new date.

[[(4) …[4]][5]

(5) In relation to an application to which …[6] […[6] the 2007 Hague Convention][7] applies, where the applicant does not already know the address of the respondent at the time the application is issued, paragraph (2) does not apply and the court will serve the application in accordance with paragraph (1).][8]

Amendment

1 Substituted by the Family Procedure (Amendment) Rules 2018, SI 2018/440, rr 2, 7, 8(a), (b)(i), (ii)(bb).
2 Substituted by the Family Procedure (Amendment No 3) Rules 2013, SI 2013/3204, rr 2, 28(b).
3 Inserted by the Family Procedure (Amendment) Rules 2018, SI 2018/440, rr 2, 8(b)(ii)(aa), (c)(i).
4 Repealed by the Family Procedure (Amendment) Rules 2018, SI 2018/440, rr 2, 8(b)(ii)(cc), (c)(ii), (d).
5 Substituted by the Family Procedure (Amendment No 4) Rules 2012, SI 2012/2806, rr 2, 3, 10(a).
6 Repealed by the Family Procedure Rules 2010 and Court of Protection Rules 2017 (Amendment) (EU Exit) Regulations 2019, SI 2019/517, rr 2, 8(1), (6).
7 Inserted by the Family Procedure (Amendment No 4) Rules 2012, SI 2012/2806, rr 2, 3, 10(b).
8 Inserted by the Family Procedure (Amendment) Rules 2011, SI 2011/1328, rr 2, 3, 10.

[9.18A Request for change of procedure

[(1) Paragraph (2) applies where the applicant wishes to seek a direction from the court that the standard procedure should apply to an application to which the fast-track procedure would otherwise apply.

(2) Where this paragraph applies, a request for a direction—

(a) must be made with the application for a financial remedy; and
(b) must state—
(i) that the applicant seeks a direction that the standard procedure should apply; and
(ii) the applicant's reasons for seeking such a direction.

(3) Paragraph (4) applies where—

(a) a respondent wishes to seek a direction from the court that the standard procedure should apply to an application to which the fast-track procedure would otherwise apply; or
(b) a respondent wishes to make representations on an application made by the applicant to which paragraph (1) applies.

(4) Where this paragraph applies, the respondent's request or representations—

(a) must be filed with the court within 7 days of service of the application for a financial remedy; and
(b) must state—
(i) which procedure (standard or fast-track) the respondent wishes the court to direct should apply to the application for a financial remedy; and
(ii) the respondent's reasons for seeking such a direction.

(5) Where a request or representations referred to in this rule have been made, the court must—

(a) determine without notice to the parties and before the first hearing whether the standard procedure or the fast-track procedure should apply to the application for a financial remedy; and
(b) notify the parties of its determination and any directions made in consequence of that determination.][1]][2]

Amendment

1 Substituted by the Family Procedure (Amendment) Rules 2018, SI 2018/440, rr 2, 9.
2 Inserted by the Family Procedure (Amendment No 3) Rules 2013, SI 2013/3204, rr 2, 29.

9.19 Procedure before the first hearing

(1) Not more than [14][1] days after the date of the issue of the application both parties must simultaneously exchange with each other and file with the court a financial statement referred to in Practice Direction 5A.

(2) The financial statement must—

(a) be verified by [a statement of truth][2]; and
(b) contain the following documents only—
(i) any documents required by the financial statement; and
(ii) any other documents necessary to explain or clarify any of the information contained in the financial statement.

[[(2A) The requirement of paragraph (2)(a) relating to verification by statement of truth does not apply to the financial statement of either party where the application has been made under—

(a) …[3]
(b) Article 10 of the 2007 Hague Convention, using the Financial Circumstances Form,

but the court may at any time direct that the financial statement of either party shall be verified by a statement of truth.][4]][5]

(3) Where a party was unavoidably prevented from sending any document required by the financial statement, that party must at the earliest opportunity—

(a) serve a copy of that document on the other party; and

(b) file a copy of that document with the court, together with a statement explaining the failure to send it with the financial statement.

(4) No disclosure or inspection of documents may be requested or given between the filing of the application for a financial remedy and the first hearing except copies sent with the financial statement or in accordance with paragraph (3).

(Rule 21.1 explains what is meant by disclosure and inspection.)

Amendment

1 Substituted by the Family Procedure (Amendment) Rules 2018, SI 2018/440, rr 2, 10.
2 Substituted by the Family Procedure (Amendment) Rules 2012, SI 2012/679, rr 2, 17(a).
3 Repealed by the Family Procedure Rules 2010 and Court of Protection Rules 2017 (Amendment) (EU Exit) Regulations 2019, SI 2019/517, rr 2, 8(1), (7).
4 Substituted by the Family Procedure (Amendment No 4) Rules 2012, SI 2012/2806, rr 2, 3, 11.
5 Inserted by the Family Procedure (Amendment) Rules 2011, SI 2011/1328, rr 2, 3, 11.

[9.20 Consideration of the application at the first hearing

(1) If the court is able to determine the application at the first hearing, it must do so unless it considers that there are good reasons not to do so.

(2) Paragraphs (3) to (7) apply where the court does not determine the application at the first hearing.

(3) The court may give directions relating to—

(a) the filing of further evidence;
(b) the production of further documents;
(c) any other matter required for the fair determination of the matter.

(4) The court may use the first hearing or part of it as a FDR appointment.

(5) Where the court uses the first hearing or part of it as a FDR appointment, rule 9.17 applies with these modifications—

(a) for paragraph (3) substitute—

'(3) At the first hearing, the applicant must produce to the court all offers and proposals and responses to them.'; and

(b) [paragraph (7) does][1] not apply.

(6) The court may direct that the application be referred to a FDR appointment.

(7) If the court decides that a referral to a FDR appointment is not appropriate it must direct one or more of the following—

(a) that a further directions appointment be fixed;
(b) that an appointment be fixed for the making of an interim order;
(c) that the case be fixed for a final hearing and, where that direction is given, the court must determine the judicial level at which the case should be heard.

(Under Part 3 the court may also direct that the case be adjourned if it considers that non-court dispute resolution is appropriate.)][2]

Amendment

1 Substituted by the Family Procedure (Amendment) Rules 2020, SI 2020/135, rr 2, 10(b).
2 Substituted by the Family Procedure (Amendment) Rules 2018, SI 2018/440, rr 2, 11.

9.21 Who the respondent is on an application under section 20 or section 20A of the 1978 Act or Part 6 of Schedule 6 to the 2004 Act

In relation to proceedings set out in column 1 of the following table, column 2 sets out who the respondents to those proceedings will be.

Proceedings	*Respondent*
Application under section 20 of the 1978 Act …[1].	The other party to the marriage; and where the order to which the application relates requires periodical payments to be made to, or in respect of, a child who is 16 years of age or over, that child.
Application under paragraphs 30 to 34 of Schedule 6 to the 2004 Act …[1].	The other party to the civil partnership; and where the order to which the application relates requires periodical payments to be made to, or in respect of, a child who is 16 years of age or over, that child.
Application for the revival of an order under section 20A of the 1978 Act or paragraph 40 of Schedule 6 to the 2004 Act.	The parties to the proceedings leading to the order which it is sought to have revived.

Amendment

1 Repealed by the Family Procedure (Amendment No 3) Rules 2013, SI 2013/3204, rr 2, 30.

[9.21A Duty to make entries in the court's register

Where a court officer receives notice of any direction made in the High Court or family court under section 28 of the 1978 Act by virtue of which an order made under that Act or the 2004 Act ceases to have effect, particulars of the direction must be noted in the court's records.][1]

Amendment

1 Inserted by the Family Procedure (Amendment No 2) Rules 2014, SI 2014/667, rr 2, 10.

[Chapter 5A
Certain applications][1]

[9.22 …[2]

…[2]][3]

Amendment

1 Inserted by the Family Procedure (Amendment No 2) Rules 2014, SI 2014/667, rr 2, 11.
2 Repealed by the Family Procedure Rules 2010 and Court of Protection Rules 2017 (Amendment) (EU Exit) Regulations 2019, SI 2019/517, rr 2, 8(1), (8).
3 Substituted by the Family Procedure (Amendment) Rules 2011, SI 2011/1328, rr 2, 3, 12.

9.23 …[1]

…[1]

Amendment

1 Repealed by the Family Procedure (Amendment No 2) Rules 2014, SI 2014/667, rr 2, 12.

Chapter 6
General procedure

9.24 Power to order delivery up of possession etc.

(1) This rule applies where the court has made an order under—

(a) section 24A of the 1973 Act;
(b) section 17(2) of the 1984 Act;
(c) Part 3 of Schedule 5 to the 2004 Act; or
(d) paragraph 9(4) of Schedule 7 to the 2004 Act.

(2) When the court makes an order mentioned in paragraph (1), it may order any party to deliver up to the purchaser or any other person—

(a) possession of the land, including any interest in, or right over, land;
(b) receipt of rents or profits relating to it; or
(c) both.

9.25 Where proceedings may be heard

(1) Paragraph (2) applies to an application—

(a) for a financial order;
(b) under Part 3 of the 1984 Act; or
(c) under Schedule 7 to the 2004 Act.

(2) An application mentioned in paragraph (1) must be heard—

(a) …[1]
(b) where the case is proceeding in the High Court—
  (i) at the Royal Courts of Justice; or
  (ii) in matrimonial or civil partnership proceedings, any court at which sittings of the High Court are authorised.

(3) …[1]

(4) …[1]

(5) …[1]

Amendment

1 Repealed by the Family Procedure (Amendment No 3) Rules 2013, SI 2013/3204, rr 2, 33.

9.26 Applications for consent orders for financial remedy

(1) Subject to paragraph (5) and to rule 35.2, in relation to an application for a consent order—

(a) the applicant must file two copies of a draft of the order in the terms sought, one of which must be endorsed with a statement signed by the respondent to the application signifying agreement; and
(b) each party must file with the court and serve on the other party, a statement of information in the form referred to in Practice Direction 5A.

(2) Where each party's statement of information is contained in one form, it must be signed by both the applicant and respondent to certify that they have read the contents of the other party's statement.

(3) Where each party's statement of information is in a separate form, the form of each party must be signed by the other party to certify that they have read the contents of the statement contained in that form.

(4) Unless the court directs otherwise, the applicant and the respondent need not attend the hearing of an application for a consent order.

(5) Where all or any of the parties attend the hearing of an application for a financial remedy the court may—

(a) dispense with the filing of a statement of information; and
(b) give directions for the information which would otherwise be required to be given in such a statement in such a manner as it thinks fit.

(6) In relation to an application for a consent order under Part 3 of the 1984 Act or Schedule 7 to the 2004 Act, the application for permission to make the application may be heard at the same time as the application for a financial remedy if evidence of the respondent's consent to the order is filed with the application.

(The following rules contain provision in relation to applications for consent orders – rule 9.32 (pension sharing order), rule 9.34 (pension attachment order), rule 9.41 (pension compensation sharing orders) and rule 9.43 (pension compensation attachment orders.)

[9.26A Questions as to the court's jurisdiction or whether the proceedings should be stayed

(1) This rule applies to applications for maintenance where a question as to jurisdiction arises under—

(a) …[1]
(b) …[1]
(c) …[1] …[2]
(d) …[1]
(e) Article 18 of the 2007 Hague Convention.][3]

(2) If at any time after the issue of the application it appears to the court that it does not or may not have jurisdiction to hear an application, or that under the instruments referred to in paragraph (1) it is or may be required to stay the proceedings or to decline jurisdiction, the court must—

(a) stay the proceedings, and
(b) fix a date for a hearing to determine jurisdiction or whether there should be a stay or other order.

(3) The court officer will serve notice of the hearing referred to at paragraph (2)(b) on the parties to the proceedings.

(4) The court must, in writing—

(a) give reasons for its decision under paragraph (2), and
(b) where it makes a finding of fact, state such finding.

(5) The court may with the consent of all the parties deal with any question as to the jurisdiction of the court, or as to whether the proceedings should be stayed, without a hearing.

(6) …[1]][4]

Amendment

1 Repealed by the Family Procedure Rules 2010 and Court of Protection Rules 2017 (Amendment) (EU Exit) Regulations 2019, SI 2019/517, rr 2, 8(1), (9).
2 Repealed by the Family Procedure (Amendment No 4) Rules 2012, SI 2012/2806, rr 2, 3, 12(a).
3 Inserted by the Family Procedure (Amendment No 4) Rules 2012, SI 2012/2806, rr 2, 3, 12(b).
4 Inserted by the Family Procedure (Amendment) Rules 2011, SI 2011/1328, rr 2, 3, 13.

[9.26AA International Maintenance Obligations: Communication with the Central Authority for England and Wales

(1) Where the Lord Chancellor requests information or a document from the court officer for the relevant court for the purposes of …[1] Articles 12 or 25(2) of the 2007 Hague Convention, the court officer shall provide the requested information or document to the Lord Chancellor forthwith.

(2) In this rule, 'relevant court' means the court at which an application under …[1] Article 10 of the 2007 Hague Convention has been filed.

(The Lord Chancellor is the Central Authority for England and Wales in relation to the 2007 Hague Convention …[1])][2]

Amendment

1 Repealed by the Family Procedure Rules 2010 and Court of Protection Rules 2017 (Amendment) (EU Exit) Regulations 2019, SI 2019/517, rr 2, 8(1), (10).
2 Inserted by the Family Procedure (Amendment No 4) Rules 2012, SI 2012/2806, rr 2, 3, 13.

[9.26B Adding or removing parties

(1) The court may direct that a person or body be added as a party to proceedings for a financial remedy if—

(a) it is desirable to add the new party so that the court can resolve all the matters in dispute in the proceedings; or
(b) there is an issue involving the new party and an existing party which is connected to the matters in dispute in the proceedings, and it is desirable to add the new party so that the court can resolve that issue.

(2) The court may direct that any person or body be removed as a party if it is not desirable for that person or body to be a party to the proceedings.

(3) If the court makes a direction for the addition or removal of a party under this rule, it may give consequential directions about—

(a) the service of a copy of the application form or other relevant documents on the new party; and
(b) the management of the proceedings.

(4) The power of the court under this rule to direct that a party be added or removed may be exercised either on the court's own initiative or on the application of an existing party or a person or body who wishes to become a party.

(5) An application for an order under this rule must be made in accordance with the Part 18 procedure and, unless the court directs otherwise, must be supported by evidence setting out the proposed new party's interest in or connection with the proceedings or, in the case of removal of a party, the reasons for removal.][1]

Amendment

1 Inserted by the Family Procedure (Amendment) Rules 2012, SI 2012/679, rr 2, 18.

[9.26C Method of making periodical payments

(1) This rule applies where under section 1(4) or (4A) of the Maintenance Enforcement Act 1991 the court orders that payments under a qualifying periodical maintenance order are to be made by a particular means.

(2) The court officer will record on a copy of the order the means of payment that the court has ordered.

(3) The court officer will notify in writing the person liable to make payments under the order how the payments are to be made.

(4) Where under section 1(4A) of the Maintenance Enforcement Act 1991 the court orders payment to the court by a method of payment under section 1(5) of that Act, the court officer will notify the person liable to make payments under the order of sufficient details of the account into which payments should be made to enable payments to be made into that account.

(5) Where payments are made to the court, the court officer will give or send a receipt to any person who makes such a payment and who asks for a receipt.

(6) Where payments are made to the court, the court officer will make arrangements to make the payments to—

(a) the person entitled to them; or
(b) if the person entitled to them is a child, to the child or to the person with whom the child has his or her home.

(7) The Part 18 procedure applies to an application under section 1(7) of the Maintenance Enforcement Act 1991 (application from an interested party to revoke, suspend, revive or vary the method of payment).

(8) Where the court makes an order under section 1(7) of the Maintenance Enforcement Act 1991 or dismisses an application for such an order, the court officer will, as far as practicable, notify in writing all interested parties of the effect of the order and will take the steps set out in paragraphs (2), (3) and (4), as appropriate.

(9) In this rule, 'interested party' and 'qualifying periodical maintenance order' have the meanings given in section 1(10) of the Maintenance Enforcement Act 1991.][1]

Amendment

1 Inserted by the Family Procedure (Amendment No 2) Rules 2014, SI 2014/667, rr 2, 13.

[9.26D Court officer to notify subsequent marriage or formation of civil partnership of a person entitled to payments under a maintenance order

(1) This rule applies where—

(a) there is an order of a type referred to in paragraph (4) which requires payments to be made to the court or to an officer of the court; and
(b) the court is notified in writing by—
 (i) the person entitled to receive payments under the order;
 (ii) the person required to make payments under the order; or
 (iii) the personal representative of such a person,

that the person entitled to receive payments under the order has subsequently married or formed a civil partnership.

(2) The court officer will, where practicable, notify in writing the courts referred to in paragraph (3) of the notification of the subsequent marriage or formation of a civil partnership.

(3) The courts to be notified are—

(a) any other court which has made an order of a type referred to in paragraph (4);
(b) in the case of a provisional order made under section 3 of the 1920 Act or section 3 of the 1972 Act, the court which confirmed the order;
(c) if an order of a type referred to in paragraph (4) has been transmitted abroad for registration under section 2 of the 1920 Act or section 2 of the 1972 Act, the court in which the order is registered; and
(d) any other court in which an application to enforce the order has been made.

(4) The orders are—

(a) those to which the following provisions apply—
  (i) section 38 of the 1973 Act;
  (ii) section 4(2) of the 1978 Act;
  (iii) paragraph 65 of Schedule 5 to the 2004 Act; and
  (iv) paragraph 26(2) of Schedule 6 to the 2004 Act; and
(b) an attachment of earnings order made to secure payments under an order referred to in sub-paragraph (a).

(5) In this rule—

'the 1920 Act' means the Maintenance Orders (Facilities for Enforcement) Act 1920; and

'the 1972 Act' means the Maintenance Orders (Reciprocal Enforcement) Act 1972.][1]

Amendment

1 Inserted by the Family Procedure (Amendment No 2) Rules 2014, SI 2014/667, rr 2, 13.

[9.26E Enforcement and apportionment where periodical payments are made under more than one order

(1) This rule applies where periodical payments are required to be made by a payer to a payee under more than one periodical payments order.

(2) Proceedings for the recovery of payments under more than one order may be made in one application by the payee, which must indicate the payments due under each order.

(3) Paragraphs (4) and (5) apply where any sum paid to the court on any date by a payer who is liable to make payments to the court under two or more periodical payments orders is less than the total sum that the payer is required to pay to the court on that date in respect of those orders.

(4) The payment made will be apportioned between the orders in proportion to the amounts due under each order over a period of one year.

(5) If, as a result of the apportionment referred to in paragraph (4), the payments under any periodical payments order are no longer in arrears, the residue shall be applied to the amount due under the other order or, if there is more than one other order, shall be apportioned between the other orders in accordance with paragraph (4).

(6) In this rule—

'payee' means a person entitled to receive payments under a periodical payments order; and

'payer' means a person required to make payments under a periodical payments order.][1]

Amendment

1 Inserted by the Family Procedure (Amendment No 2) Rules 2014, SI 2014/667, rr 2, 13.

Chapter 7
Estimates of costs

9.27 Estimates of Costs

[(1) Except where paragraph (4) applies, not less than one day before every hearing or appointment, each party must file with the court and serve on each other party an estimate of the costs incurred by that party up to the date of that hearing or appointment.

(2) Not less than one day before the first appointment, each party must file with the court and serve on each other party an estimate of the costs that party expects to incur up to the FDR appointment if a settlement is not reached.

(3) Not less than one day before the FDR appointment, each party must file with the court and serve on each other party an estimate of the costs that party expects to incur up to the final hearing if a settlement is not reached.

(4) Not less than 14 days before the date fixed for the final hearing of an application for a financial remedy, each party ('the filing party') must (unless the court directs otherwise) file with the court and serve on each other party a statement giving full particulars of all costs in respect of the proceedings which the filing party has incurred or expects to incur, to enable the court to take account of the parties' liabilities for costs when deciding what order (if any) to make for a financial remedy.

(5) A costs estimate filed and served in accordance with paragraph (1), (2) or (3) and particulars of costs filed and served in accordance with paragraph (4) must include confirmation—

(a) that they have been served on each other party; and
(b) in the case of a party who is legally represented, that they have been discussed with the party on whose behalf they are provided.

(6) Each party must bring to a hearing or appointment a copy of any estimate of costs filed and served in accordance with paragraph (1), (2) or (3) and any particulars of costs filed and served in accordance with paragraph (4).

(7) The amount of—

(a) a costs estimate filed and served in accordance with paragraph (1), (2) or (3); and
(b) particulars of costs filed and served in accordance with paragraph (4),

must be recorded in a recital to the order made at the hearing or appointment before which the estimate or particulars were filed or served.

(8) If a party fails to comply with paragraph (1), (2), (3) or (4)—

(a) this fact must be recorded in a recital to the order made at the hearing or appointment before which the costs estimate or particulars of costs should have been filed and served; and

(b) the court must direct that the relevant costs estimate or particulars of costs must be filed with the court and served on each other party within three days of the hearing or appointment or within such other time period as the court directs.

(Rule 28.3 makes provision for orders for costs in financial remedy proceedings.)

(Practice Direction 9A makes provision for statements of truth to be included in estimates of costs and particulars of costs filed and served in accordance with this rule.)][1]

Amendment

1 Substituted by the Family Procedure (Amendment) Rules 2020, SI 2020/135, rr 2, 12.

[9.27A Duty to make open proposals after a FDR appointment or where there has been no FDR appointment

(1) Where at a FDR appointment the court does not make an appropriate consent order or direct a further FDR appointment, each party must file with the court and serve on each other party an open proposal for settlement—

(a) by such date as the court directs; or
(b) where no direction is given under sub-paragraph (a), within 21 days after the date of the FDR appointment.

(2) Where no FDR appointment takes place, each party must file with the court and serve on each other party an open proposal for settlement—

(a) by such date as the court directs; or
(b) where no direction is given under sub-paragraph (a), not less than 42 days before the date fixed for the final hearing.][1]

Amendment

1 Inserted by the Family Procedure (Amendment) Rules 2020, SI 2020/135, rr 2, 13.

9.28 [Duty to make open proposals before a final hearing][1]

(1) Not less than 14 days before the date fixed for the final hearing of an application for a financial remedy, the applicant must (unless the court directs otherwise) file with the court and serve on the respondent an open statement which sets out concise details, including the amounts involved, of the orders which the applicant proposes to ask the court to make.

(2) Not more than 7 days after service of a statement under paragraph (1), the respondent must file with the court and serve on the applicant an open statement which sets out concise details, including the amounts involved, of the orders which the respondent proposes to ask the court to make.

Amendment

1 Substituted by the Family Procedure (Amendment) Rules 2020, SI 2020/135, rr 2, 14.

Chapter 8
Pensions

9.29 Application and interpretation of this Chapter

(1) This Chapter applies

(a) where an application for a financial remedy has been made; and
(b) the applicant or respondent is the party with pension rights.

(2) In this Chapter—

(a) in proceedings under the 1973 Act and the 1984 Act, all words and phrases defined in sections 25D(3) and (4) of the 1973 Act have the meaning assigned by those subsections;

(b) in proceedings under the 2004 Act—

(i) all words and phrases defined in paragraphs 16(4) to (5) and 29 of Schedule 5 to that Act have the meanings assigned by those paragraphs; and

(ii) 'the party with pension rights' has the meaning given to 'civil partner with pension rights' by paragraph 29 of Schedule 5 to the 2004 Act;

(c) all words and phrases defined in section 46 of the Welfare Reform and Pensions Act 1999 have the meanings assigned by that section.

9.30 What the party with pension rights must do when the court fixes a first appointment

(1) Where the court fixes a first appointment as required by rule 9.12(1)(a) the party with pension rights must request the person responsible for each pension arrangement under which the party has or is likely to have benefits to provide the information referred to in regulation 2(2) of the Pensions on Divorce etc (Provision of Information) Regulations 2000.

(The information referred to in regulation 2 of the Pensions on Divorce etc (Provision of Information) Regulations 2000 relates to the valuation of pension rights or benefits.)

(2) The party with pension rights must comply with paragraph (1) within 7 days beginning with the date on which that party receives notification of the date of the first appointment.

(3) Within 7 days beginning with the date on which the party with pension rights receives the information under paragraph (1) that party must send a copy of it to the other party, together with the name and address of the person responsible for each pension arrangement.

(4) A request under paragraph (1) need not be made where the party with pension rights is in possession of, or has requested, a relevant valuation of the pension rights or benefits accrued under the pension arrangement in question.

9.31 Applications for pension sharing orders

Where an application for a financial remedy includes an application for a pension sharing order, or where a request for such an order is added to an existing application for a financial remedy, the applicant must serve a copy of the application on the person responsible for the pension arrangement concerned.

9.32 Applications for consent orders for pension sharing

(1) This rule applies where—

(a) the parties have agreed on the terms of an order and the agreement includes a pension sharing order;

(b) service has not been effected under rule 9.31; and

(c) the information referred to in paragraph (2) has not otherwise been provided.

(2) The party with pension rights must—

(a) request the person responsible for the pension arrangement concerned to provide the information set out in Section C of the Pension Inquiry Form; and
(b) on receipt, send a copy of the information referred to in sub-paragraph (a) to the other party.

9.33 Applications for pension attachment orders

(1) Where an application for a financial remedy includes an application for a pension attachment order, or where a request for such an order is added to an existing application for a financial remedy, the applicant must serve a copy of the application on the person responsible for the pension arrangement concerned and must at the same time send—

(a) an address to which any notice which the person responsible is required to serve on the applicant is to be sent;
(b) an address to which any payment which the person responsible is required to make to the applicant is to be sent; and
(c) where the address in sub-paragraph (b) is that of a bank, a building society or the Department of National Savings, sufficient details to enable the payment to be made into the account of the applicant.

(2) A person responsible for a pension arrangement who receives a copy of the application under paragraph (1) may, within 21 days beginning with the date of service of the application, request the party with the pension rights to provide that person with the information disclosed in the financial statement relating to the party's pension rights or benefits under that arrangement.

(3) If the person responsible for a pension arrangement makes a request under paragraph (2), the party with the pension rights must provide that person with a copy of the section of that party's financial statement that relates to that party's pension rights or benefits under that arrangement.

(4) The party with the pension rights must comply with paragraph (3)—

(a) within the time limited for filing the financial statement by rule 9.14(1); or
(b) within 21 days beginning with the date on which the person responsible for the pension arrangement makes the request,

whichever is the later.

(5) A person responsible for a pension arrangement who receives a copy of the section of a financial statement as required pursuant to paragraph (4) may, within 21 days beginning with the date on which that person receives it, send to the court, the applicant and the respondent a statement in answer.

(6) A person responsible for a pension arrangement who files a statement in answer pursuant to paragraph (5) will be entitled to be represented at the first appointment, or such other hearing as the court may direct, and the court must within 4 days, beginning with the date on which that person files the statement in answer, give the person notice of the date of the first appointment or other hearing as the case may be.

9.34 Applications for consent orders for pension attachment

(1) This rule applies where service has not been effected under rule 9.33(1).

(2) Where the parties have agreed on the terms of an order and the agreement includes a pension attachment order, then they must serve on the person responsible for the pension arrangement concerned—

(a) a copy of the application for a consent order;
(b) a draft of the proposed order, complying with rule 9.35; and
(c) the particulars set out in rule 9.33(1).

(3) No consent order that includes a pension attachment order must be made unless either—

(a) the person responsible for the pension arrangement has not made any objection within 21 days beginning with the date on which the application for a consent order was served on that person; or
(b) the court has considered any such objection, and for the purpose of considering any objection the court may make such direction as it sees fit for the person responsible to attend before it or to furnish written details of the objection.

9.35 Pension sharing orders or pension attachment orders

An order for a financial remedy, whether by consent or not, which includes a pension sharing order or a pension attachment order, must—

(a) in the body of the order, state that there is to be provision by way of pension sharing or pension attachment in accordance with the annex or annexes to the order; and
(b) be accompanied by a pension sharing annex or a pension attachment annex as the case may require, and if provision is made in relation to more than one pension arrangement there must be one annex for each pension arrangement.

9.36 Duty of the court upon making a pension sharing order or a pension attachment order

(1) A court which varies or discharges a pension sharing order or a pension attachment order, must send, or direct one of the parties to send—

(a) to the person responsible for the pension arrangement concerned; or
(b) where the Board has assumed responsibility for the pension scheme or part of it, the Board;

the documents referred to in paragraph (4).

(2) A court which makes a pension sharing order or pension attachment order, must send, or direct one of the parties to send to the person responsible for the pension arrangement concerned, the documents referred to in paragraph (4).

(3) Where the Board has assumed responsibility for the pension scheme or part of it after the making of a pension sharing order or attachment order but before the documents have been sent to the person responsible for the pension arrangement in accordance with paragraph (2), the court which makes the pension sharing order or the pension attachment order, must send, or direct one of the parties to send to the Board the documents referred to in paragraph (4).

(4) The documents to be sent in accordance with paragraph (1) to (3) are—

(a) in the case of—
(i) proceedings under the 1973 Act, a copy of the [judicial separation order][1];
(ii) proceedings under Schedule 5 to the 2004 Act, a copy of the separation order;

(iii) proceedings under Part 3 of the 1984 Act, a copy of the document of divorce, annulment or legal separation;
(iv) proceedings under Schedule 7 to the 2004 Act, a copy of the document of dissolution, annulment or legal separation;

(b) in the case of divorce or nullity of marriage, a copy of the [final order][1] under rule [7.19][1] or [7.20][1]; or

(c) in the case of dissolution or nullity of civil partnership, a copy of the order making the conditional order final under rule [7.19][1] or [7.20][1]; and

(d) a copy of the pension sharing order or the pension attachment order, or as the case may be of the order varying or discharging that order, including any annex to that order relating to that pension arrangement but no other annex to that order.

(5) The documents referred to in [paragraph (4)][2] must be sent—

(a) in proceedings under the 1973 Act and the 1984 Act, within 7 days beginning with the date on which—
(i) the relevant pension sharing or pension attachment order[, or any order varying or discharging such an order,][3] is made; or
(ii) the [final order][1] of divorce or nullity or [judicial separation order][1] is made,
whichever is the later; and

(b) in proceedings under the 2004 Act, within 7 days beginning with the date on which—
(i) the relevant pension sharing or pension attachment order[, or any order varying or discharging such an order,][3] is made; or
(ii) the final order of dissolution or nullity or separation order is made,
whichever is the later.

Amendment

1 Substituted by the Family Procedure (Amendment) Rules 2022, SI 2022/44, rr 2, 24.
2 Substituted by the Family Procedure (Amendment) Rules 2012, SI 2012/679, rr 2, 19(a).
3 Inserted by the Family Procedure (Amendment) Rules 2012, SI 2012/679, rr 2, 19(b).

9.37 Procedure where Pension Protection Fund becomes involved with the pension scheme

(1) This rule applies where—

(a) rules 9.30 to 9.34 or 9.36 apply; and
(b) the party with the pension rights ('the member') receives or has received notification in compliance with the Pension Protection Fund (Provision of Information) Regulations 2005 ('the 2005 Regulations')—
(i) from the trustees or managers of a pension scheme, that there is an assessment period in relation to that scheme; or
(ii) from the Board that it has assumed responsibility for the pension scheme or part of it.

(2) If the trustees or managers of the pension scheme notify or have notified the member that there is an assessment period in relation to that scheme, the member must send to the other party, all the information which the Board is required from time to time to provide to the member under the 2005 Regulations including—

(a) a copy of the notification; and
(b) a copy of the valuation summary,

in accordance with paragraph (3).

(3) The member must send the information or any part of it referred to in paragraph (2)—

(a) if available, when the member sends the information received under rule 9.30(1); or
(b) otherwise, within 7 days of receipt.

(4) If the Board notifies the member that it has assumed responsibility for the pension scheme, or part of it, the member must—

(a) send a copy of the notification to the other party within 7 days of receipt; and
(b) comply with paragraph (5).

(5) Where paragraph (4) applies, the member must—

(a) within 7 days of receipt of the notification, request the Board in writing to provide a forecast of the member's compensation entitlement as described in the 2005 Regulations; and
(b) send a copy of the forecast of the member's compensation entitlement to the other party within 7 days of receipt.

(6) In this rule—

(a) 'assessment period' means an assessment period within the meaning of Part 2 of the Pensions Act 2004; and
(b) 'valuation summary' has the meaning assigned to it by the 2005 Regulations.

Chapter 9
Pension Protection Fund compensation

9.38 Application and interpretation of this Chapter

(1) This Chapter applies—

(a) where an application for a financial remedy has been made; and
(b) the applicant or respondent is, the party with compensation rights.

(2) In this Chapter 'party with compensation rights'—

(a) in proceedings under the 1973 Act and the 1984 Act, has the meaning given to it by section 25G(5) of the 1973 Act;
(b) in proceedings under the 2004 Act, has the meaning given to 'civil partner with compensation rights' by paragraph 37(1) of Schedule 5 to the 2004 Act.

9.39 What the party with compensation rights must do when the court fixes a first appointment

(1) Where the court fixes a first appointment as required by rule 9.12(1)(a) the party with compensation rights must request the Board to provide the information about the valuation of entitlement to PPF compensation referred to in regulations made by the Secretary of State under section 118 of the Pensions Act 2008.

(2) The party with compensation rights must comply with paragraph (1) within 7 days beginning with the date on which that party receives notification of the date of the first appointment.

(3) Within 7 days beginning with the date on which the party with compensation rights receives the information under paragraph (1) that party must send a copy of it to the

other party, together with the name and address of the trustees or managers responsible for each pension scheme.

(4) Where the rights to PPF Compensation are derived from rights under more than one pension scheme, the party with compensation rights must comply with this rule in relation to each entitlement.

9.40 Applications for pension compensation sharing orders

Where an application for a financial remedy includes an application for a pension compensation sharing order or where a request for such an order is added to an existing application for a financial remedy, the applicant must serve a copy of the application on the Board.

9.41 Applications for consent orders for pension compensation sharing

(1) This rule applies where—

(a) the parties have agreed on the terms of an order and the agreement includes a pension compensation sharing order;
(b) service has not been effected under rule 9.40; and
(c) the information referred to in paragraph (2) has not otherwise been provided.

(2) The party with compensation rights must—

(a) request the Board to provide the information set out in Section C of the Pension Protection Fund Inquiry Form; and
(b) on receipt, send a copy of the information referred to in sub-paragraph (a) to the other party.

9.42 Applications for pension compensation attachment orders

Where an application for a financial remedy includes an application for a pension compensation attachment order or where a request for such an order is added to an existing application for a financial remedy, the applicant must serve a copy of the application on the Board and must at the same time send—

(a) an address to which any notice which the Board is required to serve on the applicant is to be sent;
(b) an address to which any payment which the Board is required to make to the applicant is to be sent; and
(c) where the address in sub-paragraph (b) is that of a bank, a building society or the Department of National Savings, sufficient details to enable the payment to be made into the account of the applicant.

9.43 Applications for consent orders for pension compensation attachment

(1) This rule applies where service has not been effected under rule 9.42.

(2) Where the parties have agreed on the terms of an order and the agreement includes a pension compensation attachment order, then they must serve on the Board—

(a) a copy of the application for a consent order;
(b) a draft of the proposed order, complying with rule 9.44; and
(c) the particulars set out in rule 9.42.

9.44 Pension compensation sharing orders or pension compensation attachment orders

An order for a financial remedy, whether by consent or not, which includes a pension compensation sharing order or a pension compensation attachment order, must—

(a) in the body of the order, state that there is to be provision by way of pension compensation sharing or pension compensation attachment in accordance with the annex or annexes to the order; and

(b) be accompanied by a pension compensation sharing annex or a pension compensation attachment annex as the case may require, and if provision is made in relation to entitlement to PPF compensation that derives from rights under more than one pension scheme there must be one annex for each such entitlement.

9.45 Duty of the court upon making a pension compensation sharing order or a pension compensation attachment order

(1) A court which makes, varies or discharges a pension compensation sharing order or a pension compensation attachment order, must send, or direct one of the parties to send, to the Board—

(a) in the case of—
  (i) proceedings under Part 3 of the 1984 Act, a copy of the document of divorce, annulment or legal separation;
  (ii) proceedings under Schedule 7 to the 2004 Act, a copy of the document of dissolution, annulment or legal separation;

(b) in the case of—
  (i) divorce or nullity of marriage, a copy of the [final order][1] under rule [7.19][1] or [7.20][1];
  (ii) dissolution or nullity of civil partnership, a copy of the order making the conditional order final under rule [7.19][1] or [7.20][1];

(c) in the case of separation—
  (i) in the matrimonial proceedings, a copy of the [judicial separation order][1];
  (ii) in civil partnership proceedings, a copy of the separation order; and

(d) a copy of the pension compensation sharing order or the pension compensation attachment order, or as the case may be of the order varying or discharging that order, including any annex to that order relating to that PPF compensation but no other annex to that order.

(2) The documents referred to in paragraph (1) must be sent—

(a) in proceedings under the 1973 Act and the 1984 Act, within 7 days beginning with the date on which—
  (i) the relevant pension compensation sharing or pension compensation attachment order is made; or
  (ii) the [final order][1] of divorce or nullity or the [judicial separation order][1] is made,

  whichever is the later; and

(b) in proceedings under the 2004 Act, within 7 days beginning with the date on which—
  (i) the relevant pension compensation sharing or pension compensation attachment order is made; or
  (ii) the final order of dissolution or nullity or separation order is made,

whichever is the later.

Amendment

1 Substituted by the Family Procedure (Amendment) Rules 2022, SI 2022/44, rr 2, 25.

[Chapter 10
Communication of information from financial remedy proceedings

9.46 Communication of information: Practice Direction 9B

(1) For the purposes of the law relating to contempt of court, information from financial remedy proceedings may be communicated in accordance with Practice Direction 9B.

(2) Paragraph (1) is subject to any direction of the court.

(3) Nothing in this rule permits the communication to the public at large, or any section of the public, of any information relating to the proceedings.

(Rule 29.2 makes provision about disclosure of information under the 1991 Act.)][1]

Amendment

1 Inserted by the Family Procedure (Amendment No 3) Rules 2015, SI 2015/1868, rr 2, 7.

Practice Direction 9A – Application for a financial remedy (applicable to applications issued by the court on or after 6 April 2022)

This PD applies to applications issued by the court on or after 6 April 2022. For applications issued by the court before 6 April 2022 see [https://webarchive.nationalarchives.gov.uk/ukgwa/20211201114146/https://www.justice.gov.uk/courts/procedure-rules/family/practice_directions/pd_part_09a].

See also Part 9

This Practice Direction supplements FPR Part 9

Introduction

1.1 Part 9 of the Family Procedure Rules sets out the procedure applicable to the financial proceedings that are included in the definition of a 'financial remedy'.

1.2 The fast-track procedure set out in Chapter 5 of Part 9 of the Family Procedure Rules applies to—

(a) any application where the financial remedy sought is only for an order for periodical payments (as defined in rule 9.9B(1));
(b) any application made under—
  (i) the Domestic Proceedings and Magistrates' Courts Act 1978;
  (ii) Schedule 6 to the Civil Partnership Act 2004;
  (iii) Omitted
  (iv) Article 10 of the 2007 Hague Convention;
(c) any application for the variation of an order for periodical payments, except where the applicant seeks the dismissal (immediate or otherwise) of the periodical payments order and its substitution with one or more of a lump sum order, a property adjustment order, a pension sharing order or a pension compensation sharing order.

1.2A The standard procedure set out in Chapter 4 of Part 9 applies in respect of all other applications for a financial remedy. In a case to which the fast-track procedure applies any party may seek a direction from the court that the standard procedure should apply to the application. An applicant who seeks such a direction must include a request in the application for a financial remedy and give reasons; any such request by a respondent, or any representations about a request by the applicant, must be made, giving reasons, within 7 days after service of the application for a financial remedy. At any stage in the proceedings the court may order that an application proceeding under the fast-track procedure must proceed under the standard procedure.

1.3 Where an application for a financial remedy includes an application relating to land, details of any mortgagee must be included in the application.

Pre-application protocol

2.1 The 'pre-application protocol' annexed to this Direction outlines the steps parties should take to seek and provide information from and to each other prior to the commencement of any application for a financial remedy. The court will expect the parties to comply with the terms of the protocol.

Costs

3.1 Rule 9.27(1) requires each party to file with the court, and serve on each other party, not less than one day before a hearing or appointment, an estimate of the costs incurred by that party up to the date of that hearing or appointment. Rule 9.27(2) and (3) make provision for the filing and service of estimates of specified future costs not less than one day before a first appointment and a FDR appointment. The rule also makes provision for the filing and service of particulars of costs not less than 14 days before a final hearing of an application for a financial remedy. The rule makes provision to ensure that all parties are aware of all incurred and estimated future costs (including their own) and for the court to give directions as to compliance if these requirements are not satisfied.

3.1A References in rule 9.27 (and any other rule) to a time period of a day or a number of days must be read by reference to rule 2.9 (computation of time).

3.2 The purpose of this rule is to enable the court and the parties to take account of the impact of each party's costs liability on their financial situations. Parties should ensure that the information contained in the estimate is as full and accurate as possible and that any sums already paid in respect of a party's financial remedy costs are clearly set out. Where relevant, any liability arising from the costs of other proceedings between the parties should continue to be referred to in the appropriate section of a party's financial statement; any such costs should not be included in the estimates under rule 9.27.

3.2A An estimate of costs which is to be filed and served in accordance with rule 9.27(1), (2) or (3), and particulars of costs which are to be filed and served in accordance with rule 9.27(4) must be verified by a statement of truth.

3.2B Where an estimate of costs or particulars of costs are to be filed by a party who is not legally represented, the statement of truth should be as follows-

'I confirm that:

(a) to the best of my knowledge and belief, the contents of [this estimate of costs/ these particulars of costs] are true and accurate; and
(b) [this estimate of costs/ these particulars of costs] will be filed with the court and served on each other party, in accordance with rule 9.27 of the Family Procedure Rules 2010.'

3.2C Where an estimate of costs or particulars of costs are to be filed by a party's legal representative, the statement of truth should be as follows-

'I confirm that:

(a) to the best of my knowledge and belief, the contents of this [estimate of costs/ these particulars of costs] are true and accurate;
(b) I have discussed the contents of [this estimate of costs/ these particulars of costs] with my client (the [applicant/ respondent] in these proceedings);
(c) [this estimate of costs/ these particulars of costs] will be filed with the court and served on each other party, in accordance with rule 9.27 of the Family Procedure Rules 2010.

3.3 Rule 28.3 provides that the general rule in financial remedy proceedings is that the court will not make an order requiring one party to pay the costs of another party. However the court may make such an order at any stage of the proceedings where it considers it appropriate to do so because of the conduct of a party in relation to the proceedings.

3.4 Any breach of this practice direction or the pre-application protocol annexed to it will be taken into account by the court when deciding whether to depart from the general rule as to costs.

Procedure before the first appointment

4.1 In addition to the matters listed at rule 9.14(5), the parties should, if possible, with a view to identifying and narrowing any issues between the parties, exchange and file with the court –

(a) a summary of the case agreed between the parties;
(b) a schedule of assets agreed between the parties; and
(c) details of any directions that they seek, including, where appropriate, the name of any expert they wish to be appointed.

4.2 Where a party is prevented from sending the details referred to in (c) above, the party should make that information available at the first appointment.

Financial Statements and other documents

5.1 Practice Direction 22A (Written Evidence) applies to any financial statement filed in accordance with rules 9.14 or 9.19 and to any exhibits to a financial statement. In preparing a bundle of documents to be exhibited to or attached to a financial statement, regard must be had in particular to paragraphs 11.1 to 11.3 and 13.1 to 13.4 of that Direction. Whereon account of their bulk, it is impracticable for the exhibits to a financial statement to be retained on the court file after the First Appointment, the court may give directions as to their custody pending further hearings.

5.2 Where the court directs a party to provide information or documents by way of reply to a questionnaire or request by another party, the reply must be verified by a statement of truth. Unless otherwise directed, a reply to a questionnaire or request for information and documents shall not be filed with the court.

(Part 17 and Practice Direction 17Amake further provision about statements of truth)

Financial Dispute Resolution (FDR) Appointment

6.1 A key element in the procedure is the Financial Dispute Resolution (FDR) appointment. Rule 9.17 provides that the FDR appointment is to be treated as a meeting held for the purposes of discussion and negotiation.Such meetings have been developed as a means of reducing the tension which inevitably arises in family disputes and facilitating settlement of those disputes.

6.2 In order for the FDR to be effective, parties must approach the occasion openly and without reserve. Non-disclosure of the content of such meetings is vital and is an essential prerequisite for fruitful discussion directed to the settlement of the dispute between the parties. The FDR appointment is an important part of the settlement process. As a consequence of Re D (Minors) (Conciliation: Disclosure of Information) [1993] Fam 231,evidence of anything said or of any admission made in the course of an FDR appointment will not be admissible in evidence, except at the trial of a person for an offence committed at the appointment or in the very exceptional circumstances indicated in Re D.

6.3 Courts will therefore expect –

(a) parties to make offers and proposals;
(b) recipients of offers and proposals to give them proper consideration; and
(c) (subject to paragraph 6.4), that parties, whether separately or together, will not seek to exclude from consideration at the appointment any such offer or proposal.

6.4 Paragraph 6.3(c) does not apply to an offer or proposal made during non-court dispute resolution.

6.5 In order to make the most effective use of the first appointment and the FDR appointment, the legal representatives attending those appointments will be expected to have full knowledge of the case.

6.5A Where at a FDR appointment a settlement is not reached, the parties have an obligation to make open proposals for settlement in accordance with rule 9.27A. The normal direction would be that each party must file and serve their open proposals within 21 days of the FDR appointment. The court must consider whether it is appropriate to give any further directions about the filing and service of open proposals.

6.6 Omitted

Consent orders

7.1 Rule 9.26 (1)(a) requires an application for a consent order to be accompanied by two copies of the draft order in the terms sought, one of which must be endorsed with a statement signed by the respondent to the application signifying the respondent's agreement. The rule is considered to have been properly complied with if the endorsed statement is signed by solicitors on record as acting for the respondent; but where the consent order applied for contains undertakings, it should be signed by the party giving the undertakings as well as by that party's solicitor.

(Provision relating to the enforcement of undertakings is contained in the Practice Direction 33A supplementing Part 33 of the FPR)

7.2 Rule 9.26(1)(b) requires each party to file with the court and serve on the other party a statement of information. Where this is contained in one form, both parties must sign the statement to certify that each has read the contents of the other's statement.

7.3 Rule 35.2 deals with applications for a consent order in respect of a financial remedy where the parties wish to have the content of a written mediation agreement to which the Mediation Directive applies made the subject of a consent order.

Section 10(2) of the Matrimonial Causes Act 1973 and section 48(2)of the Civil Partnership Act 2004

8.1 Where a respondent who has applied under section 10(2) of the Matrimonial Causes Act 1973, or section 48(2) of the Civil Partnership Act 2004, for the court to consider his or her financial position after a divorce or dissolution elects not to proceed with the application, a notice of withdrawal of the application signed by the respondent or by the respondent's solicitor may be filed without leave of the court. In this event a formal order dismissing or striking out the application is unnecessary. Notice of withdrawal should also be given to the applicant's solicitor.

8.2 An application under section 10(2) or section 48(2) which has been withdrawn is not a bar to making the final order of divorce or dissolution.

Maintenance Orders – registration in the family court

9.1 Where periodical payments are required to be made to a child under an order registered in the family court, section 31L(3) and (4) of the1984 Act permits the payments to be made instead to the person with whom the child has his home. That person may proceed in his own name for variation, revival or revocation of the order and may enforce payment in his own name.

9.2 The registration in the family court of an order made direct to a child entails a considerable amount of work. Accordingly, when the High Court is considering the form of an order where there are children, care should be taken not to make orders for payment direct where such orders would be of no benefit to the parties.

Pensions

10.1 The phrase 'party with pension rights' is used in FPR Part 9, Chapter 8. For matrimonial proceedings, this phrase has the meaning given to it by section 25D(3) of the Matrimonial Causes Act 1973 and means'the party to the marriage who has or is likely to have benefits under a pension arrangement'. There is a definition of 'civil partner with pension rights' in paragraph 29 of Schedule 5 to the Civil Partnership Act 2004 which mirrors the definition of 'party with pension rights' in section 25D(3) of the 1973 Act. The phrase 'is likely to have benefits' in these definitions refers to accrued rights to pension benefits which are not yet in payment.

PPF Compensation

11.1 The phrase 'party with compensation rights' is used in FPR Part 9, Chapter 9.For matrimonial proceedings, the phrase has the meaning given to it by section 25G(5) of the Matrimonial Causes Act 1973 and means the party to the marriage who is or is likely to be entitled to PPF compensation. There is a definition of 'civil partner with compensation rights' in paragraph 37(1) of Schedule 5 to the Civil Partnership Act 2004 which mirrors the definition of 'party with compensation rights' in section 25G(5). The phrase 'is likely to be entitled to PPF Compensation' in those definitions refers to statutory entitlement to PPF Compensation which is not yet in payment.

Orders for payment in respect of legal services

12.1 An application for an order for payment in respect of legal services under section 22ZA of the 1973 Act or paragraph 38A of Part 8 of Schedule 5 to the 2004 Act must be made in accordance with FPR 9.7 using the Part 18 procedure. Where the application is made at the same time as an application for an order for maintenance pending suit or maintenance pending outcome, the applications may be included in one application notice, and evidence in support of or in response to the applications may be contained in one witness statement.

(Where an application is made for an order under FPR 9.7, a copy of the application notice must be served in accordance with the provisions of FPR Part 6 at least 14 days before the court is to deal with the application: FPR 18.8(1)(b).)

12.2 The evidence filed in support of an application for an order for payment in respect of legal services must, in addition to the matters referred to in rule 9.7(3), include a concise statement of the applicant's case on –

(a) the criteria set out in section 22ZA(3) and (4) of the 1974 Act or paragraph 38A(3) and (4) of Part 8 of Schedule 5 to the 2004 Act as applicable; and
(b) the matters set out in section 22ZB(1) of the 1973 Act or paragraph 38B(1) of Part 8 of Schedule 5 to the 2004 Act as applicable.

Applications to set aside a financial remedy

13.1 As set out in rule 9.9A(4), the Part 18 procedure applies to applications to set aside a financial remedy. Where such an application was made before rule 9.9A came into force, the Part 18 procedure will still apply subject to any directions that the court might make for the purpose of ensuring the proceedings are dealt with fairly (see the Family Procedure (Amendment No. 2) Rules 2016, rule 5).

13.2 If the financial remedy order was made before 22 April 2014, by any court, an application to set it aside under rule 9.9A is to be made to the family court. This is the combined effect of rule 9.9A(3), which provides that the application is made within the original proceedings, and the Crime and Courts Act 2013 (Family Court: Transitional and Savings Provision) Order 2014, which provides that any such proceedings became family court proceedings as of 22 April 2014.

13.3 If the financial remedy order was made on or after 22 April 2014, an application to set it aside under rule 9.9A is to be made to the court that made the order.

13.4 An application under rule 9.9A is to be dealt with by the same level of judge that dealt with the original application, by virtue of rule 17 of the Family Court (Composition and Distribution of Business) Rules 2014. Where reasonably possible, the application will be dealt with by the same judge that dealt with the original application.

13.5 An application to set aside a financial remedy order should only be made where no error of the court is alleged. If an error of the court is alleged, an application for permission to appeal under Part 30 should be considered. The grounds on which a financial remedy order may be set aside are and will remain a matter for decisions by judges. The grounds include (i) fraud; (ii) material non-disclosure; (iii) certain limited types of mistake; (iv) a subsequent event, unforeseen and unforeseeable at the time the order was made, which invalidates the basis on which the order was made.

13.6 The effect of rules 9.9A(1)(a) and (2) is that an application may be made to set aside all or only part of a financial remedy order, including a financial remedy order that has been made by consent.

13.7 The family court has the power under section 31F(6) of the Matrimonial and Family Proceedings Act 1984 to vary or set aside a financial remedy order. The High Court has the power under rule 9.9A and section 17(2) of the Senior Courts Act 1981 to set aside a financial remedy order. The difference in the wording of the legislative provisions is the reason that 'set aside' has been defined as it has in rule 9.9A(1)(b).

13.8 In applications under rule 9.9A, the starting point is that the order which one party is seeking to have set aside was properly made. A mere allegation that it was obtained by, eg, non-disclosure, is not sufficient for the court to set aside the order. Only once the ground for setting aside the order has been established (or admitted) can the court set aside the order and rehear the original application for a financial remedy. The court has a full range of case management powers and considerable discretion as to how to determine an application to set aside a financial remedy order, including where appropriate the power to strike out or summarily dispose of an application to set aside. If and when a ground for setting aside has been established, the court may decide to set aside the whole or part of the order there and then, or may delay doing so, especially if there are third party claims to the parties' assets. Ordinarily, once the court has decided to set aside a financial remedy order, the court would give directions for a full rehearing to re-determine the original application. However, if the court is satisfied that it has sufficient information to do so, it may proceed to re-determine the original application at the same time as setting aside the financial remedy order.

13.9 The effect of rule 28.3(9) is that the Part 28 rules relating to costs do not apply to applications under rule 9.9A.

Annex Pre-application protocol

Notes of guidance

Scope of the Protocol

1 This protocol is intended to apply to all applications for a financial remedy as defined by rule 2.3. It is designed to cover all classes of case, ranging from a simple application for periodical payments to an application for a substantial lump sum and property adjustment order. The protocol is designed to facilitate the operation of the procedure for financial remedy applications.

2 In considering the options of pre-application disclosure and negotiation, solicitors should bear in mind the advantage of having a court timetable and court managed process. There is sometimes an advantage in preparing disclosure before proceedings are commenced. However, solicitors should bear in mind the objective of controlling costs and in particular the costs of discovery and that the option of pre-application disclosure and negotiation has risks of excessive and uncontrolled expenditure and delay. This option should only be encouraged where both parties agree to follow this route and disclosure is not likely to be an issue or has been adequately dealt with in mediation or otherwise.

3 Solicitors should consider at an early stage and keep under review whether it would be appropriate to suggest mediation and/or collaborative law to the clients as an alternative to solicitor negotiation or court based litigation.

4 Making an application to the court should not be regarded as a hostile step or a last resort, rather as a way of starting the court timetable, controlling disclosure and endeavouring to avoid the costly final hearing and the preparation for it.

First letter

5 The circumstances of parties to an application for a financial remedy are so various that it would be difficult to prepare a specimen first letter. The request for information

will be different in every case. However, the tone of the initial letter is important and the guidelines in paragraphs 14 and 15 should be followed. It should be approved in advance by the client. Solicitors writing to an unrepresented party should always recommend that he seeks independent legal advice and enclose a second copy of the letter to be passed to any solicitor instructed. A reasonable time limit for an answer may be 14 days.

Negotiation and Settlement

6 In the event of pre-application disclosure and negotiation, as envisaged in paragraph 12 an application should not be issued when a settlement is a reasonable prospect.

Disclosure

7 The protocol underlines the obligation of parties to make full and frank disclosure of all material facts, documents and other information relevant to the issues. Solicitors owe their clients a duty to tell them in clear terms of this duty and of the possible consequences of breach of the duty, which may include criminal sanctions under the Fraud Act 2006. This duty of disclosure is an ongoing obligation and includes the duty to disclose any material changes after initial disclosure has been given. Solicitors are referred to the Good Practice Guides available to Resolution members at www.resolution.org.uk and can also contact the Law Society's Practice Advice Service on 0870 606 2522.

The Protocol

General principles

8 All parties must always bear in mind the overriding objective set out at rules 1.1 to 1.4 and try to ensure that applications should be resolved and a just outcome achieved as speedily as possible without costs being unreasonably incurred. The needs of any children should be addressed and safeguarded. The procedures which it is appropriate to follow should be conducted with minimum distress to the parties and in a manner designed to promote as good a continuing relationship between the parties and any children affected as is possible in the circumstances.

9 The principle of proportionality must be borne in mind at all times. It is unacceptable for the costs of any case to be disproportionate to the financial value of the subject matter of the dispute.

10 Parties should be informed that where a court is considering whether to make an order requiring one party to pay the costs of another party, it will take into account pre-application offers to settle and conduct of disclosure.

Identifying the issues

11 Parties must seek to clarify their claims and identify the issues between them as soon as possible. So that this can be achieved, they must provide full, frank and clear disclosure of facts, information and documents, which are material and sufficiently accurate to enable proper negotiations to take place to settle their differences. Openness in all dealings is essential.

Disclosure

12 If parties carry out voluntary disclosure before the issue of proceedings the parties should exchange schedules of assets, income, liabilities and other material facts, using the financial statement as a guide to the format of the disclosure. Documents should only be disclosed to the extent that they are required by the financial statement. Excessive or disproportionate costs should not be incurred.

Correspondence

13 Any first letter and subsequent correspondence must focus on the clarification of claims and identification of issues and their resolution. Protracted and unnecessary correspondence and 'trial by correspondence' must be avoided.

14 The impact of any correspondence upon the reader and in particular the parties must always be considered. Any correspondence which raises irrelevant issues or which might cause the other party to adopt an entrenched, polarised or hostile position is to be discouraged.

Summary

15 The aim of all pre-application proceedings steps must be to assist the parties to resolve their differences speedily and fairly or at least narrow the issues and, should that not be possible, to assist the court to do so.

Practice Direction 9B – Communication of information from financial remedy proceedings

This Practice Direction supplements FPR rule 9.46

1.1 Subject to any direction of the court, information from financial remedy proceedings may be communicated for the purposes of the law relating to contempt of court in accordance with this Practice Direction.

Communication of information by a party etc. for purposes relating to appeals under the Child Support Act 1991

2.1 A person specified in the first column of the following table may communicate to a person listed in the second column such information as is specified in the third column for the purpose specified in the fourth column–

A party	The Secretary of State, a McKenzie Friend, a lay adviser or the First-tier Tribunal dealing with an appeal under section 20 of the Child Support Act 1991	Any information relating to financial remedy proceedings	For the purposes of making or responding to an appeal under section 20 of the Child Support Act 1991 or the determination of such an appeal
A party or any other person lawfully in receipt of information	The Secretary of State, a McKenzie Friend, a lay adviser or the Upper Tier Tribunal dealing with an appeal under section 24 of the Child Support Act 1991 in respect of a decision of the First-tier Tribunal that was made under section 20 of that Act	Any information relating to financial remedy proceedings	For a purpose connected with an appeal under section 24 of the Child Support Act 1991 in respect of a decision of the First-tier Tribunal that was made under section 20 of that Act

Onward communication

3.1 A person in the second column of the table at paragraph 2.1 may only communicate information relating to the proceedings received from a person in the first column for the purpose for which he or she received that information.

Interpretation

4.1 In this Practice Direction-

'lay adviser' means a non-professional person who gives lay advice on behalf of an organisation in the lay advice sector; and

'McKenzie Friend' means any person permitted by the court or tribunal to sit beside an unrepresented litigant in court or in a tribunal to assist that litigant by prompting, taking notes and giving advice to that litigant.

PART 10
APPLICATIONS UNDER PART 4 OF THE FAMILY LAW ACT 1996

10.1 Scope and interpretation of this Part

The rules in this Part apply to proceedings under Part 4 of the 1996 Act.

10.2 Applications for an occupation order or a non-molestation order

(1) An application for an occupation order or a non-molestation order must be supported by a witness statement.

(2) [An][1] application for an occupation order or a non-molestation order may be made without notice.

(3) …[2]

(4) Where an application is made without notice, the witness statement in support of the application must state the reasons why notice has not been given.

(Section 45 of the 1996 Act sets out the criteria for making an order without notice.)

Amendment

1 Substituted by the Family Procedure (Amendment No 3) Rules 2013, SI 2013/3204, rr 2, 35(a).
2 Repealed by the Family Procedure (Amendment No 3) Rules 2013, SI 2013/3204, rr 2, 35(b).

10.3 Service of the application

(1) In an application made on notice, the applicant must[, subject to any order made under rule 6.35 or 6.36,][1] serve—

(a) a copy of the application together with any statement in support; and
(b) notice of any hearing or directions appointment set by the court,

on the respondent personally—

(i) not less than 2 days before the hearing; or
(ii) within such period as the court may direct.

[(1A) An application must not be served personally by the applicant himself or herself.][2]

(2) Where the applicant is acting in person, the applicant may request the court officer to serve the application on the respondent.

(3) In an application for an occupation order under section 33, 35 or 36 of the 1996 Act, the applicant must serve on the mortgagee and any landlord of the dwelling-house in question—

(a) a copy of the application; and
(b) notice of the right to make representations in writing or orally at any hearing.

(4) The applicant must file a certificate of service after serving the application.

…[3]

Amendment

1 Inserted by the Family Procedure (Amendment No 2) Rules 2021, SI 2021/875, rr 2, 7(a).
2 Inserted by the Family Procedure (Amendment) Rules 2017, SI 2017/413, rr 2, 3(1).
3 Repealed by the Family Procedure (Amendment No 2) Rules 2021, SI 2021/875, rr 2, 7(b).

10.4 …[1]

…[1]

Amendment

1 Repealed by the Family Procedure (Amendment No 3) Rules 2013, SI 2013/3204, rr 2, 36.

10.5 Privacy

[Any][1] hearing relating to an application for an occupation order or a non-molestation order will be in private unless the court directs otherwise.

Amendment

1 Substituted by the Family Procedure (Amendment No 3) Rules 2013, SI 2013/3204, rr 2, 37.

10.6 Service of an order

(1) [Subject to any order made under rule 6.35 or 6.36, the applicant][1] must, as soon as reasonably practicable, serve on the respondent personally—

(a) a copy of the order; and
[(b) where the order is made without notice—
(i) a copy of the application together with any statement supporting it; and
(ii) where the order is made by lay justices, a copy of the written record of the reasons for the court's decision.

(Rule 27.2 makes provision in respect of lay justices giving written reasons in the family court.)][2]

[(1A) The documents listed in paragraph (1) must not be served personally by the applicant himself or herself.][3]

(2) The court must serve the documents listed in paragraph (1) if—

(a) an applicant, acting in person, so requests; or
(b) the court made the order of its own initiative.

(3) In an application for an occupation order under section 33, 35 or 36 of the 1996 Act, the applicant must serve a copy of any order made on the mortgagee and any landlord of the dwelling house in question.

Amendment

1 Substituted by the Family Procedure (Amendment No 2) Rules 2021, SI 2021/875, rr 2, 8.
2 Substituted by the Family Procedure (Amendment No 2) Rules 2014, SI 2014/667, rr 2, 14.
3 Inserted by the Family Procedure (Amendment) Rules 2017, SI 2017/413, rr 2, 3(2).

10.7 Representations made by a mortgagee or landlord

The court may direct that a hearing be held in order to consider any representations made by a mortgagee or a landlord.

10.8 Applications to vary, extend or discharge an order

Rules 10.5 to 10.7 apply to applications to vary, extend or discharge an order.

10.9 Orders containing provisions to which a power of arrest is attached

Where the court makes an occupation order containing one or more provisions to which a power of arrest is attached ('relevant provisions')—

(a) each relevant provision must be set out in a separate paragraph in the order; and
(b) a paragraph containing a relevant provision must not include a provision of the order to which the power of arrest is not attached.

10.10 Service of an order on the officer for the time being in charge of a police station

(1) Where the court makes—

(a) an occupation order to which a power of arrest is attached; or
(b) a non-molestation order,

a copy of the order must be delivered to the officer for the time being in charge of—

(i) the police station for the applicant's address; or
(ii) such other police station as the court may specify.

(2) A copy of the order delivered under paragraph (1) must be accompanied by a statement showing that the respondent has been served with the order or informed of its terms (whether by being present when the order was made or by telephone or otherwise).

(3) The documentation referred to in paragraphs (1) and (2) must be delivered by—

(a) the applicant; or
(b) the court officer, where [rule 10.6(2) applies][1].

(4) Paragraph (5) applies where an order is made varying or discharging—

(a) a provision of an occupation order to which a power of arrest is attached; or
(b) a provision of a non-molestation order.

(5) The court officer must—

(a) immediately inform—
  (i) the officer who received a copy of the order under paragraph (1); and
  (ii) if the applicant's address has changed, the officer for the time being in charge of the police station for the new address; and
(b) deliver a copy of the order referred to in paragraph (4)(a) or (b) and the order referred to in paragraph (1) to any officer so informed.

Amendment

1 Substituted by the Family Procedure (Amendment No 2) Rules 2021, SI 2021/875, rr 2, 9.

10.11 Proceedings following arrest …[1]

(1) This rule applies where a person is arrested pursuant to—

(a) a power of arrest attached to a provision of an occupation order; …[2]

(b) a warrant of arrest issued on an application under section 47(8) of the 1996 Act[; or][3]

[(c) a warrant of arrest issued on an application for enforcement of an incoming protection measure.

(The Civil Jurisdiction and Judgments (Protection Measures) Regulations 2014 make provision in relation to the powers of the family court and the High Court to enforce incoming protection measures under the Protection Measures Regulation.)][4]

(2) The court before which a person is brought following arrest may—

(a) determine whether the facts, and the circumstances which led to the arrest, amounted to disobedience of the order; or

(b) adjourn the proceedings.

(3) Where the proceedings are adjourned and the arrested person is released—

(a) unless the court directs otherwise, the matter must be dealt with within 14 days beginning with the date of arrest; and

(b) the arrested person must be given not less than 2 days' notice of the hearing.

(4) An application notice seeking the committal for contempt of court of the arrested person may be issued if the arrested person is not dealt with within the period mentioned in paragraph (3)(a).

(The powers of [the court][5] to remand in custody or on bail are contained in section 47 of and Schedule 5 to the Family Law Act 1996.)

…[1]

Amendment

1 Repealed by the Family Procedure (Amendment No 3) Rules 2013, SI 2013/3204, rr 2, 38(a), (c).
2 Repealed by the Family Procedure (Amendment No 4) Rules 2014, SI 2014/3296, rr 2, 9(a).
3 Substituted by the Family Procedure (Amendment No 4) Rules 2014, SI 2014/3296, rr 2, 9(b).
4 Inserted by the Family Procedure (Amendment No 4) Rules 2014, SI 2014/3296, rr 2, 9(c).
5 Substituted by the Family Procedure (Amendment No 3) Rules 2013, SI 2013/3204, rr 2, 38(b).

[10.12 Enforcement of an order: requirement for a penal notice

At the time when the order is drawn up, the court officer will—

(a) where the order made is (or includes) a non-molestation order; or

(b) where the order made is an occupation order and the court so directs,

issue a copy of the order, endorsed with or incorporating a notice as to the consequences of disobedience, for service in accordance with rule 10.6.

(For enforcement of an order by way of committal see Part 37 [(rule 37.4(2)(c) requires a contempt application to include confirmation that any order allegedly breached or disobeyed contained a penal notice)][1].)][2]

Amendment

1 Substituted by the Family Procedure (Amendment No 2) Rules 2020, SI 2020/758, rr 2, 3(1).
2 Substituted by the Family Procedure (Amendment No 2) Rules 2014, SI 2014/667, rr 2, 15.

[10.13 Enforcement of an undertaking

…[1] Part 37 applies …[1] where an application is made to commit a person for breach of an undertaking.

(Rule 37.4(2) includes requirements for the information to be contained in a contempt application in relation to breach of an undertaking.)][3]

Amendment

1 Repealed by the Family Procedure (Amendment No 2) Rules 2020, SI 2020/758, rr 2, 3(2)(a), (b).
2 Substituted by the Family Procedure (Amendment No 2) Rules 2020, SI 2020/758, rr 2, 3(2)(c).
3 Substituted by the Family Procedure (Amendment No 2) Rules 2014, SI 2014/667, rr 2, 15.

10.14 Power to adjourn the hearing for consideration of the penalty

[The court][1] may adjourn the hearing for consideration of the penalty to be imposed for any contempt of court found proved and such a hearing may be restored if the respondent does not comply with any conditions specified by the court.

…[2]

Amendment

1 Substituted by the Family Procedure (Amendment No 3) Rules 2013, SI 2013/3204, rr 2, 39(a).
2 Repealed by the Family Procedure (Amendment No 3) Rules 2013, SI 2013/3204, rr 2, 39(b).

10.15 Hospital orders or guardianship orders under the Mental Health Act 1983

(1) Where the [court][1] makes a hospital order under the Mental Health Act 1983 the court officer must—

(a) send to the hospital any information which will be of assistance in dealing with the patient; and
(b) inform the applicant when the respondent is being transferred to hospital.

(2) Where the [court][1] makes a guardianship order under the Mental Health Act 1983, the court officer must send any information which will be of assistance in dealing with the patient to—

(a) the patient's guardian; and
(b) where the guardian is a person other than the local services authority, the local services authority.

…[2]

Amendment

1 Substituted by the Family Procedure (Amendment No 3) Rules 2013, SI 2013/3204, rr 2, 40(a).
2 Repealed by the Family Procedure (Amendment No 3) Rules 2013, SI 2013/3204, rr 2, 40(b).

10.16 Transfer directions under section 48 of the Mental Health Act 1983

(1) Where a transfer direction given by the Secretary of State under section 48 of the Mental Health Act 1983 is in force in respect of a person remanded in custody by the [court][1], the court officer must notify—

(a) the governor of the prison to which that person was remanded; and
(b) the hospital where that person is detained, of any committal hearing which that person is required to attend.

(2) The court officer must also give notice in writing of any further remand to the hospital where that person is detained.

…[2]

Amendment

1 Substituted by the Family Procedure (Amendment No 3) Rules 2013, SI 2013/3204, rr 2, 41(a).
2 Repealed by the Family Procedure (Amendment No 3) Rules 2013, SI 2013/3204, rr 2, 41(b).

10.17 Recognizances

(1) Where, in accordance with paragraph 2(1)(b)(ii) of Schedule 5 to the 1996 Act, the [court][1] fixes the amount of any recognizance with a view to it being taken subsequently, the recognizance may be taken by—

(a) a [judge of the court][1];
(b) a police officer of the rank of inspector or above or in charge of a police station; or
(c) the governor or keeper of a prison where the arrested person is in custody.

(2) The person having custody of an applicant for bail must release that applicant if satisfied that the required recognizances have been taken.

…[2]

Amendment

1 Substituted by the Family Procedure (Amendment No 3) Rules 2013, SI 2013/3204, rr 2, 42(a).
2 Repealed by the Family Procedure (Amendment No 3) Rules 2013, SI 2013/3204, rr 2, 42(b).

Practice Direction 10A – Part 4 of the Family Law Act 1996

See also Part 10

This Practice Direction supplements FPR Part 10

1.1 Omitted

Applications for an occupation order or non-molestation order made by a child under the age of sixteen

2.1 If an application for an occupation order or non-molestation order is made by a child under the age of sixteen attention is drawn to section 43 of the 1996 Act. This provides that leave of the court is required for an application made by a child under the age of sixteen. The application should be made in accordance with Part 18.

Privacy

3.1 Omitted.

3.2 Omitted.

3.3 When a person arrested under a power of arrest attached to an occupation order cannot conveniently be brought before the relevant judicial authority sitting in a place normally used as a courtroom within 24 hours after the arrest, that person may be brought before the relevant judicial authority at any convenient place. As the liberty of the subject is involved, the press and public should be permitted to be present, unless security needs make this impracticable.

Warrant of arrest on an application under section 47(8) of the 1996 Act

4.1 In accordance with section 47(9) of the 1996 Act, a warrant of arrest on an application under section 47(8) shall not be issued unless –

(a) the application is substantiated on oath; and
(b) the court has reasonable grounds for believing that the respondent has failed to comply with the order.

Attendance of arresting officer

5.1 Attention is drawn to section 47(7) of the 1996 Act. This provides that a person arrested under a power of arrest attached to an occupation order must be brought before a judge within the period of 24 hours beginning at the time of arrest.

5.2 When the arrested person is brought before the judge the attendance of the arresting officer will not be necessary, unless the arrest itself is in issue. A written statement from the arresting officer as to the circumstances of the arrest should normally be sufficient.

5.3 In those cases where the arresting officer was also a witness to the events leading to the arrest and his or her evidence regarding those events is required, arrangements should be made for the arresting officer to attend at a subsequent hearing to give evidence.

Application for Bail

6.1 An application for bail by a person arrested under –

(a) a power of arrest attached to an occupation order under section 47(2) or (3) of the 1996 Act; or
(b) a warrant of arrest issued on an application under section 47(8) or the 1996 Act,

may be made orally or in writing.

6.2 The court will require the following information, which an application in writing should therefore contain –

(a) the full name of the person making the application;
(b) the address of the place where the person making the application is detained at the time when the application is made;
(c) the address where the person making the application would reside if granted bail;
(d) the amount of the recognizance in which the person making the application would agree to be bound; and
(e) the grounds on which the application is made and, where a previous application has been refused, full particulars of any change in circumstances which has occurred since that refusal.

6.3 An application made in writing must be signed –

(a) by the person making the application or by a person duly authorised by that person in that behalf; or
(b) where the person making the application is a child or is for any reason incapable of acting, by a children's guardian or litigation friend acting on that person's behalf.

6.4 A copy of the application must be served on the person who obtained the injunction.

6.5 A copy of the bail notice must be given to a respondent who is remanded on bail.

Remand for Medical Examination and Report

7.1 Section 48(4) of the 1996 Act provides that the judge has power to make an order under section 35 of the Mental Health Act 1983 (remand to hospital for report on accused's mental condition) in certain circumstances. If the judge does so attention is drawn to section 35(8) of that Act, which provides that a person remanded to hospital under that section may obtain at his or her own expense an independent report on his or her mental condition from a registered medical practitioner or approved clinician of his or her choice and apply to the court on the basis of it for the remand to be terminated under section 35(7).

PART 11
APPLICATIONS UNDER PART 4A OF THE FAMILY LAW ACT 1996 [OR PART 1 OF SCHEDULE 2 TO THE FEMALE GENITAL MUTILATION ACT 2003][1]

11.1 Scope and interpretation

(1) The rules in this Part apply to proceedings …[2] under Part 4A of the 1996 Act [and under Part 1 of Schedule 2 to the 2003 Act][1].

(2) In this Part—

['the 2003 Act' means the Female Genital Mutilation Act 2003;
'a FGM protection order' means an order under paragraph 1(1) of Part 1 of Schedule 2 to the 2003 Act;][1]
'a forced marriage protection order' means an order under section 63A of the 1996 Act; …[3]
['an individual' means a person (whether legally represented or not) who is not applying for an order on behalf of an organisation, and includes the person who is the subject of the proceedings;][4]
['a protection order' means a forced marriage protection order or a FGM protection order; and][1]
'the person who is the subject of the proceedings' means the person who will be protected by the …[3] protection order applied for or being considered by the court of its own initiative, if that order is made, or who is being protected by [the protection][5] order.

Amendment

1 Inserted by the Family Procedure (Amendment No 2) Rules 2015, SI 2015/1420, rr 2, 3, 4(a), (b)(i), (iii).
2 Repealed by the Family Procedure (Amendment No 3) Rules 2013, SI 2013/3204, rr 2, 43.
3 Repealed by the Family Procedure (Amendment No 2) Rules 2015, SI 2015/1420, rr 2, 4(b)(ii), (iv)(aa).
4 Inserted by the Family Procedure (Amendment) Rules 2017, SI 2017/413, rr 2, 4(1).
5 Substituted by the Family Procedure (Amendment No 2) Rules 2015, SI 2015/1420, rr 2, 4(b)(iv)(bb).

11.2 Applications

(1) An application for a …[1] protection order may be made without notice.

(2) Where an application is made without notice, it must be supported by a [witness][2] statement explaining why notice has not been given.

(3) An application for a …[1] protection order made by an organisation must state—

(a) the name and address of the person submitting the application; and
(b) the position which that person holds in the organisation.

Amendment

1 Repealed by the Family Procedure (Amendment No 2) Rules 2015, SI 2015/1420, rr 2, 5(a), (c).
2 Substituted by the Family Procedure (Amendment No 2) Rules 2015, SI 2015/1420, rr 2, 5(b).

[11.2A Directions about service

(1) Where rules within this Part require the person who is the subject of proceedings to be served with any documents or informed of any action taken by the court, and that person is not the applicant and is—

(a) a child;
(b) a person, not being a party, who lacks or may lack capacity within the meaning of the 2005 Act; or
(c) a protected party;

the court must give directions about the persons who are to be served or informed.

(2) This rule applies to rules 11.3(3)(c), 11.4(1)(b), 11.6(3)(c) and 11.7(3).][1]

Amendment

1 Inserted by the Family Procedure (Amendment No 2) Rules 2015, SI 2015/1420, rr 2, 6.

11.3 Permission to apply

[(A1) An application for permission to apply for a protection order may be made without notice.][1]

(1) Where the permission of the court is required to apply for a …[2] protection order, the person seeking permission must file—

(a) a Part 18 application notice setting out—
  (i) the reasons for the application, for the making of which permission is sought ('the proposed application');
  (ii) the applicant's connection with the person to be protected;
  (iii) the applicant's knowledge of the circumstances of the person to be protected; and
  (iv) [in relation to an application for permission to apply for a forced marriage protection order only,][1] the applicant's knowledge of the wishes and feelings of the person to be protected; and
(b) a draft of the proposed application, together with sufficient copies for one to be served on each respondent and (if different) the person to be protected.

(2) As soon as practicable after receiving an application under paragraph (1), the court must—

(a) grant the application; or
(b) direct that a date be fixed for the hearing of the application and fix the date.

(3) The court officer must inform the following persons of the court's action under paragraph (2)—

(a) the applicant;
(b) the respondent;
(c) (if different) the person to be protected; and
(d) any other person directed by the court.

(4) Where permission is granted to apply for a …[2] protection order, the application must proceed in accordance with rule 11.2.

Amendment

1 Inserted by the Family Procedure (Amendment No 2) Rules 2015, SI 2015/1420, rr 2, 7(a), (b)(ii).
2 Repealed by the Family Procedure (Amendment No 2) Rules 2015, SI 2015/1420, rr 2, 7(b)(i), (c).

11.4 Service of applications on notice

(1) Subject to [paragraph (3)][1], where an application is made on notice, the applicant must serve a copy of the application, together with the notice of proceedings, personally on—

(a) the respondent;
(b) the person who is the subject of the proceedings (if that person is neither the applicant nor a respondent); and
(c) any other person directed by the court,

not less than 2 days before the date on which the application will be heard.

[(1A) Where the applicant is an individual, the application must not be served personally by the applicant himself or herself.][2]

(2) The court may abridge the period specified in paragraph (1).

(3) Service of the application must be effected by the court if the applicant[, acting in person,][3] so requests (this does not affect the court's power to order substituted service).

(4) Where the application is served on the person who is the subject of the proceedings, it must be accompanied by a notice informing that person—

(a) how to apply to become a party to the proceedings; and
(b) of that person's right to make representations in writing or orally at any hearing.

(5) …[4]

(6) Where an application is served by the applicant, the applicant must file a certificate of service stating the date and time of personal service [on each party served][3].

Amendment

1 Substituted by the Family Procedure (Amendment) Rules 2017, SI 2017/413, rr 2, 4(2)(a).
2 Inserted by the Family Procedure (Amendment) Rules 2017, SI 2017/413, rr 2, 4(2)(b).
3 Inserted by the Family Procedure (Amendment No 2) Rules 2015, SI 2015/1420, rr 2, 8(a), (c).
4 Repealed by the Family Procedure (Amendment No 2) Rules 2015, SI 2015/1420, rr 2, 8(b).

11.5 …[1]

…[1]

Amendment

1 Repealed by the Family Procedure (Amendment No 3) Rules 2013, SI 2013/3204, rr 2, 44.

11.6 Parties

[(A1) Where the person who is the subject of proceedings is not the applicant and is a child, the court must consider, at every stage in the proceedings, whether to make that child a party to proceedings.

(For when a child should be made a party to proceedings generally see paragraph 7 of Practice Direction 16A).][1]

(1) In proceedings under this Part, a person may file a Part 18 application notice for that person or another person to—

(a) be joined as a party; or
(b) cease to be a party.

(2) As soon as practicable after receiving an application under paragraph (1), the court must do one of the following—

(a) in the case only of an application under paragraph (1)(a), grant the application;
(b) order that the application be considered at a hearing, and fix a date for the hearing; or
(c) invite written representations as to whether the application should be granted, to be filed within a specified period, and upon expiry of that period act under sub-paragraph (a) or (b) as it sees fit.

(3) The court officer must inform the following persons of the court's action under paragraph (2)—

(a) the applicant under paragraph (1);
(b) (if different) the applicant for the …[2] protection order and the respondent to that application;
(c) (if different) the person who is the subject of the proceedings; and
(d) any other person directed by the court.

(4) The court may at any time direct—

(a) that a person who would not otherwise be a respondent under these rules be joined as a party to the proceedings; or
(b) that a party to the proceedings cease to be a party,

and such a direction may be made by the court of its own initiative as well as upon an application under paragraph (1).

(5) Where the court directs the addition or removal of a party, it may give consequential directions about—

(a) service on a new party of a copy of the application for the …[2] protection order and other relevant documents; and
(b) the management of the proceedings.

Amendment

1 Inserted by the Family Procedure (Amendment No 2) Rules 2015, SI 2015/1420, rr 2, 9(a).
2 Repealed by the Family Procedure (Amendment No 2) Rules 2015, SI 2015/1420, rr 2, 9(b), (c).

11.7 Hearings and service of orders

(1) Any hearing relating to an application for a …[1] protection order must be in private unless the court otherwise directs.

(2) The court may direct the withholding of any submissions made, or any evidence adduced, for or at any hearing in proceedings to which this Part applies—

(a) in order to protect the person who is the subject of the proceedings or any other person; or
(b) for any other good reason.

(3) The applicant must, as soon as reasonably practical, serve personally—

(a) a copy of the order;
(b) a copy of the record of the hearing; and
(c) where the order is made without notice, a copy of the application together with any statement supporting it,

on the respondent, the person who is the subject of the proceedings (if neither the applicant nor a respondent), and any other person named in the order.

[(3A) Where the applicant is an individual, the documents listed in paragraph (3) must not be served personally by the applicant himself or herself.][2]

(4) The court must serve the documents listed in paragraph (3) if—

(a) an applicant, acting in person, so requests; or
(b) the court made the order of its own initiative.

Amendment

1 Repealed by the Family Procedure (Amendment No 2) Rules 2015, SI 2015/1420, rr 2, 10.
2 Inserted by the Family Procedure (Amendment) Rules 2017, SI 2017/413, rr 2, 4(3).

11.8 Orders made by the court of its own initiative

(1) Where the court makes a …[1] protection order of its own initiative under section 63C of the 1996 Act [or under paragraph 2 of Part 1 of Schedule 2 to the 2003 Act][2], it must set out in the order—

(a) a summary of its reasons for making the order; and
(b) the names of the persons who are to be served with the order.

(2) The court may order service of the order on—

(a) any of the parties to the current proceedings;
(b) (if different) the person who is the subject of the proceedings; and
(c) any other person whom the court considers should be served.

(3) The court must give directions as to how the order is to be served.

Amendment

1 Repealed by the Family Procedure (Amendment No 2) Rules 2015, SI 2015/1420, rr 2, 11(a).
2 Inserted by the Family Procedure (Amendment No 2) Rules 2015, SI 2015/1420, rr 2, 11(b).

11.9 Representations in respect of orders

Where the court makes an order [of a type referred to in rule 11.7 or 11.8][1], it may direct that a hearing (or further hearing) be held in order to consider any representations made by any of the persons named in, or directed to be served with, the order.

Amendment

1 Substituted by the Family Procedure (Amendment) Rules 2012, SI 2012/679, rr 2, 21.

11.10 Applications to vary, extend or discharge an order

Rules 11.7 and 11.9 apply to applications to vary, extend or discharge a …[1] protection order.

Amendment

1 Repealed by the Family Procedure (Amendment No 2) Rules 2015, SI 2015/1420, rr 2, 12.

11.11 …[1]

…[1]

Amendment

1 Repealed by the Family Procedure (Amendment) Rules 2015, SI 2015/913, rr 2, 10.

[11.12 Service of an order on the officer for the time being in charge of a police station

(1) Where the court makes a …[1] protection order a copy of the order must be delivered to the officer for the time being in charge of—

(a) the police station for the address of the person who is the subject of the proceedings; [and][2]

(b) such other police station as the court may specify.

(2) A copy of the order delivered under paragraph (1) must be accompanied by a statement showing that the respondent(s) [and any other person whose breach of the order would be an offence][3] [have][2] been served with the order or informed of its terms (whether by being present when the order was made or by telephone or otherwise).

(3) The documents referred to in paragraphs (1) and (2) must be delivered by—

(a) the applicant; or

(b) the court officer, where the order was served following a request under rule 11.7(4).

(4) Where an order is made varying, extending or discharging a …[1] protection order the court officer must—

(a) immediately inform—

(i) the officer who received a copy of the order under paragraph (1); and

(ii) if the address of the person who is the subject of the proceedings has changed, the officer for the time being in charge of the police station for the new address; and

(b) deliver a copy of the order made varying, extending or discharging a …[1] protection order, together with a copy of the order referred to in paragraph (1) to any officer so informed.][4]

Amendment

1 Repealed by the Family Procedure (Amendment No 2) Rules 2015, SI 2015/1420, rr 2, 13(a)(i), (c).
2 Substituted by the Family Procedure (Amendment No 2) Rules 2015, SI 2015/1420, rr 2, 13(a)(ii), (b)(ii).
3 Inserted by the Family Procedure (Amendment No 2) Rules 2015, SI 2015/1420, rr 2, 13(b)(i).
4 Substituted by the Family Procedure (Amendment) Rules 2015, SI 2015/913, rr 2, 11.

11.13 Application for issue of warrant for arrest

(1) An application under section 63J(2) of the 1996 Act [or under paragraph 7(1) of Part 1 of Schedule 2 to the 2003 Act][1] for the issue of a warrant for the arrest of a person must be supported by a sworn statement.

(2) An application for the issue of a warrant for arrest made by a person who is neither the person who is the subject of the proceedings nor (if different) the person who applied

for the order, shall be treated, in the first instance, as an application for permission to apply for the warrant to be issued, and the court shall either—

(a) grant the application; or
(b) direct that a date be fixed for the hearing of the application and fix a date.

(3) The court officer must inform the following persons of the court's action under paragraph (2)—

(a) the person applying for the issue of the warrant;
(b) the person being protected by the order; and
(c) any other person directed by the court.

Amendment

1 Inserted by the Family Procedure (Amendment No 2) Rules 2015, SI 2015/1420, rr 2, 14.

11.14 Proceedings following arrest

(1) This rule applies where a person is arrested pursuant to—

(a) a power of arrest attached to a provision of a forced marriage protection order; or
(b) a warrant of arrest issued on an application under section 63J(2) of the 1996 Act [or under paragraph 7(1) of Part 1 of Schedule 2 to the 2003 Act][1].

(2) The court before whom a person is brought following his arrest may—

(a) determine whether the facts and the circumstances which led to the arrest amounted to disobedience of the order; or
(b) adjourn the proceedings.

(3) Where the proceedings are adjourned, the arrested person may be released and—

(a) unless the court directs otherwise, be dealt with within 14 days of the day on which the person was arrested; and
(b) be given not less than 2 days' notice of the adjourned hearing.

(4) An application notice seeking the committal for contempt of court of the arrested person may be issued if the arrested person is not dealt with within the period mentioned in paragraph (3)(a).

(The powers of [the court][2] to remand in custody or on bail are contained in section 47 of and Schedule 5 to the 1996 Act [and in paragraphs 8 to14 of Part 1 of Schedule 2 to the 2003 Act][1].)

Amendment

1 Inserted by the Family Procedure (Amendment No 2) Rules 2015, SI 2015/1420, rr 2, 15.
2 Substituted by the Family Procedure (Amendment No 3) Rules 2013, SI 2013/3204, rr 2, 45.

[11.15 Enforcement of orders and undertakings

(1) At the time when the order is drawn up, the court officer will, where the order made is (or includes a …[1] protection order, issue a copy of the order, endorsed with or incorporating a notice as to the consequences of disobedience, for service in accordance with rule 11.7.

(2) …[2] Part 37 applies …[2] where an application is made to commit a person for breach of an undertaking.

[(Rule 37.4(2) includes requirements for the information to be contained in a contempt application in relation to breach of an order or an undertaking.)][3]][4]

Amendment

1 Repealed by the Family Procedure (Amendment No 2) Rules 2015, SI 2015/1420, rr 2, 16(a).
2 Repealed by the Family Procedure (Amendment No 2) Rules 2020, SI 2020/758, rr 2, 4(a).
3 Substituted by the Family Procedure (Amendment No 2) Rules 2020, SI 2020/758, rr 2, 4(b).
4 Substituted by the Family Procedure (Amendment No 2) Rules 2014, SI 2014/667, rr 2, 16.

11.16 Power to adjourn the hearing for consideration of the penalty

The court may adjourn the hearing for consideration of the penalty to be imposed for any contempt of court found proved and such hearing may be restored if the contemnor does not comply with any conditions specified by the court.

11.17 Hospital orders or guardianship orders under the Mental Health Act 1983

(1) Where the court makes a hospital order under the Mental Health Act 1983, the court officer must—

(a) send to the hospital any information which will be of assistance in dealing with the patient; and
(b) inform the persons directed by the court to be informed about when the patient is being transferred to hospital.

(2) Where the court makes a guardianship order under the Mental Health Act 1983, the court officer must send any information which will be of assistance in dealing with the patient to—

(a) the patient's guardian; and
(b) where the guardian is a person other than the local services authority, the local services authority.

11.18 Transfer directions under section 48 of the Mental Health Act 1983

(1) Where a transfer direction given by the Secretary of State under section 48 of the Mental Health Act 1983 is in force in respect of a person remanded in custody by the court, the court officer must notify—

(a) the governor of the prison to which that person was remanded; and
(b) the hospital where that person is detained,

of any committal hearing which that person is required to attend.

(2) The court officer must also give notice in writing of any further remand to the hospital where that person is detained.

11.19 Recognizances

(1) Where, in accordance with paragraph 2(1)(b)(ii) of Schedule 5 to the 1996 Act [or paragraph 10(3)(b) of Part 1 of Schedule 2 to the 2003 Act][1], the court fixes the amount of any recognizance with a view to it being taken subsequently, the recognizance may be taken by—

(a) a [judge of the court][2];
(b) a police officer of the rank of inspector or above or in charge of a police station; or
(c) the governor or keeper of a prison where the arrested person is in the custody of that governor or keeper.

(2) The person having custody of an applicant for bail must release him if satisfied that the required recognizances have been taken.

Amendment

1 Inserted by the Family Procedure (Amendment No 2) Rules 2015, SI 2015/1420, rr 2, 17.
2 Substituted by the Family Procedure (Amendment No 3) Rules 2013, SI 2013/3204, rr 2, 46.

PART 12
[CHILDREN PROCEEDINGS][1] EXCEPT PARENTAL ORDER PROCEEDINGS AND PROCEEDINGS FOR APPLICATIONS IN ADOPTION, PLACEMENT AND RELATED PROCEEDINGS

Chapter 1
Interpretation and application of this Part

12.1 Application of this Part

(1) The rules in this Part apply to—

(a) emergency proceedings;
(b) private law proceedings;
(c) public law proceedings;
(d) proceedings relating to the exercise of the court's inherent jurisdiction (other than applications for the court's permission to start such proceedings);
(e) proceedings relating to child abduction and the recognition and enforcement of decisions relating to custody under the European Convention;
(f) proceedings relating to …[2] the 1996 Hague Convention in respect of children; and
(g) any other proceedings which may be referred to in a practice direction.

(Part 18 sets out the procedure for making an application for permission to bring proceedings.)

(Part 31 sets out the procedure for making applications for recognition and enforcement of judgments under …[2] the 1996 Hague Convention.)

(2) The rules in Chapter 7 of this Part also apply to family proceedings which are not within paragraph (1) but which otherwise relate wholly or mainly to the maintenance or upbringing of a minor.

[(3) This Part is subject to any provision made by or pursuant to Part 41 (proceeding by electronic means).][3]

Amendment

1 Substituted by the Family Procedure (Amendment) (No 5) Rules 2012, SI 2012/3061, rr 2, 5(a).
2 Repealed by the Family Procedure Rules 2010 and Court of Protection Rules 2017 (Amendment) (EU Exit) Regulations 2019, SI 2019/517, rr 2, 9(1), (2).
3 Inserted by the Family Procedure (Amendment) Rules 2020, SI 2020/135, rr 2, 15.

12.2 Interpretation

In this Part—

'the 2006 Act' means the Childcare Act 2006;
['activity condition' has the meaning given to it by section 11C(2) of the 1989 Act;
'activity direction' has the meaning given to it by section 11A(3) of the 1989 Act;][1]

'advocate' means a person exercising a right of audience as a representative of, or on behalf of, a party;

'care proceedings' means proceedings for a care order under section 31(1)(a) of the 1989 Act;

['Case Management Order' means an order in the form referred to in Practice Direction 12A;][2]

'child assessment order' has the meaning assigned to it by section 43(2) of the 1989 Act;

…[3]

…[3]

'contribution order' has the meaning assigned to it by paragraph 23(2) of Schedule 2 to the 1989 Act;

'education supervision order' has the meaning assigned to it by section 36(2) of the 1989 Act;

'emergency proceedings' means proceedings for—

(a) the disclosure of information as to the whereabouts of a child under section 33 of the 1986 Act;

(b) an order authorising the taking charge of and delivery of a child under section 34 of the 1986 Act;

(c) an emergency protection order;

(d) an order under section 44(9)(b) of the 1989 Act varying a direction in an emergency protection order given under section 44(6) of that Act;

(e) an order under section 45(5) of the 1989 Act extending the period during which an emergency protection order is to have effect;

(f) an order under section 45(8) of the 1989 Act discharging an emergency protection order;

(g) an order under section 45(8A) of the 1989 Act varying or discharging an emergency protection order in so far as it imposes an exclusion requirement on a person who is not entitled to apply for the order to be discharged;

(h) an order under section 45(8B) of the 1989 Act varying or discharging an emergency protection order in so far as it confers a power of arrest attached to an exclusion requirement;

(i) warrants under sections 48(9) and 102(1) of the 1989 Act and under section 79 of the 2006 Act; or

(j) a recovery order under section 50 of the 1989 Act;

'emergency protection order' means an order under section 44 of the 1989 Act;

'enforcement order' has the meaning assigned to it by section 11J(2) of the 1989 Act;

'financial compensation order' means an order made under section 11O(2) of the 1989 Act;

'interim order' means an interim care order or an interim supervision order referred to in section 38(1) of the 1989 Act;

['Part 4 proceedings' means proceedings for—

(a) a care order, or the discharge of such an order, under section 39(1) of the 1989 Act;

(b) an order giving permission to change a child's surname or remove a child from the United Kingdom under section 33(7) of the 1989 Act;

(c) a supervision order, the discharge or variation of such an order under section 39(2) of the 1989 Act, or the extension of such an order under paragraph 6(3) of Schedule 3 to that Act;

(d) an order making provision regarding contact under section 34(2) to (4) of the 1989 Act or an order varying or discharging such an order under section 34(9) of that Act;

(e) an education supervision order, the extension of an education supervision order under paragraph 15(2) of Schedule 3 to the 1989 Act, or the discharge of such an order under paragraph 17(1) of Schedule 3 to that Act;

(f) an order varying directions made with an interim care order or interim supervision order under section 38(8)(b) of the 1989 Act;

(g) an order under section 39(3) of the 1989 Act varying a supervision order in so far as it affects a person with whom the child is living but who is not entitled to apply for the order to be discharged;

(h) an order under section 39(3A) of the 1989 Act varying or discharging an interim care order in so far as it imposes an exclusion requirement on a person who is not entitled to apply for the order to be discharged;

(i) an order under section 39(3B) of the 1989 Act varying or discharging an interim care order in so far as it confers a power of arrest attached to an exclusion requirement; or

(j) the substitution of a supervision order for a care order under section 39(4) of the 1989 Act;][1]

'private law proceedings' means proceedings for—

[(a) a section 8 order except a child arrangements order to which section 9(6B) of the 1989 Act applies with respect to a child who is in the care of a local authority;][2]

(b) a parental responsibility order under sections 4(1)(c), 4ZA(1)(c) or 4A(1)(b) of the 1989 Act or an order terminating parental responsibility under sections 4(2A), 4ZA(5) or 4A(3) of that Act;

(c) an order appointing a child's guardian under section 5(1) of the 1989 Act or an order terminating the appointment under section 6(7) of that Act;

(d) an order giving permission to change a child's surname or remove a child from the United Kingdom under sections 13(1) or 14C(3) of the 1989 Act;

(e) a special guardianship order except where that order relates to a child who is subject of a care order;

(f) an order varying or discharging such an order under section 14D of the 1989 Act;

(g) an enforcement order;

(h) a financial compensation order;

(i) an order under paragraph 9 of Schedule A1 to the 1989 Act following a breach of an enforcement order;

(j) an order under Part 2 of Schedule A1 to the 1989 Act revoking or amending an enforcement order; or

(k) an order that a warning notice be attached to a [child arrangements order][2];

'public law proceedings' means [Part 4 proceedings and][1] proceedings for—

[(a) a child arrangements order to which section 9(6B) of the 1989 Act applies with respect to a child who is in the care of a local authority;][2]

(b) a special guardianship order relating to a child who is the subject of a care order;

(c) a secure accommodation order under section 25 of the 1989 Act;

(d) …[3]

(e) …[3]

(f) …[3]

(g) …[3]

(h) …[3]

(i) …[3]

(j) …[3]
(k) …[3]
(l) …[3]
(m) …[3]
(n) a child assessment order, or the variation or discharge of such an order under section 43(12) of the 1989 Act;
(o) an order permitting the local authority to arrange for any child in its care to live outside England and Wales under paragraph 19(1) of Schedule 2 to the 1989 Act;
(p) a contribution order, or revocation of such an order under paragraph 23(8) of Schedule 2 to the 1989 Act;
(q) an appeal under paragraph 8(1) of Schedule 8 to the 1989 Act;

'special guardianship order' has the meaning assigned to it by section 14A(1) of the 1989 Act;

'supervision order' has the meaning assigned to it by section 31(11) of the 1989 Act;

'supervision proceedings' means proceedings for a supervision order under section 31(1)(b) of the 1989 Act;

'warning notice' means a notice attached to an order pursuant to section 8(2) of the Children and Adoption Act 2006.

(The 1980 Hague Convention, the 1996 Hague Convention, the Council Regulation, and the European Convention are defined in rule 2.3.)

Amendment

1 Inserted by the Family Procedure (Amendment No 3) Rules 2014, SI 2014/843, rr 2, 15(a), (d), (f)(i).
2 Substituted by the Family Procedure (Amendment No 3) Rules 2014, SI 2014/843, rr 2, 15(b), (e), (f)(ii).
3 Repealed by the Family Procedure (Amendment No 3) Rules 2014, SI 2014/843, rr 2, 15(c), (f)(iii).

Chapter 2
General rules

12.3 Who the parties are

(1) In relation to the proceedings set out in column 1 of the following table, column 2 sets out who may make the application and column 3 sets out who the respondents to those proceedings will be.

Proceedings for	*Applicants*	*Respondents*
A parental responsibility order (section 4(1)(c), 4ZA(1)(c), or section 4A(1)(b) of the 1989 Act).	The child's father; the step parent; or the child's parent (being a woman who is a parent by virtue of section 43 of the Human Fertilisation and Embryology Act 2008 and who is not a person to whom section 1(3) of the Family Law Reform Act 1987 applies) (sections 4(1)(c), 4ZA(1)(c) and 4A(1)(b) of the 1989 Act).	Every person whom the applicant believes to have parental responsibility for the child; where the child is the subject of a care order, every person whom the applicant believes to have had parental responsibility immediately prior to the making of the care order;

Proceedings for	*Applicants*	*Respondents*
		in the case of an application to extend, vary or discharge an order, the parties to the proceedings leading to the order which it is sought to have extended, varied or discharged; in the case of specified proceedings, the child.
An order terminating a parental responsibility order or agreement (section 4(2A), 4ZA(5) or section 4A(3) of the 1989 Act.	Any person who has parental responsibility for the child; or with the court's permission, the child (section 4(3), 4ZA(6) and section 4A(3) of the 1989 Act).	As above.
An order appointing a guardian (section 5(1) of the 1989 Act).	An individual who wishes to be appointed as guardian (section 5(1) of the 1989 Act).	As above.
An order terminating the appointment of a guardian (section 6(7) of the 1989 Act).	Any person who has parental responsibility for the child; or with the court's permission, the child (section 6(7) of the 1989 Act).	As above.
A section 8 order.	Any person who is entitled to apply for a section 8 order with respect to the child (section 10(4) to (7) of the 1989 Act); or with the court's permission, any person (section10(2)(b) of the 1989 Act).	As above.
An enforcement order (section 11J of the 1989 Act).	A person who is, for the purposes of the [child arrangements order][1], a person with whom the child concerned lives or is to live; any person whose contact with the child concerned is provided for in the [child arrangements order][1]; any individual subject to a condition under section 11(7)(b) of the 1989 Act or [an activity][1] condition imposed by a [child arrangements order][1]; or with the court's permission, the child (section 11J(5) of the 1989 Act).	The person the applicant alleges has failed to comply with the [child arrangements order][1].

Proceedings for	*Applicants*	*Respondents*
A financial compensation order (section 11O of the 1989 Act).	Any person who is, for the purposes of the [child arrangements order][1], a person with whom the child concerned lives or is to live; any person whose contact with the child concerned is provided for in the [child arrangements order][1]; any individual subject to a condition under section 11(7)(b) of the 1989 Act or [an activity][1] condition imposed by a [child arrangements order][1]; or with the court's permission, the child (section 11O(6) of the 1989 Act).	The person the applicant alleges has failed to comply with the [child arrangements order][1].
An order permitting the child's name to be changed or the removal of the child from the United Kingdom (section 13(1), 14C(3) or 33(7) of the 1989 Act).	Any person (section 13(1), 14C(3), 33(7) of the 1989 Act).	As for a parental responsibility order.
A special guardianship order (section 14A of the 1989 Act).	Any guardian of the child; any individual [who is named in a child arrangements order as a person with whom the child is to live][1]; any individual listed in subsection (5)(b) or (c) of section 10 (as read with subsection (10) of that section) of the 1989 Act; a local authority foster parent with whom the child has lived for a period of at least one year immediately preceding the application; or any person with the court's permission (section 14A(3) of the 1989 Act) (more than one such individual can apply jointly (section 14A(3) and (5) of that Act)).	As above, and if a care order is in force with respect to the child, the child.

Proceedings for	*Applicants*	*Respondents*
Variation or discharge of a special guardianship order (section 14D of the 1989 Act).	The special guardian (or any of them, if there is more than one); any individual [who is named in a child arrangements order as a person with whom the child is to live;][1] the local authority designated in a care order with respect to the child; any individual within section 14D(1)(d) of the 1989 Act who has parental responsibility for the child; the child, any parent or guardian of the child and any step-parent of the child who has acquired, and has not lost, parental responsibility by virtue of section 4A of that Act with the court's permission; or any individual within section 14D(1)(d) of that Act who immediately before the making of the special guardianship order had, but no longer has, parental responsibility for the child with the court's permission.	As above.
A secure accommodation order (section 25 section of the 1989 Act).	The local authority which is looking after the child; or the Health Authority, [Secretary of State, National Health Service Commissioning Board, clinical commissioning group,][2] National Health Service Trust established under section 25 of the National Health Service Act 2006 or section 18(1) of the National Health Service (Wales) Act 2006, National Health Service Foundation Trust or any local authority providing [or arranging][3] accommodation for the child (unless the child is looked after by a local authority).	As above.

Proceedings for	*Applicants*	*Respondents*
A care or supervision order (section 31 of the 1989 Act).	Any local authority; the National Society for the Prevention of Cruelty to Children and any of its officers (section 31(1) of the 1989 Act);or any authorised person.	As above.
An order varying directions made with an interim care or interim supervision order (section 38(8)(b) of the 1989 Act).	The parties to proceedings in which directions are given under section 38(6) of the 1989 Act; or any person named in such a direction.	As above.
An order discharging a care order (section 39(1) of the 1989 Act).	Any person who has parental responsibility for the child; the child; or the local authority designated by the order (section 39(1) of the 1989 Act).	As above.
An order varying or discharging an interim care order in so far as it imposes an exclusion requirement (section 39(3A) of the 1989 Act).	A person to whom the exclusion requirement in the interim care order applies who is not entitled to apply for the order to be discharged (section 39(3A) of the 1989 Act).	As above.
An order varying or discharging an interim care order in so far as it confers a power of arrest attached to an exclusion requirement (section 39(3B) of the 1989 Act).	Any person entitled to apply for the discharge of the interim care order in so far as it imposes the exclusion requirement (section 39(3B) of the 1989 Act).	As above.
An order substituting a supervision order for a care order (section 39(4) of the 1989 Act).	Any person entitled to apply for a care order to be discharged under section 39(1) (section 39(4) of the 1989 Act).	As above.
A child assessment order (section 43(1) of the 1989 Act).	Any local authority; the National Society for the Prevention of Cruelty to Children and any of its officers; or any person authorised by order of the Secretary of State to bring the proceedings and any officer of a body who is so authorised (section 43(1) and (13) of the 1989 Act).	As above.

Proceedings for	*Applicants*	*Respondents*
An order varying or discharging a child assessment order (section 43(12) of the 1989 Act).	The applicant for an order that has been made under section 43(1) of the 1989 Act; or the persons referred to in section 43(11) of the 1989 Act (section 43(12) of that Act).	As above.
An emergency protection order (section 44(1) of the 1989 Act).	Any person (section 44(1) of the 1989 Act).	As for a parental responsibility order.
An order extending the period during which an emergency protection order is to have effect (section 45(4) of the 1989 Act).	Any person who— has parental responsibility for a child as the result of an emergency protection order; and is entitled to apply for a care order with respect to the child (section 45(4) of the 1989 Act).	As above.
An order discharging an emergency protection order (section 45(8) of the 1989 Act).	The child; a parent of the child; any person who is not a parent of the child but who has parental responsibility for the child; or any person with whom the child was living before the making of the emergency protection order (section 45(8) of the 1989 Act).	As above.
An order varying or discharging an emergency protection order in so far as it imposes the exclusion requirement (section 45(8A) of the 1989 Act).	A person to whom the exclusion requirement in the emergency protection order applies who is not entitled to apply for the emergency protection order to be discharged (section 45(8A) of the 1989 Act).	As above.
An order varying or discharging an emergency protection order in so far as it confers a power of arrest attached to an exclusion requirement (section 45(8B) of the 1989 Act).	Any person entitled to apply for the discharge of the emergency protection order in so far as it imposes the exclusion requirement (section 45(8B) of the 1989 Act).	As above.
An emergency protection order by the police (section 46(7) of the 1989 Act).	The officer designated for the purposes of section 46(3)(e) of the 1989 Act (section 46(7) of the 1989 Act).	As above.

Proceedings for	*Applicants*	*Respondents*
A warrant authorising a constable to assist in exercise of certain powers to search for children and inspect premises (section 48 of the 1989 Act).	Any person attempting to exercise powers under an emergency protection order who has been or is likely to be prevented from doing so by being refused entry to the premises concerned or refused access to the child concerned (section 48(9) of the 1989 Act).	As above.
A warrant authorising a constable to assist in exercise of certain powers to search for children and inspect premises (section 102 of the 1989 Act).	Any person attempting to exercise powers under the enactments mentioned in section 102(6) of the 1989 Act who has been or is likely to be prevented from doing so by being refused entry to the premises concerned or refused access to the child concerned (section 102(1) of that Act).	As above.
An order revoking an enforcement order (paragraph 4 of Schedule A1 to the 1989 Act).	The person subject to the enforcement order.	The person who was the applicant for the enforcement order; and, where the child was a party to the proceedings in which the enforcement order was made, the child.
An order amending an enforcement order (paragraphs 5 to 7 of Schedule A1 to the 1989 Act).	The person subject to the enforcement order.	The person who was the applicant for the enforcement order. (Rule 12.33 makes provision about applications under paragraph 5 of Schedule A1 to the 1989 Act.)
An order following breach of an enforcement order (paragraph 9 of Schedule A1 to the 1989 Act).	Any person who is, for [the purposes of the child arrangements order][1], the person with whom the child lives or is to live; any person whose contact with the child concerned is [provided for in the child arrangements order][1]; any individual subject to a condition under section 11(7)(b) of the 1989 Act or [an activity condition imposed by a child arrangements order;][1] or with the court's permission, the child (paragraph 9 of Schedule A1 to the 1989 Act).	The person the applicant alleges has failed to comply with the unpaid work requirement imposed by an enforcement order; and where the child was a party to the proceedings in which the enforcement order was made, the child.

Proceedings for	*Applicants*	*Respondents*
An order permitting the local authority to arrange for any child in its care to live outside England and Wales (Schedule 2, paragraph 19(1), to the 1989 Act).	The local authority (Schedule 2, paragraph 19(1), to the 1989 Act).	As for a parental responsibility order.
A contribution order (Schedule 2, paragraph 23(1), to the 1989 Act).	The local authority (Schedule 2, paragraph 23(1), to the 1989 Act).	As above and the contributor.
An order revoking a contribution order (Schedule 2, paragraph 23(8), to the 1989 Act).	The contributor; or the local authority.	As above.
An order relating to contact with the child in care and any named person (section 34(2) of the 1989 Act) or permitting the local authority to refuse contact (section 34(4) of that Act).	The local authority; or the child (section 34(2) or 34(4) of the 1989 Act).	As above; and the person whose contact with the child is the subject of the application.
An order relating to contact with the child in care (section 34(3) of the 1989 Act).	The child's parents; any guardian or special guardian of the child; any person who by virtue of section 4A of the 1989 Act has parental responsibility for the child; [where there was a child arrangements order in force with respect to the child immediately before the care order was made, any person named in that order as a person with whom the child was to live;][1] a person who by virtue of an order made in the exercise of the High Court's inherent jurisdiction with respect to children had care of the child immediately before the care order was made (section 34(3)(a) of the 1989 Act); or with the court's permission, any person (section 34(3) (b) of that Act).	As above; and the person whose contact with the child is the subject of the application.

Proceedings for	*Applicants*	*Respondents*
An order varying or discharging an order for contact with a child in care under section 34 (section 34((9) of the 1989 Act).	The local authority; the child; or any person named in the order (section 34(9) of the 1989 Act).	As above; and the person whose contact with the child is the subject of the application.
An education supervision order (section 36 of the 1989 Act).	Any local authority (section 36(1) of the 1989 Act).	As above; and the child.
An order varying or discharging a supervision order (section 39(2) of the 1989 Act).	Any person who has parental responsibility for the child; the child; or 'the supervisor (section 39(2) of the 1989 Act).	As above; and the supervisor.
An order varying a supervision order in so far as it affects the person with whom the child is living (section 39(3) of the 1989 Act).	The person with whom the child is living who is not entitled to apply for the order to be discharged (section 39(3) of the 1989 Act).	As above; and the supervisor.
An order varying a direction under section 44(6) of the 1989 Act in an emergency protection order (section 44(9)(b) of that Act).	The parties to the application for the emergency protection order in respect of which it is sought to vary the directions; the children's guardian; the local authority in whose area the child is ordinarily resident; or any person who is named in the directions.	As above, and the parties to the application for the order in respect of which it is sought to vary the directions; any person who was caring for the child prior to the making of the order; and any person [named in a child arrangements order as a person with whom the child is to spend time or otherwise have contact and who][1] is affected by the direction which it is sought to have varied.

Proceedings for	*Applicants*	*Respondents*
A recovery order (section 50 of the 1989 Act).	Any person who has parental responsibility for the child by virtue of a care order or an emergency protection order; or where the child is in police protection the officer designated forthe purposes of section 46(3)(e) of the 1989 Act (section 50(4) of the 1989 Act).	As above; and the person whom the applicant alleges to have effected or to have been or to be responsible for the taking or keeping of the child.
An order discharging an education supervision order (Schedule 3, paragraph 17(1), to the 1989 Act).	The child concerned; a parent of the child; or the local authority concerned (Schedule 3, paragraph 17(1), to the 1989 Act).	As above; and the local authority concerned; and the child.
An order extending an education supervision order (Schedule 3, paragraph, 15(2), to the 1989 Act).	The local authority in whose favour the education supervision order was made (Schedule 3, paragraph 15(2), to the 1989 Act).	As above; and the child.
An appeal under paragraph (8) of Schedule 8 to the 1989 Act.	A person aggrieved by the matters listed in paragraph 8(1) of Schedule 8 to the 1989 Act.	The appropriate local authority.
An order for the disclosure of information as to the whereabouts of a child under section 33 of the 1986 Act.	Any person with a legitimate interest in proceedings for an order under Part 1 of the 1986 Act; or a person who has registered an order made elsewhere in the United Kingdom or a specified dependent territory.	Any person alleged to have information as to the whereabouts of the child.
An order authorising the taking charge of and delivery of a child under section 34 of the 1986 Act.	The person to whom the child is to be given up under section 34(1) of the 1986 Act.	As above; and the person who is required to give up the child in accordance with section 34(1) of the 1986 Act.
An order relating to the exercise of the court's inherent jurisdiction (including wardship proceedings).	A local authority (with the court's permission); any person with a genuine interest in or relation to the child; or the child (wardship proceedings only).	The parent or guardian of the child; any other person who has an interest in or relationship to the child; and the child (wardship proceedings only and with the court's permission as described at rule 12.37).

Proceedings for	*Applicants*	*Respondents*
A warrant under section 79 of the 2006 Act authorising any constable to assist Her Majesty's Chief Inspector for Education, Children's Services and Skills in the exercise of powers conferred on him by section 77 of the 2006 Act.	Her Majesty's Chief Inspector for Education, Children's Services and Skills.	Any person preventing or likely to prevent Her Majesty's Chief Inspector for Education, Children's Services and Skills from exercising powers conferred on him by section 77 of the 2006 Act.
An order in respect of a child under the 1980 Hague Convention.	Any person, institution or body who claims that a child has been removed or retained in breach of rights of custody or claims that there has been a breach of rights of access in relation to the child.	The person alleged to have brought the child into the United Kingdom; the person with whom the child is alleged to be; any parent or guardian of the child who is within the United Kingdom and is not otherwise a party; any person in whose favour a decision relating to custody has been made if that person is not otherwise a party; and any other person who appears to the court to have sufficient interest in the welfare of the child.
An order concerning the recognition and enforcement of decisions relating to custody under the European Convention.	Any person who has a court order giving that person rights of custody in relation to the child.	As above.
An application for the High Court to request transfer of jurisdiction under …[4] Article 9 of the 1996 Hague Convention (rule 12.65).	Any person with sufficient interest in the welfare of the child and who would be entitled to make a proposed application in relation to that child, or who intends to seek the permission of the court to make such application if the transfer is agreed.	As directed by the court in accordance with rule 12.65.

Proceedings for	*Applicants*	*Respondents*
An application under rule 12.71 for a declaration as to the existence, or extent, of parental responsibility under Article 16 of the 1996 Convention.	Any interested person including a person who holds, or claims to hold, parental responsibility for the child under the law of another State which subsists in accordance with Article 16 of the 1996 Hague Convention following the child becoming habitually resident in a territorial unit of the United Kingdom.	Every person whom the applicant believes to have parental responsibility for the child; any person whom the applicant believes to hold parental responsibility for the child under the law of another State which subsists in accordance with Article 16 of the 1996 Hague Convention following the child becoming habitually resident in a territorial unit of the United Kingdom; and where the child is the subject of a care order, every person whom the applicant believes to have had parental responsibility immediately prior to the making of the care order.
A warning notice.	The person who is, for the purposes of the [child arrangements order][1], the person with whom the child concerned lives or is to live; the person whose contact with the child concerned is provided for in the [child arrangements order][1]; any individual subject to a condition under section 11(7)(b) of the 1989 Act or [an activity][1] condition imposed by the contact order; or with the court's permission, the child.	Any person who was a party to the proceedings in which the [child arrangements order][1] was made. (Rule 12.33 makes provision about applications for warning notices).

(2) The court will direct that a person with parental responsibility be made a party to proceedings where that person requests to be one.

(3) Subject to rule 16.2, the court may at any time direct that—

(a) any person or body be made a party to proceedings; or
(b) a party be removed.

(4) If the court makes a direction for the addition or removal of a party under this rule, it may give consequential directions about—

(a) the service of a copy of the application form or other relevant documents on the new party;
(b) the management of the proceedings.

(5) In this rule—

'a local authority foster parent' has the meaning assigned to it by section 23(3) of the 1989 Act; and
'care home', 'independent hospital', 'local authority' and ['Primary Care Trust'][2] have the meanings assigned to them by section 105 of the 1989 Act.

(Part 16 contains the rules relating to the representation of children.)

Amendment

1 Substituted by the Family Procedure (Amendment No 3) Rules 2014, SI 2014/843, rr 2, 16.
2 Substituted by the National Treatment Agency (Abolition) and the Health and Social Care Act 2012 (Consequential, Transitional and Saving Provisions) Order 2013, SI 2013/235, art 11, Sch 2, para 156(a)(i), (b).
3 Inserted by the National Treatment Agency (Abolition) and the Health and Social Care Act 2012 (Consequential, Transitional and Saving Provisions) Order 2013, SI 2013/235, art 11, Sch 2, para 156(a)(ii).
4 Repealed by the Family Procedure Rules 2010 and Court of Protection Rules 2017 (Amendment) (EU Exit) Regulations 2019, SI 2019/517, rr 2, 9(1), (3).

12.4 Notice of proceedings to person with foreign parental responsibility

(1) This rule applies where a child is subject to proceedings to which this Part applies and—

(a) a person holds or is believed to hold parental responsibility for the child under the law of another State which subsists in accordance with Article 16 of the 1996 Hague Convention following the child becoming habitually resident in a territorial unit of the United Kingdom; and
(b) that person is not otherwise required to be joined as a respondent under rule 12.3.

(2) [Subject to paragraph (2A),][1] the applicant shall give notice of the proceedings to any person to whom the applicant believes paragraph (1) applies in any case in which a person whom the applicant believed to have parental responsibility under the 1989 Act would be a respondent to those proceedings in accordance with rule 12.3.

[(2A) Notice shall not be given to a person to whom the applicant believes paragraph (1) applies if the court directs that such notice is not necessary.][1]

(3) [Unless a direction has been made under paragraph (2A)][1] the applicant and every respondent to the proceedings shall provide such details as they possess as to the identity and whereabouts of any person they believe to hold parental responsibility for the child in accordance with paragraph (1) to the court officer, upon making, or responding to the application as appropriate.

(4) Where the existence of a person who is believed to have parental responsibility for the child in accordance with paragraph (1) only becomes apparent to a party at a later date during the proceedings, that party must notify the court officer of those details at the earliest opportunity.

(5) Where a person to whom paragraph (1) applies receives notice of proceedings, that person may apply to the court to be joined as a party using the Part 18 procedure.

Amendment

1 Inserted by the Family Procedure (Amendment) Rules 2020, SI 2020/135, rr 2, 16.

12.5 What the court will do when the application has been issued

[(1)][1] When …[2] proceedings [other than public law proceedings][1] have been issued the court will consider—

(a) setting a date for—
  (i) a directions appointment;
  (ii) in private law proceedings, a First Hearing Dispute Resolution Appointment; [or][1]
  (iii) …[2]
  (iv) the hearing of the application …[2],

and if the court sets a date it will do so in accordance with rule 12.13 and [Practice Direction 12B][3];

(b) giving any of the directions listed in rule 12.12 or, where Chapter 6, section 1 applies, rule 12.48; and
(c) doing anything else which is set out in [Practice Direction 12B][3] or any other practice direction.

[(2) When Part 4 proceedings and in so far as practicable other public law proceedings have been issued the court will—

(a) set a date for the Case Management Hearing in accordance with Practice Direction 12A;
(b) set a date for the hearing of an application for an interim order if necessary;
(c) give any directions listed in rule 12.12; and
(d) do anything else which is set out in Practice Direction 12A.][1]

[(Practice Direction 12A sets out details relating to the Case Management Hearing. Practice Direction 12B supplementing this Part sets out details relating to the First Hearing Dispute Resolution Appointment.)][3]

Amendment

1 Inserted by the Family Procedure (Amendment No 3) Rules 2014, SI 2014/843, rr 2, 17(a), (c), (d), (i).
2 Repealed by the Family Procedure (Amendment No 3) Rules 2014, SI 2014/843, rr 2, 17(b), (e), (f).
3 Substituted by the Family Procedure (Amendment No 3) Rules 2014, SI 2014/843, rr 2, 17(g), (h), (j).

12.6 Children's guardian, solicitor and reports under section 7 of the 1989 Act

[Within a day of the issue of Part 4 proceedings or the transfer of Part 4 Proceedings to the court and as][1] soon as practicable after the issue of [other][2] proceedings or the transfer of the [other][2] proceedings to the court, the court will—

(a) in specified proceedings, appoint a children's guardian under rule 16.3(1) unless—
  (i) such an appointment has already been made by the court which made the transfer and is subsisting; or
  (ii) the court considers that such an appointment is not necessary to safeguard the interests of the child;
(b) where section 41(3) of the 1989 Act applies, consider whether a solicitor should be appointed to represent the child, and if so, appoint a solicitor accordingly;

(c) consider whether to ask an officer of the service or a Welsh family proceedings officer for advice relating to the welfare of the child;
(d) consider whether a report relating to the welfare of the child is required, and if so, request such a report in accordance with section 7 of the 1989 Act.

(Part 16 sets out the rules relating to representation of children.)

Amendment

1 Substituted by the Family Procedure (Amendment No 3) Rules 2014, SI 2014/843, rr 2, 18(a).
2 Inserted by the Family Procedure (Amendment No 3) Rules 2014, SI 2014/843, rr 2, 18(b), (c).

12.7 What a court officer will do

(1) As soon as practicable after the issue of proceedings the court officer will return to the applicant the copies of the application together with the forms referred to in Practice Direction 5A.

(2) As soon as practicable after the issue of proceedings or the transfer of proceedings to the court or at any other stage in the proceedings the court officer will—

(a) give notice of any hearing set by the court to the applicant; and
(b) do anything else set out in Practice Directions 12A or 12B or any other practice direction.

[12.8 Service

(1) After the issue of proceedings under this Part, the documents specified in paragraph (5) must be served on the respondent or respondents.

(2) In section 8 private law proceedings, service under paragraph (1) will be effected by the court officer, unless—

(a) the applicant requests to do so; or
(b) the court directs the applicant to do so.

(3) In this Rule, 'section 8 private law proceedings' are proceedings for a section 8 order except proceedings for a child arrangements order to which section 9(6B) of the 1989 Act applies with respect to a child who is in the care of a local authority.

(4) In any other proceedings to which this Part applies, service under paragraph (1) must be effected by the applicant.

(5) The documents are—

(a) the application together with the documents referred to in Practice Direction 12C; and
(b) notice of any hearing set by the court.

(6) Service under this rule must be carried out in accordance with Practice Direction 12C.

(7) The general rules about service in Part 6 apply but are subject to this rule.

[(Practice Direction 12C (Service of Application in Children Proceedings) provides that in Part 4 proceedings (except proceedings for an interim order) the minimum number of days prior to the Case Management Hearing for service of the application and accompanying documents is 7 days. The Court has discretion to extend or shorten this time (see rule 4.1(3)(a)).][1]][2]

Amendment

1 Inserted by the Family Procedure (Amendment No 3) Rules 2014, SI 2014/843, rr 2, 20.
2 Substituted by the Family Procedure (Amendment No 3) Rules 2014, SI 2014/843, rr 2, 19.

12.9 …[1]

…[1]

Amendment

1 Repealed by the Family Procedure (Amendment No 3) Rules 2013, SI 2013/3204, rr 2, 47.

12.10 …[1]

… -

Amendment

1 Repealed by the Family Procedure (Amendment No 3) Rules 2013, SI 2013/3204, rr 2, 47.

12.11 …[1]

…[1]

Amendment

1 Repealed by the Family Procedure (Amendment No 3) Rules 2013, SI 2013/3204, rr 2, 47.

12.12 Directions

(1) This rule does not apply to proceedings under Chapter 6 of this Part.

(2) At any stage in the proceedings, the court may give directions about the conduct of the proceedings including—

(a) the management of the case;
(b) the timetable for steps to be taken between the giving of directions and the final hearing;
(c) the joining of a child or other person as a party to the proceedings in accordance with rules 12.3(2) and (3);
(d) the attendance of the child;
(e) the appointment of a children's guardian or of a solicitor under section 41(3) of the 1989 Act;
(f) the appointment of a litigation friend;
(g) the service of documents;
(h) the filing of evidence including experts' reports; and
(i) the exercise by an officer of the Service, Welsh family proceedings officer or local authority officer of any duty referred to in rule 16.38(1)

(3) Paragraph (4) applies where—

(a) an officer of the Service or a Welsh family proceedings officer has filed a report or a risk assessment as a result of exercising a duty referred to in rule 16.38(1)(a); or
(b) a local authority officer has filed a report as a result of exercising a duty referred to in rule 16.38(1)(b).

(4) The court may—

(a) give directions setting a date for a hearing at which that report or risk assessment will be considered; and
(b) direct that the officer who prepared the report or risk assessment attend any such hearing.

(5) The court may exercise the powers in paragraphs (2) and (4) on an application or of its own initiative.

(6) Where the court proposes to exercise its powers of its own initiative the procedure set out in rule 4.3(2) to (6) applies.

(7) Directions of a court which are still in force immediately prior to the transfer of proceedings to another court will continue to apply following the transfer subject to—

(a) any changes of terminology which are required to apply those directions to the court to which the proceedings are transferred; and
(b) any variation or revocation of the direction.

(8) The court or court officer will—

(a) take a note of the giving, variation or revocation of a direction under this rule; and
(b) as soon as practicable serve a copy of the note on every party.

(Rule 12.48 provides for directions in proceedings under the 1980 Hague Convention and the European Convention.)

12.13 Setting dates for hearings and setting or confirming the timetable and date for the final hearing

(1) At the—

(a) transfer to a court of proceedings;
(b) postponement or adjournment of any hearing; or
(c) conclusion of any hearing at which the proceedings are not finally determined,

the court will set a date for the proceedings to come before the court again for the purposes of giving directions or for such other purposes as the court directs.

(2) At any hearing the court may—

(a) confirm a date for the final hearing or the week within which the final hearing is to begin (where a date or period for the final hearing has already been set);
(b) set a timetable for the final hearing unless a timetable has already been fixed, or the court considers that it would be inappropriate to do so; or
(c) set a date for the final hearing or a period within which the final hearing of the application is to take place.

(3) The court officer will notify the parties of—

(a) the date of a hearing fixed in accordance with paragraph (1);
(b) the timetable for the final hearing; and
(c) the date of the final hearing or the period in which it will take place.

(4) Where the date referred to in paragraph (1) is set at the transfer of proceedings, the date will be as soon as possible after the transfer.

(5) The requirement in paragraph (1) to set a date for the proceedings to come before the court again is satisfied by the court setting or confirming a date for the final hearing.

12.14 Attendance at hearings

(1) This rule does not apply to proceedings under Chapter 6 of this Part except for proceedings for a declaration under rule 12.71.

(2) Unless the court directs otherwise and subject to paragraph (3), the persons who must attend a hearing are—

(a) any party to the proceedings;
(b) any litigation friend for any party or legal representative instructed to act on that party's behalf; and
(c) any other person directed by the court or required by Practice Directions 12A or 12B or any other practice direction to attend.

(3) Proceedings or any part of them will take place in the absence of a child who is a party to the proceedings if—

(a) the court considers it in the interests of the child, having regard to the matters to be discussed or the evidence likely to be given; and
(b) the child is represented by a children's guardian or solicitor.

(4) When considering the interests of the child under paragraph (3) the court will give—

(a) the children's guardian;
(b) the solicitor for the child; and
(c) the child, if of sufficient understanding,

an opportunity to make representations.

(5) Subject to paragraph (6), where at the time and place appointed for a hearing, the applicant appears but one or more of the respondents do not, the court may proceed with the hearing.

(6) The court will not begin to hear an application in the absence of a respondent unless the court is satisfied that—

(a) the respondent received reasonable notice of the date of the hearing; or
(b) the circumstances of the case justify proceeding with the hearing.

(7) Where, at the time and place appointed for a hearing one or more of the respondents appear but the applicant does not, the court may—

(a) refuse the application; or
(b) if sufficient evidence has previously been received, proceed in the absence of the applicant.

(8) Where at the time and place appointed for a hearing neither the applicant nor any respondent appears, the court may refuse the application.

(9) Paragraphs (5) to (8) do not apply to a hearing where the court—

(a) is considering—
  (i) whether to make [an activity][1] direction or to attach [an activity][1] condition to a [child arrangements order][1]; or
  (ii) an application for a financial compensation order, an enforcement order or an order under paragraph 9 of Schedule A1 to the 1989 Act following a breach of an enforcement order; and
(b) has yet to obtain sufficient evidence from, or in relation to, the person who may be the subject of the direction, condition or order to enable it to determine the matter.

(10) …[2]

…[2]

Amendment

1 Substituted by the Family Procedure (Amendment No 3) Rules 2014, SI 2014/843, rr 2, 21.
2 Repealed by the Family Procedure Rules 2010 and Court of Protection Rules 2017 (Amendment) (EU Exit) Regulations 2019, SI 2019/517, rr 2, 9(1), (4).

12.15 Steps taken by the parties

If—

(a) the parties or any children's guardian agree proposals for the management of the proceedings (including a proposed date for the final hearing or a period within which the final hearing is to take place); and
(b) the court considers that the proposals are suitable,

it may approve them without a hearing and give directions in the terms proposed.

[(Practice Direction 12A gives guidance as to the application of this rule to Part 4 proceedings in the light of the period that is for the time being allowed under section 32(1)(a)(ii) of the 1989 Act)][1]

Amendment

1 Inserted by the Family Procedure (Amendment No 3) Rules 2014, SI 2014/843, rr 2, 22.

12.16 Applications without notice

(1) This rule applies to—

(a) proceedings for a section 8 order;
(b) emergency proceedings; and
(c) proceedings relating to the exercise of the court's inherent jurisdiction (other than an application for the court's permission to start such proceedings and proceedings for collection, location and passport orders where Chapter 6 applies).

(2) An application in proceedings referred to in paragraph (1) may …[1] be made without notice in which case the applicant must file the application—

(a) where the application is made by telephone, the next business day after the making of the application; or
(b) in any other case, at the time when the application is made.

(3) …[1]

(4) Where—

(a) a section 8 order;
(b) an emergency protection order;
(c) an order for the disclosure of information as to the whereabouts of a child under section 33 of the 1986 Act; or
(d) an order authorising the taking charge of and delivery of a child under section 34 of the 1986 Act,

is made without notice, the applicant must serve a copy of the application on each respondent within 48 hours after the order is made.

(5) Within 48 hours after the making of an order without notice, the applicant must serve a copy of the order on—

(a) the parties, unless the court directs otherwise;
(b) any person who has actual care of the child or who had such care immediately prior to the making of the order; and
(c) in the case of an emergency protection order and a recovery order, the local authority in whose area the child lives or is found.

(6) Where the court refuses to make an order on an application without notice it may direct that the application is made on notice in which case the application will proceed in accordance with rules 12.3 to 12.15.

(7) Where the hearing takes place outside the hours during which the court office is normally open, the court or court officer will take a note of the proceedings.

(Practice Direction 12E (Urgent Business) provides further details of the procedure for out of hours applications. See also Practice Direction 12D (Inherent Jurisdiction (including Wardship Proceedings).)

(Rule 12.47 provides for without-notice applications in proceedings under Chapter 6, section 1 of this Part, (proceedings under the 1980 Hague Convention and the European Convention).)

Amendment

1 Repealed by the Family Procedure (Amendment No 3) Rules 2013, SI 2013/3204, rr 2, 48.

12.17 Investigation under section 37 of the 1989 Act

(1) This rule applies where a direction is given to an appropriate authority by the court under section 37(1) of the 1989 Act.

(2) On giving the direction the court may adjourn the proceedings.

(3) As soon as practicable after the direction is given the court will record the direction.

(4) As soon as practicable after the direction is given the court officer will—

(a) serve the direction on—
  (i) the parties to the proceedings in which the direction is given; and
  (ii) the appropriate authority where it is not a party;
(b) serve any documentary evidence directed by the court on the appropriate authority.

(5) Where a local authority informs the court of any of the matters set out in section 37(3) (a) to (c) of the 1989 Act it will do so in writing.

(6) Unless the court directs otherwise, the court officer will serve a copy of any report to the court under section 37 of the 1989 Act on the parties.

(Section 37 of the 1989 Act refers to the appropriate authority and section 37(5) of that Act sets out which authority should be named in a particular case.)

12.18 Disclosure of a report under section 14A(8) or (9) of the 1989 Act

(1) In proceedings for a special guardianship order, the local authority must file the report under section 14A(8) or (9) of the 1989 Act within the timetable fixed by the court.

(2) The court will consider whether to give a direction that the report under section 14A(8) or (9) of the 1989 Act be disclosed to each party to the proceedings.

(3) Before giving a direction for the report to be disclosed, the court must consider whether any information should be deleted from the report.

(4) The court may direct that the report must not be disclosed to a party.

(5) The court officer must serve a copy of the report in accordance with any direction under paragraph (2).

(6) In paragraph (3), information includes information which a party has declined to reveal under rule 29.1(1).

12.19 Additional evidence

(1) This rule applies to proceedings for a section 8 order or a special guardianship order.

(2) Unless the court directs otherwise, a party must not—

- (a) file or serve any document other than in accordance with these rules or any practice direction;
- (b) in completing a form prescribed by these rules or any practice direction, give information or make a statement which is not required or authorised by that form; or
- (c) file or serve at a hearing—
  - (i) any witness statement of the substance of the oral evidence which the party intends to adduce; or
  - (ii) any copy of any document (including any experts' report) which the party intends to rely on.

(3) Where a party fails to comply with the requirements of this rule in relation to any witness statement or other document, the party cannot seek to rely on that statement or other document unless the court directs otherwise.

12.20 …[1]

…[1]

Amendment

1 Repealed by the Family Procedure (Amendment) (No 5) Rules 2012, SI 2012/3061, rr 2, 4.

12.21 Hearings

(1) The court may give directions about the order of speeches and the evidence at a hearing.

(2) Subject to any directions given under paragraph (1), the parties and the children's guardian must adduce their evidence at a hearing in the following order—

- (a) the applicant;
- (b) any party with parental responsibility for the child;
- (c) other respondents;
- (d) the children's guardian;
- (e) the child, if the child is a party to proceedings and there is no children's guardian.

Chapter 3
Special provisions about public law proceedings

[12.22 Timetable for the proceedings

In public law proceedings other than Part 4 proceedings, in so far as practicable the court will draw up the timetable for the proceedings or revise that timetable with a view to disposing of the application without delay and in any event within 26 weeks beginning with the date on which the application is issued.

(In relation to Part 4 proceedings, section 32(1)(a) of the 1989 Act requires the court to draw up a timetable with a view to disposing of the application without delay and in any event within 26 weeks beginning with the day on which the application is issued.)][1]

Amendment

1 Substituted by the Family Procedure (Amendment No 3) Rules 2014, SI 2014/843, rr 2, 23.

[12.23 Application of rules 12.24 to 12.26C

Rules 12.24 to 12.26C apply to Part 4 proceedings and in so far as practicable other public law proceedings.][1]

Amendment

1 Substituted by the Family Procedure (Amendment No 3) Rules 2014, SI 2014/843, rr 2, 24.

12.24 Directions

The court will direct the parties to—

(a) monitor compliance with the court's directions; and
(b) tell the court or court officer about—
  (i) any failure to comply with a direction of the court; and
  (ii) any other delay in the proceedings.

[12.25 The Case Management Hearing and the Issues Resolution Hearing

(1) The court will conduct the Case Management Hearing with the objective of—

(a) confirming the level of judge to which the proceedings have been allocated;
(b) drawing up a timetable for the proceedings including the time within which the proceedings are to be resolved;
(c) identifying the issues; and
(d) giving directions in accordance with rule 12.12 and Practice Direction 12A to manage the proceedings.

(2) The court may hold a further Case Management Hearing only where this hearing is necessary to fulfil the objectives of the Case Management Hearing set out in paragraph (1).

(3) The court will conduct the Issues Resolution Hearing with the objective of—

(a) identifying the remaining issues in the proceedings;
(b) as far as possible resolving or narrowing those issues; and
(c) giving directions to manage the proceedings to the final hearing in accordance with rule 12.12 and Practice Direction 12A.

(4) Where it is possible for all the issues in the proceedings to be resolved at the Issues Resolution Hearing, the court may treat the Issues Resolution Hearing as a final hearing and make orders disposing of the proceedings.

(5) The court may set a date for the Case Management Hearing, a further Case Management Hearing and the Issues Resolution Hearing at the times referred to in Practice Direction 12A.

(6) The matters which the court will consider at the hearings referred to in this rule are set out in Practice Direction 12A.

(Rule 25.6 (experts: when to apply for the court's permission) provides that unless the court directs otherwise, parties must apply for the court's permission as mentioned in section 13(1), (3) and (5) of the 2014 Act as soon as possible and in Part 4 proceedings and in so far as practicable other public law proceedings no later than the Case Management Hearing.)][1]

Amendment

1 Substituted by the Family Procedure (Amendment No 3) Rules 2014, SI 2014/843, rr 2, 25.

[12.26 Discussion between advocates

(1) When setting a date for the Case Management Hearing or the Issues Resolution Hearing the court will direct a discussion between the parties' advocates to—

(a) discuss the provisions of a draft of the Case Management Order; and
(b) consider any other matter set out in Practice Direction 12A.

(2) Where there is a litigant in person the court will give directions about how that person may take part in the discussions between the parties' advocates.

(3) Unless the court directs otherwise—

(a) any discussion between advocates must take place no later than 2 days before the Case Management Hearing; and
(b) a draft of the Case Management Order must be filed with the court no later than 11 a.m. on the day before the Case Management Hearing.

(4) Unless the court directs otherwise—

(a) any discussion between advocates must take place no later than 7 days before the Issues Resolution Hearing; and
(b) a draft of the Case Management Order must be filed with the court no later than 11 a.m. on the day before the Issues Resolution Hearing.

(5) For the purposes of this rule 'advocate' includes a litigant in person.][1]

Amendment

1 Substituted by the Family Procedure (Amendment No 3) Rules 2014, SI 2014/843, rr 2, 26.

[12.26A Application for extension of the time limit for disposing of the application

(1) An application requesting the court to grant an extension must state—

(a) the reasons for the request;
(b) the period of extension being requested; and
(c) a short explanation of—
  (i) why it is necessary for the request to be granted to enable the court to resolve the proceedings justly;

(ii) the impact which any ensuing timetable revision would have on the welfare of the child to whom the application relates;
(iii) the impact which any ensuing timetable revision would have on the duration and conduct of the proceedings; and
(iv) the reasons for the grant or refusal of any previous request for extension.

(2) Part 18 applies to an application requesting the grant of an extension.

(3) In this rule

'ensuing timetable revision' has the meaning given to it by section 32(6) of the 1989 Act;
'extension' means an extension of the period for the time being allowed under section 32(1)(a)(ii) of the 1989 Act which is to end no more than 8 weeks after the later of the times referred to in section 32(8) of that Act.][1]

Amendment

1 Inserted by the Family Procedure (Amendment No 3) Rules 2014, SI 2014/843, rr 2, 27.

[12.26B Disapplication of rule 4.1(3)(a) court's power to extend or shorten the time for compliance with a rule

Rule 4.1(3)(a) does not apply to any period that is for the time being allowed under section 32(1)(a)(ii) of the 1989 Act.][1]

Amendment

1 Inserted by the Family Procedure (Amendment No 3) Rules 2014, SI 2014/843, rr 2, 27.

[12.26C Extension of time limit: reasons for court's decision

(1) When refusing or granting an extension of the period that is for the time being allowed under section 32(1)(a)(ii) in the case of the application, the court will announce its decision and—

(a) the reasons for that decision; and
(b) where an extension is granted or refused, a short explanation of the impact which the decision would have on the welfare of the child.

(2) The court office will supply a copy of the order granting or refusing the extension including the reasons for the court's decision and the period of any extension and short explanation given under paragraph (1)(b) to—

(a) the parties; and
(b) any person who has actual care of the child who is the subject of the proceedings.][1]

Amendment

1 Inserted by the Family Procedure (Amendment No 3) Rules 2014, SI 2014/843, rr 2, 27.

12.27 Matters prescribed for the purposes of the Act

(1) Proceedings for an order under any of the following provisions of the 1989 Act—

(a) a secure accommodation order under section 25;
(b) an order giving permission to change a child's surname or remove a child from the United Kingdom under section 33(7);

(c) an order permitting the local authority to arrange for any child in its care to live outside England and Wales under paragraph 19(1) of Schedule 2;
(d) the extension or further extension of a supervision order under paragraph 6(3) of Schedule 3;
(e) appeals against the determination of proceedings of a kind set out in sub-paragraphs (a) to (d);

are specified for the purposes of section 41 of that Act in accordance with section 41(6)(i) of that Act.

(2) The persons listed as applicants in the table set out in rule 12.3 to proceedings for the variation of directions made with interim care or interim supervision orders under section 38(8) of the 1989 Act are the prescribed class of persons for the purposes of that section.

(3) The persons listed as applicants in the table set out in rule 12.3 to proceedings for the variation of a direction made under section 44(6) of the 1989 Act in an emergency protection order are the prescribed class of persons for the purposes of section 44(9) of that Act.

12.28 Exclusion requirements: interim care orders and emergency protection orders

(1) This rule applies where the court includes an exclusion requirement in an interim care order or an emergency protection order.

(2) The applicant for an interim care order or emergency protection order must—

(a) prepare a separate statement of the evidence in support of the application for an exclusion requirement;
(b) serve the statement personally on the relevant person with a copy of the order containing the exclusion requirement (and of any power of arrest which is attached to it);
(c) inform the relevant person of that person's right to apply to vary or discharge the exclusion requirement.

(3) Where a power of arrest is attached to an exclusion requirement in an interim care order or an emergency protection order, the applicant will deliver—

(a) a copy of the order; and
(b) a statement showing that the relevant person has been served with the order or informed of its terms (whether by being present when the order was made or by telephone or otherwise),

to the officer for the time being in charge of the police station for the area in which the dwelling house in which the child lives is situated (or such other police station as the court may specify).

(4) Rules 10.6(2) and 10.10 to 10.17 will apply, with the necessary modifications, for the service, variation, discharge and enforcement of any exclusion requirement to which a power of arrest is attached as they apply to an order made on an application under Part 4 of the 1996 Act.

(5) The relevant person must serve the parties to the proceedings with any application which that person makes for the variation or discharge of the exclusion requirement.

(6) Where an exclusion requirement ceases to have effect whether—

(a) as a result of the removal of a child under section 38A(10) or 44A(10) of the 1989 Act;
(b) because of the discharge of the interim care order or emergency protection order; or
(c) otherwise,

the applicant must inform—

(i) the relevant person;
(ii) the parties to the proceedings;
(iii) any officer to whom a copy of the order was delivered under paragraph (3); and
(iv) (where necessary) the court.

(7) Where the court includes an exclusion requirement in an interim care order or an emergency protection order of its own motion, paragraph (2) will apply with the omission of any reference to the statement of the evidence.

(8) In this rule, 'the relevant person' has the meaning assigned to it by sections 38A(2) and 44A(2) of the 1989 Act.

12.29 Notification of consent

(1) Consent for the purposes of the following provisions of the 1989 Act—

(a) section 16(3);
(b) section 38A(2)(b)(ii) or 44A(2)(b)(ii); or
(c) paragraph 19(3)(c) or (d) of Schedule 2,

must be given either—

(i) orally to the court; or
(ii) in writing to the court signed by the person giving consent.

(2) Any written consent for the purposes of section 38A(2) or 44A(2) of the 1989 Act must include a statement that the person giving consent—

(a) is able and willing to give to the child the care which it would be reasonable to expect a parent to give; and
(b) understands that the giving of consent could lead to the exclusion of the relevant person from the dwelling-house in which the child lives.

12.30 Proceedings for secure accommodation orders: copies of reports

In proceedings under section 25 of the 1989 Act, the court will, if practicable, arrange for copies of all written reports filed in the case to be made available before the hearing to—

(a) the applicant;
(b) the parent or guardian of the child to whom the application relates;
(c) any legal representative of the child;
(d) the children's guardian; and
(e) the child, unless the court directs otherwise,

and copies of the reports may, if the court considers it desirable, be shown to any person who is entitled to notice of any hearing in accordance with Practice Direction 12C.

Chapter 4
Special provisions about private law proceedings

12.31 The First Hearing Dispute Resolution Appointment

(1) The court may set a date for the First Hearing Dispute Resolution Appointment after the proceedings have been issued.

(2) The court officer will give notice of any of the dates so fixed to the parties.

(Provisions relating to the timing of and issues to be considered at the First Hearing Dispute Resolution Appointment are contained in Practice Direction 12B.)

12.32 Answer

A respondent must file and serve on the parties an answer to the application for an order in private law proceedings within 14 days beginning with the date on which the application is served.

12.33 Applications for warning notices or applications to amend enforcement orders by reason of change of residence

(1) This rule applies in relation to an application …[1] for—

(a) a warning notice to be attached to a [child arrangements][2] order; or
(b) an order under paragraph 5 of Schedule A1 to the 1989 Act to amend an enforcement order by reason of change of residence.

(2) The application must be made without notice.

(3) The court may deal with the application without a hearing.

(4) If the court decides to deal with the application at a hearing, rules 12.5, 12.7 and 12.8 will apply.

Amendment

1 Repealed by the Family Procedure (Amendment No 3) Rules 2013, SI 2013/3204, rr 2, 49.
2 Substituted by the Family Procedure (Amendment No 3) Rules 2014, SI 2014/843, rr 2, 28.

12.34 Service of a risk assessment

(1) Where an officer of the Service or a Welsh family proceedings officer has filed a risk assessment with the court, subject to paragraph (2), the court officer will as soon as practicable serve copies of the risk assessment on each party.

(2) Before serving the risk assessment, the court must consider whether, in order to prevent a risk of harm to the child, it is necessary for—

(a) information to be deleted from a copy of the risk assessment before that copy is served on a party; or
(b) service of a copy of the risk assessment (whether with information deleted from it or not) on a party to be delayed for a specified period,

and may make directions accordingly.

12.35 Service of enforcement orders or orders amending or revoking enforcement orders

(1) Paragraphs (2) and (3) apply where [the court][1] makes—

(a) an enforcement order; or
(b) an order under paragraph 9(2) of Schedule A1 to the 1989 Act (enforcement order made following a breach of an enforcement order).

(2) As soon as practicable after an order has been made, a copy of it must be served by the court officer on—

(a) the parties, except the person against whom the order is made;
(b) the officer of the Service or the Welsh family proceedings officer who is to comply with a request under section 11M of the 1989 Act to monitor compliance with the order; and
(c) the responsible officer.

(3) Unless the court directs otherwise, the applicant must serve a copy of the order personally on the person against whom the order is made.

(4) The court officer must send a copy of an order made under paragraph 4, 5, 6 or 7 of Schedule A1 to the 1989 Act (revocation or amendment of an enforcement order) to—

(a) the parties;
(b) the officer of the Service or the Welsh family proceedings officer who is to comply with a request under section 11M of the 1989 Act to monitor compliance with the order;
(c) the responsible officer; and
(d) in the case of an order under paragraph 5 of Schedule A1 to the 1989 Act (amendment of enforcement order by reason of change of residence), the responsible officer in the former local justice area.

(5) In this rule, 'responsible officer' has the meaning given in paragraph 8(8) of Schedule A1 to the 1989 Act.

Amendment

1 Substituted by the Family Procedure (Amendment No 3) Rules 2013, SI 2013/3204, rr 2, 50.

Chapter 5
Special provisions about inherent jurisdiction proceedings

12.36 Where to start proceedings

(1) An application for proceedings under the Inherent Jurisdiction of the court must be started in the High Court.

(2) Wardship proceedings, except applications for an order that a child be made or cease to be a ward of court, may be transferred to the [family court][1] unless the issues of fact or law make them more suitable for hearing in the High Court.

(The question of suitability for hearing in the High Court is explained in Practice Direction 12D (Inherent Jurisdiction (including Wardship Proceedings)).)

Amendment

1 Substituted by the Family Procedure (Amendment No 3) Rules 2013, SI 2013/3204, rr 2, 51.

12.37 Child as respondent to wardship proceedings

(1) A child who is the subject of wardship proceedings must not be made a respondent to those proceedings unless the court gives permission following an application under paragraph (2).

(2) Where nobody other than the child would be a suitable respondent to wardship proceedings, the applicant may apply without notice for permission to make the wardship application—

(a) without notice; or
(b) with the child as the respondent.

12.38 Registration requirements

The court officer will send a copy of every application for a child to be made a ward of court to the principal registry for recording in the register of wards.

12.39 Notice of child's whereabouts

(1) Every respondent, other than a child, must file with the acknowledgment of service a notice stating—

(a) the respondent's address; and
(b) either—
  (i) the whereabouts of the child; or
  (ii) that the respondent is unaware of the child's whereabouts if that is the case.

(2) Unless the court directs otherwise, the respondent must serve a copy of that notice on the applicant.

(3) Every respondent other than a child must immediately notify the court in writing of—

(a) any subsequent changes of address; or
(b) any change in the child's whereabouts,

and, unless the court directs otherwise, serve a copy of that notice on the applicant.

(4) In this rule a reference to the whereabouts of a child is a reference to—

(a) the address at which the child is living;
(b) the person with whom the child is living; and
(c) any other information relevant to where the child may be found.

12.40 Enforcement of orders in wardship proceedings

The High Court may secure compliance with any direction relating to a ward of court by an order addressed to the tipstaff.

(The role of the tipstaff is explained in Practice Direction 12D (Inherent Jurisdiction (including Wardship Proceedings)).)

12.41 Child ceasing to be ward of court

(1) A child who, by virtue of section 41(2) of the Senior Courts Act 1981, automatically becomes a ward of court on the making of a wardship application will cease to be a ward

on the determination of the application unless the court orders that the child be made a ward of court.

(2) Nothing in paragraph (1) affects the power of the court under section 41(3) of the Senior Courts Act 1981 to order that any child cease to be a ward of court.

12.42 Adoption of a child who is a ward of court

An application for permission—

(a) to start proceedings to adopt a child who is a ward of court;
(b) to place such a child for adoption with parental consent; or
(c) to start proceedings for a placement order in relation to such a child,

may be made without notice in accordance with Part 18.

[12.42A Application for a writ of habeas corpus for release in relation to a minor

(1) Part 87 of the CPR applies in respect of an application for a writ of habeas corpus for release in relation to a minor—

(a) as if—
 (i) for rule 87.2(1)(a) of the CPR there were substituted—

'(a) an application notice; and'; and
 (ii) for rule 87.2(4) of the CPR there were substituted—

'(4) The application notice must be filed in the Family Division of the High Court.'; and

(b) subject to any additional necessary modifications.

(2) Rules 12.5 to 12.8, 12.12 to 12.16, 12.21 and 12.39 do not apply to an application to which this rule applies.

(The term 'application notice' is defined in rule 2.3(1).)][1]

Amendment

1 Inserted by the Family Procedure (Amendment No 4) Rules 2014, SI 2014/3296, rr 2, 10.

[12.42B Application to set aside an inherent jurisdiction order

(1) In this rule—

'inherent jurisdiction order' means an order, declaration or judgment made under the inherent jurisdiction, and includes—

(a) a part of such an order, declaration or judgment; or
(b) a consent order; and

'set aside' means to set aside pursuant to section 17(2) of the Senior Courts Act 1981 and this rule.

(2) A party may apply under this rule to set aside an inherent jurisdiction order where no error of the court is alleged.

(3) An application under this rule must be made within the proceedings in which the inherent jurisdiction order was made.

(4) An application under this rule must be made in accordance with the Part 18 procedure, subject to the modifications contained in this rule.

(5) Where the court decides to set aside an inherent jurisdiction order, it shall give directions for a rehearing or make such other orders as may be appropriate to dispose of the application.

(6) This rule is without prejudice to any power the High Court has to vary, revoke, discharge or set aside other orders, declarations or judgments where no error of the court is alleged.][1]

Amendment

1 Inserted by the Family Procedure (Amendment) Rules 2020, SI 2020/135, rr 2, 17.

Chapter 6
Proceedings under the 1980 Hague Convention, the European Convention, …[1] and the 1996 Hague Convention

12.43 Scope

This Chapter applies to—

(a) [children proceedings][2] under the 1980 Hague Convention or the European Convention; and
(b) applications relating to …[1] the 1996 Hague Convention in respect of children.

Amendment

1 Repealed by the Family Procedure Rules 2010 and Court of Protection Rules 2017 (Amendment) (EU Exit) Regulations 2019, SI 2019/517, rr 2, 9(1), (5), (6).
2 Substituted by the Family Procedure (Amendment) (No 5) Rules 2012, SI 2012/3061, rr 2, 5(b).

Section 1
Proceedings under the 970 Hague Convention or the European Convention

12.44 Interpretation

In this section—

'the 1985 Act' means the Child Abduction and Custody Act 1985;
'Central Authority' means, in relation to England and Wales, the Lord Chancellor;
'Contracting State' has the meaning given in—

(a) section 2 of the 1985 Act in relation to the 1980 Hague Convention; and
(b) section 13 of the 1985 Act in relation to the European Convention; and

'decision relating to custody' has the same meaning as in the European Convention.

('the 1980 Hague Convention' and the 'the European Convention' are defined in rule 2.3)

12.45 Where to start proceedings

Every application under the 1980 Hague Convention or the European Convention must be—

(a) made in the High Court and issued in the principal registry; and
(b) heard by a Judge of the High Court unless the application is;
    (i) to join a respondent; or
    (ii) to dispense with service or extend the time for acknowledging service.

12.46 Evidence in support of application

Where the party making an application under this section does not produce the documents referred to in Practice Direction 12F, the court may—

(a) fix a time within which the documents are to be produced;
(b) accept equivalent documents; or
(c) dispense with production of the documents if the court considers it has sufficient information.

12.47 Without-notice applications

(1) This rule applies to applications—

(a) commencing or in proceedings under this section;
(b) for interim directions under section 5 or 19 of the 1985 Act;
(c) for the disclosure of information about the child and for safeguarding the child's welfare, under rule 12.57;
(d) for the disclosure of relevant information as to where the child is, under section 24A of the 1985 Act; or
(e) for a collection order, location order or passport order.

(2) Applications under this rule may be made without notice, in which case the applicant must file the application—

(a) where the application is made by telephone, the next business day after the making of the application; or
(b) in any other case, at the time when the application is made.

(3) Where an order is made without notice, the applicant must serve a copy of the order on the other parties as soon as practicable after the making of the order, unless the court otherwise directs.

(4) Where the court refuses to make an order on an application without notice, it may direct that the application is made on notice.

(5) Where any hearing takes place outside the hours during which the court office is usually open—

(a) if the hearing takes place by telephone, the applicant's solicitors will, if practicable, arrange for the hearing to be recorded; and
(b) in all other cases, the court or court officer will take a note of the proceedings.

(Practice Direction 12E (Urgent Business) provides further details of the procedure for out of hours applications. See also Practice Direction 12D (Inherent Jurisdiction (including Wardship Proceedings)).)

12.48 Directions

(1) As soon as practicable after an application to which this section applies has been made, the court may give directions as to the following matters, among others—

(a) whether service of the application may be dispensed with;
(b) whether the proceedings should be transferred to another court under rule 12.54;
(c) expedition of the proceedings or any part of the proceedings (and any direction for expedition may specify a date by which the court must issue its final judgment in the proceedings or a specified part of the proceedings);
(d) the steps to be taken in the proceedings and the time by which each step is to be taken;

(e) whether the child or any other person should be made a party to the proceedings;
(f) if the child is not made a party to the proceedings, the manner in which the child's wishes and feelings are to be ascertained, having regard to the child's age and maturity and in particular whether an officer of the Service or a Welsh family proceedings officer should report to the court for that purpose;
(g) where the child is made a party to the proceedings, the appointment of a children's guardian for that child unless a children's guardian has already been appointed;
(h) the attendance of the child or any other person before the court;
(i) the appointment of a litigation friend for a child or for any protected party, unless a litigation friend has already been appointed;
(j) the service of documents;
(k) the filing of evidence including expert evidence; and
(l) whether the parties and their representatives should meet at any stage of the proceedings and the purpose of such a meeting.

(Rule 16.2 provides for when the court may make the child a party to the proceedings and rule 16.4 for the appointment of a children's guardian for the child who is made a party. Rule 16.5 (without prejudice to rule 16.6) requires a child who is a party to the proceedings but not the subject of those proceedings to have a litigation friend.)

(2) Directions of a court which are in force immediately prior to the transfer of proceedings to another court under rule 12.54 will continue to apply following the transfer subject to—

(a) any changes of terminology which are required to apply those directions to the court to which the proceedings are transferred; and
(b) any variation or revocation of the directions.

(3) The court or court officer will—

(a) take a note of the giving, variation or revocation of directions under this rule; and
(b) as soon as practicable serve a copy of the directions order on every party.

12.49 Answer

(1) Subject to paragraph (2) and to any directions given under rule 12.48, a respondent must file and serve on the parties an answer to the application within 7 days beginning with the date on which the application is served.

(2) The court may direct a longer period for service where the respondent has been made a party solely on one of the following grounds—

(a) a decision relating to custody has been made in the respondent's favour; or
(b) the respondent appears to the court to have sufficient interest in the welfare of the child.

12.50 Filing and serving written evidence

(1) The respondent to an application to which this section applies may file and serve with the answer a statement verified by a statement of truth, together with any further evidence on which the respondent intends to rely.

(2) The applicant may, within 7 days beginning with the date on which the respondent's evidence was served under paragraph (1), file and serve a statement in reply verified by a statement of truth, together with any further evidence on which the applicant intends to rely.

12.51 Adjournment

The court will not adjourn the hearing of an application to which this section applies for more than 21 days at at any one time.

12.52 Stay of proceedings upon notification of wrongful removal etc.

(1) In this rule and in rule 12.53—

(a) 'relevant authority' means—
  (i) the High Court;
  (ii) [the family court][1];
  (iii) …[2]
  (iv) the Court of Session;
  (v) a sheriff court;
  [(vi) a children's hearing within the meaning of the Children's Hearings (Scotland) Act 2011;][3]
  (vii) the High Court in Northern Ireland;
  (viii) a county court in Northern Ireland;
  (ix) a court of summary jurisdiction in Northern Ireland;
  (x) the Royal Court of Jersey;
  (xi) a court of summary jurisdiction in Jersey;
  (xii) the High Court of Justice of the Isle of Man;
  (xiii) a court of summary jurisdiction in the Isle of Man; or
  (xiv) the Secretary of State; and
(b) 'rights of custody' has the same meaning as in the 1980 Hague Convention.

(2) Where a party to proceedings under the 1980 Hague Convention knows that an application relating to the merits of rights of custody is pending in or before a relevant authority, that party must file within the proceedings under the 1980 Hague Convention a concise statement of the nature of that application, including the relevant authority in or before which it is pending.

(3) On receipt of a statement filed in accordance with paragraph (2) above, a court officer will notify the relegant authority in or before which the application is pending and will subsequently notify the relevant authority of the result of the proceedings.

(4) On receipt by the relevant authority of a notification under paragraph (3) from the High Court or equivalent notification from the Court of Session, the High Court in Northern Ireland or the High Court of Justice of the Isle of Man—

(a) all further proceedings in the action will be stayed(GL) unless and until the proceedings under the 1980 Hague Convention in the High Court, Court of Session, the High Court in Northern Ireland or the High Court of Justice of the Isle of Man are dismissed; and
(b) the parties to the action will be notified by the court officer of the stay(GL) and dismissal.

Amendment

1 Substituted by the Family Procedure (Amendment No 3) Rules 2013, SI 2013/3204, rr 2, 52(a).
2 Repealed by the Family Procedure (Amendment No 3) Rules 2013, SI 2013/3204, rr 2, 52(b).
3 Substituted by the Children's Hearings (Scotland) Act 2011 (Consequential and Transitional Provisions and Savings) Order 2013, SI 2013/1465, art 17(1), Sch 1, para 28.

[12.52A Application to set aside a return order under the 1980 Hague Convention

(1) In this rule—

'return order' means an order for the return or non-return of a child made under the 1980 Hague Convention and includes a consent order;

'set aside' means to set aside a return order pursuant to section 17(2) of the Senior Courts Act 1981 and this rule.

(2) A party may apply under this rule to set aside a return order where no error of the court is alleged.

(3) An application under this rule must be made within the proceedings in which the return order was made.

(4) An application under this rule must be made in accordance with the Part 18 procedure, subject to the modifications contained in this rule.

(5) Where the court decides to set aside a return order, it shall give directions for a rehearing or make such other orders as may be appropriate to dispose of the application.

(6) This rule is without prejudice to any power the High Court has to vary, revoke, discharge or set aside other orders, declarations or judgments which are not specified in this rule and where no error of the court is alleged.][1]

Amendment

1 Inserted by the Family Procedure (Amendment) Rules 2020, SI 2020/135, rr 2, 18.

12.53 Stay of proceedings where application made under s.16 of the 1985 Act (registration of decisions under the European Convention)

(1) A person who—

(a) is a party to—

(i) proceedings under section 16 of the 1985 Act; or

(ii) proceedings as a result of which a decision relating to custody has been registered under section 16 of the 1985 Act; and

(b) knows that an application is pending under—

(i) section 20(2) of the 1985 Act;

(ii) Article 21(2) of the Child Abduction and Custody (Jersey) Law 2005; or

(iii) section 42(2) of the Child Custody Act 1987 (an Act of Tynwald),

must file within the proceedings under section 16 of the 1985 Act a concise statement of the nature of the pending application.

(2) On receipt of a statement filed in accordance with paragraph (1) above, a court officer will notify the relevant authority in or before which the application is pending and will subsequently notify the relevant authority of the result of the proceedings.

(3) On receipt by the relevant authority of a notification under paragraph (2) from the High Court or equivalent notification from the Court of Session, the High Court in Northern Ireland or the High Court of Justice of the Isle of Man, the court officer will notify the parties to the action.

12.54 Transfer of proceedings

(1) At any stage in proceedings under the 1985 Act the court may—

(a) of its own initiative; or
(b) on the application of a party with a minimum of two days' notice;

order that the proceedings be transferred to a court listed in paragraph (4).

(2) Where the court makes an order for transfer under paragraph (1)—

(a) the court will state its reasons on the face of the order;
(b) a court officer will send a copy of the order, the application and the accompanying documents (if any) and any evidence to the court to which the proceedings are transferred; and
(c) the costs of the proceedings both before and after the transfer will be at the discretion of the court to which the proceedings are transferred.

(3) Where proceedings are transferred to the High Court from a court listed in paragraph (4), a court officer will notify the parties of the transfer and the proceedings will continue as if they had been commenced in the High Court.

(4) The listed courts are the Court of Session, the High Court in Northern Ireland, the Royal Court of Jersey or the High Court of Justice of the Isle of Man.

12.55 Revocation and variation of registered decisions

(1) This rule applies to decisions which—

(a) have been registered under section 16 of the 1985 Act; and
(b) are subsequently varied or revoked by an authority in the Contracting State in which they were made.

(2) The court will, on cancelling the registration of a decision which has been revoked, notify—

(a) the person appearing to the court to have care of the child;
(b) the person on whose behalf the application for registration of the decision was made; and
(c) any other party to the application.

(3) The court will, on being informed of the variation of a decision, notify—

(a) the party appearing to the court to have care of the child; and
(b) any party to the application for registration of the decision;

and any such person may apply to make representations to the court before the registration is varied.

(4) Any person appearing to the court to have an interest in the proceedings may apply for the registration of a decision for the cancellation or variation of the decision referred to in paragraph (1).

12.56 The central index of decisions registered under the 1985 Act

A central index of decisions registered under section 16 of the 1985 Act, together with any variation of those decisions made under section 17 of that Act, will be kept by the principal registry.

12.57 Disclosure of information in proceedings under the European Convention

At any stage in proceedings under the European Convention the court may, if it has reason to believe that any person may have relevant information about the child who is the subject of those proceedings, order that person to disclose such information and may for that purpose order that the person attend before it or file affidavit(GL) evidence.

Section 2
Applications relating to …[1] the 1996 Hague Convention

12.58 Interpretation

(1) In this section—

…[2]

'Contracting State' means a State party to the 1996 Hague Convention;

['domestic Central Authority' means—

(a) …[1]

(b) where the matter relates to the 1996 Hague Convention in England, the Lord Chancellor;

(c) where the matter relates to the 1996 Hague Convention in Wales, the Welsh Ministers;][3]

…[1]

…[1]

'parental responsibility' has the meaning given in—

(a) …[1]

(b) Article 1(2) of the 1996 Hague Convention in relation to proceedings under that Convention; …[1]

…[1]

(2) In rules 12.59 to 12.70, references to the court of another …[1] Contracting State include …[1] authorities of Contracting States which have jurisdiction to take measures directed to the protection of the person or property of the child within the meaning of the 1996 Hague Convention.

Amendment

1 Repealed by the Family Procedure Rules 2010 and Court of Protection Rules 2017 (Amendment) (EU Exit) Regulations 2019, SI 2019/517, rr 2, 9(1), (7), (8).
2 Repealed by the Family Procedure (Amendment No 3) Rules 2012, SI 2012/2046, rr 2, 4(a).
3 Inserted by the Family Procedure (Amendment No 3) Rules 2012, SI 2012/2046, rr 2, 4(b).

12.59 …[1]

…[1]

Amendment

1 Repealed by the Family Procedure Rules 2010 and Court of Protection Rules 2017 (Amendment) (EU Exit) Regulations 2019, SI 2019/517, rr 2, 9(1), (9).

12.60 …[1]

…[1]

Amendment

1 Repealed by the Family Procedure Rules 2010 and Court of Protection Rules 2017 (Amendment) (EU Exit) Regulations 2019, SI 2019/517, rr 2, 9(1), (9).

12.61 Transfer of proceedings under …[1] Article 8 of the 1996 Hague Convention

(1) Where the court is considering the transfer of proceedings to the court of another …[1] Contracting State under rules 12.62 to 12.64 it will—

(a) fix a date for a hearing for the court to consider the question of transfer; and

(b) give directions as to the manner in which the parties may make representations.

(2) The court may, with the consent of all parties, deal with the question of transfer without a hearing.

(3) Directions which are in force immediately prior to the transfer of proceedings to a court in another …[1] Contracting State under rules 12.62 to 12.64 will continue to apply until the court in that other State accepts jurisdiction in accordance with the provisions of …[1] the 1996 Hague Convention …[1], subject to any variation or revocation of the directions.

(4) The court or court officer will—

(a) take a note of the giving, variation or revocation of directions under this rule; and

(b) as soon as practicable serve a copy of the directions order on every party.

(5) A register of all applications and requests for transfer of jurisdiction to or from another … Contracting State will be kept by the principal registry.

Amendment

1 Repealed by the Family Procedure Rules 2010 and Court of Protection Rules 2017 (Amendment) (EU Exit) Regulations 2019, SI 2019/517, rr 2, 9(1), (10).

12.62 Application by a party for transfer of the proceedings

(1) A party may apply to the court …[1] under Article 8(1) of the 1996 Hague Convention—

(a) to stay(GL) the proceedings or a specified part of the proceedings and to invite the parties to introduce a request before a court of another …[1] Contracting State; or

(b) to make a request to a court of …[1] another Contracting State to assume jurisdiction for the proceedings, or a specified part of the proceedings.

(2) An application under paragraph (1) must be made—

(a) to the court in which the relevant parental responsibility proceedings are pending; and

(b) using the Part 18 procedure.

(3) The applicant must file the application notice and serve it on the respondents [not less than 42 days before the hearing of the application][2].

Amendment

1 Repealed by the Family Procedure Rules 2010 and Court of Protection Rules 2017 (Amendment) (EU Exit) Regulations 2019, SI 2019/517, rr 2, 9(1), (11)(a).

2 Substituted by the Family Procedure Rules 2010 and Court of Protection Rules 2017 (Amendment) (EU Exit) Regulations 2019, SI 2019/517, rr 2, 9(1), (11)(b).

12.63 Application by a court of …[1] another Contracting State for transfer of the proceedings

(1) This rule applies where a court of …[1] another Contracting State makes an application under …[1] under Article 9 of the 1996 Hague Convention that the court having jurisdiction

in relation to the proceedings transfer the proceedings or a specific part of the proceedings to the applicant court.

(2) When the court receives the application, the court officer will—

(a) as soon as practicable, notify the [domestic Central Authority][2] of the application; and

(b) serve the application, and notice of the hearing on all other parties in England and Wales not less than 5 days before the hearing of the application.

Amendment

1 Repealed by the Family Procedure Rules 2010 and Court of Protection Rules 2017 (Amendment) (EU Exit) Regulations 2019, SI 2019/517, rr 2, 9(1), (12).

2 Substituted by the Family Procedure (Amendment No 3) Rules 2012, SI 2012/2046, rr 2, 5.

12.64 Exercise by the court of its own initiative of powers to seek to transfer the proceedings

(1) The court having jurisdiction in relation to the proceedings may exercise its powers of its own initiative under …[1] Article 8 of the 1996 Hague Convention in relation to the proceedings or a specified part of the proceedings.

(2) Where the court proposes to exercise its powers, the court officer will give the parties not less than 5 days' notice of the hearing.

Amendment

1 Repealed by the Family Procedure Rules 2010 and Court of Protection Rules 2017 (Amendment) (EU Exit) Regulations 2019, SI 2019/517, rr 2, 9(1), (13).

12.65 Application to High Court to make request under …[1] Article 9 of the 1996 Hague Convention to request transfer of jurisdiction

(1) An application for the court to request transfer of jurisdiction in a matter concerning a child from …[1] another Contracting State under …[1] Article 9 of the 1996 Hague Convention …[1] must be made to the principal registry and heard in the High Court.

(2) An application must be made without notice to any other person and the court may give directions about joining any other party to the application.

(3) Where there is agreement between the court and the court or competent authority to which the request under paragraph (1) is made to transfer the matter to the courts of England and Wales, the court will consider with that other court or competent authority the specific timing and conditions for the transfer.

(4) Upon receipt of agreement to transfer jurisdiction from the court or other competent authority in the …[1] Contracting State to which the request has been made, the court officer will serve on the applicant a notice that jurisdiction has been accepted by the courts of England and Wales.

(5) The applicant must attach the notice referred to in paragraph (3) to any subsequent application in relation to the child.

(6) Nothing in this rule requires an application with respect to a child commenced following a transfer of jurisdiction to be made to or heard in the High Court.

(7) Upon allocation, the court to which the proceedings are allocated must immediately fix a directions hearing to consider the future conduct of the case.

Amendment

1 Repealed by the Family Procedure Rules 2010 and Court of Protection Rules 2017 (Amendment) (EU Exit) Regulations 2019, SI 2019/517, rr 2, 9(1), (14).

12.66 Procedure where the court receives a request from the authorities of another …[1] Contracting State to assume jurisdiction in a matter concerning a child

(1) Where any court other than the High Court receives a request to assume jurisdiction in a matter concerning a child from a court or other authority which has jurisdiction in another …[1] Contracting State, that court must immediately refer the request to a Judge of the High Court for a decision regarding acceptance of jurisdiction to be made.

(2) Upon the High Court agreeing to the request under paragraph (1), the court officer will notify the parties to the proceedings before the other …[1] Contracting State of that decision, and the case must be allocated as if the application had been made in England and Wales.

(3) Upon allocation, the court to which the proceedings are allocated must immediately fix a directions hearing to consider the future conduct of the case.

(4) The court officer will serve notice of the directions hearing on all parties to the proceedings in the other …[1] Contracting State no later than 5 days before the date of that hearing.

Amendment

1 Repealed by the Family Procedure Rules 2010 and Court of Protection Rules 2017 (Amendment) (EU Exit) Regulations 2019, SI 2019/517, rr 2, 9(1), (15).

12.67 Service of the court's order or request relating to transfer of jurisdiction under …[1] the 1996 Hague Convention

The court officer will serve an order or request relating to transfer of jurisdiction on all parties, the Central Authority of the other …[1] Contracting State, and the [domestic Central Authority][2].

Amendment

1 Repealed by the Family Procedure Rules 2010 and Court of Protection Rules 2017 (Amendment) (EU Exit) Regulations 2019, SI 2019/517, rr 2, 9(1), (16).

2 Substituted by the Family Procedure (Amendment No 3) Rules 2012, SI 2012/2046, rr 2, 5.

12.68 Questions as to the court's jurisdiction or whether the proceedings should be stayed

(1) If at any time after issue of the application it appears to the court that under …[1] Article 13 of the 1996 Hague Convention it is or may be required to stay(GL) the proceedings or to decline jurisdiction, the court must—

(a) stay(GL) the proceedings; and

(b) fix a date for a hearing to determine jurisdiction or whether there should be a stay(GL) or other order.

(2) The court officer will serve notice of the hearing referred to at paragraph (1)(b) on the parties to the proceedings.

(3) The court must, in writing—

(a) give reasons for its decision under paragraph (1); and

(b) where it makes a finding of fact, state such finding.

(4) The court may with the consent of all the parties deal with any question as to the jurisdiction of the court, or as to whether the proceedings should be stayed(GL), without a hearing.

Amendment

1 Repealed by the Family Procedure Rules 2010 and Court of Protection Rules 2017 (Amendment) (EU Exit) Regulations 2019, SI 2019/517, rr 2, 9(1), (17).

12.69 Request for consultation as to contemplated placement of child in England and Wales

(1) This rule applies to a request made—

(a) …[1]

(b) under Article 33 of the 1996 Hague Convention by a court in another Contracting State for consultation on or consent to the contemplated placement of a child in England and Wales.

(2) Where the court receives a request directly from a court in another …[1] Contracting State, the court shall, as soon as practicable after receipt of the request, notify the [domestic Central Authority][2] of the request and take the appropriate action under paragraph (4).

(3) Where it appears to the court officer that no proceedings relating to the child are pending before a court in England and Wales, the court officer must inform the [domestic Central Authority][2] of that fact and forward to the Central Authority all documents relating to the request sent by the court in the other …[1] Contracting State.

(4) Where the court receives a request forwarded by the [domestic Central Authority][2], the court must, as soon as practicable after receipt of the request, either—

(a) where proceedings relating to the child are pending before the court, fix a directions hearing; or

(b) where proceedings relating to the child are pending before another court in England and Wales, send a copy of the request to that court.

Amendment

1 Repealed by the Family Procedure Rules 2010 and Court of Protection Rules 2017 (Amendment) (EU Exit) Regulations 2019, SI 2019/517, rr 2, 9(1), (18).

2 Substituted by the Family Procedure (Amendment No 3) Rules 2012, SI 2012/2046, rr 2, 5.

12.70 Request made by court in England and Wales for consultation as to contemplated placement of child in another …[1] Contracting State

(1) This rule applies where the court is contemplating the placement of a child in another …[1] Contracting State under Article 33 of the 1996 Hague Convention, and proposes to send a request for consultation with or for the consent of the central authority or other authority having jurisdiction in the other State in relation to the contemplated placement.

(2) In this rule, a reference to 'the request' includes a reference to a report prepared for purposes of Article 33 of the 1996 Hague Convention where the request is made under that Convention.

(3) Where the court sends the request directly to the central authority or other authority having jurisdiction in the other State, it shall at the same time send a copy of the request to the [domestic Central Authority][2].

(4) The court may send the request to the [domestic Central Authority][2] for onward transmission to the central authority or other authority having jurisdiction in the other …[1] State.

(5) The court should give consideration to the documents which should accompany the request.

(See Chapters 1 to 3 of this Part generally, for the procedure governing applications for an order under paragraph 19(1) of Schedule 2 to the 1989 Act permitting a local authority to arrange for any child in its care to live outside England and Wales.)

(Part 14 sets out the procedure governing applications for an order under section 84 (giving parental responsibility prior to adoption abroad) of the Adoption and Children Act 2002.)

Amendment

1 Repealed by the Family Procedure Rules 2010 and Court of Protection Rules 2017 (Amendment) (EU Exit) Regulations 2019, SI 2019/517, rr 2, 9(1), (19).
2 Substituted by the Family Procedure (Amendment No 3) Rules 2012, SI 2012/2046, rr 2, 5.

12.71 Application for a declaration as to the extent, or existence, of parental responsibility in relation to a child under Article 16 of the 1996 Hague Convention

(1) Any interested person may apply for a declaration—

(a) that a person has, or does not have, parental responsibility for a child; or
(b) as to the extent of a person's parental responsibility for a child,

where the question arises by virtue of the application of Article 16 of the 1996 Hague Convention.

(2) An application for a declaration as to the extent, or existence of a person's parental responsibility for a child by virtue of Article 16 of the 1996 Hague Convention must be made in the principal registry and heard in the High Court.

(3) An application for a declaration referred to in paragraph (1) may not be made where the question raised is otherwise capable of resolution in any other family proceedings in respect of the child.

Chapter 7

Communication of information: [children proceedings][1]

12.72 Interpretation

…[2] In this Chapter 'independent reviewing officer' means a person appointed in respect of a child in accordance with regulation 2A of the Review of Children's Cases Regulations 1991, or regulation 3 of the Review of Children's Cases (Wales) Regulations 2007.

Amendment

1 Substituted by the Family Procedure (Amendment) (No 5) Rules 2012, SI 2012/3061, rr 2, 5(a).
2 Repealed by the Family Procedure (Amendment) Rules 2012, SI 2012/679, rr 2, 22.

12.73 Communication of information: general

(1) For the purposes of the law relating to contempt of court, information relating to proceedings held in private (whether or not contained in a document filed with the court) may be communicated—

(a) where the communication is to—
  (i) a party;
  (ii) the legal representative of a party;
  (iii) a professional legal adviser;
  (iv) an officer of the service or a Welsh family proceedings officer;
  (v) the welfare officer;
  (vi) [the Director of Legal Aid Casework (within the meaning of section 4 of the Legal Aid, Sentencing and Punishment of Offenders Act 2012)][1];
  (vii) an expert whose instruction by a party has been authorised by the court for the purposes of the proceedings;
  (viii) a professional acting in furtherance of the protection of children;
  (ix) an independent reviewing officer appointed in respect of a child who is, or has been, subject to proceedings to which this rule applies;
(b) where the court gives permission; or
(c) subject to any direction of the court, in accordance with rule 12.75 and Practice Direction 12G.

(2) Nothing in this Chapter permits the communication to the public at large, or any section of the public, of any information relating to the proceedings.

(3) Nothing in rule 12.75 and Practice Direction 12G permits the disclosure of an unapproved draft judgment handed down by any court.

Amendment

1 Substituted by the Legal Aid, Sentencing and Punishment of Offenders Act 2012 (Consequential, Transitional and Saving Provisions) Regulations 2013, SI 2013/534, reg 14(1), Schedule, para 22(a).

12.74 …[1]

…[1]

Amendment

1 Repealed by the Family Procedure (Amendment) (No 5) Rules 2012, SI 2012/3061, rr 2, 4.

12.75 Communication of information for purposes connected with the proceedings

(1) A party or the legal representative of a party, on behalf of and upon the instructions of that party, may communicate information relating to the proceedings to any person where necessary to enable that party—

(a) by confidential discussion, to obtain support, advice or assistance in the conduct of the proceedings;
[(b) to attend a mediation information and assessment meeting, or to engage in mediation or other forms of non-court dispute resolution;][1]
(c) to make and pursue a complaint against a person or body concerned in the proceedings; or
(d) to make and pursue a complaint regarding the law, policy or procedure relating to a category of proceedings to which this Part applies.

(2) Where information is communicated to any person in accordance with paragraph (1)(a) of this rule, no further communication by that person is permitted.

(3) When information relating to the proceedings is communicated to any person in accordance with paragraphs (1)(b),(c) or (d) of this rule—

(a) the recipient may communicate that information to a further recipient, provided that—
   (i) the party who initially communicated the information consents to that further communication; and
   (ii) the further communication is made only for the purpose or purposes for which the party made the initial communication; and

(b) the information may be successively communicated to and by further recipients on as many occasions as may be necessary to fulfil the purpose for which the information was initially communicated, provided that on each such occasion the conditions in subparagraph (a) are met.

Amendment

1 Substituted by the Family Procedure (Amendment No 3) Rules 2014, SI 2014/843, rr 2, 29.

Practice Direction 12A – Care, supervision and other Part 4 proceedings: guide to case management

See also Part 12, Practice Direction 12B, Practice Direction 12C, Practice Direction 12D, Practice Direction 12E, Practice Direction 12F, Practice Direction 12G, Practice Direction 12H, Practice Direction 12I, Practice Direction 12J Practice Direction 12K, Practice Direction 12L, Practice Direction 12M, Practice Direction 12N, Practice Direction 12O, Practice Direction 12P

The key stages of the court process

1.1 The Public Law Outline set out in the Table below contains an outline of –

(1) the order of the different stages of the process;
(2) the matters to be considered at the main case management hearings;
(3) the latest timescales within which the main stages of the process should take place in order to resolve the proceedings within 26 weeks.

1.2 In the Public Law Outline –

(1) 'CMH' means the Case Management Hearing;
(2) 'FCMH' means Further Case Management Hearing;
(3) 'ICO' means interim care order;
(4) 'IRH' means the Issues Resolution Hearing;
(5) 'LA' means the Local Authority which is applying for a care or supervision order or a final order in other Part 4 proceedings;
(6) 'OS' means the Official Solicitor.

1.3 In applying the provisions of FPR Part 12 and the Public Law Outline the court and the parties must also have regard to –

(1) all other relevant rules and Practice Directions and in particular –
- FPR Part 1 (Overriding Objective);

- FPR Part 2 and Practice Direction 2C (relating to justices' legal adviser functions);
- FPR Part 4 (General Case Management Powers);
- FPR Part 15 (Representation of Protected Parties) and Practice Direction 15B (Adults Who May Be Protected Parties and Children Who May Become Protected Parties in Family Proceedings);
- FPR Part 18 (Procedure for Other Applications in Proceedings);
- FPR Part 22 (Evidence);
- FPR Part 24 (Witnesses and depositions generally);
- FPR Part 25 (Experts) and the Experts Practice Directions;
- FPR 27.6 and Practice Direction 27A (Court Bundles);
- FPR 30 (Appeals) and Practice Direction 30A (Appeals);

(2) the Allocation Rules;

(3) omitted

(4) President's Guidance issued from time to time on –
- Distribution of business of the family court;
- Judicial continuity and deployment;
- Prescribed templates and orders;

(5) International instruments –
- The 1996 Hague Convention;

(6) Guidance relating to protected parties and others with a disability –
- Protected Parties in Family Proceedings: Checklist For the Appointment of a Litigation Friend (including the Official Solicitor) (published in Family Law (January 2014);
- The Mental Capacity Act 2005 (Transfer of Proceedings) Order 2007 SI 2007/1899, relating to young people over 16 where they are likely to lack decision-making capacity at age 18.

Public Law Outline

Pre-proceedings

Pre-proceedings Checklist

Annex Documents are the documents specified in the Annex to the Application Form which are to be attached to that form and filed with the court: Social Work Chronology Social Work Statement and Genogram The current assessments relating to the child and/or the family and friends of the child to which the Social Work Statement refers and on which the LA relies Care Plan Index of Checklist Documents	Checklist documents (already existing on the LA's files) are – a. Evidential documents including – Previous court orders including foreign orders and judgments/reasons Any assessment materials relevant to the key issues including capacity to litigate, section 7 and 37 reports Single, joint or inter-agency materials (e.g., health and education/Home Office and Immigration Tribunal documents); b. Decision-making records including – Records of key discussions with the family Key LA minutes and records for the child Pre-existing care plans (e.g., child in need plan, looked after child plan and child protection plan) Letters Before Proceedings

	Only Checklist documents in (a) are to be served with the application form
	Checklist Documents in (b) are to be disclosed on request by any party
	Checklist documents are not to be – filed with the court unless the court directs otherwise; and older than 2 years before the date of issue of the proceedings unless reliance is placed on the same in the LA's evidence Evidence in support of directions sought – Evidence in support of any directions sought by Day 2 (see Stage 1 table below). Evidence in support of any directions sought by Day 2 should be filed with the court and served with the application form.

Stage 1 Issue and Allocation

Day 1 and Day 2 (see interpretation section)

On Day 1 (Day of issue):

- The LA files the Application Form and Annex Documents and sends copies to Cafcass/CAFCASS CYMRU
- The LA notifies the court of the need for an urgent preliminary case management hearing or an urgent contested ICO hearing where this is known or expected
- Court officer issues application

Within a day of issue (Day 2):

- Court considers jurisdiction in a case with an international element
- Court considers any application for directions on exceptions from notification or automatic party status rules and issues any directions for or related to further hearing
- Court considers initial allocation to specified level of judge, in accordance with the Allocation Rules and any President's Guidance on the distribution of business
- LA serves the Application Form, Annex Documents and evidential Checklist Documents on the parties together with the notice of date and time of CMH and any urgent hearing
- Court gives standard directions on Issue and Allocation including:
  - Checking compliance with Pre-Proceedings Checklist including service of any missing Annex Documents
  - Appointing Children's Guardian (to be allocated by Cafcass/CAFCASS CYMRU)
  - Appointing solicitor for the child only if necessary
  - Appointing (if the person to be appointed consents) a litigation friend for any protected party or any non subject child who is a party, including the OS where appropriate
  - Identifying whether a request has been made or should be made to a Central Authority or other competent authority in a foreign state or a consular authority in England and Wales in a case with an international element

- Filing and service of a LA Case Summary
- Filing and service of a Case Analysis by the Children's Guardian
- Filing and Serving the Parents' Response
- Sending a request for disclosure to, e.g., the police or health service body
- Filing and serving an application for permission relating to experts under Part 25 on a date prior to the advocates meeting for the CMH
- Directing the solicitor for the child to arrange an advocates' meeting no later than 2 business days before the CMH
- Listing the CMH

- Court considers any request for an urgent preliminary case management hearing or an urgent contested ICO hearing and where necessary lists the hearing and gives additional directions.
- Court officer sends copy Notice of Hearing of the CMH and any urgent hearing by email to Cafcass/ CAFCASS CYMRU.

Stage 2 – Case Management Hearing

Advocates' Meeting (including any litigants in person)	Case Management Hearing
No later than 2 business days before CMH (or FCMH if it is necessary)	CMH: Not before day 12 and not later than day 18 A FCMH is to be held only if necessary, it is to be listed as soon as possible and in any event no later than day 25
• Consider information on the Application Form and Annex documents, the LA Case Summary, and the Case Analysis • Identify the parties' positions to be recited in the draft Case Management Order • Identify the parties' positions about jurisdiction, in particular arising out of any international element • If necessary, identify proposed experts and draft questions in accordance with Part 25 and the Experts Practice Directions • Identify any disclosure that in the advocates' views is necessary • Immediately notify the court of the need for a contested ICO hearing and any issue about allocation • LA advocate to file a draft Case Management Order in prescribed form with court by 11 a.m. on the business day before the CMH and/or FCMH	• Court gives detailed case management directions, including: – Considering jurisdiction in a case with an international element; – Confirming allocation – Drawing up the timetable for the child and the timetable for the proceedings and considering if an extension is necessary – Identifying additional parties, intervenors and representation (including confirming that Cafcass/ CAFCASS CYMRU have allocated a Children's Guardian and that a litigation friend is appointed for any protected party or non-subject child) – Giving directions for the determination of any disputed issue about litigation capacity – Identifying the key issues – Identifying the evidence necessary to enable the court to resolve the key issues – Deciding whether there is a real issue about threshold to be resolved

Advocates' Meeting (including any litigants in person)	Case Management Hearing
	– Determining any application made under Part 25 and otherwise ensuring compliance with Part 25 where it is necessary for expert(s) to be instructed – Identifying any necessary disclosure and if appropriate giving directions – Giving directions for any concurrent or proposed placement order proceedings – Ensuring compliance with the court's directions – If a FCMH is necessary, directing an advocates' meeting and Case Analysis if required – Directing filing of any threshold agreement, final evidence and Care Plan and responses to those documents for the IRH – Directing a Case Analysis for the IRH – Directing an advocates' meeting for the IRH – Listing (any FCMH) IRH, Final Hearing (including early Final Hearing) – Giving directions for special measures and/or interpreters and intermediaries – Issuing the Case Management Order

Stage 3 – Issues Resolution Hearing

Advocates' Meeting (including any litigants in person)	IRH
No later than 7 business days before the IRH	As directed by the court, in accordance with the timetable for the proceedings
Review evidence and the positions of the parties Identify the advocates' views of – – the remaining key issues and how the issues may be resolved or narrowed at the IRH including by the making of final orders – the further evidence which is required to be heard to enable the key issues to be resolved or narrowed at the IRH – the evidence that is relevant and the witnesses that are required at the final hearing – the need for a contested hearing and/or time for oral evidence to be given at the IRH	Court identifies the key issue(s) (if any) to be determined and the extent to which those issues can be resolved or narrowed at the IRH Court considers whether the IRH can be used as a final hearing Court resolves or narrows the issues by hearing evidence Court identifies the evidence to be heard on the issues which remain to be resolved at the final hearing Court gives final case management directions including: – Any extension of the timetable for the proceedings which is necessary

Advocates' Meeting (including any litigants in person)	IRH
LA advocate to – – notify the court immediately of the outcome of the discussion at the meeting – file a draft Case Management Order with the court by 11a.m. on the business day before the IRH	– Filing of the threshold agreement or a statement of facts/issues remaining to be determined – Filing of – – Final evidence and Care Plan – Case Analysis for Final Hearing (if required) – Witness templates – Skeleton arguments – Judicial reading list/reading time, including time estimate and an estimate for judgment writing time – Ensuring Compliance with PD27A (the Bundles Practice Direction) – Listing the Final Hearing Court issues Case Management Order

Flexible powers of the court

2.1 Attention is drawn to the flexible powers of the court either following the issue of the application or at any other stage in the proceedings.

2.2 The court may give directions without a hearing including setting a date for the Final Hearing or a period within which the Final Hearing will take place. The steps, which the court will ordinarily take at the various stages of the proceedings provided for in the Public Law Outline, may be taken by the court at another stage in the proceedings if the circumstances of the case merit this approach.

2.3 The flexible powers of the court include the ability for the court to cancel or repeat a particular hearing. For example, if the issue on which the case turns can with reasonable practicability be crystallised and resolved by taking evidence at an IRH then such a flexible approach must be taken in accordance with the overriding objective and to secure compliance with section 1(2) of the 1989 Act and resolving the proceedings within 26 weeks or the period for the time being specified by the court.

2.4 Where a party has requested an urgent hearing a) to enable the court to give immediate directions or orders to facilitate any case management issue which is to be considered at the CMH, or b) to decide whether an ICO is necessary, the court may list such a hearing at any appropriate time before the CMH and give directions for that hearing. It is anticipated that an urgent preliminary case management hearing will only be necessary to consider issues such as jurisdiction, parentage, party status, capacity to litigate, disclosure and whether there is, or should be, a request to a Central Authority or other competent authority in a foreign state or consular authority in England and Wales in an international case. It is not intended that any urgent hearing will delay the CMH.

2.5 Where it is anticipated that oral evidence may be required at the CMH, FCMH or IRH, the court must be notified in accordance with Stages 2 and 3 of the Public Law Outline well in advance and directions sought for the conduct of the hearing.

2.6 It is expected that full case management will take place at the CMH. It follows that the parties must be prepared to deal with all relevant case management issues, as identified in Stage 2 of the Public Law Outline. A FCMH should only be directed where necessary and must not be regarded as a routine step in proceedings.

Compliance with pre-proceedings checklist

3.1 It is recognised that in a small minority of cases the circumstances are such that the safety and welfare of the child may be jeopardised if the start of proceedings is delayed until all of the documents appropriate to the case and referred to in the Pre-proceedings Checklist are available. The safety and welfare of the child should never be put in jeopardy by delaying issuing proceedings whether because of lack of documentation or otherwise. (Nothing in this Practice Direction affects an application for an emergency protection order under section 44 of the 1989 Act). Also, where an application for an interim order is urgent, then the hearing of that application is NOT expected to be postponed until the Case Management Hearing. The Case Management Hearing is still to be held not before day 12 and not later than day 18 in accordance with the Public Law Outline and guidance in this Practice Direction. If an urgent preliminary Case Management Hearing or an urgent contested ICO hearing is held before the CMH, the court should not dispense with the CMH unless all of the parties have been sufficiently prepared and the court has been able to deal with all case management issues which would have come before it at the CMH.

3.2 The court recognises that the preparation may need to be varied to suit the circumstances of the case. In cases where any of the Annex Documents required to be attached to the Application Form are not available at the time of issue of the application, the court will consider making directions on issue about when any missing documentation is to be filed. The expectation is that there must be a good reason why one or more of the documents are not available. Further directions relating to any missing documentation will also be made at the Case Management Hearing.

3.3 Directions may be sought in the initial application for an exception to notification requirements under paragraph 3.1 of Practice Direction 12C or rule 12.4, or for party status under rule 12.3, and evidence in support should as far as possible be included with the application (which would be made separately under Part 18). Before deciding whether to seek such an exception or not, the Local Authority should discuss the issue with the other parties to the proceedings, before proceedings are issued.

Allocation

4.1 The court considers the allocation of proceedings in accordance with the Allocation Rules and any Guidance issued by the President on distribution of business of the family court. The justices' legal adviser (with responsibility for gatekeeping and allocation of proceedings) and/or a district judge (with responsibility for allocation and gatekeeping of proceedings) will consider initial allocation as provided for in any Guidance issued by the President on distribution of business of the family court.

The timetable for the child and the timetable for proceedings

5.1 The timetable for the proceedings –

(1) The court will draw up a timetable for the proceedings with a view to disposing of the application –

(a) without delay; and

(b) in any event within 26 weeks beginning with the day on which the application was issued in accordance with section 32(1)(a)(ii) of the Children Act 1989.

(2) The court, when drawing up or revising a timetable under paragraph (1), will in particular have regard to –
(a) the impact which the timetable or any revised timetable would have on the welfare of the child to whom the application relates; and
(b) the impact which the timetable or any revised timetable would have on the duration and conduct of the proceedings.

5.2 The impact which the timetable for the proceedings, any revision or extension of that timetable would have on the welfare of the child to whom the application relates are matters to which the court is to have particular regard. The court will use the Timetable for the Child to assess the impact of these matters on the welfare of the child and to draw up and revise the timetable for the proceedings.

5.3 The 'Timetable for the Child is the timetable set by the court which takes into account dates which are important to the child's welfare and development.

5.4 The timetable for the proceedings is set having particular regard to the Timetable for the Child and the Timetable for the Child needs to be reviewed regularly. Where adjustments are made to the Timetable for the Child, the timetable for the proceedings will have to be reviewed consistently with resolving the proceedings within 26 weeks or the period for the time being specified by the court.

5.5 Examples of the dates the court will record and take into account when setting the Timetable for the Child are the dates of –

(1) any formal review by the Local Authority of the case of a looked after child (within the meaning of section 22(1) of the 1989 Act);
(2) any significant educational steps, including the child taking up a place at a new school and, where applicable, any review by the Local Authority of a statement of the child's special educational needs;
(3) any health care steps, including assessment by a paediatrician or other specialist;
(4) any review of Local Authority plans for the child, including any plans for permanence through adoption, Special Guardianship or placement with parents or relatives;
(5) any change or proposed change of the child's placement;
(6) any significant change in the child's social or family circumstances; or
(7) any timetable for the determination of an issue in a case with an international element.

5.6 To identify the Timetable for the Child, the applicant is required to provide the information needed about the significant steps in the child's life in the Application Form and the Social Work Statement and to update this information regularly taking into account information received from others involved in the child's life such as the parties, members of the child's family, the person who is caring for the child, the children's guardian, the Independent Reviewing Officer, the child's key social worker and any Central Authority or competent authority in a foreign state or a consular authority in England and Wales in a case with an international element.

5.7 Where more than one child is the subject of the proceedings, the court should consider and will set a Timetable for the Child for each child. The children may not all have the same timetable, and the court will consider the appropriate progress of the proceedings in relation to each child.

5.8 Where there are parallel care proceedings and criminal proceedings against a person connected with the child for a serious offence against the child, linked directions hearings should where practicable take place as the case progresses. The timing of the proceedings in a linked care and criminal case should appear in the Timetable for the Child. The time limit of resolving the proceedings within 26 weeks applies unless a longer timetable has been set by the court in order to resolve the proceedings justly in accordance with section 32(1)(a)(ii) and (5) of the 1989 Act. Early disclosure and listing of hearings is necessary in proceedings in a linked care and criminal case.

Extensions to the timetable for proceedings

6.1 The court is required to draw up a timetable for proceedings with a view to disposing of the application without delay and in any event within 26 weeks. If proceedings can be resolved earlier, then they should be. A standard timetable and process is expected to be followed in respect of the giving of standard directions on issue and allocation and other matters which should be carried out by the court on issue, including setting and giving directions for the Case Management Hearing.

6.2 Having regard to the circumstances of the particular case, the court may consider that it is necessary to extend the time by which the proceedings are to be resolved beyond 26 weeks to enable the court to resolve the proceedings justly (see section 32 (5) of the 1989 Act). When making this decision, the court is to take account of the guidance that extensions are not to be granted routinely and are to be seen as requiring specific justification (see section 32(7) of the 1989 Act). The decision and reason(s) for extending a case should be recorded in writing (in the Case Management Order) and orally stated in court, so that all parties are aware of the reasons for delay in the case (see FPR 12.26C). The Case Management Order must contain a record of this information, as well as the impact of the court's decision on the welfare of the child.

6.3 The court may extend the period within which proceedings are intended to be resolved on its own initiative or on application. Applications for an extension should, wherever possible, only be made so that they are considered at any hearing for which a date has been fixed or for which a date is about to be fixed. Where a date for a hearing has been fixed, a party who wishes to make an application at that hearing but does not have sufficient time to file an application notice should as soon as possible inform the court (if possible in writing) and, if possible, the other parties of the nature of the application and the reason for it. The party should then make the application orally at the hearing.

6.4 If the court agrees an extension is necessary, an initial extension to the time limit may be granted for up to eight weeks (or less if directed) in order to resolve the case justly (see section 32(8) of the 1989 Act). If more time is necessary, in order to resolve the proceedings justly, a further extension of up to eight weeks may be agreed by the court. There is no limit on the number of extensions that may be granted in a particular case.

6.5 If the court considers that the timetable for the proceedings will require an extension beyond the next eight week period in order to resolve the proceedings justly, the Case Management Order should –

(1) state the reason(s) why it is necessary to have a further extension;
(2) fix the date of the next effective hearing (which might be in a period shorter than a further eight weeks); and
(3) indicate whether it is appropriate for the next application for an extension of the timetable to be considered on paper.

6.6 The expectation is that, subject to paragraph 6.5, extensions should be considered at a hearing and that a court will not approve proposals for the management of a case under FPR 12.15 where the consequence of those proposals is that the case is unlikely to be resolved within 26 weeks or other period for the time being allowed for resolution of the proceedings. In accordance with FPR 4.1(3)(e), the court may hold a hearing and receive evidence by telephone or by using any other method of direct oral communication. When deciding whether to extend the timetable, the court must have regard to the impact of any ensuing timetable revision on the welfare of the child (see section 32(6) of the 1989 Act).

Interpretation

7.1 'Allocation Rules' mean any rules relating to composition of the court and distribution of business made under section 31D of the Matrimonial and Family Proceedings Act 1984;

'Care Plan' is a separate document from the evidence that is filed by the local authority. It is a 'section 31A plan' referred to in section 31A of the 1989 Act which complies with guidance as to content issued by the Secretary of State;

'Case Analysis' means a written or, if there is insufficient time for a written, an oral outline of the case from the perspective of the child's best interests prepared by the children's guardian or Welsh family proceedings officer for the CMH or FCMH (where one is necessary) and IRH or as otherwise directed by the court, incorporating an analysis of the key issues that need to be resolved in the case including –

(a) a threshold analysis;
(b) a case management analysis, including an analysis of the timetable for the proceedings, an analysis of the Timetable for the Child and the evidence which any party proposes is necessary to resolve the issues;
(c) a parenting capability analysis;
(d) a child impact analysis, including an analysis of the ascertainable wishes and feelings of the child and the impact on the welfare of the child of any application to adjourn a hearing or extend the timetable for the proceedings;
(e) an early permanence analysis including an analysis of the proposed placements and contact framework; by reference to a welfare and proportionality analysis.
(f) whether and if so what communication it is proposed there should be during the proceedings with the child by the court;

'Case Management Order' is the prescribed form of order referred to in any Guidance issued by the President from time to time on prescribed templates and orders;

'Day' means 'business day'. 'Day 1' is the day of issue and 'Day 2' is the next business day following the day of issue of proceedings. 'Day 12', 'Day 18' and 'Day 25' are respectively the 11th, 17th and the 24th business days after the day of issue of proceedings (Day 1). '26 weeks' means 26 calendar weeks beginning on the day of issue of proceedings (Day 1);

'Experts Practice Directions' mean –

(a) Practice Direction 25A (Experts – Emergencies and Pre Proceedings Instructions);
(b) Practice Direction 25B (The Duties of An Expert, The Expert's Report and Arrangements For An Expert To Attend Court);
(c) Practice Direction 25C (Children's Proceedings – The Use Of Single Joint Experts and The Process Leading to An Expert Being Instructed or Expert Evidence Being Put Before the Court);
(d) Practice Direction 25E (Discussions Between Experts in Family Proceedings);

'Genogram' means a family tree, setting out in diagrammatic form the child's family and extended family members and their relationship with the child;

'Index of Checklist Documents' means a list of Checklist Documents referred to in the Public Law Outline Pre-Proceedings Checklist which is divided into two parts with Part A being the documents referred to in column 2, paragraph (a) of the Pre-Proceedings Checklist and Part B being those referred to in column 2, paragraph (b) of the Pre-proceedings Checklist;

'International instruments'

'The 1996 Hague Convention' means the Convention on Jurisdiction, Applicable Law, Recognition, Enforcement and Co-operation in Respect of Parental Responsibility and Measures for the Protection of Children;

'Letter Before Proceedings' means any letter from the Local Authority containing written notification to the parents and others with parental responsibility for the child of the Local Authority's likely intention to apply to court for a care or supervision order and any related subsequent correspondence confirming the Local Authority's position;

'Local Authority Case Summary' means a document prepared by the Local Authority legal representative for each case management hearing in the form referred to in any Guidance issued by the President from time to time on prescribed templates and orders;

'Parents' Response' means a document from either or both of the parents containing –

(a) in no more than two pages, the parents' response to the Threshold Statement, and
(b) the parents' placement proposals including the identity and whereabouts of all relatives and friends they propose be considered by the court;
(c) Information which may be relevant to a person's capacity to litigate including information about any referrals to mental health services and adult services;

'Section 7 report' means any report under section 7 of the 1989 Act;

'Section 37 report' means any report by the Local Authority to the court as a result of a direction under section 37 of the 1989 Act;

'Social Work Chronology' means a schedule containing –

(a) a succinct summary of the length of involvement of the local authority with the family and in particular with the child;
(b) a succinct summary of the significant dates and events in the child's life in chronological order- i.e. a running record up to the issue of the proceedings; providing such information under the following headings-
  (i) serial number;
  (ii) date;
  (iii) event-detail;
  (iv) witness or document reference (where applicable);

'Social Work Statement' means a statement prepared by the Local Authority limited to the following evidence –

Summary

(a) The order sought;
(b) Succinct summary of reasons with reference as appropriate to the Welfare Checklist;

Family

(c) Family members and relationships especially the primary carers and significant adults/other children;

(d) Genogram;

Threshold

(e) Precipitating events;

(f) Background circumstances –

(i) summary of children's services involvement cross-referenced to the chronology;

(ii) previous court orders and emergency steps;

(iii) previous assessments;

(g) Summary of significant harm and or likelihood of significant harm which the LA will seek to establish by evidence or concession;

Parenting capability

(h) Assessment of child's needs;

(i) Assessment of parental capability to meet needs;

(j) Analysis of why there is a gap between parental capability and the child's needs;

(k) Assessment of other significant adults who may be carers;

Child impact

(l) Wishes and feelings of the child(ren);

(m) Timetable for the Child;

(n) Delay and timetable for the proceedings;

Permanence and contact

(o) Parallel planning;

(p) Realistic placement options by reference to a welfare and proportionality analysis;

(q) Contact framework;

Case Management

(r) Evidence and assessments necessary and outstanding;

(s) Any information about any person's litigation capacity, mental health issues, disabilities or vulnerabilities that is relevant to their capability to participate in the proceedings; and

(t) Case management proposals.

'Standard Directions on Issue and Allocation' means directions given by the court on issue and upon allocation in the prescribed form referred to in any Guidance issued by the President from time to time on prescribed templates and orders;

'Threshold Statement' means a written outline by the legal representative of the LA in the application form of the facts which the LA will seek to establish by evidence or concession to satisfy the threshold criteria under s31(2) of the 1989 Act limited to no more than 2 pages;

'Welfare Checklist' means the list of matters which is set out in section 1(3) of the 1989 Act and to which the court is to have particular regard in accordance with section (1)(3) and (4).

Practice Direction 12B – Child arrangement programme

See also Part 12, Practice Direction 12A, Practice Direction 12C, Practice Direction 12D, Practice Direction 12E, Practice Direction 12F, Practice Direction 12G, Practice Direction 12H, Practice Direction 12I, Practice Direction 12J, Practice Direction 12K, Practice Direction 12L, Practice Direction 12M, Practice Direction 12N, Practice Direction 12O, Practice Direction 12P

When does the Child Arrangements Programme Apply?

1.1 The Child Arrangements Programme (the 'CAP') applies where a dispute arises between separated parents and/or families about arrangements concerning children.

1.2 The CAP is designed to assist families to reach safe and child-focused agreements for their child, where possible out of the court setting. If parents / families are unable to reach agreement, and a court application is made, the CAP encourages swift resolution of the dispute through the court.

1.3 It is well-recognised that negotiated agreements between adults generally enhance long-term co-operation, and are better for the child concerned. Therefore, separated parents and families are strongly encouraged to attempt to resolve their disputes concerning the child outside of the court system. This may also be quicker and cheaper.

Signposting Services, Parenting Plans, & Public Funding

2.1 Services: Where a dispute arises in relation to a child, or children, parents and families are encouraged to obtain advice and support as soon as possible.

2.2 There are many services available for such families, who seek advice about resolving disputes concerning their child.

2.2 The following services are recommended –

(1) For more information about family mediation and to find the nearest mediation service (including those providing a MIAM): www.familymediationcouncil.org.uk;
(2) For a Guide about children and the family courts for separating parents (including representing yourself in court): the form 'CB7': http://www.cafcass.gov.uk/media/168195/cb7-eng.pdf
(3) For Cafcass (England): www.cafcass.gov.uk;
(4) For CAFCASS Cymru (Wales): www.wales.gov.uk/cafcasscymru;
(5) To find a legal adviser or family mediator: http://find-legal-advice.justice.gov.uk;
(6) To check whether you can get financial help (legal aid) to pay for non-court dispute resolution, &/or advice and representation at court, and to find a legal aid solicitor or mediator: https://www.gov.uk/check-legal-aid
(7) For general advice about sorting out arrangements for children, the use of post-separation mediation, &/or going to court: http://www.advicenow.org.uk; http://www.advicenow.org.uk/advicenow-guides/family/sorting-out-arrangements-for-your-children/
(8) For general advice on separation services and options for resolving disputes: www.sortingoutseparation.org.uk;
(9) For general advice about sorting out arrangements for children: http://theparentconnection.org.uk/
(10) For advice about Contact Centres, which are neutral places where children of separated families can enjoy contact with their non-resident parents and

sometimes other family members, in a comfortable and safe environment; and information about where they are: www.naccc.org.uk;

(11) For the form to apply for a child arrangements order: https://www.gov.uk/looking-after-children-divorce/apply-for-court-order;

(12) For help with taking a case to court without a lawyer, the Personal Support Unit: http://thepsu.org/;

(13) For guidance on representing yourself at court, including a list of commonly used terms that you may come across: http://www.barcouncil.org.uk/instructing-a-barrister/representing-yourself-in-court/;

(14) For advice about finding and using a family law solicitor see: Law Society http://www.lawsociety.org.uk, and Resolution (family law solicitors): http://www.resolution.org.uk;

(15) For advice about finding using a family law barrister: see http://www.barcouncil.org.uk/about-the-bar/find-a-barrister/, and for arrangements for using a barrister directly see http://www.barcouncil.org.uk/instructing-a-barrister/public-access/.

2.4 Parenting Plan: A Parenting Plan is widely recognised as being a useful tool for separated parents to identify, agree and set out in writing arrangements for their children; such a plan could appropriately be used as the basis for discussion about a dispute which has arisen. It is likely to be useful in any event for assisting arrangements between separated parents.

2.5 The Parenting Plan should cover all practical aspects of care for the child, and should reflect a shared commitment to the child and his/her future, with particular emphasis on parental communication (learning how to deal with differences), living arrangements, money, religion, education, health care and emotional well-being.

2.6 A Parenting Plan is designed to help separated parents (and their families) to work out the best possible arrangements for the child; the plan should be understood by everyone, including (where the child is of an appropriate age and understanding) the child concerned.

2.7 For help on preparing a Parenting Plan, see –

(1) Cafcass 'Putting Your Children First: A Guide for Separated Parents' (see also paragraph 4 below);

(2) A draft of a Parenting Plan for parents or families to complete: https://www.cafcass.gov.uk/download/4365

(3) A draft of a Parenting Plan prepared by CAFCASS Cymru for parents or families to complete: http://gov.wales/docs/cafcass/publications/071015ParentingPlanEn.pdf (this links to the draft plan in English) or http://gov.wales/docs/cafcass/publications/071015ParentingPlanCy.pdf (this links to the draft plan in Welsh).

2.8 Publicly funded mediation and/or legal advice: If parents need access to mediation, and legal advice in support of that mediation, they may be eligible for public funding. The Legal Aid Agency (LAA) will provide funding for Mediation Information and Assessment Meetings (MIAMs) and family mediation for all those who are eligible:

(1) Where at least one party is eligible, the LAA will cover the costs of both parties to attend a MIAM to encourage any non-eligible client to find out about the benefits and suitability of mediation without incurring any costs.

(2) The LAA will provide public funding for eligible parties to participate in family mediation and they may also receive some independent legal advice connected to the mediation process and where a settlement is reached can receive legal assistance to draft and issue proceedings to obtain a consent order.

(3) Parties may find out if they are likely to be eligible for legal aid at the following link: https://www.gov.uk/check-legal-aid

(4) To find the nearest publicly funded mediation service a client can use the search at http://find-legal-advice.justice.gov.uk. Publicly funded legal advisors can be found at: https://www.gov.uk/check-legal-aid

2.9 Public funding for legal advice and/or representation at court is available in limited circumstances. Further information can be found here: http://www.justice.gov.uk/legal-aid-for-private-family-matters

Explanation of terms

3.1 Some of the terms used in this document, and in the websites referred to above, may not be familiar to those who seek help and support.

3.2 A guide to some of the relevant terms is attached in the Annex at the end of this document.

The child in the dispute

4.1 In making any arrangements with respect to a child, the child's welfare must be the highest priority.

4.2 Children and young people should be at the centre of all decision-making. This accords with the Family Justice Young People's Board Charter (https://www.cafcass.gov.uk/media/179714/fjypb_national_charter_1013.pdf).

4.3 The child or young person should feel that their needs, wishes and feelings have been considered in the arrangements which are made for them.

4.4 Children should be involved, to the extent which is appropriate given their age and level of understanding, in making the arrangements which affect them. This is just as relevant where:

(1) the parties are making arrangements between themselves (which may be recorded in a Parenting Plan),

as when:

(2) arrangements are made in the context of dispute resolution outside away from the court,

and/or

(3) the court is required to make a decision about the arrangements for the child.

4.5 If an application for a court order has been issued, the judge may want to know the child's view. This may be communicated to the judge in one of a number of ways –

(1) By a Cafcass officer (in Wales, a Welsh Family Proceedings Officer (WFPO)) providing a report to the court which sets out the child's wishes and feelings;

(2) By the child being encouraged (by the Cafcass officer or WFPO, or a parent or relative) to write a letter to the court;

(3) In the limited circumstances described in paragraph 18 below, by the child being a party to the proceedings;

and/or:

(4) By the judge meeting with the child, in accordance with approved Guidance (currently the FJC Guidelines for Judges Meeting Children subject to Family Proceedings (April 2010)). http://www.judiciary.gov.uk/JCO%2fDocuments%2fFJC%2fvoc%2fGuidelines_+Judges_seeing_+Children.pdf

Non-court resolution of disputed arrangements for children

5.1 Dispute resolution services, including mediation, are available to provide opportunities for parents and families to work in a positive and constructive way, and should be actively considered and attempted where it is safe and appropriate to do so. Information about mediation and other non-court dispute resolution is available widely (see 'Signposting Services for Families' – paragraph 2 above).

5.2 It is not expected that those who are the victims of domestic violence should attempt to mediate or otherwise participate in forms of non-court dispute resolution. It is also recognised that drug and/or alcohol misuse and/or mental illness are likely to prevent couples from making safe use of mediation or similar services; these risk factors (which can be discussed at a MIAM – see below, paragraph 5.3) are likely to have an impact on arrangements for the child. Court Orders, including those made by consent, must be scrutinised to ensure that they are safe and take account of any risk factors, in accordance with Practice Direction 12J FPR.

5.3 Attendance at Mediation Information and Assessment Meeting ('MIAM'): Subject to paragraph 5.6 (below), before making a family application to the court (a 'relevant family application' as defined in paragraph 23 below), the person who is considering making such application must attend a family MIAM. A prospective respondent is expected to attend a MIAM – whether this is a separate MIAM or the same MIAM attended by the prospective applicant. At the MIAM, information will be provided about mediation of disputes of the kind to which the application relates, ways in which the dispute may be resolved otherwise than by the court, and the suitability of mediation (or any other way of resolving the dispute) for trying to resolve the dispute. The mediator will also assess whether there has been, or is a risk of,

(1) domestic violence, and/or
(2) harm by a prospective party to a child that would be the subject of the application.

5.4 It is the responsibility of the prospective applicant (or that person's legal representative) to contact a family mediator to arrange attendance at a MIAM.

5.5 Only an authorised family mediator can carry out a MIAM. An authorised family mediator is a person identified by the Family Mediation Council as qualified to conduct a MIAM.

5.6 A prospective applicant is not required to attend a MIAM where one of the circumstances set out in rule 3.8(1) or 3.8(2) FPR applies.

5.7 Information on how to find an authorised family mediator may be obtained from www.familymediationcouncil.org.uk website which hosts the 'find a local family mediator' database (see also 'Signposting Services for Families' – paragraph 2 above).

5.8 The prospective applicant (or the prospective applicant's legal representative) should provide the mediator with contact details for the other party or parties to the dispute ('the prospective respondent(s)'), so that the mediator can contact the prospective respondent(s) to discuss their willingness and availability to attend a MIAM.

5.9 The prospective applicant and, where they agree to do so, the prospective respondent(s), should then attend a MIAM arranged by the mediator. If the parties are willing to attend together and where it is assessed by the mediator to be safe, the meeting may be conducted jointly; otherwise, separate meetings will be held.

5.10 The Family Mediation Council sets the requirements for mediators who conduct MIAMs. In summary, a mediator who arranges a MIAM with one or more parties to a dispute should consider any risk factors present and how these should be managed, and should also consider with the party or parties concerned whether public funding may be available to meet the cost of the meeting and any subsequent mediation. Where neither of the parties is eligible for, or wishes to seek, public funding, any charge made by the mediator for the MIAM will be the responsibility of the party or parties attending, in accordance with any agreement made with the mediator.

5.11 Mediation is a confidential process; none of the parties to the mediation may provide information to the court as to the content of any discussions held in mediation and/or the reasons why agreement was not reached. Similarly, the mediator may not provide such information, unless the mediator considers that a safeguarding issue arises.

5.12 However, it is important that the parties, or either of them, introduce at the MIAM (or any subsequent court application) any other evidence of attempts to resolve a dispute and to focus on the needs of the child.

Resolution of disputed arrangements for children through the Court

6.1 The judge is obliged to consider, at every stage of court proceedings, whether non-court dispute resolution is appropriate.

6.2 The parties should also actively consider non-court dispute resolution even if proceedings are issued and are ongoing.

6.3 If the court considers that another form of dispute resolution is appropriate, the court may direct that the proceedings, or a hearing in the proceedings, be adjourned for such specified period as it considers appropriate:

(1) to enable the parties to obtain information and advice about non-court dispute resolution; and
(2) where the parties agree, to enable non-court dispute resolution to take place.

6.4 Where the court adjourns proceedings, it shall give directions about the timing and method by which the parties must tell the court if any of the issues in the proceedings have been resolved.

6.5 It is to be noted that some courts operate an at-court mediation scheme, and at-court MIAMs, with providers contracted to the Legal Aid Agency. Some mediators may prefer to conduct mediation outside of the court premises. A mediation assessment may be possible at court; alternatively, the court may help in making an appointment with a local mediator for a MIAM or for mediation. Information about mediation arrangements should be advertised in the local court.

Local Good Practice

7.1 The CAP is designed to provide a framework for a consistent approach to the resolution of the issues in private family law in England & Wales.

7.2 Local practices and initiatives can be operated in addition to, and within, the framework.

Application to court

8.1 Unless one of the MIAM exemptions applies (see rule 3.8 FPR), an application to court for determination of most issues concerning a child (see the definition of 'relevant family application' in rule 3.6 FPR and paragraphs 11 and 12 of PD3A) can be made only after a MIAM has taken place (at which meeting mediation and other forms of non-court dispute resolution will have been considered). One of the exemptions may be that the case is urgent, in which case see 'Urgent and Without Notice Applications' in paragraph 12 below. The grounds for urgency are defined in rule 3.8(c) FPR.

8.2 The application for a child arrangements order or other Children Act 1989 private law order shall be made on the relevant prescribed form.

8.3 For section 8 Children Act 1989 applications, the applicant will be required, on the form C100, to confirm attendance at a MIAM or specify that an exemption applies unless the application is for a consent order, or if the application concerns a child who is the subject of ongoing emergency proceedings, care proceedings or supervision proceedings, or if the child concerned is already the subject of an emergency protection order, care order or supervision order (see paragraphs 11 and 12 of PD3A).

8.4 The relevant part of the form C100 must be completed showing that either –

(1) the applicant has attended a MIAM; or
(2) the applicant has not attended a MIAM and claims one of the exemptions (rule 3.8(1) FPR) – exemptions include (but are not limited to) evidence of domestic violence, child protection concerns, urgency, previous MIAM attendance or exemption; or
(3) an authorised family mediator confirms in the form that he or she is satisfied that –
    (a) mediation is not suitable because the respondents is (if more than one respondent, any one of them is) unwilling to attend a MIAM;
    (b) mediation is not suitable as a means of resolving the dispute because the respondent (if more than one, any of them) failed without good reason to attend a MIAM; or
    (c) mediation is otherwise not suitable as a means of resolving the dispute.

8.5 The C100 form may be obtained from the Family Court or from www.gov.uk.

8.6 If the parties have previously prepared a Parenting Plan, this shall be attached to the Form C100.

8.7 If possible at the time of issue, and in any event by no later than one working day after issue, or in courts where applications are first considered on paper by no later than two working days after issue, the court shall send or hand to the Applicant the following –

(i) A copy of the application form C100 (together with the Supplemental Information Form C1A),
(ii) The Notice of Hearing;
(iii) The Acknowledgment Form C7;
(iv) A blank Form C1A, (if required);
(v) Information leaflets for the parties (which must include the CB7 leaflet)

8.8 Unless the applicant requests to do so, or the court directs the applicant to do so, the Court will serve the respondent(s) with –

(i) A copy of the application form C100 (together with Supplemental Information Form C1A, if provided);
(ii) The Notice of Hearing;
(iii) The Acknowledgement Form C7;
(iv) A blank form C1A;
(v) Information leaflet for the parties (which must include the CB7 leaflet).

8.9 The court shall send to Cafcass / CAFCASS Cymru a copy of the Form C100 (and the form C1A, if supplied), and the C6 Notice of Hearing no later than 2 working days after the date of issue. This will be in electronic format where possible.

8.10 The court shall not send to Cafcass / CAFCASS Cymru any other application under the Children Act 1989, or any other private law application, unless the Court has made a specific direction requesting the assistance of Cafcass/CAFCASS Cymru. Therefore, any application which is not in Form C100 or which does not contain a direction to Cafcass/ CAFCASS Cymru will be returned to the court at which the application has been issued.

8.11 The respondent(s) must send the Acknowledgement Form C7 and, where applicable, the Supplemental Information Form C1A, to the court within 14 days after receiving the application, unless the court has specified a shorter time.

8.12 On receipt of the Acknowledgement Form C7 and any Form C1A filed by the respondent(s), the court shall send a copy of each form to Cafcass / CAFCASS Cymru, in electronic format where possible, and shall send copies to the applicant.

Allocation and Gatekeeping

9.1 It is important that the form C100 is fully completed (including the provision of telephone numbers of the relevant parties), otherwise there may be a delay in processing the application; where the form is not fully completed, the court staff may request further information before the application form is accepted for issue. It is also important that the form C100, the Acknowledgement Form C7 and, where applicable, any Supplemental Information Form C1A are fully and accurately completed to enable the court to make appropriate decisions about allocation and case management.

9.2 The application shall be considered by a nominated Legal Adviser &/or nominated District Judge ('the Gatekeeper(s)') within one working day of the date of receipt in accordance with the appropriate Rules of Procedure.

9.3 An application for a relevant family order shall be allocated to a level of judge in the Family Court in accordance with the Guidance issued by the President on 'Allocation and Gatekeeping for Proceedings under Part II of the Children Act 1989 (Private Law Proceedings) and the Family Court (Composition and Distribution of Business) Rules 2014, together with the Allocation Schedule.

9.4 Gatekeepers shall be able to issue Directions on Issue in the following circumstances –

(1) where, on the basis of information provided on the application form and any additional information provided on a C1A Supplemental Information Form, the Gatekeeper finds that the exemption from attending a MIAM has not been validly been claimed, the Gatekeeper will direct the applicant, or direct the parties to attend a MIAM before the FHDRA, unless the Gatekeeper considers that in all the circumstances of the case the MIAM requirement should not apply to the application in question; the Gatekeeper will have particular regard to the matters set out in rule 3.10(3) FPR when making this decision;

(2) where it appears that an urgent issue requires determination, the Gatekeeper may give directions for an accelerated hearing;

(3) exceptionally, where it appears that directions need to be given for the service and filing of evidence, he/she may give directions for the filing of evidence.

Judicial continuity

10.1 All private law cases will be allocated to a level of judge within the Family Court upon issue.

10.2 Continuity of Judicial involvement in the conduct of proceedings from the FHDRA to the making of a final order should be the objective in all cases

10.3 Where the case has been allocated to be heard before lay justices, the expectation of judicial continuity should apply where –

(1) There has been a hearing to determine findings of fact,
(2) A decision yet to be made in the interests of a child by a court depends upon rulings or judicial assessments already made in the proceedings,

in which case, wherever possible, the hearing shall be listed before the same lay justices; alternatively, it shall be listed before the same legal adviser and at least one lay justice (preferably the chairman) to provide that continuity. Where a case is adjourned part-heard the court which resumes the hearing shall, wherever possible, be composed of the same lay justices as dealt with the previous part of the hearing (see rule 8 of the Family Court (Composition and Distribution of Business) Rules 2014).

Key welfare principles

11.1 Section 1 of the Children Act 1989 applies to all applications for orders concerning the upbringing of children. This means that –

(1) the child's welfare is the court's paramount consideration;
(2) delay is likely to be prejudicial to the welfare of the child, and
(3) a court order shall not be made unless the court considers that making an order would be better for the child than making no order at all.

11.2 Parties, and the court, must also have regard to the FPR in particular the following –

(1) FPR Rule 1. The 'overriding objective' will apply, so that the court will deal with a case justly, having regard to the welfare issues involved and specifically will –
  (a) Ensure that the case is dealt with expeditiously and fairly;
  (b) Deal with the case in ways which are proportionate to the nature, importance and complexity of the issues;
  (c) Ensure that the parties are on an equal footing;
  (d) Save expense;
  (e) Allot to each case an appropriate share of the court's resources, while taking account of the need to allot resources to other cases.
(2) Rule 3, and Practice Direction 3A;
(3) FPR Part 4 'General Case Management Powers';
(4) FPR Part 15 (Representation of Protected Parties) and Practice Direction 15B (Adults Who May Be Protected Parties and Children Who May Become Protected Parties in Family Proceedings);
(5) FPR Part 16 (Representation of Children) (and see also paragraph 18 below);
(6) FPR Part 18 (procedure for Other Applications in proceedings);
(7) FPR Part 22 (Evidence);
(8) Omitted
(9) FPR Part 25 (Experts) and the Experts Practice Directions;
(10) FPR 27.6 and Practice Direction 27A (Court Bundles).

11.3 Where a fact-finding hearing is required, this shall take place in accordance with revised Practice Direction 12J FPR.

11.4 The court shall exercise its powers flexibly. The flexible powers of the court include the ability for the court to cancel or repeat a particular hearing.

Urgent and Without Notice Applications

12.1 Urgent: Where an order is sought as a matter of urgency, an application may be made to the Court for an emergency order without the requirement for the Applicant to have attended at a MIAM. The categories of urgent application justifying such an exemption are set out in rule 3.8(c) FPR and include cases in which:

(1) There is a risk to the life, liberty, or the physical safety of the prospective applicant or his or her family, or his or her home;

(2) Any delay caused by attending a MIAM would cause:

  (A) A risk of harm to the child;

  (B) A risk of unlawful removal of a child from the United Kingdom or a risk of unlawful retention of a child who is currently outside England and Wales;

  (C) A significant risk of a miscarriage of justice;

(4) Unreasonable hardship to the prospective applicant;

(5) Irretrievable problems in dealing with the dispute (including the irretrievable loss of significant evidence).

(3) There is a significant risk that in the period necessary to schedule and attend a MIAM, proceedings relating to the dispute will be brought in another state in which a valid claim to jurisdiction may exist, such that a court in that other State would be seised of the dispute before a court in England and Wales.

12.2 'Without Notice': Applications to court made 'Without Notice' to the respondent(s) shall be allocated in accordance with the Family Court (Composition and Distribution of Business) Rules 2014, and determined by reference to the provisions of Practice Direction 18A, paragraph 5.1, with further regard to the principles set out in Practice Direction 20A, paragraph 4.3-4.5 FPR (noting particularly paragraph 4.3(c)).

12.3 Without Notice Orders should be made only exceptionally, and where –

(1) If the applicant were to give notice to the respondent(s) this would enable the respondent(s) to take steps to defeat the purpose of the injunction; cases where the application is brought without notice in order to conceal the step from the respondent(s) are very rare indeed; or

(2) The case is one of exceptional urgency; that is to say, that there has been literally no time to give notice (either by telephone, text or e-mail or otherwise) before the injunction is required to prevent the threatened wrongful act; or

(3) If the applicant gives notice to the respondent(s), this would be likely to expose the applicant or relevant child to unnecessary risk of physical or emotional harm.

12.4 Any Order which follows an emergency 'without notice' hearing should specify:

(1) the reason(s) why the order has been made without notice to the respondent(s),

(2) the outline facts alleged which have been relied upon by the court in making the order, unless the facts are clearly contained in the statement in support; and

(3) the right of the respondent(s) to apply to vary or discharge the order.

12.5 Gatekeeping decisions: Following any urgent or 'without notice' hearing, unless all issues have been determined or the application has been dismissed without any further directions given, the judge may make gatekeeping decisions, including allocation and venue of future hearing, (and if so, shall notify the Gatekeeping team responsible for the area in which the child resides), or shall refer the application to the relevant Gatekeeping team for a decision on allocation and venue of future hearing; in either event, a copy of the C100 shall be sent to Cafcass for safeguarding checks, and (depending on the Gatekeeping decision) the file shall be sent to the court where future hearings will take place (if at a different court centre from the court where the urgent hearing occurred).

Safeguarding

13.1 Where an application is made for a child arrangements order (but not necessarily for specific issue or prohibited steps orders), before the FHDRA (see paragraph 14 below) Cafcass / CAFCASS Cymru shall identify any safety issues by the steps outlined below.

13.2 Such steps shall be confined to matters of safety. The Cafcass Officer or (in Wales) the Welsh Family Proceedings Officer (WFPO) shall not discuss with either party before the FHDRA any matter other than one which relates to safety. The parties will not be invited to talk about other issues, for example relating to the substance of applications or replies or about issues concerning matters of welfare or the prospects of resolution. If such issues are raised by either party, they will be advised that such matters will be deferred to the FHDRA when there is equality between the parties and full discussion can take place which will be a time when any safety issues that have been identified can also be taken into account.

13.3 In order to inform the court of possible risks of harm to the child Cafcass / CAFCASS Cymru will carry out safeguarding enquiries. For all child arrangements orders this will include seeking information from local authorities, and carrying out police checks on the parties. For all other applications received from the court on the form C100, Cafcass / CAFCASS Cymru will carry out a screening process and will undertake those checks if in the professional judgment of the Cafcass officer, or the WFPO in Wales, such checks are necessary.

13.4 Cafcass / CAFCASS Cymru will, if possible, undertake telephone risk identification interviews with the parties and if risks of harm are identified, may invite parties to meet separately with the Cafcass Officer, or WFPO in Wales, before the FHDRA to clarify any safety issue.

13.5 Cafcass / CAFCASS Cymru shall record and outline any safety issues for the court, in the form of a Safeguarding letter (in Wales, this is called a 'Safeguarding report').

13.6 The Cafcass officer, or WFPO, will not initiate contact with the child prior to the FHDRA. If contacted by a child, discussions relating to the issues in the case will be postponed to the day of the hearing or after when the Cafcass officer or WFPO will have more knowledge of the issues.

13.7 Within 17 working days of receipt by Cafcass / CAFCASS Cymru of the application, and at least 3 working days before the hearing, the Cafcass Officer or WFPO shall report to the court, in a Safeguarding letter / report, the outcome of the risk identification work which has been undertaken. The letter / report should specify which court forms filed by the parties (C100, C7 and C1A) have been considered.

13.8 Further, Cafcass and CAFCASS Cymru are required, under section 16A Children Act 1989, to undertake (and to provide to the court) risk assessments where an officer of the Service ('Cafcass Officer' or WFPO) suspects that a child is at risk of harm.

Orders under section 91(14) of the Children Act 1989

13A.1 Under section 91(14) of the 1989 Act orders are available to prevent a person from making future applications under that Act without leave of the court. Section 91(14) leaves a discretion to the court to determine the circumstances in which an order should be made. These circumstances may be many and varied. They include circumstances where an application would put the child concerned, or another individual, at risk of harm (as provided in section 91A), such as psychological or emotional harm. The welfare of the child is paramount.

13A.2 These circumstances can also include where one party has made repeated and unreasonable applications; where a period of respite is needed following litigation; where a period of time is needed for certain actions to be taken for the protection of the child or other person; or where a person's conduct overall is such that an order is merited to protect the welfare of the child directly, or indirectly due to damaging effects on a parent carer. Such conduct could include harassment, or other oppressive or distressing behaviour beyond or within the proceedings including via social media and e-mail, and via third parties. Such conduct might also constitute domestic abuse. A future application could also be part of a pattern of coercive or controlling behaviour or other domestic abuse toward the victim, such that a section 91(14) order is also merited due to the risk of harm to the child or other individual.

13A.3 In proceedings in which domestic abuse is alleged or proven, or in which there are allegations or evidence of other harm to a child or other individual, the court should give early and ongoing consideration to whether it would be appropriate to make a section 91(14) order on disposal of the application, even if an application for such an order has not been made (since the court may make an order of its own motion – see section 91A(5)).

13A.4 Section 91(14) orders are a protective filter – not a bar on applications – and there is considerable scope for their use in appropriate cases. The court should refer to Practice Direction 12Q for guidance on section 91(14) applications and orders.

First Hearing Dispute Resolution Appointment (FHDRA)

14.1 The FHDRA may (where time for service on the respondent(s) has been abridged) take place within 4 weeks, but should ordinarily take place in week 5 following the issuing of the application; at the latest it will take place in week 6 following the issuing of the application.

14.2 The respondent(s) shall have at least 14 days' notice of the hearing where practicable, but the court may specify a shorter time.

14.3 Omitted

14.4 Unless the court otherwise directs, any party to proceedings, and any litigation friend of the parties must attend this (and any other) hearing. If a child is a party and represented by a children's guardian, the children's guardian need not attend directions hearings if represented.

14.5 A party may choose to be accompanied at this (or any) hearing by a McKenzie Friend to support them (a McKenzie Friend is someone who can provide moral support at court for the party; take notes; help with case papers; quietly give advice on any aspect of the conduct of the case.) If so, the McKenzie Friend must comply with the relevant Guidance (currently set out in the Practice Guidance: McKenzie Friends (Civil and Family Courts): July 2010: https://www.judiciary.gov.uk/wp-content/uploads/JCO/Documents/Guidance/mckenzie-friends-practice-guidance-july-2010.pdf).

14.6 A Cafcass Officer or WFPO shall attend this hearing. A mediator may attend where available.

14.7 The Cafcass Officer or WFPO shall, where practicable, speak separately to each party at court before the hearing in particular where it has not been possible to conduct a risk identification interview with either party.

14.8 The FHDRA provides an opportunity for the parties to be helped to an understanding of the issues which divide them, and to reach agreement. If agreement is reached –

(1) The Court will be able to make an order (which in many cases will be a final order) reflecting that agreement

(2) The Court will assist the parties (so far as it is able) in putting into effect the agreement/order in a co-operative way.

14.9 The FHDRA is not privileged. That is to say that what is said at the FHDRA may be referred to at later court hearings.

14.10 By the time of the hearing, the Court should have the following documents –

(a) C100 application, and C1A (if any);
(b) Notice of Hearing;
(c) C7 response and C1A (if any);
(d) Cafcass/CAFCASS Cymru safeguarding letter/report.

14.11 At the FHDRA the judge, working with the Cafcass Officer, or WFPO, will seek to assist the parties in conciliation and in resolution of all or any of the issues between them. Any remaining issues will be identified, the Cafcass Officer or WFPO will advise the court of any recommended means of resolving such issues, and directions will be given for the future resolution of such issues. At all times the decisions of the Court and the work of the Cafcass Officer or WFPO will take account of any risk or safeguarding issues that have been identified.

14.12 The court should have information obtained through safeguarding checks carried out by Cafcass / CAFCASS Cymru and, where applicable, Supplemental Information Forms C1A filed by the parties, to ensure that any agreement between the parties, or any dispute resolution process selected, is in the interests of the child and safe for all concerned.

14.13 The FHDRA will be conducted in the most appropriate way in the interests of the child. In particular the court shall consider the following matters –

Safeguarding, in this respect –

(a) The court shall inform the parties of the content of the safeguarding letter/report provided by Cafcass/CAFCASS Cymru, where it has not already been sent by Cafcass/CAFCASS Cymru to the parties, unless it considers that to do so would create a risk of harm to a party or the child. The court may need to consider whether, and if so how, any information contained in the checks should be disclosed to the parties if Cafcass/CAFCASS Cymru have not disclosed the letter/report.

The court will specifically consider, in the light of all the information before the court, including the contents of the safeguarding letter / report provided by Cafcass / CAFCASS Cymru and any Supplemental Information Form(s) C1A filed by the parties.

(b) The nature and extent of any factual issues and whether a fact-finding hearing is needed to determine allegations which are not accepted, and whose resolution is likely to affect the decision of the court.

(c) Risk identification followed by active case management including risk assessment, and compliance with the Practice Direction 12J.
(Specific provisions about directions for a fact-finding hearing are set out in Practice Direction 12J, paragraphs 16 to 20.)

Further –

(d) If the safeguarding information is (contrary to the arrangements set out in the CAP) not available at the FHDRA, the court should adjourn the application until the safeguarding checks are available. Interim orders (unless to protect the safety of a child) should not be made in the absence of safeguarding checks.

And further –

(e) Where the court so directs, a safeguarding letter/report ought to be attached to any referral to a supported or supervised child contact centre in the event the court directs supported or supervised contact.

MIAM, specifically:

(a) Whether, if a MIAM exemption has been claimed, the Applicant has validly claimed the exemption;
(b) Whether the Respondent has attended a MIAM;
(c) If the court finds that a MIAM exemption has not been validly claimed the court will direct the applicant or direct the parties to attend a MIAM and if necessary adjourn the proceedings to enable a MIAM to take place, unless the court considers that in all the circumstances of the case, the MIAM requirement should not apply to the application in question; when making the decision the court will have particular regard to the matters contained in rule 3.10(3) FPR.

Mediation, At-Court Mediation assessment, and other Dispute Resolution: allowing the parties the time and opportunity to engage in non-court dispute resolution.

(a) At the FHDRA, the judge will specifically consider whether, and the extent to which, the parties can safely resolve some or all of the issues with the assistance of the Cafcass Officer, WFPO, or a mediator.
(b) There will be, at every FHDRA, a period in which the Cafcass Officer, or WFPO, will seek to conciliate and explore with the parties the resolution of all or some of the issues between them if safe to do so. The procedure to be followed in this connection at the hearing will be determined by local arrangements between the Cafcass manager, or equivalent in Wales, and the Designated Family Judge or a justices' legal adviser where appropriate.

The court will further consider –

(c) What is the result of any such meeting at Court?
(d) What other options there are for resolution e.g. may the case be suitable for further intervention by Cafcass/CAFCASS Cymru; Should a referral for mediation be made? Is collaborative law appropriate? Should the parties be advised to complete a Parenting Plan?
(e) Would the parties be assisted by attendance at an Activity Separated Parents Information Programme, (or in Wales, Working Together For Children (WT4C)) or other Activity or intervention, whether by formal statutory provision under section 11 Children Act 1989 or otherwise;
(f) An at-court assessment of the suitability of the parties for mediation.

Consent Orders –

(a) Where agreement is reached at any hearing or submitted in writing to the court, no order will be made without scrutiny by the court.
(b) Where safeguarding checks or risk assessment work remain outstanding, the making of a final order may be deferred for such work. In such circumstances the court shall adjourn the case for no longer than 28 days to a fixed date.

A written notification of this work is to be provided by Cafcass/CAFCASS Cymru in the form of an updating Safeguarding letter/report, or if deemed relevant by Cafcass/CAFCASS Cymru, a section 16A risk assessment in accordance with the timescale specified by the court. If satisfactory information is then available, the order may be made at the adjourned hearing in the agreed terms without the need for attendance by the parties. If satisfactory information is not available, the order will not be made, and the case will be adjourned for further consideration with an opportunity for the parties to make further representations

Reports –

(a) Reports may be ordered where there are welfare issues or other specific considerations which should be addressed in a report by Cafcass/CAFCASS Cymru or the Local Authority. Before a report is ordered, the court should consider alternative ways of working with the parties such as are referred to in paragraph 5 ('non-court resolution of disputed arrangements') above.

(b) If a report is ordered in accordance with section 7 of the Children Act 1989, the Court should direct which specific matters relating to the welfare of the child are to be addressed. Welfare reports will generally only be ordered in cases where there is a dispute as to with whom the child should live, spend time, or otherwise have contact with. A report can also be ordered
   (i) If there is an issue concerning the child's wishes, and/or
   (ii) If there is an alleged risk to the child, and/or
   (iii) Where information and advice is needed which the court considers to be necessary before a decision can be reached in the case.

(c) General requests for a report on an application should be avoided; the Court should state on the face of the Order the specific factual and/or other issue which is to be addressed in the focused report.

(d) In determining whether a request for a report should be directed to the relevant local authority or to Cafcass/CAFCASS Cymru, the court should consider such information as Cafcass/CAFCASS Cymru has provided about the extent and nature of the local authority's current or recent involvement with the subject of the application and the parties, and any relevant protocol between Cafcass and the Association of Directors of Children's Services.

(e) The court may further consider whether there is a need for an investigation under section 37 Children Act 1989.

(f) A copy of the Order requesting the report and any relevant court documents are to be sent to Cafcass/CAFCASS Cymru or, in the case of the Local Authority to the Legal Adviser to the Director of the Local Authority Children's Services and, where known, to the allocated social worker by the court forthwith.

(g) Is any expert evidence required? If so, section 13 Children and Families Act 2014, and Part 25 of the FPR must be complied with. This is the latest point at which consideration should be given to the instruction of an expert in accordance with Rule 25.6(b) of the FPR; the court will need to consider carefully the future conduct of proceedings where the preparation of an expert report is necessary but where the parties are unrepresented and are unable to fund the preparation of such a report.

Wishes and feelings of the child –

(a) In line with the Family Justice Young People's Board Charter, children and young people should be at the centre of all proceedings.

(b) The child or young person should feel that their needs, wishes and feelings have been considered in the court process

(c) Each decision should be assessed on its impact on the child.
(d) The court must consider the wishes and feelings of the child, ascertainable so far as is possible in light of the child's age and understanding and circumstances. Specifically, the Court should ask –
  (i) Is the child aware of the proceedings?
  (ii) Are the wishes and feelings of the child available, and/or to be ascertained (if at all)?
  (iii) How is the child to be involved in the proceedings, and if so, how; for example, should they meet the judge/lay justices? Should they be encouraged to write to the court, or have their views reported by Cafcass/CAFCASS Cymru or by a local authority?
  (iv) Who will inform the child of the outcome of the case, where appropriate?

Case Management –

(a) What, if any, issues are agreed and what are the key issues to be determined?
(b) Should the matter be listed for a fact-finding hearing?
(c) Are there any interim orders which can usefully be made (e.g. indirect, supported or supervised contact) pending Dispute Resolution Appointment or final hearing?
(d) What directions are required to ensure the application is ready for a Dispute Resolution Appointment or final hearing – statements, reports etc?
(e) Should the application be listed for a Dispute Resolution Appointment (it is envisaged that most cases will be so listed)?
(f) Should the application be listed straightaway for a final hearing?
(g) Judicial continuity should be actively considered (especially if there has been or is to be a fact finding hearing or a contested interim hearing).

Allocation –

(a) The Allocation decision will be considered by the Court;
(b) If it is necessary to transfer the case to another court within the DFJ area or another area, or re-allocate it, the court shall state the reasons for transfer/re-allocation, and shall specifically make directions for the next hearing in the court.

Order (other than a final order) -

Where no final agreement is reached, and the court is required to give case management directions, the following shall be included on the order:

(a) the date, time and venue of the next hearing;
(b) whether the author of any section 7 report is required to attend the hearing, in order to give oral evidence. A direction for the Cafcass officer or WFPO to attend court will not be made without first considering the reason why attendance is necessary, and upon what issues the Cafcass officer or WFPO will be providing evidence;
(c) such other matters as may be included in President's guidance from time to time.

Where both parties are Litigants in Person, the court may direct HMCTS to produce a Litigant in Person bundle.

The judge will, as far as possible, provide a copy of the order to both parties before they leave the courtroom, and will, if necessary, go through and explain the contents of the order to ensure they are clearly understood by both parties. The parties should know the date, time and venue of any further hearing before they leave the court.

Timetable for the child

15.1 Court proceedings should be timetabled so that the dispute can be resolved as soon as safe and possible in the interests of the child.

15.2 The judge shall, at all times during the proceedings, have regard to the impact which the court timetable will have on the welfare and development of the child to whom the application relates. The judge and the parties shall pay particular attention to the child's age, and important landmarks in the immediate life of the child, including –

(a) the child's birthday;
(b) the start of nursery/schooling;
(c) the start/end of a school term/year;
(d) any proposed change of school;

and/or

(e) any significant change in the child's family, or social, circumstances.

15.3 While it is acknowledged that an interim order may be appropriate at an early stage of court proceedings, cases should not be adjourned for a review (or reviews) of contact or other orders/arrangements, &/or for addendum section 7 report, unless such a hearing is necessary and for a clear purpose that is consistent with the timetable for the child and in the child's best interests.

15.4 When preparing a section 7 report, Cafcass / CAFCASS Cymru (or, where appropriate, the local authority) is encouraged to make recommendations for the stepped phasing-in of child arrangements (i.e. recommendations for the medium and longer term future for the child) insofar as they are able to do so safely in the interests of the child concerned;

15.5 Where active involvement or monitoring is needed, the court may consider making –

(1) An order under section 11H Children Act 1989 (Monitoring);
(2) A Family Assistance Order under section 16 Children Act 1989) (in accordance with the Practice Direction 12M FPR, and if all the named adults in the order agree to the making of such an order and if the order is directed to a local authority, the child lives (or will live) within that local authority area or the local authority consents to the making of the order.

Capacity of Litigants

16.1 In the event that the judge has concerns about the capacity of a litigant before the court, the judge shall consider –

(1) the Guidance issued by the Family Justice Council in relation to assessing the capacity of litigants,
(2) Practice Direction 15B (Adults Who May Be Protected Parties and Children Who May Become Protected Parties In Family Proceedings)

Evidence

17.1 No evidence shall be filed in relation to an application until after the FHDRA unless –

(1) It has been filed in support of a without notice application
(2) It has been directed by the Court by the Directions on Issue;
(3) It has been directed by the Court for the purposes of determining an interim application.

Rule 16.4 children's guardians

18.1 The Court should be vigilant to identify the cases where a rule 16.4 children's guardian should be appointed. This should be considered initially at the FHDRA.

18.2 Where the court is considering the appointment of a children's guardian from Cafcass/CAFCASS Cymru, it should first ensure that enquiries have been made of the appropriate Cafcass/CAFCASS Cymru manager in accordance with paragraph 7.4, Part 4 of the Practice Direction 16A. This should either be in writing before the hearing or by way of case discussion with the relevant Cafcass service manager; for cases in Wales, the 'hotline' protocol agreed with CAFCASS Cymru will ensure that such a discussion can take place. The court should consult with Cafcass / CAFCASS Cymru, so as to consider any advice in connection with the prospective appointment, and the timescale involved.

18.3 When the court decides to appoint a children's guardian, consideration should first be given to appointing an Officer of the Service or WFPO. If Cafcass/CAFCASS Cymru is unable to provide a children's guardian without delay, or if there is some other reason why the appointment of a Cafcass officer is not appropriate, the court should (further to rule 16.24 of the FPR) appoint a person other than the Official Solicitor, unless the Official Solicitor expressly consents.

18.4 In considering whether to make such an appointment the Court shall take account of the demands on the resources of Cafcass/CAFCASS Cymru that such an appointment would make. The court should also make clear on the face of any order the purpose of the appointment and the timetable of any work to be undertaken.

Dispute Resolution Appointment (DRA)

19.1 The Court shall list the application for a Dispute Resolution Appointment ('DRA') to follow the preparation of section 7 or other expert report, or Separated Parenting Information Programme (SPIP) (or WT4C in Wales), if this is considered likely to be helpful in the interests of the child.

19.2 The author of the section 7 report will only attend this hearing if directed to do so by the Court.

19.3 At the DRA the Court will –

(1) Identify the key issue(s) (if any) to be determined and the extent to which those issues can be resolved or narrowed at the DRA;
(2) Consider whether the DRA can be used as a final hearing;
(3) Resolve or narrow the issues by hearing evidence;
(4) Identify the evidence to be heard on the issues which remain to be resolved at the final hearing;
(5) Give final case management directions including:
    (a) Filing of further evidence;
    (b) Filing of a statement of facts/issues remaining to be determined;
    (c) Filing of a witness template and / or skeleton arguments;
    (d) Ensuring Compliance with Practice Direction 27A (the Bundles Practice Direction);
    (e) Listing the Final Hearing.

Fact-finding hearing

20.1 If the court considers that a fact-finding hearing is necessary it shall conduct that hearing in accordance with revised Practice Direction 12J

20.2 Where there is an application for a section 91(14) order, the court should consider whether any particular findings of fact will be needed in order to determine the section 91(14) application.

Enforcement of Child Arrangements

21.1 On any application for enforcement of a child arrangements order, the court shall –

- consider whether the facts relevant to the alleged non-compliance are agreed, or whether it is necessary to conduct a hearing to establish the facts;
- consider the reasons for any non-compliance;
- consider how the wishes and feelings of the child are to be ascertained;
- consider whether advice is required from Cafcass/CAFCASS Cymru on the appropriate way forward;
- assess and manage any risks of making further or other child arrangements order;
- consider whether a SPIP or referral for dispute resolution is appropriate;
- consider whether an enforcement order may be appropriate, and
- consider the welfare checklist.

21.2 The Gatekeepers shall list any application for enforcement of a child arrangements order for hearing, before the previously allocated judge if possible, within 20 working days of issue. Enforcement cases should be concluded without delay.

21.3 An application made within existing proceedings in the family court shall be allocated to the level of judge in accordance with rule 17 of the Family Court (Composition and Distribution of Business) Rules 2014.

21.4 The Gatekeepers shall, if considered necessary, direct that further safeguarding checks are required from Cafcass/CAFCASS Cymru. On any application for enforcement issued more than three months after the order which is the subject of the enforcement, safeguarding checks shall be ordered.

21.5 The court has a wide range of powers in the event of a breach of a child arrangements order without reasonable excuse.

21.6 This range of powers includes (but is not limited to):

(a) referral of the parents to a SPIP, or in Wales a WT4C, or mediation;
(b) variation of the child arrangements order (which could include a more defined order and/or reconsidering the contact provision or the living arrangements of the child);
(c) a contact enforcement order or suspended enforcement order under section 11J Children Act 1989 ('Enforcement order' for unpaid work), (see paragraph 21.7 below);
(d) an order for compensation for financial loss (under section 11O Children Act 1989);
(e) committal to prison or
(f) a fine.

21.7 In the event that the court is considering an enforcement order for alleged non-compliance with a court order (under section 11J Children Act 1989) or considering a Compensation order in respect of financial loss (under section 11O Children Act 1989), the court shall (in the absence of agreement between the parties about the relevant facts) determine the facts in order to establish the cause of the alleged failure to comply.

21.8 Section 11L Children Act 1989 provides that if the court finds that a breach has occurred without reasonable excuse it may order the non-compliant party to undertake unpaid work if that is necessary to secure compliance, and if the effect on the non-compliant party is proportionate to the seriousness of the breach. The court must also consider whether unpaid work is available in the locality and the likely effect on the non-compliant party. It is good practice to ask Cafcass/CAFCASS Cymru to report on the suitability of this order. Section 11L(7) also requires the court to take into account the welfare of the child who is the subject of the order for contact.

Court timetable

22.1 Working Day 1: Paperwork received. Court office checks whether the revised form C100 has been completed correctly. The application will not be issued unless the form has been completed correctly.

22.2 Working Day 3: Case considered by Gatekeeping team. Case allocated by Gatekeepers in accordance with the President's Guidance on allocation and the Family Court (Composition and Distribution) Rules 2014. The Gatekeeper(s) undertaking allocation to check whether form C100 has been completed. If there has been no MIAM, and there are reasons to believe that the applicant should have attended a MIAM, the Gatekeeping judge can direct that a MIAM should take place before the FHDRA.

22.2A By Working Day 3 (2 working days after the date of issue): The court shall send to Cafcass / CAFCASS Cymru a copy of the Form C100 (and the Form C1A, if supplied), and the C6 Notice of Hearing. This will be in electronic format where possible.

22.2B On receipt of the Acknowledgement Form C7 and any Form C1A filed by the respondent(s), the court shall send a copy of each form to Cafcass / CAFCASS Cymru, in electronic format where possible, and shall send copies to the applicant.

22.3 17 working days from the date of its receipt of the application Cafcass/CAFCASS Cymru will provide the safeguarding letter / report to the Court (20 working days in the area of CAFCASS Cymru).

22.4 Week 5 (or latest, week 6): Case listed for FHDRA (before week 5 if requirements of notice have been abridged).

22.5 Thereafter, case may be listed for fact-finding hearing, DRA &/or final hearing.

Relevant Family Application (definition)

23.1 A relevant family application for the purposes of the CAP is an application that –

(1) Is made to the court in, or to initiate, family proceedings, and
(2) Is of a description specified in the Family Procedure Rules.

Annex
Explanation of terms

Abuse	Any behaviour which causes harm
Adjourn / Adjournment	Where the case, or a hearing, is directed to take place or continue at a later time (which might be on the same day or another day)
Allegation	A claim that someone has done something wrong
Applicant	The name given to someone who is asking the court for a court order
Application	How a person asks the court to do something

Cafcass	Cafcass stands for the 'Children and Family Court Advisory and Support Service'. Cafcass is independent of the courts, social services, education and health authorities and all similar agencies. Cafcass workers (sometimes called 'Family Court Advisers' or 'officers') are specialist social workers who help the court by making safeguarding checks, helping parties at the FHDRA to consider solutions, and if necessary writing reports for the court &/or monitoring arrangements after court.
CAFCASS Cymru	This is Cafcass in Wales. CAFCASS Cymru is part of the Department of Health and Social Services in the Welsh Government.
Child Arrangements Order	This is an order which will set out arrangements relating to (a) with whom a child is to live, spend time or otherwise have contact, and (b) when a child is to live, spend time or otherwise have contact with any other person.
Collaborative law	One of the ways of trying to sort out disputes away from court; each party appoints their own lawyer, and you and your lawyers all meet together to work things out face to face.
Consent order	When you have reached an agreement with the other parent, which resolves the dispute, the judge may agree to make that agreement into an order called a consent order
Contact centre	A place for a parent to see their child in a neutral and 'safe' environment. 'Supervised' contact centres provide a safe and neutral place for contact. 'Supported' contact centres, which are often run by volunteers, offer a neutral place for contact in cases where no safety concerns exist
Designated Family Judge	This is the judge who has responsibility to provide leadership to the family judiciary within the court centre or group of courts
Dispute Resolution	The method of solving disagreements
Domestic violence	This phrase is used to describe a wide range of behaviours including any incident or pattern of incidents of controlling, coercive or threatening behaviour, violence or abuse between those aged 16 or over who are or have been intimate partners or family members regardless of gender or sexuality. This can encompass, but is not limited to, the following types of abuse: psychological, physical, sexual, financial, or emotional. Controlling behaviour is: a range of acts designed to make a person subordinate and/or dependent by isolating them from sources of support, exploiting their resources and capacities for personal gain, depriving them of the means needed for independence, resistance and escape and regulating their everyday behaviour. Coercive behaviour is: an act or a pattern of acts of assault, threats, humiliation and intimidation or other abuse that is used to harm, punish, or frighten their victim.
DRA	Dispute Resolution Appointment. This is a court hearing which takes place towards the end of the court's involvement, and is another opportunity to see if the dispute can be sorted out with the help of a judge.

Enforcement	Making sure that an order is complied with
Expert evidence	Evidence and opinions provided by someone with special skills and knowledge (but, for these purposes, does not refer to a social worker employed by, and giving evidence on behalf of, a local authority who is a party to the case).
Fact finding hearing	A court hearing set up for the court to decide on issues of fact or allegations which are in dispute.
Family Assistance order	An order of the court which allows Cafcass or local authorities to provide social-work support to help parties to establish contact arrangements which might otherwise fail
FHDRA	First Hearing Dispute Resolution Appointment. This is a court hearing which takes place at the beginning of the court's involvement.
File	This means to send / deliver to the court office
FPR	Family Procedure Rules 2010; the rules of court which govern family cases.
Gatekeeper(s)	The nominated District Judge and/or nominated Legal Adviser responsible for deciding which level of judge in the family court should initially deal with an application
Hearing	The name given to a meeting or court appointment with a judge
Indirect contact	Any contact which is not face-to-face (for example, letters, birthday cards, phone calls).
Interim contact	Contact that takes place between the first court hearing and the final hearing
Investigation under section 37	Where it appears to a judge that a child is or may be at risk of significant harm and it may be appropriate for local authority children's services to apply for a court order giving them responsibilities towards a family, the judge can direct the local authority to investigate the child's circumstances
Judge	Where the term 'Judge' is used, this refers to any judge of the Family Court including lay justices (magistrates)and judges of the High Court
Judgment	The decision of the Judge, and the reasons why the decision has been made
LAA	Legal Aid Agency; this is the body responsible for providing public funding for legal representation.
Litigant in Person or LiP	This is the name given to a person in court proceedings who does not have a lawyer
Litigant in Person Bundle	A bundle of court documents, contained in a file, which contains the following: Section A: Applications, Section B: Orders, Section C: Statements, Section D: Cafcass safeguarding letter, analyses and any expert reports, and Section E: Police, medical, other documents
McKenzie Friend	A friend or other person who can help you prepare your case and go to court with you to give you support and take notes

MIAM	Mediation Information and Assessment Meeting. At this meeting, a trained mediator will explain what mediation is and how it works, explain the benefits of mediation and the likely costs, answer questions, assess whether the person is eligible for legal aid for mediation, assess whether mediation is suitable in the case. A MIAM should be held within 15 working days of contacting the mediator.
NACCC	National Association of Child Contact Centres: NACCC has in its membership about 350 child contact centres and services throughout England (including the Channel Isles), Wales and Northern Ireland. Child contact centres and services are neutral places where children of separated families can enjoy contact with the parent with whom the child does not live and sometimes with other family members, in a comfortable and safe environment.
Parental responsibility	All the legal rights and responsibilities normally associated with being a parent
Part-heard	Means a hearing which has started but which has not been finished within the day, and then continues on another day
Party	Someone involved in the court proceedings – either the person who has made the application, or the person(s) against whom the application has been made.
Practice Direction	This is a document which sets out good practice in supporting the FPR (Family Procedure Rules) or other Rules (see above) and /or may contain provisions which could otherwise be contained in rules of court and have same effect as rules
Private family law / private law	Family disputes between individuals about arrangements for children.
Respondent(s)	This is the name given to the person or people who receive the court application
Review	To look at something again
Rule 16.4 children's guardian	A person (usually a specialist social worker) appointed by the court to look after the interests of a child in the case
Safeguarding	Making sure that people are safe
Section 7 report	A welfare report, prepared under section 7 of the Children Act 1989; the report will be on such matters relating to the welfare of that child as are required to be dealt with in the report; the report may be in writing or oral.
Serve	Delivery of court documents
SPIP	Separated Parents Information Programme; this is available across England, and is for both parents and for grandparents.
Statement or Witness Statement	A document setting out what you want to say to the Judge about the case. You should sign it and date it. What you say in the statement must be true.
Undertaking	A solemn promise to the court to do, or not do, something
WFPO	Welsh Family Proceedings Officer. A Cafcass officer in Wales.
WT4C	The Working Together For Children programme which runs in Wales – and is the equivalent of the SPIP (see above)

Practice Direction 12C – Service of application in certain proceedings relating to children

See also Part 12, Practice Direction 12A, Practice Direction 12B, Practice Direction 12D, Practice Direction 12E, Practice Direction 12F, Practice Direction 12G, Practice Direction 12H, Practice Direction 12I, Practice Direction 12J, Practice Direction 12K, Practice Direction 12L, Practice Direction 12M, Practice Direction 12N, Practice Direction 12O, Practice Direction 12P

This Practice Direction supplements FPR Part 12 (Procedure Relating to Children except Parental Order Proceedings and Proceedings For Applications In Adoption, Placement and Related Proceedings), rule 12.8 (Service of the application)

Persons who receive copy of application form

1.1 In relation to the proceedings in column 1 of the following table, column 2 sets out the documentation which persons listed in column 3 are to receive –

Proceedings	Documentation	Who receives a copy of the documentation
1. Private law proceedings; public law proceedings; emergency proceedings (except those proceedings referred to in entries 2 and 3 of the Table below); proceedings for a declaration under rule 12.71 as to the existence, or extent, of parental responsibility under Article 16 of the 1996 Hague Convention; an order relating to the exercise of the court's inherent jurisdiction (including wardship proceedings)	Application form (including any supplementary forms); Form C6 (Notice of proceedings); and in private law proceedings, the form of answer	All the respondents to the application
2. An enforcement order (section 11J of the 1989 Act); a financial compensation order (section 11O of the 1989 Act)	As above	All the respondents to the application; and where the child was a party to the proceedings in which the child arrangements order was made – (a) the person who was the children's guardian or litigation friend in those proceedings; or

Proceedings	Documentation	Who receives a copy of the documentation
		(b) where there was no children's guardian or litigation friend, the person who was the legal representative of the child in those proceedings.
3. A care or a supervision order (section 31 of the 1989 Act) and other Part 4 proceedings	As above and such of the documents specified in the Annex to Form C110A as are available	All the respondents to the application; and Cafcass or CAFCASS CYMRU
4. Proceedings for an order for the return of a child under the 1980 Hague Convention or registration of an order under the European Convention	As above and the documents referred to in part 2 of the Practice Direction 12F (International Child Abduction)	All the respondents to the application

(Rule 12.3 sets out who the parties to the proceedings are.)

1.2 When filing the documents referred to in column 2 of the Table in paragraph 1.1, the applicant must also file sufficient copies for one to be served on each respondent and, except for Part 4 proceedings, Cafcass or CAFCASS CYMRU. In relation to Part 4 proceedings, the applicant need not file a copy of the documents for Cafcass or CAFCASS CYMRU as it is the applicant who sends copies of these documents to Cafcass or CAFCASS CYMRU in accordance with Practice Direction 12A.

1.3 Where the application for an order in proceedings referred to in column 1 of the Table in paragraph 1.1 is made in respect of more than one child all the children must be included in the same application form.

1.4 Form C6A (notice to non parties) must be served on the persons referred to in the Table in paragraph 3.1 at the same time as serving the documents in column 2 of the Table in paragraph 1.1.

Time for serving application

2.1 In relation to the proceedings in column 1 of the following table, column 2 sets out the time period within which the application and accompanying documents must be served on each respondent –

Proceedings	Minimum number of days prior to hearing or directions appointment for service
1. Private law proceedings; and proceedings for – an order relating to the exercise of the court's inherent jurisdiction (including wardship proceedings); a declaration under rule 12.71 as to the existence, or extent, of parental responsibility under Article 16 of the 1996 Hague Convention.	14 days

Proceedings	Minimum number of days prior to hearing or directions appointment for service
2. Public law proceedings except proceedings for an interim care order, an interim supervision order or other proceedings referred to in Box 3 below.	7 days
3. Proceedings for – an interim care order, or the discharge of such an order under section 39(1) of the 1989 Act; an interim supervision order under section 38 (1) of the 1989 Act, the discharge or variation of such an order under section 39(2) of the 1989 Act, or the extension or further extension of such an order under paragraph 6(3) of Schedule 3 to that Act; an order varying directions made with an interim care order or interim supervision order under section 38(8)(b) of the 1989 Act; an order under section 39(3) of the 1989 Act varying an interim supervision order in so far as it affects a person with whom the child is living but who is not entitled to apply for the order to be discharged; an order under section 39(3A) of the 1989 Act varying or discharging an interim care order in so far as it imposes an exclusion requirement on a person who is not entitled to apply for the order to be discharged; an order under section 39(3B) of the 1989 Act varying or discharging an interim care order in so far as it confers a power of arrest attached to an exclusion requirement.	3 days
4. Proceedings for an order for the return of a child under the 1980 Hague Convention or registration of an order under the European Convention.	4 days
5. Emergency proceedings.	1 day

2.2 The court may extend or shorten the time period referred to in column 2 of the table in paragraph 2.1 (see rule 4.1(3)(a)).

2.3 Where the application is to be served on a child, rule 6.33 provides that, in addition to the persons to be served in accordance with rules 6.28 and 6.32, the application must also be served on the persons or bodies listed in rule 6.33(3) unless the court orders otherwise.

Persons who receive a copy of Form C6A (Notice to Non-Parties)

3.1 Subject to paragraph 3.2, In relation to each type of proceedings in column 1 of the following table, the persons listed in column 2 are to receive a copy of Form C6A (Notice of Proceedings/Hearing/Directions Appointment to Non-Parties) –

Proceedings	Persons to whom notice is to be given
1. All applications	Subject to separate entries below: local authority providing accommodation for the child; persons who are caring for the child at the time when the proceedings are commenced; and in the case of proceedings brought in respect of a child who is alleged to be staying in a refuge which is certified under section 51(1) or (2) of the 1989 Act, the person who is providing the refuge
2. An order appointing a guardian (section 5(1) of the 1989 Act)	As for all applications; and the father or parent (being a woman who is a parent by virtue of section 43 of the Human Fertilisation and Embryology Act 2008) of the child if that person does not have parental responsibility
3. A section 8 order (section 8 of the 1989 Act)	As for all applications; and, every person whom the applicant believes – (i) to be named in a court order with respect to the same child, which has not ceased to have effect; (ii) to be party to pending proceedings in respect of the same child; or (iii) to be a person with whom the child has lived for at least 3 years prior to the application, unless, in a case to which (i) or (ii) applies, the applicant believes that the court order or pending proceedings are not relevant to the application
4. A special guardianship order (section 14A of the 1989 Act); variation or discharge of a special guardianship order (section 14D of the 1989 Act).	As for all applications; and every person whom the applicant believes – (i) to be named in a court order with respect to the same child, which has not ceased to have effect; (ii) to be party to pending proceedings in respect of the same child; or (iii) to be a person with whom the child has lived for at least 3 years prior to the application, unless, in a case to which (i) or (ii) applies, the applicant believes that the court order or pending proceedings are not relevant to the application; if the child is not being accommodated by the local authority, the local authority in whose area the applicant is ordinarily resident; and in the case of an application under section 14D of the 1989 Act, the local authority that prepared the report under section 14A(8) or (9) in the proceedings leading to the order which it is sought to have varied or discharged, if different from any local authority that will otherwise be notified

Proceedings	Persons to whom notice is to be given
5. An order permitting the local authority to arrange for any child in its care to live outside England and Wales (Schedule 2, paragraph 19(1) of the 1989 Act)	As for all applications; and the parties to the proceedings leading to the care order
6. A care or supervision order(section 31 of the 1989 Act)	As for all applications; and every person whom the applicant believes to be a party to pending relevant proceedings in respect of the same child; and every person whom the applicant believes to be a parent without parental responsibility for the child
7. A child assessment order (section 43(1) of the 1989 Act)	As for all applications; and every person whom the applicant believes to be a parent of the child; every person whom the applicant believes to be caring for the child; every person in whose favour a child arrangements order is in force with respect to the child;and every person who is allowed to have contact with the child by virtue of an order under section 34 of the 1989 Act
8. An order varying or discharging a child assessment order (section 43(12) of the 1989Act)	The persons referred to in section 43(11)(a) to (e) of the 1989 Act who were not party to the application for the order which it is sought to have varied or discharged
9. An emergency protection order (section 44(1) of the 1989 Act)	As for all applications above; and every person whom the applicant believes to be a parent of the child
10. An order varying a direction under section 44(6) in an emergency protection order (section44(9)(b) of the 1989 Act)	As for all applications; and the local authority in whose area the child is living; and any person whom the applicant believes to be affected by the direction which it is sought to have varied
11. A warrant authorising a constable to assist in the exercise of certain powers to search for children and inspect premises (section 102 of the 1989 Act)	The person referred to in section 102(1) of the 1989 Act; and any person preventing or likely to prevent such a person from exercising powers under enactments mentioned in subsection (6) of that section
12. An enforcement order (section 11J of the 1989 Act); a financial compensation order (section 11O of the 1989 Act)	Any officer of the Service or Welsh family proceedings officer who is monitoring compliance with a child arrangements order (in accordance with section 11H(2) of the 1989 Act)

Proceedings	Persons to whom notice is to be given
13. An order revoking or amending an enforcement order (Schedule A1, paragraphs 4 to 7 of the 1989 Act)(rule 12.33 makes provision regarding applications under Schedule A1, paragraph5 of the 1989 Act); an order following a breach of an enforcement order(Schedule A1, paragraph 9 of the 1989 Act)	Any officer of the Service or Welsh family proceedings officer who is monitoring compliance with the enforcement order (in accordance with section 11M(1) of the 1989Act); the responsible officer (as defined in section 197 of the Criminal Justice Act 2003, as modified by Schedule A1 to the 1989 Act)
14. A declaration under rule 12.71 as to the existence, or extent, of parental responsibility under Article16 of the 1996 Hague Convention	A person who the applicant believes is a parent of the child

3.2 A person listed in column 2 of the following table shall not receive a copy of Form C6A if the court, on application by any party, directs that such notification is not required.

Practice Direction 12D – Inherent jurisdiction (including wardship) proceedings

See also Part 12, Practice Direction 12A, Practice Direction 12B, Practice Direction 12C, Practice Direction 12E, Practice Direction 12F, Practice Direction 12G, Practice Direction 12H, Practice Direction 12I, Practice Direction 12J, Practice Direction 12K, Practice Direction 12L, Practice Direction 12M, Practice Direction 12N, Practice Direction 12O, Practice Direction 12P

This Practice Direction supplements FPR Part 12, Chapter 5

The nature of inherent jurisdiction proceedings

1.1 It is the duty of the court under its inherent jurisdiction to ensure that a child who is the subject of proceedings is protected and properly taken care of. The court may in exercising its inherent jurisdiction make any order or determine any issue in respect of a child unless limited by case law or statute. Case law establishes that such proceedings should only be commenced exceptionally where it is clear that the issues concerning the child should not be resolved under the Children Act 1989, for example, for reasons of urgency, of complexity or of the need for particular judicial expertise in the determination of a cross-border issue. For a review of the relevant case law and principles, see In the matter of NY (A Child) [2019] UKSC 49.

1.2 The court may under its inherent jurisdiction, in addition to all of the orders which can be made in family proceedings, make a wide range of injunctions for the child's protection of which the following are the most common –

(a) orders to restrain publicity;
(b) orders to prevent an undesirable association;
(c) orders relating to medical treatment;
(d) orders to protect abducted children, or children where the case has another substantial foreign element; and
(e) orders for the return of children to and from another state.

1.3 The court's wardship jurisdiction is part of and not separate from the court's inherent jurisdiction. The distinguishing characteristics of wardship are that –

(a) custody of a child who is a ward is vested in the court; and
(b) although day to day care and control of the ward is given to an individual or to a local authority, no important step can be taken in the child's life without the court's consent.

Transfer of proceedings to family court

2.1 Whilst the family court does not have jurisdiction to deal with applications that a child be made or cease to be a ward of court, consideration should be given to transferring the case in whole or in part to the family court where a direction has been given confirming the wardship and directing that the child remain a ward of court during his minority or until further order.

2.2 The family court must transfer the case back to the High Court if a decision is required as to whether the child should remain a ward of court.

2.3 The following proceedings in relation to a ward of court will be dealt with in the High Court unless the nature of the issues of fact or law makes them more suitable for hearing in the family court –

(a) those in which an officer of the Cafcass High Court Team or the Official Solicitor is or becomes the litigation friend or children's guardian of the ward or a party to the proceedings;
(b) those in which a local authority is or becomes a party;
(c) those in which an application for paternity testing is made;
(d) those in which there is a dispute about medical treatment;
(e) those in which an application is opposed on the grounds of lack of jurisdiction;
(f) those in which there is a substantial foreign element;
(g) those in which there is an opposed application for leave to take the child permanently out of the jurisdiction or where there is an application for temporary removal of a child from the jurisdiction and it is opposed on the ground that the child may not be duly returned.

Parties

3.1 Where the child has formed or is seeking to form an association, considered to be undesirable, with another person, that other person should not be made a party to the application. Such a person should be made a respondent only to an application within the proceedings for an injunction or committal. Such a person should not be added to the title of the proceedings nor allowed to see any documents other than those relating directly to the proceedings for the injunction or committal. He or she should be allowed time to obtain representation and any injunction should in the first instance extend over a few days only.

Removal from jurisdiction

4.1 A child who is a ward of court may not be removed from England and Wales without the court's permission. Practice Direction 12F (International Child Abduction) deals in detail with locating and protecting children at risk of unlawful removal.

Criminal Proceedings

5.1 Case law establishes that:

There is no requirement for the police or any other agency carrying out statutory powers of investigation or enforcement to seek the permission of the court to interview a child who is a ward of court. The fact that a child is a ward of court does not affect the powers and duties of the police or other statutory agencies in relation to their investigations. Provided that the relevant statutory requirements are complied with, the police or other agencies are under no duty to take any special steps in carrying out their functions in relation to a child who is a ward of court.

Where a child has been interviewed by the police in connection with contemplated criminal proceedings and the child is, or subsequently becomes, a ward of court, the permission of the court is not required for the child to be called as a witness in the criminal proceedings.

For a full review of the relevant case law and principles, see In the matter of a Ward of Court [2017] EWHC 1022 (Fam).

5.2 Where the police or other statutory agencies take any action in relation to a child who is a ward of court, the person(s) with day to day care and control of the child, or where applicable the local authority, should bring the relevant information to the attention of the court as soon as practicable. Where wardship proceedings are continuing, any children's guardian appointed for the child must be informed of the situation by the other parties.

Applications to the Criminal Injuries Compensation Authority

6.1 Where a child who is a ward of court has a right to make a claim for compensation to the Criminal Injuries Compensation Authority ('CICA'), an application must be made by the child's guardian, or, if no guardian has been appointed, the person with care and control of the child, for permission to apply to CICA and disclose such documents on the wardship proceedings file as are considered necessary to establish whether or not the child is eligible for an award plus, as appropriate, the amount of the award.

6.2 Any order giving permission should state that any award made by CICA should normally be paid into court immediately upon receipt and, once that payment has been made, application should made to the court as to its management and administration. If it is proposed to invest the award in any other way, the court's prior approval must be sought

The role of the tipstaff

7.1 The tipstaff is the enforcement officer for all orders made in the High Court. The tipstaff's jurisdiction extends throughout England and Wales. Every applicable order made in the High Court is addressed to the tipstaff in children and family matters (eg 'The Court hereby directs the Tipstaff of the High Court of Justice, whether acting by himself or his assistants or a police officer as follows …').

7.2 The tipstaff may effect an arrest and then inform the police. Sometimes the local bailiff or police will detain a person in custody until the tipstaff arrives to collect that person or give further directions as to the disposal of the matter. The tipstaff may also make a forced entry although there will generally be a uniformed police officer standing by to make sure there is no breach of the peace.

7.3 There is only one tipstaff (with two assistants) but the tipstaff can also call on any constable or bailiff to assist in carrying out the tipstaff's duties.

7.4 The majority of the tipstaff's work involves locating children and taking them into protective custody, including cases of child abduction abroad.

Application to set aside an inherent jurisdiction order

8.1 As set out in rule 12.42B, the Part 18 procedure applies to set aside an inherent jurisdiction order. Where such an application was made before rule 12.42B came into force, the Part 18 procedure will still apply subject to any directions that the court might make for the purpose of ensuring that the proceedings are dealt with fairly.

8.2 An application under rule 12.42B should be dealt with by the same level of judge that dealt with the original application. Where reasonably possible, the application should be dealt with by the same judge that dealt with the original application.

8.3 The application should be made promptly upon the party becoming aware of the information or upon the circumstances occurring that give rise to the application.

8.4 An application to set aside an inherent jurisdiction order should only be made where no error of the court is alleged (unless the circumstances set out in rule 18.11 apply). If an error of the court is alleged, an application for permission to appeal under Part 30 should be considered. The grounds on which an inherent jurisdiction order may be set aside are and will remain a matter for decisions by judges. The grounds may include: (i) fraud; (ii) material non-disclosure; (iii) certain limited types of mistake; (iv) a fundamental change in circumstances which undermines the basis on which the order was made; and (v) the welfare of the child requires it.

8.5 The effect of rules 12.42B(1)(a) and (2) is that an application may be made to set aside all or only part of an inherent jurisdiction order, including an inherent jurisdiction order that has been made by consent.

Inherent jurisdiction orders are defined in the rule and include any order, declaration or judgment made under the inherent jurisdiction, including but not limited to orders making a child a ward of court, orders regarding medical treatment of a child and orders for the return or non-return of a child made under the inherent jurisdiction. Inherent jurisdiction orders do not include return orders made under the 1980 Hague Convention (for those orders, see rule 12.42B and paragraphs 4.1A – 4.1B of Practice Direction 12F), but can include orders where the basis to exercise jurisdiction is found in other instruments, such as the 1996 Hague Convention (though the source of power for the return order remains the inherent jurisdiction). Inherent jurisdiction orders do not include orders or judgments made within inherent jurisdiction proceedings for which the power to make such an order or judgment is found in statute (such as the power to make return orders under section 8 of the Children Act 1989) or these Rules (and not the inherent jurisdiction). The power to set aside any such orders would, if it exists, derive either from relevant statutory provisions or from the power to vary or revoke in rule 4.1(6), or from any inherent power of the High Court to set aside its own orders. Rule 12.42B(6) clarifies that any such other power to revoke, discharge or set aside is not ousted by the rule.

8.6 The effect of rules 12.42B(1)(a) and (2) is that an application may be made to set aside all or only part of an inherent jurisdiction order, including an inherent jurisdiction order that has been made by consent.

Inherent jurisdiction orders are defined in the rule and include any order, declaration or judgment made under the inherent jurisdiction, including but not limited to orders making a child a ward of court, orders regarding medical treatment of a child and orders for the return or non-return of a child made under the inherent jurisdiction. Inherent jurisdiction orders do not include return orders made under the 1980 Hague Convention (for those orders, see rule 12.42B and paragraphs 4.1A – 4.1B of Practice Direction 12F), but can include orders where the basis to exercise jurisdiction is found in other instruments, such as the 1996 Hague Convention (though the source of power for the return order remains the inherent jurisdiction). Inherent jurisdiction orders do not include those orders or judgments made within inherent jurisdiction proceedings where the power to make such an order or judgment is found in statute (such as the power to make return orders under section 8 of the Children Act 1989) or these Rules (and not the inherent jurisdiction). The power to set aside any such orders would, if it exists, derive either from relevant statutory provisions or from the power to vary or revoke in rule 4.1(6), or from any inherent power of the High Court to set aside its own orders. Rule 12.42B(6) clarifies that any such other power to revoke, discharge or set aside is not ousted by the rule.

Practice Direction 12E – Urgent business

See also Part 12, Practice Direction 12A, Practice Direction 12B, Practice Direction 12C, Practice Direction 12D, Practice Direction 12F, Practice Direction 12G, Practice Direction 12H, Practice Direction 12I, Practice Direction 12J, Practice Direction 12K, Practice Direction 12L, Practice Direction 12M, Practice Direction 12N, Practice Direction 12O, Practice Direction 12P

This Practice Direction supplements FPR Part 12

Introduction

1.1 This Practice Direction describes the procedure to be followed in respect of urgent and out of hours cases in the Family Division of the High Court. For the avoidance of doubt, it does not relate to cases in respect of adults.

1.2 Urgent or out of hours applications, particularly those which have become urgent because they have not been pursued sufficiently promptly, should be avoided. A judge who has concerns that the urgent or out of hours facilities may have been abused may require a representative of the applicant to attend at a subsequent directions hearing to provide an explanation.

1.3 Urgent applications should whenever possible be made within court hours. The earliest possible liaison is required with the Clerk of the Rules who will attempt to accommodate genuinely urgent applications (at least for initial directions) in the Family Division applications court, from which the matter may be referred to another judge.

1.4 When it is not possible to apply within court hours, contact should be made with the security office at the Royal Courts of Justice (020 7947 6000 or 020 7947 6260) who will refer the matter to the urgent business officer. The urgent business officer can contact the duty judge. The judge may agree to hold a hearing, either convened at court or elsewhere, or by telephone.

1.5 When the hearing is to take place by telephone it should, unless not practicable, be by tape-recorded conference call arranged (and paid for in the first instance) by the applicant's solicitors. Solicitors acting for potential applicants should consider having standing arrangements with their telephone service providers under which such conference calls can be arranged. All parties (especially the judge) should be informed that the call is being recorded by the service provider. The applicant's solicitors should order a transcript of the hearing from the service provider. Otherwise the applicant's legal representative should prepare a note for approval by the judge.

General Issues

2.1 Parents, carers or other necessary respondents should whenever possible be given the opportunity to have independent legal advice or at least to have access to support or counselling.

2.2 In suitable cases, application may be made for directions providing for anonymity of the parties and others involved in the matter in any order or subsequent listing of the case. Exceptionally, a reporting restriction order may be sought.

2.3 Either the Official Solicitor or Cafcass, or CAFCASS CYMRU, as the case may be, may be invited by the court to be appointed as advocate to the court.

Medical treatment and press injunction cases

3.1 It may be desirable for a child who is the subject of such proceedings to be made a party and represented through a children's guardian (usually an officer of Cafcass or a Welsh Family Proceedings Officer). Cafcass and CAFCASS CYMRU stand ready to arrange for an officer to accept appointment as a children's guardian. They should be contacted at the earliest opportunity where an urgent application is envisaged. For urgent out of hours applications, the urgent business officer will contact a representative of Cafcass. CAFCASS CYMRU is not able to deal with cases that arise out of office hours and those cases should be referred to Cafcass who will deal with the matter on behalf of CAFCASS CYMRU until the next working day. A child of sufficient understanding to instruct his or her own solicitor should be made a party and given notice of any application.

3.2 Interim declarations/orders under the wardship jurisdiction or Children Act 1989 may be made on application either by an NHS trust, a local authority, an interested adult (where necessary with the leave of the court) or by the child if he or she has sufficient understanding to make the application.

Consultation with Cafcass, CAFCASS CYMRU and Official Solicitor

4.1 Cafcass, CAFCASS CYMRU and members of the Official Solicitor's legal staff are prepared to discuss cases before proceedings are issued. In all cases in which the urgent and out of hours procedures are to be used it would be helpful if the Official Solicitor, Cafcass or CAFCASS CYMRU have had some advance notice of the application and its circumstances.

4.2 Enquiries about children cases should be directed to the High Court Team Duty Manager at Cafcass National Office, 3rd Floor, 21 Bloomsbury Street, London, WC1B 3HF. DX: Cafcass DX 310101 Bloomsbury 11. Telephone 01753 235273 (Cafcass High Court Team) or 01753 235295 (Cafcass Legal Duty Lawyer). e-mail: HighCourtGM@Cafcassi.gov.uk (office hours only). Enquiries should be marked 'F.A.O. High Court Team' or 'F.A.O. HCT'.

4.3 Enquiries about children cases in Wales should be directed to the Social Care Team, Legal Services, Welsh Assembly Government, Cathays Park, Cardiff CF10 3NQ, telephone 02920 370888, fax 0872 437 7306.

4.4 Medical and welfare cases relating to an adult lacking capacity in relation to their medical treatment or welfare are brought in the Court of Protection. Enquiries about adult medical and welfare cases should be addressed to the Court of Protection Healthcare and Welfare Team, Office of the Official Solicitor, Victory House, 30-34 Kingsway, London, WC2B 6EX, telephone 020 3681 2751, fax 020 3681 2762, email enquiries@offsol.gsi.gov.uk. Reference should also be made to Practice Direction E, accompanying Part 9 of the Court of Protection Rules 2007, and to Practice Direction B accompanying Part 10 of those Rules. Information for parties and practitioners is available on the website of the Ministry of Justice www.justice.gov.uk and general information for members of the public is available on www.direct.gov.uk

Practice Direction 12F – Internation child abduction

See also Part 12, Practice Direction 12A, Practice Direction 12B, Practice Direction 12C, Practice Direction 12D, Practice Direction 12E, Practice Direction 12G, Practice Direction 12H, Practice Direction 12I, Practice Direction 12J, Practice Direction 12K,

Practice Direction 12L, Practice Direction 12M, Practice Direction 12N, Practice Direction 12O, Practice Direction 12P

This Practice Direction supplements FPR Part 12, Chapters 5 and 6

Part 1 Introduction

1.1 This Practice Direction explains what to do if a child has been brought to, or kept in, England and Wales without the permission of anyone who has rights of custody in respect of the child in the country where the child was habitually resident immediately before the removal or retention. It also explains what to do if a child has been taken out of, or kept out of, England and Wales[1]

1.2 If you have rights of custody in respect of a child and the child has been brought to England or Wales without your permission, or has been brought here with your permission but the person your child is staying with is refusing to return the child, then you can apply to the High Court of Justice, which covers all of England and Wales, for an order for the return of the child.

1.3 How you make an application to the High Court, what evidence you need to provide and what orders you should ask the court to make are all explained in this Practice Direction.

1.4 If your child is under 16 years of age and has been brought to England or Wales from a country which is a party (a 'State party') to the 1980 Hague Convention on the Civil Aspects of International Child Abduction ('the 1980 Hague Convention') then you can make an application to the High Court for an order under that Convention for the return of your child to the State in which he or she was habitually resident immediately before being removed or being kept away. This is explained in Part 2 below.

1.5 If your child is over 16 years of age and under 18, or has been brought to England or Wales from a country which is not a State party to the 1980 Hague Convention, then you can make an application for the return of your child under the inherent jurisdiction of the High Court with respect to children. In exercising this jurisdiction over children, the High Court will make your child's welfare its paramount consideration. How to make an application under the inherent jurisdiction of the High Court with respect to children is explained in Part 3 below.

1.6 It might be necessary for you to make an urgent application to the court if you are not sure where your child is, or you think that there is a risk that the person who is keeping your child away from you might take the child out of the United Kingdom or hide them away. Part 4 below explains how to make an urgent application to the High Court for orders to protect your child until a final decision can be made about returning the child and also how to ask for help from the police and government agencies if you think your child might be taken out of the country.

Footnote

1 The child must be taken or kept out of the United Kingdom without the permission of a parent or someone who has rights of custody for it to be an international child abduction. This practice direction relates to the law as it applies in England and Wales. If the child has been taken or kept out of the United Kingdom when the child was habitually resident in Scotland, you should contact the Central Authority for Scotland, Scottish Government Justice Directorate, Civil Law Division, St Andrew's House, Regent Road, Edinburgh EH1 3DG Tel: +44 (0) 131 244 4827/4832 Fax:: +44 (0) 131 244 4848 Website: http://www.gov.scot/Topics/Justice/law/17867/fm-children-root/18533. If the child has been taken or kept out of the United Kingdom when the child was habitually resident in Northern Ireland, you should contact the Central Authority for Northern Ireland, Northern Ireland Courts and Tribunals Service, Civil Policy and Tribunal Reform Division, 3rd Floor Laganside House, 23-27 Oxford Street, Belfast BT1 3LA Tel: + 44 (0)28 9072 8808 or + 44 (0) 28 9072 8819; fax +44

(0) 28 9072 8945. Website: http://www.nics.gov.uk/ or http://www.courtsni.gov.uk/en-GB/Services/ChildAbduction/ without the permission of a parent or someone who has rights of custody in respect of the child. These cases are called 'international child abduction cases' and are dealt with in the High Court. This Practice Direction also explains what to do if you receive legal papers claiming that you have abducted a child. You can find the legal cases which are mentioned in this Practice Direction, and other legal material, on the website http://www.bailii.org/ (British and Irish Legal Information Institute).

Rights of Access

1.7 Rights of access to children (also called contact or visitation) may be enforced in England and Wales. The 1980 Hague Convention expects State parties to comply with orders and agreements concerning access as well as rights of custody. If you have an access order and you want to enforce it in England or Wales, you should read Part 5 below.

Part 2 Hague Convention Cases

2.1 States which are party to the 1980 Hague Convention have agreed to return children who have been either wrongfully removed from, or wrongfully retained away from, the State where they were habitually resident immediately before the wrongful removal or retention. There are very limited exceptions to this obligation.

2.2 'Wrongfully removed' or 'wrongfully retained' means removed or retained in breach of rights of custody in respect of the child attributed to a person or a body or an institution. 'Rights of custody' are interpreted very widely (see paragraph 2.16 below).

2.3 The text of the 1980 Hague Convention and a list of Contracting States (that is, State parties) can be found on the website of the Hague Conference on Private International Law at http://www.hcch.net. All Member States of the European Union are State parties to the 1980 Hague Convention, and all but Denmark are bound by an EU Regulation which supplements the operation of the 1980 Hague Convention between the Member States of the EU (Council Regulation (EC) No 2201/2003, see paragraph 2.6).

2.4 In each State party there is a body called the Central Authority whose duty is to help people use the 1980 Hague Convention.

2.5 If you think that your child has been brought to, or kept in, England or Wales, and your State is a State party to the 1980 Hague Convention, then you should get in touch with your own Central Authority who will help you to send an application for the return of your child to the Central Authority for England and Wales. However, you are not obliged to contact your own Central Authority. You may contact the Central Authority for England and Wales directly, or you may simply instruct lawyers in England or Wales to make an application for you. The advantage of making your application through the Central Authority for England and Wales if you are applying from outside the United Kingdom is that you will get public funding ('legal aid') to make your application, regardless of your financial resources.

The Central Authority for England and Wales

2.6 The Child Abduction and Custody Act 1985 brings the 1980 Hague Convention into the law of England and Wales and identifies the Lord Chancellor as the Central Authority. His duties as the Central Authority are carried out by the International Child Abduction and Contact Unit (ICACU). ICACU also carries out the duties of the Central Authority for the European Convention on Recognition and Enforcement of Decisions concerning Custody of Children signed at Luxembourg on 20 May 1980 (called 'the European Convention' in this Practice Direction but sometimes also referred to as 'the Luxembourg Convention').

2.7 ICACU is open Mondays to Fridays from 9.00 a.m. to 5.00 p.m. It is located in the Office of the Official Solicitor and Public Trustee and its contact details are as follows:

International Child Abduction and Contact Unit
Office of the Official Solicitor
Victory House
30-34 Kingsway
London
WC2B 6EX
Email: ICACU@offsol.gsi.gov.uk
Tel: + 44 (20) 3681 2608 (10.00am to 4.00pm)
Fax: +44 (20) 3681 2763

In an emergency (including out of normal working hours) contact should be made with the Royal Courts of Justice on one of the following telephone numbers:
+ 44 (0)20 7947 6000, or
+ 44 (0) 20 7947 6260

In addition, in an emergency or outside normal working hours advice on international child abduction can be sought from reunite International Child Abduction Centre on + 44 (0)1162 556 234. Outside office hours you will be directed to the 24hour emergency service. You can also see information on reunite's website http://www.reunite.org/.

What ICACU Will Do

2.8 When ICACU receives your application for the return of your child, unless you already have a legal representative in England and Wales whom you want to act for you, it will send your application to a solicitor whom it knows to be experienced in international child abduction cases and ask them to take the case for you. You will then be the solicitor's client and the solicitor will make an application for public funding to meet your legal costs. The solicitor will then apply to the High Court for an order for the return of your child.

2.9 You can find out more about ICACU and about the 1980 Hague Convention and the other international instruments mentioned at paragraph 2.6 on two websites: Information for parties and practitioners is available on http://www.justice.gov.uk and general information for members of the public is available on www.gov.uk.

Applying to the High Court – the Form and Content of Application

2.10 An application to the High Court for an order under the 1980 Hague Convention must be made in the Principal Registry of the Family Division in Form C67.

2.11 The application must include –

(a) the names and dates of birth of the children;
(b) the names of the children's parents or guardians;
(c) the whereabouts or suspected whereabouts of the children;
(d) the interest of the applicant in the matter (e.g. mother, father, or person with whom the child lives and details of any order placing the child with that person);
(e) the reasons for the application;
(f) details of any proceedings (including proceedings not in England or Wales, and including any legal proceedings which have finished) relating to the children;
(g) where the application is for the return of a child, the identity of the person alleged to have removed or retained the child and, if different, the identity of the person with whom the child is thought to be.

2.12 The application should be accompanied by all relevant documents including (but not limited to) –

(a) an authenticated copy of any relevant decision or agreement;
(b) a certificate or an affidavit from a Central Authority, or other competent authority of the State of the child's habitual residence, or from a qualified person, concerning the relevant law of that State.

2.13 As the applicant you may also file a statement in support of the application, although usually your solicitor will make and file a statement for you on your instructions. The statement must contain and be verified by a statement of truth in the following terms:

> 'I make this statement knowing that it will be placed before the court, and I confirm that to the best of my knowledge and belief its contents are true.'

(Further provisions about statements of truth are contained in Part 17 of these Rules and in Practice Direction 17A.).

The Timetable for the Case

2.14 The following procedural steps are intended to ensure that applications under the 1980 Hague Convention are handled quickly –

(a) the application must be headed 'in the matter of the Child Abduction and Custody Act 1985';
(b) the court file will be marked to –
    (i) draw attention to the nature of the application; and
    (ii) state the date on which the 6 week period will expire (the 'hear-by date');
(c) listing priority will, where necessary, be given to such applications;
(d) the trial judge will expedite the transcript of the judgment and its approval and ensure that it is sent to the Central Authority without delay.

Applications for Declarations

2.15 If a child has been taken from England and Wales to another State party, the judicial or administrative authorities of that State may ask for a declaration that the removal or retention of the child was wrongful. Or it might be thought that a declaration from the High Court that a child has been wrongfully removed or retained away from the United Kingdom would be helpful in securing his return. The High Court can make such declarations under section 8 of the Child Abduction and Custody Act 1985. An application for a declaration is made in the same way as an application for a return order, the only difference being that the details of relevant legal proceedings in respect of which the declaration is sought (if any), including a copy of any order made relating to the application, should be included in the documentation.

Rights of Custody

2.16 'Rights of custody' includes rights relating to the care of the person of the child and, in particular, the right to determine the child's place of residence. Rights of custody may arise by operation of law (that is, they are conferred on someone automatically by the legal system in which they are living) or by a judicial or administrative decision or as a result of an agreement having legal effect. The rights of a person, an institution or any other body are a matter for the law of the State of the child's habitual residence, but it is for the State which is being asked to return the child to decide: if those rights amount to rights of custody for the purposes of the 1980 Hague Convention; whether at the time of the removal or retention those rights were actually being exercised; and whether there has been a breach of those rights.

2.17 In England and Wales a father who is not married to the mother of their child does not necessarily have 'rights of custody' in respect of the child. An unmarried father in

England and Wales who has parental responsibility for a child has rights of custody in respect of that child. In the case of an unmarried father without parental responsibility, the concept of rights of custody may include more than strictly legal rights and where immediately before the removal or retention of the child he was exercising parental functions over a substantial period of time as the only or main carer for the child he may have rights of custody. An unmarried father can ask ICACU or his legal representative for advice on this. It is important to remember that it will be for the State which is being asked to return the child to decide if the father's circumstances meet that State's requirements for the establishment of rights of custody.

2.18 Sometimes, court orders impose restrictions on the removal of children from the country in which they are living. These can be orders under the Children Act 1989 ('section 8' orders) or orders under the inherent jurisdiction of the High Court (sometimes called 'injunctions'). Any removal of a child in breach of an order imposing such a restriction would be wrongful under the 1980 Hague Convention.

2.19 The fact that court proceedings are in progress about a child does not of itself give rise to a prohibition on the removal of the child by a mother with sole parental responsibility from the country in which the proceedings are taking place unless:

(a) the proceedings are Wardship proceedings in England and Wales (in which case removal would breach the rights of custody attributed to the High Court and fathers with no custody rights could rely on that breach); or

(b) the court is actually considering the custody of the child, because then the court itself would have rights of custody.

Particular provisions for European Convention applications

2.20 The European Convention provides for the mutual recognition and enforcement of decisions relating to custody and access, so if a child has been brought here or retained here in breach of a custody order, then that order can be enforced. If you want to make an application under the European Convention, then you make it in the same way as is described in paragraphs 2.10 and 2.11 above, but in addition you must include a copy of the decision relating to custody (or rights of access – see paragraph 5.1 below) which you are seeking to register or enforce, or about which you are seeking a declaration by the court.

Defending Abduction Proceedings

2.21 If you are served with an application – whether it is under the 1980 Hague or the European Convention or the inherent jurisdiction of the High Court – you must not delay. You must obey any directions given in any order with which you have been served, and you should seek legal advice at the earliest possible opportunity, although neither you nor the child concerned will automatically be entitled to legal aid.

2.22 It is particularly important that you tell the court where the child is, because the child will not be permitted to live anywhere else without the permission of the court, or to leave England and Wales, until the proceedings are finished.

2.23 It is also particularly important that you present to the court any defence to the application which you or the child might want to make at the earliest possible opportunity, although the orders with which you will have been served are likely to tell you the time by which you will have to do this.

2.24 If the child concerned objects to any order sought in relation to them, and if the child is of an age and understanding at which the court will take account of their views, the court is likely to direct that the child is seen by an officer of the Children and Family

Court Advisory and Support Service (Cafcass) or in Wales CAFCASS CYMRU. You should cooperate in this process. Children are not usually made parties to abduction cases, but in certain exceptional circumstances the court can make them parties so that they have their own separate legal representation. These are all matters about which you should seek legal advice.

(Provisions about the power of the court to join parties are contained in rule 12.3 and provisions about the joining and representation of children are contained in Part 16 of these Rules and the Practice Direction 16A (Representation of Children.).

Part 3 Non-Convention Cases

3.1 Applications for the return of children wrongfully removed or retained away from States which are not parties to the 1980 Hague Convention or in respect of children to whom that Convention does not apply, can be made to the High Court under its inherent jurisdiction with respect to children. Such proceedings are referred to as 'non-Convention' cases. In proceedings under the inherent jurisdiction of the High Court with respect to children, the child's welfare is the court's paramount consideration. The extent of the court's enquiry into the child's welfare will depend on the circumstances of the case; in some cases the child's welfare will be best served by a summary hearing and, if necessary, a prompt return to the State from which the child has been removed or retained. In other cases a more detailed enquiry may be necessary (see Re J (Child Returned Abroad: Convention Rights) [2005] UKHL 40; [2005] 2 FLR 802).

3.2 Every application for the return of a child under the inherent jurisdiction must be made in the Principal Registry of the Family Division and heard in the High Court.

Provision about the inherent jurisdiction is made at Chapter 5 of Part 12 of the Rules and in Practice Direction 12D (Inherent Jurisdiction (including Wardship) Proceedings).

The Form and content of the application

3.3 An application for the return of a child under the inherent jurisdiction must be made in Form C66 and must include the information in paragraph 2.11 above.

3.4 You must file a statement in support of your application, which must exhibit all the relevant documents. The statement must contain and be verified by a statement of truth in the following terms:

> 'I make this statement knowing that it will be placed before the court, and I confirm that to the best of my knowledge and belief its contents are true.'

> (Further provisions about statements of truth are contained in Part 17 of these Rules and Practice Direction 17A.).

Timetable for Non-Convention Cases

3.5 While the 6 week deadline referred to in paragraph 2.14 is set out in the 1980 Hague Convention, non-Convention child abduction cases must similarly be completed in 6 weeks except where exceptional circumstances make this impossible. Paragraph 2.14 applies to these cases as appropriate for a non-Convention case.

Part 4 General Provisions

Urgent applications, or applications out of business hours

4.1 Guidance about urgent and out of hours applications is in Practice Direction 12E (Urgent Business).

Challenging a return order or non-return order

4.1A If you are a party to a return case and you believe that the court has made an error, it is possible to apply for permission to appeal (see Part 30 of the Rules and Practice Direction 30A).

In rare circumstances, the court might also 'set aside' its own order where it has not made an error but where new information comes to light which fundamentally changes the basis on which the order was made. The threshold for the court to set aside its decision is high, and evidence will be required – not just assertions or allegations.

If the return order or non-return order was made under the 1980 Hague Convention, the court might set aside its decision where there has been fraud, material non-disclosure or mistake (which all essentially mean that there was information that the court needed to know in order to make its decision, but was not told), or where there has been a fundamental change in circumstances which undermines the basis on which the order was made. If you have evidence of such circumstances and wish to apply to the court to set aside its decision, you should use the procedure in Part 18 of the Rules.

If the return order or non-return order was made under the inherent jurisdiction (see Part 3 of this Practice Direction), the court might set aside its decision for similar reasons as with return-non-return orders under the 1980 Hague Convention, but it also might set aside its decision because the welfare of the child or children requires it. If you have evidence of such circumstances and wish to apply to the court to set aside its decision, you should use the procedure in Part 18 of the Rules.

Any such application should be made promptly and the court will also aim to deal with the application as expeditiously as possible.

4.1B If the court has ordered the immediate implementation of the return order and you wish to apply for permission to appeal that return order or for that order to be set aside, you should also consider an application to the court for a 'stay' of the return order, or stop it being implemented.

Police assistance to prevent removal from England and Wales

4.2 The Child Abduction Act 1984 sets out the circumstances in which the removal of a child from this jurisdiction is a criminal offence. The police provide the following 24 hour service to prevent the unlawful removal of a child –

(a) they inform ports directly when there is a real and imminent threat that a child is about to be removed unlawfully from the country; and
(b) they liaise with Immigration Officers at the ports in an attempt to identify children at risk of removal.

4.3 Where the child is under 16, it is not necessary to obtain a court order before seeking police assistance. The police do not need an order to act to protect the child. If an order has already been obtained it should however be produced to the police. Where the child is between 16 and 18, an order must be obtained restricting or restraining removal before seeking police assistance.

4.4 Where the child is a ward of court (see Practice Direction 12D (Inherent Jurisdiction (including Wardship) Proceedings) the court's permission is needed to remove that child from the jurisdiction. When the court has not given that permission and police assistance is sought to prevent the removal of the ward, the applicant must produce evidence that the child is a ward such as –

(a) an order confirming wardship;
(b) an injunction; or

(c) where the matter is urgent and no order has been made, a certified copy of the wardship application.

4.5 The application for police assistance must be made by the applicant or his legal representative to the applicant's local police station except that applications may be made to any police station –

(a) in urgent cases;
(b) where the wardship application has just been issued; or
(c) where the court has just made the order relied on.

4.6 The police will, if they consider it appropriate, institute the 'port alert' system (otherwise known as 'an all ports warning') to try to prevent removal from the jurisdiction where the danger of removal is –

(a) real (i.e., not being sought merely by way of insurance); and
(b) imminent (i.e. within 24 to 48 hours).

4.7 The request for police assistance must be accompanied by as much of the following information as possible –

(a) the child: the name, sex, date of birth, physical description, nationality and passport number; if the child has more than one nationality or passport, provide details;
(b) the person likely to remove: the name, age, physical description, nationality, passport number, relationship to the child, and whether the child is likely to assist him or her; if the person has more than one nationality or passport, provide details;
(c) person applying for a port alert: the name, relationship to the child, nationality, telephone number and (if appropriate) solicitor's or other legal representative's name and contact details; if the person has more than one nationality, provide details;
(d) likely destination;
(e) likely time of travel and port of embarkation and, if known, details of travel arrangements;
(f) grounds for port alert (as appropriate) –
  (i) suspected offence under section 1 or section 2 of the Child Abduction Act 1984;
  (ii) the child is subject to a court order.
(g) details of person to whom the child should be returned if intercepted.

4.8 If the police decide that the case is one in which the port-alert system should be used, the child's name will remain on the stop list for four weeks. After that time it will be removed automatically unless a further application is made.

HM Passport Office

4.9 Where the court makes an order prohibiting or otherwise restricting the removal of a child from the United Kingdom, or from any specified part of it, or from a specified dependent territory, the court may make an order under section 37 of the Family Law Act 1986 requiring any person to surrender any UK passport which has been issued to, or contains particulars of, the child.

4.10 HM Passport Office ('HMPO') will take action to prevent a United Kingdom passport or replacement passport being issued only where HMPO has been served with a court order expressly requiring a United Kingdom passport to be surrendered, or expressly prohibiting the issue of any further United Kingdom passport facilities to the child without the consent of the court, or the holder of such an order. Accordingly, in every case in which such an order has been made, HMPO must be served the same day if possible, or at the latest the following day, with a copy of the order. It is the responsibility of the applicant to do this. The specimen form of letter set out below should be used and a copy of the court order must be attached to the letter. Delay in sending the letter to HMPO must be kept to an absolute minimum.

'Intelligence Hub
Her Majesty's Passport Office
3 Northgate
96 Milton Street
Glasgow
G4 0BT

Dear Sir/Madam

… ………………v …… ………………

Case no: … … …… …… … … ….

This is to inform you that the court has today made an order

*prohibiting the issue of a passport/passports to [name(s)] [date of birth (if known)] of [address] without the consent of the holder of the order.

*requiring [name(s)] [date of birth (if known)] of [address] to surrender the passport(s) issued to him/her/them/the following child[ren] / or which contain(s) particulars of the following child[ren]:

Name Date of Birth

*and has granted an injunction/*made an order restraining the removal of the child[ren] from the jurisdiction.

(*Delete as appropriate)

Please add these names to your records to prevent the issue of further passport facilities for the child[ren]. I enclose a copy of the court order.

Yours faithfully

Applicant's name / Applicant's Solicitor's name'

4.11 Following service on HMPO of an order either expressly requiring a United Kingdom passport to be surrendered by, or expressly prohibiting the issue of any further United Kingdom passport facilities to the child, HMPO will maintain a prohibition on issuing a passport, or further passport facilities until the child's 16th birthday. The order should state that a passport must not be granted/applied for without the consent of the court or the holder of the order.

Note: These requests may also be sent to any of the regional Passport Offices.

4.12 Omitted

4.13 Information about other circumstances, in which HMPO will agree not to issue a passport to a child if HMPO receives an application, or an order in more general terms than set out at 4.11 above, from a person who claims to have parental responsibility for the child, is available from HMPO or at www.gov.uk.

The Home Office

4.14 Information about communicating with the Home Office, where a question of the immigration status of a party arises in family proceedings, may be found in the Protocol:

Communicating with UK Visas and Immigration (UKVI) in Family Proceedings (revised and reissued May 2018). Annex 1 to this Practice Direction contains that Protocol and Annex 2 contains the current version (as at May 2018) of the relevant court form.

Press Reporting

4.15 When a child has been abducted and a judge considers that publicity may help in tracing the child, the judge may adjourn the case for a short period to enable representatives of the Press to attend to give the case the widest possible publicity.

4.16 If a Child Rescue Alert has been used concerning a child, within the UK or abroad, it will give rise to media publicity. The court should be informed that this has happened. If there are already court proceedings concerning a child, it is advisable to obtain the agreement of the court before there is publicity to trace a missing child. If the court has not given its permission for a child who is the subject of children proceedings to be identified as the subject of proceedings, to do so would be contempt of court.

Other Assistance

4.17 The Missing Persons Bureau will be participating for the UK in the European Union wide 116 000 hotline for missing children. Parents and children can ring this number for assistance. (It is primarily intended to deal with criminal matters, for example stranger kidnapping.)

4.18 It may also be possible to trace a child by obtaining a court order under the inherent jurisdiction or the wardship jurisdiction of the High Court addressed to certain government departments, as set out in Practice Direction 6C.

Part 5 – Omitted

Part 6 Child abduction cases between the United Kingdom and Pakistan

6.1 A consensus was reached in January 2003 between the President of the Family Division and the Hon. Chief Justice of Pakistan as to the principles to be applied in resolving child abduction cases between the UK and Pakistan.

The Protocol setting out that consensus can be accessed at: http://www.fco.gov.uk/resources/en/pdf/2855621/3069133

Annex 1

Communicating with the Home Office in Family Proceedings

Protocol agreed between the President of the Family Division and the Home Office issued on 16 May 2018

1 This Protocol enables the family courts (the Family Division of the High Court of Justice and the Family Court) to communicate with UK VISAS AND IMMIGRATION (UKVI), the relevant division of the Home Office, to obtain immigration and visa information for use in family court proceedings. Although it replaces and supersedes the previous guidance issued in 2002, 2004, 2006, 2010 and 2014, in particular to reflect new UKVI processes and contact details, it does not alter the nature or purpose of the Protocol.

2 There are three parts of the process:

(1) HMCTS form EX660 (rev 04/18), a copy of which is annexed to this Protocol, must be completed by the parties and approved by the judge.

(a) The EX660 must be typed, not handwritten.

(b) The EX660 must be completed in full, specifying the details of the relevant family members and their relationship to the child(ren). Details of both mother and father/adoptive parents if known should be provided, whether or not they are involved in the proceedings, as this enables UKVI to trace the child(ren)'s records.

(c) The EX660 and the order must specify the questions the court wishes to be answered by UKVI.

(d) The EX660 must contain the name and contact details of someone who has agreed and is able to provide further information if needed.

(e) The EX660 must clearly state the time by which the information is required.

Failure to do this may cause delay in the time it takes UKVI to process the request.

(2) An order in the relevant form, a copy of which is annexed to this Protocol, must be drawn up, approved by the judge and sealed by the court.

(a) The order must clearly state the time by which the information is required.

(b) The order must specify any additional information or documents, such as a synopsis, which it wishes UKVI to have and set out in the order that the leave of the court to make disclosure to UKVI has been given. (Note that it may be a contempt of court to disclose this information otherwise.)

(3) The UKVI SVEC pro-forma must be completed by the court staff utilising the information in the EX660 and the order.

(a) All relevant fields in the SVEC pro-forma must be completed:
   - i. Section A – All fields to be completed if known
   - ii. Section B – Enquiry Type – Select Standard
   - iii. Section C – Select Subject 1 and complete all fields.
   - iv. Section D – Enter 'Y' in 'Other' field only.
   - v. Section E – Enter 'Please refer to court order and EX660'.
   - vi. For more than one subject, select subject 2 and so on, completing steps C-E for each one.

(b) In Section B there are two fields, 'Court date' and 'required date', which must be completed. In both fields the date the information is required should be entered, not the court date. These fields generate the target date on UKVI systems and, as the information ordered by the court will be required before the date of the court hearing, this will ensure that the information is provided in time.

3 The EX660 and the order must contain sufficient information to enable UKVI to understand the nature of the case, to identify whether the case involves an adoption, and to identify whether the immigration issues raised relate to an asylum or a non- asylum application.

4 In order to comply with the agreed four (4) week period for UKVI to provide a response to the court, the sealed order should be available to be sent by the court staff to UKVI on the same day that the order is made. Where that is not possible, the court, when stating the required date of receipt by the court of the information requested, must allow any additional time necessary for the preparation, sealing and sending of the order. This is to ensure that UKVI has four (4) weeks to provide a response from the time it receives the order.

5 The sealed order, completed EX660 and SVEC pro-forma should be sent immediately by the court to ICESSVECWorkflow@homeoffice.gsi.gov.uk including EEREQUEST on the subject line of the email. The request for information will be rejected by UKVI if either the sealed order or the SVEC pro-forma is not provided.

6 Where the court wishes to progress a case that may be delayed, it may send an email to SVECManagement@homeoffice.gsi.gov.uk

7 The UKVI official will be personally responsible for either:

(i) answering the query themselves, by retrieving the file and preparing a statement for the court; or
(ii) forwarding to a caseworker or relevant official with carriage of the particular file.

8 UKVI will ensure that their information is received by the court in time, as instructed by the judge or court making the request.

Annex 2

Court request for information to the Home Office

Annex 2

Court request for information to the Home Office

UK Visas & Immigration (UKVI)

Please note that information provided in this form will be forwarded to the Home Office

Name of court	
Case no.	
Serial no.	
Date	

In the matter of the Act

In the matter of

To the judge: Each of the following fields must be completed to assist the Home Office find the relevant records. Once completed pass the form to your Court Clerk. The Court Clerk will then produce a separate order directed to the Home Office and using the information provided on this form, complete the Home Office application form SVEC.

Name of Judge:

Full name of each party, including relationship to child(ren)	Female/Male (please tick)	Date of birth	Country of origin	Date arrived in UK:	All relevant Home Office reference no's:
	☐ Female ☐ Male				
	☐ Female ☐ Male				
	☐ Female ☐ Male				
	☐ Female ☐ Male				
	☐ Female ☐ Male				

	☐ Female ☐ Male			

What questions would you like the UKVI to answer?	
Please provide a brief summary of case and any other information which will be useful to the UKVI in dealing with the request e.g. any details relating to immigration: (Please attach any documents, such as Case Summaries, in respect of which the Court has given leave to disclose to the Home Office).	

Has the court in the order given leave to disclose any supporting documentation to the Home Office?	☐ Yes ☐ No
Contact details of person from whom additional information can be sought:	
By what date is the information required? (Please allow a minimum of 4 weeks from the date of sending to the Home Office Liaison Team)	

Annex 3

See paragraph 5.5

Practice Note

5 March 1993
Citations: [1993] 1 FLR 804

Child Abduction Unit: Lord Chancellor's Department

Duties of the Central Authority for England and Wales under Article 21 of the Hague Convention on the Civil Aspects of International Child Abduction

Child Abduction and Custody Act 1985

In the case of Re G (A Minor) (Hague Convention: Access) [1993] 1 FLR 669 the Court of Appeal considered the duties of the Central Authority for England and Wales on receiving an application in respect of rights of access under Art 21 of the Hague Convention.

The Court of Appeal took the view that Art 21 conferred no jurisdiction to determine matters relating to access, or to recognise or enforce foreign access orders. It provides, however, for executive co-operation in the enforcement of such recognition as national law allows.

Accordingly, the duty of the Central Authority is to make appropriate arrangements for the applicant by providing solicitors to act on his behalf in applying for legal aid and instituting proceedings in the High Court under s 8 of the Children Act 1989.

If, during the course of proceedings under Art 21 of the Convention, the applicant decides to seek access instead of the return of the child, but no agreement can be reached and the provisions of the European Convention on the Recognition and Enforcement of Decisions Concerning Custody of Children and on Restoration of Custody of Children are not available, a separate application under s 8 of the Children Act 1989 will have to be made.

Central Authority for England and Wales

NOTE: The Child Abduction Unit is now called ICACU, see paragraph 2.6.

Practice Direction 12G – Communication of information

See also Part 12, Practice Direction 12A, Practice Direction 12B, Practice Direction 12C, Practice Direction 12D, Practice Direction 12E, Practice Direction 12F, Practice Direction 12H, Practice Direction 12I, Practice Direction 12J, Practice Direction 12K, Practice Direction 12L, Practice Direction 12M, Practice Direction 12N, Practice Direction 12O, Practice Direction 12P

This Practice Direction supplements FPR Part 12, Chapter 7

1.1 Chapter 7 deals with the communication of information (whether or not contained in a document filed with the court) relating to proceedings which relate to children.

1.2 Subject to any direction of the court, information may be communicated for the purposes of the law relating to contempt in accordance with paragraphs 2.1, 3.1 or 4.1.

Communication of information by a party etc. for other purposes

2.1 A person specified in the first column of the following table may communicate to a person listed in the second column such information as is specified in the third column for the purpose or purposes specified in the fourth column

A party	A lay adviser, a McKenzie Friend, or a person arranging or providing pro bono legal services	Any information relating to the proceedings	To enable the party to obtain advice or assistance in relation to the proceedings
A party	A health care professional or a person or body providing counselling services for children or families		To enable the party or any child of the party to obtain health care or counselling
A party	The Child Maintenance and Enforcement Commission, a McKenzie Friend, a lay adviser or the First-tier Tribunal dealing with an appeal made under section 20 of the Child Support Act 1991		For the purposes of making or responding to an appeal under section 20 of the Child Support Act 1991 or the determination of such an appeal
A party or other person lawfully in receipt of information	The Secretary of State, a McKenzie Friend, a lay adviser or the Upper Tier Tribunal dealing with an appeal under section 24 of the Child Support Act 1991 in respect of a decision of the First tier Tribunal that was made under section 20 of that Act		For a purpose connected with an appeal under section 24 of the Child Support Act 1991 in respect of a decision of the First-tier Tribunal that was made under section 20 of that Act
A party	An adoption panel		To enable the adoption panel to discharge its functions as appropriate
A party	A local authority's medical adviser appointed under the Adoption Agencies Regulations 2005 or the Adoption Agencies (Wales) Regulations 2005		To enable the medical adviser to discharge his or her functions as appropriate
A party	The European Court of Human Rights		For the purpose of making an application to the European Court of Human Rights

A party or any person lawfully in receipt of information	The Children's Commissioner or the Children's Commissioner for Wales		To refer an issue affecting the interests of children to the Children's Commissioner or the Children's Commissioner for Wales
A party or any person lawfully in receipt of information	The Welsh Language Commissioner		To refer an issue so that the Welsh Language Commissioner can consider whether to institute or intervene in legal proceedings or to assist a party or prospective party to legal proceedings.
A party, any person lawfully in receipt of information or a proper officer	A person or body conducting an approved research project		For the purpose of an approved research project
A legal representative or a professional legal adviser	A professional indemnity insurer		To enable the professional indemnity insurer to be notified of a claim or complaint, or potential claim or complaint, in relation to the legal representative or a professional legal adviser, and the legal representative or professional legal adviser to obtain advice in respect of that claim or complaint
A legal representative or a professional legal adviser	A person or body responsible for investigating or determining complaints in relation to legal representatives or professional legal advisers		For the purposes of the investigation or determination of a complaint in relation to a legal representative or a professional legal adviser
A legal representative or a professional legal adviser	A person or body assessing quality assurance systems		To enable the legal representative or professional legal adviser to obtain a quality assurance assessment

A legal representative or a professional legal adviser	An accreditation body	Any information relating to the proceedings providing that it does not, or is not likely to, identify any person involved in the proceedings	To enable the legal representative or professional legal adviser to obtain accreditation
A party	A police officer	The text or summary of the whole or part of a judgment given in the proceedings	For the purpose of a criminal investigation
A party or any person lawfully in receipt of information	A member of the Crown Prosecution Service		To enable the Crown Prosecution Service to discharge its functions under any enactment
A party or an adoption agency	An adoption agency	Any information relating to the proceedings	To enable the sharing of relevant information between adoption agencies for more effective undertaking of their functions

Communication for the effective functioning of Cafcass and CAFCASS CYMRU

3.1 An officer of the Service or a Welsh family proceedings officer, as appropriate, may communicate to a person listed in the second column such information as is specified in the third column for the purpose or purposes specified in the fourth column –

A Welsh family proceedings officer	A person or body exercising statutory functions relating to inspection of CAFCASS Cymru	Any information relating to the proceedings which is required by the person or body responsible for the inspection	For the purpose of an inspection of CAFCASS Cymru by a body or person appointed by the Welsh Ministers

An officer of the Service or a Welsh family proceedings officer	The Health and Care Professions Council or the Care Council for Wales	Any information relating to the proceedings providing that it does not, or is not likely to, identify any person involved in the proceedings	For the purpose of initial and continuing accreditation as a social worker of a person providing services to Cafcass or CAFCASS Cymru in accordance with section 13(2) of the Criminal Justice and Courts Services Act 2000 or section 36 of the Children Act 2004 as the case may be
An officer of the Service or a Welsh family proceedings officer	A person or body providing services relating to professional development or training to Cafcass or CAFCASS Cymru	Any information relating to the proceedings providing that it does not, or is not likely to, identify any person involved in the proceedings without that person's consent	To enable the person or body to provide the services, where the services cannot be effectively provided without such disclosure
An officer of the Service or a Welsh family proceedings officer	A person employed by or contracted to Cafcass or CAFCASS Cymru for the purposes of carrying out the functions referred to in column 4 of this row	Any information relating to the proceedings	Engagement in processes internal to Cafcass or CAFCASS Cymru which relate to the maintenance of necessary records concerning the proceedings, or to ensuring that Cafcass or CAFCASS Cymru functions are carried out to a satisfactory standard

Communication to and by Ministers of the Crown and Welsh Ministers

4.1 A person specified in the first column of the following table may communicate to a person listed in the second column such information as is specified in the third column for the purpose or purposes specified in the fourth column –

A party or any person lawfully in receipt of information relating to the proceedings	A Minister of the Crown with responsibility for a government department engaged, or potentially engaged, in an application before the European Court of Human Rights relating to the proceedings	Any information relating to the proceedings of which he or she is in lawful possession	To provide the department with information relevant, or potentially relevant, to the proceedings before the European Court of Human Rights

A Minister of the Crown	The European Court of Human Rights		For the purpose of engagement in an application before the European Court of Human Rights relating to the proceedings
A Minister of the Crown	Lawyers advising or representing the United Kingdom in an application before the European Court of Human Rights relating to the proceedings		For the purpose of receiving advice or for effective representation in relation to the application before the European Court of Human Rights
A Minister of the crown or a Welsh Minister	Another Minister, or Ministers, of the Crown or a Welsh Minister		For the purpose of notification, discussion and the giving or receiving of advice regarding issues raised by the information in which the relevant departments have, or may have, an interest

5.1 This paragraph applies to communications made in accordance with paragraphs 2.1, 3.1 and 4.1 and the reference in this paragraph to 'the table' means the table in the relevant paragraph.

5.2 A person in the second column of the table may only communicate information relating to the proceedings received from a person in the first column for the purpose or purposes –

(a) for which he or she received that information; or
(b) of professional development or training, providing that any communication does not, or is not likely to, identify any person involved in the proceedings without that person's consent.

6.1 In this Practice Direction –

'accreditation body' means –

(a) The Law Society,
(b) Resolution, or
(c) the Lord Chancellor in exercise of the Lord Chancellor's functions in relation to legal aid;

'adoption panel' means a panel established in accordance with regulation 3 of the Adoption Agencies Regulations 2005 or regulation 3 of the Adoption Agencies (Wales) Regulations 2005;

'approved research project' means a project of research-

(a) approved in writing by a Secretary of State after consultation with the President of the Family Division,
(b) approved in writing by the President of the Family Division, or
(c) conducted under section 83 of the Act of 1989 or section 13 of the Criminal Justice and Court Services Act 2000;

'body assessing quality assurance systems' includes –

(a) The Law Society,
(b) the Lord Chancellor in exercise of the Lord Chancellor's functions in relation to legal aid, or
(c) The General Council of the Bar;

'body or person responsible for investigating or determining complaints in relation to legal representatives or professional legal advisers' means –

(a) The Law Society,
(b) The General Council of the Bar,
(c) The Institute of Legal Executives,
(d) The Legal Services Ombudsman; or
(e) The Office of Legal Complaints.

'Cafcass' has the meaning assigned to it by section 11 of the Criminal Justice and Courts Services Act 2000;

'CAFCASS CYMRU' means the part of the Welsh Assembly Government exercising the functions of Welsh Ministers under Part 4 of the Children Act 2004;

'criminal investigation' means an investigation conducted by police officers with a view to it being ascertained –

(a) whether a person should be charged with an offence, or
(b) whether a person charged with an offence is guilty of it;

'health care professional' means –

(a) a registered medical practitioner,
(b) a registered nurse or midwife,
(c) a clinical psychologist, or
(d) a child psychotherapist;

'lay adviser' means a non-professional person who gives lay advice on behalf of an organisation in the lay advice sector;

'McKenzie Friend' means any person permitted by the court to sit beside an unrepresented litigant in court to assist that litigant by prompting, taking notes and giving him advice; and

'social worker' has the meaning assigned to it by section 55 of the Care Standards Act 2000.

Practice Direction 12H – Contribution orders

See also Part 12, Practice Direction 12A, Practice Direction 12B, Practice Direction 12C, Practice Direction 12D, Practice Direction 12E, Practice Direction 12F, Practice Direction 12G, Practice Direction 12I, Practice Direction 12J, Practice Direction 12K, Practice Direction 12L, Practice Direction 12M, Practice Direction 12N, Practice Direction 12O, Practice Direction 12P

This Practice Direction supplements FPR Part 12

1.1 Paragraph 23(6) of Schedule 2 to the 1989 Act provides that where–

(a) a contribution order is in force;
(b) the local authority serve another contribution notice; and
(c) the contributor and the local authority reach an agreement under paragraph 22(7) in respect of that other contribution notice,

the effect of the agreement shall be to discharge the order from the date on which it is agreed that the agreement shall take effect.

1.2 Where a local authority notifies the court of an agreement reached under paragraph 23(6) of Schedule 2 to the 1989 Act, the notification must be sent in writing to the designated officer of the court.

Practice Direction 12I – Applications for reporting restriction orders

See also Part 12, Practice Direction 12A, Practice Direction 12B, Practice Direction 12C, Practice Direction 12D, Practice Direction 12E, Practice Direction 12F, Practice Direction 12G, Practice Direction 12H, Practice Direction 12J, Practice Direction 12K, Practice Direction 12L, Practice Direction 12M, Practice Direction 12N, Practice Direction 12O, Practice Direction 12P

1.1 This direction applies to any application in the Family Division founded on Convention rights for an order restricting publication of information about children or incapacitated adults.

Applications to be heard in the High Court

2.1 Orders can only be made in the High Court and are normally dealt with by a Judge of the Family Division. If the need for an order arises in existing proceedings in the family court, judges should either transfer the application to the High Court or consult their Family Division Liaison Judge. Where the matter is urgent, it can be heard by the Urgent Applications Judge of the Family Division (out of hours contact number 020 7947 6000).

Service of Application on the National News Media

3.1 Section 12(2) of the Human Rights Act 1998 means that an injunction restricting the exercise of the right to freedom of expression must not be granted where the person against whom the application is made is neither present nor represented unless the court is satisfied–

(a) that the applicant has taken all practicable steps to notify the respondent, or
(b) that there are compelling reasons why the respondent should not be notified.

3.2 Service of applications for reporting restriction orders on the national media can now be effected via the Press Association's CopyDirect service, to which national newspapers and broadcasters subscribe as a means of receiving notice of such applications.

3.3 The court will bear in mind that legal advisers to the media–

(i) are used to participating in hearings at very short notice where necessary; and
(ii) are able to differentiate between information provided for legal purposes and information for editorial use.

Service of applications via the CopyDirect service should henceforth be the norm.

3.4 The court retains the power to make without notice orders, but such cases will be exceptional, and an order will always give persons affected liberty to apply to vary or discharge it at short notice.

Further Guidance

4.1 The Practice Note 'Applications for Reporting Restriction Orders' dated 18 March 2005 and issued jointly by the Official Solicitor and the Deputy Director of Legal Services, provides valuable guidance and should be followed.

4.2 Issued with the concurrence and approval of the Lord Chancellor.

Practice Direction 12J – Child arrangements & contact order: domestic violence and harm

See also Part 12, Practice Direction 12A, Practice Direction 12B, Practice Direction 12C, Practice Direction 12D, Practice Direction 12E, Practice Direction 12F, Practice Direction 12G, Practice Direction 12H, Practice Direction 12I, Practice Direction 12K, Practice Direction 12L, Practice Direction 12M, Practice Direction 12N, Practice Direction 12O, Practice Direction 12P

This Practice Direction supplements FPR Part 12, and incorporates and supersedes the President's Guidance in Relation to Split Hearings (May 2010) as it applies to proceedings for child arrangements orders.

Summary

1 This Practice Direction applies to any family proceedings in the Family Court or the High Court under the relevant parts of the Children Act 1989 or the relevant parts of the Adoption and Children Act 2002 in which an application is made for a child arrangements order, or in which any question arises about where a child should live, or about contact between a child and a parent or other family member, where the court considers that an order should be made.

2 The purpose of this Practice Direction is to set out what the Family Court or the High Court is required to do in any case in which it is alleged or admitted, or there is other reason to believe, that the child or a party has experienced domestic abuse perpetrated by another party or that there is a risk of such abuse.

Interpretation

2A In this Practice Direction, 'domestic abuse' has the same meaning as in the 2021 Act. Sections 1 and 2 of the 2021 Act provide that:

'1 Definition of 'domestic abuse'

(1) This section defines 'domestic abuse' for the purposes of this Act.

(2) Behaviour of a person ('A') towards another person ('B') is 'domestic abuse' if—

(a) A and B are each aged 16 or over and are personally connected to each other, and

(b) the behaviour is abusive.

(3) Behaviour is 'abusive' if it consists of any of the following—

(a) physical or sexual abuse;

(b) violent or threatening behaviour;

(c) controlling or coercive behaviour;

(d) economic abuse (see subsection (4));

(e) psychological, emotional or other abuse;

and it does not matter whether the behaviour consists of a single incident or a course of conduct.

(4) 'Economic abuse' means any behaviour that has a substantial adverse effect on B's ability to—

(a) acquire, use or maintain money or other property, or

(b) obtain goods or services.

(5) For the purposes of this Act A's behaviour may be behaviour 'towards' B despite the fact that it consists of conduct directed at another person (for example, B's child).

(6) References in this Act to being abusive towards another person are to be read in accordance with this section.

(7) For the meaning of 'personally connected', see section 2.

2 Definition of 'personally connected'

(1) For the purposes of this Act, two people are 'personally connected' to each other if any of the following applies—

(a) they are, or have been, married to each other;

(b) they are, or have been, civil partners of each other;

(c) they have agreed to marry one another (whether or not the agreement has been terminated);

(d) they have entered into a civil partnership agreement (whether or not the agreement has been terminated);

(e) they are, or have been, in an intimate personal relationship with each other;

(f) they each have, or there has been a time when they each have had, a parental relationship in relation to the same child (see subsection (2));

(g) they are relatives.

(2) For the purposes of subsection (1)(f) a person has a parental relationship in relation to a child if—

(a) the person is a parent of the child, or

(b) the person has parental responsibility for the child.

(3) In this section—

'child' means a person under the age of 18 years;

'civil partnership agreement' has the meaning given by section 73 of the Civil Partnership Act 2004;

'parental responsibility' has the same meaning as in the Children Act 1989 (see section 3 of that Act);

'relative' has the meaning given by section 63(1) of the Family Law Act 1996.

2B For the avoidance of doubt, it should be noted that 'domestic abuse' includes, but is not limited to, forced marriage, honour-based violence, dowry-related abuse and transnational marriage abandonment.

3 For the purpose of this Practice Direction 'the 2021 Act' means the Domestic Abuse Act 2021;

'abandonment' refers to the practice whereby a husband, in England and Wales, deliberately abandons or 'strands' his foreign national wife abroad, usually without financial resources, in order to prevent her from asserting matrimonial and/or residence rights and/or rights in relation to childcare in England and Wales. It may involve children who are either abandoned with, or separated from, their mother;

'coercive behaviour' means an act or a pattern of acts of assault, threats, humiliation and intimidation or other abuse that is used to harm, punish, or frighten the victim;

'controlling behaviour' means an act or pattern of acts designed to make a person subordinate and/or dependent by isolating them from sources of support, exploiting their resources and capacities for personal gain, depriving them of the means needed for independence, resistance and escape and regulating their everyday behaviour;

'development' means physical, intellectual, emotional, social or behavioural development;

'harm' means ill-treatment or the impairment of health or development including, for example, impairment suffered from seeing or hearing the ill-treatment of another, by domestic abuse or otherwise;

'harm' means ill-treatment or the impairment of health or development including, for example, impairment suffered from being a victim of domestic abuse or from seeing or hearing the ill-treatment of another, by domestic abuse or otherwise;

'health' means physical or mental health;

'ill-treatment' includes sexual abuse and forms of ill-treatment which are not physical;

'judge' includes salaried and fee-paid judges and lay justices sitting in the Family Court and, where the context permits, can include a justices' legal adviser in the Family Court; and

'victim of domestic abuse' includes, but is not limited to, a child who is a victim of domestic abuse by virtue of section 3 of the 2021 Act, which provides that-

> '3 Children as victims of domestic abuse
>
> (1) This section applies where behaviour of a person ('A') towards another person ('B') is domestic abuse.
>
> (2) Any reference in this Act to a victim of domestic abuse includes a reference to a child who—
>
> (a) sees or hears, or experiences the effects of, the abuse, and
>
> (b) is related to A or B.
>
> (3) A child is related to a person for the purposes of subsection (2) if—
>
> (a) the person is a parent of, or has parental responsibility for, the child, or
>
> (b) the child and the person are relatives.
>
> (4) In this section— 'child' means a person under the age of 18 years; 'parental responsibility' has the same meaning as in the Children Act 1989 (see section 3 of that Act); 'relative' has the meaning given by section 63(1) of the Family Law Act 1996.'

3A Reference is made at various points in this Practice Direction to making findings of fact in relation to domestic abuse. It should be noted that Part 3A FPR makes provision in relation to victims of domestic abuse in the specific context of participation in proceedings and giving evidence. In that context, it is not necessary for the court to make findings of fact in relation to domestic abuse before assuming that a party or witness is, or is at risk of being, a victim of domestic abuse carried out by a party, relative of another party, or a witness in the proceedings: see rule 3A.2A FPR.

General principles

4 Domestic abuse is harmful to children, and/or puts children at risk of harm, including where they are victims of domestic abuse for example by witnessing one of their parents being violent or abusive to the other parent, or living in a home in which domestic abuse is perpetrated (even if the child is too young to be conscious of the behaviour). Children may suffer direct physical, psychological and/or emotional harm from living with and being victims of domestic abuse, and may also suffer harm indirectly where the domestic abuse impairs the parenting capacity of either or both of their parents.

Orders under section 91(14) of the Children Act 1989

4A.1 Under section 91(14) of the 1989 Act orders are available to prevent a person from making an application under that Act without leave of the court. Section 91(14) leaves a discretion to the court to determine the circumstances in which an order should be made, which may therefore be many and varied. However, section 91A specifies certain circumstances 'among others' in which the court may make an order. These circumstances include where an application would put the child concerned, or another individual at risk of harm. This would include, but not be limited to, a risk of harm arising where an application could be used to carry out or continue domestic abuse. A future application could be part of a pattern of coercive or controlling behaviour or other domestic abuse toward the victim, such that a section 91(14) order is merited due to the risk of harm to the child or other individual.

4A.2 Where allegations of domestic abuse are alleged or proven, the court should consider whether a section 91(14) order might be appropriate even if an application for such an order has not been made. (Section 91A(5) of the 1989 Act specifies who can make an application, and provides that the court can make an order of its own motion.)

4A.3 The court should refer to Practice Direction 12Q for guidance on section 91(14) applications and orders.

5 The court must, at all stages of the proceedings, and specifically at the First Hearing Dispute Resolution Appointment ('FHDRA'), consider whether domestic abuse is raised as an issue, either by the parties or by Cafcass or CAFCASS Cymru or otherwise, and if so must –

- identify at the earliest opportunity (usually at the FHDRA) the factual and welfare issues involved;
- consider the nature of any allegation, admission or evidence of domestic abuse, and the extent to which it would be likely to be relevant in deciding whether to make a child arrangements order and, if so, in what terms;
- give directions to enable contested relevant factual and welfare issues to be tried as soon as possible and fairly;
- ensure that where domestic abuse is admitted or proven, any child arrangements order in place protects the safety and wellbeing of the child and the parent with whom the child is living, and does not expose either of them to the risk of further harm; and
- ensure that any interim child arrangements order (i.e. considered by the court before determination of the facts, and in the absence of admission) is only made having followed the guidance in paragraphs 25–27 below.

In particular, the court must be satisfied that any contact ordered with a parent who has perpetrated domestic abuse does not expose the child and/or other parent to the risk of harm and is in the best interests of the child.

6 In all cases it is for the court to decide whether a child arrangements order accords with Section 1(1) of the Children Act 1989; any proposed child arrangements order, whether to be made by agreement between the parties or otherwise must be carefully scrutinised by the court accordingly. The court must not make a child arrangements order by consent or give permission for an application for a child arrangements order to be withdrawn, unless the parties are present in court, all initial safeguarding checks have been obtained by the court, and an officer of Cafcass or CAFCASS Cymru has spoken to the parties separately, except where it is satisfied that there is no risk of harm to the child and/or the other parent in so doing.

7 In proceedings relating to a child arrangements order, the court presumes that the involvement of a parent in a child's life will further the child's welfare, unless there is evidence to the contrary. The court must in every case consider carefully whether the statutory presumption applies, having particular regard to any allegation or admission of harm by domestic abuse to the child or parent or any evidence indicating such harm or risk of harm.

8 In considering, on an application for a child arrangements order by consent, whether there is any risk of harm to the child, the court must consider all the evidence and information available. The court may direct a report under Section 7 of the Children

Act 1989 to be provided either orally or in writing, before it makes its decision; in such a case, the court must ask for information about any advice given by the officer preparing the report to the parties and whether they, or the child, have been referred to any other agency, including local authority children's services. If the report is not in writing, the court must make a note of its substance on the court file and a summary of the same shall be set out in a Schedule to the relevant order.

Before the FHDRA

9 Where any information provided to the court before the FHDRA or other first hearing (whether as a result of initial safeguarding enquiries by Cafcass or CAFCASS Cymru or on form C1A or otherwise) indicates that there are issues of domestic abuse which may be relevant to the court's determination, the court must ensure that the issues are addressed at the hearing, and that the parties are not expected to engage in conciliation or other forms of dispute resolution which are not suitable and/or safe.

10 If at any stage the court is advised by any party (in the application form, or otherwise), by Cafcass or CAFCASS Cymru or otherwise that there is a need for special arrangements to protect the party or child attending any hearing, the court must ensure so far as practicable that appropriate arrangements are made for the hearing (including the waiting arrangements at court prior to the hearing, and arrangements for entering and exiting the court building) and for all subsequent hearings in the case, unless it is advised and considers that these are no longer necessary. The court should consider Part 3A FPR, in particular the assumption at rule 3A.2A. Where practicable, the court should enquire of the alleged victim of domestic abuse how best she/he wishes to participate.

First hearing/ FHDRA

11 At the FHDRA, if the parties have not been provided with the safeguarding letter/ report by Cafcass/CAFCASS Cymru, the court must inform the parties of the content of any safeguarding letter or report or other information which has been provided by Cafcass or CAFCASS Cymru, unless it considers that to do so would create a risk of harm to a party or the child.

12 Where the results of Cafcass or CAFCASS Cymru safeguarding checks are not available at the FHDRA, and no other reliable safeguarding information is available, the court must adjourn the FHDRA until the results of safeguarding checks are available. The court must not generally make an interim child arrangements order, or orders for contact, in the absence of safeguarding information, unless it is to protect the safety of the child, and/or safeguard the child from harm (see further paragraphs 25–27 below).

13 There is a continuing duty on the Cafcass Officer/Welsh FPO which requires them to provide a risk assessment for the court under section 16A Children Act 1989 if they are given cause to suspect that the child concerned is at risk of harm. Specific provision about service of a risk assessment under section 16A of the 1989 Act is made by rule 12.34 of the FPR 2010.

14 The court must ascertain at the earliest opportunity, and record on the face of its order, whether domestic abuse is raised as an issue which is likely to be relevant to any decision of the court relating to the welfare of the child, and specifically whether the child and/or parent would be at risk of harm in the making of any child arrangements order.

Admissions

15 Where at any hearing an admission of domestic abuse toward another person or the child is made by a party, the admission must be recorded in writing by the judge and set

out as a Schedule to the relevant order. The court office must arrange for a copy of any order containing a record of admissions to be made available as soon as possible to any Cafcass officer or officer of CAFCASS Cymru or local authority officer preparing a report under section 7 of the Children Act 1989.

Directions for a fact-finding hearing

16 The court should determine as soon as possible whether it is necessary to conduct a fact-finding hearing in relation to any disputed allegation of domestic abuse –

(a) in order to provide a factual basis for any welfare report or for assessment of the factors set out in paragraphs 36 and 37 below;
(b) in order to provide a basis for an accurate assessment of risk;
(c) before it can consider any final welfare-based order(s) in relation to child arrangements; or
(d) before it considers the need for a domestic abuse-related Activity (such as a Domestic Violence Perpetrator Programme (DVPP)).

17 In determining whether it is necessary to conduct a fact-finding hearing, the court should consider –

(a) the views of the parties and of Cafcass or CAFCASS Cymru;
(b) whether there are admissions by a party which provide a sufficient factual basis on which to proceed;
(c) if a party is in receipt of legal aid, whether the evidence required to be provided to obtain legal aid provides a sufficient factual basis on which to proceed;
(d) whether there is other evidence available to the court that provides a sufficient factual basis on which to proceed;
(e) whether the factors set out in paragraphs 36 and 37 below can be determined without a fact-finding hearing;
(f) the nature of the evidence required to resolve disputed allegations;
(g) whether the nature and extent of the allegations, if proved, would be relevant to the issue before the court; and
(h) whether a separate fact-finding hearing would be necessary and proportionate in all the circumstances of the case.

18 Where the court determines that a finding of fact hearing is not necessary, the order must record the reasons for that decision.

19 Where the court considers that a fact-finding hearing is necessary, it must give directions as to how the proceedings are to be conducted to ensure that the matters in issue are determined as soon as possible, fairly and proportionately, and within the capabilities of the parties. In particular it should consider –

(a) what are the key facts in dispute;
(b) whether it is necessary for the fact-finding to take place at a separate (and earlier) hearing than the welfare hearing;
(c) whether the key facts in dispute can be contained in a schedule or a table (known as a Scott Schedule) which sets out what the applicant complains of or alleges, what the respondent says in relation to each individual allegation or complaint; the allegations in the schedule should be focused on the factual issues to be tried; and if so, whether it is practicable for this schedule to be completed at the first hearing, with the assistance of the judge;
(d) what evidence is required in order to determine the existence of coercive, controlling or threatening behaviour, or of any other form of domestic abuse;

(e) directing the parties to file written statements giving details of such behaviour and of any response;
(f) whether documents are required from third parties such as the police, health services or domestic abuse support services and giving directions for those documents to be obtained;
(g) whether oral evidence may be required from third parties and if so, giving directions for the filing of written statements from such third parties;
(h) where (for example in cases of abandonment) third parties from whom documents are to be obtained are abroad, how to obtain those documents in good time for the hearing, and who should be responsible for the costs of obtaining those documents;
(i) whether any other evidence is required to enable the court to decide the key issues and giving directions for that evidence to be provided;
(j) what evidence the alleged victim of domestic abuse is able to give and what support the alleged victim may require at the fact-finding hearing in order to give that evidence;
(k) in cases where the alleged victim of domestic abuse is unable for reasons beyond their control to be present at the hearing (for example, abandonment cases where the abandoned spouse remains abroad), what measures should be taken to ensure that that person's best evidence can be put before the court;
(l) what support the alleged perpetrator may need in order to have a reasonable opportunity to challenge the evidence; and
(m) whether a pre-hearing review would be useful prior to the fact-finding hearing to ensure directions have been complied with and all the required evidence is available.

20 Where the court fixes a fact-finding hearing, it must at the same time fix a Dispute Resolution Appointment to follow. Subject to the exception in paragraph 31 below, the hearings should be arranged in such a way that they are conducted by the same judge or, wherever possible, by the same panel of lay justices; where it is not possible to assemble the same panel of justices, the resumed hearing should be listed before at least the same chairperson of the lay justices. Judicial continuity is important.

Reports under Section 7

21(1) Subject to sub-paragraph (3), sub-paragraph (2) applies in any case where-

(a) a child being a victim of domestic abuse; or
(b) a risk of harm to a child resulting from domestic abuse,

is raised as an issue.

(2) In such a case, the court should consider directing that a report on the question of contact, or any other matters relating to the welfare of the child, including matters relating to whether a section 91(14) order would be appropriate (see Practice Direction 12Q) be prepared under section 7 of the Children Act 1989 by an Officer of Cafcass or a Welsh family proceedings officer (or local authority officer if appropriate).

(3) Sub-paragraph (2) does not apply where the court is satisfied that it is not necessary to order the preparation of such a report in order to safeguard the child's interests.

22 If the court directs that there shall be a fact-finding hearing on the issue of domestic abuse, the court will not usually request a section 7 report until after that hearing. In that event, the court should direct that any judgment is provided to Cafcass/CAFCASS Cymru; if there is no transcribed judgment, an agreed list of findings should be provided, as set out at paragraph 29.

23 Any request for a section 7 report should set out clearly the matters the court considers need to be addressed.

Representation of the child

24 Subject to the seriousness of the allegations made and the difficulty of the case, the court must consider whether it is appropriate for the child who is the subject of the application to be made a party to the proceedings and be separately represented. If the court considers that the child should be so represented, it must review the allocation decision so that it is satisfied that the case proceeds before the correct level of judge in the Family Court or High Court.

Interim orders before determination of relevant facts

25 Where the court gives directions for a fact-finding hearing, or where disputed allegations of domestic abuse are otherwise undetermined, the court should not make an interim child arrangements order unless it is satisfied that it is in the interests of the child to do so and that the order would not expose the child or the other parent to an unmanageable risk of harm (bearing in mind in particular the definition of 'victim of domestic abuse' and the impact which domestic abuse against a parent can have on the emotional well-being of the child, the safety of the other parent and the need to protect against domestic abuse).

26 In deciding any interim child arrangements question the court should–

(a) take into account the matters set out in section 1(3) of the Children Act 1989 or section 1(4) of the Adoption and Children Act 2002 ('the welfare check-list'), as appropriate; and

(b) give particular consideration to the likely effect on the child, and on the care given to the child by the parent who has made the allegation of domestic abuse, of any contact and any risk of harm, whether physical, emotional or psychological, which the child and that parent is likely to suffer as a consequence of making or declining to make an order.

27 Where the court is considering whether to make an order for interim contact, it should in addition consider –

(a) the arrangements required to ensure, as far as possible, that any risk of harm to the child and the parent who is at any time caring for the child is minimised and that the safety of the child and the parties is secured; and in particular:
   (i) whether the contact should be supervised or supported, and if so, where and by whom; and
   (ii) the availability of appropriate facilities for that purpose;

(b) if direct contact is not appropriate, whether it is in the best interests of the child to make an order for indirect contact; and

(c) whether contact will be beneficial for the child.

The fact-finding hearing or other hearing of the facts where domestic abuse is alleged

28 While ensuring that the allegations are properly put and responded to, the fact-finding hearing or other hearing can be an inquisitorial (or investigative) process, which at all times must protect the interests of all involved. At the fact-finding hearing or other hearing –

- each party can be asked to identify what questions they wish to ask of the other party, and to set out or confirm in sworn evidence their version of the disputed key facts; and

- the judge should be prepared where necessary and appropriate to conduct the questioning of the witnesses on behalf of the parties, focusing on the key issues in the case.

29 The court should, wherever practicable, make findings of fact as to the nature and degree of any domestic abuse which is established and its effect on the child, the child's parents and any other relevant person. The court must record its findings in writing in a Schedule to the relevant order, and the court office must serve a copy of this order on the parties. A copy of any record of findings of fact or of admissions must be sent by the court office to any officer preparing a report under Section 7 of the 1989 Act.

30 At the conclusion of any fact-finding hearing, the court must consider, notwithstanding any earlier direction for a section 7 report, whether it is in the best interests of the child for the court to give further directions about the preparation or scope of any report under section 7; where necessary, it may adjourn the proceedings for a brief period to enable the officer to make representations about the preparation or scope of any further enquiries. Any section 7 report should address the factors set out in paragraphs 36 and 37 below, unless the court directs otherwise.

31 Where the court has made findings of fact on disputed allegations, any subsequent hearing in the proceedings should be conducted by the same judge or by at least the same chairperson of the justices. Exceptions may be made only where observing this requirement would result in delay to the planned timetable and the judge or chairperson is satisfied, for reasons which must be recorded in writing, that the detriment to the welfare of the child would outweigh the detriment to the fair trial of the proceedings.

In all cases where domestic abuse has occurred

32 The court should take steps to obtain (or direct the parties or an Officer of Cafcass or a Welsh family proceedings officer to obtain) information about the facilities available locally (to include local domestic abuse support services) to assist any party or the child in cases where domestic abuse has occurred.

33 Following any determination of the nature and extent of domestic abuse, whether or not following a fact-finding hearing, the court must, if considering any form of contact or involvement of the parent in the child's life, consider-

(a) whether it would be assisted by any social work, psychiatric, psychological or other assessment (including an expert safety and risk assessment) of any party or the child and if so (subject to any necessary consent) make directions for such assessment to be undertaken and for the filing of any consequent report. Any such report should address the factors set out in paragraphs 36 and 37 below, unless the court directs otherwise;

(b) whether any party should seek advice, treatment or other intervention as a precondition to any child arrangements order being made, and may (with the consent of that party) give directions for such attendance.

34 Further or as an alternative to the advice, treatment or other intervention referred to in paragraph 33(b) above, the court may make an Activity Direction under section 11A and 11B Children Act 1989. Any intervention directed pursuant to this provision should be one commissioned and approved by Cafcass. It is acknowledged that acceptance on a DVPP is subject to a suitability assessment by the service provider, and that completion of a DVPP will take time in order to achieve the aim of risk-reduction for the long-term benefit of the child and the parent with whom the child is living.

Factors to be taken into account when determining whether to make child arrangements orders in all cases where domestic abuse has occurred

35 When deciding the issue of child arrangements the court should ensure that any order for contact will not expose the child to an unmanageable risk of harm and will be in the best interests of the child.

36(1) In the light of-

(a) any findings of fact,
(b) admissions; or
(c) domestic abuse having otherwise been established,

the court should apply the individual matters in the welfare checklist with reference to the domestic abuse which has occurred and any expert risk assessment obtained.

(2) In particular, the court should in every case consider any harm-

(a) which the child as a victim of domestic abuse, and the parent with whom the child is living, has suffered as a consequence of that domestic abuse; and
(b) which the child and the parent with whom the child is living is at risk of suffering, if a child arrangements order is made.

(3) The court should make an order for contact only if it is satisfied-

(a) that the physical and emotional safety of the child and the parent with whom the child is living can, as far as possible, be secured before, during and after contact; and
(b) that the parent with whom the child is living will not be subjected to further domestic abuse by the other parent.

37 In every case where a finding or admission of domestic abuse is made, or where domestic abuse is otherwise established, the court should consider the conduct of both parents towards each other and towards the child and the impact of the same. In particular, the court should consider –

(a) the effect of the domestic abuse on the child and on the arrangements for where the child is living;
(b) the effect of the domestic abuse on the child and its effect on the child's relationship with the parents;
(c) whether the parent is motivated by a desire to promote the best interests of the child or is using the process to continue a form of domestic abuse against the other parent;
(d) the likely behaviour during contact of the parent against whom findings are made and its effect on the child; and
(e) the capacity of the parents to appreciate the effect of past domestic abuse and the potential for future domestic abuse.

Orders under section 91(14) of the Children Act 1989

37A.1 In every case where a finding or admission of domestic abuse is made, or where domestic abuse is otherwise established, the court should consider whether an order under section 91(14) of the Children Act 1989 would be appropriate, even if an application for such an order has not been made. Section 91(14) orders are available to protect a victim of domestic abuse where a further application would constitute or continue domestic abuse. A future application could be part of a pattern of coercive or controlling behaviour or other domestic abuse toward the victim, such that a section 91(14) order is merited due to the risk of harm to the child or other individual. The court should refer to Practice Direction 12Q for direction on section 91(14) applications and orders.

Directions as to how contact is to proceed

38 Where any domestic abuse has occurred but the court, having considered any expert risk assessment and having applied the welfare checklist, nonetheless considers that direct contact is safe and beneficial for the child, the court should consider what, if any, directions or conditions are required to enable the order to be carried into effect and in particular should consider –

(a) whether or not contact should be supervised, and if so, where and by whom;
(b) whether to impose any conditions to be complied with by the party in whose favour the order for contact has been made and if so, the nature of those conditions, for example by way of seeking intervention (subject to any necessary consent);
(c) whether such contact should be for a specified period or should contain provisions which are to have effect for a specified period; and
(d) whether it will be necessary, in the child's best interests, to review the operation of the order; if so the court should set a date for the review consistent with the timetable for the child, and must give directions to ensure that at the review the court has full information about the operation of the order.

Where a risk assessment has concluded that a parent poses a risk to a child or to the other parent, contact via a supported contact centre, or contact supervised by a parent or relative, is not appropriate.

39 Where the court does not consider direct contact to be appropriate, it must consider whether it is safe and beneficial for the child to make an order for indirect contact.

The reasons of the court

40 In its judgment or reasons the court should always make clear how its findings on the issue of domestic abuse have influenced its decision on the issue of arrangements for the child. In particular, where the court has found domestic abuse proved but nonetheless makes an order which results in the child having future contact with the perpetrator of domestic abuse, the court must always explain, whether by way of reference to the welfare check-list, the factors in paragraphs 36 and 37 or otherwise, why it takes the view that the order which it has made will not expose the child to the risk of harm and is beneficial for the child.

This Practice Direction is issued by the President of the Family Division, as the nominee of the Lord Chief Justice, with the agreement of the Lord Chancellor.

Practice Direction 12K – Children Act 1989: exclusion requirement

See also Part 12, Practice Direction 12A, Practice Direction 12B, Practice Direction 12C, Practice Direction 12D, Practice Direction 12E, Practice Direction 12F, Practice Direction 12G, Practice Direction 12H, Practice Direction 12I, Practice Direction 12J, Practice Direction 12L, Practice Direction 12M, Practice Direction 12N, Practice Direction 12O, Practice Direction 12P

Under s 38A(5) and s 44A(5) of the Children Act 1989 the court may attach a power of arrest to an exclusion requirement included in an interim care order or an emergency protection order. In cases where an order is made which includes an exclusion requirement, the following shall apply –

1 Omitted.

2 When a person arrested under a power of arrest cannot conveniently be brought before the relevant judicial authority sitting in a place normally used as a court room within 24 hours after the arrest, he may be brought before the relevant judicial authority at any convenient place but, as the liberty of the subject is involved, the press and the public should be permitted to be present, unless security needs make this impracticable.

3 Any order of committal made otherwise than in public or in a courtroom open to the public, shall be announced in open court at the earliest opportunity. This may be either on the same day when the court proceeds to hear cases in open court or where there is no further business in open court on that day at the next listed sitting of the court. The announcement shall state –

(a) the name of the person committed,
(b) in general terms the nature of the contempt of the court in respect of which the order of committal has been made and
(c) the length of the period of committal.

Practice Direction 12L – Children Act 1989: risk assessments under section 16A

See also Part 12, Practice Direction 12A, Practice Direction 12B, Practice Direction 12C, Practice Direction 12D, Practice Direction 12E, Practice Direction 12F, Practice Direction 12G, Practice Direction 12H, Practice Direction 12I, Practice Direction 12J, Practice Direction 12K, Practice Direction 12M, Practice Direction 12N, Practice Direction 12O, Practice Direction 12P

1.1 This Practice Direction applies to any family proceedings in the High Court or the family courtin which a risk assessment is made under section 16A of the Children Act 1989 ('the 1989 Act'). It has effect from 1st October 2007.

1.2 Section 16A(2) of the 1989 Act provides that, if in carrying out any function to which the section applies (as set out in section 16A(1)), an officer of the Service or a Welsh family proceedings officer is given cause to suspect that the child concerned is at risk of harm, the officer must make a risk assessment in relation to the child and provide the risk assessment to the court.

1.3 The duty to provide the risk assessment to the court arises irrespective of the outcome of the assessment. Where an officer is given cause to suspect that the child concerned is at risk of harm and makes a risk assessment in accordance with section 16A(2), the officer must provide the assessment to the court, even if he or she reaches the conclusion that there is no risk of harm to the child.

1.4 The fact that a risk assessment has been carried out is a material fact that should be placed before the court, whatever the outcome of the assessment. In reporting the outcome to the court, the officer should make clear the factor or factors that triggered the decision to carry out the assessment.

1.5 Issued by the President of the Family Division, as the nominee of the Lord Chief Justice, with the agreement of the Lord Chancellor.

Practice Direction 12M – Family assistance order: consultation

See also Part 12, Practice Direction 12A, Practice Direction 12B, Practice Direction 12C, Practice Direction 12D, Practice Direction 12E, Practice Direction 12F, Practice Direction 12G, Practice Direction 12H, Practice Direction 12I, Practice Direction 12J, Practice Direction 12K, Practice Direction 12L, Practice Direction 12N, Practice Direction 12O, Practice Direction 12P

1.1 This Practice Direction applies to any family proceedings in the High Court or the family courtin which the court is considering whether to make a family assistance order under section 16 of the Children Act 1989, as amended ('the 1989 Act'). It has effect from 1st October 2007.

1.2 Before making a family assistance order the court must have obtained the opinion of the appropriate officer about whether it would be in the best interests of the child in question for a family assistance order to be made and, if so, how the family assistance order could operate and for what period.

1.3 The appropriate officer will be an officer of the Service, a Welsh family proceedings officer or an officer of a local authority, depending on the category of officer the court proposes to require to be made available under the family assistance order.

1.4 The opinion of the appropriate officer may be given orally or in writing (for example, it may form part of a report under section 7 of the 1989 Act).

1.5 Before making a family assistance order the court must give any person whom it proposes be named in the order an opportunity to comment upon any opinion given by the appropriate officer.

1.6 Issued by the President of the Family Division, as the nominee of the Lord Chief Justice, with the agreement of the Lord Chancellor.

Practice Direction 12N – Enforcement of Children Act 1989 child arrangements orders: disclosure of information to officers of the National Probation Service

See also Part 12, Practice Direction 12A, Practice Direction 12B, Practice Direction 12C, Practice Direction 12D, Practice Direction 12E, Practice Direction 12F, Practice Direction 12G, Practice Direction 12H, Practice Direction 12I, Practice Direction 12J, Practice Direction 12K, Practice Direction 12L, Practice Direction 12M, Practice Direction 12O, Practice Direction 12P

1.1 This Practice Direction applies to proceedings in the High Court or the family court where–

(a) the court is considering an application for an enforcement order[1] or for an order following an alleged breach of an enforcement order[2] and asks an officer of the Service or a Welsh family proceedings officer to provide information to the court in accordance with section 11L(5) of the Children Act 1989; or

(b) the court makes an enforcement order or an order following an alleged breach of an enforcement order and asks an officer of the Service or a Welsh family proceedings officer to monitor compliance with that order and to report to the court in accordance with section 11M of the Children Act 1989.

1.2 In all cases in which paragraph 1 applies, the officer of the Service or Welsh family proceedings officer will need to discuss aspects of the court case with an officer of the National Probation Service.

1.3 In order to ensure that the officer of the Service or Welsh family proceedings officer will not potentially be in contempt of court by virtue of such discussions, the court should, when making a request under section 11L(5) or section 11M of the Children Act 1989, give leave to that officer to disclose to the National Probation Service such information (whether or not contained in a document filed with the court) in relation to the proceedings as is necessary.

1 under section 11J of the Children Act 1989.

2 under paragraph 9 of Schedule A1 to the Children Act 1989.

Practice Direction 12O – Child: arrival by air

See also Part 12, Practice Direction 12A, Practice Direction 12B, Practice Direction 12C, Practice Direction 12D, Practice Direction 12E, Practice Direction 12F, Practice Direction 12G, Practice Direction 12H, Practice Direction 12I, Practice Direction 12J, Practice Direction 12K, Practice Direction 12L, Practice Direction 12M, Practice Direction 12N, Practice Direction 12P

1.1 Where a person seeks an order for the return to him of children about to arrive in England by air and desires to have information to enable him to meet the aeroplane, the judge should be asked to include in his order a direction that the airline operating the flight, and, if he has the information, the immigration officer at the appropriate airport, should supply such information to that person.

1.2 To obtain such information in such circumstances in a case where a person already has an order for the return to him of children, that person should apply to a judge ex parte for such a direction.

Practice Direction 12P – Removal from jurisdiction: issue of passports

See also Part 12, Practice Direction 12A, Practice Direction 12B, Practice Direction 12C, Practice Direction 12D, Practice Direction 12E, Practice Direction 12F, Practice Direction 12G, Practice Direction 12H, Practice Direction 12I, Practice Direction 12J, Practice Direction 12K, Practice Direction 12L, Practice Direction 12M, Practice Direction 12N, Practice Direction 12O

Removal from jurisdiction

1.1 The President has directed that on application for leave to remove from the jurisdiction for holiday periods a ward of court who has been placed by a local authority with foster-parents whose identity the court considers should remain confidential, for example because they are prospective adopters, it is important that such foster-parents should not be identified in the court's order. In such cases the order should be expressed as giving leave to the local authority to arrange for the child to be removed from England and Wales for the purpose of holidays.

1.2 It is also considered permissible, where care and control has been given to a local authority, or to an individual, for the court to give general leave to make such arrangements in suitable cases, thereby obviating the need to make application for leave each time it is desired to remove the child from the jurisdiction.

Issue of Passports

2.1 It is the practice of the Passport Department of the Home Office to issue passports for wards in accordance with the court's direction. This frequently results in passports being restricted to the holiday period specified in the order giving leave. It is the President's opinion that it is more convenient for wards' passports to be issued without such restriction.

2.2 The Passport Department has agreed to issue passports on this basis unless the court otherwise directs. It will, of course, still be necessary for the leave of the court to be obtained for the child's removal.

Practice Direction 12Q – Orders under sections 91(14) of the Children Act 1989

This Practice Direction supplements Part 12 and Part 18.

Definitions

1.1 In this Practice Direction –

'2021 Act' means the Domestic Abuse Act 2021;
'child concerned' has the same meaning as in section 91A(6) of the 1989 Act;
'domestic abuse' has the same meaning as in Practice Direction 12J;
'harm' has the same meaning as in Practice Direction 12J subject to sections 31(9) and 91A(3) of the 1989 Act;
'victim of domestic abuse' has the same meaning as in Practice Direction 12J; and
'named person' means the person named in a section 91(14) order who must seek the court's leave before making a specified application.

Key principles

2.1 Section 91(14) orders are available to prevent a person from making future applications under the 1989 Act without leave of the court. They are a protective filter made by the court, in the interests of children.

2.2 The court has a discretion to determine the circumstances in which an order would be appropriate. These circumstances may be many and varied. They include circumstances where an application would put the child concerned, or another individual, at risk of harm (as provided in section 91A), such as psychological or emotional harm. The welfare of the child is paramount.

2.3 These circumstances can also include where one party has made repeated and unreasonable applications; where a period of respite is needed following litigation; where a period of time is needed for certain actions to be taken for the protection of the child or other person; or where a person's conduct overall is such that an order is merited to protect the welfare of the child directly, or indirectly due to damaging effects on a parent carer. Such conduct could include harassment, or other oppressive or distressing behaviour beyond or within the proceedings including via social media and e-mail, and via third parties. Such conduct might also constitute domestic abuse.

2.4 A future application could also be part of a pattern of coercive or controlling behaviour or other domestic abuse toward the victim, such that a section 91(14) order is also merited due to the risk of harm to the child or other individual.

2.5 There is no definition in section 91A of who the other individual could be that could be put at risk of harm. However, it is most likely to be, but is not limited to, another person who has parental responsibility for the child and/or is living with or has contact with the child, or any other individual who would be a prospective respondent to a future application.

2.6 In proceedings in which domestic abuse is alleged or proven, or in which there are allegations or evidence of other harm to a child or other individual, the court should give early and ongoing consideration to whether it would be appropriate to make a section 91(14) order on disposal of the application, even if an application for such an order has not been made (since the court may make an order of its own motion – see section 91A(5)).

2.7 Section 91(14) orders are a protective filter – not a bar on applications – and there is considerable scope for their use in appropriate cases. Proceedings under the 1989 Act should not be used as a means of harassment or coercive control, or further abuse against a victim of domestic abuse or other person, and the court should therefore give due consideration to whether a future application would have such an impact.

2.8 The court should consider case law for further guidance and relevant principles, bearing in mind Parliament's insertion via the 2021 Act of section 91A into the 1989 Act.

Procedure

3.1 Under section 91A, a section 91(14) order may be made by the court of its own motion. If at any stage of the proceedings the court is considering making such an order of its own motion, it should record this fact in an order, together with any related directions (see, for example, paragraph 3.5).

3.2 An application for such an order may also be made by an individual who alleges a risk of harm from a future application, or by or on behalf of the child to whom the application would relate, or by another party to the application being disposed of.

3.3 If an application is made, the Part 18 procedure should be used. The application may be made in writing using Form C2, or orally during the hearing.

3.4 Under section 91(14), an order may only be made when disposing of another application under the Act, but section 91(14) is silent on when an application for such an order may be made. In proceedings in which risk of harm is alleged or proven, including but not limited to domestic abuse, the court should therefore give early and ongoing consideration to the question of whether a section 91(14) order might be appropriate on disposal of the application, and to whether any particular findings of fact will be needed to determine the section 91(14) application.

3.5 If an application is made, or the court is considering making an order of its own motion, the court should also consider what opportunity for representations should be provided to the parties. Courts should look to case law for further guidance and principles.

3.6 If the court decides to make a section 91(14) order, the court should give consideration as to the following matters:

a the duration of the order (see section 4);

b whether the order should cover all or only certain types of application under the 1989 Act;

c whether service of any subsequent application for leave should be prohibited until the court has made an initial determination of the merits of such an application (see section 6). Such an order delaying service would help to ensure that the very harm or other protective function that the order is intended to address, is not undermined; and

d 'whether upon any subsequent application for leave, the court should make an initial determination of the merits of the application without an oral hearing (see section 6).'

Duration

4.1 Sections 91(14) and 91A are silent on the duration of a section 91(14) order. The court therefore has a discretion as to the appropriate duration of the order. Any time limit imposed should be proportionate to the harm it is seeking to avoid. If the court decides to make a section 91(14) order, the court should explain its reasons for the duration ordered.

Types of application

5.1 Sections 91(14) and 91A give a discretion to the court as to the types of application under the 1989 Act that can be made subject to permission from the court. If the court decides to make a section 91(14) order, the court should consider which types of application should be specified in the order, and it should explain its reasons.

Application for leave

6.1 If, once a section 91(14) order has been made, the named person wishes to seek the court's leave to make a specified application, the Part 18 procedure applies subject to the following directions.

6.2 The application for leave must be made using Form C2, with two attachments: (i) a draft of the application for which permission is sought; and (ii) a witness statement setting out the grounds on which permission is sought, including whether there has been a material change of circumstances since the court made the section 91(14) order.

6.3 If the named person applies for leave, the Part 18 service rules apply, unless the court, when it made the section 91(14) order, prohibited service until initial determination of the merits of the application for leave (see section 3 above). In that case, the named person or court officer, as the case may be, must await that determination, and any directions from the court, before serving the respondent(s).

6.4 In determining any application for leave, the court has a discretion as to the circumstances in which leave should be granted. Section 91A(4) requires the court to consider whether there has been a material change of circumstances since the section 91(14) order was made. In other words, a material change of circumstances is not necessarily required in order for leave to be granted, but the question of whether there has been such a change, is something that the court must consider.

6.5 In determining any application for leave, the court should not ordinarily direct a report to be prepared under section 7 of the 1989 Act, in particular since, if leave were granted and the specified application were made, the court would then consider such a direction if appropriate.

6.6 The court may make an initial determination, without an oral hearing, of the merits of the application for leave. If the court does so, the applicant may, within 7 days of receipt of notice of the court's decision, request an oral hearing. If the court receives such a request, it must make directions as to service of the application and any other documents on the respondent, including the possibility that the respondent would not be served, and as to any representations or other matters in relation to the oral hearing.

PART 13
PROCEEDINGS UNDER SECTION 54 [OR SECTION 54A][1] OF THE HUMAN FERTILISATION AND EMBRYOLOGY ACT 2008

13.1 Interpretation and application

(1) A reference in this Part to the 2002 Act is a reference to that Act as applied with modifications by the Human Fertilisation and Embryology (Parental Order) Regulations 2010.

(2) In this Part—

'the other parent' means any person who is a parent of the child but is not one of the applicants or the woman who carried the child (including any man who is the father by virtue of section 35 or 36 of the 2008 Act or any woman who is a parent by virtue of section 42 or 43 of that Act);

'parental order' means an order under section 54 [or section 54A][1] of the 2008 Act;

'parental order proceedings' means proceedings for the making of a parental order under the 2008 Act or an order under any provision of the 2002 Act;

'parental order reporter' means an officer of the service or a Welsh family proceedings officer appointed to act on behalf of a child who is the subject of parental order proceedings;

['provision for contact' means—

(i) contact provision contained in a child arrangements order under section 8 of the 1989 Act, or

(ii) an order under section 34 of the 1989 Act;][2]

['contact provision' has the meaning given to it in section 26(5A) of the 2002 Act.][2]

(3) Except where the contrary intention appears, the rules in this Part apply to parental order proceedings.

Amendment

1 Inserted by the Human Fertilisation and Embryology Act 2008 (Remedial) Order 2018, SI 2018/1413, art 3(2), Sch 2, para 4(1)–(3).

2 Substituted by the Family Procedure (Amendment No 3) Rules 2014, SI 2014/843, rr 2, 30.

13.2 Application of Part 12

Rules …[1] 12.19 and 12.21 apply as appropriate, with any necessary modifications, to parental order proceedings.

Amendment

1 Repealed by the Family Procedure (Amendment No 3) Rules 2013, SI 2013/3204, rr 2, 53.

13.3 Who the parties are

(1) An application for a parental order [under section 54 of the 2008 Act][1] may be made by such of the following who satisfy the conditions set out in section 54(1) of the 2008 Act—

(a) a husband and wife;
(b) civil partners of each other; or
(c) two persons who are living as partners in an enduring family relationship and are not within the prohibited degrees of relationship in relation to each other.

[(1A) An application for a parental order under section 54A of the 2008 Act may only be made by one person who satisfies the conditions set out in subsection (1) of that section.][1]

(2) The respondents to an application for a parental order are—

(a) the woman who carried the child;
(b) the other parent (if any);
(c) any person in whose favour there is provision for contact; and
(d) any other person or body with parental responsibility for the child at the date of the application.

(3) The court will direct that a person with parental responsibility for the child be made a party to proceedings where that person requests to be one.

(4) The court may at any time direct that—

(a) any other person or body be made a respondent to the proceedings; or
(b) a respondent be removed from the proceedings.

(5) If the court makes a direction for the addition or removal of a party, it may give consequential directions about—

(a) serving a copy of the application form on any new respondent;
(b) serving relevant documents on the new party; and
(c) the management of the proceedings.

Amendment

1 Inserted by the Human Fertilisation and Embryology Act 2008 (Remedial) Order 2018, SI 2018/1413, art 3(2), Sch 2, para 4(1), (4), (5).

13.4 Notice of proceedings to person with foreign parental responsibility

(1) This rule applies where a child is subject to proceedings to which this Part applies and at the date of the application—

(a) a person holds or is believed to hold parental responsibility for the child under the law of another State which subsists in accordance with Article 16 of the 1996 Hague Convention following the child becoming habitually resident in a territorial unit of the United Kingdom; and
(b) that person is not otherwise required to be joined as a respondent under rule 13.3.

(2) The applicant shall give notice of the proceedings to any person to whom the applicant believes paragraph (1) applies.

(3) The applicant and every respondent to the proceedings shall provide such details as they possess as to the identity and whereabouts of any person they believe to hold parental responsibility for the child in accordance with paragraph (1) to the court officer, upon making, or responding to the application as appropriate.

(4) Where the existence of such a person only becomes apparent to a party at a later date during the proceedings, that party must notify the court officer of those details at the earliest opportunity.

(5) Where a person to whom paragraph (1) applies receives notice of proceedings, that person may apply to the court to be joined as a party using the Part 18 procedure.

13.5 What the court or a court officer will do when the application has been issued

(1) As soon as practicable after the issue of proceedings—

(a) the court will—

(i) if section 48(1) of the 2002 Act applies (restrictions on making parental orders), consider whether it is proper to hear the application;

(ii) subject to paragraph (2), set a date for the first directions hearing;

(iii) appoint a parental order reporter; and

(iv) set a date for the hearing of the application; and

(b) a court officer will—

(i) return to the applicants the copies of the application together with any other documents the applicant is required to serve; and

(ii) send a certified copy of the entry in the register of live births to the parental order reporter

(2) Where it considers it appropriate the court may, instead of setting a date for a first directions appointment, give the directions provided for in rule 13.9.

13.6 Service of the application and other documents

(1) The applicants must, within 14 days before the hearing or first directions hearing, serve on the respondents—

(a) the application;

(b) a form for acknowledging service; and

(c) a notice of proceedings.

(2) The applicants must serve a notice of proceedings on any local authority or voluntary organisation that has at any time provided accommodation for the child.

13.7 Acknowledgement

Within 7 days of the service of an application for a parental order, each respondent must file an acknowledgment of service and serve it on all the other parties.

13.8 Date for first directions hearing

Unless the court directs otherwise, the first directions hearing must be within 4 weeks beginning with the date on which the application is issued.

13.9 The first directions hearing

(1) At the first directions hearing in the proceedings the court will—

(a) fix a timetable for the filing of—

(i) any report from a parental order reporter;

(ii) if a statement of facts has been filed, any amended statement of facts; and

(iii) any other evidence;

(b) give directions relating to the report of the parental order reporter and other evidence;

(c) consider whether any other person should be a party to the proceedings and, if so, give directions in accordance with rule 13.3(3) or (4) joining that person as a party;

(d) give directions relating to the appointment of a litigation friend for any protected party unless a litigation friend has already been appointed;

[(e) consider, in accordance with rule 29.17, whether the case needs to be transferred to another court and, if so, give appropriate directions;][1]

(f) give directions about—

(i) tracing the other parent or the woman who carried the child;

(ii) service of documents;

(iii) subject to paragraph (2), disclosure as soon as possible of information and evidence to the parties; and

(iv) the final hearing.

(2) Rule 13.12 (reports of the parental order reporter and disclosure to parties) applies to any direction given under paragraph (1)(f)(iii) as it applies to a direction given under rule 13.12(1).

(3) The parties or their legal representatives must attend the first directions hearing unless the court directs otherwise.

(4) Directions may also be given at any stage in the proceedings—

(a) of the court's own initiative; or

(b) on the application of a party or the parental order reporter.

(5) Where the court proposes to exercise its powers in paragraph (1) of its own initiative the procedure set out in rule 4.3(2) to (7) applies.

(6) For the purposes of giving directions or for such purposes as the court directs—

(a) the court may set a date for a further directions hearing or other hearing; and

(b) the court officer will give notice of any date so fixed to the parties and to the parental order reporter.

(7) Directions of a court which are still in force immediately prior to the transfer of proceedings to another court shall continue to apply following the transfer subject to—

(a) any changes of terminology which are required to apply those directions to the court to which the proceedings are transferred; and

(b) any variation or revocation of the direction.

(8) The court or court officer will—

(a) take a note of the giving, variation or revocation of a direction under this rule; and

(b) as soon as practicable serve a copy of the note on every party.

(9) After the first directions hearing the court will monitor compliance by the parties with the court's timetable and directions.

Amendment

1 Substituted by the Family Procedure (Amendment No 3) Rules 2013, SI 2013/3204, rr 2, 54.

13.10 Where the agreement of the other parent or the woman who carried the child is not required

(1) This rule applies where the agreement of the other parent or the woman who carried the child to the making of the parental order is not required as the person in question cannot be found or is incapable of giving agreement.

(2) The applicants must—

(a) state that the agreement is not required in the application form, or at any later stage by filing a written note with the court;

(b) file a statement of facts setting out a summary of the history of the case and any other facts to satisfy the court that the other parent or the woman who carried the child cannot be found or is incapable of giving agreement.

(3) On receipt of the application form or written note—

(a) a court officer will—

(i) unless the other parent or the woman who carried the child cannot be found, inform the other parent or the woman who carried the child that their agreement is not required;

(ii) send a copy of the statement of facts filed in accordance with paragraph (2)(b) to—

(aa) the other parent unless the other parent cannot be found;

(bb) the woman who carried the child unless the woman cannot be found; and

(cc) the parental order reporter; and

(b) if the applicants consider that the other parent or the woman who carried the child is incapable of giving agreement the court will consider whether to—

(i) appoint a litigation friend for the other parent or the woman who carried the child under rule 15.6(1) or

(ii) give directions for an application to be made under rule 15.6(3),

unless a litigation friend is already appointed for the other parent or the woman who carried the child.

13.11 Agreement

(1) Unless the court directs otherwise, the agreement of the other parent or the woman who carried the child to the making of the parental order may be given in the form referred to in Practice Direction 5A or a form to the like effect.

(2) Any form of agreement executed in Scotland must be witnessed by a Justice of the Peace or a Sheriff.

(3) Any form of agreement executed in Northern Ireland must be witnessed by a Justice of the Peace.

(4) Any form of agreement executed outside the United Kingdom must be witnessed by—

(a) any person for the time being authorised by law in the place where the document is executed to administer an oath for any judicial or other legal purpose;

(b) a British Consular officer;

(c) a notary public; or

(d) if the person executing the document is serving in any of the regular armed forces of the Crown, an officer holding a commission in any of those forces.

13.12 Reports of the parental order reporter and disclosure to the parties

(1) The court will consider whether to give a direction that a confidential report of the parental order reporter be disclosed to each party to the proceedings.

(2) Before giving such a direction the court will consider whether any information should be deleted including information which discloses the particulars referred to in rule 29.1(1) where a party has given notice under rule 29.1(2) (disclosure of personal details).

(3) The court may direct that the report shall not be disclosed to a party.

13.13 Notice of final hearing

A court officer will give notice to the parties and to the parental order reporter—

(a) of the date and place where the application will be heard; and
(b) of the fact that, unless the person wishes or the court requires, the person need not attend.

13.14 The final hearing

(1) Any person who has been given notice in accordance with rule 13.13 may attend the final hearing and be heard on the question of whether an order should be made.

(2) The court may direct that any person must attend a final hearing.

13.15 Proof of identity of the child

(1) Unless the contrary is shown, the child referred to in the application will be deemed to be the child referred to in the form of agreement to the making of the parental order where the conditions in paragraph (2) apply.

(2) The conditions are—

(a) the application identifies the child by reference to a full certified copy of an entry in the registers of live-births;
(b) the form of agreement identifies the child by reference to a full certified copy of an entry in the registers of live-births attached to the form; and
(c) the copy of the entry in the registers of live-births referred to in sub-paragraph (a) is the same or relates to the same entry in the registers of live-births as the copy of the entry in the registers of live-births attached to the form of agreement.

(3) Where the precise date of the child's birth is not proved to the satisfaction of the court, the court will determine the probable date of birth.

(4) The probable date of the child's birth may be specified in the parental order as the date of the child's birth.

(5) Where the child's place of birth cannot be proved to the satisfaction of the court—

(a) the child may be treated as having been born in [the registration district and sub-district in which the court is sitting][1] where it is probable that the child may have been born in—
    (i) the United Kingdom;
    (ii) the Channel Islands; or
    (iii) the Isle of Man; or
(b) in any other case, the particulars of the country of birth may be omitted from the parental order.

Amendment

1 Substituted by the Family Procedure (Amendment No 3) Rules 2013, SI 2013/3204, rr 2, 55.

13.16 Disclosing information to an adult who was subject to a parental order

(1) Subject to paragraph (2), the person who is subject to the parental order has the right to receive from the court which made the parental order a copy of the following—

(a) the application form for a parental order (but not the documents attached to that form);
(b) the parental order and any other orders relating to the parental order proceedings;
(c) a transcript of the court's decision; and
(d) a report made to the court by the parental order reporter.

(2) The court will not provide a copy of a document or order referred to in paragraph (1) unless the person making the request has completed the certificate relating to counselling in the form for that purpose referred to in Practice Direction 5A.

(3) This rule does not apply to a person under the age of 18 years.

13.17 Application for recovery orders

[(1) An application for any of the orders referred to in section 41(2) of the 2002 Act (recovery orders) may be made without notice, in which case the applicant must file the application—

(a) where the application is made by telephone, the next business day after the making of the application; or
(b) in any other case, at the time when the application is made.][1]

(2) Where the court refuses to make an order on an application without notice it may direct that the application is made on notice in which case the application shall proceed in accordance with rules 13.1 to 13.14.

(3) The respondents to an application under this rule are—

(a) in a case where parental order proceedings are pending, all parties to those proceedings;
(b) any person having parental responsibility for the child;
(c) any person in whose favour there is provision for contact;
(d) any person who was caring for the child immediately prior to the making of the application; and
(e) any person whom the applicant alleges to have effected, or to have been or to be responsible for, the taking or keeping of the child.

Amendment

1 Substituted by the Family Procedure (Amendment No 3) Rules 2013, SI 2013/3204, rr 2, 56.

13.18 Keeping of registers, custody, inspection and disclosure of documents and information

(1) … [1]

(2) All documents relating to parental order proceedings and related proceedings under the 2002 Act … [1] must, while they are in the custody of the court, be kept in a place of special security.

(3) Any person who obtains any information in the course of, or relating to, parental order proceedings must treat that information as confidential and must only disclose it if—

(a) the disclosure is necessary for the proper exercise of that person's duties; or
(b) the information is requested by—

(i) a court or public authority (whether in Great Britain or not) having power to determine parental order proceedings and related matters, for the purpose of that court or authority discharging its duties relating to those proceedings and matters; or
(ii) a person who is authorised in writing by the Secretary of State to obtain the information for the purposes of research.

Amendment

1 Repealed by the Family Procedure (Amendment No 3) Rules 2013, SI 2013/3204, rr 2, 57.

13.19 Documents held by the court not to be inspected or copied without the court's permission

Subject to the provisions of these rules, any practice direction or any direction given by the court—

(a) no document or order held by the court in parental order proceedings and related proceedings under the 2002 Act will be open to inspection by any person; and
(b) no copy of any such document or order, or of an extract from any such document or order, shall be taken by or given to any person.

13.20 Orders

(1) A parental order takes effect from the date when it is made, or such later date as the court may specify.

(2) In proceedings in Wales a party may request that an order be drawn up in Welsh as well as English.

13.21 Copies of orders

(1) Within 7 days beginning with the date on which the final order was made in proceedings, or such shorter time as the court may direct, a court officer will send—

(a) a copy of the order to the applicant;
(b) a copy, which is sealed(GL), authenticated with the stamp of the court or certified as a true copy of a parental order, to the Registrar General;
(c) a notice of the making or refusal of—

(i) the final order; or
(ii) an order quashing or revoking a parental order or allowing an appeal against an order in proceedings,

to every respondent and, with the permission of the court, any other person.

(2) The court officer will also send notice of the making of a parental order to—

(a) any court in Great Britain which appears to the court officer to have made any such order as is referred to in section 46(2) of the 2002 Act (order relating to parental responsibility for, and maintenance of, the child); and

(b) the principal registry, if it appears to the court officer that a parental responsibility agreement has been recorded at the principal registry.

(3) A copy of any final order may be sent to any other person with the permission of the court.

(4) The court officer will send a copy of any order made during the course of the proceedings to all the parties to those proceedings unless the court directs otherwise.

(5) If an order has been drawn up in Welsh as well as in English in accordance with rule 13.20(2), any reference in this rule to sending an order is to be taken as a reference to sending both the Welsh and English orders.

13.22 Amendment and revocation of orders

(1) This rule applies to an application under paragraph 4 of Schedule 1 to the 2002 Act (amendment of a parental order and revocation of direction).

(2) …[1]

(3) Subject to paragraph (4), an application may be made without serving a copy of the application notice.

(4) The court may direct that an application notice be served on such persons as it thinks fit.

(5) Where the court makes an order granting the application, a [court officer][2] shall send the Registrar General a notice—

(a) specifying the amendments; or
(b) informing the Registrar General of the revocation,

giving sufficient particulars of the order to enable the Registrar General to identify the case.

Amendment

1 Repealed by the Family Procedure (Amendment No 3) Rules 2013, SI 2013/3204, rr 2, 58(a).
2 Substituted by the Family Procedure (Amendment No 3) Rules 2013, SI 2013/3204, rr 2, 58(b).

PART 14
PROCEDURE FOR APPLICATIONS IN ADOPTION, PLACEMENT AND RELATED PROCEEDINGS

14.1 Application of this Part and interpretation

(1) The rules in this Part apply to the following proceedings—

(a) adoption proceedings;
(b) placement proceedings; and
(c) proceedings for—
  (i) the making of [an][1] order under section 26 [or an order under section 51A(2)(a)][2] of the 2002 Act;
  [(ia) the making of an order under section 51A(2)(b) of the 2002 Act;][2]
  (ii) the variation or revocation of[—
    (aa) an order under section 27 of the 2002 Act; or
    (bb) an order under section 51A(2) of the 2002 Act in accordance with section 51B(1)(c);][1]

(iii) an order giving permission to change a child's surname or remove a child from the United Kingdom under section 28(2) and (3) of the 2002 Act;
(iv) a section 84 order;
(v) a section 88 direction;
(vi) a section 89 order; or
(vii) any other order that may be referred to in a practice direction.

[(1A) This Part is subject to any provision made by or pursuant to Part 41 (proceeding by electronic means).][3]

(2) In this Part—

'Central Authority' means—

(a) in relation to England, the Secretary of State; and
(b) in relation to Wales, the Welsh Ministers;

'Convention adoption order' means an adoption order under the 2002 Act which, by virtue of regulations under section 1 of the Adoption (Intercountry Aspects) Act 1999 (regulations giving effect to the Convention on Protection of Children and Co-operation in Respect of Intercountry Adoption, concluded at the Hague on 29th May 1993), is made as a Convention adoption order;

'guardian' means—

(a) a guardian (other than the guardian of the estate of a child) appointed in accordance with section 5 of the 1989 Act; and
(b) a special guardian within the meaning of section 14A of the 1989 Act;

['provision for contact' has the meaning given to it in rule 13.1(2);][1]

'section 88 direction' means a direction given by the High Court under section 88 of the 2002 Act that section 67(3) of that Act (status conferred by adoption) does not apply or does not apply to any extent specified in the direction.

Amendment

1 Substituted by the Family Procedure (Amendment No 3) Rules 2014, SI 2014/843, rr 2, 31(a)(i), (c), (d).
2 Inserted by the Family Procedure (Amendment No 3) Rules 2014, SI 2014/843, rr 2, 31(a)(ii), (b).
3 Inserted by the Family Procedure (Amendment) Rules 2020, SI 2020/135, rr 2, 19.

[14.2 [Assignment of][1] a serial number

(1) This rule applies where—

(a) any application in proceedings is made by a person who intends to adopt a child; or
(b) an adoption order in respect of the child has been made and an application is made for—
  (i) a contact order under section 51A(2)(a) of the 2002 Act;
  (ii) an order prohibiting contact with the child under section 51A(2)(b) of the 2002 Act; or
  (iii) the variation or revocation of an order under section 51A(2) of the 2002 Act in accordance with section 51B(1)(c).

[(2) In a case under paragraph (1)(a), a serial number must be assigned to identify the person intending to adopt the child in connection with the proceedings in order for the person's identity to be kept confidential in those proceedings.

(3) In a case under paragraph (1)(b), a serial number must be assigned to the person in whose favour the adoption order has been made to keep the identity of the person confidential in proceedings referred to in paragraph (1)(b).][1]

(4) The court may at any time direct that a serial number assigned to a person under paragraph (2) or (3) must be removed.

(5) [When][1] a serial number has been assigned to a person under paragraph (2) or (3)—

(a) the court officer will ensure that any notice sent in accordance with these rules does not contain information which discloses, or is likely to disclose, the identity of that person to any other party to that application who is not already aware of that person's identity; and

(b) the proceedings on the application will be conducted with a view to securing that the person is not seen by or made known to any party who is not already aware of the person's identity except with the person's consent.][2]

Amendment

1 Substituted by the Family Procedure (Amendment No 3) Rules 2016, SI 2016/1013, r 2.

2 Substituted by the Family Procedure (Amendment No 3) Rules 2014, SI 2014/843, rr 2, 32.

14.3 Who the parties are

(1) In relation to the proceedings set out in column 1 of the following table, column 2 sets out who the application may be made by and column 3 sets out who the respondents to those proceedings will be.

Proceedings for	*Applicants*	*Respondents*
An adoption order (section 46 of the 2002 Act).	The prospective adopters (sections 50 and 51 of the 2002 Act).	Each parent who has parental responsibility for the child unless that parent has given notice under section 20(4)(a) of the 2002 Act (statement of wish not to be informed of any application for an adoption order) which has effect; any guardian of the child unless that guardian has given notice under section 20(4)(a) of the 2002 Act (statement of wish not to be informed of any application for an adoption order) which has effect; any person in whose favour there is provision for contact; any adoption agency having parental responsibility for the child under section 25 of the 2002 Act; any adoption agency which has taken part at any stage in the arrangements for adoption of the child; any local authority to whom notice under section 44 of the 2002 Act (notice of intention to adopt or apply for a section 84 order) has been given; any local authority or voluntary organisation which has parental responsibility for, is looking after or is caring for, the child; and

Proceedings for	*Applicants*	*Respondents*
		the child where— – permission has been granted to a parent or guardian to oppose the making of the adoption order (section 47(3) or 47(5) of the 2002 Act); – the child opposes the making of an adoption order; – a children and family reporter recommends that it is in the best interests of the child to be a party to the proceedings and that recommendation is accepted by the court; – the child is already an adopted child; – any party to the proceedings or the child is opposed to the arrangements for allowing any person contact with the child, or a person not being allowed contact with the child after the making of the adoption order; – the application is for a Convention adoption order or a section 84 order; the child has been brought into the United Kingdom in the circumstances where section 83(1) of the 2002 Act applies (restriction on bringing children in); – the application is for an adoption order other than a Convention adoption order and the prospective adopters intend the child to live in a country or territory outside the British Islands after the making of the adoption order; or – the prospective adopters are relatives of the child.
A section 84 order.	The prospective adopters asking for parental responsibility prior to adoption abroad.	As for an adoption order.
A placement order (section 21 of the 2002 Act).	A local authority (section 22 of the 2002 Act).	Each parent who has parental responsibility for the child: any guardian of the child; any person in whose favour an order under the 1989 Act is in force in relation to the child; any adoption agency or voluntary organisation which has parental responsibility for, is looking after, or is caring for, the child; the child; and the parties or any persons who are or have been parties to proceedings for a care order in respect of the child where those proceedings have led to the application for the placement order.

Proceedings for	*Applicants*	*Respondents*
An order varying a placement order (section 23 of the 2002 Act).	The joint application of the local authority authorised by the placement order to place the child for adoption and the local authority which is to be substituted for that authority (section 23 of the 2002 Act).	The parties to the proceedings leading to the placement order which it is sought to have varied except the child who was the subject of those proceedings; and any person in whose favour there is provision for contact.
An order revoking a placement order (section 24 of the 2002 Act).	The child; the local authority authorised to place the child for adoption; or where the child is not placed for adoption by the authority, any other person who has the permission of the court to apply (section 24 of the 2002 Act).	The parties to the proceedings leading to the placement order which it is sought to have revoked; and any person in whose favour there is provision for contact.
[An order under section 26 of the 2002 Act][1].	The child; the adoption agency; any parent, guardian or relative; any person in whose favour there was provision for contact under the 1989 Act which ceased to have effect on an adoption agency being authorised to place a child	The adoption agency authorised to place the child for adoption or which has placed the child for adoption; the person with whom the child lives or is to live; each parent with parental responsibility for the child; any guardian of the child; and the child where— – the adoption agency authorised to place the child for adoption or which has placed the child for adoption or a parent with parental responsibility for the child opposes the making of [the order][1] under section 26 of the 2002 Act; – the child opposes the making of [the order][1] under section 26 of the 2002 Act;

Proceedings for	*Applicants*	*Respondents*
	for adoption, or placing a child for adoption who is less than six weeks old (section 26(1) of the 2002 Act); [if a child arrangements order was in force immediately before the adoption agency was authorised to place the child for adoption or (as the case may be) placed the child for adoption at a time when he or she was less than six weeks old, any person named in the order as a person with whom the child was to live][1]; a person who by virtue of an order made in the exercise of the High Court's inherent jurisdiction with respect to children had care of the child immediately before that time; or any person who has the permission of the court to make the application (section 26 of the 2002 Act).	– existing provision for contact is to be revoked; – relatives of the child do not agree to the arrangements for allowing any person contact with the child, or a person not being allowed contact with the child; or – the child is suffering or is at risk of suffering harm within the meaning of the 1989 Act.

Proceedings for	*Applicants*	*Respondents*
An order varying or revoking [an order under section 26 of the 2002 Act][1] (section 27 of the 2002 Act).	The child; the adoption agency; or any person named in [the order][1] (section 27(1) of the 2002 Act).	The parties to the proceedings leading to [the order][1] which it is sought to have varied or revoked; and any person named in [the order][1].
An order permitting the child's name to be changed or the removal of the child from the United Kingdom (section 28(2) and (3) of the 2002 Act).	Any person including the adoption agency or the local authority authorised to place, or which has placed, the child for adoption (section 28(2) of the 2002 Act).	The parties to proceedings leading to any placement order; the adoption agency authorised to place the child for adoption or which has placed the child for adoption; any prospective adopters with whom the child is living; each parent with parental responsibility for the child; and any guardian of the child.
[A contact order under section 51A(2)(a) of the 2002 Act.	The child; or any person who has obtained the court's leave to make the application.	A person who has applied for the adoption order or in whose favour the adoption order is or has been made; and Any adoption agency having parental responsibility for the child under section 25 of the 2002 Act.
An order prohibiting the person named in the order from having contact with the child (section 51A(2)(b) of the 2002 Act).	A person who has applied for the adoption order or in whose favour the adoption order is or has been made; the child; or any person who has obtained the court's leave to make the application.	A person against whom an application is made who— (but for the child's adoption) would be related to the child by blood (including halfblood), marriage or civil partnership; is a former guardian of the child; is a person who had parental responsibility for the child immediately before the making of the adoption order; is a person who was entitled to make an application for an order under section 26 of the 2002 Act in respect of the child (contact with children placed or to be placed for adoption) by virtue of subsection (3)(c), (d) or (e) of that section; is a person with whom the child has lived for a period of at least one year; and any adoption agency having parental responsibility for the child under section 25 of the 2002 Act.

Proceedings for	*Applicants*	*Respondents*
The variation or revocation of a contact order or an order prohibiting contact under section 51A(2) of the 2002 Act (section 51B(1)(c) of that Act).	The child; a person in whose favour the adoption order was made; or a person named in the order.	The parties to the proceedings leading to the contact order or an order prohibiting contact which it is sought to have varied or revoked; and any person named in the contact order or the order prohibiting contact.][2]
A section 88 direction.	The adopted child; the adopters; any parent; or any other person.	The adopters; the parents; the adoption agency; the local authority to whom notice under section 44 of the 2002 Act (notice of intention to apply for a section 84 order) has been given; and the Attorney-General.
A section 89 order.	The adopters; the adopted person; any parent; the relevant Central Authority; the adoption agency; the local authority to whom notice under section 44 of the 2002 Act (notice of intention to adopt or apply for a section 84 order) has been given; the Secretary of State for the Home Department; or any other person.	The adopters; the parents; the adoption agency; and the local authority to whom notice under section 44 of the 2002 Act (notice of intention to adopt or apply for a section 84 order) has been given.

(2) The court may at any time direct that a child, who is not already a respondent to proceedings, be made a respondent to proceedings where—

(a) the child—
 (i) wishes to make an application; or
 (ii) has evidence to give to the court or a legal submission to make which has not been given or made by any other party; or
(b) there are other special circumstances.

(3) The court may at any time direct that—

(a) any other person or body be made a respondent to proceedings; or
(b) a party be removed.

(4) If the court makes a direction for the addition or removal of a party, it may give consequential directions about—

(a) serving a copy of the application form on any new respondent;
(b) serving relevant documents on the new party; and
(c) the management of the proceedings.

Amendment

1 Substituted by the Family Procedure (Amendment No 3) Rules 2014, SI 2014/843, rr 2, 34.
2 Inserted by the Family Procedure (Amendment No 3) Rules 2014, SI 2014/843, rr 2, 33.

14.4 Notice of proceedings to person with foreign parental responsibility

(1) This rule applies where a child is subject to proceedings to which this Part applies and –

(a) a parent of the child holds or is believed to hold parental responsibility for the child under the law of another State which subsists in accordance with Article 16 of the 1996 Hague Convention following the child becoming habitually resident in a territorial unit of the United Kingdom; and
(b) that parent is not otherwise required to be joined as a respondent under rule 14.3.

(2) [Subject to paragraph (2A),][1] the applicant shall give notice of the proceedings to any parent to whom the applicant believes paragraph (1) applies in any case in which a person who was a parent with parental responsibility under the 1989 Act would be a respondent to the proceedings in accordance with rule 14.3.

[(2A) Notice shall not be given to a person to whom the applicant believes paragraph (1) applies if the court directs that such notice is not necessary.][1]

(3) [Unless a direction has been made under paragraph (2A),][1] the applicant and every respondent to the proceedings shall provide such details as they possess as to the identity and whereabouts of any parent they believe to hold parental responsibility for the child in accordance with paragraph (1) to the court officer, upon making, or responding to the application as appropriate.

(4) Where the existence of such a parent only becomes apparent to a party at a later date during the proceedings, that party must notify the court officer of those details at the earliest opportunity.

(5) Where a parent to whom paragraph (1) applies receives notice of proceedings, that parent may apply to the court to be joined as a party using the Part 18 procedure.

Amendment

1 Inserted by the Family Procedure (Amendment) Rules 2020, SI 2020/135, rr 2, 20.

14.5 Who is to serve

(1) The general rules about service in Part 6 are subject to this rule.

(2) In proceedings to which this Part applies, a document which has been issued or prepared by a court officer will be served by the court officer except where—

(a) a practice direction provides otherwise; or
(b) the court directs otherwise.

(3) Where a court officer is to serve a document, it is for the court to decide which of the methods of service specified in rule 6.23 is to be used.

14.6 What the court or a court officer will do when the application has been issued

(1) As soon as practicable after the application has been issued in proceedings—

(a) the court will—
  (i) if section 48(1) of the 2002 Act (restrictions on making adoption orders) applies, consider whether it is proper to hear the application;
  (ii) subject to paragraph (4), set a date for the first directions hearing;
  (iii) appoint a children's guardian in accordance with rule 16.3(1);
  (iv) appoint a reporting officer in accordance with rule 16.30;
  (v) consider whether a report relating to the welfare of the child is required, and if so, request such a report in accordance with rule 16.33;
  (vi) set a date for the hearing of the application; and
  (vii) do anything else that may be set out in a practice direction; and
(b) a court officer will—
  (i) subject to receiving confirmation in accordance with paragraph (2)(b)(ii), give notice of any directions hearing set by the court to the parties and to any children's guardian, reporting officer or children and family reporter;
  (ii) serve a copy of the application form (but, subject to sub-paragraphs (iii) and (iv), not the documents attached to it) on the persons referred to in Practice Direction 14A;
  (iii) send a copy of the certified copy of the entry in the register of live-births or Adopted Children Register and any health report attached to an application for an adoption order to—
    (aa) any children's guardian, reporting officer or children and family reporter; and
    (bb) the local authority to whom notice under section 44 of the 2002 Act (notice of intention to adopt or apply for a section 84 order) has been given;
  (iv) if notice under rule 14.9(2) has been given (request to dispense with consent of parent or guardian), in accordance with that rule inform the parent or guardian of the request and send a copy of the statement of facts to—
    (aa) the parent or guardian;
    (bb) any children's guardian, reporting officer or children and family reporter;

(cc) any local authority to whom notice under section 44 of the 2002 Act (notice of intention to adopt or apply for a section 84 order) has been given; and

(dd) any adoption agency which has placed the child for adoption; and

(v) do anything else that may be set out in a practice direction.

(2) In addition to the matters referred to in paragraph (1), as soon as practicable after an application for an adoption order or a section 84 order has been issued the court or the court officer will—

(a) where the child is not placed for adoption by an adoption agency—

(i) ask either the Service or the Assembly to file any relevant form of consent to an adoption order or a section 84 order; and

(ii) ask the local authority to prepare a report on the suitability of the prospective adopters if one has not already been prepared; and

(b) where the child is placed for adoption by an adoption agency, ask the adoption agency to—

(i) file any relevant form of consent to—

(aa) the child being placed for adoption;

(bb) an adoption order;

(cc) a future adoption order under section 20 of the 2002 Act; or

(dd) a section 84 order;

(ii) confirm whether a statement has been made under section 20(4)(a) of the 2002 Act (statement of wish not to be informed of any application for an adoption order) and if so, to file that statement;

(iii) file any statement made under section 20(4)(b) of the 2002 Act (withdrawal of wish not to be informed of any application for an adoption order) as soon as it is received by the adoption agency; and

(iv) prepare a report on the suitability of the prospective adopters if one has not already been prepared.

(3) In addition to the matters referred to in paragraph (1), as soon as practicable after an application for a placement order has been issued—

(a) the court will consider whether a report giving the local authority's reasons for placing the child for adoption is required, and if so, will direct the local authority to prepare such a report; and

(b) the court or the court officer will ask either the Service or the Assembly to file any form of consent to the child being placed for adoption.

(4) Where it considers it appropriate the court may, instead of setting a date for a first directions hearing, give the directions provided for by rule 14.8.

14.7 Date for first directions hearing

Unless the court directs otherwise, the first directions hearing must be within 4 weeks beginning with the date on which the application is issued.

14.8 The first directions hearing

(1) At the first directions hearing in the proceedings the court will—

(a) fix a [timetable for the proceedings including a][1] timetable for the filing of—

(i) any report relating to the suitability of the applicants to adopt a child;

(ii) any report from the local authority;
(iii) any report from a children's guardian, reporting officer or children and family reporter;
(iv) if a statement of facts has been filed, any amended statement of facts;
(v) any other evidence, and
(vi) give directions relating to the reports and other evidence;

(b) consider whether the child or any other person should be a party to the proceedings and, if so, give directions in accordance with rule 14.3(2) or (3) joining that child or person as a party;

(c) give directions relating to the appointment of a litigation friend for any protected party or child who is a party to, but not the subject of, proceedings unless a litigation friend has already been appointed;

(d) consider [in accordance with rule 29.17][2] whether the case needs to be transferred to another court and, if so, give directions to transfer the proceedings to another court ...[3];

(e) give directions about—
(i) tracing parents or any other person the court considers to be relevant to the proceedings;
(ii) service of documents;
(iii) subject to paragraph (2), disclosure as soon as possible of information and evidence to the parties; and
(iv) the final hearing.

([Under Part 3][4] the court may also direct that the case be adjourned if it considers that [non-court dispute resolution][4] is appropriate.)

(2) Rule 14.13(2) applies to any direction given under paragraph (1)(e)(iii) as it applies to a direction given under rule 14.13(1).

(3) In addition to the matters referred to in paragraph (1), the court will give any of the directions listed in Practice Direction 14B in proceedings for—

(a) a Convention adoption order;
(b) a section 84 order;
(c) a section 88 direction;
(d) a section 89 order; or
(e) an adoption order where section 83(1) of the 2002 Act applies (restriction on bringing children in).

(4) The parties or their legal representatives must attend the first directions hearing unless the court directs otherwise.

(5) Directions may also be given at any stage in the proceedings—

(a) of the court's own initiative; or
(b) on the application of a party or any children's guardian or, where the direction concerns a report by a reporting officer or children and family reporter, the reporting officer or children and family reporter.

(6) For the purposes of giving directions or for such purposes as the court directs—

(a) the court may set a date for a further directions hearing or other hearing; and
(b) the court officer will give notice of any date so fixed to the parties and to any children's guardian, reporting officer or children and family reporter.

(7) After the first directions hearing the court will monitor compliance by the parties with the court's timetable and directions.

Amendment

1 Inserted by the Family Procedure (Amendment No 3) Rules 2014, SI 2014/843, rr 2, 35(a).
2 Inserted by the Family Procedure (Amendment No 3) Rules 2013, SI 2013/3204, rr 2, 59(a).
3 Repealed by the Family Procedure (Amendment No 3) Rules 2013, SI 2013/3204, rr 2, 59(b).
4 Substituted by the Family Procedure (Amendment No 3) Rules 2014, SI 2014/843, rr 2, 35(b).

14.9 Requesting the court to dispense with the consent of any parent or guardian

(1) This rule applies where the applicant wants to ask the court to dispense with the consent of any parent or guardian of a child to—

(a) the child being placed for adoption;
(b) the making of an adoption order except a Convention adoption order; or
(c) the making of a section 84 order.

(2) The applicant requesting the court to dispense with the consent must—

(a) give notice of the request in the application form or at any later stage by filing a written request setting out the reasons for the request; and
(b) file a statement of facts setting out a summary of the history of the case and any other facts to satisfy the court that—
(i) the parent or guardian cannot be found or is incapable of giving consent; or
(ii) the welfare of the child requires the consent to be dispensed with.

(3) If a serial number has been assigned to the applicant under rule 14.2, the statement of facts supplied under paragraph (2)(b) must be framed so that it does not disclose the identity of the applicant.

(4) On receipt of the notice of the request—

(a) a court officer will—
(i) inform the parent or guardian of the request unless the parent or guardian cannot be found; and
(ii) send a copy of the statement of facts filed in accordance with paragraph (2)(b) to—
(aa) the parent or guardian unless the parent or guardian cannot be found;
(bb) any children's guardian, reporting officer or children and family reporter;
(cc) any local authority to whom notice under section 44 of the 2002 Act (notice of intention to adopt or apply for a section 84 order) has been given; and
(dd) any adoption agency which has placed the child for adoption; and
(b) if the applicant considers that the parent or guardian is incapable of giving consent, the court will consider whether to—
(i) appoint a litigation friend for the parent or guardian under rule 15.6(1); or
(ii) give directions for an application to be made under rule 15.6(3),
(iii) unless a litigation friend is already appointed for that parent or guardian.

14.10 Consent

(1) Consent of any parent or guardian of a child—

(a) under section 19 of the 2002 Act, to the child being placed for adoption; and
(b) under section 20 of the 2002 Act, to the making of a future adoption order,

must be given in the form referred to in Practice Direction 5A or a form to the like effect.

(2) Subject to paragraph (3), consent—

(a) to the making of an adoption order; or
(b) to the making of a section 84 order,

may be given in the form referred to in Practice Direction 5A or a form to the like effect or otherwise as the court directs.

(3) Any consent to a Convention adoption order must be in a form which complies with the internal law relating to adoption of the Convention country of which the child is habitually resident.

(4) Any form of consent executed in Scotland must be witnessed by a Justice of the Peace or a Sheriff.

(5) Any form of consent executed in Northern Ireland must be witnessed by a Justice of the Peace.

(6) Any form of consent executed outside the United Kingdom must be witnessed by—

(a) any person for the time being authorised by law in the place where the document is executed to administer an oath for any judicial or other legal purpose;
(b) a British Consular officer;
(c) a notary public; or
(d) if the person executing the document is serving in any of the regular armed forces of the Crown, an officer holding a commission in any of those forces.

14.11 Reports by the adoption agency or local authority

(1) The adoption agency or local authority must file the report on the suitability of the applicant to adopt a child within the timetable fixed by the court.

(2) A local authority that is directed to prepare a report on the placement of the child for adoption must file that report within the timetable fixed by the court.

(3) The reports must cover the matters specified in Practice Direction 14C.

(4) The court may at any stage request a further report or ask the adoption agency or local authority to assist the court in any other manner.

(5) A court officer will send a copy of any report referred to in this rule to any children's guardian, reporting officer or children and family reporter.

(6) A report to the court under this rule is confidential.

14.12 Health reports

(1) Reports by a registered medical practitioner ('health reports') made not more than 3 months earlier on the health of the child and of each applicant must be attached to an application for an adoption order or a section 84 order except where—

(a) the child was placed for adoption with the applicant by an adoption agency;
(b) the applicant or one of the applicants is a parent of the child; or
(c) the applicant is the partner of a parent of the child.

(2) Health reports must contain the matters set out in Practice Direction 14D.

(3) A health report is confidential.

14.13 Confidential reports to the court and disclosure to the parties

(1) The court will consider whether to give a direction that a confidential report be disclosed to each party to the proceedings.

(2) Before giving such a direction the court will consider whether any information should be deleted including information which—

(a) discloses, or is likely to disclose, the identity of a person who has been assigned a serial number under rule 14.2(2) [or (3)][1]; or
(b) discloses the particulars referred to in rule 29.1(1) where a party has given notice under rule 29.1(2) (disclosure of personal details).

(3) The court may direct that the report will not be disclosed to a party.

Amendment

1 Inserted by the Family Procedure (Amendment No 3) Rules 2014, SI 2014/843, rr 2, 36.

14.14 Communication of information relating to proceedings

For the purposes of the law relating to contempt of court, information (whether or not it is recorded in any form) relating to proceedings held in private may be communicated—

(a) where the court gives permission;
(b) unless the court directs otherwise, in accordance with Practice Direction 14E; or
(c) where the communication is to—
  (i) a party;
  (ii) the legal representative of a party;
  (iii) a professional legal adviser;
  (iv) an officer of the service or a Welsh family proceedings officer;
  (v) a welfare officer;
  (vi) [the Director of Legal Aid Casework (within the meaning of section 4 of the Legal Aid, Sentencing and Punishment of Offenders Act 2012)][1];
  (vii) an expert whose instruction by a party has been authorised by the court for the purposes of the proceedings; or
  (viii) a professional acting in furtherance of the protection of children.

Amendment

1 Substituted by the Legal Aid, Sentencing and Punishment of Offenders Act 2012 (Consequential, Transitional and Saving Provisions) Regulations 2013, SI 2013/534, reg 14(1), Schedule, para 22(b).

14.15 Notice of final hearing

A court officer will give notice to the parties, any children's guardian, reporting officer or children and family reporter and to any other person to whom a practice direction may require such notice to be given—

(a) of the date and place where the application will be heard; and
(b) of the fact that, unless the person wishes or the court requires, the person need not attend.

14.16 The final hearing

(1) Any person who has been given notice in accordance with rule 14.15 may attend the final hearing and, subject to paragraph (2), be heard on the question of whether an order should be made.

(2) A person whose application for the permission of the court to oppose the making of an adoption order under section 47(3) or (5) of the 2002 Act has been refused is not entitled to be heard on the question of whether an order should be made.

(3) Any member or employee of a party which is a local authority, adoption agency or other body may address the court at the final hearing if authorised to do so.

(4) The court may direct that any person must attend a final hearing.

(5) Paragraphs (6) and (7) apply to—

- (a) an adoption order;
- (b) a section 84 order; or
- (c) a section 89 order.

(6) Subject to paragraphs (7) and (8), the court cannot make an order unless the applicant and the child personally attend the final hearing.

(7) The court may direct that the applicant or the child need not attend the final hearing.

(8) In a case of adoption by a couple under section 50 of the 2002 Act, the court may make an adoption order after personal attendance of one only of the applicants if there are special circumstances.

(9) The court cannot make a placement order unless a legal representative of the applicant attends the final hearing.

14.17 Proof of identity of the child

(1) Unless the contrary is shown, the child referred to in the application will be deemed to be the child referred to in the form of consent—

- (a) to the child being placed for adoption;
- (b) to the making of an adoption order; or
- (c) to the making of a section 84 order,

where the conditions in paragraph (2) apply.

(2) The conditions are—

- (a) the application identifies the child by reference to a full certified copy of an entry in the registers of live-births;
- (b) the form of consent identifies the child by reference to a full certified copy of an entry in the registers of live-births attached to the form; and
- (c) the copy of the entry in the registers of live-births referred to in sub-paragraph (a) is the same or relates to the same entry in the registers of live-births as the copy of the entry in the registers of live-births attached to the form of consent.

(3) Where the child is already an adopted child paragraph (2) will have effect as if for the references to the registers of live-births there were substituted references to the Adopted Children Register.

(4) Subject to paragraph (7), where the precise date of the child's birth is not proved to the satisfaction of the court, the court will determine the probable date of birth.

(5) The probable date of the child's birth may be specified in the placement order, adoption order or section 84 order as the date of the child's birth.

(6) Subject to paragraph (7), where the child's place of birth cannot be proved to the satisfaction of the court—

(a) the child may be treated as having been born in [the registration district and sub-district in which the court sits][1] where it is probable that the child may have been born in—
 (i) the United Kingdom;
 (ii) the Channel Islands; or
 (iii) the Isle of Man; or
(b) in any other case, the particulars of the country of birth may be omitted from the placement order, adoption order or section 84 order.

(7) A placement order identifying the probable date and place of birth of the child will be sufficient proof of the date and place of birth of the child in adoption proceedings and proceedings for a section 84 order.

Amendment

1 Substituted by the Family Procedure (Amendment No 3) Rules 2013, SI 2013/3204, rr 2, 60.

14.18 Disclosing information to an adopted adult

(1) The adopted person has the right, on request, to receive from the court which made the adoption order a copy of the following—

(a) the application form for an adoption order (but not the documents attached to that form);
(b) the adoption order and any other orders relating to the adoption proceedings;
(c) orders [containing any provision for contact][1] with the child after the adoption order was made; and
(d) any other document or order referred to in Practice Direction 14F.

(2) The court will remove any protected information from any copy of a document or order referred to in paragraph (1) before the copies are given to the adopted person.

(3) This rule does not apply to an adopted person under the age of 18 years.

(4) In this rule 'protected information' means information which would be protected information under section 57(3) of the 2002 Act if the adoption agency gave the information and not the court.

Amendment

1 Substituted by the Family Procedure (Amendment No 3) Rules 2014, SI 2014/843, rr 2, 37.

14.19 Translation of documents

(1) Where a translation of any document is required for the purposes of proceedings for a Convention adoption order the translation must—

(a) unless the court directs otherwise, be provided by the applicant; and
(b) be signed by the translator to certify that the translation is accurate.

(2) … [1]

Amendment

1 Repealed by the Family Procedure Rules 2010 and Court of Protection Rules 2017 (Amendment) (EU Exit) Regulations 2019, SI 2019/517, rr 2, 10.

14.20 Application for recovery orders

[(1) An application for any of the orders referred to in section 41(2) of the 2002 Act (recovery orders) may be made without notice, in which case the applicant must file the application—

(a) where the application is made by telephone, the next business day after the making of the application; or

(b) in any other case, at the time when the application is made.][1]

(2) Where the court refuses to make an order on an application without notice it may direct that the application is made on notice in which case the application will proceed in accordance with rules 14.1 to 14.17.

(3) The respondents to an application under this rule are—

(a) in a case where—

 (i) placement proceedings;

 (ii) adoption proceedings; or

 (iii) proceedings for a section 84 order,

are pending, all parties to those proceedings;

(b) any adoption agency authorised to place the child for adoption or which has placed the child for adoption;

(c) any local authority to whom notice under section 44 of the 2002 Act (notice of intention to adopt or apply for a section 84 order) has been given;

(d) any person having parental responsibility for the child;

(e) any person in whose favour there is provision for contact;

(f) any person who was caring for the child immediately prior to the making of the application; and

(g) any person whom the applicant alleges to have effected, or to have been or to be responsible for, the taking or keeping of the child.

Amendment

1 Substituted by the Family Procedure (Amendment No 3) Rules 2013, SI 2013/3204, rr 2, 61.

14.21 [Notice to][1] fathers without parental responsibility

Where no proceedings have started an adoption agency or local authority may ask the [court][1] for directions on the need to give a father without parental responsibility notice of the intention to place a child for adoption.

Amendment

1 Substituted by the Family Procedure (Amendment) Rules 2020, SI 2020/135, rr 2, 21.

14.22 Timing of applications for section 89 order

An application for a section 89 order must be made within 2 years beginning with the date on which—

(a) the Convention adoption or Convention adoption order; or

(b) the overseas adoption or determination under section 91 of the 2002 Act,

to which it relates was made.

14.23 Custody of documents

All documents relating to proceedings under the 2002 Act must, while they are in the custody of the court, be kept in a place of special security.

14.24 Documents held by the court not to be inspected or copied without the court's permission

Subject to the provisions of these rules, any practice direction or any direction given by the court—

(a) no document or order held by the court in proceedings under the 2002 Act will be open to inspection by any person; and
(b) no copy of any such document or order, or of an extract from any such document or order, will be taken by or given to any person.

14.25 Orders

(1) An order takes effect from the date when it is made, or such later date as the court may specify.

(2) In proceedings in Wales a party may request that an order be drawn up in Welsh as well as English.

[(Rule 37.9 makes provision for the court to endorse an order prohibiting contact under section 51A(2)(b) of the 2002 Act with a penal notice on the application of the person entitled to enforce the order.)][1]

Amendment

1 Inserted by the Family Procedure (Amendment No 3) Rules 2014, SI 2014/843, rr 2, 38.

14.26 Copies of orders

(1) Within 7 days beginning with the date on which the final order was made in proceedings, or such shorter time as the court may direct, a court officer will send—

(a) a copy of the order to the applicant;
(b) a copy, which is sealed(GL), authenticated with the stamp of the court or certified as a true copy, of—
(i) an adoption order;
(ii) a section 89 order; or
(iii) an order quashing or revoking an adoption order or allowing an appeal against an adoption order,

to the Registrar General;
(c) a copy of a Convention adoption order to the relevant Central Authority;
(d) a copy of a section 89 order relating to a Convention adoption order or a Convention adoption to the—
(i) relevant Central Authority;
(ii) adopters;
(iii) adoption agency; and
(iv) local authority;
(e) unless the court directs otherwise, [a copy of an][1] under section 26 of the 2002 Act or a [variation or revocation of such][1] order under section 27 of the 2002 Act to the—
(i) person with whom the child is living;

(ii) adoption agency; and
(iii) local authority;

[(ee) unless the court directs otherwise, a copy of a contact order under section 51A(2)(a) of the 2002 Act, an order prohibiting contact under section 51A(2)(b) of that Act or a variation or revocation of such orders under section 51B(1)(c) of that Act to the parties to the proceedings; and][2]

(f) a notice of the making or refusal of—
(i) the final order; or
(ii) an order quashing or revoking an adoption order or allowing an appeal against an order in proceedings,

to every respondent and, with the permission of the court, any other person.

(2) The court officer will also send notice of the making of an adoption order or a section 84 order to—

(a) any court in Great Britain which appears to the court officer to have made any such order as is referred to in section 46(2) of the 2002 Act (order relating to parental responsibility for, and maintenance of, the child); and
(b) the principal registry, if it appears to the court officer that a parental responsibility agreement has been recorded at the principal registry.

(3) A copy of any final order may be sent to any other person with the permission of the court.

(4) The court officer will send a copy of any order made during the course of the proceedings to the following persons or bodies, unless the court directs otherwise—

(a) all the parties to those proceedings;
(b) any children and family reporter appointed in those proceedings;
(c) any adoption agency or local authority which has prepared a report on the suitability of an applicant to adopt a child;
(d) any local authority which has prepared a report on placement for adoption.

(5) If an order has been drawn up in Welsh as well as English in accordance with rule 14.25(2) any reference in this rule to sending an order is to be taken as a reference to sending both the Welsh and English orders.

Amendment

1 Substituted by the Family Procedure (Amendment No 3) Rules 2014, SI 2014/843, rr 2, 39(a).
2 Inserted by the Family Procedure (Amendment No 3) Rules 2014, SI 2014/843, rr 2, 39(b).

14.27 Amendment and revocation of orders

(1) Subject to paragraph (2), an application under—

(a) section 55 of the 2002 Act (revocation of adoptions on legitimation); or
(b) paragraph 4 of Schedule 1 to the 2002 Act (amendment of adoption order and revocation of direction),

may be made without serving a copy of the application notice.

(2) The court may direct that an application notice be served on such persons as it thinks fit.

(3) Where the court makes an order granting the application, a court officer will send the Registrar General a notice—

(a) specifying the amendments; or
(b) informing the Registrar General of the revocation,

giving sufficient particulars of the order to enable the Registrar General to identify the case.

14.28 …[1]

…[1]

Amendment

1 Repealed by the Family Procedure (Amendment No 3) Rules 2013, SI 2013/3204, rr 2, 62.

Practice Direction 14A – Who receives a copy of the application form for orders in proceedings

See also Part 14, Practice Direction 14B, Practice Direction 14C, Practice Direction 14D, Practice Direction 14E, Practice Direction 14F

This Practice Direction supplements Part 14, rule 14.6(1)(b)(ii) of the Family Procedure Rules 2010

Persons who receive copy of application form

1.1 Subject to paragraph 1.2, in relation to each type of proceedings in column 1 of the following table, column 2 sets out which persons are to receive a copy of the application form –

Proceeding for	Who Receives a Copy of the Application Form
An adoption order (section 46 of the Act); or a section 84 order	Any appointed children's guardian, children and family reporter and reporting officer; the local authority to whom notice under section 44 (notice of intention to apply to adopt or apply for a section 84 order) has been given; the adoption agency which placed the child for adoption with the applicants; any other person directed by the court to receive a copy.
A placement order (section 21 of the Act); or an order varying a placement order (section 23 of the Act)	Each parent with parental responsibility for the child or guardian of the child; any appointed children's guardian, children and family reporter and reporting officer; any other person directed by the court to receive a copy.
An order revoking a placement order (section 24 of the Act)	Each parent with parental responsibility for the child or guardian of the child; any appointed children's guardian and children and family reporter; the local authority authorised by the placement order to place the child for adoption; any other person directed by the court to receive a copy.

Proceeding for	Who Receives a Copy of the Application Form
A contact order (section 26 of the Act); an order varying or revoking a contact order (section 27 of the Act); an order permitting the child's name to be changed or the removal of the child from the United Kingdom (section 28(2) of the Act); a recovery order (section 41(2) of the Act); a contact order under section 51A(2)(a) of the Act; the making of an order prohibiting contact with the child under section 51A(2)(b) of the Act; the variation or revocation of an order under section 51A(2) of the Act in accordance with section 51B(1)(c) of the Act; a section 89 order; and a section 88 direction	All the parties; any appointed children's guardian and children and family reporter; any other person directed by the court to receive a copy.

1.2 A person listed in column 2 of the following table shall not receive a copy of the application form, if the court, on application by any party, directs that such notification is not required.

Practice Direction 14B – The first directions hearing – adoptions with a foreign element

See also Part 14, Practice Direction 14A, Practice Direction 14C, Practice Direction 14D, Practice Direction 14E, Practice Direction 14F

This Practice Direction supplements Part 14, rule 14.8(3)of the Family Procedure Rules 2010

Application

1.1 This Practice Direction applies to proceedings for–

- (a) a Convention adoption order;
- (b) a section 84 order;
- (c) a section 88 direction;
- (d) a section 89 order; and
- (e) an adoption order where the child has been brought into the United Kingdom in the circumstances where section 83(1) of the Act applies.

The first directions hearing

2.1 At the first directions hearing the court will, in addition to any matters referred to in rule 14.8(1),–

- (a) consider whether the requirements of the Act and the Adoptions with a Foreign Element Regulations 2005 (S.I.2005/392) appear to have been complied with and, if not, consider whether or not in a case in the family court, it is appropriate that the case should be considered by a puisne judge of the High Court sitting in the family court (who may in turn consider whether or not it is appropriate to transfer the case to the High Court);

(b) consider whether all relevant documents are translated into English and, if not, fix a timetable for translating any outstanding documents;

(c) consider whether the applicant needs to file an affidavit setting out the full details of the circumstances in which the child was brought to the United Kingdom, of the attitude of the parents to the application and confirming compliance with the requirements of The Adoptions with A Foreign Element Regulations 2005;

(d) give directions about–
 (i) the production of the child's passport and visa;
 (ii) the need for an officer of the Service or a Welsh family proceedings officer and a representative of the Home Office to attend future hearings; and
 (iii) personal service on the parents (via the Central Authority in the case of an application for a Convention Adoption Order) including information about the role of the officer of the Service or the Welsh family proceedings officer and availability of legal aid to be represented within the proceedings; and

(e) consider fixing a further directions appointment no later than 6 weeks after the date of the first directions appointment and timetable a date by which the officer of the Service or the Welsh family proceedings officer should file an interim report in advance of that further appointment.

Practice Direction 14C – Reports by the adoption agency or local authority

See also Part 14, Practice Direction 14A, Practice Direction 14B, Practice Direction 14D, Practice Direction 14E, Practice Direction 14F

This Practice Direction supplements Part 14, rule 14.11(3) of the Family Procedure Rules 2010

Matters to be contained in reports

1.1 The matters to be covered in the report on the suitability of the applicant to adopt a child are set out in Annex A to this Practice Direction.

1.2 The matters to be covered in a report on the placement of the child for adoption are set out in Annex B to this Practice Direction.

1.3 Where a matter to be covered in the reports set out in Annex A and Annex B does not apply to the circumstances of a particular case, the reasons for not covering the matter should be given.

Annex A

Report to the Court where there has been an Application for an Adoption Order or an Application for a Section 84 Order

Section A: The Report and matters for the Proceedings

Part 1 The Report

For each of the principal author/s of the report:

(i) name;

(ii) role in relation to this case;

(iii) sections completed in this report;
(iv) qualifications and experience;
(v) name and address of the adoption agency; and
(vi) adoption agency case reference number.

Part 2 Matters for the Proceedings

(a) Whether the adoption agency considers that any other person should be made a respondent or a party to the proceedings, including the child.
(a1) Whether the adoption agency or other party considers that any person should not receive notification of the proceedings or should not be made a party. Parties should discuss the matter before proceedings are issued.
(b) Whether any of the respondents is under the age of 18.
(c) Whether a respondent is a person who, by reason of mental disorder within the meaning of the Mental Health Act 1983, is incapable of managing and administering his or her property and affairs. If so, medical evidence should be provided with particular regard to the effect on that person's ability to make decisions in the proceedings.

Section B: The Child and the Birth Family

Part 1

i – Information about the Child

(a) Name, sex, date and place of birth and address including local authority area.
(b) Photograph and physical description.
(c) Nationality.
(d) Racial origin and cultural and linguistic background.
(e) Religious persuasion (including details of baptism, confirmation or equivalent ceremonies).
(f) Details of any siblings, half-siblings and step-siblings, including dates of birth.
(g) Whether the child is looked after by a local authority.
(h) Whether the child has been placed for adoption with the prospective adopter by a UK adoption agency.
(i) Whether the child was being fostered by the prospective adopter.
(j) Whether the child was brought into the UK for adoption, including date of entry and whether an adoption order was made in the child's country of origin.
(k) Personality and social development, including emotional and behavioural development and any related needs.
(l) Details of interests, likes and dislikes.
(m) A summary, written by the agency's medical adviser, of the child's health history, his current state of health and any need for health care which is anticipated, and date of the most recent medical examination.
(n) Any known learning difficulties or known general medical or mental health factors which are likely to have, or may have, genetic implications.
(o) Names, addresses and types of nurseries or schools attended, with dates.
(p) Educational attainments.
(q) Any special needs in relation to the child (whether physical, learning, behavioural or any other) and his emotional and behavioural development.
(r) Whether the child is subject to a statement under the Education Act 1996.
(s) Previous orders concerning the child:
    (i) the name of the court;
    (ii) the order made; and
    (iii) the date of the order.

(t) Inheritance rights and any claim to damages under the Fatal Accidents Act 1976 the child stands to retain or lose if adopted.
(u) Any other relevant information which might assist the court.

ii – Information about each Parent of the Child

(a) Name, date and place of birth and address (date on which last address was confirmed current) including local authority area.
(b) Photograph, if available, and physical description.
(c) Nationality.
(d) Racial origin and cultural and linguistic background.
(e) Whether the mother and father were married to each other at the time of the child's birth or have subsequently married.
(f) Where the parent has been previously married or entered into a civil partnership, dates of those marriages or civil partnerships.
(g) Where the mother and father are not married, whether the father has parental responsibility and, if so, how it was acquired.
(h) If the identity or whereabouts of the father are not known, the information about him that has been ascertained and from whom, and the steps that have been taken to establish paternity.
(i) Past and present relationship with the other parent.
(j) Other information about the parent, where available:
   (i) health, including any known learning difficulties or known general medical or mental health factors which are likely to have, or may have, genetic implications;
   (ii) religious persuasion;
   (iii) educational history;
   (iv) employment history; and
   (v) personality and interests.
(k) Any other relevant information which might assist the court.

Part 2

Relationships, contact arrangements and views

The Child

(a) If the child is in the care of a local authority or voluntary organisation, or has been, details (including dates) of any placements with foster parents, or other arrangements in respect of the care of the child, including particulars of the persons with whom the child has had his home and observations on the care provided.
(b) The child's wishes and feelings (if appropriate, having regard to the child's age and understanding) about adoption, the application and its consequences, including any wishes in respect of religious and cultural upbringing.
(c) The child's wishes and feelings in relation to contact (if appropriate, having regard to the child's age and understanding).
(d) The child's wishes and feelings recorded in any other proceedings.
(e) Date when the child's views were last ascertained.

The Child's Parents (or guardian) and relatives

(a) The parents' wishes and feelings before the placement, about the placement and about adoption, the application and its consequences, including any wishes in respect of the child's religious and cultural upbringing.

(b) Each parent's (or guardian's) wishes and feelings in relation to contact.
(c) Date/s when the views of each parent or guardian were last ascertained.
(d) Arrangements concerning any siblings, including half-siblings and step-siblings, and whether any are the subject of a parallel application or have been the subject of any orders. If so, for each case give:
  (i) the name of the court;
  (ii) the order made, or (if proceedings are pending) the order applied for; and
  (iii) the date of order, or date of next hearing if proceedings are pending.
(e) Extent of contact with the child's mother and father and, in each case, the nature of the relationship enjoyed.
(f) The relationship which the child has with relatives, and with any other person considered relevant, including:
  (i) the likelihood of any such relationship continuing and the value to the child of its doing so; and
  (ii) the ability and willingness of any of the child's relatives, or of any such person, to provide the child with a secure environment in which the child can develop, and otherwise to meet the child's needs.
(g) The wishes and feelings of any of the child's relatives, or of any such person, regarding the child.
(h) Whether the parents (or members of the child's family) have met or are likely to meet the prospective adopter and, if they have met, the effect on all involved of such meeting.
(i) Dates when the views of members of the child's wider family and any other relevant person were last ascertained.

Part 3

A summary of the actions of the adoption agency

(a) Brief account of the agency's actions in the case, with particulars and dates of all written information and notices given to the child and his parents and any person with parental responsibility.
(b) If consent has been given for the child to be placed for adoption, and also consent for the child to be adopted, the names of those who gave consent and the date such consents were given. If such consents were subsequently withdrawn, the dates of these withdrawals.
(c) If any statement has been made under section 20(4)(a) of the Adoption and Children Act 2002 (the '2002 Act') that a parent or guardian does not wish to be informed of any application for an adoption order, the names of those who have made such statements and the dates the statements were made. If such statements were subsequently withdrawn, the dates of these withdrawals.
(d) Whether an order has been made under section 21 of the 2002 Act, section 18 of the Adoption (Scotland) Act 1978 or Article 17(1) or 18(1) of the Northern Ireland Order 1987.
(e) Details of the support and advice given to the parents and any services offered or taken up.
(f) If the father does not have parental responsibility, details of the steps taken to inform him of the application for an adoption order.
(g) Brief details and dates of assessments of the child's needs, including expert opinions.
(h) Reasons for considering that adoption would be in the child's best interests (with date of relevant decision and reasons for any delay in implementing the decision).

Section C: The Prospective Adopter of the Child

Part 1

Information about the Prospective Adopter, including suitability to adopt

(a) Name, date and place of birth and address (date on which last address was confirmed current) including local authority area.
(b) Photograph and physical description.
(c) Whether the prospective adopter is domiciled or habitually resident in a part of the British Islands and, if habitually resident, for how long they have been habitually resident.
(d) Racial origin and cultural and linguistic background.
(e) Marital status or civil partnership status, date and place of most recent marriage (if any) or civil partnership (if any).
(f) Details of any previous marriage, civil partnership, or relationship where the prospective adopter lived with another person as a partner in an enduring family relationship.
(g) Relationship (if any) to the child.
(h) Where adopters wish to adopt as a couple, the status of the relationship and an assessment of the stability and permanence of their relationship.
(i) If a married person or a civil partner is applying alone, the reasons for this.
(j) Description of how the prospective adopter relates to adults and children.
(k) Previous experience of caring for children (including as a step-parent, foster parent, child-minder or prospective adopter) and assessment of ability in this respect, together where appropriate with assessment of ability in bringing up the prospective adopter's own children.
(l) A summary, written by the agency's medical adviser, of the prospective adopter's health history, current state of health and any need for health care which is anticipated, and date of most recent medical examination.
(m) Assessment of ability and suitability to bring up the child throughout his childhood.
(n) Details of income and comments on the living standards of the household with particulars of the home and living conditions (and particulars of any home where the prospective adopter proposes to live with the child, if different).
(o) Details of other members of the household, including any children of the prospective adopter even if not resident in the household.
(p) Details of the parents and any siblings of the prospective adopter, with their ages or ages at death.
(q) Other information about the prospective adopter:
    (i) religious persuasion;
    (ii) educational history;
    (iii) employment history; and
    (iv) personality and interests.
(r) Confirmation that the applicants have not been convicted of, or cautioned for, a specified offence within the meaning of regulation 23(3) of the Adoption Agencies Regulations 2005 (S.I. 2005/389).
(s) Confirmation that the prospective adopter is still approved.
(t) Confirmation that any referees have been interviewed, with a report of their views and opinion of the weight to be placed thereon and whether they are still valid.
(u) Details of any previous family court proceedings in which the prospective adopter has been involved (which have not been referred to elsewhere in this report.)

Part 2

Wishes, views and contact arrangements

Prospective Adopter

(a) Whether the prospective adopter is willing to follow any wishes of the child or his parents or guardian in respect of the child's religious and cultural upbringing.
(b) The views of other members of the prospective adopter's household and wider family in relation to the proposed adoption.
(c) Reasons for the prospective adopter wishing to adopt the child and extent of understanding of the nature and effect of adoption. Whether the prospective adopter has discussed adoption with the child.
(d) Any hope and expectations the prospective adopter has for the child's future.
(e) The prospective adopter's wishes and feelings in relation to contact.

Part 3

Actions of the adoption agency

(a) Brief account of the Agency's actions in the case, with particulars and dates of all written information and notices given to the prospective adopter.
(b) The Agency's proposals for contact, including options for facilitating or achieving any indirect contact or direct contact.
(c) The Agency's opinion on the likely effect on the prospective adopter and on the security of the placement of any proposed contact.
(d) Where the prospective adopter has been approved by an agency as suitable to be an adoptive parent, the agency's reasons for considering that the prospective adopter is suitable to be an adoptive parent for this child (with dates of relevant decisions).

Section D: The Placement

(a) Where the child was placed for adoption by an adoption agency (section 18 of the 2002 Act), the date and circumstances of the child's placement with prospective adopter.
(b) Where the child is living with persons who have applied for the adoption order to be made (section 44 of the 2002 Act), the date when notice of intention to adopt was given.
(c) Where the placement is being provided with adoption support, this should be summarised and should include the plan and timescales for continuing the support beyond the making of the adoption order.
(d) Where the placement is not being provided with adoption support, the reasons why.
(e) A summary of the information obtained from the Agency's visits and reviews of the placement, including whether the child has been seen separately to the prospective adopter and whether there has been sufficient opportunity to see the family group and the child's interaction in the home environment.
(f) An assessment of the child's integration within the family of the prospective adopter and the likelihood of the child's full integration into the family and community.
(g) Any other relevant information that might assist the court.

Section E: Recommendations

(a) The relative merits of adoption and other orders with an assessment of whether the child's long term interests would be best met by an adoption order or by other orders (such as child arrangements and special guardianship orders).
(b) Recommendations as to whether or not the order sought should be made (and, if not, alternative proposals).
(c) Recommendations as to whether there should be future contact arrangements (or not).

Section F: Further Information for Proceedings relating to Convention Adoption Orders, Convention Adoptions, Section 84 Orders or an Adoption where Section 83(1) of the 2002 Act applies

(a) The child's knowledge of their racial and cultural origin.
(b) The likelihood of the child's adaptation to living in the country he/she is to be placed.
(c) Where the UK is the State of origin, reasons for considering that, after possibilities for placement of the child within the UK have been given due consideration, intercountry adoption is in the child's best interests.
(d) Confirmation that the requirements of regulations made under sections 83(4), (5), (6) and (7) and 84(3) and (6) of the 2002 Act have been complied with.
(e) For a Convention adoption or a Convention Adoption Order where the United Kingdom is either the State of origin or the receiving State, confirmation that the Central Authorities of both States have agreed that the adoption may proceed.
(f) Where the State of origin is not the United Kingdom, the documents supplied by the Central Authority of the State of origin should be attached to the report, together with translation if necessary.
(g) Where a Convention adoption order is proposed, details of the arrangements which were made for the transfer of the child to the UK and that they were in accordance with the Adoptions with a Foreign Element Regulations 2005 (S.I.2005/392).

Annex B

Report to the Court where there has been an Application for a Placement Order

Section A: The Report and matters for the Proceedings

Part 1

The Report

For each of the principal author/s of the report:

(i) name;
(ii) role in relation to this case;
(iii) sections completed in this report;
(iv) qualifications and experience;
(v) name and address of the adoption agency; and
(vi) adoption agency case reference number.

Part 2

Matters for the Proceedings

(a) Whether the adoption agency considers that any other person should be made a respondent or a party to the proceedings.
(b) Whether any of the respondents is under the age of 18.
(c) Whether a respondent is a person who, by reason of mental disorder within the meaning of the Mental Health Act 1983, is incapable of managing and administering his or her property and affairs. If so, medical evidence should be provided with particular regard to the effect on that person's ability to make decisions in the proceedings.

Section B: The Child and the Birth Family

Part 1

i – Information about the Child

(a) Name, sex, date and place of birth and address including local authority area.
(b) Photograph and physical description.
(c) Nationality.
(d) Racial origin and cultural and linguistic background.
(e) Religious persuasion (including details of baptism, confirmation or equivalent ceremonies).
(f) Details of any siblings, half-siblings and step-siblings, including dates of birth.
(g) Whether the child is looked after by a local authority.
(h) Personality and social development, including emotional and behavioural development and any related needs.
(i) Details of interests, likes and dislikes.
(j) A summary, written by the agency's medical adviser, of the child's health history, his current state of health and any need for health care which is anticipated, and date of the most recent medical examination.
(k) Any known learning difficulties or known general medical or mental health factors which are likely to have, or may have, genetic implications.
(l) Names, addresses and types of nurseries or schools attended, with dates.
(m) Educational attainments.
(n) Any special needs in relation to the child (whether physical, learning, behavioural or any other) and his emotional and behavioural development.
(o) Whether the child is subject to a statement under the Education Act 1996.
(p) Previous orders concerning the child:
    (i) the name of the court;
    (ii) the order made; and
    (iii) the date of the order.
(q) Inheritance rights and any claim to damages under the Fatal Accidents Act 1976 the child stands to retain or lose if adopted.
(r) Any other relevant information which might assist the court.

ii – Information about each Parent of the Child

(a) Name, date and place of birth and address (date on which last address was confirmed current) including local authority area.
(b) Photograph, if available, and physical description.

(c) Nationality.
(d) Racial origin and cultural and linguistic background.
(e) Whether the mother and father were married to each other at the time of the child's birth, or have subsequently married.
(f) Where the parent has been previously married or entered into a civil partnership, dates of those marriages or civil partnerships.
(g) Where the mother and father are not married, whether the father has parental responsibility and, if so, how it was acquired.
(h) If the identity or whereabouts of the father are not known, the information about him that has been ascertained and from whom, and the steps that have been taken to establish paternity.
(i) Past and present relationship with the other parent.
(j) Other information about the parent, where available:
   (i) health, including any known learning difficulties or known general medical or mental health factors which are likely to have, or may have, genetic implications;
   (ii) religious persuasion;
   (iii) educational history;
   (iv) employment history; and
   (v) personality and interests.
(k) Any other relevant information which might assist the court.

Part 2

Relationships, contact arrangements and views

The Child

(a) If the child is in the care of a local authority or voluntary organisation, or has been, details (including dates) of any placements with foster parents, or other arrangements in respect of the care of the child, including particulars of the persons with whom the child has had his home and observations on the care provided.
(b) The child's wishes and feelings (if appropriate, having regard to the child's age and understanding) about the application, its consequences, and adoption, including any wishes in respect of religious and cultural upbringing.
(c) The child's wishes and feelings in relation to contact (if appropriate, having regard to the child's age and understanding).
(d) The child's wishes and feelings recorded in any other proceedings.
(e) Date when the child's views were last ascertained.

The Child's Parents (or guardian) and relatives

(a) The parents' wishes and feelings about the application, its consequences, and adoption, including any wishes in respect of the child's religious and cultural upbringing.
(b) Each parent's (or guardian's) wishes and feelings in relation to contact.
(c) Date/s when the views of each parent or guardian were last ascertained.
(d) Arrangements concerning any siblings, including half-siblings and step-siblings, and whether any are the subject of a parallel application or have been the subject of any orders. If so, for each case give:
   (i) the name of the court;
   (ii) the order made, or (if proceedings are pending) the order applied for; and
   (iii) the date of order, or date of next hearing if proceedings are pending.

(e) Extent of contact with the child's mother and father and in each case the nature of the relationship enjoyed.

(f) The relationship which the child has with relatives, and with any other person considered relevant, including:

(i) the likelihood of any such relationship continuing and the value to the child of its doing so; and

(ii) the ability and willingness of any of the child's relatives, or of any such person, to provide the child with a secure environment in which the child can develop, and otherwise to meet the child's needs.

(g) The wishes and feelings of any of the child's relatives, or of any such person, regarding the child.

(h) Dates when the views of members of the child's wider family and any other relevant person were last ascertained.

Part 3

Summary of the actions of the adoption agency

(a) Brief account of the Agency's actions in the case, with particulars and dates of all written information and notices given to the child and his parents and any person with parental responsibility.

(b) If consent has been given for the child to be placed for adoption, and also consent for the child to be adopted, the names of those who gave consent and the date such consents were given. If such consents were subsequently withdrawn, the dates of these withdrawals.

(c) If any statement has been made under section 20(4)(a) of the 2002 Act that a parent or guardian does not wish to be informed of any application for an adoption order, the names of those who have made such statements and the dates the statements were made. If such statements were subsequently withdrawn, the dates of these withdrawals.

(d) Details of the support and advice given to the parents and any services offered or taken up.

(e) If the father does not have parental responsibility, details of the steps taken to inform him of the application for a placement order.

(f) Brief details and dates of assessments of the child's needs, including expert opinions.

(g) Reasons for considering that adoption would be in the child's best interests (with date of relevant decision and reasons for any delay in implementing the decision).

Section C: Recommendations

(a) The relative merits of a placement order and other orders (such as a child arrangements or special guardianship order) with an assessment of why the child's long term interests are likely to be best met by a placement order rather than by any other order.

(b) Recommendations as to whether there should be future contact arrangements (or not), including whether a contact order under section 26 of the 2002 Act should be made.

Practice Direction 14D – Reports by a registered medical practitioner ('health reports')

See also Part 14, Practice Direction 14A, Practice Direction 14B, Practice Direction 14C, Practice Direction 14E, Practice Direction 14F

This Practice Direction supplements Part 14, rule 14.12(2) of the Family Procedure Rules 2010

Matters to be contained in health reports

1.1 Rule 14.12(1) requires that health reports must be attached to an application for an adoption order or a section 84 order except where–

(a) the child was placed for adoption with the applicant by an adoption agency;
(b) the applicant or one of the applicants is a parent of the child; or
(c) the applicant is the partner of a parent of the child.

1.2 The matters to be contained in the health reports are set out in the Annex to this Practice Direction.

1.3 Where a matter to be contained in the health report does not apply to the circumstances of a particular case, the reasons for not covering the matter should be given.

Annex

Contents of Health Reports

This information is required for reports on the health of children and their prospective adopter(s). Its purpose is to build up a full picture of each child's health history and current state of health, including strengths and weaknesses. This will enable local authorities' medical adviser to base their advice to the court on the fullest possible information when commenting on the health implications of the proposed adoption. The reports made by the examining doctor should cover, as far as practicable, the following matters.

1 The Child

Name, date of birth, sex, weight and height.

(A) A health history of each natural parent, so far as is possible, including:
  (i) name, date of birth, sex, weight and height;
  (ii) a family health history, covering the parents, the brothers and sisters and the other children of the natural parent, with details of any serious physical or mental illness and inherited and congenital disease;
  (iii) past health history, including details of any serious physical or mental illness, disability, accident, hospital admission or attendance at an out-patient department, and in each case any treatment given;
  (iv) a full obstetric history of the mother, including any problems in the ante-natal, labour and post-natal periods, with the results of any tests carried out during or immediately after pregnancy;
  (v) details of any present illness including treatment and prognosis;
  (vi) any other relevant information which might assist the medical adviser; and
  (vii) the name and address of any doctor(s) who might be able to provide further information about any of the above matters.

(B) A neo-natal report on the child, including:
  (i) details of the birth, and any complications;
  (ii) results of a physical examination and screening tests;
  (iii) details of any treatment given;
  (iv) details of any problem in management and feeding;
  (v) any other relevant information which might assist the medical adviser; and
  (vi) the name and address of any doctor(s) who might be able to provide further information about any of the above matters.

(C) A full health history and examination of the child, including:
  (i) details of any serious illness, disability, accident, hospital admission or attendance at an out-patient department, and in each case any treatment given;
  (ii) details and dates of immunisations;
  (iii) a physical and developmental assessment according to age, including an assessment of vision and hearing and of neurological, speech and language development and any evidence of emotional or conduct disorder;
  (iv) details, if relevant, of the impact of any addiction or substance use on the part of the natural mother before, during or following the pregnancy, and its impact or likely future impact on the child;
  (v) the impact, if any, on the child's development and likely future development of any past exposure to physical, emotional or sexual abuse or neglectful home conditions and/or any non-organic failure to thrive;
  (vi) for a child of school age, the school health history (if available);
  (vii) any other relevant information which might assist the medical adviser; and
  (viii) the name and address of any doctor(s) who might be able to provide further information about any of the above matters.

(D) The signature, name, address and qualifications of the registered medical practitioner who prepared the report, and the date of the report and of the examinations carried out.

2 The Applicant

(If there is more than one applicant, a report on each applicant should be supplied covering all the matters listed below.)

(A)
  (i) name, date of birth, sex, weight and height;
  (ii) a family health history, covering the parents, the brothers and sisters and the children of the applicant, with details of any serious physical or mental illness and inherited and congenital disease;
  (iii) marital history, including (if applicable) reasons for inability to have children, and any history of domestic violence;
  (iv) past health history, including details of any serious physical or mental illness, disability, accident, hospital admission or attendance at an out-patient department, and in each case any treatment given;
  (v) obstetric history (if applicable);
  (vi) details of any present illness, including treatment and prognosis;

(vii) a full medical examination;
(viii) details of any consumption of alcohol, tobacco and habit-forming drugs;
(ix) any other relevant information which might assist the medical adviser; and
(x) the name and address of any doctor(s) who might be able to provide further information about any of the above matters.

(B) The signature, name, address and qualifications of the registered medical practitioner who prepared the report, and the date of the report and of the examinations carried out.

Practice Direction 14E – Communication of information relating to proceedings

See see also Part 14, Practice Direction 14A, Practice Direction 14B, Practice Direction 14C, Practice Direction 14D, Practice Direction 14F

This Practice Direction supplements Part 14, rule 14.14(b) of the Family Procedure Rules 2010

Communication of information relating to proceedings

1.1 Rule 14.14 deals with the communication of information (whether or not it is recorded in any form)relating to proceedings.

1.2 Subject to any direction of the court, information may be communicated for the purposes of the law relating to contempt in accordance with paragraphs 1.3 or 1.4.

1.3 A person specified in the first column of the following table may communicate to a person listed in the second column such information as is specified in the third column for the purpose or purposes specified in the fourth column.

Communicated by	To	Information	Purpose
A party	A lay adviser or a McKenzie Friend	Any information relating to the proceedings	To enable the party to obtain advice or assistance in relation to the proceedings.
A party	The party's spouse, civil partner, cohabitant or close family member		For the purpose of confidential discussions enabling the party to receive support from his spouse, civil partner, cohabitant or close family member.
A party	A health care professional or a person or body providing counselling services for children or families		To enable the party or any child of the party to obtain health care or counselling.

Communicated by	To	Information	Purpose
A party	The Secretary of State, a McKenzie Friend, a lay adviser or an appeal tribunal dealing with an appeal made under section 20 of the Child Support Act 1991[1]		For the purposes of making or responding to an appeal under section 20 of the Child Support Act 1991 or the determination of such an appeal.
A party or other person lawfully in receipt of information	The Secretary of State, a McKenzie Friend, a lay adviser or the Upper Tier Tribunal dealing with an appeal under section 24 of the Child Support Act 1991 in respect of a decision of the First tier Tribunal that was made under section 20 of that Act		For a purpose connected with an appeal under section 24 of the Child Support Act 1991 in respect of a decision of the First-tier Tribunal that was made under section 20 of that Act
A party	An adoption panel		To enable the adoption panel to discharge its functions as appropriate.
A party	A local authority's medical adviser appointed under the Adoption Agencies Regulations 2005 or the Adoption Agencies (Wales) Regulations 2005		To enable the medical adviser to discharge his or her functions as appropriate
A party or any person lawfully in receipt of information	The Children's Commissioner or the Children's Commissioner for Wales		To refer an issue affecting the interests of children to the Children's Commissioner or the Children's Commissioner for Wales.
A party or any person lawfully in receipt of information	The Welsh Language Commissioner		To refer an issue so that the Welsh Language Commissioner can consider whether to institute or intervene in legal proceedings or to assist a party or prospective party to legal proceedings.

Communicated by	To	Information	Purpose
A party or a legal representative	A mediator		For the purpose of mediation in relation to the proceedings.
A party, any person lawfully in receipt of information or a proper officer	A person or body conducting an approved research project		For the purpose of an approved research project.
A party, a legal representative or a professional legal adviser	A person or body responsible for investigating or determining complaints in relation to legal representatives or professional legal advisers		For the purposes of making a complaint or the investigation or determination of a complaint in relation to a legal representative or a professional legal adviser.
A legal representative or a professional legal adviser	A professional indemnity insurer		To enable the professional indemnity insurer to be notified of a claim or complaint, or potential claim or complaint, in relation to the legal representative or a professional legal adviser, and the legal representative or professional legal adviser to obtain advice in respect of that claim or complaint
A legal representative or a professional legal adviser	A person or body assessing quality assurance systems		To enable the legal representative or professional legal adviser to obtain a quality assurance assessment.
A legal representative or a professional legal adviser	An accreditation body	Any information relating to the proceedings providing that it does not, or is not likely to, identify any person involved in the proceedings	To enable the legal representative or professional legal adviser to obtain accreditation.

Communicated by	To	Information	Purpose
A party	An elected representative or peer	The text or summary of the whole or part of a judgment given in the proceedings	To enable the elected representative or peer to give advice, investigate any complaint or raise any question of policy or procedure.
A party	The General Medical Council		For the purpose of making a complaint to the General Medical Council.
A party	A police officer		For the purpose of a criminal investigation.
A party or any person lawfully in receipt of information	A member of the Crown Prosecution Service		To enable the Crown Prosecution Service to discharge its functions under any enactment.
A party or an adoption agency that is not a party	An adoption agency	Any information relating to the proceedings	To enable the sharing of relevant information between adoption agencies for more effective undertaking of their functions

1.4 A person in the second column of the table in paragraph 1.3 may only communicate information relating to the proceedings received from a person in the first column for the purpose or purposes –

(a) for which he received that information, or
(b) of professional development or training, providing that any communication does not, or is not likely to, identify any person involved in the proceedings without that person's consent.

1.5 In this Practice Direction –

(1) 'accreditation body' means –
  (a) The Law Society,
  (b) Resolution, or
  (c) the Lord Chancellor in exercise of the Lord Chancellor's functions in relation to legal aid;

(1A) 'adoption panel' means a panel established in accordance with regulation 3 of the Adoption Agencies Regulations 2005[2] or regulation 3 of the Adoption Agencies (Wales) Regulations 2005[3];

(2) 'approved research project' means a project of research –
  (a) approved in writing by a Secretary of State after consultation with the President of the Family Division,
  (b) approved in writing by the President of the Family Division, or
  (c) conducted under section 83 of the Act of 1989 or section 13 of the Criminal Justice and Court Services Act 2000;

(3) 'body assessing quality assurance systems' includes –
  (a) The Law Society,
  (b) the Lord Chancellor in exercise of the Lord Chancellor's functions in relation to legal aid, or
  (c) The General Council of the Bar;
(4) 'body or person responsible for investigating or determining complaints in relation to legal representatives or professional legal advisers' means –
  (a) The Law Society,
  (b) The General Council of the Bar,
  (c) The Institute of Legal Executives, or
  (d) The Legal Services Ombudsman;
(5) 'cohabitant' means one of two persons who are neither married to each other nor civil partners of each other but are living together as husband and wife or as if they were civil partners;
(6) 'criminal investigation' means an investigation conducted by police officers with a view to it being ascertained –
  (a) whether a person should be charged with an offence, or
  (b) whether a person charged with an offence is guilty of it;
(7) 'elected representative' means–
  (a) a member of the House of Commons,
  (b) a member of the National Assembly for Wales, or
  (c) a member of the European Parliament elected in England and Wales;
(8) 'health care professional' means –
  (a) a registered medical practitioner,
  (b) a registered nurse or midwife,
  (c) a clinical psychologist,or
  (d) a child psychotherapist;
(9) 'lay adviser' means a non-professional person who gives lay advice on behalf of an organisation in the lay advice sector;
(10) 'McKenzie Friend' means any person permitted by the court to sit beside an unrepresented litigant in court to assist that litigant by prompting, taking notes and giving him advice;
(11) 'mediator' means a family mediator who is –
  (a) undertaking, or has successfully completed, a family mediation training course approved by the United Kingdom College of Family Mediators, or
  (b) a member of the Law Society's Family Mediation Panel;
(12) 'peer' means a member of the House of Lords as defined by the House of Lords Act 1999.

Amendment

1 1991 c.48; section 20 as originally enacted was substituted by the Social Security Act 1998 (c.14); and was further substituted by the Child Support, Pensions and Social Security Act 2000 (c.19); and modified by the Family Proceedings Appeals (Jurisdiction of Courts) Order 1993 S.I. 1993/961.
2 S.I. 2005/389.
3 S.I. 2005/1313.

Practice Direction 14F – Disclosing information to an adopted adult

See also Part 14, Practice Direction 14A, Practice Direction 14B, Practice Direction 14C, Practice Direction 14D, Practice Direction 14E

This Practice Direction supplements Part 14, rule 14.18(1)(d) of the Family Procedure Rules 2010

How to request for information

1.1 Rule 14.18 states that an adopted person who is over the age of 18 has the right to receive from the court which made the adoption order a copy of–

(a) the application form for an adoption order (but not the documents attached to that form);
(b) the adoption order and any other orders relating to the adoption proceedings; and
(c) orders allowing any person contact with the child after the adoption order was made.

1.2 An application under rule 14.18 must be made in form A64 which is contained in the practice direction supplementing Part 5 and must have attached to it a full certified copy of the entry in the Adopted Children Register relating to the applicant.

1.3 The completed application form must be taken to the court which made the adoption order along with evidence of the applicant's identity showing a photograph and signature, such as a passport or driving licence.

Additional documents that the adopted person is also entitled to receive from the court

2.1 The adopted adult is also entitled to receive the following documents–

(a) any transcript or written reasons of the court's decision; and
(b) a report made to the court by–
 (i) a children's guardian, reporting officer or children and family reporter;
 (ii) a local authority; or
 (iii) an adoption agency.

Before the documents are sent to the adopted adult

3.1 The court will remove protected information from documents before they are sent to the adopted adult.

PART 15
REPRESENTATION OF PROTECTED PARTIES

15.1 Application of this Part

This Part contains special provisions which apply in proceedings involving protected parties.

15.2 Requirement for litigation friend in proceedings

A protected party must have a litigation friend to conduct proceedings on that party's behalf.

15.3 Stage of proceedings at which a litigation friend becomes necessary

(1) A person may not without the permission of the court take any step in proceedings except—

(a) filing an application form; or
(b) applying for the appointment of a litigation friend under rule 15.6,

until the protected party has a litigation friend.

(2) If during proceedings a party lacks capacity (within the meaning of the 2005 Act) to continue to conduct proceedings, no party may take any step in proceedings without the permission of the court until the protected party has a litigation friend.

(3) Any step taken before a protected party has a litigation friend has no effect unless the court orders otherwise.

15.4 Who may be a litigation friend for a protected party without a court order

(1) This rule does not apply if the court has appointed a person to be a litigation friend.

(2) A person with authority as a deputy to conduct the proceedings in the name of a protected party or on that party's behalf is entitled to be the litigation friend of the protected party in any proceedings to which that person's authority extends.

(3) If there is no person with authority as a deputy to conduct the proceedings in the name of a protected party or on that party's behalf, a person may act as a litigation friend if that person—

(a) can fairly and competently conduct proceedings on behalf of the protected party;
(b) has no interest adverse to that of the protected party; and
(c) subject to paragraph (4), undertakes to pay any costs which the protected party may be ordered to pay in relation to the proceedings, subject to any right that person may have to be repaid from the assets of the protected party.

(4) Paragraph (3)(c) does not apply to the Official Solicitor.

('deputy' is defined in rule 2.3.)

15.5 How a person becomes a litigation friend without a court order

(1) If the court has not appointed a litigation friend, a person who wishes to act as a litigation friend must follow the procedure set out in this rule.

(2) A person with authority as a deputy to conduct the proceedings in the name of a protected party or on that party's behalf must file an official copy(GL) of the order, declaration or other document which confers that person's authority to act.

(3) Any other person must file a certificate of suitability stating that that person satisfies the conditions specified in rule 15.4(3).

(4) A person who is to act as a litigation friend must file—

(a) the document conferring that person's authority to act; or
(b) the certificate of suitability,

at the time when that person first takes a step in the proceedings on behalf of the protected party.

(5) A court officer will send the certificate of suitability to every person on whom, in accordance with rule 6.28, the application form should be served.

(6) This rule does not apply to the Official Solicitor.

15.6 How a person becomes a litigation friend by court order

(1) The court may, if the person to be appointed so consents, make an order appointing—

(a) a person other than the Official Solicitor; or
(b) the Official Solicitor,

as a litigation friend.

(2) An order appointing a litigation friend may be made by the court of its own initiative or on the application of—

(a) a person who wishes to be a litigation friend; or
(b) a party to the proceedings.

(3) The court may at any time direct that a party make an application for an order under paragraph (2).

(4) An application for an order appointing a litigation friend must be supported by evidence.

(5) Unless the court directs otherwise, a person appointed under this rule to be a litigation friend for a protected party will be treated as a party for the purpose of any provision in these rules requiring a document to be served on, or sent to, or notice to be given to, a party to the proceedings.

(6) Subject to rule 15.4(4), the court may not appoint a litigation friend under this rule unless it is satisfied that the person to be appointed complies with the conditions specified in rule 15.4(3).

15.7 Court's power to change litigation friend and to prevent person acting as litigation friend

(1) The court may—

(a) direct that a person may not act as a litigation friend;
(b) terminate a litigation friend's appointment; or
(c) appoint a new litigation friend in substitution for an existing one.

(2) An application for an order or direction under paragraph (1) must be supported by evidence.

(3) Subject to rule 15.4(4), the court may not appoint a litigation friend under this rule unless it is satisfied that the person to be appointed complies with the conditions specified in rule 15.4(3).

15.8 Appointment of litigation friend by court order – supplementary

(1) A copy of the application for an order under rule 15.6 or 15.7 must be sent by a court officer to—

(a) every person on whom, in accordance with rule 6.28, the application form should be served; and
(b) unless the court directs otherwise, the protected party.

(2) A copy of an application for an order under rule 15.7 must also be sent to—

(a) the person who is the litigation friend, or who is purporting to act as the litigation friend when the application is made; and
(b) the person, if not the applicant, who it is proposed should be the litigation friend.

15.9 Procedure where appointment of litigation friend comes to an end

(1) When a party ceases to be a protected party, the litigation friend's appointment continues until it is brought to an end by a court order.

(2) An application for an order under paragraph (1) may be made by—

(a) the former protected party;
(b) the litigation friend; or
(c) a party.

(3) On the making of an order under paragraph (1), the court officer will send a notice to the other parties stating that the appointment of the protected party's litigation friend to act has ended.

Practice Direction 15A – Protected parties

See also Part 15

This Practice Direction supplements FPR Part 15

General

1.1 A protected party must have a litigation friend to conduct proceedings on the protected party's behalf.

1.2 In the proceedings the protected party should be referred to in the title as 'A.B. (by C.D. his/her litigation friend).

Duties of the Litigation Friend

2.1 It is the duty of a litigation friend fairly and competently to conduct proceedings on behalf of a protected party. The litigation friend must have no interest in the proceedings adverse to that of the protected party and all steps and decisions the litigation friend takes in the proceedings must be taken for the benefit of the protected party.

Becoming a Litigation Friend without a court order

3.1 In order to become a litigation friend without a court order the person who wishes to act as litigation friend must–

(a) file an official copy of the order, declaration or other document which confers the litigation friend's authority as a deputy to conduct the proceedings in the name of a protected party or on his/her behalf; or
(b) file a certificate of suitability–
    (i) stating that the litigation friend consents to act;
    (ii) stating that the litigation friend knows or believes that the [applicant] [respondent] lacks capacity (within the meaning of the 2005 Act) to conduct proceedings;

(iii) stating the grounds of that belief and if the belief is based upon medical opinion attaching any relevant document to the certificate;

(iv) stating that the litigation friend can fairly and competently conduct proceedings on behalf of the protected party and has no interest adverse to that of the protected arty;

(v) undertaking to pay any costs which the protected party may be ordered to pay in relation to the proceedings, subject to any right the litigation friend may have to be repaid from the assets of the protected party; and

(vi) which the litigation friend has verified by a statement of truth.

3.2 Paragraph 3.1 does not apply to the Official Solicitor.

3.3 The court officer will send the certificate of suitability to the person who is the attorney of a registered enduring power of attorney, donee of a lasting power of attorney or deputy or, if there is no such person, to the person with whom the protected party resides or in whose care the protected party is.

3.4 The court officer is not required to send the documents referred to in paragraph 3.1(b)(iii) when sending the certificate of suitability to the person to be served under paragraph 3.3.

3.5 The litigation friend must file either the certificate of suitability or the authority referred to in paragraph 3.1(a) at a time when the litigation friend first takes a step in the proceedings on behalf of the protected party.

Application for a court order appointing a litigation friend

4.1 An application for a court order appointing a litigation friend should be made in accordance with Part 18 and must be supported by evidence.

4.2 The court officer must serve the application notice–

(a) on the persons referred to in paragraph 3.3; and

(b) on the protected party unless the court directs otherwise.

4.3 The evidence in support must satisfy the court that the proposed litigation friend–

(a) consents to act;

(b) can fairly and competently conduct proceedings on behalf of the protected party;

(c) has no interest adverse to that of the protected party; and

(d) undertakes to pay any costs which the protected party may be ordered to pay in relation to the proceedings, subject to any right the litigation friend may have to be repaid from the assets of the protected party.

4.4 Paragraph 4.3(d) does not apply to the Official Solicitor.

4.5 The proposed litigation friend may be one of the persons referred to in paragraph 3.3 where appropriate, or otherwise may be the Official Solicitor. Where it is sought to appoint the Official Solicitor, provision must be made for payment of his charges.

Change of litigation friend and prevention of person acting as litigation friend

5.1 Where an application is made for an order under rule 15.7, the application must set out the reasons for seeking it and must be supported by evidence.

5.2 Subject to paragraph 4.4, if the order sought is substitution of a new litigation friend for an existing one, the evidence must satisfy the court of the matters set out in paragraph 4.3.

5.3 The court officer will serve the application notice on–

(a) the persons referred to in paragraph 3.3; and
(b) the litigation friend or person purporting to act as litigation friend.

Procedure where the need for a litigation friend has come to an end

6.1 Where a person who was a protected party regains or acquires capacity (within the meaning of the 2005 Act) to conduct the proceedings, an application under rule 15.9(2) must be made for an order under rule 15.9(1) that the litigation friend's appointment has ceased.

6.2 The application must be supported by the following evidence–

(a) a medical report or other suitably qualified expert's report indicating that the protected party has regained or acquired capacity (within the meaning of the 2005 Act) to conduct the proceedings; and
(b) a copy of any relevant order or declaration of the Court of Protection.

Practice Direction 15B – Adults who may be protected parties and children who may become protected parties in family proceedings

This Practice Direction supplements FPR Part 15

What the court will do where an adult may be a protected party

Litigation Capacity

1.1 The court will investigate as soon as possible any issue as to whether an adult party or intended party to family proceedings lacks capacity (within the meaning of the Mental Capacity Act 2005) to conduct the proceedings. An adult who lacks capacity to conduct the proceedings is a protected party and must have a litigation friend to conduct the proceedings on his or her behalf. The expectation of the Official Solicitor is that the Official Solicitor will only be invited to act for the protected party as litigation friend if there is no other person suitable or willing to act.

Attention is drawn to the Checklist 'Protected Parties in Family Proceedings: Checklist For the Appointment of a Litigation Friend (including the Official Solicitor) (published in Family Law (January 2014)).

1.2 Any issue as to the capacity of an adult to conduct the proceedings must be determined before the court gives any directions relevant to that adult's role in the proceedings. Where a party has a solicitor, it is the solicitor who is likely to first identify that the party may lack litigation capacity. Expert evidence as to whether a party lacks such capacity is likely to be necessary for the court to make a determination relating to the party's capacity to conduct proceedings. However, there are some cases where the court may consider that evidence from a treating clinician such as a treating psychiatrist is all the evidence of lack of litigation capacity which may be necessary. There may also be cases where it will be clear that a party does not have litigation capacity such as where the party is in a coma, minimally conscious or in a persistent vegetative state. In those cases the court may well consider that a letter from a treating doctor confirming the party's condition is sufficient evidence of lack of litigation capacity and not need a report from an expert.

1.3 If at any time during the proceedings there is reason to believe that a party may lack capacity to conduct the proceedings, then the court must be notified and directions sought to ensure that this issue is investigated without delay. The presumption of capacity should not be forgotten. For example, where a person has an identified difficulty such as a learning disability or a mental illness, that difficulty should not automatically lead to an investigation about that party's capacity to litigate. Where a party has a solicitor, the starting point is whether that solicitor has concerns about the party's capacity to litigate.

Ability to give evidence as a witness

1.4 Where the court determines that a party does not have capacity to conduct the proceedings, the court may well also have to determine whether that party is able to give evidence and if so whether 'special measures' are required. Expert evidence is also likely to be necessary for the court to make such determinations. However, as in relation to the question of litigation capacity, the court may consider that evidence from a treating clinician who has a good understanding of the party's difficulties may be sufficient. If the treating clinician is provided with information about the legal framework, the clinician may be able to provide that evidence more readily and more quickly than an expert instructed to give an opinion as to the party's ability to give evidence.

1.5 Where the protected party is able to give evidence, the representative will wish to consider (and ask the expert to consider) the impact on that party of giving evidence. When making a determination as to whether that protected party should give evidence, the court may need to consider whether the impact of giving evidence would be so adverse to their condition that it would not be in that party's best interests to do so. The representative may put forward an argument on behalf of the protected party that the protected party should not give evidence.

Instruction of an expert where an adult is a protected party

2.1 Where there is concern that a party or intended party may lack capacity to conduct the proceedings, that party's representative must take the lead in any instruction of an expert for the purpose of assessment of the party's capacity to conduct the proceedings. In the event that the assessment is that the party does lack capacity to conduct the proceedings, it may be appropriate to ask that the expert advise about a party's ability to give evidence as a witness. Such expert evidence would relate to the party's particular difficulties and vulnerabilities (in particular in the context of cross-examination) including the techniques or measures which could be used to assist the party to give his or her evidence to the best of his or her ability and to ensure that the party's support needs are identified and addressed in advance of any final hearing.

Factors to be considered when the court is deciding whether to give permission as mentioned in FPR 25.4(1) or (2)

3.1 FPR 25.5 lists factors to which the court is to have particular regard when deciding whether to give permission in all family proceedings for expert evidence to be put before the court, and in children proceedings also for an expert to be instructed or for a child to be medically or psychiatrically examined or assessed for the purposes of obtaining expert evidence. In relation to children proceedings, one factor to be considered by the court is whether evidence could be given by another person on matters on which the expert would give evidence. For the avoidance of doubt this factor is not intended to suggest that evidence of another party to the proceedings is a substitute for expert evidence relating to a party's capacity to conduct the proceedings, ability to give evidence or special measures as mentioned in paragraphs 1.2, 1.4 and 2.1 above.

3.2 In addition, in children proceedings, it should be noted that expert evidence or other evidence from a treating clinician about a party's litigation capacity in previous proceedings is no substitute for such evidence in current proceedings. Litigation capacity has to be considered in relation to the proceedings before the court. For example, a parent may have been found to lack litigation capacity in care proceedings about child A three years before the current proceedings. That finding about litigation capacity in previous proceedings is not evidence that the parent lacks litigation capacity in subsequent proceedings about child B. It may be that the subsequent proceedings are simpler in terms of the issues and evidence before the court or that the parent's previous difficulty leading to lack of litigation capacity has improved.

Fluctuation in a party's capacity to conduct litigation

4.1 A party's capacity to conduct the litigation may fluctuate over the course of the proceedings. Litigation capacity may be lost or regained during the proceedings as a result of deterioration or improvement in the impairment of, or disturbance in the functioning of, the party's mind or brain. The necessity for expert evidence or evidence of a treating clinician as to a party's capacity can therefore arise at any time during the proceedings.

4.2 Fluctuation in a party's capacity to conduct litigation means that a litigation friend may not represent that party throughout the proceedings. It is expected that where the litigation friend has been appointed or reappointed, the court will be likely to make a direction in accordance with FPR 25.10(2) permitting such a litigation friend to put written questions to the expert after the 10 day period referred to in FPR 25.10(2)(c) where the 10 days referred to in that rule would be insufficient time for the litigation friend to become familiar with the case or latest developments in the case while assimilating the expert's report and formulating any questions.

Single joint experts

5.1 FPR 25.11 and 25.12 and paragraphs 2.1 to 2.7 of Practice Direction 25C and of Practice Direction 25D make provision for two or more parties to put expert evidence before the court from a single joint expert. 'Single joint expert' ('SJE') is defined by FPR 25.2(1) as a person who provides expert evidence for use in proceedings on behalf of two or more parties (including the applicant) to the proceedings. No provision of the FPR nor the Practice Directions compel the use of an SJE. Paragraph 2.1 of Practice Direction 25C and of Practice Direction 25D provide that a SJE should be used 'wherever possible'. The expectation is that expert evidence as mentioned in paragraphs 1.2, 1.4 and 2.1 above, including on whether a party lacks capacity to conduct the proceedings, would not be evidence which is likely to be appropriately given by a SJE. However, there may be circumstances where expert evidence is needed by two or more parties relating to, for example, the capacity of a party when he or she gave consent to the making of a consent order made by the court in financial remedy proceedings and such evidence may be considered by the court to be appropriately given by a SJE. But these are circumstances where the expert evidence relates to an issue in the proceedings.

Child aged 16–17 who is the subject of the proceedings likely to lack relevant decision making capacity at age 18

6.1 Where the child who is the subject of the proceedings is aged 16 to 17 consideration should be given as to whether it is necessary to obtain expert evidence on whether that child will lack capacity (within the meaning of the Mental Capacity Act 2005) to make one or more of the decisions relevant to the proceedings (for example, in relation to residence, contact with family or about care arrangements) when that child reaches 18.

6.2 Attention is drawn to the fact that the Mental Capacity Act 2005 provides for a framework for decision making in respect of persons over 16 who lack capacity to makes decisions about their own finances, health and welfare. The Mental Capacity Act 2005 (Transfer of Proceedings) Order 2007 (SI 2007/1899) includes provision for the transfer of proceedings from a court having jurisdiction under the Children Act 1989 to the Court of Protection.

Child who is not the subject of proceedings likely to lack capacity to conduct the proceedings when he or she reaches 18

7.1 Where it appears that a child is–

(a) a party to the proceedings and not the subject of them;
(b) nearing age 18; and
(c) considered likely to lack capacity to conduct the proceedings when 18,

the court will consider giving directions for the child's capacity in this respect to be investigated.

Definition of 'expert' and 'children proceedings'

8.1 The definitions of 'expert' and 'children proceedings' in FPR 25.2 (1) apply to this Practice Direction and the explanation of an expert team in paragraph 2.2 of Practice Direction 25B also applies.

PART 16
REPRESENTATION OF CHILDREN AND REPORTS IN PROCEEDINGS

Chapter 1
Application of this Part

16.1 Application of this Part

This Part—

(a) sets out when the court will make a child a party in family proceedings; and
(b) contains special provisions which apply in proceedings involving children.

Chapter 2
Child as party in family proceedings

16.2 When the court may make a child a party to proceedings

(1) The court may make a child a party to proceedings if it considers it is in the best interests of the child to do so.

(2) This rule does not apply to a child who is the subject of proceedings—

(a) which are specified proceedings; or
(b) to which Part 14 applies.

(The Practice Direction 16A sets out the matters which the court will take into consideration before making a child a party under this rule.)

Chapter 3
When a children's guardian or litigation friend will be appointed

16.3 Appointment of a children's guardian in specified proceedings or proceedings to which Part 14 applies

(1) Unless it is satisfied that it is not necessary to do so to safeguard the interests of the child, the court must appoint a children's guardian for a child who is—

(a) the subject of; and
(b) a party to,

proceedings—

(i) which are specified proceedings; or
(ii) to which Part 14 applies.

(Rules 12.6 and 14.6 set out the point in the proceedings when the court will appoint a children's guardian in specified proceedings and proceedings to which Part 14 applies respectively.)

(2) At any stage in the proceedings—

(a) a party may apply, without notice to the other parties unless the court directs otherwise, for the appointment of a children's guardian; or
(b) the court may of its own initiative appoint a children's guardian.

(3) Where the court refuses an application under paragraph (2)(a) it will give reasons for the refusal and the court or a court officer will—

(a) record the refusal and the reasons for it; and
(b) as soon as practicable, notify the parties and either the Service or the Assembly of a decision not to appoint a children's guardian.

(4) When appointing a children's guardian the court will consider the appointment of anyone who has previously acted as a children's guardian of the same child.

(5) Where the court appoints a children's guardian in accordance with this rule, the provisions of Chapter 6 of this Part apply.

16.4 Appointment of a children's guardian in proceedings not being specified proceedings or proceedings to which Part 14 applies

(1) [Except in proceedings under section 55A of the 1986 Act and without][1] prejudice to rule 8.42 or 16.6, the court must appoint a children's guardian for a child who is the subject of proceedings, which are not proceedings of a type referred to in rule 16.3(1), if—

(a) the child is an applicant in the proceedings;
(b) a provision in these rules provides for the child to be a party to the proceedings; or
(c) the court has made the child a party in accordance with rule 16.2.

[(1A) Without prejudice to rule 16.6, in proceedings under section 55A of the 1986 Act, the court must appoint a children's guardian for a child where—

(a) the court has made the child a party in accordance with rule 16.2; and
(b) the child is the person whose parentage is in dispute in those proceedings.][2]

(2) The provisions of Chapter 7 of this Part apply where the appointment of a children's guardian is required in accordance with paragraph (1) [or paragraph (1A)][2].

('children's guardian' is defined in rule 2.3.)

Amendment

1 Substituted by the Family Procedure (Amendment No 2) Rules 2016, SI 2016/901, rr 2, 5(a).
2 Inserted by the Family Procedure (Amendment No 2) Rules 2016, SI 2016/901, rr 2, 5(b), (c).

16.5 Requirement for a litigation friend

(1) [Except in proceedings under section 55A of the 1986 Act and without][1] prejudice to rule 16.6, where a child is—

(a) a party to proceedings; but
(b) not the subject of those proceedings,

the child must have a litigation friend to conduct proceedings on the child's behalf.

[(1A) Without prejudice to rule 16.6, where a child is—

(a) a party to proceedings under section 55A of the 1986 Act; but
(b) not the person whose parentage is in dispute in those proceedings,

the child must have a litigation friend to conduct proceedings on the child's behalf.][2]

(2) The provisions of Chapter 5 of this Part apply where a litigation friend is required in accordance with paragraph (1) [or paragraph (1A)][2].

Amendment

1 Substituted by the Family Procedure (Amendment No 2) Rules 2016, SI 2016/901, rr 2, 6(a).
2 Inserted by the Family Procedure (Amendment No 2) Rules 2016, SI 2016/901, rr 2, 6(b), (c).

Chapter 4
Where a children's guardian or litigation friend is not required

16.6 Circumstances in which a child does not need a children's guardian or litigation friend

(1) Subject to paragraph (2), a child may conduct proceedings without a children's guardian or litigation friend where the proceedings are proceedings—

(a) under the 1989 Act;
(b) to which Part 11 (applications under Part 4A of the Family Law Act 1996 [or Part 1 of Schedule 2 to the Female Genital Mutilation Act 2003][1]) or Part 14 (applications in adoption, placement and related proceedings) of these rules apply; …[2]
(c) relating to the exercise of the court's inherent jurisdiction with respect to children[; or][3]
[(d) under section 55A of the 1986 Act,][4]

and one of the conditions set out in paragraph (3) is satisfied.

(2) Paragraph (1) does not apply where the child is the subject of and a party to proceedings—

(a) which are specified proceedings; or
(b) to which Part 14 applies.

(3) The conditions referred to in paragraph (1) are that either—

(a) the child has obtained the court's permission; or
(b) a solicitor—

- (i) considers that the child is able, having regard to the child's understanding, to give instructions in relation to the proceedings; and
- (ii) has accepted instructions from that child to act for that child in the proceedings and, if the proceedings have begun, the solicitor is already acting.

(4) An application for permission under paragraph (3)(a) may be made by the child without notice.

(5) Where a child—

- (a) has a litigation friend or children's guardian in proceedings to which this rule applies; and
- (b) wishes to conduct the remaining stages of the proceedings without the litigation friend or children's guardian,

the child may apply to the court, on notice to the litigation friend or children's guardian, for permission for that purpose and for the removal of the litigation friend or children's guardian.

(6) The court will grant an application under paragraph (3)(a) or (5) if it considers that the child has sufficient understanding to conduct the proceedings concerned or proposed without a litigation friend or children's guardian.

(7) In exercising its powers under paragraph (6) the court may require the litigation friend or children's guardian to take such part in the proceedings as the court directs.

(8) The court may revoke any permission granted under paragraph (3)(a) where it considers that the child does not have sufficient understanding to participate as a party in the proceedings concerned without a litigation friend or children's guardian.

(9) Where a solicitor is acting for a child in proceedings without a litigation friend or children's guardian by virtue of paragraph (3)(b) and either of the conditions specified in paragraph (3)(b)(i) or (ii) cease to be fulfilled, the solicitor must inform the court immediately.

(10) Where—

- (a) the court revokes any permission under paragraph (8); or
- (b) either of the conditions specified in paragraph (3)(b)(i) or (ii) is no longer fulfilled,

the court may, if it considers it necessary in order to protect the interests of the child concerned, appoint a person to be that child's litigation friend or children's guardian.

Amendment

1 Inserted by the Family Procedure (Amendment) Rules 2017, SI 2017/413, rr 2, 5.
2 Repealed by the Family Procedure (Amendment No 2) Rules 2016, SI 2016/901, rr 2, 7(a).
3 Inserted by the Family Procedure (Amendment No 2) Rules 2016, SI 2016/901, rr 2, 7(b), (c).

Chapter 5
Litigation friend

16.7 Application of this Chapter

This Chapter applies where a child must have a litigation friend to conduct proceedings on the child's behalf in accordance with rule 16.5.

16.8 Stage of proceedings at which a litigation friend becomes necessary

(1) This rule does not apply in relation to a child who is conducting proceedings without a litigation friend in accordance with rule 16.6.

(2) A person may not without the permission of the court take any step in proceedings except—

(a) filing an application form; or
(b) applying for the appointment of a litigation friend under rule 16.11,

until the child has a litigation friend.

(3) Any step taken before a child has a litigation friend has no effect unless the court orders otherwise.

16.9 Who may be a litigation friend for a child without a court order

(1) This rule does not apply if the court has appointed a person to be a litigation friend.

(2) A person may act as a litigation friend if that person—

(a) can fairly and competently conduct proceedings on behalf of the child;
(b) has no interest adverse to that of the child; and
(c) subject to paragraph (3), undertakes to pay any costs which the child may be ordered to pay in relation to the proceedings, subject to any right that person may have to be repaid from the assets of the child.

(3) Paragraph (2)(c) does not apply to the Official Solicitor, an officer of the Service or a Welsh family proceedings officer.

16.10 How a person becomes a litigation friend without a court order

(1) If the court has not appointed a litigation friend, a person who wishes to act as such must file a certificate of suitability stating that that person satisfies the conditions specified in rule 16.9(2).

(2) The certificate of suitability must be filed at the time when the person who wishes to act as litigation friend first takes a step in the proceedings on behalf of the child.

(3) A court officer will send the certificate of suitability to every person on whom, in accordance with rule 6.28, the application form should be served.

(4) This rule does not apply to the Official Solicitor, an officer of the Service or a Welsh family proceedings officer.

16.11 Appointment of litigation friend by the court

(1) The court may, if the person to be appointed consents, make an order appointing as a litigation friend—

(a) the Official Solicitor;
(b) an officer of the Service or a Welsh family proceedings officer; or
(c) some other person.

(2) An order appointing a litigation friend may be made by the court of its own initiative or on the application of—

(a) a person who wishes to be a litigation friend; or
(b) a party to the proceedings.

(3) The court may at any time direct that a party make an application for an order under paragraph (2).

(4) An application for an order appointing a litigation friend must be supported by evidence.

(5) Unless the court directs otherwise, a person appointed under this rule to be a litigation friend for a child will be treated as a party for the purpose of any provision in these rules requiring a document to be served on, or sent to, or notice to be given to, a party to the proceedings.

(6) Subject to rule 16.9(3), the court may not appoint a litigation friend under this rule unless it is satisfied that the person to be appointed complies with the conditions specified in rule 16.9(2).

(7) This rule is without prejudice to rule 16.6.

16.12 Court's power to change litigation friend and to prevent person acting as litigation friend

(1) The court may—

(a) direct that a person may not act as a litigation friend;
(b) terminate a litigation friend's appointment; or
(c) appoint a new litigation friend in substitution for an existing one.

(2) An application for an order or direction under paragraph (1) must be supported by evidence.

(3) Subject to rule 16.9(3), the court may not appoint a litigation friend under this rule unless it is satisfied that the person to be appointed complies with the conditions specified in rule 16.9(2).

16.13 Appointment of litigation friend by court order – supplementary

(1) A copy of the application for an order under rule 16.11 or 16.12 must be sent by a court officer to every person on whom, in accordance with rule 6.28, the application form should be served.

(2) A copy of an application for an order under rule 16.12 must also be sent to—

(a) the person who is the litigation friend, or who is purporting to act as the litigation friend when the application is made; and
(b) the person, if not the applicant, who it is proposed should be the litigation friend.

16.14 Powers and duties of litigation friend

(1) The litigation friend—

(a) has the powers and duties set out in Practice Direction 16A; and
(b) must exercise those powers and duties in accordance with Practice Direction 16A.

(2) Where the litigation friend is an officer of the Service or a Welsh family proceedings officer, rule 16.20 applies as it applies to a children's guardian appointed in accordance with Chapter 6.

16.15 Procedure where appointment of litigation friend comes to an end

(1) When a child who is not a protected party reaches the age of 18, a litigation friend's appointment comes to an end.

(2) A court officer will send a notice to the other parties stating that the appointment of the child's litigation friend to act has ended.

Chapter 6
Children's guardian appointed under rule 16.3

16.16 Application of this Chapter

This Chapter applies where the court must appoint a children's guardian in accordance with rule 16.3.

16.17 Who may be a children's guardian

Where the court is appointing a children's guardian under rule 16.3 it will appoint an officer of the Service or a Welsh family proceedings officer.

16.18 What the court or a court officer will do once the court has made a decision about appointing a children's guardian

(1) Where the court appoints a children's guardian under rule 16.3 a court officer will record the appointment and, as soon as practicable, will—

(a) inform the parties and either the Service or the Assembly; and
(b) unless it has already been sent, send the children's guardian a copy of the application and copies of any document filed with the court in the proceedings.

(2) A court officer has a continuing duty to send the children's guardian a copy of any other document filed with the court during the course of the proceedings.

16.19 Termination of the appointment of the children's guardian

(1) The appointment of a children's guardian under rule 16.3 continues for such time as is specified in the appointment or until terminated by the court.

(2) When terminating an appointment in accordance with paragraph (1), the court will give reasons for doing so, a note of which will be taken by the court or a court officer.

16.20 Powers and duties of the children's guardian

(1) The children's guardian is to act on behalf of the child upon the hearing of any application in proceedings to which this Chapter applies with the duty of safeguarding the interests of the child.

(2) The children's guardian must also provide the court with such other assistance as it may require.

(3) The children's guardian, when carrying out duties in relation to specified proceedings, other than placement proceedings, must have regard to the principle set out in section 1(2) and the matters set out in section 1(3)(a) to (f) of the 1989 Act as if for the word 'court' in that section there were substituted the words 'children's guardian'.

(4) The children's guardian, when carrying out duties in relation to proceedings to which Part 14 applies, must have regard to the principle set out in section 1(3) and the matters set out in section 1(4)(a) to (f) of the 2002 Act as if for the word 'court' in that section there were substituted the words 'children's guardian'.

(5) The children's guardian's duties must be exercised in accordance with Practice Direction 16A.

(6) A report to the court by the children's guardian is confidential.

16.21 Where the child instructs a solicitor or conducts proceedings on the child's own behalf

(1) Where it appears to the children's guardian that the child—

(a) is instructing a solicitor direct; or
(b) intends to conduct and is capable of conducting the proceedings on that child's own behalf,

the children's guardian must inform the court of that fact.

(2) Where paragraph (1) applies the children's guardian—

(a) must perform such additional duties as the court may direct;
(b) must take such part in the proceedings as the court may direct; and
(c) may, with the permission of the court, have legal representation in the conduct of those duties.

Chapter 7
Children's guardian appointed under rule 16.4

16.22 Application of this Chapter

This Chapter applies where the court must appoint a children's guardian under rule 16.4.

16.23 Stage of proceedings at which a children's guardian becomes necessary

(1) This rule does not apply in relation to a child who is conducting proceedings without a children's guardian in accordance with rule 16.6.

(2) A person may not without the permission of the court take any step in proceedings except—

(a) filing an application form; or
(b) applying for the appointment of a children's guardian under rule 16.24,

until the child has a children's guardian.

(3) Any step taken before a child has a children's guardian has no effect unless the court orders otherwise.

16.24 Appointment of a children's guardian

(1) The court may make an order appointing as a children's guardian, an officer of the Service or a Welsh family proceedings officer or, if the person to be appointed consents—

(a) a person other than the Official Solicitor; or
(b) the Official Solicitor.

(2) An order appointing a children's guardian may be made by the court of its own initiative or on the application of—

(a) a person who wishes to be a children's guardian; or
(b) a party to the proceedings.

(3) The court may at any time direct that a party make an application for an order under paragraph (2).

(4) An application for an order appointing a children's guardian must be supported by evidence.

(5) The court may not appoint a children's guardian under this rule unless it is satisfied that that person—

(a) can fairly and competently conduct proceedings on behalf of the child;
(b) has no interest adverse to that of the child; and
(c) subject to paragraph (6), undertakes to pay any costs which the child may be ordered to pay in relation to the proceedings, subject to any right that person may have to be repaid from the assets of the child.

(6) Paragraph (5)(c) does not apply to the Official Solicitor, an officer of the Service or a Welsh family proceedings officer.

(7) This rule is without prejudice to rule 16.6 and rule 9.11.

(Rule 9.11 provides for a child to be separately represented in certain applications for a financial remedy.)

16.25 Court's power to change children's guardian and to prevent person acting as children's guardian

(1) The court may—

(a) direct that a person may not act as a children's guardian;
(b) terminate the appointment of a children's guardian; or
(c) appoint a new children's guardian in substitution for an existing one.

(2) An application for an order or direction under paragraph (1) must be supported by evidence.

(3) Subject to rule 16.24(6), the court may not appoint a children's guardian under this rule unless it is satisfied that the person to be appointed complies with the conditions specified in rule 16.24(5).

16.26 Appointment of children's guardian by court order – supplementary

(1) A copy of the application for an order under rule 16.24 or 16.25 must be sent by a court officer to every person on whom, in accordance with rule 6.28, the application form should be served.

(2) A copy of an application for an order under rule 16.25 must also be sent to—

(a) the person who is the children's guardian, or who is purporting to act as the children's guardian when the application is made; and
(b) the person, if not the applicant, who it is proposed should be the children's guardian.

16.27 Powers and duties of children's guardian

(1) The children's guardian—

(a) has the powers and duties set out in Practice Direction 16A; and
(b) must exercise those powers and duties in accordance with Practice Direction 16A.

(2) Where the children's guardian is an officer of the Service or a Welsh family proceedings officer, rule 16.20 applies to a children's guardian appointed in accordance with this Chapter as it applies to a children's guardian appointed in accordance with Chapter 6.

16.28 Procedure where appointment of children's guardian comes to an end

(1) When a child reaches the age of 18, the appointment of a children's guardian comes to an end.

(2) A court officer will send a notice to the other parties stating that the appointment of the child's children's guardian to act has ended.

Chapter 8
Duties of solicitor acting for the child

16.29 Solicitor for child

(1) Subject to paragraphs (2) and (4), a solicitor appointed—

(a) under section 41(3) of the 1989 Act; or
(b) by the children's guardian in accordance with the Practice Direction 16A,

must represent the child in accordance with instructions received from the children's guardian.

(2) If a solicitor appointed as mentioned in paragraph (1) considers, having taken into account the matters referred to in paragraph (3), that the child—

(a) wishes to give instructions which conflict with those of the children's guardian; and
(b) is able, having regard to the child's understanding, to give such instructions on the child's own behalf,

the solicitor must conduct the proceedings in accordance with instructions received from the child.

(3) The matters the solicitor must take into account for the purposes of paragraph (2) are—

(a) the views of the children's guardian; and
(b) any direction given by the court to the children's guardian concerning the part to be taken by the children's guardian in the proceedings.

(4) Where—

(a) no children's guardian has been appointed; and
(b) the condition in section 41(4)(b) of the 1989 Act is satisfied,

a solicitor appointed under section 41(3) of the 1989 Act must represent the child in accordance with instructions received from the child.

(5) Where a solicitor appointed as mentioned in paragraph (1) receives no instructions under paragraphs (1), (2) or (4), the solicitor must represent the child in furtherance of the best interests of the child.

(6) A solicitor appointed under section 41(3) of the 1989 Act or by the children's guardian in accordance with Practice Direction 16A must serve documents, and accept service of documents, on behalf of the child in accordance with rule 6.31 and, where the child has not been served separately and has sufficient understanding, advise the child of the contents of any document so served.

(7) Where the child wishes an appointment of a solicitor—

(a) under section 41(3) of the 1989 Act; or
(b) by the children's guardian in accordance with the Practice Direction 16A,

to be terminated—

(i) the child may apply to the court for an order terminating the appointment; and
(ii) the solicitor and the children's guardian will be given an opportunity to make representations.

(8) Where the children's guardian wishes an appointment of a solicitor under section 41(3) of the 1989 Act to be terminated—

(a) the children's guardian may apply to the court for an order terminating the appointment; and
(b) the solicitor and, if of sufficient understanding, the child, will be given an opportunity to make representations.

(9) When terminating an appointment in accordance with paragraph (7) or (8), the court will give its reasons for so doing, a note of which will be taken by the court or a court officer.

(10) The court or a court officer will record the appointment under section 41(3) of the 1989 Act or the refusal to make the appointment.

Chapter 9
Reporting officer

16.30 When the court appoints a reporting officer

In proceedings to which Part 14 applies, the court will appoint a reporting officer where—

(a) it appears that a parent or guardian of the child is willing to consent to the placing of the child for adoption, to the making of an adoption order or to a section 84 order; and
(b) that parent or guardian is in England or Wales.

16.31 Appointment of the same reporting officer in respect of two or more parents or guardians

The same person may be appointed as the reporting officer for two or more parents or guardians of the child.

16.32 The duties of the reporting officer

(1) The reporting officer must witness the signature by a parent or guardian on the document in which consent is given to—

(a) the placing of the child for adoption;
(b) the making of an adoption order; or
(c) the making of a section 84 order.

(2) The reporting officer must carry out such other duties as are set out in Practice Direction 16A.

(3) A report to the court by the reporting officer is confidential.

(4) The reporting officer's duties must be exercised in accordance with Practice Direction 16A.

Chapter 10
Children and family reporter and welfare officer

16.33 Request by court for a welfare report in respect of the child

(1) Where the court is considering an application for an order in proceedings, the court may ask—

(a) in proceedings to which Parts 12 and 14 apply, a children and family reporter; or
(b) in proceedings to which Part 12 applies, a welfare officer,

to prepare a report on matters relating to the welfare of the child, and, in this rule, the person preparing the report is called 'the officer'.

(2) It is the duty of the officer to—

(a) comply with any request for a report under this rule; and
(b) provide the court with such other assistance as it may require.

(3) A report to the court under this rule is confidential.

(4) The officer, when carrying out duties in relation to proceedings under the 1989 Act, must have regard to the principle set out in section 1(2) and the matters set out in section 1(3)(a) to (f) of that Act as if for the word 'court' in that section there were substituted the words 'children and family reporter' or 'welfare officer' as the case may be.

(5) A party may question the officer about oral or written advice tendered by that officer to the court.

(6) The court officer will notify the officer of a direction given at a hearing at which—

(a) the officer is not present; and
(b) the welfare report is considered.

(7) The officer's duties must be exercised in accordance with Practice Direction 16A

('children and family reporter' and 'welfare officer' are defined in rule 2.3)

Chapter 11
Parental order reporter

16.34 When the court appoints a parental order reporter

In proceedings to which Part 13 applies, the court will appoint a parental order reporter in accordance with rule 13.5.

16.35 Powers and duties of the parental order reporter

(1) The parental order reporter is to act on behalf of the child upon the hearing of any application in proceedings to which Part 13 applies with the duty of safeguarding the interests of the child.

(2) The parental order reporter must—

[(a) investigate in the case of a parental order under—
   (i) section 54(1) of the 2008 Act, the matters set out in section 54(1) to (8) of that Act;
   (ii) section 54A(1) of the 2008 Act, the matters set out in section 54A(1) to (7) of that Act;][1]

(b) so far as the parental order reporter considers necessary, investigate any matter contained in the application form or other matter which appears relevant to the making of the parental order; and

(c) advise the court on whether there is any reason under section 1 of the 2002 Act (as applied with modifications by the Human Fertilisation and Embryology (Parental Orders) Regulations 2010) to refuse the parental order.

(3) The parental order reporter must also provide the court with such other assistance as it may require.

(4) The parental order reporter's duties must be exercised in accordance with Practice Direction 16A.

(5) A report to the court by the parental order reporter is confidential.

Amendment

1 Substituted by the Human Fertilisation and Embryology Act 2008 (Remedial) Order 2018, SI 2018/1413, art 3(2), Sch 2, para 4(1), (6).

Chapter 12
Supplementary appointment provisions

16.36 Persons who may not be appointed as children's guardian, reporting officer or children and family reporter

(1) In [specified proceedings (except where paragraph (2) applies),][1] adoption proceedings or proceedings for a section 84 order or a section 89 order, no person may be appointed as a children's guardian, reporting officer or children and family reporter who—

(a) is a member, officer or servant of a local authority which is a party to the proceedings;

(b) is, or has been, a member, officer or servant of a local authority or voluntary organisation who has been directly concerned in that capacity in arrangements relating to the care, accommodation or welfare of the child during the 5 years prior to the start of the proceedings; or

(c) is a serving probation officer who has, in that capacity, been previously concerned with the child or the child's family.

(2) In placement proceedings, a person described in paragraph (1)(b) or (c) may not be appointed as a children's guardian, reporting officer or children and family reporter.

Amendment

1 Inserted by the Family Procedure (Amendment) Rules 2012, SI 2012/679, rr 2, 23.

16.37 Appointment of the same person as children's guardian, reporting officer and children and family reporter

The same person may be appointed to act as one or more of the following—

(a) the children's guardian;
(b) the reporting officer; and
(c) the children and family reporter.

Chapter 13
Officers of the Service, Welsh family proceedings officers and local authority officers: further duties

16.38 Officers of the Service, Welsh family proceedings officers and local authority officers acting under certain duties

(1) This rule applies when—

(a) an officer of the Service or a Welsh family proceedings officer is acting under a duty in accordance with—
  (i) section 11E(7) of the 1989 Act (providing the court with information as to the making of [an][1] activity direction or [an][1] activity condition);
  (ii) section 11G(2) of the 1989 Act (monitoring compliance with [an][1] activity direction or [an][1] activity condition);
  (iii) section 11H(2) of the 1989 Act (monitoring compliance with a [child arrangements][1] order);
  (iv) section 11L(5) of the 1989 Act (providing the court with information as to the making of an enforcement order);
  (v) section 11M(1) of the 1989 Act (monitoring compliance with an enforcement order);
  (vi) section 16(6) of the 1989 Act (providing a report to the court in accordance with a direction in a family assistance order); and
  (vii) section 16A of the 1989 Act (making a risk assessment); and
(b) a local authority officer is acting under a duty in accordance with section 16(6) of the 1989 Act (providing a report to the court in accordance with a direction in a family assistance order).

(2) In this rule,—

(a) '… [2] activity direction', '… [2] activity condition' and 'enforcement order' have the meanings given in rule 12.2; and
(b) references to 'the officer' are to the officer of the Service, Welsh family proceedings officer or local authority officer referred to in paragraph (1).

(3) In exercising the duties referred to in paragraph (1), the officer must have regard to the principle set out in section 1(2) of the 1989 Act and the matters set out in section 1(3)(a) to (f) of the 1989 Act as if for the word 'court' in that section there were substituted the words 'officer of the Service, Welsh family proceedings officer or local authority officer'.

(4) The officer's duties referred to in paragraph (1) must be exercised in accordance with Practice Direction 16A.

Amendment

1 Substituted by the Family Procedure (Amendment No 3) Rules 2014, SI 2014/843, rr 2, 40.
2 Repealed by the Family Procedure (Amendment No 3) Rules 2014, SI 2014/843, rr 2, 41.

Chapter 14
Enforcement orders and financial compensation orders: persons notified

16.39 Application for enforcement orders and financial compensation orders: duties of the person notified

(1) This rule applies where a person who was the child's children's guardian, litigation friend or legal representative in the proceedings in which a [child arrangements][1] order was made has been notified of an application for an enforcement order or for a financial compensation order as required by Practice Direction 12C.

(2) The person who has been notified of the application must—

(a) consider whether it is in the best interests of the child for the child to be made a party to the proceedings for an enforcement order or a financial compensation order (as applicable); and

(b) before the date fixed for the first hearing in the case notify the court, orally or in writing, of the opinion reached on the question, together with the reasons for this opinion.

(3) In this rule, 'enforcement order' and 'financial compensation order' have the meanings given in rule 12.2.

Amendment

1 Substituted by the Family Procedure (Amendment No 3) Rules 2014, SI 2014/843, rr 2, 42.

Practice Direction 16A – Representation of children

See also Part 16

PART 1
GENERAL

Reference in title of proceedings

1.1 Where a litigation friend represents a child in family proceedings in accordance with rule 16.5 and Chapter 5 of Part 16, the child should be referred to in the title of the proceedings as 'A.B. (a child by C.D. his/her litigation friend)'.

1.2 Where a children's guardian represents a child in family proceedings in accordance with rule 16.4 and Chapter 7 of Part 16, the child should be referred to in the title as 'A.B. (a child by C.D. his/her children's guardian)'.

1.3 A child who is conducting proceedings on that child's own behalf should be referred to in the title as 'A.B. (a child)'.

PART 2
LITIGATION FRIEND

Duties of the Litigation Friend

2.1 It is the duty of a litigation friend fairly and competently to conduct proceedings on behalf of the child. The litigation friend must have no interest in the proceedings adverse to that of the child and all steps and decisions the litigation friend takes in the proceedings must be taken for the benefit of the child.

Becoming a Litigation Friend without a court order

3.1 In order to become a litigation friend without a court order the person who wishes to act as litigation friend must file a certificate of suitability–

(a) stating that the litigation friend consents to act;
(b) stating that the litigation friend knows or believes that the [applicant] [respondent] is a child to whom rule 16.5 and Chapter 5 of Part 16 apply;
(c) stating that the litigation friend can fairly and competently conduct proceedings on behalf of the child and has no interest adverse to that of the child;
(d) undertaking to pay any costs which the child may be ordered to pay in relation to the proceedings, subject to any right the litigation friend may have to be repaid from the assets of the child; and
(e) which the litigation friend has verified by a statement of truth.

3.2 Paragraph 3.1 does not apply to the Official Solicitor, an officer of the Service or a Welsh family proceedings officer.

3.3 The court officer will send the certificate of suitability to one of the child's parents or guardians or, if there is no parent or guardian, to the person with whom the child resides or in whose care the child is.

3.4 The litigation friend must file the certificate of suitability at a time when the litigation friend first takes a step in the proceedings on behalf of the child.

Application for a court order appointing a litigation friend

4.1 An application for a court order appointing a litigation friend should be made in accordance with Part 18 and must be supported by evidence.

4.2 The court officer must serve the application notice on the persons referred to in paragraph 3.3.

4.3 The evidence in support must satisfy the court that the proposed litigation friend–

(a) consents to act;
(b) can fairly and competently conduct proceedings on behalf of the child;
(c) has no interest adverse to that of the child; and
(d) undertakes to pay any costs which the child may be ordered to pay in relation to the proceedings, subject to any right the litigation friend may have to be repaid from the assets of the child.

4.4 Paragraph 4.3(d) does not apply to the Official Solicitor, an officer of the Service of a Welsh family proceedings officer.

4.5 The proposed litigation friend may be one of the persons referred to in paragraph 3.3 where appropriate, or otherwise may be the Official Solicitor, an officer of the Service or a Welsh family proceedings officer. Where it is sought to appoint the Official Solicitor, an officer of the Service or a Welsh family proceedings officer, provision should be made for payment of that person's charges.

Change of litigation friend and prevention of person acting as litigation friend

5.1 Where an application is made for an order under rule 16.12, the application must set out the reasons for seeking it and the application must be supported by evidence.

5.2 Subject to paragraph 4.4, if the order sought is substitution of a new litigation friend for an existing one, the evidence must satisfy the court of the matters set out in paragraph 4.3.

5.3 The court officer will serve the application notice on–

(a) the persons referred to in paragraph 3.3; and
(b) the litigation friend or person purporting to act as litigation friend.

PART 3
CHILDREN'S GUARDIAN APPOINTED UNDER RULE 16.3

How the children's guardian exercises duties – investigations and appointment of solicitor

6.1 The children's guardian must make such investigations as are necessary to carry out the children's guardian's duties and must, in particular–

(a) contact or seek to interview such persons as the children's guardian thinks appropriate or as the court directs; and
(b) obtain such professional assistance as is available which the children's guardian thinks appropriate or which the court directs be obtained.

6.2 The children's guardian must–

(a) appoint a solicitor for the child unless a solicitor has already been appointed;
(b) give such advice to the child as is appropriate having regard to that child's understanding; and
(c) where appropriate instruct the solicitor representing the child on all matters relevant to the interests of the child arising in the course of proceedings, including possibilities for appeal.

6.3 Where the children's guardian is authorised in the terms mentioned by and in accordance with section 15(1) of the Criminal Justice and Court Services Act 2000 or section 37(1) of the Children Act 2004 (right of officer of the Service or Welsh family proceedings officer to conduct litigation or exercise a right of audience), paragraph 6.2(a) will not apply if the children's guardian intends to have conduct of the proceedings on behalf of the child unless–

(a) the child wishes to instruct a solicitor direct; and
(b) the children's guardian or the court considers that the child is of sufficient understanding to do so.

6.4 Where rule 16.21 (Where the child instructs a solicitor or conducts proceedings on the child's own behalf) applies, the duties set out in paragraph 6.2(a) and (c) do not apply.

How the children's guardian exercises duties – attendance at court, advice to the court and reports

6.5 The children's guardian or the solicitor appointed under section 41(3) of the 1989 Act or in accordance with paragraph 6.2(a) must attend all directions hearings unless the court directs otherwise.

6.6 The children's guardian must advise the court on the following matters–

(a) whether the child is of sufficient understanding for any purpose including the child's refusal to submit to a medical or psychiatric examination or other assessment that the court has the power to require, direct or order;
(b) the wishes of the child in respect of any matter relevant to the proceedings including that child's attendance at court;
(c) the appropriate forum for the proceedings;

(d) the appropriate timing of the proceedings or any part of them;
(e) the options available to it in respect of the child and the suitability of each such option including what order should be made in determining the application; and
(f) any other matter on which the court seeks advice or on which the children's guardian considers that the court should be informed.

6.7 The advice given under paragraph 6.6 may, subject to any direction of the court, be given orally or in writing. If the advice is given orally, a note of it must be taken by the court or the court officer.

6.8 The children's guardian must–

(a) unless the court directs otherwise, file a written report advising on the interests of the child in accordance with the timetable set by the court; and
(b) in proceedings to which Part 14 applies, where practicable, notify any person the joining of whom as a party to those proceedings would be likely, in the opinion of the children's guardian, to safeguard the interests of the child, of the court's power to join that person as a party under rule 14.3 and must inform the court–
   (i) of any notification;
   (ii) of anyone whom the children's guardian attempted to notify under this paragraph but was unable to contact; and
   (iii) of anyone whom the children's guardian believes may wish to be joined to the proceedings.

(Part 18 sets out the procedure for making an application to be joined as a party in proceedings.)

How the children's guardian exercises duties – service of documents and inspection of records

6.9 The children's guardian must serve and accept service of documents on behalf of the child in accordance with rule 6.31 and, where the child has not himself been served and has sufficient understanding, advise the child of the contents of any document so served.

6.10 Where the children's guardian inspects records of the kinds referred to in–

(a) section 42 of the 1989 Act (right to have access to local authority records); or
(b) section 103 of the 2002 Act (right to have access to adoption agency records)

the children's guardian must bring all records and documents which may, in the opinion of the children's guardian, assist in the proper determination of the proceedings to the attention of–
   (i) the court; and
   (ii) unless the court directs otherwise, the other parties to the proceedings.

How the children's guardian exercises duties – communication of a court's decision to the child

6.11 The children's guardian must ensure that, in relation to a decision made by the court in the proceedings–

(a) if the children's guardian considers it appropriate to the age and understanding of the child, the child is notified of that decision; and
(b) if the child is notified of the decision, it is explained to the child in a manner appropriate to that child's age and understanding.

PART 4
APPOINTMENT OF CHILDREN'S GUARDIAN UNDER RULE 16.4

Section 1 – When a child should be made a party to proceedings

7.1 Making the child a party to the proceedings is a step that will be taken only in cases which involve an issue of significant difficulty and consequently will occur in only a minority of cases. Before taking the decision to make the child a party, consideration should be given to whether an alternative route might be preferable, such as asking an officer of the Service or a Welsh family proceedings officer to carry out further work or by making a referral to social services or, possibly, by obtaining expert evidence.

7.2 The decision to make the child a party will always be exclusively that of the court, made in the light of the facts and circumstances of the particular case. The following are offered, solely by way of guidance, as circumstances which may justify the making of such an order–

(a) where an officer of the Service or Welsh family proceedings officer has notified the court that in the opinion of that officer the child should be made a party;
(b) where the child has a standpoint or interest which is inconsistent with or incapable of being represented by any of the adult parties;
(c) where there is an intractable dispute over residence or contact, including where all contact has ceased, or where there is irrational but implacable hostility to contact or where the child may be suffering harm associated with the contact dispute;
(d) where the views and wishes of the child cannot be adequately met by a report to the court;
(e) where an older child is opposing a proposed course of action;
(f) where there are complex medical or mental health issues to be determined or there are other unusually complex issues that necessitate separate representation of the child;
(g) where there are international complications outside child abduction, in particular where it may be necessary for there to be discussions with overseas authorities or a foreign court;
(h) where there are serious allegations of physical, sexual or other abuse in relation to the child or there are allegations of domestic violence not capable of being resolved with the help of an officer of the Service or Welsh family proceedings officer;
(i) where the proceedings concern more than one child and the welfare of the children is in conflict or one child is in a particularly disadvantaged position;
(j) where there is a contested issue about scientific testing.

7.3 It must be recognised that separate representation of the child may result in a delay in the resolution of the proceedings. When deciding whether to direct that a child be made a party, the court will take into account the risk of delay or other facts adverse to the welfare of the child. The court's primary consideration will be the best interests of the child.

7.4 When a child is made a party and a children's guardian is to be appointed–

(a) consideration should first be given to appointing an officer of the Service or Welsh family proceedings officer. Before appointing an officer, the court will cause preliminary enquiries to be made of Cafcass or CAFCASS CYMRU. For the relevant procedure, reference should be made to the practice note issued by Cafcass in June 2006 and any modifications of that practice note.

(b) If Cafcass or CAFCASS CYMRU is unable to provide a children's guardian without delay, or if for some other reason the appointment of an officer of the Service of Welsh family proceedings officer is not appropriate, rule 16.24 makes further provision for the appointment of a children's guardian.

Section 2 – Children's guardian appointed under rule 16.4

Duties of the children's guardian

7.6 It is the duty of a children's guardian fairly and competently to conduct proceedings on behalf of the child. The children's guardian must have no interest in the proceedings adverse to that of the child and all steps and decisions the children's guardian takes in the proceedings must be taken for the benefit of the child.

7.7 A children's guardian who is an officer of the Service or a Welsh family proceedings officer has, in addition, the duties set out in Part 3 of this Practice Direction and must exercise those duties as set out in that Part.

Becoming a children's guardian without a court order

7.8 In order to become a children's guardian without a court order the person who wishes to act as children's guardian must file a certificate of suitability–

(a) stating that the children's guardian consents to act;
(b) stating that the children's guardian knows or believes that the [applicant] [respondent] is a child to whom rule 16.4 and Chapter 7 of Part 16 apply;
(c) stating that the children's guardian can fairly and competently conduct proceedings on behalf of the child and has no interest adverse to that of the child;
(d) undertaking to pay any costs which the child may be ordered to pay in relation to the proceedings, subject to any right the children's guardian may have to be repaid from the assets of the child; and
(e) which the children's guardian has verified by a statement of truth.

7.9 Paragraph 7.8 does not apply to the Official Solicitor, an officer of the Service or a Welsh family proceedings officer.

7.10 The court officer will send the certificate of suitability to one of the child's parents or guardians or, if there is no parent or guardian, to the person with whom the child resides or in whose care the child is.

7.11 The children's guardian must file either the certificate of suitability at a time when the children's guardian first takes a step in the proceedings on behalf of the child.

Application for a court order appointing a children's guardian

7.12 An application for a court order appointing a children's guardian should be made in accordance with Part 18 and must be supported by evidence.

7.13 The court officer must serve the application notice on the persons referred to in paragraph 7.10.

7.14 The evidence in support must satisfy the court that the proposed children's guardian–

(a) consents to act;
(b) can fairly and competently conduct proceedings on behalf of the child;
(c) has no interest adverse to that of the child; and

(d) undertakes to pay any costs which the child may be ordered to pay in relation to the proceedings, subject to any right the children's guardian may have to be repaid from the assets of the child.

7.15 Paragraph 7.14 does not apply to the Official Solicitor, an officer of the Service of a Welsh family proceedings officer.

7.16 The proposed children's guardian may be one of the persons referred to in paragraph 7.10 where appropriate, or otherwise may be the Official Solicitor, an officer of the Service or a Welsh family proceedings officer. Where it is sought to appoint the Official Solicitor, an officer of the Service or a Welsh family proceedings officer, provision should be made for payment of that person's charges.

Change of children's guardian and prevention of person acting as children's guardian

7.17 Where an application is made for an order under rule 16.25, the application must set out the reasons for seeking it and must be supported by evidence.

7.18 Subject to paragraph 7.15, if the order sought is substitution of a new children's guardian for an existing one, the evidence must satisfy the court of the matters set out in paragraph 7.14.

7.19 The court officer will serve the application notice on–

(a) the persons referred to in paragraph 7.10; and
(b) the children's guardian or person purporting to act as children's guardian.

PART 5
REPORTING OFFICER

How the reporting officer exercises duties

8.1 The reporting officer must–

(a) ensure so far as reasonably practicable that the parent or guardian is–
 (i) giving consent unconditionally to the placing of the child for adoption or to the making of an adoption order (as defined in section 46 of the Adoption and Children Act 2002) or a section 84 order; and
 (ii) with full understanding of what is involved;
(b) investigate all the circumstances relevant to a parent's or guardian's consent; and
(c) on completing the investigations the reporting officer must–
 (i) make a report in writing to the court in accordance with the timetable set by the court, drawing attention to any matters which, in the opinion of the reporting officer, may be of assistance to the court in considering the application; or
 (ii) make an interim report to the court if a parent or guardian of the child is unwilling to consent to the placing of the child for adoption or to the making of an adoption order or section 84 order.

8.2 On receipt of an interim report under paragraph 8.1(1)(c)(ii) a court officer must inform the applicant that a parent or guardian of the child is unwilling to consent to the placing of the child for adoption or to the making of an adoption order or section 84 order.

8.3 The reporting officer may at any time before the final hearing make an interim report to the court if the reporting officer considers it necessary and ask the court for directions.

8.4 The reporting officer must attend hearings as directed by the court.

PART 6
CHILDREN AND FAMILY REPORTER AND WELFARE OFFICER

How the children and family reporter or welfare officer exercises powers and duties

9.1 In this Part, the person preparing the welfare report in accordance with rule 16.33 is called 'the officer'.

9.2 The officer must make such investigations as may be necessary to perform the officer's powers and duties and must, in particular–

(a) contact or seek to interview such persons as appear appropriate or as the court directs; and
(b) obtain such professional assistance as is available which the children and family reporter thinks appropriate or which the court directs be obtained.

9.3 The officer must–

(a) notify the child of such contents of the report (if any) as the officer considers appropriate to the age and understanding of the child, including any reference to the child's own views on the application and the recommendation; and
(b) if the child is notified of any contents of the report, explain them to the child in a manner appropriate to the child's age and understanding.

9.4 The officer must–

(a) attend hearings as directed by the court;
(b) advise the court of the child's wishes and feelings;
(c) advise the court if the officer considers that the joining of a person as a party to the proceedings would be likely to safeguard the interests of the child;
(d) consider whether it is in the best interests of the child for the child to be made a party to the proceedings, and if so, notify the court of that opinion together with the reasons for that opinion; and
(e) where the court has directed that a written report be made–
    (i) file the report; and
    (ii) serve a copy on the other parties and on any children's guardian,

in accordance with the timetable set by the court.

PART 7
PARENTAL ORDER REPORTER

How the parental order reporter exercises duties – investigations and reports

10.1 The parental order reporter must make such investigations as are necessary to carry out the parental order reporter's duties and must, in particular–

(a) contact or seek to interview such persons as the parental order reporter thinks appropriate or as the court directs; and
(b) obtain such professional assistance as is available which the parental order reporter thinks appropriate or which the court directs be obtained.

How the parental order reporter exercises duties – attendance at court, advice to the court and reports

10.2 The parental order reporter must attend all directions hearings unless the court directs otherwise.

10.3 The parental order reporter must advise the court on the following matters–

(a) the appropriate forum for the proceedings;
(b) the appropriate timing of the proceedings or any part of them;
(c) the options available to it in respect of the child and the suitability of each such option including what order should be made in determining the application; and
(d) any other matter on which the court seeks advice or on which the parental order reporter considers that the court should be informed.

10.4 The advice given under paragraph 10.3 may, subject to any direction of the court, be given orally or in writing. If the advice is given orally, a note of it must be taken by the court or the court officer.

10.5 The parental order reporter must–

(a) unless the court directs otherwise, file a written report advising on the interests of the child in accordance with the timetable set by the court; and
(b) where practicable, notify any person the joining of whom as a party to those proceedings would be likely, in the opinion of the parental order reporter, to safeguard the interests of the child, of the court's power to join that person as a party under rule 13.3 and must inform the court–
    (i) of any notification;
    (ii) of anyone whom the parental order reporter attempted to notify under this paragraph but was unable to contact; and
    (iii) of anyone whom the parental order reporter believes may wish to be joined to the proceedings.

(Part 18 sets out the procedure for making an application to be joined as a party in proceedings.)

PART 8
OFFICERS OF THE SERVICE, WELSH FAMILY PROCEEDINGS OFFICERS AND LOCAL AUTHORITY OFFICERS: FURTHER DUTIES

How officers of the Service, Welsh family proceedings officers and local authority officers exercise certain further duties

11.1 This Part applies when an officer of the Service, a Welsh family proceedings officer or a local authority officer is acting under a duty referred to in rule 16.38(1). In this Part, the person acting under a duty referred to in rule 16.38(1) is referred to as 'the officer'.

11.2 The officer must make such investigations as may be necessary to perform the officer's duties and must, in particular–

(a) contact or seek to interview such persons as the officer thinks appropriate or as the court directs; and
(b) obtain such professional assistance as the officer thinks appropriate or which the court directs.

11.3 The officer must–

(a) notify the child of such (if any) of the contents of any report or risk assessment as the officer considers appropriate to the age and understanding of the child;
(b) if the child is notified of any contents of a report or risk assessment, explain them to the child in a manner appropriate to the child's age and understanding;
(c) consider whether to recommend in any report or risk assessment that the court lists a hearing for the purposes of considering the report or risk assessment;

(d) consider whether it is in the best interests of the child for the child to be made a party to the proceedings, and, if so, notify the court of that opinion together with the reasons for that opinion.

11.4 When making a risk assessment, the officer must, if of the opinion that the court should exercise its discretion under rule 12.34(2), state in the risk assessment–

(a) the way in which the officer considers the court should exercise its discretion (including the officer's view on the length of any suggested delay in service); and
(b) the officer's reasons for that reaching that view.

11.5 The officer must file any report or risk assessment with the court–

(a) at or by the time directed by the court;
(b) in the absence of any direction, at least 14 days before a relevant hearing; or
(c) where there has been no direction from the court and there is no relevant hearing listed, as soon as possible following the completion of the report or risk assessment.

11.6 In paragraph 11.5, a hearing is relevant if the court officer has given the officer notice that a report prepared by the officer is to be considered at it.

11.7 A copy of any report prepared as a result of acting under a duty referred to in rule 16.38(1)(a)(i) to (vi) or (b) (but not any risk assessment) must, as soon as practicable, be served by the officer on the parties.

(Rule 12.34 makes provision for the service of risk assessments.)

PART 17
STATEMENTS OF TRUTH

[17.1 Interpretation

[(1)][1] In this Part 'statement of case' has the meaning given to it in Part 4 except that a statement of case does not include—

(a) …[2]
(b) …[3]
[(c) an application under Article 10 of the 2007 Hague Convention using the Financial Circumstances Form.][1]

(Rule 4.1 defines 'statement of case' for the purposes of Part 4.)

[(2) In this rule, 'Financial Circumstances Form' has the meaning given to it in rule 9.3(1).][1]][4]

Amendment

1 Inserted by the Family Procedure (Amendment No 4) Rules 2012, SI 2012/2806, rr 2, 3, 14(a), (c), (d).
2 Repealed by the Family Procedure (Amendment No 2) Rules 2017, SI 2017/741, rr 2, 8.
3 Repealed by the Family Procedure Rules 2010 and Court of Protection Rules 2017 (Amendment) (EU Exit) Regulations 2019, SI 2019/517, rr 2, 11(1), (2).
4 Substituted by the Family Procedure (Amendment) Rules 2011, SI 2011/1328, rr 2, 3, 14.

17.2 Documents to be verified by a statement of truth

(1) Subject to paragraph (9), the following documents must be verified by a statement of truth—

(a) a statement of case;
(b) a witness statement;

(c) an acknowledgement of service in a claim begun by the Part 19 procedure;
(d) a certificate of service;
(e) …[1]
(f) a statement of information filed under rule 9.26(1)(b); and
(g) any other document where a [court order,][2] rule or practice direction requires it.

(2) Where a statement of case is amended, the amendments must be verified by a statement of truth unless the court orders otherwise.

(3) [Subject to paragraph (10), if][3] an applicant wishes to rely on matters set out in the application form or application notice as evidence, the application form or notice must be verified by a statement of truth.

(4) Subject to paragraph (5), a statement of truth is a statement that—

(a) the party putting forward the document;
(b) in the case of a witness statement, the maker of the witness statement; or
(c) in the case of a certificate of service, the person who signs the certificate,

believes the facts stated in the document are true.

(5) If a party is conducting proceedings with a litigation friend, the statement of truth in—

(a) a statement of case; or
(b) an application notice,

is a statement that the litigation friend believes the facts stated in the document being verified are true.

(6) The statement of truth must be signed by—

(a) in the case of a statement of case—
  (i) the party or litigation friend; or
  (ii) the legal representative on behalf of the party or litigation friend; and
(b) in the case of a witness statement …[1], the maker of the statement.

(7) A statement of truth, which is not contained in the document which it verifies, must clearly identify that document.

(8) A statement of truth in a statement of case may be made by—

(a) a person who is not a party; or
(b) by two parties jointly,

where this is permitted by a practice direction.

(9) An application that does not contain a statement of facts need not be verified by a statement of truth.

[(10) Notwithstanding paragraph (3), and subject to any direction given under rule 9.14(2A) or rule 9.19(2A), the court may permit a party to rely upon matters set out in an application form which has not been verified by a statement of truth as evidence where the application has been made under—

(a) …[4]
(b) Article 10 of the 2007 Hague Convention on an Article 11 form.][2]

(Practice Direction 17A sets out the form of statement of truth.)

Amendment

1 Repealed by the Family Procedure (Amendment No 3) Rules 2014, SI 2014/843, rr 2, 43.
2 Inserted by the Family Procedure (Amendment No 4) Rules 2012, SI 2012/2806, rr 2, 3, 15(a), (c).
3 Substituted by the Family Procedure (Amendment No 4) Rules 2012, SI 2012/2806, rr 2, 3, 15(b).
4 Repealed by the Family Procedure Rules 2010 and Court of Protection Rules 2017 (Amendment) (EU Exit) Regulations 2019, SI 2019/517, rr 2, 11(1), (3).

17.3 Failure to verify a statement of case

(1) If a party fails to verify that party's statement of case by a statement of truth—

- (a) the statement of case shall remain effective unless struck out; but
- (b) the party may not rely on the statement of case as evidence of any of the matters set out in it.

(2) The court may strike out(GL) a statement of case which is not verified by a statement of truth.

(3) Any party may apply for an order under paragraph (2).

17.4 Failure to verify a witness statement

If the maker of a witness statement fails to verify the witness statement by a statement of truth, the court may direct that it shall not be admissible as evidence.

17.5 Power of the court to require a document to be verified

(1) The court may order a person who has failed to verify a document in accordance with rule 17.2 to verify the document.

(2) Any party may apply for an order under paragraph (1).

17.6 False statements

(1) Proceedings for contempt of court may be brought against a person who makes, or causes to be made, a false statement in a document verified by a statement of truth without an honest belief in its truth.

(2) Proceedings under this rule may be brought only—

- (a) by the Attorney General; or
- (b) with the permission of the court.

(3) … [1]

Amendment

1 Repealed by the Family Procedure (Amendment No 3) Rules 2013, SI 2013/3204, rr 2, 63.

Practice Direction 17A – Statements of truth

See also Part 17

See also Part 17

This Practice Direction supplements FPR Part 17

Documents to be verified by a statement of truth

1.1 Rule 17.2 sets out the documents which must be verified by a statement of truth.

1.2 If an applicant wishes to rely on matters set out in his application notice as evidence, the application notice must be verified by a statement of truth.

1.3 An expert's report should also be verified by a statement of truth. For the form of the statement of truth verifying an expert's report (which differs from that set out below), see paragraph 9.1(j) of Practice Direction 25B (The Duties Of An Expert, The Expert's Report and Arrangements For An Expert To Attend Court).

1.4 In addition, the following documents must be verified by a statement of truth –

(a) an application notice for –
  (i) a third party debt order (CPR Part 72 as modified by rule 33.24);
  (ii) a hardship payment order (CPR Part 72 as modified by rule 33.24); or
  (iii) a charging order (CPR Part 73 as modified by rule 33.25); and

(b) a notice of objections to an account being taken by the court, unless verified by an affidavit or witness statement.

1.5 The statement of truth may be contained in the document it verifies or it may be in a separate document served subsequently, in which case it must identify the document to which it relates.

1.6 Where the form to be used includes a jurat for the content to be verified by an affidavit, then a statement of truth is not required in addition.

1.7 In this Practice Direction, 'statement of case' has the meaning given to it by rule 17.1.

Form of the statement of truth

2.1 The form of the statement of truth verifying a statement of case or an application notice should be as follows:

> '[I understand] [the (applicant or as the case may be) understands] that proceedings for contempt of court may be brought against anyone who makes, or causes to be made, a false statement in a document verified by a statement of truth without an honest belief in its truth. [I believe] [the (applicant or as may be) believes] that the facts stated in this [name document being verified] are true.'

2.2 The form of the statement of truth verifying a witness statement should be as follows:

> 'I understand that proceedings for contempt of court may be brought against anyone who makes, or causes to be made, a false statement in a document verified by a statement of truth without an honest belief in its truth.
>
> I believe that the facts stated in this witness statement are true.'

2.3 Where the statement of truth is contained in a separate document, the document containing the statement of truth must be headed with the title of and court reference for the proceedings. The document being verified should be identified in the statement of truth as follows –

(a) application form: 'the application form issued on [date]';

(b) statement of case: 'the (application or answer as may be) served on [name of party] on [date]';

(c) application notice: 'the application notice issued on [date] for [set out the remedy sought]';

(d) witness statement: 'the witness statement filed on [date] or served on [party] on [date]'.

2.4 Practice Direction 9A makes provision in relation to statements of truth to be included in costs estimates and particulars of costs to be filed and served in accordance with rule 9.27(1), (2), (3) or (4).

Who may sign the statement of truth

3.1 In a statement of case or an application notice, the statement of truth must be signed by –

(a) the party or his litigation friend; or
(b) the legal representative of the party or litigation friend.

3.2 A statement of truth verifying a witness statement must be signed by the witness.

3.3 A statement of truth verifying a notice of objections to an account must be signed by the objecting party or his or her legal representative.

3.4 Where a document is to be verified on behalf of a company or corporation, subject to paragraph 3.7 below, the statement of truth must be signed by a person holding a senior position in the company or corporation. That person must state the office or position he or she holds.

3.5 Each of the following persons is a person holding a senior position –

(a) in respect of a registered company or corporation, a director, the treasurer, secretary, chief executive, manager or other officer of the company or corporation; and
(b) in respect of a corporation which is not a registered company, in addition to those persons set out in (a), the major, chairman, president, chief executive of a local authority or town clerk or other similar officer of the corporation.

3.6 Where the document is to be verified on behalf of a partnership, those who may sign the statement of truth are –

(a) any of the partners; or
(b) a person having the management or control of the partnership business.

3.7 Where a party is legally represented, the legal representative may sign the statement of truth on his or her behalf. The statement signed by the legal representative will refer to the client's belief, not his or her own. In signing he or she must state the capacity in which he or she signs and the name of his or her firm where appropriate.

3.8 Where a legal representative has signed a statement of truth, his or her signature will be taken by the court as his or her statement –

(a) that the client on whose behalf he or she has signed had authorised him or her to do so;
(b) that before signing he or she had explained to the client that in signing the statement of truth he or she would be confirming the client's belief that the facts stated in the document were true; and
(c) that before signing he or she had informed the client of the possible consequences to the client if it should subsequently appear that the client did not have an honest belief in the truth of those facts (see rule 17.6).

3.9 A legal representative who signs a statement of truth must print his or her full name clearly beneath his or her signature.

3.10 The individual who signs a statement of truth must sign in his or her own name and not that of his or her firm or employer.

3.11 The following are examples of the possible application of this practice direction describing who may sign a statement of truth verifying statements in documents other than a witness statement. These are only examples and not an indication of how a court might apply the practice direction to a specific situation.

Managing Agent

An agent who manages property or investments for the party cannot sign a statement of truth. It must be signed by the party or by the legal representative of the party.

Trusts

Where some or all of the trustees comprise a single party one, some or all of the trustees comprising the party may sign a statement of truth. The legal representative of the trustees may sign it.

Companies

Paragraphs 3.4 and 3.5 apply. The word 'manager' will be construed in the context of the phrase 'a person holding a senior position' which it is used to define. The court will consider the size of the company and the importance and nature of the proceedings. It would expect the manager signing the statement of truth to to have personal knowledge of the content of the document or to be responsible for those who have that knowledge of the content. A small company may not have a manager, apart from the directors, who holds a senior position. A large company will have many such managers. In a large company with specialist claims, insurance or legal departments the statement may be signed by the manager of such a department if he or she is responsible for handling the claim or managing the staff handling it.

Inability of persons to read or sign documents to be verified by a statement of truth

4.1 Where a document containing a statement of truth is to be signed by a person who is unable to read or sign the document, it must contain a certificate made by an authorised person.

4.2 An authorised person is a person able to administer oaths and take affidavits but need not be independent of the parties or their representatives.

4.3 The authorised person must certify –

(a) that the document has been read to the person signing it;
(b) that the person appeared to understand it and approved its content as accurate;
(c) that the declaration of truth has been read to that person;
(d) that that person appeared to understand the declaration and the consequences of making a false declaration; and
(e) that that person signed or made his mark in the presence of the authorised person.

4.4 The form of the certificate is set out at the Annex to this Practice Direction.

4A.1 Where

(a) a form referred to in Practice Direction 5A; or
(b) a form completed or generated by electronic means in accordance with Part 41 FPR,
(c) a document other than a form referred to in sub-paragraph (a) or (b), such as a witness statement

makes provision for an electronic signature of a statement of truth, references in this Practice Direction to 'sign', 'signs', 'signed' and 'signing' are to be read as including an electronic signature. An electronic signature could, for example, be in the form of the following being included next to a statement of truth: a tick box, a printed name, an image of a signature or a digital signature generated by commercial software. (Section 7 of the Electronic Communications Act 2000 provides for the use of an electronic signature in an electronic communication.)

4A.2 Paragraph 4A.1 is subject to any direction of the court on a case by case basis that the signature on a given statement of truth must be in a specified form, for example by being handwritten.

Consequences of failure to verify

5.1 If a statement of case is not verified by a statement of truth, the statement of case will remain effective unless it is struck out, but a party may not rely on the contents of a statement of case as evidence until it has been verified by a statement of truth.

5.2 Any party may apply to the court for an order that unless within such period as the court may specify the statement of case is verified by the service of a statement of truth, the statement of case will be struck out.

5.3 The usual order for the costs of an application referred to in paragraph 5.2 will be that the costs be paid by the party who had failed to verify, in any event and immediately.

Penalty

6 Attention is drawn to rule 17.6 which sets out the consequences of verifying a statement of case containing a false statement without an honest belief in its truth, and to the procedures set out in Part 37 (Applications and proceedings in relation to contempt of court).

Annex

Certificate to be used where a person is unable to read or sign a document to be verified by a statement of truth

> 'I certify that I [name and address of authorised person] have read the contents of this document and the declaration of truth to the person signing the document [if there are exhibits, add 'and explained the nature and effect of the exhibits referred to in it'] who appeared to understand (a) the document and approved its content as accurate and (b) the declaration of truth and the consequences of making a false declaration, and made his or her mark in my presence.'

PART 18
PROCEDURE FOR OTHER APPLICATIONS IN PROCEEDINGS

18.1 Types of application for which Part 18 procedure may be followed

(1) The Part 18 procedure is the procedure set out in this Part.

(2) An applicant may use the Part 18 procedure if the application is made—

(a) in the course of existing proceedings;
(b) to start proceedings except where some other Part of these rules prescribes the procedure to start proceedings; or
(c) in connection with proceedings which have been concluded.

(3) Paragraph (2) does not apply—

(a) to applications where any other rule in any other Part of these rules sets out the procedure for that type of application;

(b) if a practice direction provides that the Part 18 procedure may not be used in relation to the type of application in question.

[(4) This Part is subject to any provision made by or pursuant to Part 41 (proceeding by electronic means).][1]

Amendment

1 Inserted by the Family Procedure (Amendment) Rules 2020, SI 2020/135, rr 2, 22.

18.2 Applications for permission to start proceedings

An application for permission to start proceedings must be made to the court where the proceedings will be started if permission is granted.

[(Rule 5.4 makes general provision in relation to the court in which proceedings should be started.)][1]

Amendment

1 Inserted by the Family Procedure (Amendment No 3) Rules 2013, SI 2013/3204, rr 2, 64.

18.3 Respondents to applications under this Part

(1) The following persons are to be respondents to an application under this Part—

(a) where there are existing proceedings or the proceedings have been concluded—

(i) the parties to those proceedings; and

(ii) if the proceedings are proceedings under Part 11, the person who is the subject of those proceedings;

(b) where there are no existing proceedings—

(i) if notice has been given under section 44 of the 2002 Act (notice of intention to adopt or apply for an order under section 84 of that Act), the local authority to whom notice has been given; and

(ii) if an application is made for permission to apply for an order in proceedings, any person who will be a party to the proceedings brought if permission is granted; and

(c) any other person as the court may direct.

18.4 Application notice to be filed

(1) Subject to paragraph (2), the applicant must file an application notice.

(2) An applicant may make an application without filing an application notice if—

(a) this is permitted by a rule or practice direction; or

(b) the court dispenses with the requirement for an application notice.

18.5 Notice of an application

(1) Subject to paragraph (2), a copy of the application notice must be served on—

(a) each respondent;

(b) in relation to proceedings under Part 11, the person who is, or, in the case of an application to start proceedings, it is intended will be, the subject of the proceedings; and

(c) in relation to proceedings under Parts 12 and 14, the children's guardian (if any).

(2) An application may be made without serving a copy of the application notice if this is permitted by—

(a) a rule;
(b) a practice direction; or
(c) the court.

(Rule 18.8 deals with service of a copy of the application notice.)

18.6 Time when an application is made

When an application must be made within a specified time, it is so made if the court receives the application notice within that time.

18.7 What an application notice must include

(1) An application notice must state—

(a) what order the applicant is seeking; and
(b) briefly, why the applicant is seeking the order.

(2) A draft of the order sought must be attached to the application notice.

(Part 17 requires an application notice to be verified by a statement of truth if the applicant wishes to rely on matters set out in his application as evidence.)

18.8 Service of a copy of an application notice

(1) Subject to rule 2.4, a copy of the application notice must be served in accordance with the provisions of Part 6—

(a) as soon as practicable after it is filed; and
(b) in any event—
  (i) where the application is for an …[1] order under rule 9.7 at least 14 days; and
  (ii) in any other case, at least 7 days;

before the court is to deal with the application.

(2) The applicant must, when filing the application notice, file a copy of any written evidence in support.

(3) If a copy of an application notice is served by a court officer it must be accompanied by—

(a) a notice of the date and place where the application will be heard;
(b) a copy of any witness statement in support; and
(c) a copy of the draft order which the applicant has attached to the application.

(4) If—

(a) an application notice is served; but
(b) the period of notice is shorter than the period required by these rules or a practice direction,

the court may direct that, in the circumstances of the case, sufficient notice has been given and hear the application.

(5) This rule does not require written evidence—

(a) to be filed if it has already been filed; or
(b) to be served on a party on whom it has already been served.

Amendment

1 Repealed by the Family Procedure (Amendment No 2) Rules 2013, SI 2013/1472, rr 2, 5.

18.9 Applications which may be dealt with without a hearing

(1) The court may deal with an application without a hearing if—

(a) the court does not consider that a hearing would be appropriate; or
(b) the parties agree as to the terms of the order sought or the parties agree that the court should dispose of the application without a hearing and the court does not consider that a hearing would be appropriate.

(2) Where—

(a) an application is made for permission to make an application in proceedings under the 1989 Act; and
(b) the court refuses the application without a hearing in accordance with paragraph (1)(a),

the court must, at the request of the applicant, re-list the application and fix a date for a hearing.

(3) … [1]

Amendment

1 Repealed by the Family Procedure (Amendment No 3) Rules 2013, SI 2013/3204, rr 2, 65.

18.10 Service of application notice following court order where application made without notice

(1) This rule applies where the court has disposed of an application which it permitted to be made without service of a copy of the application notice.

(2) Where the court makes an order, whether granting or dismissing the application, a copy of the application notice and any evidence in support must unless the court orders otherwise, be served with the order on—

(a) all the parties in proceedings; and
(b) in relation to proceedings under Part 11, the person who is, or, in the case of an application to start proceedings, it is intended will be, the subject of the proceedings.

(3) The order must contain a statement of the right to make an application to set aside(GL) or vary the order under rule 18.11.

18.11 Application to set aside or vary order made without notice

(1) A person who was not served with a copy of the application notice before an order was made under rule 18.10 may apply to have the order set aside(GL) or varied.

(2) An application under this rule must be made within 7 days beginning with the date on which the order was served on the person making the application.

18.12 Power of the court to proceed in the absence of a party

(1) Where the applicant or any respondent fails to attend the hearing of an application, the court may proceed in the absence of that person.

(2) Where—

(a) the applicant or any respondent fails to attend the hearing of an application; and
(b) the court makes an order at the hearing,

the court may, on application or of its own initiative, re-list the application.

(3) …[1]

Amendment

1 Repealed by the Family Procedure (Amendment No 3) Rules 2013, SI 2013/3204, rr 2, 65.

18.13 Dismissal of totally without merit applications

If the …[1] court dismisses an application (including an application for permission to appeal) and it considers that the application is totally without merit—

(a) the court's order must record that fact; and
(b) the court must at the same time consider whether it is appropriate to make a civil restraint order.

Amendment

1 Repealed by the Family Procedure (Amendment No 3) Rules 2013, SI 2013/3204, rr 2, 66.

Practice Direction 18A – Other applications in proceedings

See also Part 18

This Practice Direction supplements FPR Part 18

Application of Part 18

1.1 Part 18 makes general provision for a procedure for making applications. All applications for the court's permission should be made under this Part, with the exception of applications for permission for which specific provision is made in other Parts of the FPR, in which case the application should be made under the specific provision. Examples of where specific provision has been made in another Part of the FPR for applications for permission are rule 11.3 (Permission to apply for a forced marriage protection order) and rule 30.3 (Permission to appeal).

2.1 Omitted

Additional requirements in relation to application notices

3.1 In addition to the requirements set out in rule 18.7, the following requirements apply to the applications to which the respective paragraph refers.

3.2 An application notice must be signed and include –

(a) the title of the case (if available);
(b) the reference number of the case (if available);

(c) the full name of the applicant;
(d) where the applicant is not already a party, the applicant's address for service, including a postcode. Postcode information may be obtained from www.royalmail.com or the Royal Mail Address Management Guide; and
(e) either a request for a hearing or a request that the application be dealt with without a hearing.

3.3 An application notice relating to an application under section 42(6) of the Adoption and Children Act 2002 (permission to apply for an adoption order) must include –

(a) the child's name, sex, date of birth and nationality;
(b) in relation to each of the child's parents or guardians, their name, address and nationality;
(c) the length of time that the child has had his or her home with the applicant;
(d) the reason why the child has had his or her home with the applicant;
(e) details of any local authority or adoption agency involved in placing the child in the applicant's home; and
(f) if there are or have been other court proceedings relating to the child, the nature of those proceedings, the name of the court in which they are being or have been dealt with, the date and type of any order made and, if the proceedings are still ongoing, the date of the next hearing.

3.4 An application notice relating to an application in the High Court by a local authority for permission under section 100(3) of the Children Act 1989 must include a draft of the application form.

3.5 Where permission is required to take any step under the Children Act 1989 (for example an application to be joined as a party to the proceedings) the application notice must include a draft of the application for the making of which permission is sought together with sufficient copies for one to be served on each respondent.

3.6 In an application for permission to bring proceedings under Schedule 1 of the Children Act 1989, the draft application for the making of which permission is sought must be accompanied by a statement setting out the financial details which the person seeking permission believes to be relevant to the request and contain a declaration that it is true to the maker's best knowledge and belief, together with sufficient copies for one to be served on each respondent.

3.7 The provisions in Schedule 1 which require an application for permission to bring proceedings are –

(a) paragraph 7(2) – permission is required to make an application for variation of a secured periodical payments order after the death of the parent liable to make the payments if a period of 6 months has passed from the date on which representation in regard to that parent's estate is first taken out; and
(b) paragraph 11(3) – permission is required to make an application to alter a maintenance agreement following the death of one of the parties if a period of 6 months has passed beginning with the day on which representation in regard to the estate of the deceased is first taken out.

Other provisions in relation to application notices

4.1 On receipt of an application notice containing a request for a hearing, unless the court considers that the application is suitable for consideration without a hearing, the court officer will, if serving a copy of the application notice, notify the applicant of the time and date fixed for the hearing of the application.

4.2 On receipt of an application notice containing a request that the application be dealt with without a hearing, the court will decide whether the application is suitable for consideration without a hearing.

4.3 Where the court –

(a) considers that the application is suitable for consideration without a hearing; but
(b) is not satisfied that it has sufficient material to decide the application immediately,

it may give directions for the filing of evidence and will inform the applicant and the respondent(s) of its decision. (Rule 18.11 enables a party to apply for an order made without notice to be set aside or varied.)

4.4 Where the court does not consider that the application is suitable for consideration without a hearing –

(a) it may give directions as to the filing of evidence; and
(b) the court officer will notify the applicant and the respondent of the time, date and place for the hearing of the application and any directions given.

4.5 Omitted

4.6 Every application should be made as soon as it becomes apparent that it is necessary or desirable to make it.

4.7 Applications should, wherever possible, be made so that they are considered at any directions hearing or other hearing for which a date has been fixed or for which a date is about to be fixed.

4.8 The parties must anticipate that at any hearing (including any directions hearing) the court may wish to review the conduct of the case as a whole and give any necessary directions. They should be ready to assist the court in doing so and to answer questions the court may ask for this purpose.

4.9 Where a date for a hearing has been fixed, a party who wishes to make an application at that hearing but does not have sufficient time to file an application notice should as soon as possible inform the court (if possible in writing) and, if possible, the other parties of the nature of the application and the reason for it. That party should then make the application orally at the hearing.

Applications without service of application notice

5.1 An application may be made without service of an application notice only –

(a) where there is exceptional urgency;
(b) where the overriding objective is best furthered by doing so;
(c) by consent of all parties;
(d) with the permission of the court;
(e) where paragraph 4.9 applies; or
(f) where a court order, rule or practice direction permits.

Giving notice of an application

6.1 Unless the court otherwise directs or paragraph 5.1 of this practice direction applies, the application notice must be served as soon as practicable after it has been issued and, if there is to be a hearing, at least 7 days before the hearing date.

6.2 Where an application notice should be served but there is not sufficient time to do so, informal notification of the application should be given unless the circumstances of the application require no notice of the application to be given.

Pre-action applications

7.1 All applications made before proceedings are commenced should be made under this Part.

Telephone hearings

8.1 The court may direct that an application be dealt with by a telephone hearing.

8.2 The applicant should, if seeking a direction under paragraph 8.1, indicate this on the application notice. Where the applicant has not indicated such an intention but nevertheless wishes to seek a direction the request should be made as early as possible.

8.3 A direction under paragraph 8.1 will not normally be made unless every party entitled to be given notice of the application and to be heard at the hearing has consented to the direction.

8.4 No representative of a party to an application being heard by telephone may attend the court in person while the application is being heard unless the other party to the application has agreed that the representative may do so.

8.5 If an application is to be heard by telephone the following directions will apply, subject to any direction to the contrary –

(a) the applicant's legal representative is responsible for arranging the telephone conference for precisely the time fixed by the court. The telecommunications provider used must be one of the approved panel of service providers (see HMCS website at www.hmcourts-service.gov.uk);

(b) the applicant's legal representative must tell the operator the telephone numbers of all those participating in the conference call and the sequence in which they are to be called;

(c) it is the responsibility of the applicant's legal representative to ascertain from all the other parties whether they have instructed counsel and, if so the identity of counsel, and whether the legal representative and counsel will be on the same or different telephone numbers;

(d) the sequence in which those involved are to be called will be –

  (i) the applicant's legal representative and (if on a different number) his counsel;

  (ii) the legal representative (and counsel) for all other parties; and

  (iii) the judge or justices, as the case may be;

(e) each speaker is to remain on the line after being called by the operator setting up the conference call. The call may be 2 or 3 minutes before the time fixed for the application;

(f) when the judge has been connected the applicant's legal representative (or counsel) will introduce the parties in the usual way;

(g) if the use of a 'speakerphone' by any party causes the court or any other party any difficulty in hearing what is said the judge may require that party to use a hand held telephone;

(h) the telephone charges debited to the account of the party initiating the conference call will be treated as part of the costs of the application.

Video conferencing

9.1 Where the parties to a matter wish to use video conferencing facilities, and those facilities are available in the relevant court, the parties should apply to the court for directions. (Practice Direction 22A provides guidance on the use of video conferencing)

Note of proceedings

10.1 The court or court officer should keep, either by way of a note or a tape recording, brief details of all proceedings before the court, including the dates of the proceedings and a short statement of the decision taken at each hearing.

Evidence

11.1 The requirement for evidence in certain types of applications is set out in some of the rules in the FPR and practice directions. Where there is no specific requirement to provide evidence it should be borne in mind that, as a practical matter, the court will often need to be satisfied by evidence of the facts that are relied on in support of or for opposing the application.

11.2 The court may give directions for the filing of evidence in support of or opposing a particular application. The court may also give directions for the filing of evidence in relation to any hearing that it fixes on its own initiative. The directions may specify the form that evidence is to take and when it is to be served.

11.3 Where it is intended to rely on evidence which is not contained in the application itself, the evidence, if it has not already been served, should be served with the application.

11.4 Where a respondent to an application wishes to rely on evidence, that evidence must be filed in accordance with any directions the court may have given and a court officer will serve the evidence on the other parties, unless the court directs otherwise.

11.5 If it is necessary for the applicant to serve any evidence in reply the court officer will serve it on the other parties unless the court directs otherwise.

11.6 Evidence must be filed with the court as well as served on the parties.

11.7 The contents of an application notice may be used as evidence provided the contents have been verified by a statement of truth.

Consent orders

12.1 The parties to an application for a consent order must ensure that they provide the court with any material it needs to be satisfied that it is appropriate to make the order. Subject to any rule in the FPR or practice direction a letter will generally be acceptable for this purpose.

12.2 Where a judgment or order has been agreed in respect of an application where a hearing date has been fixed, the parties must inform the court immediately.

Other applications considered without a hearing

13.1 Where rule 18.9(1)(a) applies the court will treat the application as if it were proposing to make an order on its own initiative.

13.2 Where the parties agree that the court should dispose of the application without a hearing they should so inform the court in writing and each should confirm that all evidence and other material on which he or she relies has been disclosed to the other parties to the application.

Miscellaneous

14.1 If the case is proceeding in the High Court and the draft order is unusually long or complex it should also be supplied in electronic form on such storage medium as shall be agreed with the judge or court staff, for use by the court office.

14.2 Where rule 18.12 applies the power to re-list the application in rule 18.12(2) is in addition to any other powers of the court with regard to the order (for example to set aside, vary, discharge or suspend the order).

Costs

15.1 Attention is drawn to the CPR costs practice direction and, in particular, to the court's power to make a summary assessment of costs.

15.2 Attention is also drawn to rule 44.13(1) of the CPR which provides that if an order makes no mention of costs, none are payable in respect of the proceedings to which it relates.

PART 19
ALTERNATIVE PROCEDURE FOR APPLICATIONS

19.1 Types of application for which Part 19 procedure may be followed

(1) The Part 19 procedure is the procedure set out in this Part.

(2) An applicant may use the Part 19 procedure where the Part 18 procedure does not apply and—

(a) there is no form prescribed by a rule or referred to in Practice Direction 5A in which to make the application;
(b) the applicant seeks the court's decision on a question which is unlikely to involve a substantial dispute of fact; or
(c) paragraph (5) applies.

[(2A) This Part is subject to any provision made by or pursuant to Part 41 (proceeding by electronic means).][1]

(3) The court may at any stage direct that the application is to continue as if the applicant had not used the Part 19 procedure and, if it does so, the court may give any directions it considers appropriate.

(4) Paragraph (2) does not apply if a practice direction provides that the Part 19 procedure may not be used in relation to the type of application in question.

(5) A rule or practice direction may, in relation to a specified type of proceedings—

(a) require or permit the use of the Part 19 procedure; and
(b) disapply or modify any of the rules set out in this Part as they apply to those proceedings.

Amendment

1 Inserted by the Family Procedure (Amendment) Rules 2020, SI 2020/135, rr 2, 23.

19.2 Applications for which the Part 19 procedure must be followed

(1) The Part 19 procedure must be used in an application made in accordance with—

(a) section 60(3) of the 2002 Act (order to prevent disclosure of information to an adopted person);

(b) section 79(4) of the 2002 Act (order for Registrar General to give any information referred to in section 79(3) of the 2002 Act); and

(c) rule 14.21 (directions …[1] regarding fathers without parental responsibility).

(2) The respondent to an application made in accordance with paragraph (1)(b) is the Registrar General.

Amendment

1 Repealed by the Family Procedure (Amendment) Rules 2020, SI 2020/135, rr 2, 24.

19.3 Contents of the application

Where the applicant uses the Part 19 procedure, the application must state—

(a) that this Part applies;

(b) either—

(i) the question which the applicant wants the court to decide; or

(ii) the order which the applicant is seeking and the legal basis of the application for that order;

(c) if the application is being made under an enactment, what that enactment is;

(d) if the applicant is applying in a representative capacity, what that capacity is; and

(e) if the respondent appears or is to appear in a representative capacity, what that capacity is.

(Part 17 requires a statement of case to be verified by a statement of truth.)

19.4 Issue of application without naming respondents

(1) A practice direction may set out circumstances in which an application may be issued under this Part without naming a respondent.

(2) The practice direction may set out those cases in which an application for permission must be made by application notice before the application is issued.

(3) The application for permission—

(a) need not be served on any other person; and

(b) must be accompanied by a copy of the application which the applicant proposes to issue.

(4) Where the court gives permission, it will give directions about the future management of the application.

19.5 Acknowledgment of service

(1) Subject to paragraph (2), each respondent must—

(a) file an acknowledgment of service within 14 days beginning with the date on which the application is served; and

(b) serve the acknowledgment of service on the applicant and any other party.

(2) If the application is to be served out of the jurisdiction, the respondent must file and serve an acknowledgment of service within the period set out in Practice Direction 6B.

(3) The acknowledgment of service must—

- (a) state whether the respondent contests the application;
- (b) state, if the respondent seeks a different order from that set out in the application, what that order is; and
- (c) be signed by the respondent or the respondent's legal representative.

19.6 Consequence of not filing an acknowledgment of service

(1) This rule applies where—

- (a) the respondent has failed to file an acknowledgment of service; and
- (b) the time period for doing so has expired.

(2) The respondent may attend the hearing of the application but may not take part in the hearing unless the court gives permission.

19.7 Filing and serving written evidence

(1) The applicant must, when filing the application, file the written evidence on which the applicant intends to rely.

(2) The applicant's evidence must be served on the respondent with the application.

(3) A respondent who wishes to rely on written evidence must file it when filing the acknowledgment of service.

(4) A respondent who files written evidence must also, at the same time, serve a copy of that evidence on the other parties.

(5) Within 14 days beginning with the date on which a respondent's evidence was served on the applicant, the applicant may file further written evidence in reply.

(6) An applicant who files further written evidence must also, within the same time limit, serve a copy of that evidence on the other parties.

19.8 Evidence – general

(1) No written evidence may be relied on at the hearing of the application unless—

- (a) it has been served in accordance with rule 19.7; or
- (b) the court gives permission.

(2) The court may require or permit a party to give oral evidence at the hearing.

(3) The court may give directions requiring the attendance for cross-examination(GL) of a witness who has given written evidence.

(Rule 22.1 contains a general power for the court to control evidence.)

19.9 Procedure where respondent objects to use of the Part 19 procedure

(1) A respondent who contends that the Part 19 procedure should not be used because—

- (a) there is a substantial dispute of fact; and
- (b) the use of the Part 19 procedure is not required or permitted by a rule or practice direction,

must state the reasons for that contention when filing the acknowledgment of service.

(2) When the court receives the acknowledgment of service and any written evidence, it will give directions as to the future management of the case.

(Rule 19.7 requires a respondent who wishes to rely on written evidence to file it when filing the acknowledgment of service.)

(Rule 19.1(3) allows the court to make an order that the application continue as if the applicant had not used the Part 19 procedure.)

Practice Direction 19A – Alternative procedure for applications

See also Part 19

This Practice Direction supplements FPR Part 19

Types of application in which Part 19 procedure must be used

1.1 An applicant must use the Part 19 procedure if the application is for an order under–

(a) section 60(3) of the 2002 Act, to prevent disclosure of information to an adopted person;

(b) section 79(4) of the 2002 Act, to require the Registrar General to provide information; or

(c) rule 14.21 (Inherent jurisdiction and fathers without parental responsibility) in Part 14, to request directions of the High Court regarding fathers without parental responsibility.

Types of application in which Part 19 procedure may be used

1.2 An applicant may use the Part 19 procedure if Part 18 does not apply and if–

(a) there is no prescribed form in which to make the application; or

(b) the applicant seeks the court's decision on a question which is unlikely to involve a substantial dispute of fact.

1.3 An applicant may also use the Part 19 procedure if a practice direction permits or requires its use for the type of proceedings concerned.

1.4 The practice directions referred to in paragraph 1.3 may in some respects modify or disapply the Part 19 procedure and, where that is so, it is those practice directions, rather than this one, which must be complied with.

1.5 The types of application for which the Part 19 procedure may be used include an application for an order or direction which is unopposed by each respondent before the commencement of the proceedings and the sole purpose of the application is to obtain the approval of the court to the agreement.

1.6 Where it appears to a court officer that an applicant is using the Part 19 procedure inappropriately, the officer may refer the application to the court for consideration of the point.

1.7 The court may at any stage order the application to continue as if the applicant had not used the Part 19 procedure and, if it does so, the court will give such directions as it considers appropriate (see rule 19.1(3)).

The application

2.1 Where an applicant uses the Part 19 procedure, the application form referred to in Practice Direction 5A should be used and must state the matters set out in rule 19.3 and, if paragraphs 1.3 and 1.4 apply, must comply with the requirements of the practice direction in question. In particular, the application form must state that Part 19 applies. A Part 19 application form means an application form which so states.

2.2 An application–

(a) in accordance with rule 19.4, to ask the High Court for directions on the need to give a father without parental responsibility notice of the intention to place a child for adoption; or

(b) under section 60(3) of the 2002 Act for an order to prevent disclosure of information to an adopted person,

may be issued without naming a respondent.

Responding to the application

3.1 Where a respondent who wishes to respond to a Part 19 application is required to file an acknowledgement of service, that acknowledgement of service should be in form FP5 which is referred to in Practice Direction 5A but can, alternatively be given in an informal document such as a letter.

3.2 Rule 19.5 sets out provisions relating to an acknowledgement of service of a Part 19 application.

3.3 Rule 19.6 sets out the consequence of failing to file an acknowledgement of service.

3.4 A respondent who believes that the Part 19 procedure should not be used because there is a substantial dispute of fact or, as the case may be, because its use is not authorised by any rule in the FPR or any practice direction, must state the reasons for that belief in writing when filing the acknowledgement of service (see rule 19.9). If the statement of reasons includes matters of evidence, it should be verified by a statement of truth.

Managing the application

4.1 The court may give directions immediately a Part 19 application is issued either on the application of a party or of its own initiative. The directions may include fixing a hearing date where–

(a) there is no dispute; or

(b) where there may be a dispute, but a hearing date could conveniently be given.

4.2 Where the court does not fix a hearing date when the application is issued, it will give directions for the disposal of the application as soon as practicable after the respondent has acknowledged service of the application or, as the case may be, after the period for acknowledging service has expired.

4.3 Certain applications may not require a hearing.

4.4 The court may convene a directions hearing before giving directions.

Evidence

5.1 An applicant wishing to rely on written evidence should file it when the Part 19 application form is issued.

5.2 Evidence will normally be in the form of a witness statement or an affidavit but an applicant may rely on the matters set out in the application form provided it has been verified by a statement of truth.

(For information about statements of truth see Part 17 and Practice Direction 17A, and about written evidence see Part 22 and Practice Direction 22A.)

5.3 A respondent wishing to rely on written evidence should file it with the acknowledgement of service (see rule 19.7(3)).

5.4 Rule 19.7 sets out the times and provisions for filing and serving written evidence.

5.5 A party may apply to the court for an extension of time to serve and file evidence under rule 19.7 or for permission to serve and file additional evidence under rule 19.8(1).

(For information about applications see Part 18 and Practice Direction 18A.)

5.6 The parties may, subject to paragraphs 5.7 and 5.8, agree in writing on an extension of time for serving and filing evidence under rule 19.7(3) or rule 19.7(5).

5.7 An agreement extending time for a respondent to file evidence in reply under rule 19.7(3)–

(a) must be filed by the respondent at the same time as the acknowledgement of service; and
(b) must not extend time by more than 17 days after the respondent files the acknowledgement of service.

5.8 An agreement extending time for an applicant to file evidence in reply under rule 19.7(5) must not extend time to more than 28 days after service of the respondent's evidence on the applicant.

Hearing

6.1 The court may on the hearing date–

(a) proceed to hear the case and dispose of the application;
(b) give case management directions.

PART 20
INTERIM REMEDIES AND SECURITY FOR COSTS

Chapter 1
Interim remedies

20.1 …[1]

…[1]

Amendment

1 Repealed by the Family Procedure (Amendment No 3) Rules 2013, SI 2013/3204, rr 2, 67.

20.2 Orders for interim remedies

(1) The court may grant the following interim remedies—

(a) an interim injunction(GL);
(b) an interim declaration;

(c) an order—
- (i) for the detention, custody or preservation of relevant property;
- (ii) for the inspection of relevant property;
- (iii) for the taking of a sample of relevant property;
- (iv) for the carrying out of an experiment on or with relevant property;
- (v) for the sale of relevant property which is of a perishable nature or which for any other good reason it is desirable to sell quickly; and
- (vi) for the payment of income from relevant property until an application is decided;

(d) an order authorising a person to enter any land or building in the possession of a party to the proceedings for the purposes of carrying out an order under sub-paragraph (c);

(e) an order under section 4 of the Torts (Interference with Goods) Act 1977 to deliver up goods;

(f) an order (referred to as a 'freezing injunction[GL]')—
- (i) restraining a party from removing from the jurisdiction assets located there; or
- (ii) restraining a party from dealing with any assets whether located within the jurisdiction or not;

(g) an order directing a party to provide information about the location of relevant property or assets or to provide information about relevant property or assets which are or may be the subject of an application for a freezing injunction[GL];

(h) an order (referred to as a 'search order') under section 7 of the Civil Procedure Act 1997 (order requiring a party to admit another party to premises for the purpose of preserving evidence etc.);

(i) an order under section 34 of the Senior Courts Act 1981 or section 53 of the County Courts Act 1984 (order in certain proceedings for disclosure of documents or inspection of property against a non-party);

(j) an order for a specified fund to be paid into court or otherwise secured, where there is a dispute over a party's right to the fund;

(k) an order permitting a party seeking to recover personal property to pay money into court pending the outcome of the proceedings and directing that, if money is paid into court, the property must be given up to that party;

(l) an order directing a party to prepare and file accounts relating to the dispute;

(m) an order directing any account to be taken or inquiry to be made by the court.

(2) In paragraph (1)(c) and (g), 'relevant property' means property (including land) which is the subject of an application or as to which any question may arise on an application.

(3) The fact that a particular kind of interim remedy is not listed in paragraph (1) does not affect any power that the court may have to grant that remedy.

20.3 Time when an order for an interim remedy may be made

(1) An order for an interim remedy may be made at any time, including—

(a) before proceedings are started; and
(b) after judgment has been given.

(Rule 5.3 provides that proceedings are started when the court issues an application form.)

(2) However—

(a) paragraph (1) is subject to any rule, practice direction or other enactment which provides otherwise; and

(b) the court may grant an interim remedy before an application has been started only if—
  (i) the matter is urgent; or
  (ii) it is otherwise desirable to do so in the interests of justice.

(3) Where the court grants an interim remedy before an application has been started, it will give directions requiring an application to be started.

(4) The court need not direct that an application be started where the application is made under section 33 of the Senior Courts Act 1981 or section 52 of the County Courts Act 1984 (order for disclosure, inspection etc. before starting an application).

20.4 How to apply for an interim remedy

(1) The court may grant an interim remedy on an application made without notice if it appears to the court that there are good reasons for not giving notice.

(2) An application for an interim remedy must be supported by evidence, unless the court orders otherwise.

(3) If the applicant makes an application without giving notice, the evidence in support of the application must state the reasons why notice has not been given.

(Part 4 lists general case-management powers of the court.)

(Part 18 contains general rules about making an application.)

20.5 Interim injunction to cease if application is stayed

If—

(a) the court has granted an interim injunction(GL) other than a freezing injunction(GL); and
(b) the application is stayed(GL) other than by agreement between the parties,

the interim injunction(GL) will be set aside(GL) unless the court orders that it should continue to have effect even though the application is stayed(GL).

Chapter 2
Security for costs

20.6 Security for costs

(1) A respondent to any application may apply under this Chapter of this Part for security for costs of the proceedings.

(Part 4 provides for the court to order payment of sums into court in other circumstances.)

(2) An application for security for costs must be supported by written evidence.

(3) Where the court makes an order for security for costs, it will—

(a) determine the amount of security; and
(b) direct—
  (i) the manner in which; and
  (ii) the time within which,

the security must be given.

20.7 Conditions to be satisfied

(1) The court may make an order for security for costs under rule 20.6 if—

(a) it is satisfied, having regard to all the circumstances of the case, that it is just to make such an order; and
(b) either—
 (i) one or more of the conditions in paragraph (2) applies; or
 (ii) an enactment permits the court to require security for costs.

(2) The conditions are—

(a) the applicant is—
 (i) resident out of the jurisdiction; but
 (ii) …[1]
(b) the applicant has changed address since the application was started with a view to evading the consequences of the litigation;
(c) the applicant failed to give an address in the application form, or gave an incorrect address in that form;
(d) the applicant has taken steps in relation to the applicant's assets that would make it difficult to enforce an order for costs against the applicant.

(3) The court may not make an order for security for costs under rule 20.6 in relation to the costs of proceedings under the 1980 Hague Convention.

(Rule 4.4 allows the court to strike out(GL) a statement of case.)

[…[1]][2]

Amendment

1 Repealed by the Family Procedure Rules 2010 and Court of Protection Rules 2017 (Amendment) (EU Exit) Regulations 2019, SI 2019/517, rr 2, 12.
2 Inserted by the Family Procedure (Amendment No 4) Rules 2012, SI 2012/2806, rr 2, 3, 16.

20.8 Security for costs of an appeal

The court may order security for costs of an appeal against—

(a) an appellant;
(b) a respondent who also appeals,

on the same grounds as it may order security for costs against an applicant under this Part.

Practice Direction 20A – Interim remedies

See also Part 20

This Practice Direction supplements FPR Part 20

Scope and jurisdiction

1.1 This Practice Direction does not apply to an order under section 48 (Powers to assist in discovery of children who may be in need of emergency protection), section 50 (Recovery of abducted children, etc.) of the Children Act 1989 or section 33(Power to order disclosure of child's whereabouts) or section 34 (Power to order recovery of child) of the Family Law Act 1986.

1.2 The Family Court (Composition and Distribution of Business) Rules 2014 make provision in relation to which judges may not grant certain remedies in the family court.

1.3 In a case in the High Court, district judges have the power to grant injunctions–

(a) by consent;
(b) in connection with charging orders and appointments of receivers;
(c) in aid of execution of judgments.

Making an application

2.1 The application notice must state–

(a) the order sought; and
(b) the date, time and place of the hearing.

2.2 The application notice and evidence in support must be served as soon as practicable after issue and in any event not less than 7 days before the court is due to hear the application unless the court directs otherwise.

2.3 Where the court is to serve, sufficient copies of the application notice and evidence in support for the court and for each respondent should be filed for issue and service.

2.4 Whenever possible a draft of the order sought should be filed with the application notice and an electronic version of the draft should also be available to the court in a format compatible with the word processing software used by the court and on such storage medium as shall be agreed by the court. This will enable the court officer to arrange for any amendments to be incorporated and for the speedy preparation and sealing of the order.

Evidence

3.1 Applications for search orders and freezing injunctions must be supported by affidavit evidence.

3.2 Applications for other interim injunctions must be supported by evidence set out in either–

(a) a witness statement; or
(b) the application notice provided that it is verified by a statement of truth,

unless the court, an Act, a rule in the FPR or a practice direction requires evidence by affidavit.

3.3 The evidence must set out the facts on which the applicant relies for the application being made against the respondent, including all material facts of which the court should be made aware.

3.4 Where an application is made without notice to the respondent, the evidence must also set out why notice was not given.

(See Part 22 and the practice direction that supplements it for information about evidence.)

Urgent applications and applications without notice

4.1 These fall into two categories–

(a) applications where an application in proceedings has already been issued; and
(b) applications where an application in proceedings has not yet been issued,

and, in both cases, where notice of the application has not been given to the respondent.

4.2 These applications are normally dealt with at a court hearing but cases of extreme urgency may be dealt with by telephone.

4.3 In relation to applications dealt with at a court hearing after issue of an application form–

(a) the application notice, evidence in support and a draft order (as in paragraph 2.4) should be filed with the court two hours before the hearing wherever possible;
(b) if an application is made before the application notice has been issued, a draft order (as in paragraph 2.4) should be provided at the hearing, and the application notice and evidence in support must be filed with the court on the same or next working day or as ordered by the court; and
(c) except in cases where it is essential that the respondent must not be aware of the application, the applicant should take steps to notify the respondent informally of the application.

4.4 In relation to applications made before the issue of an application–

(a) in addition to the provisions set out at paragraph 4.3, unless the court orders otherwise, either the applicant must undertake to the court to issue an application notice immediately or the court will give directions for the commencement of the application (see rule 20.3(3));
(b) where possible the application should be served with the order for the injunction;
(c) an order made before the issue of an application should state in the title after the names of the applicant and respondent 'the Applicant and Respondent in Intended Proceedings'.

4.5 In relation to applications made outside normal working hours–

(a) the applicant should either–
   (i) telephone the Royal Courts of Justice on 020 7947 6000 to be put in contact with the clerk to the appropriate duty judge in the High Court (or the appropriate area Circuit Judge where known); or
   (ii) telephone the Urgent Court Business Officer of the appropriate Circuit who will contact the local duty judge;
(b) where the facility is available it is likely that the judge will require a draft order to be faxed to him;
(c) the application notice and evidence in support must be filed with the court on the same or next working day or as ordered, together with two copies of the order for sealing;
(d) injunctions will be heard by telephone only where the applicant is acting by counsel or solicitors.

4.6 Each Designated Family Judge area of the family court will have its own scheme for out of hours applications, details of which will be given locally to–

(a) the police;
(b) any local Law Society and Bar organisation; and
(c) the local authority Social Services Department.

Orders for injunctions

5.1 Any order for an injunction, unless the court orders otherwise, must contain–

(a) an undertaking by the applicant to the court to pay any damages which the respondent sustains which the court considers the applicant should pay;

(b) if the order is made without notice to any other party, an undertaking by the applicant to the court to serve on the respondent the application notice, evidence in support and any order made as soon as practicable;

(c) if the order is made without notice to any other party, a return date for a further hearing at which the other party can be present;

(d) if the order is made before filing the application notice, an undertaking to file and pay the appropriate fee on the same or next working day; and

(e) if the order is made before issue of an application in proceedings–

(i) an undertaking to issue and pay the appropriate fee on the same or next working day; or

(ii) directions for the commencement of the application.

5.2 When the court makes an order for an injunction, it should consider whether to require an undertaking by the applicant to pay any damages sustained by a person other than the respondent, including another party to the proceedings or any other person who may suffer loss as a consequence of the order.

5.3 An order for an injunction made in the presence of all parties to be bound by it or made at a hearing of which they have had notice, may state that it is effective until final hearing or further order.

5.4 Any order for an injunction must set out clearly what the respondent must do or not do.

Search Orders

Orders for the preservation of evidence and property

6.1 The following provisions apply to search orders in addition to those listed above.

The Supervising Solicitor

6.2 The Supervising Solicitor must be experienced in the operation of search orders. A Supervising Solicitor may be contacted either through the Law Society or, for the London area, through the London Solicitors Litigation Association.

Evidence

6.3

(1) The affidavit must state the name, firm and its address, and experience of the Supervising Solicitor, also the address of the premises and whether it is a private or business address.

(2) The affidavit must disclose very fully the reason the order is sought, including the probability that relevant material would disappear if the order were not made.

Service

6.4

(1) The order must be served personally by the Supervising Solicitor, unless the court directs otherwise, and must be accompanied by the evidence in support and any documents capable of being copied.

(2) Confidential exhibits need not be served but they must be made available for inspection by the respondent in the presence of the applicant's solicitors while

the order is carried out and afterwards be retained by the respondent's solicitors on their undertaking not to permit the respondent–

(a) to see them or copies of them except in their presence; and
(b) to make or take away any note or record of them.

(3) The Supervising Solicitor may be accompanied only by the persons mentioned in the order.

(4) The Supervising Solicitor must explain the terms and effect of the order to the respondent in everyday language and advise the respondent–

(a) of the respondent's right to take legal advice, and to apply to vary or discharge the order; and
(b) that the respondent may be entitled to avail himself of–
  (i) legal professional privilege; and
  (ii) the privilege against self-incrimination.

(5) Where the Supervising Solicitor is a man and the respondent is likely to be an unaccompanied woman, at least one other person named in the order must be a woman and must accompany the Supervising Solicitor.

(6) The order may only be served between 9.30 a.m. and 5.30 p.m. Monday to Friday unless the court directs otherwise.

Search and custody of materials

6.5

(1) No material shall be removed unless clearly covered by the terms of the order.

(2) The premises must not be searched and no items shall be removed from them except in the presence of the respondent or a person who appears to be a responsible employee of the respondent.

(3) Where copies of documents are sought, the documents should be retained for no more than 2 days before return to the owner.

(4) Where material in dispute is removed pending hearing, the applicant's solicitors should place it in the custody of the respondent's solicitors on their undertaking to retain it in safekeeping and to produce it to the court when required.

(5) In appropriate cases the applicant should insure the material retained in the respondent's solicitors' custody.

(6) The Supervising Solicitor must make a list of all material removed from the premises and supply a copy of the list to the respondent.

(7) No material shall be removed from the premises until the respondent has had reasonable time to check the list.

(8) If any of the listed items exists only in computer readable form, the respondent must immediately give the applicant's solicitors effective access to the computers, with all necessary passwords, to enable them to be searched, and cause the listed items to be printed out.

(9) The applicant must take all reasonable steps to ensure that no damage is done to any computer or data.

(10) The applicant and his representatives may not themselves search the respondent's computers unless they have sufficient expertise to do so without damaging the respondent's system;

(11) the Supervising Solicitor shall provide a report on the carrying out of the order to the applicant's solicitors.

(12) As soon as the report is received the applicant's solicitors shall–

(a) serve a copy of it on the respondent; and
(b) file a copy of it with the court.

(13) Where the Supervising Solicitor is satisfied that full compliance with paragraph 6.5(7) and (8) above is impracticable, that Solicitor may permit the search to proceed and items to be removed without compliance with the impracticable requirements.

General

6.6 The Supervising Solicitor must not be an employee or member of the applicant's firm of solicitors.

6.7 If the court orders that the order need not be served by the Supervising Solicitor, the reason for so ordering must be set out in the order.

6.8 The search order must not be carried out at the same time as a police search warrant.

6.9 There is no privilege against self incrimination in proceedings in which a court is hearing an application for an order under Part 4 or 5 of the Children Act 1989 (see section 98 of the Children Act 1989).

Delivery up orders

7.1 The following provision applies to orders, other than search orders, for delivery up or preservation of evidence or property where it is likely that such an order will be executed at the premises of the respondent or a third party.

7.2 In such cases the court will consider whether to include in the order for the benefit or protection of the parties similar provisions to those specified above in relation to injunctions and search orders.

Injunctions against third parties

8.1 The following provision applies to orders which will affect a person other than the applicant or respondent, who–

(a) did not attend the hearing at which the order was made; and
(b) is served with the order.

8.2 Where such a person served with the order requests–

(a) a copy of any materials read by the court, including material prepared after the hearing at the direction of the court or in compliance with the order; or
(b) a note of the hearing,

the applicant, or the applicant's legal representative, must comply promptly with the request, unless the court directs otherwise.

PART 21
MISCELLANEOUS RULES ABOUT DISCLOSURE AND INSPECTION OF DOCUMENTS

21.1 Interpretation

(1) A party discloses a document by stating that the document exists or has existed.

(2) Inspection of a document occurs when a party is permitted to inspect a document disclosed by another person.

(3) For the purposes of disclosure and inspection—

(a) 'document' means anything in which information of any description is recorded; and
(b) 'copy' in relation to a document, means anything onto which information recorded in the document has been copied, by whatever means and whether directly or indirectly.

21.2 Orders for disclosure against a person not a party

(1) This rule applies where an application is made to the court under any Act for disclosure by a person who is not a party to the proceedings.

(2) The application—

(a) may be made without notice; and
(b) must be supported by evidence.

(3) The court may make an order under this rule only where disclosure is necessary in order to dispose fairly of the proceedings or to save costs.

(4) An order under this rule must—

(a) specify the documents or the classes of documents which the respondent must disclose; and
(b) require the respondent, when making disclosure, to specify any of those documents—
   (i) which are no longer in the respondent's control; or
   (ii) in respect of which the respondent claims a right or duty to withhold inspection.

(5) Such an order may—

(a) require the respondent to indicate what has happened to any documents which are no longer in the respondent's control; and
(b) specify the time and place for disclosure and inspection.

(6) An order under this rule must not compel a person to produce any document which that person could not be compelled to produce at the final hearing.

(7) This rule does not limit any other power which the court may have to order disclosure against a person who is not a party to proceedings.

…[1]

Amendment

1 Repealed by the Family Procedure Rules 2010 and Court of Protection Rules 2017 (Amendment) (EU Exit) Regulations 2019, SI 2019/517, rr 2, 13.

21.3 Claim to withhold inspection or disclosure of a document

(1) A person may apply, without notice, for an order permitting that person to withhold disclosure of a document on the ground that disclosure would damage the public interest.

(2) Unless the court otherwise orders, an order of the court under paragraph (1)—

(a) must not be served on any other person; and
(b) must not be open to inspection by any other person.

(3) A person who wishes to claim a right or a duty to withhold inspection of a document, or part of a document, must state in writing—

(a) the right or duty claimed; and
(b) the grounds on which that right or duty is claimed.

(4) The statement referred to in paragraph (3) must be made to the person wishing to inspect the document.

(5) A party may apply to the court to decide whether a claim made under paragraph (3) should be upheld.

(6) Where the court is deciding an application under paragraph (1) or (5) it may—

- (a) require the person seeking to withhold disclosure or inspection of a document to produce that document to the court; and
- (b) invite any person, whether or not a party, to make representations.

(7) An application under paragraph (1) or (5) must be supported by evidence.

(8) This Part does not affect any rule of law which permits or requires a document to be withheld from disclosure or inspection on the ground that its disclosure or inspection would damage the public interest.

Practice Direction 21A – Disclosure and inspection

See also Part 21

This Practice Direction supplements FPR Part 21

Chapter 1
Orders for Disclosure and Inspection of Documents

Interpretation

1.1 A party discloses a document by stating that the document exists or has existed. Inspection occurs when a party is permitted to inspect a document disclosed by another party.

1.2 For the purposes of disclosure and inspection in family proceedings–

'document' means anything in which information of any description is recorded and any copy of a document which contains a modification, obliteration or other marking or feature shall be treated as a separate document; and

'copy', in relation to a document, means anything on which information recorded in the document has been copied, by whatever means and whether directly or indirectly.

Types of order for disclosure in family proceedings

2.1 In family proceedings other than proceedings for a financial remedy, where the court orders disclosure, the normal order will be for disclosure by each party setting out, in a list or questionnaire, the documents material to the proceedings, of the existence of which that party is aware and which are or have been in that party's control. This process is known as 'standard disclosure'.

2.2 In proceedings for a financial remedy, the process of disclosure is staged. First, Form E (the financial statement referred to in rule 9.14(1)) is served together with the documents which are required to be attached to it. The second stage occurs by the parties requesting (further) disclosure of each other by a questionnaire served before the first appointment; the questionnaire can request both information and documents. With the court's permission, a further questionnaire can be served later in the proceedings.

2.3 In matrimonial and civil partnership proceedings, under rule 7.15, the court – either on its own initiative or on the application of the other party – may order a party to clarify any matter which is in dispute in the proceedings or give additional information in relation to any such matter, whether or not the matter is contained in or referred to in the application or in the answer.

2.4 In any family proceedings, the court may order 'specific disclosure', which is an order that a party must–

(a) disclose documents or classes of documents specified in the order;
(b) carry out a search to the extent stated in the order; or
(c) disclose any documents located as a result of that search.

PART 22
EVIDENCE

Chapter 1
General rules

22.1 Power of court to control evidence

(1) The court may control the evidence by giving directions as to—

(a) the issues on which it requires evidence;
(b) the nature of the evidence which it requires to decide those issues; and
(c) the way in which the evidence is to be placed before the court.

(2) The court may use its power under this rule to exclude evidence that would otherwise be admissible.

(3) The court may permit a party to adduce evidence, or to seek to rely on a document, in respect of which that party has failed to comply with the requirements of this Part.

(4) The court may limit cross-examination(GL).

22.2 Evidence of witnesses – general rule

(1) The general rule is that any fact which needs to be proved by the evidence of witnesses is to be proved—

(a) at the final hearing, by their oral evidence; and
(b) at any other hearing, by their evidence in writing.

(2) The general rule does not apply—

(a) to proceedings under Part 12 for secure accommodation orders, interim care orders or interim supervision orders; or
(b) where an enactment, any of these rules, a practice direction or a court order provides to the contrary.

(Section 45(7) of the Children Act 1989 (emergency protection orders) is an example of an enactment which makes provision relating to the evidence that a court may take into account when hearing an application.)

22.3 Evidence by video link or other means

The court may allow a witness to give evidence through a video link or by other means.

22.4 Witness statements

(1) A witness statement is a written statement signed by a person which contains the evidence which that person would be allowed to give orally.

(2) A witness statement must comply with the requirements set out in the Practice Direction 22A.

(Part 17 requires a witness statement to be verified by a statement of truth.)

22.5 Service of witness statements for use at the final hearing

(1) The court may give directions as to service on the other parties of any witness statement of the oral evidence on which a party intends to rely in relation to any issues of fact to be decided at the final hearing.

(2) The court may give directions as to—

(a) the order in which witness statements are to be served; and
(b) whether or not the witness statements are to be filed.

(3) Where the court directs that a court officer is to serve a witness statement on the other parties, any reference in this Chapter to a party serving a witness statement is to be read as including a reference to a court officer serving the statement.

22.6 Use at the final hearing of witness statements which have been served

(1) If a party—

(a) has served a witness statement; and
(b) wishes to rely at the final hearing on the evidence of the witness who made the statement,

that party must call the witness to give oral evidence unless the court directs otherwise or the party puts the statement in as hearsay evidence.

(Part 23 (miscellaneous rules about evidence) contains provisions about hearsay evidence.)

(2) The witness statement of a witness called to give oral evidence under paragraph (1) is to stand as the evidence in chief(GL) of that witness unless the court directs otherwise.

(3) A witness giving oral evidence at the final hearing may with the permission of the court—

(a) amplify his witness statement; and
(b) give evidence in relation to new matters which have arisen since the witness statement was served on the other parties.

(4) The court will give permission under paragraph (3) only if it considers that there is good reason not to confine the evidence of the witness to the contents of the witness statement.

(5) If a party who has served a witness statement does not—

(a) call the witness to give evidence at the final hearing; or
(b) put the witness statement in as hearsay evidence,

any other party may put the witness statement in as hearsay evidence.

22.7 Evidence at hearings other than the final hearing

(1) Subject to paragraph (2), the general rule is that evidence at hearings other than the final hearing is to be by witness statement unless the court, any other rule, a practice direction or any other enactment requires otherwise.

(2) At hearings other than the final hearing, a party may rely on the matters set out in that party's—

(a) application form;
(b) application notice; or
(c) answer,

if the application form, application notice or answer, as the case may be, is verified by a statement of truth [or if the court gives that party permission to do so without such verification][1].

Amendment

1 Inserted by the Family Procedure (Amendment No 4) Rules 2012, SI 2012/2806, rr 2, 3, 17.

22.8 Order for cross-examination

(1) Where, at a hearing other than the final hearing, evidence is given in writing, any party may apply to the court for permission to cross-examine[(GL)] the person giving the evidence.

(2) If the court gives permission under paragraph (1) but the person in question does not attend, that person's evidence may not be used unless the court directs otherwise.

…[1]

Amendment

1 Repealed by the Family Procedure Rules 2010 and Court of Protection Rules 2017 (Amendment) (EU Exit) Regulations 2019, SI 2019/517, rr 2, 14.

22.9 Witness summaries

(1) A party who—

(a) is required to serve a witness statement for use at any hearing; but
(b) is unable to obtain one,

may apply, without notice, for permission to serve a witness summary instead.

(2) A witness summary is a summary of—

(a) the evidence, if known, which would otherwise be included in a witness statement; or
(b) if the evidence is not known, the matters about which the party serving the witness summary proposes to question the witness.

(3) Unless the court directs otherwise, a witness summary must include the name and address of the intended witness.

(4) Unless the court directs otherwise, a witness summary must be served within the period in which a witness statement would have had to be served.

(5) Where a party serves a witness summary, so far as practicable rules 22.4(2) (form of witness statements), 22.5 (service of witness statements for use at the final hearing) and 22.6(3) (amplifying witness statements) apply to the summary.

22.10 Consequence of failure to serve witness statement

If a witness statement for use at the final hearing is not served in respect of an intended witness within the time specified by the court, then the witness may not be called to give oral evidence unless the court gives permission.

22.11 Cross-examination on a witness statement

A witness who is called to give evidence at the final hearing may be cross-examined(GL) on the witness statement, whether or not the statement or any part of it was referred to during the witness's evidence in chief(GL).

22.12 Affidavit evidence

(1) Evidence must be given by affidavit(GL) instead of or in addition to a witness statement if this is required by the court, a provision contained in any other rule, a practice direction or any other enactment.

(2) … [1]

… [1]

Amendment

1 Repealed by the Family Procedure (Amendment No 3) Rules 2013, SI 2013/3204, rr 2, 68.

22.13 Form of affidavit

An affidavit(GL) must comply with the requirements set out in the Practice Direction 22A.

22.14 Affidavit made outside the jurisdiction

A person may make an affidavit(GL) outside the jurisdiction in accordance with—

(a) this Part; or
(b) the law of the place where the affidavit(GL) is made.

22.15 Notice to admit facts

(1) A party may serve notice on another party requiring the other party to admit the facts, or the part of the case of the serving party, specified in the notice.

(2) A notice to admit facts must be served no later than 21 days before the final hearing.

(3) Where the other party makes any admission in answer to the notice, the admission may be used against that party only—

(a) in the proceedings in which the notice to admit is served; and
(b) by the party who served the notice.

(4) The court may allow a party to amend or withdraw any admission made by that party on such terms as it thinks just.

22.16 Notice to admit or produce documents

(1) A party to whom a document is disclosed is deemed to admit the authenticity of that document unless notice is served by that party that the party wishes the document to be proved at the final hearing.

(2) A notice to prove a document must be served—

(a) by the latest date for serving witness statements; or
(b) within 7 days beginning with the date of service of the document, whichever is later.

22.17 Notarial acts and instruments

A notarial act or instrument may be received in evidence without further proof as duly authenticated in accordance with the requirements of law unless the contrary is proved.

Chapter 2
Rules applying only to particular proceedings

22.18 Scope of this Chapter

This Chapter of this Part applies to affidavits(GL) and affirmations as it applies to witness statements.

22.19 Availability of witness statements for inspection during the final hearing

(1) This rule applies to proceedings under Part 7 (matrimonial and civil partnership proceedings).

(2) A witness statement which stands as evidence in chief(GL) is open to inspection during the course of the final hearing unless the court directs otherwise.

(3) Any person may ask for a direction that a witness statement is not open to inspection.

(4) The court will not make a direction under paragraph (2) unless it is satisfied that a witness statement should not be open to inspection because of—

(a) the interests of justice;
(b) the public interest;
(c) the nature of any expert medical evidence in the statement;
(d) the nature of any confidential information (including information relating to personal financial matters) in the statement; or
(e) the need to protect the interests of any child or protected party.

(5) The court may exclude from inspection words or passages in the witness statement.

22.20 Use of witness statements for other purposes

(1) This rule applies to proceedings under Part 7 (matrimonial and civil partnership proceedings) or Part 9 (financial remedies).

(2) Except as provided by this rule, a witness statement may be used only for the purpose of the proceedings in which it is served.

(3) Paragraph (2) does not apply if and to the extent that—

(a) the court gives permission for some other use; or
(b) the witness statement has been put in evidence at a hearing held in public.

Practice Direction 22A – Written evidence

See also Part 22

This Practice Direction supplements FPR Part 22

Evidence in general

1.1 Rule 22.2(1) sets out the general rule as to how evidence is to be given and facts are to be proved. This is that, at the final hearing, witnesses will normally give oral evidence and, at any hearing other than the final hearing, by evidence in writing (which under rule 22.7(1) will usually be by witness statement).

1.2 Rule 22.2(2) excludes the general rule –

(a) from proceedings under Part 12 (Children) for secure accommodation orders, interim care orders or interim supervision orders; or
(b) where an enactment, any rule in the FPR, a practice direction or a court order provides to the contrary.

1.3 Application forms, application notices and answers except an application for a matrimonial order or a civil partnership order or an answer to such an application may also be used as evidence provided that their contents have been verified by a statement of truth (see Part 17 for information about statements of truth).

(For information regarding evidence by deposition see Part 24 and the practice direction which supplements it.)

1.4 Affidavits must be used as evidence –

(a) where sworn evidence is required by an enactment, rule, order or practice direction; and
(b) in any application for an order against anyone for alleged contempt of court.

1.5 If a party believes that sworn evidence is required by a court in another jurisdiction for any purpose connected with the proceedings, he may apply to the court for a direction that evidence shall be given only by affidavit on any applications to be heard before the final hearing.

1.6 The court may give a direction under rule 22.12 that evidence shall be given by affidavit instead of or in addition to a witness statement –

(a) on its own initiative; or
(b) after any party has applied to the court for such a direction.

1.7 An affidavit, where referred to in the FPR or a practice direction, also means an affirmation unless the context requires otherwise.

Affidavits and Witness Statements

Meaning of 'deponent' and 'witness'

2.1 For the purposes of the FPR –

a 'deponent' is a person who gives evidence by affidavit, affirmation or deposition; and a 'witness' is a person who gives evidence by witness statement.

2.2 References in the following paragraphs to 'the maker of', or 'making', an affidavit, affirmation, deposition or witness statement are to be construed accordingly.

Heading and format

3.1 The affidavit/statement should be headed with the title of the proceedings where the proceedings are between several parties with the same status it is sufficient to identify the parties, subject to paragraph 4.2, as follows –

Number:

A.B. (and others)	Applicants
C.D. (and others)	Respondents

3.2 Subject to paragraph 4.2, at the top right-hand corner of the first page (and on the backsheet) there should be clearly written –

(a) the party on whose behalf it is made;
(b) the initials and surname of the maker;
(c) the number of the affidavit/statement in relation to its maker;
(d) the identifying initials and number of each exhibit referred to; and
(e) the date made.

3.3 The affidavit/statement should –

(a) be produced on durable quality A4 paper with a 3.5 cm margin;
(b) be fully legible and should normally be typed on one side of the paper only;
(c) where possible, should be bound securely in a manner which would not hamper filing or, where secure binding is not possible, each page should be endorsed with the case number and should bear the following initials –
  (i) in the case of an affidavit, of the maker and of the person before whom it is sworn; or
  (ii) in the case of a witness statement, of the maker and, where the maker is unable to read or sign the statement, of the authorised person (see paragraphs 7.3 and 7.4 below);
(d) have the pages numbered consecutively as a separate document (or as one of several documents contained in a file);
(e) be divided into numbered paragraphs;
(f) have all numbers, including dates, expressed in figures; and
(g) give the reference to any document or documents mentioned either in the margin or in bold text in the body of the affidavit/statement.

Body

4.1 Subject to paragraph 4.2 and rules 14.2 and 29.1, the affidavit/statement must, if practicable, be in the maker's own words, it should be expressed in the first person, and the maker should –

(a) commence –
  (i) in an affidavit, 'I (full name) of (residential address) state on oath. ';
  (ii) in a statement, by giving his or her full name and residential address;
(b) if giving evidence in a professional, business or other occupational capacity, give the address at which he or she works in (a) above, the position held and the name of the firm or employer;
(c) give his or her occupation or (if none) description; and
(d) if it be the case that the maker is a party to the proceedings or is employed by a party to the proceedings, state that fact.

4.2 If, in proceedings to which Part 14 (Adoption, placement and related proceedings) applies, a serial number has been assigned under rule 14.2, the affidavit/statement must be framed so that it does not disclose the identity of the applicant.

(Rule 29.1 provides that, unless the court directs otherwise, a party to family proceedings is not required to reveal the address of his or her private residence or other contact details.)

4.3 An affidavit/statement must indicate –

(a) which of the statements in it are made from the maker's own knowledge and which are matters of information and belief; and
(b) the source for any matters of information and belief.

4.4 It is usually convenient to follow the chronological sequence of events or matters dealt with. Each paragraph should as far as possible be confined to a distinct portion of the subject.

4.5 The maker should, when referring to an exhibit or exhibits, state 'there is now shown to me marked'. 'the (description of exhibit)'.

Alterations to affidavits and witness statements

5.1 Any alteration to an affidavit must be initialled by both the maker and the person before whom the affidavit is sworn.

5.2 Any alteration to a witness statement must be initialled by the maker or by the authorised person where appropriate (see paragraphs 7.3 and 7.4 below).

5.3 An affidavit/statement which contains an alteration that has not been initialled in accordance with paragraphs 5.1 and 5.2 may be filed or used in evidence only with the permission of the court.

Swearing an affidavit or verifying a witness statement

6.1 An affidavit is the testimony of the person who swears it. A witness statement is the equivalent of the oral evidence which the maker would, if called, give in evidence.

6.2 The jurat of an affidavit is a statement set out at the end of the document which authenticates the affidavit. It must –

(a) be signed by all deponents;
(b) be completed and signed by the person before whom the affidavit was sworn whose name and qualification must be printed beneath his signature;
(c) contain the full address of the person before whom the affidavit was sworn; and
(d) follow immediately on from the text and not be put on a separate page.

6.3 An affidavit must be sworn before a person independent of the parties or their representatives. Only the following may administer oaths and take affidavits –

(a) a Commissioner for Oaths (Commissioners for Oaths Acts 1889 and 1891);
(b) other persons specified by statute (sections 12 and 18 of, and Schedules 2 and 4 to, the Legal Services Act 2007);
(c) certain officials of the Senior Courts (section 2 of the Commissioners for Oaths Act 1889);
(d) a judge of the family court (section 31G(8) of the Matrimonial and Family Proceedings Act 1984);
(e) an officer of the family court appointed by a judge of the family court for the purpose (section 31G(8) of the Matrimonial and Family Proceedings Act 1984).

6.4 A witness statement must include a statement of truth by the intended maker as follows:

'I understand that proceedings for contempt of court may be brought against anyone who makes, or causes to be made, a false statement in a document verified by a statement of truth without an honest belief in its truth.

'I believe that the facts stated in this witness statement are true.'

(Attention is drawn to rule 17.6 which sets out the consequences of verifying a witness statement containing a false statement without an honest belief in its truth.)

(For information regarding statements of truth, see Part 17 (Statements of truth) and Practice Direction 17A.)

(Paragraphs 7.1 to 7.4 below set out the procedures to be followed where the intended maker of an affidavit or witness statement is unable to read or sign the affidavit/statement.)

6.5 If, in proceedings under Part 14 (Adoption, placement and related proceedings), a serial number has been assigned under rule 14.2 or the name of the maker of the affidavit/statement is not being revealed in accordance with rule 29.1, the signature of the maker will be edited from the affidavit/statement before it is served on the other party.

Inability of maker to read or sign affidavit/statement

7.1 Where an affidavit is sworn by a deponent who is unable to read or sign it, the person before whom the affidavit is sworn must certify in the jurat that –

(a) that person read the affidavit to the deponent;
(b) the deponent appeared to understand it; and
(c) the deponent signed, or made his mark, in that person's presence.

7.2 If that certificate is not included in the jurat, the affidavit may not be used in evidence unless the court is satisfied that it was read to the deponent and that the deponent appeared to understand it. Annex 1 to this practice direction sets out forms of the jurat with the certificate for an affidavit and an affirmation respectively.

7.3 Where a witness statement is made by a person who is unable to read or sign the statement, it must contain a certificate made by an authorised person. An authorised person is a person able to administer oaths and take affidavits but need not be independent of the parties or their representatives.

7.4 The authorised person must certify –

(a) that the witness statement has been read to the witness;
(b) that the witness appeared to understand it and approved its content as accurate;
(c) that the statement of truth has been read to the witness;
(d) that the witness appeared to understand the statement of truth and the consequences of making a false witness statement; and
(e) that the witness signed or made his or her mark in the presence of the authorised person.

The form of the certificate is set out at Annex 2 to this practice direction.

Filing of affidavits and witness statements

8.1 If the court directs that an affidavit/statement is to be filed, it must be filed in the court or Division, or office or Registry of the court or Division, where the action in which it was or is to be used, is proceeding or will proceed.

8.2 Where the affidavit/statement is in a foreign language –

(a) the party wishing to rely on it must –
  (i) have it translated; and
  (ii) must file the foreign language affidavit/statement with the court; and
(b) the translator must sign the translation to certify that it is accurate.

Exhibits

Manner of Exhibiting Documents

9.1 A document used in conjunction with an affidavit/statement should be –

(a) shown to and verified by the maker, and remain separate from the affidavit/statement; and

(b) identified by a declaration of the person before whom the affidavit/statement was sworn.

9.2 The declaration should be headed with the name of the proceedings in the same way as the affidavit/statement is headed.

9.3 The first page of each exhibit should be marked –

(a) as in paragraph 3.2 above; and
(b) with the exhibit mark referred to in the affidavit/statement in accordance with paragraph 4.5 above.

9.4 Where the maker makes more than one affidavit/statement, to which there are exhibits, in the same proceedings, the numbering of the exhibits should run consecutively throughout and not start again with each affidavit/statement.

Letters

10.1 Copies of individual letters should be collected together and exhibited in a bundle or bundles. They should be arranged in chronological order with the earliest at the top, and firmly secured.

10.2 When a bundle of correspondence is exhibited, the exhibit should have a front page attached stating that the bundle consists of original letters and copies. They should be arranged and secured as above and numbered consecutively.

Other documents

11.1 Photocopies instead of original documents may be exhibited provided the originals are made available for inspection by the other parties before the hearing and by the court at the hearing.

11.2 Court documents must not be exhibited (official copies of such documents prove themselves).

11.3 Where an exhibit contains more than one document, a front page should be attached setting out a list of the documents contained in the exhibit. The list should contain the dates of the documents.

Exhibits other than documents

12.1 Items other than documents should be clearly marked with an exhibit number or letter in such a manner that the mark cannot become detached from the exhibit.
12.2 Small items may be placed in a container and the container appropriately marked.

General provisions

13.1 Where an exhibit contains more than one document –

(a) the bundle should not be stapled but should be securely fastened in a way that does not hinder the reading of the documents; and
(b) the pages should be numbered consecutively at bottom centre.

13.2 Every page of an exhibit should be clearly legible; typed copies of illegible documents should be included, paginated with 'a' numbers.

13.3 Where affidavits/statements and exhibits have become numerous, they should be put into separate bundles and the pages numbered consecutively throughout.

13.4 Where on account of their bulk the service of exhibits or copies of exhibits on the other parties would be difficult or impracticable, the directions of the court should be sought as to arrangements for bringing the exhibits to the attention of the other parties and as to their custody pending trial.

Miscellaneous

Defects in affidavits, witness statement and exhibits

14.1 Where –

(a) an affidavit;
(b) a witness statement; or
(c) an exhibit to either an affidavit or a witness statement,

does not comply with Part 22 or this practice direction in relation to its form, the court may refuse to admit it as evidence and may refuse to allow the costs arising from its preparation.

14.2 Permission to file a defective affidavit or witness statement or to use a defective exhibit may be obtained from the court where the case is proceeding.

Affirmations

15.1 All provisions in this or any other practice direction relating to affidavits apply to affirmations with the following exceptions –

(a) the deponent should commence 'I (full name) of (residential address) do solemnly and sincerely affirm.'; and
(b) in the jurat the word 'sworn' is replaced by the word 'affirmed'.

Certificate of court officer

16.1 In proceedings under Part 7 (Matrimonial and Civil Partnership Proceedings), where the court has ordered that a witness statement, affidavit, affirmation or deposition is not be open to inspection by the public (see rule 22.19(2) and (3)) or that words or passages in the statement etc are not to be open to inspection (see rule 22.19(5)), the court officer will so certify on the statement etc and make any deletions directed by the court under rule 22.19(3).

Video Conferencing

17.1 Guidance on the use of video conferencing in the family courts is set out at Annex 3 to this practice direction.

A list of the sites which are available for video conferencing can be found on Her Majesty's Court Service's website at www.hm-courts-service.gov.uk.

Annex 1

Certificate to be used where a deponent to an affidavit is unable to read or sign it

> Sworn at . this . day of . Before me, I having first read over the contents of this affidavit to the deponent [if there are exhibits, add 'and explained the nature and effect of the exhibits referred to in it'] who appeared to understand it and approved its content as accurate, and made his/her* mark on the affidavit in my presence. Or, (after 'Before me') the witness to the mark of the deponent having been first sworn that the witness had read over etc. (as

above) and that the witness saw the deponent make his/her* mark on the affidavit. (Witness must sign.)

* delete as appropriate

Certificate to be used where a deponent to an affirmation is unable to read or sign it

Affirmed at . this . day of . Before me, I having first read over the contents of this affirmation to the deponent [if there are exhibits, add 'and explained the nature and effect of the exhibits referred to in it'] who appeared to understand it and approved its content as accurate, and made his/her* mark on the affirmation in my presence. Or, (after 'Before me') the witness to the mark of the deponent having been first sworn that the witness had read over etc. (as above) and that the witness saw the deponent make his/her* mark on the affirmation. (Witness must sign.)

* delete as appropriate

Annex 2

Certificate to be used where a witness is unable to read or sign a witness statement

I certify that I [name and address of authorised person] have read over the contents of this witness statement and the statement of truth to the witness [if there are exhibits, add 'and explained the nature and effect of the exhibits referred to in it'] who (a) appeared to understand the witness statement and approved its content as accurate and (b) appeared to understand the statement of truth and the consequences of making a false witness statement, and [signed the statement] [made his/her mark]* in my presence.

* delete as appropriate

Annex 3

Video Conferencing Guidance

1 This guidance is for the use of video conferencing (VCF) in proceedings to which the Family Procedure Rules apply. It is in part based, with permission, upon the protocol of the Federal Court of Australia. It is intended to provide a guide to all persons involved in the use of VCF, although it does not attempt to cover all the practical questions which might arise.

Any reference in this guide to a judge is to be taken as including any judge of the family court.

Video conferencing generally

2 The guidance covers the use of VCF equipment both (a) in a courtroom, whether via equipment which is permanently placed there or via a mobile unit, and (b) in a separate studio or conference room. In either case, the location at which the judge sits is referred to as the 'local site'. The other site or sites to and from which transmission is made are referred to as 'the remote site' and in any particular case any such site may be another courtroom. The guidance applies to cases where VCF is used for the taking of evidence and also to its use for other parts of any legal proceedings.

3 VCF may be a convenient way of dealing with any part of proceedings- it can involve considerable savings in time and cost. Its use for the taking of evidence from overseas witnesses will, in particular, be likely to achieve a material saving of costs, and such savings may also be achieved by its use for taking domestic evidence. It is, however, inevitably

not as ideal as having the witness physically present in court. Its convenience should not therefore be allowed to dictate its use. A judgment must be made in every case in which the use of VCF is being considered not only as to whether it will achieve an overall cost saving but as to whether its use will be likely to be beneficial to the efficient, fair and economic disposal of the litigation. In particular, it needs to be recognised that the degree of control a court can exercise over a witness at the remote site is or may be more limited than it can exercise over a witness physically before it.

4 When used for the taking of evidence, the objective should be to make the VCF session as close as possible to the usual practice in court where evidence is taken in open court. To gain the maximum benefit, several differences have to be taken into account. Some matters, which are taken for granted when evidence is taken in the conventional way, take on a different dimension when it is taken by VCF- for example, the administration of the oath, ensuring that the witness understands who is at the local site and what their various roles are, the raising of any objections to the evidence and the use of documents.

5 It should not be presumed that all foreign governments are willing to allow their nationals or others within their jurisdiction to be examined before a court in England or Wales by means of VCF. If there is any doubt about this, enquiries should be directed to the Foreign and Commonwealth Office (International Legal Matters Unit, Consular Division) with a view to ensuring that the country from which the evidence is to be taken raises no objection to it at diplomatic level. The party who is directed to be responsible for arranging the VCF (see paragraph 8) will be required to make all necessary inquiries about this well in advance of the VCF and must be able to inform the court what those inquiries were and of their outcome.

6 Time zone differences need to be considered when a witness abroad is to be examined in England or Wales by VCF. The convenience of the witness, the parties, their representatives and the court must all be taken into account. The cost of the use of a commercial studio is usually greater outside normal business hours.

7 Those involved with VCF need to be aware that, even with the most advanced systems currently available, there are the briefest of delays between the receipt of the picture and that of the accompanying sound. If due allowance is not made for this, there will be a tendency to 'speak over' the witness, whose voice will continue to be heard for a millisecond or so after he or she appears on the screen to have finished speaking.

8 With current technology, picture quality is good, but not as good as a television picture. The quality of the picture is enhanced if those appearing on VCF monitors keep their movements to a minimum.

Preliminary arrangements

9 The court's permission is required for any part of any proceedings to be dealt with by means of VCF. Before seeking a direction, the applicant should notify the listing officer, diary manager or other appropriate court officer of the intention to seek it, and should enquire as to the availability of court VCF equipment for the day or days of the proposed VCF. If all parties consent to a direction, permission can be sought by letter, fax or e-mail, although the court may still require an oral hearing. All parties are entitled to be heard on whether or not such a direction should be given and as to its terms. If a witness at a remote site is to give evidence by an interpreter, consideration should be given at this stage as to whether the interpreter should be at the local site or the remote site. If a VCF direction is given, arrangements for the transmission will then need to be made. The court will ordinarily direct that the party seeking permission to use VCF is to be responsible for this. That party is hereafter referred to as 'the VCF arranging party'.

10 Subject to any order to the contrary, all costs of the transmission, including the costs of hiring equipment and technical personnel to operate it, will initially be the responsibility of, and must be met by, the VCF arranging party. All reasonable efforts should be made to keep the transmission to a minimum and so keep the costs down. All such costs will be considered to be part of the costs of the proceedings and the court will determine at such subsequent time as is convenient or appropriate who, as between the parties, should be responsible for them and (if appropriate) in what proportions.

11 The local site will, if practicable, be a courtroom but it may instead be an appropriate studio or conference room. The VCF arranging party must contact the listing officer, diary manager or other appropriate officer of the court which made the VCF direction and make arrangements for the VCF transmission. Details of the remote site, and of the equipment to be used both at the local site (if not being supplied by the court) and the remote site (including the number of ISDN lines and connection speed), together with all necessary contact names and telephone numbers, will have to be provided to the listing officer, diary manager or other court officer. The court will need to be satisfied that any equipment provided by the parties for use at the local site and also that at the remote site is of sufficient quality for a satisfactory transmission. The VCF arranging party must ensure that an appropriate person will be present at the local site to supervise the operation of the VCF throughout the transmission in order to deal with any technical problems. That party must also arrange for a technical assistant to be similarly present at the remote site for like purposes.

12 It is recommended that the judge, practitioners and witness should arrive at their respective VCF sites about 20 minutes prior to the scheduled commencement of the transmission.

13 If the local site is not a courtroom, but a conference room or studio, the judge will need to determine who is to sit where. The VCF arranging party must take care to ensure that the number of microphones is adequate for the speakers and that the panning of the camera for the practitioners' table encompasses all legal representatives so that the viewer can see everyone seated there.

14 If the local site is to be a studio or conference room, the VCF arranging party must ensure that it provides sufficient accommodation to enable a reasonable number of members of the public to attend if appropriate.

15 In cases where the local site is a studio or conference room, the VCF arranging party should make arrangements, if practicable, for the royal coat of arms to be placed above the judge's seat.

16 In cases in which the VCF is to be used for the taking of evidence, the VCF arranging party must arrange for recording equipment to be provided by the court which made the VCF direction so that the evidence can be recorded. An associate will normally be present to operate the recording equipment when the local site is a courtroom. The VCF arranging party should take steps to ensure that an associate is present to do likewise when it is a studio or conference room. The equipment should be set up and tested before the VCF transmission. It will often be a valuable safeguard for the VCF arranging party also to arrange for the provision of recording equipment at the remote site. This will provide a useful back-up if there is any reduction in sound quality during the transmission. A direction from the court for the making of such a back-up recording must, however, be obtained first. This is because the proceedings are court proceedings and, save as directed by the court, no other recording of them must be made. The court will direct what is to happen to the back-up recording.

17 Some countries may require that any oath or affirmation to be taken by a witness accord with local custom rather than the usual form of oath or affirmation used in England and Wales. The VCF arranging party must make all appropriate prior inquiries and put in place all arrangements necessary to enable the oath or affirmation to be taken in accordance with any local custom. That party must be in a position to inform the court what those inquiries were, what their outcome was and what arrangements have been made. If the oath or affirmation can be administered in the manner normal in England and Wales, the VCF arranging party must arrange in advance to have the appropriate holy book at the remote site. The associate will normally administer the oath.

18 Consideration will need to be given in advance to the documents to which the witness is likely to be referred. The parties should endeavour to agree on this. It will usually be most convenient for a bundle of the copy documents to be prepared in advance, which the VCF arranging party should then send to the remote site.

19 Additional documents are sometimes quite properly introduced during the course of a witness's evidence. To cater for this, the VCF arranging party should ensure that equipment is available to enable documents to be transmitted between sites during the course of the VCF transmission. Consideration should be given to whether to use a document camera. If it is decided to use one, arrangements for its use will need to be established in advance. The panel operator will need to know the number and size of documents or objects if their images are to be sent by document camera. In many cases, a simpler and sufficient alternative will be to ensure that there are fax transmission and reception facilities at the participating sites.

The hearing

20 The procedure for conducting the transmission will be determined by the judge. He will determine who is to control the cameras. In cases where the VCF is being used for an application in the course of the proceedings, the judge will ordinarily not enter the local site until both sites are on line. Similarly, at the conclusion of the hearing, he will ordinarily leave the local site while both sites are still on line. The following paragraphs apply primarily to cases where the VCF is being used for the taking of the evidence of a witness at a remote site.

21 At the beginning of the transmission, the judge will probably wish to introduce himself or herself and the advocates to the witness. He will probably want to know who is at the remote site and will invite the witness to introduce himself or herself and anyone else who is with the witness. The judge may wish to give directions as to the seating arrangements at the remote site so that those present are visible at the local site during the taking of the evidence and to explain to the witness the method of taking the oath or of affirming, the manner in which the evidence will be taken, and who will be conducting the examination and cross-examination. The judge will probably also wish to inform the witness of the matters referred to in paragraphs 7 and 8 (co-ordination of picture with sound, and picture quality).

22 The examination of the witness at the remote site should follow as closely as possible the practice adopted when a witness is in the courtroom. During examination, cross-examination and re-examination, the witness must be able to see the legal representative asking the question and also any other person (whether another legal representative or the judge) making any statements in regard to the witness's evidence. It will in practice be most convenient if everyone remains seated throughout the transmission.

PART 23
MISCELLANEOUS RULES ABOUT EVIDENCE

23.1 Scope and interpretation of this Part

Rules 23.2 to 23.6 apply to evidence to which the Children (Admissibility of Hearsay Evidence) Order 1993 does not apply.

23.2 Notice of intention to rely on hearsay evidence

(1) Where a party intends to rely on hearsay evidence at the final hearing and either—

(a) that evidence is to be given by a witness giving oral evidence; or
(b) that evidence is contained in a witness statement of a person who is not being called to give oral evidence,

that party complies with section 2(1)(a) of the Civil Evidence Act 1995 by serving a witness statement on the other parties in accordance with the court's directions.

(2) Where paragraph (1)(b) applies, the party intending to rely on the hearsay evidence must, when serving the witness statement—

(a) inform the other parties that the witness is not being called to give oral evidence; and
(b) give the reason why the witness will not be called.

(3) In all other cases where a party intends to rely on hearsay evidence at the final hearing, that party complies with section 2(1)(a) of the Civil Evidence Act 1995 by serving a notice on the other parties which—

(a) identifies the hearsay evidence;
(b) states that the party serving the notice proposes to rely on the hearsay evidence at the final hearing; and
(c) gives the reason why the witness will not be called.

(4) The party proposing to rely on the hearsay evidence must—

(a) serve the notice no later than the latest date for serving witness statements; and
(b) if the hearsay evidence is to be in a document, supply a copy to any party who requests it.

23.3 Circumstances in which notice of intention to rely on hearsay evidence is not required

Section 2(1) of the Civil Evidence Act 1995 (duty to give notice of intention to rely on hearsay evidence) does not apply—

(a) to evidence at hearings other than final hearings;
(b) to an affidavit(GL) or witness statement which is to be used at the final hearing but which does not contain hearsay evidence; or
(c) where the requirement is excluded by a practice direction.

23.4 Power to call witness for cross-examination on hearsay evidence

(1) Where a party—

(a) proposes to rely on hearsay evidence; and
(b) does not propose to call the person who made the original statement to give oral evidence,

the court may, on the application of any other party, permit that party to call the maker of the statement to be cross-examined(GL) on the contents of the statement.

(2) An application for permission to cross-examine(GL) under this rule must be made within 14 days beginning with the date on which a notice of intention to rely on the hearsay evidence was served on the applicant.

…[1]

Amendment

1 Repealed by the Family Procedure Rules 2010 and Court of Protection Rules 2017 (Amendment) (EU Exit) Regulations 2019, SI 2019/517, rr 2, 15.

23.5 Credibility

(1) Where a party proposes to rely on hearsay evidence, but—

- (a) does not propose to call the person who made the original statement to give oral evidence; and
- (b) another party wishes to call evidence to attack the credibility of the person who made the statement,

the party who so wishes must give notice of that intention to the party who proposes to give the hearsay statement in evidence.

(2) A party must give notice under paragraph (1) within 14 days after the date on which a hearsay notice relating to the hearsay evidence was served on that party.

23.6 Use of plans, photographs and models etc as evidence

(1) This rule applies to—

- (a) evidence (such as a plan, photograph or model) which is not—
  - (i) contained in a witness statement, affidavit(GL) or expert's report;
  - (ii) to be given orally at the final hearing; or
  - (iii) evidence of which prior notice must be given under rule 23.2; and
- (b) documents which may be received in evidence without further proof under section 9 of the Civil Evidence Act 1995.

(2) Except as provided below, section 2(1)(a) of the Civil Evidence Act 1995 (notice of proposal to adduce hearsay evidence) does not apply to evidence falling within paragraph (1).

(3) Such evidence is not receivable at the final hearing unless the party intending to rely on it (in this rule, 'the party') has—

- (a) served it or, in the case of a model, a photograph of it with an invitation to inspect the original, on the other party in accordance with this rule; or
- (b) complied with such directions as the court may give for serving the evidence on, or for giving notice under section 2(1)(a) of the Civil Evidence Act 1995 in respect of the evidence to, the other party.

(4) Where the party intends to use the evidence as evidence of any fact then, except where paragraph (6) applies, the party must serve the evidence not later than the latest date for serving witness statements.

(5) The party must serve the evidence at least 21 days before the hearing at which the party proposes to rely on it if—

(a) there are not to be witness statements; or
(b) the party intends to put in the evidence solely in order to disprove an allegation made in a witness statement.

(6) Where the evidence forms part of expert evidence, the party must serve the evidence when the expert's report is served on the other party.

(7) Where the evidence is being produced to the court for any reason other than as part of factual or expert evidence, the party must serve the evidence at least 21 days before the hearing at which the party proposes to rely on it.

(8) Where the court directs a party to give notice that the party intends to put in the evidence, the court may direct that every other party be given an opportunity to inspect it and to agree to its admission without further proof.

23.7 Evidence of finding on question of foreign law

(1) This rule sets out the procedure which must be followed by a party (in this rule, 'the party') who intends to put in evidence a finding on a question of foreign law by virtue of section 4(2) of the Civil Evidence Act 1972.

(2) The party must give any other party notice of that intention.

(3) The party must give the notice—

(a) if there are to be witness statements, not later than the latest date for serving them; or
(b) otherwise, not less than 21 days before the hearing at which the party proposes to put the finding in evidence.

(4) The notice must—

(a) specify the question on which the finding was made; and
(b) enclose a copy of a document where it is reported or recorded.

23.8 Evidence of consent of trustee to act

In proceedings to which Part 9 (financial remedies) applies, a document purporting to contain the written consent of a person to act as trustee and to bear that person's signature verified by some other person is evidence of such consent.

23.9 Note of oral evidence …[1]

In proceedings [in the family court before a lay justice or lay justices][2], the [justices' legal adviser][3] or the court shall keep a note of the substance of the oral evidence given at a directions appointment or at a hearing of any proceedings.

Amendment

1 Repealed by the Family Procedure (Amendment No 2) Rules 2014, SI 2014/667, rr 2, 17(a).
2 Substituted by the Family Procedure (Amendment No 2) Rules 2014, SI 2014/667, rr 2, 17(b).
A Substituted by the Family Procedure (Amendment) Rules 2020, SI 2020/135, rr 2, 25.

PART 24
[WITNESSES AND DEPOSITIONS GENERALLY][1]

Chapter 1
Witnesses and depositions

24.1 Scope of this Chapter

(1) This Chapter provides—

(a) for the circumstances in which a person may be required to attend court to give evidence or to produce a document; and

(b) for a party to obtain evidence before a hearing to be used at the hearing.

(2) …[2]

…[3]

Amendment

1 Substituted by the Family Procedure Rules 2010 and Court of Protection Rules 2017 (Amendment) (EU Exit) Regulations 2019, SI 2019/517, rr 2, 16(1), (2).

2 Repealed by the Family Procedure (Amendment No 3) Rules 2013, SI 2013/3204, rr 2, 69.

3 Repealed by the Family Procedure Rules 2010 and Court of Protection Rules 2017 (Amendment) (EU Exit) Regulations 2019, SI 2019/517, rr 2, 16(1), (3).

24.2 Witness summonses

(1) A witness summons is a document issued by the court requiring a witness to—

(a) attend court to give evidence; or

(b) produce documents to the court.

(2) A witness summons must be in the form set out in Practice Direction 24A.

(3) There must be a separate witness summons for each witness.

(4) A witness summons may require a witness to produce documents to the court either—

(a) on the date fixed for a hearing; or

(b) on such date as the court may direct.

(5) The only documents that a summons under this rule can require a person to produce before a hearing are documents which that person could be required to produce at the hearing.

…[1]

Amendment

1 Repealed by the Family Procedure Rules 2010 and Court of Protection Rules 2017 (Amendment) (EU Exit) Regulations 2019, SI 2019/517, rr 2, 16(1), (3).

24.3 Issue of a witness summons

(1) A witness summons is issued on the date entered on the summons by the court.

(2) A party must obtain permission from the court where that party wishes to—

(a) have a summons issued less than 7 days before the date of the final hearing;

(b) have a summons issued for a witness to attend court to give evidence or to produce documents on any date except the date fixed for the final hearing; or

(c) have a summons issued for a witness to attend court to give evidence or to produce documents at any hearing except the final hearing.

(3) A witness summons must be issued by—

(a) the court where the case is proceeding; or
(b) the court where the hearing in question will be held.

(4) The court may set aside (GL) or vary a witness summons issued under this rule.

24.4 Time for serving a witness summons

(1) The general rule is that a witness summons is binding if it is served at least 7 days before the date on which the witness is required to attend before the court.

(2) The court may direct that a witness summons is binding although it is served less than 7 days before the date on which the witness is required to attend before the court.

(3) A witness summons which is—

(a) served in accordance with this rule; and
(b) requires the witness to attend court to give evidence,

is binding until the conclusion of the hearing at which the attendance of the witness is required.

…[1]

Amendment

1 Repealed by the Family Procedure Rules 2010 and Court of Protection Rules 2017 (Amendment) (EU Exit) Regulations 2019, SI 2019/517, rr 2, 16(1), (3).

24.5 Who is to serve a witness summons

(1) Subject to paragraph (2), a witness summons is to be served by the party on whose behalf it is issued unless that party indicates in writing, when asking the court to issue the summons, that that party wishes the court to serve it instead.

(2) In proceedings to which Part 14 (procedure for applications in adoption, placement and related proceedings) applies, a witness summons is to be served by the court unless the court directs otherwise.

(3) Where the court is to serve the witness summons, the party on whose behalf it is issued must deposit, in the court office, the money to be paid or offered to the witness under rule 24.6.

24.6 Right of witness to travelling expenses and compensation for loss of time

At the time of service of a witness summons the witness must be offered or paid—

(a) a sum reasonably sufficient to cover the expenses of the witness in travelling to and from the court; and
(b) such sum by way of compensation for loss of time as may be specified in Practice Direction 24A.

24.7 Evidence by deposition

(1) A party may apply for an order for a person to be examined before the hearing takes place.

(2) A person from whom evidence is to be obtained following an order under this rule is referred to as a 'deponent' and the evidence is referred to as a 'deposition'.

(3) An order under this rule is for a deponent to be examined on oath before—

(a) a judge;
(b) an examiner of the court; or
(c) such other person as the court appoints.

(Rule 24.14 makes provision for the appointment of examiners of the court.)

(4) The order may require the production of any document which the court considers is necessary for the purposes of the examination.

(5) The order must state the date, time and place of the examination.

(6) At the time of service of the order the deponent must be offered or paid—

(a) a sum reasonably sufficient to cover the expenses of the deponent in travelling to and from the place of examination; and
(b) such sum by way of compensation for loss of time as may be specified in Practice Direction 24A.

(7) Where the court makes an order for a deposition to be taken, it may also order the party who obtained the order to serve a witness statement or witness summary in relation to the evidence to be given by the person to be examined.

(Part 22 (evidence) contains the general rules about witness statements and witness summaries.)

…[1]

Amendment

1 Repealed by the Family Procedure Rules 2010 and Court of Protection Rules 2017 (Amendment) (EU Exit) Regulations 2019, SI 2019/517, rr 2, 16(1), (3).

24.8 Conduct of examination

(1) Subject to any directions contained in the order for examination, the examination must be conducted in the same way as if the witness were giving evidence at a final hearing.

(2) If all the parties are present, the examiner may conduct the examination of a person not named in the order for examination if all the parties and the person to be examined consent.

(3) In [disputed][1] proceedings under Part 7 (matrimonial and civil partnership proceedings), the examiner may conduct the examination in private if of the view that it is appropriate to do so.

(4) Save in proceedings to which paragraph (3) applies, the examiner will conduct the examination in private unless of the view that it is not appropriate to do so.

(5) The examiner must ensure that the evidence given by the witness is recorded in full.

(6) The examiner must send a copy of the deposition—

(a) to the person who obtained the order for the examination of the witness; and
(b) to the court where the case is proceeding.

(7) The court will give directions as to service of the deposition on the other party.

Amendment

1 Substituted by the Family Procedure (Amendment) Rules 2022, SI 2022/44, rr 2, 26.

24.9 Enforcing attendance of witness

(1) If a person served with an order to attend before an examiner—

(a) fails to attend; or

(b) refuses to be sworn for the purpose of the examination or to answer any lawful question or produce any document at the examination,

a certificate of that person's failure or refusal, signed by the examiner, must be filed by the party requiring the deposition.

(2) On the certificate being filed, the party requiring the deposition may apply to the court for an order requiring that person to attend or to be sworn or to answer any question or produce any document, as the case may be.

(3) An application for an order under this rule may be made without notice.

(4) The court may order the person against whom an order is made under this rule to pay any costs resulting from that person's failure or refusal.

…[1]

Amendment

1 Repealed by the Family Procedure Rules 2010 and Court of Protection Rules 2017 (Amendment) (EU Exit) Regulations 2019, SI 2019/517, rr 2, 16(1), (3).

24.10 Use of deposition at a hearing

(1) A deposition ordered under rule 24.7 may be given in evidence at a hearing unless the court orders otherwise.

(2) A party intending to put in evidence a deposition at a hearing must file notice of intention to do so on the court and the court will give directions about serving the notice on every other party.

(3) The party must file the notice at least 21 days before the day fixed for the hearing.

(4) The court may require a deponent to attend the hearing and give evidence orally.

(5) Where a deposition is given in evidence at the final hearing, it is treated as if it were a witness statement for the purposes of rule 22.19 (availability of witness statements for inspection).

…[1]

Amendment

1 Repealed by the Family Procedure Rules 2010 and Court of Protection Rules 2017 (Amendment) (EU Exit) Regulations 2019, SI 2019/517, rr 2, 16(1), (3).

24.11 Restrictions on subsequent use of deposition taken for the purpose of any hearing except the final hearing

(1) This rule applies to proceedings under Part 7 (matrimonial and civil partnership proceedings) or Part 9 (financial remedies).

(2) Where the court orders a party to be examined about that party's or any other assets for the purpose of any hearing except the final hearing, the deposition may be used only for the purpose of the proceedings in which the order was made.

(3) However it may be used for some other purpose—

(a) by the party who was examined;
(b) if the party who was examined agrees; or
(c) if the court gives permission.

24.12 Where a person to be examined is out of the jurisdiction – letter of request

(1) This rule applies where a party wishes to take a deposition from a person who is [out of the jurisdiction][1].

(2) The High Court may order the issue of a letter of request to the judicial authorities of the country in which the proposed deponent is.

(3) A letter of request is a request to a judicial authority to take the evidence of that person, or arrange for it to be taken.

(4) The High Court may make an order under this rule in relation to [family court][2] proceedings.

(5) If the government of a country allows a person appointed by the High Court to examine a person in that country, the High Court may make an order appointing a special examiner for that purpose.

(6) A person may be examined under this rule on oath or affirmation or in accordance with any procedure permitted in the country in which the examination is to take place.

(7) If the High Court makes an order for the issue of a letter of request, the party who sought the order must file—

(a) the following documents and, except where paragraph (8) applies, a translation of them—
   (i) a draft letter of request;
   (ii) a statement of the issues relevant to the proceedings; and
   (iii) a list of questions or the subject matter of questions to be put to the person to be examined; and
(b) an undertaking to be responsible for the Secretary of State's expenses.

(8) There is no need to file a translation if—

(a) English is one of the official languages of the country where the examination is to take place; or
(b) a practice direction has specified that country as a country where no translation is necessary.

…[3]

Amendment

1 Substituted by the Family Procedure Rules 2010 and Court of Protection Rules 2017 (Amendment) (EU Exit) Regulations 2019, SI 2019/517, rr 2, 16(1), (4)(a).
2 Substituted by the Family Procedure (Amendment No 3) Rules 2013, SI 2013/3204, rr 2, 70.
3 Repealed by the Family Procedure Rules 2010 and Court of Protection Rules 2017 (Amendment) (EU Exit) Regulations 2019, SI 2019/517, rr 2, 16(1), (4)(b).

24.13 Fees and expenses of examiner of the court

(1) An examiner of the court may charge a fee for the examination.

(2) The examiner need not send the deposition to the court unless the fee is paid.

(3) The examiner's fees and expenses must be paid by the party who obtained the order for examination.

(4) If the fees and expenses due to an examiner are not paid within a reasonable time, the examiner may report that fact to the court.

(5) The court may order the party who obtained the order for examination to deposit in the court office a specified sum in respect of the examiner's fees and, where it does so, the examiner will not be asked to act until the sum has been deposited.

(6) An order under this rule does not affect any decision as to the party who is ultimately to bear the costs of the examination.

24.14 Examiners of the court

(1) The Lord Chancellor will appoint persons to be examiners of the court.

(2) The persons appointed must be barristers or solicitor-advocates who have been practising for a period of not less than 3 years.

(3) The Lord Chancellor may revoke an appointment at any time.

Chapter 2

… [1]

24.15 …[1]

…[1]

Amendment

1 Repealed by the Family Procedure Rules 2010 and Court of Protection Rules 2017 (Amendment) (EU Exit) Regulations 2019, SI 2019/517, rr 2, 16(1), (5).

24.16 …[1]

…[1]

Amendment

1 Repealed by the Family Procedure Rules 2010 and Court of Protection Rules 2017 (Amendment) (EU Exit) Regulations 2019, SI 2019/517, rr 2, 16(1), (5).

Practice Direction 24A – Witnessses and depositions generally

See also Part 24

Witness Summonses

Issue of witness summons

1.1 A witness summons may require a witness to –

(a) attend court to give evidence;
(b) produce documents to the court; or
(c) both,

on either a date fixed for the hearing or such date as the court may direct (see rule 24.2).

1.2 Two copies of the witness summons should be filed with the court for sealing, one of which will be retained on the court file.

1.3 A mistake in the name or address of a person named in a witness summons may be corrected if the summons has not been served.

1.4 The corrected summons must be re-sealed by the court and marked 'Amended and Re-Sealed'.

2.1 Omitted

Travelling expenses and compensation for loss of time

3.1 When a witness is served with a witness summons the witness must be offered a sum to cover travelling expenses to and from the court and compensation for loss of time (see rule 24.6).

3.2 If the witness summons is to be served by the court, the party issuing the summons must deposit with the court –

(a) a sum sufficient to pay for the witness's expenses in travelling to the court and in returning to his or her home or place of work; and
(b) a sum in respect of the period during which earnings or benefit are lost, or such lesser sum as it may be proved that the witness will lose as a result of attendance at court in answer to the witness summons.

3.3 The sum referred to in paragraph 3.2(b) is to be based on the sums payable to witnesses attending the Crown Court (fixed pursuant to the Prosecution of Offences Act 1985 and Costs in Criminal Cases (General) Regulations 1986).

Depositions to be taken in England and Wales for use as evidence in proceedings in courts in England and Wales

4.1 A party may apply for an order for a person to be examined on oath before –

(a) a judge;
(b) an examiner of the court; or
(c) such other person as the court may appoint (see rule 24.7(3)).

4.2 The party who obtains an order for the examination of a deponent (see rule 24.7(2)) before an examiner of the court must –

(a) apply to the Foreign Process Section of the Masters' Secretary's Department at the Royal Courts of Justice for the allocation of an examiner;
(b) when allocated, provide the examiner with copies of all documents in the proceedings necessary to inform the examiner of the issues; and
(c) pay the deponent a sum to cover travelling expenses to and from the examination and compensation for loss of time (see rule 24.7(6)).

4.3 In ensuring that the deponent's evidence is recorded in full, the court or the examiner may permit it to be recorded on audiotape or videotape, but the deposition (see rule 24.7(2)) must always be recorded in writing by the examiner or by a competent shorthand writer or stenographer.

4.4 If the deposition is not recorded word for word, it must contain, as nearly as may be, the statement of the deponent. The examiner may record word for word any particular questions and answers which appear to have special importance.

4.5 If a deponent objects to answering any question or where any objection is taken to any question, the examiner must –

(a) record in the deposition or a document attached to it –
  (i) the question;
  (ii) the nature of and grounds for the objection;
  (iii) any answer given; and
(b) give the examiner's opinion as to the validity of the objection and must record it in the deposition or a document attached to it.

The court will decide as to the validity of the objection and any question of costs arising from it.

4.6 Documents and exhibits must –

(a) have an identifying number or letter marked on them by the examiner; and
(b) be preserved by the party or legal representative (see rule 2.3) who obtained the order for the examination, or as the court or the examiner may direct.

4.7 The examiner may put any question to the deponent as to –

(a) the meaning of any of the deponent's answers; or
(b) any matter arising in the course of the examination.

4.8 Where a deponent –

(a) fails to attend the examination; or
(b) refuses to –
  (i) be sworn; or
  (ii) answer any lawful question; or
  (iii) produce any document,

the examiner will sign a certificate (see rule 24.9) of such failure or refusal and may include in the certificate any comment as to the conduct of the deponent or of any person attending the examination.

4.9 The party who obtained the order for the examination must file the certificate with the court and may apply for an order that the deponent attend for examination or produce any document, as the case may be (see rule 24.9(2) and (3)). The application may be made without notice.

4.10 The court will make such order on the application as it thinks fit including an order for the deponent to pay any costs resulting from the failure or refusal (see rule 24.9(4)).

4.11 A deponent who wilfully refuses to obey an order of the High Court or the family court made under Part 24 may be proceeded against for contempt of court.

4.12 A deposition must –

(a) be signed by the examiner;
(b) have any amendments to it initialled by the examiner and the deponent;
(c) be endorsed by the examiner with –
  (i) a statement of the time occupied by the examination; and
  (ii) a record of any refusal by the deponent to sign the deposition and of the deponent's reasons for not doing so; and
(d) be sent by the examiner to the court where the proceedings are taking place for filing on the court file.

4.13 Rule 24.13 deals with the fees and expenses of an examiner.

Depositions to be taken abroad for use as evidence in proceedings before courts in England and Wales

5.1 Where a party wishes to take a deposition from a person outside the jurisdiction, the High Court may order the issue of a letter of request to the judicial authorities of the country in which the proposed deponent is (see rule 24.12).

5.2 An application for an order referred to in paragraph 5.1 should be made by application notice in accordance with Part 18 (Procedure for other applications in proceedings).

5.3 The documents which a party applying for an order for the issue of a letter of request must file with the application notice are set out in rule 24.12(7). They are as follows –

(a) a draft letter of request in the form set out in Annex A to this practice direction;
(b) a statement of the issues relevant to the proceedings;
(c) a list of questions or the subject matter of questions to be put to the proposed deponent;
(d) a translation of the documents in (a), (b) and (c), unless the proposed deponent is in a country of which English is an official language; and
(e) an undertaking to be responsible for the expenses of the Secretary of State.

In addition to the documents listed above the party applying for the order must file a draft order.

5.4 The above documents should be filed with the Masters' Secretary in Room E214, Royal Courts of Justice, Strand, London WC2A 2LL.

5.5 The application will be dealt with by the Senior Master of the Queen's Bench Division of the Senior Courts who will, if appropriate, sign the letter of request.

5.6 Attention is drawn to the provisions of rule 18.11 (Application to set aside or vary order made without notice).

5.7 If parties are in doubt as to whether a translation under paragraph 5.3(d) is required, they should seek guidance from the Foreign Process Section of the Masters' Secretary's Department.

5.8 A special examiner appointed under rule 24.12(5) may be the British Consul or the Consul-General or his deputy in the country where the evidence is to be taken if –

(a) there is in respect of that country a Civil Procedure Convention providing for the taking of evidence in that country for the assistance of proceedings in the High Court or other court in this country; or
(b) the Secretary of State has consented.

5.9 The provisions of paragraphs 4.1 to 4.12 apply to the depositions referred to in this paragraph.

Annex A

Draft Letter of Request (see paragraph 5.3(a) above)

1 To the Competent Judicial Authority of … … … in the ……… of … … … [name] Senior Master of the Queen's Bench Division of the Senior Courts of England and Wales respectfully request the assistance of your court with regard to the following matters.

2 An application is now pending in the … … … Division of the High Court of Justice in England and Wales entitled as follows [set out full title and case number] in which [name] of [address] is the applicant and [name] of [address] is the respondent.

3 The names and addresses of the representatives or agents of [set out names and addresses of representatives of the parties].

4 The application by the applicant is for –

(a) [set out the nature of the application]
(b) [the order sought] and
(c) [a summary of the facts.]

5 It is necessary for the purposes of justice between the parties that you cause the following witnesses, who are resident within your jurisdiction, to be examined. The names and addresses of the witnesses are as follows:

6 The witnesses should be examined on oath or if that is not possible within your laws or is impossible of performance by reason of the internal practice and procedure of your court or by reason of practical difficulties, they should be examined in accordance with whatever procedure your laws provide for in these matters.

7 Either/

The witnesses should be examined in accordance with the list of questions annexed hereto.

Or/

The witnesses should be examined regarding [set out full details of evidence sought] N.B. Where the witness is required to produce documents, these should be clearly identified.

8 I would ask that you cause me, or the agents of the parties (if appointed), to be informed of the date and place where the examination is to take place.

9 Finally, I request that you will cause the evidence of the said witnesses to be reduced into writing and all documents produced on such examinations to be duly marked for identification and that you will further be pleased to authenticate such examinations by the seal of your court or in such other way as is in accordance with your procedure and return the written evidence and documents produced to me addressed as follows –

Senior Master of the Queen's Bench Division
Royal Courts of Justice
Strand
London
WC2A 2LL
England

[PART 25
EXPERTS AND ASSESSORS

25.1 …[1]

…[1]][2]

Amendment

1 Repealed by the Family Procedure (Amendment No 3) Rules 2014, SI 2014/843, rr 2, 44.
2 Substituted by the Family Procedure (Amendment) (No 5) Rules 2012, SI 2012/3061, r 6, Schedule.

[25.2 Interpretation

(1) In this Part—

…[1]

'children proceedings' means—

(a) proceedings referred to in rules 12.1 and 14.1 and any other proceedings which relate wholly or mainly to the maintenance or upbringing of a minor;

(b) applications for permission to start proceedings mentioned in paragraph (a);and

(c) applications made in the course of proceedings mentioned in paragraph (a);

'expert' means a person who provides expert evidence for use in proceedings;

[(Section 13(8) of the 2014 Act provides for what is not included in reference to providing expert evidence or putting expert evidence before the court in children proceedings)][2]

…[1]

'single joint expert' means a person who provides expert evidence for use in proceedings on behalf of two or more of the parties (including the applicant) to the proceedings.

[(2) The meaning of 'children proceedings' in paragraph (1) is the prescribed meaning for the purposes of section 13(9) of the 2014 Act.][3]

(Regulation 3 of the Restriction on the Preparation of Adoption Reports Regulations 2005 (S.I. 2005/1711) sets out which persons are within a prescribed description for the purposes of section 94(1) of the 2002 Act.)][4]

Amendment

1 Repealed by the Family Procedure (Amendment No 3) Rules 2014, SI 2014/843, rr 2, 45(a), (c).
2 Inserted by the Family Procedure (Amendment No 3) Rules 2014, SI 2014/843, rr 2, 45(b).
3 Substituted by the Family Procedure (Amendment No 3) Rules 2014, SI 2014/843, rr 2, 45(d).
4 Substituted by the Family Procedure (Amendment) (No 5) Rules 2012, SI 2012/3061, r 6, Schedule.

[25.3 Experts-overriding duty to the court

(1) It is the duty of experts to help the court on matters within their expertise.

(2) This duty overrides any obligation to the person from whom experts have received instructions or by whom they are paid.

(Particular duties of an expert are set out in Practice Direction 25B (The Duties of an Expert, the Expert's Report and Arrangements for an Expert to Attend Court.)][1]

Amendment

1 Substituted by the Family Procedure (Amendment) (No 5) Rules 2012, SI 2012/3061, r 6, Schedule.

[25.4 Control of expert evidence in proceedings other than children proceedings

(1) This rule applies to proceedings other than children proceedings.

(2) A person may not without the permission of the court put expert evidence (in any form) before the court.

(3) The court may give permission as mentioned in paragraph (2) only if the court is of the opinion that the expert evidence is necessary to assist the court to resolve the proceedings.

(Provision relating to the control of expert evidence in children proceedings is contained in section 13 of the 2014 Act.)][1]

Amendment

1 Substituted by the Family Procedure (Amendment No 3) Rules 2014, SI 2014/843, rr 2, 46.

[25.5 Further provisions about the court's power to restrict expert evidence

[(1) When deciding whether to give permission as mentioned in section 13(1), (3) or (5) of the 2014 Act or to give a direction under 38(6) of the 1989 Act in children proceedings, the court is to have regard in particular to any failure to comply with rule 25.6 or any direction of the court about expert evidence.][1]

[(1A) The matter referred to in paragraph (1) is a prescribed matter for the purposes of section 13(7)(h) of the 2014 Act and section 38(7B) of the 1989 Act.][2]

(2) When deciding whether to give permission as mentioned in rule 25.4(1) in proceedings other than children proceedings, the court is to have regard in particular to—

- (a) the issues to which the expert evidence would relate;
- (b) the questions which the court would require the expert to answer;
- (c) the impact which giving permission would be likely to have on the timetable, duration and conduct of the proceedings;
- (d) any failure to comply with rule 25.6 or any direction of the court about expert evidence; and
- (e) the cost of the expert evidence.

[(3) Provision may be made in a practice direction in relation to permission to put expert evidence in relation to toxicology testing before the court.][3]][4]

Amendment

1 Substituted by the Family Procedure (Amendment No 3) Rules 2014, SI 2014/843, rr 2, 47(a).
2 Inserted by the Family Procedure (Amendment No 3) Rules 2014, SI 2014/843, rr 2, 47(b).
3 Inserted by the Family Procedure (Amendment) Rules 2020, SI 2020/135, rr 2, 26.
4 Substituted by the Family Procedure (Amendment) (No 5) Rules 2012, SI 2012/3061, r 6, Schedule.

[25.6 When to apply for the court's permission

Unless the court directs otherwise, parties must apply for the court's permission as mentioned in section 13(1), (3) or (5) of the 2014 Act or rule 25.4(2) as soon as possible and—

- (a) in Part 4 proceedings referred to in rule 12.2 and in so far as practicable other public law proceedings referred to in that rule, no later than a Case Management Hearing;
- (b) in private law proceedings referred to in rule 12.2, no later than the First Hearing Dispute Resolution Appointment;
- (c) in adoption proceedings and placement proceedings, no later than the first directions hearing;
- (d) in proceedings for a financial remedy, no later than the first appointment; and
- (e) in a [disputed][1] case referred to in rule 7.1(3), no later than any Case Management Hearing directed by the court under rule [7.14][1].][2]

Amendment

1 Substituted by the Family Procedure (Amendment) Rules 2022, SI 2022/44, rr 2, 27.
2 Substituted by the Family Procedure (Amendment No 3) Rules 2014, SI 2014/843, rr 2, 48.

[25.7 What an application notice requesting the court's permission must include

(1) Part 18 applies to an application for the court's permission as mentioned in [section 13(1), (3) or (5) of the 2014 Act or][1] rule 25.4[(2)][1].

(2) In any proceedings—

(a) the application notice requesting the court's permission as mentioned in [section 13(1), (3) or (5) of the 2014 Act or][1] rule 25.4[(2)][1] must state—
  (i) the field in which the expert evidence is required;
  (ii) where practicable, the name of the proposed expert;
  (iii) the issues to which the expert evidence is to relate;
  (iv) whether the expert evidence could be obtained from a single joint expert;
  (v) the other matters set out in Practice Direction 25C or 25D, as the case may be; and

(b) a draft of the order sought is to be attached to the application notice requesting the court's permission and that draft order must set out the matters specified in Practice Direction 25C or 25D, as the case may be.

(3) In children proceedings, an application notice requesting the court's permission as mentioned in [section 13(1), (3) or (5) of the 2014 Act][2] must, in addition to the matters specified in paragraph (2)(a), state the questions which the expert is to be required to answer.][3]

Amendment

1 Inserted by the Family Procedure (Amendment No 3) Rules 2014, SI 2014/843, rr 2, 49.
2 Substituted by the Family Procedure (Amendment No 3) Rules 2014, SI 2014/843, rr 2, 49(c).
3 Substituted by the Family Procedure (Amendment) (No 5) Rules 2012, SI 2012/3061, r 6, Schedule.

[25.8 Where permission is granted

(1) In any proceedings, where the court grants permission as mentioned in [section 13(1), (3) or (5) of the 2014 Act or][1] rule 25.4[(2)][1]—

(a) it will grant permission only in relation to the expert named or the field identified in the application notice requesting the court's permission; and

(b) the court will give directions specifying the date by which the expert is to provide a written report.

(2) In children proceedings, in addition to the directions in paragraph (1)(b), the court will give directions—

(a) approving the questions which the expert is required to answer;
(b) specifying the date by which the expert is to receive the letter of instruction.][2]

Amendment

1 Inserted by the Family Procedure (Amendment No 3) Rules 2014, SI 2014/843, rr 2, 50.
2 Substituted by the Family Procedure (Amendment) (No 5) Rules 2012, SI 2012/3061, r 6, Schedule.

[25.9 General requirement for expert evidence to be given in a written report

(1) Expert evidence is to be given in a written report unless the court directs otherwise.

(2) The court will not direct an expert to attend a hearing unless it is necessary to do so in the interests of justice.][1]

Amendment

1 Substituted by the Family Procedure (Amendment) (No 5) Rules 2012, SI 2012/3061, r 6, Schedule.

[25.10 Written questions to experts

(1) A party may put written questions about an expert's report to—

(a) an expert instructed by another party; or
(b) a single joint expert appointed under rule 25.11.

(2) Unless the court directs otherwise or a practice direction provides otherwise, written questions under paragraph (1)—

(a) must be proportionate;
(b) may be put once only;
(c) must be put within 10 days beginning with the date on which the expert's report was served;
(d) must be for the purpose only of clarification of the report; and
(e) must be copied and sent to the other parties at the same time as they are sent to the expert.

(3) An expert's answers to questions put in accordance with paragraph (1)—

(a) must be given within the timetable specified by the court; and
(b) are treated as part of the expert's report.

(4) Where—

(a) a party has put a written question to an expert instructed by another party; and
(b) the expert does not answer that question, the court may make one or both of the following orders in relation to the party who instructed the expert—
   (i) that the party may not rely on the evidence of that expert; or
   (ii) that the party may not recover the fees and expenses of that expert from any other party.][1]

Amendment

1 Substituted by the Family Procedure (Amendment) (No 5) Rules 2012, SI 2012/3061, r 6, Schedule.

[25.11 Court's power to direct that evidence is to be given by a single joint expert

(1) Where two or more parties wish to put expert evidence before the court on a particular issue, the court may direct that the evidence on that issue is to be given by a single joint expert.

(2) Where the parties who wish to put expert evidence before the court ('the relevant parties') cannot agree who should be the single joint expert, the court may—

(a) select the expert from a list prepared or identified by the relevant parties; or
(b) direct that the expert be selected in such other manner as the court may direct.][1]

Amendment

1 Substituted by the Family Procedure (Amendment) (No 5) Rules 2012, SI 2012/3061, r 6, Schedule.

[25.12 Instructions to a single joint expert

(1) Where the court gives a direction under rule 25.11(1) for a single joint expert to be used, the instructions are to be contained in a jointly agreed letter unless the court directs otherwise.

(2) Where the instructions are to be contained in a jointly agreed letter, in default of agreement the instructions may be determined by the court on the written request of any relevant party copied to the other relevant parties.

(3) Where the court permits the relevant parties to give separate instructions to a single joint expert, each instructing party must, when giving instructions to the expert, at the same time send a copy of the instructions to the other relevant parties.

(4) The court may give directions about—

(a) the payment of the expert's fees and expenses; and
(b) any inspection, examination or assessments which the expert wishes to carry out.

(5) The court may, before an expert is instructed, limit the amount that can be paid by way of fees and expenses to the expert.

(6) Unless the court directs otherwise, the relevant parties are jointly and severally liable for the payment of the expert's fees and expenses.][1]

Amendment

1 Substituted by the Family Procedure (Amendment) (No 5) Rules 2012, SI 2012/3061, r 6, Schedule.

[25.13 Power of court to direct a party to provide information

(1) Subject to paragraph (2), where a party has access to information which is not reasonably available to another party, the court may direct the party who has access to the information to—

(a) prepare and file a document recording the information; and
(b) serve a copy of that document on the other party.

(2) In proceedings under Part 14 (procedure for applications in adoption, placement and related proceedings), a court officer will send a copy of the document recording the information to the other party.][1]

Amendment

1 Substituted by the Family Procedure (Amendment) (No 5) Rules 2012, SI 2012/3061, r 6, Schedule.

[25.14 Contents of report

(1) An expert's report must comply with the requirements set out in Practice Direction 25B.

(2) At the end of an expert's report there must be a statement that the expert understands and has complied with the expert's duty to the court.

(3) The instructions to the expert are not privileged against disclosure.

(Rule 21.1 explains what is meant by disclosure.)][1]

Amendment

1 Substituted by the Family Procedure (Amendment) (No 5) Rules 2012, SI 2012/3061, r 6, Schedule.

[25.15 Use by one party of expert's report disclosed by another

Where a party has disclosed an expert's report, any party may use that expert's report as evidence at any hearing where an issue to which the report relates is being considered.][1]

Amendment

1 Substituted by the Family Procedure (Amendment) (No 5) Rules 2012, SI 2012/3061, r 6, Schedule.

[25.16 Discussions between experts

(1) The court may, at any stage, direct a discussion between experts for the purpose of requiring the experts to—

(a) identify and discuss the expert issues in the proceedings; and
(b) where possible, reach an agreed opinion on those issues.

(2) The court may specify the issues which the experts must discuss.

(3) The court may direct that following a discussion between the experts they must prepare a statement for the court setting out those issues on which—

(a) they agree; and
(b) they disagree, with a summary of their reasons for disagreeing.][1]

Amendment

1 Substituted by the Family Procedure (Amendment) (No 5) Rules 2012, SI 2012/3061, r 6, Schedule.

[25.17 Expert's right to ask court for directions

(1) Experts may file written requests for directions for the purpose of assisting them in carrying out their functions.

(2) Experts must, unless the court directs otherwise, provide copies of the proposed requests for directions under paragraph (1)—

(a) to the party instructing them, at least 7 days before they file the requests; and
(b) to all other parties, at least 4 days before they file them.

(3) The court, when it gives directions, may also direct that a party be served with a copy of the directions.][1]

Amendment

1 Substituted by the Family Procedure (Amendment) (No 5) Rules 2012, SI 2012/3061, r 6, Schedule.

[25.18 Copies of orders and other documents

Unless the court directs otherwise, a copy of any order or other document affecting an expert filed with the court after the expert has been instructed, must be served on the expert by the party who instructed the expert or, in the case of a single joint expert, the party who was responsible for instructing the expert, within 2 days of that party receiving the order or other document.][1]

Amendment

1 Substituted by the Family Procedure (Amendment) (No 5) Rules 2012, SI 2012/3061, r 6, Schedule.

[25.19 Action after final hearing

(1) Within 10 business days after the final hearing, the party who instructed the expert or, in the case of a single joint expert, the party who was responsible for instructing the expert, must inform the expert in writing about the court's determination and the use made by the court of the expert's evidence.

(2) Unless the court directs otherwise, the party who instructed the expert or, in the case of the single joint expert, the party who was responsible for instructing the expert, must send to the expert a copy of the court's final order[, any transcript or written record of the court's decision, and its reasons for reaching its decision, within 10 business days from the date when the party received the order and any such transcript or record][1] …[2]

(a) …[2]
(b) …[2]

within 10 business days from the date when that party received the order and transcript or reasons.][3]

Amendment

1 Inserted by the Family Procedure (Amendment No 3) Rules 2014, SI 2014/843, rr 2, 51(a).
2 Repealed by the Family Procedure (Amendment No 3) Rules 2014, SI 2014/843, rr 2, 51(b).
3 Substituted by the Family Procedure (Amendment) (No 5) Rules 2012, SI 2012/3061, r 6, Schedule.

[25.20 Assessors

(1) This rule applies where the court appoints one or more persons under section 70 of the Senior Courts Act 1981 …[1] as an assessor.

(2) An assessor will assist the court in dealing with a matter in which the assessor has skill and experience.

(3) The assessor will take such part in the proceedings as the court may direct and in particular the court may direct an assessor to—

(a) prepare a report for the court on any matter at issue in the proceedings; and
(b) attend the whole or any part of the hearing to advise the court on any such matter.

(4) If the assessor prepares a report for the court before the hearing has begun—

(a) the court will send a copy to each of the parties; and
(b) the parties may use it at the hearing.

(5) Unless the court directs otherwise, an assessor will be paid at the daily rate payable for the time being to a fee-paid deputy district judge of the principal registry and an assessor's fees will form part of the costs of the proceedings.

(6) The court may order any party to deposit in the court office a specified sum in respect of an assessor's fees and, where it does so, the assessor will not be asked to act until the sum has been deposited.

(7) Paragraphs (5) and (6) do not apply where the remuneration of the assessor is to be paid out of money provided by Parliament.][2]

Amendment

1 Repealed by the Family Procedure (Amendment No 2) Rules 2014, SI 2014/667, rr 2, 18.
2 Substituted by the Family Procedure (Amendment) (No 5) Rules 2012, SI 2012/3061, r 6, Schedule.

Practice Direction 25A – Experts and assessors in family proceedings

See also Part 25

This Practice Direction supplements FPR Part 25

Introduction

1.1 This Practice Direction and Practice Directions 25B to E relate to expert evidence and supplement FPR Part 25. This Practice Direction applies to children proceedings and all other family proceedings.

Emergency and urgent cases

2.1 In emergency or urgent cases – for example, where, before formal issue of proceedings, a without-notice application is made to the court during or out of business hours; or where, after proceedings have been issued, a previously unforeseen need for (further) expert evidence arises at short notice – a party may wish to put expert evidence before the court without having complied with all or any part of Practice Directions 25B to E. In such circumstances, the party wishing to put the expert evidence before the court must apply forthwith to the court – where possible or appropriate, on notice to the other parties – for directions as to the future steps to be taken in respect of the expert evidence in question.

Pre-application instruction of experts

3.1 When experts' reports are commissioned before the commencement of proceedings, it should be made clear to the expert that he or she may in due course be reporting to the court and should therefore consider himself or herself bound by the duties of an expert set out in Practice Direction 25B (The Duties of An Expert, the Expert's Report and Arrangements for An Expert To Attend Court). In so far as possible the enquiries of the expert and subsequent letter of instruction should follow either Practice Direction 25C (Children Proceedings – the Use of Single Joint Experts and the Process Leading to an Expert Being Instructed or Expert Evidence Being Put Before The Court) or 25D (Financial Remedy Proceedings and other Family Proceedings (except Children Proceedings) – the Use of Single Joint Experts and the Process Leading to Expert Evidence Being Put Before The Court).

3.2 In particular, a prospective party to children proceedings (for example, a local authority) should always write a letter of instruction when asking a potential witness for a report or an opinion, whether that request is within proceedings or pre-proceedings (for example, when commissioning specialist assessment materials, reports from a treating expert or other evidential materials); and the letter of instruction should conform to the principles set out in Practice Direction 25C.

3.3 It should be noted that the court's permission is required to put expert evidence (in any form) before the court in all family proceedings (see (see section 13(5) of the 2014 Act and FPR 25.4(2)). In children proceedings, the court's permission is also required for an expert to be instructed and for a child to be medically or psychiatrically examined or otherwise assessed for the purposes of the provision of expert evidence in the proceedings section 13(1) and (3) of the 2014 Act. Where the court's permission has not been given in accordance with section 13(1) and (3) of the 2014 Act, evidence resulting from such instructions or examination or other assessment is inadmissible unless the court rules otherwise section 13 (2) and (4) of the 2014 Act and (4)). The court's permission will be needed to put any expert evidence before the court which was obtained before proceedings have started.

3.4 Attention is drawn to Practice Direction 15B (Adults Who May Be Protected Parties and Children Who May Become Protected Parties In Family Proceedings) which gives guidance relating to proceedings where an adult party may not have capacity to conduct the litigation or to instruct an expert.

Practice Direction 25B – The duties of an expert, the expert's report and arrangements for an expert to attend court

See also Part 25, Practice Direction 25A, Practice Direction 25C, Practice Direction 25D, Practice Direction 25E, Practice Direction 25F

This Practice Direction supplements FPR Part 25

Scope of this Practice Direction

1.1 This Practice Direction focuses on the duties of an expert including the contents of the expert's report and, where an expert is to attend court, the arrangements for such attendance. Other Practice Directions supporting FPR Part 25 deal with different aspects of experts in family proceedings. The relevant Practice Directions are–

(a) Practice Direction 25A (Experts – Emergencies and Pre proceedings Instructions);

(b) Practice Direction 25C (Children Proceedings – The Use of Single Joint Experts and the Process Leading to an Expert Being Instructed or Expert Evidence Being Put Before the Court);

(c) Practice Direction 25D (Financial Remedy Proceedings and Other Family Proceedings (except Children Proceedings) – The Use of Single Joint Experts and the Process Leading to Expert Evidence Being Put Before The Court);and

(d) Practice Direction 25E (Discussions Between Experts in Family Proceedings).

1.2 Practice Direction 15B (Adults Who May Be Protected Parties and Children Who May Become Protected Parties In Family Proceedings) gives guidance relating to proceedings where an adult party may not have capacity to conduct the litigation or to instruct an expert.

1.3 In accordance with FPR 25.2(1), 'children proceedings' means–

(a) proceedings referred to in FPR 12.1 and 14.1 and any other proceedings which relate wholly or mainly to the maintenance or upbringing of a minor;

(b) applications for permission to start proceedings mentioned in paragraph (a);

(c) applications made in the course of proceedings mentioned in paragraph (a).

The meaning of 'expert'

2.1 In accordance with FPR 25.2(1), 'expert' means a person who provides expert evidence for use in family proceedings. section 13(8) of the 2014 Act expressly refers to evidence that is not expert evidence. For example, evidence given by a children's guardian is not expert evidence.

2.2 An expert includes a reference to an expert team which can include ancillary workers in addition to experts. In an expert team, an 'ancillary' worker may be, for example, a play therapist or similar who undertakes work with the child or family for the purpose of the expert assessment. It is perfectly possible that such workers will be experts in their own right and in their own field, but it would be cumbersome to name everyone in that position in an order giving permission for an expert to be instructed, a child to be medically or psychiatrically examined or otherwise assessed or expert evidence to be put before the court or in a letter of instruction to an expert. The purpose of the term 'expert team' is to enable a multi-disciplinary team to undertake the assessment without the order having to name everyone who may be involved. The final expert's report must, however, give information about those persons who have taken part in the assessment and their respective roles and who is responsible for the report.

The expert's overriding duty

3.1 An expert in family proceedings has an overriding duty to the court that takes precedence over any obligation to the person from whom the expert has received instructions or by whom the expert is paid.

Particular duties of the expert

4.1 An expert shall have regard to the following, among other, duties–

(a) to assist the court in accordance with the overriding duty;

(aa) in children proceedings, to comply with the Standards for Expert Witnesses in Children Proceedings in the Family Court which are set out in the Annex to this Practice Direction;

(b) to provide advice to the court that conforms to the best practice of the expert's profession;

(c) to answer the questions about which the expert is required to give an opinion (in children proceedings, those questions will be set out in the order of the court giving permission for an expert to be instructed, a child to be examined or otherwise assessed or expert evidence to be put before the court);

(d) to provide an opinion that is independent of the party or parties instructing the expert;

(e) to confine the opinion to matters material to the issues in the case and in relation only to the questions that are within the expert's expertise (skill and experience);

(f) where a question has been put which falls outside the expert's expertise, to state this at the earliest opportunity and to volunteer an opinion as to whether another expert is required to bring expertise not possessed by those already involved or, in the rare case, as to whether a second opinion is required on a key issue and, if possible, what questions should be asked of the second expert;

(g) in expressing an opinion, to take into consideration all of the material facts including any relevant factors arising from ethnic, cultural, religious or linguistic contexts at the time the opinion is expressed;

(h) to inform those instructing the expert without delay of any change in the opinion and of the reason for the change.

The requirement for the court's permission

5.1 The general rule in family proceedings is that the court's permission is required to put expert evidence (in any form) before the court (see section 13(5) of the 2014 Act for children proceedings and FPR 25.4(2) for other family proceedings.). The court is under a duty to restrict expert evidence to that which in the opinion of the court is necessary to assist the court to resolve the proceedings. The overriding objective in FPR1.1 applies when the court is exercising this duty. In children proceedings, the court's permission is required to instruct an expert and for a child to be medically or psychiatrically examined or otherwise assessed for the purposes of the provision of expert evidence in the proceedings section 13(1) and (3) of the 2014 Act.

Preliminary enquiries which the expert should expect to receive

6.1 In good time for the information requested to be available for–

(a) the court hearing when the court will decide whether to give permission for the expert evidence to be put before the court (or also in children proceedings, for the expert to be instructed or the child to be examined or otherwise assessed); or

(b) the advocates' meeting or discussion where one takes place before such a hearing, the party or parties intending to instruct the expert shall approach the expert with some information about the case.

6.2 The details of the information to be given to the expert are set out in Practice Direction 25C, paragraph 3.2 and Practice Direction 25D paragraph 3.3 and include the nature of the proceedings, the questions for the expert, the time when the expert's report is likely to be required, the timing of any hearing at which the expert may have to give evidence and how the expert's fees will be funded.

6.3 Children proceedings are confidential which means in thos eproceedings parties raising preliminary enquiries of an expert who has not ye tbeen instructed can only tell the expert information which he or she will need about the case to be able to answer the preliminary questions raised.

Balancing the needs of the court and those of the expert

7.1 It is essential that there should be proper co-ordination between the court and the expert when drawing up the case management timetable: the needs of the court should be balanced with the needs of the expert whose forensic work is undertaken as an adjunct to his or her main professional duties.

The expert's response to preliminary enquiries

8.1 In good time for the court hearing when the court will decide whether or not to give permission for the expert evidence to be put before the court (or also in children proceedings, for the expert to be instructed or the child to be examined or otherwise assessed) or for the advocates' meeting or discussion where one takes place before that hearing, the party or parties intending to instruct the expert will need confirmation from the expert–

(a) that acceptance of the proposed instructions will not involve the expert in any conflict of interest;
(b) that the work required is within the expert's expertise;
(c) that the expert is available to do the relevant work within the suggested time scale;
(d) when the expert is available to give evidence, of the dates and times to avoid and, where a hearing date has not been fixed, of the amount of notice the expert will require to make arrangements to come to court (or to give evidence by telephone conference or video link) without undue disruption to his or her normal professional routines;
(e) of the cost, including hourly or other charging rates, and likely hours to be spent attending experts' meetings, attending court and writing the report (to include any examinations and interviews);
(f) of any representations which the expert wishes to make to the court about being named or otherwise identified in any public judgment given by the court.

Content of the expert's report

9.1 The expert's report shall be addressed to the court and prepared and filed in accordance with the court's timetable and must–

(a) give details of the expert's qualifications and experience;
(b) include a statement identifying the document(s) containing the material instructions and the substance of any oral instructions and, as far as necessary to explain any opinions or conclusions expressed in the report, summarising the facts and instructions which are material to the conclusions and opinions expressed;

(c) state who carried out any test, examination or interview which the expert has used for the report and whether or not the test, examination or interview has been carried out under the expert's supervision;
(d) give details of the qualifications of any person who carried out the test, examination or interview;
(e) answer the questions about which the expert is to give an opinion and which relate to the issues in the case;
(f) in expressing an opinion to the court–
  (i) take into consideration all of the material facts including any relevant factors arising from ethnic, cultural, religious or linguistic contexts at the time the opinion is expressed, identifying the facts, literature and any other material, including research material, that the expert has relied upon in forming an opinion;
  (ii) describe the expert's own professional risk assessment process and process of differential diagnosis, highlighting factual assumptions, deductions from the factual assumptions, and any unusual, contradictory or inconsistent features of the case;
  (iii) indicate whether any proposition in the report is an hypothesis (in particular a controversial hypothesis), or an opinion deduced in accordance with peer-reviewed and tested technique, research and experience accepted as a consensus in the scientific community;
  (iv) indicate whether the opinion is provisional (or qualified, as the case may be), stating the qualification and the reason for it, and identifying what further information is required to give an opinion without qualification;
(g) where there is a range of opinion on any question to be answered by the expert–
  (i) summarise the range of opinion;
  (ii) identify and explain, within the range of opinions, any 'unknown cause', whether arising from the facts of the case (for example, because there is too little information to form a scientific opinion) or from limited experience or lack of research, peer review or support in the relevant field of expertise;
  (iii) give reasons for any opinion expressed: the use of a balance sheet approach to the factors that support or undermine an opinion can be of great assistance to the court;
(h) contain a summary of the expert's conclusions and opinions;
(i) contain a statement that the expert–
  (i) has no conflict of interest of any kind, other than any conflict disclosed in his or her report;
  (ii) does not consider that any interest disclosed affects his or her suitability as an expert witness on any issue on which he or she has given evidence;
  (iii) will advise the instructing party if, between the date of the expert's report and the final hearing, there is any change in circumstances which affects the expert's answers to (i) or (ii) above;
  (iv) understands their duty to the court and has complied with that duty; and
  (v) is aware of the requirements of FPR Part 25 and this practice direction;
  (vi) in children proceedings, has complied with the Standards for Expert Witnesses in Children Proceedings in the Family Court which are set out in the Annex to this Practice Direction;
(j) be verified by a statement of truth in the following form–

> 'I confirm that I have made clear which facts and matters referred to in this report are within my own knowledge and which are not. Those that are within my own knowledge I confirm to be true. The opinions I have expressed represent my true and complete professional opinions on the matters to which they refer.'

Where the report relates to children proceedings the form of statement of truth must include–

> 'I also confirm that I have complied with the Standards for Expert Witnesses in Children Proceedings in the Family Court which are set out in the Annex to Practice Direction 25B- The Duties of an Expert, the Expert's Report and Arrangements for an Expert to Attend Court'

(FPR Part 17deals with statements of truth. Rule 17.6 sets out the consequences of verifying a document containing a false statement without an honest belief in its truth.)

Arrangements for experts to give evidence

Preparation

10.1 Where the court has directed the attendance of an expert witness, the party who instructed the expert or party responsible for the instruction of the expert shall, by a date specified by the court prior to the hearing at which the expert is to give oral evidence ('the specified date') or, where in care or supervision proceedings an Issues Resolution Hearing ('the IRH') is to be held, by the IRH, ensure that–

(a) a date and time (if possible, convenient to the expert) are fixed for the court to hear the expert's evidence, substantially in advance of the hearing at which the expert is to give oral evidence and no later than a specified date prior to that hearing or, where an IRH is to be held, than the IRH;

(b) if the expert's oral evidence is not required, the expert is notified as soon as possible;

(c) the witness template accurately indicates how long the expert is likely to be giving evidence, in order to avoid the inconvenience of the expert being delayed at court;

(d) consideration is given in each case to whether some or all of the experts participate by telephone conference or video link, or submit their evidence in writing, to ensure that minimum disruption is caused to professional schedules and that costs are minimised.

Experts attending court

10.2 Where expert witnesses are to be called, all parties shall, by the specified date or, where an IRH is to be held, by the IRH, ensure that–

(a) the parties' advocates have identified (whether at an advocates' meeting or by other means) the issues which the experts are to address;

(b) wherever possible, a logical sequence to the evidence is arranged, with experts of the same discipline giving evidence on the same day;

(c) the court is informed of any circumstance where all experts agree but a party nevertheless does not accept the agreed opinion, so that directions can be given for the proper consideration of the experts' evidence and opinion;

(d) in the exceptional case the court is informed of the need for a witness summons.

Annex

Standards for Expert Witnesses in Children Proceedings in the Family Court

Subject to any order made by the court, expert witnesses involved in family proceedings (involving children) in England and Wales, whatever their field of practice or country of origin, must comply with the standards (1–11).

1 The expert's area of competence is appropriate to the issue(s) upon which the court has identified that an opinion is required, and relevant experience is evidenced in their CV.

2 The expert has been active in the area of work or practice, (as a practitioner or an academic who is subject to peer appraisal), has sufficient experience of the issues relevant to the instant case, and is familiar with the breadth of current practice or opinion.

3 The expert has working knowledge of the social, developmental, cultural norms and accepted legal principles applicable to the case presented at initial enquiry, and has the cultural competence skills to deal with the circumstances of the case.

4 The expert is up-to-date with Continuing Professional Development appropriate to their discipline and expertise, and is in continued engagement with accepted supervisory mechanisms relevant to their practice.

5 If the expert's current professional practice is regulated by a UK statutory body (See Appendix 1) they are in possession of a current licence to practise or equivalent.

6 If the expert's area of professional practice is not subject to statutory registration (e.g. child psychotherapy, systemic family therapy, mediation, and experts in exclusively academic appointments) the expert should demonstrate appropriate qualifications and/ or registration with a relevant professional body on a case by case basis. Registering bodies usually provide a code of conduct and professional standards and should be accredited by the Professional Standards Authority for Health and Social Care (See Appendix 2). If the expertise is academic in nature (e.g. regarding evidence of cultural influences) then no statutory registration is required (even if this includes direct contact or interviews with individuals) but consideration should be given to appropriate professional accountability.

7 The expert is compliant with any necessary safeguarding requirements, information security expectations, and carries professional indemnity insurance.

8 If the expert's current professional practice is outside the UK they can demonstrate that they are compliant with the FJC 'Guidelines for the instruction of medical experts from overseas in family cases'.[1]

9 The expert has undertaken appropriate training, updating or quality assurance activity – including actively seeking feedback from cases in which they have provided evidence- relevant to the role of expert in the family courts in England and Wales within the last year.

10 The expert has a working knowledge of, and complies with, the requirements of Practice Directions relevant to providing reports for and giving evidence to the family courts in England and Wales. This includes compliance with the requirement to identify where their opinion on the instant case lies in relation to other accepted mainstream views and the overall spectrum of opinion in the UK.

Amendment

1 December 2011. See www.judiciary.gov.uk/about-the-judiciary/advisory-bodies/fjc.

Expectations in relation to experts' fees

11 The expert should state their hourly rate in advance of agreeing to accept instruction, and give an estimate of the number of hours the report is likely to take. This will assist the legal representative to apply expeditiously to the Legal Aid Agency if prior authority is to be sought in a publicly funded case.

Appendix 1 to the standards

UK Health and Social Care Professions and Statutory Regulators with responsibilities within England and Wales

The Professional Standards Authority for Health and Social Care (PSA)[2] (formerly the Council for Healthcare Regulatory Excellence) oversees statutory bodies that regulate health and social care professionals in the UK. It assesses their performance, conducts audits, scrutinises their decisions and reports to Parliament. It also sets standards for organisations holding voluntary registers for health and social care occupations and accredits those that meet them. It shares good practice and knowledge, conducts research and introduces new ideas to the sector including the concept of right-touch regulation. It monitors policy developments in the UK and internationally and provides advice on issues relating to professional standards in health and social care.

The General Medical Council[3] (GMC) is the independent regulator for doctors in the UK. The GMC's statutory purpose is to protect, promote and maintain the health and safety of the public by ensuring proper standards in the practice of medicine through the Medical Register.

The General Dental Council[4] regulates dental professionals in the UK. All dentists, dental nurses, dental technicians, clinical dental technicians, dental hygienists, dental therapists and orthodontic therapists must be registered with the GDC to work in the UK.

The Nursing and Midwifery Council[5] regulates nurses and midwives in the UK, setting standards for work, education and a code of conduct for all registered nurses and midwives.

Care Council for Wales: The Care Council for Wales is the social care workforce regulator in Wales responsible for promoting and securing high standards across the social services and social care workforce. It regulates social workers in Wales and managers of care services, including residential care homes for children, care homes for adults and domiciliary care for both adults and children. It also regulates social work students and residential child care workers.

The General Optical Council[6] is the regulator for the optical professions in the UK. Its purpose is to protect the public by promoting high standards of education, performance and conduct amongst opticians.

The General Pharmacy Council[7] is the independent regulator for pharmacists, pharmacy technicians and pharmacy premises in Great Britain. Its role is to protect, promote and maintain the health, safety and wellbeing of members of the public by upholding standards and public trust in pharmacy.

The General Chiropractic Council[8] is a UK-wide statutory body with regulatory powers established by the Chiropractors Act 1994. Its duties are to protect the public by establishing and operating a scheme of statutory regulation for chiropractors, to set the standards of chiropractic education, conduct and practice and to ensure the development of the profession of chiropractic, using a model of continuous improvement in practice.

The General Osteopathic Council[9] regulates the practice of osteopathy in the United Kingdom. By law osteopaths must be registered with the Council in order to practise in the UK. It works with the public and osteopathic profession to promote patient safety by registering qualified professionals and sets, maintain and develop standards of osteopathic practice and conduct.

The Health and Care Professions Council[10] regulates health and social care professionals with protected titles. Further information is set out in the table below.

Profession	*Protected title(s)*
Arts therapist An art, music or drama therapist encourages people to express their feelings and emotions through art, such as painting and drawing, music or drama.	• Art psychotherapist • Art therapist • Dramatherapist • Music therapist
Biomedical scientist A biomedical scientist analyses specimens from patients to provide data to help doctors diagnose and treat disease.	• Biomedical scientist
Chiropodist/Podiatrist A chiropodist / podiatrist diagnoses and treats disorders, diseases and deformities of the feet.	• Chiropodist • Podiatrist
Clinical scientist A clinical scientist oversees specialist tests for diagnosing and managing disease. They advise doctors on using tests and interpreting data and they also carry out research to understand diseases.	• Clinical scientist
Dietician A dietician uses the science of nutrition to devise eating plans for patients to treat medical conditions, and to promote good health.	• Dietician
Hearing aid dispenser Hearing aid dispensers assess, fit and provide aftercare for hearing aids.	• Hearing aid dispenser
Occupational therapist An occupational therapist uses specific activities to limit the effects of disability and promote independence in all aspects of daily life.	• Occupational therapist
Operating department practitioner Operating department practitioners participate in the assessment of the patient prior to surgery and provide individualised care.	• Operating department practitioner
Orthoptist Orthoptists specialise in diagnosing and treating visual problems involving eye movement and alignment.	• Orthoptist
Paramedic Paramedics provide specialist care and treatment to patients who are either acutely ill or injured. They can administer a range of drugs and carry out certain surgical techniques.	• Paramedic

Profession	*Protected title(s)*
Physiotherapist Physiotherapists deal with human function and movement and help people to achieve their full physical potential. They use physical approaches to promote, maintain and restore wellbeing.	• Physiotherapist • Physical therapist
Practitioner psychologist Psychology is the scientific study of people, the mind and behaviour. Psychologists attempt to understand the role of mental functions in individual and social behaviour.	• Practitioner psychologist • Registered psychologist • Clinical psychologist • Counselling psychologist • Educational psychologist • Forensic psychologist • Health psychologist • Occupational psychologist • Sport and exercise psychologist
Prosthetist/Orthotist Prosthetists and orthotists are responsible for all aspects of supplying prostheses and orthoses for patients. A prosthesis is a device that replaces a missing body part. An orthosis is a device fixed to the body.	• Prosthetist • Orthotist
Radiographer Therapeutic radiographers plan and deliver treatment using radiation. Diagnostic radiographers produce and interpret high-quality images of the body to diagnose injuries and diseases.	• Radiographer • Diagnostic radiographer • Therapeutic radiographer
Social workers in England	• Social worker
Speech and language therapist Speech and language therapists assess, treat and help to prevent speech, language and swallowing difficulties.	• Speech and language therapist • Speech therapist

2 www.professionalstandards.org.uk
3 www.gmc-uk.org
4 www.gdc-uk.org
5 www.nmc-uk.org
6 www.optical.org
7 www.pharmacyregulation.org/about-us
8 www.gcc-uk.org/page.cfm
9 www.osteopathy.org.uk
10 www.hpc-uk.org/aboutregistration/protectedtitles

Appendix 2 to the standards

Examples of professional bodies / associations relating to non- statutorily regulated work

Resolution UK

www.resolution.org.uk/

Resolution's members are family lawyers committed to the constructive resolution of family disputes. Members follow a Code of Practice that promotes a non-confrontational approach to family problems, encourage solutions that consider the needs of the whole family and in particular the best interests of children.

Association of Child Psychotherapists (Psychoanalytic)

www.childpsychotherapy.org.uk

The Association of Child Psychotherapists is the professional organisation for Child and Adolescent Psychoanalytic Psychotherapy in the UK. The Association recognises and monitors five training schools in Child and Adolescent Psychotherapy (e.g. the Tavistock and Portman NHS Foundation Trust). Child Psychotherapists who have qualified in one of these trainings (minimum 4 years in-service clinical training, doctoral or doctoral equivalent) are eligible for full membership of the Association and are able to work as autonomous professionals within the NHS or in independent practice. Child Psychotherapists are appointed at similar grades to Clinical Psychologists.

The UK Council for Psychotherapy (UKCP)

www.psychotherapy.org.uk

The UKCP is a membership organisation with over 75 training and listing organisations, and over 7,000 individual practitioners. UKCP holds the national register of psychotherapists and psychotherapeutic counsellors, listing those practitioner members who meet exacting standards and training requirements. Organisational members / associations are grouped together in modality colleges representing all the main traditions in the practice of psychotherapy in the UK including

- Association for Cognitive Analytic Therapy
- Association for Family Therapy and Systemic Practice
- Gestalt Psychotherapy and Training Institute
- Institute of Transactional Analysis
- Institute for Arts in Therapy and Education

The British Association for Counselling & Psychotherapy (BACP)

www.bacp.co.uk

BACP is a membership organisation and a registered charity that sets standards for a wide variety of therapeutic practice and provides information for therapists, clients of therapy, and the general public. It has over 37,000 members and is the largest professional body representing counselling and psychotherapy in the UK. BACP accredits training courses for counsellors and psychotherapists and is dedicated to ensuring its members practice responsibly, ethically and to the highest of standards.

The British Association for Behavioural and Cognitive Psychotherapies (BABCP)

www.babcp.com

The BABCP is the lead organisation for Cognitive Behavioural Therapy in the UK. It is a multi-disciplinary interest group for people involved in the practice and theory of behavioural and cognitive psychotherapy. The BABCP maintain standards for practitioners of Behavioural & Cognitive Psychotherapy by providing the opportunity for members who meet minimum criteria to become accredited.

British Psychoanalytic Council

www.psychoanalytic-council.org

Psychoanalytic or psychodynamic psychotherapy draws on theories and practices of analytical psychology and psychoanalysis. It is a therapeutic process which helps patients understand and resolve their problems by increasing awareness of their inner world and its influence over relationships both past and present. It differs from most other therapies in aiming for deep seated change in personality and emotional development. Psychoanalytic and psychodynamic psychotherapy aim to help people with serious psychological disorders to understand and change complex, deep-seated and often unconsciously based emotional and relationship problems thereby reducing symptoms and alleviating distress.

NAGALRO

www.nagalro.com

Professional association for Family Court Advisers, Children's Guardians and Independent Social Workers.

British Association of Social Workers (BASW)

www.basw.co.uk

UK professional association of social workers.

Confederation of Independent Social Work Agencies UK (CISWA)

www.ciswa-uk.org

CISWA-UK is a not for profit organisation which brings independent social work providers together with the aim of improving the professionalism and expertise of agencies providing services to children and families.

Practice Direction 25C – Children proceedings – the use of single joint experts and the process leading to an expert being instructed or expert evidence being put before the court

See also Part 25, Practice Direction 25A, Practice Direction 25B, Practice Direction 25D, Practice Direction 25E, Practice Direction 25F

This Practice Direction supplements FPR Part 25

Scope of this Practice Direction

1.1 This Practice Direction applies to children proceedings and contains guidance on–

(a) the use of single joint experts;

(b) how to prepare for the hearing at which the court will consider whether to give permission for an expert to be instructed, a child to be medically or psychiatrically examined or otherwise assessed for the purposes of provision of expert evidence in the proceedings or for putting expert evidence (in any form) before the court including–

   (i) preliminary enquiries of experts;

   (ii) the content of an application for the court's permission in addition to matters mentioned in FPR25.7;

(iii) matters to be set out in the draft order to be attached to the application for permission; and

(c) the letter of instruction to the expert.

1.2 'Children proceedings' includes proceedings under Schedule 1 to the 1989 Act as those proceedings are proceedings which relate wholly or mainly to the maintenance or upbringing of a minor referred to in FPR25.2(1).

Single joint experts

2.1 section 13(1),(3) and (5) of the 2014 Act applies to a single joint expert ('SJE') in addition to an expert instructed by one party. This means that the court's permission is required to put expert evidence from an SJE (in any form) before the court section 13(5) of the 2014 Act. The court's permission is also required to instruct an SJE and for a child to be medically or psychiatrically examined or otherwise assessed for the purposes of provision of evidence from an SJE substitute section 13(1) and (3) of the 2014 Act. Wherever possible, expert evidence should be obtained from an SJE instructed by both or all the parties. To that end, a party wishing to instruct an expert should as soon as possible after the start of the proceedings first give the other party or parties a list of the names of one or more experts in the relevant speciality whom they consider suitable to be instructed.

2.2 Within 5 business days after receipt of the list of proposed experts, the other party or parties should indicate any objection to one or more of the named experts and, if so, supply the name(s) of one or more experts whom they consider suitable.

2.3 Each party should disclose whether they have already consulted any of the proposed experts about the issue(s) in question.

2.4 Where the parties cannot agree on the identity of the expert, each party should think carefully before seeking the permission of the court to instruct their own expert because of the costs implications. Disagreements about the use and identity of an expert may be better managed by the court in the context of the application for the court's permission to instruct the expert and for directions for the use of an SJE (see paragraph 2.6 below).

Instructing separate experts

2.5 If the parties seek the permission of the court to instruct separate experts–

(a) they should agree in advance that the reports will be disclosed; and

(b) the instructions to each expert should comply, so far as appropriate, with paragraphs 4.1 and 6.1 below (Letter of instruction).

Where two or more parties wish to instruct an SJE

2.6 If two or more parties wish to instruct an SJE, before applying to the court for permission and directions for the use of an SJE, the parties should–

(a) so far as appropriate, comply with the guidance in paragraphs 3.2 (Preliminary enquiries of the expert) and paragraphs 3.10 and 3.11 below;

(b) receive the expert's confirmation in response to preliminary enquiries referred to in paragraph 8.1 of Practice Direction 25B;

(c) have agreed in what proportion the SJE's fee is to be shared between them (at least in the first instance) and when it is to be paid; and

(d) if applicable, have obtained agreement for public funding.

2.7 The instructions to the SJE should comply, so far as appropriate, with paragraphs 4.1 and 6.1 below (Letter of instruction).

Preparation for the permission hearing

3.1 Paragraphs 3.2 to 3.11 give guidance on how to prepare for the hearing at which the court will consider whether to give permission for an expert to be instructed, a child to be examined or otherwise assessed or expert evidence to be put before the court. The purpose of the preparation is to ensure that the court has the information required to enable it to exercise its powers under section 13(1), (3), (5) and (7) of the 2014 Act and FPR 25.5.

Preliminary enquiries of the expert

3.2 In good time for the information requested to be available for the hearing at which the court will consider whether to give permission for an expert to be instructed, a child to be examined or otherwise assessed or expert evidence to be put before the court or for the advocates' meeting or discussion where one takes place before that hearing, the party or parties intending to instruct the expert shall approach the expert with the following information–

(a) the nature of the proceedings and the issues likely to require determination by the court;
(b) the issues in the proceedings to which the expert evidence is to relate;
(c) the questions about which the expert is to be asked to give an opinion (including any ethnic, cultural,religious or linguistic contexts) and which relate to the issues in the case;
(d) the date when the court is to be asked to give permission for the instruction (or if – unusually – permission has already been given, the date and details of that permission);
(e) whether permission is to be asked of the court for the instruction of another expert in the same or any related field (that is, to give an opinion on the same or related questions);
(f) the volume of reading which the expert will need to undertake;
(g) whether or not permission has been applied for or given for the expert to examine the child;
(h) whether or not it will be necessary for the expert to conduct interviews – and, if so, with whom;
(i) the likely timetable of legal and social work steps;
(j) in care and supervision proceedings, any dates in the Timetable for the Child which would be relevant to the proposed timetable for the assessment;
(k) when the expert's report is likely to be required;
(l) whether and, if so, what date has been fixed by the court for any hearing at which the expert may be required to give evidence (in particular the Final Hearing); and whether it may be possible for the expert to give evidence by telephone conference or video link: see paragraphs 10.1 and 10.2 (Arrangements for experts to give evidence) of Practice Direction 25B;
(m) the possibility of making, through their instructing solicitors, representations to the court about being named or otherwise identified in any public judgment given by the court;
(n) whether the instructing party has public funding and the legal aid rates of payment which are applicable.

Confidentiality of children proceedings and making preliminary enquiries of an expert

3.3 For the purposes of the law of contempt of court, information relating to children proceedings (whether or not contained in a document filed with the court or recorded in any form) may be communicated only to an expert whose instruction by a party has been permitted by the court (see FPR 12.73(1)(a)(vii) and 14.14(c)(vii)) as children proceedings are confidential.

3.4 Before permission is obtained from the court to instruct an expert in children proceedings, the party seeking permission needs to make the enquiries of the expert referred to above in order to provide the court with information to enable it to decide whether to give permission. In practice, enquiries may need to be made of more than one expert for this purpose. This will in turn require each expert to be given sufficient information about the case to decide whether or not he or she is in a position to accept instructions. Such preliminary enquiries, and the disclosure of information about the case which is a necessary part of such enquiries, will not require the court's permission and will not amount to a contempt of court.

Expert's response to preliminary enquiries

3.5 In good time for the hearing at which the court will consider whether to give permission for an expert to be instructed, a child to be examined or otherwise assessed or expert evidence to be put before the court, the party or parties intending to instruct the expert must obtain the confirmations from the expert referred to in paragraph 8.1 of Practice Direction 25B. These confirmations include that the work is within the expert's expertise, the expert is available to do the work within the relevant timescale and the expert's costs.

3.6 Where the parties cannot agree who should be the single joint expert before the hearing at which the court will consider whether to give permission for an expert to be instructed, a child to be examined or otherwise assessed or expert evidence to be put before the court, they should obtain the above confirmations in respect of all experts whom they intend to put to the court for the purposes of FPR 25.11(2)(a) as candidates for the appointment.

The application for the court's permission mentioned in in section 13(1), (3) and (5) of the 2014 Act

Timing and oral applications for the court's permission mentioned in in section 13(1), (3) and (5) of the 2014 Act

3.7 An application for the court's permission for an expert to be instructed, a child to be examined or otherwise assessed or expert evidence to be put before the court should be made as soon as it becomes apparent that it is necessary to make it. FPR 25.6 makes provision about the time by which applications for the court's permission should be made.

3.8 Applications should, wherever possible, be made so that they are considered at any directions hearing or other hearing for which a date has been fixed or for which a date is about to be fixed. It should be noted that one application notice can be used by a party to make more than one application for an order or direction at a hearing held during the course of proceedings. An application for the court's permission for an expert to be instructed, a child to be examined or otherwise assessed or expert evidence to be put before the court may therefore be included in an application notice requesting other orders to be made at such a hearing.

3.9 Where a date for a hearing has been fixed, a party who wishes to make an application at that hearing but does not have sufficient time to file an application notice should as soon as possible inform the court (if possible in writing) and, if possible, the other parties of the nature of the application and the reason for it. The party should provide the court and the other party with as much as possible of the information referred to in FPR 25.7 and paragraph 3.10 below. That party should then make the application orally at the hearing. An oral application of this kind should be the exception and reserved for genuine cases where circumstances are such that it has only become apparent shortly before the hearing that an expert opinion is necessary.

The application

3.10 In addition to the matters specified in FPR 25.7(2)(a)and (3), an application for the court's permission for an expert to be instructed, a child to be examined or otherwise assessed or expert evidence to be put before the court, must state–

(a) the discipline, qualifications and expertise of the expert (by way of C.V. where possible);
(b) the expert's availability to undertake the work;
(c) the timetable for the report;
(d) the responsibility for instruction;
(e) whether the expert evidence can properly be obtained by only one party (for example, on behalf of the child);
(f) why the expert evidence proposed cannot properly be given by an officer of the service, Welsh family proceedings officer or the local authority (social services undertaking a core assessment) in accordance with their respective statutory duties or any other party to the proceedings or an expert already instructed in the proceedings;
(g) the likely cost of the report on an hourly or other charging basis;
(h) the proposed apportionment (at least in the first instance) of any jointly instructed expert's fee; when it is to be paid; and, if applicable, whether public funding has been approved.

The terms of the draft order to be attached to the application for the court's permission

3.11 FPR 25.7(2)(b) provides that a draft of the order giving the court's permission as mentioned in section 13(1), (3) and (5) of the 2014 Act is to be attached to the application for the court's permission. That draft order must set out the following matters–

(a) the issues in the proceedings to which the expert evidence is to relate and which the court is to identify;
(b) the questions relating to the issues in the case which the expert is to answer and which the court is to approve ensuring that they–
    (i) are within the ambit of the expert's area of expertise;
    (ii) do not contain unnecessary or irrelevant detail;
    (iii) are kept to a manageable number and are clear, focused and direct;
(c) the party who is responsible for drafting the letter of instruction and providing the documents to the expert;
(d) the timetable within which the report is to be prepared, filed and served;
(e) the disclosure of the report to the parties and to any other expert;
(f) the organisation of, preparation for and conduct of any experts' discussion (see Practice Direction 25E – Discussions between Experts in Family Proceedings);
(g) the preparation of a statement of agreement and disagreement by the experts following an experts' discussion;

(h) making available to the court at an early opportunity the expert reports in electronic form;

(i) the attendance of the expert at court to give oral evidence (alternatively, the expert giving his or her evidence in writing or remotely by video link), whether at or for the Final Hearing or another hearing; unless agreement about the opinions given by the expert is reached at or before the Issues Resolution Hearing ('IRH') or, if no IRH is to be held, by a date specified by the court prior to the hearing at which the expert is to give oral evidence.

Letter of instruction

4.1 The party responsible for instructing the expert shall prepare (in agreement with the other parties where appropriate), a letter of instruction to the expert and shall–

(a) set out the context in which the expert's opinion is sought (including any ethnic, cultural, religious or linguistic contexts);

(b) set out the questions approved by the court and which the expert is required to answer and any other linked questions ensuring that they–
   (i) are within the ambit of the expert's area of expertise;
   (ii) do not contain unnecessary or irrelevant detail;
   (iii) are kept to a manageable number and are clear, focused and direct; and
   (iv) reflect what the expert has been requested to do by the court

   (Annex A to this Practice Direction sets out suggested questions in letters of instruction to (1) child mental health professionals or paediatricians, and (2) adult psychiatrists and applied psychologists, in Children Act 1989 proceedings);

(c) list the documentation provided,or provide for the expert an indexed and paginated bundle which shall include–
   (i) an agreed list of essential reading; and
   (ii) a copy of this Practice Direction and Practice Directions 25B and E and where appropriate Practice Direction 15B;

(d) identify any materials provided to the expert which have not been produced either as original medical (or other professional) records or in response to an instruction from a party, and state the source of that material (such materials may contain an assumption as to the standard of proof, the admissibility or otherwise of hearsay evidence, and other important procedural and substantive questions relating to the different purposes of other enquiries, for example, criminal or disciplinary proceedings);

(e) identify all requests to third parties for disclosure and their responses in order to avoid partial disclosure, which tends only to prove a case rather than give full and frank information;

(f) identify the relevant people concerned with the proceedings (for example, the treating clinicians) and inform the expert of his or her right to talk to them provided that an accurate record is made of the discussions;

(g) identify any other expert instructed in the proceedings and advise the expert of their right to talk to the other experts provided that an accurate record is made of the discussions;

(h) subject to any public funding requirement for prior authority, define the contractual basis upon which the expert is retained and in particular the funding mechanism including how much the expert will be paid (an hourly rate and overall estimate should already have been obtained), when the expert will be paid, and what limitation there might be on the amount the expert can charge for the work which they will have to do. In cases where the parties are publicly funded, there may also be a brief explanation of the costs and expenses excluded from public funding by Funding Code criterion 1.3 and the detailed assessment process.

Adult who is a protected party

5.1 Where the adult is a protected party, that party's representative shall be involved in any instruction of an expert, including the instruction of an expert to assess whether the adult, although a protected party, is competent to give evidence (see Practice Direction 15B – Adults Who May Be Protected Parties and Children Who May Become Protected Parties in Family Proceedings).

Asking the court to settle the letter of instruction to a single joint expert

6.1 Where possible, the written request for the court to consider the letter of instruction referred to in rule 25.12(2) should be set out in an e-mail to the court and copied by e-mail to the other instructing parties. The request should be sent to the relevant court or (by prior arrangement only) directly to the judge dealing with the proceedings. Where a legal adviser has been appointed as the case manager, the request should also be sent to the appointed legal adviser. The court will settle the letter of instruction, usually without a hearing to avoid delay; and will send (where practicable, by e-mail) the settled letter to the lead solicitor for transmission forthwith to the expert, and copy it to the other instructing parties for information.

Annex A

(drafted by the Family Justice Council)

Suggested questions in letters of instruction tochild mental health professional or paediatrician in Children Act 1989 proceedings

A The Child(ren)

1 Please describe the child(ren)'s current health, development and functioning (according to your area of expertise), and identify the nature of any significant changes which have occurred

- Behavioural
- Emotional
- Attachment organisation
- Social/peer/sibling relationships
- Cognitive/educational
- Physical
  - Growth, eating, sleep
  - Non-organic physical problems (including wetting and soiling)
  - Injuries
  - Paediatric conditions

2 Please comment on the likely explanation for/aetiology of the child(ren)'s problems/ difficulties/injuries

- History/experiences (including intrauterine influences, and abuse and neglect)
- Genetic/innate/developmental difficulties
- Paediatric/psychiatric disorders

3 Please provide a prognosis and risk if difficulties not addressed above.

4 Please describe the child(ren)'s needs in the light of the above

- Nature of care-giving
- Education
- Treatment

in the short and long term (subject, where appropriate, to further assessment later).

B The parents/primary carers

5 Please describe the factors and mechanisms which would explain the parents' (or primary carers) harmful or neglectful interactions with the child(ren) (if relevant).

6 What interventions have been tried and what has been the result?

7 Please assess the ability of the parents or primary carers to fulfil the child(ren)'s identified needs now.

8 What other assessments of the parents or primary carers are indicated?

- Adult mental health assessment
- Forensic risk assessment
- Physical assessment
- Cognitive assessment

9 What, if anything, is needed to assist the parents or primary carers now, within the child(ren)'s timescales and what is the prognosis for change?

- Parenting work
- Support
- Treatment/therapy

C Alternatives

10 Please consider the alternative possibilities for the fulfilment of the child(ren)'s needs

- What sort of placement
- Contact arrangements

Please consider the advantages, disadvantages and implications of each for the child(ren).

Suggested questions in letters of instruction to adult psychiatrists and applied psychologists in Children Act 1989 proceedings

1 Does the parent/adult have – whether in his/her history or presentation – a mental illness/disorder (including substance abuse) or other psychological/emotional difficulty and, if so, what is the diagnosis?

2 How do any/all of the above (and their current treatment if applicable) affect his/her functioning, including interpersonal relationships?

3 If the answer to Q1 is yes, are there any features of either the mental illness or psychological/emotional difficulty or personality disorder which could be associated with risk to others, based on the available evidence base (whether published studies or evidence from clinical experience)?

4 What are the experiences/antecedents/aetiology which would explain his/her difficulties, if any, (taking into account any available evidence base or other clinical experience)?

5 What treatment is indicated, what is its nature and the likely duration?

6 What is his/her capacity to engage in/partake of the treatment/therapy?

7 Are you able to indicate the prognosis for, time scales for achieving, and likely durability of, change?

8 What other factors might indicate positive change?

(It is assumed that this opinion will be based on collateral information as well as interviewing the adult).

Practice Direction 25D – Financial remedy proceedings and other family proceedings (except children proceedings) – the use of single joint experts and the process leading to expert evidence being put before the court

See also Part 25, Practice Direction 25A, Practice Direction 25B, Practice Direction 25C, Practice Direction 25E, Practice Direction 25F

This Practice Direction supplements FPR Part 25

Scope of this Practice Direction

1.1 This Practice Direction applies to financial remedy proceedings and other family proceedings except children proceedings and contains guidance on–

- (a) the use of single joint experts;
- (b) how to prepare for the hearing at which the court will consider whether to give permission for putting expert evidence (in any form) before the court including–
  - (i) preliminary enquiries of experts;
  - (ii) information to be given to the court before the hearing;
- (c) the letter of instruction to the expert.

Single joint experts

2.1 FPR 25.4 applies to a single joint expert ('SJE') in addition to an expert instructed by one party. This means that the court's permission is required to put expert evidence from an SJE (in any form) before the court. However, in family proceedings (except children proceedings) there is no requirement for the court's permission to be obtained before instructing an expert. Wherever possible, expert evidence should be obtained from a single joint expert instructed by both or all the parties ('SJE'). To that end, a party wishing to instruct an expert should first give the other party or parties a list of the names of one or more experts in the relevant speciality whom they consider suitable to be instructed.

2.2 Within 10 business days after receipt of the list of proposed experts, the other party or parties should indicate any objection to one or more of the named experts and, if so, supply the name(s) of one or more experts whom they consider suitable.

2.3 Each party should disclose whether they have already consulted any of the proposed experts about the issue(s) in question.

2.4 Where the parties cannot agree on the identity of the expert, each party should think carefully before instructing their own expert and seeking the permission of the court to put that expert evidence before it because of the costs implications. Disagreements about the use and identity of an expert may be better managed by the court in the context of an application for the court's permission to put the expert evidence before the court and for directions for the use of an SJE (see paragraph 2.6 below).

Agreement to instruct separate experts

2.5 If the parties agree to instruct separate experts and to seek the permission of the court to put the separate expert evidence before it–

(a) they should agree in advance that the reports will be disclosed; and
(b) the instructions to each expert should comply, so far as appropriate, with paragraphs 4.1 and 6.1 below (Letter of instruction).

Agreement to instruct an SJE

2.6 If there is agreement to instruct an SJE, before applying to the court for permission to put the expert evidence before it and directions for the use of an SJE, the parties should–

(a) so far as appropriate, comply with the guidance in paragraphs 3.3 (Preliminary enquiries of the expert) and paragraphs 3.11 and 3.12 below;
(b) receive the expert's confirmation in response to preliminary enquiries referred to in paragraph 8.1 of Practice Direction 25B;
(c) have agreed in what proportion the SJE's fee is to be shared between them (at least in the first instance) and when it is to be paid; and
(d) if applicable, have obtained agreement for public funding.

2.7 The instructions to the SJE should comply, so far as appropriate, with paragraphs 4.1 and 6.1 below (Letter of instruction).

The test for permission and preparation for the permission hearing

3.1 The test in FPR 25.4(3) which the court is to apply to determine whether permission should be given for expert evidence to be put before the court has been altered from one which refers to expert evidence being restricted by the court to that which is reasonably required to resolve the proceedings to one which refers to the expert evidence being in the opinion of the court necessary to assist the court to resolve the proceedings. The overriding objective of the FPR, which is to enable the court to deal with cases justly, having regard to any welfare issues involved, continues to apply when the court is making the decision whether to give permission. In addition, the rules (FPR 25.5(2)) now tell the court what factors it is to have particular regard to when deciding whether to give permission.

3.2 Paragraphs 3.3 to 3.12 below give guidance on how to prepare for the hearing at which the court will apply the test in FPR 25.4(3) and the factors in FPR 25.5(2) and decide whether to give permission for expert evidence to be put before the court. The purpose of the preparation is to ensure that the court has the information required to enable it to exercise its powers under FPR 25.4(2) and 25.5(2) in line with FPR 25.4(3).

Preliminary enquiries of the expert

3.3 In good time for the information requested to be available for the hearing at which the court will consider whether to give permission for expert evidence to be put before the court, the party or parties intending to instruct the expert shall approach the expert with the following information–

(a) the nature of the proceedings and the issues likely to require determination by the court;
(b) the issues in the proceedings to which the expert evidence is to relate;
(c) the questions about which the expert is to be asked to give an opinion and which relate to the issues in the case;

(d) whether permission is to be asked of the court for the use of another expert in the same or any related field (that is, to give an opinion on the same or related questions);
(e) the volume of reading which the expert will need to undertake;
(f) whether or not it will be necessary for the expert to conduct interviews and, if so, with whom;
(g) the likely timetable of legal steps;
(h) when the expert's report is likely to be required;
(i) whether and, if so, what date has been fixed by the court for any hearing at which the expert may be required to give evidence (in particular the Final Hearing); and whether it may be possible for the expert to give evidence by telephone conference or video link: see paragraphs 10.1 and 10.2 (Arrangements for experts to give evidence) of Practice Direction 25B;
(j) the possibility of making, through their instructing solicitors, representations to the court about being named or otherwise identified in any public judgment given by the court;
(k) whether the instructing party has public funding and the legal aid rates of payment which are applicable.

Expert's response to preliminary enquiries

3.4 In good time for the hearing at which the court will consider whether to give permission for expert evidence to be put before the court, the solicitors or party intending to instruct the expert must obtain the confirmations from the expert referred to in paragraph 8.1 of Practice Direction 25B. These confirmations include that the work is within the expert's expertise, the expert is available to do the work within the relevant timescale and the expert's costs.

3.5 Where parties cannot agree who should be the single joint expert before the hearing at which the court will consider whether to give permission for expert evidence to be put before the court, they should obtain the above confirmations in respect of all experts whom they intend to put to the court for the purposes of rule 25.11(2)(a) as candidates for the appointment.

The application for the court's permission to put expert evidence before the court

Timing and oral applications for the court's permission

3.6 An application for the court's permission to put expert evidence before the court should be made as soon as it becomes apparent that it is necessary to make it. FPR 25.6 makes provision about the time by which applications for the court's permission should be made.

3.7 Applications should, wherever possible, be made so that they are considered at any directions hearing or other hearing for which a date has been fixed or for which a date is about to be fixed. It should be noted that one application notice can be used by a party to make more than one application for an order or direction at a hearing held during the course of proceedings. An application for the court's permission to put expert evidence before the court may therefore be included in an application notice requesting other orders to be made at such a hearing.

3.8 Where a date for a hearing has been fixed, a party who wishes to make an application at that hearing but does not have sufficient time to file an application notice should as soon as possible inform the court (if possible in writing) and, if possible, the other parties of the nature of the application and the reason for it. The party should provide the court and the other party with as much as possible of the information referred to in FPR 25.7

and paragraph 3.11 below. That party should then make the application orally at the hearing. An oral application of this kind should be the exception and reserved for genuine cases where circumstances are such that it has only become apparent shortly before the hearing that an expert opinion is necessary.

3.9 In financial remedy proceedings, unless the court directs otherwise, parties must apply for permission to put expert evidence before the court as soon as possible and no later than the first appointment. The expectation is that the court will give directions extending the time by which permission should be obtained where there is good reason for parties to delay the decision whether to use expert evidence and make an application for the court's permission.

3.10 Examples of situations where the time for requesting permission to put expert evidence before the court is likely to be extended are where–

(a) a decision about the need for expert evidence cannot be made until replies to questionnaires in relation to Forms E have been fully considered; or
(b) valuations of property are agreed for the purposes of the Financial Dispute Resolution appointment but no agreement is reached to resolve the proceedings at that appointment and the court cannot make a consent order as mentioned in FPR 9.17(8). In these circumstances, it may become clear to a party that he or she will want to use expert valuations of property and an application for the court's permission for such valuation to be put before it may be made orally at the end of the appointment to avoid the need for a separate hearing about this issue. As with other oral applications, the party should provide the court and the other party with as much as possible of the information referred to in FPR 25.7 and paragraph 3.11 below. FPR 9.17(9) requires the court to give directions for the future course of the proceedings where it has not made a consent order including, where appropriate, the filing of evidence.

The application

3.11 In addition to the matters specified in FPR 25.7(2)(a), an application for the court's permission to put expert evidence before the court must state–

(a) the discipline, qualifications and expertise of the expert (by way of C.V. where possible);
(b) the expert's availability to undertake the work;
(c) the timetable for the report;
(d) the responsibility for instruction;
(e) whether the expert evidence can properly be obtained by only one party;
(f) why the expert evidence proposed cannot properly be given by an expert already instructed in the proceedings;
(g) the likely cost of the report on an hourly or other charging basis:
(h) the proposed apportionment (at least in the first instance) of any jointly instructed expert's fee; when it is to be paid; and, if applicable, whether public funding has been approved.

The draft order to be attached to the application for the court's permission

3.12 FPR 25.7(2)(b) provides that a draft of the order giving the court's permission to put expert evidence before the court is to be attached to the application for the court's permission. That draft order must set out the following matters–

(a) the issues in the proceedings to which the expert evidence is to relate;
(b) the party who is to be responsible for drafting the letter of instruction and providing the documents to the expert;

(c) the timetable within which the report is to be prepared, filed and served;
(d) the disclosure of the report to the parties and to any other expert;
(e) the organisation of, preparation for and conduct of any experts' discussion (see Practice Direction 25E – Discussions between Experts in Family Proceedings);
(f) the preparation of a statement of agreement and disagreement by the experts following an experts' discussion;
(g) making available to the court at an early opportunity the expert reports in electronic form;
(h) the attendance of the expert at court to give oral evidence (alternatively, the expert giving his or her evidence in writing or remotely by video link), whether at or for the Final Hearing or another hearing; unless agreement about the opinions given by the expert is reached by a date specified by the court prior to the hearing at which the expert is to give oral evidence.

Letter of instruction

4.1 The party responsible for instructing the expert shall, within 5 business days after the permission hearing, prepare (in agreement with the other parties where appropriate), file and serve a letter of instruction to the expert which shall–

(a) set out the context in which the expert's opinion is sought (including any ethnic, cultural, religious or linguistic contexts);
(b) set out the questions which thee xpert is required to answer and ensuring that they–
   (i) are within the ambit of the expert's area of expertise;
   (ii) do not contain unnecessary or irrelevant detail;
   (iii) are kept to a manageable number and are clear, focused and direct; and
   (iv) reflect what the expert has been requested to do by the court;
(c) list the documentation provided,or provide for the expert an indexed and paginated bundle which shall include–
   (i) an agreed list of essential reading; and
   (ii) a copy of this Practice Direction and Practice Directions 25B, 25E and where appropriate Practice Direction 15B;
(d) identify any materials provided to the expert which have not been produced either as original medical (or other professional) records or in response to an instruction from a party, and state the source of that material (such materials may contain an assumption as to the standard of proof, the admissibility or otherwise of hearsay evidence, and other important procedural and substantive questions relating to the different purposes of other enquiries);
(e) identify all requests to third parties for disclosure and their responses in order to avoid partial disclosure, which tends only to prove a case rather than give full and frank information;
(f) identify the relevant people concerned with the proceedings and inform the expert of his or her right to talk to them provided that an accurate record is made of the discussions;
(g) identify any other expert instructed in the proceedings and advise the expert of their right to talk to the other experts provided that an accurate record is made of the discussions;
(h) subject to any public funding requirement for prior authority, define the contractual basis upon which the expert is retained and in particular the funding mechanism including how much the expert will be paid (an hourly rate and overall estimate should already have been obtained), when the expert

will be paid, and what limitation there might be on the amount the expert can charge for the work which they will have to do. In cases where the parties are publicly funded, there may also be a brief explanation of the costs and expenses excluded from public funding by Funding Code criterion 1.3 and the detailed assessment process.

Adult who is a protected party

5.1 Where the adult is a protected party, that party's representative shall be involved in any instruction of an expert, including the instruction of an expert to assess whether the adult, although a protected party, is competent to give evidence (see Practice Direction 15B – Adults Who May Be Protected Parties and Children Who May Become Protected Parties in Family Proceedings).

Asking the court to settle the letter of instruction to a single joint expert

6.1 Where possible, the written request for the court to consider the letter of instruction referred to in rule 25.12(2) should be set out in an e-mail to the court and copied by e-mail to the other instructing parties. The request should be sent to the relevant court or (by prior arrangement only) directly to the judge dealing with the proceedings. Where a legal adviser has been appointed as the case manager, the request should also be sent to the appointed legal adviser. The court will settle the letter of instruction, usually without a hearing to avoid delay; and will send (where practicable, by e-mail) the settled letter to the party responsible for instructing the expert for transmission forthwith to the expert, and copy it to the other instructing parties for information.

Practice Direction 25E – Discussions between experts in family proceedings

See also Part 25, Practice Direction 25A, Practice Direction 25B, Practice Direction 25C, Practice Direction 25D, Practice Direction 25F

This Practice Direction supplements FPR Part 25

Scope

1.1 This Practice Direction supports FPR25.16 by providing details about how and when experts discussions are to be arranged, their purpose and content. This Practice Direction applies to children proceedings and all other family proceedings.

Experts' discussion or meeting: purpose

2.1 In accordance with FPR 25.16, the court may, at any stage, direct a discussion between experts for the purpose outlined in paragraph (1) of that rule. FPR 25.16(2) provides that the court may specify the issues which the experts must discuss. The expectation is that those issues will include–

(a) the reasons for disagreement on any expert question and what, if any, action needs to be taken to resolve any outstanding disagreement or question;
(b) an explanation of existing evidence or additional evidence in order to assist the court to determine the issues.

One of the aims of specifying the issues for discussion is to limit, wherever possible, the need for the experts to attend court to give oral evidence.

Experts' discussion or meeting: arrangements

3.1 Subject to the directions given by the court under FPR25.16, the solicitor or other professional who is given the responsibility by the court ('the nominated professional') shall within 15 business days after the experts' reports have been filed and copied to the other parties, make arrangements for the experts to have discussions. Subject to any specification by the court of the issues which experts must discuss under FPR 25.16(2), the following matters should be considered as appropriate–

(a) where permission has been given for the instruction of experts from different disciplines, a global discussion may be held relating to those questions that concern all or most of them;

(b) separate discussions may have to be held among experts from the same or related disciplines, but care should be taken to ensure that the discussions complement each other so that related questions are discussed by all relevant experts;

(c) 5 business days prior to a discussion or meeting, the nominated professional should formulate an agenda including a list of questions for consideration. The agenda should, subject always to the provisions of FPR 25.16(1), focus on those questions which are intended to clarify areas of agreement or disagreement.

Questions which repeat questions asked in the court order giving permission for an expert to be instructed or expert evidence to be put before the court or the letter of instruction or which seek to rehearse cross-examination in advance of the hearing should be rejected as likely to defeat the purpose of the meeting. The agenda may usefully take the form of a list of questions to be circulated among the other parties in advance and should comprise all questions that each party wishes the experts to consider.

The agenda and list of questions should be sent to each of the experts not later than 2 business days before the discussion;

(d) the nominated professional may exercise his or her discretion to accept further questions after the agenda with the list of questions has been circulated to the parties. Only in exceptional circumstances should questions be added to the agenda within the 2-day period before the meeting. Under no circumstances should any question received on the day of or during the meeting be accepted. This does not preclude questions arising during the meeting for the purposes of clarification. Strictness in this regard is vital, for adequate notice of the questions enables the parties to identify and isolate the expert issues in the case before the meeting so that the experts' discussion at the meeting can concentrate on those issues;

(e) the discussion should be chaired by the nominated professional. A minute must be taken of the questions answered by the experts. Where the court has given a direction under FPR 25.16(3) and subject to that direction, a Statement of Agreement and Disagreement must be prepared which should be agreed and signed by each of the experts who participated in the discussion. In accordance with FPR25.16(3) the statement must contain a summary of the experts' reasons for disagreeing. The statement should be served and filed not later than 5 business days after the discussion has taken place;

(f) in each case, whether some or all of the experts participate by telephone conference or video link to ensure that minimum disruption is caused to professional schedules and that costs are minimised.

Meetings or conferences attended by a jointly instructed expert

4.1 Jointly instructed experts should not attend any meeting or conference which is not a joint one, unless all the parties have agreed in writing or the court has directed that such a meeting may be held, and it is agreed or directed who is to pay the expert's fees for the meeting or conference. Any meeting or conference attended by a jointly instructed expert should be proportionate to the case.

(Practice Direction 25C, paragraphs 2.1 to 2.7 deals generally with single joint experts in children proceedings and Practice Direction 25D paragraphs 2.1 to 2.7 deals with single joint experts in relation to other family proceedings).

Court-directed meetings involving experts in public law Children Act cases

5.1 In public law Children Act proceedings, where the court gives a direction that a meeting shall take place between the local authority and any relevant named experts for the purpose of providing assistance to the local authority in the formulation of plans and proposals for the child, the meeting shall be arranged, chaired and minuted in accordance with the directions given by the court.

Practice Direction 25F – Assessor in family proceedings

See also Part 25, Practice Direction 25A, Practice Direction 25B, Practice Direction 25C, Practice Direction 25D, Practice Direction 25E,

This Practice Direction supplements FPR Part 25

Scope of this Practice Direction

1.1 This Practice Direction applies to the appointment of assessors in family proceedings in England and Wales.

Appointment of assessors in family proceedings

2.1 The power to appoint one or more assessors to assist the court is conferred by section 70(1) of the Senior Courts Act 1981, which applies to the family court via section 31E(1) of the Matrimonial and Family Proceedings Act 1984 (and section 31J(e) of that Act confirms that this is the case). In practice, these powers have been used in appeals from a district judge or costs judge in costs assessment proceedings – although, in principle, the statutory powers permit one or more assessors to be appointed in any family proceedings where the High Court or the family court sees fit.

2.2 Not less than 21 days before making any such appointment, the court will notify each party in writing of the name of the proposed assessor, of the matter in respect of which the assistance of the assessor will be sought and of the qualifications of the assessor to give that assistance.

2.3 Any party may object to the proposed appointment, either personally or in respect of the proposed assessor's qualifications.

2.4 Any such objection must be made in writing and filed and served within 7 business days of receipt of the notification from the court of the proposed appointment, and will be taken into account by the court in deciding whether or not to make the appointment.

Practice Direction 25G – Toxicology test evidence

This practice direction supplements Part 25 of the Family Procedure Rules 2010

1 This practice direction applies whenever a person seeks to put before the court, or to instruct a person to provide, expert evidence in the form of or based on toxicology testing

carried out on a person with a view to establishing whether such testing provides evidence of the abuse of drugs or alcohol.

2 The court will not give permission to put the evidence before the court, or as the case may be to instruct the person, unless the condition in paragraph 3 or 4 is met.

3 Where the testing has not been carried out and a person is seeking to instruct a person to carry out testing or provide evidence on the basis of such testing, the laboratory which is to carry out the testing must at the time of the application for permission to instruct be accredited to—

(a) International Organisation for Standardisation ISO/IEC 17025: 2017 General Requirements for the competence of testing and calibration laboratories; or
(b) International Organisation for Standardisation ISO 15189: Medical laboratories – Requirements for quality and competence.

4 Where the testing has been carried out and a person is seeking to put the evidence before the court—

(a) the laboratory which carried out the testing must at the time of the testing have been accredited to—
 (i) International Organisation for Standardisation ISO/IEC 17025: 2017 General Requirements for the competence of testing and calibration laboratories; or
 (ii) International Organisation for Standardisation ISO 15189: Medical laboratories – Requirements for quality and competence; or
(b) the court must be satisfied that there are exceptional circumstances justifying giving permission to put the evidence before the court.

PART 26
CHANGE OF SOLICITOR

26.1 Solicitor acting for a party

Where the address for service of a party is the business address of that party's solicitor, the solicitor will be considered to be acting for that party until the provisions of this Part have been complied with.

(Part 6 contains provisions about the address for service.)

26.2 Change of solicitor – duty to give notice

(1) This rule applies where—

(a) a party for whom a solicitor is acting wants to change solicitor;
(b) a party, after having conducted the application in person, appoints a solicitor to act for that party (except where the solicitor is appointed only to act as an advocate for a hearing); or
(c) a party, after having conducted the application by a solicitor, intends to act in person.

(2) Where this rule applies, the party or the party's solicitor (where one is acting) must—

(a) serve notice of the change on—
 (i) every other party; and
 (ii) where paragraph (1)(a) or (c) applies, the former solicitor; and
(b) file notice of the change.

(3) Except where a serial number has been assigned under rule 14.2 or the name or address of a party is not being revealed in accordance with rule 29.1, the notice must state the party's new address for service.

(4) The notice filed at court must state that notice has been served as required by paragraph (2)(a) or, where rule 2.4 applies, in accordance with the court's directions given under that rule.

(5) Subject to paragraph (6), where a party has changed solicitor or intends to act in person, the former solicitor will be considered to be the party's solicitor unless and until—

(a) notice is filed and served in accordance with paragraph (2)(a) or, where rule 2.4 applies, in accordance with the court's directions given under that rule; or

(b) the court makes an order under rule 26.3 and the order is served as required by paragraph (3) of that rule.

(6) Where the certificate of a [legally aided person][1] (in this rule 'C') [is revoked or withdrawn][1]—

(a) the solicitor who acted for C will cease to be the solicitor acting in the case as soon as the retainer is determined under [regulation 24 or 41 of the Civil Legal Aid (Procedure) Regulations 2012][1]; and

(b) if C wishes to continue—

(i) where C appoints a solicitor to act on C's behalf, paragraph (2) will apply as if C had previously conducted the application in person; and

(ii) where C wants to act in person, C must give an address for service, in accordance with rule 6.26, unless the court directs otherwise.

(7) In this rule—

…[2]

'certificate' means a certificate issued [under the Civil Legal Aid (Procedure) Regulations 2012][1]; and

…[2]

['legally aided person' means a person to whom civil legal services (within the meaning of Part 1 of the Legal Aid, Sentencing and Punishment of Offenders Act 2012) have been made available under arrangements made for the purposes of that Part of that Act).][3]

Amendment

1 Substituted by the Legal Aid, Sentencing and Punishment of Offenders Act 2012 (Consequential, Transitional and Saving Provisions) Regulations 2013, SI 2013/534, reg 14(1), Schedule, para 22(c)(i), (ii), (iii), (iv).

2 Repealed by the Legal Aid, Sentencing and Punishment of Offenders Act 2012 (Consequential, Transitional and Saving Provisions) Regulations 2013, SI 2013/534, reg 14(1), Schedule, para 22(c)(v).

3 Inserted by the Legal Aid, Sentencing and Punishment of Offenders Act 2012 (Consequential, Transitional and Saving Provisions) Regulations 2013, SI 2013/534, reg 14(1), Schedule, para 22(c)(v).

26.3 Order that a solicitor has ceased to act

(1) A solicitor may apply for an order declaring that that solicitor has ceased to be the solicitor acting for—

(a) a party; or

(b) a children's guardian.

(2) Where an application is made under this rule—

(a) notice of the application must be given to the party, or children's guardian, for whom the solicitor is acting, unless the court directs otherwise; and
(b) the application must be supported by evidence.

(3) Where the court makes an order declaring that a solicitor has ceased to act, a court officer will serve a copy of the order on—

(a) every party to the proceedings; and
(b) where applicable, a children's guardian.

26.4 Removal of solicitor who has ceased to act on application of another party

(1) Where—

(a) a solicitor who has acted for a party—
  (i) has died;
  (ii) has become bankrupt;
  (iii) has ceased to practise; or
  (iv) cannot be found; and
(b) the party has not given notice of a change of solicitor or notice of intention to act in person as required by rule 26.2(2),

any other party may apply for an order declaring that the solicitor has ceased to be the solicitor acting for the other party in the case.

(2) Where an application is made under this rule, notice of the application must be given to the party to whose solicitor the application relates unless the court directs otherwise.

(3) Where the court makes an order made under this rule, a court officer will serve a copy of the order on every other party to the proceedings.

Practice Direction 26A – Change of solicitor

See also Part 26

This Practice Direction supplements FPR Part 26

Solicitor acting for a party

1.1 Rule 26.1 states that where the address for service of a party is the business address of his solicitor, the solicitor will be considered to be acting for that party until the provisions of Part 26 have been complied with.

1.2 Subject to rule 26.2(6) (where the certificate of a legally aided person or assisted person is revoked or withdrawn), where a party has changed his solicitor or intends to act in person, the former solicitor will be considered to be the party's solicitor unless or until–

(a) a notice of the change is–
  (i) served on every other party (see rule 26.2(2)(a)); and
  (ii) filed with the court (see rule 26.2(2)(b)); or
(b) the court makes an order under rule 26.3 and the order is served on the former solicitor and every other party in accordance with directions of the court (see rule 26.2(5)).

1.3 A solicitor appointed to represent a party only as an advocate at a hearing will not be considered to be acting for that party within the meaning of Part 26.

Notice of change of solicitor

2.1 Rule 26.2(1) sets out the circumstances following which a notice of the change must be filed and served.

2.2 A notice of the change giving the last known address of the former assisted person must also be filed and served on every party where, under rule 26.2(6)–

(a) the certificate of a legally aided person or assisted person is revoked or withdrawn; and

(b) the legally aided person or the assisted person wishes either to act in person or appoint another solicitor to act on his behalf.

2.3 Where a solicitor has given notice that he or she acts for a child directly, and an officer of the Service, a Welsh family proceedings officer or the Official Solicitor continues with the permission of the court to have legal representation, notice of that legal representation must be given to the court.

2.4 In addition, where a party or solicitor changes his address for service, a notice of that change should be filed and served on every party.

2.5 A party who, having conducted an application by a solicitor, intends to act in person must give in his notice an address for service that is within the United Kingdom (see rule 6.26).

2.6 The form giving notice of any change is referred to in Practice Direction 5A. The notice should be filed in the court office in which the application is proceeding.

Application for an order that a solicitor has ceased to act

3.1 A solicitor may apply under rule 26.3 for an order declaring that he has ceased to be the solicitor acting for a party.

3.2 The application should be made in accordance with Part 18 and must be supported by evidence (see Part 18 and the Practice Direction 18A). Unless the court directs otherwise the application notice must be served on the party (see rule 26.3(2)).

3.3 An order made under rule 26.3 will be served on every party by the court officer and takes effect when it is served.

Application by another party to remove a solicitor

4.1 Rule 26.4 sets out circumstances in which any other party may apply for an order declaring that a solicitor has ceased to be the solicitor acting for another party in the proceedings.

4.2 The application should be made in accordance with Part 18 and must be supported by evidence. Unless the court directs otherwise the application notice must be served on the party to whose solicitor the application relates.

4.3 An order made under rule 26.4 will be served on every party by the court officer.

New address for service where order made under rules 26.3 or 26.4

5.1 Where the court has made an order under rule 26.3 that a solicitor has ceased to act or under rule 26.4 declaring that a solicitor has ceased to be the solicitor for a party, the party for whom the solicitor was acting must give a new address for service to comply with rule 6.26.

(Rule 6.26 provides that a party must give an address for service within the United Kingdom, or where a solicitor is acting for a party, an address for service either in the United Kingdom or any other EEA state, at which that party resides or carries on business. Where that party does not have such an address, an address within the United Kingdom must generally be given (see rule 6.26(3) and (4)).

(Until such time as a new address for service is given directions may be needed under rule 6.19.)

PART 27
HEARINGS AND DIRECTIONS APPOINTMENTS

27.1 Application of this Part

This Part is subject to any enactment, any provision in these rules or a practice direction.

> (Rule 27.4(7) makes additional provision in relation to requirements to stay proceedings where the respondent does not appear and a relevant European regulation or international convention applies)

27.2 Reasons for a decision[: proceedings before a lay justice or justices][1]

(1) This rule applies to proceedings [in the family court before a lay justice or justices][1].

(2) After a hearing, the court will make its decision as soon as is practicable.

(3) The court must give written reasons for its decision.

(4) Paragraphs (5) and (6) apply where the functions of the court are being performed by—

(a) two or three lay justices; or
(b) by a single lay justice in accordance with these rules and Practice Direction 2A.

(5) The [justices' legal adviser][2] must, before the court makes an order or refuses an application or request, make notes of—

(a) the names of the [lay][3] justice or justices constituting the court by which the decision is made; and
(b) in consultation with the [lay][3] justice or justices, the reasons for the court's decision.

(6) The [justices' legal adviser][2] must make a written record of the reasons for the court's decision.

(7) When making an order or refusing an application, the court, or one of the [lay][3] justices constituting the court by which the decision is made, will announce its decision and—

(a) the reasons for that decision; or
(b) a short explanation of that decision.

(8) Subject to any other rule or practice direction, the court officer will supply a copy of the order and the reasons for the court's decision to the persons referred to in paragraph (9)—

(a) by close of business on the day when the court announces its decision; or
(b) where that time is not practicable and the proceedings are on notice, no later than 72 hours from the time when the court announced its decision.

(9) The persons referred to in paragraph (8) are—

- (a) the parties (unless the court directs otherwise);
- (b) any person who has actual care of a child who is the subject of proceedings, or who had such care immediately prior to the making of the order;
- (c) in the case of an emergency protection order and a recovery order, the local authority in whose area the child lives or is found;
- (d) in proceedings to which Part 14 applies—
  - (i) an adoption agency or local authority which has prepared a report on the suitability of the applicant to adopt a child;
  - (ii) a local authority which has prepared a report on the placement of the child for adoption;
- (e) any other person who has requested a copy if the court is satisfied that it is required in connection with an appeal or possible appeal.

(10) …[4]

(Rule 12.16(5) provides for the applicant to serve a section 8 order and an order in emergency proceedings made without notice within 48 hours after the making of the order. Rule 10.6(1) provides for the applicant to serve the order in proceedings under Part 4 of the 1996 Act. Rule 4.1(3)(a) permits the court to extend or shorten the time limit for compliance with any rule. Rule 6.33 provides for other persons to be supplied with copy documents under paragraph (8).)

Amendment

1 Substituted by the Family Procedure (Amendment No 2) Rules 2014, SI 2014/667, rr 2, 19(a), (b).
2 Substituted by the Family Procedure (Amendment) Rules 2020, SI 2020/135, rr 2, 27.
3 Inserted by the Family Procedure (Amendment No 2) Rules 2014, SI 2014/667, rr 2, 19(c), (d).
4 Repealed by the Family Procedure (Amendment No 2) Rules 2014, SI 2014/667, rr 2, 19(e).

27.3 Attendance at hearing or directions appointment

Unless the court directs otherwise, a party shall attend a hearing or directions appointment of which that party has been given notice.

27.4 Proceedings in the absence of a party

(1) Proceedings or any part of them shall take place in the absence of any party, including a party who is a child, if—

- (a) the court considers it in the interests of the party, having regard to the matters to be discussed or the evidence likely to be given; and
- (b) the party is represented by a children's guardian or solicitor,

and when considering the interests of a child under sub-paragraph (a) the court shall give the children's guardian, the solicitor for the child and, if of sufficient understanding and the court thinks it appropriate, the child, an opportunity to make representations.

(2) Subject to paragraph (3), where at the time and place appointed for a hearing or directions appointment the applicant appears but one or more of the respondents do not, the court may proceed with the hearing or appointment.

(3) The court shall not begin to hear an application in the absence of a respondent unless—

- (a) it is proved to the satisfaction of the court that the respondent received reasonable notice of the date of the hearing; or
- (b) the court is satisfied that the circumstances of the case justify proceeding with the hearing.

(4) Where, at the time and place appointed for a hearing or directions appointment, one or more of the respondents appear but the applicant does not, the court may refuse the application or, if sufficient evidence has previously been received, proceed in the absence of the applicant.

(5) Where, at the time and place appointed for a hearing or directions appointment, neither the applicant nor any respondent appears, the court may refuse the application.

(6) Paragraphs (2) to (5) do not apply to a hearing to which paragraphs (5) to (8) of rule 12.14 do not apply by virtue of paragraph (9) of that rule.

(7) Nothing in this rule affects any provision of [an][1] international convention by which the United Kingdom is bound which requires a court to stay proceedings where a respondent in another State has not been adequately served with proceedings in accordance with the requirements of that …[2] convention.

Amendment

1 Substituted by the Family Procedure Rules 2010 and Court of Protection Rules 2017 (Amendment) (EU Exit) Regulations 2019, SI 2019/517, rr 2, 17(1), (2)(a).
2 Repealed by the Family Procedure Rules 2010 and Court of Protection Rules 2017 (Amendment) (EU Exit) Regulations 2019, SI 2019/517, rr 2, 17(1), (2)(b).

27.5 Application to set aside judgment or order following failure to attend

(1) Where a party does not attend a hearing or directions appointment and the court gives judgment or makes an order against him, the party who failed to attend may apply for the judgment or order to be set aside[(GL)].

(2) An application under paragraph (1) must be supported by evidence.

(3) Where an application is made under paragraph (1), the court may grant the application only if the applicant—

(a) acted promptly on finding out that the court had exercised its power to enter judgment or make an order against the applicant;
(b) had a good reason for not attending the hearing or directions appointment; and
(c) has a reasonable prospect of success at the hearing or directions appointment.

(4) …[1]

Amendment

1 Repealed by the Family Procedure (Amendment No 3) Rules 2013, SI 2013/3204, rr 2, 71.

27.6 Court bundles and place of filing of documents and bundles

(1) The provisions of Practice Direction 27A must be followed for the preparation of court bundles and for other related matters in respect of hearings and directions appointments.

(2) …[1]

(3) …[1]

…[1]

Amendment

1 Repealed by the Family Procedure (Amendment No 3) Rules 2013, SI 2013/3204, rr 2, 71.

27.7 Representation of companies or other corporations

A company or other corporation may be represented at a hearing or directions appointment by an employee if—

(a) the employee has been authorised by the company or corporation to appear at the hearing or directions appointment on its behalf; and
(b) the court gives permission.

27.8 Impounded documents

(1) Documents impounded by order of the court must not be released from the custody of the court except in compliance with—

(a) a court order; or
(b) a written request made by a Law Officer or the Director of Public Prosecutions.

(2) A document released from the custody of the court under paragraph (1)(b) must be released into the custody of the person who requested it.

(3) Documents impounded by order of the court, while in the custody of the court, may not be inspected except by a person authorised to do so by a court order.

[27.9 Recording, transcription and informal notes of proceedings

(1) At any hearing, the proceedings will be tape recorded or digitally recorded unless the court directs otherwise.

(2) No party or member of the public may use unofficial recording equipment in any court without the permission of the court. (To do so without permission constitutes a contempt of court under section 9 of the Contempt of Court Act 1981.)

(3) Unless the court directs otherwise, a person to whom paragraph (4) applies may require a transcript of the recording of any hearing in proceedings to be supplied to them, upon payment of the charges authorised by any scheme in force for the making of the recording or the transcript.

(4) This paragraph applies to—

(a) a party to the proceedings;
(b) the Queen's Proctor; and
(c) where a declaration of parentage has been made under section 55A of the 1986 Act, the Registrar General.

(5) A person to whom paragraph (4) does not apply may be provided with a transcript of the recording of any hearing—

(a) with the permission of the court; and
(b) upon payment of the charges authorised by any scheme in force for the making of the recording or the transcript.

(6) At any hearing, the court may give appropriate directions to assist a party, in particular one who is or has been or may become unrepresented, for the compilation and sharing of a note or other informal record of the proceedings made by another party.][1]

Amendment

1 Substituted by the Family Procedure (Amendment) Rules 2020, SI 2020/135, rr 2, 28.

27.10 Hearings in private

(1) Proceedings to which these rules apply will be held in private, except—

(a) where these rules or any other enactment provide otherwise;
(b) subject to any enactment, where the court directs otherwise.

(2) For the purposes of these rules, a reference to proceedings held 'in private' means proceedings at which the general public have no right to be present.

27.11 Attendance at private hearings

(1) This rule applies when proceedings are held in private, except in relation to—

(a) hearings conducted for the purpose of judicially assisted conciliation or negotiation;
(b) proceedings to which the following provisions apply—
(i) Part 13 (proceedings under section 54 [or section 54A][1] of the Human Fertilisation and Embryology Act 2008);
(ii) Part 14 (procedure for applications in adoption, placement and related proceedings); and
(iii) any proceedings identified in a practice direction as being excepted from this rule.

(2) When this rule applies, no person shall be present during any hearing other than—

(a) an officer of the court;
(b) a party to the proceedings;
(c) a litigation friend for any party, or legal representative instructed to act on that party's behalf;
(d) an officer of the service or Welsh family proceedings officer;
(e) a witness;
(f) duly accredited representatives of news gathering and reporting organisations; …[2]
[(ff) a duly authorised lawyer attending for journalistic, research or public legal educational purposes; and][3]
(g) any other person whom the court permits to be present.

(3) At any stage of the proceedings the court may direct that persons within paragraph (2)(f) [and (ff)][3] shall not attend the proceedings or any part of them, where satisfied that—

(a) this is necessary—
(i) in the interests of any child concerned in, or connected with, the proceedings;
(ii) for the safety or protection of a party, a witness in the proceedings, or a person connected with such a party or witness; or
(iii) for the orderly conduct of the proceedings; or
(b) justice will otherwise be impeded or prejudiced.

(4) The court may exercise the power in paragraph (3) of its own initiative or pursuant to representations made by any of the persons listed in paragraph (5), and in either case having given to any person within paragraph (2)(f) [or (ff)][3] who is in attendance an opportunity to make representations.

(5) At any stage of the proceedings, the following persons may make representations to the court regarding restricting the attendance of persons within paragraph (2)(f) [and (ff)][3] in accordance with paragraph (3)—

(a) a party to the proceedings;
(b) any witness in the proceedings;
(c) where appointed, any children's guardian;
(d) where appointed, an officer of the service or Welsh family proceedings officer, on behalf of the child the subject of the proceedings;
(e) the child, if of sufficient age and understanding.

(6) This rule does not affect any power of the court to direct that witnesses shall be excluded until they are called for examination.

[(7) In this rule—

'duly accredited' refers to accreditation in accordance with any administrative scheme for the time being approved for the purposes of this rule by the Lord Chancellor; and

'duly authorised lawyer' means a person who meets the criteria specified in Practice Direction 27B.][4]

Amendment

1 Inserted by the Human Fertilisation and Embryology Act 2008 (Remedial) Order 2018, SI 2018/1413, art 3(2), Sch 2, para 4(1), (7).
2 Repealed by the Family Procedure (Amendment No 2) Rules 2021, SI 2021/875, rr 2, 10(a)(i).
3 Inserted by the Family Procedure (Amendment No 2) Rules 2021, SI 2021/875, rr 2, 10(a)(ii), (b), (c).
4 Substituted by the Family Procedure (Amendment No 2) Rules 2021, SI 2021/875, rr 2, 10(d).

Practice Direction 27A – Family proceedings: court bundles (universal practice to be applied in the High Court and Family Court)

See also Part 27, Practice Direction 27B

This Practice Direction supplements FPR Part 27

1.1 The President of the Family Division has issued this practice direction to achieve consistency across the country in the Family Court and the Family Division of the High Court in the preparation of court bundles and in respect of other related matters.

Application of the practice direction

2.1 Except as specified in paragraph 2.4, subject to specific directions given in any particular case and, in relation to electronic bundles, subject to such directions in relation to local arrangements ('the local arrangements') as have been specified by the designated family judge for the relevant area with the agreement of the President of the Family Division, the following practice applies to:

(a) all hearings before a judge sitting in the Family Division of the High Court wherever the court may be sitting; and
(b) all hearings in the Family Court.

2.2 'Hearing' includes all appearances before the court, whether with or without notice to other parties, whether at first instance or (subject to paragraph 5.2A.3) on appeal and whether for directions or for substantive relief.

2.3 This practice direction applies whether a bundle is being lodged for the first time or is being re-lodged for a further hearing (see paragraph 9.2).

2.4 This practice direction does not apply to the hearing of any urgent application if and to the extent that it is impossible to comply with it.

2.5 This practice direction applies whether the bundle is prepared and presented in paper or in electronic format. In relation to a hearing before a High Court Judge an electronic bundle may be used with the permission of the judge and in accordance with directions given by the judge. In relation to all other hearings an electronic bundle may be used only -

(a) in such cases or classes of case as have been approved by the designated family judge for the relevant area with the agreement of the President of the Family Division; and

(b) in accordance with the local arrangements.

2.6 In this practice direction, the term 'lodged with the Court' and any comparable expression in respect of an electronic bundle means making the electronic bundle available to the Court or Judge (and, where required, to the other parties) in accordance with the local arrangements.

Responsibility for the preparation of the bundle

3.1 A bundle for the use of the court at the hearing shall be provided by the party in the position of applicant at the hearing (or, if there are cross-applications, by the party whose application was first in time) or, if that person is a litigant in person, by the first listed respondent who is not a litigant in person. Where all the parties are litigants in person none of them shall, unless the court otherwise directs, be obliged to provide a bundle, but any bundle which they choose to lodge must be prepared and lodged so as to comply with this practice direction.

3.2 The party preparing the bundle shall paginate it using Arabic numbering throughout. If possible the contents of the bundle shall be agreed by all parties.

Contents of the bundle

4.1 The bundle shall contain copies of only those documents which are relevant to the hearing and which it is necessary for the court to read or which will actually be referred to during the hearing. In particular, copies of the following classes of documents must not be included in the bundle unless specifically directed by the court:

(a) correspondence (including letters of instruction to experts);

(b) medical records (including hospital, GP and health visitor records);

(c) bank and credit card statements and other financial records;

(d) notes of contact visits;

(e) foster carer logs;

(f) social services files (with the exception of any assessment being relied on by any of the parties);

(g) police disclosure.

This does not prevent the inclusion in the bundle of specific documents which it is necessary for the court to read or which will actually be referred to during the hearing.

4.2 The documents in the bundle shall be arranged in chronological order from the front of the bundle, paginated individually and consecutively (starting with page 1 and using Arabic numbering throughout), indexed and divided into separate sections (each section being separately paginated) as follows:

(a) preliminary documents (see paragraph 4.3) and any other case management documents required by any other practice direction;

(b) applications and orders;

(c) statements and affidavits (which must be dated in the top right corner of the front page) but without exhibiting or duplicating documents referred to in para 4.1;
(d) care plans (where appropriate);
(e) experts' reports and other reports (including those of a guardian, children's guardian or litigation friend); and
(f) other documents, divided into further sections as may be appropriate.

All statements, affidavits, care plans, experts' reports and other reports included in the bundle must be copies of originals which have been signed and dated.

4.3 At the commencement of the bundle there shall be inserted the following documents (the preliminary documents):

(a) an up to date case summary of the background to the hearing confined to those matters which are relevant to the hearing and the management of the case and limited, if practicable, to four A4 pages;
(b) a statement of the issue or issues to be determined (1) at that hearing and (2) at the final hearing;
(c) a position statement by each party including a summary of the order or directions sought by that party (1) at that hearing and (2) at the final hearing;
(d) an up to date chronology, if it is a final hearing or if the summary under (a) is insufficient, each entry being limited, if practicable, to one sentence and cross-referenced to the relevant page(s) in the bundle;
(e) skeleton arguments, if appropriate;
(f) a list of essential reading for that hearing; and
(g) the time estimate (see paragraph 10.1).

4.3A.1 Copies of all authorities relied on must be contained in a separate composite bundle agreed between the advocates. Unless the court has specifically directed otherwise, being satisfied that such direction is necessary to enable the proceedings to be disposed of justly, the bundle shall not contain more than 10 authorities. Where a case is reported in a law report which contains a headnote, such a report shall be used and transcripts (including transcripts on BAILII) shall not be used. Where the bundle is in electronic format an appropriate hyperlink to each authority should be provided.

4.3A.2 Attention is drawn to paragraph 6 of Practice Direction (Citation of Authorities) [2001] 1 WLR 1001 and to Practice Direction (Citation of Authorities) [2012] 1 WLR 780 (both set out in The Family Court Practice) which must be complied with. The reference to 'county court cases' in para 6.1 of the first practice direction should be read as including family court cases decided by a judge other than a judge of High Court judge level. Therefore, a judgment on an application attended by one party only, or on an application for permission to appeal, or that only decides that the application is arguable, or by the county court, or in the family court of a judge other than a judge of High Court judge level, may not be cited or included in the bundle of authorities unless either (i) the judgment clearly indicates that it purports to establish a new principle or to extend the present law or (ii) the court for good reason has specifically directed otherwise.

4.4 Each of the preliminary documents shall be as short and succinct as possible and shall state on the front page immediately below the heading the date when it was prepared and the date of the hearing for which it was prepared. Where proceedings relating to a child are being heard by magistrates the summary of the background shall be prepared in anonymised form, omitting the names and identifying information of every person referred to other than the parties' legal representatives, and stating the number of pages contained in the bundle. Identifying information can be contained in all other preliminary documents.

4.5 The summary of the background, statement of issues, chronology, position statement and any skeleton arguments shall be cross-referenced to the relevant pages of the bundle.

4.6 The summary of the background, statement of issues, chronology and reading list shall in the case of a final hearing, and shall so far as practicable in the case of any other hearing, each consist of a single document in a form agreed by all parties. Where the parties disagree as to the content the fact of their disagreement and their differing contentions shall be set out at the appropriate places in the document.

4.7 Where the nature of the hearing is such that a complete bundle of all documents is unnecessary, the bundle (which need not be repaginated) may comprise only those documents necessary for the hearing, but

(a) the summary of the background must commence with a statement that the bundle is limited or incomplete; and
(b) the bundle shall if reasonably practicable be in a form agreed by all parties.

4.8 Where the bundle is re-lodged in accordance with paragraph 9.2, before it is re-lodged:

(a) the bundle shall be updated as appropriate; and
(b) all superseded documents (and in particular all outdated summaries, statements of issues, chronologies, skeleton arguments and similar documents) shall be removed from the bundle.

Format of the bundle

5.1 Unless the court has specifically directed otherwise, being satisfied that such direction is necessary to enable the proceedings to be disposed of justly, the bundle (if a paper bundle) shall be contained in one A4 size ring binder or lever arch file limited to no more than 350 sheets of A4 paper and 350 sides of text and (if an electronic bundle) shall be limited to 350 pages of text.

5.2 All documents in the bundle (including statements, affidavits, care plans and experts' reports and other reports) shall (a) in the case of a paper bundle be copied on one side of paper only, unless the court has specifically directed otherwise, (b) be divided by the author into numbered paragraphs and (c) be typed or printed in a font no smaller than 12 point and with 1 ½ or double spacing.

5.2A.1 Unless the court has specifically directed otherwise, being satisfied that such direction is necessary to enable the proceedings to be disposed of justly, and subject to paragraph 5.2A.2 below, any of the following documents included in the bundle shall be limited to no more than the number of sheets of A4 paper and sides of text specified below:

Case summary	6
Statement of issues	2
Position statement	3
Chronology	10
Skeleton argument	20
List of essential reading	1
Witness statement or affidavit (exclusive of exhibits)	25
Expert's or other report	40 (including executive summary at the beginning of no more than 4 pages)
Care plan	10

5.2A.2 The length and content of skeleton arguments in financial remedy cases which have been allocated to a High Court Judge shall continue to be governed by paragraph 15 of the Statement on the Efficient Conduct of Financial Remedy Hearings dated 1 February 2016.

5.2A.3 In the case of an appeal the bundle must comply with the relevant paragraphs of PD 30A.

5.3 The ring binder or lever arch file in the case of a paper bundle shall have clearly marked on the front and the spine:

(a) the title and number of the case;
(b) the place where the case has been listed;
(c) the hearing date and time;
(d) if known, the name of the judge hearing the case; and
(e) where in accordance with a direction of the court there is more than one ring binder or lever arch file, a distinguishing letter (A, B, C etc).

In the case of an electronic bundle the bundle must be clearly identifiable with the title and number of the case and as much of the information set out above as is practical should also be provided in accordance with the local arrangements.

Timetable for preparing and lodging the bundle

6.1 The party preparing the bundle shall, whether or not the bundle has been agreed, provide a paginated index to all other parties not less than 4 working days before the hearing.

6.2 Where counsel is to be instructed at any hearing, a paginated bundle shall (if not already in counsel's possession) be delivered to counsel by the person instructing that counsel not less than 3 working days before the hearing.

6.3 The bundle (with the exception of the preliminary documents if and insofar as they are not then available) shall be lodged with the court not less than 2 working days before the hearing, or at such other time as may be specified by the court.

6.4 The preliminary documents shall be lodged with the court no later than 11 am on the day before the hearing and, where the hearing is before a judge of the High Court and the name of the judge is known, shall (with the exception of the authorities, which are to be lodged in hard copy and not sent by email) at the same time be sent by email to the judge's clerk.

Lodging the bundle

7.1 The bundle shall be lodged at the appropriate office. If the bundle is lodged in the wrong place the court may:

(a) treat the bundle as having not been lodged; and
(b) take the steps referred to in paragraph 12.

7.2 Unless the court has given some other direction as to where the bundle in any particular case is to be lodged (for example a direction that the bundle is to be lodged with the judge's clerk) the bundle shall be lodged:

(a) for hearings at the RCJ, in the office of the Clerk of the Rules, 1st Mezzanine (Rm 1M), Queen's Building, Royal Courts of Justice, Strand, London WC2A 2LL (DX 44450 Strand);

(b) for hearings at any other place, at such place as may be designated by the designated family judge responsible for that place and in default of any such designation at the court office for the place where the hearing is to take place.

7.3 Any bundle sent to the court by post, DX or courier shall be clearly addressed to the appropriate office and shall show the date and place of the hearing on the outside of any packaging as well as on the bundle itself.

7.4 Unless the court has given some other direction or paragraph 7.5 applies only one copy of the bundle shall be lodged with the court but the party who is responsible for lodging the bundle shall bring to court at each hearing at which oral evidence may be called a copy of the bundle for use by the witnesses (or in the case of an electronic bundle make appropriate arrangements in accordance with the local arrangements for the use by the witnesses of the electronic bundle).

7.5 In the case of a hearing listed before a bench of magistrates where a paper bundle is to be used four copies of the bundle shall be lodged with the court.

7.6 In the case of hearings at the RCJ or at any other place where the designated family judge responsible for that place has directed that this paragraph shall apply, parties shall:

(a) if the bundle or preliminary documents are delivered personally, ensure that they obtain a receipt from the clerk accepting it or them; and

(b) if the bundle or preliminary documents are sent by post or DX or electronically, ensure that they obtain proof of posting or despatch.

The receipt (or proof of posting or despatch, as the case may be) shall be brought to court on the day of the hearing and must be produced to the court if requested. If the receipt (or proof of posting or despatch) cannot be produced to the court the judge may: (a) treat the bundle as having not been lodged; and (b) take the steps referred to in paragraph 12.

Lodging the bundle – additional requirements for Family Division or Family Court cases being heard at the RCJ

8.1 Bundles or preliminary documents delivered after 11 am on the day before the hearing may not be accepted by the Clerk of the Rules and if not shall be delivered:

(a) in a case where the hearing is before a judge of the High Court, directly to the clerk of the judge hearing the case;

(b) in a case where the hearing is before any other judge, to such place as may be specified by the Clerk of the Rules.

8.2 Upon learning before which judge a hearing is to take place, the clerk to counsel, or other advocate, representing the party in the position of applicant shall no later than 3 pm the day before the hearing:

(a) in a case where the hearing is before a judge of the High Court, telephone the clerk of the judge hearing the case;

(b) in a case where the hearing is before any other judge email the Clerk of the Rules at RCJ.familyhighcourt@hmcts.gsi.gov.uk;

to ascertain whether the judge has received the bundle (including the preliminary documents) and, if not, shall organise prompt delivery by the applicant's solicitor.

Removing and re-lodging the bundle

9.1 Unless either the court wishes to retain the bundle or specific alternative arrangements have been agreed with the court, the party responsible for the bundle shall, following completion of the hearing, retrieve the bundle from the court immediately or, if that is not practicable, collect it from the court within 5 working days. Bundles which are not collected in due time are liable to be destroyed without further notice. The local arrangements will specify the length of time that an electronic bundle will remain available to the court following a hearing.

9.2 The bundle shall be re-lodged for the next and any further hearings in accordance with the provisions of this practice direction and in a form which complies with para 4.7.

Time estimates

10.1 In every case a time estimate (which shall be inserted at the front of the bundle) shall be prepared which shall so far as practicable be agreed by all parties and shall:

(a) specify separately: (i) the time estimated to be required for judicial pre-reading; and (ii) the time required for hearing all evidence and submissions; and (iii) the time estimated to be required for preparing and delivering judgment;
(b) be prepared on the basis that before they give evidence all witnesses will have read all relevant filed statements and reports; and
(c) take appropriate account of any additional time likely to be incurred by the use of interpreters or intermediaries.

10.2 Once a case has been listed, any change in time estimates shall be notified immediately by telephone (and then immediately confirmed in writing):

(a) in the case of hearings in the RCJ, to the Clerk of the Rules; and
(b) in the case of hearings elsewhere, to the relevant listing officer.

Taking cases out of the list

11.1 As soon as it becomes known that a hearing will no longer be effective, whether as a result of the parties reaching agreement or for any other reason, the parties and their representatives shall immediately notify the court by telephone and email which shall be confirmed by letter. The letter, which shall wherever possible be a joint letter sent on behalf of all parties with their signatures applied or appended, shall include:

(a) a short background summary of the case;
(b) the written consent of each party who consents and, where a party does not consent, details of the steps which have been taken to obtain that party's consent and, where known, an explanation of why that consent has not been given;
(c) a draft of the order being sought; and
(d) enough information to enable the court to decide (i) whether to take the case out of the list and (ii) whether to make the proposed order.

Penalties for failure to comply with the practice direction

12.1 Failure to comply with any part of this practice direction may result in the judge removing the case from the list or putting the case further back in the list and may also result in a 'wasted costs' order or some other adverse costs order.

Commencement of the practice direction and application of other practice directions

13.1 This practice direction shall have effect from 23 July 2018.

14.1 This practice direction should where appropriate be read in conjunction with the Public Law Outline 2014 (PD12A) and the Child Arrangements Programme 2014 (PD12B). In particular, nothing in this practice direction is to be read as removing or altering any obligation to comply with the requirements of the Public Law Outline 2014 and the Child Arrangements Programme 2014.

This Practice Direction is issued –

(a) in relation to family proceedings, by the President of the Family Division, as the nominee of the Lord Chief Justice, with the agreement of the Lord Chancellor; and

(b) to the extent that it applies to proceedings to which section 5 of the Civil Procedure Act 1997 applies, by the Master of the Rolls as the nominee of the Lord Chief Justice, with the agreement of the Lord Chancellor

Practice Direction 27B – Attendance of media representatives at hearings in family proceedings

See also Part 27, Practice Direction 27A

Introduction

1.1 This Practice Direction supplements rule 10.28 of the Family Proceedings Rules 1991('FPR 1991') and deals with the right of representatives of news gathering and reporting organisations ('media representatives') and of duly authorised lawyers to attend at hearings of family proceedings which take place in private subject to the discretion of the court to exclude such representatives or such lawyers from the whole or part of any hearing on specified grounds[1]. It takes effect on 27 April 2009.

Matters unchanged by the rule

2.1 Rule 10.28(1) contains an express exception in respect of hearings which are conducted for the purpose of judicially assisted conciliation or negotiation and media representatives or duly authorised lawyers do not have a right to attend these hearings. Financial Dispute Resolution hearings will come within this exception. First Hearing Dispute Resolution appointments in private law Children Act cases will also come within this exception to the extent that the judge plays an active part in the conciliation process. Where the judge plays no part in the conciliation process or where the conciliation element of a hearing is complete and the judge is adjudicating upon the issues between the parties, media representatives or duly authorised lawyers should be permitted to attend, subject to the discretion of the court to exclude them on the specified grounds. Conciliation meetings or negotiation conducted between the parties with the assistance of an officer of the service or a Welsh Family Proceedings officer, and without the presence of the judge, are not 'hearings' within the meaning of this rule and media representatives or duly authorised lawyers have no right to attend such appointments.

The exception in rule 10.28(1) does not operate to exclude media representatives or duly authorised lawyers from –

(a) Hearings to consider applications brought under Parts IV and V of the Children Act 1989, including Case Management Hearings, any Further Case Management Hearings and Issues Resolution Hearings

(b) Hearings relating to findings of fact

(c) Interim hearings

(d) Final hearings.

The rights of media representatives or duly authorised lawyers to attend such hearings are limited only by the powers of the court to exclude such attendance on the limited grounds and subject to the procedures set out in paragraphs (4)–(6) of rule 10.28.

2.2 During any hearing, courts should consider whether the exception in rule 10.28(1) becomes applicable so that media representatives or duly authorised lawyers should be directed to withdraw.

2.3 The provisions of the rules permitting the attendance of media representatives or duly authorised lawyers and the disclosure to third parties of information relating to the proceedings do not entitle a media representative to receive or peruse court documents referred to in the course of evidence, submissions or judgment without the permission of the court or otherwise in accordance with Part 11 of the FPR 1991 (rules relating to disclosure to third parties). (This is in contrast to the position in civil proceedings, where the court sits in public and where members of the public are entitled to seek copies of certain documents[2])

2.4 The question of attendance of media representatives or duly authorised lawyers at hearings in family proceedings to which rule 10.28 and this guidance apply must be distinguished from statutory restrictions on publication and disclosure of information relating to proceedings, which continue to apply and are unaffected by the rule and this guidance.

2.5 The prohibition in section 97(2) of the Children Act 1989, on publishing material intended to or likely to identify a child as being involved in proceedings or the address or school of any such child, is limited to the duration of the proceedings[3]. However, the limitations imposed by section 12 of the Administration of Justice Act 1960 on publication of information relating to certain proceedings in private[4] apply during and after the proceedings. In addition, in proceedings to which s.97(2) of the Children Act 1989 applies the court should continue to consider at the conclusion of the proceedings whether there are any outstanding welfare issues which require a continuation of the protection afforded during the course of the proceedings by that provision.

Aims of the guidance

3.1 This Practice Direction is intended to provide guidance regarding –

(a) the handling of applications to exclude media representatives or duly authorised lawyers from the whole or part of a hearing: and

(b) the exercise of the court's discretion to exclude media representatives or duly authorised lawyers whether upon the court's own motion or any such application

3.2 While the guidance does not aim to cover all possible eventualities, it should be complied with so far as consistent in all the circumstances with the just determination of the proceedings.

Identification of media representatives or duly authorised lawyers as 'accredited'

4.1 Media representatives or duly authorised lawyers will be expected to carry with them identification sufficient to enable court staff, or if necessary the court itself, to verify that they are 'accredited' representatives of news gathering or reporting organisations within the meaning of the rule.

4.2 By virtue of paragraph (8) of the rule, it is for the Lord Chancellor to approve a scheme which will provide for accreditation. The Lord Chancellor has decided that the scheme operated by the UK Press Card Authority provides sufficient accreditation; a card issued under that scheme will be the expected form of identification, and production of the Card will be both necessary and sufficient to demonstrate accreditation.

4.3 A media representative unable to demonstrate accreditation in accordance with the UK Press Card Authority scheme, so as to be able to attend by virtue of paragraph (3)

(f) of the rule, may nevertheless be permitted to attend at the court's discretion under paragraph (3)(g).

Meaning of 'duly authorised lawyer'

4A.1 In rule 27.11 FPR and in this practice direction-

'duly authorised lawyer' means-

(a) a person who is authorised by a practising certificate to conduct litigation or exercise a right of audience in the family court;

(b) a lawyer working for the Law School, Faculty or Department of a Higher Education Institution designated as a recognised body pursuant to section 216 of the Education Reform Act 1988; or

(c) a lawyer attending on behalf of a registered educational charity the name, objects and registered charity number of which have been provided to the President of the Family Division; and

'lawyer' means a person who—

(a) holds a qualifying law degree as defined by the Bar Standards Board or Solicitors Regulation Authority;

(b) holds or has completed—

(i) the Common Professional Examination (CPE);

(ii) an approved Graduate Diploma in Law (GDL) course or the Solicitors Qualifying Examination (SQE);

(iii) a postgraduate legal qualification; or

(iv) the CILEx Level 6 Diploma in Law and Practice or the CILEx Graduate Fast Track Diploma.

Identification of lawyers as 'authorised'

5A.1 Lawyers will be expected to carry with them identification sufficient to enable court staff, or if necessary the court itself, to verify that they are 'authorised' lawyers within the meaning of the rule.

5A.2 The following forms of identification provide sufficient information, and production of such identification will be both necessary and sufficient to demonstrate that the lawyer is 'authorised' within the meaning of rule 27.11(7)(b)(i), (ii) and (iii) respectively-

(a) a current practising certificate accompanied by picture identification of the lawyer and a signed written statement by the lawyer which complies with paragraph 5A.3;

(b) confirmation on headed notepaper from the relevant Higher Education Institution (or Law School, Faculty or Department of that Institution) of the lawyer's position and qualification, accompanied by picture identification of the lawyer and a signed written statement by the lawyer which complies with paragraph 5A.3;

(c) confirmation on headed notepaper from the relevant registered educational charity (specifying the registered charity number) of the lawyer's position and qualification, accompanied by picture identification of the lawyer and a signed written statement by the lawyer which complies with paragraph 5A.3.

5A.3 The signed written statement required by paragraph 5A.2 must—

(a) confirm that the lawyer's attendance is for journalistic, research or public legal educational purposes and that the lawyer has no personal interest in the proceedings and that he or she is not attending in the capacity of agent or instructed lawyer for any client; and

(b) confirm that the lawyer is aware of and will abide by any restrictions on publication, whether arising by operation of law (for example under section 97 of the Children Act 1989 and section 12 of the Administration of Justice Act 1960) or imposed by order of the court, which follow from the proceedings being in private.

5A.4 The information about a registered educational charity required by rule 27.11(7)(b)(iii) is to be submitted using Form FP300 (Request by educational charity to attend family proceedings for authorisation by the President of the Family Division) by e-mail to pfd.office@judiciary.uk, or by post to: The Office of the President of the Family Division, Royal Courts of Justice, Strand, London WC2A 2LL. It will be entered on a list maintained by that office, and therefore need be submitted only once.

Exercise of the discretion to exclude media representatives or duly authorised lawyers from all or part of the proceedings

5.1 The rule anticipates and should be applied on the basis that media representatives or duly authorised lawyers have a right to attend family proceedings throughout save and to the extent that the court exercises its discretion to exclude them from the whole or part of any proceedings on one or more of the grounds set out in paragraph (4) of the rule.

5.2 When considering the question of exclusion on any of the grounds set out in paragraph (4) of the rule the court should –

(a) specifically identify whether the risk to which such ground is directed arises from the mere fact of media presence or the attendance of duly authorised lawyers at the particular hearing or hearings the subject of the application or whether the risk identified can be adequately addressed by exclusion of media representatives or duly authorised lawyers from a part only of such hearing or hearings;

(b) consider whether the reporting or disclosure restrictions which apply by operation of law, or which the court otherwise has power to order will provide sufficient protection to the party on whose behalf the application is made or any of the persons referred to in paragraph (4)(a) of the rule;

(c) consider the safety of the parties in cases in which the court considers there are particular physical or health risks against which reporting restrictions may be inadequate to afford protection;

(d) in the case of any vulnerable adult or child who is unrepresented before the court, consider the extent to which the court should of its own motion take steps to protect the welfare of that adult or child.

5.3 Paragraph (4)(a)(iii) of the rule permits exclusion where necessary 'for the orderly conduct of proceedings'. This enables the court to address practical problems presented by media attendance or the attendance of duly authorised lawyers. In particular, it may be difficult or even impossible physically to accommodate all (or indeed any) media representatives or duly authorised lawyers who wish to attend a particular hearing on the grounds of the restricted size or layout of the court room in which it is being heard. Court staff will use their best efforts to identify more suitable accommodation in advance of any hearing which appears likely to attract particular media attention or the particular attention of duly authorised lawyers, and to move hearings to larger court rooms where possible. However, the court should not be required to adjourn a hearing in order for larger accommodation to be sought where this will involve significant disruption or delay in the proceedings.

5.4 Paragraph (4)(b) of the rule permits exclusion where, unless the media and duly authorised lawyers are excluded, justice will be impeded or prejudiced for some reason other than those set out in sub-paragraph (a). Reasons of administrative inconvenience are not sufficient. Examples of circumstances where the impact on justice of continued attendance might be sufficient to necessitate exclusion may include –

(a) a hearing relating to the parties' finances where the information being considered includes price sensitive information (such as confidential information which could affect the share price of a publicly quoted company); or

(b) any hearing at which a witness (other than a party) states for credible reasons that he or she will not give evidence in front of media representatives or duly authorised lawyers, or where there appears to the court to be a significant risk that a witness will not give full or frank evidence in the presence of media representatives or duly authorised lawyers.

5.5 In the event of a decision to exclude media representatives or duly authorised lawyers, the court should state brief reasons for the decision.

Applications to exclude media representatives or duly authorised lawyers from all or part of proceedings

6.1 The court may exclude media representatives or duly authorised lawyers on the permitted grounds of its own motion or after hearing representations from the interested persons listed at paragraph (6) of the rule. Where exclusion is proposed, any media representatives or duly authorised lawyers who are present are entitled to make representations about that proposal. There is, however, no requirement to adjourn proceedings to enable media representatives or duly authorised lawyers who are not present to attend in order to make such representations, and in such a case the court should not adjourn unless satisfied of the necessity to do so having regard to the additional cost and delay which would thereby be caused.

6.2 Applications to exclude media representatives or duly authorised lawyers should normally be dealt with as they arise and by way of oral representations, unless the court directs otherwise.

6.3 When media representatives or duly authorised lawyers are expected to attend a particular hearing (for example, where a party is encouraging media or duly authorised lawyers interest and attendance) and a party intends to apply to the court for the exclusion of the media or duly authorised lawyers, that party should, if practicable, give advance notice to the court, to the other parties and (where appointed) any children's guardian, officer of the service or Welsh Family Proceedings officer, NYAS or other representative of the child of any intention to seek the exclusion of media representatives or duly authorised lawyers from all or part of the proceedings. Equally, legal representatives and parties should ensure that witnesses are aware of the right of media representatives or duly authorised lawyers to attend and should notify the court at an early stage of the intention of any witness to request the exclusion of media representatives or duly authorised lawyers.

6.4 Prior notification by the court of a pending application for exclusion will not be given to media interests or to any duly authorised lawyers unless the court so directs. However, where such an application has been made, the applicant must where possible, notify the relevant media organisations.

Footnotes

1 It does not, accordingly, apply where hearings are held in open court where the general public including media representatives or duly authorised lawyers may attend as of right, such as committal hearings or the hearing of matrimonial or civil partnership causes.
2 See *GIO Services Ltd v Liverpool and London Ltd* [1999] 1 WLR 984
3 See *Clayton v Clayton* [2006] EWCA Civ 878
4 In particular proceedings which –
(a) relate to the exercise of the inherent jurisdiction of the High Court with respect to minors;
(b) are brought under the Children Act 1989; or
(c) otherwise relate wholly or mainly to the maintenance or upbringing of a minor

PART 28
COSTS

28.1 Costs

The court may at any time make such order as to costs as it thinks just.

28.2 Application of other rules

(1) Subject to rule 28.3 …[1], [Parts 44 (except rules 44.2(2) and (3) and 44.10(2) and (3)), 46 and 47 and rule 45.8][2] of the CPR apply to costs in proceedings, with the following modifications—

[(a) in the definition of 'authorised court officer' in rule 44.1(1), for the words in sub-paragraph (i) substitute 'the family court';][3]
(b) …[1]
(c) in accordance with any provisions in Practice Direction 28A; and
(d) any other necessary modifications.

(2) …[1]

Amendment

1 Repealed by the Family Procedure (Amendment No 3) Rules 2013, SI 2013/3204, rr 2, 72(a)(i), (iii), (b).
2 Substituted by the Family Procedure (Amendment) Rules 2013, SI 2013/530, rr 2, 3(a)(i).
3 Substituted by the Family Procedure (Amendment No 3) Rules 2013, SI 2013/3204, rr 2, 72(a)(ii).

28.3 Costs in financial remedy proceedings

(1) This rule applies in relation to financial remedy proceedings.

(2) Rule [44.2][1](1), (4) and (5)] of the CPR do not apply to financial remedy proceedings.

(3) [Rules 44.2(6) to (8) and 44.12][1] of the CPR apply to an order made under this rule as they apply to an order made under rule 44.3 of the CPR.

(4) In this rule—

(a) 'costs' has the same meaning as in rule [44.1(1)(c)][1] of the CPR; and
(b) 'financial remedy proceedings' means proceedings for—
(i) a financial order except an order for maintenance pending suit, an order for maintenance pending outcome of proceedings, an interim periodical payments order[, an order for payment in respect of legal services][2] or any other form of interim order for the purposes of rule 9.7(1)(a), (b), (c) and (e);
(ii) an order under Part 3 of the 1984 Act;
(iii) an order under Schedule 7 to the 2004 Act;

(iv) an order under section 10(2) of the 1973 Act;
(v) an order under section 48(2) of the 2004 Act.

(5) Subject to paragraph (6), the general rule in financial remedy proceedings is that the court will not make an order requiring one party to pay the costs of another party.

(6) The court may make an order requiring one party to pay the costs of another party at any stage of the proceedings where it considers it appropriate to do so because of the conduct of a party in relation to the proceedings (whether before or during them).

(7) In deciding what order (if any) to make under paragraph (6), the court must have regard to—

(a) any failure by a party to comply with these rules, any order of the court or any practice direction which the court considers relevant;
(b) any open offer to settle made by a party;
(c) whether it was reasonable for a party to raise, pursue or contest a particular allegation or issue;
(d) the manner in which a party has pursued or responded to the application or a particular allegation or issue;
(e) any other aspect of a party's conduct in relation to proceedings which the court considers relevant; and
(f) the financial effect on the parties of any costs order.

(8) No offer to settle which is not an open offer to settle is admissible at any stage of the proceedings, except as provided by rule 9.17.

[(9) For the purposes of this rule 'financial remedy proceedings' do not include an application under rule 9.9A.][3]

Amendment

1 Substituted by the Family Procedure (Amendment) Rules 2013, SI 2013/530, rr 2, 4.
2 Inserted by the Family Procedure (Amendment No 2) Rules 2013, SI 2013/1472, rr 2, 6.
3 Inserted by the Family Procedure (Amendment No 2) Rules 2016, SI 2016/901, rr 2, 8.

28.4 …[1]

…[1]

Amendment

1 Repealed by the Family Procedure (Amendment No 3) Rules 2013, SI 2013/3204, rr 2, 73.

Practice Direction 28A – Costs

See also Part 28

This Practice Direction supplements FPR Part 28

Application and modification of the CPR

1.1 Rule 28.2 provides that subject to rule 28.3 of the FPR, Parts 44 (except rules 44.2(2) and (3) and 44.10(2) and (3)), 46 and 47 and rule 45.8 of the CPR apply to costs in family proceedings with the modifications listed in rule 28.2(1)(a), (c) and (d). Rule 28.2(1)(c) refers to modifications in accordance with this Practice Direction.

Application and modification of the Practice Directions supplementing CPR Parts 44 to 47

2.1 For the purpose of proceedings to which these Rules apply, the Practice Directions which supplement Parts 44 to 47 of the CPR will apply, but with the exclusions and modifications explained below to reflect the exclusions and modifications to those Parts of the CPR as they are applied by Part 28 of these Rules.

2.2 Rule 28.2(1) applies, with modifications and certain exceptions, Parts 44 to 47 of the CPR to costs in family proceedings. Rule 28.3, by way of exception, disapplies CPR rule 44.2(1), (4) and (5) in the case of financial remedy proceedings.

2.3 CPR Practice Directions 44 to 47 do not, therefore, apply in their entirety but with the exclusion of Practice Direction 45 and of certain sections of the other Practice Directions, reflecting the non-application of Part 45 and of certain rules of the CPR which those sections of the other Practice Directions supplement.

2.4 CPR Practice Directions 44, 46 and 47 apply as follows –

- to family proceedings including financial remedy proceedings with the exception of paragraphs 3.1 to 3.5 of Practice Direction 44 and paragraphs 7.1 and 9.1 to 9.12 of Practice Direction 46;

2.5 All subsequent editions of CPR Practice Directions 44, 46 and 47 as and when they are published and come into effect shall in the same way extend to all family proceedings.

2.6 CPR Practice Directions 44, 46, 47 and 48 include provisions applicable to proceedings following changes in the manner in which legal services are funded pursuant to the Access to Justice Act 1999. It should be noted that family proceedings (within section 58A(2) of the Courts and Legal Services Act 1990) cannot be the subject of an enforceable conditional fee agreement.

2.7 Paragraph 1.1 of CPR Practice Direction 44 shall be modified as follows –

- in the definition of 'counsel' for 'High Court or in the county courts' substitute 'High Court or in the family court.'

2.8 Paragraphs 4.1 and 4.2 of CPR Practice Direction 47 shall be modified as follows –

- for paragraphs 4.1 and 4.2 substitute:

'4.1 For the purposes of rule 47.4(1), 'appropriate office' means the court office of the Designated Family Court for the Designated Family Judge area in which the case was being dealt with when the judgment or order was made, or the event occurred which gave rise to the right to assessment, or to which the case has subsequently been moved.

(Her Majesty's Courts and Tribunals Service will publish information to enable Designated Family Judge areas and Designated Family Courts to be identified).'.

General Interpretation of references in CPR

3.1 References in the costs practice direction to 'claimant' and 'defendant' are to be read as references to equivalent terms used in proceedings to which these Rules apply and other terms and expressions used in the costs practice direction shall be similarly treated.

3.2 References in CPR Parts 44 to 47 to other rules or Parts of the CPR shall be read, where there is an equivalent rule or Part in these Rules, to that equivalent rule or Part.

Costs in financial remedy proceedings

4.1 Rule 28.3 relates to the court's power to make costs orders in financial remedy proceedings. For the purposes of rule 28.3, 'financial remedy proceedings' are defined in accordance with rule 28.3(4)(b). That definition, which is more limited than the principal definition in rule 2.3(1), includes –

(a) an application for a financial order, except –
  (i) an order for maintenance pending suit or an order for maintenance pending outcome of proceedings;
  (ii) an interim periodical payments order or any other form of interim order for the purposes of rule 9.7(1)(a),(b),(c) and (e);
  (iii) an order for payment in respect of legal services.
(b) an application for an order under Part 3 of the Matrimonial and Family Proceedings Act 1984 or Schedule 7 to the Civil Partnership Act 2004; and
(c) an application under section 10(2) of the Matrimonial Causes Act 1973 or section 48(2) of the Civil Partnership Act 2004.

4.2 Accordingly, it should be noted that –

(a) while most interim financial applications are excluded from rule 28.3, the rule does apply to an application for an interim variation order within rule 9.7(1)(d),
(b) rule 28.3 does not apply to an application for any of the following financial remedies –
  (i) an order under Schedule 1 to the Children Act 1989;
  (ii) an order under section 27 of the Matrimonial Causes Act 1973 or Part 9 of Schedule 5 to the Civil Partnership Act 2004;
  (iii) an order under section 35 of the Matrimonial Causes Act 1973 or paragraph 69 of Schedule 5 to the Civil Partnership Act 2004; or
  (iv) an order under Part 1 of the Domestic Proceedings and Magistrates' Courts Act 1978 or Schedule 6 to the Civil Partnership Act 2004.

4.3 Under rule 28.3 the court only has the power to make a costs order in financial remedy proceedings when this is justified by the litigation conduct of one of the parties. When determining whether and how to exercise this power the court will be required to take into account the list of factors set out in that rule. The court will not be able to take into account any offers to settle expressed to be 'without prejudice' or 'without prejudice save as to costs' in deciding what, if any, costs orders to make.

4.4 In considering the conduct of the parties for the purposes of rule 28.3(6) and (7) (including any open offers to settle), the court will have regard to the obligation of the parties to help the court to further the overriding objective (see rules 1.1 and 1.3) and will take into account the nature, importance and complexity of the issues in the case. This may be of particular significance in applications for variation orders and interim variation orders or other cases where there is a risk of the costs becoming disproportionate to the amounts in dispute.The court will take a broad view of conduct for the purposes of this rule and will generally conclude that to refuse openly to negotiate reasonably and responsibly will amount to conduct in respect of which the court will consider making an order for costs. This includes in a 'needs' case where the applicant litigates unreasonably resulting in the costs incurred by each party becoming disproportionate to the award made by the court. Where an order for costs is made at an interim stage the court will not usually allow any resulting liability to be reckoned as a debt in the computation of the assets.

4.5 Parties who intend to seek a costs order against another party in proceedings to which rule 28.3 applies should ordinarily make this plain in open correspondence or in skeleton arguments before the date of the hearing. In any case where summary assessment of costs awarded under rule 28.3 would be appropriate parties are under an obligation to file a statement of costs in CPR Form N260.

4.6 An order for payment in respect of legal services under section 22ZA of the Matrimonial Causes Act 1973 or paragraph 38A of Part 8 of Schedule 5 to the Civil Partnership Act 2004 is not a 'costs order' within the meaning of rule 28.3.

4.7 By virtue of rule 28.2(1), where rule 28.3 does not apply, the exercise of the court's discretion as to costs is governed by the relevant provisions of the CPR and in particular rule 44.2 (excluding r 44.2(2) and (3)).

PART 29
MISCELLANEOUS

29.1 Personal details

(1) Unless the court directs otherwise, a party is not required to reveal—

- (a) the party's home address or other contact details;
- (b) the address or other contact details of any child;
- (c) the name of a person with whom the child is living, if that person is not the applicant; or
- (d) in relation to an application under section 28(2) of the 2002 Act (application for permission to change the child's surname), the proposed new surname of the child.

(2) Where a party does not wish to reveal any of the particulars in paragraph (1), that party must give notice of those particulars to the court and the particulars will not be revealed to any person unless the court directs otherwise.

(3) Where a party changes home address during the course of proceedings, that party must give notice of the change to the court.

29.2 Disclosure of information under the 1991 Act

Where the [Secretary of State][1] requires a person mentioned in regulation 3(1), 4(2) or 6(2)(a) of the Child Support Information Regulations 2008 to furnish information or evidence for a purpose mentioned in regulation 4(1) of those Regulations, nothing in these rules will—

- (a) prevent that person from furnishing the information or evidence sought; or
- (b) require that person to seek permission of the court before doing so.

Amendment

1 Substituted by the Public Bodies (Child Maintenance and Enforcement Commission: Abolition and Transfer of Functions) Order 2012, SI 2012/2007, art 3(2), Schedule, para 125(c).

29.3 Method of giving notice

(1) Unless directed otherwise, a notice which is required by these rules to be given to a person must be given—

- (a) in writing; and
- (b) in a manner in which service may be effected in accordance with Part 6.

(2) Rule 6.33 applies to a notice which is required by these rules to be given to a child as it applies to a document which is to be served on a child.

29.4 Withdrawal of applications in proceedings

(1) This rule applies to applications in proceedings—

(a) under Part 7;
(b) under Parts 10 to 14 or under any other Part where the application relates to the welfare or upbringing of a child or;
(c) where either of the parties is a protected party.

(2) Where this rule applies, an application may only be withdrawn with the permission of the court.

(3) Subject to paragraph (4), a person seeking permission to withdraw an application must file a written request for permission setting out the reasons for the request.

(4) The request under paragraph (3) may be made orally to the court if the parties are present.

(5) A court officer will notify the other parties of a written request.

(6) The court may deal with a written request under paragraph (3) without a hearing if the other parties, and any other persons directed by the court, have had an opportunity to make written representations to the court about the request.

29.5 The Human Rights Act 1998

(1) In this rule—

'the 1998 Act' means the Human Rights Act 1998;
'Convention right' has the same meaning as in the 1998 Act; and
'declaration of incompatibility' means a declaration of incompatibility under section 4 of the 1998 Act.

(2) A party who seeks to rely on any provision of or right arising under the 1998 Act or seeks a remedy available under that Act must inform the court in that party's application or otherwise in writing specifying—

(a) the Convention right which it is alleged has been infringed and details of the alleged infringement; and
(b) the relief sought and whether this includes a declaration of incompatibility.

(3) The High Court may not make a declaration of incompatibility unless 21 days' notice, or such other period of notice as the court directs, has been given to the Crown.

(4) Where notice has been given to the Crown, a Minister, or other person permitted by the 1998 Act, will be joined as a party on giving notice to the court.

(5) Where a claim is made under section 7(1) of the 1998 Act (claim that public authority acted unlawfully) in respect of a judicial act—

(a) that claim must be set out in the application form or the appeal notice; and
(b) notice must be given to the Crown.

(6) Where paragraph (4) applies and the appropriate person (as defined in section 9(5) of the 1998 Act) has not applied within 21 days, or such other period as the court directs, beginning with the date on which the notice to be joined as a party was served, the court may join the appropriate person as a party.

(7) On any application concerning a committal order, if the court ordering the release of the person concludes that that person's Convention rights have been infringed by the making of the order to which the application or appeal relates, the judgment or order should so state, but if the court does not do so, that failure will not prevent another court from deciding the matter.

(8) Where by reason of a rule, practice direction or court order the Crown is permitted or required—

(a) to make a witness statement;
(b) to swear an affidavit(GL);
(c) to verify a document by a statement of truth; or
(d) to discharge any other procedural obligation,

that function will be performed by an appropriate officer acting on behalf of the Crown, and the court may if necessary nominate an appropriate officer.

(Practice Direction 29A (Human Rights – Joining the Crown) makes provision for the notices mentioned in this rule.)

29.6 Documents in proceedings concerning gender recognition

(1) This rule applies to all documents in proceedings brought under—

(a) [section 12(1)(g) or (h)][1] of, or paragraph 11(1)(e) of Schedule 1 to, the 1973 Act; …[2]
[(aa) section 12A(3) of the 1973 Act in a case where section 12(1)(g) or (h) of the 1973 Act applies; …[3]][4]
[(ab) section 50(1)(d) of the 2004 Act;
(ac) section 50(1)(e) of the 2004 Act; or][5]
(b) the Gender Recognition Act 2004.

(2) Documents to which this rule applies must, while they are in the custody of the court, be kept in a place of special security.

[(In relation to paragraph (1)(aa), section 9(6) of the Marriage (Same Sex Couples) Act 2013 provides that where a civil partnership is converted into a marriage, the civil partnership ends on the conversion, and the resulting marriage is to be treated as having subsisted since the date the civil partnership was formed.)][4]

Amendment

1 Substituted by the Family Procedure (Amendment) Rules 2015, SI 2015/913, rr 2, 12(a)(i)(aa).
2 Repealed by the Family Procedure (Amendment) Rules 2015, SI 2015/913, rr 2, 12(a)(i)(bb).
3 Repealed by the Family Procedure (Amendment No 2) Rules 2021, SI 2021/875, rr 2, 11(a).
4 Inserted by the Family Procedure (Amendment) Rules 2015, SI 2015/913, rr 2, 12(a)(ii), (b).
5 Inserted by the Family Procedure (Amendment No 2) Rules 2021, SI 2021/875, rr 2, 11(b).

29.7 Stamping or sealing court documents

(1) A court officer must, when issuing the following documents, seal(GL), or otherwise authenticate them with the stamp of the court—

(a) the application form;
(b) an order; and
(c) any other document which a rule or practice direction requires the court officer to seal(GL) or stamp.

(2) The court officer may place the seal(GL) or the stamp on the document—

(a) by hand; or
(b) by printing a facsimile of the seal(GL) on the document whether electronically or otherwise.

(3) A document purporting to bear the court's seal(GL) or stamp will be admissible in evidence without further proof.

29.8 Applications for relief which is precluded by the 1991 Act

(1) This rule applies where an application is made for an order which, in the opinion of the court, it would be prevented from making under section 8 or 9 of the 1991 Act and in this rule, 'the matter' means the question of whether or not the court would be so prevented.

(2) The court will consider the matter without holding a hearing.

(3) Where the court officer receives the opinion of the court, as mentioned in paragraph (1), the court officer must send a notice to the applicant of that opinion.

(4) Paragraphs (5) to (11) apply where the court officer sends a notice under paragraph (3).

(5) Subject to paragraph (6), no requirement of these rules apply except the requirements—

(a) of this rule;
(b) as to service of the application by the court officer; and
(c) as to any procedural step to be taken following the making of an application of the type in question.

(6) The court may direct that the requirements of these rules apply, or apply to such extent or with such modifications as are set out in the direction.

(7) If the applicant informs the court officer, within 14 days of the date of the notice, that the applicant wishes to persist with the application, the court will give appropriate directions for the matter to be heard and determined and may provide for the hearing to be without notice.

(8) Where directions are given in accordance with paragraph (7), the court officer must—

(a) inform the applicant of the directions;
(b) send a copy of the application to the other parties;
(c) if the hearing is to be without notice, inform the other parties briefly—
    (i) of the nature and effect of the notice given to the applicant under paragraph (3);
    (ii) that the matter is being resolved without a hearing on notice; and
    (iii) that they will be notified of the result; and
(d) if the hearing is to be on notice, inform the other parties of—
    (i) the circumstances which led to the directions being given; and
    (ii) the directions.

(9) If the applicant does not inform the court officer as mentioned in paragraph (7), the application shall be treated as having been withdrawn.

(10) Where—

(a) the matter is heard in accordance with directions given under paragraph (7); and

(b) the court determines that it would be prevented, under section 8 or 9 of the 1991 Act, from making the order sought by the applicant,

the court will dismiss the application.

(11) Where the court dismisses the application—

(a) the court must give its reasons in writing; and
(b) the court officer must send a copy of the reasons to the parties.

29.9 Modification of rule 29.8 where the application is not freestanding

(1) Where the court officer sends a notice under rule 29.8(3) in relation to an application which is contained in another document ('the document') which contains material extrinsic to the application—

(a) subject to paragraph (2), the document will be treated as if it did not contain the application in respect of which the notice was served; and
(b) the court officer, when sending copies of the documents to the respondents under any provision of these rules, must attach—
  (i) a copy of the notice under rule 29.8(3); and
  (ii) a notice informing the respondents of the effect of paragraph (1)(a).

(2) If the court determines that it is not prevented by section 8 or 9 of the 1991 Act from making the order sought by the application, the court—

(a) must direct that the document shall be treated as if it contained the application; and
(b) may give such directions as it considers appropriate for the subsequent conduct of the proceedings.

29.10 Standard requirements

(1) Every judgment or order must state the name and judicial title of the person who made it.

(2) Every judgment or order must—

(a) bear the date on which it is given or made; and
(b) be sealed(GL) by the court.

29.11 Drawing up and filing of judgments and orders

(1) Except as provided by a rule or a practice direction, every judgment or order will be drawn up by the court unless—

(a) the court orders a party to draw it up;
(b) a party, with the permission of the court, agrees to draw it up; or
(c) the court dispenses with the need to draw it up.

(2) The court may direct that—

(a) a judgment or an order drawn up by a party must be checked by the court before it is sealed(GL); or
(b) before a judgment or an order is drawn up by the court, the parties must file an agreed statement of its terms.

(3) Where a judgment or an order is to be drawn up by a party—

(a) that party must file it no later than 7 days after the date on which the court ordered or gave permission for the order to be drawn up so that it can be sealed by the court; and
(b) if that party fails to file it within that period, any other party may draw it up and file it.

[29.12 Access to and inspection of documents retained in court

(1) Except as provided by this rule or by any other rule or Practice Direction, no document [or copy of a document][1] filed or lodged in the court office shall be open to inspection by any person without the permission of the court, and no copy of any such document [or copy][1] shall be taken by, or issued to, any person without such permission.

(2) A copy of an order made in open court will be issued to any person who requests it.

(3) Subject to rules 14.24 and 29.1(2) and to any direction given by the court, a party to any family proceedings, or the legal representative, children's guardian or litigation friend for a party in any family proceedings, may have a search made for, and may inspect, and obtain a copy of, any document [or copy of a document][1] filed or lodged in the court office in those proceedings.

(4) Any person who intends to make an application in relation to a child under the 1980 Hague Convention in a Contracting State (as defined in rule 12.44) other than the United Kingdom shall, if the court is satisfied that that person intends to make such an application, be entitled to obtain a copy bearing the seal[(GL)] of the court of any order made in relation to the child under the 1989 Act or under the inherent jurisdiction, whether or not that person was a party to the proceedings in which the order was made.

[(5) For the purposes of this rule, 'document' and 'copy' have the meanings given in rule 21.1(3).][1]][2]

Amendment

1 Inserted by the Family Procedure (Amendment No 3) Rules 2015, SI 2015/1868, rr 2, 8.
2 Substituted by the Family Procedure (Amendment) Rules 2012, SI 2012/679, rr 2, 25.

29.13 Service of judgments and orders

(1) The court officer must, unless the court directs otherwise, serve a copy of a judgment or an order made in family proceedings to every party affected by it.

(2) Where a judgment or an order has been drawn up by a party and is to be served by the court officer the party who drew it up must file a copy to be retained at court and sufficient copies for service on all the parties.

(3) A party in whose favour an order is made need not prove that a copy of the order has reached a party to whom it is required to be sent under this rule.

(4) This rule does not affect the operation of any rule or enactment which requires an order to be served in a particular way

29.14 Power to require judgment or order to be served on a party as well as the party's solicitor

Where the party on whom a judgment or order is served is acting by a solicitor, the court may order the judgment or order to be served on the party as well as on the party's solicitor.

29.15 When judgment or order takes effect

A judgment or order takes effect from the day when it is given or made, or such later date as the court may specify.

29.16 Correction of errors in judgments and orders

(1) The court may at any time correct an accidental slip or omission in a judgment or order.

(2) A party may apply for a correction without notice.

[29.17 Transfer of proceedings

(1) Subject to paragraph (3), a court may transfer a case to another court, either of its own initiative or on the application of one of the parties if—

(a) the parties consent to the transfer;
(b) the court has held a hearing to determine whether a transfer should be ordered; or
(c) paragraph (2) applies.

(2) A court may transfer a case without a hearing if—

(a) the court has notified the parties in writing that it intends to order a transfer; and
(b) no party has, within 14 days of the notification being sent, requested a hearing to determine whether a transfer should be ordered.

(3) A case may not be transferred from the family court to the High Court unless—

(a) the decision to transfer was made by a judge sitting in the family court who is a person to whom paragraph (4) applies; or
(b) one or more of the circumstances specified in Practice Direction 29C applies.

(4) This paragraph applies to a person who is—

(a) the President of the Family Division;
(b) an ordinary judge of the Court of Appeal (including the vice-president, if any, of either division of that court);
(c) a puisne judge of the High Court.][1]

Amendment

1 Inserted by the Family Procedure (Amendment No 3) Rules 2013, SI 2013/3204, rr 2, 74.

[29.18 Application for change of area

The Part 18 procedure applies to an application to the family court for existing proceedings to be heard in a different Designated Family Judge area.

(Her Majesty's Courts and Tribunals Service publishes information to enable Designated Family Judge areas to be identified.)][1]

Amendment

1 Inserted by the Family Procedure (Amendment No 3) Rules 2013, SI 2013/3204, rr 2, 74.

[29.19 Allocation of proceedings to another level of judge

(1) Paragraphs (2) and (3) apply where there has been allocation without a hearing.

(2) A party may request the court to reconsider allocation at a hearing.

(3) Unless the court directs otherwise, a party may make a request referred to in paragraph (2)—

(a) at any hearing where that party first has notice of allocation; or
(b) in writing no later than 2 days before the first hearing in the proceedings after the party receives notice of allocation.

(4) When the party requests the court to reconsider allocation in accordance with paragraph (3)(b), the party must at the same time notify other parties of the request in writing.

(5) The court may reconsider allocation of its own initiative.

(6) Rule 4.3 does not apply to allocation without a hearing.

(7) In this rule 'allocation' means allocation of proceedings other than appeal proceedings to a level of judge.][1]

Amendment

1 Inserted by the Family Procedure (Amendment No 2) Rules 2014, SI 2014/667, rr 2, 20.

Practice Direction 29A – Human rights, joining the Crown

See also Part 29, Practice Direction 29B, Practice Direction 29C

This Practice Direction supplements FPR Part 29, rule 29.5 (The Human Rights Act 1998)

Section 4 of the Human Rights Act 1998

1.1 Where a party has informed the court about–

(a) a claim for a declaration of incompatibility in accordance with section 4 of the Human Rights Act 1998; or
(b) an issue for the court to decide which may lead to the court considering making a declaration,

then the court may at any time consider whether notice should be given to the Crown as required by that Act and give directions for the content and service of the notice. The rule allows a period of 21 days before the court will make the declaration but the court may vary this period of time.

1.2 The court will normally consider the issues and give the directions referred to in paragraph 1.1 at a directions hearing.

1.3 The notice must be served on the person named in the list published under section 17 of the Crown Proceedings Act 1947.

1.4 The notice will be in the form directed by the court and will normally include the directions given by the court. The notice will also be served on all the parties.

1.5 The court may require the parties to assist in the preparation of the notice.

1.6 Unless the court orders otherwise, the Minister or other person permitted by the Human Rights Act 1998 to be joined as a party must, if he or she wishes to be joined, give notice of his or her intention to be joined as a party to the court and every other party. Where the Minister has nominated a person to be joined as a party the notice must be accompanied by the written nomination.

(Section 5(2)(a) of the Human Rights Act 1998 permits a person nominated by a Minister of the Crown to be joined as a party. The nomination may be signed on behalf of the Minister.)

Section 9 of the Human Rights Act 1998

2.1 The procedure in paragraphs 1.1 to 1.6 also applies where a claim is made under sections 7(1)(a) and 9(3) of the Human Rights Act 1998 for damages in respect of a judicial act.

2.2 Notice must be given to the Lord Chancellor and should be served on the Treasury Solicitor on his behalf.

2.3 The notice will also give details of the judicial act, which is the subject of the claim for damages, and of the court that made it.

(Section 9(4) of the Human Rights Act 1998 provides that no award of damages may be made against the Crown as provided for in section 9(3) unless the appropriate person is joined in the proceedings. The appropriate person is the Minister responsible for the court concerned or a person or department nominated by him or her (section 9(5) of the Act).

Practice Direction 29B – Human Rights Act 1998

See also Part 29, Practice Direction 29A, Practice Direction 29C

Human Rights Act 1998

1.1 It is directed that the following practice shall apply as from 2 October 2000 in all family proceedings:

Citation of authorities

2.1 When an authority referred to in s 2 of the Human Rights Act 1998 ('the Act') is to be cited at a hearing–

(a) the authority to be cited shall be an authoritative and complete report;

(b) the court must be provided with a list of authorities it is intended to cite and copies of the reports–

  (i) in cases to which Practice Direction (Family Proceedings: Court Bundles) (10 March 2000) [2000] 1 FLR 536 applies, as part of the bundle;

  (ii) otherwise, not less than 2 clear days before the hearing; an

(c) copies of the complete original texts issued by the European Court and Commission, either paper based or from the Court's judgment database (HUDOC) which is available on the internet, may be used.

Allocation to judges

3.1 The hearing and determination of the following will be confined to a High Court judge–

(a) a claim for a declaration of incompatibility under s 4 of the Act; or

(b) an issue which may lead to the court considering making such a declaration.

3.2 The hearing and determination of a claim made under the Act in respect of a judicial act shall be confined in the High Court to a High Court judge and in the family court to a judge of High Court level.

Practice Direction 29C – Transfer of proceedings from the Family Court to the High Court

See also Part 29, Practice Direction 29A, Practice Direction 29B

This Practice Direction supplements rule 29.17(3)(b) FPR.

1.1 Rule 29.17(3)(b) FPR provides that a judge other than one to whom rule 29.17(4) applies may make a decision to transfer proceedings from the family court to the High Court where the circumstances specified in this Practice Direction apply.

1.2 The circumstances are that the proceedings are to be transferred solely for the purpose of making an order under the inherent jurisdiction of the High Court to require a Government Department or agency to disclose an address to the court.

Practice Direction 29D – Court officers making corrections to orders

This practice direction supplements rule 29.16 FPR 2010

1.1 Rule 29.10 FPR p6ovides that the court may correct an accidental slip or omission in a judgment or order. Corrections under that rule must be approved by a judge, or by a Justices' Legal Adviser where Practice Direction 2C so provides.

1.2 A court officer may make an amendment to an order, without prior reference to a judge or Justices' Legal Adviser (as applicable), in the following circumstances-

(a) where a court officer has wrongly transposed details in the draft order approved by the court;
(b) where the error is obviously typographical such as-
  (i) the spelling of a party's name, a date of birth, a place of birth or marriage, where that can be corrected by reference to the application or supporting evidence on the court file such as a birth or marriage certificate; or
  (ii) a nonsensical word clearly included in error (but see paragraph 1.4);
(c) changes to references in the order to the venue at which a hearing took place, where this can be verified from the court file, court diary or cause list;
(d) the date of the order, where this can be verified from the court file, court diary or cause list;
(e) details of a party's legal representatives at a hearing when this can be verified from the court file or other record of hearing;
(f) the date of a hearing, where the court officer has listed a matter for hearing but transposed the details incorrectly into the order that notifies the parties of the hearing date;
(g) to improve the formatting (but not the numbering) of an order.

1.3 If a court officer concludes that-

(a) it would be inappropriate to make an amendment to an order even where they consider that a case falls within paragraph 1.2; or
(b) they are not certain whether or not a case falls within paragraph 1.2 (for example whether an error is obviously typographical),

the court officer must refer the matter to a judge to determine whether to make the amendment.

1.4 Save as specified in paragraph 1.2, a court officer must never make linguistic, grammatical or textual amendments to an order, or alter its numbering, without reference to a judge or, where Practice Direction 2C applies, to a Justices' Legal Adviser.

1.5 A court officer must never make an amendment to a judgment or written ruling without reference to a judge or, where Practice Direction 2C applies, to a Justices' Legal Adviser.

PART 30
APPEALS

30.1 Scope and interpretation

(1) The rules in this Part apply to appeals to—

(a) the High Court; and
(b) [the family court][1].

(2) This Part does not apply to an appeal in detailed assessment proceedings against a decision of an authorised court officer.

(Rules [47.21 to 47.24][1] of the CPR deal with appeals against a decision of an authorised court officer in detailed assessment proceedings.)

(3) In this Part—

'appeal court' means the court to which an appeal is made;
'appeal notice' means an appellant's or respondent's notice;
'appellant' means a person who brings or seeks to bring an appeal;
['costs judge' means—
(a) the Chief Taxing Master;
(b) a taxing master of the Senior Courts; or
(c) a person appointed to act as deputy for the person holding office referred to in paragraph (b) or to act as temporary additional officer for any such office;

'district judge' means—
(a) the Senior District Judge of the Family Division
(b) a district judge of the Principal Registry of the Family Division;
(c) a person appointed to act as deputy for the person holding office referred to in paragraph (b) or to act as temporary additional officer for any such office;
(d) a district judge;
(e) a deputy district judge appointed under section 102 of the Senior Courts Act 1981 or section 8 of the County Courts Act 1984; or
(f) a District Judge (Magistrates' Courts);][2]

'lower court' means the court from which, or the person from whom, the appeal lies; and
'respondent' means—
(a) a person other than the appellant who was a party to the proceedings in the lower court and who is affected by the appeal; and
(b) a person who is permitted by the appeal court to be a party to the appeal.

(4) This Part is subject to any rule, enactment or practice direction which sets out special provisions with regard to any particular category of appeal.

Amendment

1 Substituted by the Family Procedure (Amendment No 2) Rules 2014, SI 2014/667, rr 2, 21(a), (b).
2 Inserted by the Family Procedure (Amendment No 2) Rules 2014, SI 2014/667, rr 2, 21(c).

30.2 Parties to comply with the practice direction

All parties to an appeal must comply with Practice Direction 30A.

30.3 Permission

[(1) Paragraphs (1B) and (2) of this rule set out when permission to appeal is, or is not, required under these rules to appeal against a decision or order of the family court.

(1A) This rule does not apply where the route of appeal from a decision or order of the family court is to the Court of Appeal, namely where the appeal is against a decision or order made by a circuit judge or Recorder—

(a) in proceedings under—
 (i) Part 4 of the 1989 Act (care and supervision);
 (ii) Part 5 of the 1989 Act (protection of children);
 (iii) paragraph 19(1) of Schedule 2 to the 1989 Act (approval by the court of local authority arrangements to assist children to live abroad); or
 (iv) the 2002 Act (adoption, placement etc.);
(b) in exercise of the family court's jurisdiction in relation to contempt of court where that decision or order was made in, or in connection with, proceedings referred to in sub-paragraph (a); or
(c) where that decision or order was itself made on an appeal to the family court.

(Appeals in the cases referred to in this paragraph are outside the scope of these rules. The CPR make provision requiring permission to appeal in those cases.)

(1B) Permission to appeal is required under these rules—
(a) unless paragraph (2) applies, where the appeal is against a decision made by a circuit judge, Recorder, district judge or costs judge; or
(b) as provided by Practice Direction 30A.][1]

(2) Permission to appeal is not required where the appeal is against—

(a) a committal order; …[2]
(b) a secure accommodation order under section 25 of the 1989 Act[; or][3]
[(c) a refusal to grant habeas corpus for release in relation to a minor.][4]

(3) An application for permission to appeal may be made—

(a) to the lower court at the hearing at which the decision to be appealed was made [or, if the hearing is adjourned to a later date, the hearing on that date][5]; or
(b) to the appeal court in an appeal notice.

(Rule 30.4 sets out the time limits for filing an appellant's notice at the appeal court. Rule 30.5 sets out the time limits for filing a respondent's notice at the appeal court. Any application for permission to appeal to the appeal court must be made in the appeal notice (see rules 30.4(1) and 30.5(3).)

(4) Where the lower court refuses an application for permission to appeal, a further application for permission to appeal may be made to the appeal court.

(5) [Subject to paragraph (5A), where][6] the appeal court, without a hearing, refuses permission to appeal, the person seeking permission may request the decision to be reconsidered at a hearing.

[(5A) Where a judge of the High Court or [in the family court, a judge of the High Court or][7] a Designated Family Judge refuses permission to appeal without a hearing and considers that the application is totally without merit, the judge may make an order that the person seeking permission may not request the decision to be reconsidered at a hearing.

(5B) Rule 4.3(5) will not apply to an order that the person seeking permission may not request the decision to be reconsidered at a hearing made under paragraph (5A).][8]

(6) A request under paragraph (5) must be filed within 7 days beginning with the date on which the notice that permission has been refused was served.

(7) Permission to appeal may be given only where—

(a) the court considers that the appeal would have a real prospect of success; or
(b) there is some other compelling reason why the appeal should be heard.

(8) An order giving permission may—

(a) limit the issues to be heard; and
(b) be made subject to conditions.

(9) … [9]

Amendment

1 Substituted by the Access to Justice Act 1999 (Destination of Appeals) (Family Proceedings) (Amendment) Order 2016, SI 2016/891, art 3.
2 Repealed by the Family Procedure (Amendment No 4) Rules 2014, SI 2014/3296, rr 2, 11(a).
3 Substituted by the Family Procedure (Amendment No 4) Rules 2014, SI 2014/3296, rr 2, 11(b).
4 Inserted by the Family Procedure (Amendment No 4) Rules 2014, SI 2014/3296, rr 2, 11(c).
5 Inserted by the Family Procedure (Amendment) Rules 2022, SI 2022/44, rr 2, 28(1).
6 Substituted by the Family Procedure (Amendment) Rules 2013, SI 2013/530, rr 2, 5(a).
7 Inserted by the Family Procedure (Amendment No 2) Rules 2014, SI 2014/667, rr 2, 22(a).
8 Inserted by the Family Procedure (Amendment) Rules 2013, SI 2013/530, rr 2, 5(b).
9 Repealed by the Family Procedure (Amendment No 2) Rules 2014, SI 2014/667, rr 2, 22(b).

30.4 Appellant's notice

(1) Where the appellant seeks permission from the appeal court it must be requested in the appellant's notice.

(2) Subject to paragraph (3), the appellant must file the appellant's notice at the appeal court within—

(a) such period as may be directed by the lower court [at the hearing at which the decision to be appealed was made or, if the hearing is adjourned to a later date, the hearing on that date][1] (which may be longer or shorter than the period referred to in sub-paragraph (b)); or
(b) where the court makes no such direction, 21 days after the date of the decision of the lower court against which the appellant wishes to appeal.

[(3) Where the appeal is against—

(a) a case management decision; or
(b) an order under section 38(1) of the 1989 Act,

the appellant must file the appellant's notice within 7 days beginning with the date of the decision of the lower court.][2]

(4) Unless the appeal court orders otherwise, an appellant's notice must be served on each respondent and the persons referred to in paragraph (5)—

(a) as soon as practicable; and
(b) in any event not later than 7 days,

after it is filed.

(5) The persons referred to in paragraph (4) are—

(a) any children's guardian, welfare officer, or children and family reporter;
(b) a local authority who has prepared a report under section 14A(8) or (9) of the 1989 Act;
(c) an adoption agency or local authority which has prepared a report on the suitability of the applicant to adopt a child;
(d) a local authority which has prepared a report on the placement of the child for adoption; and
(e) …[3]

Amendment

1 Inserted by the Family Procedure (Amendment) Rules 2022, SI 2022/44, rr 2, 28(2).
2 Substituted by the Family Procedure (Amendment No 2) Rules 2014, SI 2014/667, rr 2, 23(a).
3 Repealed by the Family Procedure (Amendment No 2) Rules 2014, SI 2014/667, rr 2, 23(b).

30.5 Respondent's notice

(1) A respondent may file and serve a respondent's notice.

(2) A respondent who—

(a) is seeking permission to appeal from the appeal court; or
(b) wishes to ask the appeal court to uphold the order of the lower court for reasons different from or additional to those given by the lower court,

must file a respondent's notice.

(3) Where the respondent seeks permission from the appeal court it must be requested in the respondent's notice.

(4) [Subject to paragraph (4A), a respondent's notice][1] must be filed within—

(a) such period as may be directed by the lower court [at the hearing at which the decision to be appealed was made or, if the hearing is adjourned to a later date, the hearing on that date][2]; or
(b) where the court makes no such direction, 14 days beginning with the date referred to in paragraph (5).

[(4A) Where the appeal is against a case management decision, a respondent's notice must be filed within—

(a) such period as may be directed by the lower court; or
(b) where the court makes no such direction, 7 days beginning with the date referred to in paragraph (5).][3]

(5) The date referred to in paragraph (4) is—

(a) the date on which the respondent is served with the appellant's notice where—
  (i) permission to appeal was given by the lower court; or
  (ii) permission to appeal is not required;
(b) the date on which the respondent is served with notification that the appeal court has given the appellant permission to appeal; or
(c) the date on which the respondent is served with notification that the application for permission to appeal and the appeal itself are to be heard together.

(6) Unless the appeal court orders otherwise, a respondent's notice must be served on the appellant, any other respondent and the persons referred to in rule 30.4(5)—

(a) as soon as practicable; and
(b) in any event not later than 7 days,

after it is filed.

(7) Where there is an appeal against an order under section 38(1) of the 1989 Act—

(a) a respondent may not, in that appeal, bring an appeal from the order or ask the appeal court to uphold the order of the lower court for reasons different from or additional to those given by the lower court; and
(b) paragraphs (2) and (3) do not apply.

Amendment

1 Substituted by the Family Procedure (Amendment No 2) Rules 2014, SI 2014/667, rr 2, 24(a).
2 Inserted by the Family Procedure (Amendment) Rules 2022, SI 2022/44, rr 2, 28(3).
3 Inserted by the Family Procedure (Amendment No 2) Rules 2014, SI 2014/667, rr 2, 24(b).

30.6 Grounds of appeal

The appeal notice must state the grounds of appeal.

30.7 Variation of time

(1) An application to vary the time limit for filing an appeal notice must be made to the appeal court.

(2) The parties may not agree to extend any date or time limit set by—

(a) these rules;
(b) Practice Direction 30A; or
(c) an order of the appeal court or the lower court.

(Rule 4.1(3)(a) provides that the court may extend or shorten the time for compliance with a rule, practice direction or court order (even if an application for extension is made after the time for compliance has expired).)

(Rule 4.1(3)(c) provides that the court may adjourn or bring forward a hearing.)

30.8 Stay

Unless the appeal court or the lower court orders otherwise, an appeal does not operate as a stay(GL) of any order or decision of the lower court.

30.9 Amendment of appeal notice

An appeal notice may not be amended without the permission of the appeal court.

30.10 Striking out appeal notices and setting aside or imposing conditions on permission to appeal

(1) The appeal court may—

(a) strike out(GL) the whole or part of an appeal notice;
(b) set aside(GL) permission to appeal in whole or in part;
(c) impose or vary conditions upon which an appeal may be brought.

(2) The court will only exercise its powers under paragraph (1) where there is a compelling reason for doing so.

(3) Where a party was present at the hearing at which permission was given that party may not subsequently apply for an order that the court exercise its powers under paragraphs (1)(b) or (1)(c).

30.11 Appeal court's powers

(1) In relation to an appeal the appeal court has all the powers of the lower court.

(Rule 30.1(4) provides that this Part is subject to any enactment that sets out special provisions with regard to any particular category of appeal.)

(2) The appeal court has power to—

(a) affirm, set aside(GL) or vary any order or judgment made or given by the lower court;
(b) refer any application or issue for determination by the lower court;
(c) order a new hearing;
(d) make orders for the payment of interest;
(e) make a costs order.

(3) The appeal court may exercise its powers in relation to the whole or part of an order of the lower court.

(Rule 4.1 contains general rules about the court's case management powers.)

(4) If the appeal court—

(a) refuses an application for permission to appeal;
(b) strikes out an appellant's notice; or
(c) dismisses an appeal,

and it considers that the application, the appellant's notice or the appeal is totally without merit, the provisions of paragraph (5) must be complied with.

(5) Where paragraph (4) applies—

(a) the court's order must record the fact that it considers the application, the appellant's notice or the appeal to be totally without merit; and
(b) the court must at the same time consider whether it is appropriate to make a civil restraint order.

30.12 Hearing of appeals

(1) Every appeal will be limited to a review of the decision of the lower court unless—

(a) an enactment or practice direction makes different provision for a particular category of appeal; or
(b) the court considers that in the circumstances of an individual appeal it would be in the interests of justice to hold a re-hearing.

(2) Unless it orders otherwise, the appeal court will not receive—

(a) oral evidence; or
(b) evidence which was not before the lower court.

(3) The appeal court will allow an appeal where the decision of the lower court was—

(a) wrong; or
(b) unjust because of a serious procedural or other irregularity in the proceedings in the lower court.

(4) The appeal court may draw any inference of fact which it considers justified on the evidence.

(5) At the hearing of the appeal a party may not rely on a matter not contained in that party's appeal notice unless the appeal court gives permission.

[30.12A Appeal court's power to order that hearing of appeal be held in public

(1) This rule applies where by virtue of rule 27.10 the hearing of an appeal is to be held in private.

(2) The appeal court may make an order—

(a) for the hearing of the appeal to be in public;
(b) for a part of the hearing of the appeal to be in public; or
(c) excluding any person or class of persons from attending a public hearing of an appeal or any part of it.

(3) Where the appeal court makes an order under paragraph (2), it may in the same order or in a subsequent order—

(a) impose restrictions on the publication of the identity of—
  (i) any party;
  (ii) any child (whether or not a party);
  (iii) any witness; or
  (iv) any other person;
(b) prohibit the publication of any information which may lead to any such person being identified;
(c) prohibit the publication of any information relating to the proceedings from such date as the court may specify; or
(d) impose such other restrictions on the publication of information relating to the proceedings as the court may specify.

(4) A practice direction may provide for—

(a) circumstances (which may be of general application or applicable only to specified appeal courts or proceedings) in which the appeal court will ordinarily make an order under paragraph (2); and
(b) the terms of the order under paragraph (3) which the court will ordinarily make in such circumstances.][1]

Amendment

1 Inserted by the Family Procedure (Amendment No 2) Rules 2018, SI 2018/1172, rr 2, 6.

30.13 Assignment of appeals to the Court of Appeal

(1) Where the court from or to which an appeal is made or from which permission to appeal is sought ('the relevant court') considers that—

(a) an appeal which is to be heard by a county court or the High Court would raise an important point of principle or practice; or

(b) there is some other compelling reason for the Court of Appeal to hear it,

the relevant court may order the appeal to be transferred to the Court of Appeal.

[(2) Paragraph (1) does not allow an application for permission to appeal to be transferred to the Court of Appeal.][1]

Amendment

1 Substituted by the Family Procedure (Amendment No 2) Rules 2014, SI 2014/667, rr 2, 25.

30.14 Reopening of final appeals

(1) The High Court will not reopen a final determination of any appeal unless—

(a) it is necessary to do so in order to avoid real injustice;

(b) the circumstances are exceptional and make it appropriate to reopen the appeal; and

(c) there is no alternative effective remedy.

(2) In paragraphs (1), (3), (4) and (6), 'appeal' includes an application for permission to appeal.

(3) This rule does not apply to appeals to [the family court][1].

(4) Permission is needed to make an application under this rule to reopen a final determination of an appeal.

(5) There is no right to an oral hearing of an application for permission unless, exceptionally, the judge so directs.

(6) The judge will not grant permission without directing the application to be served on the other party to the original appeal and giving that party an opportunity to make representations.

(7) There is no right of appeal or review from the decision of the judge on the application for permission, which is final.

(8) The procedure for making an application for permission is set out in Practice Direction 30A.

Amendment

1 Substituted by the Family Procedure (Amendment No 2) Rules 2014, SI 2014/667, rr 2, 26.

Practice Direction 30A – Appeals

See also Part 30

This Practice Direction supplements FPR Part 30

Application and interpretation

1.1 This practice direction applies to all appeals to which Part 30 applies.

1.2 In this Practice Direction in relation to the family court –

'the 1984 Act' means the Matrimonial and Family Proceedings Act 1984;

'authorised' means authorised by the President of the Family Division or nominated by or on behalf of the Lord Chief Justice to conduct particular business in the family court, in accordance with Part 3 of rules relating to the composition of the court and distribution of business made in accordance with section 31 D of the 1984 Act;

'costs judge means –

(a) the Chief Taxing Master;
(b) a taxing master of the Senior Courts; or
(c) a person appointed to act as deputy for the person holding office referred to in paragraph (b) or to act as a temporary additional officer for any such office;

'judge of circuit judge level means –

(a) a circuit judge who, where applicable, is authorised;
(b) a Recorder who, where applicable, is authorised;
(c) any other judge of the family court authorised to sit as a judge of circuit judge level in the family court;

'judge of district judge level' means –

(a) the Senior District Judge of the Family Division;
(b) a district judge of the Principal Registry of the Family Division ('PRFD');
(c) a person appointed to act as deputy for the person holding office referred to in paragraph (b) or to act as a temporary additional officer for any such office;
(d) a district judge who, where applicable, is authorised;
(e) a deputy district judge appointed under section 102 of the Senior Courts Act 1981 or section 8 of the County Courts Act 1984 who, where applicable, is authorised;
(f) an authorised District Judge (Magistrates' Courts);
(g) any other judge of the family court authorised to sit as a judge of district judge level in the family court.

'judge of High Court judge level' means –

(a) a deputy judge of the High Court;
(b) a puisne judge of the High Court;
(c) a person who has been a judge of the Court of Appeal or a puisne judge of the High Court who may act as a judge of the family court by virtue of section 9 of the Senior Courts Act 1981;
(d) the Senior President of Tribunals;
(e) the Chancellor of the High Court;
(f) an ordinary judge of the Court of Appeal (including the vice-president, if any, of either division of that court);
(g) the President of the Queen's Bench Division;
(h) the President of the Family Division;
(i) the Master of the Rolls;
(j) the Lord Chief Justice;

'justices' legal adviser' means a person authorised to exercise functions under section 67B of the Courts Act 2003 who has such qualifications as are prescribed by the Authorised Court Staff (Legal Advice Functions) Qualifications Regulations 2020; and

'lay justice' means an authorised justice of the peace who is not a District Judge (Magistrates' Courts).

Routes of appeal

2.1 The following table sets out to which court or judge an appeal is to be made (subject to obtaining any necessary permission) from decisions of the family court –

Decision of judge sitting in the family court	*Permission generally required (subject to exception in rules of court, for example, no permission required to appeal against a committal order)*	*Appeal to*
1. A bench of – two or three lay magistrates; or a lay justice	No	a judge of circuit judge level sitting in the family court; a judge of High Court judge level sitting in the family court where a Designated Family Judge or a judge of High Court Judge level considers that the appeal would raise an important point of principle or practice. (NB a judge of High Court judge level may hear the appeal in interests of effective and efficient use of local judicial resource and the resource of the High Court bench)
2. A judge of district judge level (except the Senior District Judge of the Family Division in proceedings for a financial remedy)	Yes	As above
3. Omitted		
4. Senior District Judge of the Family Division in proceedings for financial remedy	Yes	Judge of High Court judge level sitting in the family court
4A. Circuit judge or Recorder, except where paragraph 5 of this table applies.	Yes	High Court Judge (sitting in the High Court)

Decision of judge sitting in the family court	*Permission generally required (subject to exception in rules of court, for example, no permission required to appeal against a committal order)*	*Appeal to*
5. Circuit judge or Recorder, where the appeal is from: (a) a decision or order in proceedings under— (i) Part 4 or 5 of, or paragraph 19(1) of Schedule 2 to, the Children Act 1989; or (ii) the Adoption and Children Act 2002; (b) a decision or order in exercise of the court's jurisdiction in relation to contempt of court, where that decision or order was made in, or in connection with, proceedings of a type referred to in sub-paragraph (a); or (c) a decision or order made on appeal to the family court.	Yes	Court of Appeal
6. Costs Judge	Yes	Judge of High Court judge level sitting in the family court
7. Judge of High Court judge level	Yes	Court of Appeal
8. Any other judge of the family court not referred to in paragraphs 1 to 7 of	Yes	Court of Appeal

(Provisions setting out routes of appeal include section 31K(1) of the 1984 Act for appeals against decisions from the family court and section 13(2A) of the Administration of Justice Act 1960 for appeals against decisions or orders from the family court relating to contempt of court.

The Access to Justice Act 1999 (Destination of Appeals) (Family Proceedings) Order 2014 (S. I. 2014/602) routes appeals from certain judges and office holders to the family court instead of to the Court of Appeal and rules relating to the composition of the court and distribution of business made in accordance with section 31 D of the 1984 Act make provision for appeals within the family court.

Amendments to the 2014 Order (made by the Access to Justice Act 1999 (Destination of Appeals) (Family Proceedings) (Amendment) Order 2016) route certain appeals from Circuit Judges or Recorders to the High Court instead of the Court of Appeal. These appeals are heard by a High Court judge sitting in the High Court (see paragraph 8.4 below).

The leapfrogging provision in section 57 of the Access to Justice Act 1999 applies to appeals where in any proceedings in the family court a person appeals or seeks permission to appeal to a court other than the Court of Appeal or the Supreme Court.)

2.2 The following table sets out to which court or judge an appeal is to be made (subject to obtaining any necessary permission) from decisions of the High Court –

Decision of judge	*Permission generally required (subject to exception in rules of court, for example, no permission required to appeal against a committal order)*	*Appeal to*
1. District Judge of the High Court; or a deputy district judge appointed under section 102 of the Senior Courts Act 1981	Yes	High Court Judge
2. The Senior District Judge of the Family Division; District Judge of the PRFD; or a person appointed to act as deputy for a District Judge of the PRFD or to act as a temporary additional officer for such office	Yes	High Court Judge
3. Costs judge; or a person appointed to act as deputy for a costs judge who is a taxing master of the senior courts or to act as a temporary additional officer for such office	Yes	High Court Judge
4. Judge of the High Court (including a person acting as a judge of the High Court in accordance with section 9(1) or section 9(4) of the Senior Courts Act 1981)	Yes	Court of Appeal

(Provisions setting out routes of appeal include section 16(1) of the Senior Courts Act 1981 (as amended) for appeals against decisions from the High Court and section 13 of the Administration of Justice Act 1960 for appeals against an order or decision of the High Court relating to contempt of court. The Access to Justice Act 1999 (Destination of Appeals)(Family Proceedings) Order 2011 (S. I. 2011/1044) routes appeals against decisions of certain judges to the High Court instead of the Court of Appeal. The leapfrogging provision in section 57 of the Access to Justice Act 1999 referred to above applies.

The general rule is that appeals under section 8(1) of the Gender Recognition Act 2004 must be started in the family court as both the High Court and the family court have jurisdiction to hear the appeal (see section 8 of the 2004 Act and FPR 5.4). The procedure for appeals to the Court of Appeal is governed by the Civil Procedure Rules 1998, in particular CPR Part 52.).

2.3 Justices' legal advisers are not judges of the family court but they are authorised to exercise functions under section 67B of the Courts Act 2003. Appeals against decisions of a justices' legal adviser are to a judge of circuit judge level sitting in the family court. However, it is expected that such appeals will be rare as a justices' legal adviser may refer a matter to the court as appropriate before making a decision.

2.4 Where the decision to be appealed is a decision in a Part 19 (Alternative Procedure For Applications) application on a point of law in a case which did not involve any substantial dispute of fact, the court to which the appeal lies, where that court is the High Court or the family court and unless the appeal would lie to the Court of Appeal in any event, must consider whether to order the appeal to be transferred to the Court of Appeal under FPR 30.13 (Assignment of Appeals to the Court of Appeal).

Grounds for appeal

3.1 Rule 30.12 (hearing of appeals) sets out the circumstances in which the appeal court will allow an appeal.

3.2 The grounds of appeal should –

(a) set out clearly the reasons why rule 30.12 (3)(a) or (b) is said to apply; and
(b) specify in respect of each ground, whether the ground raises an appeal on a point of law or is an appeal against a finding of fact.

Permission to appeal

4.1 FPR 30.3 (Permission) sets out the circumstances when permission to appeal is required. At present permission to appeal is required where the decision of the family court appealed against was made by a district judge (including a District Judge (Magistrates' Courts)) or a costs judge. Permission to appeal is required where the decision of the High Court appealed against is a decision of a district judge or a costs judge. However, no permission is required where FPR 30.3(2) (appeals against a committal order or a secure accommodation order under section 25 of the Children Act 1989) applies.

(The requirement of permission to appeal may be imposed by a practice direction – see FPR 30.3(1)(b) (Permission). 'District judge' and 'costs judge' are defined in FPR 30.1(3)).

4.1A FPR Part 30 does not apply to an appeal against the decision or order of a Circuit Judge or Recorder in the family court where the decision or order was made-

(a) in proceedings under-
 (i) Part 4 or 5 of, or paragraph 19(1) of Schedule 2 to, the Children Act 1989; or
 (ii) the Adoption and Children Act 2002;
 (b) in exercise of the court's jurisdiction in relation to contempt of court, where that decision or order was made in, or in connection with, proceedings of a type referred to in paragraph (a); or
(c) on appeal to the family court.

(An appeal against a decision by a Circuit Judge or Recorder, where the appeal is from a decision or order referred to in paragraph 4.1A, is to the Court of Appeal and the Civil Procedure Rules 1998 apply.)

4.1B 4.1B The court should not ordinarily grant permission to appeal where the matters complained of would be better dealt with on an application to set aside a financial remedy order under rule 9.9A, an inherent jurisdiction order under rule 12.42B or a return order or non-return order under rule 12.52A. Such an application would be appropriate if the proposed appeal does not in fact allege an error of the court on the materials that were before the court at the time the order was made. However, by way of exception, permission to appeal may still be given where (i) a litigant alleges both that the court erred on the materials before it and that a ground for setting aside exists; or (ii) as the case may be, the order which it is sought to set aside includes a pension sharing order or pension compensation sharing order and the court may be asked to consider making orders under s 40A(5) or s 40B(2) of the Matrimonial Causes Act 1973.

Court to which permission to appeal application should be made

4.2 An application for permission should be made orally at the hearing at which the decision to be appealed against is made.

4.3 Where –

(a) no application for permission to appeal is made at the hearing; or
(b) the lower court refuses permission to appeal,

an application for permission to appeal may be made to the appeal court in accordance with rules 30.3(3) and (4) (Permission).

(Rule 30.1(3) defines 'lower court'.)

4.4 Where no application for permission to appeal has been made in accordance with rule 30.3(3)(a) (Permission) but a party requests further time to make such an application the court may adjourn the hearing to give that party an opportunity to do so.

4.5 There is no appeal from a decision of the appeal court to allow or refuse permission to appeal to that court. However, where the appeal court, without a hearing, refuses permission to appeal, the person seeking permission may request that decision to be reconsidered at a hearing, unless an order has been made under rule 30.3(5A) that the person seeking permission may not do so (where the application for permission is considered to be totally without merit) – see section 54(4) of the Access to Justice Act 1999 and rule 30.3(5), (5A) (Permission).

Permission and case management decisions

4.5A Where the application is for permission to appeal from a case management decision, the factors to which the court is to have particular regard include whether –

(a) the issue is of sufficient significance to justify an appeal;
(b) the procedural consequences of an appeal (e.g. the impact upon the timetable) outweigh the significance of the case management decision;
(c) it would be more convenient to adjourn the determination of the issue.

4.5B Case management decisions include decisions made under FPR 4.1(3) and decisions about disclosure, filing of witness statements or experts' reports, directions about the timetable of the proceedings and adding a party to the proceedings.

Material omission from a judgment of the lower court

4.6 Where a party's advocate considers that there is a material omission from a judgment of the lower court or, where the decision is made by a lay justice or justices, the written reasons for the decision of the lower court (including inadequate reasons for the lower court's decision), the advocate should before the drawing of the order give the lower court which made the decision the opportunity of considering whether there is an omission and should not immediately use the omission as grounds for an application to appeal.

4.7 Paragraph 4.8 below applies where there is an application to the lower court for permission to appeal on the grounds of a material omission from a judgment or written reasons (where a decision is made in the family court by a lay justice or justices) of the lower court. Paragraph 4.9 below applies where there is an application for permission to appeal to the appeal court on the grounds of a material omission from a judgment or written reasons (where a decision is made in the family court by a lay justice or justices) of the lower court.

4.8 Where the application for permission to appeal is made to the lower court, the court which made the decision must –

(a) consider whether there is a material omission and adjourn for that purpose if necessary; and
(b) where the conclusion is that there has been such an omission, provide additions to the judgment.

4.9 Where the application for permission to appeal is made to the appeal court, the appeal court –

(a) must consider whether there is a material omission; and
(b) where the conclusion is that there has been such an omission, may adjourn the application and remit the case to the lower court with an invitation to provide additions to the judgment.

Consideration of Permission without a hearing

4.10 An application for permission to appeal may be considered by the appeal court without a hearing.

4.11 If permission is granted without a hearing the parties will be notified of that decision and the procedure in paragraphs 6.1 to 6.8 will then apply.

4.12 If permission is refused without a hearing the parties will be notified of that decision with the reasons for it. The decision is subject to the appellant's right to have it reconsidered at an oral hearing. This may be before the same judge. However the appellant has no right to have the application considered at an oral hearing where a High Court Judge or Designated Family Judge refused permission to appeal without a hearing and made an order under rule 30.3(5A) that the appellant may not request the decision to be reconsidered at a hearing because he or she considered the application for permission to be totally without merit.

4.13 A request for the decision to be reconsidered at an oral hearing must be filed at the appeal court within 7 days after service of the notice that permission has been refused. A copy of the request must be served by the appellant on the respondent at the same time. This does not apply where an order has been made under rule 30.3(5A) that the appellant may not request the decision to be reconsidered at a hearing.

Permission hearing

4.14 Where an appellant, who is represented, makes a request for a decision to be reconsidered at an oral hearing, the appellant's advocate must, at least 4 days before the hearing, in a brief written statement –

(a) inform the court and the respondent of the points which the appellant proposes to raise at the hearing;

(b) set out the reasons why permission should be granted notwithstanding the reasons given for the refusal of permission; and
(c) confirm, where applicable, that the requirements of paragraph 4.17 have been complied with (appellant in receipt of legal aid).

4.15 The respondent will be given notice of a permission hearing, but is not required to attend unless requested by the court to do so.

4.16 If the court requests the respondent's attendance at the permission hearing, the appellant must supply the respondent with a copy of the appeal bundle (see paragraph 5.9 or 5.9A, as applicable) within 7 days of being notified of the request, or such other period as the court may direct. The costs of providing that bundle shall be borne by the appellant initially, but will form part of the costs of the permission application.

Appellants in receipt of services funded by legal aid: applying for permission to appeal

4.17 Where the appellant is in receipt of legal aid and permission to appeal has been refused by the appeal court without a hearing, the appellant must send a copy of the reasons the appeal court gave for refusing permission to the Director of legal aid casework as soon as it has been received from the court. The court will require confirmation that this has been done if a hearing is requested to re-consider the question of permission.

Limited permission

4.18 Where a court under rule 30.3 (Permission) gives permission to appeal on some issues only, it will –

(a) refuse permission on any remaining issues; or
(b) reserve the question of permission to appeal on any remaining issues to the court hearing the appeal.

4.19 If the court reserves the question of permission under paragraph 4.18(b), the appellant must, within 14 days after service of the court's order, inform the appeal court and the respondent in writing whether the appellant intends to pursue the reserved issues. If the appellant does intend to pursue the reserved issues, the parties must include in any time estimate for the appeal hearing, their time estimate for the reserved issues.

4.20 If the appeal court refuses permission to appeal on the remaining issues without a hearing and the applicant wishes to have that decision reconsidered at an oral hearing, the time limit in rule 30.3(6) (Permission) shall apply. Any application for an extension of this time limit should be made promptly. The court hearing the appeal on the issues for which permission has been granted will not normally grant, at the appeal hearing, an application to extend the time limit in rule 30.3 (6) for the remaining issues.

4.21 If the appeal court refuses permission to appeal on remaining issues at or after an oral hearing, the application for permission to appeal on those issues cannot be renewed at the appeal hearing (see section 54(4) of the Access to Justice Act 1999).

Respondents' costs of permission applications

4.22 In most cases, applications for permission to appeal will be determined without the court requesting –

(a) submissions from; or
(b) if there is an oral hearing, attendance by,

the respondent.

4.23 Where the court does not request submissions from or attendance by the respondent, costs will not normally be allowed to a respondent who volunteers submissions or attendance.

4.24 Where the court does request –

(a) submissions from; or
(b) attendance by the respondent,

the court will normally allow the costs of the respondent if permission is refused.

Allocation-appropriate procedure

4A.1 Where a party is dissatisfied with allocation that party may appeal or request the court to reconsider allocation at a hearing under FPR 29.19.

4A.2 Where allocation was made at a hearing, the party who is dissatisfied may appeal.

4A.3 Where allocation was made without a hearing, the party who is dissatisfied should request the court to reconsider allocation at a hearing.

Appellant's notice

5.1 An appellant's notice must be filed and served in all cases. Where an application for permission to appeal is made to the appeal court it must be applied for in the appellant's notice.

Practice Direction 5A specifies the forms to be used to make an appeal: different forms are to be used, depending on the court to which the appeal lies.

Human Rights

5.2 Where the appellant seeks –

(a) to rely on any issue under the Human Rights Act 1998; or
(b) a remedy available under that Act,

for the first time in an appeal the appellant must include in the appeal notice the information required by rule 29.5(2).

5.3 Practice Direction 29A (Human Rights, Joining the Crown) will apply as if references to the directions hearing were to the application for permission to appeal.

Extension of time for filing appellant's notice

5.4 If an extension of time is required for filing the appellant's notice the application must be made in that notice. The notice should state the reason for the delay and the steps taken prior to the application being made.

5.5 Where the appellant's notice includes an application for an extension of time and permission to appeal has been given or is not required the respondent has the right to be heard on that application and must be served with a copy of the appeal bundle (see paragraph 5.9). However, a respondent who unreasonably opposes an extension of time runs the risk of being ordered to pay the appellant's costs of that application.

5.6 If an extension of time is given following such an application the procedure at paragraphs 6.1 to 6.8 applies.

Applications

5.7 Notice of an application to be made to the appeal court for a remedy incidental to the appeal (e.g. an interim injunction under rule 20.2 (Orders for interim remedies)) may be included in the appeal notice or in a Part 18 (Procedure For Other Applications in Proceedings) application notice.

(Paragraph 13 of this practice direction contains other provisions relating to applications.).

Documents: appeals to the family court

5.8 Where the appeal lies to the family court, the appellant must file the following documents together with an appeal bundle (see paragraph 5.9) with his or her appellant's notice –

(a) Omitted
(b) one copy of the appellant's notice for each of the respondents;
(c) one copy of the appellant's skeleton argument for each of the respondents;
(d) Omitted
(e) Omitted
(f) any witness statements or affidavits in support of any application included in the appellant's notice.

5.9 Where the appeal lies to the family court, an appellant must include the following documents in his or her appeal bundle –

(a) a sealed or stamped copy of the appellant's notice;
(b) a sealed or stamped copy of the order being appealed, or a copy of the notice of the making of an order;
(c) a copy of any order giving or refusing permission to appeal, together with a copy of the court's reasons for allowing or refusing permission to appeal;
(d) any affidavit or witness statement filed in support of any application included in the appellant's notice;
(e) where the appeal is against a consent order, a statement setting out the change in circumstances since the order was agreed or other circumstances justifying a review or re-hearing;
(f) a copy of the appellant's skeleton argument;
(g) a transcript or note of judgment or, in a magistrates' court, written reasons for the court's decision (see paragraph 5.23), and in cases where permission to appeal was given by the lower court or is not required those parts of any transcript of evidence which are directly relevant to any question at issue on the appeal;
(h) the application form;
(i) any application notice (or case management documentation) relevant to the subject of the appeal;
(j) any other documents which the appellant reasonably considers necessary to enable the appeal court to reach its decision on the hearing of the application or appeal; and
(k) such other documents as the court may direct.

5.10 All documents that are extraneous to the issues to be considered on the application or the appeal must be excluded. The appeal bundle may include affidavits, witness statements, summaries, experts' reports and exhibits but only where these are directly relevant to the subject matter of the appeal.

Documents: appeals to the High Court

5.10A Where an appeal lies to the High Court, the appellant must file the following documents, in the following sequence, as the appeal bundle:

(a) a sealed or stamped copy of the appellant's notice (including the grounds of appeal);
(b) a sealed or stamped copy of the order being appealed [or a copy of the notice of the making of an order];
(c) a transcript or note of the judgment (see also paragraphs 5.23 and 5.24);
(d) copies of any documents specifically referred to in the judgment;
(e) a copy of the appellant's skeleton argument (see also paragraphs 5.14 and 5.15).

5.10B Subject to paragraphs 5.11 and 6.4(1) and (c), no further documents may be included in the appeal bundle without an order of a High Court Judge sitting in the High Court.

5.10C In addition to the appeal bundle, the appellant must file the following duplicate documents-

(a) one copy of the appellant's notice for each of the respondents;
(b) one copy of the appellant's skeleton argument for each of the respondents (see also paragraphs 5.14 and 5.15).

Documents: appeals to the family court or the High Court

5.11 Where the appellant is represented, the appeal bundle must contain a certificate signed by the appellant's solicitor, counsel or other representative to the effect that the appellant has read and understood paragraph 5.10 and that the composition of the appeal bundle complies with it.

5.12 Where it is not possible to file all the above documents, the appellant must indicate which documents have not yet been filed and the reasons why they are not currently available. The appellant must then provide a reasonable estimate of when the missing document or documents can be filed and file them as soon as reasonably practicable.

Skeleton arguments

5.13 As noted in paragraphs 5.9 and 5.10A, the appellant's notice must, subject to paragraphs 5.14 and 5.15, be accompanied by a skeleton argument. Alternatively the skeleton argument may be included in the appellant's notice. Where the skeleton argument is so included it will not form part of the notice for the purposes of rule 30.9 (Amendment of appeal notice).

5.14 Subject to paragraph 5.14A, where it is impracticable for the appellant's skeleton argument to accompany the appellant's notice it must be filed and served on all respondents within 14 days of filing the notice.

5.14A In appeals against case management decisions, where the appellant's skeleton argument cannot accompany the appellant's notice it must be filed as soon as practicable or as directed by the court, but in any event not less than 3 days before the hearing of the appeal.

5.15 An appellant who is not represented need not file a skeleton argument but is encouraged to do so since this will be helpful to the court.

5.16 A skeleton argument must contain a numbered list of the points which the party wishes to make. These should both define and confine the areas of controversy. Each point should be stated as concisely as the nature of the case allows.

5.17 A numbered point must be followed by a reference to any document on which the party wishes to rely.

5.18 A skeleton argument must state, in respect of each authority cited –

(a) the proposition of law that the authority demonstrates; and
(b) the parts of the authority (identified by page or paragraph references) that support the proposition.

5.19 If more than one authority is cited in support of a given proposition, the skeleton argument must briefly state the reason for taking that course.

5.20 The statement referred to in paragraph 5.19 should not materially add to the length of the skeleton argument but should be sufficient to demonstrate, in the context of the argument –

(a) the relevance of the authority or authorities to that argument; and
(b) that the citation is necessary for a proper presentation of that argument.

5.21 The cost of preparing a skeleton argument which –

(a) does not comply with the requirements set out in this paragraph; or
(b) was not filed within the time limits provided by this Practice Direction (or any further time granted by the court),

will not be allowed on assessment except to the extent that the court otherwise directs.

5.22 The appellant should consider what other information the appeal court will need. This may include a list of persons who feature in the case or glossaries of technical terms. A chronology of relevant events will be necessary in most appeals.

Suitable record of the judgment

5.23 Where the judgment to be appealed has been officially recorded by the court, an approved transcript of that record should accompany the appellant's notice. Photocopies will not be accepted for this purpose. However, where there is no officially recorded judgment, the following documents will be acceptable –

Written judgments – where a decision is made by a lay justice or justices in the family court, a copy of the written reasons for the court's decision.

Written reasons – where a decision is made by a lay justice or justices in the family court, a copy of the written reasons for the court's decision.

Note of judgment – When judgment was not officially recorded or made in writing a note of the judgment (agreed between the appellant's and respondent's advocates) should be submitted for approval to the judge whose decision is being appealed. If the parties cannot agree on a single note of the judgment, both versions should be provided to that judge with an explanatory letter. For the purpose of an application for permission to appeal the note need not be approved by the respondent or the lower court judge.

Advocates' notes of judgments where the appellant is unrepresented – When the appellant was unrepresented in the lower court it is the duty of any advocate for the respondent to make the advocate's note of judgment promptly available, free of charge to the appellant where there is no officially recorded judgment or if the court so directs. Where the appellant was represented in the lower court it is the duty of the appellant's own former advocate to make that advocate's note available in these circumstances. The appellant should submit the note of judgment to the appeal court.

5.24 An appellant may not be able to obtain an official transcript or other suitable record of the lower court's decision within the time within which the appellant's notice must be filed. In such cases the appellant's notice must still be completed to the best of the appellant's ability on the basis of the documentation available. However it may be amended subsequently with the permission of the appeal court in accordance with rule 30.9 (Amendment of appeal notice).

Advocates' notes of judgments

5.25 Advocates' brief (or, where appropriate, refresher) fee includes –

(a) remuneration for taking a note of the judgment of the court;
(b) having the note transcribed accurately;
(c) attempting to agree the note with the other side if represented;
(d) submitting the note to the judge for approval where appropriate;
(e) revising it if so requested by the judge,
(f) providing any copies required for the appeal court, instructing solicitors and lay client; and
(g) providing a copy of the note to an unrepresented appellant.

5.26 Omitted

Appeals under section 8(1) of the Gender Recognition Act 2004

5.27 Paragraph 5.28 to 5.30 apply where the appeal is brought under section 8(1) of the Gender Recognition Act 2004 on a point of law against a decision by the Gender Recognition Panel to reject the application under sections 1(1), 5(2), 5(A)(2) or 6(1) of the 2004 Act. The appeal is to the High Court or to the family court. However, FPR 5.4 provides that where the family court has jurisdiction to deal with a matter, the proceedings relating to that matter must be started in the family court except where the court otherwise directs, any rule, other enactment or Practice Direction provides otherwise or proceedings relating to the same parties are already being heard by the High Court. Most appeals under section 8(1) of the Gender Recognition Act 2004 are therefore likely to be to the family court and be heard by a judge of High Court Judge level sitting in that court in accordance with the rules relating to the composition of the court and distribution of business made in accordance with section 31 D of the 1984 Act.

5.28 Where the appeal is to the High Court, the appeal notice must be –

(a) filed in the PRFD; and
(b) served on the Secretary of State and the President of the Gender Recognition Panels.

5.28A Where the appeal is to the family court the appeal notice must be served on the Secretary of State and the President of the Gender Recognition Panels.

5.29 The Secretary of State may appear and be heard in the proceedings on the appeal.

5.30 Where the High Court issues a gender recognition certificate under section 8(3)(a) of the Gender Recognition Act 2004, the court officer must send a copy of that certificate to the Secretary of State.

Transcripts or Notes of Evidence

5.31 When the evidence is relevant to the appeal an official transcript of the relevant evidence must be obtained. Transcripts or notes of evidence are generally not needed for the purpose of determining an application for permission to appeal.

Notes of evidence

5.32 If evidence relevant to the appeal was not officially recorded, a typed version of the judge's or justices' legal adviser's notes of evidence must be obtained.

Transcripts at public expense

5.33 Where the lower court or the appeal court is satisfied that –

(a) an unrepresented appellant; or
(b) an appellant whose legal representation is provided free of charge to the appellant and not funded by the Community Legal Service,

is in such poor financial circumstances that the cost of a transcript would be an excessive burden the court may certify that the cost of obtaining one official transcript should be borne at public expense.

5.34 In the case of a request for an official transcript of evidence or proceedings to be paid for at public expense, the court must also be satisfied that there are reasonable grounds for appeal. Whenever possible a request for a transcript at public expense should be made to the lower court when asking for permission to appeal.

Filing and service of appellant's notice

5.35 Rule 30.4 (Appellant's notice) sets out the procedure and time limits for filing and serving an appellant's notice. Subject to paragraph 5.36, the appellant must file the appellant's notice at the appeal court within such period as may be directed by the lower court, which should not normally exceed 14 days or, where the lower court directs no such period within 21 days of the date of the decision that the appellant wishes to appeal.

5.36 Rule 30.4(3) (Appellant's notice) provides that unless the appeal court orders otherwise, where the appeal is against an order under section 38(1) of the 1989 Act or a case management decision in any proceedings, the appellant must file the appellant's notice within 7 days beginning with the date of the decision of the lower court.

5.37 Where the lower court announces its decision and reserves the reasons for its judgment or order until a later date, it should, in the exercise of powers under rule 30.4 (2)(a))(Appellant's notice), fix a period for filing the appellant's notice at the appeal court that takes this into account.

5.38 Except where the appeal court orders otherwise a sealed or stamped copy of the appellant's notice, including any skeleton arguments must be served on all respondents and other persons referred to in rule 30.4(5) (Appellant's notice) in accordance with the timetable prescribed by rule 30.4(4)) (Appellant's notice) except where this requirement is modified by paragraph 5.14 or 5.14A in which case the skeleton argument should be served as soon as it is filed.

5.39 Where the appellant's notice is to be served on a child, then rule 6.33 (supplementary provision relating to service on children) applies and unless the appeal court orders otherwise a sealed or stamped copy of the appellant's notice, including any skeleton arguments must be served on the persons or bodies mentioned in rule 6.33(3). For example, the appeal notice must be served on any children's guardian, welfare officer or children and family reporter who is appointed in the proceedings.

5.40 Unless the court otherwise directs, a respondent need not take any action when served with an appellant's notice until such time as notification is given to the respondent that permission to appeal has been given.

5.41 The court may dispense with the requirement for service of the notice on a respondent.

5.42 Unless the appeal court directs otherwise, the appellant must serve on the respondent the appellant's notice and skeleton argument (but not the appeal bundle),where the appellant is applying for permission to appeal in the appellant's notice.

5.43 Where permission to appeal –

(a) has been given by the lower court; or
(b) is not required,

the appellant must serve the appeal bundle on the respondent and the persons mentioned in paragraph 5.39 with the appellant's notice.

Amendment of Appeal Notice

5.44 An appeal notice may be amended with permission. Such an application to amend and any application in opposition will normally be dealt with at the hearing unless that course would cause unnecessary expense or delay in which case a request should be made for the application to amend to be heard in advance.

Procedure after permission is obtained

6.1 This paragraph sets out the procedure where –

(a) permission to appeal is given by the appeal court; or
(b) the appellant's notice is filed in the appeal court and –
    (i) permission was given by the lower court; or
    (ii) permission is not required.

6.2 If the appeal court gives permission to appeal, the appeal bundle must be served on each of the respondents within 7 days of receiving the order giving permission to appeal.

6.3 The appeal court will send the parties –

(a) notification of the date of the hearing or the period of time (the 'listing window') during which the appeal is likely to be heard;
(b) where permission is granted by the appeal court a copy of the order giving permission to appeal; and
(c) any other directions given by the court.

6.4 Where the appeal court grants permission to appeal, the appellant must add the following documents to the appeal bundle –

(a) the respondent's notice and skeleton argument (if any);
(b) those parts of the transcripts of evidence which are directly relevant to any question at issue on the appeal;
(c) the order granting permission to appeal and, where permission to appeal was granted at an oral hearing, the transcript (or note) of any judgment which was given; and
(d) any document which the appellant and respondent have agreed to add to the appeal bundle in accordance with paragraph 7.16.

6.5 Where permission to appeal has been refused on a particular issue, the appellant must remove from the appeal bundle all documents that are relevant only to that issue.

Time estimates

6.6 If the appellant is legally represented, the appeal court must be notified, in writing, of the advocate's time estimate for the hearing of the appeal.

6.7 The time estimate must be that of the advocate who will argue the appeal. It should exclude the time required by the court to give judgment.

6.8 A court officer will notify the respondent of the appellant's time estimate and if the respondent disagrees with the time estimate the respondent must inform the court within 7 days of the notification. In the absence of such notification the respondent will be deemed to have accepted the estimate proposed on behalf of the appellant.

Respondent

7.1 A respondent who wishes to ask the appeal court to vary the order of the lower court in any way must appeal and permission will be required on the same basis as for an appellant.

(Paragraph 3.2 applies to grounds of appeal by a respondent.).

7.2 A respondent who wishes to appeal or who wishes to ask the appeal court to uphold the order of the lower court for reasons different from or additional to those given by the lower court must file a respondent's notice.

7.3 A respondent who does not file a respondent's notice will not be entitled, except with the permission of the court, to rely on any reason not relied on in the lower court. This paragraph and paragraph 7.2 do not apply where the appeal is against an order under section 38(1) of the 1989 Act (see rule 30.5(7) (Respondent's notice)).

7.4 Paragraphs 5.3 (Human Rights and extension for time for filing appellant's notice) and 5.4 to 5.6 (extension of time for filing appellant's notice) of this practice direction also apply to a respondent and a respondent's notice.

Time limits

7.5 The time limits for filing a respondent's notice are set out in rule 30.5(4) and (5) (Respondent's notice).

7.6 Where an extension of time is required the extension must be requested in the respondent's notice and the reasons why the respondent failed to act within the specified time must be included.

7.7 Except where paragraphs 7.8 7.9A and 7.10 apply, the respondent must file a skeleton argument for the court in all cases where the respondent proposes to address arguments to the court. The respondent's skeleton argument may be included within a respondent's notice. Where a skeleton argument is included within a respondent's notice it will not form part of the notice for the purposes of rule 30.9 (Amendment of appeal notice).

7.8 Subject to paragraph 7.9A, a respondent who –

(a) files a respondent's notice; but
(b) does not include a skeleton argument with that notice,

must file the skeleton argument within 14 days of filing the notice.

7.9 Subject to paragraph 7.9A, a respondent who does not file a respondent's notice but who files a skeleton argument must file that skeleton argument at least 7 days before the appeal hearing.

(Rule 30.5(4) (Respondent's notice) sets out the period for filing a respondent's notice.).

7.9A In appeals against case management decisions, where –

(a) the respondent's skeleton argument cannot accompany the respondent 's notice; or

(b) a respondent does not file a respondent's notice but files a skeleton argument,

the skeleton argument must be filed as soon as practicable or as directed by the court, but in any event not less than 3 days before the hearing of the appeal.

7.10 A respondent who is not represented need not file a skeleton argument but is encouraged to do so in order to assist the court.

7.11 The respondent must serve the skeleton argument on –

(a) the appellant; and
(b) any other respondent;

at the same time as the skeleton argument is filed at court. Where a child is an appellant or respondent the skeleton argument must also be served on the persons listed in rule 6.33(3) unless the court directs otherwise.

7.12 A respondent's skeleton argument must conform to the directions at paragraphs 5.16 to 5.22 with any necessary modifications. It should, where appropriate, answer the arguments set out in the appellant's skeleton argument.

Applications within respondent's notices

7.13 A respondent may include an application within a respondent's notice in accordance with paragraph 5.7.

Filing respondent's notices and skeleton arguments

7.14 The respondent must file the following documents with the respondent's notice in every case –

(a) two additional copies of the respondent's notice for the appeal court; and
(b) one copy each for the appellant, any other respondents and any persons referred to in paragraph 5.39.

7.15 The respondent may file a skeleton argument with the respondent's notice and –

(a) where doing so must file two copies; and
(b) where not doing so must comply with paragraph 7.8.

7.16 If the respondent considers documents in addition to those filed by the appellant to be necessary to enable the appeal court to reach its decision on the appeal and wishes to rely on those documents, any amendments to the appeal bundle should be agreed with the appellant if possible.

7.17 If the representatives for the parties are unable to reach agreement, the respondent may prepare a supplemental bundle.

7.18 The respondent must file any supplemental bundle so prepared, together with the requisite number of copies for the appeal court, at the appeal court –

(a) with the respondent's notice; or
(b) if a respondent's notice is not filed, within 21 days after the respondent is served with the appeal bundle.

7.19 The respondent must serve –

(a) the respondent's notice;
(b) the skeleton argument (if any); and
(c) the supplemental bundle (if any), on –
  (i) the appellant; and
  (ii) any other respondent;

at the same time as those documents are filed at the court. Where a child is an appellant or respondent the documents referred to in paragraphs (a) to (c) above must also be served on the persons listed in rule 6.33(2) unless the court directs otherwise.

Appeals to the High Court

Application

8.1 The appellant's notice must be filed at the Family Division of the High Court at the Royal Courts of Justice, Strand, London, WC2A 2LL.

8.2 A respondent's notice must be filed at the court where the appellant's notice was filed.

8.3 In the case of appeals from district judges of the High Court, applications for permission and any other applications in the appeal, appeals may be heard and directions in the appeal may be given by a High Court Judge.

8.4 In cases where paragraph 8.5 applies, appeals, applications for permission to appeal and any other applications in the appeal may be heard, and directions in the appeal or application may be given, by a High Court judge only.

8.5 This paragraph applies in the case of appeals from a Circuit judge or Recorder, except where the appeal is from:

(a) a decision or order in proceedings under—
  (i) Part 4 or 5 of, or paragraph 19(1) of Schedule 2 to, the Children Act 1989; or
  (ii) the Adoption and Children Act 2002;
(b) a decision or order in exercise of the court's jurisdiction in relation to contempt of court, where that decision or order was made in, or in connection with, proceedings of a type referred to in sub-paragraph (a); or
(c) a decision or order made on appeal to the family court.'.

Appeals to a county court

9.1 Omitted

9.2 Omitted

Appeals to the family court from decisions in child support proceedings under section 111A of the Magistrates' Courts Act 1980 ('the 1980 Act')

9.3 Section 111A of the 1980 Act, provides that in proceedings under the Child Support Act 1991 a person may appeal to the family court on the ground that a decision is wrong in law or is in excess of jurisdiction. Section 111A(3)(a) provides that no appeal may be brought under section 111A if there is a right of appeal to the family court against the decision otherwise than under that section. Such an appeal is usually heard by a judge of circuit judge level court in accordance with the rules relating to the composition of the court and distribution of business made in accordance with section 31 D of the 1984 Act.

9.4 Subject to section 111A of the 1980 Act and any other enactment, the following rules in Part 30 apply to appeals under section 111A of the 1980 Act –

(a) 30.1 (scope and interpretation);
(b) 30.2 (parties to comply with the practice direction);
(c) 30.4 (appellant's notice);
(d) 30.6 (grounds of appeal);
(e) 30.8 (stay); and
(f) 30.9 (amendment of appeal notice).

9.5 Section 111A(4) of the 1980 Act provides that the notice of appeal must be filed within 21 days after the day on which the decision of the magistrates' court was given. The notice of appeal should also be served within this period of time. The time period for filing the appellant's notice in rule 30.4 (2) and (3) does not apply. There can be no extension of this 21 day time limit under rule 4.1(3)(a).

Other statutory rights of appeal from a magistrates court and the court at which the appellants notice is to be filed-provisions applying to those appeals and appeals under section 111A of the 1980 Act.

9.6 Omitted

9.7 Omitted

9.8 Subject to any enactment, a district judge may –

(a) dismiss an appeal;
  (i) for want of prosecution; or
  (ii) with the consent of the parties; or
(b) give leave for the appeal to be withdrawn,

and may deal with any question of costs arising out of the dismissal or withdrawal.

Unless the court directs otherwise, any interlocutory application in an appeal under section 111A of the 1980 Act may be made to a district judge sitting in the family court in accordance with the rules relating to the composition of the court and distribution of business made in accordance with section 31 D of the 1984 Act.

9.9 Omitted

9.10 Omitted

9.11 Omitted

9.12 This practice direction applies to appeals under section 111A of the 1980 Act with the following modifications and any other necessary modifications –

(a) after paragraph 5.6 insert –
  '5.6A Paragraphs 5.4 to 5.6 do not apply to the family court under section 111A of the Magistrates' Courts Act 1980.'
(b) in paragraph 5.35, insert 'and 5.36A' after 'subject to paragraph 5.36';
(c) after paragraph 5.36 insert –
  '5.36A Where the appeal is to a judge of a family court under section 111A of the Magistrates' Courts Act 1980, the appellant's notice must be filed and served within 21 days after the day on which the decision of the lower court was given.'.

Appeals to the family court from the Secretary of State: Deduction order appeals

9.13 A 'deduction order appeal' is an appeal under regulation 25AB(1)(a) to (d) of the Child Support (Collection and Enforcement) Regulations 1992 (S.I. 1992/1989) ('the Collection and Enforcement Regulations'). A deduction order appeal is an appeal against –

(a) the making of a regular deduction order under section 32A of the Child Support Act 1991 ('the 1991 Act');
(b) a decision on an application to review a regular deduction order;
(c) a decision to withhold consent to the disapplication of sections 32G(1) and 32H(2)(b) of the 1991 Act which has the effect of unfreezing funds in the liable person's account; or
(d) the making of a final lump sum deduction order under section 32F of the 1991 Act.

A deduction order appeal lies to the family court from the Secretary of State as a result of regulation 25AB(1) of the Collection and Enforcement Regulations.

9.14 The rules in Part 30 apply to deduction order appeals with the amendments set out in paragraphs 9.15 to 9.27 and 9.29 and 9.30 below. The rules in Part 30 also apply to appeals against the decision of a district judge in proceedings relating to a deduction order appeal with the amendments set out in paragraph 9.28 below.

9.15 'The respondent' means –

(a) the Secretary of State and any person other than the appellant who was served with an order under section 32A(1), 32E(1) or 32F(1) of the 1991 Act; and
(b) a person who is permitted by the appeal court to be a party to the appeal.

9.16 The appellant will serve the appellant's notice on the Secretary of State and any other respondent.

9.17 The appellant shall file and serve the appellant's notice, within 21 days of –

(a) where the appellant is a deposit-taker, service of the order;
(b) where the appellant is a liable person, receipt of the order; or
(c) where the appellant is either a deposit-taker or a liable person, the date of receipt of notification of the decision.

9.18 For the purposes of paragraph 9.17 –

(a) references to 'liable person' and 'deposit-taker' are to be interpreted in accordance with section 32E of the 1991 Act and regulation 25A(2) of the Collection and Enforcement Regulations and section 54 of the 1991 Act, respectively; and
(b) the liable person is to be treated as having received the order or notification of the decision 2 days after it was posted by the Secretary of State.

9.19 Rule 4.1(3)(a) (court's power to extend or shorten the time for compliance with a rule, practice direction or court order) does not apply to an appeal against the making of a lump sum deduction order under section 32F of the 1991 Act in so far as that rule gives the court power to extend the time set out in paragraph 9.17 for filing and serving an appellant's notice after the time for filing and serving the that notice set out in paragraph 9.17 has expired.

9.20 The Secretary of State shall provide to the court and serve on all other parties to the appeal any information and evidence relevant to the making of the decision or order being appealed, within 14 days of receipt of the appellant's notice.

9.21 Subject to paragraph 9.23, a respondent who wishes to ask the appeal court to uphold the order or decision of the Secretary of State for reasons different from or in additional to those given by the Secretary of State must file a respondent's notice.

9.22 A respondent's notice must be filed within 14 days of receipt of the appellant's notice.

9.23 Where the Secretary of State as a respondent, wishes to contend that its order or decision should be –

(a) varied, either in any event or in the event of the appeal being allowed in whole or in part; or

(b) affirmed on different grounds from those on which it relied when making the order or decision,

it shall, within 14 days of receipt of the appellant's notice, file and serve on all other parties to the appeal a respondent's notice.

9.24 In so far as rule 30.7 (Variation of time) may permit any application for variation of the time limit for filing an appellant's notice after the time for filing the appellant's notice has expired, that rule shall not apply to an appeal made against an order under section 32F(1) of the Act of 1991.

9.25 Rule 30.8 (stay) shall not apply to an appeal made against an order under section 32F(1) of the Act of 1991.

9.26 Omitted

9.27 Rule 30.11 (appeal court's powers) does not apply to deduction order appeals.

9.28 Rule 30.11(2)(d) (making orders for payment of interest) does not apply in the case of an appeal against a decision of a district judge in proceedings relating to a deduction order appeal.

9.29 In the case of a deduction order appeal –

(a) the appeal court has power to –
  (i) affirm or set aside the order or decision;
  (ii) remit the matter to the Secretary of State for the order or decision to be reconsidered, with appropriate directions;
  (iii) refer any application or issue for determination by the Secretary of State;
  (iv) make a costs order; and

(b) the appeal court may exercise its powers in relation to the whole or part of an order or decision of the Secretary of State.

9.30 In rule 30.12 (Hearing of appeals) –

(a) at the beginning of paragraph (1), for 'Every' substitute 'Subject to paragraph (2A), every';

(b) at the beginning of paragraph (2), for 'Unless' substitute 'Subject to paragraph (2A), unless';

(c) after paragraph (2), insert –
  '(2A) In the case of a deduction order appeal, the appeal will be a re-hearing, unless the appeal court orders otherwise.';

(d) in paragraph (3), after 'lower court' insert 'or, in a deduction order appeal, the order or decision of the Secretary of State'; and

(e) for sub-paragraph (b) of paragraph (3), substitute –
'(b) unjust because of a serious procedural or other irregularity in –
(i) the proceedings in the lower court; or
(ii) the making of an order or decision by the Secretary of State.'

Information about the Secretary of State's decision

9.31 In relation to the deduction order appeals listed in column 1 of the table in Schedule 2 to this Practice Direction –

(a) the documents to be filed and served by the appellant include the documents set out in Column 3; and
(b) the relevant information to be provided by the Secretary of State in accordance with paragraph 9.20 above includes the information set out in Column 4.

The court at which the appeal notice is to be filed

9.32 In relation to a deduction order appeal, the appellant's notice and other documents required to be filed with that notice shall be filed in the family court (the Collection and Enforcement Regulations 25AB(1)).

In accordance with the rules relating to the composition of the court and distribution of business made in accordance with section 31D of the 1984 Act, deduction order appeals will be heard at district judge level.

The Secretary of State's address for service

9.33 For the purposes of a deduction order appeal, the Secretary of State's address for service is –

Freepost
DWP Child Support Agency 19

All notices or other documents for Secretary of State relating to a deduction order appeal should be sent to the above address.

9.34 This practice direction applies to deduction order appeals and appeals against the decision of a district judge in proceedings relating to a deduction order appeal with the following modifications and any other necessary modifications –

(a) in paragraph 5.35, insert 'and 5.36B' after 'subject to paragraph 5.36A';
(b) after paragraph 5.36A insert –
'5.36A Where the appeal is a deduction order appeal, the appellant's notice must be filed and served within 21 days of –
(a) where the appellant is a deposit-taker, service of the order;
(b) where the appellant is a liable person, receipt of the order; or
(c) where the appellant is either a deposit-taker or a liable person, the date of receipt of notification of the decision the lower court was given.'.

Appeal against the court's decision under rules 31.10, 31.11 or 31.14

10.1 The rules in Part 30 apply to appeals against the court's decision under rules 31.10, 31.11 or 31.14 with the amendments set out in paragraphs 10.2 to 10.5 below. Rules 31.15 and 31.16 apply to these appeals. These modifications do not apply to appeals against the decision made on appeal under rule 31.15.

10.2 Rule 30.3 (permission to appeal) does not apply.

10.3 The time for filing an appellant's notice at the appeal court in rule 30.4(2) does not apply. Rule 31.15 sets out the time within which an appeal against the court's decision under rules 31.10, 31.11 or 31.14 must be made to a judge of the High Court.

10.4 Rule 4.1(3)(a) (court's power to extend or shorten the time for compliance with a rule, practice direction or court order) does not apply to an appeal against the court's decision under rules 31.10, 31.11 or 31.14 in so far as that rule gives the court power to extend the time set out in rule 31.15 for filing an appellant's notice.

10.5 Rules 30.7 (variation), 30.8 (stay of proceedings), 30.10 (striking out appeal notices, setting aside or imposing conditions on permission to appeal) and 30.12 (hearing of appeals) do not apply.

Appeals against pension orders and pension compensation sharing orders

11.1 Paragraph 11.2 below applies to appeals against –

(a) a pension sharing order under section 24B of the Matrimonial Causes Act 1973 or the variation of such an order under section 31 of that Act;
(b) a pension sharing order under Part 4 of Schedule 5 to the Civil Partnership Act 2004 or the variation of such an order under Part 11 of Schedule 5 to that Act;
(c) a pension compensation sharing order under section 24E of the Matrimonial Causes Act 1973 or a variation of such an order under section 31 of that Act; and
(d) a pension compensation sharing order under Part 4 of Schedule 5 to the Civil Partnership Act 2004or a variation of such an order under Part 11 of Schedule 5 to that Act.

11.2 In appeals to which this paragraph applies, the court may extend the time set out in rule 30.4 for filing and serving an appellant's notice in accordance with rule 4.1(3)(a) (court's power to extend or shorten the time for compliance with a rule, practice direction or court order) or rule 30.7 (Variation of time), even if the pension sharing order or pension compensation sharing order has taken effect. However, where an application is made for variation of the time limit for filing or serving an appellant's notice after the order has taken effect, the court should have particular regard to the matters referred to in sections 40A and 40B of the Matrimonial Causes Act 1973 and paragraphs 79 and 80 of Schedule 5 to the Civil Partnership Act 2004 (which restrict the appeal court's power to set aside or vary an order in certain circumstances where an appeal is begun on or after the day on which the order takes effect but which also allow the appeal court in those circumstances to make such further orders as it thinks fit for putting the parties in the position it considers appropriate).

11.3 Omitted

Appeals to a court under section 20 of the 1991 Act (appeals in respect of parentage determinations)

12.1 The rules in Chapters 1 and 5 of Part 8 will apply as appropriate to an appeal under section 20(1) of the 1991 Act where that appeal must be made to a court in accordance with the Child Support Appeals (Jurisdiction of Courts) Order 2002.

12.2 The respondent to such an appeal will be the Secretary of State.

In accordance with the rules relating to the composition of the court and distribution of business made in accordance with section 31D of the 1984 Act, appeals under section 20 of the 1991 Act will be heard at district judge level.

Applications

13.1 Where a party to an appeal makes an application whether in an appeal notice or by Part 18 (Procedure For Other Applications in Proceedings) application notice, the provisions of Part 18 will apply.

Appeals against consent orders

14.1 The rules in Part 30 and the provisions of this Practice Direction apply to appeals relating to orders made by consent in addition to orders which are not made by consent.

Disposing of applications or appeals by consent

15.1 An appellant who does not wish to pursue an application or an appeal may request the appeal court for an order that the application or appeal be dismissed. Such a request must state whether the appellant is a child, or a protected person.

15.2 The request must be accompanied by a consent signed by the other parties stating whether the respondent is a child, or a protected person and consents to the dismissal of the application or appeal.

Allowing unopposed appeals or applications on paper

16.1 The appeal court will not normally make an order allowing an appeal unless satisfied that the decision of the lower court was wrong, but the appeal court may set aside or vary the order of the lower court with consent and without determining the merits of the appeal, if it is satisfied that there are good and sufficient reasons for doing so. Where the appeal court is requested by all parties to allow an application or an appeal the court may consider the request on the papers. The request should state whether any of the parties is a child, or protected person and set out the relevant history of the proceedings and the matters relied on as justifying the proposed order and be accompanied by a copy of the proposed order.

Summary assessment of costs

17.1 Costs are likely to be assessed by way of summary assessment at the following hearings –

(a) contested directions hearings;
(b) applications for permission to appeal at which the respondent is present;
(c) appeals from case management decisions or decisions made at directions hearings; and
(d) appeals listed for one day or less.

(Provision for summary assessment of costs is made by section 13 of the Practice Direction supplementing CPR Part 44)

17.2 Parties attending any of the hearings referred to in paragraph 17.1 should be prepared to deal with the summary assessment.

Reopening of final appeals

18.1 This paragraph applies to applications under rule 30.14 (Reopening of final appeals) for permission to reopen a final determination of an appeal.

18.2 In this paragraph, 'appeal' includes an application for permission to appeal.

18.3 Permission must be sought from the court whose decision the applicant wishes to reopen.

18.4 The application for permission must be made by application notice and supported by written evidence, verified by a statement of truth.

18.5 A copy of the application for permission must not be served on any other party to the original appeal unless the court so directs.

18.6 Where the court directs that the application for permission is to be served on another party, that party may within 14 days of the service on him or her of the copy of the application file a written statement either supporting or opposing the application.

18.7 The application for permission, and any written statements supporting or opposing it, will be considered on paper by a single judge, and will be allowed to proceed only if the judge so directs.

Schedule 1

Omitted

Schedule 2

Appeal	*Relevant Legislation*	*Appellant Information*	*Secretary of State Information*
Appeal against the making of a regular deduction order (under section 32A of the 1991 Act)	Section 32C(4)(a) of the 1991 Act The Collection and Enforcement Regulations 25AB(1)(a) (appeals)	A copy of the order; A covering letter explaining that the order has been made and the reasons for the order namely that there are arrears of child maintenance and/or no other arrangements have been made for the payment of child maintenance, including arrears	The amount of the current maintenance calculation, the period of debt and the total amount of arrears (including account breakdown if appropriate) and the reasons for the Secretary of State's decision, details of all previous attempts to negotiate payment i.e. phone calls and letters to the non resident parent, details of any previous enforcement action taken
Appeal against a decision on an application for a review of a regular deduction order	Sections 32C(4)(b) 32C(2)(k) of the 1991 Act The Collection and Enforcement Regulations 25G (review of a regular deduction order) and 25AB(1)(b) (appeals)	A decision notification setting out whether or not the review has been agreed by the Secretary of State and the resulting action to be taken if agreed; with an enclosure setting out the specific reasons for the Secretary of State's decision	The reasons for the Secretary of State's decision in respect of the application for review and any evidence supporting that decision

Appeal	*Relevant Legislation*	*Appellant Information*	*Secretary of State Information*
Appeal against the withholding of consent to the disapplication of sections 32G(1) and 32H(2)(b) of the 1991 Act	Section 32I(4) of the 1991 Act The Collection and Enforcement Regulations 25N (disapplication of sections 32G(1) and 32H(2)(b) of the 1991 Act) and 25AB(1)(c) (appeals)	A decision notification setting out that either: (a) consent has been refused; or (b) consent has been given in relation to part of the application i.e. that only some of the funds which were requested to be released have been agreed to be released (the right of appeal will lie in respect of the part of the application which has been refused) There will be an enclosure with the notification setting out the reasons for the decision on the application	The reasons for the Secretary of State's decision in respect of the application for consent and any evidence supporting that decision
Appeal against the making of a final lump sum deduction order (under section 32F of the 1991 Act)	Section 32J(5) of the 1991 Act The Collection and Enforcement Regulations 25AB(1)(d) (appeals)	A copy of the order; A covering letter explaining that the order has been made and the reasons for the order namely that there are arrears of child maintenance and/or no other arrangements have been made for the payment of child maintenance, including arrears	The amount of the current maintenance calculation (if applicable), the period of debt and the total amount of arrears (including account breakdown if appropriate) and the reasons for the Secretary of State's decision, details of all previous attempts to negotiate payment i.e. phone calls and letters to the non resident parent, details of any previous enforcement action taken.

Practice Direction 30B – Appeals – transparency

This practice direction supplements Part 30 of the Family Procedure Rules 2010

NOTE: This Practice Direction refers to orders made under FPR rule 30.12A(2), and terms of orders made under FPR rule 30.12A(3). Those references are correct. Rule 30.12A itself, however, refers in paragraphs (3) and (4)(a) to an order under paragraph (1) of the rule, and in paragraph (4)(b) to the terms of an order under paragraph (2) of the rule. Those references are incorrect and should respectively be to an order under paragraph (2), and the terms of an order under paragraph (3) of the rule. The references in the rule are being corrected, but pending correction, they should be read as referring in paragraphs (3) and (4)(a) to an order under paragraph (2) of the rule, and in paragraph (4)(b) to the terms of an order under paragraph (3) of the rule.

Introduction

1.1 This practice direction is made under rule 30.12A(4). It provides for circumstances in which the appeal court will ordinarily make an order under rule 30.12A(2) and for the terms of the order under 30.12A(3) which the court will ordinarily make in such circumstances.

1.2 This practice direction applies to all hearings in appeals within the scope of rule 30.12A(1) from the family court to the High Court.

Standard order

2.1 Subject to paragraph 2.3, the appeal court will ordinarily (and so without any application being made)—

(a) make an order under rule 30.12A (3)(a) that the hearing of the appeal shall be in public; and

(b) in the same order, impose restrictions under rule 30.12A(3) in relation to the publication of information about the proceedings.

2.2 An order pursuant to paragraph 2.1 will ordinarily be in the terms of the standard order approved by the President of the Family Division and published on the judicial website at https://www.judiciary.uk/publication-jurisdiction/family-2/, using the variant appropriate to the nature of the proceedings.

2.3 In the case of an appeal against a decision or order made in proceedings for a financial remedy where no minor children are involved, the court will not normally impose restrictions under rule 30.12A(3).

2.4 The court may decide not to make an order pursuant to paragraph 2.1 if it appears to the court that there is good reason for not making the order, but will consider whether it would be appropriate instead to make an order (under rule 30.12A (2)(b) or (c))—

(a) for a part only of the hearing to be held in public; or

(b) excluding any persons, or class of persons from the hearing, or from such part of the hearing as is held in public.

2.5 In deciding whether there is good reason not to make an order pursuant to paragraph 2.1 and whether to make an order pursuant to paragraph 2.3 instead, the court will have regard in particular to—

(a) the need to protect any child or another person involved in the proceedings;

(b) the nature of the evidence in the proceedings;

(c) whether earlier hearings in the proceedings have taken place in private;
(d) whether there is any risk of disruption to the hearing if there is general public access to it.

Documents to be provided to court reporters at the hearing of an appeal

3.1 The court will make available to the usher or other court official present in court two copies of the judgment under appeal for provision to accredited law reporters and accredited media reporters in accordance with the provisions of this paragraph.

3.2 Where a party is legally represented at the hearing of an appeal, the legal representative must bring to the hearing two additional copies of the party's skeleton argument (including any supplementary skeleton argument) for provision to accredited law reporters and accredited media reporters in accordance with the provisions of this paragraph.

3.3 The additional copies of skeleton arguments must be supplied before the commencement of the hearing to the usher or other court official present in court.

3.4 The usher or other court official to whom the copies of the judgment and skeleton arguments are supplied under paragraphs 3.1 and 3.3 must provide one copy of each to an accredited law reporter (upon production of their Royal Courts of Justice security pass) and one copy of each to an accredited media reporter (upon production of their press pass), if so requested by them. Those copies are to be provided only for the purpose of reporting the court proceedings and on the basis that the recipients may remove them from the court and make further copies of them for distribution to other accredited reporters in court, again only for the purpose of reporting the court proceedings.

3.5 Any party may apply orally to the court at the commencement of the hearing for a direction lifting or varying the obligations imposed by paragraph 3.4. Where a party intends to make such an application or is notified by another party of the intention to make one, the operation of paragraph 3.4 is suspended pending the ruling of the court.

3.6 In deciding whether to make a direction under paragraph 3.5, the court must take into account all the circumstances of the case and have regard in particular to—

(a) the interests of justice;
(b) the public interest;
(c) the protection of the interests of any child, vulnerable adult or protected party;
(d) the protection of the identity of any person intended to be protected by an order or direction relating to anonymity; and
(e) the nature of any private or confidential information (including information relating to personal financial matters) in the document.

A direction may permit a skeleton argument to be supplied in redacted or anonymised form.

3.7 For the purposes of this paragraph, 'the hearing of an appeal' includes a hearing listed as an application for permission to appeal with the appeal to follow immediately if permission is granted.

3.8 Paragraphs 3.1 to 3.7 apply to duly authorised lawyers who are attending court for journalistic, research or public legal educational purposes, in the same way as those paragraphs apply to accredited law reporters and accredited media reporters.

3.9 For the purposes of paragraph 3.4, a duly authorised lawyer is only to be provided with copies of the documents referred to in that paragraph upon production to the usher or other court official of a form of identification specified in paragraph 5A.2 of Practice Direction 27B.

3.10 In this Practice Direction, 'duly authorised lawyer' has the same meaning as in rule 27.11.

PART 31
REGISTRATION OF ORDERS UNDER …[1] THE HAGUE CONVENTION 1996

31.1 Scope

This Part applies to proceedings for the recognition, non-recognition and registration of—

(a) …[1]
(b) measures to which the 1996 Hague Convention applies; …[2]
(c) …[1]
[(d) …[1]][3]

Amendment

1 Repealed by the Family Procedure Rules 2010 and Court of Protection Rules 2017 (Amendment) (EU Exit) Regulations 2019, SI 2019/517, rr 2, 18(1)–(3).
2 Repealed by the Family Procedure (Amendment) Rules 2014, SI 2014/524 rr 2, 6(a).
3 Inserted by the Family Procedure (Amendment) Rules 2014, SI 2014/524 rr 2, 6(c).

31.2 Interpretation

(1) In this Part—
(a) 'judgment' is to be construed—
(i) …[1]
(ii) …[1] …[2]
(iii) as meaning any measure taken by an authority with jurisdiction under Chapter II of the 1996 Hague Convention where that Convention applies; […[1]][3]
[(iv) …[1]][3]
(b) …[1]
[(ba) …[1]][3]
(c) …[1]
(d) 'Contracting State' means a State …[1] in relation to which the 1996 Hague Convention is in force as between that State and the United Kingdom; and
(e) 'parental responsibility'—
(i) …[1]
(ii) where the 1996 Hague Convention applies, has the meaning given in Article 1(2) of that Convention.

(2) References in this Part to registration are to the registration of a judgment in accordance with the provisions of this Part.

Amendment

1 Repealed by the Family Procedure Rules 2010 and Court of Protection Rules 2017 (Amendment) (EU Exit) Regulations 2019, SI 2019/517, rr 2, 18(1), (4).
2 Repealed by the Family Procedure (Amendment) Rules 2014, SI 2014/524 rr 2, 7(a).
3 Inserted by the Family Procedure (Amendment) Rules 2014, SI 2014/524 rr 2, 7(b), (c), (d), (e).

31.3 Where to start proceedings

(1) Every application under this Part, except for an application under rule 31.18 for a certified copy of a judgment …[1] must be made to the principal registry.

(2) …[1]

(3) Notwithstanding paragraph (1), where recognition of a judgment is raised as an incidental question in proceedings under the 1996 Hague Convention[,][2] …[1] the court hearing those proceedings may determine the question of recognition.

Amendment

1 Repealed by the Family Procedure Rules 2010 and Court of Protection Rules 2017 (Amendment) (EU Exit) Regulations 2019, SI 2019/517, rr 2, 18(1), (5).
2 Substituted by the Family Procedure (Amendment) Rules 2014, SI 2014/524 rr 2, 8(a).

31.4 Application for registration, recognition or non-recognition of a judgment

(1) Any interested person may apply to the court for an order that the judgment be registered, recognised or not recognised.

(2) [An][1] application for registration, recognition or nonrecognition must be—

(a) made to a district judge of the principal registry; and
(b) in the form, and supported by the documents and the information required by a practice direction.

Amendment

1 Substituted by the Family Procedure Rules 2010 and Court of Protection Rules 2017 (Amendment) (EU Exit) Regulations 2019, SI 2019/517, rr 2, 18(1), (6).

31.5 Documents – supplementary

(1) [Where][1] the person making an application under this Part does not produce the documents required by rule 31.4(2)(b) the court may—

(a) fix a time within which the documents are to be produced;
(b) accept equivalent documents; or
(c) dispense with production of the documents if the court considers it has sufficient information.

(2) …[2]

Amendment

1 Substituted by the Family Procedure Rules 2010 and Court of Protection Rules 2017 (Amendment) (EU Exit) Regulations 2019, SI 2019/517, rr 2, 18(1), (7)(a).
2 Repealed by the Family Procedure Rules 2010 and Court of Protection Rules 2017 (Amendment) (EU Exit) Regulations 2019, SI 2019/517, rr 2, 18(1), (7)(b).

31.6 Directions

(1) As soon as practicable after an application under this Part has been made, the court may …[1] give such directions as it considers appropriate, including as regards the following matters—

(a) whether service of the application may be dispensed with;
(b) expedition of the proceedings or any part of the proceedings (and any direction for expedition may specify a date by which the court must give its decision);

(c) the steps to be taken in the proceedings and the time by which each step is to be taken;
(d) the service of documents; and
(e) the filing of evidence.

(2) The court or court officer will—

(a) record the giving, variation or revocation of directions under this rule; and
(b) as soon as practicable serve a copy of the directions order on every party.

Amendment

1 Repealed by the Family Procedure Rules 2010 and Court of Protection Rules 2017 (Amendment) (EU Exit) Regulations 2019, SI 2019/517, rr 2, 18(1), (8).

31.7 …[1]

…[1]

Amendment

1 Repealed by the Family Procedure Rules 2010 and Court of Protection Rules 2017 (Amendment) (EU Exit) Regulations 2019, SI 2019/517, rr 2, 18(1), (9).

31.8 Registration for enforcement or order for non-recognition of a judgment

(1) This rule applies where an application is made for an order that a judgment given in another …[1] Contracting State, should be registered, or should not be recognised …[1].

(2) where the application is made for an order that the judgment should be registered—

(a) upon receipt of the application, and subject to any direction given by the court under rule 31.6, the court officer will serve the application on the person against whom registration is sought;
(b) the court will not accept submissions from either the person against whom registration is sought or any child in relation to whom the judgment was given.

(3) Where the application is for an order that the judgment should not be recognised—

(a) upon receipt of the application, and subject to any direction given by the court under rule 31.6, the court officer will serve the application on the person in whose favour judgment was given;
(b) the person in whose favour the judgment was given must file an answer to the application and serve it on the applicant—
  (i) within 1 month of service of the application; …[1]
  (ii) …[1]

(4) [The][2] court may extend the time set out in subparagraph (3)(b)(ii) on account of distance.

(5) The person in whose favour the judgment was given may request recognition or registration of the judgment in their answer, and in that event must comply with 31.4(2) (b), to the extent that such documents, information and evidence are not already contained in the application for nonrecognition.

(6) …[1]

(7) [The][2] person in whose favour the judgment was given fails to file a answer as required by paragraph (3)—

(a) where the Hague Convention of 15th November 1965 on the service abroad of judicial and extrajudicial documents in civil or commercial matters applies, the court shall apply Article 15 of that Convention; and

(b) in all other cases, the court will not consider the application unless—

(i) it is proved to the satisfaction of the court that the person in whose favour judgment was given was served with the application within a reasonable period of time to arrange his or her response; or

(ii) the court is satisfied that the circumstances of the case justify proceeding with consideration of the application.

(8) …[1]

Amendment

1 Repealed by the Family Procedure Rules 2010 and Court of Protection Rules 2017 (Amendment) (EU Exit) Regulations 2019, SI 2019/517, rr 2, 18(1), (10)(a), (b), (d), (f).

2 Substituted by the Family Procedure Rules 2010 and Court of Protection Rules 2017 (Amendment) (EU Exit) Regulations 2019, SI 2019/517, rr 2, 18(1), (10)(c), (e).

31.9 Stay of recognition proceedings by reason of an appeal

Where recognition or non-recognition of a judgment given in another …[1] Contracting State is sought, or is raised as an incidental question in other proceedings, the court may stay the proceedings—

(a) if an ordinary appeal against the judgment has been lodged; or

(b) if the judgment was given in the Republic of Ireland, if enforcement of the judgment is suspended there by reason of an appeal.

Amendment

1 Repealed by the Family Procedure Rules 2010 and Court of Protection Rules 2017 (Amendment) (EU Exit) Regulations 2019, SI 2019/517, rr 2, 18(1), (11).

31.10 Effect of refusal of application for a decision that a judgment should not be recognised

Where the court refuses an application for a decision that a judgment should not be recognised, the court may—

(a) direct that the decision to refuse the application is to be treated as a decision that the judgment be recognised; or

(b) treat the answer under paragraph (3)(b) of rule 31.8 as an application that the judgment be registered for enforcement if paragraph (5) of that rule is complied with and order that the judgment be registered for enforcement in accordance with rule 31.11.

31.11 Notification of the court's decision on an application for registration or non-recognition

(1) Where the court has—

(a) made an order on an application for an order that a judgment should be registered for enforcement; or

(b) refused an application that a judgment should not be recognised and ordered under rule 31.10 that the judgment be registered for enforcement, the court officer will as soon as practicable take the appropriate action under paragraph (2) or (3).

(2) If the court refuses the application for the judgment to be registered for enforcement, the court officer will serve the order on the applicant and the person against whom judgment was given in the state of origin.

(3) If the court orders that the judgment should be registered for enforcement, the court officer will—

- (a) register the judgment in the central index of judgments kept by the principal registry;
- (b) confirm on the order that the judgment has been registered; and
- (c) serve on the parties the court's order endorsed with the court officer's confirmation that the judgment has been registered.

(4) A sealed order of the court endorsed in accordance with paragraph (3)(b) will constitute notification that the judgment has been registered under …[1] Article 26 of the 1996 Hague Convention …[1], and in this Part 'notice of registration'. means a sealed order so endorsed.

(5) The notice of registration must state—

- (a) full particulars of the judgment registered and the order for registration;
- (b) the name of the party making the application and his address for service within the jurisdiction;
- (c) the right of the person against whom judgment was given to appeal against the order for registration; and
- (d) the period within which an appeal against the order for registration may be made.

Amendment

1 Repealed by the Family Procedure Rules 2010 and Court of Protection Rules 2017 (Amendment) (EU Exit) Regulations 2019, SI 2019/517, rr 2, 18(1), (12).

31.12 Effect of registration under rule 31.11

Registration of a judgment under rule 31.11 will serve for the purpose of …[1] Article 24 of the 1996 Hague Convention[,][2] …[1] as a decision that the judgment is recognised.

Amendment

1 Repealed by the Family Procedure Rules 2010 and Court of Protection Rules 2017 (Amendment) (EU Exit) Regulations 2019, SI 2019/517, rr 2, 18(1), (13).
2 Substituted by the Family Procedure (Amendment) Rules 2014, SI 2014/524 rr 2, 10(a).

31.13 The central index of judgments registered under rule 31.11

The central index of judgments registered under rule 31.11 will be kept by the principal registry.

31.14 Decision on recognition of a judgment only

(1) Where an application is made seeking recognition of a judgment only, the provisions of rules 31.8 and 31.9 apply to that application as they do to an application for registration for enforcement.

(2) Where the court orders that the judgment should be recognised, the court officer will serve a copy of the order on each party as soon as practicable.

(3) A sealed order of the court will constitute notification that the judgment has been recognised under …[1] Article 24 of the 1996 Hague convention …[1].

(4) The sealed order shall indicate—

- (a) full particulars of the judgment recognised;
- (b) the name of the party making the application and his address for service within the jurisdiction;
- (c) the right of the person against whom judgment was given to appeal against the order for recognition; and
- (d) the period within which an appeal against the order for recognition may be made.

Amendment

1 Repealed by the Family Procedure Rules 2010 and Court of Protection Rules 2017 (Amendment) (EU Exit) Regulations 2019, SI 2019/517, rr 2, 18(1), (14).

31.15 Appeal against the court's decision under rules 31.10, 31.11 or 31.14

(1) An appeal against the court's decision under rules 31.10, 31.11 or 31.14 must be made to a judge of the High Court—

- (a) within one month of the date of service of the notice of registration; or
- (b) if the party bringing the appeal is habitually resident in another …[1] Contracting State, within two months of the date of service.

(2) …[1]

(3) If …[1], the appeal is brought by the applicant for a declaration of enforceability or registration and the respondent fails to appear—

- (a) where the Hague Convention of 15th November 1965 on the service abroad of judicial and extrajudicial documents in civil or commercial matters applies, the court shall apply Article 15 of that Convention; and
- (b) in all other cases, the court will not consider the appeal unless—
  - (i) it is proved to the satisfaction of the court that the respondent was served with notice of the appeal within a reasonable period of time to arrange his or her response; or
  - (ii) the court is satisfied that the circumstances of the case justify proceeding with consideration of the appeal.

(4) This rule is subject to rule 31.16.

(The procedure for applications under rule 31.15 is set out in Practice Direction 30A (Appeals).)

Amendment

1 Repealed by the Family Procedure Rules 2010 and Court of Protection Rules 2017 (Amendment) (EU Exit) Regulations 2019, SI 2019/517, rr 2, 18(1), (15).

31.16 Stay of enforcement where appeal pending in state of origin

(1) A party against whom enforcement is sought of a judgment which has been registered under rule 31.11 may apply to the court with which an appeal is lodged under rule 31.15 for the proceedings to be stayed where—

- (a) that party has lodged an ordinary appeal in the …[1] Contracting State of origin; or
- (b) the time for such an appeal has not yet expired.

(2) Where an application for a stay is filed in the circumstances described in paragraph (1)(b), the court may specify the time within which an appeal must be lodged.

Amendment

1 Repealed by the Family Procedure Rules 2010 and Court of Protection Rules 2017 (Amendment) (EU Exit) Regulations 2019, SI 2019/517, rr 2, 18(1), (16).

31.17 Enforcement of judgments registered under rule 31.11

(1) [Subject to paragraph (1A),][1] the court will not enforce a judgment registered under rule 31.11 until after—

(a) the expiration of any applicable period under rules 31.15 or 31.16; or
(b) if that period has been extended by the court, the expiration of the period so extended.

[(1A) The court may enforce a judgment registered under rule 31.11 before the expiration of a period referred to in paragraph (1) where urgent enforcement of the judgment is necessary to secure the welfare of the child to whom the judgment relates.][1]

(2) A party applying to the court for the enforcement of a registered judgment must produce to the court a certificate of service of—

(a) the notice of registration of the judgment; and
(b) any order made by the court in relation to the judgment.

(Service out of the jurisdiction …[2] is dealt with in chapter 4 of Part 6 and in Practice Direction 6B.)

Amendment

1 Inserted by the Family Procedure (Amendment) (No 2) Rules 2012, SI 2012/1462, rr 2, 3.
2 Repealed by the Family Procedure Rules 2010 and Court of Protection Rules 2017 (Amendment) (EU Exit) Regulations 2019, SI 2019/517, rr 2, 18(1), (17).

31.18 Request for a certificate or a certified copy of a judgment

(1) An application for a certified copy of a judgment …[1] must be made to the court which made the order or judgment in respect of which certification is sought and without giving notice to any other party.

(2) The application must be made in the form, and supported by the documents and information required by a practice direction.

(3) The certified copy of the judgment will be an office copy sealed with the seal of the court and signed by [a court officer][2]. It will be issued with a certified copy of any order which has varied any of the terms of the original order.

(4) Where the application is made for the purposes of applying for recognition or recognition and enforcement of the order in another Contracting State, the court must indicate on the certified copy of the judgment the grounds on which it based its jurisdiction to make the order, for the purposes of Article 23(2)(a) of the 1996 Hague Convention.

Amendment

1 Repealed by the Family Procedure Rules 2010 and Court of Protection Rules 2017 (Amendment) (EU Exit) Regulations 2019, SI 2019/517, rr 2, 18(1), (18).
2 Substituted by the Family Procedure (Amendment No 3) Rules 2013, SI 2013/3204, rr 2, 75.

31.19 …[1]

…[1]

Amendment

1 Repealed by the Family Procedure Rules 2010 and Court of Protection Rules 2017 (Amendment) (EU Exit) Regulations 2019, SI 2019/517, rr 2, 18(1), (19).

31.20 …[1]

…[1]

Amendment

1 Repealed by the Family Procedure Rules 2010 and Court of Protection Rules 2017 (Amendment) (EU Exit) Regulations 2019, SI 2019/517, rr 2, 18(1), (19).

31.21 …[1]

…[1]

Amendment

1 Repealed by the Family Procedure Rules 2010 and Court of Protection Rules 2017 (Amendment) (EU Exit) Regulations 2019, SI 2019/517, rr 2, 18(1), (19).

31.22 Application for provisional, including protective measures.

An application for provisional, including protective, measures under …[1] Articles 11 or 12 of the 1996 Hague Convention may be made notwithstanding that the time for appealing against an order for registration of a judgment has not expired or that a final determination of any issue relating to enforcement of the judgment is pending.

Amendment

1 Repealed by the Family Procedure Rules 2010 and Court of Protection Rules 2017 (Amendment) (EU Exit) Regulations 2019, SI 2019/517, rr 2, 18(1), (20).

Practice Direction 31A – Registration of orders under the 1996 Hague Convention

See also Part 31

Form of application

1.1 An application under rule 31.4 must be made using the Part 19 procedure, except that the provisions of rules 31.8 to 31.14 and of this Practice Direction shall apply in place of rules 19.4 to 19.9.

1.2 Where the application is for recognition only of an order, it should be made clear that the application does not extend to registration for enforcement.

Evidence in support of all applications for registration, recognition or non-recognition

2.1 Omitted

2.2 All applications to which rule 31.4(2) applies must be supported by a statement that is sworn to be true or an affidavit, exhibiting the judgment, or a verified, certified or otherwise duly authenticated copy of the judgment. In the case of an application under the 1996 Hague Convention, a translation of the judgment should be supplied.

2.3 Where any other document required by this Practice Direction or by direction of the court under rule 31.5 is not in English, the applicant must supply a translation of that document into English certified by a notary public or a person qualified for the purpose, or accompanied by witness statement or affidavit confirming that the translation is accurate.

Evidence required in support of an application for registration, recognition or non-recognition of a judgment under the 1996 Hague Convention

4.1 An application for an order for a judgment to be registered under Article 26 or not recognised under Article 24 of the 1996 Hague Convention must be accompanied by a witness statement or affidavit exhibiting the following documents and giving the information required by 4.2, 4.3 or 4.4 below as appropriate.

4.2 In the case of an application for registration –

(a) those documents necessary to show that the judgment is enforceable according to the law of the Contracting State in which it was given;
(b) a description of the opportunities provided by the authority which gave the judgment in question for the child to be heard, except where that judgment was given in a case of urgency;
(c) where the judgment was given in a case of urgency, a statement as to the circumstances of the urgency that led to the child not having the opportunity to be heard;
(d) details of any measures taken in the non-Contracting State of the habitual residence of the child, if applicable, specifying the nature and effect of the measure, and the date on which it was taken;
(e) in as far as not apparent from the copy of the judgment provided, a statement of the grounds on which the authority which gave the judgment based its jurisdiction, together with any documentary evidence in support of that statement;
(f) where appropriate, a statement regarding whether Article 33 of the 1996 Hague Convention has been complied with, and the identity and address of the authority or authorities from which consent has been obtained, together with evidence of that consent; and
(g) the information referred to at 3.2 (c) to (e) above.

4.3 In the case of an application for an order that a judgment should not be recognised –

(a) a statement of the ground or grounds under Article 23 of the 1996 Hague Convention on which it is requested that the judgment be not recognised, the reasons why the applicant asserts that such ground or grounds is or are made out, and any documentary evidence on which the Applicant relies; and
(b) an address within the jurisdiction of the court for service of process on the applicant and stating, in so far as is known to the applicant, the name and usual or last known address or place of business of the person in whose favour judgment was given.

4.4 Where is it sought to apply for recognition only of a judgment under the 1996 Hague Convention, the provisions of paragraph 4.2 apply with the exception that the applicant is not required to produce the document referred to in subparagraph 4.2 (a).

Evidence in support of application for a certified copy of a judgment

6.6 An application for a certified copy of a judgment for the purposes of recognition and enforcement of the judgment under the 1996 Hague Convention must –

(a) provide a statement of the grounds on which the court based its jurisdiction to make the orders in question;
(b) indicate the age of the child at the time of the judgment and the measures taken, if any, for the child's wishes and feelings to be ascertained; and
(c) indicate which persons were provided with notice of the proceedings and, where such persons were served with the proceedings, attach evidence of such service.

PART 32
REGISTRATION AND ENFORCEMENT OF ORDERS

Chapter 1
Scope and interpretation of this Part

32.1 Scope and interpretation

(1) This Part contains rules about the registration and enforcement of maintenance orders and custody orders.

[(2) In this Part, 'the 1950 Act' means the Maintenance Orders Act 1950.][1]

(3) Chapter 2 of this Part relates to—

(a) the registration of a maintenance order, made in the High Court or [the family court][2], in a court in Scotland or Northern Ireland in accordance with the 1950 Act; and
(b) the registration of a maintenance order, made in Scotland or Northern Ireland, in the High Court in accordance with the 1950 Act.

…[3]

[(4) Chapter 3 of this Part contains rules to be applied in the family court in relation to the registration in the family court of a maintenance order made in the High Court, in accordance with the 1958 Act.][2]

(5) Chapter 4 of this Part relates to the registration and enforcement of custody orders in accordance with the 1986 Act.

[(6) Chapter 5 of this Part relates to the ability of a court officer to take enforcement proceedings in relation to certain orders for periodical payments.][4]

Amendment

1 Substituted by the Family Procedure (Amendment) Rules 2011, SI 2011/1328, rr 2, 3, 16.
2 Substituted by the Family Procedure (Amendment No 3) Rules 2013, SI 2013/3204, rr 2, 76(a)(i), (b).
3 Repealed by the Family Procedure (Amendment No 3) Rules 2013, SI 2013/3204, rr 2, 76(a)(ii).
4 Inserted by the Family Procedure (Amendment No 3) Rules 2013, SI 2013/3204, rr 2, 76(c).

Chapter 2
Registration etc. of orders under the 1950 Act

Section 1
Interpretation of this Chapter

32.2 Interpretation

In this Chapter—

'the clerk of the Court of Session' means the deputy principal clerk in charge of the petition department of the Court of Session;

['the clerk of the court which made the order' means, in the case of a county court in Northern Ireland, the Chief Clerk for the appropriate court in Northern Ireland;][1]

…[2]

['family court order' means a maintenance order made in the family court;][1]

'High Court order' means a maintenance order made in the High Court;

'maintenance order' means a maintenance order to which section 16 of the 1950 Act applies;

['Northern Irish order' means a maintenance order made by a court in Northern Ireland;][3]

'the register' means the register kept for the purposes of the 1950 Act;

'the registrar in Northern Ireland' means the chief registrar of the Queen's Bench Division (Matrimonial) of the High Court of Justice in Northern Ireland;

'registration' means registration under Part 2 of the 1950 Act and 'registered' is to be construed accordingly; and

['Scottish order' means a maintenance order made by a court in Scotland][3].

Amendment

1 Inserted by the Family Procedure (Amendment No 3) Rules 2013, SI 2013/3204, rr 2, 77(a), (c).
2 Repealed by the Family Procedure (Amendment No 3) Rules 2013, SI 2013/3204, rr 2, 77(b).
3 Substituted by the Family Procedure (Amendment No 3) Rules 2013, SI 2013/3204, rr 2, 77(d), (e).

Section 2
Registration etc of High Court and [family court][1] orders

32.3 Registration of a High Court order

(1) An application for the registration of a High Court order may be made by sending to a court officer at the court which made the order—

(a) a certified copy of the order; and
(b) a statement which—
  (i) contains the address in the United Kingdom, and the occupation, of the person liable to make payments under the order;
  (ii) contains the date on which the order was served on the person liable to make payments, or, if the order has not been served, the reason why service has not been effected;
  (iii) contains the reason why it is convenient for the order to be enforced in Scotland or Northern Ireland, as the case may be;
  (iv) contains the amount of any arrears due to the applicant under the order;
  (v) confirms that the order is not already registered; and
  (vi) is verified by a statement of truth.

(2) If it appears to the court that—

(a) the person liable to make payments under the order resides in Scotland or Northern Ireland; and
(b) it is convenient for the order to be enforced there,

the court officer will send the documents filed under paragraph (1) to the clerk of the Court of Session or to the registrar in Northern Ireland, as the case may be.

(3) On receipt of a notice of the registration of a High Court order in the Court of Session or the Court of Judicature of Northern Ireland, the court officer (who is the prescribed officer for the purposes of section 17(4) of the 1950 Act) will—

(a) enter particulars of the notice of registration in the register;
(b) note the fact of registration in the court records; and
(c) send particulars of the notice to the principal registry.

Amendment

1 Substituted by the Family Procedure (Amendment No 3) Rules 2013, SI 2013/3204, rr 2, 78.

32.4 Notice of Variation etc. of a High Court order

(1) This rule applies where a High Court order, which is registered in the Court of Session or the Court of Judicature of Northern Ireland, is discharged or varied.

(2) A court officer in the court where the order was discharged or varied will send a certified copy of that order to the clerk of the Court of Session or the registrar in Northern Ireland, as the case may be.

32.5 Cancellation of registration of a High Court order [by the court of registration][1]

(1) This rule applies where—

(a) the registration of a High Court order registered in the Court of Session or the Court of Judicature of Northern Ireland is cancelled under section 24(1) of the 1950 Act; and
(b) notice of the cancellation is given to a court officer in the court in which the order was made (who is the prescribed officer for the purposes of section 24(3)(a) of the 1950 Act).

(2) On receipt of a notice of cancellation of registration, the court officer will enter particulars of the notice in …[2] the register.

Amendment

1 Inserted by the Family Procedure (Amendment No 3) Rules 2013, SI 2013/3204, rr 2, 79(a).
2 Repealed by the Family Procedure (Amendment No 3) Rules 2013, SI 2013/3204, rr 2, 79(b).

[32.5A Cancellation of registration of a High Court order by the High Court

The Part 19 procedure applies to an application to the High Court under section 24(2) of the 1950 Act.][1]

Amendment

1 Inserted by the Family Procedure (Amendment No 3) Rules 2013, SI 2013/3204, rr 2, 80.

32.6 Application of this Chapter to a [family court][1] order

Rules 32.3 to [32.5A][1] apply to [a family court order][1] as if—

(a) references to a High Court order were references to a [family court][1] order;

[(aa) in rule 32.5A, references to the High Court were to the family court;][2]

(b) where the order is to be registered in Scotland, references to the Court of Session and the clerk of the Court of Session were references to the sheriff court and the sheriff-clerk of the sheriff court respectively; and

(c) where the order is to be registered in Northern Ireland, references to the Court of Judicature of Northern Ireland and the registrar of Northern Ireland were references to the court of summary jurisdiction and the clerk of the court of summary jurisdiction respectively.

Amendment

1 Substituted by the Family Procedure (Amendment No 3) Rules 2013, SI 2013/3204, rr 2, 81(a), (b), (c), (d).

2 Inserted by the Family Procedure (Amendment No 3) Rules 2013, SI 2013/3204, rr 2, 81(e).

[32.6A Variation of a family court order: section 22(1) of the 1950 Act

Where a family court order, which is registered in a court in Scotland or Northern Ireland, is varied under section 22(1) of the 1950 Act by the court in which it is registered—

(a) the court officer for the court which made the order will be the prescribed officer to whom notice of the variation must be given under section 23(1) of the 1950 Act; and

(b) on receipt of a notice under section 23(1) of the 1950 Act, the court officer will enter particulars of the notice in the register.][1]

Amendment

1 Inserted by the Family Procedure (Amendment No 3) Rules 2013, SI 2013/3204, rr 2, 82.

[32.6B Application to adduce evidence: section 22(5) of the 1950 Act

(1) The Part 18 procedure applies to an application under section 22(5) of the 1950 Act where a maintenance order was made by the family court.

(2) The family court will send a transcript or summary of any evidence taken to the clerk of the court in which the order is registered.

(3) The court officer for the court in England and Wales which made the maintenance order will be the prescribed officer to whom any transcript or summary of evidence adduced in the court in Scotland or Northern Ireland must be sent under section 22(5) of the 1950 Act.][1]

Amendment

1 Inserted by the Family Procedure (Amendment No 3) Rules 2013, SI 2013/3204, rr 2, 82.

Section 3

Registration etc. of Scottish and Northern Irish orders

32.7 Registration of Scottish and Northern Irish orders

On receipt of a certified copy of a Scottish order or a Northern Irish order for registration, a court officer in the principal registry (who is the prescribed officer [in the High Court][1] for the purposes of section 17(2) of the 1950 Act) [or a court officer in the family court (who is the prescribed officer in the family court for the purposes of section 17(2) of the 1950 Act)][1] will—

(a) enter particulars of the order in …[2] the register;

(b) notify the clerk of [the court which made the order][3] or the registrar in Northern Ireland, as the case may be, that the order has been registered; and

(c) file the certified copy of the order and any statutory declaration, affidavit[(GL)] or statement as to the amount of any arrears due under the order.

[(Section 17(3) of the 1950 Act makes provision as to the court in England and Wales to which a Northern Irish order or a Scottish order should be sent, which depends on which court originally made the order.)][1]

Amendment

1 Inserted by the Family Procedure (Amendment No 3) Rules 2013, SI 2013/3204, rr 2, 83(a), (b), (e).
2 Repealed by the Family Procedure (Amendment No 3) Rules 2013, SI 2013/3204, rr 2, 83(c).
3 Substituted by the Family Procedure (Amendment No 3) Rules 2013, SI 2013/3204, rr 2, 83(d).

[32.8 Application to adduce evidence: sections 21(2) and 22(5) of the 1950 Act

(1) The Part 18 procedure applies to the applications under these provisions of the 1950 Act—

(a) an application to the High Court to adduce evidence under section 21(2) by a person liable to make payments under a Scottish order registered in the High Court;

(b) an application to the family court to adduce evidence under section 21(2) by a person liable to make payments under a Scottish order registered in the High Court under the 1950 Act and registered in the family court under Part 1 of the 1958 Act; and

(c) an application to the family court to adduce evidence under section 22(5) by a person entitled to payments or a person liable to make payments under a Scottish order or a Northern Irish order registered in the family court under Part 1 of the 1950 Act.

(2) The court officer for the family court (being the court in which the order is registered) will be the prescribed officer under section 22(5) of the 1950 Act to whom any transcript or summary of evidence adduced in the court in Scotland or Northern Ireland by which the order was made must be sent.][1]

Amendment

1 Substituted by the Family Procedure (Amendment No 3) Rules 2013, SI 2013/3204, rr 2, 84.

32.9 Notice of variation etc. of Scottish and Northern Irish orders

(1) This rule applies where—

(a) a Scottish order or a Northern Irish order, which is registered in the High Court [or the family court][1], is discharged or varied [by the court in Scotland or Northern Ireland][1]; and

(b) notice of the discharge or variation is given to [the court officer in the High Court or in the family court, as the case may be][2] (who is the prescribed officer for the purposes of section 23(1)(a) of the 1950 Act).

(2) On receipt of a notice of discharge or variation, the court officer will enter particulars of the notice in …[3] the register.

Amendment

1 Inserted by the Family Procedure (Amendment No 3) Rules 2013, SI 2013/3204, rr 2, 85(a).
2 Substituted by the Family Procedure (Amendment No 3) Rules 2013, SI 2013/3204, rr 2, 85(b).
3 Repealed by the Family Procedure (Amendment No 3) Rules 2013, SI 2013/3204, rr 2, 85(c).

[32.9A Variation of Scottish and Northern Irish orders by the family court

(1) The Part 18 procedure applies to an application to the family court under section 22(1) of the 1950 Act to vary a Scottish order or a Northern Irish order which is registered in the family court.

(2) Where a Scottish order or a Northern Irish order is varied by the family courton an application under section 22(1) of the 1950 Act, the court officer will give notice of the variation to the clerk of the court in Scotland or Northern Ireland which made the order by sending a certified copy of the order of variation.][1]

Amendment

1 Inserted by the Family Procedure (Amendment No 3) Rules 2013, SI 2013/3204, rr 2, 86.

32.10 Cancellation of registration of Scottish and Northern Irish orders

(1) The Part 18 procedure applies to an application [under section 24(1) of the 1950 Act][1] for the cancellation of the registration of a Scottish order or a Northern Irish order in the High Court [or the family court][1].

(2) The application must be made without notice to the person liable to make payments under the order.

(3) If the registration of the order is cancelled, the court officer will—

(a) note the cancellation in …[2] the register; and
(b) send written notice of the cancellation to—
  (i) the clerk of the [court which made the order][3] or the registrar in Northern Ireland, as the case may be; and
  (ii) the court officer [of the family court if the order has been registered in the family court][3] in accordance with section 2(5) of the 1958 Act.

[(4) Where a maintenance order is registered under the 1950 Act in the family court, the court officer for the family court is the prescribed officer for the purposes of section 24(2) of the 1950 Act, and in paragraphs (5) and (6) references to the court officer are to the court officer of the family court.

(5) If a notice under section 24(2) of the 1950 Act is received, the court officer will—

(a) cancel the registration of the order; and
(b) send written notice of the cancellation to the clerk of the court which made the order.

(6) Where a maintenance order is registered in the family court under Part 1 of the 1958 Act and the court officer receives a notice of cancellation under section 24(3) of the 1950 Act from the appropriate officer of the High Court, the court officer will—

(a) enter the details of the notice in the register;
(b) cancel the registration under Part 1 of the 1958 Act; and

(c) give notice of the cancellation to the appropriate officer of the court which made the order, being—
   (i) the Deputy Principal Clerk of Session, in the case of the Court of Session; or
   (ii) the Chief Registrar of the Queen's Bench Division (Matrimonial), in the case of the High Court of Justice in Northern Ireland.][1]

Amendment

1 Inserted by the Family Procedure (Amendment No 3) Rules 2013, SI 2013/3204, rr 2, 87(a), (c).
2 Repealed by the Family Procedure (Amendment No 3) Rules 2013, SI 2013/3204, rr 2, 87(b)(i).
3 Substituted by the Family Procedure (Amendment No 3) Rules 2013, SI 2013/3204, rr 2, 87(b)(ii), (iii).

[32.10A Payments under a maintenance order registered in the family court

(1) This rule applies where section 22(1A) of the 1950 Act applies and the family court orders that payments under a maintenance order registered in the family court are to be made by a particular means.

(2) The court officer will record on a copy of the order the means of payment that the court has ordered.

(3) The court officer will notify, in writing, the person liable to make payments under the order how the payments are to be made.

(4) Where [under section 1(4A) of the Maintenance Enforcement Act 1991][1] the family court orders payment to the court by a method of payment specified in [section 1(5) of that Act][2], the court officer will notify the person liable to make payments under the order of sufficient details of the account into which the payments should be made to enable payments to be made into that account.

(5) The Part 18 procedure applies to an application under section 1(7) of the Maintenance Enforcement Act 1991 [(application from an interested party to revoke, suspend, revive or vary a means of payment order)][2].

[(6) Where the court makes an order under section 1(7) of the Maintenance Enforcement Act 1991 or dismisses an application for such an order, the court officer will, as far as practicable, notify in writing all interested parties of the effect of the order and will take the steps set out in paragraphs (2), (3) and (4), as appropriate.

(7) In this rule, 'interested party' has the meaning given in section 1(10) of the Maintenance Enforcement Act 1991.][2]][3]

Amendment

1 Inserted by the Family Procedure (Amendment No 2) Rules 2014, SI 2014/667, rr 2, 27(a)(i).
2 Substituted by the Family Procedure (Amendment No 2) Rules 2014, SI 2014/667, rr 2, 27(a)(ii), (b), (c).
3 Inserted by the Family Procedure (Amendment No 3) Rules 2013, SI 2013/3204, rr 2, 88.

32.11 Enforcement

(1) [Subject to paragraph (2), Part 33][1] applies to an application for or with respect to the enforcement of a Scottish order or a Northern Irish order registered in the High Court [or the family court][2].

(2) The application may be made without notice to the person liable to make payments under the order.

Amendment

1 Substituted by the Family Procedure (Amendment No 3) Rules 2013, SI 2013/3204, rr 2, 89(a).
2 Inserted by the Family Procedure (Amendment No 3) Rules 2013, SI 2013/3204, rr 2, 89(b).

32.12 Inspection of register and copies of order

Any person—

(a) who is entitled to receive, or liable to make, payments under [a Scottish order or a Northern Irish order registered in the High Court or the family court under the 1950 Act][1]; or
(b) with the permission of the court,

may—

(i) inspect the register; or
(ii) request a copy of any order registered in the High Court [or the family court][2] under Part 2 of the 1950 Act and any statutory declaration, affidavit(GL) or statement filed with the order.

Amendment

1 Substituted by the Family Procedure (Amendment No 3) Rules 2013, SI 2013/3204, rr 2, 90(a).
2 Inserted by the Family Procedure (Amendment No 3) Rules 2013, SI 2013/3204, rr 2, 90(b).

[32.12A Notices and certificates: section 19(4), 20(1) and 24(5) and (5A) of the 1950 Act

(1) Practice Direction 32A contains the form of—

(a) a notice under section 19(4) of the 1950 Act that payments under a maintenance order made by a sheriff court in Scotland or a court of summary jurisdiction in Northern Ireland have become payable through or to any officer or person;
(b) a notice under section 19(4) of the 1950 Act that the payments under a maintenance order made by the family court have, on its registration under Part 2 of the 1950 Act in a court in Scotland or Northern Ireland, ceased to be payable to or through the court or any person;
(c) a certificate lodged under section 20(1) of the 1950 Act as to the amount of any arrears due under a maintenance order made by the family court; and
(d) a notice under section 24(5) or (5A) of the 1950 Act of the cancellation of the registration under Part 2 of the 1950 Act of a maintenance order in the family court.

(2) The court officer will send a notice referred to in paragraph (1)(a), (b) or (d) to the person liable to make the payments under the order at that person's last known address.][1]

Amendment

1 Inserted by the Family Procedure (Amendment No 3) Rules 2013, SI 2013/3204, rr 2, 91.

Chapter 3
Registration of maintenance orders under the 1958 Act

32.13 Interpretation

In this Chapter 'the register' means the register kept for the purposes of the 1958 Act.

32.14 Registration of orders – prescribed period

The prescribed period for the purpose of section 2(2) of the 1958 Act is 14 days.

(Section 2(2) sets out the period during which an order, which is to be registered in a magistrates' court, may not be enforced)

32.15 Application for registration of a maintenance order in [the family court – procedure in the High Court][1]

(1) An application under section 2(1) of the 1958 Act may be made by sending to the court officer at the court which made the order—

(a) a certified copy of the maintenance order; and
(b) two copies of the application.

(2) When, on the grant of an application, the court officer sends the certified copy of the maintenance order to the [family court][1] in accordance with section 2(2), the court officer must—

(a) note on the order that the application for registration has been granted; and
(b) send to the [family court][1] a copy of the application for registration of the order.

(3) On receiving notice that the [family court][1] has registered the order, the court officer [of the High Court][2] must enter particulars of the registration in the court records.

Amendment

1 Substituted by the Family Procedure (Amendment No 3) Rules 2013, SI 2013/3204, rr 2, 92(a), (b).
2 Inserted by the Family Procedure (Amendment No 3) Rules 2013, SI 2013/3204, rr 2, 92(c).

[32.15A Application for registration of a maintenance order in the family court – procedure in the family court

(1) This rule applies where the court officer for the family court receives from the court officer of the High Court a certified copy of a High Court order, in accordance with section 2(2)(b) of the 1958 Act.

(2) The court officer of the family court will—

(a) register the order in the family court by entering particulars in the register; and
(b) send notice to the court officer of the High Court that the order has been registered.][1]

Amendment

1 Inserted by the Family Procedure (Amendment No 3) Rules 2013, SI 2013/3204, rr 2, 93.

32.16 Registration in [the family court][1] of an order registered in the High Court [– procedure in the High Court][2]

(1) This rule applies where—

(a) a maintenance order is registered in the High Court in accordance with section 17(4) of the 1950 Act; and
(b) the court officer [of the High Court][2] receives notice that the [family court][1] has registered the order in accordance with section 2(5) of the 1958 Act.

(2) The court officer [of the High Court][2] must enter particulars of the registration in …[3] the register.

Amendment

1 Substituted by the Family Procedure (Amendment No 3) Rules 2013, SI 2013/3204, rr 2, 94(a)(i), (c).
2 Inserted by the Family Procedure (Amendment No 3) Rules 2013, SI 2013/3204, rr 2, 94(a)(ii), (b).
3 Repealed by the Family Procedure (Amendment No 3) Rules 2013, SI 2013/3204, rr 2, 94(d).

[32.16A Registration in the family court of an order registered in the High Court – procedure in the family court

(1) This rule applies where—

(a) a maintenance order is registered in the High Court in accordance with section 17(4) of the 1950 Act; and
(b) the court officer of the family court, in accordance with section 2(2)(b) of the 1958 Act, receives from the appropriate officer of the original court in Scotland or Northern Ireland a certified copy of an order made by the court in Scotland or Northern Ireland.

(2) The court officer of the family court will—

(a) register the order in the family court by entering particulars in the register; and
(b) send written notice to the court officer of the High Court and to the appropriate officer of the original court in Scotland or in Northern Ireland that the order has been registered.][1]

Amendment

1 Inserted by the Family Procedure (Amendment No 3) Rules 2013, SI 2013/3204, rr 2, 95.

32.17 …[1]

…[1]

Amendment

1 Repealed by the Family Procedure (Amendment No 3) Rules 2013, SI 2013/3204, rr 2, 96.

32.18 …[1]

…[1]

Amendment

1 Repealed by the Family Procedure (Amendment No 3) Rules 2013, SI 2013/3204, rr 2, 96.

32.19 Variation or discharge of an order registered in [the family court – procedure in the High Court][1]

(1) This rule applies where a maintenance order is registered in [the family court][1] under Part 1 of the 1958 Act.

(2) If the court which made the order makes an order varying or discharging that order the court officer [of the High Court][2] must send a certified copy of the order of variation or discharge to [the family court][1].

(3) If the court officer [of the High Court][2] receives from [the family court][1] a certified copy of an order varying the maintenance order the court officer must—

(a) file the copy of the order; and
(b) enter the particulars of the variation in the place where the details required by rule 32.15(3) were entered.

Amendment

1 Substituted by the Family Procedure (Amendment No 3) Rules 2013, SI 2013/3204, rr 2, 97(a), (b), (c)(ii), (d)(ii).
2 Inserted by the Family Procedure (Amendment No 3) Rules 2013, SI 2013/3204, rr 2, 97(c)(i), (d)(i).

[32.19A Variation, remission, discharge or cancellation of registration of an order registered in the family court – procedure in the family court

(1) Where under section 4(2) of the 1958 Act a High Court order registered in the family court is varied by the family court, the court officer for the family court will give notice of the variation to the High Court.

(2) Where under section 4(4) of the 1958 Act an application for the variation of a High Court order registered in the family court is remitted to the High Court by the family court, the court officer for the family court will give notice of its having been remitted to the High Court.

(3) Where under section 5(4) of the 1958 Act the registration of a High Court order in the family court is cancelled by the family court, the court officer for the family court will give notice of cancellation to the High Court, stating (if applicable) that the cancellation is a result of a notice given under section 5(1) of the 1958 Act.

(4) Where under section 5(4) of the 1958 Act the registration in the family court of an order made in Scotland or Northern Ireland is cancelled by the family court, the court officer for the family court will give notice of the cancellation to—

(a) the appropriate officer of the court which made the order; and
(b) where the order is registered under Part 2 of the 1950 Act, to the appropriate officer of the High Court.

(5) Where under section 5(4) of the 1958 Act the registration in the family court of an order under Part 2 of the 1950 Act is cancelled by the family court, the court officer for the family court will give notice of the cancellation to the appropriate officer of the original court.

(6) Where under section 5 of the 1958 Act the cancellation of the registration of a High Court order means that any order which requires payment to be made to the family court is to cease to have effect, the court officer will give notice to the defendant in the form set out in Practice Direction 32A (Form 7).][1]

Amendment

1 Inserted by the Family Procedure (Amendment No 3) Rules 2013, SI 2013/3204, rr 2, 98.

32.20 …[1]

…[1]

Amendment

1 Repealed by the Family Procedure (Amendment No 3) Rules 2013, SI 2013/3204, rr 2, 99.

32.21 …[1]

…[1]

Amendment

1 Repealed by the Family Procedure (Amendment No 3) Rules 2013, SI 2013/3204, rr 2, 99.

32.22 Cancellation of registration – orders registered in [the family court][1]

(1) Where the court gives notice under section 5(2) of the 1958 Act, the court officer must endorse the notice on the certified copy of the order of variation or discharge sent to the [family court][1] in accordance with rule 32.19(2).

(2) Where notice is received from [the family court][1] that registration of an order made by the High Court …[2] under Part 1 of the 1958 Act has been cancelled, the court officer must enter particulars of the cancellation in the place where the details required by rule 32.15(3) were entered.

Amendment

1 Substituted by the Family Procedure (Amendment No 3) Rules 2013, SI 2013/3204, rr 2, 100(a), (b).
2 Repealed by the Family Procedure (Amendment No 3) Rules 2013, SI 2013/3204, rr 2, 100(c).

[32.22A Notices: payments made through the family court

(1) Paragraph (2) applies where a notice is given under section 2(6ZC) of the 1958 Act that payments under an order registered in the family court are payable to the family court.

(2) The notice will be in the form set out in Practice Direction 32A (Form 5) and will be given by the court officer of the family court.

(3) Paragraph (4) applies where a notice is given under section 2(6ZC) of the 1958 Act that payments under an order registered in the family court have ceased to be payable to the family court.

(4) The notice will be in the form set out in Practice Direction 32A (Form 6) and will be given by the court officer of the family court.][1]

Amendment

1 Inserted by the Family Procedure (Amendment No 3) Rules 2013, SI 2013/3204, rr 2, 101.

[32.22B Method of payment

(1) This rule applies where the family court exercises its duties or powers under section 4A(2) of the 1958 Act to make, revive or vary any means of payment order within the meaning of section 1(7) of the Maintenance Enforcement Act 1991.

(2) Where the court orders that payments under a registered order are to be made by a particular means—

(a) the court will record on a copy of the order the means of payment which the court has ordered; and
(b) the court officer will notify, in writing, the person liable to make payments under the order how the payments are to be made.

(3) Paragraph (4) applies where the court orders that payments be made—

(a) by the debtor to the creditor; or
(b) by the debtor to the court;

by a method falling within section 1(5) of the Maintenance Enforcement Act 1991.

(4) The court officer will notify the person liable to make payments under the order of sufficient details of the account into which payments should be made to enable payments to be made into that account.][1]

Amendment

1 Inserted by the Family Procedure (Amendment No 3) Rules 2013, SI 2013/3204, rr 2, 101.

[32.22C Variation of method of payment

(1) The Part 18 procedure applies to an application under section 1(3)(a) of the Maintenance Enforcement Act 1991 received from an interested party for the method of payment to be varied under section 4A of the 1958 Act.

(2) The court will notify the interested party who made the application and, where practicable, any other interested party, of the result of the application.

(3) The court will record any variation on a copy of the order.][1]

Amendment

1 Inserted by the Family Procedure (Amendment No 3) Rules 2013, SI 2013/3204, rr 2, 101.

[32.22D Notices received from another court or from a person entitled to payments

(1) This rule applies where any notice is received—

(a) of the discharge or variation by the High Court of a High Court order registered in the family court;

(b) of the discharge or variation by a court in Scotland or Northern Ireland of an order made by such a court and registered in the family court; or

(c) under section 5(1) or (2) of the 1958 Act.

(2) The court officer for the family court will enter details of any such notice in the register.

(3) In the case of a notice under section 5(1) or (2) of the 1958 Act, the court officer for the family court will ensure that the person in possession of any warrant of commitment, issued but not executed, for the enforcement of the order is informed of the giving of that notice.][1]

Amendment

1 Inserted by the Family Procedure (Amendment No 3) Rules 2013, SI 2013/3204, rr 2, 101.

Chapter 4
Registration and enforcement of custody orders under the 1986 Act

32.23 Interpretation

In this Chapter—

'appropriate court' means, in relation to—

(a) Scotland, the Court of Session;

(b) Northern Ireland, the High Court in Northern Ireland; and

(c) a specified dependent territory, the corresponding court in that territory;

'appropriate officer' means, in relation to—

(a) the Court of Session, the Deputy Principal Clerk of Session;

(b) the High Court in Northern Ireland, the Master (Care and Protection) of that court; and

(c) the appropriate court in a specified dependent territory, the corresponding officer of that court;

'Part 1 order' means an order under Part 1 of the 1986 Act;
'the register' means the register kept for the purposes of Part 1 of the 1986 Act; and
'specified dependent territory' means a dependent territory specified in column 1 of Schedule 1 to the Family Law Act 1986 (Specified Dependent Territories) Order 1991.

32.24 Prescribed officer and functions of the court

(1) The prescribed officer for the purposes of sections 27(4) and 28(1) of the 1986 Act is the family proceedings department manager of the principal registry.

(2) The function of the court under sections 27(3) and 28(1) of the 1986 Act shall be performed by a court officer.

32.25 Application for the registration of an order made by the High Court or [the family court][1]

(1) An application under section 27 of the 1986 Act for the registration of an order made in the High Court or [the family court][1] may be made by sending to a court officer at the court which made the order—

(a) a certified copy of the order;
(b) a copy of any order which has varied the terms of the original order;
(c) a statement which—
 (i) contains the name and address of the applicant and the applicant's interest under the order;
 (ii) contains—
  (aa) the name and date of birth of the child in respect of whom the order was made;
  (bb) the whereabouts or suspected whereabouts of the child; and
  (cc) the name of any person with whom the child is alleged to be;
 (iii) contains the name and address of any other person who has an interest under the order and states whether the order has been served on that person;
 (iv) states in which of the jurisdictions of Scotland, Northern Ireland or a specified dependent territory the order is to be registered;
 (v) states that to the best of the applicant's information and belief, the order is in force;
 (vi) states whether, and if so where, the order is already registered;
 (vii) gives details of any order known to the applicant which affects the child and is in force in the jurisdiction in which the order is to be registered;
 (viii) annexes any document relevant to the application; and
 (ix) is verified by a statement of truth; and
(d) a copy of the statement referred to in paragraph (c).

(2) On receipt of the documents referred to in paragraph (1), the court officer will, subject to paragraph (4)—

(a) keep the original statement and send the other documents to the appropriate officer;
(b) record in the court records the fact that the documents have been sent to the appropriate officer; and
(c) file a copy of the documents.

(3) On receipt of a notice that the document has been registered in the appropriate court the court officer will record that fact in the court records.

(4) The court officer will not send the documents to the appropriate officer if it appears to the court officer that—

(a) the order is no longer in force; or
(b) the child has reached the age of 16.

(5) Where paragraph (4) applies—

(a) the court officer must, within 14 days of the decision, notify the applicant of the decision of the court officer in paragraph (4) and the reasons for it; and
(b) the applicant may apply to [the court][1], in private for an order that the documents be sent to the appropriate court.

Amendment

1 Substituted by the Family Procedure (Amendment No 3) Rules 2013, SI 2013/3204, rr 2, 102.

32.26 Registration of orders made in Scotland, Northern Ireland or a specified dependent territory

(1) This rule applies where the prescribed officer receives, for registration, a certified copy of an order made in Scotland, Northern Ireland or a specified dependent territory.

(2) The prescribed officer will—

(a) enter in the register—
   (i) the name and address of the applicant and the applicant's interest under the order;
   (ii) the name and date of birth of the child and the date the child will attain the age of 16;
   (iii) the whereabouts or suspected whereabouts of the child; and
   (iv) the terms of the order, its date and the court which made it;
(b) file the certified copy and accompanying documents; and
(c) notify—
   (i) the court which sent the order; and
   (ii) the applicant,

that the order has been registered.

32.27 Revocation and variation of an order made in the High Court or [the family court][1]

(1) Where a Part 1 order, registered in an appropriate court, is varied or revoked, the court officer of the court making the order of variation or revocation will—

(a) send a certified copy of the order of variation or revocation to—
   (i) the appropriate officer; and
   (ii) if a different court, the court which made the Part 1 order;
   (b) record in the court records the fact that a copy of the order has been sent; and
(c) file a copy of the order.

(2) On receipt of notice from the appropriate court that its register has been amended, this fact will be recorded by the court officer of—

(a) the court which made the order of variation or revocation; and
(b) if different, the court which made the Part 1 order.

Amendment

1 Substituted by the Family Procedure (Amendment No 3) Rules 2013, SI 2013/3204, rr 2, 103.

32.28 Registration of varied, revoked or recalled orders made in Scotland, Northern Ireland or a specified dependent territory

(1) This rule applies where the prescribed officer receives a certified copy of an order made in Scotland, Northern Ireland or a specified dependent territory which varies, revokes or recalls a registered Part 1 order.

(2) The prescribed officer shall enter particulars of the variation, revocation or recall in the register and give notice of the entry to—

(a) the court which sent the certified copy;
(b) if different, the court which made the Part 1 order;
(c) the applicant for registration; and
(d) if different, the applicant for the variation, revocation of recall of the order.

(3) An application under section 28(2) of the 1986 Act must be made in accordance with the Part 19 procedure.

(4) The applicant for the Part 1 order, if not the applicant under section 28(2) of the 1986 Act, must be made a defendant to the application.

(5) Where the court cancels a registration under section 28(2) of the 1986 Act, the court officer will amend the register and give notice of the amendment to the court which made the Part 1 order.

32.29 Interim directions

The following persons will be made parties to an application for interim directions under section 29 of the 1986 Act—

(a) the parties to the proceedings for enforcement; and
(b) if not a party to those proceedings, the applicant for the Part 1 order.

32.30 Staying and dismissal of enforcement proceedings

(1) The following persons will be made parties to an application under section 30(1) or 31(1) of the 1986 Act—

(a) the parties to the proceedings for enforcement which are sought to be stayed(GL); and
(b) if not a party to those proceedings, the applicant for the Part 1 order.

(2) Where the court makes an order under section 30(2) or (3) or section 31(3) of the 1986 Act, the court officer will amend the register and give notice of the amendment to—

(a) the court which made the Part 1 order; and
(b) the applicants for—
  (i) registration;
  (ii) enforcement; and
  (iii) stay(GL) or dismissal of the enforcement proceedings.

32.31 Particulars of other proceedings

A party to proceedings for or relating to a Part 1 order who knows of other proceedings which relate to the child concerned (including proceedings out of the jurisdiction and concluded proceedings) must file a witness statement which—

(a) states in which jurisdiction and court the other proceedings were begun;
(b) states the nature and current state of the proceedings and the relief claimed or granted;
(c) sets out the names of the parties to the proceedings and their relationship to the child;
(d) if applicable and if known, states the reasons why relief claimed in the proceedings for or relating to the Part 1 order was not claimed in the other proceedings; and
(e) is verified by a statement of truth.

32.32 Inspection of register

The following persons may inspect any entry in the register relating to a Part 1 order and may request copies of the order any document relating to it—

(a) the applicant for registration of the Part 1 order;
(b) a person who, to the satisfaction of a district judge, has an interest under the Part 1 order; and
(c) a person who obtains the permission of a district judge.

[Chapter 5
Ability of a court officer to take enforcement proceedings in relation to certain orders for periodical payments

32.33 Court officers and enforcement proceedings

(1) In this rule—

'the 1972 Act' means the Maintenance Orders (Reciprocal Enforcement) Act 1972;
'relevant order' means—

(a) any order made by the family court for periodical payments, other than an order made by virtue of Part 2 of the 1972 Act;
(b) any order for periodical payments made by the High Court (including an order deemed to be made by the High Court by virtue of section 1(2) of the 1958 Act) and registered under Part 1 of the 1958 Act in the family court; and
(c) an order made by a court in Scotland or in Northern Ireland which is registered in the family court under Part 2 of the 1950 Act; and

'the payee' means the person for whose benefit payments under a relevant order are required to be made.

(2) Where—

(a) payments under a relevant order are required to be made periodically to the family court; and
(b) any sums payable under the order are in arrears,

a court officer will, if the payee so requests in writing, and unless it appears to the court officer that it is unreasonable in the circumstances to do so, proceed in the officer's own name for the recovery of those sums.

(3) Where payments under a relevant order are required to be made periodically to the court, the payee may, at any time during the period in which the payments are required to be so made, give authority in writing to a court officer for the officer to proceed as mentioned in paragraph (4).

(4) Where authority is given under paragraph (3) to a court officer, that officer will, unless it appears unreasonable in the circumstances to do so, proceed in the officer's own name for the recovery of any sums payable to the court under the order in question which, on or after the date of the giving of the authority, fall into arrears.

(5) In any case where—

(a) authority under paragraph (3) has been given to a court officer; and

(b) the payee gives notice in writing to that court officer cancelling the authority,

the authority will cease to have effect and so the court officer will not continue any proceedings already commenced by virtue of the authority.

(6) The payee shall have the same liability for all of the costs properly incurred in, or in relation to, proceedings taken under paragraph (2) at the payee's request, or under paragraph (3) by virtue of the payee's authority, including any court fees and any costs incurred as a result of any proceedings commenced not being continued, as if the proceedings had been commenced by the payee.

(7) Nothing in paragraph (2) or (4) shall affect any right of a payee to proceed in his or her own name for the recovery of sums payable under an order of any court.][1]

Amendment

1 Inserted by the Family Procedure (Amendment No 3) Rules 2013, SI 2013/3204, rr 2, 104.

Practice Direction 32A – Forms relating to Part 32

See also Part 32

This Practice Direction supplements rules 32.12A(1)(a), (b), (c) and (d), 32.19A(6) and 32.22A(2) and (4)

1 The form referred to in rule 32.12A(1)(a) is–

Form 1

Notice to person liable to make payments that sums payable under a maintenance order registered in the family court become payable through the court: Maintenance Orders Act 1950

Family Court sitting at ……………………

Date:

To:

Address:

You are given notice that the sums payable by you under (insert particulars of maintenance order) made on the …. day of … …. 20 …, by (state court in Scotland or Northern Ireland by which order was made) and registered in this Court under Part 2 of the Maintenance Orders Act 1950, have, under an order of this Court dated the …. day of … … 20 …., become payable through (or to) this Court.

From the date of this notice, payments under the order (including payments in respect of any sums due at the date of the receipt by you of this notice) should be only sent to (state address).

If payments are not sent in this way, then, unless the contrary is proved, you may be assumed not to have made the payments under the order.

A.B,

[Court Officer]

2 The form referred to in rule 32.12A(1)(b) is–

Form 2

Notice to person liable to make payments that sums payable under a maintenance order made by the family court have ceased to be payable to or through the court: Maintenance Orders Act 1950

Family Court sitting at ……………………… (Code)

Date:

To:

Address:

You are given notice that the sums payable by you under (insert particulars of maintenance order) made on the … …. day of … … 20 …, by this Court have, by reason of the registration of the said order in (state court in Scotland or Northern Ireland in which order is registered), ceased to be payable through (or to) the court.

From the date of this notice, payments under the order (including payments in respect of any sums due at the date of the receipt by you of this notice) should be only paid to (state name and address of person entitled to payments under the order) (, unless you receive, or have meanwhile received, notice from the clerk of the said court in Scotland or Northern Ireland that they are to be paid to any other person).

If payments are not paid in this way, then, unless the contrary is proved, you may be assumed not to have made the payments under the order.

A.B,

Court Officer

3 The form referred to in rule 32.12A(1)(c) is–

Form 3

Certificate of arrears: Maintenance Orders Act 1950

I hereby certify that the arrears due at the date of this certificate under (insert particulars of maintenance order) made on the … …. day of …… 20 …., by the family court sitting at …… …., the payments under which are at present required to be made to (or through) the court, amount to …… … …

Dated the … …. day of … …. 20 ….

A.B.

Court officer

4 The form referred to in rule 32.12A(1)(d) is–

Form 4

Notice of cancellation of registration of maintenance order in the family court

Family court sitting at …………………….. (Code)

Date:

To:

Address:

You are given notice that the registration in this Court under Part 2 of the Maintenance Orders Act 1950 of (insert particulars of maintenance order) made on the … …. day of …. 20 …, by (state court in Scotland or Northern Ireland by which order was made) has been cancelled.

(Sums payable by you under the order have, by reason of the cancellation of the registration of the order, ceased to be payable through the court (by the following method of payment falling within section 1 of the Maintenance Enforcement Act 1991 (standing order etc.), namely … … … ….), (by an attachment of earnings order).

From the date of this notice, payments under the order (including payments in respect of any sums due at the date of receipt by you of this notice) should be only paid to (state name and address of person entitled to payments under the order), unless you receive, or meanwhile have received, notice from the court officer for a competent court that they are to be paid to any other person.

If payments are not paid in this way, then, unless the contrary is proved, you may be assumed not to have made the payments under the order.

A.B.

Court officer

5 The form referred to in rule 32.22A(2) is–

Form 5

Notice that payments have become payable through the family court (Maintenance Orders Act 1958, section 2(6ZC))

Family Court sitting at … … … (Code)

Date:

To:

Address:

You are given notice that the sums payable by you under (insert particulars of maintenance order) made on the … … …… day of …… …. 20 …. by the (High Court) (Court of Session) (High Court in Northern Ireland) and registered in this Court under Part 1 of the Maintenance Orders Act 1958, have under an order of this Court dated the ……. day of … … … 20 …., become payable through the family court.

From the date of this notice, payments under the order (including payments in respect of any sums due at the date of the receipt by you of this notice) should be only sent to the court at (state address).

If payments are not sent in this way, then, unless the contrary is proved, you may be assumed not to have made the payments under the order.

A.B.

Court officer, family court

6 The form referred to in rule 32.22A(4) is–

Form 6

Notice to person liable to make payments that sums payable under a maintenance order made by the family court have ceased to be payable to or through the court: Maintenance Orders Act 1958

Family Court sitting at … … … (Code)

Date:

To:

Address:

You are given notice that the sums payable by you under (insert particulars of maintenance order) made on the … …. day of …… 20 …, by the (High Court) (Court of Session) (High Court in Northern Ireland) and registered in this Court under Part 1 of the Maintenance Orders Act 1958, have under an Order of this Court dated the …… … day of … … …. 20 …., ceased to be payable to or through the family court.

From the date of this notice, payments under the order (including payments in respect of any sums due at the date of the receipt by you of this notice) should be paid only to (state name and address of person entitled to payments under the order) (, unless you receive, or have meanwhile received, notice from the clerk of the said High Court, Court of Session or High Court in Northern Ireland that they are to be paid to any other person).

If payments are not made in this way, then, unless the contrary is proved, you may be assumed not to have made the payments under the order.

A.B,

Court Officer

7 The form referred to at rule 32.19A(6) is–

Form 7

Notice of cancellation of registration (Maintenance Orders Act 1958, section 5(5))

Family Court sitting at ………………………..

Date:

To:

Address:

You are hereby given notice that the registration in this Court under Part 1 of the Maintenance Orders Act 1958, of (insert particulars of maintenance order) made on the … … … day of … …. 20 …., by the (High Court) (Court of Session) (High Court in Northern Ireland) has been cancelled.

Sums payable by you under the said order have by reason of the cancellation of the registration of the order ceased to be payable through the family court, (by the following method of payment falling within section 1 of the Maintenance Enforcement Act 1991 (standing order etc), namely … … …….), (by an attachment of earnings order) (by direct payment to …… … ….).

From the date of this notice, payments under the order (including payments in respect of any sums due on the date of the receipt by you of this notice) should be paid only to (state name and address of person entitled to payments under the order).

If payments are not sent in this way, then, unless the contrary is proved, you may be assumed not to have made the payments under the order.

A.B.

Court officer.

PART 33
ENFORCEMENT

Chapter 1
General rules

33.1 Application

(1) The rules in this Part apply to an application made in the High Court and [the family court][1] to enforce an order made in family proceedings.

(2) [Parts 50, 83 and 84][1] of, and Schedules 1 and 2 to, the CPR apply, as far as they are relevant and with necessary modification …[2], to an application made in the High Court and [the family court][1] to enforce an order made in family proceedings.

Amendment

1 Substituted by the Family Procedure (Amendment No 2) Rules 2014, SI 2014/667, rr 2, 28(a), (b)(i), (iii).
2 Repealed by the Family Procedure (Amendment No 2) Rules 2014, SI 2014/667, rr 2, 28(b)(ii).

Section 1
Enforcement of orders for the payment of money

33.2 Application of the Civil Procedure Rules

Part 70 of the CPR applies to proceedings under this Section as if—

(a) in rule 70.1, in paragraph (2)(d), 'but does not include a judgment or order for the payment of money into court' is omitted; …[1]
[(a1) in rule 70.3(1), for 'County Court' there is substituted 'family court'; and][2]
(b) rule 70.5 is omitted.

Amendment

1 Repealed by the Family Procedure (Amendment No 2) Rules 2014, SI 2014/667, rr 2, 29(a).
2 Inserted by the Family Procedure (Amendment No 2) Rules 2014, SI 2014/667, rr 2, 29(b).

33.3 How to apply

(1) Except where a rule or practice direction otherwise requires, an application for an order to enforce an order for the payment of money must be made in a notice of application accompanied by a statement which must—

(a) state the amount due under the order, showing how that amount is arrived at; and
(b) be verified by a statement of truth.

(2) The notice of application may either—

(a) apply for an order specifying the method of enforcement; or
(b) apply for an order for such method of enforcement as the court may consider appropriate.

(3) If an application is made under paragraph (2)(b), an order to attend court will be issued and rule 71.2 (6) and (7) of the CPR will apply as if the application had been made under that rule.

33.4 Transfer of orders

(1) This rule applies to an application for the transfer—

(a) to the High Court of an order made in [the family court][1]; and
(b) to [the family court][1] of an order made in the High Court.

(2) The application must be—

(a) made without notice; and
(b) accompanied by a statement which complies with rule 33.3(1).

(3) The transfer will have effect upon the filing of the application.

(4) Where an order is transferred from [the family court][1] to the High Court—

(a) it will have the same force and effect; and
(b) the same proceedings may be taken on it,

as if it were an order of the High Court.

(5) This rule does not apply to the transfer of orders for periodical payments or for the recovery of arrears of periodical payments.

Amendment

1 Substituted by the Family Procedure (Amendment No 2) Rules 2014, SI 2014/667, rr 2, 30.

Section 2
Committal and injunction

[33.5 Enforcement of orders by way of committal

Part 37 applies as appropriate for the enforcement by way of committal of an order made in family proceedings.][1]

Amendment

1 Substituted by the Family Procedure (Amendment No 2) Rules 2014, SI 2014/667, rr 2, 31.

33.6 …[1]

…[1]

Amendment

1 Repealed by the Family Procedure (Amendment No 2) Rules 2014, SI 2014/667, rr 2, 31.

33.7 …[1]

…[1]

Amendment

1 Repealed by the Family Procedure (Amendment No 2) Rules 2014, SI 2014/667, rr 2, 31.

33.8 …[1]

…[1]

Amendment

1 Repealed by the Family Procedure (Amendment No 2) Rules 2014, SI 2014/667, rr 2, 31.

Chapter 2
Committal by way of judgment summons

33.9 Interpretation

In this Chapter, unless the context requires otherwise—

'order' means an order made in family proceedings for the payment of money;

'judgment creditor' means a person entitled to enforce an order under section 5 of the Debtors Act 1869;

'debtor' means a person liable under an order; and

'judgment summons' means a summons under [section 5 of the Debtors Act 1869][1] requiring a debtor to attend court.

Amendment

1 Substituted by the Family Procedure (Amendment No 2) Rules 2015, SI 2015/1420, rr 2, 18.

33.10 Application

[(1) An application for the issue of a judgment summons may be made—

(a) in the case of an order of the High Court, to—
(i) the principal registry;
(ii) a district registry; or
(iii) the family court,

whichever in the opinion of the judgment creditor is most convenient, and if to the family court, to whichever Designated Family Judge area is in the opinion of the judgment creditor most convenient; and

(b) in the case of an order of the family court, to whichever Designated Family Judge area is in the opinion of the judgment creditor most convenient,

having regard (in any case) to the place where the debtor resides or carries on business and irrespective of the location of the court or registry in which the order was made.

(For the way in which information will be provided to enable Designated Family Judge areas and Designated Family Courts to be identified, see Practice Direction 34E.)][1]

(2) An application must be accompanied by a statement which—

(a) complies with rule 33.3(1);
(b) contains all the evidence on which the judgment creditor intends to rely; and
(c) has exhibited to it a copy of the order.

Amendment

1 Substituted by the Family Procedure (Amendment No 2) Rules 2014, SI 2014/667, rr 2, 32.

33.11 Judgment summons

(1) If the debtor is in default under an order of committal made on a previous judgment summons in respect of the same order, a judgment summons must not be issued without the court's permission.

[(2) A judgment summons must be accompanied by the statement referred to in rule 33.10(2).

(3) A judgment summons must be served on the debtor—

- (a) personally; or
- (b) by the court sending it to the debtor by first class post—
  - (i) at the address stated in the application for the issue of a judgment summons; or
  - (ii) in a case where a court officer is proceeding for the recovery of a debt in accordance with rule 32.33, at the last known address for the debtor shown on court records.

(4) In a case to which paragraph (3)(b)(i) applies, the judgment creditor must file with the court a certificate for postal service.

(5) A judgment summons must be served on the debtor not less than 14 days before the hearing.

(6) Paragraph (3) is subject to any direction of the court that the judgment summons must be served personally on the debtor.][1]

Amendment

1 Substituted by the Family Procedure (Amendment No 2) Rules 2015, SI 2015/1420, rr 2, 19.

33.12 Successive judgment summonses

Subject to rule 33.11(1), successive judgment summonses may be issued even if the debtor has ceased to reside or carry on business at the address stated in the application for the issue of a judgment summons since the issue of the original judgment summons.

[33.13 Order or summons to attend adjourned hearing: requirement for personal service

(1) Paragraph (2) applies in proceedings for committal by way of judgment summons where—

- (a) the family court has ordered under section 110(1) of the County Courts Act 1984 that the debtor must attend an adjourned hearing; or
- (b) the High Court has summonsed the debtor to attend an adjourned hearing following the debtor's failure to attend the hearing of the judgment summons.

(2) The following documents must be served personally on the debtor—

- (a) the notice of the date and time fixed for the adjourned hearing; and
- (b) copies of the judgment summons and the documents mentioned in rule 33.10(2).][1]

Amendment

1 Substituted by the Family Procedure (Amendment No 2) Rules 2015, SI 2015/1420, rr 2, 20.

[33.14 Committal on application for judgment summons

(1) Subject to paragraph (2), on a hearing of an application for a judgment summons the debtor may be committed for making default on payment of a debt if the judgment creditor proves that the debtor—

(a) has, or has had, since the date of the order the means to pay the sum in respect of which the debtor has made default; and

(b) has refused or neglected, or refuses or neglects, to pay that sum.

(2) A debtor may not be committed in accordance with paragraph (1) where the judgment summons was served by post, unless the debtor attends the hearing.

(3) Where the debtor has been ordered or summonsed to attend an adjourned hearing in accordance with rule 33.13, the debtor may be committed—

(a) for failure to attend the adjourned hearing; or

(b) for making default on payment of a debt, if the judgment creditor proves that the debtor—

   (i) has, or has had, since the date of the order the means to pay the sum in respect of which the debtor has made default; and

   (ii) has refused or neglected, or refuses or neglects, to pay that sum.

(4) The debtor may not be compelled to give evidence.][1]

Amendment

1 Substituted by the Family Procedure (Amendment No 2) Rules 2015, SI 2015/1420, rr 2, 21.

[33.14A Expenses

(1) A debtor must not be committed to prison under section 110(2) of the County Courts Act 1984 unless the debtor has been paid or offered a sum reasonably sufficient to cover the expenses of travelling to and from the court building at which the debtor is summoned or ordered to appear.

(2) The sum must be paid or offered at the time of service of—

(a) the judgment summons; or

(b) the order to attend under section 110(1) of the County Courts Act 1984.][1]

Amendment

1 Inserted by the Family Procedure (Amendment No 2) Rules 2015, SI 2015/1420, rr 2, 22.

33.15 Orders for the benefit of different persons

Where an applicant has obtained one or more orders in the same application but for the benefit of different persons—

(a) where the judgment creditor is a child, the applicant may apply for the issue of a judgment summons in respect of those orders on behalf of the judgment creditor without seeking permission to act as the child's litigation friend; and

(b) only one judgment summons need be issued in respect of those orders.

33.16 Hearing of judgment summons

(1) On the hearing of the judgment summons the court may—

(a) where the order is for lump sum provision or costs; or

(b) where the order is an order for maintenance pending suit, an order for maintenance pending outcome of proceedings or an order for other periodical payments and it appears to the court that the order would have been varied or suspended if the debtor had made an application for that purpose,

make a new order for payment of the amount due under the original order, together with the costs of the judgment summons, either at a specified time or by instalments.

(2) If the court makes an order of committal, it may direct its execution to be suspended on terms that the debtor pays to the judgment creditor—

(a) the amount due;
(b) the costs of the judgment summons; and
(c) any sums accruing due under the original order,

either at a specified time or by instalments.

(3) All payments under a new order or an order of committal must be made to the judgment creditor unless the court directs otherwise.

(4) Where an order of committal is suspended on such terms as are mentioned in paragraph (2)—

(a) all payments made under the suspended order will be deemed to be made—
  (i) first, in or towards the discharge of any sums from time to time accruing due under the original order; and
  (ii) secondly, in or towards the discharge of a debt in respect of which the judgment summons was issued and the costs of the summons; and
(b) the suspended order must not be executed until the judgment creditor has filed a statement of default on the part of the debtor.

33.17 Special provisions as to judgment summonses in the High Court

(1) [The High Court][1] may summons witnesses to give evidence to prove the means of the debtor and may issue a witness summons for that purpose.

(2) Where the debtor appears at the hearing, [the High Court][1] may direct that the travelling expenses paid to the debtor be allowed as expenses of a witness.

(3) Where the debtor appears at the hearing and no order of committal is made, [the High Court][1] may allow the debtor's proper costs including compensation for any loss of earnings.

(4) When [the High Court][1] makes—

(a) a new order; or
(b) an order of committal,

a court officer must send notice of the order to the debtor and, if the original order was made in another court, to that court.

(5) An order of committal must be directed—

(a) where the order is to be executed by the tipstaff, to the tipstaff; or
(b) where the order is to be executed by a deputy tipstaff, to the [Designated Family Judge area within][2] which the debtor is to be found.

Amendment

1 Substituted by the Family Procedure (Amendment No 2) Rules 2015, SI 2015/1420, rr 2, 23.
2 Substituted by the Family Procedure (Amendment No 2) Rules 2014, SI 2014/667, rr 2, 35.

33.18 …[1]

…[1]

Amendment

1 Repealed by the Family Procedure (Amendment No 2) Rules 2014, SI 2014/667, rr 2, 36.

Chapter 3
Attachment of earnings

[33.19 Enforcement by attachment of earnings order

Part 39 applies to applications for an attachment of earnings order to secure payments under a maintenance order.][1]

Amendment

1 Substituted by the Family Procedure (Amendment) Rules 2016, SI 2016/355, rr 2, 4.

Chapter 4
Warrant of [control][1]

33.20 Applications to vary existing orders

Where an application is pending for a variation of—

(a) a financial order;
(b) an order under section 27 of the 1973 Act; or
(c) an order under Part 9 of Schedule 5 to the 2004 Act,

no warrant of [control][1] may be issued to enforce payment of any sum due under those orders, except with the permission of the [court][1].

Amendment

1 Substituted by the Family Procedure (Amendment No 2) Rules 2014, SI 2014/667, rr 2, 38, 39.

33.21 …[1]

…[1]

Amendment

1 Repealed by the Family Procedure (Amendment No 2) Rules 2014, SI 2014/667, rr 2, 40.

Chapter 5
Court's power to appoint a receiver

33.22 Application of the CPR

Part 69 of the CPR applies to proceedings under this Part.

Chapter 6
Orders to obtain information from judgment debtors

[33.23 Application of the CPR

(1) Part 71 of the CPR applies to proceedings under this Part with the following modifications.

(2) In rule 71.2, for sub-paragraph (b) substitute—

(b) must be—
  (i) issued in the High Court if the High Court made the judgment or order which it is sought to enforce; or
  (ii) made to the Designated Family Court for the Designated Family Judge area within which the judgment or order was made,

except that if the proceedings have since been transferred to a different court or Designated Family Judge area, it must be issued in that court or made to that area.][1]

Amendment

1 Substituted by the Family Procedure (Amendment No 2) Rules 2014, SI 2014/667, rr 2, 41.

Chapter 7
Third party debt orders

33.24 Application of the CPR

(1) Part 72 of the CPR applies to proceedings under this Part with the following modifications.

[(1A) In rule 72.3, for paragraph (1)(b) there is substituted—

'(b) must be issued in the court which made the judgment or order which it is sought to enforce, or made to the Designated Family Judge area within which that judgment or order was made, except that if the proceedings have since been transferred to a different court or Designated Family Judge area, it must be issued in that court or made to that area.'][1]

(2) In rule 72.4—

(a) in paragraph (1), for 'a judge' there is substituted 'the court'; and
(b) in paragraph (2), for 'judge' there is substituted 'court'.

[(3) In rule 72.7—

(a) in paragraph (2)(a), after 'the Royal Courts of Justice' there is inserted 'or the principal registry'; and
(b) in paragraph (2)(b), for 'in County Court proceedings, to any County Court hearing centre' there is substituted 'in family court proceedings, to any Designated Family Judge area'.][2]

(4) Rule 72.10 is omitted.

Amendment

1 Inserted by the Family Procedure (Amendment No 2) Rules 2014, SI 2014/667, rr 2, 42(a).
2 Substituted by the Family Procedure (Amendment No 2) Rules 2014, SI 2014/667, rr 2, 42(b).

Chapter 8
Charging order, stop order, stop notice

[33.25 Application for a charging order, stop order or stop notice

Part 40 applies for the enforcement of a judgment or order made in family proceedings by way of a charging order, stop order or stop notice.][1]

Amendment

1 Substituted by the Family Procedure (Amendment) Rules 2016, SI 2016/355, rr 2, 5.

Practice Direction 33A – Enforcement of undertakings

See also Part 33

This Practice Direction supplements FPR Part 33

Enforcement of undertaking to do or abstain from doing any act other than the payment of money

1 Attention is drawn to the provisions of Part 37 (in particular rule 37(2)) about contempt applications for the enforcement of undertakings.

Enforcement of undertaking for the payment of money

2.1 Any undertaking for the payment of money that has effect as if it was an order made under Part 2 of the Matrimonial Causes Act 1973 may be enforced as if it was an order and Part 33 and Part 37 apply accordingly.

2.2 The form of an undertaking for the payment of money that has effect as if it were an order under Part 2 of the Matrimonial Causes Act 1973 must be endorsed with a notice setting out the consequences of disobedience, as follows:

> 'If you fail to pay any sum of money which you have promised the court that you will pay, a person entitled to enforce the undertaking may apply to the court for an order. You may be sent to prison if it is proved that you–
>
> (a) have, or have had since the date of your undertaking, the means to pay the sum; and
>
> (b) have refused or neglected, or are refusing or neglecting, to pay that sum'.

2.3 The person giving the undertaking must make a signed statement to the effect that he or she understands the terms of the undertaking being given and the consequences of failure to comply with it, as follows:

> 'I understand the undertaking that I have given, and that if I break my promise to the court to pay any sum of money, I may be sent to prison'.

2.4 The statement need not be given before the court in person. It may be endorsed on the court copy of the undertaking or may be filed in a separate document such as a letter.

PART 34
RECIPROCAL ENFORCEMENT OF MAINTENANCE ORDERS

34.1 Scope and interpretation of this Part

(1) This Part contains rules about the reciprocal enforcement of maintenance orders.

(2) In this Part—

'the 1920 Act' means the Maintenance Orders (Facilities for Enforcement) Act 1920;
'the 1972 Act' means the Maintenance Orders (Reciprocal Enforcement) Act 1972;
…[1]
…[1]
…[1]
…[1]

(3) Chapter 1 of this Part relates to the enforcement of maintenance orders in accordance with the 1920 Act.

(4) Chapter 2 of this Part relates to the enforcement of maintenance orders in accordance with [Parts 1 and 2][2] of the 1972 Act.

(5) Chapter 3 of this Part relates to the enforcement of maintenance orders in accordance with—

(a) …[1]
(b) …[1] …[3]
(c) …[1] […[4]][5]
[(d) …[1]][6]
[(e) the 2007 Hague Convention.][7]

Amendment

1 Repealed by the Family Procedure Rules 2010 and Court of Protection Rules 2017 (Amendment) (EU Exit) Regulations 2019, SI 2019/517, rr 2, 19(1), (2).
2 Substituted by the Family Procedure (Amendment No 3) Rules 2013, SI 2013/3204, rr 2, 105.
3 Repealed by the Family Procedure (Amendment) Rules 2011, SI 2011/1328, rr 2, 3, 17(a).
4 Repealed by the Family Procedure (Amendment No 4) Rules 2012, SI 2012/2806, rr 2, 3, 18(a).
5 Substituted by the Family Procedure (Amendment) Rules 2011, SI 2011/1328, rr 2, 3, 17(b).
6 Inserted by the Family Procedure (Amendment) Rules 2011, SI 2011/1328, rr 2, 3, 17(c).
7 Substituted by the Family Procedure (Amendment No 4) Rules 2012, SI 2012/2806, rr 2, 3, 18(b).

34.2 Meaning of prescribed officer in [the family court][1]

(1) For the purposes of the 1920 Act, the prescribed officer in relation to [the family court is the court officer][1].

(2) For the purposes of Part 1 of the 1972 Act …[2], the prescribed officer in relation to [the family court is the court officer][1].

[(3) For the purposes of an application under …[2] Article 23(2) or (3) of the 2007 Hague Convention for registration of a maintenance order, the prescribed officer in relation to the family court is the court officer.][3]

Amendment

1 Substituted by the Family Procedure (Amendment No 3) Rules 2013, SI 2013/3204, rr 2, 106(a), (b), (c).
2 Repealed by the Family Procedure Rules 2010 and Court of Protection Rules 2017 (Amendment) (EU Exit) Regulations 2019, SI 2019/517, rr 2, 19(1), (3).
3 Inserted by the Family Procedure (Amendment No 3) Rules 2013, SI 2013/3204, rr 2, 106(d).

34.3 Registration of maintenance orders in [the family court][1]

Where [the family court][1] is required by any of the enactments referred to in rule 34.1(2) [or by virtue of …[2]][3] […[2] the 2007 Hague Convention][4] to register a foreign order the court officer must—

(a) enter …[5] a memorandum of the order in the register …[6]; and
(b) state on the memorandum the statutory provision [or international instrument][4] under which the order is registered.

Amendment

1 Substituted by the Family Procedure (Amendment No 3) Rules 2013, SI 2013/3204, rr 2, 107(a), (b).
2 Repealed by the Family Procedure Rules 2010 and Court of Protection Rules 2017 (Amendment) (EU Exit) Regulations 2019, SI 2019/517, rr 2, 19(1), (4).
3 Inserted by the Family Procedure (Amendment) Rules 2011, SI 2011/1328, rr 2, 3, 18.
4 Inserted by the Family Procedure (Amendment No 4) Rules 2012, SI 2012/2806, rr 2, 3, 19.
5 Repealed by the Family Procedure (Amendment) Rules 2012, SI 2012/679, rr 2, 27.
6 Repealed by the Family Procedure (Amendment No 3) Rules 2013, SI 2013/3204, rr 2, 107(c).

Chapter 1
Enforcement of maintenance orders under the Maintenance Orders (Facilities for Enforcement) Act 1920

34.4 Interpretation

(1) In this Chapter—

'payer', in relation to a maintenance order, means the person liable to make the payments for which the order provides; and
'reciprocating country' means a country or territory to which the 1920 Act extends.

(2) In this Chapter, an expression defined in the 1920 Act has the meaning given to it in that Act.

34.5 Confirmation of provisional orders made in a reciprocating country

(1) This rule applies where, in accordance with section 4(1) of the 1920 Act, the court officer receives a provisional maintenance order.

(2) The court must fix the date, time and place for a hearing.

(3) The court officer must register the order in accordance with rule 34.3.

(4) The court officer must serve on the payer—

(a) certified copies of the provisional order and accompanying documents; and
(b) a notice—
  (i) specifying the time and date fixed for the hearing; and
  (ii) stating that the payer may attend to show cause why the order should not be confirmed.

(5) The court officer must inform—

(a) the court which made the provisional order; and
(b) the Lord Chancellor,

whether the court confirms, with or without modification, or decides not to confirm, the order.

34.6 Payment of sums due under registered orders

Where an order made by a reciprocating country is registered in [the family court under section 1 of the 1920 Act][1], the court must order payments due to be made to the court …[2].

(Practice Direction 34A contains further provisions relating to the payment of sums due under registered orders.)

Amendment

1 Substituted by the Family Procedure (Amendment No 3) Rules 2013, SI 2013/3204, rr 2, 108(a).
2 Repealed by the Family Procedure (Amendment No 3) Rules 2013, SI 2013/3204, rr 2, 108(b).

34.7 [Collection and enforcement][1] of sums due under registered orders

(1) [This rule applies to—

(a) an order made in a reciprocating county which is registered in the family court; and
(b) a provisional order made in a reciprocating country which has been confirmed by the family court,

where the court has ordered that payments due under the order be made to the court.][1]

(2) The court officer must—

(a) collect the monies due under the order …[2]; and
(b) send the monies collected to—
  (i) the court in the reciprocating country which made the order; or
  (ii) such other person or authority as that court or the Lord Chancellor may from time to time direct.

(3) The court officer may take proceedings in that officer's own name for enforcing payment of monies due under the order.

[(Rule 32.33 makes provision in relation to a court officer taking such proceedings.)][3]

Amendment

1 Substituted by the Family Procedure (Amendment No 3) Rules 2013, SI 2013/3204, rr 2, 109(a), (b).
2 Repealed by the Family Procedure (Amendment No 3) Rules 2013, SI 2013/3204, rr 2, 109(c).
3 Inserted by the Family Procedure (Amendment No 3) Rules 2013, SI 2013/3204, rr 2, 109(d).

34.8 Prescribed notice for the taking of further evidence

(1) This rule applies where a court in a reciprocating country has sent a provisional order to [the family court][1] for the purpose of taking further evidence.

(2) The court officer must send a notice to the person who applied for the provisional order specifying—

(a) the further evidence required; and
(b) the time and place fixed for taking the evidence.

Amendment

1 Substituted by the Family Procedure (Amendment No 3) Rules 2013, SI 2013/3204, rr 2, 110.

34.9 Transmission of maintenance orders made in a reciprocating country to the High Court

A maintenance order to be sent by the Lord Chancellor to the High Court in accordance with section 1(1) of the 1920 Act will be—

(a) sent to the senior district judge who will register it in the register kept for the purpose of the 1920 Act; and
(b) filed in the principal registry.

34.10 Transmission of maintenance orders made in the High Court to a reciprocating country

(1) This rule applies to maintenance orders made in the High Court.

(2) An application for a maintenance order to be sent to a reciprocating country under section 2 of the 1920 Act must be made in accordance with this rule.

(3) The application must be made to a district judge in the principal registry unless paragraph (4) applies.

(4) If the order was made in the course of proceedings in a district registry, the application may be made to a district judge in that district registry.

(5) The application must be—

(a) accompanied by a certified copy of the order; and
(b) supported by a record of the sworn written evidence.

(6) The written evidence must give—

(a) the applicant's reason for believing that the payer resides in the reciprocating country;
(b) such information as the applicant has as to the whereabouts of the payer; and
(c) such other information as may be set out in Practice Direction 34A.

34.11 Inspection of the register in the High Court

(1) A person may inspect the register and request copies of a registered order and any document filed with it if the district judge is satisfied that that person is entitled to, or liable to make, payments under a maintenance order made in—

(a) the High Court; or
(b) a court in a reciprocating country.

(2) The right to inspect the register referred to in paragraph (1) may be exercised by—

(a) a solicitor acting on behalf of the person entitled to, or liable to make, the payments referred to in that paragraph; or
(b) with the permission of the district judge, any other person.

Chapter 2
Enforcement of maintenance orders under Part 1 of the 1972 Act

34.12 Interpretation

(1) In this Chapter—

(a) 'reciprocating country' means a country to which Part 1 of the 1972 Act extends; and

(b) 'relevant court in the reciprocating country' means, as the case may be—
   (i) the court which made the order which has been sent to England and Wales for confirmation;
   (ii) the court which made the order which has been registered in a court in England and Wales;
   (iii) the court to which an order made in England and Wales has been sent for registration; or
   (iv) the court to which a provisional order made in England and Wales has been sent for confirmation.

(2) In this Chapter, an expression defined in the 1972 Act has the meaning given to it in that Act.

(3) In this Chapter, 'Hague Convention Countries' means the countries listed in Schedule 1 to the Reciprocal Enforcement of Maintenance Orders (Hague Convention Countries) Order [1993][1].

Amendment

1 Substituted by the Family Procedure (Amendment) Rules 2011, SI 2011/1328, rr 2, 3, 19.

34.13 Scope

(1) Section 1 of this Chapter contains rules relating to the reciprocal enforcement of maintenance orders under Part 1 of the 1972 Act.

(2) Section 2 of this Chapter modifies the rules contained in Section 1 of this Chapter in their application to—

(a) …[1]
(b) the Hague Convention Countries; and
(c) the United States of America.

(Practice Direction 34A sets out in full the rules for …[1] the Hague Convention Countries and the United States of America as modified by Section 2 of this Chapter.)

[(3) Section 3 of this Chapter contains a rule in relation to notification of proceedings in a Hague Convention Country or the United States of America.

(4) Section 4 of this Chapter contains rules in relation to proceedings under Part 2 of the 1972 Act (reciprocal enforcement of claims for the recovery of maintenance).][2]

Amendment

1 Repealed by the Family Procedure (Amendment) Rules 2011, SI 2011/1328, rr 2, 3, 20.
2 Inserted by the Family Procedure (Amendment No 3) Rules 2013, SI 2013/3204, rr 2, 111.

Section 1
Reciprocal enforcement of maintenance orders under Part 1 of the 1972 Act

34.14 Application for transmission of maintenance order to reciprocating country

An application for a maintenance order to be sent to a reciprocating country under section 2 of the 1972 Act must be made in accordance with Practice Direction 34A.

34.15 Certification of evidence given on provisional orders

A document setting out or summarising evidence is authenticated by a court in England and Wales by a certificate signed [by the judge][1] before whom that evidence was given.

(Section 3(5)(b), 5(4) and 9(5) of the 1972 Act require a document to be authenticated by the court.)

Amendment

1 Substituted by the Family Procedure (Amendment No 3) Rules 2013, SI 2013/3204, rr 2, 112.

34.16 Confirmation of a provisional order made in a reciprocating country

(1) This rule applies to proceedings for the confirmation of a provisional order made in a reciprocating country[, including proceedings in the family court for the confirmation of a provisional order made in a reciprocating country varying a maintenance order to which section 5(5) or 9(6) of the 1972 Act applies][1].

(2) Paragraph (3) applies on receipt by the court of—

(a) a certified copy of the order; and
(b) the documents required by the 1972 Act to accompany the order.

(3) On receipt of the documents referred to in paragraph (2)—

(a) the court must fix the date, time and place for a hearing or a directions appointment; and
(b) the court officer must send to the payer notice of the date, time and place fixed together with a copy of the order and accompanying documents.

(4) The date fixed for the hearing must be not less than 21 days beginning with the date on which the court officer sent the documents to the payer in accordance with paragraph (2).

(5) The court officer will send to the relevant court in the reciprocating country a certified copy of any order confirming or refusing to confirm the provisional order.

(6) … [2]

(Section 5(5) and 7 of the 1972 Act provide for proceedings for the confirmation of a provisional order.)

…[2]

(Rule 34.22 provides for the transmission of documents to a court in a reciprocating country.)

Amendment

1 Inserted by the Family Procedure (Amendment No 3) Rules 2013, SI 2013/3204, rr 2, 113(a).
2 Repealed by the Family Procedure (Amendment No 3) Rules 2013, SI 2013/3204, rr 2, 113(b), (c).

34.17 Consideration of revocation of a provisional order made by [the family court][1]

(1) This rule applies where—

(a) [the family court][1] has made a provisional order by virtue of section 3 of the 1972 Act;
(b) before the order is confirmed, evidence is taken by the court or received by it as set out in section 5(9) of the 1972 Act; and
(c) on consideration of the evidence the court considers that the order ought not to have been made.

(Section 5(9) of the 1972 Act provides that [the family court][1] may revoke a provisional order made by it, before the order has been confirmed in a reciprocating country, if it receives new evidence.)

(2) The court officer must serve on the person who applied for the provisional order ('the applicant') a notice which must—

- (a) set out the evidence taken or received by the court;
- (b) inform the applicant that the court considers that the order ought not to have been made; and
- (c) inform the applicant that the applicant may—
  - (i) make representations in relation to that evidence either orally or in writing; and
  - (ii) adduce further evidence.

(3) If an applicant wishes to adduce further evidence—

- (a) the applicant must notify the court officer at the court which made the order;
- (b) the court will fix a date for the hearing of the evidence; and
- (c) the court officer will notify the applicant in writing of the date fixed.

Amendment

1 Substituted by the Family Procedure (Amendment No 3) Rules 2013, SI 2013/3204, rr 2, 114.

34.18 Notification of variation or revocation of a maintenance order by the High Court or [the family court][1]

(1) This rule applies where—

- (a) a maintenance order has been sent to a reciprocating country in pursuance of section 2 of the 1972 Act; and
- (b) the court makes an order, not being a provisional order, varying or revoking that order.

(2) The court officer must send a certified copy of the order of variation or revocation to the relevant court in the reciprocating country.

(Rule 34.22 provides for the transmission of documents to a court in a reciprocating country.)

Amendment

1 Substituted by the Family Procedure (Amendment No 3) Rules 2013, SI 2013/3204, rr 2, 115.

34.19 Notification of confirmation[, variation][1] or revocation of a maintenance order by [the family court][2]

(1) This rule applies where [the family court][2] makes an order—

- (a) not being a provisional order, revoking [or varying][1] a maintenance order to which section 5 of the 1972 Act applies;
- (b) under section 9 of the 1972 Act, revoking [or varying][1] a registered order; or
- (c) under section 7(2) of the 1972 Act, confirming an order to which section 7 of that Act applies.

(2) The court officer must send written notice of the making, [variation,][1] revocation or confirmation of the order, as appropriate, to the relevant court in the reciprocating country.

(3) …[3]

(Section 5 of the 1972 Act applies to a provisional order made by [the family court][2] in accordance with section 3 of that Act which has been confirmed by a court in a reciprocating country.)

…[3]

(Rule 34.22 provides for the transmission of documents to a court in a reciprocating country.)

Amendment

1 Inserted by the Family Procedure (Amendment No 3) Rules 2013, SI 2013/3204, rr 2, 116(a)(i), (b)(ii), (c).
2 Substituted by the Family Procedure (Amendment No 3) Rules 2013, SI 2013/3204, rr 2, 116(a)(ii), (b)(i), (e)(i).
3 Repealed by the Family Procedure (Amendment No 3) Rules 2013, SI 2013/3204, rr 2, 116(d), (e)(ii).

34.20 Taking of evidence for court in reciprocating country

(1) This rule applies where a request is made by or on behalf of a court in a reciprocating country for the taking of evidence for the purpose of proceedings relating to a maintenance order to which Part 1 of the 1972 Act applies.

(Section 14 of the 1972 Act makes provision for the taking of evidence needed for the purpose of certain proceedings.)

(2) The High Court has power to take the evidence where—

(a) the request for evidence relates to a maintenance order made by a superior court in the United Kingdom; and
(b) the witness resides in England and Wales.

[(3) The family court has power to take evidence where—

(a) the request for evidence relates to a maintenance order—
 (i) made by the family court; or
 (ii) registered in the family court; or
(b) the Lord Chancellor sends to the family court a request to take evidence.

(Practice Direction 34E makes further provision on this matter)][1]

(4) …[2]
(5) …[2]

(6) The evidence is to be taken in accordance with Part 22.

Amendment

1 Substituted by the Family Procedure (Amendment No 3) Rules 2013, SI 2013/3204, rr 2, 117.
2 Repealed by the Family Procedure (Amendment No 3) Rules 2013, SI 2013/3204, rr 2, 117.

34.21 Request for the taking of evidence by a court in a reciprocating country

(1) This rule applies where a request is made by [the family court][1] for the taking of evidence in a reciprocating country in accordance with section 14(5) of the 1972 Act.
(2) The request must be made in writing to the court in the reciprocating country.

(Rule 34.22 provides for the transmission of documents to a court in a reciprocating country.)

Amendment

1 Substituted by the Family Procedure (Amendment No 3) Rules 2013, SI 2013/3204, rr 2, 118.

34.22 Transmission of documents

(1) This rule applies to any document, including a notice or request, which is required to be sent to a court in a reciprocating country by—

(a) Part 1 of the 1972 Act; or
(b) Section 1 of Chapter 2 of this Part of these rules.

(2) The document must be sent to the Lord Chancellor for transmission to the court in the reciprocating country.

34.23 Method of payment under registered orders

(1) Where an order is registered in [the family court][1] in accordance with section 6(3) of the 1972 Act, the court must order that the payment of sums due under the order be made—

(a) to the …[2] registering court; and
(b) at such time and place as the court officer directs.

(Section 6(3) of the 1972 Act makes provision for the registration of maintenance orders made in a reciprocating country.)

(2) Where the court orders payments to be made [to the court][1], whether in accordance with paragraph (1) or otherwise, the court officer must send the payments—

(a) by post to either—
(i) the court which made the order; or
(ii) such other person or authority as that court, or the Lord Chancellor, directs; or

(b) if the court which made the order is a country or territory specified in the Practice Direction 34A—

(i) to the Crown Agents for Overseas Governments and Administrations for transmission to the person to whom they are due; or
(ii) as the Lord Chancellor directs.

(Practice Direction 34A contains further provisions relating to the payment of sums due under registered orders.)

Amendment

1 Substituted by the Family Procedure (Amendment No 3) Rules 2013, SI 2013/3204, rr 2, 119(a)(i), (b).
2 Repealed by the Family Procedure (Amendment No 3) Rules 2013, SI 2013/3204, rr 2, 119(a)(ii).

34.24 Enforcement of payments under registered orders

(1) This rule applies where a court has ordered periodical payments under a registered maintenance order to be made to the court …[1].

(2) The court officer must take reasonable steps to notify the payee of the means of enforcement available.

(3) Paragraph (4) applies where periodical payments due under a registered order are in arrears.

(4) The court officer, on that officer's own initiative—

- (a) may; or
- (b) if the sums due are more than 4 weeks in arrears, must,

proceed in that officer's own name for the recovery of the sums due unless of the view that it is unreasonable to do so.

Amendment

1 Repealed by the Family Procedure (Amendment No 3) Rules 2013, SI 2013/3204, rr 2, 120.

34.25 Notification of registration and cancellation

(1) The court officer must send written notice to the Lord Chancellor of the due registration of orders registered in accordance with section 6(3), 7(5), or 10(4) of the 1972 Act.

(2) The court officer must, when registering an order in accordance with section 6(3), 7(5), 9(10), 10(4) or (5) or 23(3) of the 1972 Act, send written notice to the payer stating—

- (a) that the order has been registered;
- (b) that payments under the order should be made to the court officer; and
- (c) the hours during which and the place at which the payments should be made.

(3) The court officer must, when cancelling the registration of an order in accordance with section 10(1) of the 1972 Act, send written notice of the cancellation to the payer.

Section 2
Modification of rules in Section 1 of this Chapter
Sub-section 1

…[1]

34.26 …[1]

…[1]

Amendment

1 Repealed by the Family Procedure (Amendment) Rules 2011, SI 2011/1328, rr 2, 3, 22.

Sub-section 2
Hague Convention Countries

34.27 Application of Section 1 of this Chapter to the Hague Convention Countries

(1) In relation to the Hague Convention Countries, Section 1 of this Chapter has effect as modified by this rule.

(2) A reference in this rule, and in any rule which has effect in relation to the Hague Convention Countries by virtue of this rule to—

(a) the 1972 Act is a reference to the 1972 Act as modified by Schedule 2 to the Reciprocal Enforcement of Maintenance Orders (Hague Convention Countries) Order 1993; and
(b) a section under the 1972 Act is a reference to the section so numbered in the 1972 Act as so modified.

(3) A reference to a reciprocating country in rule 34.12(1) and Section 1 of this Chapter is a reference to a Hague Convention Country.

(4) Rules 34.15 (certification of evidence given on provisional orders), 34.16 (confirmation of provisional orders), 34.19 (notification of confirmation[, variation][1] or revocation of a maintenance order by [the family court][2]) and 34.21 (request for the taking of evidence by a court in a reciprocating country) do not apply.

(5) For rule 34.17 (consideration of revocation of a provisional order made by [the family court][2]) substitute—

'[34.17 Consideration of variation or revocation of a maintenance order made by the family court][2]

(1) This rule applies where—

(a) an application has been made to [the family court by a payee for the variation or revocation][2] of an order to which section 5 of the 1972 Act applies; and
(b) the payer resides in a Hague Convention Country.

(2) The court officer must serve on the payee, by post, a copy of any representations or evidence adduced by or on behalf of the payer.

...[3]'

(6) For rule 34.18 (notification of variation or revocation of a maintenance order by the High Court or [the family court][2]) substitute—

'34.18 Notification of variation or revocation of a maintenance order by the High Court or [the family court][2]

(1) This rule applies if the High Court or [the family court][2] makes an order varying or revoking a maintenance order to which section 5 of the 1972 Act applies.
(2) If the time for appealing has expired without an appeal having been entered, the court officer will send to the Lord Chancellor—

(a) the documents required by section 5(8) of the 1972 Act; and
(b) a certificate signed by [a judge][2] stating that the order of variation or evocation is enforceable and no longer subject to the ordinary forms of review.

(3) A party who enters an appeal against the order of variation or revocation must, at the same time, give written notice to the court officer.'.

(7) For rule 34.23(2) (method of payment under registered orders) substitute—

'(2) Where the court orders payment to be [made to the court][2], the court officer must send the payments by post to the payee under the order.'

(8) For rule 34.25 (notification of registration and cancellation) substitute—

'34.25 Notification of registration and cancellation

The court officer must send written notice to—

(a) the Lord Chancellor, on the due registration of an order under section 10(4) of the 1972 Act; and

(b) the payer under the order, on—
   (i) the registration of an order under section 10(4) of the 1972 Act; or
   (ii) the cancellation of the registration of an order under section 10(1) of the 1972 Act.'.

(9) After rule 34.25 insert—

'34.25A General provisions as to notices

(1) A notice to a payer of the registration of an order in [the family court][2] in accordance with section 6(3) of the 1972 Act must be in the form referred to in a practice direction.

(Section 6(8) of the 1972 Act requires notice of registration to be given to the payer.)

(2) If the court sets aside the registration of a maintenance order following an appeal under section 6(9) of the 1972 Act, the court officer must send written notice of the decision to the Lord Chancellor.

(3) A notice to a payee that the court officer has refused to register an order must be in the form referred to in a practice direction.

(Section 6(11) of the 1972 Act requires notice of refusal of registration to be given to the payee.)

(4) Where, under any provision of Part 1 of the 1972 Act, a court officer serves a notice on a payer who resides in a Hague Convention Country, the court officer must send to the Lord Chancellor a certificate of service.'.

Amendment

1 Inserted by the Family Procedure (Amendment No 3) Rules 2013, SI 2013/3204, rr 2, 122(a)(i).
2 Substituted by the Family Procedure (Amendment No 3) Rules 2013, SI 2013/3204, rr 2, 122(a)(ii), (b)(i), (ii)(aa), (bb), (c), (d), (e).
3 Repealed by the Family Procedure (Amendment No 3) Rules 2013, SI 2013/3204, rr 2, 122(b)(ii)(cc).

Sub-section 3
United States of America

34.28 Application of Section 1 of this Chapter to the United States of America

(1) In relation to the United States of America, Section 1 of this Chapter has effect as modified by this rule.

(2) A reference in this rule and in any rule which has effect in relation to the United States of America by virtue of this rule to—

(a) the 1972 Act is a reference to the 1972 Act as modified by Schedule 1 to the Reciprocal Enforcement of Maintenance Orders (United States of America) Order 2007; and
(b) a section under the 1972 Act is a reference to the section so numbered in the 1972 Act as so modified.

(3) A reference to a reciprocating country in rule 34.12(1) and Section 1 of this Chapter is a reference to the United States of America.

(4) Rules 34.15 (certification of evidence given on provisional orders), 34.16 (confirmation of provisional orders), 34.19 (notification of confirmation[, variation][1] or revocation of a maintenance order made by [the family court][2]) and 34.21 (request for the taking of evidence in a reciprocating country) do not apply.

(5) For rule 34.17 (consideration of revocation of a provisional order made by [the family court][2]) substitute—

'[34.17 Consideration of variation or revocation of a maintenance order made by the family court][2]

(1) This rule applies where—

(a) an application has been made to [the family court by a payee for the variation or revocation][2] of an order to which section 5 of the 1972 Act applies; and

(b) the payer resides in the United States of America.

(2) The court officer must serve on the payee by post a copy of any representations or evidence adduced by or on behalf of the payer.

…[3]'

(6) For rule 34.18 (notification of variation or revocation), substitute—

'34.18 Notification of variation or revocation

If the High Court or [the family court][2] makes an order varying or revoking a maintenance order to which section 5 of the 1972 Act applies, the court officer will send to the Lord Chancellor the documents required by section 5(7) of that Act.'.

(7) For rule 34.23(2)(method of payment under registered orders) substitute—

'(2) Where the court orders payment to be [made to the court][2], the court officer must send the payments by post to the payee under the order.'.

(8) For rule 34.25 (notification of registration and cancellation) substitute—

'34.25 Notification of registration and cancellation

The court officer must send written notice to—

(a) the Lord Chancellor, on the due registration of an order under section 10(4) of the 1972 Act; or

(b) the payer under the order, on—

(i) the registration of an order under section 10(4) of the 1972 Act; or

(ii) the cancellation of the registration of an order under section 10(1) of that Act.'

Amendment

1 Inserted by the Family Procedure (Amendment No 3) Rules 2013, SI 2013/3204, rr 2, 123(a)(i).
2 Substituted by the Family Procedure (Amendment No 3) Rules 2013, SI 2013/3204, rr 2, 123(a)(ii), (b)(i), (ii)(aa), (bb), (c), (d).
3 Repealed by the Family Procedure (Amendment No 3) Rules 2013, SI 2013/3204, rr 2, 123(b)(ii)(cc).

[Section 3
Proceedings in a Hague Convention Country or in the United States of America

34.28ZA Notification of proceedings in a Hague Convention Country or in the United States of America

Practice Direction 34E applies where the court officer receives from the Lord Chancellor notice of the institution of proceedings, including notice of the substance of a claim, in a Hague Convention Country or in the United States of America in relation to the making, variation or revocation of a maintenance order.][1]

Amendment

1 Inserted by the Family Procedure (Amendment No 3) Rules 2013, SI 2013/3204, rr 2, 124.

[Section 4
Reciprocal enforcement of claims for the recovery of maintenance

34.28ZB Interpretation

In this Section—

'convention country' means a country or territory specified in an Order in Council made under section 25 of the 1972 Act; and

an expression defined in the 1972 Act has the meaning given to it in that Act.][1]

Amendment

1 Inserted by the Family Procedure (Amendment No 3) Rules 2013, SI 2013/3204, rr 2, 124.

[34.28ZC Dismissal of an application under section 27A of the 1972 Act or application for variation

(1) Where the family court dismisses an application under—

(a) section 27A of the 1972 Act (application for recovery of maintenance); or
(b) an application by a person in a convention country for the variation of a registered order,

the court officer will send a written notice of the court's decision to the Lord Chancellor.

(2) The notice will include a statement of the court's reasons for its decision.][1]

Amendment

1 Inserted by the Family Procedure (Amendment No 3) Rules 2013, SI 2013/3204, rr 2, 124.

[34.28ZD Application for recovery of maintenance in England and Wales: section 27B of the 1972 Act

(1) Where the family court receives an application for the recovery of maintenance sent from the Lord Chancellor under section 27B of the 1972 Act, the court will—

(a) fix the date, time and place for a hearing or directions appointment, allowing sufficient time for service under this rule to be effected at least 21 days before the date fixed; and
(b) serve copies of the application and any accompanying documents, together with a notice stating the date, time and place so fixed, on the respondent.

(2) Within 14 days of service under this rule, the respondent must file an answer to the application in the form referred to in Practice Direction 5A.][1]

Amendment

1 Inserted by the Family Procedure (Amendment No 3) Rules 2013, SI 2013/3204, rr 2, 124.

[34.28ZE Application under section 26(1) or (2) of the 1972 Act and certificate under section 26(3A) of the 1972 Act: registration

Where—

(a) an application under section 26(1) or (2) of the 1972 Act; or
(b) a certificate under section 26(3A) of the 1972 Act,

is required to be registered in the family court by virtue of the Recovery of Maintenance (United States of America) Order 2007, the court officer will enter a minute or memorandum of the application or certificate in the register.][1]

Amendment

1 Inserted by the Family Procedure (Amendment No 3) Rules 2013, SI 2013/3204, rr 2, 124.

[34.28ZF Registration of an order: sections 27C(7) and 32(3) and (6) of the 1972 Act

(1) Where the family court makes an order which is required under section 27C(7) of the 1972 Act to be registered, the court officer will enter a minute or memorandum of the order in the register.

(2) Where a court officer receives under section 32(3) of the 1972 Act a certified copy of an order, the court officer will register the order by means of a minute or memorandum in the register.

(3) Every minute or memorandum entered under paragraph (1) or (2) will specify the section and subsection of the 1972 Act under which the order in question is registered.

(4) Where a court officer registers an order as required by section 27C(7) or 32(3) of the 1972 Act, the court officer will send written notice to the Lord Chancellor that the order has been registered.

(5) Where a court officer is required by section 32(6) of the 1972 Act to give notice of the registration of an order, the court officer will do this by sending written notice to the officer specified in that subsection that the order has been registered.][1]

Amendment

1 Inserted by the Family Procedure (Amendment No 3) Rules 2013, SI 2013/3204, rr 2, 124.

[34.28ZG Payments made to the family court

(1) Where payments are made to the family court by virtue of section 27C or 34A of the 1972 Act, the court officer will send those payments by post to such person or authority as the Lord Chancellor may from time to time direct.

(2) Subject to paragraph (3), if it appears to a court officer that any sums payable under a registered order are in arrears, the officer may proceed in the officer's own name for the recovery of those sums.

(3) Where it appears to the officer that sums payable under the order are in arrears to an amount equal—

(a) in the case of payments to be made monthly or less frequently, to twice the sum payable periodically; or

(b) in any other case, to four times the sum payable periodically,

the officer will proceed in the officer's own name for the recovery of those sums, unless it appears to the officer that it is unreasonable in the circumstances to do so.][1]

Amendment

1 Inserted by the Family Procedure (Amendment No 3) Rules 2013, SI 2013/3204, rr 2, 124.

[34.28ZH Method of payment

(1) This rule applies where the family court exercises its duties or powers under section 27C or 34A of the 1972 Act.

(2) Where the court orders that payments under the order are to be made by a particular means—

(a) the court will record on the copy of the order the means of payment that the court has ordered; and

(b) the court officer will, as soon as practicable, notify, in writing, the person liable to make the payments under the order how payments are to be made.

(3) Paragraph (4) applies where the court orders that payments be made to the court by a method of payment falling within section 1(5) of the Maintenance Enforcement Act 1991.

(4) The court officer will notify the person liable to make the payments under the order of sufficient details of the account into which the payments should be made to enable payments to be made into that account.][1]

Amendment

1 Inserted by the Family Procedure (Amendment No 3) Rules 2013, SI 2013/3204, rr 2, 124.

[34.28ZI Application under section 34 of the 1972 Act: variation or revocation

(1) This rule applies in relation to an application under section 34 of the 1972 Act for the variation or revocation of a registered order.

(2) An application which is made directly to the registering court must be filed in the form referred to in Practice Direction 5A.

(3) Where the court receives an application, either filed in accordance with paragraph (2) or sent from the Lord Chancellor under section 34(3) of the 1972 Act—

(a) the court will set the date, time and place for a hearing or directions appointment; and

(b) the court officer will notify the applicant of the date, time and place.][1]

Amendment

1 Inserted by the Family Procedure (Amendment No 3) Rules 2013, SI 2013/3204, rr 2, 124.

[34.28ZJ Application under section 35 of the 1972 Act: variation or revocation

(1) This rule applies in relation to an application under section 35 of the 1972 Act for the variation or revocation of a registered order.

(2) Notice under section 35(3)(b) of the 1972 Act of the time and place appointed for the hearing of the application will be in the form specified in Practice Direction 34D.

(3) The court officer will send the notice by post to the Lord Chancellor for onward transmission to the appropriate authority in the convention country in which the respondent is residing.

(4) The time appointed for the hearing of the application will not be less than six weeks later than the date on which the notice is sent to the Lord Chancellor.][1]

Amendment

1 Inserted by the Family Procedure (Amendment No 3) Rules 2013, SI 2013/3204, rr 2, 124.

[34.28ZK Request under section 38(1) of the 1972 Act to the family court

(1) This rule applies where the family court receives from the Lord Chancellor a request under section 38(1) of the 1972 Act (taking evidence at the request of a court in a convention country) to take the evidence of any person.

(2) Subject to paragraph (3)—

(a) the evidence will be taken in the same manner as if the person concerned were a witness in family proceedings;

(b) any oral evidence so taken will be put into writing and read to the person who gave it, who must sign the document; and

(c) the judge who takes any such evidence of any person will certify at the foot of the document setting out the evidence of, or produced in evidence by, that person that such evidence was taken, or document received in evidence, as the case may be, by that judge.

(3) Where the request referred to in section 38(2) of the 1972 Act includes a request that the evidence be taken in a particular manner, the court by which the evidence is taken will, so far as circumstances permit, comply with that request.][1]

Amendment

1 Inserted by the Family Procedure (Amendment No 3) Rules 2013, SI 2013/3204, rr 2, 124.

[34.28ZL Request under section 38(1) of the 1972 Act to the officer of the court

(1) This rule applies where an officer of the court receives from the Lord Chancellor a request under section 38(1) of the 1972 Act to take the evidence of any person.

(2) Subject to paragraph (3)—

(a) the person whose evidence is to be taken will be examined on oath by or before a [justices' legal adviser][1] or any other court officer determined by the Lord Chancellor;

(b) any oral evidence will be put into writing and read to the person who gave it, who must sign the document; and

(c) the [justices' legal adviser][1] or other officer will certify at the foot of the document setting out the evidence of, or produced by, that person, that such evidence was taken, or document received in evidence, as the case may be, by that [justices' legal adviser][1] or other officer.

(3) Where the request referred to in section 38(1) of the 1972 Act includes a request that the evidence be taken in a particular manner, the [justices' legal adviser][1] or other officer by whom the evidence is taken will, so far as circumstances permit, comply with that request.

(4) For the purposes of this rule, the [justices' legal adviser][1] or other officer has the same power to administer oaths as a single justice of the peace.][2]

Amendment

1 Substituted by the Family Procedure (Amendment) Rules 2020, SI 2020/135, rr 2, 29.
2 Inserted by the Family Procedure (Amendment No 3) Rules 2013, SI 2013/3204, rr 2, 124.

[34.28ZM Onward transmission of documents

Any document mentioned in rule 34.28ZK(2)(c) or rule 34.28ZL(2)(c) will be sent to the Lord Chancellor for onward transmission to the appropriate authority in the convention country in which the request referred to in section 38(1) of the 1972 Act originated.][1]

Amendment

1 Inserted by the Family Procedure (Amendment No 3) Rules 2013, SI 2013/3204, rr 2, 124.

Chapter 3
Enforcement of maintenance orders under [the 2007 Hague Convention][1]

[34.28A Application of this Chapter

(1) In this Chapter—

[(a) references to a maintenance order include—

(i) …[2]

(ii) a maintenance decision to which Chapter V of the 2007 Hague Convention applies by virtue of Article 19(1) of that Convention;

(iii) a maintenance arrangement (as defined in Article 3(e) of the 2007 Hague Convention) which is to be recognised and enforceable in the same way as a maintenance decision by virtue of Article 30 of that Convention;][3]

(b) references to the Hague Protocol are to the Protocol on the Law Applicable to Maintenance Obligations done at The Hague on 23 November 2007[;][4]

[(c) …[2]][5]

(2) …[2]

…[6]][7]

Amendment

1 Substituted by the Family Procedure Rules 2010 and Court of Protection Rules 2017 (Amendment) (EU Exit) Regulations 2019, SI 2019/517, rr 2, 19(1), (5).
2 Repealed by the Family Procedure Rules 2010 and Court of Protection Rules 2017 (Amendment) (EU Exit) Regulations 2019, SI 2019/517, rr 2, 19(1), (6).
3 Substituted by the Family Procedure (Amendment No 4) Rules 2012, SI 2012/2806, rr 2, 3, 21.
4 Substituted by the Family Procedure (Amendment) Rules 2012, SI 2012/679, rr 2, 28(a).
5 Inserted by the Family Procedure (Amendment) Rules 2012, SI 2012/679, rr 2, 28(b).
6 Repealed by the Family Procedure (Amendment No 3) Rules 2013, SI 2013/3204, rr 2, 125.
7 Inserted by the Family Procedure (Amendment) Rules 2011, SI 2011/1328, rr 2, 3, 23, 24.

Section 1
Registration and enforcement in a magistrates' court of maintenance order made in [a State bound by the 2007 Hague Convention][1]

34.29 …[2]

…[2]

Amendment

1 Substituted by the Family Procedure Rules 2010 and Court of Protection Rules 2017 (Amendment) (EU Exit) Regulations 2019, SI 2019/517, rr 2, 19(1), (7).
2 Repealed by the Family Procedure Rules 2010 and Court of Protection Rules 2017 (Amendment) (EU Exit) Regulations 2019, SI 2019/517, rr 2, 19(1), (8).

[34.29A …[1]

…[1]][2]

Amendment

1 Repealed by the Family Procedure (Amendment No 3) Rules 2013, SI 2013/3204, rr 2, 126.
2 Inserted by the Family Procedure (Amendment) Rules 2011, SI 2011/1328, rr 2, 3, 26.

34.30 Registration of maintenance orders

(1) …[1]

(2) [This rule and Practice Direction 34E apply where the family court][2] receives—

(a) …[3]
(b) …[3]
[(c) …[3] …[4]][5]
(d) …[3] […[3]
(e) an application under Article 23 of the 2007 Hague Convention for registration of a maintenance order made in a State bound by that Convention …[3].][6]

(3) …[1]

(4) …[1]

(5) …[1]

(6) Except where [Practice Direction 34E provides otherwise, the court][2] must register the order unless—

(a) …[3] …[4]
(b) …[3] […[3]
(c) in the case of an application under Article 23(2) or (3) of the 2007 Hague Convention, Article 22(a) of that Convention applies.][6]

(7) If the court …[1] refuses to register an order to which this rule relates the court officer must notify the applicant.

(8) If the court …[1] registers an order the court officer must send written notice of that fact to—

(a) the Lord Chancellor;
(b) the payer; and
(c) the applicant.

(9) …[1]

Amendment

1 Repealed by the Family Procedure (Amendment No 3) Rules 2013, SI 2013/3204, rr 2, 127(a), (c), (e), (f).
2 Substituted by the Family Procedure (Amendment No 3) Rules 2013, SI 2013/3204, rr 2, 127(b), (d).
3 Repealed by the Family Procedure Rules 2010 and Court of Protection Rules 2017 (Amendment) (EU Exit) Regulations 2019, SI 2019/517, rr 2, 19(1), (9).
4 Repealed by the Family Procedure (Amendment No 4) Rules 2012, SI 2012/2806, rr 2, 3, 24(a)(i), (b)(i).
5 Substituted by the Family Procedure (Amendment) Rules 2011, SI 2011/1328, rr 2, 3, 27.
6 Substituted by the Family Procedure (Amendment No 4) Rules 2012, SI 2012/2806, rr 2, 3, 24(a)(ii), (b)(ii).

34.31 Appeal from a decision relating to registration

(1) This rule applies to an appeal under—

(a) …[1]
(b) …[1]
[(c) …[1] …[2]][3]
(d) …[1] […[1]
(e) Article 23(5) of the 2007 Hague Convention.][4]

[(2) The appeal must be to the family court.

(Practice Direction 34E makes provision in relation to such cases.)][5]

Amendment

1 Repealed by the Family Procedure Rules 2010 and Court of Protection Rules 2017 (Amendment) (EU Exit) Regulations 2019, SI 2019/517, rr 2, 19(1), (10).
2 Repealed by the Family Procedure (Amendment No 4) Rules 2012, SI 2012/2806, rr 2, 3, 25(a).
3 Substituted by the Family Procedure (Amendment) Rules 2011, SI 2011/1328, rr 2, 3, 28.
4 Substituted by the Family Procedure (Amendment No 4) Rules 2012, SI 2012/2806, rr 2, 3, 25(b).
5 Substituted by the Family Procedure (Amendment No 3) Rules 2013, SI 2013/3204, rr 2, 128.

34.32 Payment of sums due under a registered order

(1) Where an order is registered in [Article 23 of the 2007 Hague Convention][1], the court [may][2] order that payment of sums due under the order be made [to the court, at such time and place as directed.][2]

(2) Where the court orders payments to be made to the court …[3], whether in accordance with paragraph (1) or otherwise, the court officer must send the payments by post either—

(a) to the court which made the order; or
(b) to such other person or authority as that court, or the Lord Chancellor, directs.

(Practice Direction 34A contains further provisions relating to the payment of sums due under registered orders.)

Amendment

1 Substituted by the Family Procedure Rules 2010 and Court of Protection Rules 2017 (Amendment) (EU Exit) Regulations 2019, SI 2019/517, rr 2, 19(1), (11).
2 Substituted by the Family Procedure (Amendment No 3) Rules 2013, SI 2013/3204, rr 2, 129(a).
3 Repealed by the Family Procedure (Amendment No 3) Rules 2013, SI 2013/3204, rr 2, 129(b).

34.33 Enforcement of payments under registered orders

(1) This rule applies where a court has ordered periodical payments under a registered maintenance order to be made to the [the family court][1].

(2) The court officer must take reasonable steps to notify the payee of the means of enforcement available.

(3) Paragraph (4) applies where periodical payments due under a registered order are in arrears.

(4) The court officer, on that officer's own initiative—

(a) may; or
(b) if the sums due are more than 4 weeks in arrears, must,

proceed in that officer's own name for the recovery of the sums due unless of the view that it is unreasonable to do so.

Amendment

1 Substituted by the Family Procedure (Amendment No 3) Rules 2013, SI 2013/3204, rr 2, 130.

34.34 Variation and revocation of registered orders

(1) This rule applies where the court officer for a registering court receives notice that a registered maintenance order has been varied or revoked by a competent court in [a State bound by the 2007 Hague Convention][1].

(2) The court officer for the registering court must—

(a) register the order of variation or revocation; and
(b) send notice of the registration by post to the payer and payee under the order.

[(3) … [2]][3]

Amendment

1 Substituted by the Family Procedure Rules 2010 and Court of Protection Rules 2017 (Amendment) (EU Exit) Regulations 2019, SI 2019/517, rr 2, 19(1), (12)(a).
2 Repealed by the Family Procedure Rules 2010 and Court of Protection Rules 2017 (Amendment) (EU Exit) Regulations 2019, SI 2019/517, rr 2, 19(1), (12)(b).
3 Inserted by the Family Procedure (Amendment) Rules 2011, SI 2011/1328, rr 2, 3, 30.

[34.35 Registered order: payer residing in an area covered by a different Maintenance Enforcement Business Centre

Practice Direction 34E makes provision for cases where a court officer in the Maintenance Enforcement Business Centre for the Designated Family Judge area where an order is registered considers that the payer is residing in a Designated Family Judge area covered by a different Maintenance Enforcement Business Centre.

(For the way in which information will be provided to enable Maintenance Enforcement Business Centres to be identified, see Practice Direction 34E.)][1]

Amendment

1 Substituted by the Family Procedure (Amendment No 2) Rules 2015, SI 2015/1420, rr 2, 24.

34.36 Cancellation of registered orders

[(1) Where the court officer for the registering court—

(a) has no reason to send papers to another Maintenance Enforcement Business Centre under Practice Direction 34E; and
(b) considers that the payer under the registered order is not residing within the area covered by the Maintenance Enforcement Business Centre for the Designated Family Judge area where the order is registered and has no assets in England and Wales,

the court officer must cancel the registration.][1]
(2) The court officer must—

(a) give notice of cancellation to the payee; and
[(b) send to the Lord Chancellor—
   (i) the information and documents relating to the registration;
   (ii) a certificate of arrears, if applicable, signed by the court officer;
   (iii) a statement giving such information as the court officer possesses as to the whereabouts of the payer and the nature and location of the payer's assets; and
   (iv) any other relevant documents which the court officer has relating to the case.

(Practice Direction 34E makes further provision on this matter.)][2]

Amendment

1 Substituted by the Family Procedure (Amendment No 2) Rules 2015, SI 2015/1420, rr 2, 25.
2 Substituted by the Family Procedure (Amendment) Rules 2015, SI 2015/913, rr 2, 13.

[34.36A Directions as to stays, documents and translations

At any stage in proceedings for registration of a maintenance order under this Section of this Chapter, the court may give directions about the conduct of the proceedings, including—

(a) staying of proceedings in accordance with—
   (i) …[1]
   (ii) …[1]
   (iii) …[1], …[2]
   (iv) …[1] [...[1]
   (v) Article 30(6) of the 2007 Hague Convention;][3]

(b) the provision of documents in accordance with—
   (i) …[1]
   (ii) …[1]
   (iii) …[1] …[2]
   (iv) …[1] […[1]
   (v) Article 25 or 30 of the 2007 Hague Convention;][3]

(c) the provision of translations in accordance with—
   (i) …[1]
   (ii) …[1]
   (iii) …[1] …[2]
   (iv) …[1] […[1]
   (v) in relation to an application under this Section relating to the 2007 Hague Convention, without prejudice to Article 44 of that Convention.][3]][4]

Amendment

1 Repealed by the Family Procedure Rules 2010 and Court of Protection Rules 2017 (Amendment) (EU Exit) Regulations 2019, SI 2019/517, rr 2, 19(1), (13).
2 Repealed by the Family Procedure (Amendment No 4) Rules 2012, SI 2012/2806, rr 2, 3, 29(a)(i), (b)(i), (c)(i).
3 Inserted by the Family Procedure (Amendment No 4) Rules 2012, SI 2012/2806, rr 2, 3, 29(a)(ii), (b)(ii), (c)(ii).
4 Inserted by the Family Procedure (Amendment) Rules 2011, SI 2011/1328, rr 2, 3, 32.

[34.36B International Maintenance Obligations; Communication with the Central Authority for England and Wales

(1) Where the Lord Chancellor requests information or a document from the court officer for the relevant court for the purposes of …[1] Article 12 or 25(2) of the 2007 Hague Convention, the court officer shall provide the requested information or document to the Lord Chancellor forthwith.

(2) In this rule, 'relevant court' means the court at which an application under …[1] Article 10 of the 2007 Hague Convention has been filed.

(The Lord Chancellor is the Central Authority for the 2007 Hague Convention …[1])][2]

Amendment

1 Repealed by the Family Procedure Rules 2010 and Court of Protection Rules 2017 (Amendment) (EU Exit) Regulations 2019, SI 2019/517, rr 2, 19(1), (14).
2 Inserted by the Family Procedure (Amendment No 4) Rules 2012, SI 2012/2806, rr 2, 3, 30.

[34.36C …[1]

…[1]][2]

Amendment

1 Repealed by the Family Procedure Rules 2010 and Court of Protection Rules 2017 (Amendment) (EU Exit) Regulations 2019, SI 2019/517, rr 2, 19(1), (15).
2 Inserted by the Family Procedure (Amendment No 3) Rules 2013, SI 2013/3204, rr 2, 133.

Section 2
Reciprocal enforcement in a Contracting State …[1] […[1]][2] of orders of a court in England and Wales

34.37 …[3]

…[3]

Amendment

1 Repealed by the Family Procedure Rules 2010 and Court of Protection Rules 2017 (Amendment) (EU Exit) Regulations 2019, SI 2019/517, rr 2, 19(1), (16).
2 Substituted by the Family Procedure (Amendment) Rules 2011, SI 2011/1328, rr 2, 3, 33.
3 Repealed by the Family Procedure (Amendment) Rules 2011, SI 2011/1328, rr 2, 3, 34.

34.38 Admissibility of Documents

(1) This rule applies to a document, referred to in paragraph (2) and authenticated in accordance with paragraph (3), which comprises, records or summarises evidence given in, or information relating to, proceedings in a court in another part of the UK [or another Contracting State to][1] [the 2007 Hague Convention,][2] and any reference in this rule to 'the court', without more, is a reference to that court.

(2) The documents referred to at paragraph (1) are documents which purport to—

- (a) set out or summarise evidence given [to][3] the court;
- (b) have been received in evidence [to][4] the court;
- (c) set out or summarise evidence taken in the court for the purpose of proceedings in a court in England and Wales to which …[5] […[5] the 2007 Hague Convention][2] applies; or
- (d) record information relating to payments made under an order of the court.

(3) A document to which paragraph (1) applies shall, in any proceedings in [the family court][6] relating to a maintenance order to which …[5] […[5] the 2007 Hague Convention][2] applies, be admissible as evidence of any fact stated in it to the same extent as oral evidence of that fact is admissible in those proceedings.

(4) A document to which paragraph (1) applies shall be deemed to be authenticated—

- (a) in relation to the documents listed at paragraph 2(a) or (c), if the document purports to be—
  - (i) certified by the judge or official before whom the evidence was given or taken; or
  - (ii) the original document recording or summarising the evidence, or a true copy of that document;
- (b) in relation to a document listed at paragraph (2)(b), if the document purports to be certified by a judge or official of the court to be, or to be a true copy of, the document received in evidence; and

(c) in relation to the document listed at paragraph (2)(d), if the document purports to be certified by a judge or official of the court as a true record of the payments made under the order.

(5) It shall not be necessary in any proceedings in which evidence is to be received under this rule to prove the signature or official position of the person appearing to have given the certificate referred to in paragraph (4).

(6) Nothing in this rule shall prejudice the admission in evidence of any document which is admissible in evidence apart from this rule.

[[(7) Any request by the family court for the taking or providing of evidence by a court in a State bound by the 2007 Hague Convention for the purposes of proceedings to which that Convention applies, or by a court in another part of the United Kingdom, shall be communicated in writing to the court in question.][1]

(8) …[5]][7]

…[5]

Amendment

1 Substituted by the Family Procedure Rules 2010 and Court of Protection Rules 2017 (Amendment) (EU Exit) Regulations 2019, SI 2019/517, rr 2, 19(1), (17)(a) (d).
2 Inserted by the Family Procedure (Amendment No 4) Rules 2012, SI 2012/2806, rr 2, 3, 31(a), (b)(ii), (c)(ii).
3 Substituted by the Family Procedure (Amendment) Rules 2011, SI 2011/1328, rr 2, 3, 35(a), (b)(i), (e).
4 Inserted by the Family Procedure (Amendment) Rules 2011, SI 2011/1328, rr 2, 3, 35(b)(ii), (iii), (c).
5 Repealed by the Family Procedure Rules 2010 and Court of Protection Rules 2017 (Amendment) (EU Exit) Regulations 2019, SI 2019/517, rr 2, 19(1), (17)(b), (c), (e).
6 Substituted by the Family Procedure (Amendment No 3) Rules 2013, SI 2013/3204, rr 2, 134.
7 Substituted by the Family Procedure (Amendment No 4) Rules 2012, SI 2012/2806, rr 2, 3, 31(b)(i), (c)(i), (d).

34.39 Enforcement of orders of [the family court][1]

[[(1) A person who wishes to enforce a maintenance order obtained in the family court in a State bound by the 2007 Hague Convention must apply for a certified copy of the order and, where required by Practice Direction 34A, a certificate giving particulars relating to the judgment and proceedings in which it was given.][2]

(2) …[3]][4]

(3) An application under this rule must be made in writing to the court officer and must specify—

(a) the names of the parties to the proceedings;
(b) the date, or approximate date, of the proceedings in which the maintenance order was made and the nature of those proceedings;
(c) the [State][5] in which the application for recognition or enforcement has been made or is to be made; and
(d) the postal address of the applicant.

(4) The court officer must, on receipt of the application, send a copy of the order to the applicant certified in accordance with …[6] practice direction [34A][7][, [together with a copy of any certificate required by that practice direction][4]][8].

(5) Paragraph (6) applies where—

(a) a maintenance order is registered in [the family court][1]; and

(b) a person wishes to obtain a certificate giving details of any payments made or arrears accrued under the order while it has been registered, for the purposes of an application made or to be made in connection with that order in—

(i) …[3]
(ii) …[3]
(iii) …[3]
(iv) …[3] …[6]
(v) another part of the United Kingdom[; or
(vi) another State bound by the 2007 Hague Convention …[3].][4]

(6) The person wishing to obtain the certificate referred to in paragraph (5) may make a written application to the court officer for the registering court.

(7) On receipt of an application under paragraph (6) the court officer must send to the applicant a certificate giving the information requested.

(Rule 74.12 (application for certified copy of a judgment) and 74.13 (evidence in support) of the CPR apply in relation to the application for a certified copy of a judgment obtained in the High Court or a county court.)

Amendment

1 Substituted by the Family Procedure (Amendment No 3) Rules 2013, SI 2013/3204, rr 2, 135.
2 Substituted by the Family Procedure Rules 2010 and Court of Protection Rules 2017 (Amendment) (EU Exit) Regulations 2019, SI 2019/517, rr 2, 19(1), (18)(a).
3 Repealed by the Family Procedure Rules 2010 and Court of Protection Rules 2017 (Amendment) (EU Exit) Regulations 2019, SI 2019/517, rr 2, 19(1), (18)(b), (c).
4 Substituted by the Family Procedure (Amendment No 4) Rules 2012, SI 2012/2806, rr 2, 3, 32(a), (b)(iii), (c)(ii).
5 Substituted by the Family Procedure (Amendment) Rules 2012, SI 2012/679, rr 2, 29.
6 Repealed by the Family Procedure (Amendment No 4) Rules 2012, SI 2012/2806, rr 2, 3, 32(b)(i), (c)(i).
7 Inserted by the Family Procedure (Amendment No 4) Rules 2012, SI 2012/2806, rr 2, 3, 32(b)(ii).
8 Inserted by the Family Procedure (Amendment) Rules 2011, SI 2011/1328, rr 2, 3, 36(d).

[34.40 Enforcement of orders of the High Court or [the family court][1]

(1) This rule applies where a person wishes to enforce a maintenance order obtained in the High Court or [the family court][1] in …[2] or a State bound by the 2007 Hague Convention …[2].

(2) Subject to the requirements of Practice Direction 34A, rules 74.12 (application for a certified copy of a judgment) and 74.13 (evidence in support) of the CPR apply in relation to—

(a) …[2]
(b) an application for a certified copy of a judgment and a certificate giving particulars relating to the judgment and the proceedings in which it was given.][3]

Amendment

1 Substituted by the Family Procedure (Amendment No 3) Rules 2013, SI 2013/3204, rr 2, 136.
2 Repealed by the Family Procedure Rules 2010 and Court of Protection Rules 2017 (Amendment) (EU Exit) Regulations 2019, SI 2019/517, rr 2, 19(1), (19).
3 Substituted by the Family Procedure (Amendment No 4) Rules 2012, SI 2012/2806, rr 2, 3, 33.

Practice Direction 34A – Reciprocal enforcement of maintenance orders

See also Part 34, Practice Direction 34B, Practice Direction 34C, Practice Direction 34D, Practice Direction 34E

This Practice Direction supplements FPR Part 34

Noting Record of Means of Payment

1.1 Where the family court orders payments under a maintenance order to which Part 34 applies to be made in a particular way, the court must record that on a copy of the order.

1.2 If the court orders payment to be made to the court by a method referred to in section 1(5) of the Maintenance Enforcement Act 1991, the court may vary the method of payment on the application of an interested party and where it does so the court must record the variation on a copy of the order.

(Section 1(5) refers to payment by standing order or other methods which require transfer between accounts of a specific amount on a specific date during the period for which the authority to make the payment is in force.)

Notification by court officer

2.1 The court officer must, as soon as practicable, notify in writing the person liable to make the payments of the method by which they must be made.

2.2 If the court orders payment to be made to the court by a method referred to in section 1(5) of the Maintenance Enforcement Act 1991 the court officer must inform the person liable to make the payments of the number and location of the account to which the payments must be made.

2.3 If, on application, the court varies the method of payment, the court officer will notify all parties of the result of the application, in writing and as soon as possible.

Applications under section 2 of the 1920 Act

3.1 This paragraph refers to an application for the transmission of a maintenance order to a reciprocating country under section 2of the 1920 Act in accordance with rule 34.10.

3.2 The applicant's written evidence must include such information as may be required by the law of the reciprocating country for the purpose of enforcement of the order.

3.3 If, in accordance with section 2 of the 1920 Act, the court sends a maintenance order to the Lord Chancellor for transmission to a reciprocating country, it shall record the fact in the court records.

Applications under section 2 of the 1972 Act (rule 34.14)

Introduction

4.1 An application for a maintenance order to be sent to a reciprocating country under section 2 of the 1972 Act is made by lodging specified documents with the court. The documents to be lodged vary according to which country it is intended that the maintenance order is be sent and the requirements are set out in this paragraph.

General provision

4.2 The general requirement is that the following documents should be lodged with the court –

(a) an affidavit by the applicant stating –
  (i) the reason that the applicant has for believing that the payer under the maintenance order is residing in the reciprocating country; and
  (ii) the amount of any arrears due to the applicant under the order, the date to which those arrears have been calculated and the date on which the next payment under the order falls due;
(b) a certified copy of the maintenance order;
(c) a statement giving such information as the applicant has as to the whereabouts of the payer;
(d) a statement giving such information as the applicant has for facilitating the identification of the payer, (including, if known to the applicant, the name and address of any employer of the payer, his occupation and the date and place of issue of any passport of the payer); and
(e) if available to the applicant, a photograph of the payer.

4.3 Omitted

4.4 Omitted

Hague Convention Country

4.5 If the country to which it is intended to send the maintenance order is a Hague Convention country (as defined in rule 34.12), then the following changes to the general requirements apply.

4.6 In addition to the matters stated in that paragraph, the affidavit referred to in paragraph 4.2(a) must also state whether the time for appealing against the maintenance order has expired and whether an appeal is pending.

4.7 The applicant must lodge the following documents with the court in addition to those set out in paragraph 4.2 –

(a) a statement as to whether or not the payer appeared in the proceedings in which the maintenance order was made;
(b) if the payer did not so appear –
  (i) the original of a document which establishes that notice of the institution of proceedings, including notice of the substance of the claim, was served on the payer; or
  (ii) a copy of such a document certified by the applicant or the applicant's solicitor to be a true copy;
(c) a document which establishes that notice of the order was sent to the payer;
(d) a written statement as to whether or not the payee received legal aid in the proceedings in which the order was made, or in connection with the application under section 2 of the 1972 Act; and
(e) if the payee did receive legal aid, a copy certified by the applicant or the applicant's solicitor to be a true copy of the legal aid certificate.

United States of America

4.8 If the country to which it is intended to send the maintenance order is the United States of America, then the following changes to the general requirements apply.

4.9 There is no requirement to lodge a statement giving information as to the whereabouts of the payer since this information must be contained in the affidavit as mentioned in paragraph 4.10.

4.10 In addition to the matters stated in that paragraph, the affidavit referred to in paragraph 4.2(a) must also state –

(a) the address of the payee;
(b) such information as is known as to the whereabouts of the payer; and
(c) a description, so far as is known, of the nature and location of any assets of the payer available for execution.

4.11 The applicant must lodge three certified copies of the maintenance order.

Transitional Provision in respect of the United States of America

4A.1 Where, by virtue of article 6(2) of the Reciprocal Enforcement of Maintenance Orders (United States of America) Order 2007, the Reciprocal Enforcement of Maintenance Orders (United States of America) Order 1995 continues in full force and effect, the FPR shall apply with such modifications as are necessary.

Notification to the Lord Chancellor

5.1 Where, in accordance with Part 1 of the 1972 Act, the family court registers a maintenance order sent to it from a Hague Convention Country, the court officer must send written notice of the registration to the Lord Chancellor.

Notification of means of enforcement

6.1 The court officer of the family court must take reasonable steps to notify the person to whom payments are due under a registered order of the means of enforcement available in respect of it.

Certified copies of orders issued under rules 34.39 and 34.40

7.1 In an application under rule 34.39 or 34.40 by a person wishing to enforce abroad a maintenance order, the certified copy of the order will be a sealed copy and will be accompanied by a certificate signed by the court officer.

7.2 In an application under the 1982 Act, the certificate signed by the court officer must state that it is a true copy of the order concerned and must give particulars of the proceedings in which it was made.

7.6 In an application under the 2007 Hague Convention, the certificate will be comprised of the following Article 11 forms duly completed by the court officer –

(a) the Abstract of a Decision;
(b) the Statement of Enforceability; and
(c) the Statement of Proper Notice.

7.7 In an application under the 2007 Hague Convention, the certificate will additionally state the jurisdictional basis upon which the order was made, with reference to the jurisdictional criteria in Article 20(1) of that Convention to be applied by the State in which recognition and/or enforcement is to be sought.

Countries and Territories in which Sums are Payable through Crown Agents for Overseas Governments and Territories (rule 34.23)

8.1 Gibraltar, Barbados, Bermuda, Ghana, Kenya, Fiji, Hong Kong, Singapore, Turks and Caicos Islands, United Republic of Tanzania (except Zanzibar), Anguilla, Falkland Islands and Dependencies, St Helena.

Part 1 of the 1972 Act – Modified Rules

9.1 The annexes to this Practice Direction set out rules 34.14 to 34.25 as they are modified –

(a) in relation to the Republic of Ireland, by rule 34.26 (Annex 1) (but see the note in that Annex regarding the ongoing relevance of those rules following revocation of rule 34.26);
(b) in relation to the Hague Convention Countries, by rule 34.27 (Annex 2); and
(c) in relation to the United States of America, by rule 34.28 (Annex3).

9.2 The statutory references in the annexes are construed in accordance with rule 34.26(2), 34.27(2) or 34.28(2) as the case may be.

Annex 1
Application of Section 1 of Chapter 2 of Part 34 to the Republic of Ireland

NOTE – rule 34.26 was revoked by S.I.2011/1328. Reciprocal enforcement of maintenance as between the UK and the Irish Republic was governed by the Maintenance Regulation (Council Regulation (EC) no 4/2009) from 18th June 2011 until exit day (as defined in the European Union (Withdrawal) Act 2018), and by the 2007 Hague Convention thereafter and the relevant rules for that Regulation were, and for that Convention are contained in Chapter 3 of Part 34 of the Rules. The provisions of this Annex are therefore of relevance only where either –

(a) the application for registration of an order relating to an Irish maintenance order was made on or before the 18th June 2011 and was still pending on that date; or
(b) the order was registered prior to the 18th June 2011.

34.14 Application for transmission of maintenance order to the Republic of Ireland
An application for a maintenance order to be sent to the Republic of Ireland under section 2 of the 1972 Act must be made in accordance with Practice Direction 34A.

34.15 Certification of evidence given on provisional orders

A document setting out or summarising evidence is authenticated by a court in England and Wales by a certificate signed, as appropriate, by –

(a) one of the justices; or
(b) the District Judge (Magistrates' Courts),

before whom that evidence was given.

(Section 3(5)(b) or 5(3) of the1972 Act require a document to be authenticated by the court.)

34.16 Confirmation of a provisional order ….

[This rule does not apply to the Republic of Ireland]

34.17 Consideration of confirmation of a provisional order made by a magistrates' court

(1) This rule applies where –

(a) a magistrates' court has made a provisional order by virtue of section 3 of the 1972 Act;
(b) the payer has made representations or adduced evidence to the court; and
(c) the court has fixed a date for the hearing at which it will consider confirmation of the order.

(2) The court officer must serve on the applicant for the provisional order –

(a) a copy of the representations or evidence; and
(b) written notice of the date fixed for the hearing.

34.18 Notification of variation or revocation of a maintenance order by the High Court

Where the High Court makes an order varying or revoking an order to which section 5 of the 1972 Act applies the court officer must send –

(a) a certified copy of the order of variation or revocation; and
(b) a statement as to the service on the payer of the documents mentioned in section 5(3) of the 1972 Act;

to the court in the Republic of Ireland.

(Rule 34.22 provides for the transmission of documents to a court in a reciprocating country.)

34.19 Notification of variation or revocation of a maintenance order by the High Court

Where a magistrates' court makes an order revoking an order to which section 5 of the 1972 Act applies, the court officer must send written notice of the making of the order to the Lord Chancellor.

(Section 5 of the 1972 Act applies to a maintenance order sent to the Republic of Ireland in accordance with section 2 of that Act and a provisional order made by a magistrates' court in accordance with section 3 of that Act which has been confirmed by such a court.)

(Provision in respect of notification of variation of a maintenance order by a magistrates' court under the 1972 Act is made in Rules made under section 144 of the Magistrates' Courts Act 1980.)

34.20 Taking of evidence for court in the Republic of Ireland

(1) This rule applies where a request is made by or on behalf of a court in the Republic of Ireland for the taking of evidence for the purpose of proceedings relating to a maintenance order to which Part 1 of the 1972 Act applies.

(Section 14 of the 1972 Act makes provision for the taking of evidence needed for the purpose of certain proceedings.)

(2) The High Court has power to take the evidence where –

(a) the request for evidence relates to a maintenance order made by a superior court in the United Kingdom; and
(b) the witness resides in England and Wales.

(3) The county court has power to take the evidence where –

(a) the request for evidence relates to a maintenance order made by a county court; and

(b) the maintenance order has not been registered in a magistrates' court under the 1958 Act.

(4) The following magistrates' courts have power to take the evidence, that is –

(a) where the proceedings in the Republic of Ireland relate to a maintenance order made by a magistrates' court, the court which made the order;

(b) where the proceedings relate to an order which is registered in a magistrates' court, the court in which the order is registered; and

(c) a magistrates' court to which the Secretary of State sends the request to take evidence.

(5) A magistrates' court not mentioned in paragraph (4) has power to take the evidence if the magistrates' court which would otherwise have that power consents because the evidence could be taken more conveniently.

(6) The evidence is to be taken in accordance with Part 22.

34.21 Request for the taking of evidence by a court ….

[This rule does not apply to the Republic of Ireland]

34.22 Transmission of documents

(1) This rule applies to any document, including a notice or request, which is required to be sent to a court in the Republic of Ireland by –

(a) Part 1 of the 1972 Act; or

(b) Section1 of Chapter 2 of this Part of these Rules.

(2) The document must be sent to the Lord Chancellor for transmission to the court in the Republic of Ireland.

34.23 Method of payment under registered orders

(1) Where an order is registered in a magistrates' court in accordance with section 6(3) of the 1972 Act, the court must order that the payment of sums due under the order be made–

(a) to the court officer for the registering court; and

(b) at such time and place as the court officer directs.

(Section 6(3) of the 1972 Act makes provision for the registration of maintenance orders made in the Republic of Ireland.)

(2) Where the court orders payment to be made to the court officer, the court officer must send the payments by post –

(a) to the payee under the order; or

(b) where a public authority has been authorised by the payee to receive the payments, to that public authority.

(Practice Direction 34A contains further provisions relating to the payment of sums due under registered orders.)

34.24 Enforcement of payments under registered orders

(1) This rule applies where periodical payments under a registered order are in arrears.

(2) The court officer must, on the written request of the payee, proceed in that officer's own name for the recovery of the sums due unless of the view that it is unreasonable to do so.

(3) If the sums due are more than 4 weeks in arrears the court officer must give the payee notice in writing of that fact stating the particulars of the arrears.

34.25 Notification of registration and cancellation

The court officer must send written notice to –

(a) the Lord Chancellor, on the due registration of an order under section 6(3) or 10(4) of the 1972 Act; and
(b) to the payer under the order, on –
  (i) the registration of an order under section 10(4) of the 1972 Act; or
  (ii) the cancellation of the registration of an order under section 10(1) of that Act.

34.25A Other notices under section 6 of the 1972 Act

(1) A notice required under section 6(6) or (10) of the 1972 Act must be in the form referred to in a practice direction.

(2) Where a magistrates' court sets aside the registration of an order following an appeal under section 6(7)of the 1972 Act, the court officer must send written notice of the court's decision to the payee.

(Section 6(6) of the 1972 Act provides for notice of registration in a United Kingdom court of a maintenance order made in the Republic of Ireland, and section 6(10) of that Act for notice that a maintenance order made in the Republic of Ireland has not been registered in a United Kingdom court.)

Annex 2

Application of Section 1 of Chapter 2 of Part 34 to the Hague Convention Countries

34.14 Application for transmission of maintenance order to a Hague Convention Country

An application for a maintenance order to be sent to a Hague Convention Country under section 2 of the 1972 Act must be made in accordance with Practice Direction 34A.

34.15 Certification of evidence given on provisional orders

[This rule does not apply to the Hague Convention Countries]

34.16 Confirmation of a provisional order made in a reciprocating country

[This rule does not apply to the Hague Convention Countries]

34.17 Consideration of revocation of a maintenance order made by a magistrates' court

(1) This rule applies where –

(a) an application has been made to a magistrates' court by a payee for the revocation of an order to which section 5 of the 1972 Act applies; and
(b) the payer resides in a Hague Convention Country.

(2) The court officer must serve on the payee, by post, a copy of any representations or evidence adduced by or on behalf of the payer.

(Provision relating to consideration of variation of a maintenance order made by a magistrates' court to which section 5 of the 1972 Act applies is made in Rules made under section 144 of the Magistrates' Courts Act 1980.)

34.18 Notification of variation or revocation of a maintenance order by the High Court or a county court

(1) This rule applies if the High Court or a county court makes an order varying or revoking a maintenance order to which section 5 of the 1972 Act applies.

(2) If the time for appealing has expired without an appeal having been entered, the court officer will send to the Lord Chancellor –

(a) the documents required by section 5(8) of the 1972 Act; and
(b) a certificate signed by the district judge stating that the order of variation or revocation is enforceable and no longer subject to the ordinary forms of review.

(3) A party who enters an appeal against the order of variation or revocation must, at the same time, give written notice to the court officer.

34.19 Notification of confirmation or revocation of a maintenance order by a magistrates' court

[This rule does not apply to the Hague Convention Countries]

34.20 Taking of evidence for court in a Hague Convention Country

(1) This rule applies where a request is made by or on behalf of a court in a Hague Convention Country for the taking of evidence for the purpose of proceedings relating to a maintenance order to which Part 1 of the 1972 Act applies.

(Section 14 of the 1972 Act makes provision for the taking of evidence needed for the purpose of certain proceedings.)

(2) The High court has power to take the evidence where –

(a) the request for evidence relates to a maintenance order made by a superior court in the United Kingdom: and
(b) the witness resides in England and Wales.

(3) The county court has power to take the evidence where –

(a) the request for evidence relates to a maintenance order made by a county court; and
(b) the maintenance order has not been registered in a magistrates' court under the 1958 Act.

(4) The following magistrates' courts have power to take the evidence, that is –

(a) where the proceedings in the Hague Convention Country relate to a maintenance order made by a magistrates' court, the court which made the order;
(b) where the proceedings relate to an order which is registered in a magistrates' court, the court in which the order is registered; and
(c) a magistrates' court to which the Secretary of State sends the request to take evidence.

(5) A magistrates' court not mentioned in paragraph (4) has power to take the evidence if the magistrates' court which would otherwise have that power consents because the evidence could be taken more conveniently.

(6) The evidence is to be taken in accordance with Part 22.

34.21 Request for the taking of evidence by a court in a Hague Convention country

[This rule does not apply to the Hague Convention countries.]

34.22 Transmission of documents

(1) This rule applies to any document, including a notice or request, which is required to be sent to a court in a Hague Convention country by –

(a) Part 1 of the 1972 Act; or
(b) Section1 of Chapter 2 of this Part of these Rules.

(2) The document must be sent to the Lord Chancellor for transmission to the court in the Hague Convention country.

34.23 Method of payment under registered orders

(1) Where an order is registered in a magistrates' court in accordance with section 6(3) of the 1972 Act, the court must order that the payment of sums due under the order be made –

(a) to the court officer for the registering court; and
(b) at such time and place as the court officer directs.

(Section 6(3) of the 1972 Act makes provision for the registration of maintenance orders made in a Hague Convention country.)

(2) Where the court orders payment to be made to the court officer, the court officer must send the payments by post to the payee under the order.

(Practice Direction 34A contains further provision relating to the payment of sums due under registered orders.)

34.24 Enforcement of payments under registered orders

(1) This rule applies where a court has ordered periodical payments under a registered maintenance order to be made to the court officer.

(2) The court officer must take reasonable steps to notify the payee of the means of enforcement available.

(3) Paragraph (4) applies where periodical payments due under a registered order are in arrears.

(4) The court officer, on that officer's own initiative –

(a) may; or
(b) if the sums due are more than 4 weeks in arrears, must,

proceed in that officer's own name for the recovery of the sums due unless of the view that it is unreasonable to do so.

34.25 Notification of registration and cancellation

The court officer must send written notice to –

(a) the Lord Chancellor, on the due registration of an order under section 10(4) of the 1972 Act; and

(b) the payer under the order, on –

(i) the registration of an order under section 10(4) of the 1972 Act; or

(ii) the cancellation of the registration of an order under section 10(1) of the 1972 Act.

34.25A General provisions as to notices

(1) A notice to a payer of the registration of an order in a magistrates' court in accordance with section 6(3) of the 1972 Act must be in the form referred to in a practice direction.

(Section 6(8) of the 1972 Act requires notice of registration to be given to the payer.)

(2) If the court sets aside the registration of a maintenance order following an appeal under section 6(9) of the 1972 Act, the court officer must send written notice of the decision to the Lord Chancellor.

(3) A notice to a payee that the court officer has refused to register an order must be in the form referred to in a practice direction.

(Section 6(11) of the 1972 Act requires notice of refusal of registration to be given to the payee.)

(4) Where, under any provision of Part 1 of the 1972 Act, a court officer serves a notice on a payer who resides in a Hague Convention Country, the court officer must send to the Lord Chancellor a certificate of service.

Annex 3

Application for Section 1 of Chapter 2 of Part 34 to the United States of America

34.14 Application for transmission of maintenance order to the United States of America

An application for a maintenance order to be sent to the United States of America under section 2 of the 1972 Act must be made in accordance with Practice Direction 34A.

34.15 Certification of evidence given on provisional orders

[This rule does not apply to the United States of America]

34.16 Confirmation of a provisional order made in a reciprocating country

[This rule does not apply to the United States of America]

34.17 Consideration of revocation of a maintenance order made by a magistrates' court

(1) This rule applies where –

(a) an application has been made to a magistrates' court by a payee for the revocation of an order to which section 5 of the 1972 Act applies; and

(b) the payer resides in the United States of America.

(2) The court officer must serve on the payee by post a copy of any representations or evidence adduced by or on behalf of the payer.

(Provision relating to consideration of variation of a maintenance order made by a magistrates' court to which section 5 of the 1972 Act applies is made in rules made under section 144 of the Magistrates' Courts Act 1980.)

34.18 Notification of variation or revocation

If the High Court or a county court makes an order varying or revoking a maintenance order to which section 5 of the 1972 Act applies, the court officer will send to the Lord Chancellor the documents required by section 5(7) of that Act.

34.19 Notification of confirmation or revocation of a maintenance order by a magistrates' court

[This rule does not apply to the United States of America]

34.20 Taking of evidence for court in United States of America

(1) This rule applies where a request is made by or on behalf of a court in the United States of America for the taking of evidence for the purpose of proceedings relating to a maintenance order to which Part 1 of the 1972 Act applies.

(Section 14 of the1972 Act makes provision for the taking of evidence needed for the purpose of certain proceedings.)

(2) The High Court has power to take the evidence where –

(a) the request for evidence relates to a maintenance order made by a superior court in the United Kingdom; and
(b) the witness resides in England and Wales.

(3) The county court has power to take the evidence where –

(a) the request for evidence relates to a maintenance order made by a county court; and
(b) the maintenance order has not been registered in a magistrates' court under the 1958 Act.

(4) The following magistrates' courts have power to take the evidence, that is –

(a) where the proceedings in the United States of America relate to a maintenance order made by a magistrates' court, the court which made the order;
(b) where the proceedings relate to an order which is registered in a magistrates' court, the court in which the order is registered; and
(c) a magistrates' court to which the Secretary of State sends the request to take evidence.

(5) A magistrates' court not mentioned in paragraph (4) has power to take the evidence if the magistrates' court which would otherwise have that power consents because the evidence could be taken more conveniently.

(6) The evidence is to be taken in accordance with Part 22.

34.21 Request for the taking of evidence by a court in a reciprocating country

[This rule does not apply to the United States of America]

34.22 Transmission of documents

(1) This rule applies to any document, including a notice or request, which is required to be sent to a court in the United States of America by –

(a) Part 1 of the 1972 Act; or
(b) Section 1 of Chapter 2 of this Part of these Rules.

(2) The document must be sent to the Lord Chancellor for transmission to the court in the United States of America.

34.23 Method of payment under registered orders

(1) Where an order is registered in a magistrates' court in accordance with section 6(3) of the 1972 Act, the court must order that the payment of sums due under the order be made –

(a) to the court officer for the registering court; and
(b) at such time and place as the court officer directs.

(Section 6(3) of the 1972 Act makes provision for the registration of maintenance orders made in the United States of America.)

(2) Where the court orders payment to be made to the court officer, the court officer must send the payments by post to the payee under the order.

(Practice Direction 34A contains further provisions relating to the payment of sums due under registered orders.)

34.24 Enforcement of payments under registered orders

(1) This rule applies where a court has ordered periodical payments under a registered maintenance order to be made to the court officer.

(2) The court officer must take reasonable steps to notify the payee of the means of enforcement available.

(3) Paragraph (4) applies where periodical payments due under a registered order are in arrears.

(4) The court officer, on that officer's own initiative –

(a) may; or
(b) if the sums due are more than 4 weeks in arrears, must,

proceed in that officer's own name for the recovery of the sums due unless of the view that it is unreasonable to do so.

34.25 Notification of registration and cancellation

The court officer must send written notice to –

(a) the Lord Chancellor, on the due registration of an order under section 10(4) of the 1972 Act; or
(b) the payer under the order, on –
 (i) the registration of an order under section 10(4) of the 1972 Act; or
 (ii) the cancellation of the registration of an order under section 10(1) of that Act.

Practice Direction 34B – Tracing payers overseas

See also Part 34, Practice Direction 34A, Practice Direction 34C, Practice Direction 34D, Practice Direction 34E

Practice Note –10 February 1976

Difficulties can arise where a person in this country wishes to take proceedings under the Maintenance Orders (Facilities for Enforcement) Act 1920 or Part I of the Maintenance Orders (Reciprocal Enforcement) Act 1972 to obtain or enforce a maintenance order against a payer living overseas whose address is unknown to the applicant.

To mitigate those difficulties, arrangements have now been made with the appropriate authorities in Australia, Canada, New Zealand and South Africa, whereby the court may on request ask the authorities in those countries to make enquiries with a view to tracing the whereabouts of the payer. The following procedure should be followed.

On or before an application is made for a provisional maintenance order, or for transmission of an absolute maintenance order under the above Acts by an applicant who does not know the payer's actual address in either Australia, Canada, New Zealand or South Africa, there should be completed and lodged with the [court] a questionnaire, in duplicate, ([Principal] Registry Form D312 or family court Form D85 as appropriate) obtainable from the registry or court office, together with a written undertaking from the solicitor (or from the applicant if acting in person) that any address of the payer received in response to the enquiries will not be disclosed or used except for the purpose of proceedings.

This Note is issued [in its original form] with the concurrence of the Lord Chancellor.

Practice Direction 34C – Revoked

Practice Direction 34D – Form relating to Part 34

See also Part 34, Practice Direction 34A, Practice Direction 34B, Practice Direction 34C, Practice Direction 34E

This Practice Direction supplements rule 34.28ZJ.

1 The form referred to in rule 34.28ZJ is–

Form of Notice

Notice under section 35(3) of the Maintenance Orders (Reciprocal Enforcement) Act 1972

Family Court sitting at……………………..

Date:

To the defendant…………

of……………

…………….

[application] has been made by

The applicant…………

of.................

.....who states that by an order made on.......................
...... under the............... Act

...... by the family court

...... you were ordered as follows:-

...... and applies for that order to be [revoked] [varied by an order requiring ....]

...... on the ground that

The hearing of the application will be on:

Date of hearing.............. at .... [am/pm]

at the family court sitting at ....

A.B.

Court officer

Note: if you do not appear at the time and place specified above the court may proceed in your absence. If you wish to make written representations to the court you may do so on the enclosed form.

Practice Direction 34E – Reciprocal enforcement of maintenance orders – Designated Family Judge areas

See also Part 34, Practice Direction 34A, Practice Direction 34B, Practice Direction 34C, Practice Direction 34D

This Practice Direction supplements FPR Part 34

Maintenance Enforcement Business Centres, Designated Family Judge areas and Designated Family Courts

1.1 Her Majesty's Courts and Tribunals Service will publish information to enable the family court Maintenance Enforcement Business Centres of the family court, Designated Family Judge areas and Designated Family Courts to be identified.

Taking of evidence for court in reciprocating country

2.1 Rule 34.20(3) FPR sets out where the family court has power to take evidence when a request is made by or on behalf of a court in a reciprocating country for the taking of evidence for the purpose of proceedings relating to a maintenance order to which Part 1 of the 1972 Act applies.

2.2 Where rule 34.20(3) applies, the evidence will be taken by the family court sitting in the Designated Family Judge area in which the maintenance order is made or registered, or to which the Lord Chancellor sends the request to take evidence.

Notification of proceedings in a Hague Convention Country or in the United States of America

3.1 Rule 34.28ZA FPR applies where the court officer receives from the Lord Chancellor a notice of the institution of proceedings, including notice of the substance of a claim, in a Hague Convention Country or in the United States of America in relation to the making, variation or revocation of a maintenance order.

3.2 Where rule 34.28ZA applies –

(a) if it appears to the court officer that the person against whom the proceedings were instituted is residing within the area covered by the Maintenance Enforcement Business Centre in which the court officer acts, the court officer will serve the notice on that person by sending it to that person's last known or usual address;

(b) if it appears to the court officer that the person concerned is not residing within that area, the court officer must inform the Lord Chancellor and return the notice.

Registration of maintenance orders

4.1 Paragraphs 4.2 to 4.5 apply where the family court receives an application of a type referred to in rule 34.30 FPR.

4.2 The court officer will –

(a) take such steps as appear appropriate for ascertaining whether the payer resides within the area covered by the Maintenance Enforcement Business Centre to which the application has been sent; and

(b) consider any available information as to the nature and location of the payer's assets.

4.3 If the court officer is satisfied that the payer –

(a) does not reside within the area covered by the Maintenance Enforcement Business Centre to which the application has been sent; and

(b) does not have assets in that area against which the maintenance order could be enforced,

the court officer will refuse the application and return the application to the Lord Chancellor stating the information the court officer has as to the whereabouts of the payer and the nature and location of the payer's assets.

4.4 Paragraph 4.5 applies if the court officer is satisfied that the payer –

(a) does not reside within the area covered by the Maintenance Enforcement Business Centre to which the application has been sent; but

(b) has assets in that area against which the maintenance order could be enforced.

4.5 Where this paragraph applies, then either –

(a) the court officer must register the order; or

(b) if the court officer believes that the payer is residing in an area covered by a different Maintenance Enforcement Business Centre, the court officer may refuse the application and return the documents to the Lord Chancellor stating the information the court officer has as to the whereabouts of the payer and the nature and location of the payer's assets

Appeal from a decision relating to registration

5.A1 Where rule 34.31(2) FPR applies (certain appeals to be to the family court), the appeal should be sent to the Maintenance Enforcement Business Centre that has been in most recent communication with the parties.

5.1 Where rule 34.31(2) FPR applies (certain appeals to be to the family court), the appeal should be heard in the same Designated Family Judge area in which –

(a) the order is registered; or
(b) the application for registration has been refused,

as the case may be.

Registered order: payer residing in an area covered by a different Maintenance Enforcement Business Centre

6.1 Paragraphs 6.2 to 6.5 apply where a court officer in the Maintenance Enforcement Business Centre for the Designated Family Judge area where an order is registered considers that the payer is residing in a Designated Family Judge area covered by a different Maintenance Enforcement Business Centre (rule 34.35 refers).

6.2 The court officer will send to the Maintenance Enforcement Business Centre for that other area –

(a) the information and documents relating to the registration;
(b) a certificate of arrears, if applicable, signed by the court officer;
(c) a statement giving such information as the court officer possesses as to the whereabouts of the payer and the nature and location of the payer's assets; and
(d) any other relevant documents which the court officer has relating to the case.

6.3 The information and documents referred to in paragraph 6.2(a) are those required, as appropriate, under –

(a) Articles 46 and 47 of the 1968 Convention;
(b) Articles 46 and 47 of the 1988 Convention;
(c) Article 53 of the Judgments Regulation;
(d) Article 53 of the Lugano Convention;
(e) Article 28 or 29 of the Maintenance Regulation; or
(f) Article 25 or 30 of the 2007 Hague Convention.

6.4 The court officer must give notice to the payee and the Lord Chancellor that the papers have been sent to the Maintenance Enforcement Business Centre for another area.

6.5 If the papers are sent to the Maintenance Enforcement Business Centre for another area, the court officer in that Maintenance Enforcement Business Centre must note that the order has been, and remains, registered in the family court.

PART 35

...[1]

...[1]

Amendment

1 Repealed by the Family Procedure Rules 2010 and Court of Protection Rules 2017 (Amendment) (EU Exit) Regulations 2019, SI 2019/517, rr 2, 20.

PART 36
TRANSITIONAL ARRANGEMENTS AND PILOT SCHEMES

36.1 Transitional provisions

Practice Direction 36A shall make provision for the extent to which these rules shall apply to proceedings started before the day on which they come into force.

36.2 Pilot schemes

Practice directions may modify or disapply any provision of these rules—

(a) for specified periods; and
(b) in relation to proceedings in specified courts,

during the operation of pilot schemes for assessing the use of new practices and procedures in connection with proceedings.

[36.3 Temporary modifications for coronavirus or other emergency

Practice Directions may modify or disapply any provision of these rules—

(a) for specified periods; and
(b) in relation to proceedings in specified courts,

in order to address issues for the work of the courts arising from the coronavirus (SARS-CoV-2) outbreak or any other public emergency.][1]

Amendment

1 Inserted by the Family Procedure (Amendment) Rules 2021, SI 2021/155, rr 2, 4.

Practice Direction 36A – Transitional arrangements

See also Part 36, Practice Direction 36C

This Practice Direction supplements FPR Part 36

Chapter 1
Content of this Practice Direction

1.1 This Chapter deals with the application of the FPR to proceedings started before 6th April 2011 ('existing proceedings').

1.2 In this Practice Direction 'the previous rules' means, as appropriate, the Rules of the Supreme Court 1965 and County Court Rules 1981 as in force immediately before 26 April 1999, and–

the Maintenance Orders (Facilities for Enforcement) Rules 1922;
the Magistrates' Courts (Guardianship of Minors) Rules 1974;
the Magistrates' Courts (Reciprocal Enforcement of Maintenance Orders) Rules 1974;
the Magistrates' Courts (Reciprocal Enforcement of Maintenance Orders) (Republic of Ireland) Rules 1975;
the Magistrates' Courts (Reciprocal Enforcement of Maintenance Orders) (Hague Convention Countries) Rules 1980;
the Magistrates' Courts (Child Abduction and Custody) Rules 1986;
the Magistrates' Courts (Civil Jurisdiction and Judgments Act 1982) Rules 1986;
the Family Proceedings Rules 1991;
the Family Proceedings Courts (Children Act 1989) Rules 1991;
the Family Proceedings Courts (Matrimonial Proceedings etc.) Rules 1991 (in so far as those rules do not relate to enforcement or variation of orders);
the Magistrates' Courts (Costs Against Legal Representatives in Civil Proceedings) Rules 1991 (in so far as those rules relate to family proceedings);
the Family Proceedings Courts (Child Support Act 1991) Rules 1993;

the Magistrates' Courts (Reciprocal Enforcement of Maintenance Orders) (United States of America) Rules 1995 (subject to the saving in paragraph 3.6 of this Practice Direction);

the Magistrates' Courts (Hearsay Evidence in Civil Proceedings) Rules 1999 (in so far as those rules relate to family proceedings); and

the Family Procedure (Adoption) Rules 2005,

as in force immediately before 6th April 2011.

1.3 Insofar as they relate to family proceedings, the previous rules are revoked with effect from 6 April 2011 by operation of law and necessary implication. This is the case except where the previous rules continue to apply to existing family proceedings in accordance with this Practice Direction. The revocation of the previous rules arises from–

the repeal of the powers under which the previous rules were made (by section 109(1) and (3) of, and paragraph 245(2) of Schedule 8 and Schedule 10 to, the Courts Act 2003) or in the case of the Family Procedure (Adoption) Rules 2005 by remaking the rules in the FPR, and

the fact that the FPR are stated in terms to be a new procedural code and to apply to family proceedings in the High Court, a county court and a magistrates' court (FPR rules 1.1 and 2.1).

General scheme of transitional arrangements

2.1 The general scheme is–

(a) to apply the FPR to existing proceedings so far as is practicable; but
(b) where this is not practicable, to apply the previous rules to such proceedings.

Where the previous rules will normally apply

General principle

3.1 Where an initiating step has been taken in a case before 6th April 2011, in particular a step using forms or other documentation required by the previous rules, the case will proceed in the first instance under the previous rules. Where a party must take a step in response to something done by another party in accordance with the previous rules, that step must also be in accordance with those rules.

Responding to old process

3.2 A party who is served with an old type of originating process (for example, an originating summons) on or after 6th April 2011 must respond in accordance with the previous rules and the instructions on any forms received.

Filing and service of pleadings where old process served

3.3 Where a case has been begun by an old type of originating process (whether served before or after 6th April 2011), filing and service of pleadings will continue according to the previous rules.

Pre-commencement order inconsistent with FPR

3.4 Where a court order has been made before 6th April 2011, that order must still be complied with on or after that date.

Steps taken before commencement

3.5 Where a party has, before 6th April 2011, taken any step in the proceedings in accordance with the previous rules, that step will remain valid on or after that date, and a party will not normally be required to take any action that would amount to taking such a step again under the FPR.

Where the FPR will normally apply

General principle

4.1 Where a new step is to be taken in any existing proceedings on or after 6th April 2011, it is to be taken under the FPR.

Part 1 (Overriding objective) to apply

4.2 Part 1 of the FPR (Overriding objective) will apply to all existing proceedings from 6th April 2011 onwards.

Issuing of application forms after the FPR come into force

4.3 (1) The general rule is that–

(a) only application forms under the FPR will be issued by the court on or after 6th April 2011; and

(b) if a request to issue an old type of form or originating process (summons, etc.) is received at the court on or after 6th April 2011, it will be returned unissued.

(2) By way of exception to the general rule, the court may in cases of urgency direct that the form or process is to be issued as if the request to issue it had been a request to issue an application form under the FPR and, if it does so, the court may make such supplementary directions as it considers appropriate.

First time before a court on or after 6th April 2011

4.4 (1) When proceedings come before a court (whether at a hearing or on paper) for the first time on or after 6th April 2011, the court may direct how the FPR are to apply to the proceedings and may disapply certain provisions of the FPR. The court may also give case management directions.

(2) The general presumption will be that the FPR will apply to the proceedings from then on unless the court directs or this practice direction provides otherwise.

(3) If an application has been issued before 6th April 2011 and the hearing of the application has been set on or after that date, the general presumption is that the application will be decided having regard to the FPR.

(4) When the first occasion on which existing proceedings are before a court on or after 6th April 2011 is a hearing of a substantive issue, the general presumption is that the hearing will be conducted according to the FPR.

Costs

4.5 (1) Any assessment of costs that takes place on or after 6th April 2011 will be in accordance with FPR Part 28 and the provisions of the Civil Procedure Rules as applied by that Part.

(2) However, the general presumption is that no costs for work undertaken before 6th April 2011 will be disallowed if those costs would have been allowed on detailed assessment before that date.

(3) The decision as to whether to allow costs for work undertaken on or after 6th April 2011 will generally be taken in accordance with FPR Part 28 and the provisions of the Civil Procedure Rules as applied by that Part.

Chapter 2

4.6 (1) Subject to paragraph (3), the following forms will be returned unissued if received by the court on or after 22nd April 2014–

Name	*Name*
A (except version 04/14)	Notice of [intention to proceed with] an application for a financial order
A1 (except version 04/14)	Notice of [intention to proceed with] an application for a financial remedy (other than a financial order) in the county or high court
B (except version 04/14)	An application for an order for special protection for respondent in certain separation cases (under section 10(2) of the Matrimonial Causes Act 1973 or under section 48(2) of the Civil Partnership Act 2004
C11	Supplement for an application for an Emergency Protection Order
C110	Application under the Children Act 1989 for a care or supervision order
C110A (except version 04/14)	Application for a Care or Supervision Order and Applications for Other Orders under Part 4 of the Children Act 1989

(2) Subject to paragraph (3), the following forms, if used to request that the proceedings listed in column B are issued, will be returned unissued if received by the court on or after 22nd April 2014–

Number	*Proceedings requested to be issued*
C1 (Application for an order)	Private law proceedings for– • parental responsibility order (under sections 4(1)(c), 4ZA(1)(c) or 4A(1)(b) of the Children Act 1989) or an order terminating parental responsibility (under sections 4(2A), 4ZA(5) or 4A(3) of that Act);
	• an order appointing a child's guardian (under section 5(1) of the Children Act 1989) or an order terminating the appointment (under section 6(7) of that Act); • an order giving permission to change a child's surname or remove a child from the United Kingdom (under sections 13(1) or 14C of the Children Act 1989); • a special guardianship order; and • an order varying or discharging such an order (under section 14D of the Children Act 1989), • unless a separate Form FM1 of version 04/14 has been filed with the C1 application.

C2 (Application: for permission to start proceedings; for an order or directions in existing proceedings; to be joined as, or cease to be, a party in existing family proceedings under the Children Act 1989)	Private law proceedings for– • a parental responsibility order (under sections 4(1)(c), 4ZA(1)(c) or 4A(1)(b) of the Children Act 1989) or an order terminating parental responsibility (under sections 4(2A), 4ZA(5) or 4A(3) of that Act); • an order appointing a child's guardian (under section 5(1) of the Children Act 1989) or an order terminating the appointment (under section 6(7) of that Act); • an order giving permission to change a child's surname or remove a child from the United Kingdom (under sections 13(1) or 14C of the Children Act 1989); • a special guardianship order; and • an order varying or discharging such an order (under section 14D of the Children Act 1989), unless a separate Form FM1 of version 04/14 has been filed with the C2 application.
C100 (Application under the Children Act 1989 for a residence, contact, prohibited steps, specific issue section 8 order or to vary or discharge a section 8 order	Private law proceedings. Proceedings under section 51A of the Adoption and Children Act 2002.
C100 (Application under the Children Act 1989 for a child arrangements, prohibited steps, specific issue section 8 order or to vary or discharge a section 8 order) (version 04/14)	Proceedings under section 51A of the Adoption and Children Act 2002.

(3) Subject to paragraph (4), the court may in cases of urgency direct that a form specified in paragraph 4.6(1) or 4.6(2) is to be issued as if the request to issue had been made on the form applicable on or after 22nd April 2014, and if it does so, may make any supplementary directions as it considers appropriate.

(4) Paragraph (3) does not apply if a form specified in paragraph 4.6(1) or 4.62(3) is issued after a period of six months beginning with the 22nd April 2014 has elapsed.

Practice Direction 36C – Pilot scheme: care and supervision proceedings and other proceedings under Part 4 of the Children Act 1989

See also Part 36, Practice Direction 36A

This Practice Direction supplements FPR Part 36, rule 36.2 (Transitional Arrangements and Pilot Schemes)

Scope

1.1 This Practice Direction is made under rule 36.2 and sets up a Pilot Scheme. The Pilot Scheme applies to Part 4 proceedings (defined in FPR 12.2 as modified by paragraph 6.1 below) which are started–

(1) in any magistrates' court, county court and the High Court in accordance with the Allocation Order and the Guidance on allocation of proceedings issued from time to time by the President of the Family Division;
(2) on the Relevant Start Date in relation to that court (see paragraph 2.1 below) or any time from that date until 31st March 2014;

The relevant start date

2.1

(1) 1st July 2013;
(2) 5th August 2013;
(3) 2nd September 2013; or
(4) 7th October 2013,

on which the court will start to operate the Pilot Scheme.

Publication of relevant start date

3.1 The list of courts choosing to start operating the Pilot Scheme from 1st July 2013 may be found (from 25th June 2013) at http://www.justice.gov.uk/protecting-the-vulnerable/care-proceedings-reform. Courts joining the Pilot Scheme after 1st July will be added to the list of courts on the website not less than 7 working days before the Relevant Start Date.

Purpose of the pilot scheme

4.1 The purpose of the Pilot Scheme is to assess the use of new practices and procedures to support the 26 week time limit for Part 4 proceedings in the amendments made to section 32 of the Children Act 1989 by clause 14 of the Children and Families Bill, as introduced into Parliament on 4th February 2013.

http://www.education.gov.uk/aboutdfe/departmentalinformation/childrenandfamiliesbill/a00221161/children-families-bill

Modification of the FPR and Practice Directions during operation of the pilot scheme

5.1 During the operation of the Pilot Scheme the Family Procedure Rules 2010 and the Practice Directions supporting those Rules will apply as modified by paragraphs 6.1 to 14.1.

Modification of FPR Part 12

6.1 In rule 12.2–

(1) for the definition of 'Case Management Order', substitute–
"Case Management Order' means an order in the form referred to in Practice Direction 12A or Pilot Practice Direction 12A;';

(2) after the definition of 'interim order' insert–
"Part 4 proceedings' means proceedings for–

(a) a care order except an interim care order, or the discharge of such an order under section 39(1) of the 1989 Act;

(b) an order giving permission to change a child's surname or remove a child from the United Kingdom under section 33(7) of the 1989 Act whle a care order is in force with respect to the child;

(c) a supervision order except an interim supervision order, the discharge or variation of such an order under section 39(2) of the 1989 Act, or the extension or further extension of such an order under paragraph 6(3) of Schedule 3 to that Act;

(d) an order making provision regarding contact under section 34(2) to (4) of the 1989 Act made at the same time as the making of a care order other than an interim care order or later or an order varying or discharging such an order under section 34(9) of that Act;

(e) an education supervision order, the extension of an education supervision order under paragraph 15(2) of Schedule 3 to the 1989 Act, or the discharge of such an order under paragraph 17(1) of Schedule 3 to that Act;

(f) an order under section 39(3) of the 1989 Act varying a supervision order in so far as it affects a person with whom the child is living but who is not entitled to apply for the order to be discharged; or

(g) the substitution of a supervision order for a care order under section 39(4) of the 1989 Act;';

(3) In the definition of 'public law proceedings'–

(a) after "public law proceedings' means', insert 'Part 4 proceedings and';

(b) in paragraph (d) of the definition, for 'a care order' substitute 'an interim care order';

(c) in paragraph (e) of the definition, after '1989 Act' insert 'while an interim care order is in force with respect to the child';

(d) in paragraph (f) of the definition, for 'a supervision order under section 31(1)(b)' substitute 'an interim supervision order under section 38(1)';

(e) in paragraph (g) of the definition, after '1989 Act' insert 'made at the same time as the making of an interim care order or later';

(f) in paragraph (j) of the definition, for 'a supervision order' substitute 'an interim supervision order';

(g) omit paragraphs (h) and (m) of the definition.

6.2 In rule 12.5–

(1) for paragraph (a)(iii), substitute '(iii) in Part 4 proceedings, the Case Management Hearing;';

(2) at the end of paragraph (a)(iii) omit 'or';

(3) after paragraph (a)(iii), insert '(iiia) in so far as practicable in public law proceedings other than Part 4 proceedings, the First Appointment; or';

(4) in paragraph (a) after 'Practice Directions 12A or B', insert 'and Pilot Practice Direction 12A';

(5) in paragraph (c) after 'Practice Directions 12A or B', insert ', Pilot Practice Direction 12A';

(6) at the beginning of the words in parentheses following the rule, insert 'Pilot Practice Direction 12A sets out the details relating to the Case Management Hearing and'.

6.3 In rule 12.7(2)(b)–

after 'Practice Directions 12A or B', insert ', Pilot Practice Direction 12A'.

6.4 After rule 12.8, insert–

'(Practice Direction 12C (Service of Application in Certain Children Proceedings) provides that in Part 4 proceedings the minimum number of days prior to the Case Management Hearing for service of the application and accompanying documents is 7 days. The Court has discretion to extend or shorten this time (see rule 4.1(3) (a)).)'.

6.5 After the heading to Chapter 3 'Special provisions about public law proceedings', insert–

'12.21A Application of rules 12.21B to 12.21E

Rules 12.21B to 12.21E apply to Part 4 proceedings.

12.21B The timetable for the proceedings

The court will draw up the timetable for the proceedings or revise that timetable with a view to disposing of the proceedings without delay.

12.21C Directions

(1) The court will direct the parties to–

(a) monitor compliance with the court's directions; and
(b) tell the court or court officer about–
  (i) any failure to comply with a direction of the court; and
  (ii) any other delay in the proceedings.

12.21D The Case Management Hearing and the Issues Resolution Hearing

(1) The court will conduct the Case Management Hearing with the objective of–

(a) confirming the court to which the proceedings have been allocated or, if necessary, considering transfer of the proceedings in accordance with the Allocation Order;
(b) drawing up a timetable for the proceedings in accordance with rule 12.21B including the time within which the proceedings are to be resolved;
(c) identifying the issues;
(d) giving directions in accordance with rule 12.12 and Pilot Practice Direction 12A to manage the proceedings.

(2) The court may hold a Further Case Management Hearing only where this hearing is necessary to fulfil the objectives of the Case Management Hearing set out in paragraph (1).

(3) The court will conduct the Issues Resolution Hearing with the objective of–

(a) identifying the remaining issues in the proceedings;
(b) as far as possible resolving or narrowing those issues;
(c) giving directions to manage the proceedings to the final hearing in accordance with rule 12.12 and Pilot Practice Direction 12A.

(4) Where it is possible for all the issues in the proceedings to be resolved at the Issues Resolution Hearing, the court may treat the Issues Resolution Hearing as a final hearing and make orders disposing of the proceedings.

(5) The court may set the date for the Case Management Hearing, a Further Case Management Hearing and the Issues Resolution Hearing at the times referred to in Pilot Practice Direction 12A.

(6) The matters which the court will consider at the hearings referred to in this rule are set out in Pilot Practice Direction 12A.

(Rule 25.6 (experts: when to apply for the court's permission) provides that unless the court directs otherwise, parties must apply for the court's permission as mentioned in rule 25.4 as soon as possible and in Part 4 Proceedings no later than the Case Management Hearing.)

12.21E Discussion between advocates

(1) When setting a date for the Case Management Hearing or the Issues Resolution Hearing the court will direct a discussion between the parties' advocates to–

(a) discuss the provisions of a draft of the Case Management Order; and
(b) consider any other matter set out in Pilot Practice Direction 12A.

(2) Where there is a litigant in person the court will give directions about how that person may take part in the discussions between the parties' advocates.

(3) Unless the court directs otherwise–

(a) any discussion between advocates must take place no later than 2 days before the Case Management Hearing; and
(b) a draft of the Case Management Order must be filed with the court no later than 11 a.m. on the day before the Case Management Hearing.

(4) Unless the court directs otherwise–

(a) any discussion between advocates must take place no later than 7 days before the Issues Resolution Hearing; and
(b) a draft of the Case Management Order must be filed with the court no later than 11 a.m. on the day before the Issues Resolution Hearing.

(5) For the purposes of this rule 'advocate' includes a litigant in person.'.

6.6 For rule 12.22, substitute–

'12.22 Rules 12.23 to 12.26 apply in so far as practicable to public law proceedings other than Part 4 proceedings.'.

Modification of FPR Part 25

7.1 For FPR 25.6, substitute–

'25.6 When to apply for the court's permission

Unless the court directs otherwise, parties must apply for the court's permission as mentioned in rule 25.4 as soon as possible and–

(a) in Part 4 proceedings referred to in rule 12.2, no later than the Case Management Hearing;
(b) in public law proceedings other than Part 4 proceedings referred to in rule 12.2, no later than the Case Management Conference;
(c) in public law proceedings referred to in rule 12.2, no later than the First Hearing Dispute Resolution Appointment;
(d) in adoption proceedings and placement proceedings, no later than the first directions hearing;
(e) in proceedings for a financial remedy, no later than the first appointment;
(f) in a defended case referred to in rule 7.1(3), no later than any case management hearing directed by the court under rule 7.20.'.

Modification of FPR Part 27

8.1 Omit the words in parentheses following FPR27.6.

Modification of Practice Direction 5A (Forms)

9.1 In Table 1(Index to forms), in the box in column 2 which applies to FPR Part 12–

(1) omit 'C17' and 'C17A';
(2) for 'C110' substitute 'C110A', and
(3) after 'PLP 10' insert, '(PL08 and PL09 do not apply to Part 4 proceedings)'.

9.2 In Table 2 (List of Forms)–

(1) omit the entries for Forms C17 and C17A;
(2) for the entry for Form C110, substitute 'C110A Application for a Care or Supervision Order and Applications for other orders under Part 4 of the Children Act 1989.'.

Application of Practice Direction 12A (Public Law Proceedings: Guide to Case Management) and Pilot Practice Direction 12A (Care, Supervision and Other Part 4 Proceedings: Guide to Case Management)

10.1 In relation to public law proceedings other than Part 4 proceedings, Practice Direction 12A will apply, so far as practicable, without modification.

10.2 In relation to Part 4 proceedings, Pilot Practice Direction 12A as set out in the Annex to this Practice Direction will apply in place of Practice Direction 12A.

Modification of Practice Direction 12C (Service of Application in Children Proceedings)

11.1 In the Table in paragraph 1.1–

(1) in Box 3,column 1, after '(section 31 of the 1989 Act)' insert 'and other Part 4 proceedings';
(2) in Box 3, column 2, for 'Form C110' substitute 'Form C110A'.

11.2 For paragraph 1.2, substitute–

> '1.2 When filing the documents referred to in column 2 of the Table in paragraph 1.1, the applicant must also file sufficient copies for one to be served on each respondent and, except for Part 4 proceedings, Cafcass or CAFCASS CYMRU. In relation to Part 4 proceedings, the applicant need not file a copy of the documents for Cafcass or CAFCASS CYMRU as it is the applicant who sends copies of these documents to Cafcass or CAFCASS CYMRU in accordance with Pilot Practice Direction 12A.'.

11.3 In the table in paragraph 2.1

(1) in Box 1,column 1, after '(s 33(7) of the 1989 Act)' insert 'while an interim care order is in force with respect to the child';
(2) in Box 2, column 1, after '(section 14A of the 1989 Act)' insert–

'care or supervision order (section 31 of the 1989 Act) except an interim care order or an interim supervision order (section 38 (1) of the 1989 Act);
an order permitting the child's name to be changed or the removal of the child from the United Kingdom (s 33(7) of the 1989 Act) while a care order is in force with respect to the child';
an order making provision for contact under section 34(2) to (4) of the 1989 Act made at the same time as the making of a care order other than an

interim care order or later or an order varying or discharging such an order under section 34(9) of the 1989 Act;';

(3) in Box 3, column 1–
  (a) for 'care or supervision order (section 31 of the 1989 Act)' substitute 'an interim care order or an interim supervision order (section 38 (1) of the 1989 Act)';
  (b) after 'section 34(2) to (4) of the 1989 Act', insert 'made at the same time as the making of an interim care order or later'.

Modifications to Practice Direction 27A (Family Proceedings: Court Bundles: (Universal Practice to be Applied in all Courts other than the Family Proceedings Court)

12.1 In Practice Direction 27A–

(1) in the heading omit 'Other than the Family Proceedings Court';
(2) in paragraph 1.1 omit '(other than the Family Proceedings Court)';
(3) in paragraph 2.1(d) omit 'except for Family Proceedings Courts';
(4) for paragraph 2.2 substitute–

"Hearings' includes–

  (a) all appearances before a judge, district judge or a magistrates' court, whether with or without notice to other parties and whether for directions or for substantive relief; and
  (b) in a magistrates' court, references to a directions appointment whether conducted by the justices, a district judge (magistrates' court) or a justices' clerk.';

(5) at the beginning of paragraph 2.5, insert 'In relation to a county court or the High Court,';
(6) in paragraph 4.1, for 'a judge' substitute 'the court';
(7) in paragraph 6.1, for the references to 'case management conference' substitute 'Case Management Hearing';
(8) in paragraphs 6.3, 7.1,and 12.1, for 'judge' substitute 'court';
(9) in paragraph 7.2–
  (a) for 'Unless the judge' substitute 'Unless the court';
  (b) in sub paragraph (c) for 'for hearings at any other court' substitute 'for hearings in a county court or the High Court';
  (c) after sub paragraph (c) insert '(d) in the magistrates' court, at the court office of the court where the hearing is to take place.';
(10) the reference to–
  (a) the 'Public Law Protocol (2003) 2 FLR 719' in paragraph 6.1;
  (b) the 'Practice Direction: Care Cases: Judicial Continuity and Judicial Case Management appended to the Public Law Protocol (2003) 2FLR 719' in paragraph 15; and
  (c) 'the Public Law Protocol' in paragraph 15,

shall be read as if it were a reference to Pilot Practice Direction 12A Care Supervision and Other Part 4 Proceedings: Guide to Case Management contained in Practice Direction 36C.

Modifications to Practice Direction 27B (Attendance of Media Representatives at Hearings in Family Proceedings)

13.1 In paragraph 2.1(a), after 'Case Management Conferences' insert 'Case Management Hearings, any Further Case Management Hearings'.

Modifications to Practice Direction 27C (Attendance of Media Representatives at Hearings in Family Proceedings)

14.1 In paragraph 2.1(a), after 'Case Management Conferences' insert 'Case Management Hearings, any Further Case Management Hearings'.

Annex 1

Pilot Practice Direction 12A – Care, supervision and other Part 4 proceedings: guide to case management

The key stages of the court process

1.1 The Public Law Outline set out in the Table below contains an outline of–

(1) the order of the different stages of the process;
(2) the matters to be considered at the main case management hearings;
(3) the latest timescales within which the main stages of the process should take place in order to achieve the aim of resolving the proceedings within 26 weeks.

1.2 In the Public Law Outline–

(1) 'CMH' means the Case Management Hearing;
(2) 'FCMH' means Further Case Management Hearing;
(3) 'ICO' means interim care order;
(4) 'IRH' means the Issues Resolution Hearing;
(5) 'LA' means the Local Authority which is applying for a care or supervision order or a final order in other Part 4 Proceedings;
(6) 'OS' means the Official Solicitor.

1.3 In applying the provisions of FPR Part 12 and the Public Law Outline the court and the parties must also have regard to–

(1) all other relevant rules and Practice Directions and in particular–

- FPR Part 1 (Overriding Objective);
- FPR Part 4 (General Case Management Powers);
- FPR Part 15 (Representation of Protected Parties) and Practice Direction 15B (Adults Who May Be Protected Parties and Children Who May Become Protected Parties in Family Proceedings);
- FPR Part 22 (Evidence);
- FPR Part 25 (Experts) and the Experts Practice Directions;
- FPR 27.6 and Practice Direction 27A (Court Bundles);

(2) President's Guidance issued from time to time on

- Allocation and Gatekeeping;
- Judicial continuity and deployment;
- Prescribed templates and orders;

(3) Justices' Clerks Rules 2005 and FPR Practice Direction 2A (Functions of the Court In The Family Procedure Rules 2010 And Practice Directions Which May Be Performed By a Single Justice of the Peace).

Pro-preceedings

Pro-preceedings Checklist;

Annex Documents are the documents specified in the Annex to the Application Form which are to be attached to that form and filed with the court: • Social Work Chronology • Social Work Statement and genogram • The current assessments relating to the child and/or the family and friends of the child to which the Social Work Statement refers and on which the LA relies	Checklist documents (already existing on the LA's files) are– (a) Evidential documents including– • Previous court orders and judgments/reasons • Any assessment materials relevant to the key issues including Section 7 and 37 reports • Single, joint or inter-agency materials (e.g., health & education/ Home Office and Immigration Tribunal documents);
• Threshold Statement • Care Plan • Allocation Proposal Form • Index of Checklist Documents	(b) Decision-making records including– • Records of key discussions with the family • Key LA minutes and records for the child • Pre-existing care plans (e.g., child in need plan, looked after child plan and child protection plan) • Letters Before Proceedings
	Only Checklist documents in (a) are to be served with the application form
	Checklist Documents in (b) are to be disclosed on request by any party
	Checklist documents are not to be– • filed with the court unless the court directs otherwise; and • older than 2 years before the date of issue of the proceedings unless reliance is placed on the same in the LA's evidence

Stage 1 – Issue and Allocation

Day 1 and day 2

On Day 1 (Day of issue):

- The LA files the Application Form and Annex Documents and sends copies to Cafcass/CAFCASS CYMRU
- The LA notifies the court of the need for a contested ICO hearing where this is known or expected
- Court officer issues application

Within a day of issue (Day 2):

- Court considers allocation, and if appropriate, transfers proceedings in accordance with the President's Guidance on Allocation and Gatekeeping
- LA serves the Application Form, Annex Documents and evidential Checklist Documents on the parties together with the notice of date and time of CMH

- Court gives standard directions on Issue and Allocation including:
  - Checking compliance with Pre-Proceedings Checklist including service of any missing Annex Documents
  - Appointing Children's Guardian (to be allocated by Cafcass/CAFCASS CYMRU)
  - Appointing solicitor for the child only if necessary
  - Appointing (if the person to be appointed consents) a litigation friend for any protected party or any non subject child who is a party, including the OS where appropriate
  - Filing and service of a LA Case Summary
  - Filing and service of a Case Analysis by the Children's Guardian
  - Making arrangements for a contested ICO hearing (if necessary)
  - Filing and Serving the Parents' Response
  - Sending a request for disclosure to, e.g., the police
  - Filing and serving an application for permission relating to experts under Part 25 on a date prior to the advocates meeting for the CMH
  - Directing the solicitor for the child to arrange an advocates' meeting 2 days before the CMH
  - Listing the CMH
- Court officer sends copy Notice of Hearing of the CMH by email to Cafcass/ CAFCASS CYMRU

Stage 2 – Case Management Hearing

Advocates' Meeting (including any litigants in person (FPR12.21E(5))	*Case Management Hearing*
No later than 2 clear days before CMH (or FCMH if it is necessary) • Consider information on the Application Form and Annex documents, the LA Case Summary, and the Case Analysis • Identify the parties' positions to be recited in the draft Case Management Order • If necessary, identify proposed experts and draft questions in accordance with Part 25 and the Experts Practice Directions • Identify any disclosure that in the advocates' views is necessary • Immediately notify the court of the need for a contested ICO hearing LA advocate to file a draft Case Management Order in prescribed form with court by 11 a.m. on the working day before the CMH and/or FCMH	CMH: by Day 12 A FCMH is to be held only if necessary, it is to be listed as soon as possible and in any event no later than day 20 (week 4) • Court gives detailed case management directions, including: – Confirming allocation and/or considering transfer – Drawing up the timetable for the child and the timetable for the proceedings and considering if an extension is necessary – Identifying additional parties and representation (including confirming that Cafcass/ CAFCASS CYMRU have allocated a Children's Guardian) – Identifying the key issues – Identifying the evidence necessary to enable the court to resolve the key issues – Deciding whether there is a real issue about threshold to be resolved

Advocates' Meeting (including any litigants in person (FPR12.21E(5))	*Case Management Hearing*
	– Determining any application made under Part 25 and otherwise ensuring compliance with Part 25 where it is necessary for expert(s) to be instructed – Identifying any necessary 3rd party disclosure and if appropriate giving directions – Giving directions for any concurrent or proposed placement order proceedings – Ensuring compliance with the court's directions – If a FCMH is necessary, directing an advocates' meeting and Case Analysis if required – Directing filing of any threshold agreement, final evidence and Care Plan and responses to those documents for the IRH – Directing a Case Analysis for the IRH – Directing an advocates' meeting for the IRH – Listing (any FCMH) IRH, Final Hearing (including early Final Hearing) – Giving directions for special measures and/or interpreters • Issuing the Case Management Order

Stage 3 – Issues Resolution Hearing

Advocates' Meeting (including any litigants in person (FPR12.21E(5))	*Case Management Hearing*
No later than 7 days before the IRH	As directed by the court, in accordance with the timetable for the proceedings
• Review evidence and the positions of the parties • Identify the advocates' views of– – the remaining key issues and how the issues may be resolved or narrowed at the IRH including by the making of final orders	

Advocates' Meeting (including any litigants in person (FPR12.21E(5))	*Case Management Hearing*
– the further evidence which is required to be heard to enable the key issues to be resolved or narrowed at the IRH – the evidence that is relevant and the witnesses that are required at the final hearing – the need for a contested hearing and/or time for oral evidence to be given at the IRH • LA advocate to– – notify the court immediately of the outcome of the discussion at the meeting – file a draft Case Management Order with the court by 11 a.m. on the working day before the IRH	
	• Court identifies the key issue(s) (if any) to be determined and the extent to which those issues can be resolved or narrowed at the IRH • Court considers whether the IRH can be used as a final hearing • Court resolves or narrows the issues by hearing evidence • Court identifies the evidence to be heard on the issues which remain to be resolved at the final hearing • Court gives final case management directions including: – Any extension of the timetable for the proceedings which is necessary – Filing of the threshold agreement or a statement of facts/issues remaining to be determined – Filing of: • Final evidence & Care Plan • Case Analysis for Final Hearing (if required) • Witness templates • Skeleton arguments – Judicial reading list/reading time, including time estimate and an estimate for judgment writing time – Ensuring Compliance with PD27A (the Bundles Practice Direction) – Listing the Final Hearing • Court issues Case Management Order

Flexible powers of the court

2.1 Attention is drawn to the flexible powers of the court either following the issue of the application in that court, the transfer of the case to that court or at any other stage in the proceedings.

2.2 The court may give directions without a hearing including setting a date for the Final Hearing or a period within which the Final Hearing will take place. The steps, which the court will ordinarily take at the various stages of the proceedings provided for in the Public Law Outline, may be taken by the court at another stage in the proceedings if the circumstances of the case merit this approach.

2.3 The flexible powers of the court include the ability for the court to cancel or repeat a particular hearing. For example, if the issue on which the case turns can with reasonable practicability be crystallised and resolved by taking evidence at an IRH then such a flexible approach must be taken in accordance with the overriding objective and to secure compliance with section 1(2) of the 1989 Act and achieving the aim of resolving the proceedings within 26 weeks or the period for the time being specified by the court.

2.4 Where it is anticipated that oral evidence may be required at the CMH, FCMH or IRH, the court must be notified in accordance with Stages 2 and 3 of the Public Law Outline well in advance and directions sought for the conduct of the hearing.

2.5 It is expected that full case management will take place at the CMH. It follows that the parties must be prepared to deal with all relevant case management issues, as identified in Stage 2 of the Public Law Outline. A FCMH should only be directed where necessary and must not be regarded as a routine step in proceedings.

Compliance with Pre-proceedings Checklist

3.1 It is recognised that in a small minority of cases the circumstances are such that the safety and welfare of the child may be jeopardised if the start of proceedings is delayed until all of the documents appropriate to the case and referred to in the Pre-proceedings Checklist are available. The safety and welfare of the child should never be put in jeopardy because of lack of documentation. (Nothing in this Practice Direction affects an application for an emergency protection order under section 44 of the 1989 Act).

3.2 The court recognises that the preparation may need to be varied to suit the circumstances of the case. In cases where any of the Annex Documents required to be attached to the Application Form are not available at the time of issue of the application, the court will consider making directions on issue about when any missing documentation is to be filed. The expectation is that there must be a good reason why one or more of the documents are not available. Further directions relating to any missing documentation will also be made at the Case Management Hearing.

Allocation

4.1 The court considers the allocation of proceedings in accordance with the Allocation Order and whether transfer is appropriate in accordance with this Order and the Guidance issued by the President on Allocation and Gatekeeping. When proceedings are issued in the magistrates' court the justices' clerk or assistant justices' clerk (with responsibility for gatekeeping and allocation of proceedings) will discuss allocation and transfer with a district judge of the county court (with responsibility for allocation and gatekeeping of proceedings as provided for in the Guidance issued by the President on Allocation and Gatekeeping) and will, where appropriate, transfer the case.

The timetable for the child and the timetable for proceedings

5.1 The timetable for the proceedings–

(1) The court will draw up a timetable for the proceedings with a view to disposing of the application–

(a) without delay; and

(b) in any event with the aim of doing so within 26 weeks beginning with the day on which the application was issued.

(2) The court, when drawing up or revising a timetable under paragraph (1), will in particular have regard to–

(a) the impact which the timetable or any revised timetable would have on the welfare of the child to whom the application relates; and

(b) the impact which the timetable or any revised timetable would have on the duration and conduct of the proceedings.

5.2 The impact which the timetable for the proceedings, any revision or extension of that timetable would have on the welfare of the child to whom the application relates are matters to which the court is to have particular regard. The court will use the Timetable for the Child to assess the impact of these matters on the welfare of the child and to draw up and revise the timetable for the proceedings.

5.3 The 'Timetable for the Child' is the timetable set by the court which takes into account dates which are important to the child's welfare and development.

5.4 The timetable for the proceedings is set having particular regard to the Timetable for the Child and the Timetable for the Child needs to be reviewed regularly. Where adjustments are made to the Timetable for the Child, the timetable for the proceedings will have to be reviewed consistently with the aim of resolving the proceedings within 26 weeks or the period for the time being specified by the court.

5.5 Examples of the dates the court will record and take into account when setting the Timetable for the Child are the dates of–

(1) any formal review by the Local Authority of the case of a looked after child (within the meaning of section 22(1) of the 1989 Act);

(2) any significant educational steps, including the child taking up a place at a new school and, where applicable, any review by the Local Authority of a statement of the child's special educational needs;

(3) any health care steps, including assessment by a paediatrician or other specialist;

(4) any review of Local Authority plans for the child, including any plans for permanence through adoption, Special Guardianship or placement with parents or relatives;

(5) any change or proposed change of the child's placement; or

(6) any significant change in the child's social or family circumstances.

5.6 To identify the Timetable for the Child, the applicant is required to provide the information needed about the significant steps in the child's life in the Application Form and the social work statement and to update this information regularly taking into account information received from others involved in the child's life such as the parties, members of the child's family, the person who is caring for the child, the children's guardian and the child's key social worker.

5.7 Where more than one child is the subject of the proceedings, the court should consider and will set a Timetable for the Child for each child. The children may not all have the same timetable, and the court will consider the appropriate progress of the proceedings in relation to each child.

5.8 Where there are parallel care proceedings and criminal proceedings against a person connected with the child for a serious offence against the child, linked directions hearings should where practicable take place as the case progresses. The timing of the proceedings in a linked care and criminal case should appear in the Timetable for the Child. The aim of resolving the proceedings within 26 weeks applies unless a longer timetable has been set by the court in order to resolve the proceedings justly. In these proceedings, early disclosure and listing of hearings is necessary.

Extensions to the timetable for proceedings

6.1 The court is required to draw up a timetable for proceedings with a view to disposing of the application without delay and with the aim of doing so within 26 weeks. If proceedings can be resolved earlier, then they should be. A standard timetable and process is expected to be followed in respect of the giving of standard directions on issue and allocation and other matters which should be carried out by the court on issue, including setting and giving directions for the Case Management Hearing.

6.2 Having regard to the circumstances of the particular case, the court may consider that it is necessary to extend the time by which the proceedings are intended to be resolved beyond 26 weeks to enable the court to resolve the proceedings justly. When making this decision, the court is to take account of the guidance that extensions are not to be granted routinely and are to be seen as requiring specific justification. The decision and reason(s) for extending a case should be recorded in writing (in the Case Management Order) and orally stated in court, so that all parties are aware of the reasons for delay in the case. The Case Management Orders must contain a record of this information, as well as the impact of the court's decision on the welfare of the child.

6.3 The court may extend the period within which proceedings are intended to be resolved on its own initiative or on application. Applications for an extension should, wherever possible, only be made so that they are considered at any hearing for which a date has been fixed or for which a date is about to be fixed. Where a date for a hearing has been fixed, a party who wishes to make an application at that hearing but does not have sufficient time to file an application notice should as soon as possible inform the court (if possible in writing) and, if possible, the other parties of the nature of the application and the reason for it. The party should then make the application orally at the hearing.

6.4 If the court agrees an extension is necessary, the intention is that an initial extension to the time limit may be granted for up to eight weeks (or less if directed) in order to resolve the case justly, meaning that the maximum time limit for proceedings will be 34 weeks. If more time is necessary, in order to resolve the proceedings justly, a further extension of up to eight weeks may be agreed by the court. There is no limit on the number of extensions that may be granted in a particular case.

6.5 If the court considers that the timetable for the proceedings will require an extension beyond the next eight week period in order to resolve the proceedings justly, the Case Management Order should–

(1) state the reason(s) why it is necessary to have a further extension;
(2) fix the date of the next effective hearing (which might be in a period shorter than a further eight weeks); and
(3) indicate whether it is appropriate for the next application for an extension of the timetable to be considered on paper.

6.6 The expectation is that, subject to paragraph 6.5, extensions should be considered at a hearing and that a court will not approve proposals for the management of a case under FPR 12.15 where the consequence of those proposals is that the case is unlikely to be resolved within 26 weeks or other period for the time being allowed for resolution of the proceedings. In accordance with FPR 4.1(3)(e), the court may hold a hearing and receive evidence by telephone or by using any other method of direct oral communication. When deciding whether to extend the timetable, the court must have regard to the impact of any ensuing timetable revision on the welfare of the child.

Interpretation

7.1 In this Practice Direction–

'Allocation Proposal Form' is the proposal in the prescribed form referred to in any Guidance issued by the President from time to time on prescribed templates and orders;

'Care Plan' means a 'section 31A plan' referred to in section 31A of the 1989 Act;

'Case Analysis' means a written or, if there is insufficient time for a written, an oral outline of the case from the perspective of the child's best interests prepared by the children's guardian or Welsh family proceedings officer for the CMH or FCMH (where one is necessary) and IRH or as otherwise directed by the court, incorporating an analysis of the key issues that need to be resolved in the case including–

(a) a threshold analysis;
(b) a case management analysis, including an analysis of the timetable for the proceedings, an analysis of the Timetable for the Child and the evidence which any party proposes is necessary to resolve the issues;
(c) a parenting capacity analysis;
(d) a child impact analysis, including an analysis of the ascertainable wishes and feelings of the child and the impact on the welfare of the child of any application to adjourn a hearing or extend the timetable for the proceedings; and
(e) an early permanence analysis including an analysis of the proposed placements and contact framework;

'Case Management Order' is the prescribed form of order referred to in any Guidance issued by the President from time to time on prescribed templates and orders;

'Day' means 'business day';

'Experts Practice Directions' mean–

(a) Practice Direction 25A (Experts – Emergencies and Pre Proceedings Instructions);
(b) Practice Direction 25B (The Duties of An Expert, The Expert's Report and Arrangements For An Expert To Attend Court);
(c) Practice Direction 25C (Children's Proceedings – The Use Of Single Joint Experts and The Process Leading to An Expert Being Instructed or Expert Evidence Being Put Before the Court);
(d) Practice Direction 25E (Discussions Between Experts in Family Proceedings).

'Genogram' means a family tree, setting out in diagrammatic form the child's family and extended family members and their relationship with the child;

'Index of Checklist Documents' means a list of Checklist Documents referred to in the Public Law Outline Pre-Proceedings Checklist which is divided into two parts with Part A being the documents referred to in column 2, paragraph (a) of the Pre-Proceedings Checklist and Part B being those referred to in column 2, paragraph (b) of the Pre-proceedings Checklist;

'Letter Before Proceedings' means any letter from the Local Authority containing written notification to the parents and others with parental responsibility for the child of the Local Authority's plan to apply to court for a care or supervision order and any related subsequent correspondence confirming the Local Authority's position;

'Local Authority Case Summary' means a document prepared by the Local Authority legal representative for each case management hearing in the form referred to in any Guidance issued by the President from time to time on prescribed templates and orders;

'Parents' Response' means a document from either or both of the parents containing–

(a) in no more than two pages, the parents' response to the Threshold Statement, and

(b) the parents' placement proposals including the identity of all relatives and friends they propose be considered by the court;

'Section 7 report' means any report under section 7 of the 1989 Act;

'Section 37 report' means any report by the Local Authority to the court as a result of a direction under section 37 of the 1989 Act;

'Social Work Chronology' means a schedule containing–

(a) a succinct summary of the significant dates and events in the child's life in chronological order- a running record up to the issue of the proceedings;

(b) information under the following headings–

(i) serial number;

(ii) date;

(iii) event-detail;

(iv) witness or document reference (where applicable);

'Social Work Statement' means a statement prepared by the Local Authority limited to the following evidence–

Summary

(a) The order sought;

(b) Succinct summary of reasons with reference as appropriate to the Welfare Checklist;

Family

(c) Family members and relationships especially the primary carers and significant adults/other children;

(d) Genogram;

Threshold

(e) Precipitating events;

(f) Background circumstances;

(i) summary of children's services involvement cross-referenced to the chronology;

(ii) previous court orders and emergency steps;

(iii) previous assessments;

(g) Summary of significant harm and or likelihood of significant harm which the LA will seek to establish by evidence or concession;

Parenting capacity

(h) Assessment of child's needs;
(i) Assessment of parental capacity to meet needs;
(j) Analysis of why there is a gap between parental capacity and the child's needs;
(k) Assessment of other significant adults who may be carers;

Child impact

(l) Wishes and feelings of the child(ren);
(m) Timetable for the Child;
(n) Delay and timetable for the proceedings;

Early permanence and contact

(o) Parallel planning;
(p) Placement options;
(q) Contact framework;

Case Management

(r) Evidence and assessments necessary and outstanding;
(s) Case management proposals;

'Standard Directions on Issue and Allocation' means directions given by the court on issue and upon allocation and/or transfer in the prescribed form referred to in any Guidance issued by the President from time to time on prescribed templates and orders;

'Threshold Statement' means a written outline by the legal representative of the LA of the facts which the LA will seek to establish by evidence or concession to satisfy the threshold criteria under s 31(2) of the 1989 Act limited to no more than 2 pages;

'Welfare Checklist' means the list of matters which is set out in section 1(3) of the 1989 Act and to which the court is to have particular regard in accordance with section (1)(3) and (4).

Annex 2
Keeling schedule

Keeling schedule showing (in bold, using underlining to denote insertions and strikethrough to denote deletions) how FPR Part 12, Chapters 1 to 3 is modified for the pilot scheme set up by Practice Direction 3C (pilot scheme: care and supervision proceedings and other proceedings under u Part 4 of the Children Act 1989) and how the modified version differs from the existing (pre-pilot) version

This Keeling Schedule has been prepared by the Ministry of Justice. It is intended for illustrative purposes only to assist the reader of the Pilot Practice Direction 36C to understand the rule changes made in that Practice Direction for the purposes of the Pilot. While care has been taken in its preparation it may not be full and complete in every respect.

The Keeling Schedule does not add footnotes to pilot rules and footnotes to existing rules have not been updated.

PART 12
CHILDREN PROCEEDINGS AND PROCEEDINGS FOR APPLICATIONS IN ADOPTION, PLACEMENT AND RELATED PROCEEDINGS

Chapter 1
Interpretation and application of this Part

12.1 Application of this Part

(1) The rules in this Part apply to–

(a) emergency proceedings;
(b) private law proceedings;
(c) public law proceedings;
(d) proceedings relating to the exercise of the court's inherent jurisdiction (other than applications for the court's permission to start such proceedings);
(e) proceedings relating to child abduction and the recognition and enforcement of decisions relating to custody under the European Convention;
(f) proceedings relating to the Council Regulation or the 1996 Hague Convention in respect of children; and
(g) any other proceedings which may be referred to in a practice direction.

(Part 18 sets out the procedure for making an application for permission to bring proceedings.)

(Part 31 sets out the procedure for making applications for recognition and enforcement ofjudgments under the Council Regulation or the 1996 Hague Convention.)

(2) The rules in Chapter 7 of this Part also apply to family proceedings which are not within paragraph (1) but which otherwise relate wholly or mainly to the maintenance or upbringing of a minor.

12.2 Interpretation

In this Part–

'the 2006 Act' means the Childcare Act 2006[1]
'advocate' means a person exercising a right of audience as a representative of, or on behalf of, a party;
'care proceedings' means proceedings for a care order under section 31(1)(a) of the 1989 Act;
~~'Case Management Order' means an order in the form referred to in Practice Direction 12A which may contain such of the provisions listed in that practice direction as may be appropriate to the proceedings;~~
'Case Management Order' means an order in the form referred to in Practice Direction 12A or Pilot Practice Direction 12A;
'child assessment order' has the meaning assigned to it by section 43(2) of the 1989 Act;
'contact activity condition' has the meaning assigned to it by section 11C(2) of the 1989 Act;
'contact activity direction' has the meaning assigned to it by section 11A(3) of the 1989 Act;
'contribution order' has the meaning assigned to it by paragraph 23(2) of Schedule 2 to the 1989 Act;
'education supervision order' has the meaning assigned to it by section 36(2) of the 1989 Act;

'emergency proceedings' means proceedings for–

(a) the disclosure of information as to the whereabouts of a child under section 33 of the 1986 Act[2]

(b) an order authorising the taking charge of and delivery of a child under section 34 of the 1986 Act[3,4];

(c) an emergency protection order;

(d) an order under section 44(9)(b) of the 1989 Act varying a direction in an emergency protection order given under section 44(6) of that Act;

(e) an order under section 45(5) of the 1989 Act extending the period during which an emergency protection order is to have effect;

(f) an order under section 45(8)of the 1989 Act discharging an emergency protection order;

(g) an order under section 45(8A) of the 1989[4] Act varying or discharging an emergency protection order in so far as it imposes an exclusion requirement on a person who is not entitled to apply for the order to be discharged;

(h) an order under section 45(8B)of the 1989 Act[5] varying or discharging an emergency protection order in so far as it confers a power of arrest attached to an exclusion requirement;

(i) warrants under sections 48(9)and 102(1) of the 1989 Act and under section 79 of the 2006 Act[6]; or

(j) a recovery order under section 50 of the 1989 Act[7];

'emergency protection order' means an order under section 44 of the 1989 Act;

'enforcement order' has the meaning assigned to it by section 11J(2) of the 1989 Act;

'financial compensation order' means an order made under section 11O(2) of the 1989 Act;

'interim order' means an interim care order or an interim supervision order referred to in section 38(1) of the 1989 Act;

'Part 4 proceedings' means proceedings for—

(a) a care order except an interim care order, or the discharge of such an order under section 39(1) of the 1989 Act;

(b) an order giving permission to change a child's surname or remove a child from the United Kingdom under section 33(7) of the 1989 Act whle a care order is in force with respect to the child;

(c) a supervision order except an interim supervision order, the discharge or variation of such an order under section 39(2) of that Act, or the extension or further extension of such an order under paragraph 6(3) of Schedule 3 to that Act;

(d) an order making provision regarding contact under section 34(2) to (4) of the 1989 Act made at the same time as the making of a care order other than an interim care order or later or an order varying or discharging such an order under section 34(9) of that Act;

(e) an education supervision order, the extension of an education supervision order under paragraph 15(2) of Schedule 3 to the 1989 Act, or the discharge of such an order under paragraph 17(1) of Schedule 3 to that Act;

(f) an order under section 39(3) of the 1989 Act varying a supervision order in so far as it affects a person with whom the child is living but who is not entitled to apply for the order to be discharged; or

(g) the substitution of a supervision order for a care order under section 39(4) of the 1989 Act;

'private law proceedings' means proceedings for—

(a) a section 8 order except a residence order under section 8 of the 1989 Act relating to a child who is the subject of a care order;
(b) a parental responsibility order under sections 4(1)(c)[8], 4ZA(1)(c)[9] or 4A(1)(b) of the 1989 Act[10] or an order terminating parental responsibility under sections 4(2A), 4ZA(5) or 4A(3) of that Act;
(c) an order appointing a child's guardian under section 5(1) of the 1989 Act or an order terminating the appointment under section 6(7) of that Act;
(d) an order giving permission to change a child's surname or remove a child from the United Kingdom under sections 13(1) or 14C(3) of the 1989 Act;
(e) a special guardianship order except where that order relates to a child who is subject of a care order;
(f) an order varying or discharging such an order under section 14D of the 1989 Act[11];
(g) an enforcement order;
(h) a financial compensation order;
(i) an order under paragraph 9 of Schedule A1 to the 1989 Act following a breach of an enforcement order;
(j) an order under Part 2 of Schedule A1 to the 1989 Act revoking or amending an enforcement order; or
(k) an order that a warning notice be attached to a contact order;

'public law proceedings' means Part 4 proceedings and proceedings for—

(a) a residence order under section 8 of the 1989 Act relating to a child who is the subject of a care order;
(b) a special guardianship order relating to a child who is the subject of a care order;
(c) a secure accommodation order under section 25 of the 1989 Act[12];
(d) an interim care order, or the discharge of such an order under section 39(1) of the 1989 Act;
(e) an order giving permission to change a child's surname or remove a child from the United Kingdom under section 33(7) of the 1989 Act while an interim care order is in force with respect to the child;
(f) ~~a supervision order under section 31(1)(b)~~ an interim supervision order under section 38(1) of the 1989 Act[13], the discharge or variation of such an order under section 39(2) of that Act, or the extension or further extension of such an order under paragraph 6(3) of Schedule 3 to that Act;
(g) an order making provision regarding contact under section 34(2) to (4) of the 1989 Act made at the same time as the making of an interim care order or later or an order varying or discharging such an order under section 34(9) of that Act;
~~(h) an education supervision order, the extension of an education supervision order under paragraph 15(2) of Schedule 3 to the 1989 Act, or the discharge of such an order under paragraph17(1) of Schedule 3 to that Act[14]~~;
(i) an order varying directions made with an interim care order or interim supervision order under section 38(8)(b) of the 1989 Act;
(j) an order under section 39(3)of the 1989 Act varying ~~a supervision order~~ an interim supervision order in so far as it affects a person with whom the child is living but who is not entitled to apply for the order to be discharged;
(k) an order under section 39(3A)of the 1989[15] Act varying or discharging an interim care order in so far as it imposes an exclusion requirement on a person who is not entitled to apply for the order to be discharged;

(l) an order under section 39(3B)[16] of the 1989 Act varying or discharging an interim care order in so far as it confers a power of arrest attached to an exclusion requirement;

~~(m) the substitution of a supervision order for a care order under section 39(4) of the 1989 Act;~~

(n) a child assessment order, or the variation or discharge of such an order under section 43(12) of the 1989 Act;

(o) an order permitting the local authority to arrange for any child in its care to live outside England and Wales under paragraph 19(1) of Schedule 2 to the 1989 Act;

(p) a contribution order, or revocation of such an order under paragraph 23(8) of Schedule 2 to the 1989 Act;

(q) an appeal under paragraph 8(1)of Schedule 8 to the 1989 Act;

'special guardianship order' has the meaning assigned to it by section 14A(1) of the 1989 Act[17];

'supervision order' has the meaning assigned to it by section 31(11) of the 1989 Act;

'supervision proceedings' means proceedings for a supervision order under section 31(1)(b) of the 1989 Act;

'warning notice' means a notice attached to an order pursuant to section 8(2) of the Children and Adoption Act 2006.

(The 1980 Hague Convention, the 1996 Hague Convention, the Council Regulation, and the European Convention are defined in rule 2.3.)

1 2006 c.21.

2 Section 33 was amended by section 108(5) of and paragraph 62 of Schedule 13 to the Children Act 1989 and section 261(1) of and paragraph 124 of Schedule 27 to the Civil Partnership Act 2004.

3 Section 34 was amended by section 108(5) of and paragraphs 62 and 70 of Schedule 13 to the Children Act 1989 and article 12(3) of Children (Northern Ireland Consequential Amendments) Order 1995 (S.I. 1995/756).

4 Section 45(8A) was inserted by section 52 of and paragraph 4 of Schedule 6 to the Family Law Act 1996.

5 Section 45(8B) was inserted by section 52 of and paragraph 4 of Schedule 6 to the Family Law Act 1996.

6 Section 79 was amended by section 157 of and paragraphs 108 and 114(1) and (2) and (3)(b) of Schedule 14 to the Education and Inspections Act 2006 (c.40).

7 Section 50 was amended by section 261(1) of and paragraph 131 of Schedule 27 to the Civil Partnership Act 2004.

8 Section 4(1)(c) was amended by section 111(1) and (2) of the Adoption and Children Act 2002 and section 56 of and paragraphs 21(1) and (2) of Schedule 6 to the Welfare Reform Act 2009 (c.29).

9 Section 4ZA was inserted by section 56 of and paragraph 2 of Schedule 6 to the Human Fertilisation and Embryology Act 2008.

10 Section 4A(1)(b) was amended by section 75(1) and (2) of the Civil Partnership Act 2004.

11 Section 14D was inserted by section 115(1) of the Adoption and Children Act 2002.

12 Section 25 was amended by section 39 of and paragraphs 1 and 15 of Schedule 3 to the Children and Young Persons Act 2008 and section 24 of and paragraph 45 of Schedule 4 to the Access to Justice Act 1999.

13 Section 31(1)(b) was amended by sections 74 and 75 of and paragraphs 87 and 90 of Schedule 7 to the Criminal Justice and Court Services Act 2000 (c.43).

14 Paragraph 17(1) was amended by article 5(1) of and paragraphs 37(1) and (14)(a) of Schedule 2 to the Local Education Authorities and Children's Services Authorities (Intergration of Functions) Order 2010 (S.I. 2010/1158).

15 Section 39(3A) was inserted by section 52 of and paragraph 2 of Schedule 6 to the Family Law Act 1996.

16 Section 39(3B) was inserted by section 56 of and paragraph 2 of Schedule to the Family Law Act 1996.

17 Section 14A(1) was inserted by section 115(1) of the Adoption and Children Act 2002.

Chapter 2
General rules

12.3 Who the parties are

(1) In relation to the proceedings set out in column 1 of the following table, column 2 sets out who may make the application and column 3 sets out who the respondents to those proceedings will be.

Proceedings for	*Applicants*	*Respondents*
A parental responsibility order (section 4(1)(c), 4ZA(1)(c), or section 4A(1)(b) of the 1989 Act).	The child's father; the step parent; or the child's parent (being a woman who is a parent by virtue of section 43 of the Human Fertilisation and Embryology Act 2008 and who is not a person to whom section 1(3) of the Family Law Reform Act 1987[16] applies) (sections 4(1)(c), 4ZA(1)(c) and 4A(1)(b) of the 1989 Act).	Every person whom the applicant believes to have parental responsibility for the child; where the child is the subject of a care order, every person whom the applicant believes to have had parental responsibility immediately prior to the making of the care order; in the case of an application to extend, vary or discharge an order, the parties to the proceedings leading to the order which it is sought to have extended, varied or discharged; in the case of specified proceedings, the child.
An order terminating a parental responsibility order or agreement (section 4(2A), 4ZA(5) or section 4A(3) of the 1989 Act[17].	Any person who has parental responsibility for the child; or with the court's permission, the child (section 4(3), 4ZA(6) and section 4A(3) of the 1989 Act).	As above.
An order appointing a guardian (section 5(1) of the 1989 Act[18]).	An individual who wishes to be appointed as guardian (section 5(1) of the 1989 Act).	As above.
An order terminating the appointment of a guardian (section 6(7) of the 1989 Act).	Any person who has parental responsibility for the child; or with the court's permission, the child (section 6(7) of the 1989 Act).	As above.

Proceedings for	*Applicants*	*Respondents*
A section 8 order.	Any person who is entitled to apply for a section 8 order with respect to the child (section 10(4) to (7) of the 1989 Act[19]); or with the court's permission, any person (section 10(2)(b) of the 1989 Act).	As above.
An enforcement order (section 11J of the 1989 Act[20]).	A person who is, for the purposes of the contact order, a person with whom the child concerned lives or is to live; any person whose contact with the child concerned is provided for in the contact order; any individual subject to a condition under section 11(7)(b) of the 1989 Act or a contact activity condition imposed by a contact order; or with the court's permission, the child (section 11J(5) of the 1989 Act).	The person the applicant alleges has failed to comply with the contact order.
A financial compensation order (section 11O of the 1989 Act).	Any person who is, for the purposes of the contact order, a person with whom the child concerned lives or is to live; any person whose contact with the child concerned is provided for in the contact order; any individual subject to a condition under section 11(7)(b) of the 1989 Act or a contact activity condition imposed by a contact order; or with the court's permission, the child (section 11O(6) of the 1989 Act).	The person the applicant alleges has failed to comply with the contact order.
An order permitting the child's name to be changed or the removal of the child from the United Kingdom (section 13(1), 14C(3) or 33(7) of the 1989 Act).	Any person (section 13(1), 14C(3), 33(7) of the 1989 Act).	As for a parental responsibility order.

Proceedings for	*Applicants*	*Respondents*
A special guardianship order (section 14A of the 1989 Act).	Any guardian of the child; any individual in whose favour a residence order is in force with respect to the child; any individual listed in subsection (5)(b) or (c) of section 10 (as read with subsection (10) of that section) of the 1989 Act; a local authority foster parent with whom the child has lived for a period of at least one year immediately preceding the application; or any person with the court's permission (section 14A(3) of the 1989 Act) (more than one such individual can apply jointly (section 14A(3) and (5) of that Act)).	As above, and if a care order is in force with respect to the child, the child.
Variation or discharge of a special guardianship order (section 14D of the 1989 Act[21]).	The special guardian (or any of them, if there is more than one); any individual in whose favour a residence order is in force with respect to the child; the local authority designated in a care order with respect to the child; any individual within section 14D(1)(d) of the 1989 Act who has parental responsibility for the child; the child, any parent or guardian of the child and any step-parent of the child who has acquired, and has not lost, parental responsibility by virtue of section 4A of that Act with the court's permission; or any individual within section 14D(1)(d) of that Act who immediately before the making of the special guardianship order had, but no longer has, parental responsibility for the child with the court's permission.	As above.

Proceedings for	*Applicants*	*Respondents*
A secure accommodation order (section 25 section of the 1989 Act).	The local authority which is looking after the child; or the Health Authority, Secretary of State, National Health Service Commissioning Board, clinical commissioning group, National Health Service Trust established under section 25 of the National Health Service Act 2006[22] or section 18(1) of the National Health Service (Wales) Act 2006[23], National Health Service Foundation Trust or any local authority providing or arranging accommodation for the child (unless the child is looked after by a local authority).	As above.
A care or supervision order (section 31 of the 1989 Act).	Any local authority; the National Society for the Prevention of Cruelty to Children and any of its officers (section 31(1) of the 1989 Act);or any authorised person.	As above.
An order varying directions made with an interim care or interim supervision order (section 38(8)(b) of the 1989 Act).	The parties to proceedings in which directions are given under section 38(6) of the 1989 Act; or any person named in such a direction.	As above.
An order discharging a care order (section 39(1) of the 1989 Act).	Any person who has parental responsibility for the child; the child; or the local authority designated by the order (section 39(1) of the 1989 Act).	As above.

Proceedings for	*Applicants*	*Respondents*
An order varying or discharging an interim care order in so far as it imposes an exclusion requirement (section 39(3A) of the 1989 Act).	A person to whom the exclusion requirement in the interim care order applies who is not entitled to apply for the order to be discharged (section 39(3A) of the 1989 Act).	As above.
An order varying or discharging an interim care order in so far as it confers a power of arrest attached to an exclusion requirement (section 39(3B) of the 1989 Act).	Any person entitled to apply for the discharge of the interim care order in so far as it imposes the exclusion requirement (section 39(3B) of the 1989 Act).	As above.
An order substituting a supervision order for a care order (section 39(4) of the 1989 Act).	Any person entitled to apply for a care order to be discharged under section 39(1) (section 39(4) of the 1989 Act).	As above.
A child assessment order (section 43(1) of the 1989 Act).	Any local authority; the National Society for the Prevention of Cruelty to Children and any of its officers; or any person authorised by order of the Secretary of State to bring the proceedings and any officer of a body who is so authorised (section 43(1) and (13) of the 1989 Act).	As above.

Proceedings for	*Applicants*	*Respondents*
An order varying or discharging a child assessment order (section 43(12) of the 1989 Act).	The applicant for an order that has been made under section 43(1) of the 1989 Act; or the persons referred to in section 43(11) of the 1989 Act (section 43(12) of that Act).	As above.
An emergency protection order (section 44(1) of the 1989 Act).	Any person (section 44(1) of the 1989 Act).	As for a parental responsibility order.
An order extending the period during which an emergency protection order is to have effect (section 45(4) of the 1989 Act).	Any person who— has parental responsibility for a child as the result of an emergency protection order; and is entitled to apply for a care order with respect to the child (section 45(4) of the 1989 Act).	As above.
An order discharging an emergency protection order (section 45(8) of the 1989 Act).	The child; a parent of the child; any person who is not a parent of the child but who has parental responsibility for the child; or any person with whom the child was living before the making of the emergency protection order (section 45(8) of the 1989 Act).	As above.
An order varying or discharging an emergency protection order in so far as it imposes the exclusion requirement (section 45(8A) of the 1989 Act).	A person to whom the exclusion requirement in the emergency protection order applies who is not entitled to apply for the emergency protection order to be discharged (section 45(8A) of the 1989 Act).	As above.

Proceedings for	*Applicants*	*Respondents*
An order varying or discharging an emergency protection order in so far as it confers a power of arrest attached to an exclusion requirement (section 45(8B) of the 1989 Act).	Any person entitled to apply for the discharge of the emergency protection order in so far as it imposes the exclusion requirement (section 45(8B) of the 1989 Act).	As above.
An emergency protection order by the police (section 46(7) of the 1989 Act).	The officer designated for the purposes of section 46(3)(e) of the 1989 Act (section 46(7) of the 1989 Act).	As above.
A warrant authorising a constable to assist in exercise of certain powers to search for children and inspect premises (section 48 of the 1989 Act).	Any person attempting to exercise powers under an emergency protection order who has been or is likely to be prevented from doing so by being refused entry to the premises concerned or refused access to the child concerned (section 48(9) of the 1989 Act).	As above.
A warrant authorising a constable to assist in exercise of certain powers to search for children and inspect premises (section 102 of the 1989 Act).	Any person attempting to exercise powers under the enactments mentioned in section 102(6) of the 1989 Act who has been or is likely to be prevented from doing so by being refused entry to the premises concerned or refused access to the child concerned (section 102(1) of that Act).	As above.
An order revoking an enforcement order (paragraph 4 of Schedule A1 to the 1989 Act).	The person subject to the enforcement order.	The person who was the applicant for the enforcement order; and, where the child was a party to the proceedings in which the enforcement order was made, the child.

Proceedings for	*Applicants*	*Respondents*
An order amending an enforcement order (paragraphs 5 to 7 of Schedule A1 to the 1989 Act).	The person subject to the enforcement order.	The person who was the applicant for the enforcement order. (Rule 12.33 makes provision about applications under paragraph 5 of Schedule A1 to the 1989 Act.)
An order following breach of an enforcement order (paragraph 9 of Schedule A1 to the 1989 Act).	Any person who is, for the purposes of the contact order, the person with whom the child lives or is to live; any person whose contact with the child concerned is provided for in the contact order; any individual subject to a condition under section 11(7)(b) of the 1989 Act or a contact activity condition imposed by a contact order; or with the court's permission, the child (paragraph 9 of Schedule A1 to the 1989 Act).	The person the applicant alleges has failed to comply with the unpaid work requirement imposed by an enforcement order; and where the child was a party to the proceedings in which the enforcement order was made, the child.
An order permitting the local authority to arrange for any child in its care to live outside England and Wales (Schedule 2, paragraph 19(1), to the 1989 Act).	The local authority (Schedule 2, paragraph 19(1), to the 1989 Act).	As for a parental responsibility order.
A contribution order (Schedule 2, paragraph 23(1), to the 1989 Act).	The local authority (Schedule 2, paragraph 23(1), to the 1989 Act).	As above and the contributor.

Proceedings for	*Applicants*	*Respondents*
An order revoking a contribution order (Schedule 2, paragraph 23(8), to the 1989 Act).	The contributor; or the local authority.	As above.
An order relating to contact with the child in care and any named person (section 34(2) of the 1989 Act) or permitting the local authority to refuse contact (section 34(4) of that Act).	The local authority; or the child (section 34(2) or 34(4) of the 1989 Act).	As above; and the person whose contact with the child is the subject of the application.
An order relating to contact with the child in care (section 34(3) of the 1989 Act).	The child's parents; any guardian or special guardian of the child; any person who by virtue of section 4A of the 1989 Act has parental responsibility for the child; a person in whose favour there was a residence order in force with respect to the child immediately before the care order was made; a person who by virtue of an order made in the exercise of the High Court's inherent jurisdiction with respect to children had care of the child immediately before the care order was made (section 34(3)(a) of the 1989 Act); or with the court's permission, any person (section 34(3)(b) of that Act).	As above; and the person whose contact with the child is the subject of the application.

Proceedings for	*Applicants*	*Respondents*
An order varying or discharging an order for contact with a child in care under section 34 (section 34((9) of the 1989 Act).	The local authority; the child; or any person named in the order (section 34(9) of the 1989 Act).	As above; and the person whose contact with the child is the subject of the application.
An education supervision order (section 36 of the 1989 Act).	Any local authority (section 36(1) of the 1989 Act).	As above; and the child.
An order varying or discharging a supervision order (section 39(2) of the 1989 Act).	Any person who has parental responsibility for the child; the child; or the supervisor (section 39(2) of the 1989 Act).	As above; and the supervisor.
An order varying a supervision order in so far as it affects the person with whom the child is living (section 39(3) of the 1989 Act).	The person with whom the child is living who is not entitled to apply for the order to be discharged (section 39(3) of the 1989 Act).	As above; and the supervisor.
An order varying a direction under section 44(6) of the 1989 Act in an emergency protection order (section 44(9)(b) of that Act).	The parties to the application for the emergency protection order in respect of which it is sought to vary the directions; the children's guardian; the local authority in whose area the child is ordinarily resident; or any person who is named in the directions.	As above, and the parties to the application for the order in respect of which it is sought to vary the directions; any person who was caring for the child prior to the making of the order; and any person whose contact with the child is affected by the direction which it is sought to have varied.

Proceedings for	*Applicants*	*Respondents*
A recovery order (section 50 of the 1989 Act).	Any person who has parental responsibility for the child by virtue of a care order or an emergency protection order; or where the child is in police protection the officer designated for the purposes of section 46(3)(e) of the 1989 Act (section 50(4) of the 1989 Act).	As above; and the person whom the applicant alleges to have effected or to have been or to be responsible for the taking or keeping of the child.
An order discharging an education supervision order (Schedule 3, paragraph 17(1), to the 1989 Act).	The child concerned; a parent of the child; or the local authority concerned (Schedule 3, paragraph 17(1), to the 1989 Act).	As above; and the local authority concerned; and the child.
An order extending an education supervision order (Schedule 3, paragraph, 15(2), to the 1989 Act).	The local authority in whose favour the education supervision order was made (Schedule 3, paragraph 15(2), to the 1989 Act).	As above; and the child.
An appeal under paragraph (8) of Schedule 8 to the 1989 Act.	A person aggrieved by the matters listed in paragraph 8(1) of Schedule 8 to the 1989 Act.	The appropriate local authority.
An order for the disclosure of information as to the whereabouts of a child under section 33 of the 1986 Act.	Any person with a legitimate interest in proceedings for an order under Part 1 of the 1986 Act; or a person who has registered an order made elsewhere in the United Kingdom or a specified dependent territory.	Any person alleged to have information as to the whereabouts of the child.
An order authorising the taking charge of and delivery of a child under section 34 of the 1986 Act.	The person to whom the child is to be given up under section 34(1) of the 1986 Act.	As above; and the person who is required to give up the child in accordance with section 34(1) of the 1986 Act.

Proceedings for	*Applicants*	*Respondents*
An order relating to the exercise of the court's inherent jurisdiction (including wardship proceedings).	A local authority (with the court's permission); any person with a genuine interest in or relation to the child; or the child (wardship proceedings only).	The parent or guardian of the child; any other person who has an interest in or relationship to the child; and the child (wardship proceedings only and with the court's permission as described at rule 12.37).
A warrant under section 79 of the 2006 Act authorising any constable to assist Her Majesty's Chief Inspector for Education, Children's Services and Skills in the exercise of powers conferred on him by section 77 of the 2006 Act.	Her Majesty's Chief Inspector for Education, Children's Services and Skills.	Any person preventing or likely to prevent Her Majesty's Chief Inspector for Education, Children's Services and Skills from exercising powers conferred on him by section 77 of the 2006 Act.
An order in respect of a child under the 1980 Hague Convention.	Any person, institution or body who claims that a child has been removed or retained in breach of rights of custody or claims that there has been a breach of rights of access in relation to the child.	The person alleged to have brought the child into the United Kingdom; the person with whom the child is alleged to be; any parent or guardian of the child who is within the United Kingdom and is not otherwise a party; any person in whose favour a decision relating to custody has been made if that person is not otherwise a party; and any other person who appears to the court to have sufficient interest in the welfare of the child.

Proceedings for	*Applicants*	*Respondents*
An order concerning the recognition and enforcement of decisions relating to custody under the European Convention.	Any person who has a court order giving that person rights of custody in relation to the child.	As above.
An application for the High Court to request transfer of jurisdiction under Article 15 of the Council Regulation or Article 9 of the 1996 Hague Convention (rule 12.65).	Any person with sufficient interest in the welfare of the child and who would be entitled to make a proposed application in relation to that child, or who intends to seek the permission of the court to make such application if the transfer is agreed.	As directed by the court in accordance with rule 12.65.
An application under rule 12.71 for a declaration as to the existence, or extent, of parental responsibility under Article 16 of the 1996 Convention.	Any interested person including a person who holds, or claims to hold, parental responsibility for the child under the law of another State which subsists in accordance with Article 16 of the 1996 Hague Convention following the child becoming habitually resident in a territorial unit of the United Kingdom.	Every person whom the applicant believes to have parental responsibility for the child; any person whom the applicant believes to hold parental responsibility for the child under the law of another State which subsists in accordance with Article 16 of the 1996 Hague Convention following the child becoming habitually resident in a territorial unit of the United Kingdom; and where the child is the subject of a care order, every person whom the applicant believes to have had parental responsibility immediately prior to the making of the care order.

Proceedings for	*Applicants*	*Respondents*
A warning notice.	The person who is, for the purposes of the contact order, the person with whom the child concerned lives or is to live; the person whose contact with the child concerned is provided for in the contact order; any individual subject to a condition under section 11(7)(b) of the 1989 Act or a contact activity condition imposed by the contact order; or with the court's permission, the child.	Any person who was a party to the proceedings in which the contact order was made. (Rule 12.33 makes provision about applications for warning notices).

(2) The court will direct that a person with parental responsibility be made a party to proceedings where that person requests to be one.

(3) Subject to rule 16.2, the court may at any time direct that—

(a) any person or body be made a party to proceedings; or
(b) a party be removed.

(4) If the court makes a direction for the addition or removal of a party under this rule, it may give consequential directions about—

(a) the service of a copy of the application form or other relevant documents on the new party;
(b) the management of the proceedings.

(5) In this rule–

'a local authority foster parent' has the meaning assigned to it by section 23(3) of the 1989 Act; and

'care home', 'independent hospital', 'local authority' and 'clinical commissioning group' have the meanings assigned to them by section 105 of the 1989 Act.

(Part 16 contains the rules relating to the representation of children.)

16 Section 1(3) was inserted by section 56 of and paragraphs 24(1) and (2) of Schedule 6 to the Human Fertilisation and Embryology Act 2008.

17 Section 4A(3) was inserted by section 112 of the Adoption and Children Act 2002.

18 Section 5(1) was amended by section 115(2), and (4)(a)(i) and (ii) of the Adoption and Children Act 2002.

19 Section 10(4) was amended by section 139(1) of and paragraphs 54, 56(a) and (b) of Schedule 3 to the Adoption and Children Act 2002. Section 10(5) was inserted by section 77 of the Civil Partnership Act 2004. Section 10(5A) was inserted by section 139(1) and paragraphs 54 and 56(c) of Schedule 3 to the Adoption and Children Act 2002. Section 10(5B) was inserted by section 36 of the Children and Young Persons Act 2008. Section 10(7A) was inserted by section 139(1) of and paragraphs 54 and 56(d) of Schedule 3 to the Adoption and Children Act 2002.

20 Section 11J was inserted by section 4(1) of the Children and Adoption Act 2006 (c.20).

21 Section 14D was inserted by section 115(1) of the Adoption and Children Act 2002.

22 2006 c.4.

23 2006 c.42.

12.4 Notice of proceedings to person with foreign parental responsibility

(1) This rule applies where a child is subject to proceedings to which this Part applies and—

(a) a person holds or is believed to hold parental responsibility for the child under the law of another State which subsists in accordance with Article 16 of the 1996 Hague Convention following the child becoming habitually resident in a territorial unit of the United Kingdom; and
(b) that person is not otherwise required to be joined as a respondent under rule 12.3.

(2) The applicant shall give notice of the proceedings to any person to whom the applicant believes paragraph (1) applies in any case in which a person whom the applicant believed to have parental responsibility under the 1989 Act would be a respondent to those proceedings in accordance with rule 12.3.

(3) The applicant and every respondent to the proceedings shall provide such details as they possess as to the identity and whereabouts of any person they believe to hold parental responsibility for the child in accordance with paragraph (1) to the court officer, upon making, or responding to the application as appropriate.

(4) Where the existence of a person who is believed to have parental responsibility for the child in accordance with paragraph (1) only becomes apparent to a party at a later date during the proceedings, that party must notify the court officer of those details at the earliest opportunity.

(5) Where a person to whom paragraph (1) applies receives notice of proceedings, that person may apply to the court to be joined as a party using the Part 18 procedure.

12.5 What the court will do when the application has been issued
When the proceedings have been issued the court will consider—

(a) setting a date for—
  (i) a directions appointment;
  (ii) in private law proceedings, a First Hearing Dispute Resolution Appointment;
  (iii) ~~in care and supervisionproceedings and in so far as practicable other public law proceedings, the First Appointment~~ in Part 4 proceedings, the Case Management Hearing; ~~or~~
  (iiiA) in so far as practicable in public law proceedings other than Part 4 proceedings, the First Appointment; or
  (iv) the hearing of the application or an application for an interim order,

and if the court sets a date it will do so in accordance with rule 12.13 and Practice Directions 12A and 12B and Pilot Practice Direction 12A;

(b) giving any of the directions listed in rule 12.12 or, where Chapter 6, section 1 applies, rule 12.48; and
(c) doing anything else which is set out in Practice Directions 12A or 12B, Pilot Practice Direction 12A or any other practice direction.

(Pilot Practice Direction 12A sets out the details relating to the Case Management Hearing and Practice Directions 12A and 12B supplementing this Part set out details relating to the First Hearing Dispute Resolution Appointment and the First Appointment.)

12.6 Children's guardian, solicitor and reports under section 7 of the 1989 Act

As soon as practicable after the issue of proceedings or the transfer of the proceedings to the court, the court will—

(a) in specified proceedings, appoint a children's guardian under rule 16.3(1) unless—
  (i) such an appointment has already been made by the court which made the transfer and is subsisting; or
  (ii) the court considers that such an appointment is not necessary to safeguard the interests of the child;

(b) where section 41(3) of the 1989 Act applies, consider whether a solicitor should be appointed to represent the child, and if so, appoint a solicitor accordingly;

(c) consider whether to ask an officer of the service or a Welsh family proceedings officer for advice relating to the welfare of the child;

(d) consider whether a report relating to the welfare of the child is required, and if so, request such a report in accordance with section 7 of the 1989 Act.

(Part 16 sets out the rules relating to representation of children.)

12.7 What a court officer will do

(1) As soon as practicable after the issue of proceedings the court officer will return to the applicant the copies of the application together with the forms referred to in Practice Direction 5A.

(2) As soon as practicable after the issue of proceedings or the transfer of proceedings to the court or at any other stage in the proceedings the court officer will—

(a) give notice of any hearing set by the court to the applicant; and

(b) do anything else set out in Practice Directions 12A or 12B, Pilot Practice Direction 12A or any other practice direction.

12.8 Service of the application

The applicant will serve—

(a) the application together with the documents referred to in Practice Direction 12C on the persons referred to and within the time specified in that Practice Direction; and

(b) notice of any hearing set by the court on the persons referred to in Practice Direction 12C at the same time as serving the application.

(Practice Direction 12C (Service of Application in Children Proceedings) provides that in Part 4 Proceedings the minimum number of days prior to the Case Management Hearing for service of the application and accompanying documents is 7 days. The Court has discretion to extend or shorten this time (see rule 4.1(3)(a))

12.9 Request for transfer from magistrates' court to county court or to another magistrates' court

(1) In accordance with the Allocation Order, a magistrates' court may order proceedings before the court (or any part of them) to be transferred to another magistrates' court or to a county court.

(2) Where any request to transfer proceedings to another magistrates' court or to a county court is refused, the court officer will send a copy of the written record of the reasons for refusing the transfer to the parties.

12.10 Procedure following refusal of magistrates' court to order transfer

(1) Where a request under rule 12.9 to transfer proceedings to a county court in accordance with the provisions of the Allocation Order is refused, a party to the proceedings may apply to a county court for an order transferring proceedings from the magistrates' court.

(2) Such an application must be made in accordance with Part 18 and the Allocation Order.

12.11 Transfer of proceedings from one court to another court

Where proceedings are transferred from one court to another court in accordance with the provisions of the Allocation Order, the court officer from the transferring court will notify the parties of any order transferring the proceedings.

12.12 Directions

(1) This rule does not apply to proceedings under Chapter 6 of this Part.

(2) At any stage in the proceedings, the court may give directions about the conduct of the proceedings including–

(a) the management of the case;
(b) the timetable for steps to be taken between the giving of directions and the final hearing;
(c) the joining of a child or other person as a party to the proceedings in accordance with rules 12.3(2) and (3);
(d) the attendance of the child;
(e) the appointment of a children's guardian or of a solicitor under section 41(3) of the 1989 Act;
(f) the appointment of a litigation friend;
(g) the service of documents;
(h) the filing of evidence including experts' reports; and
(i) the exercise by an officer of the Service, Welsh family proceedings officer or local authority officer of any duty referred to in rule 16.38(1)

(3) Paragraph (4) applies where–

(a) an officer of the Service or a Welsh family proceedings officer has filed a report or a risk assessment as a result of exercising a duty referred to in rule 16.38(1)(a); or
(b) a local authority officer has filed a report as a result of exercising a duty referred to in rule 16.38(1)(b).

(4) The court may—

(a) give directions setting a date for a hearing at which that report or risk assessment will be considered; and
(b) direct that the officer who prepared the report or risk assessment attend any such hearing.

(5) The court may exercise the powers in paragraphs (2) and (4) on an application or of its own initiative.

(6) Where the court proposes to exercise its powers of its own initiative the procedure set out in rule 4.3(2) to (6) applies.

(7) Directions of a court which are still in force immediately prior to the transfer of proceedings to another court will continue to apply following the transfer subject to—

(a) any changes of terminology which are required to apply those directions to the court to which the proceedings are transferred; and
(b) any variation or revocation of the direction.

(8) The court or court officer will–

(a) take a note of the giving, variation or revocation of a direction under this rule; and
(b) as soon as practicable serve a copy of the note on every party.

(Rule 12.48 provides for directions in proceedings under the 1980 Hague Convention and the European Convention.)

12.13 Setting dates for hearings and setting or confirming the timetable and date for the final hearing

(1) At the—

(a) transfer to a court of proceedings;
(b) postponement or adjournment of any hearing; or
(c) conclusion of any hearing at which the proceedings are not finally determined,

the court will set a date for the proceedings to come before the court again for the purposes of giving directions or for such other purposes as the court directs.

(2) At any hearing the court may–

(a) confirm a date for the final hearing or the week within which the final hearing is to begin (where a date or period for the final hearing has already been set);
(b) set a timetable for the final hearing unless a timetable has already been fixed, or the court considers that it would be inappropriate to do so; or
(c) set a date for the final hearing or a period within which the final hearing of the application is to take place.

(3) The court officer will notify the parties of—

(a) the date of a hearing fixed in accordance with paragraph (1);
(b) the timetable for the final hearing; and
(c) the date of the final hearing or the period in which it will take place.

(4) Where the date referred to in paragraph (1) is set at the transfer of proceedings, the date will be as soon as possible after the transfer.

(5) The requirement in paragraph (1) to set a date for the proceedings to come before the court again is satisfied by the court setting or confirming a date for the final hearing.

12.14 Attendance at hearings

(1) This rule does not apply to proceedings under Chapter 6 of this Part except for proceedings for a declaration under rule 12.71.

(2) Unless the court directs otherwise and subject to paragraph (3), the persons who must attend a hearing are–

(a) any party to the proceedings;
(b) any litigation friend for any party or legal representative instructed to act on that party's behalf; and

(c) any other person directed by the court or required by Practice Directions 12A or 12B or any other practice direction to attend.

(3) Proceedings or any part of them will take place in the absence of a child who is a party to the proceedings if–

(a) the court considers it in the interests of the child, having regard to the matters to be discussed or the evidence likely to be given; and
(b) the child is represented by a children's guardian or solicitor.

(4) When considering the interests of the child under paragraph (3) the court will give—

(a) the children's guardian;
(b) the solicitor for the child; and
(c) the child, if of sufficient understanding,

an opportunity to make representations.

(5) Subject to paragraph (6), where at the time and place appointed for a hearing, the applicant appears but one or more of the respondents do not, the court may proceed with the hearing.

(6) The court will not begin to hear an application in the absence of a respondent unless the court is satisfied that–

(a) the respondent received reasonable notice of the date of the hearing; or
(b) the circumstances of the case justify proceeding with the hearing.

(7) Where, at the time and place appointed for a hearing one or more of the respondents appear but the applicant does not, the court may—

(a) refuse the application; or
(b) if sufficient evidence has previously been received, proceed in the absence of the applicant.

(8) Where at the time and place appointed for a hearing neither the applicant nor any respondent appears, the court may refuse the application.

(9) Paragraphs (5) to (8) do not apply to a hearing where the court—

(a) is considering—
 (i) whether to make a contact activity direction or to attach a contact activity condition to a contact order; or
 (ii) an application for a financial compensation order, an enforcement order or an order under paragraph 9 of Schedule A1 to the 1989 Act following a breach of an enforcement order; and
(b) has yet to obtain sufficient evidence from, or in relation to, the person who may be the subject of the direction, condition or order to enable it to determine the matter.

(10) Nothing in this rule affects the provisions of Article 18 of the Council Regulation in cases to which that provision applies.

(The Council Regulation makes provision in Article 18 for the court to stay proceedings where the respondent is habitually resident in another Member State of the European Union and has not been adequately served with the proceedings as required by that provision.)

12.15 Steps taken by the parties

If—

(a) the parties or any children's guardian agree proposals for the management of the proceedings (including a proposed date for the final hearing or a period within which the final hearing is to take place); and
(b) the court considers that the proposals are suitable,

it may approve them without a hearing and give directions in the terms proposed.

12.16 Applications without notice

(1) This rule applies to—

(a) proceedings for a section 8 order;
(b) emergency proceedings; and
(c) proceedings relating to the exercise of the court's inherent jurisdiction (other than an application for the court's permission to start such proceedings and proceedings for collection, location and passport orders where Chapter 6 applies).

(2) An application in proceedings referred to in paragraph (1) may, in the High Court or a county court, be made without notice in which case the applicant must file the application—

(a) where the application is made by telephone, the next business day after the making of the application; or
(b) in any other case, at the time when the application is made.

(3) An application in proceedings referred to in paragraph (1)(a) or (b) may, in a magistrates' court, be made with the permission of the court, without notice, in which case the applicant must file the application at the time when the application is made or as directed by the court.

(4) Where—

(a) a section 8 order;
(b) an emergency protection order;
(c) an order for the disclosure of information as to the whereabouts of a child under section 33 of the 1986 Act; or
(d) an order authorising the taking charge of and delivery of a child under section 34 of the 1986 Act,

is made without notice, the applicant must serve a copy of the application on each respondent within 48 hours after the order is made.

(5) Within 48 hours after the making of an order without notice, the applicant must serve a copy of the order on–

(a) the parties, unless the court directs otherwise;
(b) any person who has actual care of the child or who had such care immediately prior to the making of the order; and
(c) in the case of an emergency protection order and a recovery order, the local authority in whose area the child lives or is found.

(6) Where the court refuses to make an order on an application without notice it may direct that the application is made on notice in which case the application will proceed in accordance with rules 12.3 to 12.15.

(7) Where the hearing takes place outside the hours during which the court office is normally open, the court or court officer will take a note of the proceedings.

(Practice Direction 12E (Urgent Business) provides further details of the procedure for out of hours applications. See also Practice Direction 12D (Inherent Jurisdiction (including Wardship Proceedings).)

(Rule 12.47 provides for without-notice applications in proceedings under Chapter 6, section 1 of this Part, (proceedings under the 1980 Hague Convention and the European Convention).)

12.17 Investigation under section 37 of the 1989 Act

(1) This rule applies where a direction is given to an appropriate authority by the court under section 37(1) of the 1989 Act.

(2) On giving the direction the court may adjourn the proceedings.

(3) As soon as practicable after the direction is given the court will record the direction.

(4) As soon as practicable after the direction is given the court officer will—

(a) serve the direction on–
 (i) the parties to the proceedings in which the direction is given; and
 (ii) the appropriate authority where it is not a party;
(b) serve any documentary evidence directed by the court on the appropriate authority.

(5) Where a local authority informs the court of any of the matters set out in section 37(3)(a) to (c) of the 1989 Act it will do so in writing.

(6) Unless the court directs otherwise, the court officer will serve a copy of any report to the court under section 37 of the 1989 Act on the parties.

(Section 37 of the 1989 Act refers to the appropriate authority and section 37(5) of that Act sets out which authority should be named in a particular case.)

12.18 Disclosure of a report under section 14A(8) or (9) of the 1989 Act

(1) In proceedings for a special guardianship order, the local authority must file the report under section 14A(8) or (9) of the 1989 Act[24] within the timetable fixed by the court.

(2) The court will consider whether to give a direction that the report under section 14A(8) or (9) of the 1989 Act be disclosed to each party to the proceedings.

(3) Before giving a direction for the report to be disclosed, the court must consider whether any information should be deleted from the report.

(4) The court may direct that the report must not be disclosed to a party.

(5) The court officer must serve a copy of the report in accordance with any direction under paragraph (2).

(6) In paragraph (3), information includes information which a party has declined to reveal under rule 29.1(1).

24 Sections 14A(8) and (9) were inserted by section 115(1) of the Adoption and Children Act 2002.

12.19 Additional evidence

(1) This rule applies to proceedings for a section 8 order or a special guardianship order.

(2) Unless the court directs otherwise, a party must not—

(a) file or serve any document other than in accordance with these rules or any practice direction;
(b) in completing a form prescribed by these rules or any practice direction, give information or make a statement which is not required or authorised by that form; or
(c) file or serve at a hearing–
  (i) any witness statement of the substance of the oral evidence which the party intends to adduce; or
  (ii) any copy of any document (including any experts' report) which the party intends to rely on.

(3) Where a party fails to comply with the requirements of this rule in relation to any witness statement or other document, the party cannot seek to rely on that statement or other document unless the court directs otherwise.

12.20 Omitted

12.21 Hearings

(1) The court may give directions about the order of speeches and the evidence at a hearing.

(2) Subject to any directions given under paragraph (1), the parties and the children's guardian must adduce their evidence at a hearing in the following order—

(a) the applicant;
(b) any party with parental responsibility for the child;
(c) other respondents;
(d) the children's guardian;
(e) the child, if the child is a party to proceedings and there is no children's guardian.

Chapter 3
Special provisions about public law proceedings

12.21A Application of rules 12.21B to 12.21E

Rules 12.21B to 12.21E apply to Part 4 proceedings.

12.21B The timetable for the proceedings

The court will draw up the timetable for the proceedings or revise that timetable with a view to disposing of the proceedings without delay.

12.21C Directions

(1) The court will direct the parties to—

(a) monitor compliance with the court's directions; and
(b) tell the court or court officer about—
  (i) any failure to comply with a direction of the court; and
  (ii) any other delay in the proceedings.

12.21D The Case Management Hearing and the Issues Resolution Hearing

(1) The court will conduct the Case Management Hearing with the objective of—

(a) confirming the court to which the proceedings have been allocated or, if necessary, considering transfer of the proceedings in accordance with the Allocation Order;
(b) drawing up a timetable for the proceedings in accordance with rule 12.21B including the time within which the proceedings are to be resolved;
(c) identifying the issues;
(d) giving directions in accordance with rule 12.12 and Pilot Practice Direction 12A to manage the proceedings.

(2) The court may hold a Further Case Management Hearing only where this hearing is necessary to fulfil the objectives of the Case Management Hearing set out in paragraph (1).

(3) The court will conduct the Issues Resolution Hearing with the objective of—

(a) identifying the remaining issues in the proceedings;
(b) as far as possible resolving or narrowing those issues;
(c) giving directions to manage the proceedings to the final hearing in accordance with rule 12.12 and Pilot Practice Direction 12A.

(4) Where it is possible for all the issues in the proceedings to be resolved at the Issues Resolution Hearing, the court may treat the Issues Resolution Hearing as a final hearing and make orders disposing of the proceedings.

(5) The court may set the date for the Case Management Hearing, a Further Case Management Hearing and the Issues Resolution Hearing at the times referred to in Pilot Practice Direction 12A.

(6) The matters which the court will consider at the hearings referred to in this rule are set out in Pilot Practice Direction 12A.

(Rule 25.6 (experts: when to apply for the court's permission) provides that unless the court directs otherwise, parties must apply for the court's permission as mentioned in rule 25.4 as soon as possible and in Part 4 Proceedings no later than the Case Management Hearing.)

12.21E Discussion between advocates

(1) When setting a date for the Case Management Hearing or the Issues Resolution Hearing the court will direct a discussion between the parties' advocates to—

(a) discuss the provisions of a draft of the Case Management Order; and
(b) consider any other matter set out in Pilot Practice Direction 12A.

(2) Where there is a litigant in person the court will give directions about how that person may take part in the discussions between the parties' advocates.

(3) Unless the court directs otherwise—

(a) any discussion between advocates must take place no later than 2 days before the Case Management Hearing; and
(b) a draft of the Case Management Order must be filed with the court no later than 11 a.m. on the day before the Case Management Hearing.

(4) Unless the court directs otherwise—

(a) any discussion between advocates must take place no later than 7 days before the Issues Resolution Hearing; and
(b) a draft of the Case Management Order must be filed with the court no later than 11 a.m. on the day before the Issues Resolution Hearing.

(5) For the purposes of this rule 'advocate' includes a litigant in person.

12.22 Application of rules 12.23 to 12.26

~~Rules 12.23 to 12.26 apply to care and supervision proceedings and in so far as practicable other public law proceedings~~ Rules 12.23 to 12.26 apply in so far as practicable to public law proceedings other than Part 4 proceedings.

12.23 Timetable for the Child

(1) The court will set the timetable for the proceedings in accordance with the Timetable for the Child.

(2) The 'Timetable for the Child' means the timetable set by the court in accordance with its duties under section 1 and 32 of the 1989 Act[25] and will—

(a) take into account dates of the significant steps in the life of the child who is the subject of the proceedings; and
(b) be appropriate for that child.

25 Section 1 was amended by section 115(2) and (3) of the Adoption and Children Act 2002.

12.24 Directions

(1) The court will direct the parties to–

(a) monitor compliance with the court's directions; and
(b) tell the court or court officer about—
   (i) any failure to comply with a direction of the court; and
   (ii) any other delay in the proceedings.

12.25 First Appointment, Case Management Conference and Issues Resolution Hearing

(1) The court may set the date for the First Appointment, Case Management Conference and Issues Resolution Hearing at the times and in the circumstances referred to in Practice Direction 12A.

(2) The matters which the court will consider at the hearings referred to in paragraph (1) are set out in Practice Direction 12A.

12.26 Discussion between advocates

(1) When setting a date for a Case Management Conference or an Issues Resolution Hearing the court will direct a discussion between the parties' advocates to—

(a) discuss the provisions of a draft of the Case Management Order; and
(b) consider any other matter setout in Practice Direction 12A.

(2) Where there is a litigant in person the court will give directions about how that person may take part in the discussions between the parties' advocates.

(3) The court will direct that following a discussion between advocates they must prepare or amend a draft of the Case Management Order for the court to consider.

(4) Where it is not possible for the advocates to agree the terms of a draft of the Case Management Order, the advocates should specify on a draft of the Case Management Order or on a separate document if more practicable—

(a) those provisions on which they agree; and
(b) those provisions on which they disagree.

(5) Unless the court directs otherwise–

(a) any discussion between advocates must take place no later than 2 days; and
(b) a draft of the Case Management Order must be filed with the court no later than 1 day,

before the Case Management Conference or the Issues Resolution Hearing whichever may be appropriate.

(6) For the purposes of this rule 'advocate' includes a litigant in person.

12.27 Matters prescribed for the purposes of the Act

(1) Proceedings for an order under any of the following provisions of the 1989 Act—

(a) a secure accommodation order under section 25;
(b) an order giving permission to change a child's surname or remove a child from the United Kingdom under section 33(7);
(c) an order permitting the local authority to arrange for any child in its care to live outside England and Wales under paragraph 19(1) of Schedule 2;
(d) the extension or further extension of a supervision order under paragraph 6(3) of Schedule 3;
(e) appeals against the determination of proceedings of a kind set out in sub-paragraphs (a) to (d);

are specified for the purposes of section 41 of that Act in accordance with section 41(6)(i) of that Act.

(2) The persons listed as applicants in the table set out in rule 12.3 to proceedings for the variation of directions made with interim care or interim supervision orders under section 38(8) of the 1989 Act are the prescribed class of persons for the purposes of that section.

(3) The persons listed as applicants in the table set out in rule 12.3 to proceedings for the variation of a direction made under section 44(6) of the 1989 Act in an emergency protection order are the prescribed class of persons for the purposes of section 44(9) of that Act.

12.28 Exclusion requirements: interim care orders and emergency protection orders

(1) This rule applies where the court includes an exclusion requirement in an interim care order or an emergency protection order.

(2) The applicant for an interim care order or emergency protection order must—

(a) prepare a separate statement of the evidence in support of the application for an exclusion requirement;

(b) serve the statement personally on the relevant person with a copy of the order containing the exclusion requirement (and of any power of arrest which is attached to it);
(c) inform the relevant person of that person's right to apply to vary or discharge the exclusion requirement.

(3) Where a power of arrest is attached to an exclusion requirement in an interim care order or an emergency protection order, the applicant will deliver—

(a) a copy of the order; and
(b) a statement showing that the relevant person has been served with the order or informed of its terms (whether by being present when the order was made or by telephone or otherwise),

to the officer for the time being in charge of the police station for the area in which the dwelling-house in which the child lives is situated (or such other police station as the court may specify).

(4) Rules 10.6(2) and 10.10 to 10.17 will apply, with the necessary modifications, for the service, variation, discharge and enforcement of any exclusion requirement to which a power ofarrest is attached as they apply to an order made on an application under Part 4 of the 1996 Act.

(5) The relevant person must serve the parties to the proceedings with any application which that person makes for the variation or discharge of the exclusion requirement.

(6) Where an exclusion requirement ceases to have effect whether—

(a) as a result of the removal of a child under section 38A(10) or 44A(10) of the 1989 Act[26];
(b) because of the discharge of the interim care order or emergency protection order; or
(c) otherwise,

the applicant must inform—
(i) the relevant person;
(ii) the parties to the proceedings;
(iii) any officer to whom a copy of the order was delivered under paragraph (3); and
(iv) (where necessary) the court.

(7) Where the court includes an exclusion requirement in an interim care order or an emergency protection order of its own motion, paragraph (2) will apply with the omission of any reference to the statement of the evidence.

(8) In this rule, 'the relevant person' has the meaning assigned to it by sections 38A(2) and 44A(2) of the 1989 Act.

26 Sections 38A(10) and 44A(10) were inserted by section 52 of and paragraphs 1 and 3 of Schedule 6 to the Family Law Act 1996.

12.29 Notification of consent

(1) Consent for the purposes of the following provisions of the 1989 Act—

(a) section 16(3)[27];
(b) section 38A(2)(b)(ii) or 44A(2)(b)(ii); or
(c) paragraph 19(3)(c) or (d) of Schedule 2,

must be given either—

(i) orally to the court; or
(ii) in writing to the court signed by the person giving consent.

(2) Any written consent for the purposes of section 38A(2) or 44A(2) of the 1989 Act must include a statement that the person giving consent—

(a) is able and willing to give to the child the care which it would be reasonable to expect a parent to give; and
(b) understands that the giving of consent could lead to the exclusion of the relevant person from the dwelling-house in which the child lives.

27 Paragraph (a) was repealed by sections 6(1), (2), 15(2) of and Schedule 3 to the Children and Adoption Act 2006.

12.30 Proceedings for secure accommodation orders: copies of reports

In proceedings under section 25 of the 1989 Act, the court will, if practicable, arrange for copies of all written reports filed in the case to be made available before the hearing to—

(a) the applicant;
(b) the parent or guardian of the child to whom the application relates;
(c) any legal representative of the child;
(d) the children's guardian; and
(e) the child, unless the court directs otherwise,

and copies of the reports may, if the court considers it desirable, be shown to any person who is entitled to notice of any hearing in accordance with Practice Direction 12C.

Practice Direction 36D – Pilot scheme: procedure for using an online system to generate applications in certain proceedings for a matrimonial order

This Practice Direction supplements rule 36.2 FPR (Transitional arrangements and pilot schemes).

Scope and interpretation

1.1 This Practice Direction is made under rule 36.2 FPR and sets up a Pilot Scheme to allow for certain applications to be filled in via an online process.

1.2 The Pilot Scheme applies to applications where all of the following conditions are met:

(a) the application is for a matrimonial order which is a decree of divorce made under section 1 of the 1973 Act;
(b) access to the online system for making such applications is permitted;
(c) all stages of the process provided for in the online system can be fully completed;
(d) the application is started in the family court; and
(e) the application is filed in the period commencing 25 January 2017 and ending 27 October 2017.

1.3 In this Practice Direction, 'the online system' means Her Majesty's Courts and Tribunal Service's online system to allow for specified stages in for matrimonial proceedings to be dealt with online.

Purpose of the Pilot Scheme

2.1 The purpose of this Pilot Scheme is to assess new practices and procedures to allow for certain applications for certain matrimonial orders to be generated via the online system. For the purposes of this Pilot Scheme, once the application has been generated the applicant will need to save or print off the generated application. It will then need to be filed at court, in accordance with the procedure currently provided for in the FPR and Practice Directions. It is intended that future Practice Directions will establish other Pilot Schemes which will allow for later stages in matrimonial proceedings to take place via the online system, for example for making the application online.

Modification of the FPR and Practice Directions during the operation of the Pilot Scheme

3.1 During the operation of the Pilot Scheme, the FPR and the Practice Directions supporting the FPR will apply to cases falling within the Pilot Scheme as modified by paragraphs 4.1 to 5.4.

Modification of Part 5 FPR

4.1 For rule 5.1, substitute-

'5.1 Where the Pilot Scheme referred to in Practice Direction 36D applies, the applicant must-

(a) complete all sections of the application process set out in the online system referred to in that Practice Direction;
(b) print or save the resulting application form which is generated by the online system;
(c) when filing that application, include all of the information, including any additional documents, that the online system requires to be included.'.

4.2 Omit rule 5.2.

Modification of Part 17 FPR

4A.1 In rule 17.2(6), for 'The statement of truth' substitute 'Subject to paragraph (6A), the statement of truth'.

4A.2 After rule 17.2(6) insert-

'(6A) Where a statement of truth is included in an application for a matrimonial order to which the pilot scheme referred to in Practice Direction 36D applies-

(a) the applicant must file with the court an application which includes the name of the person who the online system requires to sign a statement of truth printed underneath the statement of truth; and
(b) the court may require the applicant to produce a copy of the application containing the signature of the person referred to in sub-paragraph (a) at a later date.'.

Modification of PD7A

5.1 For paragraph 1.1, substitute-

'1.1 Where the pilot scheme referred to in Practice Direction 36D applies, an application for a matrimonial order must be made in the form generated by the online system referred to in that Practice Direction. The online system sets out the documents which must accompany the application.'.

5.2 For paragraph 1.2 substitute-

'1.2 The application must be completed according to the detailed guidance contained in the online system. It is especially important that the particulars provide evidence to show why the applicant is entitled to a decree of divorce. The particulars should, however, be as concise as possible consistent with providing the necessary evidence.'.

5.3 In paragraph 3.1-

(a) for the heading and the first sentence of paragraph 3.1 substitute-

'Proof of marriage

3.1 The online system referred to in Practice Direction 36D sets out the documents which must accompany the application for a matrimonial order.';

(b) in the second sentence of paragraph 3.1 omit 'or civil partnership';

(c) in sub-paragraph (a)(i)-

(i) for 'marriage or civil partnership to' substitute 'marriage to'; and

(ii) omit 'or civil partnership registration'; and

(d) in sub-paragraph (a) (ii), omit 'or civil partnership registration'.

5.4 In paragraph 4.1–

(a) for 'An applicant for a matrimonial or civil partnership order' substitute

'Where the pilot scheme referred to in Practice Direction 36D applies, an applicant'; and

(b) omit 'form'.

Modification of Practice Direction 17A

6.1 Omit paragraphs 1.5 and 2.3.

6.2 In the heading to paragraph 3.1 and in paragraphs 3.1, 3.7, 3.8 and 3.10 references to 'sign', 'signs', 'signed' and 'signing' are to be read as references to the name of the person being, or having been, printed under the statement of truth included in an application for a matrimonial order to which the pilot scheme referred to in Practice Direction 36D applies.

6.3 For paragraph 4.1 substitute–

'4.1 Where an application (being an application for a matrimonial order to which the pilot scheme referred to in Practice Direction 36D applies) contains a statement of truth with the printed name of a person who is unable to read or sign the document, the application must be accompanied by a certificate made by an authorised person.'.

6.4 In paragraph 4.3–

(a) for sub-paragraph (a) substitute 'that the content of the online application has been read to the person before completion of the statement of truth required by the online system;'; and

(b) for sub-paragraph (e) substitute 'that that person confirmed in the presence of the authorised person that it was their belief that the contents of the application were true.'

6.5 For the Annex substitute–

'Certificate to be used where a person is unable to read or sign an application for a matrimonial order to which the pilot scheme in Practice Direction 36D applies.

I certify that I [name and address of authorised person] have read the contents of the application and the statement of truth to the person whose name is printed under the statement of truth in the application, who appeared to understand (a) the application and approved its contents as accurate and (b) the statement of truth and the consequences of making a false statement, and orally confirmed that this was the case in my presence.'.

Practice Direction 36E – Pilot scheme: procedure for online filing of applications in certain proceedings for a matrimonial order

This Practice Direction supplements rule 36.2 FPR (Transitional arrangements and pilot schemes).

Scope and interpretation

1.1 This Practice Direction is made under rule 36.2 FPR and sets up a Pilot Scheme to allow for certain applications to be filed via a HMCTS online application system.

1.2 This Practice Direction comes into force on 16 January 2018.

1.3 Subject to paragraph 1.4, this Practice Direction supersedes Practice Direction 36D, which is revoked from the date this Practice Direction comes into force.

1.4 Practice Direction 36D will remain in force in relation to any applications commenced under the Pilot Scheme referred to in that Practice Direction, and this Practice Direction (and any that supersede it) will not apply in relation to such applications.

1.5 This Pilot Scheme applies to applications where all of the following conditions are met:

(a) the application is for a matrimonial order which is a decree of divorce made under section 1 of the 1973 Act;
(b) access to the online system for making such applications is permitted;
(c) all stages of the process provided for in the online system can be fully completed;
(d) the application is started in the family court; and
(e) the application is filed in the period commencing on 16 January 2018 and ending on 29 March 2019.

1.6 In this Practice Direction, 'the online system' means Her Majesty's Courts and Tribunal Service's online system to allow for specified stages in matrimonial proceedings to be dealt with online.

Purpose of this Pilot Scheme

2.1 The purpose of this Pilot Scheme is to assess new practices and procedures to allow for certain applications for certain matrimonial orders to be filed via an online system. It is intended that future Practice Directions will establish other Pilot Schemes which will allow for specified later stages in matrimonial proceedings to take place via the online system.

Modification or disapplication of the FPR and Practice Directions during the operation of the Pilot Scheme

3.1 During the operation of the Pilot Scheme, the FPR and the Practice Directions supporting the FPR will apply to cases falling within the Pilot Scheme as modified, or disapplied, by paragraphs 4.1 to 10.5.

Modification of Part 5 FPR

4.1 For rule 5.1, substitute-

'5.1 Where the Pilot Scheme referred to in Practice Direction 36E applies, the applicant must-

(a) complete all sections of the application process; and
(b) provide all the information, including any additional documents, that the online application system referred to in that Practice Direction requires, or that the court requires, in a manner specified by the online application system, or required by the court. '.

4.2 Omit rule 5.2.

Modification of Part 7 FPR

5.1 For rule 7.6(1) FPR substitute-

'7.6(1) Where the applicant is legally represented, the legal representative must complete and provide with the application, in a manner specified in the online system referred to in Practice Direction 36E, a statement certifying whether the legal representative has discussed with the applicant the possibility of a reconciliation and given the applicant the names and addresses of persons qualified to help effect a reconciliation.'.

Modification of Part 17 FPR

6.1 In rule 17.2(6), for 'The statement of truth' substitute 'Subject to paragraph (6A), the statement of truth'.

6.2 After rule 17.2(6) insert-

'(6A) Where a statement of truth is included in an application for a matrimonial order to which the pilot scheme referred to in Practice Direction 36E applies-

(a) the applicant must file with the court an application which includes the name of the person who the online system requires to sign a statement of truth printed underneath the statement of truth; and
(b) the court may require the applicant to produce a copy of the application containing the signature of the person referred to in sub-paragraph (a) at a later date.'.

Modification of Practice Direction 6A

7.1 In paragraph 4.2(b)-

(a) in paragraph (iii) for '; or' substitute ';';
(b) in paragraph (iv) for the full-stop substitute '; or'; and
(c) after paragraph (iv) insert-

'(v) confirmation given, by the party to be served, within the application made via the online system referred to in PD36E that that party is willing to accept service by email and stating the email address for such service.'

Disapplication of Practice Direction 5B

8.1 Practice Direction 5B does not apply in relation to an application which can be made online under the Pilot Scheme referred to in Practice Direction 36E.

Modification of Practice Direction 7A

9.1 For paragraph 1.1 substitute-

'1.1 Where the Pilot Scheme referred to in Practice Direction 36E applies, an application for a matrimonial order must be made as required by the online system referred to in that Practice Direction and in accordance with rule 5.1.'.

9.2 For paragraph 1.2 substitute-

'1.2 The application must be completed according to the detailed guidance contained in the online system. It is especially important that the particulars provide evidence to show why the applicant is entitled to a decree of divorce. The particulars should, however, be as concise as possible consistent with providing the necessary evidence.'.

9.3 After paragraph 1.3 insert-

'Applications for matrimonial orders received via the online system: timing

1A.1 When an application is received via the online system referred to in Practice Direction 36E and is recorded by Her Majesty's Courts and Tribunals Service software has having been received at or after 4.31pm and before or at 11.59pm, the date of filing will not be before the next day that the court location to which the application has been sent via the online system is open for business.

1A.2 When an application is received via the online system referred to in Practice Direction 36E, an acknowledgement of receipt will automatically be sent to the applicant. This acknowledgement of receipt does not constitute a notice that the application has been issued.'.

9.4 In paragraph 3.1-

(a) for the heading of, and first sentence of, paragraph 3.1, substitute-

'*Proof of marriage*

3.1 The online system referred to in Practice Direction 36E sets out the documents which must accompany an application for a matrimonial order and the way in which those documents may be provided (for example, the online system may allow for documents to be posted, or to be uploaded and submitted online with the application).';

(b) in the second sentence of paragraph 3.1 omit 'or civil partnership';

(c) in sub-paragraph (a)(i)-

(i) for 'marriage or civil partnership to' substitute 'marriage to'; and

(ii) omit 'or civil partnership registration'; and

(d) in sub-paragraph (a) (ii), omit 'or civil partnership registration'.

9.5 In paragraph 4.1-

(a) for 'An applicant for a matrimonial or civil partnership order' substitute 'Where the Pilot Scheme referred to in Practice Direction 36E applies, an applicant'; and

(b) omit 'form'.

Modification of Practice Direction 17A

10.1 Omit paragraphs 1.5 and 2.3.

10.2 In the heading to paragraph 3.1 and in paragraphs 3.1, 3.7, 3.8 and 3.10 references to 'sign', 'signs', 'signed' and 'signing' are to be read as references to the name of the person being, or having been, printed under the statement of truth included in an application for a matrimonial order to which the pilot scheme referred to in Practice Direction 36E applies.

10.3 For paragraph 4.1 substitute-

'4.1 Where an application (being an application for a matrimonial order to which the pilot scheme referred to in Practice Direction 36E applies) contains a statement of truth with the printed name of a person who is unable to read or sign the document, the application must be accompanied by a certificate made by an authorised person.'.

10.4 In paragraph 4.3-

(a) for sub-paragraph (a) substitute 'that the content of the online application has been read to the person before completion of the statement of truth required by the online system;'; and

(b) for sub-paragraph (e) substitute 'that that person confirmed in the presence of the authorised person that it was their belief that the contents of the application were true.'

10.5 For the Annex substitute-

'Certificate to be used where a person is unable to read or sign an application for a matrimonial order to which the pilot scheme in Practice Direction 36E applies.

I certify that I [name and address of authorised person] have read the contents of the application and the statement of truth to the person whose name is printed under the statement of truth in the application, who appeared to understand (a) the application and approved its contents as accurate and (b) the statement of truth and the consequences of making a false statement, and orally confirmed that this was the case in my presence.'.

Practice Direction 36F – Pilot scheme: procedure for using structured interventions before a first hearing dispute resolution appointment in certain private law proceedings relating to children

This Practice Direction supplements FPR Part 36, rule 36.2 (Transitional Arrangements and Pilot Schemes).

Scope and interpretation

1.1 This Practice Direction is made under rule 36.2 and sets up a Pilot Scheme.

1.2 The Pilot Scheme applies to certain private law proceedings relating to children (as defined in FPR 12.2) where the following conditions are met:

a) The application is for either a section 8 order or an enforcement order; and

b) The application is filed at the Manchester Civil and Family Justice Centre between 22 January 2018 and 23 July 2018.

Purpose of the Pilot Scheme

2.1 The purpose of the Pilot Scheme is to assess the use of new practices and procedures to allow for structured interventions to take place before a First Hearing Dispute Resolution Appointment (FHDRA). The aim of the Pilot Scheme is to help families resolve disputes involving children without the need to attend Court, thus easing the burden of the Family Courts and benefiting the children and families involved.

2.2 The Pilot Scheme involves the following key stages:

(1) An assessment and screening stage, within which applications may be deemed as unsuitable to remain within the Pilot Scheme; and

(2) The intervention stage, within which parties participate in a tailored package of dispute resolution services before the FHDRA.

Modification of the FPR and Practice Directions during operation of the Pilot Scheme

3.1 During the operation of the Pilot Scheme the Family Procedure Rules 2010 and the Practice Direction supporting the Rules will apply to cases falling within the Pilot Scheme as modified by paragraphs 4.1 to 6.1.

Modification of Part 12 FPR

4.1 In Rule 12.2 insert –

"Pilot Scheme' means the Pilot Scheme described in Practice Direction 36F.'

4.2 In Rule 12.32 substitute –

'Where an application has exited the Pilot Scheme described in Practice Direction 36F the respondent must file and serve on the parties an answer to the application for an order in private law proceedings at least 3 working days before the FHDRA is scheduled to take place.'

Modification of FPR Practice Direction 12B – 'Child Arrangements Programme'

5.1 After paragraph 5.11, insert –

'5.11A Where parties attend mediation which has been arranged by a Cafcass officer as part of the Pilot Scheme, the mediator shall provide such information as the Cafcass officer may request in accordance with paragraph 24.8 provided the parties give their consent to do so.'

5.2 In paragraph 5.12, omit the word 'however'.

5.3 For paragraph 8.9 substitute –

'The court shall send electronically to Cafcass a copy of the Form C100/C79 (and Form C1A if supplied) within one working day of receipt of a properly completed application, whereupon the safeguarding checks referred to in paragraph 13.3 will be commenced where appropriate. The C6 Notice of Hearing shall be sent electronically to Cafcass no later than 2 working days after the date of issue of the application.'

5.4 For paragraph 9.2 substitute –

'Within three working days of the date of receipt, applications shall be considered in accordance with the following procedure:

(1) There shall be an initial screening by a Cafcass officer to determine whether it would be appropriate for the application to remain within the Pilot Scheme;

(2) Thereafter there shall be a joint assessment of suitability for the intervention stage of the Pilot Scheme by the Cafcass officer and a nominated Legal Adviser and/or nominated District Judge in accordance with paragraph 24.1.

5.5 After paragraph 9.2 insert:

'9.2A Applications which exit the Pilot Scheme at step (1) above shall be considered by a nominated legal advisor and/or nominated District Judge ('the Gatekeepers') in accordance with the appropriate Rules of Procedure.'

5.6 Paragraph 13.2 is omitted.

5.7 In paragraph 13.3 after the word 'parties' insert –

'such safeguarding checks to be requested immediately upon receipt of the application by Cafcass.'.

5.8 For paragraph 13.5 substitute –

'Cafcass shall record and outline any safety issues for the court. Where agreement is reached between the parties before the FHDRA, the Cafcass officer shall provide the court with a written endorsement of this agreement which will include the outcome of safeguarding checks. Where the application has exited the Pilot Scheme, the Cafcass officer shall file a safeguarding letter at court at least 3 working days before the FHDRA.'

5.9 Paragraph 13.7 is omitted.

5.10 For paragraph 14.3 substitute –

'For cases which have exited the Pilot Scheme, the respondent should file the response no later than 3 working days before the FHDRA.'

5.11 After paragraph 22.1 insert –

'22.1A Working Day 2: Initial screening of application by a Cafcass officer to determine whether it would be appropriate for the application to remain within the Pilot Scheme. Applications deemed to be inappropriate will exit the Pilot Scheme and will be considered by the Gatekeeping team in accordance with paragraph 22.2.'

5.12 In paragraph 22.2 substitute 'Working Day 3' for 'Working Day 2'

5.13 For paragraph 22.3 substitute –

'Cafcass shall prepare a safeguarding letter if the application exits the Pilot Scheme and will file this at court no later than 3 working days before the FHDRA.'

6.1 After paragraph 23.1 insert –

'Pilot Scheme Procedure

24.1 In order to determine suitability for remaining within the Pilot Scheme, applications will be jointly assessed by a Cafcass officer and a nominated Legal Advisor (and/or nominated District Judge). The assessment will be based on suitability threshold criteria. The Cafcass officer will thereafter make the final decision as to whether the application remains within the Pilot Scheme once the Police and Local Authority safeguarding checks have been returned and the safeguarding interview with the parties has been carried out. A Cafcass officer may withdraw the suitability decision as a result of any subsequent information received.

24.2 Parties will be sent information about the Pilot Scheme by the court and Cafcass. Participation in the Pilot Scheme is voluntary and the parties may withdraw their consent at any stage of the process. If consent is withdrawn, the application will exit the Pilot Scheme. A Cafcass officer may withdraw an application from the Pilot Scheme at any time if in their professional judgment they consider it appropriate to do so.

24.3 Parties who have consented to participate in the Pilot Scheme will be invited to compete an online self-assessment survey, the results of which will be provided to an allocated Cafcass officer.

24.4 The Cafcass officer will contact the parties to conduct a telephone assessment and triage. Such assessment and triage is to be undertaken as soon as practicable upon return of the safeguarding checks.

24.5 If, following the assessment and triage, the Cafcass officer considers that the application remains suitable for the Pilot Scheme, the officer will prepare a package of structured interventions that are tailored to the needs of the parties. Interventions may include (but shall not be limited to):

(1) Attendance at a SPIP;
(2) Mediation (including where appropriate a MIAM);
(3) Supported or supervised contact referral;
(4) A Parenting Plan meeting.

24.6 The Cafcass officer will contact the parties to confirm which interventions, if any, the parties wish to utilise and will provide specific information on those selected. In the event either party declines to participate with any of the interventions, the application will exit the Pilot Scheme.

24.7 The Cafcass officer will assist the parties with booking the interventions.

24.8 Where interventions are provided by organisations other than Cafcass, those external providers will share feedback on the interventions with the Cafcass officer within 2 working days of the last session with the parties in accordance with paragraph 5.11A.

24.9 The Cafcass officer will undertake such further work with the parties as is considered necessary in their professional judgment to assist the parties resolve their dispute. Such work may involve convening a Parenting Plan meeting, drafting a Parenting Plan or otherwise facilitating another form of agreement.

24.10 Any Parenting Plan or other form of agreement must be endorsed in writing by the Cafcass officer. This written endorsement must confirm the outcome of the safeguarding checks.

24.11 Once the Parenting Plan or agreement is endorsed, the applicant may apply to withdraw the application. The application to withdraw must include a copy of the Parenting Plan or agreement, and the written endorsement of the Cafcass officer. The application to withdraw must be made by no later than 5 working days before the FHDRA. If so advised, the parties may include a draft consent order within the application to withdraw.

24.12 The application to withdraw may be made by email and not on Form C2 provided that the facts contained within the email are verified by a statement of truth in accordance with paragraph 2.1 of PD17A.

24.13 A Judge will consider any application to withdraw on paper and if permission to withdraw is granted, the FHDRA will be vacated. If the application to withdraw is received less than 5 working days before the FHDRA or if the Judge so requires for any other reason, the parties may be required to attend the FHDRA in any event.

24.14 If the parties do not reach an agreement, or if the application exits the Pilot Scheme for any other reason, the respondent must file a response on form C7 at least 3 working days before the FHDRA. The parties must attend the FHDRA and the procedure described in paragraphs 14.4 onwards will apply thereafter.

24.15 If the application has exited the Pilot Scheme, the Cafcass officer shall prepare the safeguarding letter and file this at court at least 3 working days before the FHDRA.

24.16 Where the Cafcass officer determines the parties are making sufficient progress towards resolving their dispute, but require further time to reach an agreement, the

Cafcass officer may request that the FHDRA be adjourned to enable further work to take place. Such request may only be made with the consent of the parties and if possible will be made no later than 5 working days before the FHDRA. Where this is not possible the parties or Cacass officer may request an adjournment at the start of the FHDRA.'

Practice Direction 36G – Pilot scheme: procedure for using an online system to generate applications in certain private law proceedings relating to children

This Practice Direction supplements FPR Part 36, rule 36.2 (Transitional Arrangements and Pilot Schemes).

Scope and interpretation

1.1 This Practice Direction is made under rule 36.2 and sets up a Pilot Scheme to allow for certain applications to be filled in via an online process.

1.2 The Pilot Scheme applies to applications where all of the following conditions are met:

a) the application is for-
   (i) an order under section 8 of the Children Act 1989 ('section 8 order'); or
   (ii) permission to apply for a section 8 order ('permission application');
b) access to the online system for making such applications is permitted;
c) the application is started in the Family Court; and
d) the application is filed in the period commencing 26 March 2018 and ending at the end of the day on 31 December 2022.

1.3 In this Practice Direction, the 'online system' means the Her Majesty's Courts and Tribunals Service's online system to allow for applications for section 8 orders and for permission applications to be filled in online.

Purpose of the Pilot Scheme

2.1 The purpose of this Pilot Scheme is to assess the use of new practices and procedures to allow for certain applications for section 8 orders, and certain permission applications, to be generated via the online system. For the purposes of this Pilot Scheme, once the application has been generated the applicant will need to save or print that application, which will then need to be filed at court in accordance with the procedure currently provided for in the FPR and Practice Directions. Alternatively, the applicant may file the application by an email generated by the online system.

2.2 It is intended that future Practice Directions will establish other Pilot Schemes which will allow for later stages in applications for section 8 orders or permission applications to be completed via the online system, for example making the application online.

Modification of the FPR and Practice Directions during operation of the Pilot Scheme

3.1 During the operation of the Pilot Scheme the Family Procedure Rules 2010 and the Practice Directions supporting the Rules will apply to cases falling within the Pilot Scheme as modified by paragraphs 4.1 to 10.3.

Modification of Part 3 FPR

4.1 For Rule 3.7 substitute:

> '3.7 Where the Pilot Scheme referred to in Practice Direction 36G applies, the application must include from the prospective applicant:
>
> (a) confirmation that the applicant has attended a MIAM;
> (b) a claim that one of the MIAM exemptions applies; or
> (c) confirmation that a mediator's exemption applies.'

4.2 In Rule 3.8(2) for 'has provided signed confirmation' substitute 'confirms in the relevant form.

Modification of Part 5 FPR

5.1 For Rule 5.1 substitute:

> '5.1 Where the Pilot Scheme referred to in Practice Direction 36G applies, the applicant must:
>
> (a) complete all sections of the application process set out in the online system referred to in that Practice Direction;
> (b) Omitted
> (c) file the application generated by the online system at court-
>   (i) in accordance with the procedure currently provided for in the FPR and Practice Directions; or
>   (ii) by an email generated by the online system.

5.2 Omit Rule 5.2.

Modification of Part 17 FPR

6.1 In Rule 17.2(6) for 'The statement of truth' substitute 'Subject to paragraph (6A), the statement of truth'.

6.2 After Rule 17.2(6) insert:

> '(6A) Where a statement of truth is included in an application for a section 8 order to which the Pilot Scheme referred to in Practice Direction 36G applies –
>
> (a) the applicant must file with the court an application which includes the name of the person who the online system requires to sign a statement of truth printed underneath the statement of truth; and
> (b) the court may require the applicant to produce a copy of the application containing the signature of the person referred to in sub-paragraph (a) at a later date.'

Modification of FPR Practice Direction 3A

7.1 For paragraph 6 substitute:

> '6 Where the pilot scheme referred to in Practice Direction 36G applies, the applicant must provide within the application one of the following:
>
> (i) confirmation that she or he has attended a MIAM including the date attended, the name of the authorised family mediator (and/or Family Mediation Service) and their FMC registration number;
> (ii) confirmation that a 'mediator's exemption' applies; or
> (iii) a claim that a MIAM exemption applies.'

7.2 After paragraph 6 insert:

'6A An applicant who provides confirmation or makes a claim in accordance with (i) – (iii) above is not required to attach any supporting evidence with their application, but should bring any supporting evidence, including where appropriate the signed confirmation by the authorised family mediator, to the first hearing.'

7.3 Omit paragraphs 14, 15 and 16.

7.4 In paragraph 18, for 'on the relevant form' substitute 'in the relevant section of the online system.'

7.5 In paragraph 34, omit the words after 'MIAM exemption' and substitute 'and signed confirmation should then be returned to the applicant.'

Modification of FPR Practice Direction 5B

8.1 Omit paragraphs 3.3(a), 6.1 and 6.2.

Modification of FPR Practice Direction 12B – 'Child Arrangements Programme'

9.1 For paragraph 8.2 substitute:

'8.2 Where the pilot scheme referred to in Practice Direction 36G applies, the application for a section 8 order must be made in the form generated by the online system referred to in Practice Direction 36G. For the purposes of the pilot scheme, references in this Practice Direction to 'form C100' and 'form C1A' are to be read as including those versions of the forms generated by the online system.'

9.2 For paragraph 8.4 substitute:

'8.4 The applicant must provide in the application one of the following:
(i) confirmation that she or he has attended a MIAM including the date attended, the contact details of the authorised family mediator and their FMC registration number;
(ii) confirmation that a 'mediator's exemption' applies; or
(iii) a claim that a MIAM exemption applies.'

9.3 Omit paragraph 8.5.

9.4 In paragraph 8.6 for 'shall be attached to the Form C100' substitute 'should be provided at the first hearing.'

Modification of FPR Practice Direction 17A

10.1 In the heading to paragraph 3.1 and in paragraphs 3.1, 3.7, 3.8 and 3.10 references to 'sign', 'signs', 'signing' and 'signed' are to be read as references to the name of the person being, or having been, printed under the statement of truth included in an application to which the Pilot Scheme referred to in Practice Direction 36G applies.

10.2 For paragraph 4.1 substitute:

'4.1 Where an application (being an application to which the Pilot Scheme referred to in Practice Direction 36G applies) contains a statement of truth with the printed name of a person who is unable to read or sign the document, the application must be accompanied by a certificate made by an authorised person.'

10.3 In paragraph 4.3:

a) for sub-paragraph (a) substitute 'that the content of the application generated by the online system has been read to the person before completion of the statement of truth required by the online system;'
b) for sub-paragraph (e) substitute 'that that person confirmed in the presence of the authorised person that it was their belief that the contents of the application were true.'

10.4 For the Annex substitute:

'Certificate to be used where a person is unable to read or sign an application to which the Pilot Scheme referred to in Practice Direction 36G applies.

I certify that I [name and address of authorised person' have read the contents of the application and the statement of truth to the person whose name is printed under the statement of truth in the application, who appeared to understand (a) the application and approved its contents as accurate and (b) the statement of truth and the consequences of making a false statement, and orally confirmed that this was the case in my presence.'.

Practice Direction 36H – Revoked

Practice Direction 36I – Pilot scheme: procedure for online filing of certain applications for consent orders for a financial remedy in connection with matrimonial proceedings

This Practice Direction supplements FPR Part 36, rule 36.2 (Transitional Arrangements and Pilot Schemes).

Scope and interpretation

1.1 This Practice Direction is made under rule 36.2 and sets up a Pilot Scheme to allow for certain applications for a consent order for a financial remedy in connection with matrimonial proceedings to be completed and filed via an HMCTS online application system.

1.2 This Practice Direction comes into force on 6 August 2018.

1.3 Subject to paragraph 1.3A, the Pilot Scheme applies to applications where each of the following conditions are met:

a) the application is for a financial remedy in connection with an application for a matrimonial order which is a decree of divorce made under section 1 of the 1973 Act;
b) the application is for a consent order only;
c) the applicant is legally represented;
d) access to the online system for making such applications is permitted;
e) the application is started in the Family Court; and
f) the application is filed in the period commencing 6 August 2018 and ending 31 March 2020.

1.3A The exception referred to in paragraph 1.3 is where the application is for a variation order.

1.4 In this Practice Direction, 'the online system' means HM Courts and Tribunals Service's online system to allow for specified stages in financial remedy proceedings to be dealt with online.

Purpose of the Pilot Scheme

2.1 The purpose of this Pilot Scheme is to assess the use of new practices and procedures to allow for certain applications for financial remedy in connection with matrimonial proceedings to be completed and filed via an online system.

2.2 It is intended that future Practice Directions will establish other Pilot Schemes which will allow for other specified stages in financial remedy proceedings to take place via the online system.

Modification or disapplication of the FPR and Practice Directions during operation of the Pilot Scheme

3.1 During the operation of the Pilot Scheme the Family Procedure Rules 2010 and the Practice Directions supporting the Rules will apply to cases falling within the Pilot Scheme as modified by paragraphs 4.1 to 9.2.

Modification of Part 5 FPR

4.1 For rule 5.1, substitute–

'5.1 Where the Pilot Scheme referred to in Practice Direction 36I applies, the applicant must-

(a) complete all sections of the online application; and
(b) provide all the information, including any additional documents, that the online application system referred to in that Practice Direction requires, or that the court requires, in a manner specified by the online application system or required by the court.'.

Modification of Part 9 FPR

5.1 For rule 9.26(1)(a) substitute-

'(a) the applicant must file a draft of the order in the terms sought which must be signed by both parties.'.

Modification of Part 29

6.1 In rule 29.13, paragraph (2) is omitted.

Modification of Practice Direction 6A

7.1 In paragraph 4.2(b)-

(a) in paragraph (iii) for '; or' substitute ';';
(b) in paragraph (iv) for the full-stop substitute '; or'; and
(c) after paragraph (iv) insert-

'(v) confirmation given within the application for a consent order for a financial remedy in connection with matrimonial proceedings made via the online system referred to in Practice Direction 36I that the applicant is willing to accept service by email and stating the email address for such service.'

Disapplication of Practice Direction 5B

8.1 Practice Direction 5B does not apply in relation to an application which can be made online under the pilot scheme referred to in Practice Direction 36I.

Modification of Practice Direction 9A

9.1 For paragraph 7.1, substitute-

'7.1 Rule 9.26(1)(a) is considered to be properly complied with if the draft order is signed by solicitors on record as acting for a party. However, where the consent order applied for contains undertakings, it should be signed by the party giving the undertakings as well as by that party's solicitor.

(Provision relating to the enforcement of undertakings is contained in the Practice Direction 33A supplementing Part 33 of the FPR)'.

9.2 After paragraph 7.3, insert-

'Applications for a consent order for a financial remedy in connection with matrimonial proceedings received via the online system: timing

7A.1 When an application for a consent order for a financial remedy in connection with matrimonial proceedings is received via the online system referred to in Practice Direction 36I and is recorded by HM Courts and Tribunals Service software as having been received at or after 4.31pm and before or at 11.59pm, the date of filing will not be before the next day that the court location to which the application has been sent via the online system is open for business.

7A.2 When an application for a consent order for a financial remedy in connection with matrimonial proceedings is received via the online system referred to in Practice Direction 36I, an acknowledgment of receipt will automatically be sent to the email address given as the address for service in the online system. This acknowledgment of receipt does not constitute a notice that the application has been issued.'

Practice Direction 36J – Pilot scheme: transparency (attendance at hearings in private)

This Practice Direction supplements FPR Part 36 (Transitional Arrangements and Pilot Schemes).

Scope and interpretation

1.1 This Practice Direction is made under rule 36.2 and sets up a Pilot Scheme.

1.2 The Pilot Scheme applies in relation to any proceedings to which rule 27.11 applies.

1.3 The Pilot Scheme operates from 1 October 2018 to the end of the day on 30 September 2021.

Purpose of the Pilot Scheme

2.1 The purpose of the Pilot Scheme is to assess the use of new practices and procedures to allow for attendance at hearings in private by certain lawyers with a view to their being able to report on proceedings (as 'legal bloggers') in addition to duly accredited representatives of news gathering and reporting organisations.

Modification of the Family Procedure Rules and supporting practice directions during operation of the Pilot Scheme

3.1 During the operation of the Pilot Scheme the Family Procedure Rules 2010 will apply to cases falling within the Pilot Scheme as modified by paragraphs 4.1 to 4.5; and the practice directions supporting the rules will apply to such cases as modified by paragraph 5.1.

Modification of rule 27.11 of the Family Procedure Rules 2010

4.1 In rule 27.11(2)—

(a) at the end of sub-paragraph (f), omit 'and';
(b) after sub-paragraph (f), insert—

'(ff) duly authorised lawyers attending for journalistic, research or public legal educational purposes; and'.

4.2 In rule 27.11(3), after 'paragraph (2)(f)' insert 'and (ff)'.

4.3 In rule 27.11(4), after 'paragraph (2)(f)' insert 'or (ff)'.

4.4 In rule 27.11(5), after 'paragraph (2)(f)' insert 'and (ff)'.

4.5 For rule 27.11(7) substitute—

'(7) In this rule—

(a) 'duly accredited' refers to accreditation in accordance with any administrative scheme for the time being approved for the purposes of this rule by the Lord Chancellor;
(b) 'duly authorised lawyer' means—
(i) a person who is authorised by a practising certificate to conduct litigation or exercise a right of audience in the family court;
(ii) a lawyer working for the Law School, Faculty or Department of a Higher Education Institution designated as a recognised body pursuant to section 216 of the Education Reform Act 1988; or
(iii) a lawyer attending on behalf of a registered educational charity the name, objects and registered charity number of which have been provided to the President of the Family Division;
(c) 'lawyer' means a person who—
(i) holds a qualifying law degree as defined by the Bar Standards Board or Solicitors Regulation Authority;
(ii) holds or has completed—
(aa) the Common Professional Examination (CPE);
(bb) an approved Graduate Diploma in Law (GDL) course or the Solicitors Qualifying Examination (SQE);
(cc) a postgraduate legal qualification; or
(dd) the CILEx Level 6 Diploma in Law and Practice or the CILEx Graduate Fast Track Diploma.'

Modification of Practice Direction 27C

5.1 In Practice Direction PD27B, after paragraph 4 insert—

'Identification of lawyers as 'authorised'

4A.1 Lawyers will be expected to carry with them identification sufficient to enable court staff, or if necessary the court itself, to verify that they are 'authorised' lawyers within the meaning of the rule.

4A.2 The following forms of identification provide sufficient information, and production of such identification will be both necessary and sufficient to demonstrate that the lawyer is 'authorised' within the meaning of rule 27.11(7)(b)(i), (ii) and (iii) respectively—

(a) a current practising certificate accompanied by picture identification of the lawyer and a signed written statement by the lawyer which complies with paragraph 4A.3;

(b) confirmation on headed notepaper from the relevant Higher Education Institution (or Law School, Faculty or Department of that Institution) of the lawyer's position and qualification, accompanied by picture identification of the lawyer and a signed written statement by the lawyer which complies with paragraph 4A.3;

(c) confirmation on headed notepaper from the relevant registered educational charity (specifying the registered charity number) of the lawyer's position and qualification, accompanied by picture identification of the lawyer and a signed written statement by the lawyer which complies with paragraph 4A.3.

4A.3 The signed written statement required by paragraph 4A.2 must—

(a) confirm that the lawyer's attendance is for journalistic, research or public legal educational purposes and that the lawyer has no personal interest in the proceedings and that he or she is not attending in the capacity of agent or instructed lawyer for any client; and

(b) confirm that the lawyer is aware of and will abide by any restrictions on publication, whether arising by operation of law (for example under section 97 of the Children Act 1989 and section 12 of the Administration of Justice Act 1960) or imposed by order of the court, which follow from the proceedings being in private.

4A.4 The information about a registered educational charity required by rule 27.11(7)(b)(iii) is to be submitted using Form FP300 (Request by educational charity to attend family proceedings for authorisation by the President of the Family Division) by e-mail to pfd.office@judiciary.uk, or by post to: The Office of the President of the Family Division, Royal Courts of Justice, Strand, London WC2A 2LL. It will be entered on a list maintained by that office, and therefore need be submitted only once.'

Practice Direction 36K – Pilot scheme: procedure for the bulk scanning of certain private law applications

This Practice Direction supplements FPR Part 36, rule 36.2 (Transitional Arrangements and Pilot Schemes).

Scope and interpretation

1.1 This Practice Direction is made under rule 36.2 and sets up a Pilot Scheme to allow for the bulk scanning of certain private law applications and supporting documents.

1.2 The Pilot Scheme applies in relation to an application where all of the following conditions are met:

a) the application is for an order in private law proceedings, as defined in rule 12.2 FPR;
b) the application does not state that it should be considered within 48 hours;
c) any application fee will be paid by means other than postal order or cash;
d) the application is to be made in the family court;
e) the application is filed in the period commencing 29 October 2018 and ending at the end of the day on 3 April 2022; and
(f) Her Majesty's Courts and Tribunals Service indicates (whether via information given online, in correspondence or otherwise) that the application must be filed by sending it to C100 Applications, PO Box 4936, 69 Buckingham Avenue, Slough, SL1 0JR.

Purpose of the Pilot Scheme

2.1 The purpose of this Pilot Scheme is to assess the use of new practices and procedures to allow for certain applications and supporting documents to be scanned by a third-party company and sent to court and to Cafcass by email within 24 hours, with the aim of reducing the administrative burden on court staff and improving efficiency.

Modification of the FPR and Practice Directions during operation of the Pilot Scheme

3.1 During the operation of the Pilot Scheme the Family Procedure Rules 2010 and the Practice Directions supporting the Rules will apply to cases falling within the Pilot Scheme as modified by paragraphs 4.1 to 5.3.

Modification of Practice Direction 5B

4.1 In paragraph 1.3, at end insert ', but not to those companies specified in Rule 3A.1'

4.2 After paragraph 1.3 insert-

'1.3A Chapter 3A applies to the companies specified in Rule 3A.1.'

4.3 After paragraph 3.4 insert-

'Chapter 3A: Bulk scanning of court documents

3A.1 Where the pilot scheme described in Practice Direction 36K applies, the following third-party companies may e-mail the court or attach a specified document to an e-mail to the court:

(a) Quadient, C100 Applications, PO Box 4936, 69 Buckingham Avenue, Slough, SL1 0JR

3A.2 If the application fee is paid by cheque, the third-party company will be responsible for accounting for the fee in accordance with its contractual obligations. The court will retain responsibility for collecting credit/debit card payments.

3A.3 Chapter 6 of Practice Direction 5B does not apply to a document which has been scanned by a third-party company and sent to court in accordance with this chapter.'

4.4 Omit paragraph 5.1.

4.5 In paragraph 5.2(a) for 'or chapter 3' substitute ', chapter 3 or chapter 3A'.

4.6 Omit paragraphs 5.3 and 5.4.

Modification of Practice Direction 12B

5.1 Omitted

5.2 In paragraph 8.9, omit the words 'a copy of the Form C100 (and the form C1A, if supplied), and'.

5.2A After paragraph 8.10 insert-

'Modifications where the pilot scheme in Practice Direction 36K applies

8A.1 Where the pilot scheme described in Practice Direction 36K applies and the application is to be made on Form C100, the applicant must send the Form C100, Form C1A and any supporting documents ('the C100 application pack') plus any documents relating to fee payment to Quadient at the address specified in paragraph 3A.1(a) of Practice Direction 5B.

8A.2 Where the pilot scheme described in Practice Direction 36K applies and the application is to be made on a form other than Form C100, the applicant must send the relevant application form and any supporting documents plus any documents relating to fee payment to Quadient at the address specified in paragraph 3A.1(a) of Practice Direction 5B.

8A.3 If the applicant fails to comply with paragraph 8A.1 or 8A.2 and instead sends the application form and any supporting documents plus any documents relating to fee payment to the court (rather than to Quadient), the court may send the application form and any supporting documents, plus any documents relating to fee payment, to Quadient.

8A.4 Subject to paragraphs 8A.6 and 8A.8, where paragraph 8A.1 or 8A.3 applies and Quadient receives a C100 application pack, Quadient will email-

(a) the C100 application pack plus any documents relating to fee payment to the court; and
(b) the C100 application pack only to Cafcass,

within 24 hours of receipt at the specified address.

8A.5 Where-

(a) either –
  (i) paragraph 8A.2 applies; or
  (ii) paragraph 8A.3 applies in respect of an application on a form other than Form C100; and
(b) Quadient receives an application form and any supporting documents, plus any documents relating to fee payment, Quadient will email the application form and any supporting documents, plus any documents relating to fee payment, to the court, within 24 hours of receipt at the specified address.

8A.7 For the purposes of paragraph 8A.6 the documents submitted will contain relevant errors if-

(a) Quadient is unable to comply with its obligations under paragraph 3A.2 of Practice Direction 5B;
(b) they are not accompanied by –
  (i) a cheque for the application fee;
  (ii) a completed Form EX160; or
  (iii) confirmation on Form C100 that the fee will be paid by debit card or credit card or via a legal representative's fee account held with Her Majesty's Courts and Tribunals Service;
(c) the correct court to whom the C100 application pack and supporting documents should be sent cannot be identified;

(d) Form C100 is omitted in its entirety or there are pages missing;
(e) there is no address given for the respondent(s);
(f) the applicant has not confirmed attendance at a MIAM or claimed an exemption from attendance; or
(g) the statement of truth is not signed on Form C100 and/or Form C1A, if supplied.

8A.8 Paragraph 8A.4(b) (Quadient emailing to Cafcass) does not apply where the application is to be filed at a family court location which has been specified to Quadient by Her Majesty's Courts and Tribunals Service as one where C100 application packs should not be emailed to Cafcass.

8A.9 The email from Quadient to the court to which the C100 application pack or other application form is attached will record the date of receipt at the specified address.

8A.10 Subject to paragraph 8A.11, for the purposes of Article 16(1)(a) of Council Regulation (EC) 2201/2003, the date of receipt recorded in accordance with paragraph 8A.9 is to be treated as the date that the application was 'lodged' with the court.

8A.11 If the applicant fails to comply with paragraph 8A.1 or 8A.2 and instead sends the C100 application pack or other application form and any supporting documents, plus any documents relating to fee payment, to the court (rather than to Quadient), paragraph 8A.10 does not apply.

8A.12 After 30 days have passed from the date of receipt of any application form and accompanying documents, the application form and those documents must be destroyed by Quadient.

8A.13 A scan of a document received by the court by email from Quadient shall be treated by the court as a true copy of the original document.'

5.3 In paragraph 13.3-

(a) after 'enquiries' insert 'on receipt of a valid C100 application.'; and
(b) in the third sentence omit 'from the court'.

Practice Direction 36L – Pilot scheme: procedure for using an online system to complete certain stages of certain proceedings for a matrimonial order

This Practice Direction supplements FPR Part 36, rule 36.2 (Transitional Arrangements and Pilot Schemes).

Scope and interpretation

1.1 This Practice Direction is made under rule 36.2 and sets up a Pilot Scheme to allow for certain applications and stages in certain matrimonial proceedings to be completed using the online system.

1.2 This Practice Direction comes into force on 14 January 2019.

1.3 Subject to paragraph 1.4, this Practice Direction supersedes Practice Direction 36E, which is revoked from the date this Practice Direction comes into force.

1.4 Practice Direction 36E will remain in force in relation to any applications commenced under the Pilot Scheme referred to in that Practice Direction, and this Practice Direction (and any that supersede it) will not apply in relation to such applications.

1.5 The Pilot Scheme applies where all of the following conditions are met:

a) the application is for a matrimonial order which is a decree of divorce made under section 1 of the 1973 Act;
b) the application is not unsuitable for the online system (as explained in paragraph 1.6);
c) the applicant chooses to use the online system as described in this Practice Direction;
d) the application does not at any time become a defended case (should the application become a defended case it will exit the Pilot Scheme and this Practice Direction will no longer apply to it);
e) the application is started in the family court; and
f) the application is filed in the period commencing 14 January 2019 and ending 5 April 2020.

1.6 HMCTS may conclude that certain individual or categories of applications are not suitable for the online system, and such categories are to be specified in guidance issued by HMCTS and published on GOV.UK.

1.7 Following the making of an application online, certain other stages under Part 7 of the Rules (including an applicant's application for decree nisi under FPR 7.19(1)) may be completed online where HMCTS selects the application to test new features of the online system. The online system will notify the applicant straight away if the application has been selected. The technical capacity of the system will widen in stages and so, while some types of applications made online in accordance with paragraph 1.5(a) may not be selected to test new features at the outset, they may be selected for testing as the system develops.

1.8 For the avoidance of doubt, where an application has not been selected to test new features under paragraph 1.7 then an applicant will be asked to complete relevant further stages under Part 7 of the Rules using the paper forms prescribed in PD 5A.

1.9 In this Practice Direction-

a) the 'online system' means Her Majesty's Courts and Tribunals Service's online system to allow for specified applications and stages in matrimonial proceedings to be completed online;
b) 'new features' means any features of the online system that are in an earlier stage of development, and that are only available for certain applications as described in paragraph 1.7.

Purpose of the Pilot Scheme

2.1 The purpose of this Pilot Scheme is to assess the use of new practices and procedures to allow for certain stages in certain matrimonial proceedings to be completed using the online system. It is intended that future Practice Directions will establish other Pilot Schemes to allow for other specified stages in those proceedings, and for other types of matrimonial proceedings, to also be completed using the online system.

Modification of the FPR and Practice Directions during operation of the Pilot Scheme

3.1 During the operation of the Pilot Scheme the Family Procedure Rules 2010 and the Practice Directions supporting the Rules will apply to cases falling within the Pilot Scheme as modified by paragraphs 4.1 to 12.7. This Practice Direction contains provisions that apply generally to applications in the Pilot Scheme, and also specific additional provisions that apply to applications selected to test new features.

Modifications that apply generally to applications in the pilot scheme

Modification of Part 5 FPR

4.1 For rule 5.1, substitute-

'5.1(1) Where the Pilot Scheme referred to in Practice Direction 36L applies, and subject to that Practice Direction, the following stages in matrimonial proceedings shall be completed online by the parties in the manner specified by the online system-

(a) the application for a decree of divorce (including an amended application if relevant);
(b) the acknowledgment of service;
(c) the applicant's application for a decree nisi; and
(d) the notice that the applicant wishes the decree nisi to be made absolute.

(2) Each party must at each stage provide all the information requested, including any documents that the online system or court requires, in a manner specified by the online system or by the court.'.

4.2 Omit rule 5.2.

Modification of Part 6 FPR

5.1 In Rule 6.15-

(a) For paragraph (1) substitute-

'(1) An application is deemed to be served if-

(a) subject to paragraph (2), a paper acknowledgment of service, signed by the party served or the solicitor acting on that party's behalf, is returned to the court office; or
(b) the respondent or co-respondent completes the acknowledgment of service using the online system referred to in Practice Direction 36L.'

Modification of Part 7 FPR

6.1 For rule 7.6(1) substitute-

'7.6(1) Where the applicant is legally represented, the legal representative must complete and provide with the application, in a manner specified in the online system referred to in Practice Direction 36L, a statement certifying whether the legal representative has discussed with the applicant the possibility of a reconciliation and given the applicant the names and addresses of persons qualified to help effect a reconciliation.'.

6.2 For Rule 7.8(2)(a) substitute-

'(a) details of how to respond to the application; and'

6.3 In Rule 7.12-

(a) in paragraph (1) for 'The' substitute 'Subject to paragraphs (2A) to (2C), the';
(b) after paragraph (2) insert-

'(2A) A respondent and co-respondent may choose whether or not to use the online system to complete and file an acknowledgment of service. Details of how to respond online will be provided in the letter sent to them in accordance with 7.8(2)(a).

(2B) If a respondent or co-respondent chooses not to use the online system then they must contact HMCTS (using the details provided in the letter sent to them) to request a paper form for acknowledging service.

(2C) Where paragraph (2B) applies, the acknowledgment of service must be filed within 7 days beginning with the date on which the respondent or co-respondent received the paper form for acknowledging service. The amended deadline for filing the acknowledgment will be notified to all parties.'.

(c) in paragraphs 3(a) and 4 references to 'signed' and 'sign' are to be read as references to the name of the individual being, or having been, recorded against the statement of truth included in an acknowledgment of service which has been completed online in accordance with paragraph (2A).

Modification of Part 17 FPR

7.1 In rule 17.2(6), for 'The statement of truth' substitute 'Subject to paragraph (6A), the statement of truth'.

7.2 After rule 17.2(6) insert-

'(6A) Where a statement of truth is included in an application or acknowledgment of service completed using the online system referred to in Practice Direction 36L-

(a) the party must file with the court an application or acknowledgment of service which includes the name of the person who the online system requires to sign a statement of truth recorded against the statement of truth; and
(b) the court may require the party to produce a copy of the application or acknowledgment of service containing the signature of the person referred to in sub-paragraph (a) at a later date.'.

Modification of Part 29 FPR

8.1 After rule 29.13(1) insert-

'(1A) Where the pilot scheme referred to in Practice Direction 36L applies, service under paragraph (1) or otherwise may be effected by the court sending each party an email, to the address given for service in accordance with Practice Direction 6A, containing a weblink from which the order may be accessed and downloaded.'

Disapplication of Practice Direction 5B

9.1 Practice Direction 5B does not apply in relation to an application which can be made online under the Pilot Scheme referred to in Practice Direction 36L.

Modification of Practice Direction 6A

10.1 In paragraph 4.2(b)-

(a) in paragraph (iii) for '; or' substitute ';';
(b) in paragraph (iv) for the full-stop substitute '; or'; and
(c) after paragraph (iv) insert-

'(v) confirmation given, by the party to be served, within the online system referred to in Practice Direction 36L that that party is willing to accept service by email and stating the email address for such service.'

10.2 In paragraph 10.1-

(a) for 'send' substitute 'provide'; and
(b) omit 'photographic or scanned'.

Modification of Practice Direction 7A

11.1 For paragraph 1.1 substitute-

'1.1 Where the Pilot Scheme referred to in Practice Direction 36L applies, an application for a matrimonial order must be made as required by the online system referred to in that Practice Direction and in accordance with rule 5.1.'.

11.2 For paragraph 1.2 substitute-

'1.2 The application must be completed according to the detailed guidance contained in the online system. It is especially important that the particulars provide evidence to show why the applicant is entitled to a decree of divorce. The particulars should, however, be as concise as possible consistent with providing the necessary evidence.'.

11.3 After paragraph 1.3 insert-

'Applications for matrimonial orders received via the online system: timing

1A.1 When an application is received via the online system referred to in Practice Direction 36L and is recorded by Her Majesty's Courts and Tribunals Service software has having been received at or after 4.31pm and before or at 11.59pm, the date of filing will not be before the next day that the court location to which the application has been sent via the online system is open for business.

1A.2 When an application is received via the online system referred to in Practice Direction 36L, an acknowledgement of receipt will automatically be sent to the applicant. This acknowledgement of receipt does not constitute a notice that the application has been issued.'.

11.4 In paragraph 3.1-

(a) for the heading of, and first sentence of, paragraph 3.1, substitute-

'Proof of marriage

3.1 The online system referred to in Practice Direction 36L sets out the documents which must accompany an application for a matrimonial order and the way in which those documents may be provided (for example, the online system may allow for documents to be posted, or to be uploaded and submitted online with the application).';

(b) in the second sentence of paragraph 3.1 omit 'or civil partnership';
(c) in sub-paragraph (a)(i)-
  (i) omit 'or civil partnership'; and
  (ii) omit 'or civil partnership registration'; and
(d) in sub-paragraph (a)(ii), omit 'or civil partnership registration'.

11.5 In paragraph 4.1-

(a) for 'An applicant for a matrimonial or civil partnership order' substitute 'Where the Pilot Scheme referred to in Practice Direction 36L applies, an applicant'; and
(b) omit 'form'.

Modification of Practice Direction 17A

12.1 Omit paragraphs 1.5 and 2.3.

12.2 In the heading to paragraph 3.1 and in paragraphs 3.1, 3.7, 3.8 and 3.10 references to 'sign', 'signs', 'signed' and 'signing' are to be read as references to the name of the person being, or having been, recorded against the statement of truth included in an application or acknowledgment of service filed in matrimonial proceedings to which the pilot scheme referred to in Practice Direction 36L applies.

12.3 For paragraph 4.1 substitute-

'4.1 Where an application or acknowledgment of service completed using the online system referred to in Practice Direction 36L contains a statement of truth, with the name of a person who is unable to read or sign the document recorded against it, the application or acknowledgment of service must be accompanied by a certificate made by an authorised person.'.

12.4 In paragraph 4.3-

(a) for sub-paragraph (a) substitute-

'(a) that the content of the online application or acknowledgment of service has been read to the person before completion of the statement of truth required by the online system;'; and

(b) for sub-paragraph (e) substitute-

'(e) that that person confirmed in the presence of the authorised person that it was their belief that the contents of the online application or acknowledgment of service were true.'

12.5 For the Annex substitute-

'Certificate to be used where a person is unable to read or sign an online application or acknowledgment of service filed in matrimonial proceedings to which the pilot scheme in Practice Direction 36L applies.

I certify that I [name and address of authorised person] have read the contents of the online [application][acknowledgment of service] and the statement of truth to the person whose name is recorded against the statement of truth, who appeared to understand (a) the [application][acknowledgment of service] and approved its contents as accurate and (b) the statement of truth and the consequences of making a false statement, and orally confirmed that this was the case in my presence.'.

Additional modifications that apply to applications selected for the testing of new features

Additional modification of Part 7 FPR

12.6 In Rule 7.19-

(a) for paragraph (1) substitute-

'(1) An application may be made to the court, using the online system described in Practice Direction 36L, for it to consider the making of a decree nisi in the proceedings –

(b) in subparagraph (b) omit 'or civil partnership'.
(c) in paragraph (2)(b) omit 'or civil partnership';
(d) in paragraph (3)–
  (i) omit 'form'; and
  (ii) for 'be accompanied by a statement setting' substitute 'set'.
(e) in paragraph (4)–
  (i) omit ', conditional order, a decree of judicial separation or a separation order';
  (ii) for 'be accompanied by' substitute 'include';
  (iii) in subparagraph (c) for 'the' substitute 'a paper'.

12.7 In Rule 7.32(1)(a) -

(a) after 'court' insert ', using the online system described in Practice Direction 36L,

Practice Direction 36M – Pilot scheme: online system for certain public law proceedings and emergency proceedings relating to children

This Practice Direction supplements FPR Part 36, rule 36.2 (Transitional Arrangements and Pilot Schemes).

Scope and interpretation

1.1 This Practice Direction is made under rule 36.2 and sets up a Pilot Scheme to allow for certain applications and stages in the proceedings specified in paragraph 1.3(a) of this Practice Direction to be completed using an online system.

1.2 This Practice Direction comes into force on 31 January 2019.

1.3 The Pilot Scheme applies where all of the following conditions are met:

(a) the application is -
   (i) for an order in public law proceedings, as defined in rule 12.2 FPR;
   (ii) for a secure accommodation order under section 119 of the Social Services and Wellbeing (Wales) Act 2014;
   (iii) for an order in emergency proceedings, as defined in rule 12.2 FPR; or
   (iv) made within proceedings for an order referred to in paragraph (i), (ii) or (iii);
(aa) the application is made by-
   (i) a Local Authority;
   (ii) Cafcass or Cafcass Cymru; or
   (iii) a legally represented party to proceedings;
(b) access to the online system for making and continuing such applications is permitted;
(c) the process provided for in the online system can be completed;
(d) the application is started in the family court; and
(e) the application is filed in the period commencing 31 January 2019 and ending 31 October 2022.

1.4 In this Practice Direction, 'the online system' means Her Majesty's Courts and Tribunals Service's online system to allow for certain stages in applications specified in paragraph 1.3(a) of this Practice Direction to be dealt with online.

Purpose of the Pilot Scheme

2.1 The purpose of this Pilot Scheme is to assess the use of new practices and procedures to allow for certain stages in applications specified in paragraph 1.3(a) of this Practice Direction to be completed using the online system.

2.2 This Pilot Scheme enables a person or body referred to in paragraph 1.3(aa) to start, progress and participate in proceedings via the online system, to include taking the following steps -

(a) to create and file an application referred to in paragraph 1.3(a)(i), (ii) or (iii) to commence proceedings;
(b) to file an application referred to in paragraph 1.3(a)(iv);

(c) in respect of an application referred to in sub-paragraph (a) or (b), to-
  (i) file documents;
  (ii) amend the application;
  (iii) indicate willingness to accept service of documents relating to the application via email containing a weblink from which a document may be accessed and downloaded; and
  (iv) accept service of any documents relating to the application;
(d) to view an electronic record of the progress of the application and of applications within proceedings that are progressing using the online system.

2.2A Subject to paragraph 2.2C, a Local Authority which is a party to proceedings started-

(a) on or after a date specified in paragraph 2.2D; and
(b) in a court listed in paragraph 2.2D, must use the procedure provided for by this Practice Direction to start, progress and participate in proceedings, to include taking any of the steps specified in paragraph 2.2(a) to (d).

2.2B Subject to paragraph 2.2C, where existing proceedings are progressing via the online system-

(a) on a date specified in paragraph 2.2D; and
(b) in a court listed in paragraph 2.2D, a Local Authority which is a party to those proceedings must continue to use the procedure provided for by this Practice Direction to progress and participate in those proceedings.

2.2C Paragraph 2.2A or 2.2B does not apply-

(a) where proceedings are transferred from the family court to the High Court; or
(b) when the online system is not available for use because of-
  (i) planned 'down time' for system maintenance or upgrades; or
  (ii) unplanned 'down-time' because of, for example, a system failure or power outage or some other unplanned circumstance.

2.2D The dates and courts referred to in paragraph 2.2A and 2.2B are-

(a) from 26 July 2021, the family court sitting at-
  (i) Worcester;
  (ii) Coventry;
  (iii) Swansea;
(b) from 20 September 2021, the family court sitting at-
  (i) Cardiff;
  (ii) Kingston Upon Hull;
  (iii) Newcastle;
  (iv) Kent;
  (v) Bristol;
  (vi) Leicester;
  (vii) Taunton.
(c) from 18 October 2021, the family court sitting at-
  (i) Derby;
  (ii) Oxford;
  (iii) Reading;
  (iv) Swindon;
  (v) Truro.
(d) from 15 November 2021, the family court sitting at-
  (i) Barrow in Furness;
  (ii) Blackpool;

(iii) Bournemouth;
(iv) Carlisle;
(v) Exeter;
(vi) Lancaster;
(vii) Lincoln;
(viii) Milton Keynes;
(ix) Nottingham;
(x) Plymouth;
(xi) Preston;
(xii) West Cumbria.

(e) from 29 November 2021, the family court sitting at-
(i) Bradford;
(ii) Brighton;
(iii) Caernarfon;
(iv) Chester;
(v) Crewe;
(vi) Durham;
(vii) Guildford;
(viii) Leeds;
(ix) Liverpool;
(x) Manchester;
(xi) Northampton;
(xii) Norwich;
(xiii) Portsmouth;
(xiv) Teesside;
(xv) Wakefield;
(xvi) West London;
(xvii) Wrexham;
(xviii) York.

(f) from 20 December 2021, the family court sitting at-
(i) Birmingham;
(ii) Chelmsford;
(iii) Luton;
(iv) Peterborough;
(v) Sheffield;
(vi) Stoke on Trent;
(vii) Watford;
(viii) Wolverhampton.

(g) from 28 February 2022 the family court sitting at any location not already referred to in sub-paragraphs (a) to (f).

2.3 For the avoidance of doubt, it should not be assumed that an application of a type specified in paragraph 1.3(a), or any or all stages of such an application, will always be able to be dealt with on the online system. This is because Her Majesty's Courts and Tribunals Service will be gradually rolling out the types of application that can be dealt with via the online system. Her Majesty's Courts and Tribunals Service will indicate via the online system which applications can be dealt with on the online system at any point in time.

Modification of the FPR and Practice Directions during the operation of the Pilot Scheme

3.1 During the operation of the Pilot Scheme, the Family Procedure Rules 2010 and the Practice Directions supporting the rules will apply to cases falling within the Pilot Scheme as modified by paragraphs 3A.1 to 7.2.

Modification of rule 2.3(1) FPR

3A.1 In rule 2.3(1) FPR, the definition of 'filing' is modified by inserting after 'office'-

'or, where the Pilot Scheme referred to in Practice Direction 36M applies, by creating and submitting, or by or uploading, the document on the online system referred to in that Practice Direction'.

Modification of Part 5 FPR

4.1 For rule 5.1, substitute-

'5.1 Where the Pilot Scheme referred to in Practice Direction 36M applies, the applicant must-

(a) either-
(i) complete all sections of the application process set out in the online system referred to in that Practice Direction; or
(ii) upload the application to the online system in the manner specified by the online system;
(b) provide all the information, including any additional documents, that the online application system referred to in that Practice Direction requires, or that the court requires, in a manner specified by the online application system, or required by the court.'.

4.2 In rule 5.2 for 'Subject' substitute 'Where rule 5.1(a)(ii) applies, subject

4.3 After rule 5.2 FPR insert-

'Timing of receipt of applications
5.3 An application that is submitted via the online system in accordance with rule 5.1 is lodged with the court on the date and at the time that HMCTS software records the application as received, provided that the application is subsequently issued by the court.
Timing of receipt of documents other than applications
5.3A A document, other than an application, that is submitted via the online system is filed with or otherwise received by the court on the date and at the time that HMCTS software records the document as received.'

Modification of Part 17 FPR

5.1 In rule 17.2(6), for 'The statement of truth' substitute 'Subject to paragraph (6A), the statement of truth'.

5.2 After rule 17.2(6) insert-

'(6A) Where a statement of truth is included in an application completed using the online system referred to in Practice Direction 36M applies, the applicant must file with the court an application which includes the name of the person who the online system requires to sign a statement of truth recorded against the statement of truth.'

Modification of Part 29 FPR

5A.1 After rule 29.13(1) insert-

'(1A) Where the pilot scheme referred to in Practice Direction 36M applies, service under paragraph (1) or otherwise may be effected by the court sending each party an email, to the address given for service in accordance with Practice Direction 6A, containing a weblink from which the judgment or order may be accessed and downloaded.'

Disapplication of Practice Direction 5B

Modification of Practice Direction 6A

6A.1 After paragraph 4.1 insert-

'4.1A Paragraphs 4.2 to 4.6 also apply where-

(a) the pilot scheme referred to in Practice Direction 36M applies; and
(b) service of a judgment or order by the court is to be effected in accordance with rule 29.13(1A), as inserted by Practice Direction 36M.

4.1B Where paragraph 4.1A applies, references in paragraphs 4.2 to 4.5 to service of a document by email include service of a judgment or order by the court sending by email a weblink from which the judgment or order may be accessed and downloaded.'

6B.1 In paragraph 4.2(b)-

(a) in paragraph (iii) for '; or' substitute ';';
(b) in paragraph (iv) for the full-stop substitute '; or'; and
(c) after paragraph (iv) insert-

'(v) confirmation given, by the party to be served, within the online system referred to in Practice Direction 36M that that party is willing to accept service by email and stating the email address for such service.'

Modification of Practice Direction 17A

7.1 Omit paragraphs 1.5 and 2.3.

7.2 In the heading to paragraph 3.1 and in paragraphs 3.1, 3.4, 3.7, 3.8 and 3.10 references to 'sign', 'signs', 'signed' and 'signing' are to be read as references to checking a box next to the statement of truth included in applications to which the pilot scheme referred to in Practice Direction 36M applies.

Practice Direction 36N – Pilot scheme: procedure for online filing and progression of certain applications for a financial remedy in connection with proceedings for a matrimonial order or for a civil partnership order

This PD applies to applications issued by the court on or after 6 April 2022. For applications issued by the court before 6 April 2022 see [https://webarchive.nationalarchives.gov.uk/ukgwa/20211201113641/https:/www.justice.gov.uk/courts/procedure-rules/family/practice_directions/practice-direction-36n-pilot-scheme-procedure-for-online-filing-and-progression-of-certain-applications-for-a-financial-remedy-in-connection-with-certain-proceedings-for-a-matrimonial-order].

This Practice Direction supplements rule 36.2 FPR (Transitional arrangements and pilot schemes).

Scope and interpretation

1.1 This Practice Direction is made under rule 36.2 FPR and sets up a Pilot Scheme to allow for certain applications for a financial remedy in connection with proceedings for a matrimonial order or for a civil partnership order to be filed and progressed via a HMCTS online application system.

(It should be noted that, while a presumption of death order under the 2004 Act is a form of 'civil partnership order' as defined in rule 2.3 FPR, no application for a financial remedy may be made under the 2004 Act in connection with an application for such a presumption of death order.)

1.2 This Practice Direction comes into force on 27th May 2019.

1.3 This Pilot Scheme applies to applications where all of the following conditions are met:

(a) subject to the exception in paragraph 1.4, the application is-
  (i) for a financial remedy in connection with an application for a matrimonial order or for a civil partnership order; or
  (ii) a notice of intention to proceed with an application for a financial remedy that was made in an application for a matrimonial order or for a civil partnership order;
(b) the application is not for a consent order;
(c) either –
  (i) the applicant is legally represented; or
  (ii) the applicant and the respondent are legally represented;
(d) access by the party's legal representative to the online system for creating, starting or progressing such applications is permitted;
(e) the application is started in the family court; and
(f) the application is made in the period commencing on 27th May 2019 and at the end of the day on 31 December 2022.

1.4 The exception referred to in paragraph 1.3 is where the application is for-

(a) an order for payment in respect of legal services; or
(b) a variation order in respect of a financial remedy order that was not made as a result of an application made via the online system.

1.5 In this Practice Direction, 'the online system' means Her Majesty's Courts and Tribunal Service's online system to allow for specified stages in specified financial remedy proceedings to be dealt with online.

Purpose of this Pilot Scheme

2.1 The purpose of this Pilot Scheme is to assess new practices and procedures to allow for certain applications for a financial remedy, made in connection with certain proceedings for a matrimonial order or for a civil partnership order, to be created, started and progressed via an online system.

2.2 It is intended that future Practice Directions will establish other Pilot Schemes which will allow for other specified stages in specified financial remedy proceedings to take place via the online system.

2.3 For the avoidance of doubt-

(a) it should not be assumed that all stages of an application will always be able to be dealt with on the online system or that all legal representatives of parties will have access to the online system. This is because Her Majesty's Courts and Tribunals Service will be gradually rolling out new stages and features on the online system. Her Majesty's Courts and Tribunals Service will indicate via the online system who can access the online system, and which stages in proceedings can be dealt with on the online system, at any point in time; and

(b) filing a document via the online system does not mean that service of that document has been effected.

Modification or disapplication of the FPR and Practice Directions during the operation of the Pilot Scheme

3.1 During the operation of the Pilot Scheme, the FPR and the Practice Directions supporting the FPR will apply in respect of the applicant to cases falling within the Pilot Scheme as modified, or disapplied, by paragraphs 3A.1 to 11.2.

Modification of Part 2 FPR

3A.1 In rule 2.3(1), for the definition of 'filing' substitute-

'filing' in relation to supplying a document or information means-

(a) delivering it, by post or otherwise, to the court office; or
(b) where Practice Direction 36N applies, by-
(i) uploading the document to the online system referred to in that Practice Direction; or
(ii) submitting the information via that online system.

Modification of Part 3 FPR

4.1 For rule 3.7 substitute-

'3.7 Where the Pilot Scheme referred to in Practice Direction 36N applies, the application must include from the prospective applicant -

(a) confirmation that the prospective applicant has attended a MIAM;
(b) a claim that one of the MIAM exemptions applies; or
(c) confirmation that a mediator's exemption applies.'.

4.2 In rule 3.8(2) for 'confirms in the relevant form' substitute 'has provided signed confirmation'.

Modification of Part 5 FPR

5.1 For rule 5.1, substitute-

'5.1 Where the Pilot Scheme referred to in Practice Direction 36N applies-

(a) the applicant must complete all sections of the online application; and
(b) the applicant and the respondent must provide all the information, including any additional documents, that the online application system referred to in that Practice Direction requires, or that the court requires, in a manner-
(i) specified by the online application system;
(ii) specified in guidance relating to the online application system; or
(iii) required by the court.'

5.2 Omit rule 5.2.

Modification of Part 9 FPR

6.1 After rule 9.9B insert-

'Pilot Scheme cases: filing of documents

9.9C(1) In this rule, 'document' means anything in which information of any description is recorded.

(2) Where-

(a) the Pilot Scheme referred to in Practice Direction 36N applies;
(b) the court, a rule in this Part or a provision in Practice Direction 9A requires a party to file a document with the court; and
(c) the court or the online system requires that that document be filed with the court in a specified manner;

the party must comply with that requirement by filing the document in the specified manner.

(See also Practice Direction 9A.)'.

6.2 In rule 9.17, after paragraph (5) insert-

'(5A) Where the Pilot Scheme referred to in Practice Direction 36N applies and a document has been filed in a manner specified by the online system referred to in that Practice Direction, paragraph (5) does not apply.

(5B) Where paragraph (5A) applies, the document will not be retained on the online system or on the court file following the conclusion of the FDR appointment.'.

6.3 For rule 9.26(1)(a) substitute-

'(a) the applicant must file a draft of the order in the terms sought, which must be signed by both parties; and'.

Modification of Part 29 FPR

7.1 After rule 29.13(1) insert-

'(1A) Where the Pilot Scheme referred to in Practice Direction 36N applies, service on a party under paragraph (1) or otherwise may be effected by the court sending the party an email, to the address given for service in accordance with Practice Direction 6A, containing a weblink from which the order may be accessed and downloaded.'.

Modification of Practice Direction 3A

8.1 For paragraph 6 substitute-

'6 Where the Pilot Scheme referred to in Practice Direction 36N applies, the application must include from the applicant one of the following-

(a) confirmation that the applicant has attended a MIAM, including the date attended, the name of the authorised family mediator (and/or Family Mediation Service) and their FMC registration number;
(b) a claim that one of the MIAM exemptions applies; or
(c) confirmation that a mediator's exemption applies.'.

8.2 After paragraph 6 insert-

'6A An applicant who provides confirmation or makes a claim in accordance with paragraph 6(a), (b) or (c) above is not required to provide any supporting evidence with their application, but should bring any supporting evidence (including where applicable the signed confirmation by the authorised family mediator that a mediator's exemption applies) to the first appointment.'.

8.3 Omit paragraphs 14 and 15.

8.4 In paragraph 18 for 'on the relevant form' substitute 'in the relevant section of the online system'.

8.5 In paragraph 34, for the words after 'MIAM exemption' substitute 'and signed confirmation should then be returned to the applicant.'.

Disapplication of Practice Direction 5B

9.1 Omitted

Modification of Practice Direction 6A

10.1 In paragraph 4.2(b)-

(a) in paragraph (iii) for '; or' substitute ';';
(b) in paragraph (iv) for the full-stop substitute '; or'; and
(c) after paragraph (iv) insert-

'(v) confirmation given, by the party to be served, within the online system referred to in Practice Direction 36N, that that applicant is willing to accept service by email and stating the email address for such service.'.

Modification of Practice Direction 9A

11.1 After paragraph 2.1, insert-

'Application for a financial remedy received via the online system: timing

2A.1 An application for a financial remedy that is submitted via the online system referred to in Practice Direction 36N is lodged with the court on the date and at the time that HMCTS software records the application as received, provided that the application is subsequently issued by the court.

2A.1A A document, other than an application, that is submitted via the online system referred to in Practice Direction 36N is filed with or otherwise received by the court on the date and at the time that HMCTS software records the document as received.'; and

2A.2 When an application for a financial remedy to which the Pilot Scheme referred to in Practice Direction 36N applies is received via the online system referred to in that Practice Direction, an acknowledgement of receipt will automatically be sent to the email address given as the address for service in the online system. This acknowledgement of receipt does not constitute a notice that the application has been issued.

Application for a financial remedy received via the online system: filing of subsequent documents (etc)

2B.1 Rule 9.9C makes provision in relation to cases to which the Pilot Scheme referred to in Practice Direction 36N applies. The term 'document' is defined widely in the rule. The reference in rule 9.9C to a 'document' includes all statements, evidence, notices and other documents that a party may be required to file in accordance with a direction or order of the court, a rule in Part 9 of the FPR or a provision of this Practice Direction, to include:

rule 9.14 – a financial statement, documents accompanying the financial statement, a statement of issues, chronology, questionnaire, notice of readiness, confirmation of who has been served;

rule 9.15 – further documents to be filed, as directed by the court at the first appointment;
rule 9.16 – documents to be filed, as directed by the court after the first appointment;
rule 9.17(3) – details of offers and proposals;
rule 9.17(9) – evidence directed at the conclusion of an FDR appointment to be filed;
rule 9.18(2)(c)(iii) – certificate of service;
rule 9.19(1), (2) and (3) – financial statement and specified supporting documents;
rule 9.20(3)(a) and (b) – further evidence or documents to be filed, as directed by the court at the first hearing;
rule 9.28(1) – an open statement which sets out concise details, including the amounts involved, of the orders which the applicant proposes to ask the court to make;
paragraph 4.1 of this Practice Direction – a summary of the case agreed between the parties, a schedule of assets agreed between the parties and details of any directions that they seek, including, where appropriate, the name of any expert they wish to be appointed; and
paragraph 5.2 of Practice Direction 9A – documents or information filed by way of reply to a questionnaire, where the court has directed that these be filed with the court.'.

11.2 For paragraph 7.1 substitute-

'7.1 Rule 9.26(1)(a) is considered to be properly complied with if the draft order is signed by solicitors on record as acting for a party. However, where the consent order applied for contains undertakings, it should be signed by the party giving the undertakings as well as by that party's solicitor.

(Provision relating to the enforcement of undertakings is contained in Practice Direction 33A supplementing Part 33 of the FPR.)'

Practice Direction 36O – Pilot scheme: procedure for bulk scanning of certain documents

This Practice Direction supplements rule 36.2 FPR (Transitional arrangements and pilot schemes).

Scope and interpretation

1.1 This Practice Direction is made under rule 36.2 FPR and sets up a Pilot Scheme to allow for the bulk scanning by a specified third-party company of certain documents which are required to be filed with or otherwise sent to the court.

1.2 This Practice Direction comes into force on 1st July 2019.

1.3 This Pilot Scheme applies where all of the following conditions are met-

(a) a document is to be filed with or otherwise sent to the family court;
(b) Her Majesty's Courts and Tribunals Service indicates (whether via information given online, in correspondence or otherwise) that the document must be filed with or sent to the court by sending it to a specified third-party company; and
(c) the document is filed or sent in the period commencing on 1st July 2019 and at the end of the day on 3 April 2022.

1.4 Nothing in this Practice Direction precludes a document being sent to the court by email where that would be in accordance with rule 5.5 FPR and Practice Direction 5B.

1.5 In this Practice Direction-

'document' means anything in which information of any description is recorded and includes (but is not limited to) an application, a notice, a statement or a letter; and

'specified third-party company' means-

(a) Exela Technologies Limited.'

Purpose of this Pilot Scheme

2.1 The purpose of this Pilot Scheme is to assess new practices and procedures to allow for certain documents to be filed with or otherwise sent to the court by being sent by post to a specified third-party company, and for such a company to scan those documents and send them electronically to a secure cloud-based system which is accessible by Her Majesty's Courts and Tribunals Service. This is with the aim of reducing the administrative burden on court staff and improving efficiency.

Modification or disapplication of the FPR and Practice Directions, and application of this Practice Direction, during the operation of the Pilot Scheme

3.1 During the operation of the Pilot Scheme, where the Pilot Scheme applies, the FPR and the Practice Directions supporting the FPR will apply-

(a) subject to the provisions of this Practice Direction; and
(b) as modified by paragraphs 7.1 and 8.1.

Sending documents to a specified-third party company

4.1 Where this Pilot Scheme applies, subject to paragraph 4.5, any document to be filed with, or otherwise sent to, the court must be sent by post to the address for a specified third-party company to which Her Majesty's Courts and Tribunals Service has indicated that the document should be sent.

(The indication from Her Majesty's Courts and Tribunals Service of the address to which a document should be sent may be via information provided online, in correspondence, or otherwise.)

4.2 An application sent to a specified third-party company in accordance with paragraph 4.1 is treated as lodged with the court on the date of receipt recorded as required by paragraph 5.2(a), provided that the application is subsequently issued by the court.

4.2A A document other than an application sent to a specified third-party company in accordance with paragraph 4.1 is treated as filed with or otherwise received by the court on the date of receipt recorded as required by paragraph 5.2(a).

4.3 If a person fails to send a document to a specified third-party company in accordance with paragraph 4.1 and instead sends a document to the court (other than by way of email in accordance with rule 5.5 FPR and Practice Direction 5B), the court may send the document to the specified third-party company.

4.3A The court may also send a document to the specified third-party company where the court considers it appropriate to do so.

4.4 Where paragraph 4.3 or 4.3A applies and the court sends a document to the specified third-party company, paragraph 4.2 does not apply.

4.5 Nothing in this Practice Direction precludes a document being sent to the court by email, where that is permitted under rule 5.5 FPR and Practice Direction 5B.

Action to be taken by a specified third-party company

5.1 Paragraph 5.2 applies where-

(a) this Pilot Scheme applies; and
(b) documents are sent to a specified third-party company in accordance with paragraph 4.1 or 4.3.

5.2 The specified third-party company must-

(a) record the date of receipt of the document;
(b) scan the document;
(c) send the scanned document, with any necessary attached information, electronically to a secure cloud-based storage system which is accessible by Her Majesty's Courts and Tribunals Service.

5.3 After taking the steps outlined in paragraph 5.2, any original document other than a court form or an item of correspondence addressed to the court must be returned to the sender by the specified third-party company.

5.4 After 30 days have passed from the date of receipt, any original document that is a court form or item of correspondence addressed to the court must be destroyed by the specified third-party company.

Documents scanned by a specified third-party company

6.1 A scan of a document from a specified third-party company shall be treated by the court as a true copy of the original document.

Modification of rule 2.3(1) of the FPR

7.1 In cases to which this Pilot Scheme applies, in rule 2.3(1) of the FPR, the definition of 'filing' is modified by inserting after 'office'-

'(or, where the Pilot Scheme referred to in Practice Direction 36O applies, to the address to which HMCTS indicates that a document should be sent)'.

Modification of Practice Direction 27A – Family Proceedings: Court Bundles (Universal Practice to be applied in the High Court and Family Court)

8.1 In cases to which this Pilot Scheme applies, Practice Direction 27A is modified as follows-

(a) in paragraph 7.1, for 'The bundle' substitute 'Subject to paragraph 7.2A, the bundle';
(b) in paragraph 7.2(b), for 'Unless' substitute 'Subject to paragraph 7.2A, unless';
(c) after paragraph 7.2, insert-

'7.2A Where the Pilot Scheme referred to in Practice Direction 36O applies, if Her Majesty's Courts and Tribunals Service has indicated to a litigant in person that the bundle should be sent to an address for a specified third-party company, the bundle shall be lodged with the court by sending it to that address.'; and

(d) after paragraph 7.3 insert-

'7.3A Any bundle lodged in accordance with paragraph 7.2 shall show the date and place of the hearing on the bundle.

Practice Direction 36P – Pilot scheme: placement proceedings: procedure for specified steps to be taken via the online system

This Practice Direction supplements rule 36.2 FPR (transitional arrangements and pilot schemes)

Scope and interpretation

1.1 This Practice Direction is made under rule 36.2 and sets up a Pilot Scheme to allow-

(a) for applications in placement proceedings, and all required accompanying documents, to be filed with the court via uploading them to the online system; and

(b) for applications, judgments and orders in such proceedings to be served by the court via the online system.

1.2 This Practice Direction comes into force on 9th March 2020.

1.3 The Pilot Scheme applies where all of the following conditions are met:

(a) the application is in placement proceedings (as defined in rule 2.3(1) FPR);

(b) access to the online system for filing via uploading such applications and all required accompanying documents is permitted;

(c) the application is started in the family court; and

(d) the application and all required accompanying documents are filed in the period commencing 9th March 2020 and at the end of the day on 1 September 2022.

1.4 In this Practice Direction, 'the online system' means Her Majesty's Courts and Tribunals Service's online system to allow for applications for placement proceedings to be filed with the court by being uploaded, and for applications, judgments and orders in those proceedings to be served via that system.

Purpose of the Pilot Scheme

2.1 The purpose of this Pilot Scheme is to assess the use of new practices and procedures to allow for certain stages in applications specified in paragraph 1.3(a) of this Practice Direction to be completed using the online system.

Modification of the FPR and Practice Directions during the operation of the Pilot Scheme

3.1 During the operation of the Pilot Scheme, the Family Procedure Rules 2010 and the Practice Directions supporting the rules will apply to cases falling within the Pilot Scheme as modified by paragraphs 4.1 to 6.3.

Modification of rule 2.3(1) of the FPR

4.1 In cases to which this Pilot Scheme applies, in rule 2.3(1) of the FPR, the definition of 'filing' is modified by inserting after 'office'-

> 'or, where the Pilot Scheme referred to in Practice Direction 36P applies by creating and submitting or by uploading the document on the online system referred to in that Practice Direction'.

Modification of Part 5 FPR

4AA.1 In rule 5.1-

(a) in paragraph (1) after 'Subject to' insert 'paragraph (7) and to'; and
(b) after paragraph (6) insert-

'(7) Where the pilot scheme referred to in Practice Direction 36P applies, the requirement in rule 26.2(2)(b) FPR to file notice of a change must be met by completing the relevant section on the online service, not by using the form referred to in a practice direction.'

4A.1 After rule 5.1 insert-

'Timing of receipt of applications

5.1A An application that is submitted via the online system referred to in Practice Direction 36P is lodged with the court on the date and at the time that HMCTS software records the application as received, provided that the application is subsequently issued by the court.'

Modification of Part 29 FPR

5.1 After rule 29.13(1) insert-

'(1A) Where the pilot scheme referred to in Practice Direction 36P applies, service under paragraph (1) or otherwise may be effected by the court sending to a party an email, to the address given for service in accordance with Practice Direction 6A, containing a weblink from which the judgment or order may be accessed and downloaded.'.

Modification of Practice Direction 6A

6.1 After paragraph 4.1 insert-

'4.1A Paragraphs 4.2 to 4.6 also apply where-

(a) the pilot scheme referred to in Practice Direction 36P applies; and
(b) service by the court-
(i) of an application is to be effected in accordance with paragraph 4.7; or
(ii) of a judgment or order is to be effected in accordance with rule 29.13(1A) FPR.

4.1B Where paragraph 4.1A applies, references in paragraphs 4.2 to 4.5 to service of a document by email include service of an application, judgment or order by the court sending by email a weblink from which the application, judgment or order may be accessed and downloaded.'.

6.2 In paragraph 4.2(b)-

(a) in paragraph (iii) for '; or' substitute ';';
(b) in paragraph (iv) for the full-stop substitute '; or'; and
(c) after paragraph (iv) insert-

'(v) confirmation given, by the party to be served, within the online system referred to in Practice Direction 36M or 36P that that party is willing to accept service by email and stating the email address for such service.'.

6.3 After paragraph 4.6 insert-

'4.7 Where the pilot scheme referred to in Practice Direction 36P applies, service of an application to which that pilot scheme applies may be effected by the court sending to a party an email, to the address given for service in accordance with paragraph 4.2, containing a weblink from which the application may be accessed and downloaded.'.

Practice Direction 36Q – Expired on 31 March 2022

Practice Direction 36R – Expired on 31 March 2022

Practice Direction 36S – Pilot provision: announcements in open court (suspension of certain requirements)

This practice direction supplements rule 36.2 FPR (transitional arrangements and pilot schemes)

1.1 This practice direction is made under rule 36.2 FPR. It is intended to assess modifications to Practice Directions 10A and 12K to remove current requirements to make specified announcements in open court.

1.2 This practice direction ceases to have effect on 31 March 2021.

1.3 Practice Direction 10A (Part 4 of the Family Law Act 1996) is modified by omitting paragraphs 3.1 and 3.2.

1.4 Practice Direction 12K (Children Act: Exclusion Requirement) is modified by omitting paragraph (1).

Practice Direction 36T – Expired on 31 May 2021

Practice Direction 36U – Pilot provision: service and notification of applications and orders under Part 4 of the Family Law Act 1996

This practice direction supplements rule 36.2 FPR (transitional arrangements and pilot schemes).

1.1 This practice direction is made under rule 36.2 FPR. It is intended to assess modifications to Part 10 FPR in relation to methods of serving applications and orders made under Part 4 of the 1996 Act. It also makes a minor modification to rule 10.10 FPR which deals with notification of such orders to the police.

1.2 This practice direction expires at the end of the day on 30 September 2021.

1.4 While this practice direction is in force, the FPR apply as modified by paragraphs 1.7 to 1.10.

1.5 This practice direction applies to all applications and orders made under Part 4 of the 1996 Act, whether made before or after this practice direction comes into force.

1.6 Nothing in this practice direction affects any power to order alternative service, or dispense with service, of orders and applications made under Part 4 of the 1996 Act that may exist under the FPR as they apply prior to the coming into force of this practice direction.

Modifications of Part 10 FPR

1.7 In rule 10.3(1) after 'must' insert ', subject to any order made under rule 6.35 or 6.36,'.

1.8 Omit the words in brackets after rule 10.3(4).

1.9 In rule 10.6(1) for 'The applicant' substitute 'Subject to any order made under rule 6.35 or 6.36, the applicant'.

1.10 In rule 10.10(3)(b) for 'the order was served following a request under rule 10.6(2)' substitute 'rule 10.6(2) applies'.

Practice Direction 36V – Pilot scheme: family mediation voucher scheme

This Practice Direction supplements rule 36.2 FPR (transitional arrangements and pilot schemes).

Scope and interpretation

1.1 This Practice Direction is made under rule 36.2 and modifies the FPR and Practice Directions to support the Family Mediation Voucher Scheme.

1.2 This Practice Direction-

(a) comes into force on the day after the date on which Practice Direction Update No.2 of 2021 is approved; and
(b) expires at the end of 30 September 2022.

1.3 Terms which are defined in rule 3.1 FPR have the same meaning in this Practice Direction.

1.4 In this Practice Direction, 'the Family Mediation Voucher Scheme' means the Ministry of Justice's pilot scheme for £500 of financial assistance to be provided towards the costs of attendance at mediation. A person is eligible for this assistance where-

(a) they have attended a MIAM, whether because-
  (i) the MIAM requirement, applies; or
  (ii) the court has directed that they attend a MIAM;
(b) they are a party to proceedings, or prospective proceedings, which are-
  (i) private law proceedings relating to children, as specified in paragraph 12 of Practice Direction 3A; or
  (ii) proceedings for a financial remedy, as specified in paragraph 13 of Practice Direction 3A, where the person is also a party to proceedings, or prospective proceedings, relating to children, as specified in paragraph 12 of Practice Direction 3A; and
(c) funding within the pilot scheme remains available.

1.5 The modifications made to the FPR and Practice Directions in this Practice Direction apply in cases where eligibility for the Family Mediation Voucher Scheme arises.

Purpose of the Family Mediation Voucher Scheme

2.1 The purpose of the Family Mediation Voucher Scheme is to offer a financial contribution of £500 towards mediation costs for eligible cases. The aims of this are two-fold. Firstly, as an immediate measure to try to reduce the backlogs in family proceedings which have been exacerbated by the coronavirus pandemic. Secondly, to provide an evidence base around the effectiveness of providing a financial incentive to encourage disputes to be resolved via mediation rather than through the courts.

Modification of the FPR and Practice Directions during the operation of the Family Mediation Voucher Scheme

3.1 During the operation of the Family Mediation Voucher Scheme, the FPR and the Practice Directions supporting the FPR, will apply as modified by paragraphs 4.1 to 5.3.

Modification of rule 3.9 of the FPR

4.1 After paragraph (2)(a) of rule 3.9 insert-

'(aa) provide information about the Family Mediation Voucher Scheme, if the authorised family mediator considers that the person attending the MIAM might be eligible for assistance under that scheme;'

Modification of Practice Direction 12B

5.1 After paragraph 2.9 insert-

'2A.1 The Family Mediation Voucher Scheme: Assistance of £500 towards the costs of mediation may also be available via the Family Mediation Voucher Scheme referred to in Practice Direction 36V. Where parties may be eligible for such assistance, information about this will be provided at a MIAM.'

5.2 In paragraph 5.3 after 'resolve the dispute' insert-

'Information will also be provided about the Family Mediation Voucher Scheme, if the mediator considers that the person attending the MIAM might be eligible for assistance under that scheme.'

5.3 In paragraph 5.10-

(a) after 'subsequent mediation' insert-

'The mediator should also consider with the party or parties whether they might be eligible for assistance under the Family Mediation Voucher Scheme.'; and

(b) after 'seek, public funding' insert-

'or assistance under the Family Mediation Voucher Scheme'.

Practice Direction 36W – Pilot scheme: procedure for notification of certain protection orders to the police by email

This practice direction supplements FPR Part 36 (Transitional Arrangements and Pilot Schemes)

Scope and interpretation

1.1 This Practice Direction is made under rule 36.2 FPR and sets up a Pilot Scheme to allow for notification to the police of certain orders to be sent to a centralised email address. It also pilots a change to the timescale within which protection orders must be served, and the removal of a requirement to serve a record of a hearing when serving certain orders.

1.2 This Practice Direction comes into force on 26 April 2021.

1.3 This Pilot Scheme applies where all of the following conditions are met-

(a) the order is a protection order or an order varying, discharging or extending a protection order;
(b) the protection order was made in the High Court or family court; and
(c) the protection order, or the order varying, discharging or extending a protection order, was made in the period commencing on 26 April 2021 and ending at the end of the day on 30 September 2022.

Purpose of this Pilot Scheme

2.1 The purpose of this Pilot Scheme is to assess:

(a) the use of new practices and procedures to allow for-
  (i) the court to email certain protection orders,
  (ii) the court to email certain further orders extending, varying or discharging such orders; and
  (iii) the applicant or the court to email confirmation that an order or further order referred to in sub-paragraph (a) or (b) has been served, or that the person to whom it applies has been informed of its terms,

  to a centralised email address for the police; and
(b) a change to the timescale within which protection orders must be served and the removal of a current requirement to serve a copy of a record of a hearing when serving a protection order.

2.2 Orders or other information received at the centralised email address referred to in this Practice Direction will be automatically forwarded to-

(a) the local and regional policing lead for the address of the person who is the subject of the proceedings, where that address is in England and Wales; and
(b) to the local and regional policing lead for the address of the respondent(s) to the order, where that address is in England and Wales and where the court has directed that the policing lead for that address should be informed.

2.3 This Practice Direction supersedes Practice Direction 36H, which is revoked from the date this Practice Direction comes into force.

Modification of the FPR and Practice Directions, and application of this Practice Direction, during the operation of the Pilot Scheme

3.1 During the operation of the Pilot Scheme, where the Pilot Scheme applies, the FPR and the Practice Directions supporting the FPR will apply-

(a) subject to the provisions of this Practice Direction; and
(b) as modified by paragraphs 4.1 and 4.2.

Modification of Part 11 FPR

4.1 In rule 11.7(3)–

(a) for 'as soon as reasonably practical' substitute 'within 2 days of an order being made (unless otherwise directed by the court)'; and
(b) omit sub-paragraph (b).

4.2 For rule 11.12 substitute—

'Notifying the police by email when a protection order is made, varied, extended or discharged

11.12(1) Where the court makes a protection order, notification must be given to the police force for the address of-

(a) the person who is the subject of the protection order; and

(b) if the court so directs, the respondent(s),

by the court officer emailing notification, together with a copy of the protection order, to Protectionorders@pds.police.uk.cjsm.net.

(2) Where an order is made varying, extending or discharging a protection order, notification must be given to any police force notified of the protection order under paragraph (1), by the court officer emailing notification, together with a copy of the protection order and a copy of any order varying, extending or discharging the protection order, to Protectionorders@pds.police.uk.cjsm.net.

(3) Paragraphs (1) and (2) only apply where the address of the person who is the subject of the protection order or of the respondent (as the case may be) is in England and Wales.

(4) The email referred to in paragraph (1) or (2) must be sent within 1 day of the order being sealed by the court officer.

Notifying the police by email when an order is served or a person is informed of its terms

11.12A(1) Paragraph (2) applies when the respondent(s) and any other person whose breach of the order would be an offence has been-

(a) served with; or

(b) informed (whether by being present when the order was made or by telephone or otherwise) of the terms of,

an order referred to in rule 11.12(1) or (2).

(2) A notification showing that the person has been served with, or has been informed of the terms of, the order must be sent by email -

(a) where the sender has access to the 'cjsm' network, to Protectionorders@pds.police.uk.cjsm.net

(b) where the sender does not have access to the 'cjsm' network, to Protectionorders@pds.police.uk.

(3) The notification referred to in paragraph (2) must be sent by-

(a) the applicant, where rule 11.7(3) applies; or

(b) the court officer, where rule 11.7(4) applies.

(4) Where paragraph (3)(a) applies-

(a) the email referred to in paragraph (2) must be sent within 2 days of the person being served with, or informed of the terms of, the order; and

(b) the applicant must also send a statement of service confirming that the person has been served with, or has otherwise been informed of the terms of, the order by email to the court.

(5) Where paragraph (3)(b) applies, the notification referred to in paragraph (2) must be sent within 1 day of receipt by the court officer of confirmation of service, or of the person having been informed of the terms of the order, from the court bailiff.

Practice Direction 36X – Pilot provision: proceeding by electronic means: certain proceedings for a matrimonial order

PLEASE NOTE THIS PD COMES INTO FORCE ON 13 SEPTEMBER 2021

This practice direction supplements rule 36.2 FPR (transitional arrangements and pilot schemes)

1.1 This practice direction is made under rule 36.2 FPR. It is intended to assess modifications to Practice Direction 41A to make the use of electronic means via the online system referred to in Practice Direction 41A mandatory for an applicant who is legally represented.

1.2 This practice direction comes into force on 13th September 2021 and expires at the end of the day on 5th April 2022.

1.3 While this practice direction is in force, Practice Direction 41A is modified as follows-

(a) in the heading to paragraph 2.1 after 'may' insert 'or must';

(b) in paragraph 2.1, for 'An application' substitute 'Subject to paragraph 2.1A, an application';

(c) after paragraph 2.1 insert-

'2.1A Subject to paragraph 2.1B, an application must proceed by electronic means where-

(a) all of the conditions in paragraph 2.1(a), (b), (d) and (e) are met; and

(b) the applicant is legally represented.

2.1B Paragraph 2.1A does not apply when the online system is not available for use because of-

(a) planned 'down time' for system maintenance or upgrades; or

(b) unplanned 'down-time' because of, for example, a system failure or power outage or some other unplanned circumstance.';

(d) in paragraph 3.1 after 'enables' insert '(or, where paragraph 2.1A applies, this practice direction requires)';

(e) after paragraph 7.1 insert-

'7.1A Where paragraph 2.1A applies, an application for a matrimonial order must be created via the online system.';

(f) at the end of paragraph 10.4 insert-

'Where paragraph 2.1A applies, the applicant must use the online system to take further steps in the proceedings.';

(g) after paragraph 13.1 insert-

'13.1A Where paragraph 2.1A applies, any application made by the applicant for the court to consider the making of a decree nisi in the proceedings must be made-

(a) using the online system; and

(b) at a point in time specified in paragraph 13.1(a) or (b).'; and

(h) after paragraph 15.1 insert-

'15.1A Where paragraph 2.1A and 15.1 both apply, the applicant must give the notice referred to in paragraph 15.1 using the online system.'.

Practice Direction 36Y – Pilot provision: temporary modification of Practice Directions 2C, 5B, 12A and 12B – in light of and following coronavirus

Please note not yet in force and will only come into force when PD36Q and PD36R expire

This practice direction supplements rule 36.2 FPR (transitional arrangements and pilot schemes)

1.1 This practice direction is made under rule 36.2 of the Family Procedure Rules. It is intended to assess modifications to Practice Directions 2C, 5B, 12A and 12B in light of and following the coronavirus pandemic to ensure that the administration of justice is carried out and so as to take account of available resources.

1.2 This Practice Direction-

(a) comes into force immediately on the expiry of Practice Directions 36Q and 36R; and

(b) expires at the end of the day 12 months after the date on which it comes into force.

Modification of Practice Directions

2.1 During the period in which this Practice Direction is in force, the Practice Directions supporting the FPR will apply as modified by paragraphs 3.1 to 6.1.

Modification of Practice Direction 2C

3.1 Practice Direction 2C (justices' legal adviser) is modified as follows-

(a) in the table, in the row where the first column reads FPR 12.3(2), delete the wording in the second column; and

(b) at the end of the table, insert the following new rows-

'FPR rule 3A.4, 3A.5 and 3A.6	Only where: 1. the proceedings are allocated within the family court to lay justices or when the justices' legal adviser is acting as a gatekeeper at the allocation stage; and 2. the measure specified is under rule 3A.8(1)(a) to 3A.8(1)(c).
Practice Direction 6C	Only where the proceedings are allocated within the family court to lay justices or when the justices' legal adviser is acting as a gatekeeper at the allocation stage.
the 1989 Act, section 10(1)(a)	Only where: 1. the proceedings are allocated within the family court to lay justices or when the justices' legal adviser is acting as a gatekeeper at the allocation stage; 2. all parties consent to the order being made; 3. CAFCASS has confirmed that no safeguarding issues have been identified which require further enquiry or would preclude the parties agreeing a consent order; and 4. the principles of PD12J have been applied and the justices' legal adviser determines it is consistent with PD12J and the child's welfare to make the order in the terms sought.

the 1989 Act, sections 11A(2), 11A(2B), 11C(2), 11E(7), 11G(2), 11H(2), 11H(5) and 11H(8)	Only where the proceedings are allocated within the family court to lay justices or when the justices' legal adviser is acting as a gatekeeper at the allocation stage.'

Modification of Practice Direction 5B

4.1 Practice Direction 5B (communication and filing of documents by email) is modified as follows-

(a) for the heading to Chapter 2 substitute-

'Specified organisations and adoption agencies'; and

(b) after paragraph 2.1 insert-

'2.1A Subject to this Chapter-

(a) a specified organisation;
(b) an adoption agency (other than a local authority) which has taken part at any stage in the arrangements for the adoption of the child; or
(c) a legal representative of a specified organisation or of an adoption agency referred to in sub-paragraph (b),

may email a court at the court's specified email address and attach or include one or more documents related to adoption proceedings.

2.1B Paragraph 2.1A does not apply to an application for an adoption order (section 46 of the 2002 Act).'.

Modification of Practice Direction 12A

5.1 Practice Direction 12A (care, supervision and other Part 4 proceedings: guide to case management) is modified by substituting the second sentence in paragraph 4.1 with the following-

'The justices' legal adviser (with responsibility for gatekeeping and allocation of proceedings) and/or a district judge (with responsibility for allocation and gatekeeping of proceedings) will consider initial allocation as provided for in any Guidance issued by the President on distribution of business of the family court.'.

Modification of Practice Direction 12B

6.1 Practice Direction 12B (child arrangements programme) is modified by inserting after paragraph 7.2-

'7.3 Local practices and initiatives can be operated differently to the framework where such practices or initiatives are-

(a) operated to ensure the administration of justice is carried out and so as to take account of available resources;
(b) approved by the local Designated Family Judge, after consultation with Her Majesty's Courts and Tribunals Service and with Cafcass or Cafcass Cymru.

7.4 Where any local practices and initiatives are put in place under paragraph 7.2 or 7.3, the local Designated Family Judge working with Her Majesty's Courts and Tribunals

Service must ensure that parties, their legal representatives, relevant local support organisations and Local Authorities are given information about the detail of those local practices and initiatives.'

Practice Direction 36Z – Pilot scheme: private law reform: investigative approach

This Practice Direction supplements FPR Part 36, rule 36.2 (Transitional Arrangements and Pilot Schemes).

Scope and interpretation

1.1 This Practice Direction is made under rule 36.2 and establishes a Pilot Scheme (referred to as 'the Pilot Scheme') to allow certain applications, and stages in proceedings relating to such applications, to follow a procedure different to that specified in the Family Procedure Rules 2010 ('the FPR') and supporting Practice Directions.

1.2 This Practice Direction comes into force on 21 February 2022.

1.3 The Pilot Scheme applies where all of the following conditions are met-

(a) the application is for-
  (i) a section 8 order;
  (ii) an enforcement order;
(b) the application is started in the family court sitting at a location specified in paragraph 1.4; and
(c) the application is filed in the period commencing 21 February 2022 and ending at the end of 21 February 2024.

1.4 The locations of the family court referred to in paragraph 1.3(b) are-

(a) Bournemouth;
(b) Caernarfon;
(c) Mold;
(d) Prestatyn;
(e) Weymouth;
(f) Wrexham.

1.5 In this Practice Direction, 'enforcement order' has the meaning given in rule 12.2 FPR.

Purpose of the Pilot Scheme

2.1 The purpose of the Pilot Scheme is to assess the use of new practices and procedures to allow for applications specified in paragraph 1.3(a) of this Practice Direction to follow a revised court process. The revised process has been designed for all court users, but with a particular focus on improving the experience of the family court and outcomes for survivors of domestic abuse, including children and litigants in person. The pilot seeks to test a more investigative approach, featuring earlier gatekeeping and information gathering to enable earlier triaging decisions and to front-load engagement with parties rather than engaging through multiple hearings. The court will also seek to hear the voice of the child more clearly through each case in this pilot, with the aim that appropriate engagement and communication are considered throughout proceedings. A more holistic, multi-agency approach is planned, with the court engaging and developing positive working relationships with key local partners such as mediators and local authorities.

A review stage during the pilot process will aim to ensure that court orders meet the welfare needs of the child and reduce the number of cases which come back to court.

Modification of the FPR and Practice Directions during operation of the Pilot Scheme

3.1 During the operation of the Pilot Scheme the FPR and supporting Practice Directions will apply to cases falling within the Pilot Scheme as modified by paragraphs 4.1 to 7.2.

Modification of rules in the FPR

4.1 In rule 12.5-

(a) for paragraph (1) substitute-

'(1) When proceedings have been issued to which pilot Practice Direction 36Z applies, the court will consider the appropriate steps to take in accordance with Practice Direction 12B (Pilot) and rule 12.12.'; and

(b) In the words in parentheses at the end of the rule, for the second sentence substitute-

'Practice Direction 12B (Pilot) sets out the procedure for cases under the Pilot Scheme referred to in Practice Direction 36Z.'.

4.2 In rule 12.7-

(a) in paragraph (1), after '5A' insert 'and in accordance with Practice Direction 12B (Pilot)'; and

(b) in paragraph (2), for '12B' substitute '12B (Pilot)'.

4.3 In rule 12.13-

(a) for 'final hearing', in each place those words appear, substitute 'Decision Hearing'; and

(b) after sub-paragraph (5) insert-

'(Details in relation to Decision Hearings are set out in Practice Direction 12B (Pilot).)'.

4.4 In rule 12.14, in paragraph (2)(c) for '12B' substitute '12B (Pilot)'.

4.5 In rule 12.15-

(a) for 'final hearing', in both places those words appear, substitute 'Decision Hearing'; and

(b) at the end of the rule insert-

'(Details in relation to Decision Hearings are set out in Practice Direction 12B (Pilot).)'.

4.6 Omit rule 12.31.

4.7 In rule 25.6 for 'the First Hearing Dispute Resolution Appointment' substitute 'the Safeguarding Gatekeeping Appointment/ Case Management stage'.

Modification of Practice Directions

5.1 In Practice Direction 2C, in the Table-

(a) after the row relating to FPR rule 12.73(1)(b) insert-

'Practice Direction 12B (Pilot) – paragraphs: 9.3 13.2 13.3 13.4 13.6 13.7 14.4 15.1 16.1 17.1(c)	Where: (a) the proceedings have not yet been allocated to a level of judge in the family court; (b) the proceedings have been allocated to lay justices; or (c) the proceedings have been allocated to a judge of District Judge level, Circuit Judge level or High Court judge level and the allocated judge indicates that a justices' legal adviser may carry out the function in question.
Practice Direction 12B (Pilot) – paragraphs 9.1 9.2 9.4 14.1 17.1(a)	Where the function is described as being capable of being carried out by a Gatekeeper, and where the justices' legal adviser is acting as a Gatekeeper.'

; and

(b) omit the row relating to FPR rule 12.31.

5.2 In Practice Direction 12J-

(a) in paragraph 3, after the definition of 'abandonment' insert-

"Child Impact Report' means such a report as referred to in Practice Direction 12B (Pilot);';

(b) in paragraph 5-
  (i) for 'at the First Hearing Dispute Resolution appointment ('FHDRA')' substitute 'when giving directions for the preparation of a Child Impact Report and when considering the content of a Child Impact Report';
  (ii) for 'or CAFCASS Cymru' substitute 'Cafcass Cymru, a local authority'; and
  (iii) in the first indented bullet point omit '(usually at the FHDRA)'; and
  (iv) in the third indented bullet point for 'tried' substitute 'determined';

(c) in paragraph 6 for 'are present in court' substitute 'have been suitably engaged (which may be at a hearing, if the court considers that essential')';

(d) in paragraph 8 after 'information available' insert 'in the Child Impact Report';

(e) for the heading to paragraph 9 substitute-

'Consideration at the Information Gathering and Assessment Stage';

(f) in paragraph 9-
  (i) for 'before the FHDRA or other first hearing' substitute 'at the Information Gathering and Assessment Stage (Stage 1, PD12B (Pilot))';
  (ii) after 'Cymru' insert 'as part of the completion of the Child Impact Report'; and
  (iii) for 'at the hearing' substitute 'in the Child Impact Report';

(g) omit the heading to paragraph 11;

(h) omit paragraph 11;

(i) omit the first sentence of paragraph 12;

(j) in paragraph 15-

(i) after 'at any hearing' insert ', or during any other contact with the court';

(ii) for 'judge' substitute 'court';

(iii) for 'a report under section 7 of the Children Act 1989' substitute 'the Child Impact Report';

(k) in paragraph 16-

(i) in the first sentence for 'The court' substitute 'As outlined in paragraph 14.2 of Practice Direction 12B (Pilot), the court';

(ii) in sub-paragraph (a) for 'any welfare report' substitute 'the Child Impact Report, any section 7 or section 37 Children Act 1989 report';

(iii) in sub-paragraph (d)-

(aa) for 'Violence' substitute 'Abuse'; and

(bb) for 'DVPP' substitute 'DAPP';

(l) in paragraph 17(a) after 'Cymru' insert 'or others, including as recorded in any Child Impact Report';

(m) in paragraph 18 after 'decision' insert ', and this should be noted in the Child Impact Report';

(n) in paragraph 19-

(i) in the opening paragraph after 'should consider' insert 'taking into account any information already included in any Child Impact Report';

(ii) for sub-paragraph (a) substitute-

'(a) what are the key factual issues in dispute and how should they be set out so that any complaints or allegations made by a party, and the other party's replies to these complaints or allegations, are clear;';

(iii) in sub-paragraph (b) for 'welfare hearing' substitute 'Decision Hearing (see Practice Direction 12B (Pilot) Stage 2)';

(iv) omit sub-paragraph (c);

(v) for sub-paragraph (e) substitute-

'(e) directing the parties to describe in short terms the overall experience of being in a relationship and parenting with each other (this may be provided in a written statement or orally at a preliminary hearing if the court considers such a hearing to be essential);'; and

(vi) in sub-paragraph (m)-

(aa) for 'useful' substitute 'essential'; and

(bb) after 'available' insert ', in the event that any such matters have not already been addressed as part of the Information Gathering and Assessment Stage set out in Practice Direction 12B (Pilot).';

(o) for paragraph 20 substitute-

'When conducting any fact finding (or other) hearing, the court should consider the guidance on hearings as set out in paragraphs 23.1 to 23.5 of Practice Direction 12B (Pilot).';

(p) in paragraph 21(2) after 'if appropriate)' insert 'as part of a Child Impact Report';

(q) for paragraph 22 substitute-

'If the court directs that there shall be a fact-finding hearing on the issue of domestic abuse, the Child Impact Report should contain information needed for that hearing, and should be updated after the hearing, to take account of the findings of fact made by the court.';

(r) in paragraph 28-
   (i) for 'inquisitorial (or investigative)' substitute 'investigative'; and
   (ii) after 'all involved' insert '(see also the guidance on the conduct of hearings at paragraphs 23.1 to 23.5 of Practice Direction 12B (Pilot)')';

(s) in paragraph 29 after 'preparing a' insert 'Child Impact Report or';

(t) in paragraph 30-
   (i) after 'earlier direction for a' insert 'Child Impact Report or';
   (ii) for 'any report under section 7' substitute 'any such report'; and
   (iii) for 'Any section 7 report' substitute 'Any such report';

(u) in paragraph 32 for 'an Officer of Cafcass or a Welsh family proceedings officer' substitute 'the involved Cafcass officer, Welsh Family Proceedings Officer or local authority officer';

(v) in paragraph 33(a) after 'consequent report' insert 'as part of the Child Impact Report';

(w) in paragraph 34 for 'DVPP' both times it appears substitute 'DAPP'; and

(x) in paragraph 38(d) for 'set a date for the review consistent with' substitute 'make provision for the review consistent with Stage 3 of Practice Direction 12B (Pilot) and with'.

5.3 In Practice Direction 27A

(a) in paragraph 4.2 for sub-paragraph (b) to the end of the paragraph substitute-

'(b) the Child Impact Report, which must contain:
   (i) applications and orders;
   (ii) statements and affidavits (which must be dated in the top right corner of the front page) but without exhibiting or duplicating documents referred to in para 4.1; and
   (iii) experts' reports and other reports (including those of a guardian, children's guardian or litigation friend); and

(c) other documents, divided into further sections as may be appropriate.

All statements, affidavits, experts' reports and other reports included in the bundle must be copies of originals which have been signed and dated.';

(b) in paragraphs 4.3(b), (c) and (d) and 4.6 for 'final hearing', in each place those words appear, substitute 'Decision Hearing'; and

(c) in paragraph 14.1-
   (i) in the first sentence, for 'and the Child Arrangements Programme 2014 (PD12B)' substitute 'and PD12B (Pilot)'; and
   (ii) in the second sentence, for 'and the Child Arrangements Programme 2014' substitute 'and of PD12B (Pilot)

5.4 In Practice Direction 36G-

(a) for the heading to paragraph 9.1 substitute-

'Modification of FPR Practice Direction 12B (Pilot) – Private Law Reform: Investigative Approach'; and

(b) in paragraph 9.4 for 'should be provided at the first hearing' substitute 'should be sent with the application or provided during the Information Gathering and Assessment stage'; and

5.5 In Practice Direction 36V, in the heading to paragraph 5.1, after '12B' insert '(Pilot)'.

Application of Practice Direction 12B and Practice Direction 12B (Pilot)

6.1 Practice Direction 12B (Pilot) (Private Law Reform: Investigative Approach) as set out in the Annex to this Practice Direction will apply in place of Practice Direction 12B (Child Arrangements Programme).

Disapplication of PD36Q and aspects of PD36Y

7.1 PD36Q (Pilot Provision: Modification of Practice Direction 12B – Coronavirus) does not apply in cases to which this Practice Direction 36Z applies.

7.2 Paragraph 6.1 of PD36Y (Pilot Provision: Temporary modification of Practice Directions 2C, 5B, 12A and 12B – Post-coronavirus) does not apply in cases to which this Practice Direction 36Z applies.

Annex to Practice Direction 36Z: Practice Direction 12B (pilot) – Private law reform: investigative approach

Chapter (I): Introduction and context

When this Practice Direction applies and Interpretation.

1.1 The procedure set out in this Practice Direction applies where separated parents and/or families cannot agree about arrangements concerning children.

1.2 The procedure is designed to assist families to reach safe and child-focused agreements for their child, where possible out of the court setting. If parents / families are unable to reach agreement, and a court application is made, this procedure encourages swift resolution through the court.

1.3 It is well-recognised that negotiated agreements between adults generally enhance long-term co-operation, and are better for the child concerned. Therefore, separated parents and families are strongly encouraged to attempt to try and reach agreement concerning the child outside of the court system. This may also be quicker and cheaper and any future issues that may arise could be easier to resolve.

1.4 In this Practice Direction, reference is made to 'non-court resolution'. Any such reference is to be read as if it were to 'non-court dispute resolution' as used in Part 3 FPR.

Signposting Services, Parenting Plans, & Public Funding

2.1 Services: If parents and families cannot agree arrangements for children, they are encouraged to obtain advice and support as soon as possible. Information about the impact of separation on children can be found at:

(a) Voice of the Child of Divorce https://www.youtube.com/watch?app=desktop&v=lbTFZ8cvHo4

(b) Fegans and Wells Mediation https://www.wellsfamilymediation.co.uk/blog/Co-parenting%20film/

(c) Supporting healthy family relationships Warwickshire County Council https://www.youtube.com/watch?app=desktop&v=1ZUWbIBOyL8

(d) https://www.cafcass.gov.uk/2021/03/02/responding-to-feedback-fjypb-top-tips-for-separated-parents-updated/

2.2 There are many services available for such families, who seek advice about resolving disputes concerning their child.

2.3 The following services are recommended –

(a) For more information about family mediation and to find the nearest mediation service (including those providing a MIAM): www.familymediationcouncil.org.uk;

(b) For a Guide about children and the family courts for separating parents (including representing yourself in court): the form 'CB7': https://www.gov.uk/government/publications/guide-for-separated-parents-children-and-the-family-courts-cb7/guide-for-separated-parents-children-and-the-family-courts-cb7

(c) For Cafcass (England): Parenting together – Cafcass – Children and Family Court Advisory and Support Service;

(d) For Cafcass Cymru (Wales):Cafcass Cymru: Information about separated parents | GOV.WALES;

(e) To find a legal adviser or family mediator: http://find-legal-advice.justice.gov.uk;

(f) To check whether you can get financial help (legal aid) to pay for non-court dispute resolution, &/or advice and representation at court, and to find a legal aid solicitor or mediator: https://www.gov.uk/check-legal-aid

(g) For general advice about sorting out arrangements for children, the use of post-separation mediation, &/or going to court: http://www.advicenow.org.uk; http://www.advicenow.org.uk/advicenow-guides/family/sorting-out-arrangements-for-your-children/

(h) For general advice about sorting out arrangements for children: http://theparentconnection.org.uk/

(i) For advice about Contact Centres, which are neutral places where children of separated families can enjoy contact with their non-resident parents and sometimes other family members, in a comfortable and safe environment; and information about where they are: www.naccc.org.uk;

(j) For the form to apply for a child arrangements order: https://www.gov.uk/looking-after-children-divorce/apply-for-court-order;

(k) For help with taking a case to court without a lawyer, the Personal Support Unit: http://thepsu.org/;

(l) For guidance on representing yourself at court, including a list of commonly used terms that you may come across: https://www.advicenow.org.uk/family-court;

(m) For advice about finding and using a family law solicitor see: Law Society https://www.lawsociety.org.uk/, and Resolution (family law solicitors): http://www.resolution.org.uk;

(n) For advice about finding using a family law barrister: see https://www.barcouncil.org.uk/find-a-barrister.html and for arrangements for using a barrister directly see https://www.directaccessportal.co.uk/.

2.4 Parenting Plan: A Parenting Plan is widely recognised as being a useful tool for separated parents to identify, agree and set out in writing arrangements for their children; such a plan could appropriately be used as the basis for discussion about child arrangements and how parents wish to decide issues concerning their child.

2.5 The Parenting Plan should cover all practical aspects of care for the child, and should reflect a shared commitment to the child and his/her future, with particular emphasis on parental communication (learning how to deal with differences), living arrangements, money, religion, education, health care and emotional well-being.

2.6 A Parenting Plan is designed to help separated parents (and their families) to work out the best possible arrangements for the child; the plan should be understood by everyone, including (where the child is of an appropriate age and understanding) the child concerned.

2.7 For help on preparing a Parenting Plan, see –

(a) Cafcass 'Putting Your Children First: A Guide for Separated Parents';

(b) A draft of a Parenting Plan for parents or families to complete:https://www.cafcass.gov.uk/grown-ups/parents-and-carers/divorce-and-separation/parenting-together/parenting-plan/

(c) A draft of a Parenting Plan prepared by Cafcass Cymru for parents or families to complete: The Parenting Plan: Cafcass Cymru | GOV.WALES (this links to the draft plan in English) or Y Cynllun Rhianta: Cafcass Cymru | LLYW.CYMRU (this links to the draft plan in Welsh).

2.8 Publicly funded mediation and/or legal advice: If parents need access to mediation, and legal advice in support of that mediation, they may be eligible for public funding. The Legal Aid Agency (LAA) will provide funding for Mediation Information and Assessment Meetings (MIAMs) and family mediation for all those who are eligible:

(a) where at least one party is eligible, the LAA will cover the costs of both parties to attend a MIAM to encourage any non-eligible client to find out about the benefits and suitability of mediation without incurring any costs;

(b) the LAA will provide public funding for eligible parties to participate in family mediation and they may also receive some independent legal advice connected to the mediation process and where a settlement is reached can receive legal assistance to draft and issue proceedings to obtain a consent order;

(c) parties may find out if they are likely to be eligible for legal aid at the following link: https://www.gov.uk/check-legal-aid;

(d) to find the nearest publicly funded mediation service a client can use the search at http://find-legal-advice.justice.gov.uk. Publicly funded legal advisors can be found at: https://www.gov.uk/check-legal-aid.

2.9 Public funding for legal advice and/or representation at court is available in limited circumstances. Further information can be found here: http://www.justice.gov.uk/legal-aid-for-private-family-matters.

Explanation of terms

3.1 Some of the terms used in this document, and in the websites referred to above, may not be familiar to those who seek help and support.

3.2 A guide to some of the relevant terms is attached in the Annex at the end of this document.

Including the child

4.1 In making any arrangements with respect to a child, the child's welfare must be the highest priority.

4.2 Children and young people should be at the centre of all decision-making. This accords with the Family Justice Young People's Board Charter (https://www.cafcass.gov.uk/family-justice-young-peoples-board/). Each decision should be assessed on its impact on the child.

4.3 The child or young person should feel that their needs, wishes and feelings have been considered in the arrangements which are made for them. They should be informed how their needs, wishes and feelings were considered in arriving at any order or reaching any agreement.

4.4 Children should be involved, to the extent which is appropriate given their expressed desire for involvement, any welfare concerns, and their age and level of understanding, in making the arrangements which affect them. This is just as relevant where the parties are making arrangements between themselves (which may be recorded in a Parenting Plan) as when:

(a) arrangements are made away from the court; and/or
(b) the court is required to make a decision about the arrangements for the child.

4.5 If an application for a court order has been issued, the judge will want to know the child's view, where it is possible and appropriate to ascertain this in light of the child's age and understanding. This could be communicated to the judge in one of a number of ways, guided primarily by the child's preferences (where these can be ascertained)–

(a) by a Cafcass officer (in Wales, a Welsh Family Proceedings Officer (WFPO)) providing a report to the court which sets out the child's wishes and feelings;
(b) by the child being supported (by, for example, the Cafcass officer, WFPO or local authority social worker) to write a letter to the court;
(c) in the limited circumstances described in section 13 below, by the child being a party to the proceedings;
(d) by the judge meeting with the child, in accordance with approved Guidance (currently the FJC Guidelines for Judges Meeting Children subject to Family Proceedings (April 2010)). http://www.judiciary.gov.uk/JCO%2fDocuments%2fFJC%2fvoc%2fGuidelines_+Judges_seeing_+Children.pdf; and/or
(e) through a third-party professional trusted by the child, such as a teacher, social worker or support worker (enabled by, for example, the Cafcass officer, WFPO or local authority social worker).

Non-court resolution of arrangements for children

5.1 Services, including mediation, are available to provide opportunities for parents and families to work in a positive and constructive way to resolve arrangements for children. These should be actively considered and attempted where it is safe and appropriate to do so. Information about mediation and other means of resolving issues away from court is available widely (see Signposting Services – paragraph 2 above – and see also Part 3 FPR).

5.2 It is not expected that those who are the victims of domestic abuse should attempt to mediate or otherwise participate in forms of non-court dispute resolution. It is also recognised that drug and/or alcohol misuse and/or mental illness are likely to prevent parents and families from making safe use of mediation or similar services; these risk factors (which can be discussed at a MIAM – see below, paragraph 5.3) are likely to have an impact on arrangements for the child. Court Orders, including those made by consent, must be scrutinised to ensure that they are safe and take account of any risk factors, in accordance with Practice Direction 12J FPR.

5.3 Attendance at Mediation Information and Assessment Meeting ('MIAM'): Subject to paragraph 5.6, before making a family application to the court (a 'relevant family application' as defined in paragraph 28.1 below), the person who is considering making such application must attend a family MIAM. A prospective respondent is also expected to attend a MIAM. At the MIAM, the mediator will assess whether there has been, or is a risk of,

(a) domestic abuse; and/or
(b) harm by a prospective party to a child that would be the subject of the application.

Subject to this initial risk of harm assessment, information will be provided by the mediator as appropriate about ways in which arrangements may be resolved otherwise than by the court, and the suitability of mediation (or any other service) for trying to reach resolution.

5.4 It is the responsibility of the prospective applicant (or that person's legal representative) to contact a family mediator to arrange attendance at a MIAM.

5.5 Only an authorised family mediator can carry out a MIAM. An authorised family mediator is a person identified by the Family Mediation Council as qualified to conduct a MIAM.

5.6 A prospective applicant is not required to attend a MIAM where one of the circumstances set out in rule 3.8(1) or 3.8(2) FPR applies.

5.7 Information on how to find an authorised family mediator may be obtained from www.familymediationcouncil.org.uk website which hosts the 'find a local family mediator' database (see also 'Signposting Services' – paragraph 2 above).

5.8 The prospective applicant (or their legal representative) should provide the mediator with contact details for the other party or parties involved ('the prospective respondent(s)'), so that the mediator can contact the prospective respondent(s) to discuss their willingness and availability to attend a MIAM.

5.9 The prospective applicant and, where they agree to do so, the prospective respondent(s), should then attend a MIAM arranged by the mediator.

5.10 The Family Mediation Council sets the requirements for mediators who conduct MIAMs. In summary, a mediator who arranges a MIAM should consider any risk factors present and how these should be managed, and should also consider with the party or parties concerned whether public funding may be available to meet the cost of the meeting and any subsequent mediation. Where neither of the parties is eligible for, or wishes to seek, public funding, any charge made by the mediator for the MIAM will be the responsibility of the party or parties attending, in accordance with any agreement made with the mediator.

5.11 Mediation is a confidential process; none of the parties to the mediation may provide information to the court as to the content of any discussions held in mediation and/or the reasons why agreement was not reached. Similarly, the mediator may not provide such information, unless the mediator considers that a safeguarding issue arises.

5.12 However, it is important that the parties, or either of them, introduce at the MIAM (or any subsequent court application) any other evidence of attempts to reach resolution and to focus on the needs of the child.

Resolution of arrangements for children through the Court

6.1 The judge is obliged to consider, at every stage of court proceedings, whether non-court resolution is appropriate.

6.2 The parties should also actively consider non-court resolution even if proceedings are issued and are ongoing.

6.3 If the court considers that another form of non-court resolution is appropriate, the court may direct that the proceedings, or a hearing in the proceedings, be adjourned for such specified period as it considers appropriate:

(a) to enable the parties to obtain information and advice about non-court resolution; and
(b) where the parties agree, to enable non-court resolution to take place.

6.4 Where the court adjourns proceedings, it shall give directions about the timing and method by which the parties must tell the court if any of the issues in the proceedings have been resolved.

6.5 Some courts operate an at-court mediation scheme, and at-court MIAMs, with providers contracted to the Legal Aid Agency. Some mediators may prefer to conduct mediation outside of the court premises. A mediation assessment may be possible at court; alternatively, the court may help in making an appointment with a local mediator for a MIAM or for mediation. Information about mediation arrangements should be advertised in the local court.

Local Good Practice: Pilot Scheme

7.1 Local practices and initiatives can be operated within the framework provided for in this Practice Direction. It is expected that local practices will include the development of indicative timescales for cases to proceed from application to conclusion.

Chapter (II): Procedure

Application to court

8.1 Unless one of the MIAM exemptions applies (see rule 3.8 FPR), an application to court for determination of most issues concerning a child (see the definition of 'relevant family application' in rule 3.6 FPR and paragraphs 11 and 12 of PD3A) can be made only after a MIAM has taken place (at which meeting mediation and other forms of non-court resolution will have been considered). One of the exemptions may be that the case is urgent, in which case see 'Urgent and Without Notice Applications' in paragraph 10 below. The grounds for urgency are defined in rule 3.8(c) FPR.

8.2 The application must be made on the relevant prescribed form.

8.3 For section 8 Children Act 1989 applications, the applicant will be required, on the form C100, to confirm attendance at a MIAM or specify that an exemption applies unless the application is for a consent order, or if the application concerns a child who is the subject of ongoing emergency proceedings, care proceedings or supervision proceedings, or if the child concerned is already the subject of an emergency protection order, care order or supervision order (see paragraphs 11 and 12 of PD3A).

8.4 The relevant part of the form C100 must be completed showing that either –

(a) the applicant has attended a MIAM; or

(b) the applicant has not attended a MIAM and claims one of the exemptions (rule 3.8(1) FPR) – exemptions include (but are not limited to) evidence of domestic abuse, child protection concerns, urgency, previous MIAM attendance or exemption; or

(c) an authorised family mediator confirms in the form that he or she is satisfied that–

   (i) mediation is not suitable because the respondent is (if more than one respondent, any one of them is) unwilling to attend a MIAM;

   (ii) mediation is not suitable as a means of resolving the dispute because the respondent (if more than one, any of them) failed without good reason to attend a MIAM; or

   (iii) mediation is otherwise not suitable as a means of resolving the dispute.

8.5 The C100 form may be obtained from the Family Court or from www.gov.uk.

8.6 If the parties have previously prepared a Parenting Plan, this shall be attached to the Form C100.

8.7 It is important that the form C100 is completed in full (including the provision of telephone numbers, e-mail and postal address of the relevant parties), otherwise there may be a delay in processing the application. Where the form is not fully completed, the court staff may request further information before the application form is accepted for issue. It is also important that the form C100, the Acknowledgement Form C7 and, where applicable, any Supplemental Information Form C1A are fully and accurately completed to enable the court to make appropriate decisions about allocation and case management.

8.8 If possible at the time of issue, and in any event ideally by no later than one working day after issue, or in courts where applications are first considered on paper ideally by no later than two working days after issue, the court shall send or hand to the Applicant the following –

(a) in the case of an application being made on a form C100:
  (i) a copy of the application form C100 (together with the Supplemental Information Form C1A);
  (ii) information leaflets for the parties;
  (iii) directions on issue;
(b) in the case of an application being made on a form C79:
  (i) a copy of the application form C79;
  (ii) information leaflets for the parties;
  (iii) directions on issue.

8.9 Unless the applicant requests to do so, or the court directs the applicant to do so, the court will serve the respondent(s) with the following–

(a) in the case of an application being made on a form C100:
  (i) a copy of the application form C100 (together with Supplemental Information Form C1A, if provided);
  (ii) the Acknowledgement Form C7;
  (iii) a blank form C1A;
  (iv) information leaflet for the parties;
  (v) directions on issue;
(b) in the case of an application being made on form C79:
  (i) a copy of the application form C79;
  (ii) the Acknowledgement Form C7;
  (iii) information leaflet for the parties;
  (iv) directions on issue.

8.10 As soon as possible after completing initial gatekeeping (see section 9 below), the court staff shall contact the applicant by telephone to acknowledge receipt of the application and provide information to the applicant on the process which is to be undertaken. This telephone contact should also be attempted with the respondent a reasonable period of time after the acknowledgement form C7 has been sent to the respondent.

8.11 As soon as reasonably possible after the court has carried out initial gatekeeping (see section 9) and has attempted to make contact with the applicant as set out in paragraph 8.10, the court shall send to Cafcass / Cafcass Cymru copies of-

(a) the Form C100 (and the form C1A, if supplied) or the Form C79, as applicable; and
(b) any Form C8 or other document stating that contact details are to be kept confidential.

These will be sent in electronic format where possible.

8.12 The respondent(s) must send the Acknowledgement Form C7 and, where applicable, the Supplemental Information Form C1A, to the court as soon as possible and in any event within 14 days after receiving the application, unless the court has specified a shorter time.

8.13 On receipt of the Acknowledgement Form C7 and any Form C1A filed by the respondent(s), the court shall send a copy of each form to Cafcass/ Cafcass Cymru, in electronic format where possible, and shall send copies to the applicant.

Initial Gatekeeping

9.1 The question of the level of judge to whom an application should be allocated can be made by a nominated Justices' Legal Adviser and/or nominated District Judge ('the Gatekeeper(s)') in accordance with the Family Court (Composition and Distribution of Business) Rules 2014, either –

(a) as soon as possible after receipt of the application, at this initial gatekeeping stage; or

(b) at any point until and including the Safeguarding Gatekeeping Appointment/ Case Management stage (see paragraph 14 below).

It is for the Gatekeeper(s) to decide at what point it is appropriate to make the allocation decision, within the parameters set out above. Making an allocation decision at the initial gatekeeping stage could be appropriate where, for example, the case is a returning case (see paragraph 9.4 below) or a case of particular complexity.

9.2 A Gatekeeper (or two Gatekeepers, acting jointly) or the judge (where one has been allocated) shall be able to-

(a) issue Directions on Issue;

(b) direct that the applicant or the parties attend a MIAM before the case progresses to the next Stage, where, on the basis of information provided on the application form and any additional information provided on a C1A Supplemental Information Form, the court considers that the exemption from attending a MIAM has not been validly claimed, unless the court considers that in all the circumstances of the case the MIAM requirement should not apply to the application in question (the court will have particular regard to the matters set out in rule 3.10(3) FPR when making this decision);

(c) give directions for an accelerated hearing, where it appears that an urgent issue requires determination;

(d) give directions for the service and filing of evidence.

9.3 Following consideration of compliance with the MIAMs requirement, in any case that the court has determined does not require an urgent determination, the court must refer the application to the persons or bodies who are to undertake the Information Gathering and Assessment and contribute to the Child Impact Report.

9.4 Returning and related cases. Cases should be checked for previous or ongoing proceedings relating to the same child, and any related injunction proceedings, prior to gatekeeping. (It should be noted that court staff cannot search for placement and adoption proceedings, given there is restricted access to such files.) If a case is flagged as returning, the Gatekeeper should engage with the last judge (if possible) to determine the appropriate approach in light of the risk profile, case details and length of time since the last application. If the last judge is not available, the Gatekeeper should engage with another judge of equivalent level for instruction on what approach should be taken.

Urgent and Without Notice Applications

10.1 Urgent: Where an order is sought as a matter of urgency, an application may be made to the Court for an emergency order without the requirement for the Applicant to have attended at a MIAM. The categories of urgent application justifying such an exemption are set out in rule 3.8(c) FPR and include cases in which:

(a) there is a risk to the life, liberty, or the physical safety of the prospective applicant or his or her family, or his or her home;

(b) any delay caused by attending a MIAM would cause:

- (i) a risk of harm to the child;
- (ii) a risk of unlawful removal of a child from the United Kingdom or a risk of unlawful retention of a child who is currently outside England and Wales;
- (iii) a significant risk of a miscarriage of justice;
- (iv) unreasonable hardship to the prospective applicant;
- (v) irretrievable problems in dealing with the dispute (including the irretrievable loss of significant evidence);

(c) there is a significant risk that in the period necessary to schedule and attend a MIAM, proceedings relating to the dispute will be brought in another state in which a valid claim to jurisdiction may exist, such that a court in that other State would be seised of the dispute before a court in England and Wales.

10.2 'Without Notice': Applications to court made 'Without Notice' to the respondent(s) shall be allocated in accordance with the Family Court (Composition and Distribution of Business) Rules 2014, and determined by reference to the provisions of Practice Direction 18A, paragraph 5.1, with further regard to the principles set out in Practice Direction 20A, paragraph 4.3-4.5 FPR (noting particularly paragraph 4.3(c)).

10.3 Without Notice Orders should be made only exceptionally, and where –

(a) if the applicant were to give notice to the respondent(s) this would enable the respondent(s) to take steps to defeat the purpose of the injunction; cases where the application is brought without notice in order to conceal the step from the respondent(s) are very rare indeed; or

(b) the case is one of exceptional urgency; that is to say, that there has been literally no time to give notice (either by telephone, text or e-mail or otherwise) before the injunction is required to prevent the threatened wrongful act; or

(c) if the applicant gives notice to the respondent(s), this would be likely to expose the applicant or relevant child to unnecessary risk of physical or emotional harm.

10.4 Any Order which follows an emergency 'without notice' hearing should specify:

(a) the reason(s) why the order has been made without notice to the respondent(s);

(b) the outline facts alleged which have been relied upon by the court in making the order, unless the facts are clearly contained in the statement in support; and

(c) the right of the respondent(s) to apply to vary or discharge the order.

10.5 Gatekeeping decisions in urgent and without notice cases: Following any urgent hearing or any return hearing following an initial 'without notice' hearing, unless all issues have been determined or the application has been dismissed without any further directions given, the judge may either:

(a) make the necessary gatekeeping decisions in order to move the case forward to Stage 1 (below); or

(b) alternatively, refer the application to the relevant Gatekeeping team to make the necessary gatekeeping decisions.

10.6 In either event, a copy of the C100 or C79, as applicable, shall be sent to Cafcass/ Cafcass Cymru for safeguarding checks, and (depending on the Gatekeeping decision) the file shall be sent to the court where any future hearings will take place (if at a different court centre from the court where the urgent hearing occurred).

Stages of the Pilot Scheme

11.1 Following the initial gatekeeping referred to above, all applications to which this Practice Direction applies (other than those resolved via an urgent or without notice hearing) must follow these Stages:

Stage 1: Information Gathering and Assessment
Stage 2: Interventions and/or Decision Hearing
Stage 3: Review.

Details in relation to each of these Stages are set out below. Specific provision about applications for enforcement orders is set out at paragraphs 17.1 to 17.4.

Stage 1: Information Gathering and Assessment

12.1 The purpose of this Stage is to take a proportionate, child welfare focussed approach to actively investigate the impact of issues presented in the application (and any additional information requested as part of this Stage) on the child – through engagement and assessment. This Stage comprises the following steps:

Child Impact Report

13.1 This Stage must begin with the gathering of information to complete a Child Impact Report. This will involve, at a minimum:

(a) safeguarding checks (see paragraph 13.8);
(b) parental/party engagement – to involve initial contact to understand from parties what their circumstances are and get their perspectives on what they consider to be in the best interests of the child;
(c) direct or indirect (for example, via digital means or through a third party) engagement with the child (in a means consistent with their welfare needs and determined as appropriate in accordance with their age and understanding), to determine their circumstances, preferences for engagement and initial wishes and feelings;
(d) a DASH (or equivalent) risk assessment where Domestic Abuse is a feature of the case;
(e) consideration of any other cases involving the child or parties that are relevant to the case management of the case which could include whether a section 91(14) order would be appropriate upon disposal of the proceedings (see paragraph 24A and Practice Direction 12Q).

13.2 The court will determine who should be involved in this information gathering. This may involve, for example, officers of Cafcass or Cafcass Cymru, local authority officers, Independent Domestic Abuse Advisers or Domestic Abuse Support Workers.

13.3 Cafcass or Cafcass Cymru will undertake safeguarding checks (see paragraph 13.8 below) and will likely lead on other work for the Information Gathering and Assessment stage. However, if the court determines that a local authority has relevant recent involvement with the family involved in the proceedings, then the court may consider the local authority should lead on other work for the Information Gathering and Assessment stage. The court may reach this conclusion at the outset of the proceedings, or upon receipt of information collected during the course of the preparation of the Child Impact Report.

13.4 Content of the Child Impact Report. There should be liaison between those undertaking the Information Gathering and Assessment stage and the court: see paragraph 13.6 below. Ultimately, the content of the Child Impact Report will be determined by the court. The court may consider it appropriate for the Child Impact Report to be relatively 'light touch', depending on the circumstances of the case, for example in a case which is returning recently after a final order was made. In any event, the Child Impact Report may include any or all of the following:

- (a) the application form and any response filed with the court;
- (b) information obtained from each party, and the child, on their circumstances, background, wishes and other relevant information;
- (c) safeguarding information;
- (d) evidence ordered by the court;
- (e) details of any information obtained from external sources relevant to the child/parties;
- (f) any 'DASH' or other risk assessment, where domestic abuse is a feature of the case;
- (g) details of any requested participation directions ahead of any court hearings (see Part 3A FPR);
- (h) any previous orders made in the proceedings;
- (ha) consideration of any risk of harm from future applications, and whether a section 91(14) order would be appropriate (see paragraph 24A and Practice Direction 12Q);
- (i) recommendations for next steps, made by those involved in compiling the Child Impact Report, which may include:
  - (i) referral to out-of-court services such as mediation;
  - (ii) referral to support services such as a WT4C, SPIP or DAPP before a Decision Hearing;
  - (iii) recommendation to fix a fact finding hearing, if not already completed;
  - (iv) recommendation about what is in the best welfare interests of the child;
  - (v) recommendation to fix a Decision Hearing.

13.5 The Child Impact Report must be filed with the court once it is complete.

13.6 Communication with the court. During the course of the preparation of the Child Impact Report, those involved in its preparation will exercise their professional judgment in considering what should be included in the Child Impact Report. They must communicate with the court to the extent that they, or the court, consider appropriate in order to ensure that the Child Impact Report can be completed and to ensure that the court retains oversight of what information is being sought. This communication should take place in the manner determined by the court, for example, in writing or, if essential, at a directions hearing. The court should also determine the extent (if any) to which the parties should be involved in any such communication between those preparing the Child Impact Report and the court.

13.7 In the event of any communication with the court as referred to at paragraph 13.6 which takes place during the preparation of the Child Impact Report in the absence of the parties, the court must keep a clear record of the matters considered and discussed during that communication and must consider whether, and if so how, to share such a record with the parties. Any communication by the parties with the court must be in accordance with rule 5.7 FPR.

13.8 Safeguarding checks. In order to inform the court of possible risks of harm to the child Cafcass / Cafcass Cymru will carry out safeguarding enquiries as part of the Information Gathering and Assessment stage. A record and outline of any safety issues must be included in the Child Impact Report.

13.9 For all applications for child arrangements orders, safeguarding checks will include seeking information from local authorities and carrying out police checks on the parties. They may include seeking information from others if that is necessary in the professional judgment of the Cafcass Officer or the Welsh Family Proceedings Officer. For all other applications, Cafcass / Cafcass Cymru will carry out a screening process and will undertake those safeguarding checks if in the professional judgment of the Cafcass officer or the Welsh Family Proceedings Officer such checks are necessary. Safeguarding checks must be undertaken in any case where domestic abuse has been raised as an issue.

13.10 Reports which are to form part of the Child Impact Report may be ordered where there are welfare issues or other specific considerations which should be addressed in a report by Cafcass/Cafcass Cymru or the local authority. Before a report is ordered, the court should consider alternative ways of working with the parties such as are referred to in paragraph 5.1 ('Non-court resolution of arrangements for children').

13.11 If a report is ordered in accordance with section 7 of the Children Act 1989, the court should direct which specific matters relating to the welfare of the child are to be addressed. Welfare reports will generally only be ordered in cases where there is an issue as to with whom the child should live, spend time, or otherwise have contact with. A report can also be ordered:

(a) if there is an issue concerning the child's wishes;
(b) if there is an alleged risk to the child; and/or
(c) where information and advice is needed which the court considers to be necessary before a decision can be reached in the case.

13.12 General requests for a report on an application should be avoided; the court should state on the face of the order the specific factual and/or other issue which is to be addressed in the focused report.

13.13 In determining whether a request for a report should be directed to the relevant local authority or to Cafcass/Cafcass Cymru, the court should consider such information as Cafcass/Cafcass Cymru has provided about the extent and nature of the local authority's current or recent involvement with the subject of the application and the parties, and any relevant protocol between Cafcass and the Association of Directors of Children's Services.

13.14 The court may consider whether there is a need for an investigation under section 37 Children Act 1989.

13.15 A copy of the order requesting the report and any relevant court documents are to be sent to Cafcass/Cafcass Cymru or, in the case of the local authority to the Legal Adviser to the Director of the local authority Children's Services and, where known, to the allocated social worker by the court forthwith.

13.16 Is any expert evidence required? If so, section 13 Children and Families Act 2014, and Part 25 of the FPR must be complied with. The court will need to consider carefully the future conduct of proceedings where the preparation of an expert report is necessary but where the parties are unrepresented and are unable to fund the preparation of such a report.

Rule 16.4 children's guardians

13.17 The court should be vigilant to identify the cases where a rule 16.4 children's guardian should be appointed.

13.18 Where the court is considering the appointment of a children's guardian from Cafcass/Cafcass Cymru, it should first ensure that enquiries have been made of the appropriate Cafcass/Cafcass Cymru manager in accordance with paragraph 7.4, Part 4 of the Practice Direction 16A. This should either be in writing or by way of case discussion with the relevant Cafcass service manager; for cases in Wales, the 'hotline' protocol agreed with Cafcass Cymru will ensure that such a discussion can take place. The court should consult with Cafcass / Cafcass Cymru, so as to consider any advice in connection with the prospective appointment, and the timescale involved.

13.19 When the court decides to appoint a children's guardian, consideration should first be given to appointing an Officer of the Service or WFPO. If Cafcass/Cafcass Cymru is unable to provide a children's guardian without delay, or if there is some other reason why the appointment of a Cafcass officer is not appropriate, the court should (further to rule 16.24 of the FPR) appoint a person other than the Official Solicitor, unless the Official Solicitor expressly consents.

13.20 In considering whether to make such an appointment the Court shall take account of the demands on the resources of Cafcass/Cafcass Cymru that such an appointment would make. The court should also make clear on the face of any order the purpose of the appointment and the timetable of any work to be undertaken.

13.21 Any children's guardian appointed should carry out their duties and functions in accordance with the provisions of the FPR, and contribute to the Child Impact Report accordingly.

Safeguarding Gatekeeping Appointment/ Case Management following the filing of the Child Impact Report

14.1 Allocation: following receipt of the Child Impact Report, the Gatekeepers must decide to which level of judge the application is to be allocated (if not already allocated – see paragraph 9.1). The allocation decision must be made in accordance with the Family Court (Composition and Distribution of Business) Rules 2014, together with Guidance issued by the President on 'Allocation and Gatekeeping for Proceedings under Part II of the Children Act 1989 (Private Law Proceedings) and the Allocation Schedule.

14.2 Further steps: following receipt of the Child Impact Report, the judge to whom the case has been allocated must determine what steps are necessary to enable the application to proceed to Stage 2. This may involve consideration of any or all of the following:

(a) what, if any, issues are agreed and what are the key issues to be determined?

(b) Is there a need for findings of fact to be made? What are the specific issues where finding of fact is required? If fact-finding is determined to be required, a decision should be made on-

   (i) whether a preliminary hearing is essential (see also Practice Direction 12J in relation to cases where domestic abuse is in issue);

   (ii) the timing and nature of the fact-finding hearing, for example whether there should be a standalone fact-finding hearing or whether fact finding should this take place at the same time as the Decision Hearing.

   Parties, and any other necessary people or agencies, should then be engaged to gather the necessary evidence and information for the fact-finding hearing to take place.

If fact-finding is required, the court will need to consider, following the fact finding hearing, whether further information is required to be added to the Child Impact Report, although this may not be required for all cases. (See paragraphs 23.1 to 23.5 below for information on hearings).

(ba) Has an application been made for an order under section 91(14) of the Children Act 1989, or might such an order be appropriate? Are any specific findings of fact necessary? (See paragraph 24A and Practice Direction 12Q.)

(c) Is further engagement with external agencies, such as schools, nurseries, the local authority and GPs, required to determine matters relating to the child?

(d) Are there any interim orders which can usefully be made (e.g. indirect, supported or supervised contact) pending any Decision Hearing?

(e) What, if any, directions are required to ensure the application is ready for any Decision Hearing – any further statements, disclosure from bodies such as Local Authorities or the police, reports etc (see paragraph 14.2)?

(f) Should the application be listed straight away for a Decision Hearing?

(g) The case should be managed by the allocated judge unless there is good reason for it to be re-allocated (especially if there has been or is to be a fact finding hearing or a contested interim hearing). This is also important for returning cases.

(h) Should the child be engaged further to ensure the court remains aware of their preferences and wishes and feelings?

(i) Is input, or further input, required from an IDVA or Domestic Abuse Support Worker?

14.3 If an updated Child Impact Report is prepared as a result of any directions of the court as outlined above, this must be filed with the court. In any event, at the end of Stage 1 the Child Impact Report must be updated and filed with the court.

14.4 Disclosure of the Child Impact Report. When considering this, the court must take into account safeguarding issues. In this respect –

(a) the court must consider whether to inform the parties of the content of the Child Impact Report. The parties must be informed of the content, unless the court considers that to do so would create a risk of harm to a party or the child. The court may determine that only part of the content should be disclosed. In determining any such risk of harm, the court will specifically consider all the information before the court, including the safeguarding information in the Child Impact Report, including any Supplemental Information Form(s) C1A filed by the parties.

(b) The court must consider whether the content of the Child Impact Report (or part of it) ought to be attached to any referral to a supported or supervised child contact centre in the event the court directs supported or supervised contact.

(c) The court must consider whether the content of the Child Impact Report (or part of it) ought to be attached to any other referral to local support services, such as mediation or therapeutic support for the child or parties.

Stage 2: Interventions and/or Decision Hearing

15.1 At this Stage, the court must exercise its discretion as to how to enable the application to proceed to a conclusion. This may involve, for example:

(a) the court using its powers under section 11A of the Children Act 1989 to make an activity direction (being a direction requiring an individual who is a party to the proceedings to take part in an activity that would, in the court's opinion, help to establish, maintain or improve the involvement in the life of the child concerned of (i) that individual or (ii) another party to the proceedings;

(b) recommending to the parties that they pursue suitable and appropriate alternative means of non-court resolution, such as mediation or arbitration, or interventions such as counselling or parenting programmes, to arrive at an agreement or narrow the issues between the parties ahead of any future Decision Hearing;

(c) considering the appropriate means of monitoring and review of any agreement that is made between the parties;

(d) considering whether it would be appropriate to make a Consent Order where any agreement is made between the parties (see paragraphs 24.1 and 24.2 below);

(e) holding a Decision Hearing.

15.2 At a Decision Hearing, the court will-

(a) investigate the issues and make decisions on those issues which are not agreed and do so by encouraging the parties to focus on the best interests of the child;

(b) exercise its discretion as to what order (if any) to make on the application including a section 91(14) order if appropriate (see paragraph 24A and Practice Direction 12Q);

(c) give directions about the Review stage (see paragraphs 16.1 to 16.3 below); and

(d) consider how the decision of the court should be communicated to the child.

Stage 3: Review

16.1 When determining what directions to make about the Review stage, the court must take into account any recommendations made in the Child Impact Report and its statutory powers to require further involvement with the parties to the case, including:

(a) section 11H of the Children Act 1989 (monitoring contact);

(b) section 16 of the Children Act 1989 (family assistance orders);

(c) making interim orders on the application, with provision for a further report or hearing (or both).

16.2 The question of what provision to make for the Review Stage is a matter for the court's discretion. In exercising that discretion, the court should consider the following guidance:

(a) the intention is that the Review should be a means of contacting the parties, including the child where appropriate, to determine how the order is working for them;

(b) the focus of the Review should be on the safety of parties and children, post-order support to parties and follow up or signposting to sources of support, not on providing legal advice or dealing with complaints regarding the court process;

(c) the focus of the Review should not be on checking on order adherence, unless the court considers that appropriate, for example, in the context of an order under section 11H of the Children Act 1989;

(d) the Review would normally take place 3 to12 months from the point at which the order is made;

(e) the risk profile of the case will likely be relevant in determining the format of the Review;

(f) the Review is not intended to be ongoing support over a period, rather specific instances of contact at agreed times;

(g) a Review is likely to be suitable for the majority of cases, although there is the potential that it may not be required or suitable for every case;

(h) the Review will not usually involve a hearing, unless the court so determines, having received advice from those who have made contact with the parties. In such cases, the court will wish to consider making an interim order on the application, to facilitate a return hearing after the Review;

(i) if the court makes an order under section 11H or section 16 of the Children Act 1989, the court has discretion to determine the extent of any engagement by the officer involved: this might be 'light touch' or more in-depth, depending on the facts of the case.

16.3 A summary of the Review outcome should be added to the Child Impact Report.

Enforcement of Child Arrangements

17.1 On any application for an enforcement order, the court shall follow the steps and Stages outlined above, subject to the following–

(a) the Gatekeepers must allocate the case to a level of judge at the initial gatekeeping step, in accordance with rule 17 of the Family Court (Composition and Distribution of Business) Rules 2014;

(b) if possible, the case should be allocated to the judge who made the order to which the application for an enforcement order relates;

(c) the Information Gathering and Assessment stage should include further safeguarding checks if determined by the court to be required and, in any event, for any application for an enforcement order issued more than three months after the order to which the application for an enforcement order relates;

(d) the Information Gathering and Assessment stage should seek to determine the circumstances and allow the court to consider which of the following are required to complete the Information Gathering and Assessment Stage:

(i) in respect of the enforcement order application:

(aa) whether the facts relevant to the alleged non-compliance are agreed, or whether it is necessary to conduct a hearing to establish the facts;

(bb) the reasons for any non-compliance;

(cc) whether an enforcement order may be appropriate (see section 11L Children Act 1989);

(ii) in respect of any other order in relation to the Child Arrangements Order that the court may consider making:

(aa) how the wishes and feelings of the child are to be ascertained;

(bb) whether further advice is required from Cafcass/Cafcass Cymru on the appropriate way forward;

(cc) how to assess and manage any risks of making a further or other child arrangements order;

(dd) whether a SPIP or referral for non-court resolution is appropriate;

(ee) the welfare checklist.

17.2 Once the Child Impact Report is complete, the court shall list any application for enforcement of a child arrangements order for hearing, before the previously allocated judge if possible, within 20 working days of issue. Enforcement cases should be concluded without delay.

17.3 The court has a wide range of powers in the event of a breach of a child arrangements order without reasonable excuse. This range of powers includes (but is not limited to):

(a) referral of the parents to a SPIP, or in Wales a WT4C, or mediation;

(b) variation of the child arrangements order (which could include a more defined order and/or reconsidering the contact provision or the living arrangements of the child);

(c) an enforcement order or suspended enforcement order for unpaid work to be undertaken by the person in breach (see paragraph 17.1);
(d) an order for compensation for financial loss (under section 11O Children Act 1989) to be paid by the person in breach;
(e) committal to prison or a fine for contempt of court.

17.4 Section 11L Children Act 1989 provides that if the court finds that a breach has occurred without reasonable excuse it may order the non-compliant party to undertake unpaid work if that is necessary to secure compliance, and if the effect on the non-compliant party is proportionate to the seriousness of the breach. The court must also consider whether unpaid work is available in the locality and the likely effect on the non-compliant party. It is good practice to ask Cafcass/Cafcass Cymru to report on the suitability of this order. Section 11L(7) also requires the court to take into account the welfare of the child who is the subject of the order for contact.

Chapter (III): General provisions

18.1 The remaining sections of this Practice Direction cover points that may be relevant at any or all stages of proceedings.

Timetable for the child

19.1 Court proceedings should be timetabled so that they can be resolved as soon as safe and possible in the interests of the child.

19.2 The court shall, at all times during the proceedings, have regard to the impact which the court timetable will have on the welfare and development of the child to whom the application relates. The court and the parties shall pay particular attention to the child's age, and important landmarks in the immediate life of the child, including –

(a) the child's birthday;
(b) the start of nursery/schooling;
(c) the start/end of a school term/year;
(d) any proposed change of school; and/or
(e) any significant change in the child's family, or social, circumstances.

19.3 While it is acknowledged that an interim order may be appropriate at an early stage of court proceedings, cases should not be adjourned for a review (or reviews) of contact or other orders/arrangements, &/or for addendum section 7 report, unless such a hearing is necessary and for a clear purpose that is consistent with the timetable for the child and in the child's best interests. This might be the case, for example, where the court has determined that a further hearing is required to complete the Review stage.

19.4 When preparing a Child Impact Report, Cafcass / Cafcass Cymru (or, where appropriate, the local authority) is encouraged to make recommendations for the stepped phasing-in of child arrangements (i.e. recommendations for the medium and longer term future for the child) insofar as they are able to do so safely in the interests of the child concerned.

19.5 Where active involvement or monitoring is needed, the court may consider making –

(a) an order under section 11H Children Act 1989 (Monitoring);
(b) a Family Assistance Order under section 16 Children Act 1989) (in accordance with the Practice Direction 12M FPR, and if all the named adults in the order agree to the making of such an order and if the order is directed to a local authority, the child lives (or will live) within that local authority area or the local authority consents to the making of the order.

Key welfare principles

20.1 Section 1 of the Children Act 1989 applies to all applications for orders concerning the upbringing of children. This means that –

(a) the child's welfare is the court's paramount consideration;
(b) delay is likely to be prejudicial to the welfare of the child; and
(c) a court order shall not be made unless the court considers that making an order would be better for the child than making no order at all.

20.2 Parties, and the court, must also have regard to the FPR in particular the following –

(a) FPR Rule 1. The 'overriding objective' will apply, so that the court will deal with a case justly, having regard to the welfare issues involved and specifically will –
   (i) ensure that the case is dealt with expeditiously and fairly;
   (ii) deal with the case in ways which are proportionate to the nature, importance and complexity of the issues;
   (iii) ensure that the parties are on an equal footing;
   (iv) save expense;
   (v) allot to each case an appropriate share of the court's resources, while taking account of the need to allot resources to other cases.
(b) rule 3, and Practice Direction 3A;
(c) FPR Part 4 'General Case Management Powers';
(d) FPR Part 15 (Representation of Protected Parties) and Practice Direction 15B (Adults Who May Be Protected Parties and Children Who May Become Protected Parties in Family Proceedings);
(e) FPR Part 16 (Representation of Children) (and see also paragraph 13.17);
(f) FPR Part 18 (procedure for Other Applications in proceedings);
(g) FPR Part 22 (Evidence);
(h) FPR Part 25 (Experts) and the Experts Practice Directions;
(i) FPR 27.6 and Practice Direction 27A (Court Bundles).

20.3 Where a fact-finding hearing is required, this shall take place in accordance with Practice Direction 12J FPR.

20.4 The court shall exercise its powers flexibly.

Mediation and other non-court resolution: allowing the parties the time and opportunity to engage in non-court dispute resolution

21.1 Throughout the proceedings, the court will consider whether, and the extent to which, the parties can safely resolve some or all of the issues by means of non-court resolution (see Part 3A FPR).

21.2 The court should consider what options there are for resolution, for example:

(a) may the case be suitable for intervention by Cafcass/Cafcass Cymru?
(b) Should a referral for mediation be made?
(c) Is collaborative law appropriate?
(d) Should the parties be advised to complete a Parenting Plan?
(e) Would the parties be assisted by attendance at a Separated Parents Information Programme, (or in Wales, Working Together For Children (WT4C)) or other Activity or intervention, whether by formal statutory provision under section 11A Children Act 1989 or otherwise?

Judicial continuity

22.1 All cases will be allocated to a level of judge within the Family Court as set out in this Practice Direction (see paragraph 9.1).

22.2 Continuity of judicial involvement in the conduct of proceedings from the initial allocation to the making of a final order should be the objective in all cases, including where the judge is a Deputy District Judge or Recorder.

22.3 Where the case has been allocated to be heard before lay justices, the expectation of judicial continuity should apply where –

(a) there has been a hearing to determine findings of fact; or
(b) a decision yet to be made in the interests of a child by a court depends upon rulings or judicial assessments already made in the proceedings,

in which case, wherever possible, the hearing shall be listed before the same lay justices; alternatively, it shall be listed before the same the legal adviser and at least one lay justice (preferably the chairman) to provide that continuity. Where a case is adjourned part-heard the court which resumes the hearing shall, wherever possible, be composed of the same lay justices as dealt with the previous part of the hearing (see rule 8 of the Family Court (Composition and Distribution of Business) Rules 2014).

Hearings: attendance and conduct

23.1 Unless the court otherwise directs, any party to proceedings, and any litigation friend of the parties must attend any hearing. If a child is a party and represented by a children's guardian, the children's guardian need not attend directions hearings if represented.

23.2 A party may choose to be accompanied at a hearing by a McKenzie Friend to support them. A McKenzie Friend is someone who can provide moral support at court for the party; take notes; help with case papers; quietly give advice on any aspect of the conduct of the case.) If so, the McKenzie Friend must comply with the relevant Guidance (currently set out in the Practice Guidance: McKenzie Friends (Civil and Family Courts): July 2010: https://www.judiciary.uk/wp-content/uploads/JCO/Documents/Guidance/mckenzie-friends-practice-guidance-july-2010.pdf).

23.3 A Cafcass Officer, WFPO or local authority officer shall attend any hearing, subject to any direction of the court. A mediator, IDVA or Domestic Abuse Support Worker may attend where available and subject to any direction of the court.

23.4 If the court considers that a fact-finding hearing is necessary, it must conduct that hearing in accordance with revised Practice Direction 12J.

23.5 In respect of a hearing, consideration must be given by the court to:

(a) Part 3A of the FPR (vulnerable persons: participation in proceedings and giving evidence);
(b) whether to hold a fact finding hearing separately to, or at the same time as, a Decision Hearing;
(c) the witnesses needed to resolve the issues;
(d) how to minimise any risk of undue confrontation, harm or trauma occurring at, or resulting from, the hearing, while also ensuring that the hearing is fair to all parties, for example by:
    (i) clearly identifying the issues that the court needs to investigate in order to make a welfare decision for the child;

(ii) the court considering how evidence is to be given and tested to ensure that the quality of a person's evidence is not diminished and that participants do not suffer significant distress;

(iii) the court (or Justices' Legal Adviser) putting questions to a party, rather than another party doing so;

(iv) setting clear ground rules for the conduct of the case and for how the hearing will be structured.

Consent orders

24.1 Where agreement is reached at any hearing or submitted in writing to the court, no order will be made without scrutiny by the court.

24.2 Where safeguarding checks or risk assessment work remain outstanding, the making of a final order may be deferred for such work. In such circumstances the court shall adjourn the case, ideally for no longer than 28 days, to a fixed date. A written notification of this work is to be provided by Cafcass/Cafcass Cymru in the form of an updating Child Impact Report (which may include, if deemed relevant by Cafcass/Cafcass Cymru), a section 16A Children Act 1989 risk assessment). If satisfactory information is then available, the order may be made at the adjourned hearing in the agreed terms without the need for attendance by the parties. If satisfactory information is not available, the order will not be made, and the case will be adjourned for further consideration with an opportunity for the parties to make further representations.

Orders under section 91(14) of the Children Act 1989

24A.1 Under section 91(14) of the Children Act 1989, orders are available to prevent a person from making an application under that Act without leave of the court. Section 91(14) leaves a discretion to the court to determine the circumstances in which an order should be made, which may therefore be many and varied. They include circumstances where an application would put the child concerned, or another individual, at risk of harm (as provided in section 91A), such as psychological or emotional harm. The welfare of the child is paramount.

24A.2 These circumstances can also include where one party has made repeated and unreasonable applications; where a period of respite is needed following litigation; where a period of time is needed for certain actions to be taken for the protection of the child or other person; or where a person's conduct overall is such that an order is merited to protect the welfare of the child directly, or indirectly due to damaging effects on a parent carer. Such conduct could include harassment, or other oppressive or distressing behaviour beyond or within the proceedings including via social media and e-mail, and via third parties. Such conduct might also constitute domestic abuse.

24A.3 A future application could be part of a pattern of coercive or controlling behaviour or other domestic abuse toward the victim, such that a section 91(14) order is also merited due to the risk of harm to the child or other individual.

24A.4 In proceedings in which domestic abuse is alleged or proven, or in which there are allegations or evidence of other harm to a child or other individual, the court should give early and ongoing consideration to whether it would be appropriate to make a section 91(14) order on disposal of the application, even if an application for such an order has not been made (since the court may make an order of its own motion – see section 91A(5)).

24A.5 Section 91(14) orders are a protective filter – not a bar on applications – and there is considerable scope for their use in appropriate cases

Capacity of Litigants

25.1 In the event that the judge has concerns about the capacity of a litigant before the court, the judge shall consider –

(a) the Guidance issued by the Family Justice Council in relation to assessing the capacity of litigants Capacity to Litigate in Proceedings involving Children (judiciary.uk); and
(b) Practice Direction 15B (Adults Who May Be Protected Parties and Children Who May Become Protected Parties In Family Proceedings).

Evidence

26.1 No evidence shall be filed in relation to an application until after the court has issued any case management decisions following the filing of the Child Impact Report, unless –

(a) it has been filed in support of a without notice application; or
(b) it has been directed by the court.

Using the court process appropriately

27.1 Consideration must be given by the court as to whether an application (including a repeat application) could be a sign of a party using the court process as a form of ongoing coercion or abuse against another party.

Relevant Family Application (definition)

28.1 A relevant family application for the purposes of this Practice Direction is an application that –

(a) is made to the court in, or to initiate, family proceedings; and
(b) is of a description specified in the Family Procedure Rules.

Annex
Explanation of terms

Abuse	Any behaviour which causes harm
Adjourn / Adjournment	Where the case, or a hearing, is directed to take place or continue at a later time (which might be on the same day or another day)
Allegation	A claim that someone has done something wrong
Applicant	The name given to someone who is asking the court for a court order
Application	How a person asks the court to do something
Cafcass	Cafcass stands for the 'Children and Family Court Advisory and Support Service' Cafcass is independent of the courts, social services, education and health authorities and all similar agencies. Cafcass workers (sometimes called 'Family Court Advisers' or 'officers') are specialist social workers who help the court by making safeguarding checks, helping parties at the FHDRA to consider solutions, and if necessary writing reports for the court &/or monitoring arrangements after court.

Cafcass Cymru	This is Cafcass in Wales. Cafcass Cymru is part of the Department of Health and Social Services in the Welsh Government.
Child Arrangements Order	This is an order which will set out arrangements relating to (a) with whom a child is to live, spend time or otherwise have contact, and (b) when a child is to live, spend time or otherwise have contact with any other person.
Collaborative law	One of the ways of trying to sort out disputes away from court; each party appoints their own lawyer, and you and your lawyers all meet together to work things out face to face.
Consent order	When you have reached an agreement with the other parent, which resolves the dispute, the judge may agree to make that agreement into an order called a consent order
Contact centre	A place for a parent to see their child in a neutral and 'safe' environment. 'Supervised' contact centres provide a safe and neutral place for contact. 'Supported' contact centres, which are often run by volunteers, offer a neutral place for contact in cases where no safety concerns exist
Domestic abuse	This term has the meaning given in Practice Direction 12J.
Expert evidence	Evidence and opinions provided by someone with special skills and knowledge (but, for these purposes, does not refer to a social worker employed by, and giving evidence on behalf of, a local authority who is a party to the case).
Fact finding hearing	A court hearing set up for the court to decide on issues of fact or allegations which are in dispute.
Family Assistance order	An order of the court which allows Cafcass or local authorities to provide social-work support to help parties to establish contact arrangements which might otherwise fail
File	This means to send / deliver to the court office
FPR	Family Procedure Rules 2010; the rules of court which govern family cases.
Gatekeeper	The nominated District Judge and/or nominated Legal Adviser responsible for deciding which level of judge in the family court should initially deal with an application, acting alone or jointly
Hearing	The name given to a meeting or court appointment with a judge
Indirect contact	Any contact which is not face-to-face (for example, letters, birthday cards, phone calls).
IDVA	Independent Domestic Violence Advisors (IDVAs) are trained specialists who act as a single point of contact to help victims of domestic abuse who are at the most risk of serious injury or death to become safe, ensuring their voice is heard by statutory agencies. An IDVA carries out a risk-assessment to identify a victim's level of risk of abuse (high, medium or standard) and supports them with immediate safety plans, such as accompanying them to court hearings, and implementing longer-term interventions to ensure their safety, such as accessing counselling or mental health services.

Investigation under section 37	Where it appears to a judge that a child is or may be at risk of significant harm and it may be appropriate for local authority children's services to apply for a court order giving them responsibilities towards a family, the judge can direct the local authority to investigate the child's circumstances
Judge	Where the term 'Judge' is used, this refers to any judge of the Family Court including lay justices (magistrates)and judges of the High Court
LAA	Legal Aid Agency; this is the body responsible for providing public funding for legal representation.
McKenzie Friend	A friend or other person who can help you prepare your case and go to court with you to give you support and take notes
MIAM	Mediation Information and Assessment Meeting. At this meeting, a trained mediator will explain what mediation is and how it works, explain the benefits of mediation and the likely costs, answer questions, assess whether the person is eligible for legal aid for mediation, assess whether mediation is suitable in the case. A MIAM should be held within 15 working days of contacting the mediator.
Non-court resolution	A method of solving disagreements outside of court proceedings.
Part-heard	Means a hearing which has started but which has not been finished within the day, and then continues on another day
Party	Someone involved in the court proceedings – either the person who has made the application, or the person(s) against whom the application has been made.
Practice Direction	This is a document which sets out good practice in supporting the FPR (Family Procedure Rules) or other Rules (see above) and /or may contain provisions which could otherwise be contained in rules of court and have same effect as rules
Respondent(s)	This is the name given to the person or people who receive the court application
Rule 16.4 children's guardian	A person (usually a specialist social worker) appointed by the court to look after the interests of a child in the case
Safeguarding	Making sure that people are safe
Section 7 report	A welfare report, prepared under section 7 of the Children Act 1989; the report will be on such matters relating to the welfare of that child as are required to be dealt with in the report; the report may be in writing or oral.
Section 91(14) order	An order made under section 91(14) of the Children Act 1989 which requires a person to seek the court's permission before making a further application.
Serve	Delivery of court documents
SPIP	Separated Parents Information Programme; this is available across England, and is for both parents and for grandparents.

Statement	A document setting out what you want to say to the Judge about the case. You should sign it and date it. What you say in the statement must be true.
WFPO	Welsh Family Proceedings Officer. A Cafcass officer in Wales.
WT4C	The Working Together For Children programme which runs in Wales – and is the equivalent of the SPIP (see above)

Practice Direction 36ZA – Pilot scheme: procedure for notification to the police by email of certain orders made under Part 4 of the Family Law Act 1996

This practice direction supplements FPR Part 36 (Transitional Arrangements and Pilot Schemes)

Scope and interpretation

1.1 This Practice Direction is made under rule 36.2 FPR and sets up a Pilot Scheme to allow for emails to be sent to the police notifying them when a notifiable order has been made or when a notifiable order has been served or the respondent has been otherwise informed of its terms.

1.2 This Practice Direction comes into force on 28 February 2022.

1.3 This Pilot Scheme applies where all of the following conditions are met-

(a) there is a notifiable order made by a court sitting at a location specified in paragraph 1.4; and
(c) that notifiable orderwas made in the period commencing on 28 February 2022 and ending at the end of the day on 28 February 2023.

1.4 The specified locations are the family court or the High Court District Registry sitting at-

(a) York;
(b) Harrogate;
(c) Scarborough;
(d) Skipton.

1.5 In this Practice Direction, 'notifiable order' means-

(a) a non-molestation order;
(b) an occupation order to which a power of arrest has been attached pursuant to section 47(2) or (3) of the 1996 Act; or
(c) an order varying, discharging or extending an order of a type mentioned in sub-paragraph (a) or (b).

Purpose of this Pilot Scheme

2.1 The purpose of this Pilot Scheme is to assess the use of new practices and procedures to allow for-

(a) the court to email notifiable orders to the police;
(b) the applicant or the court to email to the police a statement of service to confirm that a notifiable order has been served, or that the respondent to whom the order applies has been informed of order's terms.

Modification of the FPR and Practice Directions, and application of this Practice Direction, during the operation of the Pilot Scheme

3.1 During the operation of the Pilot Scheme, where the Pilot Scheme applies, the FPR and the Practice Directions supporting the FPR will apply-

(a) subject to the provisions of this Practice Direction; and
(b) as modified by paragraphs 4.1 and 4.2.

Modification of Part 10 FPR

4.1 In rule 10.1-

(a) the current wording shall form paragraph (1); and
(b) after paragraph (1) insert-

'(2) In this Part, in cases to which the Pilot Scheme in Practice Direction 36ZA applies, 'notifiable order' has the meaning given in paragraph 1.5 of that Practice Direction.'.

4.2 For rule 10.10 substitute—

'Notifying the police by email when a notifiable order is made

10.10(1) Where the court makes a notifiable order, notification must be given to the police force for the address of-

(a) the applicant; and
(b) if the court so directs, the respondent,

by the court officer emailing a copy of the order to the email address for that police force.

(2) Paragraph (1) only applies where the address of the applicant for notifiable order, or of the respondent to the application for that order (as the case may be), is in-

(a) the North Yorkshire Police Area.

(3) The email referred to in paragraph (1) must be sent-

(a) in the case of the North Yorkshire Police area-
    (i) where the sender has access to the cjsm network, to PNCBureau@northyorkshire.police.uk.cjsm.net; or
    (ii) where the sender does not have access to the cjsm network, to PNCBureau@northyorkshire.police.uk.

(4) The email referred to in paragraph (1) must be sent within 1 day of whichever is the earliest of-

(a) the order being sealed; or
(b) the order being approved by the judge, where the order states that it has effect despite not bearing the seal of the court.

Notifying the police by email when an order is served or the respondent is informed of its terms

10.10A(1) Subject to paragraph (2), paragraph (3) applies when the respondent has been-

(a) served with a notifiable order; or
(b) informed (whether by being present when the order was made or by telephone or otherwise) of the terms of a notifiable order.

(2) Paragraph (3) does not apply where the order states that the court has dispensed for the need for service of the order, because the court is satisfied that the respondent is aware of the terms of the order without the need for such service to be effected.

(3) A statement of service showing that the respondent has been served with, or has been informed of the terms of, the notifiable order must be sent by email to the police force to which the order was sent, in accordance with rule 10.10(3).

(4) The email referred to in paragraph (3) must be sent by-

(a) the applicant, where rule 10.6(1) applies; or
(b) the court officer, where rule 10.6(2) applies.

(5) Where paragraph (4)(a) applies-

(a) the email referred to in paragraph (3) must be sent within 2 days of the respondent being served with, or informed of the terms of, the notifiable order; and
(b) the applicant must also send the statement of service by email to the court.

(5) Where paragraph (4)(b) applies, the email referred to in paragraph (3) must be sent within 1 day of receipt by the court officer of confirmation of service, or of the person having been informed of the terms of the order, from the court bailiff.'

Practice Direction 36ZB – Pilot scheme: procedure for using an online system to complete and file certain applications for an adoption order

PLEASE NOTE THIS PD COMES INTO FORCE 6 APRIL 2022

This Practice Direction supplements FPR Part 36, rule 36.2 (Transitional Arrangements and Pilot Schemes).

Scope and interpretation

1.1 This Practice Direction is made under rule 36.2 and sets up a Pilot Scheme to allow certain applications and stages in proceedings for an adoption order to be completed using the online system.

1.2 This Practice Direction comes into force on 6 April 2022.

1.3 The Pilot Scheme applies where all of the following conditions are met-

(a) the application is for an adoption order under the Adoption and Children Act 2002 made in relation to a child who is habitually resident in the British Islands;
(b) the application is not for a 'Convention adoption order' as defined in Rule 14.1(2);
(c) one of the following applies –
   (i) the child to whom the application for an adoption order relates is made has been placed for adoption under section 19 of the 2002 Act;
   (ii) a placement order under the 2002 Act is in force in respect of the child to whom the application for an adoption order relates;
   (iii) the child is the subject of a Scottish permanence order (which term has the meaning given in section 47(10) of the 2002 Act) which includes provision granting authority for the child to be adopted; or
   (iv) the child is free for adoption by virtue of an order made under Article 17(1) or 18(1) of the Adoption (Northern Ireland) Order 1987;

(d) access to the online system for making and continuing such applications is permitted;
(e) the process provided for in the online system can be completed;
(f) the application is started in the family court sitting at-
  (i) Chelmsford;
  (ii) Leeds;
  (iii) Medway;
  (iv) Newport (Gwent);
  (v) Northampton;
  (vi) Oxford;
  (vii) Portsmouth; or
  (viii) Worcester;
(g) the application is filed in the period commencing 6 April 2022 and ending 31 October 2022.

1.4 In this Practice Direction the 'online system' means Her Majesty's Courts and Tribunals Service's online system to allow for certain stages in applications specified in paragraph 1.3 of this Practice Direction to be dealt with online.

Purpose of the Pilot Scheme

2.1 The purpose of this Pilot Scheme is to assess the use of new practices and procedures to allow for certain stages in the applications specified in paragraph 1.3 of this Practice Direction to be completed using the online system.

2.2 Where the conditions in paragraph 1.3 are met, this Pilot Scheme enables-

(a) prospective adopters;
(b) local authorities; and
(c) adoption agencies;

to engage in proceedings via the online system, to include taking the steps specified in paragraph 2.3.

2.3 The specified steps are-

(a) to create and file an application referred to in paragraph 1.3 to commence proceedings;
(b) in respect of an application referred to in sub-paragraph (a), to-
  (i) file documents, including draft orders, further applications and reports at the same time as filing the application;
  (ii) amend the application;
  (iii) indicate willingness to accept service by the court of documents relating to the application via email; and
  (iv) accept service by the court by email of any documents relating to the application; and
(c) to view an electronic record of the progress of the application that is progressing using the online system.

2.4 For the avoidance of doubt-

(a) it should not be assumed that an application of a type specified in paragraph 1.3, or any or all stages of such an application, will always be dealt with on the online system. For example, Her Majesty's Courts and Tribunals Service may gradually roll-out provision for the online service. Her Majesty's Courts and

Tribunals Service will indicate via the online system which applications and stages in proceedings can be dealt with on the online system at any point in time;

(b) parties to proceedings may not effect service of applications or other documents on other parties via the online service; and

(c) the online service cannot be accessed by those referred to at paragraph 2.2, but they will be able to view an electronic record of the progress of an application that is progressing using the online system;

(d) parents (even if parties to the proceedings) and any other parties not referred to in paragraph 2.2 will not have access to the online system and nor will they be able to view the electronic record referred to in sub-paragraph (c): they will be kept informed in accordance with the provisions of the FPR.

Modification of the FPR and Practice Directions during operation of the Pilot Scheme

3.1 During the operation of the Pilot Scheme the Family Procedure Rules 2010 and the Practice Directions supporting the Rules will apply to cases falling within the Pilot Scheme as modified by paragraphs 4.1 to 11.5.

Modification of rule 2.3(1) FPR

4.1 In rule 2.3(1) FPR, the definition of 'filing' is modified by inserting after 'office'-

'or, where the Pilot Scheme referred to in Practice Direction 36ZB applies, by creating and submitting, or by uploading, the document on the online system referred to in that Practice Direction.'.

Modification of Part 5 FPR

5.1 For 5.1, substitute-

'5.1 Where the Pilot Scheme referred to in Practice Direction 36ZB applies, the applicant must-

(a) complete all sections of the application process to apply for an adoption order in a manner set out in the online system referred to in that Practice Direction;

(b) provide all the information, including any additional documents, that the online application system referred to in that Practice Direction requires, or that the court requires, in a manner specified by the online application system, or required by the court.'.

5.2 In rule 5.2, for 'Subject' substitute 'Where rule 5.1(a)(ii) applies and a form is uploaded to the online system, subject'.

5.3 After rule 5.2 FPR insert-

'Timing and receipt of applications

5.3 An application that is submitted via the online system in accordance with rule 5.1 is lodged with the court on the date and at the time that HMCTS software records the application as received, provided that the application is subsequently issued by the court.

Timing of receipt of documents other than applications

5.3A A document, other than an application, that is submitted via the online system is filed with or otherwise received by the court on the date and at the time that HMCTS software records the document as received.'.

Modification of Part 14 FPR

6.1 In rule 14.5 after paragraph (3) insert-

'(4) In a case where-

(a) the Pilot Scheme referred to in Practice Direction 36ZB applies; and
(b) the court officer is to serve a document by email,

the court may either attach the document to be served to the email or include within the email a link to the document.'.

6.2 In rule 14.17 after paragraph (2) insert-

'(2A) In a case where-

(a) the Pilot Scheme referred to in Practice Direction 36ZB applies; and
(b) any document referred to in paragraph (2) has been provided to the court by being uploaded to the online system,

the court may require that the document also be provided in hard copy by a date specified by the court.'.

6.3 In rule 14.23 after 'special security.' insert 'Where any information or document is held electronically by the court, such as on the online system referred to in Practice Direction 36ZB, special security arrangements must be in place, in particular in relation to restrictions on access to any such information or document by the court, court staff or others.'

Modification of Part 17 FPR

7.1 In rule 17.2(6), for 'The statement of truth' substitute 'Subject to paragraph (6A), the statement of truth'.

7.2 After rule 17.2(6) insert-

'(6A) Where a statement of truth is included in an application completed using the online system referred to in Practice Direction 36ZB the party must file with the court an application which includes the name of the person who the online system requires to sign a statement of truth recorded against the statement of truth.'.

Modification of rule 29.13(1) FPR

8.1 After rule 29.13(1) insert-
'(1A) Where-

(a) the Pilot Scheme referred to in Practice Direction 369ZB applies; and
(b) the court is to serve order or judgment on a party by email,

service under paragraph (1) or otherwise may be effected by the court sending the party an email, to the address given for service in accordance with Practice Direction 6A, with the judgment or order attached to the email or with a link to the judgment or order included within the email.'.

Disapplication of Practice Direction 5B as modified by Practice Direction 36R or by Practice Direction 36Y

9.1(1) Subject to paragraph (2), where the Pilot Scheme referred to in Practice Direction 36ZB applies, the modifications to Practice Direction 5B made by Practice Direction 36R or by Practice Direction 36Y do not apply.

(2) Paragraph (1) does not apply if it is not possible to upload a given document to the online system referred to in Practice Direction 36ZB, for example because the online system is not accessible because of planned system maintenance or unplanned circumstances.

Modification of Practice Direction 6A

10.1 After paragraph 4.1 insert-

'4.1A Paragraphs 4.2 to 4.6 also apply where

(a) the pilot scheme referred to in Practice Direction 36ZB applies; and
(b) service of a judgment or order by the court is to be effected in accordance with rule 29.13(1A), as inserted by Practice Direction 36ZB.

4.1B Where paragraph 4.1A applies, references in paragraphs 4.2 to 4.5 to service of a document by email include service of a judgment or order by the court sending an email with the judgment or order attached to the email or with a link to the judgment or order included within the email.'.

10.2 In paragraph 4.2(b)-

(a) in paragraph (iii) for '; or' substitute ';';
(b) in paragraph (iv) for the full-stop substitute '; or'; and
(c) after paragraph (iv) insert-

'(v) confirmation given, by the party to be served, within the online system referred to in Practice Direction 36ZB that that party is willing to accept service by email and stating the email address for such service.'.

Modification of Practice Direction 17A

11.1 Omit paragraphs 1.5 and 2.3.

11.2 In the heading to paragraph 3.1 and in paragraphs 3.1, 3.7, 3.8 and 3.10 references to 'sign', 'signs', 'signed' and 'signing' are to be read as references to the name of the person being, or having been, recorded against the statement of truth included in an application for an adoption order to which the Pilot Scheme referred to in Practice Direction 36ZB applies.

11.3 For paragraph 4.1 substitute-

'4.1 Where an application completed using the online system referred to in Practice Direction 36ZB contains a statement of truth with the name of a person who is unable to read or sign the document recorded against it, the application must be accompanied by a certificate made by an authorised person.'.

11.4 In paragraph 4.3-

(a) for sub-paragraph (a) substitute-

'(a) that the content of the online application has been read to the person before completion of the statement of truth required by the online system;'

(b) for sub-paragraph (e) substitute-

'(e) that that person confirmed in the presence of the authorised person that it was their belief that the contents of the online application were true.'.

11.5 For the Annex substitute-

'Certificate to be used where a person is unable to read or sign an online application for an adoption order to which the Pilot Scheme in Practice Direction 36ZB applies.

I certify that I [name and address of authorised person] have read the contents of the online application and the statement of truth to the person whose name is recorded against the statement of truth, who appeared to understand (a) the application and approved its contents as accurate and (b) the statement of truth and the consequences of making a false statement, and orally confirmed that this was the case in my presence.

Practice Direction 36ZC – Pilot scheme: procedure for using an online system to complete certain proceedings for a matrimonial order or civil partnership order (new law)

PLEASE NOTE THIS PD COMES INTO FORCE 6 APRIL 2022

This Practice Direction supplements FPR Part 36, rule 36.2 (Transitional Arrangements and Pilot Schemes).

Scope and interpretation

1.1 This Practice Direction is made under rule 36.2 and sets up a Pilot Scheme to allow for an application for a matrimonial order or civil partnership order to proceed by electronic means via the online system.

1.2 This Practice Direction comes into force on 6 April 2022.

1.3 Subject to paragraph 1.4, this Practice Direction applies to all applications made on the online system from 6 April 2022.

1.4 Practice Direction 41A will remain in force in relation to any applications commenced under that Practice Direction, and this Practice Direction (and any that supersede it) will not apply in relation to such applications.

1.5 Subject to paragraph 1.6, the Pilot Scheme applies where the following conditions are met:

1 the application is for a matrimonial order which is an order of divorce made under section 1 of the 1973 Act;

2 the application is for a civil partnership order which is an order of dissolution made under section 1 of the 2004 Act;

3 the application is not unsuitable for the online system (as explained in paragraph 1.8);

4 in a sole application, either party chooses to proceed with the application by electronic means;

5 in a joint application, the parties each choose to proceed with the application by electronic means;

6 the application is started in the family court; and

7 the application is filed in the period commencing 6April 2022 and ending 5 April 2023.

1.6 Subject to paragraph 1.7, an application must proceed by electronic means where-

(a) all of the conditions in paragraph 1.5(a), (b), (c), (f) and (g) are met; and

(b) the applicant is legally represented.

1.7 Paragraph 1.6 does not apply when the online system is not available for use because of-

(a) planned 'down time' for system maintenance or upgrades;
(b) unplanned 'down-time' because of, for example, a system failure or power outage or some other unplanned circumstance.'; or
(c) in a joint application, the same legal representative is acting for both applicants.

1.8 Her Majesty's Courts and Tribunals Service may conclude that certain individual or categories of applications are not suitable for the online system, and such categories are to be specified in guidance issued by Her Majesty's Courts and Tribunals Service and published on GOV.UK.

1.9 In this Practice Direction the 'online system' means Her Majesty's Courts and Tribunals Service's online system to allow for specified applications in matrimonial and civil partnership proceedings to be completed online. The online system is accessible at https://www.gov.uk/apply-for-divorce.

Purpose of the Pilot Scheme

2.1 The purpose of this Pilot Scheme is to assess the use of new practices and procedures to allow for an application for a matrimonial order or civil partnership order to proceed by electronic means via the online system.

Modification of the FPR and Practice Directions during operation of the Pilot Scheme

3.1 During the operation of the Pilot Scheme the Family Procedure Rules 2010 and the Practice Directions supporting the Rules will apply to cases falling within the Pilot Scheme as modified by paragraphs 4.1 to 13.5. This Practice Direction contains provisions that apply generally to applications in the Pilot Scheme.

3.2 There are certain steps that cannot be taken by electronic means via the online system and which must be taken offline and in accordance with the FPR and supporting practice directions. (In turn, rule 5.5 and PD5B will apply to determine whether any of the steps can be taken via email.)

3.3 The Pilot Scheme does not make provision in relation to steps that can already be undertaken by email (via rule 5.5 FPR and PD5B) or in relation to procedures to enable documents to be held electronically by HMCTS via bulk scanning (PD5D).

Modification of Part 2 FPR

4.1 In rule 2.3(1) FPR, for the definition of 'filing' substitute-

"'filing' in relation to supplying a document or information, means-

(a) delivering it, by post or otherwise, to the court office; or
(b) where Practice Direction 36ZC applies, by-
    (i) uploading the document on the online system referred in that Practice Direction; or
    (ii) submitting the information via that online system;'.

Modification of Part 5 FPR

5.1 For rule 5.1, substitute-

'5.1(1) Where the Pilot Scheme referred to in Practice Direction 36ZC applies, and subject to that Practice Direction, the following stages in matrimonial or civil partnership proceedings shall be completed online by the applicant, or applicants jointly, in the manner specified by the online system-

(a) create and start certain types of application for a matrimonial order or civil partnership order;

(b) in respect of such an application-

(i) file documents;

(ii) in the case of joint applicants, file an acknowledgement of receipt;

(iii) indicate willingness to accept service of any documents relating to the application by email;

(iv) accept service of any documents relating to the application;

(v) serve any documents relating to the application (but not serve the application itself);

(vi) make an application for a conditional order; and

(vii) make an application for a final order (and give notice of such application where required);

(c) view an electronic record of the progress of the application.

(2) Where the Pilot Scheme referred to in Practice Direction 36ZC applies, and subject to that Practice Direction, the respondent may take the following steps by electronic means via the online system in respect of an application for a matrimonial order or civil partnership order which is progressing via the online system-

(a) file an acknowledgement of service;

(b) indicate willingness to accept service of any documents relating to the application (but not the application itself) by email;

(c) accept service of any documents relating to the application;

(d) make an application for a final order (where applicable); and

(d) view an electronic record of the progress of the application.

(3) Each party must at each stage provide all the information requested, including any documents that the online system or court requires, in a manner specified by the online system or by the court.'.

5.2 Omit rule 5.2.

Modification of Part 6 FPR

6.1 In rule 6.15 for paragraph (1) substitute-

'(1) An application is deemed to be served if-

(a) subject to paragraph (2), a paper acknowledgment of service, signed by the party served or the solicitor acting on that party's behalf, is returned to the court office; or

(b) the respondent completes the acknowledgment of service using the online system referred to in Practice Direction 36ZC.'

Modification of Part 7 FPR

7.1 For rule 7.3(1) substitute-

'7.3(1) Where an applicant is legally represented, the legal representative must complete and provide with the application, in a manner specified in the online system referred to in Practice Direction 36ZC, a statement certifying whether the legal representative has discussed with the applicant the possibility of reconciliation and given the applicant the names and addresses of persons qualified to help effect a reconciliation.'.

7.2 For rule 7.5(2)(a) substitute-

'(a) details of how to respond to the application; and'.

7.3 In rule 7.7-

(a) in paragraph (1) for 'The' substitute 'Subject to paragraphs (2A) to (2C), the';
(b) after paragraph (2) insert-

'(2A) A respondent may choose whether or not to use the online system to complete and file an acknowledgment of service. Details of how to respond online will be sent to them in accordance with 7.5(2)(a).

(2B) If a respondent chooses not to use the online system then they must contact Her Majesty's Courts and Tribunals Service (using the details sent to them in accordance with 7.5(2)(a)) to request a paper form for acknowledging service.

(2C) Where paragraph (2B) applies, the acknowledgment of service must be filed within 14 days beginning with the date on which the respondent received the paper form for acknowledging service. The amended deadline for filing the acknowledgment will be notified to all parties.';

(c) in paragraph (3)(a) reference to 'signed' is to be read as reference to the name of the individual being, or having been, recorded against the statement of truth included in an acknowledgment of service which has been completed online in accordance with paragraph (2A);
(d) in paragraph (4) after 'proceedings', the second time it appears, insert 'using the online system described in Practice Direction 36ZC'.

7.4 In rule 7.9-

(a) in paragraph (1) after 'court' insert 'using the online system described in Practice Direction 36ZC';
(b) after paragraph (3) insert—

'(3A) An application made under paragraph (3)(c) may be made offline and in accordance with Part 7 of the FPR or using the online system described in Practice Direction 36ZC.';

(c) in paragraph (4)–
 (i) for 'be accompanied by' substitute 'include';
 (ii) in subparagraph (c) for 'the', the first time it appears, substitute 'a paper';
(d) in paragraph (6) for 'must be served on the other party to the marriage or civil partnership' substitute 'using the online system described in Practice Direction 36ZC will be automatically sent to the other party to the marriage or civil partnership'.

7.5 In rule 7.19 -

(a) in paragraph (1) after 'court', each time it appears, insert ', using the online system described in Practice Direction 36ZC';
(b) in paragraph (2)–
 (i) after '(1)(c)' insert 'using the online system described in Practice Direction 36ZC';
 (ii) after 'notice', the second time it appears, insert 'using the online system described in Practice Direction 36ZC';

(c) after paragraph (2) insert—

'(2A) An application made under (1)(c) may be made offline and in accordance with Part 7 of the FPR or using the online system described in Practice Direction 36ZC.';

(d) omit paragraph (3).

Modification of Part 17 FPR

8.1 In rule 17.2(6), for 'The statement of truth' substitute 'Subject to paragraph (6A), the statement of truth'.

8.2 After rule 17.2(6) insert-

'(6A) Where a statement of truth is included in an application or acknowledgment of service completed using the online system referred to in Practice Direction 36ZC-

(a) the party must file with the court an application or acknowledgment of service which includes the name of the person who the online system requires to sign a statement of truth recorded against the statement of truth; and

(b) the court may require the party to produce a copy of the application or acknowledgment of service containing the signature of the person referred to in sub-paragraph (a) at a later date.'.

Modification of Part 29 FPR

9.1 After rule 29.13(1) insert-

'(1A) Where the pilot scheme referred to in Practice Direction 36ZC applies, service under paragraph (1) or otherwise may be effected by the court sending each party an email, to the address given for service in accordance with Practice Direction 6A, containing a weblink from which the order may be accessed and downloaded.'.

Disapplication of Practice Direction 5B

10.1 Practice Direction 5B does not apply in relation to an application made online under the Pilot Scheme referred to in Practice Direction 36ZC.

Modification of Practice Direction 6A

11.1 In paragraph 4.2(b)-

(a) in paragraph (iii) for '; or' substitute ';';

(b) in paragraph (iv) for the full-stop substitute '; or'; and

(c) after paragraph (iv) insert-

'(v) confirmation given, by the party to be served, within the online system referred to in Practice Direction 36ZC that that party is willing to accept service by email and stating the email address for such service.'

11.2 In paragraph 10.1-

(a) for 'send' substitute 'provide'; and

(b) omit 'photographic or scanned'.

Modification of Practice Direction 7A

12.1 For paragraph 1.1 substitute-

'1.1 Where the Pilot Scheme referred to in Practice Direction 36ZC applies, an application for a matrimonial order or civil partnership order must be made as required by the online system referred to in that Practice Direction and in accordance with rule 5.1.'.

12.2 For paragraph 1.2 substitute-

'1.2 The application must be completed according to the detailed guidance contained in the online system.'.

12.3 After paragraph 1.2 insert-

'Applications for matrimonial or civil partnership orders received via the online system: timing

'1A.1 An application for a matrimonial or civil partnership order that is submitted via the online system is lodged with the court on the date and at the time that HMCTS software records the application as received, provided that the application is subsequently issued by the court.

1A.2 A document, other than an application for a matrimonial or civil partnership order, that is submitted via the online system is filed with or otherwise received by the court on the date and at the time that HMCTS software records the document as received.

1A.3 When an application is received via the online system referred to in Practice Direction 36ZC, an acknowledgement of receipt will automatically be sent to the applicant or applicants. This acknowledgement of receipt does not constitute a notice that the application has been issued.'.

12.4 In paragraph 3.1-

(a) for the heading of, and first sentence of, paragraph 3.1, substitute-

'Proof of marriage

3.1 The online system referred to in Practice Direction 36ZC sets out the documents which must accompany an application for a matrimonial order or civil partnership order and the way in which those documents may be provided (for example, the online system may allow for documents to be posted, or to be uploaded and submitted online with the application).'.

Modification of Practice Direction 17A

13.1 Omit paragraphs 1.5 and 2.3.

13.2 In the heading to paragraph 3.1 and in paragraphs 3.1, 3.7, 3.8 and 3.10 references to 'sign', 'signs', 'signed' and 'signing' are to be read as references to the name of the person being, or having been, recorded against the statement of truth included in an application or acknowledgment of service filed in matrimonial or civil partnership proceedings to which the pilot scheme referred to in Practice Direction 36ZC applies.

13.3 For paragraph 4.1 substitute-

'4.1 Where an application or acknowledgment of service completed using the online system referred to in Practice Direction 36ZC contains a statement of truth, with the name of a person who is unable to read or sign the document recorded against it, the application or acknowledgment of service must be accompanied by a certificate made by an authorised person.'.

13.4 In paragraph 4.3-

(a) for sub-paragraph (a) substitute-

'(a) that the content of the online application or acknowledgment of service has been read to the person before completion of the statement of truth required by the online system;'; and

(b) for sub-paragraph (e) substitute-

'(e) that that person confirmed in the presence of the authorised person that it was their belief that the contents of the online application or acknowledgment of service were true.'

13.5 For the Annex substitute-

'Certificate to be used where a person is unable to read or sign an online application or acknowledgment of service filed in matrimonial or civil partnership proceedings to which the pilot scheme in Practice Direction 36ZC applies.

I certify that I [name and address of authorised person] have read the contents of the online [application][acknowledgment of service] and the statement of truth to the person whose name is recorded against the statement of truth, who appeared to understand (a) the [application][acknowledgment of service] and approved its contents as accurate and (b) the statement of truth and the consequences of making a false statement, and orally confirmed that this was the case in my presence.

Practice Direction 36ZD – Pilot scheme: online system for certain private law proceedings relating to children and for certain protective orders

PLEASE NOTE THIS PD COMES INTO FORCE 20 APRIL 2022

This Practice Direction supplements FPR Part 36, rule 36.2 (Transitional Arrangements and Pilot Schemes).

Chapter 1
Introductory provisions

Scope and interpretation

1.1 This Practice Direction is made under rule 36.2 FPR and sets up a Pilot Scheme to allow for certain applications and certain stages in the proceedings relating to those applications to proceed via an online system.

1.2 The Pilot Scheme applies to applications where all of the following conditions are met:

(a) the application is for-

(i) an order under section 8 of the 1989 Act;

(ii) permission to apply for an order under section 8 of the 1989 Act; or

(iii) an order under Part 4 of the 1996 Act;

(b) the applicant is legally represented;
(c) access by the applicant's legal representative to the online system for making such applications is permitted;
(d) the application is to be started in the family court; and
(e) the application is filed in the period commencing 20 April 2022 and ending at the end of the day on 19 April 2023.

1.3 In this Practice Direction-

'HMCTS' means Her Majesty's Courts and Tribunals Service; and
'online system' means the HMCTS's online system to allow for certain applications and certain stages in the proceedings relating to those applications to proceed online.

Purpose of the Pilot Scheme

2.1 The initial purpose of this Pilot Scheme is to assess the use of new practices and procedures to allow, where the conditions specified in paragraph 1.2 are met, for applications be created and submitted via an online system.

2.2 It is intended that this Practice Direction will be amended in future to allow for later stages in those applications to be completed via the online system.

2.3 For the avoidance of doubt-

(a) HMCTS will determine who may have access to the online system (as per paragraph 1.2(c)). For example, it may be that initially access is only permitted to selected legal representatives or that, in time, access is permitted to a party's legal representative who is registered in accordance with requirements specified by HMCTS;
(b) it should not be assumed that an application of a type specified in paragraph 1.2(a), or any or all stages of such an application, will always be able to be dealt with on the online system. This is because HMCTS will be gradually rolling out the types of application that can be dealt with via the online system. There may also be times when the online system is not available, for example because of planned or unplanned down-time. HMCTS will indicate via the online system which applications can be dealt with on the online system at any point in time;
(c) it should be noted that Practice Direction 36G makes provision for a Pilot Scheme for generating an application for a section 8 order online (with the application then usually being filed by email). If a party or their legal representative does not have access to the online system referred to in this Practice Direction 36ZD, then they can instead access the online system referred to in Practice Direction 36G.

Modification of the FPR and Practice Directions during operation of the Pilot Scheme

3.1 During the operation of the Pilot Scheme the FPR and the Practice Directions supporting the FPR will apply-

(a) as modified by Chapter 2, to all cases falling within the Pilot Scheme;
(b) as modified by Chapter 3, to applications for an order under section 8 of the 1989 Act; and
(c) as modified by Chapter 4, to applications for an order under Part 4 of the 1996 Act.

Chapter 2
Modifications applicable to all cases within the pilot scheme

Modification of Part 2 FPR

4.1 In rule 2.3(1) FPR, for the definition of 'filing' substitute-

"filing' in relation to supplying a document or information, means-

(a) delivering it, by post or otherwise, to the court office; or
(b) where Practice Direction 36ZD applies, by-
  (i) uploading the document on the online system referred in that Practice Direction; or
  (ii) submitting the information via that online system;'

Modification of Part 5 FPR

5.1 For rule 5.1 FPR substitute:

'5.1 Where the Pilot Scheme referred to in Practice Direction 36ZD applies, the applicant must:

(a) complete all relevant sections of the application process set out in the online system;
(b) submit the completed application via the online system;
(c) provide all the information, including any additional documents, that the online system or the court requires, in the manner specified by the online system or required by the court.'.

5.2 Omit rule 5.2 FPR.

5.3 After rule 5.2 FPR insert-

'Timing of receipt of applications

5.3 An application that is submitted via the online system in accordance with rule 5.1 is lodged with the court on the date and at the time that HMCTS software records the application as received, provided that the application is subsequently issued by the court.

Timing of receipt of documents other than applications

5.3A A document, other than an application, that is submitted via the online system is filed with or otherwise received by the court on the date and at the time that HMCTS software records the document as received.'.

Modification of Part 17 FPR

6.1 In rule 17.2(6) FPR for 'The statement of truth' substitute 'Subject to paragraph (6A), the statement of truth'.

6.2 After rule 17.2(6) FPR insert:

'(6A) Where a statement of truth is included in an application to which the Pilot Scheme referred to in Practice Direction 36ZD applies –

(a) the applicant must file with the court an application which includes the name of the person who the online system requires to sign a statement of truth printed underneath the statement of truth; and
(b) the court may require the applicant to produce a copy of the application containing the signature of the person referred to in sub-paragraph (a) at a later date.'

Modification of FPR Practice Direction 17A

7.1 In the heading to paragraph 3.1 and in paragraphs 3.1, 3.7, 3.8 and 3.10 references to 'sign', 'signs', 'signing' and 'signed' are to be read as references to the name of the person being, or having been, printed under the statement of truth included in an application to which the Pilot Scheme referred to in Practice Direction 36ZD applies.

7.2 For paragraph 4.1 substitute-

'4.1 Where an application (being an application to which the Pilot Scheme referred to in Practice Direction 36ZD applies) contains a statement of truth with the printed name of a person who is unable to read or sign the document, the application must be accompanied by a certificate made by an authorised person.'

7.3 In paragraph 4.3-

(a) for sub-paragraph (a) substitute-

'(a) that the content of the application generated by the online system has been read to the person before completion of the statement of truth required by the online system;'; and

(b) for sub-paragraph (e) substitute-

'(e) that that person confirmed in the presence of the authorised person that it was their belief that the contents of the application were true.'.

7.4 For the Annex substitute-

'Certificate to be used where a person is unable to read or sign an application to which the Pilot Scheme referred to in Practice Direction 36ZD applies.

I certify that I [name and address of authorised person' have read the contents of the application and the statement of truth to the person whose name is printed under the statement of truth in the application, who appeared to understand (a) the application and approved its contents as accurate and (b) the statement of truth and the consequences of making a false statement, and orally confirmed that this was the case in my presence.'.

Chapter 3

Modifications applicable to applications for an order under section 8 of the 1989 Act

Modification of Part 3 FPR

8.1 For rule 3.7 substitute-

'3.7 An application to initiate any of the proceedings specified in Rule 3.8 must either-

(a) be accompanied by a form (uploaded to the online system) which includes confirmation from an authorised family mediator that –
  (i) the prospective applicant has attended a MIAM; or
  (ii) a mediator's exemption applies; or

(b) contain a claim by the prospective applicant that one of the MIAM exemptions applies.

(A list of MIAM exemptions is set out in Rule 3.8(1) below. A list of mediator's exemptions is set out in Rule 3.8(2) below.)'.

Modification of FPR Practice Direction 3A

9.1 For paragraph 6 substitute-

'6 When making certain kinds of applications (see paragraphs 12 and 13 below), an applicant must therefore either-

(a) provide on a separate form uploaded to the online system confirmation from a mediator that-
(i) the applicant has attended a MIAM; or
(ii) a 'mediator's exemption' applies; or
(b) include in the application a claim that a MIAM exemption applies.

An applicant who claims an exemption from the MIAM requirement is not required to attach any supporting evidence with their application, but should bring any supporting evidence to the first hearing.'.

9.2 Omit paragraphs 14 to 16.

9.3 In paragraph 18, for 'on the relevant form' substitute 'in the relevant section of the online system.'

9.4 In paragraph 34, omit the words after 'MIAM exemption' and substitute 'and signed confirmation should then be returned to the applicant.'

Modification of FPR Practice Direction 12B

10.1 For paragraph 8.2 substitute-

'8.2 Where the pilot scheme referred to in Practice Direction 36ZD applies, the application for a section 8 order must be created and submitted on the online system referred to in Practice Direction 36ZD. For the purposes of that pilot scheme, references in this Practice Direction to 'form C100' and 'form C1A' are to be read as including those versions of the forms generated by the online system.'

10.2 In paragraph 8.3 for 'on the form C100' substitute 'on the application submitted on the online system referred to in Practice Direction 36ZD'.

10.3 In paragraph 8.4-

(a) for 'the form C100' substitute 'application'; and
(b) in sub-paragraph (3) for 'in the form' substitute 'on a form uploaded to the online system by the applicant'.

10.4 Omit paragraph 8.5.

10.5 In paragraph 8.6 for 'attached to the Form C100' substitute 'filed with the court by email'.

Modification of FPR Practice Direction 12B (Pilot), annexed to Practice Direction 36Z

11.1 Omit paragraph 8.2.

11.2 In paragraph 8.3 for 'on the form C100' substitute 'in the application created and submitted on the online system referred to in Practice Direction 36ZD'.

11.3 In paragraph 8.4 for 'form C100' substitute 'the application'.

11.4 Omit paragraph 8.5.

11.5 In paragraph 8.6 for 'attached to the Form C100' substitute 'filed with the court by email'.

11.6 In paragraph 8.7 for 'form C100' both times those words appear substitute 'the application'.

11.7 In paragraph 8.8-

(a) in sub-paragraph (a) for 'being made on a form C100' substitute 'for an order under section 8 of the 1989 Act which is created and submitted on the online system referred to in Practice Direction 36ZD'; and

(b) in sub-paragraph (a)(i) after 'Form C1A)' insert 'as generated by the online system'.

11.8 In paragraph 8.9-

(a) in sub-paragraph (a) for 'being made on a form C100' substitute 'for an order under section 8 of the 1989 Act which is created and submitted on the online system referred to in Practice Direction 36ZD'; and

(b) in sub-paragraph (a)(i) for '(together with Supplemental Information Form C1A, if provided)' substitute '(together with any Supplemental Information Form C1A) as generated by the online system'.

11.9 In paragraph 8.11-

(a) in sub-paragraph (a) for '(and the form C1A, if supplied)' substitute '(and any Form C1A) as generated by the online system'; and

(b) in sub-paragraph (b) after 'Form C8' insert '(as generated by the online system)'.

Chapter 4

Modifications applicable to applications for an order under Part 4 of the 1996 Act

12.1 In rule 10.2(1) after 'statement' inserted 'which must be uploaded to the online system referred to in Practice Direction 36ZD'.

[[PART 37
APPLICATIONS AND PROCEEDINGS IN RELATION TO CONTEMPT OF COURT

37.1 Scope

(1) This Part sets out the procedure to be followed in proceedings for contempt of court ('contempt proceedings').

(2) This Part does not alter the scope and extent of the jurisdiction of courts determining contempt proceedings, whether inherent, statutory or at common law.

(3) This Part has effect subject to and to the extent that it is consistent with the substantive law of contempt of court.][1]][2]

Amendment

1 Substituted by the Family Procedure (Amendment No 2) Rules 2020, SI 2020/758, rr 2, 5, Schedule.
2 Inserted by the Family Procedure (Amendment No 2) Rules 2014, SI 2014/667, rr 2, 44, Schedule.

[[37.2 Interpretation

In this Part—

'claimant' means a person making a contempt application;

'contempt application' means an application to the court for an order determining contempt proceedings;

'defendant' means the person against whom the application is made;

'order of committal' means the imposition of a sentence of imprisonment (whether immediate or suspended) for contempt of court;

'penal notice' means a prominent notice on the front of an order warning that if the person against whom the order is made (and, in the case of a corporate body, a director or officer of that body) disobeys the court's order, the person (or director or officer) may be held in contempt of court and punished by a fine, imprisonment, confiscation of assets or other punishment under the law.][1]][2]

Amendment

1 Substituted by the Family Procedure (Amendment No 2) Rules 2020, SI 2020/758, rr 2, 5, Schedule.

2 Inserted by the Family Procedure (Amendment No 2) Rules 2014, SI 2014/667, rr 2, 44, Schedule.

[[37.3 How to make a contempt application

(1) A contempt application made in existing High Court or family court proceedings is made by an application under Part 18 in those proceedings, whether or not the application is made against a party to those proceedings.

(2) If the application is made in the High Court, it shall be determined by a High Court judge of the Division in which the case is proceeding. If it is made in the family court, it shall be determined by a judge of the family court.

(The Family Court (Composition and Distribution of Business) Rules 2014 make provision for which level of judge may determine a contempt application.)

(3) A contempt application in relation to alleged interference with the due administration of justice, otherwise than in existing High Court or family court proceedings, is made by an application to the High Court under Part 19.

(4) Where an application under Part 19 is made under paragraph (3), the rules in Part 19 apply except as modified by this Part and the defendant is not required to acknowledge service of the application.

(5) Permission to make a contempt application is required where the application is made in relation to—

(a) interference with the due administration of justice, except in relation to existing High Court or family court proceedings;

(b) an allegation of knowingly making a false statement in any affidavit, affirmation or other document verified by a statement of truth or in a disclosure statement.

(6) If permission to make the application is needed, the application for permission shall be included in the contempt application, which will proceed to a full hearing only if permission is granted.

(7) If permission is needed and the application relates to High Court proceedings, the question of permission shall be determined by a single judge of the High Court. If permission is granted the contempt application shall be determined by a single judge or Divisional Court of that Division.][1]][2]

Amendment

1 Substituted by the Family Procedure (Amendment No 2) Rules 2020, SI 2020/758, rr 2, 5, Schedule.
2 Inserted by the Family Procedure (Amendment No 2) Rules 2014, SI 2014/667, rr 2, 44, Schedule.

[[37.4 Requirements of a contempt application

(1) Unless and to the extent that the court directs otherwise, every contempt application must be supported by written evidence given by affidavit or affirmation.

(2) A contempt application must include statements of all the following, unless (in the case of (b) to (g)) wholly inapplicable—

(a) the nature of the alleged contempt (for example, breach of an order or undertaking or contempt in the face of the court);
(b) the date and terms of any order allegedly breached or disobeyed;
(c) confirmation that any such order was personally served, and the date it was served, unless the court or the parties dispensed with personal service;
(d) if the court dispensed with personal service, the terms and date of the court's order dispensing with personal service;
(e) confirmation that any order allegedly breached or disobeyed included a penal notice;
(f) the date and terms of any undertaking allegedly breached;
(g) confirmation of the claimant's belief that the person who gave any undertaking understood its terms and the consequences of failure to comply with it;
(h) a brief summary of the facts alleged to constitute the contempt, set out numerically in chronological order;
(i) that the defendant has the right to be legally represented in the contempt proceedings;
(j) that the defendant is entitled to a reasonable opportunity to obtain legal representation and to apply for legal aid which may be available without any means test;
(k) that the defendant may be entitled to the services of an interpreter;
(l) that the defendant is entitled to a reasonable time to prepare for the hearing;
(m) that the defendant is entitled but not obliged to give written and oral evidence in their defence;
(n) that the defendant has the right to remain silent and to decline to answer any question the answer to which may incriminate the defendant;
(o) that the court may proceed in the defendant's absence if they do not attend but (whether or not they attend) will only find the defendant in contempt if satisfied beyond reasonable doubt of the facts constituting contempt and that they do constitute contempt;
(p) that if the court is satisfied that the defendant has committed a contempt, the court may punish the defendant by a fine, imprisonment, confiscation of assets or other punishment under the law;
(q) that if the defendant admits the contempt and wishes to apologise to the court, that is likely to reduce the seriousness of any punishment by the court;
(r) that the court's findings will be provided in writing as soon as practicable after the hearing; and
(s) that the court will sit in public, unless and to the extent that the court orders otherwise, and that its findings will be made public.][1]][2]

Amendment

1 Substituted by the Family Procedure (Amendment No 2) Rules 2020, SI 2020/758, rr 2, 5, Schedule.
2 Inserted by the Family Procedure (Amendment No 2) Rules 2014, SI 2014/667, rr 2, 44, Schedule.

[[37.5 Service of a contempt application

(1) Unless the court directs otherwise in accordance with Part 6 and except as provided in paragraph (2), a contempt application and evidence in support must be served on the defendant personally.

(2) Where a legal representative for the defendant is on the record in the proceedings in which, or in connection with which, an alleged contempt is committed—

- (a) the contempt application and evidence in support may be served on the representative for the defendant unless the representative objects in writing within seven days of receipt of the application and evidence in support;
- (b) if the representative does not object in writing, they must at once provide to the defendant a copy of the contempt application and the evidence supporting it and take all reasonable steps to ensure the defendant understands them;
- (c) if the representative objects in writing, the issue of service shall be referred to a judge of the court dealing with the contempt application; and the judge shall consider written representations from the parties and determine the issue on the papers, without (unless the judge directs otherwise) an oral hearing.][1]][2]

Amendment

1 Substituted by the Family Procedure (Amendment No 2) Rules 2020, SI 2020/758, rr 2, 5, Schedule.
2 Inserted by the Family Procedure (Amendment No 2) Rules 2014, SI 2014/667, rr 2, 44, Schedule.

[[37.6 Cases where no application is made

(1) If the court considers that a contempt of court (including a contempt in the face of the court) may have been committed, the court on its own initiative shall consider whether to proceed against the defendant in contempt proceedings.

(2) Where the court does so, any other party in the proceedings may be required by the court to give such assistance to the court as is proportionate and reasonable, having regard to the resources available to that party.

(3) If the court proceeds of its own initiative, it shall issue a summons to the defendant which includes the matters set out in rule 37.4(2)(a)-(s) (in so far as applicable) and requires the defendant to attend court for directions to be given.

(4) A summons issued under this rule shall be served on the defendant personally and on any other party, unless the court directs otherwise. If rule 37.5(2) applies, the procedure there set out shall be followed unless the court directs otherwise.][1]][2]

Amendment

1 Substituted by the Family Procedure (Amendment No 2) Rules 2020, SI 2020/758, rr 2, 5, Schedule.
2 Inserted by the Family Procedure (Amendment No 2) Rules 2014, SI 2014/667, rr 2, 44, Schedule.

[[37.7 Directions for hearing of contempt proceedings

(1) The court shall give such directions as it thinks fit for the hearing and determination of contempt proceedings, including directions for the attendance of witnesses and oral evidence, as it considers appropriate.

(2) The court may issue a bench warrant to secure the attendance of the defendant at a directions hearing or at the substantive hearing.

(3) The court may not give any direction compelling the defendant to give evidence either orally or in writing.][1]][2]

Amendment

1 Substituted by the Family Procedure (Amendment No 2) Rules 2020, SI 2020/758, rr 2, 5, Schedule.
2 Inserted by the Family Procedure (Amendment No 2) Rules 2014, SI 2014/667, rr 2, 44, Schedule.

[[37.8 Hearings and judgments in contempt proceedings

(1) All hearings of contempt proceedings shall, irrespective of the parties' consent, be listed and heard in public unless the court otherwise directs, applying the provisions of paragraph (4).

(2) In deciding whether to hold a hearing in private, the court must consider any duty to protect or have regard to a right to freedom of expression which may be affected.

(3) The court shall .take reasonable steps to ensure that all hearings are of an open and public character, save when a hearing is held in private.

(4) A hearing, or any part of it, must be held in private if, and only to the extent that, the court is satisfied of one or more of the matters set out in sub-paragraphs (a) to (g) and that it is necessary to sit in private to secure the proper administration of justice—

(a) publicity would defeat the object of the hearing;
(b) it involves matters relating to national security;
(c) it involves confidential information (including information relating to personal financial matters) and publicity would damage that confidentiality;
(d) a private hearing is necessary to protect the interests of any child or protected party;
(e) it is a hearing of an application made without notice and it would be unjust to any respondent for there to be a public hearing;
(f) it involves uncontentious matters arising in the administration of trusts or in the administration of a deceased person's estate; or
(g) the court for any other reason considers this to be necessary to secure the proper administration of justice.

(5) The court must order that the identity of any party or witness shall not be disclosed if, and only if, it considers non-disclosure necessary to secure the proper administration of justice and in order to protect the interests of that party or witness.

(6) Unless and to the extent that the court otherwise directs, where the court acts under paragraph (4) or (5), a copy of the court's order shall be published on the website of the Judiciary of England and Wales (which may be found at www.judiciary.uk). Any person who is not a party to the proceedings may apply to attend the hearing and make submissions, or apply to set aside or vary the order.

(7) Advocates and the judge shall appear robed in all hearings of contempt proceedings, whether or not the court sits in public.

(8) Before deciding to sit in private for all or part of the hearing, the court shall notify the national print and broadcast media, via the Press Association.

(9) The court shall consider any submissions from the parties or media organisations before deciding whether and if so to what extent the hearing should be in private.

(10) If the court decides to sit in private it shall, before doing so, sit in public to give a reasoned public judgment setting out why it is doing so.

(11) At the conclusion of the hearing, whether or not held in private, the court shall sit in public to give a reasoned public judgment stating its findings and any punishment.

(12) The court shall inform the defendant of the right to appeal without permission, the time limit for appealing and the court before which any appeal must be brought.

(13) The court shall be responsible for ensuring that judgments in contempt proceedings are transcribed and published on the website of the judiciary of England and Wales.][1][2]

Amendment

1 Substituted by the Family Procedure (Amendment No 2) Rules 2020, SI 2020/758, rr 2, 5, Schedule.
2 Inserted by the Family Procedure (Amendment No 2) Rules 2014, SI 2014/667, rr 2, 44, Schedule.

[[37.9 Powers of the court in contempt proceedings

(1) If the court finds the defendant in contempt of court, the court may impose a period of imprisonment (an order of committal), a fine, confiscation of assets or other punishment permitted under the law.

(2) Execution of an order of committal requires issue of a warrant of committal. An order of committal and a warrant of committal have immediate effect unless and to the extent that the court decides to suspend execution of the order or warrant.

(3) An order or warrant of committal must be personally served on the defendant unless the court directs otherwise.

(4) To the extent that the substantive law permits, a court may attach a power of arrest to a committal order.

(5) An order or warrant of committal may not be enforced more than two years after the date it was made unless the court directs otherwise.][1][2]

Amendment

1 Substituted by the Family Procedure (Amendment No 2) Rules 2020, SI 2020/758, rr 2, 5, Schedule.
2 Inserted by the Family Procedure (Amendment No 2) Rules 2014, SI 2014/667, rr 2, 44, Schedule.

[37.10 Applications to discharge committal orders

(1) A defendant against whom a committal order has been made may apply to discharge it.

(2) Any such application shall be made by an application notice under Part 18 in the contempt proceedings.

(3) The court hearing such an application shall consider all the circumstances and make such order under the law as it thinks fit.][1][2]

Amendment

1 Substituted by the Family Procedure (Amendment No 2) Rules 2020, SI 2020/758, rr 2, 5, Schedule.
2 Inserted by the Family Procedure (Amendment No 2) Rules 2014, SI 2014/667, rr 2, 44, Schedule.

Practice Direction 37A – Applications and proceedings in relation to contempt of court

See also Part 37

Directions for hearings of contempt proceedings

1 Evidence adduced by defendant. Rule 37.7(3) provides that the court may not give any direction compelling the defendant to give evidence either orally or in writing. The court

may, however, direct that, if the defendant wishes to adduce evidence in response to the contempt application, the defendant file and serve witness statements of the witnesses (including himself or herself) on which reliance is intended. Such statements may not be used against the defendant in the contempt application unless and until the defendant deploys them in support of the defendant's case against the contempt application.

2 Striking out and procedural defects.

(1) On application by the defendant or on its own initiative, the court may strike out a contempt application if it appears to the court—

(a) that the application and the evidence served in support of it disclose no reasonable ground for alleging that the defendant is guilty of a contempt of court;

(b) that the application is an abuse of the court's process or, if made in existing proceedings, is otherwise likely to obstruct the just disposal of those proceedings; or

(c) that there has been a failure to comply with a rule, practice direction or court order.

(2) The court may waive any procedural defect in the commencement or conduct of a contempt application if satisfied that no injustice has been caused to the defendant by the defect.

Hearings and judgments in contempt proceedings

3 Informing the defendant of right to appeal, etc. Paragraph (12) of rule 37.8 does not require the court to inform a defendant who has been acquitted of contempt of the right to appeal and the other matters listed in that paragraph.

4 Responsibility of court for publication of judgments. While paragraph (13) of rule 37.8 makes the court responsible for the publication of transcripts of judgments in contempt proceedings, it does not require the court to publish a transcript of every judgment, but only in a case where the court makes an order for committal.

[PART 38
RECOGNITION AND ENFORCEMENT OF PROTECTION MEASURES

Chapter 1
Scope and interpretation of this Part

38.1 Scope and interpretation

(1) This Part contains rules about the …[1] recognition and enforcement of [incoming][2] protection measures between England and Wales and Member States of the European Union other than the United Kingdom and Denmark.

(2) In this Part—

…[1]

…[1]

'Article 11 notice' means the notification required by Article 11 of the Protection Measures Regulation;

'Article 14 certificate' means a certificate issued under Article 14 of the Protection Measures Regulation;

…[1]

'person causing the risk' has the meaning given to it in the Protection Measures Regulation; and

'protected person' has the meaning given to it in the Protection Measures Regulation.][3]

Amendment

1 Repealed by the Family Procedure Rules 2010 and Court of Protection Rules 2017 (Amendment) (EU Exit) Regulations 2019, SI 2019/517, rr 2, 21(1), (2)(a)(i), (iii), (b).
2 Inserted by the Family Procedure Rules 2010 and Court of Protection Rules 2017 (Amendment) (EU Exit) Regulations 2019, SI 2019/517, rr 2, 21(1), (2)(a)(ii).
3 Inserted by the Family Procedure (Amendment No 4) Rules 2014, SI 2014/3296, rr 2, 14.

[Chapter 2
…[1]

38.2 …[1]

…[1]][2]

Amendment

1 Repealed by the Family Procedure Rules 2010 and Court of Protection Rules 2017 (Amendment) (EU Exit) Regulations 2019, SI 2019/517, rr 2, 21(1), (3).
2 Inserted by the Family Procedure (Amendment No 4) Rules 2014, SI 2014/3296, rr 2, 14.

[38.3 …[1]

…[1]][2]

Amendment

1 Repealed by the Family Procedure Rules 2010 and Court of Protection Rules 2017 (Amendment) (EU Exit) Regulations 2019, SI 2019/517, rr 2, 21(1), (3).
2 Inserted by the Family Procedure (Amendment No 4) Rules 2014, SI 2014/3296, rr 2, 14.

[38.4 …[1]

…[1]][2]

Amendment

1 Repealed by the Family Procedure Rules 2010 and Court of Protection Rules 2017 (Amendment) (EU Exit) Regulations 2019, SI 2019/517, rr 2, 21(1), (3).
2 Inserted by the Family Procedure (Amendment No 4) Rules 2014, SI 2014/3296, rr 2, 14.

[38.5 …[1]

…[1]][2]

Amendment

1 Repealed by the Family Procedure Rules 2010 and Court of Protection Rules 2017 (Amendment) (EU Exit) Regulations 2019, SI 2019/517, rr 2, 21(1), (3).
2 Inserted by the Family Procedure (Amendment No 4) Rules 2014, SI 2014/3296, rr 2, 14.

[38.6 …[1]

…[1]][2]

Amendment

1 Repealed by the Family Procedure Rules 2010 and Court of Protection Rules 2017 (Amendment) (EU Exit) Regulations 2019, SI 2019/517, rr 2, 21(1), (3).
2 Inserted by the Family Procedure (Amendment No 4) Rules 2014, SI 2014/3296, rr 2, 14.

[38.7 …[1]

…[1]][2]

Amendment

1 Repealed by the Family Procedure Rules 2010 and Court of Protection Rules 2017 (Amendment) (EU Exit) Regulations 2019, SI 2019/517, rr 2, 21(1), (3).
2 Inserted by the Family Procedure (Amendment No 4) Rules 2014, SI 2014/3296, rr 2, 14.

[38.8 …[1]

…[1]][2]

Amendment

1 Repealed by the Family Procedure Rules 2010 and Court of Protection Rules 2017 (Amendment) (EU Exit) Regulations 2019, SI 2019/517, rr 2, 21(1), (3).
2 Inserted by the Family Procedure (Amendment No 4) Rules 2014, SI 2014/3296, rr 2, 14.

[38.9 …[1]

…[1]][2]

Amendment

1 Repealed by the Family Procedure Rules 2010 and Court of Protection Rules 2017 (Amendment) (EU Exit) Regulations 2019, SI 2019/517, rr 2, 21(1), (3).
2 Inserted by the Family Procedure (Amendment No 4) Rules 2014, SI 2014/3296, rr 2, 14.

[38.10 …[1]

…[1]][2]

Amendment

1 Repealed by the Family Procedure Rules 2010 and Court of Protection Rules 2017 (Amendment) (EU Exit) Regulations 2019, SI 2019/517, rr 2, 21(1), (3).
2 Inserted by the Family Procedure (Amendment No 4) Rules 2014, SI 2014/3296, rr 2, 14.

[38.11 …[1]

…[1]][2]

Amendment

1 Repealed by the Family Procedure Rules 2010 and Court of Protection Rules 2017 (Amendment) (EU Exit) Regulations 2019, SI 2019/517, rr 2, 21(1), (3).
2 Inserted by the Family Procedure (Amendment No 4) Rules 2014, SI 2014/3296, rr 2, 14.

[Chapter 3
Incoming protection measures

38.12 Application for adjustment under Article 11

A protected person may apply to the court under Article 11 of the Protection Measures Regulation [(as it has effect in the law of England and Wales)][1] to adjust the factual elements of an incoming protection measure.][2]

Amendment

1 Inserted by the Family Procedure Rules 2010 and Court of Protection Rules 2017 (Amendment) (EU Exit) Regulations 2019, SI 2019/517, rr 2, 21(1), (4).
2 Inserted by the Family Procedure (Amendment No 4) Rules 2014, SI 2014/3296, rr 2, 14.

[38.13 Notification of the adjustment under Article 11

(1) Subject to paragraph (2), the court officer must give Article 11 notice to the person causing the risk by serving it in accordance with Chapter 3 of Part 6 and the rules in that Chapter apply to service of the notice as they apply to any other document to be served by a court officer.

(2) If the person causing the risk resides [outside the United Kingdom][1], the court officer must give Article 11 notice by sending it by registered letter with acknowledgment of receipt or other confirmation of delivery or equivalent to the last known place of residence of that person.][2]

Amendment

1 Substituted by the Family Procedure Rules 2010 and Court of Protection Rules 2017 (Amendment) (EU Exit) Regulations 2019, SI 2019/517, rr 2, 21(1), (5).
2 Inserted by the Family Procedure (Amendment No 4) Rules 2014, SI 2014/3296, rr 2, 14.

[38.14 Application for refusal of recognition or enforcement under Article 13

An application by a person causing the risk for refusal of recognition or enforcement under Article 13 of the Protection Measures Regulation [(as it has effect in the law of England and Wales)][1] must be made to—

(a) the family court if—
  (i) there are proceedings relating to the same protection measure before the family court; or
  (ii) proceedings relating to the same protection measure were dealt with by the family court;
(b) the High Court if—
  (i) there are proceedings relating to the same protection measure before the High Court; or
  (ii) proceedings relating to the same protection measure were dealt with by the High Court; or
(c) the family court, unless, applying rule 5.4, the application should be made to the High Court.][2]

Amendment

1 Inserted by the Family Procedure Rules 2010 and Court of Protection Rules 2017 (Amendment) (EU Exit) Regulations 2019, SI 2019/517, rr 2, 21(1), (6).
2 Inserted by the Family Procedure (Amendment No 4) Rules 2014, SI 2014/3296, rr 2, 14.

[38.15 Application under Article 14(2)

(1) This rule applies where an Article 14 certificate has been issued in a Member State of the European Union other than …[1] Denmark.

(2) A protected person or person causing the risk may apply to the court to stay, suspend or withdraw the effects of recognition or, where applicable, the enforcement of the protection measure.

(3) An application under this rule must include a copy of the Article 14 certificate issued in the …[1] Member State.

(4) On an application under this rule, the court must make such orders or give such directions as may be necessary to give effect to the Article 14 certificate.][2]

Amendment

1 Repealed by the Family Procedure Rules 2010 and Court of Protection Rules 2017 (Amendment) (EU Exit) Regulations 2019, SI 2019/517, rr 2, 21(1), (7).
2 Inserted by the Family Procedure (Amendment No 4) Rules 2014, SI 2014/3296, rr 2, 14.

Practice Direction 38A – Recognition and enforcement of protection measures

This Practice Direction supplements Part 38

The Protection Measures Regulation

1.1 The Protection Measures Regulation is an EU law[1] which helps a person who has a 'protection measure' obtained in one Member State to have it recognised and enforced in any other EU Member State (except Denmark). The protection can continue in the other Member State for the length of time the 'protection measure' has been ordered, except it cannot continue for longer than twelve months. The Protection Measures Regulation forms part of retained EU law in the United Kingdom by virtue of the European Union (Withdrawal) Act 2018, and provision is made in the Mutual Recognition of Protection Measures in Civil Matters (Amendment) (EU Exit) Regulations 2019 for its provisions in relation to 'incoming' protection measures to continue to have effect so that incoming measures can be enforced in England and Wales.

1.2 The Protection Measures Regulation applies across the United Kingdom. Part 38 and this Practice Direction apply in England and Wales only. If you need information about Scotland you should contact the Scottish Government[2]. If you need information about Northern Ireland you should contact the Northern Ireland Department for Justice[3].

1.3 A 'protection measure' is a decision that says the 'person causing the risk' must comply with one or more of the three kinds of obligation set out below, to protect another person, the 'protected person', from physical or psychological harm.

The obligations[4] are:

- a ban or controls on entering the place where the protected person lives or works, or regularly visits or stays;
- a ban or controls on contact, in any form, with the protected person, including by telephone, post, e-mail, text or social media or any other means;
- a ban or controls on approaching the protected person closer than a stated distance.

1.4 A 'protected person' is the individual who is protected by the obligation in the protection measure. A 'person causing the risk' is the individual on whom the obligation has been imposed.

Footnotes

1 EU Regulation No 606/2013 OJ L 181/4 of 29 June 2013.

2 Simon Stockwell, Family and Property Law, Scottish Government, St Andrew's House, Regent Road, Edinburgh, EH1 3DG. simon.stockwell@scotland.gsi.gov.uk 0131 244 3322.

3 Naomi Callaghan, Civil Justice Policy Division, Department of Justice, Massey House, Stormont Estate, Belfast BT4 3SX. Naomi.Callaghan@dojni.x.gsi.gov.uk.

4 See Article 3(1) of the Protection Measures Regulation.

Incoming protection measures

3.1 An incoming protection measure for which an Article 5 certificate has been issued in another Member State, is automatically recognised by the court in England and Wales. This section sets out actions the protected person can take in relation to an incoming protection measure, and the points at which the incoming protection measure and Article 5 certificate must be provided to the court. The applications set out below can be made to the family court, the county court and sometimes to the Family Division of the High Court (see rule 5.4 of the Family Procedure Rules 2010). This practice direction and the Family Procedure Rules apply to the family court and Family Division of the High Court only. Applications to the county court are covered by the Civil Procedure Rules[7].

3.2 The protected person and the person causing the risk can make applications in relation to incoming protection measures using the procedure in Part 18 (or Part 19 if applicable) of the Family Procedure Rules. There is more information in Practice Directions 18A and 19A. These Practice Directions set out the documents the applicant must provide with the application, in addition to any requirements set out in this Practice Direction. When making an application the protected person or the person causing the risk must also provide a copy of the order containing the incoming protection measure and the Article 5 certificate issued in the Member State of origin. (Explanations of the terms used in the Protection Measures Regulation and the certificates are set out in section 1 above.)

Footnotes

7 http://www.justice.gov.uk/courts/procedure-rules/civil/rules

Adjustment of 'factual elements' in the protection measure

3.3 The protected person can apply to the court for the adjustment of 'factual elements' in the incoming protection measure to make it effective in England and Wales. 'Factual elements' can, for example, include the address or location the person causing the risk must stay away from, such as the location where the protected person lived or worked in the Member State of origin, or the minimum distance the person causing the risk must keep away from the protected person[8]. To make the protection measure work in England and Wales the protected person can apply for the protection measure to be adjusted to show an address in England or Wales. ANY ADDRESS OR LOCATION IN THE ADJUSTED PROTECTION MEASURE WILL BE DISCLOSED TO THE PERSON CAUSING THE RISK, BECAUSE THE ADJUSTMENT MUST BE NOTIFIED TO THE PERSON CAUSING THE RISK.

3.4 The protected person can apply to the court under rule 38.12 using the appropriate form for an adjustment to the factual elements to be made. If you are the protected person, you will need to provide an address for notification. You can decide what address to provide and it does not have to be your own home address. IF YOU ARE THE

PROTECTED PERSON, AND THE ADDRESS YOU PROVIDE IS ALSO IN THE ADJUSTED PROTECTION MEASURE, THAT ADDRESS WILL BE DISCLOSED TO THE PERSON CAUSING THE RISK, BECAUSE THE PERSON CAUSING THE RISK MUST BE NOTIFIED OF THE ADJUSTMENT TO BE ABLE TO COMPLY WITH IT. When the court adjusts the facts in the protection measure the court officer must notify the person causing the risk of the adjustment in accordance with rule 38.13 (Article 11 notice). A protected person may choose not to apply for an adjustment of a protection measure that contains a specific address or location, and may choose to apply only for adjustments of the factual elements of a protection measure that do not contain such information.

Footnotes

8 Article 11.

Enforcement of the protection measure

3.5 If the protected person has an incoming protection measure accompanied by an Article 5 certificate from the Member State of origin and they believe the person causing the risk has disobeyed the protection measure, the protected person can apply to the court under rule 10.11 for the issue of a civil warrant for the arrest of the person causing the risk[9]. IF YOU ARE THE PROTECTED PERSON AND YOU BELIEVE THE PERSON CAUSING THE RISK HAS COMMITTED A CRIMINAL OFFENCE UNDER THE LAW OF ENGLAND AND WALES YOU SHOULD CONTACT THE POLICE. If this has happened, the person causing the risk may be subject to criminal punishment under the law of England and Wales.

3.6 Incoming protection measures can be enforced by the family court and the High Court in England and Wales as if they had been ordered by those courts. IF YOU ARE THE PERSON CAUSING THE RISK AND YOU DISOBEY THE PROTECTION MEASURE, YOU MAY BE HELD TO BE IN CONTEMPT OF COURT IN ENGLAND AND WALES AND YOU MAY BE IMPRISONED OR FINED. Part 10 and Part 37 of the FPR provide more information.

Footnotes

9 This is a civil warrant for arrest and would lead to civil enforcement proceedings for contempt of court only, not criminal proceedings. Contempt of court can be punished by the defendant being sent to prison or fined, but it is not a criminal offence.

Application for refusal to recognise or enforce the protection measure

3.7 The person causing the risk can apply under rule 38.14 using the appropriate form for the court to refuse to recognise an incoming protection measure or to refuse to enforce it against them. Under the Protection Measures Regulation, the court will only refuse to recognise or enforce the protection measure when to do so would be 'manifestly contrary to public policy' or if recognition of the incoming protection measure is 'irreconcilable' with a judgment that has been given or recognised in the United Kingdom.

Suspension or withdrawal of recognition or enforcement

3.8 When a protection measure from another Member State has been suspended, limited or withdrawn in the Member State of origin or an Article 5 certificate has been withdrawn there, and an Article 14 certificate has been issued to confirm this, the protected person or the person causing the risk can apply under rule 38.15 using the appropriate form to the court in England and Wales which dealt or is dealing with the incoming protection measure to ask the court to stay, suspend or withdraw the effects of recognition or enforcement. The applicant must provide a copy of the Article 14 certificate. When the court has made orders or given directions to give effect to the Article 14 certificate the court officer will inform the other party.

Appeals

4.1 All decisions made by the court in England and Wales under the Protection Measures Regulation are subject to ordinary appeal procedures. In most cases permission to appeal will be required, but there is no need to get permission to appeal a decision made by lay justices. (The issue of an Article 5 certificate is separate and cannot be appealed.) Either the protected person or the person causing the risk can seek permission to appeal using the Part 30 procedure.

[PART 39
ATTACHMENT OF EARNINGS

Chapter 1
General

39.1 Application of this Part

(1) Chapter 2 of this Part applies where an attachment of earnings order is sought in the family court to secure payments under a family court or High Court maintenance order whether or not arrears have accrued.

(2) Chapter 3 of this Part applies where an attachment of earnings order is sought in the High Court to secure payments under a High Court maintenance order whether or not arrears have accrued.

(Section 1 of the 1971 Act makes provision for when the family court or the High Court may make an attachment of earnings order.)][1]

Amendment

1 Inserted by the Family Procedure (Amendment) Rules 2016, SI 2016/355, r 8(a), Sch 1.

[39.2 Interpretation of this Part

In this Part—

'the 1971 Act' means the Attachment of Earnings Act 1971 and unless the context otherwise requires or this Part otherwise provides, expressions used in that Act, including the term 'maintenance order', have the same meaning as in that Act;

'creditor' means the person who is entitled to enforce a maintenance order; and

'debtor' means the person against whom a maintenance order was made.][1]

Amendment

1 Inserted by the Family Procedure (Amendment) Rules 2016, SI 2016/355, r 8(a), Sch 1.

[39.3 Search of court records

If requested to do so by any person having a maintenance order against a debtor, the court officer must—

(a) cause a search to be made in the court records to determine whether there is an attachment of earnings order in force in relation to that debtor; and

(b) issue a certificate of the result of the search.][1]

Amendment

1 Inserted by the Family Procedure (Amendment) Rules 2016, SI 2016/355, r 8(a), Sch 1.

[Chapter 2
Securing payments under a maintenance order in the family court – attachment of earnings order

39.4 Where to apply

An application for an attachment of earnings order to which this Chapter applies must be sent to the family court.

(Her Majesty's Courts and Tribunals Service publishes information to identify the appropriate location to which an application for an attachment of earnings order should be sent.)][1]

Amendment

1 Inserted by the Family Procedure (Amendment) Rules 2016, SI 2016/355, r 8(a), Sch 1.

[39.5 Application for an attachment of earnings order

(1) Where an application is made for an attachment of earnings order on the making of the maintenance order or of an order varying the maintenance order, the remainder of this rule and rule 39.6 do not apply.

(2) A creditor who wishes to apply for an attachment of earnings order must file—

(a) an application in accordance with rule 33.3(1); and
(b) a copy of the sealed [(GL)] maintenance order.

(3) When the documents mentioned in paragraph (2) are filed with the court, the court officer must fix a day for the hearing of the application.][1]

Amendment

1 Inserted by the Family Procedure (Amendment) Rules 2016, SI 2016/355, r 8(a), Sch 1.

[39.6 Service and reply

(1) Notice of the application and a reply form must be served by the court on the debtor in accordance with Chapter 3 of Part 6.

(2) The notice of application must include an instruction to the debtor to file the reply form within 8 days after service, and that instruction constitutes a requirement imposed under section 14(4) of the 1971 Act.

(3) No proceedings may be brought for an alleged offence under section 23(2)(c) or (f) of the 1971 Act in relation to the requirement to reply unless—

(a) the notice of application and reply form have been served personally on the debtor; or
(b) the court is satisfied that those documents came to the debtor's knowledge in sufficient time to comply with the requirement.

(4) The court officer must send to the creditor a copy of any reply form received from the debtor.][1]

Amendment

1 Inserted by the Family Procedure (Amendment) Rules 2016, SI 2016/355, r 8(a), Sch 1.

[39.7 Notice to the debtor's employer

(1) Without prejudice to the power conferred by section 14(1) of the 1971 Act, a court officer may, at any stage of the proceedings, send to any person appearing to be the debtor's employer a notice requesting that person to give to the court a statement of the debtor's earnings.

(2) The statement of the debtor's earnings must—

(a) state the debtor's earnings;
(b) state the debtor's anticipated earnings;
(c) include such particulars as requested in the notice from the court; and
(d) be given to the court within such period as is specified in the notice.][1]

Amendment

1 Inserted by the Family Procedure (Amendment) Rules 2016, SI 2016/355, r 8(a), Sch 1.

[39.8 Attachment of earnings order

An application for an attachment of earnings order to secure payments under a maintenance order must be heard in private, unless the court directs otherwise.

(Rule 39.21 modifies this rule and sets out steps for a court officer of the family court to take when an attachment of earnings order made by the High Court designates the court officer of the family court as the collecting officer.)][1]

Amendment

1 Inserted by the Family Procedure (Amendment) Rules 2016, SI 2016/355, r 8(a), Sch 1.

[39.9 Failure by debtor

(1) If the debtor has failed to comply with rule 39.6(2) or to make payment to the creditor, the court officer may issue an order under section 14(1) of the 1971 Act which must, in addition to meeting the requirements of rule 39.18(1), direct that any payments made after the date of service of the order must be paid to the court and not direct to the creditor.

(2) Without prejudice to rule 39.19, if the person served with an order referred to in paragraph (1) fails—

(a) to obey the order;
(b) to complete and file the form of reply, including the statement of means; or
(c) make payment,

the court officer must issue a notice to the person to attend a hearing at which the court will consider whether an offence has been committed under section 23(2)(c) of the 1971 Act and whether the person should be imprisoned or fined as a result.

(3) A notice of a type referred to in paragraph (2) must be served on the debtor personally not less than 5 days before the hearing.

(4) In this rule, 'statement of means' means a statement given under section 14(1) of the 1971 Act.][1]

Amendment

1 Inserted by the Family Procedure (Amendment) Rules 2016, SI 2016/355, r 8(a), Sch 1.

[39.10 Enforcement under section 23(1) of the 1971 Act

(1) An order under section 23(1) of the 1971 Act for the attendance of the debtor at an adjourned hearing for an attachment of earnings order to secure payments under a maintenance order—

(a) must be served on the debtor personally not less than 5 days before the day fixed for the adjourned hearing; and

(b) may direct that any future payments made after the date of service of the order under section 23(1) of the 1971 Act must be paid into the court and not direct to the creditor.

(2) An application by a debtor for the revocation of an order committing the debtor to prison and (if already in custody) for discharge under section 23(7) of the 1971 Act must—

(a) be made to court in writing without notice to any other party, stating the reasons for the debtor's failure to attend the court or refusal to be sworn or to give evidence (as the case may be) and containing an undertaking by the debtor to attend the court or be sworn or to give evidence when required to do so; and

(b) if the debtor has already been lodged in prison, be attested by the governor of the prison (or any other officer of the prison not below rank of principal officer), and in any other case be made in a witness statement or affidavit,

and before dealing with the application the court may, if it thinks fit, cause notice to be given to the creditor that the application has been made and of a date and time when the creditor may attend and be heard.][1]

Amendment

1 Inserted by the Family Procedure (Amendment) Rules 2016, SI 2016/355, r 8(a), Sch 1.

[39.11 Suspended committal order

(1) If the debtor fails to attend an adjourned hearing of an application for an attachment of earnings order and a committal order is made, the court making the committal order may direct that its execution be suspended for such period or on such terms or conditions as it may specify.

(2) Unless the court otherwise directs, the creditor must serve on the debtor personally a copy of any order made under paragraph (1).

(3) Where a committal order is suspended under paragraph (1) and the debtor fails to attend at the time and place specified in the committal order, a certificate to that effect given by the court officer is sufficient authority for the issue of a warrant of committal.

(4) If execution of a committal order is suspended under paragraph (1), the debtor may apply for a further suspension.

(5) The debtor may apply for a further suspension by attending at, or writing to, the court office and explaining why they have been unable to comply with the terms of the original suspension.

(6) If the debtor applies for a further suspension in accordance with paragraph (5), the court must—

(a) fix a date for the hearing of the application; and
(b) give the debtor and creditor at least 3 days' notice of the hearing.

(7) The court may suspend execution of the committal order pending the hearing of the application under paragraph (5).][1]

Amendment

1 Inserted by the Family Procedure (Amendment) Rules 2016, SI 2016/355, r 8(a), Sch 1.

[39.12 Costs

(1) Where costs are allowed to the creditor on an application for an attachment of earnings order, there may be allowed—

(a) a charge of a legal representative for preparing the application, attending the hearing and, if applicable, for serving the application; and
(b) the court fee for issuing the application.

(2) The costs may be fixed and allowed without detailed assessment under CPR Part 47.][1]

Amendment

1 Inserted by the Family Procedure (Amendment) Rules 2016, SI 2016/355, r 8(a), Sch 1.

[39.13 Contents and service of the order

(1) An attachment of earnings order must contain such of the following information about the debtor as is known to the court—

(a) the debtor's full name and address;
(b) the debtor's place of work;
(c) the nature of the debtor's work and works number, if any.

(2) That information will be the prescribed particulars for the purposes of section 6(3) of the 1971 Act.

(3) An attachment of earnings order and any order varying or discharging such an order must be served on the parties and on the person to whom the order is directed.

(4) Where—

(a) the order is directed to a corporation; and
(b) that corporation has requested that the court serve on the corporation documents relating to the debtor or to the class of persons to whom the debtor belongs at a particular address,

service may be effected on the corporation at that address, if the court thinks fit.

(5) Where an attachment of earnings order is made by the family court to secure payments under a maintenance order made by the High Court, a copy of the attachment of earnings order and of any order discharging or varying it must be sent by the court officer of the family court to the court officer of the High Court.][1]

Amendment

1 Inserted by the Family Procedure (Amendment) Rules 2016, SI 2016/355, r 8(a), Sch 1.

[39.14 Application to determine whether particular payments are earnings

(1) An application to the court under section 16 of the 1971 Act to determine whether payments to the debtor of a particular class or description are earnings for the purposes of an attachment of earnings order may be made to the court in accordance with Part 18.

(2) If such an application is made, the court officer must fix a date for the hearing of the application by the court and give notice of that hearing to the persons mentioned in section 16(2)(a), (b) and (c) of the 1971 Act.][1]

Amendment

1 Inserted by the Family Procedure (Amendment) Rules 2016, SI 2016/355, r 8(a), Sch 1.

[39.15 Notice that an order has ceased to have effect

Where an attachment of earnings order made by the family court to secure payments under a maintenance order ceases to have effect under section 8(3) of the 1971 Act and—

(a) the related maintenance order was made by that court; or
(b) the related maintenance order was made by the High Court; and—
  (i) the court officer has received notice of the cessation from the court officer of the High Court; or
  (ii) a committal order has been made in the family court for the enforcement of the related maintenance order,

the court officer of the family court must give notice of the cessation to the person to whom the attachment of earnings order was directed.][1]

Amendment

1 Inserted by the Family Procedure (Amendment) Rules 2016, SI 2016/355, r 8(a), Sch 1.

[39.16 Variation and discharge by the court of its own initiative

(1) The powers conferred by section 9(1) of the 1971 Act may be exercised by the court of its own initiative in the circumstances specified in this rule.

(2) Where it appears to the court that a person served with an attachment of earnings order does not employ the debtor, the court must discharge the order.

(3) Where an attachment of earnings order which has lapsed under section 9(4) of the 1971 Act is again directed to a person who appears to the court to employ the debtor, the court may make such consequential variations in the order as it thinks fit.

(4) Where the court has made an attachment of earnings order and it appears to the court that the related maintenance order has ceased to have effect (whether by virtue of the terms of the maintenance order or under section 28 of the 1973 Act or otherwise), the court may discharge or vary the attachment of earnings order.

(5) The court may discharge the attachment of earnings order where an attachment of earnings order has been made to secure payments under a maintenance order and—

(a) the court makes an order for another form of enforcement for the recovery of payments under the maintenance order; or
(b) there is no further sum payable under the maintenance order.

(6) Before varying or discharging an attachment of earnings order of its own initiative under any of the paragraphs of this rule, the court must, unless it thinks it unnecessary in

the circumstances to do so, give the debtor, and the person on whose application the order was made, an opportunity of being heard on the question of whether the order should be varied or discharged.

(7) The court officer must give those people mentioned in paragraph (6) notice of the date, time and place fixed for the hearing.][1]

Amendment

1 Inserted by the Family Procedure (Amendment) Rules 2016, SI 2016/355, r 8(a), Sch 1.

[39.17 Change of Designated Family Judge area

If, in the opinion of the family court sitting in a Designated Family Judge area in which an attachment of earnings order has been made, the matter could more conveniently proceed in another Designated Family Judge area (whether by reason of the debtor having become resident in that other Designated Family Judge area or otherwise), the court may order that the matter should proceed in that other area.][1]

Amendment

1 Inserted by the Family Procedure (Amendment) Rules 2016, SI 2016/355, r 8(a), Sch 1.

[39.18 Exercise of power to obtain statement of earnings etc.

(1) An order under section 14(1) of the 1971 Act must—

(a) be endorsed with or incorporate a notice warning the person to whom it is directed of the consequences of disobeying the order; and

(b) be served on that person personally.

(2) Rule 37.35 applies, with the necessary modifications in relation to any penalty for failure to comply with an order under section 14(1) of the 1971 Act as it applies in relation to a fine under section 31G of the 1984 Act.][1]

Amendment

1 Inserted by the Family Procedure (Amendment) Rules 2016, SI 2016/355, r 8(a), Sch 1.

[39.19 Offences

(1) Paragraph (2) applies where—

(a) it is alleged that a person has committed any offence mentioned in section 23(2) (a), (b), (d), (e) or (f) of the 1971 Act in relation to proceedings in, or to an attachment of earnings order made by, the family court; and

(b) the alleged offender is not being proceeded against summarily.

(2) The court may issue a notice to the alleged offender to attend a hearing at which the court will consider whether the alleged offence has been committed and whether the alleged offender should be imprisoned or fined as a result.

(3) The notice must be served on the alleged offender personally not less than 14 days before the hearing.

(4) Rules 37.36 and 37.37 apply to proceedings for an offence under section 23(2) of the 1971 Act as they apply to proceedings for offences under the County Courts Act 1984.

(5) Where a person other than a debtor is committed for an offence under section 23(2) of the 1971 Act, rule 37.30 applies to an application by that person to be discharged from custody.][1]

Amendment

1 Inserted by the Family Procedure (Amendment) Rules 2016, SI 2016/355, r 8(a), Sch 1.

[39.20 Permission to enforce arrears

(1) This rule applies where a creditor applies for an attachment of earnings order to enforce the payment of arrears which became due more than 12 months before the date of the application for an attachment of earnings order.

(2) Where the creditor requires the permission of the court under—

(a) section 32 of the 1973 Act;
(b) section 32(4) of the 1978 Act; or
(c) paragraph 63 of Schedule 5 to the 2004 Act,

to enforce the payment of such arrears, the permission application must be made in the application for the attachment of earnings order.

(3) Notice of the application, together with a form of reply in the appropriate form, must be served on the debtor in the manner set out in rule 6.23 and the notice must be served not less than 14 days before the hearing.][1]

Amendment

1 Inserted by the Family Procedure (Amendment) Rules 2016, SI 2016/355, r 8(a), Sch 1.

[Chapter 3
Securing payments under a maintenance order in the High Court – attachment of earnings order

39.21

Where an application is made to the High Court under this Chapter, the rules in Chapter 2 apply with the following modifications—

(a) for rule 39.4 there is substituted—

'(1) Subject to paragraph (2), an application for an attachment of earnings order must be sent to the District Registry of the High Court for the district in which the debtor resides.

(2) If the debtor resides outside of England and Wales, or if the debtor's place of residence is not known to the creditor, an application for an attachment of earnings order must be sent to the District Registry of the High Court for the district in which the proceedings which resulted in the maintenance order being made took place.';

(b) for rule 39.8 there is substituted—

'(1) An application for an attachment of earnings order to secure payments under a maintenance order must be heard in private, unless the court directs otherwise.

(2) Where an attachment of earnings order made by the High Court designates the court officer of the family court as the collecting officer, that officer must, on receipt of a certified copy of the order from the court officer of the High Court, send to the person to whom the order is directed a notice as to the mode of payment.';

(c) rule 39.13(5) is omitted;

(d) for rule 39.15 there is substituted—

'Where an attachment of earnings order made by the High Court to secure payments under a High Court maintenance order ceases to have effect under section 8(3) of the 1971 Act, the court officer of the High Court must give notice of the cessation to the person to whom the attachment of earnings order was directed.'

(e) for rule 39.17, including the heading to that rule, there is substituted—

'39.17 Change of District Registry

If, in the opinion of the High Court sitting in a District Registry in which an attachment of earnings order has been made, the matter could more conveniently proceed in another District Registry (whether by reason of the debtor having become resident in the area of that District Registry or otherwise), the court may order that the matter should proceed in that other District Registry.';

(f) in rule 39.19(1)(a), for 'family court' there is substituted 'High Court'; and

(g) in rule 39.20(2), sub-paragraph (b) is omitted.][1]

Amendment

1 Inserted by the Family Procedure (Amendment) Rules 2016, SI 2016/355, r 8(a), Sch 1.

[PART 40
CHARGING ORDER, STOP ORDER, STOP NOTICE

Chapter 1
General

40.1 Application of this Part

This Part contains rules which provide for a creditor to enforce a judgment or order by obtaining—

(a) a charging order (Chapter 2);

(b) a stop order (Chapter 3); or

(c) a stop notice (Chapter 4),

over or against the debtor's interest in an asset.][1]

Amendment

1 Inserted by the Family Procedure (Amendment) Rules 2016, SI 2016/355, r 8(b), Sch 2.

[40.2 Interpretation of this Part

In this Part—

'the 1979 Act' means the Charging Orders Act 1979;

'creditor' means the person to whom payment of a sum of money is due under a judgment or order or a person who is entitled to enforce such a judgment or order;

'debtor' means the person against whom a judgment or other order for payment of a sum of money was given, made or ordered, as the case may be;

'interim charging order' means an interim charging order made in accordance with rule 40.5; and

'securities' means securities of any of the kinds specified in section 2(2)(b) of the 1979 Act.][1]

Amendment

1 Inserted by the Family Procedure (Amendment) Rules 2016, SI 2016/355, r 8(b), Sch 2.

[Chapter 2
Charging orders

40.3 Scope of this Chapter

This Chapter applies to an application by a creditor for a charging order under section 1 of the 1979 Act.][1]

Amendment

1 Inserted by the Family Procedure (Amendment) Rules 2016, SI 2016/355, r 8(b), Sch 2.

[40.4 Application for a charging order

(1) An application for a charging order may be made without notice.

(2) An application must be made to the family court or to the High Court, as appropriate and as specified in section 1 of the 1979 Act.

(Her Majesty's Courts and Tribunals Service publishes information to identify the appropriate location of the family court or High Court to which an application for a charging order should be sent.)

(3) A creditor may apply for a single charging order in respect of more than one judgment or order against the same debtor.

(4) The application must—

(a) be in the form and contain the information required by Practice Direction 40A; and

(b) be verified by a statement of truth.][1]

Amendment

1 Inserted by the Family Procedure (Amendment) Rules 2016, SI 2016/355, r 8(b), Sch 2.

[40.5 Interim charging order

(1) An application for a charging order will initially be dealt with by the court without a hearing.

(2) The court may make an interim charging order—

(a) imposing a charge over the debtor's interest in the asset to which the application relates; and
(b) fixing a hearing to consider whether to make a final charging order as provided by rule 40.8.][1]

Amendment

1 Inserted by the Family Procedure (Amendment) Rules 2016, SI 2016/355, r 8(b), Sch 2.

[40.6 Service of an interim charging order

(1) Copies of the interim charging order, the application and any documents filed in support of it must, not less than 21 days before the hearing, be served by the creditor on the persons listed in paragraph (3).

(2) The creditor must either—

(a) file a certificate of service in relation to each person served not less than 2 days before the hearing; or
(b) produce a certificate of service at the hearing.

(3) The persons to be served in accordance with paragraph (1) are—

(a) the debtor;
(b) if the order relates to an interest in land, any co-owner;
(c) the debtor's spouse or civil partner (if known);
(d) such other creditors as are identified in the application or as the court directs;
(e) if the order relates to an interest under a trust, on such of the trustees as the court directs; and
(f) if the interest charged is securities, then—
  (i) in the case of stock for which the Bank of England keeps the register, the Bank of England;
  (ii) in the case of government stock to which sub-paragraph (f)(i) does not apply, the keeper of the register;
  (iii) in the case of stock of any body incorporated within England and Wales, that body;
  (iv) in the case of stock of any body incorporated outside England and Wales or of any state or territory outside the United Kingdom, which is registered in a register kept in England and Wales, the keeper of that register; and
  (v) in the case of units of any unit trust in respect of which a register of the unit holders is kept in England and Wales, the keeper of that register.][1]

Amendment

1 Inserted by the Family Procedure (Amendment) Rules 2016, SI 2016/355, r 8(b), Sch 2.

[40.7 Effect of interim charging order in relation to securities

(1) If a debtor disposes of their interest in any securities while they are subject to an interim charging order which has been served on them, that disposition will not, so long as that order remains in force, be valid as against the creditor.

(2) A person served under rule 40.6(3)(f) with an interim charging order relating to securities must not, unless the court gives permission—

(a) permit any transfer of any of the securities; or
(b) pay any dividend, interest or redemption payment relating to them.

(3) If a person acts in breach of paragraph (2), that person will be liable to pay to the creditor—

(a) the value of the securities transferred or the amount of the payment made (as the case may be); or
(b) if less, the amount necessary to satisfy the debt in relation to which the interim charging order was made.][1]

Amendment

1 Inserted by the Family Procedure (Amendment) Rules 2016, SI 2016/355, r 8(b), Sch 2.

[40.8 Further consideration of the application

(1) If any person objects to the court making a final charging order, that person must—

(a) file; and
(b) serve on the creditor,

written evidence stating the grounds of objection, not less than 7 days before the hearing.

(2) At the hearing, the court may—

(a) make a final charging order confirming that the charge imposed by the interim charging order continues, with or without modification;
(b) discharge the interim charging order and dismiss the application;
(c) decide any issues in dispute between the parties, or between any of the parties and any other person who objects to the court making a final charging order;
(d) direct a trial of any such issues, and if necessary give directions; or
(e) make such other order as the court considers appropriate.

(3) If the court makes a final charging order which charges securities, the order must include a stop notice unless the court otherwise orders.

(Chapter 4 of this Part contains provision about stop notices.)

(4) Any order made at the hearing must be served by the creditor on all the persons on whom the interim charging order was served.][1]

Amendment

1 Inserted by the Family Procedure (Amendment) Rules 2016, SI 2016/355, r 8(b), Sch 2.

[40.9 Discharge or variation of order

(1) Where an application is made to discharge or vary a charging order, the court may direct that—

(a) any interested person be joined as a party to such an application; or
(b) the application be served on any such person.

(2) An order discharging or varying a charging order must be served, by the person who applied for that order, on all the persons on whom the charging order was required to be served.][1]

Amendment

1 Inserted by the Family Procedure (Amendment) Rules 2016, SI 2016/355, r 8(b), Sch 2.

[Chapter 3
Stop orders

40.10 Interpretation

In this Chapter, 'stop order' means an order of the High Court not to take, in relation to securities specified in the order, any of the steps listed in section 5(5) of the 1979 Act.][1]

Amendment

1 Inserted by the Family Procedure (Amendment) Rules 2016, SI 2016/355, r 8(b), Sch 2.

[40.11 Application for a stop order

(1) The High Court may make a stop order relating to securities, on the application of any person claiming to be beneficially entitled to an interest in the securities.

(2) An application for a stop order must be made—

- (a) by application in existing proceedings; or
- (b) by a Part 19 application if there are no existing proceedings in the High Court.

(3) The application must be served on—

- (a) every person whose interest may be affected by the order applied for; and
- (b) the person specified in rule 40.6(3)(f).][1]

Amendment

1 Inserted by the Family Procedure (Amendment) Rules 2016, SI 2016/355, r 8(b), Sch 2.

[40.12 Stop order relating to securities

(1) A stop order relating to securities may prohibit all or any of the following steps—

- (a) the registration of any transfer of the securities;
- (b) the making of any payment by way of dividend, interest or otherwise in respect of the securities; and
- (c) in the case of units of a unit trust, any acquisition of, or other dealing with, the units by any person or body exercising functions under the trust.

(2) The order must specify—

- (a) the securities to which it relates;
- (b) the name in which the securities stand;
- (c) the steps which may not be taken; and
- (d) whether the prohibition applies to the securities only or to the dividends or interest as well.][1]

Amendment

1 Inserted by the Family Procedure (Amendment) Rules 2016, SI 2016/355, r 8(b), Sch 2.

[40.13 Variation or discharge of order

(1) The court may, on the application of any person claiming to have a beneficial interest in the securities to which a stop order relates, make an order discharging or varying the order.

(2) An application seeking the variation or discharge of a stop order must be served on the person who obtained the order.][1]

Amendment

1 Inserted by the Family Procedure (Amendment) Rules 2016, SI 2016/355, r 8(b), Sch 2.

[Chapter 4
Stop notices

40.14 General

In this Chapter, 'stop notice' means a notice issued by the court which requires a person or body not to take, in relation to securities specified in the notice, any of the steps listed in section 5(5) of the 1979 Act, without first giving notice to the person who obtained the notice.

(Her Majesty's Courts and Tribunals Service publishes information to identify the appropriate court location to which to send a request under rule 40.15 or rule 40.18 or an application under rule 40.19.)][1]

Amendment

1 Inserted by the Family Procedure (Amendment) Rules 2016, SI 2016/355, r 8(b), Sch 2.

[40.15 Request for a stop notice

(1) The High Court may, on the request of any person claiming to be beneficially entitled to an interest in securities, issue a stop notice.

(A stop notice may also be included in a final charging order, by either the High Court or the family court under rule 40.8(3).)

(2) A request for a stop notice must be made by filing—

(a) a draft stop notice; and
(b) written evidence which—
 (i) identifies the securities in question;
 (ii) describes the applicant's interest in the securities; and
 (iii) gives an address for service for the applicant.

(A sample form of stop notice is annexed to Practice Direction 40A.)

(3) If a court officer considers that the request complies with paragraph (2), the court officer must issue a stop notice.

(4) The applicant must serve copies of the stop notice and the applicant's written evidence on the person to whom the stop notice is addressed.][1]

Amendment

1 Inserted by the Family Procedure (Amendment) Rules 2016, SI 2016/355, r 8(b), Sch 2.

[40.16 Effect of a stop notice

(1) A stop notice—

(a) takes effect when it is served in accordance with rule 40.15(4); and
(b) remains in force unless it is withdrawn or discharged in accordance with rule 40.18 or 40.19.

(2) While a stop notice is in force, the person on whom it is served—

(a) must not—
(i) register a transfer of the securities described in the notice; or
(ii) take any other step restrained by the notice,

without first giving 14 days' notice to the person who obtained the stop notice; but

(b) must not, by reason only of the notice, refuse to register a transfer or to take any other step, after the person has given 14 days' notice under paragraph (2)(a) and that period has expired.][1]

Amendment

1 Inserted by the Family Procedure (Amendment) Rules 2016, SI 2016/355, r 8(b), Sch 2.

[40.17 Amendment of a stop notice

(1) If any securities are incorrectly described in a stop notice which has been obtained and served in accordance with rule 40.15, the applicant may request an amended stop notice in accordance with that rule.

(2) The amended stop notice takes effect when it is served.][1]

Amendment

1 Inserted by the Family Procedure (Amendment) Rules 2016, SI 2016/355, r 8(b), Sch 2.

[40.18 Withdrawal of a stop notice

(1) A person who has obtained a stop notice may withdraw it by serving a request for its withdrawal on—

(a) the person or body on whom the stop notice was served; and
(b) the court which issued the stop notice.

(2) The request must be signed by the person who obtained the stop notice, and that person's signature must be witnessed by a practising solicitor.][1]

Amendment

1 Inserted by the Family Procedure (Amendment) Rules 2016, SI 2016/355, r 8(b), Sch 2.

[40.19 Discharge or variation of a stop notice

(1) The court may, on the application of any person claiming to be beneficially entitled to an interest in the securities to which a stop notice relates, make an order varying or discharging the notice.

(2) An application to discharge or vary a stop notice must be made to the court which issued the notice.

(3) The application must be served on the person who obtained the stop notice.][1]

Amendment

1 Inserted by the Family Procedure (Amendment) Rules 2016, SI 2016/355, r 8(b), Sch 2.

[40.20 Practice Direction

Practice Direction 40A makes provision for the procedure to be followed when applying for an order under section 23 of the Partnership Act 1890.][1]

Amendment

1 Inserted by the Family Procedure (Amendment) Rules 2016, SI 2016/355, r 8(b), Sch 2.

Practice Direction 40A – Charging orders, stop orders and stop notices

This Practice Direction supplements Part 40

Section I
Charging orders

Applicant and application notice – rules 40.2 and 40.4

1.1 A creditor may apply for a charging order. The term 'creditor' is defined in rule 40.2 to mean 'the person to whom payment of a sum of money is due under a judgment or order, or a person who is entitled to enforce such a judgment or order'. A person who is entitled to enforce such a judgment or order would include a court officer who is able to take enforcement proceedings by virtue of rule 32.33.

1.2 An application for a charging order must be made by filing an application in Practice Form N379 if the application relates to land, or N380 if the application relates to securities.

1.3 The application notice must contain the following information–

(1) the name and address of the debtor;
(2) details of the judgment or order sought to be enforced;
(3) the amount of money remaining due under the judgment or order;
(4) if the judgment debt is payable by instalments, the amount of any instalments which have fallen due and remain unpaid;
(5) if the judgment creditor knows of the existence of any other creditors of the judgment debtor, their names and (if known) their addresses;
(6) identification of the asset or assets which it is intended to charge including, where applicable, the title number under which any land upon which it is sought to impose a charge is registered;
(7) details of the debtor's interest in the asset; and
(8) the names and addresses of the persons on whom an interim charging order must be served under rule 40.6.

1.4 A creditor may apply in a single application notice for charging orders over more than one asset, but if the court makes interim charging orders over more than one asset, it will draw up a separate order relating to each asset.

High Court and family court jurisdiction

2.1 The jurisdiction of the High Court and the family court to make charging orders is set out in section 1(2) of the 1979 Act.

Change of location

3.1 The court may, on an application by a debtor who wishes to oppose an application for a charging order, direct that the matter be dealt with in a court building serving the address where the debtor resides or carries on business, or in another location (see rule 29.18 FPR).

Enforcement of charging orders by sale

4.1 The High Court or, subject to the county court limit, the county court can enforce a charging order by an order for sale. Provision in respect of applications for an order for sale is made in rule 73.10C CPR.

Charging Orders made against partnership property

5.1 A charging order or interim charging order may be made against any property, within the jurisdiction, belonging to–

(1) a debtor that is a partnership, or
(2) a debtor who is in a partnership.

5.2 Where paragraph 5.1(1) applies, then for the purposes of rule 40.6 (service of the interim order), the specified documents must be served on–

(1) a member of the partnership within the jurisdiction;
(2) a person authorised by a partner; or
(3) some other person having the control or management of the partnership business.

5.3 Where an order requires a partnership to appear before the court, it will be sufficient for a partner to appear before the court.

Section II
Stop notices

6 A sample form of stop notice is set out in the Appendix to this Practice Direction.

Section III
Applications for orders made under section 23 of the Partnership Act 1890

7.1 This paragraph relates to orders made under section 23 of the Partnership Act 1890 ('Section 23').

7.2 The following applications must be made in accordance with Part 18:

(1) an application for an order under Section 23 of the 1890 Act made by a creditor of a partner;
(2) an application for any order by a partner of the debtor in consequence of any application made by the creditor under Section 23.

7.3 Every application notice filed under this paragraph by a creditor, and every order made following such an application, must be served on the debtor and on any of the other partners that are within the jurisdiction.

7.4 Every application notice filed under this paragraph by a partner of a debtor, and every order made following such an application, must be served–

(1) on the creditor and the debtor; and
(2) on the other partners of the debtor who are not joined in the application and who are within the jurisdiction.

7.5 An application notice or order served under this paragraph on one or more, but not all, of the partners of a partnership is deemed to have been served on all the partners of that partnership.

Appendix
Stop notice

To [insert name of person or body to whom the notice is addressed]

TAKE NOTICE that

[insert name and address]

claims to be beneficially entitled to an interest in the following securities—

[specify the securities, giving the name(s) in which they stand]

This Notice requires you to refrain from–

(1) registering a transfer of the securities specified above; or
(2) paying any dividend or interest in respect of the securities [delete if inappropriate];

without first giving 14 days' notice in writing to the said [insert name] of the above address.

[PART 41
PROCEEDING BY ELECTRONIC MEANS

41.1 Provision for proceeding by electronic means

(1) A practice direction may make provision for proceedings to proceed by electronic means.

(2) Proceedings proceed by electronic means if they are—

(a) created;
(b) started;
(c) progressed; or
(d) disposed of,

by electronic means.

(3) The practice direction may, in particular—

(a) specify the types of proceedings which may proceed by electronic means;
(b) specify the conditions which must be met before proceedings may proceed by electronic means;
(c) provide for the filing of documents by electronic means;
(d) specify any requirements that must be fulfilled for any document to be filed by electronic means; and
(e) provide for how any fee payable in respect of a document filed by electronic means is to be paid.

(4) The practice direction may disapply or modify these Rules or any other practice direction supporting these Rules in relation to cases to which the practice direction applies.

(5) These Rules and any other practice direction supporting these Rules apply—

(a) subject to the provisions of a practice direction made pursuant to paragraph (1); and

(b) as modified in accordance with paragraph (3).

(6) In this Part—

'document' means anything in which information of any description is recorded and includes, but is not limited to, an application, a notice, a statement or a letter; and

'proceedings' includes one or more aspects of proceedings.][1]

Amendment

1 Inserted by the Family Procedure (Amendment) Rules 2020, SI 2020/135, rr 2, 30.

Practice Direction 41A – Proceeding by electronic means: certain proceedings for a matrimonial order

This practice direction supplements rule 41.1 of the Family Procedure Rules 2010.

A Scope of this practice direction

Introduction and interpretation

1.1 This practice direction provides for the procedure by which, in the circumstances set out in this practice direction, an application for a matrimonial order may proceed by electronic means via the online system.

1.2 References in this practice direction to 'the online system' mean Her Majesty's Courts and Tribunal Service's online system to allow for specified applications and stages in matrimonial proceedings to be completed online. The online system is accessible at https://www.gov.uk/apply-for-divorce.

Types of applications which may proceed by electronic means

2.1 An application may proceed by electronic means where all of the following conditions are met-

(a) the application is for a matrimonial order which is a decree of divorce made under section 1 of the 1973 Act;

(b) the application is not unsuitable to proceed by electronic means, as explained in paragraph 2.2;

(c) the parties each choose to proceed with the application by electronic means;

(d) the application does not at any time become a defended case (should the application become a defended case it will cease to proceed by electronic means and will instead proceed in accordance with Part 7 of the FPR); and

(e) the application is started in the family court.

2.2 Her Majesty's Courts and Tribunals Service may conclude that certain individual or categories of applications are not suitable to proceed by electronic means, and such categories are to be specified in guidance issued by Her Majesty's Courts and Tribunals Service and published on GOV.UK.

Steps which may be taken by electronic means: outline

3.1 This practice direction enables an applicant to, in the circumstances set out in this practice direction, take the following steps by electronic means via the online system-

(a) create and start certain types of application for a matrimonial order;

(b) in respect of such an application-

(i) file documents;

(ii) make an application for an order for costs;

(iii) amend the application;

(iv) indicate willingness to accept service of any documents relating to the application by email;

(v) accept service of any documents relating to the application;

(vi) serve any documents relating to the application (but not serve the application itself);

(vii) make an application for a decree nisi; and

(viii) make an application for a decree absolute;

(c) view an electronic record of the progress of the application.

3.2 This practice direction enables a respondent, in the circumstances set out in this practice direction, take the following steps by electronic means via the online system in respect of an application for a matrimonial order which is progressing via the online system -

(a) file an acknowledgement of service;

(b) indicate willingness to accept service of any documents relating to the application (but not the application itself) by email;

(c) accept service of any documents relating to the application (but not the application itself); and

(d) view an electronic record of the progress of the application.

3.3 This practice direction enables a co-respondent to, in the circumstances set out in this practice direction, take the following steps by electronic means via the online system in respect of an application for a matrimonial order which is progressing via the online system-

(a) file an acknowledgment of service;

(b) indicate willingness to accept service of any documents relating to the application (but not the application itself) by email;

(c) accept service of any documents relating to the application (but not the application itself); and

(d) view an electronic record of the certificate of entitlement to a decree nisi, the decree nisi and any relevant order for costs.

3.4 This practice direction does not make provision for a respondent or co-respondent to file an answer via the online system. If an application for a matrimonial order becomes defended (for any reason) then it cannot proceed via the online system and must proceed offline and in accordance with Part 7 FPR.

3.5 This practice direction does not make provision in relation to steps that can already be undertaken by email (via rule 5.5 FPR and PD5B) or in relation to procedures to enable documents to be held electronically by HMCTS via bulk scanning (via pilot PD36O).

B Relationship between the Family Procedure Rules and this practice direction

Application of the Family Procedure Rules 2010

4.1 The Family Procedure Rules 2010 ('FPR') and supporting practice directions apply to proceedings to which this practice direction applies, subject to the provisions of this practice direction.

4.2 In particular, certain provisions of Part 7 FPR and certain provisions in Practice Direction 7A apply to proceedings to which this practice direction applies. These are set out in the table below.

(It should be noted that this table relates only to Part 7 FPR and Practice Direction 7A, so is not an exhaustive list of all provisions in the FPR and supporting practice directions which apply to proceedings to which this practice direction applies.)

Rule in Part 7 FPR or paragraph in Practice Direction 7A	Subject matter of provision
Rule 7.7	Limitation on applications in respect of the same marriage
Rule 7.10	Who the parties are
Rule 7.15 (except insofar as it relates to an application being made for further information, as referred to in Practice Direction 7A, paragraphs 6.1 to 6.5)	Further information about the contents of the application
Practice Direction 7A, paragraph 2.1	Respondents: restrictions
Practice Direction 7A, paragraph 3.5	Other methods of proof of marriage
Practice Direction 7A, paragraph 4.1	Information required where evidence of a conviction or a finding is to be relied on

4.3 In particular, certain provisions of Part 7 FPR and certain provisions in Practice Direction 7A do not apply to proceedings to which this practice direction applies but provisions of this practice direction apply instead. These are detailed in the table below.

(It should be noted that this table relates only to Part 7 FPR and Practice Direction 7A, so is not an exhaustive list of all provisions in the FPR and supporting practice directions which do not apply to proceedings to which this practice direction applies.)

Rule in Part 7 FPR or paragraph in Practice Direction 7A	Provision of this practice direction which applies instead
Rule 7.6(1) (statement of reconciliation)	Paragraph 8.1
Rule 7.8 (service of application)	Paragraphs 9.1 and 9.2
Rule 7.12(1) to (6) (what the respondent and co-respondent should do on receiving the application)	Paragraphs 10.1 to 10.13
Rule 7.13 (insofar as it relates to amending an application in the circumstances specified in this practice direction)	Paragraphs 12.1 to 12.4
Rule 7.19 (application for decree nisi)	Paragraphs 13.1 to 13.5

Rule 7.20, except for paragraph (8) (what the court will do on an application for a decree nisi)	Paragraphs 14.1 to 14.6
Rule 7.32(1) and (2) (making decrees nisi absolute by giving notice)	Paragraphs 15.1 to 15.4
Rule 7.34 (what the court officer must do when a decree nisi is made absolute)	Paragraph 16.1
Practice Direction 7A, paragraphs 1.1 and 1.2	Paragraph 7.3
Practice Direction 7A, paragraph 3.1	Paragraphs 7.5 and 7.6

4.4 There are certain steps that cannot be taken by electronic means via the online system and which must be taken offline and in accordance with the FPR and supporting practice directions. (In turn, rule 5.5 and PD5B will apply to determine whether any of the steps can be taken via email.) In particular, the table below sets out the provisions in Part 7 FPR and Practice Direction 7A which cannot apply to cases proceeding by electronic means via the online system.

(It should be noted that this table relates only to Part 7 FPR and Practice Direction 7A, so is not an exhaustive list of all provisions in the FPR and supporting practice directions which cannot apply to proceedings to which this practice direction applies.)

Rule in Part 7 FPR or paragraph in Practice Direction 7A which cannot apply to an application proceeding by electronic means via the online system	Subject matter of provision
Rule 7.9	Withdrawal of application before service
Rule 7.11	Nullity: interim and full gender recognition certificates
Rule 7.12(8) to (15)	Certain steps which may be taken by a respondent or co-respondent on receiving the application
Rule 7.13 FPR and Practice Direction 7A paragraph 1.3	Supplemental application and amendment of application and answer (save insofar as paragraphs 11.1 to 11.5 of this practice direction apply)
Rule 7.14	How the respondent can make an application
Rule 7.15, insofar as it relates to an application being made for the disclosure of further information, as referred to in Practice Direction 7A, paragraphs 6.1 to 6.5)	Further information about the contents of the application
Rule 7.16	General rule – hearing to be in public
Rule 7.18	Notice of hearing
Rule 7.20(8)	Inspection of certificate of entitlement to a decree and any connected evidence filed
Rule 7.21	Further provision about costs

Rule 7.22	What the court must do in a case management hearing
Rule 7.26	Medical examination in proceedings for nullity of a marriage of an opposite sex couple
Rule 7.27	Stay of proceedings
Rule 7.28	Circumstances in which an order may be set aside (rescission)
Rule 7.29	Applications under section 10(2) of 1973 Act or section 48(2) of 2004 Act
Rule 7.30	Orders under section 10A(2) of the 1973 Act
Rule 7.31	Applications to prevent decrees nisi being made absolute
Rule 7.32(3) and (4)	Making decree nisi absolute where the notice is received more than 12 months after the making of the decree nisi
Rule 7.33	Applications to make decrees nisi absolute
Rule 7.36	Records of decrees absolute and final orders
Practice Direction 7A, paragraph 3.2	Filing without accompanying proof of marriage
Practice Direction 7A paragraphs 5.1 to 5.4	Supplemental applications and amendments to applications and answers, where permission is needed
Practice Direction 7A paragraphs 8.1 to 8.4	Decrees absolute: need for expedition

4.5 In addition, there are certain applications referred to in provisions of the FPR or practice directions other than Part 7 FPR and Practice Direction 7A which cannot be made by electronic means via the online system and which must be made in accordance with the FPR and supporting practice directions. In particular, the table below sets out the applications under Part 6 FPR which cannot be made by electronic means via the online system.

(It should be noted that this table relates only to Part 6 FPR so is not an exhaustive list of all provisions in the FPR and supporting practice directions which cannot apply to proceedings to which this practice direction applies.)

Rule in Part 6 FPR in respect of which an application cannot be made by electronic means via the online system	Subject matter of provision
Rule 6.9	Request for bailiff service
Rule 6.16	Request that the court directs that the application is deemed to be served
Rule 6.20	Application for an order to dispense with service

4.6 Subject to paragraph 4.7, this practice direction supersedes Practice Directions 36D, 36E and 36L.

4.7 Practice Directions 36D, 36E and 36L will each remain in force in relation to any application for a matrimonial order commenced under the pilot scheme referred to in each of those practice directions, and this practice direction (and any that supersede it) will not apply in relation to such an application.

C Procedure when proceeding by electronic means via the online system

Security

5.1 Her Majesty's Courts and Tribunals Service will take such measures as it thinks fit to ensure the security of steps taken in cases proceeding by electronic means or in respect of information stored electronically. These may include requiring parties to cases which are proceeding by electronic means-

(a) to use a unique identification code or password;
(b) to provide personal information for identification purposes; and
(c) to comply with any other security measures,

before taking any of the steps mentioned in paragraphs 3.1, 3.2 or 3.3.

Providing information requested

6.1 Where proceedings are progressing by electronic means via the online system, each party must at each stage provide all the information requested, including any documents that the online system or the court requires, in the manner specified by the online system or by the court.

Creating and starting an application by electronic means

7.1 Where paragraph 2.1 applies, an application for a matrimonial order can be created via the online system.

Contents of the application

7.2 Where an application for a matrimonial order is created via the online system, the application must be completed according to the detailed guidance contained in the online system.

7.3 It is especially important that the particulars provide evidence to show why the applicant is entitled to a decree of divorce. The particulars should, however, be as concise as possible consistent with providing the necessary evidence.

7.4 The online system sets out the documents which must accompany an application for a matrimonial order and the way in which those documents may be provided (for example, the online system may allow for documents to be posted, or to be uploaded and submitted online with the application).

Proof of validity of marriage

7.5 Where the existence and validity of a marriage is not disputed, its validity will be proved by the application for a matrimonial order being accompanied by-

(a) one of the following-
  (i) a certificate of the marriage to which the application relates issued under the law in force in the country where the marriage took place;
  (ii) a similar document issued under the law in force in the country where the marriage took place; or

(iii) a certified copy of such a certificate or document obtained from the appropriate register office; and

(b) where the certificate, document or certified copy is not in English, or is not in both English and Welsh, a translation of that document certified by a notary public or authenticated by a statement of truth.

Submitting the application

7.6 An application for a matrimonial order created on the online system is submitted to the court via the online system. Once submitted in this way, the proceedings are started when they are issued by the court.

Timing

7.7 An application for a matrimonial order that is submitted via the online system is lodged with the court on the date and at the time that HMCTS software records the application as received, provided that the application is subsequently issued by the court.

7.7A A document, other than an application for a matrimonial order, that is submitted via the online system is filed with or otherwise received by the court on the date and at the time that HMCTS software records the document as received.

7.8 When an application for a matrimonial order is received via the online system, an acknowledgment of receipt is automatically sent to the applicant. This acknowledgement of receipt does not constitute a notice that the application has been issued.

Statement of reconciliation

8.1 Where the applicant is legally represented, the legal representative must complete and provide with the application for a matrimonial order, in a manner specified in the online system, a statement certifying whether the legal representative has discussed with the applicant the possibility of a reconciliation and given the applicant the names and addresses of persons qualified to help effect a reconciliation.

Service of an application for a matrimonial order

9.1 After an application for a matrimonial order made via the online system has been issued by the court, a copy of it must be served on the respondent and on any co-respondent.

(Rule 6.5 FPR provides for who may serve such an application. Provision about methods of service is made in Chapters 2 and 4 of Part 6 FPR and in supporting practice directions. It should be noted that an application for a matrimonial order cannot be served by email or on or via the online system.)

9.2 When the application for a matrimonial order is served on a respondent or co-respondent, it must be accompanied by-

(a) details of what steps to take to respond to the application; and

(b) a notice of proceedings.

What the respondent and co-respondent should do on receiving the application

10.1 On receiving an application for a matrimonial order, the respondent, and any co-respondent, must file an acknowledgment of service.

10.2 The respondent, and any co-respondent, may choose whether or not to use the online system to complete and file an acknowledgement of service. Details of how to respond via the online system will be included in the letter provided in accordance with paragraph 9.2(a).

10.3 If the respondent or co-respondent chooses to use the online system, the acknowledgment of service must be filed within 7 days beginning with the date on which the application for a matrimonial order was served.

10.4 If the respondent or co-respondent chooses not to use the online system, they must contact Her Majesty's Courts and Tribunals Service (using the details included in the letter provided in accordance with paragraph 9.2(a)) to request a paper form for acknowledging service. If the respondent or co-respondent then files that paper form, this Practice Direction no longer applies and the applicant can no longer use the online system to take further steps in the proceedings. Instead, the further stages of the proceedings will be completed under Part 7 of the FPR.

10.5 Where paragraph 10.4 applies, the acknowledgment of service must be filed within 7 days beginning with the date on which the respondent or co-respondent received the paper form for acknowledging service. The amended deadline for filing the acknowledgment of service will be notified to all parties.

10.6 Paragraphs 10.3 and 10.5 are subject to rule 6.42 FPR (which specify how the period for filing an acknowledgment of service is calculated where the application is served out of the jurisdiction).

10.7 The acknowledgment of service completed by the respondent or, as the case may be, the co-respondent, must-

(a) include the respondent's or, as the case may be, the co-respondent's address for service of further documents in the proceedings; and
(b) where it is filed by the respondent, indicate whether or not the respondent intends to defend the case.

(Should the application for a matrimonial order become a defended case it will cease to proceed by electronic means via the online system and will instead proceed offline and in accordance with Part 7 of the FPR).

10.8 The acknowledgment of service must include a statement of truth. Where the acknowledgment of service has been completed via the online system, the name of the person giving the statement of truth must be recorded against it.

10.9 Subject to paragraph 10.10, the name of the person giving the statement of truth must be that of the respondent or the respondent's legal representative, or (as the case may be) the co-respondent or the co-respondent's legal representative.

10.10 Where paragraph 10.11 or 10.12 applies, the name of the person giving the statement of truth must be the respondent's.

10.11 This paragraph applies where-

(a) the application alleges that the respondent has committed adultery; and
(b) the respondent admits the adultery.

10.12 This paragraph applies where-

(a) the application alleges that the parties to the marriage have been separated for more than 2 years; and
(b) the respondent consents to the making of the matrimonial order.

10.13 Where the respondent or co-respondent completes an acknowledgement of service via the online system-

(a) an acknowledgment of receipt is automatically sent to the respondent or the co-respondent, as the case may be, via the online system;
(b) the application is deemed to be served; and
(c) a notification must be sent to the applicant via an email attaching a link from which the acknowledgement of service may be accessed and downloaded.

Service by email (documents other than an application for a matrimonial order)

11.1 Paragraph 9.1 makes provision in relation to service of an application for a matrimonial order which this practice direction applies. Paragraphs 11.2 to 11.5 make provision in relation to service of documents other than such an application in cases which are proceeding by electronic means via the online system.

11.2 Practice Direction 6A makes provision about methods of service, including by email. That practice direction applies to proceedings to which this practice direction applies, subject to paragraphs 11.3 to 11.5.

11.3 Where paragraph 4(2)(a) of Practice Direction 6A applies, confirmation given on or via the online system that a party is willing to accept service by email, and stating the email address for such service, is to be taken as sufficient written indication for the purposes of paragraph 4.2(a) of Practice Direction 6A, in addition to the means of confirmation specified in paragraph 4.2(b) of Practice Direction 6A.

11.4 Where a party has indicated willingness to accept service by email (as set out in paragraph 11.3), service of a document may be effected by the court sending the party an email, to the address given for service by email, containing a link from which the document may be accessed and downloaded.

11.5 References in paragraphs 4.2 to 4.5 of Practice Direction 6A to service of a document by email include service by the court acting in accordance with paragraph 11.4 of this practice direction.

Amendment of an application for a matrimonial order

12.1 It is not possible to make a supplemental application for a matrimonial order via the online system. It is not possible to amend an application for a matrimonial order via the online system except where paragraph 12.2 or 12.3 applies. A party wishing to make a supplemental application, or to amend an application where paragraph 12.2 or 12.3 does not apply, may only do so in accordance with rule 7.13 FPR.

12.2 This paragraph applies where the court is considering an application made under paragraph 13.1 for a decree nisi and makes a direction, as referred to in paragraph 14.3, that an amended application for a matrimonial order must be filed.

12.3 This paragraph applies where-

(a) the application for a matrimonial order states that the respondent has committed adultery, but the respondent does not admit that adultery in the acknowledgement of service; or
(b) the application for a matrimonial order states that the parties to the marriage have lived apart for a continuous period of two years, but the respondent does not consent in the acknowledgement of service to a decree being granted.

12.4 Where paragraph 12.3 applies, the applicant may amend the application for a matrimonial order via the online system, to cite a different fact under section 1(2) of the 1973 Act.

Application for a decree nisi

13.1 An application may be made by the applicant to the court, using the online system, for it to consider the making of a decree nisi in the proceedings-

(a) at any time after the time for filing the acknowledgement of service has expired, provided that no party has filed an acknowledgement of service indicating an intention to defend the case; and
(b) in any other case, at any time after the time for filing an answer to the application for a matrimonial order has expired.

13.2 An application under paragraph 13.1 must, if the information which was required to be provided by the application is no longer correct, set out particulars of the change.

13.3 If no party has filed an answer opposing the making of a decree nisi on another party's application for a matrimonial order, then an application under paragraph 13.1 must include a statement-

(a) stating whether there have been any changes in the information given in the application;
(b) confirming that, subject to any changes stated, the contents of the application are true; and
(c) where a paper acknowledgement of service has been signed by the other party to the marriage, confirming that party's signature on the acknowledgement of service.

13.4 A statement under paragraph 13.3 must be verified by a statement of truth.

13.5 Where an application under paragraph 13.1 is received via the online system, an acknowledgment of receipt is automatically sent to the applicant.

What the court will do on an application for a decree nisi

14.1 Paragraphs 14.2 to 14.6 apply where an application is made under paragraph 13.1 in relation to an application for a matrimonial order that is progressing on the online system.

14.2 The court must, if satisfied that the applicant is entitled to a decree nisi, so certify and direct that the application be listed before a judge for the making of the decree at the next available date.

14.3 If the court is not satisfied that the applicant is entitled to a decree nisi, it must direct–

(a) that any party to the proceedings provide such further information, or take such other steps, as the court may specify, for example requiring an amended application for a matrimonial order to be filed; or
(b) that the case be listed for a case management hearing.

(Should the case be listed for a case management hearing, the case will cease to proceed by electronic means via the online system and will instead proceed offline and in accordance with Part 7 of the FPR).

14.4 The court may, when giving a direction under paragraph 14.3 direct that the further information provided be verified by an affidavit or a statement of truth.

14.5 If the applicant has applied for costs, the court may, on making a direction under paragraph 14.2 –

(a) if satisfied that the applicant is entitled to an order for costs, so certify; or
(b) if not so satisfied, make no direction about costs.

14.6 The court must not give directions under paragraph 14.2 or 14.3 unless at the relevant time it is satisfied –

(a) that a copy of the application for a matrimonial order (including any amended application) has been properly served on each party on whom it is required to be served; and
(b) that the application for a decree nisi was made at a time permitted by paragraph 13.1.

(In this paragraph 'the relevant time' means the time at which the court is considering an application made under paragraph 13.1).

Making a decree nisi absolute by giving notice

15.1 Unless rule 7.33 FPR applies, an applicant in whose favour a decree nisi has been made may give notice to the court, using the online system, that he or she wishes the decree nisi to be made absolute.

(Where rule 7.33 FPR applies, the case cannot proceed via the online system and must instead proceed under Part 7 FPR.)

15.2 Subject to paragraph 15.3, where the court receives a notice under paragraph 15.1 it will make the decree nisi absolute if it is satisfied that –

(a) no application for rescission of the decree nisi is pending;
(b) no appeal against the making of the decree nisi is pending;
(c) no order has been made by the court extending the time for bringing an appeal of the kind mentioned in sub-paragraph (b), or if such an order has been made, that the time so extended has expired;
(d) no application for an order of the kind mentioned in sub-paragraph (c) is pending;
(e) no application to prevent the decree nisi being made absolute is pending;
(f) the provisions of section 10(2) to (4) of the 1973 Act or section 48(2) to (4) of the 2004 Act do not apply or have been complied with; and
(g) any order under section 10A(2) of the 1973 Act has been complied with.

15.3 Where a notice would be received more than 12 months after the making of the decree nisi, the notice cannot be given via the online system. Rule 7.32(3) and (4) FPR will apply to such cases.

15.4 Where a notice referred to in paragraph 15.1 is received via the online system, an acknowledgment of receipt is automatically sent to the applicant.

What must happen when a decree nisi is made absolute

16.1 When a decree nisi is made absolute in a case proceeding via the online system-

(a) the date and time on which the decree nisi is made absolute must be recorded on the online system; and

(b) a notification must be sent to each of the parties that the decree nisi has been made absolute.

Statements of Truth

17.1 In paragraphs 17.2 and 17.3, 'document' means anything in which information of any description is recorded.

17.2 Where a statement of truth is included in any document completed or generated using the online system-

(a) the document must include the name of the person who the online system requires to give the statement of truth recorded against the statement of truth; and

(b) the court may require the party to produce a copy of the document containing the signature of the person referred to in sub-paragraph (a) at a later date.

17.3 Practice Direction 17A applies to a statement of truth given in a document completed or generated via the online system, except that-

(a) paragraphs 1.5 and 2.3 of Practice Direction 17A do not apply;

(b) in the heading to paragraph 3 and in paragraphs 3.1, 3.7, 3.8 and 3.10 of Practice Direction 17A, references to 'sign', 'signs', 'signed' and 'signing' are to be read as references to the name of the person being, or having been, recorded against the statement of truth included in the document completed or generated via the online system;

(c) paragraph 4.3(a) is substituted with-

'(a) that the content of the document completed or generated via the online system has been read to the person before completion of the statement of truth required by the online system;';

(d) paragraph 4.3(e) is substituted with-

'(e) that the person confirmed in the presence of the authorised person that it was their belief that the contents of the document completed or generated via the online system were true.'; and

(e) the Annex is substituted with-

'Certificate to be used where a person is unable to read or sign a document completed or generated in matrimonial proceedings to which the online scheme in Practice Direction 41A applies.

I certify that I [name and address of authorised person] have read the contents of the [name of document completed via the online system] and the statement of truth to the person whose name is recorded against the statement of truth, who appeared to understand (a) the [name of document] and approved its contents as accurate and (b) the statement of truth and the consequences of making a false statement, and orally confirmed that this was the case in my presence.'

Practice Direction 41B – Proceeding by electronic means: procedure for an application for a consent order for a financial remedy in connection with matrimonial or civil partnership proceedings

This PD applies to applications issued by the court on or after 6 April 2022. For applications issued by the court before 6 April 2022 see [https://webarchive.nationalarchives.gov.uk/ukgwa/20211201114213/https://www.justice.gov.uk/courts/procedure-rules/family/practice_directions/practice-direction-41a-proceeding-by-electronic-means-certain-proceedings-for-a-matrimonial-order/practice-direction-41b-proceeding-by-electronic-means-procedure-for-an-application-for-a-consent-order-for-a-financial-remedy-in-connection-with-divorce-proceedings].

This practice direction supplements rule 41.1 of the Family Procedure Rules 2010.

A Scope of this practice direction

Introduction and interpretation

1.1 This practice direction provides for the procedure by which, in the circumstances set out in this practice direction, an application for a consent order for a financial remedy in connection with proceedings for a matrimonial order or for a civil partnership order may proceed by electronic means.

> (It should be noted that, while a presumption of death order under the 2004 Act is a form of 'civil partnership order' as defined in rule 2.3 FPR, no application for a financial remedy may be made under the 2004 Act in connection with an application for such a presumption of death order.)

1.2 References in this practice direction to 'the online system' mean Her Majesty's Courts and Tribunal Service's online system known as the Online Financial Remedy Consent Order Service, which allows for applications to which this practice direction applies to proceed by electronic means.

1.3 References in this practice direction to 'applicant' and 'respondent' are to the applicant and the respondent in financial remedy proceedings. The applicant for a financial remedy could be either the applicant (petitioner) or the respondent in the connected proceedings for a matrimonial or civil partnership order and, in turn, the respondent in the financial remedy proceedings could be either the applicant (petitioner) or the respondent in the connected proceedings for a matrimonial or civil partnership order.

Types of applications which must proceed by electronic means

2.1 An application must proceed by electronic means where all of the following conditions are met-

- (a) subject to the exceptions in paragraph 2A.1, the application is for a financial remedy in connection with proceedings for a matrimonial or civil partnership order;
- (b) a decree nisi or a conditional order (as applicable) has been made in that application for a matrimonial or civil partnership order;
- (c) the application is for a consent order only;
- (d) either-
  - (i) the applicant for a financial remedy is legally represented; or
  - (ii) the applicant and the respondent in the financial remedy proceedings are legally represented;

(e) Omitted
(f) the application is started in the family court.

2A.1 The exceptions referred to in paragraph 2.1 are where the application is for-

(a) an order for payment in respect of legal services; or
(b) a variation order in respect of a financial remedy order that was not made as a result of an application made via the online system

2.2 For the avoidance of doubt-

(a) Omitted
(b) filing a document via the online system does not mean that service of that document has been effected.

Steps that may be taken by electronic means: outline

3.1 This practice direction enables applicants to, in the circumstances set out in this practice direction, take the following steps by electronic means via the online system-

(a) create and start an application for a consent order for a financial remedy where all of the criteria in paragraph 2.1 are satisfied;
(b) in respect of such an application-
  (i) file documents, if requested by the court to do so;
  (ii) amend the application, if requested by the court to do so;
  (iii) indicate willingness to accept service by the court of any documents relating to the application by email;
  (iv) accept service of any documents relating to the application; and
  (v) give notice of a change of solicitor to the court;
(c) view an electronic record of the progress and outcome of the application and download copies of documents.

3.2 This practice direction enables respondents to, in the circumstances set out in this practice direction, take the steps at paragraph 3.1(b) and (c) via the online system.'.

B Relationship between the Family Procedure Rules and this practice direction

Application of the Family Procedure Rules 2010 and supporting practice directions

4.1 The Family Procedure Rules 2010 ('the FPR') apply to proceedings to which this practice direction applies, subject to the provisions of this practice direction.

4.2 In particular, certain provisions of the FPR and supporting practice directions do not apply to proceedings to which this practice direction applies, but provisions of this practice direction apply instead. The key such provisions are detailed in the table below.

Provision in the FPR or supporting practice direction which does not apply	Provision of this practice direction which applies instead
Rule 5.1 FPR (forms)	Paragraph 6.1
Rule 9.26 FPR (applications for consent orders for financial remedy)	Paragraphs 6.2 to 6.9
Practice Direction 9A, paragraph 7.1 (consent orders)	Paragraph 6.4

C Procedure when proceeding by electronic means via the online system

Security

5.1 Her Majesty's Courts and Tribunals Service will take such measures as it thinks fit to ensure the security of steps taken in cases proceeding by electronic means or in respect of information stored electronically. These may include requiring parties to cases which are proceeding by electronic means-

(a) to use a unique identification code or password;
(b) to provide personal information for identification purposes; and
(c) to comply with any other security measures,

before taking any of the steps mentioned in paragraph 3.1.

Application for a consent order for financial remedy

6.1 Where the criteria in paragraph 2.1 are all met, an application must be created, started and progressed via the online system, and the progress and outcome can be viewed, as specified in this practice direction.

6.2 The applicant must-

(a) complete all relevant sections of the application on the online system; and
(b) provide, in the manner specified, any information, any additional documents or amended application that this practice direction, the online system or the court requires.

6.2A The respondent must provide, in the manner specified, any information or documents that this practice direction, the online system or the court requires.'.

6.3 Subject to paragraph 6.8 and to rule 35.2 FPR, in relation to an application for a consent order –

(a) the applicant must file a draft of the order in the terms sought which must be signed by both parties; and
(b) each party must file with the court and serve on the other party, a statement of information in the form referred to in Practice Direction 5A.

6.4 Paragraph 6.3(a) is considered to be properly complied with if the draft order is signed by solicitors on record as acting for a party. However, where the consent order applied for contains undertakings, it should be signed by the party giving the undertakings as well as by that party's solicitor.

(Provision in relation to the enforcement of undertakings is contained in Practice Direction 33A supplementing Part 33 of the FPR).

6.5 Where each party's statement of information is contained in one form, it must be signed by both the applicant and respondent to certify that they have read the contents of the other party's statement.

6.6 Where each party's statement of information is in a separate form, the form of each party must be signed by the other party to certify that they have read the contents of the statement contained in that form.

6.7 Unless the court directs otherwise, the applicant and the respondent need not attend the hearing of an application for a consent order.

6.8 Where all or any of the parties attend the hearing of an application for a financial remedy the court may –

(a) dispense with the filing of a statement of information; and
(b) give directions for the information which would otherwise be required to be given in such a statement in such a manner as it thinks fit.

6.9 The following rules in the FPR contain provision in relation to applications for consent orders – rule 9.32 (pension sharing order), rule 9.34 (pension attachment order), rule 9.41 (pension compensation sharing orders) and rule 9.43 (pension compensation attachment orders.)

Timing of applications

7.1 An application for a consent order for a financial remedy that is submitted via the online system is lodged with the court on the date and at the time that HMCTS software records the application as received, provided that the application is subsequently issued by the court.

7.1A A document, other than an application for a consent order for a financial remedy, that is submitted via the online system is filed with or otherwise received by the court on the date and at the time that HMCTS software records the document as received.

7.2 When an application for a consent order is received via the online system, an acknowledgment of receipt will automatically be sent to the email address given as the address for service in the online system. This acknowledgment of receipt does not constitute a notice that the application has been issued.

Service by email

8.1 Practice Direction 6A makes provision about methods of service, including by email. That practice direction applies to proceedings to which this practice direction applies, subject to the modification made in paragraphs 8.2 to 8.4.

8.2 Where paragraph 4.2(a) of Practice Direction 6A applies, confirmation given on or via the online system that a party is willing to accept service by email and stating the email address for such service is also to be taken as sufficient written indication for the purposes of paragraph 4.2(a) of Practice Direction 6A, in addition to the means of confirmation specified in paragraph 4.2(b) of Practice Direction 6A.

8.3 Where a party has indicated willingness to accept service by email (as set out in paragraph 8.2), service of a document may be effected by the court sending the party an email, to the address given for service by email, containing a link from which the document may be accessed and downloaded.

8.4 References in paragraphs 4.2 to 4.5 of Practice Direction 6A to service of a document by email include service by the court acting in accordance with paragraph 8.3 of this practice direction.

Statements of Truth

9.1 In paragraphs 9.2 and 9.3, 'document' means anything in which information of any description is recorded.

9.2 Where a statement of truth is included in any document completed or generated using the online system-

(a) the document must include the name of the person who the online system requires to give the statement of truth recorded against the statement of truth; and

(b) the court may require the party to produce a copy of the document containing the signature of the person referred to in sub-paragraph (a) at a later date.

9.3 Practice Direction 17A applies to a statement of truth given in a document completed or generated via the online system, except that-

(a) paragraphs 1.5 and 2.3 of Practice Direction 17A do not apply;

(b) in the heading to paragraph 3 and in paragraphs 3.1, 3.7, 3.8 and 3.10 of Practice Direction 17A, references to 'sign', 'signs', 'signed' and 'signing' are to be read as references to the name of the person being, or having been, recorded against the statement of truth included in the document completed or generated via the online system;

(c) paragraph 4.3(a) is substituted with-

'(a) that the content of the document completed or generated via the online system has been read to the person before completion of the statement of truth required by the online system;';

(d) paragraph 4.3(e) is substituted with-

'(e) that the person confirmed in the presence of the authorised person that it was their belief that the contents of the document completed or generated via the online system were true.'; and

(e) the Annex is substituted with-

'Certificate to be used where a person is unable to read or sign a document completed or generated in proceedings to which the online scheme in Practice Direction 41B applies.

I certify that I [name and address of authorised person] have read the contents of the [name of document completed via the online system] and the statement of truth to the person whose name is recorded against the statement of truth, who appeared to understand (a) the [name of document] and approved its contents as accurate and (b) the statement of truth and the consequences of making a false statement, and orally confirmed that this was the case in my presence.'.

Change of solicitor

10.1 When an application for a consent order is proceeding on the online system, rule 26.2(2)(b) FPR does not apply. Instead, notice of a change of solicitor must be given to the court by a party or a party's solicitor (where one is acting) submitting information in relation to that change on the online system.

Practice Direction 41C – Proceeding by electronic means: appeals in family proceedings heard in the High Court

This Practice Direction comes into force on 1 February 2021.

This Practice Direction supplements rule 41.1 of the Family Procedure Rules 2010

General

1.1 This practice direction provides for the procedure by which, in the circumstances set out in this practice direction, appeal proceedings may be proceed by electronic means using an online case management system.

1.2 This practice direction comes into force on 1st February 2021.

1.3 In this practice direction-

'appeal proceedings' means -

(a) an application for permission to appeal; and
(b) an appeal;

'document' has the meaning given in rule 41.1 FPR;
'FPR' means the Family Procedure Rules 2010;
'HMCTS' means Her Majesty's Courts and Tribunal Service;
'online case management system' means HMCTS's online case management system which allows for specified steps in appeal proceedings to be undertaken online.

Types of appeal proceedings which may proceed by electronic means

2.1 On or after the date that is practice direction comes into force, appeal proceedings may proceed by electronic means using the online case management system where all of the following conditions are met-

(a) the proceedings were commenced on or after 7th October 2019; and
(b) the appeal would be heard by a High Court Judge sitting in the High Court.

(Practice Direction 30A, paragraph 2.1 and 2.2, summarise which decisions are appealed to a High Court Judge sitting in the High Court.)

Steps which may be taken by electronic means: outline

3.1 This practice direction enables a party to, in the circumstances set out in this practice direction, take the following steps by electronic means using the online case management system on or after the date on which this practice direction comes into force-

(a) file an application for permission to appeal;
(b) file an appeal notice;
(c) file documents in respect of an application referred to in sub-paragraph (a) or (b);
(d) file any other information requested or required by the court in respect of an application referred to in sub-paragraph (a) or (b);
(e) pay court fees; and
(f) view an electronic record of the progress of the application.

Application of the FPR and supporting practice directions

4.1 The FPR and practice directions supporting the FPR apply to proceedings to which this practice direction applies, subject to the provisions of this practice direction.

4.2 In particular, paragraph 8.1 of Practice Direction 30A (a requirement to file appellant's notices at a postal address for the Family Division of the High Court) does not apply to proceedings to which this practice direction applies. Instead, paragraph 5.2 of this practice direction applies.

Proceeding by electronic means

5.1 Where this practice direction applies, parties may take a step outlined at paragraph 3.1 using the online case management system 24 hours a day every day all year round, including during out of normal court office opening hours and on weekends and bank holidays, except—

(a) where there is planned 'down-time': as with all electronic systems, there will be some planned periods for system maintenance and upgrades when the online case management system will not be available;
(b) where there is unplanned 'down-time': periods during which the online case management system will not be available due, for example, to a system failure or power outage, or some other unplanned circumstance.

5.2 Where this practice direction applies, documents that a party is permitted or required to file may be filed with the court by uploading them to the online case management system.

5.3 To file a document on the online case management system, a party must—

(a) access the online case management system via the website address specified by HMCTS ('the Website');
(b) register for an account or log on to an existing account;
(c) enter details of a new case or use the details of an existing case;
(d) upload the appropriate document; and
(e) pay the appropriate fee.

5.4 Proceedings issued will be stored by the court as an electronic case file.

5.5 The Website contains further details, updated from time to time, on how to complete a filing, including in the event of down-time or where a particular document format is not compatible with the online case management system, information about the timing of any planned down-time, and a support email address to contact in the event of any down-time or when experiencing any other technical difficulty in using the Website.

The online case management system and alternative filing methods

6.1 Any document which is filed using the online case management system must not also be filed by some other means unless this is required by a rule, this or another practice direction, or by the court.

6.2 If the court has requested or permitted the submission of a document by e-mail then it must be so submitted as well as being filed through the online case management system.

6.3 Where an original document is required by a court order, rule or Practice Direction to be filed, such original document cannot be filed using the online case management system and must instead be physically filed with the court.

6.4 Proceedings commenced on or after 7th October 2019 which have not been started using the online case management system may be continued using the online case management system after documents originally submitted in those proceedings have been converted to PDF format. The proceedings will then continue as if they had been started using the online case management system.

6.5 Where paragraph 6.4 applies, the court may refuse to convert a document to PDF format where that document was originally submitted by some other means and may instead require a party to provide the document in PDF format.

Original documents

7.1 Where parties file documents using the online case management system, the original signed documents, including the original exhibits to any witness statement filed, must be preserved and must be made available for inspection if required by another party to the proceedings or by order of the court.

General rules regarding issue and filing

8.1 Any document which is filed using the online case management system must—

(a) consist of one copy only unless required by a court order, rule or practice direction;

(b) be in PDF format (or in Excel format if appropriate) unless the court directs otherwise or unless the document is a draft order, in which case it shall be in 'Word' format;

(c) not exceed 50 (fifty) megabytes or such other limit that may be specified by HMCTS; and

(d) be categorised or labelled as to the type of document that it is (e.g. 'Witness Statement', 'Exhibit'); and

(e) be numbered sequentially.

8.2 Paragraph 8.1(c) is subject to any direction of the court restricting the number or length of documents to be filed.

8.3 In the event that a document exceeds the maximum limit specified in paragraph 8.1(c), the party seeking to file the document must divide the document into parts and file each part separately.

8.4 Parties can, in one filing, file up to 10 (ten) documents with each document not exceeding 50 (fifty) megabytes or such other limit specified by HMCTS.

8.5 In the event that a document is confidential and is required to be filed, it must, when filed in the electronic case file, be filed as a confidential document, using the process set up in the online case management system, in order to ensure that it is not visible to everyone.

8.6 Submission of any document using the online case management system generates an automated notification acknowledging that the document has been submitted and is being reviewed by the court prior to being accepted (the 'Acceptance').

8.6 The court may make an order to remedy an error of procedure made while using the online case management system, in accordance with rule 4.7 FPR. When the court makes such an order, a document filing will not fail Acceptance because of the error of procedure made.

8.8 Court staff may refuse to include a submitted document in its corresponding electronic case file if the document has been scanned and saved upside down or is otherwise illegible or incomplete.

8.9 Where court staff has not included a submitted document on its corresponding electronic case file for one of the reasons listed above, the submission will not have failed Acceptance, but the party that made the submission must upload the document again in accordance with court staff instructions in order for the document to be properly included on the corresponding electronic case file.

8.10 Where payment of a court fee is required to accompany the filing of a document, the date and time of filing on the online case management system is deemed to be the date and time at which payment of the court fee is made.

8.11 The date and time of payment is the date and time of issue for all applications submitted using the online case management system.

8.12 For all other document filed using the online case management system, the date and time of filing is the submission date and time for the purposes of any direction under the appropriate rules or for the purposes of complying with an order of the court, unless expressly provided otherwise by the court.

8.13 Once a document filing is accepted, a notification will appear on the online case management system account registered to the filing party to confirm that the document has been accepted and to confirm the date and time of issue or the date and time of filing in accordance with paragraphs 8.10 to 8.12.

8.13 The date and time of issue or the date and time of filing of a document submitted using the online case management system must not be delayed by Acceptance, unless the submission fails Acceptance because the filing error is more serious than an error of procedure, or the court orders that it has failed Acceptance for some other reason.

8.14 If the submission fails Acceptance, notice of the reasons for failure must be given to the party on that party's account for the online case management system and if the submission was of a claim form or other document requiring to be issued, it will be deemed not to have been issued.

8.15 In cases where payment of the court fee has already been made and an appeal notice or other application fails Acceptance, the fee will be refunded and a corrected notice or application must be submitted and the court fee paid again in order for proceedings to be issued. In such cases, the new submission will generate a new date and time of issue or date and time of filing in accordance with paragraphs 8.10 to 8.12.

8.16 An appeal notice or other application filed by a party using the online case management system must, subject to Acceptance and fee payment, be issued by the High Court, and the case claim will proceed in that court unless it is transferred to another court.

8.17 If any documents that are not required by any rule, practice direction, order or direction to be filed are submitted using the online case management system, they may not be retained on the online account and/or electronic case file.

8.18 Filing of a document with the court using the online case management system does not mean that service of that document has been effected. The provisions of the FPR and supporting practice directions relating to service will apply to a case on the online case management system as they would apply to any other case.

Payment of fees

9.1 Where any fee must be paid, a party filing a document using the online case management system must, except in circumstances specified in paragraph 9.4, pay the appropriate fee by account or by credit/debit card or by any other online method specified by HMCTS.

9.2 When a party enters its payment by account number into the online case management system when prompted by the online case management system to do so, that party will be deemed to have made the payment. The party will thereby owe the relevant court fee to HMCTS.

9.3 The court must keep a record of when payment was made or deemed to have been made.

9.4 For filings other than the issue of an application which incurs payment of a fee, a party who is not legally represented and who wishes to pay that fee by account or by credit/debit card must make the filing and the payment through the online case management system.

9.5 A party who has applied or wishes to apply for Help with Fees or partial Help with Fees must contact the court to obtain a Help with Fees payment by account number, prior to using the online case management system to issue appeal proceedings which require the payment of a court fee.

Electronic sealing

10.1 When the court issues an appeal notice or other application which has been submitted using the online case management system and has been accepted by the court, the court must electronically seal the notice or application with the date on which the relevant court fee was paid, and this shall be the issue date, as per the provisions of paragraphs 8.10 to 8.16.

10.2 The electronic seal may differ in appearance to the seal used on paper.

Service

11.1 The court must electronically return the sealed and issued appeal notice or other application to the relevant party's account on the online case management system and notify the party that it is ready for service.

(Rules 30.4(4) and 30.5(6) FPR and Part 6 FPR make provision regarding service.)

Transfer of proceedings and file transmission

12.1 If appeal proceedings which have used the online case management system are subsequently transferred to a court which does not operate the online case management system, no documents will be able to be filed in those proceedings through the online case management system after the date of transfer and this practice direction will cease to apply to those proceedings.

12.2 HMCTS must make arrangements for a version of the electronic case file of any transferred proceedings to be made available to the receiving court in a format requested by the receiving court.

Applications in proceedings

13.1 Where a party to appeal proceedings files an application for an order or other relief using the online case management system and the court determines that a hearing is required, the party filing the application must lodge an application bundle with the court.

13.2 The application bundle may be lodged in electronic format.

13.3 The application bundle must—

(a) also be filed as a paper copy, unless ordered otherwise;
(b) contain the application notice and any evidence filed in the application, including exhibits together with such other documents as may be required by any rule, practice direction or order of the court; and
(c) be filed in accordance with the time limits required by any applicable rule, practice direction or order of the court or, in the absence of such a requirement, 3 (three) days before the hearing.

13.4 The electronic copy of the application bundle must—

(a) be filed using the online case management system;
(b) be formatted as one PDF document with bookmarks as appropriate for each document and with section headings within the document, unless its size exceeds 50 (fifty) megabytes, in which case it can be divided into up to 10 (ten) documents of that size, each bearing bookmarks as appropriate; and
(c) be updated as required and filed in compliance with paragraphs (a) and (b) above.

13.5 The copy in paper format should be indexed and should correspond exactly to the electronic version of the bundle including sequential pagination.

Case and cost management and other directions

14.1 Where—

(a) a rule, practice direction or order of the court requires—
  (i) the court to give case management or other directions, whether at a hearing or not; and
  (ii) a bundle to be filed with the court in connection with case management or other directions; and
(b) a party wishes to file the bundle using the online case management system,

the bundle must contain such documents as are required by any rule, practice direction or order of the court.

14.2 The bundle must be filed in paper copy as well, unless the court orders otherwise.

14.3 The applicant is responsible for ensuring the electronic copy of the bundle complies with the requirements specified in paragraph 13.4.

14.4 The applicant is responsible for ensuring the paper copy is indexed and corresponds exactly with the electronic version of the bundle with sequential pagination.

Bundles for hearings

15.1 Subject to any direction of the court, the bundle for the hearing of-

(a) a contested permission application; or
(b) an appeal,

must be filed with the court in paper format and must comply with paragraph 13.5.

15.2 Subject to any direction of the court, an electronic version of the bundle must also be filed, in which case it must comply with the requirements of paragraph 13.4.

15.3 The court must retain any electronic copy of the bundle for a period of 2 (two) months after judgment has been delivered, after which it may be deleted.

15.4 The time in paragraph 15.3 may be extended by order of the court at the request of a party or on the court's own initiative.

Security

16.1 HMCTS must take such measures as it thinks fit to ensure the security of information communicated or stored electronically. These may include requiring persons using the online case management system to follow security steps such as—

(a) entering an email address as their customer identification and/or password;

(b) providing personal information for identification purposes; and
(c) complying with any other security measures as may from time to time be required before using the online case management system.

Glossary

Scope

This glossary is a guide to the meaning of certain legal expressions as used in these rules, but it does not give the expressions any meaning in the rules which they do not otherwise have in the law.

Expression	*Meaning*
Affidavit	A written, sworn, statement of evidence.
Cross-examination	Questioning of a witness by a party other than the party who called the witness.
Evidence in chief	The evidence given by a witness for the party who called him.
Injunction	A court order prohibiting a person from doing something or requiring a person to do something.
Official copy	A copy of an official document, supplied and marked as such by the office which issued the original.
Pre-action protocol	Statements of best practice about pre-action conduct which have been approved by the President of the Family Division and which are annexed to a Practice Direction.
Privilege	The right of a party to refuse to disclose a document or produce a document or to refuse to answer questions on the ground of some special interest recognised by law.
Seal	A seal is a mark which the court puts on document to indicate that the document has been issued by the court.
Service	Steps required by rules of court to bring documents used in court proceedings to a person's attention.
Set aside	Cancelling a judgment or order or a step taken by a party in the proceedings.
Stay	A stay imposes a halt on proceedings, apart from the taking of any steps allowed by the rules or the terms of the stay. Proceedings can be continued if a stay is lifted.
Strike out	Striking out means the court ordering written material to be deleted so that it may no longer be relied upon.
Without prejudice	Negotiations with a view to settlement are usually conducted 'without prejudice' which means that the circumstances in which the content of those negotiations may be revealed to the court are very restricted.

APPENDIX E

INTERNATIONAL INSTRUMENTS

(1) Convention on Jurisdiction, Applicable Law, Recognition, Enforcement and Co-operation In Respect of Parental Responsibility and Measures for the Protection of Children (19 October 1996)

(2) Council Regulation (EC) No 2201/2003

(3) Convention on the International Recovery of Child Support and Other Forms of Family Maintenance (23 November 2007)

(4) President's Guidance: Liaison between Courts in England and Wales and British Embassies and High Commissions Abroad

(5) Practice Guidance (Case Management and Mediation of International Child Abduction Proceedings) (13 March 2018)

(6) Other useful references

 (a) Link for lists and status of contracting parties to relevant conventions

 (b) Link for HCCH Emerging Guidance on Direct Judicial Communications

(1) Convention on Jurisdiction, Applicable Law, Recognition, Enforcement and Co-operation in Respect of Parental Responsibility and Measures for the Protection of Children

(Concluded 19 October 1996)

The States signatory to the present Convention,

Considering the need to improve the protection of children in international situations,

Wishing to avoid conflicts between their legal systems in respect of jurisdiction, applicable law, recognition and enforcement of measures for the protection of children,

Recalling the importance of international co-operation for the protection of children,

Confirming that the best interests of the child are to be a primary consideration,

Noting that the *Convention of 5 October 1961 concerning the powers of authorities and the law applicable in respect of the protection of minors* is in need of revision,

Desiring to establish common provisions to this effect, taking into account the *United Nations Convention on the Rights of the Child* of 20 November 1989,

Have agreed on the following provisions -

Chapter I – Scope of the Convention

Article 1

(1) The objects of the present Convention are -

a) to determine the State whose authorities have jurisdiction to take measures directed to the protection of the person or property of the child;

b) to determine which law is to be applied by such authorities in exercising their jurisdiction;

c) to determine the law applicable to parental responsibility;

d) to provide for the recognition and enforcement of such measures of protection in all Contracting States;

e) to establish such co-operation between the authorities of the Contracting States as may be necessary in order to achieve the purposes of this Convention.

(2) For the purposes of this Convention, the term 'parental responsibility' includes parental authority, or any analogous relationship of authority determining the rights, powers and responsibilities of parents, guardians or other legal representatives in relation to the person or the property of the child.

Article 2

The Convention applies to children from the moment of their birth until they reach the age of 18 years.

Article 3

The measures referred to in Article 1 may deal in particular with -

a) the attribution, exercise, termination or restriction of parental responsibility, as well as its delegation;

b) rights of custody, including rights relating to the care of the person of the child and, in particular, the right to determine the child's place of residence, as well as rights of access including the right to take a child for a limited period of time to a place other than the child's habitual residence;

c) guardianship, curatorship and analogous institutions;

d) the designation and functions of any person or body having charge of the child's person or property, representing or assisting the child;

e) the placement of the child in a foster family or in institutional care, or the provision of care by *kafala* or an analogous institution;

f) the supervision by a public authority of the care of a child by any person having charge of the child;

g) the administration, conservation or disposal of the child's property.

Article 4

The Convention does not apply to -

a) the establishment or contesting of a parent-child relationship;

b) decisions on adoption, measures preparatory to adoption, or the annulment or revocation of adoption;

c) the name and forenames of the child;

d) emancipation;

e) maintenance obligations;

f) trusts or succession;

g) social security;

h) public measures of a general nature in matters of education or health;
i) measures taken as a result of penal offences committed by children;
j) decisions on the right of asylum and on immigration.

Chapter II – Jurisdiction

Article 5

(1) The judicial or administrative authorities of the Contracting State of the habitual residence of the child have jurisdiction to take measures directed to the protection of the child's person or property.

(2) Subject to Article 7, in case of a change of the child's habitual residence to another Contracting State, the authorities of the State of the new habitual residence have jurisdiction.

Article 6

(1) For refugee children and children who, due to disturbances occurring in their country, are internationally displaced, the authorities of the Contracting State on the territory of which these children are present as a result of their displacement have the jurisdiction provided for in paragraph 1 of Article 5.

(2) The provisions of the preceding paragraph also apply to children whose habitual residence cannot be established.

Article 7

(1) In case of wrongful removal or retention of the child, the authorities of the Contracting State in which the child was habitually resident immediately before the removal or retention keep their jurisdiction until the child has acquired a habitual residence in another State, and

a) each person, institution or other body having rights of custody has acquiesced in the removal or retention; or

b) the child has resided in that other State for a period of at least one year after the person, institution or other body having rights of custody has or should have had knowledge of the whereabouts of the child, no request for return lodged within that period is still pending, and the child is settled in his or her new environment.

(2) The removal or the retention of a child is to be considered wrongful where -

a) it is in breach of rights of custody attributed to a person, an institution or any other body, either jointly or alone, under the law of the State in which the child was habitually resident immediately before the removal or retention; and

b) at the time of removal or retention those rights were actually exercised, either jointly or alone, or would have been so exercised but for the removal or retention.

The rights of custody mentioned in sub-paragraph *a* above, may arise in particular by operation of law or by reason of a judicial or administrative decision, or by reason of an agreement having legal effect under the law of that State.

(3) So long as the authorities first mentioned in paragraph 1 keep their jurisdiction, the authorities of the Contracting State to which the child has been removed or in which he or she has been retained can take only such urgent measures under Article 11 as are necessary for the protection of the person or property of the child.

Article 8

(1) By way of exception, the authority of a Contracting State having jurisdiction under Article 5 or 6, if it considers that the authority of another Contracting State would be better placed in the particular case to assess the best interests of the child, may either

– request that other authority, directly or with the assistance of the Central Authority of its State, to assume jurisdiction to take such measures of protection as it considers to be necessary, or
– suspend consideration of the case and invite the parties to introduce such a request before the authority of that other State.

(2) The Contracting States whose authorities may be addressed as provided in the preceding paragraph are

a) a State of which the child is a national,
b) a State in which property of the child is located,
c) a State whose authorities are seised of an application for divorce or legal separation of the child's parents, or for annulment of their marriage,
d) a State with which the child has a substantial connection.

(3) The authorities concerned may proceed to an exchange of views.

(4) The authority addressed as provided in paragraph 1 may assume jurisdiction, in place of the authority having jurisdiction under Article 5 or 6, if it considers that this is in the child's best interests.

Article 9

(1) If the authorities of a Contracting State referred to in Article 8, paragraph 2, consider that they are better placed in the particular case to assess the child's best interests, they may either

– request the competent authority of the Contracting State of the habitual residence of the child, directly or with the assistance of the Central Authority of that State, that they be authorised to exercise jurisdiction to take the measures of protection which they consider to be necessary, or
– invite the parties to introduce such a request before the authority of the Contracting State of the habitual residence of the child.

(2) The authorities concerned may proceed to an exchange of views.

(3) The authority initiating the request may exercise jurisdiction in place of the authority of the Contracting State of the habitual residence of the child only if the latter authority has accepted the request.

Article 10

(1) Without prejudice to Articles 5 to 9, the authorities of a Contracting State exercising jurisdiction to decide upon an application for divorce or legal separation of the parents of a child habitually resident in another Contracting State, or for annulment of their marriage, may, if the law of their State so provides, take measures directed to the protection of the person or property of such child if

a) at the time of commencement of the proceedings, one of his or her parents habitually resides in that State and one of them has parental responsibility in relation to the child, and
b) the jurisdiction of these authorities to take such measures has been accepted by the parents, as well as by any other person who has parental responsibility in relation to the child, and is in the best interests of the child.

(2) The jurisdiction provided for by paragraph 1 to take measures for the protection of the child ceases as soon as the decision allowing or refusing the application for divorce, legal separation or annulment of the marriage has become final, or the proceedings have come to an end for another reason.

Article 11

(1) In all cases of urgency, the authorities of any Contracting State in whose territory the child or property belonging to the child is present have jurisdiction to take any necessary measures of protection.

(2) The measures taken under the preceding paragraph with regard to a child habitually resident in a Contracting State shall lapse as soon as the authorities which have jurisdiction under Articles 5 to 10 have taken the measures required by the situation.

(3) The measures taken under paragraph 1 with regard to a child who is habitually resident in a non-Contracting State shall lapse in each Contracting State as soon as measures required by the situation and taken by the authorities of another State are recognised in the Contracting State in question.

Article 12

(1) Subject to Article 7, the authorities of a Contracting State in whose territory the child or property belonging to the child is present have jurisdiction to take measures of a provisional character for the protection of the person or property of the child which have a territorial effect limited to the State in question, in so far as such measures are not incompatible with measures already taken by authorities which have jurisdiction under Articles 5 to 10.

(2) The measures taken under the preceding paragraph with regard to a child habitually resident in a Contracting State shall lapse as soon as the authorities which have jurisdiction under Articles 5 to 10 have taken a decision in respect of the measures of protection which may be required by the situation.

(3) The measures taken under paragraph 1 with regard to a child who is habitually resident in a non-Contracting State shall lapse in the Contracting State where the measures were taken as soon as measures required by the situation and taken by the authorities of another State are recognised in the Contracting State in question.

Article 13

(1) The authorities of a Contracting State which have jurisdiction under Articles 5 to 10 to take measures for the protection of the person or property of the child must abstain from exercising this jurisdiction if, at the time of the commencement of the proceedings, corresponding measures have been requested from the authorities of another Contracting State having jurisdiction under Articles 5 to 10 at the time of the request and are still under consideration.

(2) The provisions of the preceding paragraph shall not apply if the authorities before whom the request for measures was initially introduced have declined jurisdiction.

Article 14

The measures taken in application of Articles 5 to 10 remain in force according to their terms, even if a change of circumstances has eliminated the basis upon which jurisdiction was founded, so long as the authorities which have jurisdiction under the Convention have not modified, replaced or terminated such measures.

Chapter III – Applicable Law

Article 15

(1) In exercising their jurisdiction under the provisions of Chapter II, the authorities of the Contracting States shall apply their own law.

(2) However, in so far as the protection of the person or the property of the child requires, they may exceptionally apply or take into consideration the law of another State with which the situation has a substantial connection.

(3) If the child's habitual residence changes to another Contracting State, the law of that other State governs, from the time of the change, the conditions of application of the measures taken in the State of the former habitual residence.

Article 16

(1) The attribution or extinction of parental responsibility by operation of law, without the intervention of a judicial or administrative authority, is governed by the law of the State of the habitual residence of the child.

(2) The attribution or extinction of parental responsibility by an agreement or a unilateral act, without intervention of a judicial or administrative authority, is governed by the law of the State of the child's habitual residence at the time when the agreement or unilateral act takes effect.

(3) Parental responsibility which exists under the law of the State of the child's habitual residence subsists after a change of that habitual residence to another State.

(4) If the child's habitual residence changes, the attribution of parental responsibility by operation of law to a person who does not already have such responsibility is governed by the law of the State of the new habitual residence.

Article 17

The exercise of parental responsibility is governed by the law of the State of the child's habitual residence. If the child's habitual residence changes, it is governed by the law of the State of the new habitual residence.

Article 18

The parental responsibility referred to in Article 16 may be terminated, or the conditions of its exercise modified, by measures taken under this Convention.

Article 19

(1) The validity of a transaction entered into between a third party and another person who would be entitled to act as the child's legal representative under the law of the State where the transaction was concluded cannot be contested, and the third party cannot be held liable, on the sole ground that the other person was not entitled to act as the child's legal representative under the law designated by the provisions of this Chapter, unless the third party knew or should have known that the parental responsibility was governed by the latter law.

(2) The preceding paragraph applies only if the transaction was entered into between persons present on the territory of the same State.

Article 20

The provisions of this Chapter apply even if the law designated by them is the law of a non-Contracting State.

Article 21

(1) In this Chapter the term "law" means the law in force in a State other than its choice of law rules.

(2) However, if the law applicable according to Article 16 is that of a non-Contracting State and if the choice of law rules of that State designate the law of another non-Contracting State which would apply its own law, the law of the latter State applies. If that other non-Contracting State would not apply its own law, the applicable law is that designated by Article 16.

Article 22

The application of the law designated by the provisions of this Chapter can be refused only if this application would be manifestly contrary to public policy, taking into account the best interests of the child.

Chapter IV – Recognition and Enforcement

Article 23

(1) The measures taken by the authorities of a Contracting State shall be recognised by operation of law in all other Contracting States.

(2) Recognition may however be refused -

a) if the measure was taken by an authority whose jurisdiction was not based on one of the grounds provided for in Chapter II;

b) if the measure was taken, except in a case of urgency, in the context of a judicial or administrative proceeding, without the child having been provided the opportunity to be heard, in violation of fundamental principles of procedure of the requested State;

c) on the request of any person claiming that the measure infringes his or her parental responsibility, if such measure was taken, except in a case of urgency, without such person having been given an opportunity to be heard;

d) if such recognition is manifestly contrary to public policy of the requested State, taking into account the best interests of the child;

e) if the measure is incompatible with a later measure taken in the non-Contracting State of the habitual residence of the child, where this later measure fulfils the requirements for recognition in the requested State;

f) if the procedure provided in Article 33 has not been complied with.

Article 24

Without prejudice to Article 23, paragraph 1, any interested person may request from the competent authorities of a Contracting State that they decide on the recognition or non-recognition of a measure taken in another Contracting State. The procedure is governed by the law of the requested State.

Article 25

The authority of the requested State is bound by the findings of fact on which the authority of the State where the measure was taken based its jurisdiction.

Article 26

(1) If measures taken in one Contracting State and enforceable there require enforcement in another Contracting State, they shall, upon request by an interested party, be declared enforceable or registered for the purpose of enforcement in that other State according to the procedure provided in the law of the latter State.

(2) Each Contracting State shall apply to the declaration of enforceability or registration a simple and rapid procedure.

(3) The declaration of enforceability or registration may be refused only for one of the reasons set out in Article 23, paragraph 2.

Article 27

Without prejudice to such review as is necessary in the application of the preceding Articles, there shall be no review of the merits of the measure taken.

Article 28

Measures taken in one Contracting State and declared enforceable, or registered for the purpose of enforcement, in another Contracting State shall be enforced in the latter State as if they had been taken by the authorities of that State. Enforcement takes place in accordance with the law of the requested State to the extent provided by such law, taking into consideration the best interests of the child.

Chapter V – Co-operation

Article 29

(1) A Contracting State shall designate a Central Authority to discharge the duties which are imposed by the Convention on such authorities.

(2) Federal States, States with more than one system of law or States having autonomous territorial units shall be free to appoint more than one Central Authority and to specify the territorial or personal extent of their functions. Where a State has appointed more than one Central Authority, it shall designate the Central Authority to which any communication may be addressed for transmission to the appropriate Central Authority within that State.

Article 30

(1) Central Authorities shall co-operate with each other and promote co-operation amongst the competent authorities in their States to achieve the purposes of the Convention.

(2) They shall, in connection with the application of the Convention, take appropriate steps to provide information as to the laws of, and services available in, their States relating to the protection of children.

Article 31

The Central Authority of a Contracting State, either directly or through public authorities or other bodies, shall take all appropriate steps to -

a) facilitate the communications and offer the assistance provided for in Articles 8 and 9 and in this Chapter;

b) facilitate, by mediation, conciliation or similar means, agreed solutions for the protection of the person or property of the child in situations to which the Convention applies;

c) provide, on the request of a competent authority of another Contracting State, assistance in discovering the whereabouts of a child where it appears that the child may be present and in need of protection within the territory of the requested State.

Article 32

On a request made with supporting reasons by the Central Authority or other competent authority of any Contracting State with which the child has a substantial connection, the Central Authority of the Contracting State in which the child is habitually resident and present may, directly or through public authorities or other bodies,

a) provide a report on the situation of the child;
b) request the competent authority of its State to consider the need to take measures for the protection of the person or property of the child.

Article 33

(1) If an authority having jurisdiction under Articles 5 to 10 contemplates the placement of the child in a foster family or institutional care, or the provision of care by *kafala* or an analogous institution, and if such placement or such provision of care is to take place in another Contracting State, it shall first consult with the Central Authority or other competent authority of the latter State. To that effect it shall transmit a report on the child together with the reasons for the proposed placement or provision of care.
(2) The decision on the placement or provision of care may be made in the requesting State only if the Central Authority or other competent authority of the requested State has consented to the placement or provision of care, taking into account the child's best interests.

Article 34

(1) Where a measure of protection is contemplated, the competent authorities under the Convention, if the situation of the child so requires, may request any authority of another Contracting State which has information relevant to the protection of the child to communicate such information.
(2) A Contracting State may declare that requests under paragraph 1 shall be communicated to its authorities only through its Central Authority.

Article 35

(1) The competent authorities of a Contracting State may request the authorities of another Contracting State to assist in the implementation of measures of protection taken under this Convention, especially in securing the effective exercise of rights of access as well as of the right to maintain direct contacts on a regular basis.
(2) The authorities of a Contracting State in which the child does not habitually reside may, on the request of a parent residing in that State who is seeking to obtain or to maintain access to the child, gather information or evidence and may make a finding on the suitability of that parent to exercise access and on the conditions under which access is to be exercised. An authority exercising jurisdiction under Articles 5 to 10 to determine an application concerning access to the child, shall admit and consider such information, evidence and finding before reaching its decision.
(3) An authority having jurisdiction under Articles 5 to 10 to decide on access may adjourn a proceeding pending the outcome of a request made under paragraph 2,

in particular, when it is considering an application to restrict or terminate access rights granted in the State of the child's former habitual residence.

(4) Nothing in this Article shall prevent an authority having jurisdiction under Articles 5 to 10 from taking provisional measures pending the outcome of the request made under paragraph 2.

Article 36

In any case where the child is exposed to a serious danger, the competent authorities of the Contracting State where measures for the protection of the child have been taken or are under consideration, if they are informed that the child's residence has changed to, or that the child is present in another State, shall inform the authorities of that other State about the danger involved and the measures taken or under consideration.

Article 37

An authority shall not request or transmit any information under this Chapter if to do so would, in its opinion, be likely to place the child's person or property in danger, or constitute a serious threat to the liberty or life of a member of the child's family.

Article 38

(1) Without prejudice to the possibility of imposing reasonable charges for the provision of services, Central Authorities and other public authorities of Contracting States shall bear their own costs in applying the provisions of this Chapter.

(2) Any Contracting State may enter into agreements with one or more other Contracting States concerning the allocation of charges.

Article 39

Any Contracting State may enter into agreements with one or more other Contracting States with a view to improving the application of this Chapter in their mutual relations. The States which have concluded such an agreement shall transmit a copy to the depositary of the Convention.

Chapter VI – General Provisions

Article 40

(1) The authorities of the Contracting State of the child's habitual residence, or of the Contracting State where a measure of protection has been taken, may deliver to the person having parental responsibility or to the person entrusted with protection of the child's person or property, at his or her request, a certificate indicating the capacity in which that person is entitled to act and the powers conferred upon him or her.

(2) The capacity and powers indicated in the certificate are presumed to be vested in that person, in the absence of proof to the contrary.

(3) Each Contracting State shall designate the authorities competent to draw up the certificate.

Article 41

Personal data gathered or transmitted under the Convention shall be used only for the purposes for which they were gathered or transmitted.

Article 42

The authorities to whom information is transmitted shall ensure its confidentiality, in accordance with the law of their State.

Article 43

All documents forwarded or delivered under this Convention shall be exempt from legalisation or any analogous formality.

Article 44

Each Contracting State may designate the authorities to which requests under Articles 8, 9 and 33 are to be addressed.

Article 45

(1) The designations referred to in Articles 29 and 44 shall be communicated to the Permanent Bureau of the Hague Conference on Private International Law.

(2) The declaration referred to in Article 34, paragraph 2, shall be made to the depositary of the Convention.

Article 46

A Contracting State in which different systems of law or sets of rules of law apply to the protection of the child and his or her property shall not be bound to apply the rules of the Convention to conflicts solely between such different systems or sets of rules of law.

Article 47

In relation to a State in which two or more systems of law or sets of rules of law with regard to any matter dealt with in this Convention apply in different territorial units -

(1) any reference to habitual residence in that State shall be construed as referring to habitual residence in a territorial unit;

(2) any reference to the presence of the child in that State shall be construed as referring to presence in a territorial unit;

(3) any reference to the location of property of the child in that State shall be construed as referring to location of property of the child in a territorial unit;

(4) any reference to the State of which the child is a national shall be construed as referring to the territorial unit designated by the law of that State or, in the absence of relevant rules, to the territorial unit with which the child has the closest connection;

(5) any reference to the State whose authorities are seised of an application for divorce or legal separation of the child's parents, or for annulment of their marriage, shall be construed as referring to the territorial unit whose authorities are seised of such application;

(6) any reference to the State with which the child has a substantial connection shall be construed as referring to the territorial unit with which the child has such connection;

(7) any reference to the State to which the child has been removed or in which he or she has been retained shall be construed as referring to the relevant territorial unit to which the child has been removed or in which he or she has been retained;

(8) any reference to bodies or authorities of that State, other than Central Authorities, shall be construed as referring to those authorised to act in the relevant territorial unit;

(9) any reference to the law or procedure or authority of the State in which a measure has been taken shall be construed as referring to the law or procedure or authority of the territorial unit in which such measure was taken;

(10) any reference to the law or procedure or authority of the requested State shall be construed as referring to the law or procedure or authority of the territorial unit in which recognition or enforcement is sought.

Article 48

For the purpose of identifying the applicable law under Chapter III, in relation to a State which comprises two or more territorial units each of which has its own system of law or set of rules of law in respect of matters covered by this Convention, the following rules apply -

a) if there are rules in force in such a State identifying which territorial unit's law is applicable, the law of that unit applies;

b) in the absence of such rules, the law of the relevant territorial unit as defined in Article 47 applies.

Article 49

For the purpose of identifying the applicable law under Chapter III, in relation to a State which has two or more systems of law or sets of rules of law applicable to different categories of persons in respect of matters covered by this Convention, the following rules apply -

a) if there are rules in force in such a State identifying which among such laws applies, that law applies;

b) in the absence of such rules, the law of the system or the set of rules of law with which the child has the closest connection applies.

Article 50

This Convention shall not affect the application of the *Convention of 25 October 1980 on the Civil Aspects of International Child Abduction*, as between Parties to both Conventions. Nothing, however, precludes provisions of this Convention from being invoked for the purposes of obtaining the return of a child who has been wrongfully removed or retained or of organising access rights.

Article 51

In relations between the Contracting States this Convention replaces the *Convention of 5 October 1961 concerning the powers of authorities and the law applicable in respect of the protection of minors*, and the *Convention governing the guardianship of minors*, signed at The Hague 12 June 1902, without prejudice to the recognition of measures taken under the Convention of 5 October 1961 mentioned above.

Article 52

(1) This Convention does not affect any international instrument to which Contracting States are Parties and which contains provisions on matters governed by the Convention, unless a contrary declaration is made by the States Parties to such instrument.

(2) This Convention does not affect the possibility for one or more Contracting States to conclude agreements which contain, in respect of children habitually resident in any of the States Parties to such agreements, provisions on matters governed by this Convention.

(3) Agreements to be concluded by one or more Contracting States on matters within the scope of this Convention do not affect, in the relationship of such States with other Contracting States, the application of the provisions of this Convention.

(4) The preceding paragraphs also apply to uniform laws based on special ties of a regional or other nature between the States concerned.

Article 53

(1) The Convention shall apply to measures only if they are taken in a State after the Convention has entered into force for that State.

(2) The Convention shall apply to the recognition and enforcement of measures taken after its entry into force as between the State where the measures have been taken and the requested State.

Article 54

(1) Any communication sent to the Central Authority or to another authority of a Contracting State shall be in the original language, and shall be accompanied by a translation into the official language or one of the official languages of the other State or, where that is not feasible, a translation into French or English.

(2) However, a Contracting State may, by making a reservation in accordance with Article 60, object to the use of either French or English, but not both.

Article 55

(1) A Contracting State may, in accordance with Article 60,

a) reserve the jurisdiction of its authorities to take measures directed to the protection of property of a child situated on its territory;

b) reserve the right not to recognise any parental responsibility or measure in so far as it is incompatible with any measure taken by its authorities in relation to that property.

(2) The reservation may be restricted to certain categories of property.

Article 56

The Secretary General of the Hague Conference on Private International Law shall at regular intervals convoke a Special Commission in order to review the practical operation of the Convention.

Chapter VII – Final Clauses

Article 57

(1) The Convention shall be open for signature by the States which were Members of the Hague Conference on Private International Law at the time of its Eighteenth Session.

(2) It shall be ratified, accepted or approved and the instruments of ratification, acceptance or approval shall be deposited with the Ministry of Foreign Affairs of the Kingdom of the Netherlands, depositary of the Convention.

Article 58

(1) Any other State may accede to the Convention after it has entered into force in accordance with Article 61, paragraph 1.

(2) The instrument of accession shall be deposited with the depositary.

(3) Such accession shall have effect only as regards the relations between the acceding State and those Contracting States which have not raised an objection to its accession in the six months after the receipt of the notification referred to in sub-paragraph *b* of Article 63. Such an objection may also be raised by States at the time when they ratify, accept or approve the Convention after an accession. Any such objection shall be notified to the depositary.

Article 59

(1) If a State has two or more territorial units in which different systems of law are applicable in relation to matters dealt with in this Convention, it may at the time of signature, ratification, acceptance, approval or accession declare that the Convention shall extend to all its territorial units or only to one or more of them and may modify this declaration by submitting another declaration at any time.

(2) Any such declaration shall be notified to the depositary and shall state expressly the territorial units to which the Convention applies.

(3) If a State makes no declaration under this Article, the Convention is to extend to all territorial units of that State.

Article 60

(1) Any State may, not later than the time of ratification, acceptance, approval or accession, or at the time of making a declaration in terms of Article 59, make one or both of the reservations provided for in Articles 54, paragraph 2, and 55. No other reservation shall be permitted.

(2) Any State may at any time withdraw a reservation it has made. The withdrawal shall be notified to the depositary.

(3) The reservation shall cease to have effect on the first day of the third calendar month after the notification referred to in the preceding paragraph.

Article 61

(1) The Convention shall enter into force on the first day of the month following the expiration of three months after the deposit of the third instrument of ratification, acceptance or approval referred to in Article 57.

(2) Thereafter the Convention shall enter into force -

a) for each State ratifying, accepting or approving it subsequently, on the first day of the month following the expiration of three months after the deposit of its instrument of ratification, acceptance, approval or accession;

b) for each State acceding, on the first day of the month following the expiration of three months after the expiration of the period of six months provided in Article 58, paragraph 3;

c) for a territorial unit to which the Convention has been extended in conformity with Article 59, on the first day of the month following the expiration of three months after the notification referred to in that Article.

Article 62

(1) A State Party to the Convention may denounce it by a notification in writing addressed to the depositary. The denunciation may be limited to certain territorial units to which the Convention applies.

(2) The denunciation takes effect on the first day of the month following the expiration of twelve months after the notification is received by the depositary. Where a longer period for the denunciation to take effect is specified in the notification, the denunciation takes effect upon the expiration of such longer period.

Article 63

The depositary shall notify the States Members of the Hague Conference on Private International Law and the States which have acceded in accordance with Article 58 of the following -

a) the signatures, ratifications, acceptances and approvals referred to in Article 57;
b) the accessions and objections raised to accessions referred to in Article 58;
c) the date on which the Convention enters into force in accordance with Article 61;
d) the declarations referred to in Articles 34, paragraph 2, and 59;
e) the agreements referred to in Article 39;
f) the reservations referred to in Articles 54, paragraph 2, and 55 and the withdrawals referred to in Article 60, paragraph 2;
g) the denunciations referred to in Article 62.

In witness whereof the undersigned, being duly authorised thereto, have signed this Convention.

Done at The Hague, on the 19th day of October 1996, in the English and French languages, both texts being equally authentic, in a single copy which shall be deposited in the archives of the Government of the Kingdom of the Netherlands, and of which a certified copy shall be sent, through diplomatic channels, to each of the States Members of the Hague Conference on Private International Law at the date of its Eighteenth Session.

(2) Council Regulation (EC) No 2201/2003

of 27 November 2003

concerning jurisdiction and the recognition and enforcement of judgments in matrimonial matters and the matters of parental responsibility, repealing Regulation (EC) No 1347/2000

THE COUNCIL OF THE EUROPEAN UNION,

Having regard to the Treaty establishing the European Community, and in particular Article 61(*c*) and Article 67(1) thereof,

Having regard to the proposal from the Commission,

Having regard to the opinion of the European Parliament,

Having regard to the opinion of the European Economic and Social Committee,

Whereas:

(1) The European Community has set the objective of creating an area of freedom, security and justice, in which the free movement of persons is ensured. To this end, the Community is to adopt, among others, measures in the field of judicial cooperation in civil matters that are necessary for the proper functioning of the internal market.

(2) The Tampere European Council endorsed the principle of mutual recognition of judicial decisions as the cornerstone for the creation of a genuine judicial area, and identified visiting rights as a priority.

(3) Council Regulation (EC) No 1347/2000 sets out rules on jurisdiction, recognition and enforcement of judgments in matrimonial matters and matters of parental responsibility for the children of both spouses rendered on the occasion of the

matrimonial proceedings. The content of this Regulation was substantially taken over from the Convention of 28 May 1998 on the same subject matter.

(4) On 3 July 2000 France presented an initiative for a Council Regulation on the mutual enforcement of judgments on rights of access to children.

(5) In order to ensure equality for all children, this Regulation covers all decisions on parental responsibility, including measures for the protection of the child, independently of any link with a matrimonial proceeding.

(6) Since the application of the rules on parental responsibility often arises in the context of matrimonial proceedings, it is more appropriate to have a single instrument for matters of divorce and parental responsibility.

(7) The scope of this Regulation covers civil matters, whatever the nature of the court or tribunal.

(8) As regards judgments on divorce, legal separation or marriage annulment, this Regulation should apply only to the dissolution of matrimonial ties and should not deal with issues such as the grounds for divorce, property consequences of the marriage or any other ancillary measures.

(9) As regards the property of the child, this Regulation should apply only to measures for the protection of the child, i.e. (i) the designation and functions of a person or body having charge of the child's property, representing or assisting the child, and (ii) the administration, conservation or disposal of the child's property. In this context, this Regulation should, for instance, apply in cases where the parents are in dispute as regards the administration of the child's property. Measures relating to the child's property which do not concern the protection of the child should continue to be governed by Council Regulation (EC) No 44/2001 of 22 December 2000 on jurisdiction and the recognition and enforcement of judgments in civil and commercial matters.

(10) This Regulation is not intended to apply to matters relating to social security, public measures of a general nature in matters of education or health or to decisions on the right of asylum and on immigration. In addition it does not apply to the establishment of parenthood, since this is a different matter from the attribution of parental responsibility, nor to other questions linked to the status of persons. Moreover, it does not apply to measures taken as a result of criminal offences committed by children.

(11) Maintenance obligations are excluded from the scope of this Regulation as these are already covered by Council Regulation No 44/2001. The courts having jurisdiction under this Regulation will generally have jurisdiction to rule on maintenance obligations by application of Article 5(2) of Council Regulation No 44/2001.

(12) The grounds of jurisdiction in matters of parental responsibility established in the present Regulation are shaped in the light of the best interests of the child, in particular on the criterion of proximity. This means that jurisdiction should lie in the first place with the Member State of the child's habitual residence, except for certain cases of a change in the child's residence or pursuant to an agreement between the holders of parental responsibility.

(13) In the interest of the child, this Regulation allows, by way of exception and under certain conditions, that the court having jurisdiction may transfer a case to a court of another Member State if this court is better placed to hear the case. However, in this case the second court should not be allowed to transfer the case to a third court.

(14) This Regulation should have effect without prejudice to the application of public international law concerning diplomatic immunities. Where jurisdiction under this Regulation cannot be exercised by reason of the existence of diplomatic immunity in accordance with international law, jurisdiction should

be exercised in accordance with national law in a Member State in which the person concerned does not enjoy such immunity.

(15) Council Regulation (EC) No 1348/2000 of 29 May 2000 on the service in the Member States of judicial and extrajudicial documents in civil or commercial matters should apply to the service of documents in proceedings instituted pursuant to this Regulation.

(16) This Regulation should not prevent the courts of a Member State from taking provisional, including protective measures, in urgent cases, with regard to persons or property situated in that State.

(17) In cases of wrongful removal or retention of a child, the return of the child should be obtained without delay, and to this end the Hague Convention of 25 October 1980 would continue to apply as complemented by the provisions of this Regulation, in particular Article 11. The courts of the Member State to or in which the child has been wrongfully removed or retained should be able to oppose his or her return in specific, duly justified cases. However, such a decision could be replaced by a subsequent decision by the court of the Member State of habitual residence of the child prior to the wrongful removal or retention. Should that judgment entail the return of the child, the return should take place without any special procedure being required for recognition and enforcement of that judgment in the Member State to or in which the child has been removed or retained.

(18) Where a court has decided not to return a child on the basis of Article 13 of the 1980 Hague Convention, it should inform the court having jurisdiction or central authority in the Member State where the child was habitually resident prior to the wrongful removal or retention. Unless the court in the latter Member State has been seised, this court or the central authority should notify the parties. This obligation should not prevent the central authority from also notifying the relevant public authorities in accordance with national law.

(19) The hearing of the child plays an important role in the application of this Regulation, although this instrument is not intended to modify national procedures applicable.

(20) The hearing of a child in another Member State may take place under the arrangements laid down in Council Regulation (EC) No 1206/2001 of 28 May 2001 on cooperation between the courts of the Member States in the taking of evidence in civil or commercial matters.

(21) The recognition and enforcement of judgments given in a Member State should be based on the principle of mutual trust and the grounds for non-recognition should be kept to the minimum required.

(22) Authentic instruments and agreements between parties that are enforceable in one Member State should be treated as equivalent to "judgments" for the purpose of the application of the rules on recognition and enforcement.

(23) The Tampere European Council considered in its conclusions (point 34) that judgments in the field of family litigation should be "automatically recognised throughout the Union without any intermediate proceedings or grounds for refusal of enforcement". This is why judgments on rights of access and judgments on return that have been certified in the Member State of origin in accordance with the provisions of this Regulation should be recognised and enforceable in all other Member States without any further procedure being required. Arrangements for the enforcement of such judgments continue to be governed by national law.

(24) The certificate issued to facilitate enforcement of the judgment should not be subject to appeal. It should be rectified only where there is a material error, i.e. where it does not correctly reflect the judgment.

(25) Central authorities should cooperate both in general matter and in specific cases, including for purposes of promoting the amicable resolution of family disputes, in matters of parental responsibility. To this end central authorities shall participate in the European Judicial Network in civil and commercial matters created by Council Decision 2001/470/EC of 28 May 2001 establishing a European Judicial Network in civil and commercial matters.

(26) The Commission should make publicly available and update the lists of courts and redress procedures communicated by the Member States.

(27) The measures necessary for the implementation of this Regulation should be adopted in accordance with Council Decision 1999/468/EC of 28 June 1999 laying down the procedures for the exercise of implementing powers conferred on the Commission.

(28) This Regulation replaces Regulation (EC) No 1347/2000 which is consequently repealed.

(29) For the proper functioning of this Regulation, the Commission should review its application and propose such amendments as may appear necessary.

(30) The United Kingdom and Ireland, in accordance with Article 3 of the Protocol on the position of the United Kingdom and Ireland annexed to the Treaty on European Union and the Treaty establishing the European Community, have given notice of their wish to take part in the adoption and application of this Regulation.

(31) Denmark, in accordance with Articles 1 and 2 of the Protocol on the position of Denmark annexed to the Treaty on European Union and the Treaty establishing the European Community, is not participating in the adoption of this Regulation and is therefore not bound by it nor subject to its application.

(32) Since the objectives of this Regulation cannot be sufficiently achieved by the Member States and can therefore be better achieved at Community level, the Community may adopt measures, in accordance with the principle of subsidiarity as set out in Article 5 of the Treaty. In accordance with the principle of proportionality, as set out in that Article, this Regulation does not go beyond what is necessary in order to achieve those objectives.

(33) This Regulation recognises the fundamental rights and observes the principles of the Charter of Fundamental Rights of the European Union. In particular, it seeks to ensure respect for the fundamental rights of the child as set out in Article 24 of the Charter of Fundamental Rights of the European Union,

HAS ADOPTED THE PRESENT REGULATION:

Chapter I
Scope and Definitions

Article 1
Scope

1 This Regulation shall apply, whatever the nature of the court or tribunal, in civil matters relating to:

(a) divorce, legal separation or marriage annulment;

(b) the attribution, exercise, delegation, restriction or termination of parental responsibility.

2 The matters referred to in paragraph 1(b) may, in particular, deal with:

(a) rights of custody and rights of access;

(b) guardianship, curatorship and similar institutions;

(c) the designation and functions of any person or body having charge of the child's person or property, representing or assisting the child;
(d) the placement of the child in a foster family or in institutional care;
(e) measures for the protection of the child relating to the administration, conservation or disposal of the child's property.

3 This Regulation shall not apply to:

(a) the establishment or contesting of a parent-child relationship;
(b) decisions on adoption, measures preparatory to adoption, or the annulment or revocation of adoption;
(c) the name and forenames of the child;
(d) emancipation;
(e) maintenance obligations;
(f) trusts or succession;
(g) measures taken as a result of criminal offences committed by children.

Article 2
Definitions

For the purposes of this Regulation:

1 the term "court" shall cover all the authorities in the Member States with jurisdiction in the matters falling within the scope of this Regulation pursuant to Article 1;
2 the term "judge" shall mean the judge or an official having powers equivalent to those of a judge in the matters falling within the scope of the Regulation;
3 the term "Member State" shall mean all Member States with the exception of Denmark;
4 the term "judgment" shall mean a divorce, legal separation or marriage annulment, as well as a judgment relating to parental responsibility, pronounced by a court of a Member State, whatever the judgment may be called, including a decree, order or decision;
5 the term "Member State of origin" shall mean the Member State where the judgment to be enforced was issued;
6 the term "Member State of enforcement" shall mean the Member State where enforcement of the judgment is sought;
7 the term "parental responsibility" shall mean all rights and duties relating to the person or the property of a child which are given to a natural or legal person by judgment, by operation of law or by an agreement having legal effect. The term shall include rights of custody and rights of access;
8 the term "holder of parental responsibility" shall mean any person having parental responsibility over a child;
9 the term "rights of custody" shall include rights and duties relating to the care of the person of a child, and in particular the right to determine the child's place of residence;
10 the term "rights of access" shall include in particular the right to take a child to a place other than his or her habitual residence for a limited period of time;
11 the term "wrongful removal or retention" shall mean a child's removal or retention where:

(a) it is in breach of rights of custody acquired by judgment or by operation of law or by an agreement having legal effect under the law of the Member State where the child was habitually resident immediately before the removal or retention; and

(b) provided that, at the time of removal or retention, the rights of custody were actually exercised, either jointly or alone, or would have been so exercised but for the removal or retention. Custody shall be considered to be exercised jointly when, pursuant to a judgment or by operation of law, one holder of parental responsibility cannot decide on the child's place of residence without the consent of another holder of parental responsibility.

Chapter II
Jurisdiction

Section 1
Divorce, legal separation and marriage annulment

Article 3
General jurisdiction

1 In matters relating to divorce, legal separation or marriage annulment, jurisdiction shall lie with the courts of the Member State

(a) in whose territory:

- the spouses are habitually resident, or
- the spouses were last habitually resident, insofar as one of them still resides there, or
- the respondent is habitually resident, or
- in the event of a joint application, either of the spouses is habitually resident, or
- the applicant is habitually resident if he or she resided there for at least a year immediately before the application was made, or
- the applicant is habitually resident if he or she resided there for at least six months immediately before the application was made and is either a national of the Member State in question or, in the case of the United Kingdom and Ireland, has his or her "domicile" there;

(b) of the nationality of both spouses or, in the case of the United Kingdom and Ireland, of the "domicile" of both spouses.

2 For the purpose of this Regulation, "domicile" shall have the same meaning as it has under the legal systems of the United Kingdom and Ireland.

Article 4
Counterclaim

The court in which proceedings are pending on the basis of Article 3 shall also have jurisdiction to examine a counterclaim, insofar as the latter comes within the scope of this Regulation.

Article 5
Conversion of legal separation into divorce

Without prejudice to Article 3, a court of a Member State that has given a judgment on a legal separation shall also have jurisdiction for converting that judgment into a divorce, if the law of that Member State so provides.

Article 6
Exclusive nature of jurisdiction under Articles 3, 4 and 5

A spouse who:

(a) is habitually resident in the territory of a Member State; or
(b) is a national of a Member State, or, in the case of the United Kingdom and Ireland, has his or her "domicile" in the territory of one of the latter Member States,

may be sued in another Member State only in accordance with Articles 3, 4 and 5.

Article 7
Residual jurisdiction

1 Where no court of a Member State has jurisdiction pursuant to Articles 3, 4 and 5, jurisdiction shall be determined, in each Member State, by the laws of that State.

2 As against a respondent who is not habitually resident and is not either a national of a Member State or, in the case of the United Kingdom and Ireland, does not have his "domicile" within the territory of one of the latter Member States, any national of a Member State who is habitually resident within the territory of another Member State may, like the nationals of that State, avail himself of the rules of jurisdiction applicable in that State.

Section 2
Parental responsibility

Article 8
General jurisdiction

1 The courts of a Member State shall have jurisdiction in matters of parental responsibility over a child who is habitually resident in that Member State at the time the court is seised.

2 Paragraph 1 shall be subject to the provisions of Articles 9, 10 and 12.

Article 9
Continuing jurisdiction of the child's former habitual residence

1 Where a child moves lawfully from one Member State to another and acquires a new habitual residence there, the courts of the Member State of the child's former habitual residence shall, by way of exception to Article 8, retain jurisdiction during a three-month period following the move for the purpose of modifying a judgment on access rights issued in that Member State before the child moved, where the holder of access rights pursuant to the judgment on access rights continues to have his or her habitual residence in the Member State of the child's former habitual residence.

2 Paragraph 1 shall not apply if the holder of access rights referred to in paragraph 1 has accepted the jurisdiction of the courts of the Member State of the child's new habitual residence by participating in proceedings before those courts without contesting their jurisdiction.

Article 10
Jurisdiction in cases of child abduction

In case of wrongful removal or retention of the child, the courts of the Member State where the child was habitually resident immediately before the wrongful removal or retention shall retain their jurisdiction until the child has acquired a habitual residence in another Member State and:

(a) each person, institution or other body having rights of custody has acquiesced in the removal or retention; or

(b) the child has resided in that other Member State for a period of at least one year after the person, institution or other body having rights of custody has had or should have had knowledge of the whereabouts of the child and the child is settled in his or her new environment and at least one of the following conditions is met:

 (i) within one year after the holder of rights of custody has had or should have had knowledge of the whereabouts of the child, no request for return has been lodged before the competent authorities of the Member State where the child has been removed or is being retained;

 (ii) a request for return lodged by the holder of rights of custody has been withdrawn and no new request has been lodged within the time limit set in paragraph (i);

 (iii) a case before the court in the Member State where the child was habitually resident immediately before the wrongful removal or retention has been closed pursuant to Article 11(7);

 (iv) a judgment on custody that does not entail the return of the child has been issued by the courts of the Member State where the child was habitually resident immediately before the wrongful removal or retention.

Article 11

Return of the child

1 Where a person, institution or other body having rights of custody applies to the competent authorities in a Member State to deliver a judgment on the basis of the Hague Convention of 25 October 1980 on the Civil Aspects of International Child Abduction (hereinafter "the 1980 Hague Convention"), in order to obtain the return of a child that has been wrongfully removed or retained in a Member State other than the Member State where the child was habitually resident immediately before the wrongful removal or retention, paragraphs 2 to 8 shall apply.

2 When applying Articles 12 and 13 of the 1980 Hague Convention, it shall be ensured that the child is given the opportunity to be heard during the proceedings unless this appears inappropriate having regard to his or her age or degree of maturity.

3 A court to which an application for return of a child is made as mentioned in paragraph 1 shall act expeditiously in proceedings on the application, using the most expeditious procedures available in national law.

Without prejudice to the first subparagraph, the court shall, except where exceptional circumstances make this impossible, issue its judgment no later than six weeks after the application is lodged.

4 A court cannot refuse to return a child on the basis of Article 13b of the 1980 Hague Convention if it is established that adequate arrangements have been made to secure the protection of the child after his or her return.

5 A court cannot refuse to return a child unless the person who requested the return of the child has been given an opportunity to be heard.

6 If a court has issued an order on non-return pursuant to Article 13 of the 1980 Hague Convention, the court must immediately either directly or through its central authority, transmit a copy of the court order on non-return and of the

relevant documents, in particular a transcript of the hearings before the court, to the court with jurisdiction or central authority in the Member State where the child was habitually resident immediately before the wrongful removal or retention, as determined by national law. The court shall receive all the mentioned documents within one month of the date of the non-return order.

7 Unless the courts in the Member State where the child was habitually resident immediately before the wrongful removal or retention have already been seised by one of the parties, the court or central authority that receives the information mentioned in paragraph 6 must notify it to the parties and invite them to make submissions to the court, in accordance with national law, within three months of the date of notification so that the court can examine the question of custody of the child.

Without prejudice to the rules on jurisdiction contained in this Regulation, the court shall close the case if no submissions have been received by the court within the time limit.

8 Notwithstanding a judgment of non-return pursuant to Article 13 of the 1980 Hague Convention, any subsequent judgment which requires the return of the child issued by a court having jurisdiction under this Regulation shall be enforceable in accordance with Section 4 of Chapter III below in order to secure the return of the child.

Article 12

Prorogation of jurisdiction

1 The courts of a Member State exercising jurisdiction by virtue of Article 3 on an application for divorce, legal separation or marriage annulment shall have jurisdiction in any matter relating to parental responsibility connected with that application where:

(a) at least one of the spouses has parental responsibility in relation to the child; and

(b) the jurisdiction of the courts has been accepted expressly or otherwise in an unequivocal manner by the spouses and by the holders of parental responsibility, at the time the court is seised, and is in the superior interests of the child.

2 The jurisdiction conferred in paragraph 1 shall cease as soon as:

(a) the judgment allowing or refusing the application for divorce, legal separation or marriage annulment has become final;

(b) in those cases where proceedings in relation to parental responsibility are still pending on the date referred to in (a), a judgment in these proceedings has become final;

(c) the proceedings referred to in (a) and (b) have come to an end for another reason.

3 The courts of a Member State shall also have jurisdiction in relation to parental responsibility in proceedings other than those referred to in paragraph 1 where:

(a) the child has a substantial connection with that Member State, in particular by virtue of the fact that one of the holders of parental responsibility is habitually resident in that Member State or that the child is a national of that Member State; and

(b) the jurisdiction of the courts has been accepted expressly or otherwise in an unequivocal manner by all the parties to the proceedings at the time the court is seised and is in the best interests of the child.

4 Where the child has his or her habitual residence in the territory of a third State which is not a contracting party to the Hague Convention of 19 October 1996 on jurisdiction, applicable law, recognition, enforcement and cooperation in respect of parental responsibility and measures for the protection of children, jurisdiction under this Article shall be deemed to be in the child's interest, in particular if it is found impossible to hold proceedings in the third State in question.

Article 13

Jurisdiction based on the child's presence

1 Where a child's habitual residence cannot be established and jurisdiction cannot be determined on the basis of Article 12, the courts of the Member State where the child is present shall have jurisdiction.

2 Paragraph 1 shall also apply to refugee children or children internationally displaced because of disturbances occurring in their country.

Article 14

Residual jurisdiction

Where no court of a Member State has jurisdiction pursuant to Articles 8 to 13, jurisdiction shall be determined, in each Member State, by the laws of that State.

Article 15

Transfer to a court better placed to hear the case

1 By way of exception, the courts of a Member State having jurisdiction as to the substance of the matter may, if they consider that a court of another Member State, with which the child has a particular connection, would be better placed to hear the case, or a specific part thereof, and where this is in the best interests of the child:

(a) stay the case or the part thereof in question and invite the parties to introduce a request before the court of that other Member State in accordance with paragraph 4; or
(b) request a court of another Member State to assume jurisdiction in accordance with paragraph 5.

2 Paragraph 1 shall apply:

(a) upon application from a party; or
(b) of the court's own motion; or
(c) upon application from a court of another Member State with which the child has a particular connection, in accordance with paragraph 3.

A transfer made of the court's own motion or by application of a court of another Member State must be accepted by at least one of the parties.

3 The child shall be considered to have a particular connection to a Member State as mentioned in paragraph 1, if that Member State:

(a) has become the habitual residence of the child after the court referred to in paragraph 1 was seised; or
(b) is the former habitual residence of the child; or
(c) is the place of the child's nationality; or
(d) is the habitual residence of a holder of parental responsibility; or
(e) is the place where property of the child is located and the case concerns measures for the protection of the child relating to the administration, conservation or disposal of this property.

4 The court of the Member State having jurisdiction as to the substance of the matter shall set a time limit by which the courts of that other Member State shall be seised in accordance with paragraph 1.

If the courts are not seised by that time, the court which has been seised shall continue to exercise jurisdiction in accordance with Articles 8 to 14.

5 The courts of that other Member State may, where due to the specific circumstances of the case, this is in the best interests of the child, accept jurisdiction within six weeks of their seisure in accordance with paragraph 1(*a*) or 1(*b*). In this case, the court first seised shall decline jurisdiction. Otherwise, the court first seised shall continue to exercise jurisdiction in accordance with Articles 8 to 14.

6 The courts shall cooperate for the purposes of this Article, either directly or through the central authorities designated pursuant to Article 53.

Section 3
Common provisions

Article 16
Seising of a Court

1 A court shall be deemed to be seised:

(a) at the time when the document instituting the proceedings or an equivalent document is lodged with the court, provided that the applicant has not subsequently failed to take the steps he was required to take to have service effected on the respondent; or

(b) if the document has to be served before being lodged with the court, at the time when it is received by the authority responsible for service, provided that the applicant has not subsequently failed to take the steps he was required to take to have the document lodged with the court.

Article 17
Examination as to jurisdiction

Where a court of a Member State is seised of a case over which it has no jurisdiction under this Regulation and over which a court of another Member State has jurisdiction by virtue of this Regulation, it shall declare of its own motion that it has no jurisdiction.

Article 18
Examination as to admissibility

1 Where a respondent habitually resident in a State other than the Member State where the action was brought does not enter an appearance, the court with jurisdiction shall stay the proceedings so long as it is not shown that the respondent has been able to receive the document instituting the proceedings or an equivalent document in sufficient time to enable him to arrange for his defence, or that all necessary steps have been taken to this end.

2 Article 19 of Regulation (EC) No 1348/2000 shall apply instead of the provisions of paragraph 1 of this Article if the document instituting the proceedings or an equivalent document had to be transmitted from one Member State to another pursuant to that Regulation.

3 Where the provisions of Regulation (EC) No 1348/2000 are not applicable, Article 15 of the Hague Convention of 15 November 1965 on the service abroad of judicial and extrajudicial documents in civil or commercial matters shall

apply if the document instituting the proceedings or an equivalent document had to be transmitted abroad pursuant to that Convention.

Article 19
Lis pendens and dependent actions

1 Where proceedings relating to divorce, legal separation or marriage annulment between the same parties are brought before courts of different Member States, the court second seised shall of its own motion stay its proceedings until such time as the jurisdiction of the court first seised is established.

2 Where proceedings relating to parental responsibility relating to the same child and involving the same cause of action are brought before courts of different Member States, the court second seised shall of its own motion stay its proceedings until such time as the jurisdiction of the court first seised is established.

3 Where the jurisdiction of the court first seised is established, the court second seised shall decline jurisdiction in favour of that court.

In that case, the party who brought the relevant action before the court second seised may bring that action before the court first seised.

Article 20
Provisional, including protective, measures

1 In urgent cases, the provisions of this Regulation shall not prevent the courts of a Member State from taking such provisional, including protective, measures in respect of persons or assets in that State as may be available under the law of that Member State, even if, under this Regulation, the court of another Member State has jurisdiction as to the substance of the matter.

2 The measures referred to in paragraph 1 shall cease to apply when the court of the Member State having jurisdiction under this Regulation as to the substance of the matter has taken the measures it considers appropriate.

Chapter III
Recognition and Enforcement

Section 1
Recognition

Article 21
Recognition of a judgment

1 A judgment given in a Member State shall be recognised in the other Member States without any special procedure being required.

2 In particular, and without prejudice to paragraph 3, no special procedure shall be required for updating the civil-status records of a Member State on the basis of a judgment relating to divorce, legal separation or marriage annulment given in another Member State, and against which no further appeal lies under the law of that Member State.

3 Without prejudice to Section 4 of this Chapter, any interested party may, in accordance with the procedures provided for in Section 2 of this Chapter, apply for a decision that the judgment be or not be recognised.

The local jurisdiction of the court appearing in the list notified by each Member State to the Commission pursuant to Article 68 shall be determined by the internal law of the Member State in which proceedings for recognition or non-recognition are brought.

4 Where the recognition of a judgment is raised as an incidental question in a court of a Member State, that court may determine that issue.

Article 22
Grounds of non-recognition for judgments relating to divorce, legal separation or marriage annulment

A judgment relating to a divorce, legal separation or marriage annulment shall not be recognised:

(a) if such recognition is manifestly contrary to the public policy of the Member State in which recognition is sought;
(b) where it was given in default of appearance, if the respondent was not served with the document which instituted the proceedings or with an equivalent document in sufficient time and in such a way as to enable the respondent to arrange for his or her defence unless it is determined that the respondent has accepted the judgment unequivocally;
(c) if it is irreconcilable with a judgment given in proceedings between the same parties in the Member State in which recognition is sought; or
(d) if it is irreconcilable with an earlier judgment given in another Member State or in a non-Member State between the same parties, provided that the earlier judgment fulfils the conditions necessary for its recognition in the Member State in which recognition is sought.

Article 23
Grounds of non-recognition for judgments relating to parental responsibility

A judgment relating to parental responsibility shall not be recognised:

(a) if such recognition is manifestly contrary to the public policy of the Member State in which recognition is sought taking into account the best interests of the child;
(b) if it was given, except in case of urgency, without the child having been given an opportunity to be heard, in violation of fundamental principles of procedure of the Member State in which recognition is sought;
(c) where it was given in default of appearance if the person in default was not served with the document which instituted the proceedings or with an equivalent document in sufficient time and in such a way as to enable that person to arrange for his or her defence unless it is determined that such person has accepted the judgment unequivocally;
(d) on the request of any person claiming that the judgment infringes his or her parental responsibility, if it was given without such person having been given an opportunity to be heard;
(e) if it is irreconcilable with a later judgment relating to parental responsibility given in the Member State in which recognition is sought;
(f) if it is irreconcilable with a later judgment relating to parental responsibility given in another Member State or in the non-Member State of the habitual residence of the child provided that the later judgment fulfils the conditions necessary for its recognition in the Member State in which recognition is sought; or
(g) if the procedure laid down in Article 56 has not been complied with.

Article 24
Prohibition of review of jurisdiction of the court of origin

The jurisdiction of the court of the Member State of origin may not be reviewed. The test of public policy referred to in Articles 22(*a*) and 23(*a*) may not be applied to the rules relating to jurisdiction set out in Articles 3 to 14.

Article 25
Differences in applicable law

The recognition of a judgment may not be refused because the law of the Member State in which such recognition is sought would not allow divorce, legal separation or marriage annulment on the same facts.

Article 26
Non-review as to substance

Under no circumstances may a judgment be reviewed as to its substance.

Article 27
Stay of proceedings

1 A court of a Member State in which recognition is sought of a judgment given in another Member State may stay the proceedings if an ordinary appeal against the judgment has been lodged.

2 A court of a Member State in which recognition is sought of a judgment given in Ireland or the United Kingdom may stay the proceedings if enforcement is suspended in the Member State of origin by reason of an appeal.

Section 2
Application for a declaration of enforceability

Article 28
Enforceable judgments

1 A judgment on the exercise of parental responsibility in respect of a child given in a Member State which is enforceable in that Member State and has been served shall be enforced in another Member State when, on the application of any interested party, it has been declared enforceable there.

2 However, in the United Kingdom, such a judgment shall be enforced in England and Wales, in Scotland or in Northern Ireland only when, on the application of any interested party, it has been registered for enforcement in that part of the United Kingdom.

Article 29
Jurisdiction of local courts

1 An application for a declaration of enforceability shall be submitted to the court appearing in the list notified by each Member State to the Commission pursuant to Article 68.

2 The local jurisdiction shall be determined by reference to the place of habitual residence of the person against whom enforcement is sought or by reference to the habitual residence of any child to whom the application relates.

Where neither of the places referred to in the first subparagraph can be found in the Member State of enforcement, the local jurisdiction shall be determined by reference to the place of enforcement.

Article 30
Procedure

1 The procedure for making the application shall be governed by the law of the Member State of enforcement.
2 The applicant must give an address for service within the area of jurisdiction of the court applied to. However, if the law of the Member State of enforcement does not provide for the furnishing of such an address, the applicant shall appoint a representative ad litem.
3 The documents referred to in Articles 37 and 39 shall be attached to the application.

Article 31
Decision of the court

1 The court applied to shall give its decision without delay. Neither the person against whom enforcement is sought, nor the child shall, at this stage of the proceedings, be entitled to make any submissions on the application.
2 The application may be refused only for one of the reasons specified in Articles 22, 23 and 24.

Article 32
Notice of the decision

The appropriate officer of the court shall without delay bring to the notice of the applicant the decision given on the application in accordance with the procedure laid down by the law of the Member State of enforcement.

Article 33
Appeal against the decision

1 The decision on the application for a declaration of enforceability may be appealed against by either party.
2 The appeal shall be lodged with the court appearing in the list notified by each Member State to the Commission pursuant to Article 68.
3 The appeal shall be dealt with in accordance with the rules governing procedure in contradictory matters.
4 If the appeal is brought by the applicant for a declaration of enforceability, the party against whom enforcement is sought shall be summoned to appear before the appellate court. If such person fails to appear, the provisions of Article 18 shall apply.
5 An appeal against a declaration of enforceability must be lodged within one month of service thereof. If the party against whom enforcement is sought is habitually resident in a Member State other than that in which the declaration of enforceability was given, the time for appealing shall be two months and shall run from the date of service, either on him or at his residence. No extension of time may be granted on account of distance.

Article 34
Courts of appeal and means of contest

The judgment given on appeal may be contested only by the proceedings referred to in the list notified by each Member State to the Commission pursuant to Article 68.

Article 35
Stay of proceedings

1 The court with which the appeal is lodged under Articles 33 or 34 may, on the application of the party against whom enforcement is sought, stay the proceedings if an ordinary appeal has been lodged in the Member State of origin, or if the time for such appeal has not yet expired. In the latter case, the court may specify the time within which an appeal is to be lodged.

2 Where the judgment was given in Ireland or the United Kingdom, any form of appeal available in the Member State of origin shall be treated as an ordinary appeal for the purposes of paragraph 1.

Article 36
Partial enforcement

1 Where a judgment has been given in respect of several matters and enforcement cannot be authorised for all of them, the court shall authorise enforcement for one or more of them.

2 An applicant may request partial enforcement of a judgment.

Section 3
Provisions common to Sections 1 and 2

Article 37
Documents

1 A party seeking or contesting recognition or applying for a declaration of enforceability shall produce:

(a) a copy of the judgment which satisfies the conditions necessary to establish its authenticity; and

(b) the certificate referred to in Article 39.

2 In addition, in the case of a judgment given in default, the party seeking recognition or applying for a declaration of enforceability shall produce:

(a) the original or certified true copy of the document which establishes that the defaulting party was served with the document instituting the proceedings or with an equivalent document; or

(b) any document indicating that the defendant has accepted the judgment unequivocally.

Article 38
Absence of documents

1 If the documents specified in Article 37(1)(*b*) or (2) are not produced, the court may specify a time for their production, accept equivalent documents or, if it considers that it has sufficient information before it, dispense with their production.

2 If the court so requires, a translation of such documents shall be furnished. The translation shall be certified by a person qualified to do so in one of the Member States.

Article 39

Certificate concerning judgments in matrimonial matters and certificate concerning judgments on parental responsibility

The competent court or authority of a Member State of origin shall, at the request of any interested party, issue a certificate using the standard form set out in Annex I (judgments in matrimonial matters) or in Annex II (judgments on parental responsibility).

Section 4

Enforceability of certain judgments concerning rights of access and of certain judgments which require the return of the child

Article 40

Scope

1 This Section shall apply to:

(a) rights of access; and

(b) the return of a child entailed by a judgment given pursuant to Article 11(8).

2 The provisions of this Section shall not prevent a holder of parental responsibility from seeking recognition and enforcement of a judgment in accordance with the provisions in Sections 1 and 2 of this Chapter.

Article 41

Rights of access

1 The rights of access referred to in Article 40(1)(*a*) granted in an enforceable judgment given in a Member State shall be recognised and enforceable in another Member State without the need for a declaration of enforceability and without any possibility of opposing its recognition if the judgment has been certified in the Member State of origin in accordance with paragraph 2.

Even if national law does not provide for enforceability by operation of law of a judgment granting access rights, the court of origin may declare that the judgment shall be enforceable, notwithstanding any appeal.

2 The judge of origin shall issue the certificate referred to in paragraph 1 using the standard form in Annex III (certificate concerning rights of access) only if:

(a) where the judgment was given in default, the person defaulting was served with the document which instituted the proceedings or with an equivalent document in sufficient time and in such a way as to enable that person to arrange for his or her defense, or, the person has been served with the document but not in compliance with these conditions, it is nevertheless established that he or she accepted the decision unequivocally;

(b) all parties concerned were given an opportunity to be heard; and

(c) the child was given an opportunity to be heard, unless a hearing was considered inappropriate having regard to his or her age or degree of maturity.

The certificate shall be completed in the language of the judgment.

3 Where the rights of access involve a cross-border situation at the time of the delivery of the judgment, the certificate shall be issued ex officio when the judgment becomes enforceable, even if only provisionally. If the situation subsequently acquires a cross-border character, the certificate shall be issued at the request of one of the parties.

Article 42
Return of the child

1 The return of a child referred to in Article 40(1)(*b*) entailed by an enforceable judgment given in a Member State shall be recognised and enforceable in another Member State without the need for a declaration of enforceability and without any possibility of opposing its recognition if the judgment has been certified in the Member State of origin in accordance with paragraph 2.

Even if national law does not provide for enforceability by operation of law, notwithstanding any appeal, of a judgment requiring the return of the child mentioned in Article 11(*b*)(8), the court of origin may declare the judgment enforceable.

2 The judge of origin who delivered the judgment referred to in Article 40(1)(*b*) shall issue the certificate referred to in paragraph 1 only if:

(a) the child was given an opportunity to be heard, unless a hearing was considered inappropriate having regard to his or her age or degree of maturity;
(b) the parties were given an opportunity to be heard; and
(c) the court has taken into account in issuing its judgment the reasons for and evidence underlying the order issued pursuant to Article 13 of the 1980 Hague Convention.

In the event that the court or any other authority takes measures to ensure the protection of the child after its return to the State of habitual residence, the certificate shall contain details of such measures.

The judge of origin shall of his or her own motion issue that certificate using the standard form in Annex IV (certificate concerning return of the child(ren)).

The certificate shall be completed in the language of the judgment.

Article 43
Rectification of the certificate

1 The law of the Member State of origin shall be applicable to any rectification of the certificate.

2 No appeal shall lie against the issuing of a certificate pursuant to Articles 41(1) or 42(1).

Article 44
Effects of the certificate

The certificate shall take effect only within the limits of the enforceability of the judgment.

Article 45
Documents

1 A party seeking enforcement of a judgment shall produce:

(a) a copy of the judgment which satisfies the conditions necessary to establish its authenticity; and
(b) the certificate referred to in Article 41(1) or Article 42(1).

2 For the purposes of this Article,

– the certificate referred to in Article 41(1) shall be accompanied by a translation of point 12 relating to the arrangements for exercising right of access,

– the certificate referred to in Article 42(1) shall be accompanied by a translation of its point 14 relating to the arrangements for implementing the measures taken to ensure the child's return.

The translation shall be into the official language or one of the official languages of the Member State of enforcement or any other language that the Member State of enforcement expressly accepts. The translation shall be certified by a person qualified to do so in one of the Member States.

Section 5
Authentic instruments and agreements

Article 46

Documents which have been formally drawn up or registered as authentic instruments and are enforceable in one Member State and also agreements between the parties that are enforceable in the Member State in which they were concluded shall be recognised and declared enforceable under the same conditions as judgments.

Section 6
Other provisions

Article 47
Enforcement procedure

1 The enforcement procedure is governed by the law of the Member State of enforcement.

2 Any judgment delivered by a court of another Member State and declared to be enforceable in accordance with Section 2 or certified in accordance with Article 41(1) or Article 42(1) shall be enforced in the Member State of enforcement in the same conditions as if it had been delivered in that Member State.

In particular, a judgment which has been certified according to Article 41(1) or Article 42(1) cannot be enforced if it is irreconcilable with a subsequent enforceable judgment.

Article 48
Practical arrangements for the exercise of rights of access

1 The courts of the Member State of enforcement may make practical arrangements for organising the exercise of rights of access, if the necessary arrangements have not or have not sufficiently been made in the judgment delivered by the courts of the Member State having jurisdiction as to the substance of the matter and provided the essential elements of this judgment are respected.

2 The practical arrangements made pursuant to paragraph 1 shall cease to apply pursuant to a later judgment by the courts of the Member State having jurisdiction as to the substance of the matter.

Article 49
Costs

The provisions of this Chapter, with the exception of Section 4, shall also apply to the determination of the amount of costs and expenses of proceedings under this Regulation and to the enforcement of any order concerning such costs and expenses.

Article 50
Legal aid

An applicant who, in the Member State of origin, has benefited from complete or partial legal aid or exemption from costs or expenses shall be entitled, in the procedures provided for in Articles 21, 28, 41, 42 and 48 to benefit from the most favourable legal aid or the most extensive exemption from costs and expenses provided for by the law of the Member State of enforcement.

Article 51
Security, bond or deposit

No security, bond or deposit, however described, shall be required of a party who in one Member State applies for enforcement of a judgment given in another Member State on the following grounds:

(a) that he or she is not habitually resident in the Member State in which enforcement is sought; or
(b) that he or she is either a foreign national or, where enforcement is sought in either the United Kingdom or Ireland, does not have his or her "domicile" in either of those Member States.

Article 52
Legalisation or other similar formality

No legalisation or other similar formality shall be required in respect of the documents referred to in Articles 37, 38 and 45 or in respect of a document appointing a representative ad litem.

Chapter IV
Cooperation between Central Authorities in Matters of Parental Responsibility

Article 53
Designation

Each Member State shall designate one or more central authorities to assist with the application of this Regulation and shall specify the geographical or functional jurisdiction of each. Where a Member State has designated more than one central authority, communications shall normally be sent direct to the relevant central authority with jurisdiction. Where a communication is sent to a central authority without jurisdiction, the latter shall be responsible for forwarding it to the central authority with jurisdiction and informing the sender accordingly.

Article 54
General functions

The central authorities shall communicate information on national laws and procedures and take measures to improve the application of this Regulation and strengthening their cooperation. For this purpose the European Judicial Network in civil and commercial matters created by Decision No 2001/470/EC shall be used.

Article 55
Cooperation on cases specific to parental responsibility

The central authorities shall, upon request from a central authority of another Member State or from a holder of parental responsibility, cooperate on specific cases to achieve the purposes of this Regulation. To this end, they shall, acting directly or through public authorities or other bodies, take all appropriate steps in accordance with the law of that Member State in matters of personal data protection to:

(a) collect and exchange information:
   (i) on the situation of the child;
   (ii) on any procedures under way; or
   (iii) on decisions taken concerning the child;
(b) provide information and assistance to holders of parental responsibility seeking the recognition and enforcement of decisions on their territory, in particular concerning rights of access and the return of the child;
(c) facilitate communications between courts, in particular for the application of Article 11(6) and (7) and Article 15;
(d) provide such information and assistance as is needed by courts to apply Article 56; and
(e) facilitate agreement between holders of parental responsibility through mediation or other means, and facilitate cross-border cooperation to this end.

Article 56
Placement of a child in another Member State

1 Where a court having jurisdiction under Articles 8 to 15 contemplates the placement of a child in institutional care or with a foster family and where such placement is to take place in another Member State, it shall first consult the central authority or other authority having jurisdiction in the latter State where public authority intervention in that Member State is required for domestic cases of child placement.
2 The judgment on placement referred to in paragraph 1 may be made in the requesting State only if the competent authority of the requested State has consented to the placement.
3 The procedures for consultation or consent referred to in paragraphs 1 and 2 shall be governed by the national law of the requested State.
4 Where the authority having jurisdiction under Articles 8 to 15 decides to place the child in a foster family, and where such placement is to take place in another Member State and where no public authority intervention is required in the latter Member State for domestic cases of child placement, it shall so inform the central authority or other authority having jurisdiction in the latter State.

Article 57
Working method

1 Any holder of parental responsibility may submit, to the central authority of the Member State of his or her habitual residence or to the central authority of the Member State where the child is habitually resident or present, a request for assistance as mentioned in Article 55. In general, the request shall include all available information of relevance to its enforcement. Where the request for assistance concerns the recognition or enforcement of a judgment on parental responsibility that falls within the scope of this Regulation, the holder of parental responsibility shall attach the relevant certificates provided for in Articles 39, 41(1) or 42(1).
2 Member States shall communicate to the Commission the official language or languages of the Community institutions other than their own in which communications to the central authorities can be accepted.

3 The assistance provided by the central authorities pursuant to Article 55 shall be free of charge.

4 Each central authority shall bear its own costs.

Article 58

Meetings

1 In order to facilitate the application of this Regulation, central authorities shall meet regularly.

2 These meetings shall be convened in compliance with Decision No 2001/470/EC establishing a European Judicial Network in civil and commercial matters.

Chapter V
Relations with Other Instruments

Article 59

Relation with other instruments

1 Subject to the provisions of Articles 60, 63, 64 and paragraph 2 of this Article, this Regulation shall, for the Member States, supersede conventions existing at the time of entry into force of this Regulation which have been concluded between two or more Member States and relate to matters governed by this Regulation.

2

(a) Finland and Sweden shall have the option of declaring that the Convention of 6 February 1931 between Denmark, Finland, Iceland, Norway and Sweden comprising international private law provisions on marriage, adoption and guardianship, together with the Final Protocol thereto, will apply, in whole or in part, in their mutual relations, in place of the rules of this Regulation. Such declarations shall be annexed to this Regulation and published in the Official Journal of the European Union. They may be withdrawn, in whole or in part, at any moment by the said Member States.

(b) The principle of non-discrimination on the grounds of nationality between citizens of the Union shall be respected.

(c) The rules of jurisdiction in any future agreement to be concluded between the Member States referred to in subparagraph (a) which relate to matters governed by this Regulation shall be in line with those laid down in this Regulation.

(d) Judgments handed down in any of the Nordic States which have made the declaration provided for in subparagraph (a) under a forum of jurisdiction corresponding to one of those laid down in Chapter II of this Regulation, shall be recognised and enforced in the other Member States under the rules laid down in Chapter III of this Regulation.

3 Member States shall send to the Commission:

(a) a copy of the agreements and uniform laws implementing these agreements referred to in paragraph 2(a) and (c);

(b) any denunciations of, or amendments to, those agreements or uniform laws.

Article 60
Relations with certain multilateral conventions

In relations between Member States, this Regulation shall take precedence over the following Conventions in so far as they concern matters governed by this Regulation:

(a) the Hague Convention of 5 October 1961 concerning the Powers of Authorities and the Law Applicable in respect of the Protection of Minors;
(b) the Luxembourg Convention of 8 September 1967 on the Recognition of Decisions Relating to the Validity of Marriages;
(c) the Hague Convention of 1 June 1970 on the Recognition of Divorces and Legal Separations;
(d) the European Convention of 20 May 1980 on Recognition and Enforcement of Decisions concerning Custody of Children and on Restoration of Custody of Children; and
(e) the Hague Convention of 25 October 1980 on the Civil Aspects of International Child Abduction.

Article 61

Relation with the Hague Convention of 19 October 1996 on Jurisdiction, Applicable law, Recognition, Enforcement and Cooperation in Respect of Parental Responsibility and Measures for the Protection of Children.

As concerns the relation with the Hague Convention of 19 October 1996 on Jurisdiction, Applicable law, Recognition, Enforcement and Cooperation in Respect of Parental Responsibility and Measures for the Protection of Children, this Regulation shall apply:

(a) where the child concerned has his or her habitual residence on the territory of a Member State;
(b) as concerns the recognition and enforcement of a judgment given in a court of a Member State on the territory of another Member State, even if the child concerned has his or her habitual residence on the territory of a third State which is a contracting Party to the said Convention.

Article 62
Scope of effects

1 The agreements and conventions referred to in Articles 59(1), 60 and 61 shall continue to have effect in relation to matters not governed by this Regulation.
2 The conventions mentioned in Article 60, in particular the 1980 Hague Convention, continue to produce effects between the Member States which are party thereto, in compliance with Article 60.

Article 63
Treaties with the Holy See

1 This Regulation shall apply without prejudice to the International Treaty (Concordat) between the Holy See and Portugal, signed at the Vatican City on 7 May 1940.
2 Any decision as to the invalidity of a marriage taken under the Treaty referred to in paragraph 1 shall be recognised in the Member States on the conditions laid down in Chapter III, Section 1.

3 The provisions laid down in paragraphs 1 and 2 shall also apply to the following international treaties (Concordats) with the Holy See:

(a) "Concordato lateranense" of 11 February 1929 between Italy and the Holy See, modified by the agreement, with additional Protocol signed in Rome on 18 February 1984;

(b) Agreement between the Holy See and Spain on legal affairs of 3 January 1979.

(c) Agreement between the Holy See and Malta on the recognition of civil effects to canonical marriages and to decisions of ecclesiastical authorities and tribunals on those marriages of 3 February 1993, including the Protocol of application of the same date, with the second Additional Protocol of 6 January 1995.

4 Recognition of the decisions provided for in paragraph 2 may, in Spain, Italy or Malta, be subject to the same procedures and the same checks as are applicable to decisions of the ecclesiastical courts handed down in accordance with the international treaties concluded with the Holy See referred to in paragraph 3.

5 Member States shall send to the Commission:

(a) a copy of the Treaties referred to in paragraphs 1 and 3;

(b) any denunciations of or amendments to those Treaties.

Chapter VI
Transitional Provisions

Article 64

1 The provisions of this Regulation shall apply only to legal proceedings instituted, to documents formally drawn up or registered as authentic instruments and to agreements concluded between the parties after its date of application in accordance with Article 72.

2 Judgments given after the date of application of this Regulation in proceedings instituted before that date but after the date of entry into force of Regulation (EC) No 1347/2000 shall be recognised and enforced in accordance with the provisions of Chapter III of this Regulation if jurisdiction was founded on rules which accorded with those provided for either in Chapter II or in Regulation (EC) No 1347/2000 or in a convention concluded between the Member State of origin and the Member State addressed which was in force when the proceedings were instituted.

3 Judgments given before the date of application of this Regulation in proceedings instituted after the entry into force of Regulation (EC) No 1347/2000 shall be recognised and enforced in accordance with the provisions of Chapter III of this Regulation provided they relate to divorce, legal separation or marriage annulment or parental responsibility for the children of both spouses on the occasion of these matrimonial proceedings.

4 Judgments given before the date of application of this Regulation but after the date of entry into force of Regulation (EC) No 1347/2000 in proceedings instituted before the date of entry into force of Regulation (EC) No 1347/2000 shall be recognised and enforced in accordance with the provisions of Chapter III of this Regulation provided they relate to divorce, legal separation or marriage annulment or parental responsibility for the children of both spouses on the occasion of these matrimonial proceedings and that jurisdiction was founded on rules which accorded with those provided for either in Chapter II of this Regulation or in Regulation (EC) No 1347/2000 or in a convention concluded

between the Member State of origin and the Member State addressed which was in force when the proceedings were instituted.

Chapter VII
Final Provisions

Article 65
Review

No later than 1 January 2012, and every five years thereafter, the Commission shall present to the European Parliament, to the Council and to the European Economic and Social Committee a report on the application of this Regulation on the basis of information supplied by the Member States. The report shall be accompanied if need be by proposals for adaptations.

Article 66
Member States with two or more legal systems
With regard to a Member State in which two or more systems of law or sets of rules concerning matters governed by this Regulation apply in different territorial units:

(a) any reference to habitual residence in that Member State shall refer to habitual residence in a territorial unit;
(b) any reference to nationality, or in the case of the United Kingdom "domicile", shall refer to the territorial unit designated by the law of that State;
(c) any reference to the authority of a Member State shall refer to the authority of a territorial unit within that State which is concerned;
(d) any reference to the rules of the requested Member State shall refer to the rules of the territorial unit in which jurisdiction, recognition or enforcement is invoked.

Article 67
Information on central authorities and languages accepted

The Member States shall communicate to the Commission within three months following the entry into force of this Regulation:

(a) the names, addresses and means of communication for the central authorities designated pursuant to Article 53;
(b) the languages accepted for communications to central authorities pursuant to Article 57(2); and
(c) the languages accepted for the certificate concerning rights of access pursuant to Article 45(2).

The Member States shall communicate to the Commission any changes to this information.

The Commission shall make this information publicly available.

Article 68
Information relating to courts and redress procedures

The Member States shall notify to the Commission the lists of courts and redress procedures referred to in Articles 21, 29, 33 and 34 and any amendments thereto.

The Commission shall update this information and make it publicly available through the publication in the Official Journal of the European Union and any other appropriate means.

Article 69
Amendments to the Annexes

Any amendments to the standard forms in Annexes I to IV shall be adopted in accordance with the consultative procedure set out in Article 70(2).

Article 70
Committee

1 The Commission shall be assisted by a committee (committee).
2 Where reference is made to this paragraph, Articles 3 and 7 of Decision 1999/468/EC shall apply.
3 The committee shall adopt its rules of procedure.

Article 71
Repeal of Regulation (EC) No 1347/2000

1 Regulation (EC) No 1347/2000 shall be repealed as from the date of application of this Regulation.
2 Any reference to Regulation (EC) No 1347/2000 shall be construed as a reference to this Regulation according to the comparative table in Annex V.

Article 72
Entry into force

This Regulation shall enter into force on 1 August 2004.

The Regulation shall apply from 1 March 2005, with the exception of Articles 67, 68, 69 and 70, which shall apply from 1 August 2004.

This Regulation shall be binding in its entirety and directly applicable in the Member States in accordance with the Treaty establishing the European Community.

Done at Brussels, 27 November 2003.

For the Council

The President

R. CASTELLI

Annex I

Certificate Referred to in Article 39 Concerning Judgments in Matrimonial Matters[1]

1 Member State of origin
2 Court or authority issuing the certificate
  2.1 Name
  2.2 Address
  2.3 Tel./fax/e-mail
3 Marriage
  3.1 Wife
    3.1.1 Full name
    3.1.2 Address
    3.1.3 Country and place of birth
    3.1.4 Date of birth

3.2 Husband

3.2.1 Full name
3.2.2 Address
3.2.3 Country and place of birth
3.2.4 Date of birth

3.3 Country, place (where available) and date of marriage

3.3.1 Country of marriage
3.3.2 Place of marriage (where available)
3.3.3 Date of marriage

4 Court which delivered the judgment

4.1 Name of Court
4.2 Place of Court

5 Judgment

5.1 Date
5.2 Reference number
5.3 Type of judgment

5.3.1 Divorce
5.3.2 Marriage annulment
5.3.3 Legal separation

5.4 Was the judgment given in default of appearance?

5.4.1 No
5.4.2 Yes[2]

6 Names of parties to whom legal aid has been granted

7 Is the judgment subject to further appeal under the law of the Member State of origin?

7.1 No
7.2 Yes

8 Date of legal effect in the Member State where the judgment was given

8.1 Divorce
8.2 Legal separation

Done at …, date …

Signature and/or stamp

1 Council Regulation (EC) No 2201/2003 of 27 November 2003 concerning jurisdiction and the recognition and enforcement of judgments in matrimonial matters and the matters of parental responsibility, repealing Regulation (EC) No 1347/2000.

2 Documents referred to in Article 37(2) must be attached.

Annex II

Certificate Referred to in Article 39 Concerning Judgments on Parental Responsibility[1]

1 Member State of origin

2 Court or authority issuing the certificate

2.1 Name
2.2 Address
2.3 Tel./Fax/e-mail

3 Person(s) with rights of access

3.1 Full name
3.2 Address
3.3 Date and place of birth (where available)

4 Holders of parental responsibility other than those mentioned under 3[2]

4.1

4.1.1 Full name
4.1.2 Address
4.1.3 Date and place of birth (where available)

4.2

4.2.1 Full Name
4.2.2 Address
4.2.3 Date and place of birth (where available)

4.3

4.3.1 Full name
4.3.2 Address
4.3.3 Date and place of birth (where available)

5 Court which delivered the judgment

5.1 Name of Court
5.2 Place of Court

6 Judgment

6.1 Date
6.2 Reference number
6.3 Was the judgment given in default of appearance?

6.3.1 No
6.3.2 Yes[3]

7 Children who are covered by the judgment[4]

7.1 Full name and date of birth
7.2 Full name and date of birth
7.3 Full name and date of birth
7.4 Full name and date of birth

8 Names of parties to whom legal aid has been granted

9 Attestation of enforceability and service

9.1 Is the judgment enforceable according to the law of the Member State of origin?

9.1.1 Yes
9.1.2 No

9.2 Has the judgment been served on the party against whom enforcement is sought?

9.2.1 Yes

9.2.1.1 Full name of the party
9.2.1.2 Address
9.2.1.3 Date of service

9.2.2 No

10 Specific information on judgments on rights of access where "exequatur" is requested under Article 28. This possibility is foreseen in Article 40(2).

10.1 Practical arrangements for exercise of rights of access (to the extent stated in the judgment)

10.1.1 Date and time

10.1.1.1 Start
10.1.1.2 End

10.1.2 Place
10.1.3 Specific obligations on holders of parental responsibility
10.1.4 Specific obligations on the person with right of access
10.1.5 Any restrictions attached to the exercise of rights of access

11 Specific information for judgments on the return of the child in cases where the "exequatur" procedure is requested under Article 28. This possibility is foreseen under Article 40(2).

11.1 The judgment entails the return of the child
11.2 Person to whom the child is to be returned (to the extent stated in the judgment)

11.2.1 Full name
11.2.2 Address

Done at …, date ….

Signature and/or stamp

1 Council Regulation (EC) No 2201/2003 of 27 November 2003 concerning jurisdiction and the recognition and enforcement of judgments in matrimonial matters and the matters of parental responsibility, repealing Regulation (EC) No 1347/2000.
2 In cases of joint custody, a person already mentioned under item 3 may also be mentioned under item 4.
3 Documents referred to in Article 37(2) must be attached.
4 If more than four children are covered, use a second form.

Annex III

Certificate Referred to in Article 41(1) Concerning Judgments on Rights of Access[1]

1 Member State of origin
2 Court or authority issuing the certificate

2.1 Name
2.2 Address
2.3 Tel./fax/e-mail

3 Person(s) with rights of access

3.1 Full name
3.2 Address
3.3 Date and place of birth (where available)

4 Holders of parental responsibility other than those mentioned under 3[2,3]

4.1

4.1.1 Full name
4.1.2 Address
4.1.3 Date and place of birth (where available)

4.2

4.2.1 Full name
4.2.2 Address
4.2.3 Date and place of birth (where available)

4.3 Other

4.3.1 Full name
4.3.2 Address
4.3.3 Date and place of birth (where available)

5 Court which delivered the judgment

5.1 Name of Court
5.2 Place of Court

6 Judgment

6.1 Date
6.2 Reference number

7 Children who are covered by the judgment[4]

7.1 Full name and date of birth
7.2 Full name and date of birth
7.3 Full name and date of birth
7.4 Full name and date of birth

8 Is the judgment enforceable in the Member State of origin?

8.1 Yes
8.2 No

9 Where the judgment was given in default of appearance, the person defaulting was served with the document which instituted the proceedings or with an equivalent document in sufficient time and in such a way as to enable that person to arrange for his or her defence, or the person has been served with the document but not in compliance with these conditions, it is nevertheless established that he or she accepted the decision unequivocally

10 All parties concerned were given an opportunity to be heard

11 The children were given an opportunity to be heard, unless a hearing was considered inappropriate having regard to their age or degree of maturity

12 Practical arrangements for exercise of rights of access (to the extent stated in the judgment)

12.1 Date and time

12.1.1 Start
12.1.2 End

12.2 Place
12.3 Specific obligations on holders of parental responsibility
12.4 Specific obligations on the person with right of access
12.5 Any restrictions attached to the exercise of rights of access

13 Names of parties to whom legal aid has been granted

Done at …, date ….

Signature and/or stamp

1 Council Regulation (EC) No 2201/2003 of 27 November 2003 concerning jurisdiction and the recognition and enforcement of judgments in matrimonial matters and the matters of parental responsibility, repealing Regulation (EC) No 1347/2000.
2 In cases of joint custody, a person already mentioned under item 3 may also be mentioned in item 4.
3 Please put a cross in the box corresponding to the person against whom the judgment should be enforced.
4 If more than four children are concerned, use a second form.

Annex IV

Certificate Referred to in Article 42(1) Concerning the Return of the Child[1]

1 Member State of origin

2 Court or authority issuing the certificate

2.1 Name

2.2 Address

2.3 Tel./fax/e-mail

3 Person to whom the child has to be returned (to the extent stated in the judgment)

3.1 Full name

3.2 Address

3.3 Date and place of birth (where available)

4 Holders of parental responsibility[2]

4.1 Mother

4.1.1 Full name

4.1.2 Address (where available)

4.1.3 Date and place of birth (where available)

4.2 Father

4.2.1 Full name

4.2.2 Address (where available)

4.2.3 Date and place of birth (where available)

4.3 Other

4.3.1 Full name

4.3.2 Address (where available)

4.3.3 Date and place of birth (where available)

5 Respondent (where available)

5.1 Full name

5.2 Address (where available)

6 Court which delivered the judgment

6.1 Name of Court

6.2 Place of Court

7 Judgment

7.1 Date

7.2 Reference number

8 Children who are covered by the judgment[3]

8.1 Full name and date of birth

8.2 Full name and date of birth

8.3 Full name and date of birth

8.4 Full name and date of birth

9 The judgment entails the return of the child

10 Is the judgment enforceable in the Member State of origin?

10.1 Yes

10.2 No

11 The children were given an opportunity to be heard, unless a hearing was considered inappropriate having regard to their age or degree of maturity

12 The parties were given an opportunity to be heard

13 The judgment entails the return of the children and the court has taken into account in issuing its judgment the reasons for and evidence underlying the decision issued pursuant to Article 13 of the Hague Convention of 25 October 1980 on the Civil Aspects of International Child Abduction

14 Where applicable, details of measures taken by courts or authorities to ensure the protection of the child after its return to the Member State of habitual residence

15 Names of parties to whom legal aid has been granted

Done at …, date ….

Signature and/or stamp

1 Council Regulation (EC) No 2201 of 27 November 2003 concerning jurisdiction and the recognition and enforcement of judgments in matrimonial matters and the matters of parental responsibility, repealing Regulation (EC) No 1347/2000.

2 This item is optional.

3 If more than four children are covered, use a second form.

Annex V

Comparative Table with Regulation (EC) No 1347/2000

Articles repealed	Corresponding Articles of new text
1	1, 2
2	3
3	12
4	
5	4
6	5
7	6
8	7
9	17
10	18
11	16, 19
12	20
13	2, 49, 46
14	21
15	22, 23
16	
17	24
18	25
19	26
20	27
21	28
22	21, 29
23	30
24	31
25	32
26	33

Articles repealed	Corresponding Articles of new text
27	34
28	35
29	36
30	50
31	51
32	37
33	39
34	38
35	52
36	59
37	60, 61
38	62
39	
40	63
41	66
42	64
43	65
44	68, 69
45	70
46	72
Annex I	68
Annex II	68
Annex III	68
Annex IV	Annex I
Annex V	Annex II

Annex VI
Declarations by Sweden and Finland pursuant to Article 59(2)(a) of the Council Regulation concerning jurisdiction and the recognition and enforcement of judgments in matrimonial matters and matters of parental responsibility, repealing Regulation (EC) No 1347/2000

Declaration by Sweden:

Pursuant to Article 59(2)(*a*) of the Council Regulation concerning jurisdiction and the recognition and enforcement of judgments in matrimonial matters and matters of parental responsibility, repealing Regulation (EC) No 1347/2000, Sweden hereby declares that the Convention of 6 February 1931 between Denmark, Finland, Iceland, Norway and Sweden comprising international private law provisions on marriage, adoption and guardianship, together with the Final Protocol thereto, will apply in full in relations between Sweden and Finland, in place of the rules of the Regulation.

Declaration by Finland:

Pursuant to Article 59(2)(*a*) of the Council Regulation concerning jurisdiction and the recognition and enforcement of judgments in matrimonial matters and matters of parental responsibility, repealing Regulation (EC) No 1347/2000, Finland hereby declares that the Convention of 6 February 1931 between Finland, Denmark, Iceland, Norway and Sweden comprising international private law provisions on marriage, adoption and guardianship, together with the Final Protocol thereto, will apply in full in relations between Finland and Sweden, in place of the rules of the Regulation.

Date:

Signature and/or stamp:

(3) Convention on the International Recovery of Child Support and Other Forms of Family Maintenance

(*Concluded 23 November 2007*)

The States signatory to the present Convention,

Desiring to improve co-operation among States for the international recovery of child support and other forms of family maintenance,

Aware of the need for procedures which produce results and are accessible, prompt, efficient, cost-effective, responsive and fair,

Wishing to build upon the best features of existing Hague Conventions and other international instruments, in particular the United Nations Convention on the Recovery Abroad of Maintenance of 20 June 1956,

Seeking to take advantage of advances in technologies and to create a flexible system which can continue to evolve as needs change and further advances in technology create new opportunities, Recalling that, in accordance with Articles 3 and 27 of the United Nations Convention on the Rights of the Child of 20 November 1989,

- in all actions concerning children the best interests of the child shall be a primary consideration,
- every child has a right to a standard of living adequate for the child's physical, mental, spiritual, moral and social development,
- the parent(s) or others responsible for the child have the primary responsibility to secure, within their abilities and financial capacities, the conditions of living necessary for the child's development, and
- States Parties should take all appropriate measures, including the conclusion of international agreements, to secure the recovery of maintenance for the child from the parent(s) or other responsible persons, in particular where such persons live in a State different from that of the child,

Have resolved to conclude this Convention and have agreed upon the following provisions –

Chapter I – Object, Scope and Definitions

Article 1 Object

The object of the present Convention is to ensure the effective international recovery of child support and other forms of family maintenance, in particular by –

a) establishing a comprehensive system of co-operation between the authorities of the Contracting States;

b) making available applications for the establishment of maintenance decisions;
c) providing for the recognition and enforcement of maintenance decisions; and
d) requiring effective measures for the prompt enforcement of maintenance decisions.

Article 2 Scope

(1) This Convention shall apply –
 a) to maintenance obligations arising from a parent-child relationship towards a person under the age of 21 years;
 b) to recognition and enforcement or enforcement of a decision for spousal support when the application is made with a claim within the scope of sub-paragraph a); and
 c) with the exception of Chapters II and III, to spousal support.

(2) Any Contracting State may reserve, in accordance with Article 62, the right to limit the application of the Convention under sub-paragraph 1 a), to persons who have not attained the age of 18 years. A Contracting State which makes this reservation shall not be entitled to claim the application of the Convention to persons of the age excluded by its reservation.

(3) Any Contracting State may declare in accordance with Article 63 that it will extend the application of the whole or any part of the Convention to any maintenance obligation arising from a family relationship, parentage, marriage or affinity, including in particular obligations in respect of vulnerable persons. Any such declaration shall give rise to obligations between two Contracting States only in so far as their declarations cover the same maintenance obligations and parts of the Convention.

(4) The provisions of this Convention shall apply to children regardless of the marital status of the parents.

Article 3 Definitions

For the purposes of this Convention –

a) "creditor" means an individual to whom maintenance is owed or is alleged to be owed;
b) "debtor" means an individual who owes or who is alleged to owe maintenance;
c) "legal assistance" means the assistance necessary to enable applicants to know and assert their rights and to ensure that applications are fully and effectively dealt with in the requested State. The means of providing such assistance may include as necessary legal advice, assistance in bringing a case before an authority, legal representation and exemption from costs of proceedings;
d) "agreement in writing" means an agreement recorded in any medium, the information contained in which is accessible so as to be usable for subsequent reference;
e) "maintenance arrangement" means an agreement in writing relating to the payment of maintenance which –
 i) has been formally drawn up or registered as an authentic instrument by a competent authority; or
 ii) has been authenticated by, or concluded, registered or filed with a competent authority, and may be the subject of review and modification by a competent authority;
f) "vulnerable person" means a person who, by reason of an impairment or insufficiency of his or her personal faculties, is not able to support him or herself.

Chapter II – Administrative Co-operation

Article 4 Designation of Central Authorities

(1) A Contracting State shall designate a Central Authority to discharge the duties that are imposed by the Convention on such an authority.

(2) Federal States, States with more than one system of law or States having autonomous territorial units shall be free to appoint more than one Central Authority and shall specify the territorial or personal extent of their functions. Where a State has appointed more than one Central Authority, it shall designate the Central Authority to which any communication may be addressed for transmission to the appropriate Central Authority within that State.

(3) The designation of the Central Authority or Central Authorities, their contact details, and where appropriate the extent of their functions as specified in paragraph 2, shall be communicated by a Contracting State to the Permanent Bureau of the Hague Conference on Private International Law at the time when the instrument of ratification or accession is deposited or when a declaration is submitted in accordance with Article 61. Contracting States shall promptly inform the Permanent Bureau of any changes.

Article 5 General functions of Central Authorities

Central Authorities shall –

a) co-operate with each other and promote co-operation amongst the competent authorities in their States to achieve the purposes of the Convention;

b) seek as far as possible solutions to difficulties which arise in the application of the Convention.

Article 6 Specific functions of Central Authorities

(1) Central Authorities shall provide assistance in relation to applications under Chapter III. In particular they shall –

  a) transmit and receive such applications;

  b) initiate or facilitate the institution of proceedings in respect of such applications.

(2) In relation to such applications they shall take all appropriate measures –

  a) where the circumstances require, to provide or facilitate the provision of legal assistance;

  b) to help locate the debtor or the creditor;

  c) to help obtain relevant information concerning the income and, if necessary, other financial circumstances of the debtor or creditor, including the location of assets;

  d) to encourage amicable solutions with a view to obtaining voluntary payment of maintenance, where suitable by use of mediation, conciliation or similar processes;

  e) to facilitate the ongoing enforcement of maintenance decisions, including any arrears;

  f) to facilitate the collection and expeditious transfer of maintenance payments;

  g) to facilitate the obtaining of documentary or other evidence;

  h) to provide assistance in establishing parentage where necessary for the recovery of maintenance;

i) to initiate or facilitate the institution of proceedings to obtain any necessary provisional measures that are territorial in nature and the purpose of which is to secure the outcome of a pending maintenance application;

j) to facilitate service of documents.

(3) The functions of the Central Authority under this Article may, to the extent permitted under the law of its State, be performed by public bodies, or other bodies subject to the supervision of the competent authorities of that State. The designation of any such public bodies or other bodies, as well as their contact details and the extent of their functions, shall be communicated by a Contracting State to the Permanent Bureau of the Hague Conference on Private International Law. Contracting States shall promptly inform the Permanent Bureau of any changes.

(4) Nothing in this Article or Article 7 shall be interpreted as imposing an obligation on a Central Authority to exercise powers that can be exercised only by judicial authorities under the law of the requested State.

Article 7 Requests for specific measures

(1) A Central Authority may make a request, supported by reasons, to another Central Authority to take appropriate specific measures under Article 6(2) b), c), g), h), i) and j) when no application under Article 10 is pending. The requested Central Authority shall take such measures as are appropriate if satisfied that they are necessary to assist a potential applicant in making an application under Article 10 or in determining whether such an application should be initiated.

(2) A Central Authority may also take specific measures on the request of another Central Authority in relation to a case having an international element concerning the recovery of maintenance pending in the requesting State.

Article 8 Central Authority costs

(1) Each Central Authority shall bear its own costs in applying this Convention.

(2) Central Authorities may not impose any charge on an applicant for the provision of their services under the Convention save for exceptional costs arising from a request for a specific measure under Article 7.

(3) The requested Central Authority may not recover the costs of the services referred to in paragraph 2 without the prior consent of the applicant to the provision of those services at such cost.

Chapter III – Applications through Central Authorities

Article 9 Application through Central Authorities

An application under this Chapter shall be made through the Central Authority of the Contracting State in which the applicant resides to the Central Authority of the requested State. For the purpose of this provision, residence excludes mere presence.

Article 10 Available applications

(1) The following categories of application shall be available to a creditor in a requesting State seeking to recover maintenance under this Convention –

a) recognition or recognition and enforcement of a decision;

b) enforcement of a decision made or recognised in the requested State;

c) establishment of a decision in the requested State where there is no existing decision, including where necessary the establishment of parentage;
d) establishment of a decision in the requested State where recognition and enforcement of a decision is not possible, or is refused, because of the lack of a basis for recognition and enforcement under Article 20, or on the grounds specified in Article 22 b) or e);
e) modification of a decision made in the requested State;
f) modification of a decision made in a State other than the requested State.

(2) The following categories of application shall be available to a debtor in a requesting State against whom there is an existing maintenance decision –

a) recognition of a decision, or an equivalent procedure leading to the suspension, or limiting the enforcement, of a previous decision in the requested State;
b) modification of a decision made in the requested State;
c) modification of a decision made in a State other than the requested State.

(3) Save as otherwise provided in this Convention, the applications in paragraphs 1 and 2 shall be determined under the law of the requested State, and applications in paragraphs 1 c) to f) and 2 b) and c) shall be subject to the jurisdictional rules applicable in the requested State.

Article 11 Application contents

(1) All applications under Article 10 shall as a minimum include –

a) a statement of the nature of the application or applications;
b) the name and contact details, including the address and date of birth of the applicant;
c) the name and, if known, address and date of birth of the respondent;
d) the name and date of birth of any person for whom maintenance is sought;
e) the grounds upon which the application is based;
f) in an application by a creditor, information concerning where the maintenance payment should be sent or electronically transmitted;
g) save in an application under Article 10(1) a) and (2) a), any information or document specified by declaration in accordance with Article 63 by the requested State;
h) the name and contact details of the person or unit from the Central Authority of the requesting State responsible for processing the application.

(2) As appropriate, and to the extent known, the application shall in addition in particular include –

a) the financial circumstances of the creditor;
b) the financial circumstances of the debtor, including the name and address of the employer of the debtor and the nature and location of the assets of the debtor;
c) any other information that may assist with the location of the respondent.

(3) The application shall be accompanied by any necessary supporting information or documentation including documentation concerning the entitlement of the applicant to free legal assistance. In the case of applications under Article 10(1) a) and (2) a), the application shall be accompanied only by the documents listed in Article 25.

(4) An application under Article 10 may be made in the form recommended and published by the Hague Conference on Private International Law.

Article 12 Transmission, receipt and processing of applications and cases through Central Authorities

(1) The Central Authority of the requesting State shall assist the applicant in ensuring that the application is accompanied by all the information and documents known by it to be necessary for consideration of the application.

(2) The Central Authority of the requesting State shall, when satisfied that the application complies with the requirements of the Convention, transmit the application on behalf of and with the consent of the applicant to the Central Authority of the requested State. The application shall be accompanied by the transmittal form set out in Annex 1. The Central Authority of the requesting State shall, when requested by the Central Authority of the requested State, provide a complete copy certified by the competent authority in the State of origin of any document specified under Articles 16(3), 25(1) a), b) and d) and (3) b) and 30(3).

(3) The requested Central Authority shall, within six weeks from the date of receipt of the application, acknowledge receipt in the form set out in Annex 2, and inform the Central Authority of the requesting State what initial steps have been or will be taken to deal with the application, and may request any further necessary documents and information. Within the same six-week period, the requested Central Authority shall provide to the requesting Central Authority the name and contact details of the person or unit responsible for responding to inquiries regarding the progress of the application.

(4) Within three months after the acknowledgement, the requested Central Authority shall inform the requesting Central Authority of the status of the application.

(5) Requesting and requested Central Authorities shall keep each other informed of –

a) the person or unit responsible for a particular case;

b) the progress of the case, and shall provide timely responses to enquiries.

(6) Central Authorities shall process a case as quickly as a proper consideration of the issues will allow.

(7) Central Authorities shall employ the most rapid and efficient means of communication at their disposal.

(8) A requested Central Authority may refuse to process an application only if it is manifest that the requirements of the Convention are not fulfilled. In such case, that Central Authority shall promptly inform the requesting Central Authority of its reasons for refusal.

(9) The requested Central Authority may not reject an application solely on the basis that additional documents or information are needed. However, the requested Central Authority may ask the requesting Central Authority to provide these additional documents or information. If the requesting Central Authority does not do so within three months or a longer period specified by the requested Central Authority, the requested Central Authority may decide that it will no longer process the application. In this case, it shall inform the requesting Central Authority of this decision.

Article 13 Means of communication

Any application made through Central Authorities of the Contracting States in accordance with this Chapter, and any document or information appended thereto or provided by a Central Authority, may not be challenged by the respondent by reason only of the medium or means of communication employed between the Central Authorities concerned.

Article 14 Effective access to procedures

(1) The requested State shall provide applicants with effective access to procedures, including enforcement and appeal procedures, arising from applications under this Chapter.

(2) To provide such effective access, the requested State shall provide free legal assistance in accordance with Articles 14 to 17 unless paragraph 3 applies.

(3) The requested State shall not be obliged to provide such free legal assistance if and to the extent that the procedures of that State enable the applicant to make the case without the need for such assistance, and the Central Authority provides such services as are necessary free of charge.

(4) Entitlements to free legal assistance shall not be less than those available in equivalent domestic cases.

(5) No security, bond or deposit, however described, shall be required to guarantee the payment of costs and expenses in proceedings under the Convention.

Article 15 Free legal assistance for child support applications

(1) The requested State shall provide free legal assistance in respect of all applications by a creditor under this Chapter concerning maintenance obligations arising from a parent-child relationship towards a person under the age of 21 years.

(2) Notwithstanding paragraph 1, the requested State may, in relation to applications other than those under Article 10(1) a) and b) and the cases covered by Article 20(4), refuse free legal assistance if it considers that, on the merits, the application or any appeal is manifestly unfounded.

Article 16 Declaration to permit use of child-centred means test

(1) Notwithstanding Article 15(1), a State may declare, in accordance with Article 63, that it will provide free legal assistance in respect of applications other than under Article 10(1) a) and b) and the cases covered by Article 20(4), subject to a test based on an assessment of the means of the child.

(2) A State shall, at the time of making such a declaration, provide information to the Permanent Bureau of the Hague Conference on Private International Law concerning the manner in which the assessment of the child's means will be carried out, including the financial criteria which would need to be met to satisfy the test.

(3) An application referred to in paragraph 1, addressed to a State which has made the declaration referred to in that paragraph, shall include a formal attestation by the applicant stating that the child's means meet the criteria referred to in paragraph 2. The requested State may only request further evidence of the child's means if it has reasonable grounds to believe that the information provided by the applicant is inaccurate.

(4) If the most favourable legal assistance provided for by the law of the requested State in respect of applications under this Chapter concerning maintenance obligations arising from a parent-child relationship towards a child is more favourable than that provided for under paragraphs 1 to 3, the most favourable legal assistance shall be provided.

Article 17 Applications not qualifying under Article 15 or Article 16

In the case of all applications under this Convention other than those under Article 15 or Article 16 – a) the provision of free legal assistance may be made subject to a means or a merits test; b) an applicant, who in the State of origin has benefited from free legal assistance, shall be entitled, in any proceedings for recognition or enforcement, to benefit, at least to the same extent, from free legal assistance as provided for by the law of the State addressed under the same circumstances.

Chapter IV – Restrictions on Bringing Proceedings

Article 18 Limit on proceedings

(1) Where a decision is made in a Contracting State where the creditor is habitually resident, proceedings to modify the decision or to make a new decision cannot be brought by the debtor in any other Contracting State as long as the creditor remains habitually resident in the State where the decision was made.

(2) Paragraph 1 shall not apply –

a) where, except in disputes relating to maintenance obligations in respect of children, there is agreement in writing between the parties to the jurisdiction of that other Contracting State;

b) where the creditor submits to the jurisdiction of that other Contracting State either expressly or by defending on the merits of the case without objecting to the jurisdiction at the first available opportunity;

c) where the competent authority in the State of origin cannot, or refuses to, exercise jurisdiction to modify the decision or make a new decision; or

d) where the decision made in the State of origin cannot be recognised or declared enforceable in the Contracting State where proceedings to modify the decision or make a new decision are contemplated.

Chapter V – Recognition and Enforcement

Article 19 Scope of the Chapter

(1) This Chapter shall apply to a decision rendered by a judicial or administrative authority in respect of a maintenance obligation. The term "decision" also includes a settlement or agreement concluded before or approved by such an authority. A decision may include automatic adjustment by indexation and a requirement to pay arrears, retroactive maintenance or interest and a determination of costs or expenses.

(2) If a decision does not relate solely to a maintenance obligation, the effect of this Chapter is limited to the parts of the decision which concern maintenance obligations.

(3) For the purpose of paragraph 1, "administrative authority" means a public body whose decisions, under the law of the State where it is established –

a) may be made the subject of an appeal to or review by a judicial authority; and

b) have a similar force and effect to a decision of a judicial authority on the same matter.

(4) This Chapter also applies to maintenance arrangements in accordance with Article 30.

(5) The provisions of this Chapter shall apply to a request for recognition and enforcement made directly to a competent authority of the State addressed in accordance with Article 37.

Article 20 Bases for recognition and enforcement

(1) A decision made in one Contracting State ("the State of origin") shall be recognised and enforced in other Contracting States if –

a) the respondent was habitually resident in the State of origin at the time proceedings were instituted;

b) the respondent has submitted to the jurisdiction either expressly or by defending on the merits of the case without objecting to the jurisdiction at the first available opportunity;
c) the creditor was habitually resident in the State of origin at the time proceedings were instituted;
d) the child for whom maintenance was ordered was habitually resident in the State of origin at the time proceedings were instituted, provided that the respondent has lived with the child in that State or has resided in that State and provided support for the child there;
e) except in disputes relating to maintenance obligations in respect of children, there has been agreement to the jurisdiction in writing by the parties; or
f) the decision was made by an authority exercising jurisdiction on a matter of personal status or parental responsibility, unless that jurisdiction was based solely on the nationality of one of the parties.

(2) A Contracting State may make a reservation, in accordance with Article 62, in respect of paragraph 1 c), e) or f).
(3) A Contracting State making a reservation under paragraph 2 shall recognise and enforce a decision if its law would in similar factual circumstances confer or would have conferred jurisdiction on its authorities to make such a decision.
(4) A Contracting State shall, if recognition of a decision is not possible as a result of a reservation under paragraph 2, and if the debtor is habitually resident in that State, take all appropriate measures to establish a decision for the benefit of the creditor. The preceding sentence shall not apply to direct requests for recognition and enforcement under Article 19(5) or to claims for support referred to in Article 2(1) b).
(5) A decision in favour of a child under the age of 18 years which cannot be recognised by virtue only of a reservation in respect of paragraph 1 c), e) or f) shall be accepted as establishing the eligibility of that child for maintenance in the State addressed.
(6) A decision shall be recognised only if it has effect in the State of origin, and shall be enforced only if it is enforceable in the State of origin.

Article 21 Severability and partial recognition and enforcement

(1) If the State addressed is unable to recognise or enforce the whole of the decision, it shall recognise or enforce any severable part of the decision which can be so recognised or enforced.
(2) Partial recognition or enforcement of a decision can always be applied for.

Article 22 Grounds for refusing recognition and enforcement

Recognition and enforcement of a decision may be refused if –

a) recognition and enforcement of the decision is manifestly incompatible with the public policy ("ordre public") of the State addressed;
b) the decision was obtained by fraud in connection with a matter of procedure;
c) proceedings between the same parties and having the same purpose are pending before an authority of the State addressed and those proceedings were the first to be instituted;
d) the decision is incompatible with a decision rendered between the same parties and having the same purpose, either in the State addressed or in another State, provided that this latter decision fulfils the conditions necessary for its recognition and enforcement in the State addressed;

e) in a case where the respondent has neither appeared nor was represented in proceedings in the State of origin –
   i) when the law of the State of origin provides for notice of proceedings, the respondent did not have proper notice of the proceedings and an opportunity to be heard; or
   ii) when the law of the State of origin does not provide for notice of the proceedings, the respondent did not have proper notice of the decision and an opportunity to challenge or appeal it on fact and law; or

f) the decision was made in violation of Article 18.

Article 23 Procedure on an application for recognition and enforcement

(1) Subject to the provisions of the Convention, the procedures for recognition and enforcement shall be governed by the law of the State addressed.

(2) Where an application for recognition and enforcement of a decision has been made through Central Authorities in accordance with Chapter III, the requested Central Authority shall promptly either –
   a) refer the application to the competent authority which shall without delay declare the decision enforceable or register the decision for enforcement; or
   b) if it is the competent authority take such steps itself.

(3) Where the request is made directly to a competent authority in the State addressed in accordance with Article 19(5), that authority shall without delay declare the decision enforceable or register the decision for enforcement.

(4) A declaration or registration may be refused only on the ground set out in Article 22 a). At this stage neither the applicant nor the respondent is entitled to make any submissions.

(5) The applicant and the respondent shall be promptly notified of the declaration or registration, made under paragraphs 2 and 3, or the refusal thereof in accordance with paragraph 4, and may bring a challenge or appeal on fact and on a point of law.

(6) A challenge or an appeal is to be lodged within 30 days of notification under paragraph 5. If the contesting party is not resident in the Contracting State in which the declaration or registration was made or refused, the challenge or appeal shall be lodged within 60 days of notification.

(7) A challenge or appeal may be founded only on the following –
   a) the grounds for refusing recognition and enforcement set out in Article 22;
   b) the bases for recognition and enforcement under Article 20;
   c) the authenticity or integrity of any document transmitted in accordance with Article 25(1) a), b) or d) or (3) b).

(8) A challenge or an appeal by a respondent may also be founded on the fulfilment of the debt to the extent that the recognition and enforcement relates to payments that fell due in the past.

(9) The applicant and the respondent shall be promptly notified of the decision following the challenge or the appeal.

(10) A further appeal, if permitted by the law of the State addressed, shall not have the effect of staying the enforcement of the decision unless there are exceptional circumstances.

(11) In taking any decision on recognition and enforcement, including any appeal, the competent authority shall act expeditiously.

Article 24 Alternative procedure on an application for recognition and enforcement

(1) Notwithstanding Article 23(2) to (11), a State may declare, in accordance with Article 63, that it will apply the procedure for recognition and enforcement set out in this Article.

(2) Where an application for recognition and enforcement of a decision has been made through Central Authorities in accordance with Chapter III, the requested Central Authority shall promptly either –

a) refer the application to the competent authority which shall decide on the application for recognition and enforcement; or

b) if it is the competent authority, take such a decision itself.

(3) A decision on recognition and enforcement shall be given by the competent authority after the respondent has been duly and promptly notified of the proceedings and both parties have been given an adequate opportunity to be heard.

(4) The competent authority may review the grounds for refusing recognition and enforcement set out in Article 22 a), c) and d) of its own motion. It may review any grounds listed in Articles 20, 22 and 23(7) c) if raised by the respondent or if concerns relating to those grounds arise from the face of the documents submitted in accordance with Article 25.

(5) A refusal of recognition and enforcement may also be founded on the fulfilment of the debt to the extent that the recognition and enforcement relates to payments that fell due in the past.

(6) Any appeal, if permitted by the law of the State addressed, shall not have the effect of staying the enforcement of the decision unless there are exceptional circumstances.

(7) In taking any decision on recognition and enforcement, including any appeal, the competent authority shall act expeditiously.

Article 25 Documents

(1) An application for recognition and enforcement under Article 23 or Article 24 shall be accompanied by the following –

a) a complete text of the decision;

b) a document stating that the decision is enforceable in the State of origin and, in the case of a decision by an administrative authority, a document stating that the requirements of Article 19(3) are met unless that State has specified in accordance with Article 57 that decisions of its administrative authorities always meet those requirements;

c) if the respondent did not appear and was not represented in the proceedings in the State of origin, a document or documents attesting, as appropriate, either that the respondent had proper notice of the proceedings and an opportunity to be heard, or that the respondent had proper notice of the decision and the opportunity to challenge or appeal it on fact and law;

d) where necessary, a document showing the amount of any arrears and the date such amount was calculated;

e) where necessary, in the case of a decision providing for automatic adjustment by indexation, a document providing the information necessary to make the appropriate calculations;

f) where necessary, documentation showing the extent to which the applicant received free legal assistance in the State of origin.

(2) Upon a challenge or appeal under Article 23(7) c) or upon request by the competent authority in the State addressed, a complete copy of the document concerned, certified by the competent authority in the State of origin, shall be provided promptly –

a) by the Central Authority of the requesting State, where the application has been made in accordance with Chapter III;

b) by the applicant, where the request has been made directly to a competent authority of the State addressed.

(3) A Contracting State may specify in accordance with Article 57 –

a) that a complete copy of the decision certified by the competent authority in the State of origin must accompany the application;

b) circumstances in which it will accept, in lieu of a complete text of the decision, an abstract or extract of the decision drawn up by the competent authority of the State of origin, which may be made in the form recommended and published by the Hague Conference on Private International Law; or

c) that it does not require a document stating that the requirements of Article 19(3) are met.

Article 26 Procedure on an application for recognition

This Chapter shall apply mutatis mutandis to an application for recognition of a decision, save that the requirement of enforceability is replaced by the requirement that the decision has effect in the State of origin.

Article 27 Findings of fact

Any competent authority of the State addressed shall be bound by the findings of fact on which the authority of the State of origin based its jurisdiction.

Article 28 No review of the merits

There shall be no review by any competent authority of the State addressed of the merits of a decision.

Article 29 Physical presence of the child or the applicant not required

The physical presence of the child or the applicant shall not be required in any proceedings in the State addressed under this Chapter.

Article 30 Maintenance arrangements

(1) A maintenance arrangement made in a Contracting State shall be entitled to recognition and enforcement as a decision under this Chapter provided that it is enforceable as a decision in the State of origin.

(2) For the purpose of Article 10(1) a) and b) and (2) a), the term "decision" includes a maintenance arrangement.

(3) An application for recognition and enforcement of a maintenance arrangement shall be accompanied by the following –

a) a complete text of the maintenance arrangement; and

b) a document stating that the particular maintenance arrangement is enforceable as a decision in the State of origin.

(4) Recognition and enforcement of a maintenance arrangement may be refused if –

a) the recognition and enforcement is manifestly incompatible with the public policy of the State addressed;

b) the maintenance arrangement was obtained by fraud or falsification;

c) the maintenance arrangement is incompatible with a decision rendered between the same parties and having the same purpose, either in the State addressed or in another State, provided that this latter decision fulfils the conditions necessary for its recognition and enforcement in the State addressed.

(5) The provisions of this Chapter, with the exception of Articles 20, 22, 23(7) and 25(1) and (3), shall apply mutatis mutandis to the recognition and enforcement of a maintenance arrangement save that –

a) a declaration or registration in accordance with Article 23(2) and (3) may be refused only on the ground set out in paragraph 4 a);

b) a challenge or appeal as referred to in Article 23(6) may be founded only on the following –

i) the grounds for refusing recognition and enforcement set out in paragraph 4;

ii) the authenticity or integrity of any document transmitted in accordance with paragraph 3;

c) as regards the procedure under Article 24(4), the competent authority may review of its own motion the ground for refusing recognition and enforcement set out in paragraph 4 a) of this Article. It may review all grounds listed in paragraph 4 of this Article and the authenticity or integrity of any document transmitted in accordance with paragraph 3 if raised by the respondent or if concerns relating to those grounds arise from the face of those documents.

(6) Proceedings for recognition and enforcement of a maintenance arrangement shall be suspended if a challenge concerning the arrangement is pending before a competent authority of a Contracting State.

(7) A State may declare, in accordance with Article 63, that applications for recognition and enforcement of a maintenance arrangement shall only be made through Central Authorities.

(8) A Contracting State may, in accordance with Article 62, reserve the right not to recognise and enforce a maintenance arrangement.

Article 31 Decisions produced by the combined effect of provisional and confirmation orders

Where a decision is produced by the combined effect of a provisional order made in one State and an order by an authority in another State ("the confirming State") confirming the provisional order –

a) each of those States shall be deemed for the purposes of this Chapter to be a State of origin;

b) the requirements of Article 22 e) shall be met if the respondent had proper notice of the proceedings in the confirming State and an opportunity to oppose the confirmation of the provisional order;

c) the requirement of Article 20(6) that a decision be enforceable in the State of origin shall be met if the decision is enforceable in the confirming State; and

d) Article 18 shall not prevent proceedings for the modification of the decision being commenced in either State.

Chapter VI – Enforcement by the State Addressed

Article 32 Enforcement under internal law

(1) Subject to the provisions of this Chapter, enforcement shall take place in accordance with the law of the State addressed.

(2) Enforcement shall be prompt.

(3) In the case of applications through Central Authorities, where a decision has been declared enforceable or registered for enforcement under Chapter V, enforcement shall proceed without the need for further action by the applicant.

(4) Effect shall be given to any rules applicable in the State of origin of the decision relating to the duration of the maintenance obligation.

(5) Any limitation on the period for which arrears may be enforced shall be determined either by the law of the State of origin of the decision or by the law of the State addressed, whichever provides for the longer limitation period.

Article 33 Non-discrimination

The State addressed shall provide at least the same range of enforcement methods for cases under the Convention as are available in domestic cases.

Article 34 Enforcement measures

(1) Contracting States shall make available in internal law effective measures to enforce decisions under this Convention.

(2) Such measures may include –

a) wage withholding;

b) garnishment from bank accounts and other sources;

c) deductions from social security payments;

d) lien on or forced sale of property;

e) tax refund withholding;

f) withholding or attachment of pension benefits;

g) credit bureau reporting;

h) denial, suspension or revocation of various licenses (for example, driving licenses);

i) the use of mediation, conciliation or similar processes to bring about voluntary compliance.

Article 35 Transfer of funds

(1) Contracting States are encouraged to promote, including by means of international agreements, the use of the most cost-effective and efficient methods available to transfer funds payable as maintenance.

(2) A Contracting State, under whose law the transfer of funds is restricted, shall accord the highest priority to the transfer of funds payable under this Convention.

Chapter VII – Public Bodies

Article 36 Public bodies as applicants

(1) For the purposes of applications for recognition and enforcement under Article 10(1) a) and b) and cases covered by Article 20(4), "creditor" includes a public body acting in place of an individual to whom maintenance is owed or one to which reimbursement is owed for benefits provided in place of maintenance.

(2) The right of a public body to act in place of an individual to whom maintenance is owed or to seek reimbursement of benefits provided to the creditor in place of maintenance shall be governed by the law to which the body is subject.

(3) A public body may seek recognition or claim enforcement of –

a) a decision rendered against a debtor on the application of a public body which claims payment of benefits provided in place of maintenance;

b) a decision rendered between a creditor and debtor to the extent of the benefits provided to the creditor in place of maintenance.

(4) The public body seeking recognition or claiming enforcement of a decision shall upon request furnish any document necessary to establish its right under paragraph 2 and that benefits have been provided to the creditor.

Chapter VIII – General Provisions

Article 37 Direct requests to competent authorities

(1) The Convention shall not exclude the possibility of recourse to such procedures as may be available under the internal law of a Contracting State allowing a person (an applicant) to seise directly a competent authority of that State in a matter governed by the Convention including, subject to Article 18, for the purpose of having a maintenance decision established or modified.

(2) Articles 14(5) and 17 b) and the provisions of Chapters V, VI, VII and this Chapter, with the exception of Articles 40(2), 42, 43(3), 44(3), 45 and 55, shall apply in relation to a request for recognition and enforcement made directly to a competent authority in a Contracting State.

(3) For the purpose of paragraph 2, Article 2(1) a) shall apply to a decision granting maintenance to a vulnerable person over the age specified in that sub-paragraph where such decision was rendered before the person reached that age and provided for maintenance beyond that age by reason of the impairment.

Article 38 Protection of personal data

Personal data gathered or transmitted under the Convention shall be used only for the purposes for which they were gathered or transmitted.

Article 39 Confidentiality

Any authority processing information shall ensure its confidentiality in accordance with the law of its State.

Article 40 Non-disclosure of information

(1) An authority shall not disclose or confirm information gathered or transmitted in application of this Convention if it determines that to do so could jeopardise the health, safety or liberty of a person.

(2) A determination to this effect made by one Central Authority shall be taken into account by another Central Authority, in particular in cases of family violence.

(3) Nothing in this Article shall impede the gathering and transmitting of information by and between authorities in so far as necessary to carry out the obligations under the Convention.

Article 41 No legalisation

No legalisation or similar formality may be required in the context of this Convention.

Article 42 Power of attorney

The Central Authority of the requested State may require a power of attorney from the applicant only if it acts on his or her behalf in judicial proceedings or before other authorities, or in order to designate a representative so to act.

Article 43 Recovery of costs

(1) Recovery of any costs incurred in the application of this Convention shall not take precedence over the recovery of maintenance.
(2) A State may recover costs from an unsuccessful party.
(3) For the purposes of an application under Article 10(1) b) to recover costs from an unsuccessful party in accordance with paragraph 2, the term "creditor" in Article 10(1) shall include a State.
(4) This Article shall be without prejudice to Article 8.

Article 44 Language requirements

(1) Any application and related documents shall be in the original language, and shall be accompanied by a translation into an official language of the requested State or another language which the requested State has indicated, by way of declaration in accordance with Article 63, it will accept, unless the competent authority of that State dispenses with translation.
(2) A Contracting State which has more than one official language and cannot, for reasons of internal law, accept for the whole of its territory documents in one of those languages shall, by declaration in accordance with Article 63, specify the language in which such documents or translations thereof shall be drawn up for submission in the specified parts of its territory.
(3) Unless otherwise agreed by the Central Authorities, any other communications between such Authorities shall be in an official language of the requested State or in either English or French. However, a Contracting State may, by making a reservation in accordance with Article 62, object to the use of either English or French.

Article 45 Means and costs of translation

(1) In the case of applications under Chapter III, the Central Authorities may agree in an individual case or generally that the translation into an official language of the requested State may be made in the requested State from the original language or from any other agreed language. If there is no agreement and it is not possible for the requesting Central Authority to comply with the requirements of Article 44(1) and (2), then the application and related documents may be transmitted with translation into English or French for further translation into an official language of the requested State.
(2) The cost of translation arising from the application of paragraph 1 shall be borne by the requesting State unless otherwise agreed by Central Authorities of the States concerned.
(3) Notwithstanding Article 8, the requesting Central Authority may charge an applicant for the costs of translation of an application and related documents, except in so far as those costs may be covered by its system of legal assistance.

Article 46 Non-unified legal systems – interpretation

(1) In relation to a State in which two or more systems of law or sets of rules of law with regard to any matter dealt with in this Convention apply in different territorial units –

a) any reference to the law or procedure of a State shall be construed as referring, where appropriate, to the law or procedure in force in the relevant territorial unit;

b) any reference to a decision established, recognised, recognised and enforced, enforced or modified in that State shall be construed as referring, where appropriate, to a decision established, recognised, recognised and enforced, enforced or modified in the relevant territorial unit;

c) any reference to a judicial or administrative authority in that State shall be construed as referring, where appropriate, to a judicial or administrative authority in the relevant territorial unit;

d) any reference to competent authorities, public bodies, and other bodies of that State, other than Central Authorities, shall be construed as referring, where appropriate, to those authorised to act in the relevant territorial unit;

e) any reference to residence or habitual residence in that State shall be construed as referring, where appropriate, to residence or habitual residence in the relevant territorial unit;

f) any reference to location of assets in that State shall be construed as referring, where appropriate, to the location of assets in the relevant territorial unit;

g) any reference to a reciprocity arrangement in force in a State shall be construed as referring, where appropriate, to a reciprocity arrangement in force in the relevant territorial unit;

h) any reference to free legal assistance in that State shall be construed as referring, where appropriate, to free legal assistance in the relevant territorial unit;

i) any reference to a maintenance arrangement made in a State shall be construed as referring, where appropriate, to a maintenance arrangement made in the relevant territorial unit;

j) any reference to recovery of costs by a State shall be construed as referring, where appropriate, to the recovery of costs by the relevant territorial unit.

(2) This Article shall not apply to a Regional Economic Integration Organisation.

Article 47 Non-unified legal systems – substantive rules

(1) A Contracting State with two or more territorial units in which different systems of law apply shall not be bound to apply this Convention to situations which involve solely such different territorial units.

(2) A competent authority in a territorial unit of a Contracting State with two or more territorial units in which different systems of law apply shall not be bound to recognise or enforce a decision from another Contracting State solely because the decision has been recognised or enforced in another territorial unit of the same Contracting State under this Convention.

(3) This Article shall not apply to a Regional Economic Integration Organisation.

Article 48 Co-ordination with prior Hague Maintenance Conventions

In relations between the Contracting States, this Convention replaces, subject to Article 56(2), the Hague Convention of 2 October 1973 on the Recognition and Enforcement of Decisions Relating to Maintenance Obligations and the Hague Convention of 15 April 1958 concerning the recognition and enforcement of decisions relating to maintenance obligations towards children in so far as their scope of application as between such States coincides with the scope of application of this Convention.

Article 49 Co-ordination with the 1956 New York Convention

In relations between the Contracting States, this Convention replaces the United Nations Convention on the Recovery Abroad of Maintenance of 20 June 1956, in so far as its scope of application as between such States coincides with the scope of application of this Convention.

Article 50 Relationship with prior Hague Conventions on service of documents and taking of evidence

This Convention does not affect the Hague Convention of 1 March 1954 on civil procedure, the Hague Convention of 15 November 1965 on the Service Abroad of Judicial and Extrajudicial Documents in Civil or Commercial Matters and the Hague Convention of 18 March 1970 on the Taking of Evidence Abroad in Civil or Commercial Matters.

Article 51 Co-ordination of instruments and supplementary agreements

(1) This Convention does not affect any international instrument concluded before this Convention to which Contracting States are Parties and which contains provisions on matters governed by this Convention.

(2) Any Contracting State may conclude with one or more Contracting States agreements, which contain provisions on matters governed by the Convention, with a view to improving the application of the Convention between or among themselves, provided that such agreements are consistent with the objects and purpose of the Convention and do not affect, in the relationship of such States with other Contracting States, the application of the provisions of the Convention. The States which have concluded such an agreement shall transmit a copy to the depositary of the Convention.

(3) Paragraphs 1 and 2 shall also apply to reciprocity arrangements and to uniform laws based on special ties between the States concerned.

(4) This Convention shall not affect the application of instruments of a Regional Economic Integration Organisation that is a Party to this Convention, adopted after the conclusion of the Convention, on matters governed by the Convention provided that such instruments do not affect, in the relationship of Member States of the Regional Economic Integration Organisation with other Contracting States, the application of the provisions of the Convention. As concerns the recognition or enforcement of decisions as between Member States of the Regional Economic Integration Organisation, the Convention shall not affect the rules of the Regional Economic Integration Organisation, whether adopted before or after the conclusion of the Convention.

Article 52 Most effective rule

(1) This Convention shall not prevent the application of an agreement, arrangement or international instrument in force between the requesting State and the requested State, or a reciprocity arrangement in force in the requested State that provides for –

a) broader bases for recognition of maintenance decisions, without prejudice to Article 22 f) of the Convention;

b) simplified, more expeditious procedures on an application for recognition or recognition and enforcement of maintenance decisions;

c) more beneficial legal assistance than that provided for under Articles 14 to 17; or

d) procedures permitting an applicant from a requesting State to make a request directly to the Central Authority of the requested State.

(2) This Convention shall not prevent the application of a law in force in the requested State that provides for more effective rules as referred to in paragraph 1 a) to c). However, as regards simplified, more expeditious procedures referred to in paragraph 1 b), they must be compatible with the protection offered to the parties under Articles 23 and 24, in particular as regards the rights of the parties to be duly notified of the proceedings and be given adequate opportunity to be heard and as regards the effects of any challenge or appeal.

Article 53 Uniform interpretation

In the interpretation of this Convention, regard shall be had to its international character and to the need to promote uniformity in its application.

Article 54 Review of practical operation of the Convention

(1) The Secretary General of the Hague Conference on Private International Law shall at regular intervals convene a Special Commission in order to review the practical operation of the Convention and to encourage the development of good practices under the Convention.

(2) For the purpose of such review, Contracting States shall co-operate with the Permanent Bureau of the Hague Conference on Private International Law in the gathering of information, including statistics and case law, concerning the practical operation of the Convention.

Article 55 Amendment of forms

(1) The forms annexed to this Convention may be amended by a decision of a Special Commission convened by the Secretary General of the Hague Conference on Private International Law to which all Contracting States and all Members shall be invited. Notice of the proposal to amend the forms shall be included in the agenda for the meeting.

(2) Amendments adopted by the Contracting States present at the Special Commission shall come into force for all Contracting States on the first day of the seventh calendar month after the date of their communication by the depositary to all Contracting States.

(3) During the period provided for in paragraph 2 any Contracting State may by notification in writing to the depositary make a reservation, in accordance with Article 62, with respect to the amendment. The State making such reservation shall, until the reservation is withdrawn, be treated as a State not Party to the present Convention with respect to that amendment.

Article 56 Transitional provisions

(1) The Convention shall apply in every case where –

a) a request pursuant to Article 7 or an application pursuant to Chapter III has been received by the Central Authority of the requested State after the Convention has entered into force between the requesting State and the requested State;

b) a direct request for recognition and enforcement has been received by the competent authority of the State addressed after the Convention has entered into force between the State of origin and the State addressed.

(2) With regard to the recognition and enforcement of decisions between Contracting States to this Convention that are also Parties to either of the Hague Maintenance Conventions mentioned in Article 48, if the conditions for the recognition and enforcement under this Convention prevent the recognition and enforcement of a decision given in the State of origin before the entry into force of this Convention for that State, that would otherwise have been recognised and enforced under the terms of the Convention that was in effect at the time the decision was rendered, the conditions of that Convention shall apply.

(3) The State addressed shall not be bound under this Convention to enforce a decision or a maintenance arrangement, in respect of payments falling due prior to the entry into force of the Convention between the State of origin and the State addressed, except for maintenance obligations arising from a parent-child relationship towards a person under the age of 21 years.

Article 57 Provision of information concerning laws, procedures and services

(1) A Contracting State, by the time its instrument of ratification or accession is deposited or a declaration is submitted in accordance with Article 61 of the Convention, shall provide the Permanent Bureau of the Hague Conference on Private International Law with –

a) a description of its laws and procedures concerning maintenance obligations;

b) a description of the measures it will take to meet the obligations under Article 6;

c) a description of how it will provide applicants with effective access to procedures, as required under Article 14;

d) a description of its enforcement rules and procedures, including any limitations on enforcement, in particular debtor protection rules and limitation periods;

e) any specification referred to in Article 25(1) b) and (3).

(2) Contracting States may, in fulfilling their obligations under paragraph 1, utilise a country profile form recommended and published by the Hague Conference on Private International Law.

(3) Information shall be kept up to date by the Contracting States.

Chapter IX – Final Provisions

Article 58 Signature, ratification and accession

(1) The Convention shall be open for signature by the States which were Members of the Hague Conference on Private International Law at the time of its Twenty-First Session and by the other States which participated in that Session.

(2) It shall be ratified, accepted or approved and the instruments of ratification, acceptance or approval shall be deposited with the Ministry of Foreign Affairs of the Kingdom of the Netherlands, depositary of the Convention.

(3) Any other State or Regional Economic Integration Organisation may accede to the Convention after it has entered into force in accordance with Article 60(1).

(4) The instrument of accession shall be deposited with the depositary.

(5) Such accession shall have effect only as regards the relations between the acceding State and those Contracting States which have not raised an objection to its accession in the 12 months after the date of the notification referred to in Article 65. Such an objection may also be raised by States at the time when they ratify, accept or approve the Convention after an accession. Any such objection shall be notified to the depositary.

Article 59 Regional Economic Integration Organisations

(1) A Regional Economic Integration Organisation which is constituted solely by sovereign States and has competence over some or all of the matters governed by this Convention may similarly sign, accept, approve or accede to this Convention. The Regional Economic Integration Organisation shall in that case have the rights and obligations of a Contracting State, to the extent that the Organisation has competence over matters governed by the Convention.

(2) The Regional Economic Integration Organisation shall, at the time of signature, acceptance, approval or accession, notify the depositary in writing of the matters governed by this Convention in respect of which competence has been transferred to that Organisation by its Member States. The Organisation shall promptly notify the depositary in writing of any changes to its competence as specified in the most recent notice given under this paragraph.

(3) At the time of signature, acceptance, approval or accession, a Regional Economic Integration Organisation may declare in accordance with Article 63 that it exercises competence over all the matters governed by this Convention and that the Member States which have transferred competence to the Regional Economic Integration Organisation in respect of the matter in question shall be bound by this Convention by virtue of the signature, acceptance, approval or accession of the Organisation.

(4) For the purposes of the entry into force of this Convention, any instrument deposited by a Regional Economic Integration Organisation shall not be counted unless the Regional Economic Integration Organisation makes a declaration in accordance with paragraph 3.

(5) Any reference to a "Contracting State" or "State" in this Convention shall apply equally to a Regional Economic Integration Organisation that is a Party to it, where appropriate. In the event that a declaration is made by a Regional Economic Integration Organisation in accordance with paragraph 3, any reference to a "Contracting State" or "State" in this Convention shall apply equally to the relevant Member States of the Organisation, where appropriate.

Article 60 Entry into force

(1) The Convention shall enter into force on the first day of the month following the expiration of three months after the deposit of the second instrument of ratification, acceptance or approval referred to in Article 58.

(2) Thereafter the Convention shall enter into force –

a) for each State or Regional Economic Integration Organisation referred to in Article 59(1) subsequently ratifying, accepting or approving it, on the first day of the month following the expiration of three months after the deposit of its instrument of ratification, acceptance or approval;

b) for each State or Regional Economic Integration Organisation referred to in Article 58(3) on the day after the end of the period during which objections may be raised in accordance with Article 58(5);

c) for a territorial unit to which the Convention has been extended in accordance with Article 61, on the first day of the month following the expiration of three months after the notification referred to in that Article.

Article 61 Declarations with respect to non-unified legal systems

(1) If a State has two or more territorial units in which different systems of law are applicable in relation to matters dealt with in the Convention, it may at the time of signature, ratification, acceptance, approval or accession declare in accordance with Article 63 that this Convention shall extend to all its territorial units or only to one or more of them and may modify this declaration by submitting another declaration at any time.

(2) Any such declaration shall be notified to the depositary and shall state expressly the territorial units to which the Convention applies.

(3) If a State makes no declaration under this Article, the Convention shall extend to all territorial units of that State.

(4) This Article shall not apply to a Regional Economic Integration Organisation.

Article 62 Reservations

(1) Any Contracting State may, not later than the time of ratification, acceptance, approval or accession, or at the time of making a declaration in terms of

Article 61, make one or more of the reservations provided for in Articles 2(2), 20(2), 30(8), 44(3) and 55(3). No other reservation shall be permitted.

(2) Any State may at any time withdraw a reservation it has made. The withdrawal shall be notified to the depositary.

(3) The reservation shall cease to have effect on the first day of the third calendar month after the notification referred to in paragraph 2.

(4) Reservations under this Article shall have no reciprocal effect with the exception of the reservation provided for in Article 2(2).

Article 63 Declarations

(1) Declarations referred to in Articles 2(3), 11(1) g), 16(1), 24(1), 30(7), 44(1) and (2), 59(3) and 61(1), may be made upon signature, ratification, acceptance, approval or accession or at any time thereafter, and may be modified or withdrawn at any time.

(2) Declarations, modifications and withdrawals shall be notified to the depositary.

(3) A declaration made at the time of signature, ratification, acceptance, approval or accession shall take effect simultaneously with the entry into force of this Convention for the State concerned.

(4) A declaration made at a subsequent time, and any modification or withdrawal of a declaration, shall take effect on the first day of the month following the expiration of three months after the date on which the notification is received by the depositary.

Article 64 Denunciation

(1) A Contracting State to the Convention may denounce it by a notification in writing addressed to the depositary. The denunciation may be limited to certain territorial units of a multi-unit State to which the Convention applies.

(2) The denunciation shall take effect on the first day of the month following the expiration of 12 months after the date on which the notification is received by the depositary. Where a longer period for the denunciation to take effect is specified in the notification, the denunciation shall take effect upon the expiration of such longer period after the date on which the notification is received by the depositary.

Article 65 Notification

The depositary shall notify the Members of the Hague Conference on Private International Law, and other States and Regional Economic Integration Organisations which have signed, ratified, accepted, approved or acceded in accordance with Articles 58 and 59 of the following –

a) the signatures, ratifications, acceptances and approvals referred to in Articles 58 and 59;

b) the accessions and objections raised to accessions referred to in Articles 58(3) and (5) and 59;

c) the date on which the Convention enters into force in accordance with Article 60; d) the declarations referred to in Articles 2(3), 11(1) g), 16(1), 24(1), 30(7), 44(1) and (2), 59(3) and 61(1);

e) the agreements referred to in Article 51(2);

f) the reservations referred to in Articles 2(2), 20(2), 30(8), 44(3) and 55(3), and the withdrawals referred to in Article 62(2);

g) the denunciations referred to in Article 64.

In witness whereof the undersigned, being duly authorised thereto, have signed this Convention.

Done at The Hague, on the 23rd day of November 2007, in the English and French languages, both texts being equally authentic, in a single copy which shall be deposited in the archives of the Government of the Kingdom of the Netherlands, and of which a certified copy shall be sent, through diplomatic channels, to each of the Members of the Hague Conference on Private International Law at the date of its Twenty-First Session and to each of the other States which have participated in that Session.

(4) President's Guidance: Liaison between Courts in England and Wales and British Embassies and High Commissions Abroad

(1) This guidance note describes procedures which are to be followed when a court in England and Wales exercising family jurisdiction seeks to invoke consular assistance. The procedures have been agreed between the President of the Family Division and the Foreign, Commonwealth and Development Office (FCDO).

(2) Courts exercising family jurisdiction in England and Wales regularly deal with cases where children have been wrongfully removed to a foreign country or have been retained there wrongfully, most commonly by a parent or relative. Such cases may involve abduction or removal by one or both parents with a view to forced marriage or female genital mutilation, in which case a Forced Marriage Protection Order (FMPO) or Female Genital Mutilation Protection Order (FGMPO) may be appropriate.

(3) When the court is exercising family jurisdiction in such circumstances, consular assistance may be sought, via the FCDO in London, from the relevant British Embassies, High Commissions or Consulates abroad.

(4) Where the country to which the child has been taken is a party to the Convention on the Civil Aspects of International Child Abduction signed at The Hague on 25 October 1980 (1980 Hague Convention), established procedures apply for the making of applications for the return of the child, via the central authority, which for England and Wales is The International Child Abduction and Contact Unit (ICACU), situated in the office of the Official Solicitor and Public Trustee at Post Point 0.53, 102 Petty France, London, SW1H 9AJ, telephone +44 (0)20 3681 2756, email icacu@ospt.gov.uk.

(5) Where the country to which the child has been taken is a party to either of the following Conventions, the court will need to consider the Convention when deciding what steps to take:

- 1980 European Convention on Recognition and Enforcement of Decisions concerning Custody of Children and on the Restoration of Custody of Children (a Convention of the Council of Europe, also known as the 1980 Luxembourg Convention);
- 1996 Hague Convention on jurisdiction, applicable law, recognition, enforcement and cooperation in respect of parental responsibility and measures for the protection of children. Please note that for the 1996 Hague Convention, ICACU is the (operational) central authority for England and the Welsh Government is separately the central authority for Wales (Tel.: +44 (29) 23000 61500) Email: WalesCAHague1996@gov.wales.

(6) ICACU has published explanatory guidance and application forms regarding the assistance which can be provided in respect of the above-named Conventions. The relevant forms for the 1980 and 1996 Hague Conventions can be found at: https://www.gov.uk/government/publications/international-child-abduction-andcontact-unit-application-form https://www.gov.uk/government/publications/international-child-abduction-unitrequest-for-co-operation-form.

(7) Where, however, the country concerned is not a party to any of the above Conventions, consideration will need to be given in each case as to what orders if any should be made to seek to secure the return of the child to England and Wales.

(8) It may be possible in appropriate cases for representatives from the relevant British Embassy, High Commission or Consulate to follow-up with the competent safeguarding authority to check the child[ren]'s welfare, engage local police to ascertain what efforts have been made to locate the child[ren], to host consular appointments involving the child[ren], and to advise on travel arrangements for the return of the child[ren] to England and Wales. Such activities will however always be subject to the requirements of the domestic law of the country in question. The Foreign Secretary has discretion in deciding how to conduct international affairs, and the court cannot order the FCDO to exercise consular assistance. There is no general duty for the FCDO to provide consular assistance to British nationals. There may be limits to what the FCDO can do to help when a dual national child is in the country of their other nationality.

(9) Before the court requests assistance from the FCDO, contact should be made with the Child Policy Unit in Consular Directorate (Consular.ChildrensPolicyOfficer@fcdo.gov.uk), or the Forced Marriage Unit (FMU@fcdo.gov.uk) if the case involves forced marriage or female genital mutilation. This is to provide the FCDO with an opportunity to clarify what level of assistance it may be in a position to offer in the country concerned. The FCDO will be able to identify the relevant Embassy, High Commission or Consulate to which any order or request for assistance should be directed, and to forward documents.

(10) The FCDO provides a facilitative role in relation to the return of the child but is not able to care for, take control of, or assist in procuring the return of the child. The naming of specific officials (for example Ambassadors, High Commissioners or other FCDO officials) must be avoided. Instead reference should be made to 'The Consular Directorate of the Foreign, Commonwealth and Development Office'.

(11) Consular staff are not trained to assess the welfare of a child as a professional Social Worker would be. Accordingly, the FCDO cannot conduct welfare visits or safe and well checks. The FCDO can provide information and contact details for the competent safeguarding authority/ies and Non-Governmental Organisations (NGOs) in the relevant country who may be able to undertake welfare checks on the child[ren].

(12) The FCDO will take practical steps to co-operate in any way which is appropriate on UK passport handling. It should be noted that:

(a) The FCDO is dependent upon the co-operation of the parent or adult to comply with an order. The FCDO is unable to authorise or enforce compliance.

(b) The FCDO or UK diplomatic premises should not be used as a depositary for the return of UK passports.

(c) The FCDO is not in a position to carry passports across international borders via the diplomatic bag or other means. Arrangements to transport a UK Passport should be made by the passport holder or, if a child passport, those with parental responsibility.

(d) On return of the child[rens]'s passport/s no further responsibility lies with the FCDO in relation to the parties' future movements.

(13) The FCDO can provide information and contact details for the competent safeguarding authority and NGOs in the relevant country to assist the court and other parties. Authorities and NGOs in the relevant country may be able to assist in locating the child[ren], and arranging to return the child[ren]. However, Social Services in England and Wales are not authorised to work outside the UK and as such the primary work of returning the child will require the cooperation of in-country authorities.

(14) The FCDO can issue Emergency Travel Documents (ETDs) to British citizens or those with a claim to British nationality providing they meet the eligibility criteria. ETDs do not replace full validity passports, but in issuing them the FCDO is providing consular assistance to a person who urgently needs to travel. ETDs are only issued to those who have not held a British passport before in exceptional circumstances. Ordinarily, first time applicants should apply for a passport to travel. FCDO policy states that ETDs can only be issued to those who are 15 years old and younger when all those with parental responsibility have given consent. This policy is deviated from only in exceptional circumstances. It is helpful to the FCDO if the court can make it clear when an ETD may be issued with the consent of only one person with parental responsibility or, where necessary, without the consent of anyone with parental responsibility. Foreign nationals looking to travel to the UK will need to make the necessary visa arrangements with UK Visas and Immigration (UKVI).

(15) The FCDO can provide advice on the repatriation of a child, including options for financing travel. Financial assistance (such as a loan) can be considered in exceptional circumstances, but will be considered on a case by case basis. The court or those with parental responsibility may contact the FCDO before an order is made to discuss these options.

(16) Whilst the FCDO stands ready to assist the court in any way which is appropriate, the repatriation of foreign nationals from the UK to a third country is outside the scope of consular assistance. Likewise, the submission of visa applications to a third country is the responsibility of the applicant.

(17) In a case where assistance can be given by the FCDO, the order should provide for disclosure of the specific documents required in order for the FCDO to provide the necessary assistance. A copy of all such orders should be sent to the Child Policy Unit, Foreign, Commonwealth and Development Office, King Charles Street, London, SW1A 2AH; Consular.ChildrensPolicyOfficer@fcdo.gov.uk.

(18) If the order relates to the 2003 UK-Pakistan Protocol on Child Contact and Abduction, a copy should in addition be sent by email to the International Family Justice Office IFJOffice@Justice.gov.uk.

(19) The FCDO has published guidance on the assistance which can be provided in respect to international parental child abductions: https://www.gov.uk/government/publications/international-parental-childabduction/international-parental-child-abduction.

(20) Attached is a Schedule of specimen provisions which may be included in orders principally directed to cases where a child has been wrongfully removed to/retained in a foreign country.

The Rt Hon Sir Andrew McFarlane President of the Family Division

14 March 2022

Schedule
Specimen Provisions for Orders

AND WHEREAS [AB] is a Ward of the High Court of England and Wales and is a British citizen; and currently [believed to be] travelling outside England and Wales with a United Kingdom passport

AND WHEREAS in consequence of the fact that this Court has ordered that [AB] remain a Ward of this Court, the High Court of England and Wales, while (until [s]he attains the age of 18 years on [date]) [s]he remains a minor, this Court is empowered and required to exercise its custodial jurisdiction over him/her and to ascertain his/her best interests and to facilitate and protect those best interests

AND WHEREAS it appears from an order made in [details of proceedings] on [date] (of which a copy is attached) that [AB] was habitually resident in England and Wales [on[date]/at the time [s]he was removed from this jurisdiction]

AND WHEREAS the High Court of England and Wales is anxious to protect and secure his/her wellbeing and best interests and to ensure that he/she may freely express his/her wishes concerning his/her country and place of residence

AND WHEREAS the High Court of England and Wales is anxious to ensure that [s]he is not induced or coerced into contracting any marriage or betrothal against his/her will

AND WHEREAS the High Court of England and Wales is satisfied that all interested parties are before the Court including Cafcass (the Children and Family Court Advisory and Support Service) appointed by the Court to represent the Ward

AND WHEREAS the High Court of England and Wales having heard oral evidence from [ ] is of the view that serious grounds exist in the present circumstances to question whether this Court's Ward [AB] is able freely to express his/her views and wishes and in particular with regard to his/her country of residence

AND WHEREAS the High Court of England and Wales has in the interests of [AB] determined that [s]he should so soon as practicable return/be returned to England and Wales

IT IS ORDERED that every person within the jurisdiction of this Court who is in a position to do so shall co-operate in assisting and securing the immediate return to England and Wales of [AB], a Ward of the High Court of England and Wales

AND NOW THEREFORE THIS COURT RESPECTFULLY REQUESTS any person not within the jurisdiction of this Court who is in a position to do so to co-operate in assisting and securing the immediate return to England and Wales of the Ward [AB]

AND THIS COURT RESPECTFULLY REQUESTS all judicial and administrative bodies in the State of [ ] to consider what assistance may be provided pursuant to the exercise of their respective powers, and to provide such assistance that they consider appropriate, with a view to establishing the whereabouts of the Ward of the High Court of England and Wales.

AND NOW THEREFORE THIS COURT RESPECTFULLY REQUESTS all judicial, administrative and law enforcement authorities to consider what assistance may be provided pursuant to the exercise of their respective powers, and to provide such assistance that they consider appropriate, with a view to locating, safeguarding and facilitating the return to England and Wales of the said minor child[ren] pursuant to the laws of England and Wales [and in accordance with the Protocol made on 17 January 2003 in London and signed by the Honourable Chief Justice of the Supreme Court of Pakistan and by the Right Honourable The President of the Family Division of the High Court of Justice of England and Wales].

Other Examples of Helpful Wording

FOR THE AVOIDANCE OF DOUBT the Foreign, Commonwealth and Development Office and/or Her Majesty's Passport Office may grant a passport, travel document or emergency travel document to [names of child/ren] without the consent of [name of parent/mother/father]

PERMISSION IS HEREBY GIVEN to the Foreign, Commonwealth and Development Office of the United Kingdom to share the information disclosed to them in accordance with paragraph [X] above with [named bodies/persons] [and any other relevant agency]

(5) Practice Guidance (Case Management and Mediation of International Child Abduction Proceedings)

13 March 2018

1 Introduction

1.1 For the purposes of this Practice Guidance, 'international child abduction proceedings' are proceedings in which the return of a child is sought under any of the following:

(a) The Convention on the Civil Aspects of International Child Abduction of 25 October 1980 ('the 1980 Hague Convention');

(b) The Convention on Jurisdiction, Applicable Law, Recognition, Enforcement and Cooperation in Respect of Parental Responsibility and Measures for the Protection of Children ('the 1996 Hague Convention');

(c) Council Regulation (EC) No 2201/2003 of 27 November 2003 on jurisdiction and the recognition and enforcement of judgments in matrimonial matters and matters of parental responsibility ('the Council Regulation');

(d) The High Court's power to make an order returning the child to another jurisdiction or to make an order for the return of the child to this jurisdiction ('the inherent jurisdiction')

1.2 International child abduction proceedings dealt with under the 1980 Hague Convention must be completed within six weeks of the date of the application. FPR PD12F paragraph 3.5 applies the same time limit to non-Convention cases under the inherent jurisdiction, save where exceptional circumstances make this impossible. This Practice Guidance is issued to ensure all applications are case managed in a manner that facilitates these time limits, both in cases that commence with a without notice application and cases that commence on notice.

1.3 Chapter 6 of Part 12 of the FPR 2010 and PD12F provide the procedural framework for proceedings under the 1980 Hague Convention, the 1996 Hague Convention and the Council Regulation. The rules provide for case management directions in child abduction proceedings to be given 'as soon as practicable' after the application has been made. In particular, the rules provide for:

(a) Directions for the production of the applicant's evidence (r. 12.46)

(b) The giving of case management directions generally (r 12.48) (c) The filing and service of an answer (r 12.49)

(d) The filing and service of written evidence (r 12.50)

2 Case Management – Procedure

(a) Without notice applications

Use of without notice applications

2.1 Commencing proceedings by way of a without notice application pursuant to FPR r 12.47 will be justified only where

(a) the case is one of exceptional urgency or

(b) there is a compelling case that the child's welfare will be compromised if the other party is alerted in advance or

(c) where the whereabouts of the child and the proposed respondent are unknown.

An urgent out of hours without notice application will be justified only where an order is necessary to regulate the position between the moment the order is made and the next available sitting of the court.

Evidence in support of without notice applications

2.2 The evidence in support of a without notice application must be as detailed and precise as possible having regard to the material provided by the applicant and transmitted by the Central Authority of the Requesting State. Unparticularised generalities will not suffice. Sources of hearsay must be identified and expressions of opinion must be supported by evidence and proper reasoning. The evidence should set out the orders sought, together with fully particularised reasons. Specifically, with respect to the narrow circumstances justifying a without notice application set out in para 2.1 above:

(a) Where the justification for proceeding without notice is said to be exceptional urgency, the evidence in support of the without notice application must identify why the case is exceptionally urgent and why no notice, even short informal notice, can be given to the respondent (with respect to short, informal notice see para 2.8 below).

(b) Where the justification for proceeding without notice is said to be a compelling case that the child's welfare will be compromised if notice is given, the evidence in support of the without notice application must demonstrate a real risk that if the respondent is alerted in advance the welfare of the child will be compromised, whether by the respondent thwarting the court's order or otherwise. Where the risk is said to be removal of the child from the jurisdiction, the evidence must address (i) the magnitude of the risk that the respondent will be minded to remove, (ii) the magnitude of the risk that, if the respondent is minded to remove, he or she will be able to evade protective measures put in place by the court and (iii) the magnitude of the consequences for the children if the protective measures are evaded.

(c) Where the justification for proceeding without notice is said to be that the whereabouts of the child and the proposed respondent are unknown, the evidence in support of the without notice application must explain what steps have been taken to locate them, what disclosure orders are required against an identified agency and why there is reason to believe that that agency may be able to provide information which may lead to the location of the child.

Without notice orders

2.3 Before seeking a without notice Tipstaff order the applicant or their legal representative must speak to the Tipstaff. The Tipstaff can be contacted by telephone on 01622 858035.

2.4 Passport orders, location orders and collection orders constitute an interference with the child's and the respondent's fundamental rights. On a without notice application, parties should only seek, and the court can only be expected to grant, such orders as are necessary and proportionate having regard to the risks assessed to exist on the evidence. Where a court makes more than one disclosure order, it may provide for the sequential service of those orders.

Case management directions at without notice hearings

2.5 Where a without notice application is justified and the court grants a Tipstaff or other substantive order, or where a without notice application is justified but the court refuses to grant a Tipstaff or other substantive order on the merits, the court will in each case proceed to give case management directions to progress the matter, which directions may be varied and/or supplemented at the first on notice hearing where appropriate. The directions given will include the following:

(a) A direction that at the first on notice hearing the applicant and the respondent shall each be given the opportunity to speak separately with a mediator, who will be present at the Royal Courts of Justice, to enable the mediator to discuss with the parties the possibility of mediation under the Child Abduction Mediation Scheme and, where appropriate, undertake a screening interview.

(b) A direction pursuant to FPR r 12.46(a) for the filing of any further evidence to be relied on by the applicant in support of the application including, where it is not already contained in the evidence supporting the application, a description of any protective measures (including orders that may be subject to a declaration of enforceability or registration under Art 11 of the 1996 Hague Convention or, where appropriate, undertakings) the applicant is prepared, without prejudice to his or her case, to offer for the purpose of securing the child's return.

(c) A direction pursuant to FPR r 12.50(2)(a) for the filing and serving of the respondent's answer.

(d) A direction pursuant to FPR r 12.50(1) for the filing of the respondent's evidence in support of the answer, to include details of any protective measures the respondent seeks (including, where appropriate, undertakings) in the event that the court orders the child's return.

(e) An order listing the matter for hearing for summary resolution, or in the alternative, further directions, no more than seven days from the date on which the without notice order is made (where a collection order is made the Tipstaff will return the matter to court within 3 days of the order being executed) with a direction that the respondent shall attend this hearing.

(f) A direction for the provision by HMCTS of an interpreter for the hearing where Section 11 of Form C67 indicates that the respondent does not speak English and indicates the language and dialect spoken by the respondent.

(g) Such further or other case management directions that are appropriate in the circumstances of the case. Where it is clear on the face of the application and supporting evidence that it will be appropriate for the child to be heard during the proceedings the court may make directions to ensure the child is given the opportunity to be heard (see paragraph 3.5 below).

(h) Unless the court directs otherwise, a direction pursuant to FPR r 12.47(3) that the applicant is to effect personal service of the standard directions order together with a record of the without notice hearing (note that where an order provides for service by the Tipstaff it is not sufficient for the order to be served by the applicant).

2.6 It is important that any without notice application is prepared in a manner that maximises the chances of the on notice hearing being effective. To this end, the without notice application and the evidence in support must contain all the information in the possession of the applicant that will or may assist in the prompt execution of any orders made. To further assist in achieving an effective on notice hearing, the directions order resulting from the without notice hearing will be served together with an information sheet, detailing how the respondent can obtain legal advice, public funding from the Legal Aid Agency and, if necessary, pro bono assistance, and a copy of the Child Abduction Mediation Scheme.

2.7 Where the application has been commenced by way of a without notice hearing, at the first effective on notice hearing the court will make further case management directions with input from both parties with a view to addressing each of the matters set out in paragraph 2.11 of this Practice Guidance where those matters have not already been dealt with by way of directions at the without notice hearing.

(b) On notice applications

Notice periods for on notice applications

2.8 FPR r 12.8 and PD12C provide that, in proceedings under the 1980 Hague Convention, service of the application on the respondent must be effected a minimum of 4 days before the first hearing and that, in proceedings under the inherent jurisdiction, service on the respondent must be effected a minimum of 14 days before the first hearing. Pursuant to PD12C para 2.2 the court may extend or shorten these periods for service. Whilst the courts have endorsed the practice of giving short, informal notice of proceedings in preference to proceeding without notice, where short, informal notice is given there must be evidence identifying why it was not possible to serve the application in accordance with the rules or to make an application to abridge time for service.

Standard directions on issue

2.9 Where the application is made on notice (and, accordingly, there is no without notice hearing immediately following the issuing of the application) there is a risk that valuable time will be lost between issue and the first on notice hearing. To minimise this risk, upon the court issuing an on notice application the court will, of its own motion, make standard directions upon issue pursuant to FPR r 12.5(1)(b), to include:

(a) A direction that at the first on notice hearing the applicant and the respondent shall each be given the opportunity to speak separately with the mediator present at the Royal Courts of Justice to enable the mediator to discuss with the parties the possibility of mediation under the Child Abduction Mediation Scheme and, where appropriate, undertake a screening interview.

(b) A direction pursuant to FPR r 12.46(a) for the filing of any further evidence to be relied on by the applicant in support of the application including, where it is not already contained in the evidence supporting the application, a description of any protective measures (including orders that may be subject to registration under Art 11 of the 1996 Hague Convention or, where appropriate, undertakings) the applicant is prepared, without prejudice to his or her case, to offer for the purpose of securing the child's return.

(c) A direction pursuant to FPR r 12.50(2)(a) for the filing and serving of the respondent's answer not less than 2 days prior to the first hearing.
(d) A direction pursuant to FPR r 12.50(1) for the filing of the respondent's evidence in support of the answer, to include details of any protective measures the respondent seeks (including, where appropriate, undertakings) in the event that the court orders the child's return not less than 2 days prior to the first hearing.
(e) A direction that upon service of the application the respondent file with the court a notice confirming the respondent's address and the whereabouts of the child (or that they are unaware of the child's whereabouts) and, where the respondent subsequently changes his or her address or becomes aware of any change in the child's whereabouts, a notice of the new address or of the new whereabouts of the child.
(f) A direction that upon service of the application the respondent serve on the applicant the notice confirming the respondent's address and the whereabouts of the child (or that they are unaware of the child's whereabouts) or file with the court a notice indicating that the respondent objects to serving on the applicant with notice confirming the respondent's address and the whereabouts of the child and the reasons for that objection.
(g) An order listing the matter for hearing for summary resolution or in the alternative further directions, seven days from the date the application is issued with a direction that the respondent shall attend this hearing.
(h) A direction for the provision by HMCTS of an interpreter for the hearing where Section 11 of Form C67 indicates that the respondent does not speak English and indicates the language and dialect spoken by the respondent.
(i) Such further or other case management directions that are appropriate in the circumstances of the case. Where it is clear on the face of the application and supporting evidence that it will be appropriate for the child to be heard during the proceedings the court may make directions to ensure the child is given the opportunity to be heard (see paragraph 3.5 below).
(j) A direction that the applicant is to effect personal service of the standard directions order.

2.10 The resulting directions order will be served together with an information sheet, detailing how the respondent can obtain legal advice, public funding from the Legal Aid Agency and, if necessary, pro bono assistance, and a copy of the Child Abduction Mediation Scheme.

Directions at first on notice hearing

2.11 At the first hearing, the parties should attend fully prepared to deal with the case management matters that have not been dealt with by way of standard directions upon issue or which have been so dealt with but require variation, together with any additional case management matters that may arise in the circumstances of the case. The court will expect the parties to be able to deal with the following case management issues if applicable:

(a) Further directions with respect to mediation or other non-court dispute resolution procedure.
(b) Allocation.
(c) Any directions required to deal with further disclosure.
(d) Any further directions with respect to the filing and service of an answer and evidence in support, to include details of any protective measures the respondent seeks (including, where appropriate, undertakings) in the event that the court orders the child's return.

(e) Any further directions with respect to the filing and service of the applicant's evidence in reply to the answer, including, where it is not already contained in the evidence supporting the application, a description of any protective measures (including orders that may be subject to a declaration of enforceability or registration under Art 11 of the 1996 Hague Convention or, where appropriate, undertakings) the applicant is prepared, without prejudice to his or her case, to offer to secure the child's return. Where the respondent's answer raises a defence under Art 13(b) the applicant should give immediate consideration to, and take steps, in the most expeditious way available, to ensure that information is obtained, whether from the Central Authority of the Requesting State or otherwise, as to the protective measures that are available, or could be put in place to meet the alleged identified risks.

(f) Directions in respect of expert evidence, if appropriate. Where a party seeks to adduce expert evidence, that party must comply with the requirements of FPR Part 25.

(g) Directions in respect of oral evidence, if appropriate (in respect of directions for oral evidence see para 3.8 below).

(h) Directions with respect to ensuring that the child is given the opportunity to be heard during the proceedings, unless this appears inappropriate having regard to his or her age or degree of maturity, including consideration of joinder and separate representation (see paragraph 3.5 below). Any application for joinder and separate representation should be made on notice prior to the first on notice hearing, to be dealt with at that hearing.

(i) The timetabling of the final hearing prior to the expiry of the six-week deadline, including the appropriate time estimate for the hearing, incorporating time for judicial reading and judgment writing.

(j) The arrangements for the provision of a court bundle that complies with FPR 2010 PD27A.

(k) The arrangements for the provision, where appropriate, of skeleton arguments and an agreed bundle of authorities in compliance with PD27A.

(l) Ancillary directions making provision where necessary for the attendance of a party not in the jurisdiction, the provision of video-links and the provision for interpreters at the final hearing. Where a video-link it sought, it is the responsibility of the parties to ensure appropriate arrangements are made for the video link and that the connection is made to the court via an ISDN line or, where an ISDN line is not available, that a 'bridging link' is arranged to ensure that a connection with the court can take place.

3 Case Management – Related Matters

(a) Child Abduction Mediation Scheme

3.1 The requirement in FPR r 1.4(2)(f)) that case management includes encouraging the parties to use a non-court dispute resolution procedure if the court considers that appropriate and facilitating the use of such procedure, and the obligation imposed by FPR r 3.3(1) to consider whether non-court dispute resolution is appropriate at every stage of the proceedings, applies to international child abduction proceedings. The Lord Chancellor has set out in regulations provision on the of grant of non-means non-merit tested legal aid for mediation for applicant parents in cases under the 1980 Hague Convention.

3.2 Within this context, the court will, where appropriate, encourage the parties to engage in mediation of their dispute through participation in the Child Abduction Mediation Scheme (see Appendix). In any case where it is alleged or admitted, or there is other reason to believe, that the child or a parent has experienced domestic abuse or that there is a risk of such abuse, the court will have regard to these matters when deciding whether it is appropriate to encourage the parties to mediate. Participation in the Child Abduction Mediation Scheme is voluntary and without prejudice to the parties' right to invite the court to determine the issues between them. An unwillingness to enter into mediation will not have an effect on the outcome of the proceedings. It is important that parties and their representatives note that entering into a process of mediation will not ground a defence of acquiescence (see In Re H (Minors) (Abduction: Acquiescence) [1998] AC 72 at 88–89).

3.3 The Child Abduction Mediation Scheme will operate in parallel with, but independent from, the proceedings. Where parties agree to enter into mediation, the court will give any directions required to facilitate the mediation. The parties or the parties' representatives must be in a position to address the court on the question of mediation at the relevant hearing to enable the court to consider the appropriateness of such directions. The mediation will proceed with the aim of completing that mediation within the applicable timescales. Where the mediation is successful, the resulting Memorandum of Understanding will be drawn up into a consent order for approval by the court. If the mediation is not successful, the court will proceed to determine the application.

(b) Issue Identification

3.4 Key to ensuring that the final hearing is dealt with in a manner commensurate with the summary nature of most international child abduction hearings is the identification at the case management stage of what matters are truly in issue between the parties. It is particularly important that the directions hearing(s) preceding the final hearing be used to identify the real issues in the case, so that the judge can give firm and focused case management directions, including as to the form that the hearing will take. Parties can expect the court to be rigorous and robust at the case management stage in requiring parties to consider and identify the issues that the court is required to determine and to make concessions in respect of issues that are capable of agreement.

(c) Participation of the Child

3.5 Art 11(3) of the Council Regulation requires the court to ensure that child is given the opportunity to be heard during the proceedings unless this appears inappropriate having regard to his or her age or degree of maturity. Where it is clear on the face of the application and supporting evidence that it will be appropriate for the child to be heard during the proceedings the court may give directions to facilitate this at a without notice hearing or by way of standard directions on issue. Where directions have not already been given, the question of whether the child is to be given an opportunity to be heard in proceedings having regard to his or her age and degree of maturity, and if so how, must be considered and determined at the first on notice hearing. The methods by which a child may be heard during the proceedings comprise a report from an Officer of the Cafcass High Court Team or party status with legal representation. In most cases where it is appropriate for the child to be given an opportunity to be heard in proceedings an interview of the child by an officer of the Cafcass High Court Team will be sufficient to ensure that the child's wishes and feelings are placed before the court. In only a very few cases will party status be necessary. Where the exception relied on is that of settlement pursuant to Art 12 of the 1980 Hague Convention, the separate point of view of the child will be particularly important. The court should record on the face of any final order the manner in which the child has been heard in the proceedings.

(d) Witness Statements

3.6 Paragraph 2.13 of Practice Direction PD12F recognises that, to avoid delay, the initial statement in support of the application may be in the form of a statement given by the applicant's solicitor based on information transmitted by the Central Authority of the Requesting State. The applicant's initial statement of evidence must however, include the applicant's evidence establishing the necessary requirements for a return, a description of any protective measures (including orders that may be subject to a declaration of enforceability or registration under Art 11 of the 1996 Hague Convention or, where appropriate, undertakings) the applicant is prepared, without prejudice to his or her case, to offer for the purpose of securing the child's return and full details of any proceedings in the Requesting State or in England and Wales of which the applicant is aware.

3.7 Witness statements filed in support of the answer and in reply to the answer should be as economical as possible and should deal only with those factual matters relevant to the issues raised in the answer. The court will rarely be assisted by a detailed account of the history of the parents' relationship. Appropriate translations of exhibits should be provided with the statement. Where the maker of the statement does not speak English, the statement should be prepared and served in the maker's own language and then certified translation into English provided by the party concerned.

(e) Oral Evidence

3.8 The court will rarely make a direction for oral evidence to be given. Any party seeking such direction for oral evidence will need to demonstrate to the satisfaction of the court that oral evidence is necessary to assist the court to resolve the proceedings justly. Any party seeking to rely on oral evidence should raise the issue at the earliest available opportunity and no later than the pre-hearing review.

(f) Bundles

3.9 The court bundle for any hearing must comply with FPR PD 27A. PD27A limits the size of the bundle to a single file containing no more than 350 pages (PD 27A para 5.1). The limit of 350 pages includes the skeleton arguments. Only those documents which are relevant to the hearing and which it is necessary for the court to read, or which will be referred to during the hearing, may be included (PD 27A para 4.1). It will not generally be necessary to include in the bundle the application sent from the home country's Central Authority to ICACU. Where an issue arises as to the inclusion of this document, that issue will be dealt with by direction of the court. Skeleton arguments and other preliminary materials prepared for use in relation to earlier hearings should be excluded. Any separate bundle of all authorities relied on for any hearing must comply with PD 27A para 4.3. Each authority relied on must be provided with the relevant passages highlighted by means of a vertical line in the margin. Skeleton arguments must be filed by no later than 11am on the working day before the hearing (PD 27A para 6.4).

3.10 The time limits set out in FPR PD 27A para 6 for preparing and delivering the bundle and case management documents represent the minimum time limits applicable to this task. Where the hearing is on notice and the respondent is a litigant in person, the applicant should prepare and deliver the bundle pursuant to PD27A para 6 in a timeframe that ensures that the bundle and the case management documents are provided to the litigant in person at least three working days prior to the hearing.

(g) Time estimates

3.11 The time estimate for the final hearing should make reasonable allowance for judicial reading time and judgment writing. In those cases where permission for oral evidence has been given a witness template for the final hearing should also be completed at the time that the direction for oral evidence is made to ensure that the time estimate for the final hearing is accurate.

(h) International Judicial Liaison

3.12 The following matters may appropriately be the subject of direct international judicial liaison:

(a) information concerning the scheduling of the case in the foreign jurisdiction,
(b) seeking to establish whether protective measures are available for the child or other parent in the State to which the child would be returned,
(c) ascertaining whether the foreign court can accept and enforce orders made or undertakings offered by the parties in the initiating jurisdiction,
(d) ascertaining whether the foreign court can make a 'mirror order',
(e) confirming whether orders were made by the foreign court and
(f) verifying whether findings about domestic violence were made by the foreign court.

This is not an exhaustive list. It is important to remember that international judicial liaison is not intended to be a substitute for obtaining legal advice, a means to avoid having to seek expert evidence as to foreign law or procedure, a mechanism for judges to settle welfare disputes or a means of making submissions to a foreign court. All requests for international judicial liaison should be made through the International Family Justice Office (IFJOffice@hmcts.gsi.gov.uk) and should be accompanied by a (preferably agreed) concise case summary and a set of focused questions to be put to the network judge which ask for information of a practical and non-legal nature, phrased in a neutral, non-tactical way.

(i) Final Hearing

3.13 Article 11 of the 1980 Hague Convention requires the judicial or administrative authorities of Contracting States to act expeditiously in proceedings for the return of children. Article 11(3) of the Council Regulation also requires a court to which a return application is made to act expeditiously and stipulates that, unless exceptional circumstances make this impossible, the court must issue its judgment no later than six weeks after the application is lodged. Within this context, whilst the quantity and nature of the evidential material required to reach a proper determination of the application at final hearing will depend on the individual case, as will the format of the final hearing, including the extent to which oral evidence is permitted, the final hearing will be dealt with summarily and in most cases based on the written material then available to the court.

(j) Orders

3.14 The Tipstaff passport, location and collection orders are in a standard format that has been arrived at after careful consultation and revision. It is for the court to draw the relevant Tipstaff order once granted. Legal representatives should not provide a draft of the passport order, location order or collection order sought. Legal representatives should provide drafts of any disclosure orders sought and a separate draft of the case management directions sought alongside the Tipstaff and/or disclosure order(s) applied for. Orders which discharge Tipstaff orders, including orders for the release of passports held by the Tipstaff, will only be accepted by the Tipstaff if they are sealed.

3.15 Where one of the parties is a litigant in person, the advocate for the represented party will need to ensure that any case management and disclosure orders made by court are drafted and submitted for approval by the judge. When the solicitor for the represented party sends a copy of the order to the litigant in person, the solicitor should highlight in writing to the litigant in person any case management steps that the order requires them to take. Counsel instructed on a Direct Access basis cannot conduct litigation on behalf of their client. The obligation on Direct Access counsel ends once the order has been submitted to the court. Case management directions made against the client must accordingly be met by them as a litigant in person.

3.16 Where an order refusing the return of the child (a 'non-return' order) has been made in respect of an applicant from an EU member state on the grounds set out in Art 13 of the 1980 Hague Convention, the procedure set out in Art 11(6) of the Council Regulation, requiring the transmission of certain documents to the court with jurisdiction or Central Authority in the Member State where the child was habitually resident within one month of the date of the nonreturn order, must be complied with.

(k) Appeals and Applications for Stay

3.17 Any application for a stay pending an application for permission to appeal and the application for permission to appeal should be made expeditiously. Any application for permission to appeal and any stay should be made to the judge if possible and, if not possible or if refused, to the Court of Appeal. The filing of the notice of appeal should not be delayed until the appellant has received a copy of the approved transcript of the judgment under appeal.

Sir James Munby
President of the Family Division
13 March 2018

Appendix
Child Abduction Mediation Scheme

Introduction

1 The requirement in FPR r 1.4(2)(f)) that case management includes encouraging the parties to use a non-court dispute resolution procedure if the court considers that appropriate and facilitating the use of such procedure, and the obligation imposed by FPR r 3.3(1) to consider whether non-court dispute resolution is appropriate at every stage of the proceedings, applies to international child abduction proceedings. The 1980 Hague Convention itself, by Arts 7(c) and 10, places weight on the desirability of a negotiated or voluntary return or the amicable resolution of the issues.

2 In 2006, a child abduction Mediation Pilot Scheme run by Reunite, with funding from the Nuffield Foundation, found, in the context of twenty-eight cases which progressed to a concluded mediation, that there is a clear role for mediation in resolving cases of alleged child abduction and that parents were willing to embrace the use of mediation. Seventy-five percent of cases resulted in the parents concerned reaching a Memorandum of Understanding.

3 The Child Abduction Mediation Scheme is a mediation scheme that aims to ensure that parties engaged in child abduction proceedings are able, in an appropriate case, to access a mediation service as an integral part of the court process and in parallel with, but independent from, the proceedings. Whilst mediation will not be appropriate, or suitable, in every case, it is an option that should be explored by the court in all cases of alleged international child abduction.

Child Abduction Mediation Scheme – Key Principles

4 The Child Abduction Mediation Scheme is an independent mediation scheme run with the assistance of Reunite, which organisation provides mediators with specialised knowledge of international child abduction, trained and experienced in mediating cases of this nature. The following key principles apply to the operation of the Child Abduction Mediation Scheme:

- (a) The mediation will run in parallel with, but independent from, the proceedings in court, with the aim of completing the mediation within the timescale applicable to the proceedings.
- (b) Mediation is voluntary and will only be undertaken with the consent of both parents. An unwillingness to enter into mediation will not have an effect on the outcome of the proceedings.
- (c) Mediation will only be undertaken if the mediator considers that it is appropriate and safe to do so, and following an assessment of the parties and their situation during the required screening stage.
- (d) Participation by the parties in mediation is without prejudice to the applicant's right to pursue the return of the child, and without prejudice to the respondent's right to defend the proceedings.
- (e) Participation by the parties in mediation does not prevent the parties from requesting that the court determine the issues between them.
- (f) If the mediation is not successful in resolving the issues then the matter will return to the court arena for determination.

5 The Child Abduction Mediation Scheme complements the proceedings and is only embarked upon once proceedings have been issued (Reunite also runs a mediation scheme that operates independent of court proceedings. Full details of this scheme can be found at http://www.reunite.org/pages/mediation.asp).

6 The operation of the Child Abduction Mediation Scheme will be facilitated by the presence at the Royal Courts of Justice of mediators from Reunite with specialised knowledge of international child abduction who will be available to speak with parties on child abduction matters.

Child Abduction Mediation Scheme – Operation

7 The scheme has three key stages, namely (i) identification, (ii) screening and (iii) mediation. The three key stages operate as follows:

Identification

8 Participation in the Child Abduction Mediation Scheme is voluntary. Mediation will only be undertaken with the consent of both parents and where it can be undertaken safely. However, it is also important that parties to child abduction proceedings are aware of, and have the proper opportunity to indicate their willingness to participate in the Child Abduction Mediation Scheme.

9 Within this context, the following steps will be taken by the court in each case, with a view to identifying those cases in which the parties are willing to consider mediation of their dispute:

(a) At the first without notice hearing, or by way of standard directions following an on notice application, the court will, where appropriate, direct that the applicant and the respondent shall each be given the opportunity at the first on notice hearing to speak with a mediator.

(b) At the first on notice hearing, the court will, where appropriate, encourage the parties to consider the option of mediation and, in an appropriate case, will invite the parties to speak with a mediator.

(c) Where the parties agree to speak with the mediator, the mediator will discuss with the parties the possibility of participating in mediation under the Child Abduction Mediation Scheme and will carry out an initial screening interview (see paragraph 11 below).

(d) Where the parties consent to mediate and the case is suitable for mediation, the court will give any directions necessary to facilitate the mediation and will record on the face of the order the proposed outline timetable for the mediation, in consultation with the parties and the mediator.

10 Where one party is outside the jurisdiction, the steps set out at Paragraph 9 will be accomplished by telephone at the first on notice hearing. Where this is not possible, for example due to a time difference, they will be accomplished on an agreed date shortly after the hearing. If these steps are accomplished on an agreed date shortly after the hearing, the parties will inform the court of the outcome and, where necessary, the court will either approve agreed directions to facilitate any agreement to mediate or list the matter for the purposes of giving any such directions. In any event, the mediator will ensure that the required screening and assessment is carried out prior to the mediation commencing.

11 It is important to note that entering into a process of mediation will not ground a defence of acquiescence (see In Re H (Minors) (Abduction: Acquiescence) [1998] AC 72 at 88–89).

Screening

12 In addition to the parents being willing to mediate, the case must be suitable for mediation. Mediators have a responsibility to ensure that the parents take part in any mediation process willingly, and without fear of violence or harm. The mediator will undertake a screening procedure to confirm that this can be achieved. The mediator will have particular regard to the welfare of the child or children. The mediator will also have particular regard to any allegation or admission of domestic abuse (as defined in FPR PD12J paragraph 3), or other reason to believe that the child or a parent has experienced domestic abuse or is at risk of such abuse.

13 Within this context, an initial screening interview will be undertaken individually with each of the parents prior to undertaking mediation, in order to ensure that the parent is willing to take part in mediation and to assess whether the case is suitable and safe for mediation. The screening interview will also allow the mediator to confirm to each parent at the conclusion of the interview whether it is appropriate for mediation to be offered and, if so, to ensure that each parent understand the purpose of the mediation and to provide an opportunity for any concerns relevant to mediation to be further discussed.

14 As provided for at paragraphs 8(c) and 10, where possible, the screening interviews will take place at the first on notice hearing when the parents speak with the mediator, either in person or by telephone. However, where the screening interview takes place at a later agreed date, the parties will inform the court of the outcome and, where necessary, the court will either approve agreed directions to facilitate any agreement to mediate or list the matter for the purposes of giving any such directions.

15 Where both parents indicate a willingness to engage in mediation, during the screening interview the mediator will deal with the following matters:

(a) Whether or not the case is one that is suitable for mediation.
(b) Whether or not both parents are willing to mediate and to attend mediation with an open mind.
(c) Whether or not the subject child appears to be of an age and level of maturity at which their voice should be heard.
(d) Provide information about the mediation and how the mediation process will work in parallel with, but independent from, the proceedings.
(e) Address any concerns that either parent may have relevant to the conduct of the mediation.

16 Within the context of the matters set out in paragraph 12, the assessment of the suitability of a case for mediation will include an assessment of whether the mediation can be conducted safely. In any case in which the parents are willing to mediate but it is alleged or admitted, or there is other reason to believe, that the child or a parent has experienced domestic abuse (as defined in FPR PD12J paragraph 3) or that there is a risk of such abuse, the mediator will assess, through the screening procedure, whether a mediation can be conducted safely having regard to the matters set out in FPR PD12B paragraphs 5.1 and 5.2 and FPR PD12J. A mediation will take place in such circumstances only after the mediator has undertaken a risk assessment and is satisfied that appropriate measures are in place to protect the safety of those participating in the mediation process.

17 If, during the screening interview, it is identified that the subject child appears to be of an age and level of maturity at which their voice should be heard, the court will direct that the child be interviewed by a member of the Cafcass High Court Team and a report filed with the court and provided to the parents and mediators.

Mediation

18 Where the parties agree to mediate and the case is suitable for mediation, the mediation will be timetabled so as to ensure that the timescales applicable to the proceedings are met.

19 Reunite will contact both parents to arrange appropriate dates for mediation. Where it proves impossible for an applicant to come to this jurisdiction for the purposes of mediation, the mediator will conduct the mediation with the applicant attending by way of a telecommunications application such as Skype.

20 In some circumstances public funding from the Legal Aid Agency may be available to cover the costs of flights and hotel for the applicant parent to come to this jurisdiction for the purposes of mediation, in which case Reunite will co-ordinate travel and accommodation arrangements.

21 Where the parent has requested the services of an interpreter, this will be provided throughout the mediation session(s).

22 Parents are free at any stage during the course of the mediation to consult their respective legal representatives in this jurisdiction or overseas, or any other individual they wish to consult and the mediator may encourage them, as appropriate, to consult.

23 Where a safeguarding issue concerning a child or an adult arises during the course of the mediation, the mediator will, where appropriate, terminate the mediation and will notify the relevant agencies.

24 Where the mediation is successful, the agreement reached between the parents will be set down in the form of a Memorandum of Understanding. Parents will be encouraged to seek advice on the Memorandum of Understanding from their respective legal representatives if they have them. The court will be informed of the outcome of the mediation and the Memorandum of Understanding will be reduced to a consent order which will be placed before the court for approval. Any consent order will explain how the child has been heard in the context of the mediation process.

25 Where the mediation is not successful, the court will proceed to determine the case. Ordinarily, there will be no further reference to the mediation or to anything said during the mediation, save where child protection concerns have been revealed or a report has been prepared by the Cafcass High Court Team pursuant to paragraph 17 above.

(6) Other useful references

(a) Lists and status of contracting parties to relevant conventions can be found as follows:

Convention of 25 October 1980 on the Civil Aspects of International Child Abduction	https://www.hcch.net/en/instruments/conventions/status-table/?cid=24 (Last accessed 4 August 2022.)
Convention of 19 October 1996 on Jurisdiction, Applicable Law, Recognition, Enforcement and Co-operation in Respect of Parental Responsibility and Measures for the Protection of Children	https://www.hcch.net/en/instruments/conventions/status-table/?cid=70 (Last accessed 4 August 2022.)
European Convention on Recognition and Enforcement of Decisions concerning Custody of Children and on Restoration of Custody of Children (ETS No. 105)	https://www.coe.int/en/web/conventions/full-list?module=signatures-by-treaty&treatynum=105 (Last accessed 4 August 2022.)

(b) HCCH Emerging Guidance on Direct Judicial Communications can be found as follows:

https://assets.hcch.net/docs/62d073ca-eda0-494e-af66-2ddd368b7379.pdf (last accessed 4 August 2022).

INDEX

[*all references are to paragraph number*]